the Writer's Handbook 2004

Preface by
Natalie Goldberg

Edited by Elfrieda Abbe

the Writer books

The Writer Books is an imprint of Kalmbach Trade Press, a division of Kalmbach Publishing Co. These books are distributed to the book trade by Watson-Guptill. For all other inquiries, including individual orders or details on special quantity discounts for groups or conferences, contact:

Kalmbach Publishing Co.
21027 Crossroads Circle
Waukesha, WI 53187
(800) 533-6644

Visit our website at http://www.writermag.com to learn more about *The Writer* magazine, view current articles, or order copies of *The Writer's Handbook*. Secure online ordering available.

Printed in the United States of America
03 04 05 06 07 08 09 10 11 12   10 9 8 7 6 5 4 3 2 1

Publisher's Cataloging-in-Publication
(Provided by Quality Books, Inc.)

The writer's handbook 2004 / edited by Elfrieda Abbe ;
    preface by Natalie Goldberg.
        p. cm.
        Includes bibliographical references and index.
        ISBN 0-87116-200-8

        1. Authorship—Handbooks, manuals, etc.
    2. Publishers and publishing. I. Abbe, Elfrieda.

    PN137.W733 2002   808'.02
                         QBI03-200399

Project Editor: Philip Martin
Assistant Editor: Amy Glander

Art Director: Kristi Ludwig
Cover Design: Lisa Zehner

Acknowledgments

Thanks to Philip Martin, project editor, for his assistance in assembling this volume. Thanks also to many others at Kalmbach Publishing Co. who helped with the preparation of this 68th edition, especially to those who helped to verify information in the market listings section, in particular Amy Glander, as well as Jeff Reich and Sally VanDenburg of *The Writer* magazine staff. Thanks also to Mary Algozin and Julia Gerlach for their tireless copy-editing of this thousand-page tome.

We all know that the publishing world is in a constant state of flux, and some information in the market listings may have changed since last updated. We would greatly appreciate any feedback from readers, with corrections or comments on how better to improve the usefulness of the information presented. Kalmbach Publishing Co. has a tradition of outstanding customer service, and we look forward to continuing to improve and refine this long-standing resource to writers in coming years by incorporating your feedback.

If you know of new or overlooked markets of significance to aspiring writers that you wish to recommend for future volumes, please forward those ideas to Philip Martin, The Writer Books, 21027 Crossroads Circle, P.O. Box 1612, Waukesha, WI 53187-1612, or send an e-mail directly to the attention of books@kalmbach.com.

CONTENTS

ARTICLES

ARTICLES (cont.)

MARKETS

Nonfiction Magazines

MARKETS (cont.)

PREFACE

Pen, paper, and the human mind

by Natalie Goldberg

Though I did not pick up a pen and attempt to write a word until I was 24 years old, working as a cook at Naked Lunch, the first natural foods restaurant in Ann Arbor, Michigan, the true heart of a writer was born in me in ninth grade in Mr. Clemente's class. One March afternoon our English teacher suddenly flipped off the lights at the beginning of class and said, "Listen to the rain." He didn't ask us to write an essay nor was there going to be any test on "rain." We could even put our heads down on our desks, if we wanted.

For a few moments in the regulated school day, we experienced a moment of space, also a recognition that something existed outside the classroom. A torrent was hitting pavement and bouncing, sinking into the grass, pounding on the window. It was an acknowledgment that an element unknowable, mysterious, could be encountered with our senses beyond our thinking brains. I felt and smelled rain. It coursed through my blood.

After four minutes Mr. Clemente once again switched on the light and we abruptly moved into analyzing *Portrait of the Artist* by James Joyce, removing ourselves from the true source of inspiration: the breath and a rootedness in the body. Though I'm certain Joyce imbued those pages with essential connections, we used the novel as a tool to dislodge ourselves from the writer's work by dissecting it, rather than staying close to it.

Perhaps the power of those four minutes was intensified because they were suspended—like dashes hold a dangling clause in the middle of a very different sentence—but whatever the circumstances, I never forgot the incident. From then on dreaming became legitimate. Intuiting something beyond the ordinary, but at the same time centered in the familiar, eventually grew into my life's work. Certainly this wasn't my first rainfall. I lived on Long Island in the '50s and early '60s. We had abundant precipitation. But that one afternoon—I think it was a Wednesday—liberated me, the downpour was mine.

And isn't that the writer's task? To claim experience, even if we write about things we've never done and by characters who are not us. Writing is a physical activity. It comes from our whole body, from our lungs, shoulders, hands, kidneys—and from beyond the corporeal, from memory, vision, imagination, the fusing of what is and what isn't, a coalescing of time.

And every writer knows in order to leap into the unknown, we need to ignite and ground ourselves in the specifics. In my early 20s when I realized I wanted to write, I took on the task of learning the names of things: not car, but Cadillac, not tree, but sycamore, not fruit but pear. Over the last 30 years, I have walked down the streets and roads of every place I have ever lived and discovered peony, gardenia, petunia, oak, sage, chamisa, pinon, ponderosa, lilac, redwood, elm, forsythia, cedar, juniper, English ivy, black locust. I was proud of my identification. I noticed sky—big and deep blue in New Mexico, a consistent gray in the midwest, more white on the east coast—distant mountains, the look of flat land, humidity, a rough river. The world opened to me, the fine edge of the seen and the unseen revealed itself. Writing became religious. The place I went to meet myself, to come home to all my running thoughts.

I fell in love with story. If someone told me a tale while I was in a restaurant, my food grew cold, the bite of potato was suspended at the edge of my fork. In my mind one event began to link with another. I understood how to weave incidents together to create structure. I built plot—whether for fiction or nonfiction—through dialogue, action, the visual world. I made sure to take into account weather—nothing happened devoid of a season. What did the trees look like? Any insects? Heavy jackets? I wanted people I wrote about to have coughs, flu, sneezes, yawns. Things that are never mentioned. We're quick to write about sex, but what about blowing our nose or low back pain? I needed to stand witness and become intimate with the truth of our aching, inspired human lives.

What are the tools of a writer?—pen, paper (of course, computer, if you are so inclined), and the human mind. What crannies of untouched perception could I explore? I grew "strong minded," not stubborn, but I began to know what I thought. Writing gave me a confidence, a training in waking up.

Alongside writing, I practiced Zen. The two naturally went together. From 1978-1990 I studied with a Japanese Zen Master, living in Minnesota. His name was Katagiri Roshi. From all the all-day, early-morning, week-long practices I did, the bowing, chanting, the general fierce regimentation and challenge, I came away with three clear things that have become the backbone for the long life of my writing:

1. *Continue Under All Circumstances.* No excuses.

2. *Don't Be Tossed Away.* If your kid falls and needs stitches, write in the waiting room.

3. *Make Positive Effort for the Good.* Roshi told me this when I was going through a divorce. Positive effort doesn't mean hauling a mountain to Iowa. Sometimes it just means getting out of bed, brushing your teeth. Picking up the pen. Even if you write about rape, poverty, cancer, it's a positive act. You are speaking; you are standing up.

It is not an easy thing to be a writer. Layers of skin are yanked off. Roshi's three dictums gave me a skeleton, a form.

Four of Jack Kerouac's essentials for prose provided me with heart for the path:

> Accept loss forever.
> Be submissive to everything, open, listening.
> No fear or shame in the dignity of your experience, language,
>   and knowlodge.
> Be in love with your life.

For those with the desire to venture out into the world, grab this *Writer's Handbook* as a guide and talisman. There's a great mixture here of solid, nitty-gritty information about places to publish alongside the sound advice and care of experienced writers.

Believe me, you, too, can find your place inside the huge terrain of writing. No one is too odd that they are left out.

Natalie Goldberg, of Taos, N.M., is the author of *Writing Down the Bones: Freeing the Writer Within* (1986), one of the most popular books ever written on creativity and writing. It has sold over one million copies and been translated into nine languages. Her book *Thunder and Lightning: Cracking Open the Writer's Craft* takes writers beyond practice to focus on more finished work. She is also a poet; her newest collection, *Top of My Lungs*, includes poems, paintings, and an essay, "How Poetry Saved My Life." She practices Zen meditation and teaches seminars in writing, including week-long courses at the Mabel Dodge House, a historic site on the edge of Pueblo land in the shadow of Taos Mountain. More information is available at her Web site, www.nataliegoldberg.com

INTRODUCTION

by Elfrieda Abbe

As editor of *The Writer's Handbook*, it's my pleasure to select essays from *The Writer* magazine to be included in each edition. While looking for suitable articles in recent issues, I was reminded of the willingness of writers to help one another by sharing what they have learned. With so much material to choose from, I always start off with far more articles than we could possibly use, then face the challenge of pruning the list, looking for the right mix of nuts-and-bolts advice, inspiration, and market tips that writers can use in their day-to-day endeavors.

What helps me in this process is to imagine writers like you, thumbing through *The Handbook*, looking for answers to questions about the craft and business of writing, seeking inspiration to help them through a rough patch, or finding the perfect markets for their manuscripts.

The Handbook is a tool for working writers. We send it off to bookstores, shiny and new, its pages pristine. I hope it doesn't stay that way. I imagine it a few months from now, sitting on your desk, pages worn from use. I hope you will take it with you to your writers groups, jot notes in the margins, bookmark the markets you want to query, and draw from it the ideas and tips that will help you achieve your goals.

Maybe you're looking for an agent, but don't know where to begin. You're writing a book proposal and need some tips on what that entails. You're plotting your novel and wonder what journeys your characters might take. Perhaps you're out of fresh ideas and need some prompts, or are writing your first young-adult book and could use some guidance. You'll find help on all those topics and more in this volume.

Writing may be a solitary act, but as a writer you are not alone. *The Writer* magazine and *The Writer's Handbook* are your connection to some of our most accomplished writers—such as Natalie Goldberg, Elizabeth Berg, Robert Bly, Lois Lowry, Anne Lamott, Janet Evanonvich, Ray Bradbury—as well as agents and editors who generously share a wealth of knowledge and experiences to help you succeed.

Having *The Writer's Handbook* on your desk is like having a group of writing mentors at your fingertips to consult 24 hours a day. If you feel stuck, there is someone in this book who will encourage you to keep going. If you're making excuses, someone will else will gently chide, "Quit griping and start writing." And if you doubt you have something to say, a fellow writer will remind you to "believe in yourself."

We hope that this annual book will give you the inside track you need to navigate the competitive publishing world. Along with the many successful bestselling authors who share their advice here, all of us on *The Writer* team want you to succeed—to start writing, keep writing, and achieve your writing dreams.

Since 1887, this has been *The Writer*'s mission, and you'll find it reflected on these pages. I know that this rich collection of writing expertise, business savvy, and inspiration will speed you on your way.

Elfrieda Abbe is Editor of *The Writer*.

WELCOME TO THE WONDERFUL WORLD OF FREELANCING

Getting started as a professional writer

by Kelly James-Enger

So, you're a writer—or want to be one. You may have started out writing for yourself, but now you think you'd like to take the next step and publish your work. Or maybe you've already seen your writing in print, and want to explore new markets or different types of writing. That's probably why you picked up this book.

When you're writing only for your own satisfaction, there are no rules dictating what you can and can't do. You can scribble on the back of a legal pad, scratch a poem on a bar napkin with a leaky ballpoint pen, or hammer out your novel on a dusty old typewriter with an aging ribbon.

But when you decide to write for publication, things change. You can't just toss your wonderful new essay in the mail, and hope someone will buy it. You must first find potential markets for your work and determine what kind of material they're looking for. That's rule number one when writing for publication—remember that you're writing for someone other than (or in addition to) yourself.

While your essay may be wonderful, it's unlikely to be read if it's printed in crayon—or if it's three times too long. Rule number two—follow the standards for the proper way to approach editors and submit your work. New writers sometimes ignore the basics when it comes to submitting their writing to publishers, assuming that it's only the writing itself that's important. The truth is that even the most stellar work is likely to be ignored when it's submitted to an inappropriate market or is nearly impossible to read.

Finally, there are other aspects to writing for publication—like what editors expect from writers—that new freelancers may be unaware of. Most of them can be summed up by rule number three: be professional.

Assuming you already have basic writing skills, you needn't have a journalism or English degree to write for publication. You do have to learn about the basics of freelancing and submitting your work. If you dream of taking the next step—and becoming a *published* writer—read on.

Part 1: Before You Begin

Make the commitment

If you're writing for yourself, you can write whenever you feel like it—and skip it when you don't. You may go days, even weeks, without putting a word down on the page, but if you're going to write for publication, you need to make a commitment to yourself. Writing for publication involves more than simply writing. It means spending time researching potential markets, analyzing what they're looking for, preparing work for submission, and oh yeah, writing. It's a time-consuming job and it takes dedication, desire, and determination to stick with it.

Decide now when you will spend time to further your goal of having your writing published. Will you write three mornings a week before you go to work? Will you carve out a half-hour each night after dinner? On your calendar or day planner, write down when you'll write—in *ink*. Treat your writing as you would any other obligation—otherwise, it's likely to end up at the bottom of an already crowded to-do list.

Decide *what* you want to write

Maybe you already know what you want to write—a children's book, humorous essays, nonfiction articles, the Great American Novel. Then again, you may not be sure of what you want to say. You have all these great ideas, but when you sit down to capture them, they fly right out of your head.

If that's the case, imagine this. You receive word that you've won a weeklong, all-expenses-paid trip to a writer's retreat. Not only that, but if you have children, the conference will pay for the cost of a nanny or house husband to care for them while you're gone. Your partner, your pets, even your plants will all be cared for in your absence. Your place of employment will give you a week's vacation pay, and you'll have no repercussions for taking off to spend a week—an entire week!—writing. (Kind of scary, isn't it?)

Now that time isn't an excuse, what types of writing do you want to explore during this week? How do you want to spend your time? What will you write about? Make a list here:

_____
_____
_____
_____
_____
_____
_____
_____
_____

If you're stuck, consider your interests and the things you feel strongly about—you may find subjects that appeal to you there. Think about what you read for pleasure. Often we want to write the type of work we enjoy reading. List any other ideas here:

_____
_____
_____
_____
_____
_____
_____

Take a look at your list, and choose which type of writing and which subject most appeals to you. It's fine to have more than one writing project going at a time, but if your time is limited, you also need to decide which one is more important to you and work on that first. If appropriate, make a list of your writing priorities here:

_____
_____
_____
_____
_____
_____
_____
_____

Part 2: Get Ready to Write and Submit

Act the part

First things first. If you're writing for yourself, you needn't worry about being professional—after all, who do you need to impress? But when you're writing for publication, you need to consider the impression you make with your approach and your work.

That means not apologizing for your writing. Claim yourself as a freelancer—someone who writes for pay and publication. If you're asked what you do, don't mumble, "Oh, I'm trying to be a writer." "I'm a chiropractor/parent/dentist/software analyst/fill-in-the-blank and freelance writer" is a much more businesslike, self-assured answer. Be prepared to answer questions about your writing—many people *say* they want to write (that is, until they realize how much time and effort is involved!)

You may never meet any of your editors in person. That's the good news—you can toil away in pajamas or sweatpants and no one's the wiser! That means, though, that the first impression you make will be through your letterhead, business card, or the way you answer your phone.

Is your letterhead professional, simple, and free of cutesy drawings or cartoons? If you're a children's author, a childlike design might be appropriate or even eye-catching. Most writers, however, want to present a more polished image. It needn't be fancy or expensive—you can produce a template letterhead with your contact information on your computer, or spend a few more dollars for printed letterhead. Matching business cards and preprinted envelopes round out the package.

Your telephone message on your voicemail should also be friendly but brief. If you share a phone line with family members, leave a professional message on your answering machine, and teach your kids how to answer the phone. And you should check your voicemail—and e-mail—at least once a day.

Editors expect to be able to reach writers quickly. They also expect you to be professional, resourceful, and (hopefully) easy to work with. You'll have a leg up on other writers if you keep these tips in mind:

• Be pleasant. Say you write an essay, and an editor buys it. Five months later when you've practically forgotten about it, she calls and asks you to review the galleys ASAP. Don't whine about the short notice—do them immediately (and graciously) to help make her job easier. An editor trying to close an issue has plenty on her mind already; she wants to work with writers who won't give her a hard time.

• Be able to disagree without making it personal. You can argue a point without getting nasty. Your editor's rewritten lead weakens the piece considerably? Remain calm and point out why you're not happy with the new version. You don't have to be a jellyfish, but you can disagree respectfully and thus maintain your relationship.

• Deliver what you promise. This goes beyond meeting the deadline. It means that you turn in a story that the editor asked for as closely as you can. If she wants 1,500 words and two sidebars, that's what you write—not 2,500 words, figuring that she can cut it down.

• Treat deadlines seriously. If you discover that you're going to need more time to finish a piece (say, one of your critical sources is unavailable until after the piece is due), talk to your editor immediately. Ask for an extension so she can plan for the late story. The worst thing you can do is simply not turn it in, and then dodge your editor who's wondering where the story is.

A Room of one's own (or not)

You don't need a separate office when you start freelancing, but you do need a computer (or regular access to one). Twenty years ago, a typewriter and a telephone were all a writer needed—today, editors expect writers to have a computer and e-mail. While the advent of e-mail has made owning a fax machine less important, fax access is still helpful. (If you don't have a fax, use a friend's fax number or a fax at a Mail Boxes Etc., Kinko's, or Office Max store.)

You'll also need a way to keep track of your submissions. While there are software programs available for this purpose, a simple notebook system is probably the easiest. Keep track of what you sent out, when, how (i.e., e-mail or snail mail), markets, and responses. A typical entry might look like this:

Date	Piece/topic	Market	Response
02/27/03	Using yoga to lose weight (e-mail query)	*Oxygen*	Assigned 03/25/03
02/28/03	Essay on writer's hats (e-mail)	*The Writer*	

When you get an assignment or sell a piece, you can make a new entry that details the assignment:

Date	Piece/topic	Market	Word Count/$$	Deadline
03/25/03	Yoga & weight loss	*Oxygen*	1,500/$1,275	04/20/03

When you receive an assignment, make a note of it in your assignment log, and write down the deadline in your calendar or daily planner. That way you have the deadline noted in two places—using a "double diary" system helps prevent you from missing one.

Finally, when you turn a piece in or an editor notifies you that he or she wants to purchase rights to it, ask if you need to send an invoice. Some publications require invoices; others will simply put a request for payment through. While software programs like Quickbooks include invoices, a short letter that includes your mailing address and social security number can serve as an invoice. A sample is shown below:

February 25, 2003 [always include the date]

Re: INVOICE #401 [an invoice number makes it easy to track]

Dear Lisa,

Please let this letter serve as my invoice for **$1,275.00** for the rights to "The Perfect Tan" per written contract of February 5, 2003. My social security number is xxx-xx-xxxx.

Thank you very much!

Best,
Kelly James-Enger
6911 Waterfall Place
Downers Grove, IL 60516
630/795-1288
kellyjames@pop.net

[Note: This invoice was sent via e-mail; otherwise, it would have included the editor's full name, title, and mailing address. In addition to the date and invoice number, it sets out the amount of money billed; the title of the piece; the contract date; writer's social security number; and writer's name and contact information of the writer. If there is no written contract, make sure to state in the invoice what rights are being purchased (such as "reprint rights" or "first North American serial rights")].

Is Your Writing a Business or a Hobby?

The fact that you're trying to publish your work and get paid for it rather than writing for yourself can have tax benefits as well. If your writing is considered a *business* rather than a *hobby*, the IRS will allow you to deduct legitimate business deductions—and that means a lower net income at the end of the year, which translates into less out of your pocket and into Uncle Sam's. The key is to have a "profit motive," meaning that you're writing to make money, not just satisfy your creative muse.

What's a legitimate expense? According to IRS regulations, you can deduct expenses that are both ordinary and necessary. An "ordinary" expense is one that is "common and accepted in your trade or business" and a "necessary" expense is one that is "helpful and appropriate for your trade or business."

Assuming you meet the IRS's standards for writing as a business, you're entitled to take deductions such as:

• Telephone expenses (while you can't deduct the cost of your primary phone line, you can deduct long-distance calls related to your writing as well as a second business-only phone line)
• Postage and mailing costs
• Office supplies (including paper, printer supplies, computer and peripherals)
• Travel expenses (you can deduct business-related transportation and lodging along with 50% of business-related meals)
• Computer used for work and peripherals such as a printer, scanner, and a fax machine
• Subscriptions to writing magazines and the cost of writing-related books (like this one!)
• Fees for attending writer's conferences

Keep receipts for your business expenses, and plan to file a Schedule C at the end of the year. Remember, the more expenses you have, the less you'll pay in taxes.

Want more info? The IRS's guide for small businesses (Publication 334) and sections 1, 8, and 13 of the IRS's guide to business expenses (Publication 535) are available at http://www.irs.gov.

Copyright: A Quick Q & A

Perhaps no concept is as confusing to beginning writers as copyright—what it is, how it's created, and how to protect your own.

What is copyright?

"Copyright" refers to a form of protection provided by U.S. law to the authors of "original works of authorship" including literary, dramatic, musical, artistic, and other intellectual works. The owner of copyrighted material has the exclusive right to (and the right to authorize others to) reproduce, distribute, and display the work.

When is copyright created?

Copyright protection exists from the time the work is created "in fixed form." Once you complete a draft of a poem, novel, or article, you automatically own the copyright and it's yours until you sell or license it to someone else.

What does the copyright symbol do?

Many writers mistakenly believe that you must include a copyright symbol © on your work, but the symbol doesn't *create* copyright. It merely gives notice of the copyright to others who might steal it and defend their actions under the so-called "innocent infringement" doctrine.

Say you write a poem and give it to a friend, sans notice. If your friend relies in good faith on the fact that there's no copyright notice—and distributes your poem to 693 of his closest confidants—he may not be liable for damages and may even be permitted to continue copying the work! The notice required is the copyright symbol ©, followed by the date the work was first published, and the author's name—e.g., © 2001, Kelly James-Enger.

Why register your work?

The answer is simple—to be able to effectively protect your copyrights in the future. While you don't have to register your copyright to bring an action for infringement, any infringement that occurs prior to registration will not give rise to attorneys' fees or statutory damages.

That may not seem like a big deal, but attorneys' fees and statutory damages are two of your best remedies in a copyright infringement suit. The fact that you registered your work can be used as evidence that you're the legal copyright owner at trial. Better yet, if you've registered the work within 3 months of publication and you win an infringement suit, you're entitled to attorneys' fees and statutory damages—a specified amount of money set out by law. If you haven't registered your work within 3 months, you may still have a cause of action for infringement, but you'll be limited to injunctive relief (meaning that the violator can be prohibited from using your copyrighted work) and/or actual damages—i.e., the amount of money you have lost because of the violator's actions. But proving actual damages can be difficult, especially in the relatively new area of electronic rights.

How do I register my work?

You can register unpublished work at any time; once it's published, you have three months in which to register it. That time period is retroactive, meaning that if you register within those three months, you're protected back to the date of publication. Currently it costs $30 to register work with the U.S. Copyright Office, but you can include more than one piece of writing on the same application. Published or unpublished work created in the same calendar year can be registered under one application as long as it's grouped together. (For more information about copyright registration procedures, visit the Copyright Office Web site at www.loc.gov/copyright; forms are available at www.loc.gov/copyright/forms/)

What Rights Are You Selling?

When you create a written work, you own a "bundle of rights," including the right to reproduce and sell the work in every conceivable kind of media. A brief run-down on some of the rights publishers commonly ask for:

First North American serial rights—this is the right to publish the story for the first time in a North American magazine; magazines often purchase first N.A. serial rights along with other (i.e., electronic) rights.

Electronic rights—the right to publish, disseminate, and store your article electronically (such as on a Web site or in an online database); more publishers are insisting on electronic rights, although many writers ask for additional compensation for these rights.

All rights—what it sounds like. The publisher buys all rights to the piece; bad news for writers because it prevents you from reselling the story later.

Work-for-hire—technically, it means the publisher owns the copyright to the piece, which by definition includes all rights. Again, this is bad news for writers because you're giving up all rights to the story.

Reprint rights (also called second rights)—the right to publish an article after it has already been published elsewhere. You can offer reprint or second rights as many times as you like to increase the amount you make from one particular story.

Exclusive rights—many publishers will ask for exclusive rights to the story for a period of time like 90 days or 6 months. You're prohibited from reprinting or otherwise offering the story to any other publishers during the exclusivity period.

Locate Potential Markets

Since you're writing for publication, your next step is to determine which markets may be right for your work. This book lists thousands of markets for nonfiction books, novels, short stories, articles, essays, and poetry. While reviewing guidelines is helpful, it's no substitute for actually looking at books, magazines, newspapers, or Web sites themselves to get a better feel for the kind of material they publish.

The type of market you're pitching to will determine your approach. Here's a quick rundown on potential markets:

Magazines

Thousands of magazines purchase freelance work. Consumer magazines are those you can find on the newsstands; trade publications are aimed at people in a particular industry or profession and are often available by subscription only. With magazine articles, you usually send a query letter first, and then write the piece after you receive an assignment. (Or an editor may offer to look at the piece "on spec," or on speculation, meaning that he's willing to read it with no guarantees of purchasing it.) Essays and humorous pieces are the exceptions to the rule—with them, you send in the completed work with a brief cover letter introducing it.

Newspapers

Newspapers are a great place for new writers to gather writing experience and gain clips. Most local publications pay modestly (ranging from $5-10 to $125 for features), but they're often looking for freelancers, or "stringers," and it's a good way to hone your reporting and writing skills. Call your local newspaper with a list of story ideas and express your interest in freelancing for the publication. (Ask the editor if she's on deadline before you start your spiel.) She may want you to write about an idea you've pitched or send you out to cover another story.

Books

If you want to publish a novel, you'll want to have the manuscript completed before you start looking for a publisher or agent. (Many larger publishers only want "agented submissions," while smaller publishers are more likely to look at manuscripts sent directly from writers.) Depending on the publisher or agent, you may send a query letter; a query letter with a synopsis or outline; or a synopsis and the first two or three chapters of your manuscript.

With nonfiction books, you usually write a book proposal designed to sell the editor or agent on your idea before you complete the entire manuscript. You may use a query letter and/or the proposal when pitching an editor or agent.

Web sites

With Web sites, you'll make your approach via e-mail. Depending on the site, you may send a query or the completed manuscript. Many Web sites don't pay for submissions and many more pay very little, so you may want to make online publishing your last resort.

Corporate/business writing

Writing for businesses gives you a chance to sell your writing and "publish" your work. Unless you have a copywriting background, however, you'll probably want to read up on sales writing techniques. For example, you'll need to know the difference between a feature and a benefit and how to write customer oriented copy before your take on your first gig.

The Copywriter's Handbook (Henry Holt, 1985) and *Secrets of a Freelance Writer: How to Make $85,000 a Year* (Henry Holt, 1997), both by Robert Bly, cover the basics of writing pieces like brochures, ads, and sales letters and include suggestions on marketing your services and running your freelance business; *The Well-Fed Writer: Financial Self-Sufficiency as a Freelance Writer in Six Months or Less* by Peter Bowerman (Fanove Publishing, 2000) is another excellent resource.

Analyzing Markets

When looking for potential markets, consider their guidelines. First stop: this book. Many publishers now have writers' guidelines available online; you can also obtain a copy of guidelines by sending a SASE (self-addressed stamped envelope) to the magazine or book publisher and requesting them.

Guidelines in hand, you should also consider these factors when analyzing potential markets:

- What type of material do they accept?
- How many words do they want?
- Who's their audience? (This is particularly important with magazines, which tend to have a specific readership in mind.)
- How do they want you to submit material? For example, a nonfiction book publisher may want a book proposal as opposed to a full-length manuscript; a magazine may specifically request query letters, not completed articles.

• What do they pay for material?
• What's their response time?
When you're starting out, keep all your market information in one place. Then you'll have it to refer to when you're preparing your work for submission.

Submission Samples

Magazine query

While some magazines will accept completed manuscripts, most prefer query letters. A query introduces your idea, demonstrates why readers of the publication will be interested in the story, outlines how you'll approach the story, and convinces the editor that you're uniquely qualified to write the piece. Note: Many magazines accept queries by e-mail, but if you e-mail a query, include it in the body of the message, not as an attachment.

A sample query appears below. Note that the query:

• Catches the editor's attention with a first-person anecdotal lead in the first two paragraphs.
• Demonstrates why readers of the magazine will be interested in the idea in paragraph #3 by including the fact that 4 out 5 Americans experience back pain.
• Describes the approach the writer will take with the story, the type of experts that will be interviewed, and a possible sidebar in paragraph #4.
• Demonstrates familiarity with the market (by mentioning the "Physical Health" section of the magazine) and highlights the writer's relevant writing qualifications (and here, the writer's personal experience will bring a unique perspective to the piece).

February 12, 2002

Ms. Erin Eagan
Managing Editor
Bally Total Fitness
RB Publishing Inc.
2424 American Lane
Madison, WI 53704

Dear Ms. Eagan:
As a long-time runner, I compete in a half-dozen races every year. Last March, I signed up for one of the first 5Ks of the season. It was a perfect Sunday spring morning, clear, cool, and windless, and I was rested, fit, and ready to race. Until I pinned on my race number, stretched,

and bent over to tie my shoe just before the race—and felt a flash of pain streak up my back. I straightened up to discover that running was out of the question—I could barely walk and even a slow jog brought tears to my eyes. My race was over before it had begun.

After spending the rest of the day alternating between ice packs and heating pads, I still hadn't improved. I made an appointment with a sports medicine specialist Monday morning and explained what had happened. "It's not fair!" I cried. "I could see if I was overweight or stressed or was lifting something wrong. But I didn't do anything!"

Yet my doc told me that this kind of injury isn't unusual, even in fit men and women. No matter how healthy you are, a back injury can occur at any time, and more than 80% of Americans will experience back pain at least once in their lives. Happily, with the right drugs, rest, and gentle stretches—not to mention a few massages—my back is now on the mend. Now I'm determined to not let another back injury sideline me. I'm religiously performing my back exercises and am going to incorporate regular stretching into my routine as well.

"Back to Basics. Reduce Your Risk of Injury" will explain why back injuries are so common and describe how readers can avoid them and maintain back flexibility and strength. I'll interview respected physicians and sports medicine experts about prevention and treatment options including stress reduction techniques (stress appears to contribute to and aggravate back injuries); a possible sidebar might list simple back exercises to do as "preventive maintenance." While I estimate 1,200 words for this story, that's flexible depending on your needs.

Interested in this topic for your "Physical Health" section? I'm a full-time freelancer who's written about health, fitness, and nutrition for magazines including *Fitness, Shape, Self, Oxygen, Energy for Women, Redbook, Family Circle, Marie Claire*, and *Woman's Day*; clips are enclosed.

Let me know if you have any questions about this story idea; I look forward to hearing from you soon.

Very truly yours,
Kelly James-Enger

Magazine cover letter

If you're submitting a completed piece—say an essay, a humorous piece, a poem, or an article that's previously been published—a simple cover letter will suffice. You can use a brief lead and include information about where the piece has been published before:

March 19, 1999

Ms. Lynn Varacalli
Editor-in-Chief
Woman's Own
Harris Publications, Inc.
1115 Broadway, 8th Floor
New York, NY 10010

Dear Ms. Varacalli:
So you'd love to lose that last five pounds before summer . . . but you can't stick to a diet. Your best friend, on the other hand, gets so stressed at work that she actually forgets to eat lunch. Why? Because what you eat, and why, and when are all heavily influenced by your "eating personality." Want insight into your eating habits? Take the ten-question quiz contained in "What's Your Eating Personality?" for a better understanding of your unique food behavior.

Offered [Kelly, do you mean interested?] in reprint rights for this story? "What's Your Eating Personality?" was originally published in the March/April, 1999 issue of *Fit*; a copy is enclosed.

Let me know if you're interested in purchasing reprint rights to this story for *Woman's Own*. Thank you for your time; I look forward to hearing from you soon.

Very truly yours,
Kelly James-Enger

Nonfiction book letter

For a nonfiction book, you'll want to describe what makes your book unique, demonstrate that there's a market for it, and mention your relevant qualifications, regardless of whether you're sending it to an agent or an editor. If you can, demonstrate familiarity with the agent or editor's work. Mentioning a book he or she has published or represented or using a referral (if you have one) is a good way to start.

Note that this query:

• Explains why the agent is being contacted.
• Describes the idea behind the book and proves that there's a market for it with relevant statistics.
• Outlines what types of information the book will include.
• Briefly summarizes the writer's unique qualifications.

July 21, 2000

Laurie Harper
The Sebastian Agency
172 East Sixth Street, Suite 2005
St. Paul, MN 55101

Dear Ms. Harper:

I've heard good things about you from fellow ASJA member Tina Tessina and am writing to query you about a nonfiction book proposal you may be interested in:

Falling in love is the easy part—it's the day-to-day challenges that really put a relationship to the test. But while maintaining a strong, loving bond is difficult for even the most committed couples, those in long-distance relationships face an even greater challenge.

According to recent statistics, at least 1 million Americans currently have commuter marriages and maintain two separate households. Millions more—including the more than 1,300,000 men and women in the U.S. armed services— face extended time away from each other because of jobs that require frequent travel. And every fall as students leave to attend college and graduate school, hundreds of thousands of dating and engaged couples face the prospect of long-distance love as well.

Any couple faced with a long-distance relationship faces a multitude of concerns. Will distance threaten their relationship? How will they maintain intimacy? What kind of financial burden will it cause? How will it affect the couple's future? Is infidelity more likely? What if children are involved? How do they know if this is the right decision? How will they cope with the inevitable stress of being apart?

My book, *Make the Heart Grow Fonder: How to Survive—and Thrive in—Your Long-Distance Relationship,* will answer all of the questions and concerns that these couples face. *Heart* will include the experiences of hundreds of long-distance relationship "veterans" as well as expert advice from psychologists and relationship experts. The book will also feature quizzes and activities for couples to use to determine whether a long-distance relationship is a healthy option for their relationship as well as ways to cope with loneliness and separation, tips on dealing with the financial burden these relationships can cause, and advice for parents who want to maintain a close relationship with their children regardless of physical distance. *Heart* will also look at the reasons for the growing trend in long-distance relationships and report on recent research on the factors that influence the success and stability of such relationships.

This down-to-earth, anecdote-filled book will be both a source of strength and encouragement as well as a wealth of practical information for the millions of people facing this increasingly common challenge. As a fulltime freelance journalist and a veteran of three long-distance relationships, I can bring a unique perspective to this timely subject.

I hope you'll be in interested reviewing my book proposal for *Heart*— please let me know if I may send it to you immediately. Thank you very much for your time; I look forward to hearing from you soon.

Very truly yours,
Kelly James-Enger

Nonfiction book proposal

If an editor or agent is interested in your nonfiction book idea, most will ask to see a completed book proposal. Proposals differ in length and format, but the typical one sets out the premise of the book, provides an outline of the material that will be covered, lists competing titles and explains how your book differs from the competition, offers marketing and promotion ideas, describes your relevant background and experience, and includes one or more sample chapters. The purpose of the proposal is to convince the publisher that the book will sell enough copies for it to make a profit. It will also help you research and organize your material before you begin the book itself.

There are several excellent books to help guide you through the process, including Elizabeth Lyon's *Nonfiction Book Proposals Anybody Can Write: How to Get a Contract and Advance Before Writing your Book* (Blue Heron, 2000) and *How to Write a Book Proposal* by Michael Larsen (Writer's Digest Books, 1997) and *Write the Perfect Book Proposal: 10 Proposals That Sold and Why* (John Wiley and Sons, 1993). Before you start on the proposal itself, research the market to see what other titles are available on your subject; for a speedy search, type in some keywords on either www.amazon.com or www.barnesandnoble.com to see how many books you find.

While this will give you a general idea of what's out there, you'll want to read the titles that seem closest to yours. That way you can briefly describe them and explain how your book is better than/different from these titles; this "competition analysis" is important. Another critical part of the proposal is the marketing/promotion section. What will you, as the author, do to promote and publicize the book once it comes out? Think beyond author signings and media interviews—the more creative you are here, the better.

In addition to an outline of the book itself, the proposal should include chapter summaries and at least one complete chapter. The proposal should also have a brief "about the author" section that highlights your relevant experience, and a paragraph describing the format of the book, i.e., number of pages, possible appendixes, and the like. If this is your first book, you may also want to include clips with the proposal.

Novel query letter

With book-length fiction, most editors and agents want to see a query letter first. Then they'll ask for a synopsis and sample chapters or the complete manuscript. With a novel query, you want to sell your book idea and give the editor a feel for your writing style. The query below:

- Introduces the "hook" of the book at the beginning of the letter.
- Gives a brief overview of the main characters and the book's plot.
- Explains what type of novel it is and the likely readership.
- Briefly mentions the writer's background.

August 16, 2002

Mr. John Scognamiglio
Kensington Books
850 Third Avenue
New York, NY 10022

Dear Mr. Scognamiglio:

Have you ever gotten the Vibe? You know, that feeling when you meet a woman, and you know that you're attracted to each other?

Kate, 28, has based her dating life on the Vibe. If there's a Vibe there, the guy is worth pursuing—it not, forget it. The trouble is that the too-beautiful-for-her Andrew just dumped her, and now she can hardly fit into her favorite jeans. And she hates her job, but everyone keeps telling her how great it is to be a lawyer. Yeah, right.

At least she has Tracy, her best friend from law school. Both live in Chicago's up-and-coming Lakeview neighborhood. Tracy's gorgeous, smart, and has a great job, a great apartment, and a great live-in boyfriend, Tom, to go along with it all. She also has an eating disorder she's managed to keep secret from even her closest friend. Tracy doesn't believe in the Vibe—until she experiences it for the first time, and it turns her life upside down.

Will Kate find lasting love, meaningful work, and be able to squeeze back into her clothes? Will Tracy give up the man who loves her to experience sexual fulfillment—and come to grips with what she's doing to her body and her spirit? *Did You Get the Vibe?* explores the lives of these two best friends as they love, work, diet, laugh, and bond over their boyfriends, jobs, diets, and sex lives. Readers of women's contemporary fiction will enjoy their stories, and relate to their experiences, struggles, and insights.

Did You Get the Vibe? is 78,855 words and is my first novel. I've been a fulltime freelance journalist for the past five years. My work has appeared in more than 40 magazines including *Marie Claire, Woman's Day, Family Circle, Self*, and *Redbook*; I'm also a contributing editor at *Oxygen, The Writer*, and *For the Bride*. My first nonfiction book, *Ready, Aim, Specialize! How to Create Your Writing Specialty and Make More Money* will be published by The Writer Books in the winter of 2003. I'm also a frequent speaker at writers' conferences, and not surprisingly, a big believer in the Vibe.

Please let me know if you're interested in seeing a synopsis and three chapters or the complete manuscript of *Vibe*. I'm contacting a handful of editors and agents who I think might be interested in this book, and hope to find a home for it soon.

Thank you very much for your time.

Sincerely,
Kelly James-Enger

Part 3: Surviving as a Freelancer

Now you've been introduced to the basics of submitting work for publication. That's not all there is to it, though. As a freelancer, you'll need to know how to overcome rejection, stay motivated, meet deadlines, and overcome writer's anxiety, among other things.

Set your own deadlines

As a new writer, you may not be working on anyone's schedule but your own. However, the time may come when an editor gives you a deadline you'll have to meet. Get used to writing on deadline by setting your own targets for the writing that you're working on. If you're working on a big project, like a book, break it into smaller chunks—say, chapter by chapter—and set deadlines for each one, plus a deadline for completing the whole thing.

Become a sponge

In the same way you want to gather information about potential markets, you want to gather information about the type of writing you're interested in. This book contains articles about a variety of types of writing, but you may find it helpful to read books specifically devoted to craft, and check out *The Writer* or other magazines dedicated to writing and publishing. You'll improve your own work—and your chances of getting published—in the process.

Overcome rejection

Trust me, you will get rejected. All writers do. The first step to coping with rejection is expecting it. That *doesn't* mean that you shouldn't have faith in your work. It does mean that you that realize your odds of having work turned down are high, especially if you're a new writer. By remembering that it's normal, you ease its sting.

Second, treat rejections as opportunities. When you receive a rejection, or "bong," act immediately. If you have another idea that's right for the market, start your new query or cover letter with language like, "Thank you very much for your response to [the essay or query]. While I'm sorry you can't use it at this time, I have another idea for you to consider…" and mail it to the market. In the meantime, tweak the original query if necessary and resubmit it to another publication or agent. Your work won't sell sitting on your hard drive. You've got to get it out there.

And don't take it personally. Any rejection you receive is only of that particular piece by that particular editor at that particular publisher. It's not a reflection on you or your abilities as a writer. The timing may be wrong, the editor may not care for the idea, or she may already have something similar in the works. A rejection can even be a positive sign if the editor took time to write a personal note like "Sorry, not quite right for us" or "Nice essay, but we're overstocked." Instead of stewing over *why* your work was turned down, find another market for it—taking action is the best way to overcome rejection.

Calm writer's anxiety

Call it writer's block, performance anxiety, or plain old-fashioned self-doubt—every writer suffers from it at one time or another. Anxiety is common, normal, and part of the writing process for all of us. When you're beginning work on a piece, some nervousness is normal and to be expected. If you're afraid you don't know enough to write what you intend to write, then you'll naturally be anxious. Maybe you don't have a handle on your subject yet. But if your research is almost complete and you're still too anxious to write, your fear may be due to a number of factors.

Are you afraid to offend someone? Do you continually worry that what you write isn't good enough? That means your internal censor is at work—the nasty little critic that's always telling you you're not good enough.

Perfectionism is another major source of writing-related anxiety. If you expect your first draft to be perfect, you're setting yourself up for disappointment. Good writing is rewriting—and sometimes rewriting again (and again). Give these techniques a try next time you're feeling anxious, stuck, or blocked:

• Schedule your writing. Having a regular writing habit works for nearly everyone. You'll start training your brain to turn on and get creative every morning at 6 a.m. or each night at 9:00 p.m. Instead of worrying about when you'll write, you simply stick to the schedule.

• Just do it. Sometimes you just need to write. You can't write and angst at the same time.

• Switch gears. Do something different—vacuum, walk, read, do a crossword puzzle. Or write something else for a while.

• Break it up. When an assignment appears overwhelming, you're likely to feel anxious. Break the work up into smaller steps—conducting research, doing interviews, transcribing notes, writing a draft, and so on—and focus on one step at a time.

• Move your body. Nothing conquers writers' anxiety like physical exercise. Take brief movement breaks away from the computer even if it's only five minutes to get up, stretch, and take some deep breaths. You'll feel calmer and more able to focus on your work.

• Be gentle. Writers are often their own harshest critics. Be nice to yourself. If you picture an audience for your work, think of someone who gets it—your best friend, spouse, or someone who thinks like you do.

Stay connected

Just because writing is a solitary activity doesn't mean you have to go it alone. In fact, hooking up with other writers can help you find new markets for your work, improve your chances of publication, and stay motivated through the tough times. If you have friends who write, you can ask for help with a particularly tricky lead or use them as a sounding board for story ideas. You also have someone to share the inevitable ups (you got the assignment!) and the downs (after three months, the publisher turned down your book proposal) of freelancing.

Your freelancing friends can also introduce you to markets you may not have considered for your work. No matter how many hours you devote to market research, you can't keep up on all the magazines, newspapers, and Web sites that might be interested in your work. Sharing information with other writers about possible markets can give you the inside track into netting assignments.

So where do you find your fellow writers?

• Check with your local library, Borders, or Barnes and Noble. Many libraries and bookstores have writers' groups already in place; if not, offer to help create one.

• Go back to school. Community colleges and local universities offer a variety of writing-related classes. Look for workshop-type classes that will give you a chance to get to know your fellow students.

• Get online. There's a number of e-mail lists, electronic bulletin boards. and newsgroups where you can meet other writers and share information. Do a www.google.com search or visit   http://freelancewrite.about.com/careers/freelancewrite/cs/newsgroupslists/index.htm for a list of links.

• Join up. Consider joining a writer's organization like the National Writers' Union (www.nwu.org), Society of Children's Book Writers & Illustrators (http://www.scbwi.org/) or attend a writers' conference (check out the online directory at http://writing.shawguides.com/ to search for conferences and workshops). You'll meet writers who share your interests, hone your skills, and learn more about the publishing process as well.

Stay motivated

Writing well is a demanding job, and sending out work and getting published, even tougher. The writers who succeed are resilient, dedicated, and more than a little bit stubborn. Those qualities will help you survive the ups and downs of freelancing.

One of the most effective ways to stay motivated is to set two types of goals for your writing. Set an outcome goal and then design production goals to get you there. An outcome goal is often what you're striving for in terms of publishing your work. It might be "I'll publish my work in a national magazine" or "I'll write and sell my novel." A production goal, on the other hand, is a small, measurable, specific goal that will help you reach your overall or outcome goal—like "I will send out three queries each month" or "I will write for 30 minutes every day."

When you're writing for publication, you need both. The production goals, although seemingly minor, will help keep you on target to reach your overall or outcome goals. They also give you a way to track your progress. After six months of working on your novel, for example, you may not have achieved your goal of publishing it (yet), but you will have met your production goals of writing every day. That kind of success helps keep you on track—while making you a better writer and improving your chance of getting published in the process.

Take the next step

You may feel nervous, maybe even terrified, the first time you mail off an essay or hit "send" to e-mail an article query. That's normal. Remember, though, to become a published writer you have to take the first step and actually submit work to a publication. Chances are slim that you'll run into an editor at the grocery store, who after staring at you for several minutes, will approach you with the words, "You appear to be a writer of some talent. Would you like to write for me?" You might laugh at the idea, but many writers secretly hope that they won't have to make the effort to publish their work. They'll know someone, or meet someone who knows someone (who knows someone) and magically be "discovered."

Hey, you can be discovered, but it won't be in the grocery, dry cleaners, or even the bookstore. You'll be discovered by making yourself visible—by honing your writing skills, researching the best markets for your work, and getting your work in front of editors. There's no mystery to how unpublished writers become published writers—it simply takes time, work, and a refusal to give up. But the reward of seeing your first byline (and your tenth, and your fiftieth) makes it well worth it.

SECTION ONE

Professional Basics

KEEP IN WRITING SHAPE

10 commandments for getting your work published

by Michael P. Geffner

Every successful writer I ever met, I'd ultimately find out, had, at some critical point, a mentor. Usually an older writer whom they greatly admired, who not only freely offered advice on the art and craft but helped navigate them through the tricky ins and outs of the business. Strangely, my mentor wasn't a writer at all. He was, of all things, a retired salesman for *The Wall Street Journal,* a tall, white-haired man in his 60s named Al.

For years, all over Manhattan, Al gave free lectures on how to effectively find work in the increasingly competitive marketplace. While hunting down a couple of research books in the New York Public Library one day, I accidentally ran into one of his talks. It was infinitely eye-opening. I was immediately sucked in by the core of his philosophy: that the secret to finding work, no matter what type, lay in nothing but simple sales techniques in aggressively selling yourself.

Before I knew it, I was following Al everywhere he spoke, four days a week, mornings and afternoons, uptown and downtown, East Side and West, to libraries and churches. Traipsing through rain, sleet, and snow. I just couldn't get enough of him. His approach was so novel, and it made so much sense. All I had to do was translate it into the business of freelance writing. That ended up being so incredibly easy, I remember letting out a slight giggle.

The results of my initial efforts came shockingly fast and were nothing less than overwhelming. Like a huge wave. Within two months, I'd attracted so much work I was actually forced to turn things away.

Its magic continues to this day—the gift that keeps on giving. I'm always working on two assignments at a time, with a third waiting not far away in the wings.

When I asked Al how I could ever thank him for what he taught me, if I could repay him in some way, he threw me a gentle, if not embarrassed, half-smile. He said he didn't want a thing. "The best way to thank me," he said, "is to pass it on—just pass it on."

And so here, in these pages, all these years later, Al-inspired, I am passing it on.

1. Network.

You need to seek out contacts, preferably the power brokers at the top of the masthead or high-level editors, and cultivate them as "allies." Networking is a must-have tool in your writing existence. If you ignore this aspect of the business, believe me, you'll suffer the consequences. I hear all the time from writers, "But I don't like to mingle. I'm too shy. I'm not a good talker." My response is matter-of-fact: "This is the way the game is played. If you don't want to play, don't expect to win." Which means: Don't expect editors to come to *you*. They won't. Like Mohammed, you need to go to the mountain. I don't care how much talent you *think* you have. It's not enough, all by itself, to "make your career." And remember: If you're not cultivating contacts, some other writer out there is.

2. Learn to work under deadline pressure.

Deadlines are what separate the professional from the hobbyist. Pros can't wait for inspiration to propel their creativity. They write because they have to, because someone on the other end is waiting for their work. They write all hours of the day and night. I've tortured myself over the years to hit deadlines, from five-minute ones to monthlies. That's the nature of the beast. It's where the tough get tougher. So either get assigned to something with a due date or create an artificial one. If nothing else, it's good practice to see how well you function in such a situation. You may actually find that you're not cut out to write professionally, that in reality, you're merely a dabbler. Not that there's anything wrong with that. It's just good to know where you stand.

3. Build a portfolio.

Before you start hitting the major newspapers/magazines/publishers, you will need some clips. Mind you, I'm not even remotely suggesting that you work for free. I'm really not. In fact, I insist on writers *always* getting paid at least something for their hard work.

What I am saying is this: You can't expect to be published in *The New York Times* or sell a book for a $400,000 advance or get a major assignment from *Sports Illustrated* or *People Magazine* with little or no experience. You must pay your dues, as in any other profession. You won't go from singing in the shower to headlining in Vegas. That's not realistic, and you'll be hitting your head against a brick wall if you try.

Instead, move up the publishing ladder a step at a time. Before going for the majors, get five to eight sizable clips together, ones that show off your writing.

Begin with local newspapers, small magazines, or trade publications. Make your "bones" there, where there is less competition and where you'll have the freedom and opportunity to develop your own voice. And consider each story you write an audition for something better and higher paying. In other words, write the heck out of it. Make it brilliant!

4. Read something every day.

Magazines, newspapers, books. But try to be choosy. Read things written by great writers. If you're a magazine writer, get a copy of *The Best American Magazine Writing 2002*. If you're a sportswriter, pick up *The Best American Sports Writing 2002*. And don't be a passive reader: Analyze what the writer is doing, what the writer does to achieve a certain effect, what the writer does with plot, characters, dialogue, action, and exposition.

Read, read, and read. The theory: Whatever goes into your brain is likely, in time, to find its way out. It's called "filling your cup." By mere osmosis, you'll absorb the craft without even knowing it. Great writing will be inside you, dying to get back out. In pop-psychology parlance, this is called "modeling."

5. Write something every day.

No matter what. Forget that you're tired or don't feel like it. You're supposedly a writer. So write. Don't be a pretender. And don't even think about that dreaded aspect of all things creative: writer's block. If you're convinced you have writer's block, just write about it. Write about why you think you're blocked. Trust me, this'll snap you out of it in a hurry. Remember, all writers, from Tolstoy to Hemingway to Stephen King, have written badly before they wrote well.

6. Make friends with writers.

It'll inspire you to be around other wonderfully creative people and to be able to share ideas back and forth. Seek out happy, positive, and successful writers. Afterward, your energy will fly off the chart.

7. Turn in clean copy.

Make sure you spell correctly and are grammatical in your dealings with editors. I can't tell you how many letters/notes/e-mails I get from "writers" with grossly ungrammatical sentences and a slew of misspellings. I cringe. It turns me off immediately—as I'm sure it would editors. These are the tools of your craft. Learn how to use them—or else. Buy a grammar/spelling book. Get a good "spell/grammar check" computer program. There's no excuse for sloppy English. One misstep can sink your chances of selling a story.

8. Study the publication.

You need to know as much as you can about the editor, magazine, or publishing house before firing off a proposal. The more you know, the more you can "target" your approach. It'll likely also give you a step up on the competition, since most writers don't do this extra homework (at least, they didn't until they read it here). A great example of someone going that extra yard for success is the great golfer Jack Nicklaus. Before playing in tournaments, the "Golden Bear" would arrive in town a few days early just to scout out the course. Taking a golf cart, he'd ride around, jotting down observations and ideas in a small notebook on how to play certain holes. No wonder he won more major tournaments than anyone else did. One time, playing in the Masters, another golfer noticed that Nicklaus looked decidedly perplexed. "What's wrong, Jack?" To which Nicklaus responded, "There's supposed to be a telephone pole there." The pole had been removed a day earlier. Jack knew it was there!

9. Find a mentor.

Someone who's a successful writer can teach you the ropes and keep you from making the same mistakes he or she did—a tour guide to lead you down this dark, mysterious tunnel called the writing business. It'll not only save you a ton of time reaching your goals as a writer, but will also keep you from climbing the wall with frustration. A mentor can be your answer person on all problems.

10. Stay on the case.

Don't be a lazy slug even for a moment. Be relentless in your writing and your search for work. Do something toward furthering your writing career every day. Read a book on writing. Write a pitch letter. Apply for a writing job. Set up a job interview. Write a networking letter. Arrange a meeting with an editor. Read a book by a great writer (not so much for entertainment but analyzing what the author does to achieve a certain effect).

Read articles about the industry (at Inside.com or Mediaweek.com, for example, or in *The New York Observer's* Off the Record column) and general interest magazines where you'd like your work to appear one day.

You need to be proactive and be it daily. Action breeds action! It also adds up: A single "positive" every day builds to 365 in a year!

Bottom line: Fight for your writing dreams with all your might and never let go!

Michael P. Geffner of New York City has been a successful freelance writer for more than 20 years. He is a former Contributing Editor at *Details* and *Maximum Golf*, a Contributing Writer at *The Village Voice* and *The Sporting News*, and a frequent contributor to *Texas Monthly*. His work has appeared in *USA Today*, *Gear*, *Los Angeles Magazine*, *Men's Health*, and in three editions of *The Best American Sports Writing*. This article is from *The Writer*, January 2003.

A CRITIQUE GROUP THAT WORKS

Four writers share their blueprint for success

by WritersX4

Don't read this article unless you're determined to finish that short story you filed away, the family memoir you promised everyone, or the screenplay you storyboarded months ago. You yearn to write "The End," but it never happens. WritersX4, an Oregon writers group, guarantees that if you implement our critique process, you will become a better writer and find support and camaraderie with your fellow professionals.

Insist on going it alone? There's always spell-check, a dog-eared copy of *The Elements of Style,* and *Roget's Thesaurus* hiding on a shelf somewhere. A reputable book doctor may be hard to find and expensive. Or you might ask your spouse or neighbor to read a troublesome passage and make suggestions—on second thought, don't! There is an easier way.

Critique groups probably existed even before the Declaration of Independence, but most are short-lived or contentious. Members' writing goals may clash, and opinions often can be unfounded and tactless. Meetings become social gatherings where gregarious participants consistently seize the spotlight. Serious writers demand and deserve objective assessment of their work.

Frustrated over half-completed manuscripts and insecure about the quality of our writing, four of us joined forces about three years ago. We realized that in today's marketplace, being a good writer isn't enough. We needed grammar police, objective editing, and unbridled encouragement to make our work the best it could be.

Our backgrounds, publishing credits, and genres are varied. Betty Henshaw has written a memoir and Lucia Smith, women's fiction. Marlene King has finished a religious novel and Richard Boich has written a political thriller. As our well-crafted, well-written, and professionally presented work makes the rounds to editors and agents, we're confident we have a better chance of acceptance than most writers.

To tell you our success stories, let's take you back to the beginning.

Why did you join a critique group?
Marlene: To realize my 35-year dream of writing a particular story, I needed structure and qualified guidance. I understood the benefits of group process, so I began looking for like-minded writers.

Betty: It was clear to me that if I wanted to become a writer and learn more, I had to be willing to put my work out there for others to see and hear.

Lucia: I longed to hear a reader say, "Yes, I've felt that way. I know what your character is experiencing." I needed input about whether my writing was amateurish or editor-ready before I mailed the query.

Dick: I wanted someone to edit my grammar, but found that it's priceless to have knowledgeable people identify problems *before* my manuscript is submitted to an agent or editor.

How does your critique group work?
Dick: Initially, we discussed our individual writing needs, considered key questions about how to formulate the group, and decided on various guidelines. (See "Our Ten Commandments" sidebar.)

An Author's Bill of Rights: The right of the author to accept, reject, or incorporate the fair and respectful opinions of others regarding his or her manuscript shall not be violated.

Who should be in the group?
Dick: Imagine that you're recruiting employees. Interview them as if you were hiring them—in a way, you are! Are they serious writers? Will their goals be compatible with yours? Do you want them in the writing foxhole with you?

Betty: Go where the writers are. Check locally for a writing class or attend a writer's conference. Run an ad in your local newspaper and ask at the library.

How big should the group be?
Marlene: Four members are ideal; that allows adequate feedback time for each member at the meeting. Factor in the time commitment to evaluate others' work between sessions, as well as to polish and produce your own material. Group size is crucial, so consider it carefully.

How often should you meet?

Dick: A lot depends on the objectives of your group. We find biweekly works best, but are flexible about meeting more often when personal deadlines demand it. We meet mid-morning and spend up to an hour per manuscript. And we show up *on time*.

What about the location?

Lucia: My house, because I'm centrally located. I don't play hostess, but provide a clean table for our brown bag lunches. Don't choose a noisy place to meet. Explore your community—libraries, or spacious bookstores, even rest homes.

What limits should you set?

Dick: Establish guidelines based on the time needed for editing the manuscripts at home. We give each other about 10 pages each session. I spend about an hour's homework per manuscript for reading and noting suggestions and corrections, adding up to about three hours total. Our meeting is an important appointment; we don't often call in sick and we always come prepared. There's no limit to what we can learn or how much we enjoy doing it.

What about the process?

Lucia: The critique method is the key. Each member comments about the manuscript at hand. What did I like about it? What worked is as important as what didn't. Were the characters' motivations compatible with their dialogue, actions? Was the voice intrusive, the point of view effective? Was the description vivid, the language clichéd, or the content compelling? And there's always grammar—it's a tedious but gratifying exercise. And I trust my colleagues endure the same process with my manuscript.

What is your commitment?

Betty: The four of us have been together for more than three years. We put our time and effort into each manuscript and it comes back to us in the form of honest, serious criticism for our own work.

Critique groups have been around for many years. How is yours different?

Dick: It's word-by-word, line-by-line, red-pencil editing, three times over. Wouldn't you like to have an objective review of every sentence you wrote? To hear why someone liked a segment or why a change was suggested?

Lucia: I'm a veteran of many critique groups. Some do not pre-distribute manuscripts for review; others don't pass around copies at meeting time but depend on the author to read several pages and expect the audience to render spontaneous and intelligent feedback. Attendance is inconsistent and critiquing is often heartless and hurtful. These formats work for some, but I appreciate that WritersX4 knows my project and is genuinely dedicated to my success.

Marlene: We don't appoint a leader or facilitator—we take turns allowing for a natural ebb and flow to determine where the work takes us.

How do you handle negative feedback from your peers after working so hard to perfect your writing?

Marlene: I take it in the spirit it is intended. Without criticism, I would never perfect my skills. There are disappointments and frustrations, but I know my peers are critiquing my work, not me.

Dick: It's tough to see a piece you thought you had nailed covered with blood-red ink. But if my group didn't like it, chances are an agent wouldn't either.

Lucia: It's a therapeutic exercise for me. As I pass out my manuscript, I'm humble enough to say, "Here's my last chapter, tell me what needs improve-

Our Ten Commandments

I. We commit to the ground rules of the group.

II. We respect the talent, potential, and work-product of fellow writers.

III. We evaluate the manuscript, not the person, with sensitivity and integrity.

IV. We pledge a thorough reading and a line-by-line edit.

V. We support our fellow writers' efforts to reach their goals.

VI. We labor to become professional writers.

VII. We critique with an attitude of giving; receiving is the natural byproduct.

VIII. We accept feedback in the spirit of learning and improving our craft.

IX. We appreciate the courage it takes to share written work.

X. We never show up without our sense of humor.

ment." I'm also thinking, "Here's my best effort and I dare you to find something wrong with it." I'm always surprised. I can be defensive, stubborn, even argumentative. If my "truth-sayers" didn't get my point or agree with the way I stated it, I'd be a fool not to reconsider or rework. The choice is mine, but it won't be a blind one.

Betty: The comments of my peers are meant to help me become a better writer. I am free to take or leave their suggestions, but most of the time, I take them.

How can you be an expert in someone else's genre?

Marlene: The answer is: We're not! The genre is not the important issue; good writing is, and it crosses all lines of subject matter. I think critiquing outside of your genre can be more valuable, focusing on the mechanics of language and the intent of the writer.

Dick: Our group is not about genres, but about helping each other write more effectively. Authors of romance, sci-fi, and thrillers all have challenges with dialogue, points of view, tense, and character development. We focus on those fundamentals.

You've each finished a project since you've been working together and started new ones. What's the secret to your success?

Betty: This group has kept me from giving up. Last year, I visited my home town, where my memoir takes place, and stood on a bridge watching muddy water swirl beneath me and flow down around the bend; it reminded me of how much murky writing my group has helped me wash away.

Dick: I don't think a critique group can help anyone if the person doesn't have a passion to write better. Success results when persistent people form a team and create a synergy that fosters mentoring and encouragement.

Marlene: The commitment to each writer's project, and respecting and practicing the principles of our Ten Commandments, has engendered everyone's success.

How do you keep it fresh? How do you handle writer's block? How do you deal with rejections?

Lucia: A show-and-tell period opens all of our meetings. Our agenda is always full. There's marketing news, grammar, a book report, community events, writing exercises, invited guests. When I want to wallow in self-pity, my fellow writers insist that I keep on writing. After all, we're on the road to publication. We'd better be ready when we get there.

Dick: We take time to give personal updates on our various projects. Frequently, the discussion becomes a pep talk, which energizes everyone.

Marlene: Our sense of humor is legion! We have fun and appreciate the process!

You're cheerleaders for critique groups. What has your group done for you?

Dick: It's an advanced class in better writing, but positive reinforcement is the main thing. Someone always gives me the verbal transfusion I need to get back to my keyboard. My polished 80,000-word manuscript is the result.

Betty: I owe so much to the group. Dick taped a PBS documentary because he thought it might be helpful to my memoir, and the information in it was invaluable. That's just one example of our support for one another.

Marlene: Being a member of this group has made my novel a *fait accompli*. I learned more than I ever would have on my own.

Lucia: Each meeting is like a mini writer's conference. I'm enthused about my own potential, and in sharing my expertise, I always take away more than I give.

Any last words or comments?

Marlene: The personality mix of a group is vital. Once the right chemistry and ground rules are established, it can be the best experience of your writing career. Three other compatible people are out there just waiting for you!

Betty: I'm a much better writer and feel ready to talk with an agent. Without Lucia, Dick, and Marlene, I couldn't have done it.

Lucia: Support group or writing seminar, whatever you call it, WritersX4 works! Remember these words when you see our names on book jackets.

Writing can be a lonely profession fraught with insecurity and tunnel vision. When we send out our heartfelt words to powerful strangers in the publishing world, whose first priority is the bottom line, the odds are never in our favor, so why do it alone? Try a critique group that *works*. You'll finish that project and become part of a professional network. We guarantee you'll find out what a good writer you can be.

WritersX4 is an Oregon writers group. Members include Richard Boich, a retired banking executive, who has completed his first novel, a contemporary thriller. Betty Henshaw has published newspaper articles and spent several years compiling her family history to complete a Dust Bowl memoir. Marlene King has had several essays published in the *Chocolate for a Woman's Soul* series and is a columnist for *Dream Network Journal*. Lucia Smith has published two children's books and several short stories and is writing her third novel. All four live in Oregon. This article is from *The Writer*, October 2002.

TOP 5 FICTION MISTAKES

Editors tell you how to get published

by Moira Allen

Ask most fiction editors how to avoid rejection, and you'll hear the same thing: Read the guidelines. Review the publication. Don't send a science fiction story to a literary magazine, and vice versa. Don't send a 10,000-word manuscript to a magazine that never publishes anything longer than 5,000 words. Spell-check. Proofread. Check your grammar. Format your manuscript correctly. Be professional. Failure to observe these basics, many editors say, accounts for more than 80 percent of all short fiction rejections.

But what if you've done all that, and your stories are still coming back with polite form-rejection letters? I surveyed dozens of fiction editors of publications ranging from traditional literary journals to flash-fiction e-zines about what types of problems resulted in the *other* 20 percent of rejections. They cited the following problems with stories that meet all the basic requirements—but still don't quite make the grade—and suggested solutions.

1. Bad beginnings

"A story needs a beginning that grabs the reader," says Lida Quillen, publisher of the digital journal *Twilight Times*. If you can't hook the editor with your opening line or first paragraph, the editor will assume that it won't hook the reader either. David Switzer, editor of *Challenging Destiny*, looks for "something new on the first page. Something unique about the character or situation that makes me want to continue reading."

One reason for weak beginnings is "taking too long to cut to the chase," according to Diane Walton, editor of *On Spec*. "When the writer spends three pages explaining the entire history of the planet, we know we are in trouble."

A story, however, must do more than begin well; it must also fulfill the promise of that beginning. "Some new fiction writers create a very good beginning, but then don't fulfill the expectations of the reader," says Quillen. "As a writer, you want to raise the reader's expectations, create a need to know what happens next, and then satisfactorily fulfill that need." Once you've "grabbed" the editor with your first sentence, your second has to keep him reading—right on to the end of the story. Andrew Gulli, an editor at *The Strand Magazine,* says, "The writers I resent are those who hook you with the first sentence, then the whole story turns out to be boring. Often, writers will write something with a beginning and an ending. There is no middle."

Solution. Be sure that your story begins where it should. Does it begin with action or conflict that draws the reader into the story? Or have you provided too much background, character description, or other information that may seem important to you but could be bogging down your readers? Opening with a bang, however, doesn't necessarily mean launching your story with an adrenaline-pumping action scene involving characters your readers haven't even met or care about yet. If you find that you have to backtrack to explain your opening paragraph (i.e., to account for who your characters are and how they got there), you may have begun your story too far into the action or conflict. Back up and start your story where it *really* begins.

2. Wordiness

Another pervasive problem cited by editors was the use of too many words. Editors advise that new writers cut their stories by 10 to 50 percent. "The most obvious error we encounter in fiction is overwriting," say Anthony Brown and Darrin English of the online *Stickman Review.* "Young writers, full of energy, throw everything and the kitchen sink into their work to impress editors." Excess verbiage can result from several fundamental writing errors:

• *Too many adjectives and adverbs.* If the copy reads: "When the 'yellow, round orb of the sun stealthily and smoothly creeps into the azure blue early morning sky,' one may wonder why the sun didn't simply rise; it would have saved a good deal of trouble for all concerned," says Max Keele, editor of *Fiction Inferno.* If you feel the need to modify every verb with an adverb (or two), or every noun with an adjective, chances are you're not picking the right words to begin with. Look for stronger nouns and verbs that can stand alone.

• *Using big words when simple ones would do just as well.* "To me, 'ascended' sounds inappropriate to describe a man walking up a few steps," says Adam Golaski, editor of *New Genre.* Seeking alternatives to "said" is another common error; too often, characters "expostulate" or "riposte."

• *Too much detail or backstory.* Many writers fall into the trap of trying to add too much detail or description. "Describing the color and length of a protagonist's hair is great if it's relevant; otherwise, it's fluff you can cut," says Don Muchow, editor of the historical science fiction e-zine *Would That It Were.*

SEVEN DEADLY SINS

Several editors had their own pet peeves to share. Here are seven that can speed your story to the rejection pile:

1. *Preachiness.* "Stories that present an obvious moral, without nuances, subtlety, or complexity, are the first to hit the [reject] pile," says Skylar Burris of *Ancient Paths*.

2. *Clichés.* "I actually received a story that began, 'It was a dark, stormy night,' " says Tom Rice of *Elbow Creek Magazine*. "It shows that a writer is not particularly careful with the quality of the story."

3. *Outlandish names.* Don't be cute. "When I see Mercutio or Hezekiah, I drop the story. Write about real people," says Tommy Zurhellen of *Black Warrior Review*.

4. *Lack of knowledge.* "If your story revolves around hacking into computers, it's best that you at least know your way around your own computer," says Rice. "If you are writing a story about the Old West and you want to include an Indian character, make sure that the tribe he/she was from actually existed within the confines of the territory you are using."

5. *Autobiographical stories.* "Leave the baggage in your own house; don't put it in an envelope to send to an editor," says Andrew Gulli of *The Strand Magazine*. "The great writer is the one who, despite having bad parents and despite all the difficulty, is able to create something so completely opposite that it is very believable. It is easier said than done."

6. *Cute titles.* "If we get another title like 'Getting Vanessa' or 'Moving Shane,' we will sue somebody," says Zurhellen. "Don't be cute. Keep it simple and short."

7. *Unprofessional cover letters.* Stick to the pertinent information, says Zurhellen. "Give us your name, some previous pubs, and sign off. Editors don't want to know what the story is about, or how long you worked on it, or what someone semifamous said about your writing, or who rejected your last story." Keep your cover letter to one page.

Make it interesting, says Don Muchow of *Would That It Were*. "I do not like authors who are scared, humble, diffident, or otherwise unsure of themselves. Send me the kind of biographies you'd tell me at a party, not the kind you'd put on your resume. If you don't think you're interesting, no one else will either."

—M.A.

Editors like Walton of *On Spec* deplore "long exposition 'lumps' that stop the action dead in its tracks, so one character can explain to another that their society has been operating in a certain way for centuries, or the long speech where the bad guy explains why he has to kill the good guy."

Solution. Put your story aside for a week after it's finished. Then go back over it and hunt down excess adverbs and adjectives. Add stronger nouns and verbs that can do the job alone. Try trimming your final draft by at least 10 percent.

3. Poor plots

Editors complained of two basic plot problems: Trite, hackneyed plots—or no plot. Ian Randal Strock, editor of *Artemis*, says many of his rejections are the result of "the author sending me a really old, lame idea that's been done to death for decades, and the author hasn't done anything new with it." Editors complain that too many writers seem to derive plots from television rather than real life.

David Ingle, assistant editor of *The Georgia Review*, says that at best, only 10 stories in a thousand that cross his desk manage to escape "the doldrums of convention." The most beautiful prose in the world, he notes, can't compensate for stock characters and plots. "My main gripe is with the so-called 'domestic story'—stories of bad childhoods, bad parents, abusive or straying spouses." He asks writers to consider how to make their stories stand out from the pile on the editor's desk. While some stories have bad plots, others have no plot. "One I received was about a woman shopping for a hat. That was it," bemoans Paul Taylor, editor of *Cenotaph*.

Solution. The way to resolve "plotless" or "hackneyed" stories is to focus on characters. If the characters are believable, with interesting goals and motivations, their interactions will drive the plot.

"Most of the *ideas* for stories have already been used; it's up to the writer to put a new spin on it to make it fresh," says Dave Felts, publisher of *SFReader.Com*. "If the characters are real enough, then a recycled plot can work, because if the character is new, the story is too."

4. Undeveloped characters

While your story may have begun with an interesting idea (e.g., "What would happen if . . . ?"), it's characters that keep people reading. Editors look for stories that are driven by interesting, believable characters. "Could you imagine the movie *Gladiator* without the scene where Maximus loses his family?" asks Doyle Wilmoth, Jr., editor of *SpecFicWorld.com*. "*Gladiator* has action, but we also have a character that moves us deeply. Someone we want to cheer for." Problems with characters include:

• *Characters the reader won't care about.* "It is especially bad news when the protagonist is someone with no redeeming social value, because we have to care about what happens to *someone* in the story, or why bother to read it?" says *On Spec*'s Walton.

• *Characters who do not grow.* Editors see too many "cardboard" characters whose motivations are unclear, or who simply react to story events rather than being the source of the story's plot or conflict. "Ultimately, the main character must decide his or her own fate; it can't be decided for them," says Felts. Skylar Burns, editor of *Ancient Paths,* a journal of Christian literature, notes that "an even greater problem is the character who undergoes a rapid and unrealistic transformation in a very short span of prose."

• *Stereotypes.* "Why can't a rich businessman be kind and compassionate? Why are unemployed men always lazy and sit around in their vests swigging out of cans? Why can't one or two learn Latin or take up line dancing?" asks Sally Zigmond, assistant editor of *QWF Magazine.*

Solution. "Know your characters, particularly the narrator," suggests Victoria Esposito-Shea, editor of the online *HandHeldCrime.* That doesn't mean you have to give the reader every detail of your character's history, but you should know that history yourself. "That's where voice is going to come from," she says.

5. No point

Editors—and readers—aren't just looking for great action and strong characters. They also want a sense of "why"—Why should I read this? What is the point?

"This is not to say that every work should address an Aesop-like moral or a grand theme, but rather that every story should contain at its core a reason to be," says Keele. "My single personal demand from a story is that it add up to something, that it shock me, scare me, unnerve me, make me think or cry."

"If we come away with the peculiar feeling that we don't really know why we've just read what we've read, or our first thought is that the washer has finished and the clothes are ready to be put in the dryer, then the writer hasn't conveyed the 'why' of the story as strongly as she could—and should—have," says Rhonna J. Robbins-Sponaas, editor of *Net Author.*

Solution. "Were I to tell a writer one thing, I'd tell her to go back and be certain what her story *is*, then be sure that she's answered the 'why' of the story, so that the reader comes away from the experience with as much a sense of its importance as the writer had," says Robbins-Sponaas.

Brown and English, editors of *The Stickman Review,* urge writers to "Write sincerely. Write stories about those things that matter the most to you. If you're writing about something you don't really care about, it'll be obvious to your readers, and they won't care either."

Moira Allen of Chantilly, Va., is a freelance writer, the editor of the Web site WritingWorld.com, and a contributing editor to *The Writer.* Her books include *Writing.com: Creative Internet Strategies to Advance Your Writing Career* and *The Writer's Guide to Queries, Pitches & Proposals.* This article appeared in *The Writer,* September 2002.

WHAT CAN YOU DO?

The one piece of advice nearly every editor had to offer was "Read, read, read." Read widely. Read the authors who have won awards in your genre or field. Read classic literature in the field to find out what has already been done, so that you don't end up offering old, trite plots without even realizing it.

"Read about three tons of short stories by different authors who have written in the past 50 years, until you find someone whose work and style turns you on and whom you'd like to emulate," says Ray Foreman of *Clark Street Review*.

Then, "Write!" says Max Keele of *Fiction Inferno*. "And keep writing. And write some more. Rejected? So what. Write another story. Rejected again? Who cares, write two this time."

When you're finished, "Let the story sit for a few days or a week," says Richard Freeborn of *Oceans of the Mind*. "Come back to it and read it aloud to yourself. I am still surprised at all the inconsistencies and bad transitions I catch when I do that."

Once your story has "aged" a bit, seek someone else's opinion. "Find an educated reader who can provide valuable feedback as to how they feel as the story unfolds," suggests *Twilight Times*' Lida Quillen. "Find readers who can mention segments that were unbelievable, let you know where the story left them cold, and sections where they were pulled into the story."

Finally, make sure you don't make the ultimate fatal mistake, cited by Tony Venables of *Ad Hoc*: "Thinking that people should read what you write simply because you write it. Writers need to understand that they have to earn their audience, to make their audience feel it's worthwhile to read their work. This does not mean pandering to populist ideas or sugar-coating what you have to say—it means choosing not to be boring."

—M.A.

TOOLS FOR SELLING YOUR BOOK

Follow a good query with a proposal
to get into print

by Elizabeth Lyon

Many artists emerge from the safe cocoon of writing their book into the foreign realm of marketing, a realm that can seem hostile, confusing, and mercenary. At one time or another, every writer I've worked with in my career as a book editor and writing instructor has probably said, "I don't like marketing. If only I could focus on writing and have someone else sell my work."

Marketing can seem like a daunting task, but mastering the basics, such as how to write a query and a book proposal, will help you get your work into print.

First, develop a marketing strategy. Make a list of the best agents for your particular book. You may send your query to more than one literary agent at the same time (simultaneous submission). If you are rejected, don't take it personally; just use the opportunity to refine your query letter.

The query letter is an amazing document that can be your entrée into publishing. Queries go to agents or acquisition editors who work for publishers. Literary agents sell about 90 percent of all published books. As the middle person in the chain from writer to publisher, agents select the most promising book ideas, offer editorial advice for polishing a manuscript, and take over the task of marketing your proposal to editors.

Even though many books are sold through literary agents, they are not your only choice. You may decide to query editors directly.

Acquisition editors, whether full time or freelance, are employees of the publishers. They are the ones who communicate with agents and writers and make the initial decision about whether to accept or reject your query. Some of the largest publishers now consider only those proposals submitted by agents, but many—if not most—North American publishers still will review query letters sent directly by writers. If the query piques their interest, these editors will request and seriously consider a proposal—a longer, more detailed description of your project. At small or even mid-size publishers, the acquisition editor also may be part or full owner of the company. In some cases, this editor has 100 percent control over which books get published. At larger houses, the decision usually falls to the editorial committee.

To research literary agents and publishing houses, study *The Writer's Handbook* (The Writer Books) and *Literary Market Place* (R.R. Bowker; www.literarymarketplace.com).

Most agents and editors prefer query letters as the first step in considering book-length manuscripts. Do not phone an agent or editor to pitch your book idea. And do not e-mail your query unless the agent or publishing house indicates a preference for e-mail queries.

By volume of mail alone (30 to 50 queries per day), most agents must reject the majority of queries and manuscripts they receive. Obviously, if you have a terrific book but can't write a compelling query letter, you'll never get a chance to have it read.

A query letter is much more than a simple letter asking an agent or editor to consider your idea or writing. A well-written query showcases your talent, describes your qualifications, and stimulates interest—in addition to describing your book idea.

Take time to write and revise your query as if it were a contest entry. Proofread it! For insurance, get another writer or freelance editor to edit your query before you send it. Use paper, font, and formatting befitting a letter to a king or queen. Don't make a good first impression; make a great first impression.

Fiction queries

Open with a straightforward business lead, such as this one by Bill Lynch:

"*Ice Ax* is a 33,000-word adventure story for fifth- and sixth-grade readers . . ."

Milt Cunningham wrote this enticing hook:

"When two men, both of them good and honest, conscientious and strong, have a dream, and the quest for the dream brings them into conflict because disparate cultures are at war, the result is *Dream and Destiny.*"

Make clear exactly what kind of book you are writing: historical, contemporary mainstream, fantasy, suspense, romance, women's fiction, etc. State the number of words or manuscript pages (using the standard 250 words per page).

Offer two or three paragraphs of story synopsis in the present tense. State your setting and time period. Identify your protagonist and the story goals—both the inner thematic yearning and the outer plot goal. For example:

"Seeking redemption for the neglect of twin baby girls, now wards of the court, Janice Doe moves across the country and opens a child-care center, hoping to put the past behind her. But then . . ."

QUERY PACKAGE

While the query letter persists as the accepted communication between writers seeking to sell their works and literary agents and editors, some writers have had good results with a query package.

It contains: a one-page query letter, a separate page of author biography, and a one-page synopsis (single-spaced) or a five-page synopsis (double-spaced), and it may contain a one-page excerpt from the book.

Successful query packages often display professional graphic arts, including, in some cases, mock full-color book covers.

This query package can be sent, with correct SASE postage for its return, to any literary agent who specifies in the agent directories that he or she wishes to see a "query plus synopsis or outline."

—E.L.

See how I grab the reader with this sample synopsis based on J.A. Jance's *Devil's Claw:*

"The disappearance of a girl, the murder of her mother, and the death of an elderly neighbor just one week before Sheriff Joanne Brady's wedding propel her into the heart of mother-daughter relationships, challenging her to heal the rift with her own mother and to protect her own daughter."

Take a full paragraph to characterize your protagonist, highlighting the wound that must be healed and the past that must be reconciled. Include a description of the protagonist's core weaknesses as well as heroic strengths.

As you summarize the plot, select emotional turning points relevant to the protagonist's struggle to reach the story goal and resolve the past. Integrate characterization into your summary of the plot. Be brief.

Add a line or two that compares your book's subject, setting, or protagonist and your writing style with other published authors. If you include the writer of a classic, add a comparison of your work to a contemporary writer, as well. This "positioning statement" shows that you read the kind of books you write.

Present your qualifications for writing your book. Mention publications, awards for writing, participation in critique groups or classes, education, if relevant, and research or experience directly related to your novel. If you have outstanding accomplishments, position them in your lead. Here's the tricky part: You should limit your query length to no more than one page. Make sure you provide contact information, including: address, phone and fax numbers, e-mail and Web addresses. Include a self-addressed, stamped envelope.

Nonfiction queries

Open your query with a straightforward business lead or craft an attention-getting hook. Follow with a clear statement about the subject of your book. Present your strongest author qualifications or your most compelling reason for seeking publication.

Present your book idea, emphasizing how it's different or better than what already exists in print. Be specific and support general statements. Use facts, statistics, and authoritative quotes to convince an agent or editor that your book is timely, needed, and unique. For example, Carolyn Korge's query for *The Spirited Walker* began:

" 'Walking is the nation's most popular fitness activity, five times as popular as jogging,' *New York Times* health writer Jane Brody reported."

Make clear how readers will benefit from your book and emphasize some of the most unique features you intend to offer. Briefly compare your book to one or two competitive titles. Do all of the above in two or three paragraphs.

For nonfiction, your credentials must be strong, so take several paragraphs, if necessary, to expand on why you are the best person to write your book. The agent or editor will also want to know what experience you have had in making presentations, giving speeches, or writing that shows you can reach a national audience.

In your closing paragraph, offer to send a proposal (see below). Don't send queries until you have drafted a proposal that can be sent within two weeks, if requested.

Elizabeth Lyon of Eugene, Ore., is a veteran editor and consultant to authors, a frequent speaker at writer's conferences, and the author of *Nonfiction Book Proposals Anybody Can Write; The Sell Your Novel Toolkit; A Writer's Guide to Nonfiction*, and *A Writer's Guide to Fiction*. This article, from *The Writer*, September 2002, is adapted from one of her books and from her presentation on queries and proposals at the 2002 Author's Venue Journey Conference, sponsored by *The Writer*. For more information, visit her Web site, Editing International, LLC, at www.4-edit.com.

FAQ: NONFICTION BOOK PROPOSALS

What is a proposal?
A proposal is a professional report—10 to 40 pages long, depending on the complexity of your book—that outlines your book idea, answers questions about its viability, and demonstrates how you can promote your published book.

What are a proposal's functions?
Proposals supply the protocol for agents to present book concepts to editors and for editors to present book concepts to editorial committees.

Writing your proposal will make the job of writing the book easier, because a proposal provides the organizational framework you need to sort, clarify, and develop your book ideas, audience, and approach.

Publishers use parts of a proposal while the author is completing the book to create catalogue descriptions and marketing materials.

What are the parts of a proposal?
Title page: Shows clearly what the book is about and reflects a specific slant or hook.
Concept statement: Describes in marketing terms your book's subject and why it's different or better than previously published books on the topic.
Table of contents (for the proposal): Lists the sections of your proposal.
About the book: Introduces the subject of your book, featuring its timeliness and originality.
About the author: Presents your qualifications.
About the market: Describes your targeted reader, potential market size, and how you propose to reach your intended audience.
About the competition: Compares and contrasts your book to others like it.
Promotion: Lists ways you can market the book—possible radio and TV shows, author readings, organizations that might bring you in as a speaker.
Production details: Discusses the book's length, time of delivery, illustrations (if any), permissions (if it includes excerpts from other sources), front matter (foreword), back matter (appendix), bibliography, and index.
Table of contents: The book's contents.
Chapter summaries: Summarizes the topics of each chapter in specific terms—facts, figures, statistics, dates, terms, places, persons, and concepts.
Sample chapters: Includes chapters that showcase your book and sell your proposal package.

[cont. on next page]

[sidebar, cont.]

Appendices: Lists materials that supplement your proposal, such as published writing samples, published material about you or your subject, copies of promotional materials about yourself or your business, awards, reviews of previous books, your resume.

How long is a proposal?
How much time does it take to write one?
The report part of the proposal, excluding the sample chapters, may be anywhere from 15 to 25 pages long. I advise giving yourself a minimum of three months to research, write, and revise your proposal, including your sample chapters. These three months include periods of gestation, as well as some time to put the proposal away to gain perspective prior to revision. An estimate of an average amount of measured time you might spend directly on a proposal project is 120 hours.

10 questions to answer before taking on a book project
• Can you write well enough for publishing standards? If your answer is no or uncertain, are you willing to learn how to improve your writing to a professional quality?
• Do you have sufficient enthusiasm for a project that may take years to write?
• Are you qualified to write your book? Can you strengthen your qualifications and your promotional skills?
• Will publication of your book satisfy your long-term career goals?
• Is your book idea different from or better than existing books on your subject?
• How large is your market?
• Do you have enough material for an entire book? Would one or several magazine articles or personal essays suffice?
• Does your subject have staying power? Will it sell copies in three, five, or 10 years?
• Does your idea spark enthusiasm? As you share it, do your friends, booksellers, and prospective readers get excited?
• Is your slant—your approach to your subject—fresh? Well-defined? Reflected in your title?

—*Elizabeth Lyon*

GET YOUR WORK PAST THE FIRST READER

9 ways to improve your chances of getting published

by Michael A. Banks

Each year, book editors and agents get thousands of nonfiction book proposals and manuscripts on a wide range of topics. They can't possibly read them all, and in some cases, they don't have the expertise to evaluate the subject matter.

For this reason, they use freelance reviewers to evaluate submissions for content and writing style. The reviewer is a writer or editor who has expertise in specific fields.

The reviewer reads the proposal or manuscript, then writes a report for the editor. In the report—about three single-spaced pages—the reviewer focuses on the content and accuracy of the manuscript, organization, readability, and suitability for the market. The reviewer's report plays a major role in determining whether or not a book is published.

As a reviewer, I've evaluated dozens of nonfiction manuscripts and proposals on such diverse topics as computer applications, writing, remote sensing devices and the Soviet manned space program. As I did more reviews, I started to recognize common problems. Amazingly, I've even found some of the same problems in my own work. These were mistakes I may never have spotted if I hadn't noticed them in other writers' manuscripts.

Some may seem trivial, but little problems can add up to big stumbling blocks. Fix the small things before you submit your work and give yourself a better chance.

Based on my experience and observations, here are nine tips for making your manuscript or proposal stand up to critical review:

1. Use a professional format.

It should go without saying that you must use the conventional manuscript format. But since I've seen so many manuscripts that don't follow this basic rule, I think it bears repeating. If you don't submit a professional-looking manuscript, it can cast a shadow over your work.

Make sure your manuscript pages are double-spaced. Set the margins to 65 characters per line, with 50 to 55 lines per 66-line page. That should give you margins of an inch and a half for the top, bottom, and sides of the page. Use a common font, such as Times New Roman or Courier. Avoid gRaTuitUs or flashy text effects, and don't change typefaces. Editors find such tricks as annoying to read as you probably found the previous passage. Remember that in nonfiction, the medium is not the message.

2. Be accurate.

Triple-check your facts. Better you find errors than the reviewer, because even one factual error will erode his confidence in your expertise. I've found factual errors that were so obvious I knew the writer would have found them had he or she done some basic checking. Once I reviewed the outline and two chapters of a basic book on astronomy in which the writer got sloppy with numbers. At one point, he stated that the Earth's moon was 93 million miles away. The correct distance is 250,000 miles (rounded off). Another error was a reference to the third moon of the planet Mars. Mars has two moons. This type of error endangers your manuscript.

3. Back up your statements.

Avoid stating opinion as fact in nonfiction. If you cannot support a statement with references, it is not a fact—not even if "everyone knows" it's true.

For example, if I were to write, "Of all compact American-made sedans on the road today, Brand X is the safest," I would need to follow that statement with supporting facts. The facts might be accident statistics from the Highway Safety Council or an analysis from *Consumer Reports*. If I couldn't find supporting facts, and there are no facts to the contrary, I would need to qualify the statement with "It is my opinion that, of all compacts . . ." or "Based solely on my observations, I believe that, of all compacts . . ."

4. Be concise.

In perhaps 20 percent of the nonfiction manuscripts I've reviewed, the authors used a formal "academic" style. Apparently, they thought it was expected. Such writing is burdened with weak nouns and passive verbs (the result of attempting to come across as well-informed by using far more words than necessary).

As with fiction, effective nonfiction relies on descriptive nouns and active verbs. Wherever you find a noun and adjective (or a rarely used noun), replace the combination with a stronger, more descriptive noun. For example, "ivy" rather than "leafy vine," or "house" rather than "domicile." Use verbs in the active voice to add strength to statements. "Astronomers accept this theory" is stronger than "The theory is accepted by astronomers."

Another kind of overwriting involves the writer using far too many words in order to say something that he or she could or might have said in a smaller number of words than the number of words used (as in this example).

Take a fierce pen to your copy and trim the excess. Be merciless.

5. Be precise.

Whenever possible, eliminate ambiguity in your writing. "Some people," "many times," and "that may be" are vague phrases.

Take the time to search out uncertain terminology in your manuscript. Search for these words: few, frequent, less, lots, many, more, most, often, and some. Replace vague phrasing with descriptive words. Here are some examples:

Imprecise: Researchers found that the technique failed quite often.

Precise: Researchers found that the technique failed 67 percent of the time.

Imprecise: After removing the housing from the sensor unit, clean it thoroughly.

Precise: After removing the housing from the sensor unit, clean the housing thoroughly.

Or—Clean the housing thoroughly after removal.

6. Use proper punctuation for dialogue.

Improper punctuation and formatting of dialogue (including the placement of quote marks) is one of the most common problems I see in submissions. If you use quote marks incorrectly, it forces a reader to stop and try to figure out what is being said by whom. Here are some mistakes I've spotted in manuscripts:

"I thought, Jim said, "that you were wrong."

Or, "Susanne burst into the room and shouted what can we do?"

If you do not feel confident about your punctuation, the best thing you can do is look at published works for examples of dialogue that are similar to yours.

Style manuals, such as *The Elements of Style, The Chicago Manual of Style,* or the *Associated Press Stylebook*, also are useful in determining the correct punctuation and formatting for dialogue.

7. Review your manuscript.

More writers than you might imagine dash off manuscripts and submit them without first reviewing them. It is almost as if they want to get their work out before they lose confidence in it, or something changes their minds.

I sometimes get the feeling that the writer simply figured the quality of his or her book proposal was not important, because it was not the "real" book.

Indications of overall sloppiness include missing words ("I'll be in car then"), duplicated words ("how how"), obvious wrong words ("The dog's hand . . .") and hasty changes without editing ("I went ran over to the desk, then stopped").

Don't send off your manuscript or proposal package as soon as it's finished. Set it aside for a few days and work on something else. Then review the hard copy. Read the manuscript from beginning to end. Try to read it as if it were not your work, but someone else's. If you find that you miss errors because you've read it so much that you only see what should be there instead of what is there, get a good copy editor to help you.

During this process, you will likely find errors and text that cry out to be rewritten. Revise and rewrite as necessary.

8. Check for spelling errors.

Misspelled words in a manuscript are jarring. Given the wide availability of spell checkers, there are no excuses for them. (I am not referring only to homonym errors such as "ad" versus "add," or "weak" and "week," but outright misspellings.)

Remember that last-minute changes can cause mistakes, so be sure to go back and check your spelling every time you make an editing change.

9. Use a checklist.

Before you send your manuscript or proposal to a publisher or agent, make certain that everything you intend to send is in the package: cover letter, outline, sample chapters, and so forth.

I've received manuscripts that were missing pages, outlines, and even entire chapters. These omissions were disruptive to the review, and all were preventable. And since they were preventable—like misspellings—these errors made me wonder whether the author was equally careless about the content and organization of the book. Make a submission checklist, and use it with every submission.

You'll have a better chance of getting your proposal or manuscript past the first reader and into the hands of a publisher if you take some extra time to carefully review, polish, and organize your work before you submit it.

Michael A. Banks of Oxford, Ohio, has, in addition to evaluating manuscripts, written more than 40 nonfiction books and novels and some 2,000 magazine articles and short stories. His most recent book, *How to Become a Fulltime Freelance Writer* (The Writer Books, 2003), offers advice on how to successfully make the transition from a part-time to a full-time writer.

HOW TO SNAG A GOOD AGENT

Believe in yourself and know why
the world needs your book

by Katharine Sands

You could have the imagination of J.K. Rowling, the wit of Frank McCourt, and the economy of Hemingway and still need help getting published. Editors rarely look at unsolicited manuscripts. Of course, there are exceptions, but if you have a great idea for a nonfiction book or have completed a fiction or non-fiction manuscript, an agent can open doors for you.

As a literary agent and frequent conference speaker, I'm often asked by writers: How do I get an agent? I surveyed several of my colleagues, and we've come up with 10 things you need to know about getting an agent and developing a successful relationship.

1. Believe in your dream.

If you don't believe in yourself, how can you expect a literary agent to believe in you? Until you find the right representation, you are, in essence, your own agent. You have to sell yourself and your book, so you need to prepare mentally for the process. Keep trying until you find an agent who suits your needs.

2. Prepare to enter the literary marketplace.

If you have a manuscript, you already are deeply committed to the craft of writing. But once your project is finished, you have to take it to the literary marketplace. This calls for a mental shift. You have to start thinking about the publishing business, not the craft.

"Publishing must tread the tightrope between art and commerce," says Michael Larsen of the Michael Larsen and Elizabeth Pomada agency in San Francisco. "Publishers want books that they can publish with pride and with passion, but to survive, they must publish books that sell."

An agent wants to know from the outset why anyone would read your book. So put aside your emotional attachment to your writing and start thinking about your manuscript's selling points.

3. Perfect your pitch.

OK, you know you've written the best book on how to trim your thighs, make better love, or make money in a bear market, but now you have to convince an agent of that. The best way to get an agent's attention is with a smashing query letter. The query is essentially your interview for the coveted job of book author.

"A good query answers the three questions," says Anna Ghosh with Scovil Chichak Galen Literary Agency, Inc., in New York City: "Why (the writer) is uniquely qualified, who the audience is for the (nonfiction) book, and what the competing books are. For fiction, I'm really looking for good writing. I think the letter should pique my interest in some way. If the letter isn't well written, it is unlikely that I'll believe that the novel will hold my interest."

Don't try to reduce your entire novel to one paragraph, says Donald Maass, author of *Writing the Breakout Novel.* "Tell the beginning of your story, which requires only three elements: the setting, your protagonist, and the problem that he or she faces. Convey these elements succinctly and colorfully, and your prospective agent may well wonder, 'Gee, what happens next?' To find out, he may ask for your manuscript. Bingo. Your fiction query has done its job."

4. Understand the agent's role in the publishing industry.

Many agents become agents because they love literature, but this is not why an agent succeeds in the book business. An agent succeeds by having an ability described by P.T. Barnum: ". . . to see what is all around you just waiting to be seen."

Agents see the potential of raw material. We envision how it could grow into a book. When reviewing new writers, we ask ourselves how the writing—as a literary property—will succeed in its bid for publication.

5. Know the lingo.

When you talk to an agent, you need to understand the language of bookselling. Look at the publishing climate for your book. What other books like yours are in bookstores? Can you identify who your primary readers will be? How does it fit into the zeitgeist? Renowned editor Max Perkins asked a question that editors continue to ask today: "Why does the world need this book?" Make sure you can answer this question.

6. Learn about the process before submitting material.

Writing is solitary, publishing is collaborative. You need to get others excited about your work. "One of the things that surprises me is that many writers don't research or learn about the proposal process before they submit their materials," says Tonianne Robino, associate literary agent with the Jeff Herman Literary Agency. "We receive a lot of query letters and proposals that are very well done, but the number of poorly prepared submission packages is unbelievable. . . . It is obvious that [the writers] really want to be published, but it's equally obvious that they haven't taken the time to learn anything about the way the submission process works.

"Before submitting to a literary agency, do your homework," she says. Find a book [such as *Writer's Guide to Book Editors, Publishers, and Literary Agents* by Jeff Herman, now being annually published by The Writer Books under the title *Jeff Herman's Guide to Book Publishers, Editors, and Literary Agents*] that walks you through the process of writing a proposal. Talk to other writers who have gone through the process. Go to workshops and conferences. The time and energy spent to prepare a professional query letter and proposal will pay off."

7. Know that agents believe writing talent can come from anywhere.

Agents know that many books on the bestseller lists are the ones nobody could have predicted. Surprisingly, a New York City high school teacher [Frank McCourt] spent 20 years telling stories of his impoverished childhood in Limerick during World War II, published his memoir, *Angela's Ashes,* became a much-loved literary figure, and won the Pulitzer Prize. And who could have imagined a single mother on the dole would spend 10 years conjuring up a world of wizardry that would set the publishing world on its ear, as J.K. Rowling did with her phenomenally successful Harry Potter series?

8. Understand why you want an agent.

Why would you want a complete stranger (who may not even sound very nice!) to take 15 percent of the revenue you might generate as an author? Here is one reason: publishers. You may be able to name a major publisher, such as HarperCollins—but do you know the many imprints under the HarperCollins corporate umbrella, including Ecco, Amistad Press, William Morrow, and ReganBooks? How could you possibly know which editor at each imprint would want to acquire and publish your book? Agents know this. They learn lunch by lunch, call by call, which editor is looking for which kind of book and who doesn't want to acquire certain categories. That's their job.

Agents are, in effect, a screening service for publishers. Editors want agents to do the representing and to bring them writers whose works fit their publishing program.

9. Contact agents.

If you have followed steps 1-8, you are now ready to find the right agent. You will have to do a bit of research. Go to the library and read up on literary agencies. *The Writer's Handbook* and *Jeff Herman's Guide to Book Publishers,*

Editors, and Literary Agents (The Writer Books) offer detailed information about literary agencies and what they are looking for.

The Association of Authors' Representatives (AAR), an organization of experienced, reputable literary agents, will send you a list of its members. Send a $7 check or money order and a SASE with 99 cents postage on a #10 envelope. (P.O. Box 237201, Ansonia Sta., New York, NY 10023. 212-252-3695. The AAR's Web site is at www. aar-online.org)

The National Writers Union, a trade union for writers of all genres, gives members access to its agent database. It also has resource materials that cover topics such as "Understanding the agent-author relationship." (113 University Pl., 6th Fl., New York, NY 10003. 212-254-0279. www.nwu.org)

10. Remember that agents are always looking for writers.

"Now is the most exciting time ever to be alive, and it's the best time ever to be a writer," says Larsen. "Information is doubling every 18 months, and the age of information is also the age of the writer. There are more subjects to write about, more media, more agents, more options for getting your books published, more ways to learn about writing and publishing, and more ways to promote your books and profit from them than ever before."

It is indeed an exciting time to be writing. Machines cannot produce content. We need hearts and minds for that. We need writers.

Katharine Sands is a literary agent with the Sarah Jane Freymann Literary Agency in New York City. She frequently speaks on writing and publishing topics for conferences and organizations, such as The American Society of Journalists and Authors. This article is from *The Writer*, March 2003.

BEFORE YOU SIGN ON THE DOTTED LINE

6 tips to boost your contract savvy

by Kelly James-Enger

As a freelancer, you're probably more interested in writing than tending to the business side of self-employment. Dealing with contracts is one aspect of the business many writers would like to ignore, but they do so at their own peril. A few simple tips can take you a long way when venturing into the murky world of publishing contracts, especially if you're new to the freelancing game.

1. Get the contract before you begin.

You query a magazine with an idea. The editor calls; he loves it and wants to assign the piece. You discuss angle, word count, deadline, and pay. You even agree to first North American serial rights, with additional money for Web rights. Everything sounds great. "I'll send you the contract in a few days," your editor tells you.

With a tight deadline, you have no choice but to start on the story. You research and write the piece, and are preparing to turn it in when . . . the contract arrives. It includes a broadly written indemnification agreement that requires you to insure the publisher against *any* claim arising out of the story (regardless of fault)—and the editor says he can't allow any changes to it. What do you do now? You don't want to sign the contract, but you've already invested significant time in the story. You're up the proverbial creek without a paddle.

To avoid this situation, tell the editor you'll start work after you receive the contract. If that's not possible—for example, if you're writing "on spec" (on speculation, with contract and payment sent on acceptance)—ask the editor to fax a copy of the publication's standard agreement so you can check for any objectionable provisions beforehand.

2. Read the contract.

Sounds obvious, right? When you're busy, though, taking an extra 20 minutes (or more) to read a contract closely—and confirm that you understand all the language it contains—can seem like a luxury.

Even if you've written for the publication before, remember that contracts can change. I'd been writing for a major magazine for years when they slipped in a one-sentence addition (on page 4, paragraph 15) that negated any previous contract amendments. I just glanced at the contract, which I had signed a dozen times before, and signed again. Was it unfair to bury that additional clause in the contract? Probably. Whose fault was it for not seeing it? Mine.

Remember, contracts are written by lawyers for *publishers*. They're not in the business of making things clear (I should know—I used to be a lawyer), and they certainly are not trying to protect *your* rights or make things more attractive for the average freelancer. Their job is to protect the publishers' interests. Your job is to make sure you understand everything you sign.

3. Beware of tricky terms and clauses.

Some contracts are relatively straightforward. But most have at least one clause or section that confuses and misleads most writers. Pay special attention to provisions involving:

Exclusivity. Many publishers request exclusive rights to a story for a certain period of time—e.g., 90 days or six months after the story is published. But others may preclude you from writing about "the same or similar subject" during that time; this hamstrings you from covering the subject until the period of exclusivity runs out.

Electronic rights. When publishers use language like "in all its forms" or "in any other media," they're grabbing your electronic rights as well. Make sure the publisher pays you for that privilege, or strike the language.

Indemnification. As I mentioned earlier, many contracts contain indemnification language that requires you to shoulder the responsibility should a claim or lawsuit arise out of your actions (such as plagiarizing material or libeling someone). Others require the writer to indemnify the publisher for "any claim" resulting from a story. I usually don't mind agreeing to indemnify a publisher if I'm found to have breached the contract (because that is within my control), but I'm not going to protect the publisher from the possibility that a bogus claim or lawsuit is filed as a result of my story.

4. Hang on to your rights.

When you create a written work, you automatically own the copyright—until you sell, transfer, or give the copyright to someone else. If you sign a work-for-hire agreement, you transfer the copyright to the publisher, which means you no longer have any legal right to the piece.

An all-rights contract, while legally different (you retain copyright but transfer all rights to the publisher), has the same effect: You no longer have any rights to the story. Selling first or one-time rights is a better deal because you can offer reprint rights to other publishers in the future.

Your job is to sell as few rights as possible and retain all others. Even if you don't sell the piece again, if the publisher wants additional rights—say, the right to include the article in a book or post it on its Web site—you want the publisher to come back and pay you more money for those rights. (Or, sell those rights in the original contract—just make sure you're compensated fairly for them.)

5. No contract?

Get it in writing. Occasionally, you may work with smaller publishers that don't use written contracts (although this seems to be increasingly rare). If that's the case, when you turn in a story, indicate on your invoice what rights you're selling—e.g., "Please consider this my invoice for one-time rights to 'Six ways to boost your bliss' per our telephone conversation of Jan. 15, 2003." Also, note on the manuscript itself what rights are being transferred. For long, complicated contracts, I often include the words "rights per written contract."

6. Offer your own language.

Finally, remember that when the publisher sends you a contract to sign, there is nothing to prevent you from suggesting different wording. For example, I was offered an all-rights contract by a magazine several years ago. I expressed my reservations about signing it, and suggested that the editor purchase first North American serial rights instead, leaving me the remaining rights. Because she was concerned about exclusivity, I offered to include "writer will not write about the same subject for another women's fitness publication for three months after publication" on the contract. She agreed, and we used the same language for other assignments.

The moral of the story? Don't be afraid to inquire about changes. Your editor may refuse, forcing you to decide whether to walk away from an objectionable contract, but it never hurts to ask.

Kelly James-Enger is a freelance journalist, writing instructor, and Contributing Editor at *The Writer*. She is also author of the recent book, *Ready, Aim, Specialize!: Create Your Own Writing Speciality and Make More Money* (The Writer Books, 2003), with advice to freelance writers on how to increase their income by focusing on top niche markets. She may be reached at her Web site: www.kellyjamesenger.com. This article appeared in *The Writer*, February 2003.

FREELANCER'S GUIDE TO FINANCIAL INDEPENDENCE

Dip your toe in—before you dive headfirst

by Ray Dreyfack

Whenever someone tells me that they are quitting their job to freelance, I remember an encounter with a friend who was freelancing full time. He looked worried, and with good reason. He wasn't getting as many assignments as he once had. His favorite editor, a primary source of income, had retired, shutting the tap when he needed it most.

No wonder he was worried. Married, with two kids and a pregnant wife, Jim saw his income vanishing while expenses kept rising. The proverbial well threatened to run dry.

Jim had quit his job as an associate editor on a trade magazine to freelance full time. It hadn't been a great job, but it was steady. "The biggest mistake I ever made," Jim groused. Three months later, he was back at the same kind of job he had left.

It still saddens me to think of it. I had made the same decision several years earlier: quitting a steady, dependable job to freelance. I regarded it then, and do now, as the smartest career move I ever made.

How much security do I need?

Why is it that one writer turns freelance, only to become beset with panic-level anxiety, while another is delighted with the outcome? More important, what steps can one take to avoid the devastating effects of financial insecurity, and at the same time cash in on the satisfactions of independence as a freelance writer? Here's what I've learned in my long career.

Economic considerations aside, it would be hard to overstate the psychological importance of a steady, dependable income. The saddest thing about Jim's surrender is that during his year or so as a freelancer, he had obtained and successfully completed above-average-paying writing assignments. In short, Jim proved he was able to compete with the best of them. Still, he couldn't survive. Financial insecurity did him in.

We all have varying degrees of financial insecurity, depending on our particular circumstances. Jim had failed to calculate the amount of security that he needed.

Facing this need squarely is the first step in constructing a practical plan to become a psychologically secure freelance writer. (Following through with an effective career strategy with this goal in mind is step two.)

It boils down to arithmetic. You have to come up with a hard figure, an income level you can get by on given your personal situation. Obviously, a writer who's 26 and single is better positioned psychologically than a writer who's 40 with two or three children, one of whom will soon enter college. Similarly, the 40-year-old family man or woman with a bank balance of $200,000 and a spouse who is employed is better placed than the writer with $5,000 in the bank and a baby on the way.

In a nutshell, the less pressing your financial obligations at the time you decide to turn freelance, the lower the level of financial security you will need to keep yourself psychologically intact when you make the change. One writer may be comfortable with a projected annual income of $20,000; another may need $40,000 or more.

Does this mean that if your realistically calculated bottom-line requirement is high, a freelance career's not for you? Not at all. Not if you play your financial cards right.

When I decided to go freelance full time three decades ago, I set myself a double earnings standard. One was for the must-earn income I absolutely had to have to achieve a tolerable way of life for myself and my family. The other was my future projection—the much more ambitious income I was shooting for down the pike. To accomplish this, I could not afford to make the plunge prematurely.

If you are a proven writer who has not yet made the leap into full-time freelancing, this section is especially important for you. When St. Augustine described patience as a "companion of wisdom," he must have had freelance writing in mind. Unless you're young and single with minimal obligations and in a position to "take a shot" at going freelance, patience is the one virtue you cannot afford to sell short.

If you are burdened with financial responsibilities—as most of us are—the best advice is to avoid the deep water until it is thoroughly tested. View that must-earn annual income as a base. For example, let's say you're a proven writer who would like to go freelance with a must-earn annual income of $20,000. Assume further that you can count on $10,000 a year from interest, dividends, or other sources. That means you must earn the other $10,000 from freelance writing fees. It may not sound like much, but that money won't come out of the blue.

That's pretty much the situation I faced when I decided to freelance back in the '60s. I had done considerable writing, had my fair share of rejections interspersed with some good hits and some valuable contacts, but few I could count on as repetitive. I was employed at a nonwriting job for a cosmetics company, my wife was a homemaker, and I had two young children to support.

From a financial standpoint, I had a dependable job. But I didn't like what I was doing, and I had caught the writing bug. I'd had some success as a nonfiction writer; I knew I could put words together and make them sell. But bills for everything from clothes to shelter to the kids' dental work and music lessons kept pouring in like rain through a leaky roof. Could I count on income from freelance writing to do the same? Too much of a gamble. At least at that point. When? That's where patience comes in.

Make a gradual transition

In making the switch to self-employed freelancer, exercising patience involved these three simple rules:
• Don't quit your job impulsively.
• Turn out copy and develop contacts while you're still employed.
• And ease yourself gradually into a full-time freelance career.
If you have recurrent financial obligations, you can't afford to take the giant step until you have a comfortable number of repeat freelance assignments. Any other course automatically generates financial insecurity, wipes you out psychologically, and explains why so many writers chicken out after freelancing for only a short period of time.

No one said it was easy. Working full time and extending your work week 10 or 15 hours writing evenings and weekends can be a grind. Is it worth it? It depends on how much you want the pot of shekels at the end. As my own and many other writers' experiences show, it is an anxiety-free way to develop the sources that you will need to achieve financial security as a freelancer. You will build up a cash reserve while doing it, and it needn't take you that long.

The idea, after developing a few sources of dependably repetitive freelance writing assignments, is to ease gradually into a freelance writing career. At the outset, when I decided to make the switch, I spent less than a year developing three contacts I could depend on for steady assignments. For me, the cash-in was promising from the outset: regular monthly features for a secondary magazine; regular contributions for a bimonthly newsletter; and regular monthly booklets for a mail-order marketer.

Fulfilling these assignments took less than one week per month and yielded 30 percent of my must-have income. Before leaving my full-time employer, I was able to land a part-time job with a small PR firm. By then, I was taking in 120 percent of my must-have income (about 80 percent of my previous full-

GETTING EXPOSURE

How do you spread the word about yourself? Among the ways:

• Send out letters and e-mail messages to all possible sources.

• Make hundreds of phone calls offering your services and soliciting work.

• Sign up for a professional association or two, like the American Society of Journalists and Authors (www. asja.org) and its second-to-none Writer's Referral Service, which links writers and clients.

• Comb the want ads regularly.

• Set up your own Web page.

It you are burdened with financial responsibilities, as most of us are, the best advice is to avoid the deep water until it is thoroughly tested.

time nonwriting job). My work consisted solely of writing, and I still had several free hours per month in which to continue expanding my sources and building my income. And I was diversifying and solidifying my experience. I was on my way.

Spread the word

I know a writer who left an advertising job to go freelance. He started modestly enough, his first year out earning 70 percent of his former income. Today he's a millionaire, an entrepreneur who farms out as much work as he handles himself. He has a stable of freelance "stringers" on call and takes 15 percent off the top of the fee. How does he do it?

He spreads the word. Makes his presence, capabilities, and availability known throughout the marketplace. The address file in his computer contains hundreds of names: writers, editors, publishers, literary agents, PR firms, corporate executives, professional associations.

More important, they have his name, phone number, and e-mail address. They're familiar with his personal Web page. They know what he can do. When a CEO needs a good speech written yesterday, the word is out that he's the guy to call. He can deliver in a pinch.

"The trouble with most writers," this savvy businessman says, "is that they're too busy writing." Right on! I should know, because I've been too busy writing for years, too busy in my earlier years to take the time and effort needed to spread the word adequately, until I finally woke up to the importance of this. So don't be shy. Blow your horn. Loud and clear.

Ray Dreyfack of Coconut Creek, Fla., has had a long career as a free-lancer. His 20 published books include *The Art of Mismanagement*. This article, which appeared in *The Writer*, June 2002, is excerpted from *Achieving Financial Independence as a Freelance Writer* by Ray Dreyfack, with permission of the author. Copyright © Ray Dreyfack 2002.

SELF-PUBLISHING: IS IT FOR YOU?

What to know and ask about doing it yourself

by Arlene S. Uslander

Are you a person easily dejected by rejection? Impatient when publishers or agents don't respond to you in a timely manner—*or not at all*? Do you like to be "captain of your own ship," always in control of your own fate? Do you have some extra cash and time you can invest in a worthy project—your very own book? If you answered "yes" to all four questions, you may be a candidate for self-publishing.

I self-published two of the 12 books I have had published. No, I didn't get rich, but I came out ahead financially, sold about 8,000 copies, and had a wonderful time promoting the books. In addition, a trade publisher saw them, liked what she saw, and recently published the two as one book, *That's What Grandparents Are For.*

Rusty Fischer of Orlando, Fla., author of *Beyond the Bookstore: 101 (Other) Places to Sell Your Self-Published Book,* says that he grew frustrated with regular publishing houses making arbitrary decisions about the new book ideas he thought were "great"—and which, he contends, have since been proven great through self-sales. "Besides," he says, "I had already been published by two traditional publishers and was unimpressed, not only with their promotional activities on my behalf (i.e., none), but with the royalty checks, which were outrageously small, considering how many copies they had sold."

Greg Ferguson, editor of *Self-Publisher's Digest,* a must for anyone contemplating self-publishing, points out that self-publishing has grown exponentially in the last several years for the following reasons: Technological advances have made it much cheaper. Mergers and other financial issues in the traditional publishing business have caused major publishers to focus on a very small

number of superstar authors and generally ignore new writers, or fail to properly promote midlist writers; and some writers see self-publishing as a way to
attract the attention of big publishers.

There are two ways to go about self-publishing. The first is with a self-
publishing book-packaging company, which puts together an entire package,
from the cover design to the typesetting, printing, marketing, and order fulfillment. A packager provides as many or as few services as a self-publisher (the
author) requires.

The other route is to use a book printer, who generally just prints the book
and offers few, if any, additional services.

A book packager knows every aspect of the book business, from design to
sales, notes Dorothy Kavka, president of Evanston Publishing, a self-publishing
book-packaging company. Kavka, who has been in the business for 16 years and
has packaged more than 500 books, adds, "Usually, a printer cannot supply
design options or an ISBN [International Standard Book Number] or copyright. Although some printers do have staff who will typeset the book, most do
not offer that service. If you do use a printer," she advises, "make sure he or she
specializes in printing books, and is not just a general printer."

Self-published author Walter Allen of Orlando (*When You Least Expect Me,
LuLu and the Palma Ceia Boy, Bellemere,* and *A Place for Me*) uses a book
printer, BookMasters. "BookMasters has cover-design people," he points out.
"You have to supply them with camera-ready material, which means you must
have someone format your book and provide laser copies of your manuscript."

How much self-publishing will cost you varies a lot. Kavka, for example,
notes, "We base prices on how much the self-publisher does himself/herself,
and how much we do. An average price for 1,000 copies of an average-size book
(128 pages, 5½ by 8½ inches) can range from about $3.20 a book (just for the
printing) to $6 a book (if we do all the production). The price goes down per
book the more books that are printed and for reprints.

"Vanity/subsidy presses charge more per book when you add in all their costs,
and a few companies charge a little less, but those are our averages."

While the costs of self-publishing may vary a lot, there is a general rule in the
industry about sales. "A successful self-published book is one that makes its
costs back plus a little more," according to Kavka. "Five thousand or 8,000 is a
bestseller for any press, let alone a self-publisher! As a rule of thumb, we figure
that a successful self-published book sells between 1,500 and 2,000 copies. Any
sales beyond that are considered 'bestseller' by everyone in the business."

Choose the right company

If you do feel that self-publishing is an attractive option for you, you'll have
to choose a company. There are many, many different companies out there,
all promising great things, "so you will really need to do your homework,"
Fischer says.

"There are lots of directories that specialize in providing such information. It also helps to visit the companies' Web sites and scour them for information. And if you belong to writers' groups—either on or offline—ask them about a particular publisher and listen to the responses you get."

In addition, talk to any friends who have self-published and see the list of resources accompanying this article.

Ralph Morales Jr., the author of four self-published books (*Jenna's Song, Out of the Darkness, Hope Amid the Shadows,* and *Love Never Dies*) says he asked self-publishing companies a number of important questions before he made his final selection. Could their company:

• Produce a reasonable number of books within his limited budget?

• Produce a book that would meet his high expectations of quality and professionalism?

• Provide the necessary support to allow him to have a voice in the book's layout and design?

• Provide an end product he'd be proud of?

Morales, of Isabela, Puerto Rico, made his decision based upon how a particular company answered these questions, as well as samples of books the company had published and the recommendation of a friend whose books it had published. Obviously, Morales was pleased with the results, since after his first book was published, he went on to have the same company (Evanston Publishing) do several more.

Get the jump on promotion

Let's say you have decided on the company, you've paid your money, and they've printed your book. Now what?

The time to start thinking about how to sell your book is not when the heavy cartons are delivered to your front door. The key is in promotion, and the key to promotion is the planning.

Allen, who has sold 2,000 copies each of two of his books and 500 of another and says he expects to sell at least 3,000 of his latest novel, *A Place for Me,* offers excellent advice for promoting and marketing your self-published book:

• Send a personal letter to everyone you know announcing the publication of your book with a brief description and ordering information. Most impersonal printed matter is never read.

• Send a free autographed copy of your book to anyone who helped you with research.

• Send a review copy to local libraries and the book editor at your local newspaper.

• Ask for opportunities to do book signings and reviews at the library, church and synagogue, ladies' groups, men's fraternal orders, etc. Offer these groups part of your profit—a percentage of each book sold at their event.

• Be sure to always personalize your autographs.

• Include a "How to Order" page in your book.

Kavka, of Evanston Publishing, offered some additional promotional advice:

• Set up a Web site for your book, and give out your Web address to every-one you know.

• Get other Web sites to sell your books by offering a referral fee. Amazon.com does this and so can you. Or better yet, try to exchange links with other Web sites, which you can do free of charge.

• Include a press release or flyer about your book in every piece of snail mail you send out.

• Be sure to let Amazon.com, Barnes & Noble, and Borders know about your book. They do sell self-published books.

• Ask friends who have indicated they like your book to send in reviews to the online booksellers.

In addition to these points, here is some other advice, based on my own experience:

Consider using a publicist.

If you can afford to hire a publicist, do so. Most of the publicists I contacted were way out of my reach cost-wise, but fortunately, I hooked up with a writer on the Internet who told me about a company called KSB Promotions. I feel that their prices are reasonable for what they do, which includes advising you on the best avenues for publicity and choosing from a database of more than 14,500 national magazine and newspaper editors and columnists, from which they handpick the best media to contact about your book.

Make the most of the Internet.

The Internet is undoubtedly the best promotional tool that has come along since the printing press to help sell books. Log onto all the writer's groups you can find, and let them know about your book for their newsletter. The editors of writer's-group newsletters are always looking for information about new books. Include the name of your book and ordering information at the bottom of every e-mail you send out.

Check search engines for appropriate publications that might be interested in knowing about your book. If you've written a book about parenting or gar-dening, for example, you'll want to find publications in those areas. You will be amazed at how many references come up. Send these publications a press release. (And for a print version of this same type of search, find a library that carries the huge *Bacon's Magazine Directory* and look for your subject area under the "Alphabetical Cross Index of Market Classifications." The listings offer a mini-profile of each magazine as well as its Web site, contact informa-tion, names of editors, and other information.)

Other tips

Ask your friends in other cities to hype your book to their local papers. Because many of my friends were kind enough to do that, I had write-ups in towns I had never even visited (and in some cases, never even heard of!).

SOME KEY ISSUES TO CONSIDER ABOUT SELF-PUBLISHING

• Decide whether you have the time and dedication to promote your book.

• Decide what services you actually need and can afford before looking for a company. For example: marketing help, cover design, ISBN, number of books, and cost per book.

• Make sure you have in writing from the publisher or printer the exact cost of each book, and the exact cost of the total number of books.

• Carefully examine samples of books produced by companies you are considering.

• Contact other writers whose books have been published by these companies to learn whether the company fulfilled all their promises.

• Check with the Better Business Bureau to make sure there are no complaints lodged against a company you are seriously considering.

• Use your gut feeling!

Because the cost of postage can quickly get out of hand, try to team up with another self-published author who has written in the same general subject area to mail joint press releases and other promotional material. I shared expenses with a woman I met on the Internet who had written a book on a subject similar to mine, but the two books were different enough not to be competitive.

Always have a photo of yourself handy because newspaper editors and columnists usually ask for one. Make sure your book is visible in the photo.

Resources on self-publishing

Here are some resources mentioned earlier in this story:

• BookMasters, 2541 Ashland Road, Mansfield, OH 44905. 800-5337-6727. www.bookmasters.com.

• Evanston Publishing, Inc.,4824 Brownsboro Center Arcade, Louisville, KY 40207. 800-594-5190. www.evanstonpublishing.com.

• KSB Promotions, 55 Honey Creek Ave. NE, Ada, MI 49301. 800-304-3269. www.ksbpromotions.com.

• *Self-Publisher's Digest*: Send a note with address to Titan Beach Publishing, 14493 S. Padre Island Dr., A-404, Corpus Christi, TX 78418 (free subscription). info@titanbeach.com.

Some helpful organizations

• Publishers Marketing Association (PMA): 627 Aviation Way, Manhattan Beach, CA 90266. 310-372-2732. info@pma-online.org. www.pmaonline.org.

• Small Publishers Association of North America (SPAN): P.O. Box 1306, 425 Cedar St., Buena Vista, CO 81211. 719-395-4790. span@ spannet.org. www.spannet.org.

Some excellent books

• *Beyond the Bookstore: 101 (Other) Places to Sell Your Self-Published Book* by Rusty Fischer (a self-published resource; available at the website, www.bookbooters.com/b00062.asp).

• *The Self-Publishing Manual: How to Write, Print and Sell Your Own Book* by Dan Poynter (Para Publishing).

Ultimately, the reason why an author self-publishes is, in a word, empowerment, says Ferguson.

"Self-publishers are a self-selecting group," he explains. "It requires a real entrepreneurial spirit. You need to believe that selling your book is just as noble as writing it, and you need to believe that all the hassles are worth the control you get over your book."

You also need to be willing to devote the necessary time and effort to promoting your book. Yes, entrepreneurial spirit and belief are certainly important, but they are not enough without the hard work to promote it.

Arlene S. Uslander of Glenview, Ill., is a freelance editor and the author of 12 nonfiction books. This article is from *The Writer,* February 2003.

A MINI-GLOSSARY OF TERMS

Publishing terms can be confusing, as many of them overlap. The following explanations may help.

Co-op publishing. This can be a group of authors who self-publish a collection of stories or poems in an anthology and share all costs of printing and marketing the book, or it can just be another name for subsidy publishing.

Electronic publishing. Any work that is available electronically, typically for download from the Internet.

POD (print on demand). The author can get anywhere from one to 100 or more books printed, and then request more books as he or she wishes. There is no inventory. As the order comes in, the book gets printed. Bookstores may or may not carry these books.

Self-publishing. The author performs or arranges and pays the cost of all aspects of the book, from the manuscript to the cover design to the marketing.

Subsidy publishing. The author and publishing company share the costs of printing and marketing the book. It is rare, however, that there is an even division of costs, and the author usually ends up paying for most of them.

Vanity publishing. The author pays all the costs in producing and marketing a book, yet the publishing company owns all or some of the rights to the book. Most bookstores will not carry this type of book.

—A.S.U.

CHAPBOOKS SHOWCASE YOUR WORK

This traditional format works well for poets

by Rita Moe

In poetry circles, the term "chapbook" often has an almost holy connotation. If you have a chapbook—a booklet of poems—published as an award for winning a competition, it can be a prestigious occasion that includes a cash prize, a supply of numbered, limited-edition chapbooks, and a gala reading in your honor.

On the other hand, publishing a chapbook could mean taking your typewritten poems to the neighborhood copy center and producing a stapled booklet, which you then hawk at every open-mike poetry slam in town.

For those who are pursuing poetry with audience and reputation in mind, winning a chapbook competition can be a boost.

Some poets, though, may opt for self-publication, because they want complete artistic control of the publishing process; they consider their work too radical for the mainstream; they want to print a small number of chapbooks for friends and family; or they simply want the satisfaction of seeing their work in print.

Either way, chapbooks are an effective way for poets to circulate their work.

What is a chapbook?

The term "chapbook" dates from the 16th century and refers to a small book or pamphlet that peddlers, or "chapmen," sold for a penny or sixpence. Chapbooks were popular literature covering a wide range of topics: fairy tales, witchcraft, murder cases, political tracts, and travel adventures.

At one time, the publishing of chapbooks was a costly and time-consuming undertaking due to the costs of printing. Thanks to digital technology, the publishing process is now streamlined and affordable.

Chapbooks still can refer to almost any small pamphlet or book. I use the term here, however, to refer to small books of poetry containing the work of one author. They typically sell for $4 to $10. Chapbooks are comprised of sheets of paper (from as few as three to as many as 18), folded in the middle and stapled. Most chapbooks are made from standard 8-by-11-inch sheets, folded to make a book size of 5 by 8 inches. Usually, the cover is of heavier stock and can include art, multicolor graphics, line drawings, or photographs.

Chapbooks generally have fewer preliminaries, such as an introduction, than larger volumes and often have no end matter (indexes and appendices). At a minimum, chapbooks have a title page on a right-hand (recto) page, including the title, author, and publishing house. Then, following on the left-hand page (verso) is a copyright notice that includes year of publication and country in which the book is published. Acknowledgments are often printed on this page, too. Additional front matter can include a blank page and/or a half title page (appearing before the main title), a dedication or epigraph, a table of contents, and a preface.

To keep costs down, some presses cut back on the preliminaries, deeming a half title page, for instance, a waste of money. I find, however, that these extras add to the appearance and quality of the finished product. Opening the cover to find a blank page or half title page gives a sense of anticipation as one enters the world of the book and a perception that care has been taken in its presentation. On the other hand, too many preliminaries can seem pretentious in a small volume—too much introduction and not enough substance. Likewise, a chapbook seldom warrants extensive end matter; one might typically find, at most, biographical notes on the author and/or printing and typesetting information (called the colophon).

The physical appearance of your book is important because the outside is the first thing readers notice. When choosing a contest, take some time to check the quality of the previous winners' chapbooks.

If you decide to enter a contest, what should you know before submitting your work? To help you, I asked chapbook editors what they look for when judging manuscripts.

What judges want

We look for "cohesion—thematically or structurally," says Ander Monson, editor and designer of New Michigan Press, publisher of the online journal *Diagram* and sponsor of a chapbook contest. "A good chapbook should hold together—maybe even more so than a book-length manuscript."

Rory Golden, executive director of the Center for Book Arts in New York City, and Sharon Dolin, coordinator and co-judge of the center's chapbook contest, agree that a good chapbook may consist of one long poem or a sequence of linked shorter poems. It may also just be a collection of poems written in a strong voice with a powerful use of language.

Robert Bixby, editor and publisher of March Street Press, which publishes

four to five chapbooks a year and *Parting Gifts,* a semi-annual literary magazine, says he looks for reasons to reject a submission. "A cliché, an idiotic rhyme
scheme," and he's on to the next manuscript.

Economics is one reason publishers (and self-publishers) gravitate to chapbooks. Publishing a full-length manuscript is a costly, time-consuming enterprise requiring orders in the thousands, something few can afford or expect to
sell. In contrast, a typical run of a contest-winning chapbook may be 50 to
500 copies.

March Street Press prints only about 20 copies at a time, printing more as
demand arises. This makes it possible to make revisions at the request of the
poet and, as Bixby points out, avoids dog-eared, sun-bleached covers.

But there are other reasons besides economics to publish poetry in chapbooks. The chapbook is "the natural length of a book of verse," Bixby says. "It's
the amount of material a reader would naturally read in one sitting, or that a
poet could present at a good reading; the amount of work needed to reflect on
a period of one's life."

How contests work

Typically, publishers charge a contest reading or entry fee ($10 to $15), which
is used to cover expenses such as advertising, printing costs, prizes, a reading/
reception, judging fees, postage, and administrative costs.

None of the publishers I interviewed find chapbooks to be a moneymaking
proposition, but all find it satisfying. New Michigan Press has printed chapbooks since 1999 and began its competition in 2001. Monson says the press
enjoys "getting the word out on our authors, many whose reputations are on
the rise."

At March Street Press, Bixby has been publishing chapbooks since 1988 and
is "closing in on 80 titles, all still in print." He does the page layout himself,
drives to the print shop, and carries the printed pages home, where he collates,
staples, trims, wraps, addresses, and delivers them to the post office. Bixby says
the reading fee he charges "ensures that people who send me work are serious
enough to cut a $10 check."

The budget may be more substantial at the Center for Book Arts than it is
at many small literary presses. With a $15 entry fee for its annual contest and
500 to 700 entrants each year, the contest can bring in $7,000 to $10,000. But
the expenses for this prestigious contest are considerable, too—a letterpress-
printed chapbook designed, printed, and bound by artists at the center; fees
for nationally known judges (Billy Collins and Sharon Dolin judged the 2001
contest); prizes; advertising; and a reception and reading honoring the winning poet.

The annual chapbook competition brings the center and the poets to the
attention of the literary community. "The combination of a gorgeously printed
book and a reading at our center in New York is enormously gratifying to the
poets and, vicariously, to us," says Dolin.

Winning the annual competition at the Center for Book Arts may not be in the stars for all of us, but if you (like me) are an intermediate poet—one who has taken a number of classes, who has had individual poems published in literary journals, who may not have enough poems for a full-length manuscript—why not enter a chapbook contest?

We can learn from organizing our work for submission and publication—and, in the process, we just might improve our poetry.

Rita Moe of Roseville, Minn., received her MFA in poetry from Hamline University. Her nonfiction and poetry have appeared in a number of publications, including *Minnesota Women's Press, A View from the Loft, Poet Lore,* and *Water~Stone.* She works full time for an investment firm. This article is from *The Writer,* February 2003.

CHAPBOOK BASICS

Get to know the beast.
There's no substitute for reading chapbooks and holding them in hand to get an idea of the quality you might expect. You can find chapbooks at independent bookstores, libraries, and literary centers. Check online (search word "chapbooks") and literary magazine listings for information about contests and publishers.

Be clear on your reasons for creating a chapbook.
If success to you depends on winning a contest, realize there is stiff competition. Be willing to invest time (researching, waiting for contest results) and money (postage, copying, and entry fees). Realize you are dependent on the whims of judges over whom you have no control.

If what matters to you is seeing your work in print, consider self-publishing.

If success means the satisfaction of creating an artistic whole, you may not feel the need to submit or publish; creating a chapbook could be an end in itself or a step in learning how to build a full-length manuscript.

[cont. on next page]

[sidebar, cont.]

Feed and groom your own winged and wooly poems.
This is your chance to create a mini-book. Look beyond the excellence of
individual poems and consider placement, pacing, and narrative arc to create an artistic whole.

Investigate publishing options.
Familiarize yourself with chapbook publishers and contests and check the
quality of both content and production before you submit. Follow the
guidelines: entry/reading fees, page count, acknowledgments, deadlines.
   You might want to self-publish or use a print-on-demand publisher.
When you self-publish, you control choice of paper, cover, artwork, and
press run. The more copies you make, the cheaper per copy, but consider
how many copies you can realistically sell. With print-on-demand, make
sure you understand all the costs before you commit to the project.

Sweat the details.
If you do it yourself, be sure your copy is clean and the pages are properly
numbered. Use good-quality paper and a crisp font.

Be prepared to market your baby.
Sometimes a press will promote its chapbooks through announcements or
readings, but often marketing is left to the poet. It's a long shot that bookstores will handle your chapbook, but it's worth inquiring at independents.
Set up a Web site, sell your chapbook at poetry readings, and try placing it
in gift or other specialty shops.

—*Rita Moe*

A MANUSCRIPT CHECKLIST

9 ways to sharpen and safety-check your writing

by Beverly Lauderdale

Whether you're a beginner or a pro, a basic checklist helps in the final revision process. It'll help you approach your manuscript with a professional eye and spot the kind of problems that can weaken your piece. Here are nine items from my checklist, with applications to both fiction and nonfiction:

Beginnings

In fiction, establish time, setting, mood, dominant tense, the main character, and an indication of the problem in the first eighth of your story. Here, for example, is how Raymond Carver's short story "Where I'm Calling From" begins: "We are on the front porch at Frank Martin's drying-out facility. Like the rest of us at Frank Martin's, J.P. is first and foremost a drunk. But he's also a chimney sweep. It's his first time here, and he's scared."

"Start with the day that's different" remains classic advice as a way to get your fiction off to a quick start.

Pick your best anecdote, fact, quote, or example for nonfiction leads (or your second best, saving your prize for the conclusion). When *Biography* assigned me a profile of singer Lena Horne, the editor suggested, "Open with the incident in her life that affected you most strongly."

Tip: The lead holds seeds for your ending.

Organization

Count the number of quotes, facts, examples, and anecdotes. Are they interwoven throughout the article? Fiction, too, depends upon alternating dialogue, exposition, action, and reaction.

Think peaks/valleys; heaviness/lightness; emotional contrasts.

Mention possible opposition to your article's premise somewhere in the text. That often defuses negative reader reaction, shows your research, and demonstrates your open-mindedness. This technique also works for fiction when characters do something "out of character." A character's admission of, "OK, it was stupid, but . . ." or "I don't know why I did that" can allay readers' doubts.

In a first-person account, balance the use of "I" against necessary information. In fiction, judge the amount of space allotted to events, characters, and descriptions. Is the allotment proportionate to its importance in the story?

Tip: Ask, "What is the minimum my audience must know at this point in my story?" Then, take out extraneous material.

Accuracy

Keep all notes and check every quote, statistic, name, etc., against finished copy. One misstep weakens the trust of an editor or reader. Example: An otherwise well-done novel I read depicted the protagonist's winter arrival in San Francisco. Yet when she drove east on the Bay Bridge toward the "brown" Contra Costa hills, Northern California purists shook their heads. East Bay hills are green in winter.

Depend on primary sources whenever possible.

Accumulate more research than needed. The more authoritative you feel, the stronger will be your voice.

Capture the vernacular of a character's speech; the vocabulary of a job and region.

Stay in viewpoint.

Tip: Correct word selection creates tone. Subtle, implied meanings may contradict your intent. Remember this slogan: "Every inappropriate word counts against you."

Redundancies

Cross out repeated words such as "free" gift, "daylight" sun and "softly" whispered.

Eliminate padding or inserting data your audience knows. What's significant about "The room has a door, a floor, a window, and four walls"? When the room's *not* conventional, that's new.

Guard against "creeping" clichés. "If a phrase comes too easily," goes the classic advice, "be suspicious. Likely you've heard it somewhere."

Choose intentional redundancies occasionally to create a special effect.

Tip: In your journal, list words you like. Amazingly, they'll turn into synonyms in future projects.

Sensory impressions

Evoke a complete world in your writing by supplying sound, taste, smell, touch. That duplicates our everyday world where we use multiple senses.

Stick with one adjective, rather than a string of descriptive words. When I asked a prolific reader how she completed so many books, she said, "Just skip over descriptions and find the good stuff."

Tip: Imagery may reflect how the writer observes the world. It's one way he or she puts a personal stamp on writing.

Verbs

Push paragraphs forward with action verbs. They help shorten sentences and give an impression of strength, motion, and vitality.

Rely on action verbs to cut your use of adjectives and adverbs. Somewhere in a verb's imagery or sound lies a suggestion of what it means.

Tip: On paper, itemize the verbs in your draft. This pinpoints passive verbs and calls attention to repetitions and weak sentences.

Transitions

"Place the emphatic words of a sentence at the end," write William Strunk Jr. and E.B. White in *The Elements of Style.* An emphatic final word may also furnish a bridge—a transition—to the next sentence, paragraph, or chapter.

Clarify changes in time, setting, and thought by choosing transitional phrases or words such as "however," "suddenly," "first," "then," and "conversely."

Vary sentence lengths. The same subject/verb pattern can be monotonous. Try an incomplete or one-word sentence. Insert a question. Join short sentences. Cut long ones. Invert a statement. Can staccato sentences illustrate action? Can complex/compound ones represent introspection? Can you employ the "emotion-first" rule, as in "Angry, he began to speak"? Read your piece aloud (yes, to an empty room). Listen for cadence, smoothness, those places where you gasp before the end punctuation.

Analyze sentences for concrete images, diverse sounds, clarity.

Avoid starting consecutive paragraphs with the same word—especially if writing in the first person.

Tip: Each sentence must carry its own weight. If omitted, would the manuscript suffer?

Grammar, spelling

Edit for mechanical problems. If necessary, recruit someone else to proof for spelling and grammar.

Master the difference between it's and its, lay and lie.

Read sentences backward to pick out misspellings or transpositions.

Become aware of your own grammatical weaknesses. For instance, certain mistakes recur among my writing students:

Dangling participles: "Walking down the street on a windy day, my hat blew off." Revised: "Walking down the street on a windy day, I felt my hat blow off."

The I/me dilemma in a prepositional phrase: "I need a reservation for my wife and I." Revised: "I need a reservation for my wife and me."

Parallelism within a sentence: "He told me either to ask for a raise or quit my job." Revised: "He told me either to ask for a raise or to quit my job."

Tip: A Writer's Reference and *The Harbrace College Handbook* are fast tools.

Endings

Conclude, in fiction, when the problem is resolved; in nonfiction, when the point is made.

Stay away from coincidences and predictability. Don't box yourself in with only two choices. Does Jane have to marry either Tom or Stephen? Are there other options for the basketball team besides winning or losing? Since solutions rarely come easily in life, readers distrust easy solutions on the printed page.

"Stop when you're ready to stop," recommends William Zinsser in *On Writing Well.* Take "your reader slightly by surprise," as Zinsser demonstrates in his feature on Woody Allen:

> "If people come away relating to me as a person," Allen says, "rather than just enjoying my jokes; if they come away wanting to hear me again, no matter what I might talk about, then I'm succeeding." Judging by the returns, he is. Woody Allen is Mr. Related-To, Mr. Pop Therapy, and he seems a good bet to hold the franchise for many years. Yet he does have a problem all his own, unshared by, unrelated to, the rest of America. "I'm obsessed," he says, "by the fact that my mother genuinely resembles Groucho Marx."

Tip: The traditional full-circle technique, in which the ending reinforces the beginning of a piece and echoes points or themes made at the start, is a satisfactory device for wrapping up your manuscript.

Beverly Lauderdale of Martinez, Calif., writes fiction and nonfiction. Her work has appeared in magazines, literary journals, and newspapers. This article appeared in *The Writer*, May 2003.

HOW TO GET YOUR SHORT STORY PUBLISHED

Getting published in a literary magazine is an important step for fiction writers

by C.M. Mayo

Beginning writers often imagine publishing their short story to be a glamorous event, Hemingwayesque in a wear-your-sunglasses-and-knock-back-the-grappa-as-agents-ring-your-phone-off kind of way. But for most writers, it's an experience on par with, say, folding laundry. Unless you make one of the majors—*Atlantic Monthly, Esquire, GQ, Harper's, The New Yorker*—most likely your payment will be two copies of the magazine. These will arrive in your mailbox in a plain brown envelope. Some editors jot a thank-you note, but most don't bother. Chances are your friends and family will not have heard of the magazine. Even the best literary journals often have only a modest circulation—500 to 5,000—and may not be on the newsstand.

In short, if you want money, you'd do better to flip burgers, and if you want attention, go fight bulls. Knock back that grappa, heck, wear a spangled pink tutu and splash in the city hall fountain during lunch hour. Scream obscenities in Swahili.

So, what's the benefit of getting published in the literary press? Consider that when your story is published, it is no longer one copy printed out from your printer, but 500 or more. Perhaps one is lying on someone's coffee table in Peterborough, N.H., or on a poet's broad oak desk overlooking the beach at La Jolla, Calif. Maybe one sits on the shelves at the University of Chicago's Joseph Regenstein Library, or on a side table in the lobby at Yaddo. Perhaps one day, a hundred years from now, a high school student will find it on a shelf in the basement of the Reno, Nev., public library, and she will sit down Indian-style on the cold linoleum floor and read it, her eyes wide with wonder. Your story, once published, lives its own life—potentially forever.

And of course, it is validating to have your work published. It also helps to mention it in your cover letters when you try to get other work published, apply for grants and fellowships, or try to attract the attention of an agent. Indeed, publishing one's stories in literary journals is (with a very few notable exceptions) a prerequisite to securing a publisher for a collection.

If you can keep your focus on the story, however, and what the story merits—rather than the warm fuzzies for your ego—the process will be easier. Your ego may take some punches, but it will be worth it.

First, rejections

From a breezy foray through the local mall's bookstore, one might guess that Americans write little beyond bodice-rippers, paperbacks with nuclear warheads on their shiny red covers, or teensy gift books with angels and cats on them. So where are all the literary markets?

Millions of Americans are scribbling, and bravely (if often furtively), thousands and thousands are sending their work to literary magazines. Yes, thousands and thousands. According to the listings in the *2001 Directory of Literary Magazines*, *The Paris Review* receives 20,000 unsolicited submissions a year (including poetry), of which it publishes 35; *The North American Review* receives 3,000 prose submissions and publishes 55 to 65. *Tameme*, my annual bilingual literary magazine with a mere three issues to date, has received hundreds of submissions. Most litmags publish only 2 to 3 percent of the manuscripts they receive. As for the top literary publications, getting into one of them is much less likely, even for the most outstanding and recognized writers (including National Book Award winners).

In short, you've got some competition. So when you receive the unsigned form rejection note that says "Sorry," it could mean your story sucks and you should do yourself a favor and burn it, but it also could mean that it's a fine story and they simply didn't have room for it. Or they already had a story about a dying alcoholic grandmother, the heartbreak of losing the family dairy farm, or for that matter, a flying monkey in a business suit. (You'd be amazed.) Equally, it could mean it's one of the best short stories ever written—better than Anton Chekhov's "The Lady with the Pet Dog," better than Flannery O'Connor's "A Good Man is Hard to Find," better than A. Manette Ansay's "Read This and Tell Me What It Says"—and the editor, or more likely some slush-pile squeegee, is an aesthetically blind Philistine pinhead who was probably hung over. Or jealous. Who knows? The point is, the little unsigned rejection note is not a Judgment From On High. It means nothing except that this particular magazine's editor at this particular time has chosen not to publish this particular story.

Sometimes editors write personal notes explaining why they didn't take your story. Indeed, anything handwritten and/or signed by an editor of a prestigious publication can mean that he or she has taken an interest in your work, and you can interpret this as both validation and an invitation to send more. If you get a note from an assistant, who is unacquainted with the toughening rigors of plowing down towering slush piles and is merely attempting to be nice, it's not so meaningful. Thus, it behooves you to research the magazines and their editors.

Research, research, research

The most basic level of research is to get an overall feel for the short fiction market. You can usually find a reasonably interesting selection of literary magazines at your local library. If you can afford it, however, I recommend you go to a bookstore and buy a bunch—at my local Barnes & Noble, I've spotted *Chelsea, Calyx, McSweenies, The Paris Review, The Southwest Review, Tin House,* and *Witness,* all of which would be worth your while to read. Read all you can, including the contributors page. If you read a story by, say, Dan Doe, whom you admire, and you read in Dan Doe's bio that he's also published in *The Seattle Review, High Plains Literary Review,* and *DoubleTake*—check 'em out!

Another good way to spot worthy litmags is to pick up anthologies of stories that have won prizes, such as the Bakeless Literary Prize for fiction, the Iowa Award for short fiction, the National Book Award, the Flannery O'Connor Award for short fiction, or the Pulitzer Prize. Check out the acknowledgments page to see where stories have been previously published and then have a look on the Internet for guidelines.

An excellent place to start your search is the Web site of the Council of Literary Magazines and Presses (www.clmp.org), which has information about and links to the sites of dozens of outstanding journals. Publications without a Web site will usually send guidelines if you send an SASE. *The Writer* lists hundreds of literary magazines on its Web site (www.writermag.com). Books such as the *Directory of Literary Magazines, The International Directory of Little Magazines and Small Presses,* and *The Writer's Handbook* can be helpful, but there is no substitute for actually seeing—and carefully reading—a magazine and its guidelines before you submit.

Guidelines not only give an idea of the types of writing the editors are looking for, but reading periods. Many litmags read only during the fall, or during the winter. Some read September to May, others October to June. Litmags often have special topic issues, such as "the body," "mothers and daughters," "love in America," "overcoming loss," "borderlands." Your manuscript will have a better chance if you can aim it at a special issue.

Calls for submissions are often listed in the classified ads of *The Writer.* Other good sources are *AWP Chronicle, Poets & Writers,* and *The Writer's Carousel,* which is the newsletter of The Writer's Center (www.writer.org) in Washington, D.C.

The mechanics of submission

First, your cover letter. This should have your name, address, telephone number, and e-mail address. Address the letter to a specific person, if you can. If you address it to "Fiction Editor," you're signaling that you don't know the magazine.

Tell them what you're submitting—e.g., "Please find enclosed for your consideration a short story, 'Down the Well.' " Do not explain the story—"This is a story about a young girl who falls down a well." You are not selling a nonfiction article—the literary short story is art, and you must let it speak for itself. Explaining and introducing is blather and it annoys most editors (the experienced ones skip over it and reach for the rejection notes).

Editors are human, however, so it helps—if you can do it honestly—to say something generous about their litmag, such as, "I bought a copy of ABC at the Bethesda Book Festival, and I really admired the story by Dan Doe." If you can't say anything, don't. Brief and businesslike is fine.

Not all but most editors appreciate it if you include something about yourself—a few sentences, a paragraph at the most—that could be used as your contributor's note if your story is taken. I find them easier to both write and read in the third person. (I put mine at the bottom of the page, under the title "Brief Bio.") This is your opportunity to signal that you're serious. You could write, for example: "Dan Doe's stories have been published in Fence and South Dakota Review" or "Dan Doe was recently awarded a scholarship at the Bread Loaf Writers' Conference."

If you don't have big-gun literary credentials, not to worry; a simple note will do—e.g., "Dan Doe is a statistician who lives in Grand Forks, N.D., with his wife, four children, and pack of seven Alpo-guzzling huskies. He is at work on his first novel." Anything more—your five-page resume, a previously published poem, a newspaper article about your amazing recovery after being simultaneously hit by a cement truck and an estimated 3,976 volts of lightning—is clutter. The editor has limited time and attention, so don't take it up with the nonessential. End the cover letter with a "Thank you for considering my work" and sign it.

The manuscript itself should have your name, address, telephone number, and e-mail address in the upper left-hand corner. Include a word count, preferably in the upper right-hand corner. Double-space the text (or else!). Fasten the whole thing—manuscript, SASE, and cover letter—with a paper clip. (Do not staple it, because if editors do seriously consider your story, they may need to make copies for other editorial readers.)

Finally—and this is crucial—enclose a SASE for the reply, because without it, you may not get one. If you also want your manuscript returned, be sure to include enough postage; otherwise, the editors will recycle it.

A note on electronic submissions

There are a burgeoning number of Internet journals that publish short stories, and these prefer, and indeed most only accept, electronic submissions. There are also an some print journals that accept electronic submissions; however, be forewarned that print editors' attitudes and philosophies on this matter vary enormously. Some encourage electronic submissions, while most refuse to read them. So again, check the guidelines.

As a writer, I think the explosion of e-journals is wonderful, and I myself have published poetry, book reviews, and even a brief bit of creative nonfiction in www.brevity.com. However, I have not yet submitted a short story to an e-journal because I believe the form, which is usually several pages long and meant to be savored, is unwieldy for a computer screen.

As editor of *Tameme*, I do not read and usually do not acknowledge unsolicited electronic submissions. My electronic mailbox would be easily overwhelmed and I am leery of opening attachments that might carry a virus.

The question of multiple submissions

A dismaying number of litmag editors state that they do not accept multiple submissions. My view is, with the odds so stacked against writers, to expect one-at-a-time submissions is not only unfair but about as realistic as insisting, say, that highschool seniors apply to only one college. According to my own informal poll, 90% of serious, already well-published short-story writers multiple submit, even to such journals, and without compunction. That means that much of the best work in any given slush pile—*regardless of the editors' stated policy*—is in fact being multiply submitted.

Thus, if you submit your stories one at a time it may take years—toe-curling, shoulder-sagging years—to find them homes. Even some of the most distinguished litmags have been known to sometimes take as long as a year to reply. That's right, *a year*. On two occasions a litmag lost my manuscript—as I found out when I queried eight months later. And I could name several that never replied. Ever.

Rather than get steamed about that, keep in mind that litmag publishing is not a profit-generating business, but a labor of love. Most editors are not paid for their time. If they are, they are so poorly paid that if you tallied all the hours, the money would amount to a fraction of the minimum wage. And they're only human; they have to take the kids to the dentist, grade papers, walk the dog, and write their own short stories, poems, or novel—and the slush pile is growing ever taller, what with all those multiple submissions!

If you have your story accepted, you should immediately inform the other editors that you are withdrawing it. A simple postcard will do: "Dear Editor: This is to let you know that I am withdrawing my story 'Down the Well,' Sincerely, Dan Doe."

To do otherwise—to wait in hopes of a bigger bite from, say, *The New Yorker*—is both dishonorable and unfair to the editor who has taken your story. The literary world is small, and it seems to me that in a somewhat random but inexorable way, what goes around comes around.

Submitting your work to two or four publications is a good place to start. With each rejection, send out another. If after three months you haven't received a reply from a given journal, it could mean your story is under serious consideration. On the other hand, it could mean your story is sitting behind some junior assistant's couch, and he or she still hasn't read it. It's a tough call whether to withdraw the manuscript or keep waiting. All I can say is, go with your gut.

Aside from the secretarial hassle and expense of postage, another reason not to send out more than a very few submissions of a given story at a time is that most likely, with a fresh look a few months later, you will want to revise it. You may even, with a bright red face, wish to hide it under a rock. (I speak from experience.)

Keep learning, keep writing

I doubt there are many serious short-story writers who don't have a brick-thick file of rejections. It's part of the game, so don't let them fluster you. Some of the best short stories have five, eight, even 15 rejections behind them. One prize-winning story by a major contemporary writer racked up 48 rejections before it was taken. Some amazing stories are never published—until they show up in a collection.

A writer must continually work to balance on the razor's edge of arrogance and humility—the arrogance to continue sending out work when it has been rejected and rejected and rejected, and the humility to recognize when one needs to rewrite or even (oh, well) discard. Trying to publish can be a discouraging and disorienting experience, like entering a dark, dense forest with no marked trails. The trick is, keep your chin up and your ego in check. Stay focused on maintaining a balance. When your story is accepted for publication, let your ego, for a few private minutes, tingle and shine.

When, some months or perhaps more than a year later, your two contributors' copies arrive in their plain brown envelope, sit down and read one. Get to know the company your story is in. Write the editors a thank-you note. Be generous, if you honestly can, with kind comments about the other contributors' work. Update your resume and bio. And then, plunk the thing on a shelf and wish your story a sweet *bon voyage*.

C.M. Mayo of Mexico City is the author of *Sky Over El Nido*, which won the Flannery O'Connor Award for Short Fiction, and *Miraculous Air: Journey of a Thousand Miles Through Baja California, the Other Mexico*. Her short fiction has appeared recently in *Chelsea, Natural Bridge*, and *Turnrow*. A version of this article appeared in *The Writer*, April 2003, reprinted from *The Part-Times*, a newsletter of the M.A. in Writing Program, Johns-Hopkins University, Fall 2001. It is reprinted here in an updated version, by permission of the author. © 2003, C.M. Mayo.

SECTION TWO

The Craft
of Writing

FOCUS ON WHAT MATTERS

Keep the core of your story center stage

by Fraser Sherman

This is terrible!" a friend complained recently. "My novel's supposed to be a dark occult thriller. So why are my protagonists going all mushy and romantic?"

Eventually, she figured it out: Although the idea of a supernatural thriller with a unique variation on werewolves had first inspired her book, it was the characters' relationship that had come to interest her most. She started over, approaching her novel as a paranormal romance and focusing on the relationship as the center of the story. The werewolves were still important, but secondary to the love affair.

The same problem my friend faced can bedevil any writer. You began by writing a bio-terrorism thriller, but you've become fascinated by the hardships that shaped your hero. How much of his coming-of-age trauma will deepen his character? How much will put thriller readers to sleep?

Conversely, you may discover the interplanetary war you conceived as the backdrop to your paranormal romance intrigues you at least as much as your romantic leads. How much of the war can you include without detracting from the core romance—or should you start over and write a science-fiction epic instead?

Knowing which part of your story to focus on is essential to holding your book together. When you've accumulated more background detail on your setting than you can use, when your computer bulges with biographical details on your leads that you just have to work in, when you can't decide if you're writing a love story with a mystery subplot or a mystery with a romance subplot, learning to focus in on the core of your story will keep your writing on track and your readers satisfied.

Whether you're writing serious literature, police procedurals, or a direct-to-video vampire film, there are only so many things you can focus on in your story.

Action: Will the terrorists blow up the White House? Will vampires rule the Earth? Will Darth Vader crush the rebellion? In action-focused stories, the characters may be believable and the settings colorful, but the heart of the story is the sequence of events that keeps readers wondering "what happens next?"

Character: In character-focused stories, on the other hand, it's the heart and mind of the protagonist that the writer focuses upon. The Oscar-winning film *The Apartment,* for example, isn't the story of Jack Lemmon's climb up the corporate ladder as much as his climb from office suck-up to a mensch willing to do the decent thing, even at the risk of his career.

Puzzle: Who killed Roger Ackroyd? Who shot JFK? What really causes cattle mutilations? Why did mom leave the family 10 years ago? The focus is on watching your protagonists solve the mystery, whether the protagonist is a complex character or a stick figure.

Setting: Setting-focused stories are the ones reviewers say "reveal the world of"—whether that world is rave clubs or pre-Raphaelite painters, Scotland Yard or daily life among the Mongol hordes.

Theme: Jesus saves. Rich people are scum. War is hell. The writer's focus is on the message she wants to spread. Romance and suspense writer Vicki Hinze, for example, says she decides on a theme, then chooses the characters, plot, and setting that will let her develop it.

Feelings: You focus on making your readers shudder in terror, start weeping, or laugh out loud. P.G. Wodehouse's inspired comic novels don't have complex characters and the plots are wildly implausible, but once I start his stories, I don't stop laughing until the end.

While this isn't a comprehensive list, it offers good guidelines that can apply to any genre. In mysteries, for instance, the classic writers—Agatha Christie, Dorothy Sayers—wrote puzzle stories in which characterization took a back seat to solving the mystery. Other detective stories give character a much stronger role: The resolution of *The Maltese Falcon* isn't Sam Spade unmasking his girlfriend as a murderer, but the revelation that he won't "play the sap" for her by covering up the truth, even though he loves her.

In a police procedural such as TV's classic *Hill Street Blues*, even though the characters are strong, the individual characters and cases don't matter as much as the world of the police. Some cases aren't solved, some criminals get off scot-free, some cops die, but the story is about the force, and it keeps going.

In science fiction, Harry Turtledove's alternate-history novels focus on setting, such as the world resulting from an alien invasion during World War II in the In the Balance series. L. Neil Smith's novels center on his libertarian themes; Poul Anderson's "Hoka" stories focus on making readers laugh their heads off at his outrageous science-fiction parodies; Kurt Busiek's *The Tarnished Angel* focuses on a petty super-criminal's struggle to find meaning in his life.

Once you know your focus, you know the narrative spine of your tale. If, like my friend, it's the characters that really captivate you, make it about them. Even as they fight lycanthropes, Vikings, or terrorists, their love story (or battles with alcoholism, or coming-of-age drama) has to be what's kept in mind; the resolution your readers expect will be a personal one, not victory over an outside force.

The Tarnished Angel, for example, is set in a colorful comic-book world where the protagonist, Steeljack, has to overcome a murderous criminal. The focus, though, isn't on the battle but on Steeljack's personal journey. The story doesn't end with his victory, but when he finally gains self-respect.

If you're focusing on action more than character, however, your readers will expect the climax to focus on the battle with the neo-Nazi conspiracy, not the hero's personal torments (unless the hero overcomes his personal torments while simultaneously beating the neo-Nazis). A puzzle story ends by wrapping up the mystery. Stories that focus on theme are resolved when the theme is proven true (to the characters, if not the reader), as in Isaac Asimov's "In a Good Cause," which ends with the unlikely hero showing how his philosophy saved the Earth.

Focusing can also help if you get lost in the middle of the book. In a good puzzle story, even when the villain is trying to murder the hero, the author never forgets that the protagonist's goal is to gather clues and find answers. In an action-centered mystery novel, gathering clues may be just an excuse for the hardboiled hero to bust heads and take names.

If you fill up the middle of your puzzle-solving story with action, or your action story with graphic autopsy scenes, the readers might feel you've pulled a bait-and-switch.

I used focusing to hammer my novel *Questionable Minds* (which I recently submitted to a publisher) into workable shape. In the early drafts, I couldn't decide what to focus on: the colorful setting of a Victorian England where psychic powers work; a mystery involving the identity and methods of a psychic serial killer; my hero Simon's inner struggle to choose between love and revenge; or Simon's efforts to destroy the villain before he kills again. The story wandered across the map, and trying to resolve all my plot threads in the last chapter, not surprisingly, made for a clunky finish.

After several more drafts, I realized the mystery wasn't that important. The setting was, but I cared about my hero's personal struggles and his exciting adventures more. I reworked the story to shift from unmasking the killer and explaining his strange powers (a puzzle) to simply stopping him (plot), with my hero's emotional drama as a secondary focus. The setting stayed a colorful backdrop to *Questionable Minds* rather than center stage; I used scenes of psychics in action only where it tied into my plot, and I trimmed away supporting cast members who added color but didn't advance the story.

Questionable Minds might have been finished sooner if I'd had a clear idea of my focus a few drafts earlier. Here are some questions that might help you shave off some rewriting time:

What inspires you? What excites you about your new story—the fascinating, ne'er-do-well lead? Exploring the world of day traders? Sharing your faith in Jesus? What you want to write about may indicate where you should focus.

Don't hesitate to dig beyond your first answer, either. If you want to write about small-town life years ago, is it to capture the setting, as Robert McCammon does brilliantly in *Boy's Life*? Or to tell a coming-of-age story (character), as Wally Lamb does in *She's Come Undone*?

How would you sum up your book? Suppose you're inspired to write a detective novel based on your own time on the force. If, in describing the book, you say, "It's about a crooked cop trying to straighten out his life," this suggests a character focus; "It's about compromises cops have to make to get the job done," might be a theme story; and "A crooked cop takes down a serial rapist" implies the focus will be on plot.

What do you want for your readers? Horror legend H.P. Lovecraft believed "wonder stories" should and could only be "a vivid picture of a human mood"— in most of his stories, fear. His characters aren't deep and the plots often have holes, but his best work focuses on building a nightmarish world of unearthly, unspeakable terrors that made Lovecraft the most influential horror writer of the last century.

> Knowing which part of your story to focus on is essential to holding your book together.

Do you want your readers to laugh? Shudder? Contemplate the pain of the human condition? Gasp in excitement or wonder? That's a big clue to your focus.

What pulls focus? In theater, "pulling focus" means drawing attention away from the characters or conversation the audience is supposed to watch. If, like my friend, you find the characters more interesting than the plot, or your Byzantine setting more fascinating than the protagonist, you may need to shift your focus.

Alternatively, the problem may be that part of your book doesn't pull focus enough. Perhaps the reason you find Byzantium more interesting than your hero is because you haven't created a strong enough character to match the color of that amazing historical setting. If you still want to create a character-focused story, rewrite your protagonist until Byzantium's religious schisms and chariot races can't steal the spotlight.

In *Questionable Minds*, I chose to focus on action over puzzle because the mystery elements were too weak to pull focus (e.g., unmasking the villain as someone who'd never appeared before). If I'd had my heart set on writing a mystery, I could have done it—added clues, given the suspects a bigger role—but it would have been much more work than the path I chose. Since I wasn't hooked on the mystery, shifting focus made more sense.

So focus is the key, not only to giving your readers satisfaction, but to satisfying yourself, keeping your book on track and figuring out, like my friend, when it's time to go back and start over instead of fighting against the tide.

Fraser Sherman of Fort Walton Beach, Fla., is a reporter for the *Destin [Fla.] Log*. His publications include a film reference book, *Cyborgs, Santa Claus, and Satan*. This article is from *The Writer*, November 2002.

MULTI-DIMENSIONAL CHARACTERS

Readers bond emotionally
with characters with depth

by Hal Blythe and Charlie Sweet

"Story is something happening to someone you've been led to care about," writes John D. MacDonald in his introduction to Stephen King's *Night Shift*.

There it is in a nutshell, the best advice we've come across on writing fiction. If your readers don't have emotional interest vested in your protagonist, nothing else matters—not a clever plot, not a minutely detailed setting, not a consistent and believable point of view, not a finely tuned tone. Nothing.

And there's a corollary to MacDonald's theory. If your readers don't connect to your character *immediately*, they probably won't connect at all.

How, then, do you build an early emotional bridge between your main character and your audience? How do you lead your readers to be concerned right away about your creation's joys and fears, successes and failures?

The answer lies in a number of choices you make as you fashion your protagonist and his or her fictional world. Before you can begin to make these choices, though, you must get to know your main character better than you know any real-life person.

To this end, we suggest that before you begin your story, you establish a fictional biography for your main character. At one extreme, you might think of this bio as a job application for an intelligence agency—providing a full spectrum of detailed information, from physical appearance to educational background, favorite hobbies to preferred authors. Or you may choose to profile only those major traits that define your character's essence—things that might appear in a eulogy. Regardless of which approach you take, you must make one essential decision: You must determine what lies at your character's emotional core.

Ask yourself, what is the one thing that defines my character? What is that character's primary goal in life? Knowing this goal will determine the subsequent choices you make as you create the story in which this character takes center stage.

Once you have a solid understanding of your character and his or her goal (to make the soccer team, to bring Mommy and Daddy back together, to realize her potential as an adult woman), you can begin to devise a plot that reveals your character's attempts to achieve this goal—the struggles, the successes, the failures, the lessons learned. Each choice you make concerning your character's traits, situations, and relationships should draw readers to your character emotionally and make them care.

Your first choice grows directly out of the character's emotional core. Do you see your protagonist as basically strong or weak, honest or dishonest, intelligent or dull? What is it about him or her that will affect a reader immediately on an emotional level?

It's important to note here that readers don't have to *like* your character to care for him or her. After all, some of literature's most memorable characters are villains. Remember Iago (*Othello*), or Lady Macbeth, Kurtz in Joseph Conrad's *Heart of Darkness,* The Misfit in Flannery O'Connor's "A Good Man Is Hard to Find"? We don't like them, but we're certainly drawn to them emotionally. We care what happens to them, even if it's that we're concerned they get their just desserts. Like all well-drawn characters, these classic villains have goals, and their struggles to achieve these goals reveal their emotional core, thus drawing readers to them from the start.

Lady Macbeth has at least two admirable qualities—her love of her husband and her ambition, while O'Connor's Misfit, who was mistreated by his father, searches desperately for a parent figure.

Film critic Roger Ebert made a similar point about the movie adaptation of Thomas Harris' *Red Dragon.* Audiences care about Hannibal Lecter and are even willing to somewhat forgive him because the doctor's trespasses are forced upon him by his strong nature, he is usually imprisoned, he aids the FBI, and his personality is partially appealing (e.g., he is literate, droll, and well-mannered).

What you as a writer must do immediately in your story, then, is provide your main character (even if that character is not altogether admirable) with at least one attractive characteristic. Perhaps it is best to think of your character's goal as a desire, which gives it an emotional context. Here are some specific character traits that create a bond with readers.

One is *curiosity*. In Sherwood Anderson's "I Want to Know Why," an uneducated young man wants to do something he knows is wrong, and basically he tells us his story so we understand the reason for his anger.

John Updike's "Flight" is narrated by Allan Dow, who immediately commands our sympathy because of an incident in his youth involving his mother. She took them both to the top of a hill overlooking their little town and said,

"Allan. You're going to fly." Like Allan, Updike's audience wants to know what Lillian Dow meant.

Conflicted conscience is another appealing trait. Readers relate to fictional people who try to do the right thing, even if they don't always succeed. William Faulkner's "Barn Burning" begins with an illiterate 10-year-old trapped in a makeshift courtroom during late Southern Reconstruction. The justice of the peace commands Sarty to tell the truth, while his father threatens him, telling him he must stick to his family even if it means lying. The narrator of Herman Melville's "Bartleby the Scrivener" is also torn by his conscience. He tells us his story of a recalcitrant copyist who worked for him, then refused to, thus becoming a nuisance. The narrator tries to help his employee, but eventually abandons him. Readers sympathize with this attempt to help a fellow human being in distress, even though the ultimate result is failure.

Readers also find themselves drawn to *altruism*—selfless characters who try to help others on an individual basis or involve themselves in worthy causes. In Ernest Hemingway's "The Killers," Nick Adams is threatened by a duo of hit men. While the easy thing for him to do would be to remain silent or flee, he immediately tries to warn Ole Anderson, the man the killers seek. We sympathize with Nick because he is less concerned with his own safety than that of another human. Popular-fiction heroes, such as Robert B. Parker's Spenser, constantly risk their lives to save ordinary citizens.

Perhaps the most attractive trait in Western culture is *love*. If a fictional character demonstrates the ability to love someone, readers will put up with many sins. Macbeth is a killer, but he deeply loves his wife. In Nathaniel Hawthorne's *The Scarlet Letter,* Arthur Dimmesdale is a sinner and a hypocrite, but he genuinely loves someone the Puritan code of Salem tells him he shouldn't, Hester Prynne. Allan Dow, though he comes to resent the dying town and his dysfunctional family, still loves and respects his mother.

Sometimes you might appeal to your readers' natural sympathies for the underdog. Many of the aforementioned characters are also *victims*, powerless pawns to larger forces that to some extent control them. Anderson's young man is a victim of a class system that rewards upward mobility and even looks down at those who don't ascend. Allan Dow and Sarty are victims of powerful parents who tyrannize them.

In general, audiences care for women and children, groups who traditionally have been seen as less powerful than adult males. But even adult males can be victims. Witness Hemingway's old man (*The Old Man and the Sea*), who constantly returns to a sea that defeats him day after day. Since Greek tragedy, audiences have especially sympathized with people who encounter overwhelming odds.

Given your choice of the "emotional magnet," you can now decide on a plot that will best reveal this trait. Perhaps you will fashion a conflict that involves an inner struggle, such as the remainder of "Barn Burning," where the opposing forces of justice and family blood continually pull young Sarty apart. You might even decide on a more physical conflict centering on some personal or professional relationship. Think of Edgar Allan Poe's unnamed narrator trying to save his childhood friend Roderick Usher ("The Fall of the House of Usher") from the mysterious maladies of that gloomy house and his sister Madeline. You might even decide on a more physical conflict that will draw your readers to your character's struggle to triumph over a disability or a seemingly superior opponent. Whatever your choice, you must tailor your conflict to your character's essential trait.

Ultimately in fiction, one major truth is proven time after time—create not just characters, but *care*-acters. If you establish an emotional bridge between your chief character and your readers early on, your audience will willingly cross into your fictional universe and want to stay.

Hal Blythe and **Charlie Sweet,** who often write under the pseudonym Hal Charles, are professors of English at Eastern Kentucky University. Collaborators for 30 years, they have published some 650 pieces and several books. This article is from *The Writer*, March 2003.

CHARACTER TRAITS

• Make the desire believable. Even in the most complex of thrillers, the simplest emotions fare best. Be sure to fashion a believable reason for that desire.

• Avoid creating robotic characters who move toward their goal with machine-like precision. Only in the best of fantasy do we care about lifeless beings.

• Shun using stereotypes and caricatures, for though they may have emotional lives, those emotions are so hackneyed and trite that readers, like overfed fish, won't bite on that hook.

• Don't overdo the emotion, either. Excessive emotions seem unreal; when in one story your main character is torn emotionally by a bullying father, an overbearing mother, a doting aunt, and a much-too-concerned big brother, you drown your readers in a sea of love.

—Hal Blythe and Charlie Sweet

WRITING ABOUT LOVE

by Sharon Oard Warner

"What do any of us really know about love?" So asks Mel McGinnis, the main character in one of Raymond Carver's finest stories, "What We Talk About When We Talk About Love."

Mel's question is rhetorical, of course, simply his way of introducing the subject to the three other people at the table. Like the rest of us, Mel considers himself an expert. As Scottish novelist and poet George MacDonald said, "There is no feeling in the human heart which exists in that heart alone—which is not, in some form or degree, in every heart." We all recognize love when we see it, know it when we feel it, cherish its presence, and grieve its loss.

No wonder writers come to the subject with a certain degree of confidence. Write about what you know, we're admonished. Well, we all know about love, don't we? Sure we do. Since all of us are experts, then why is it so damned difficult to write a good love story? Why do stories about love and the lovelorn so often leave us cold?

In my quest for answers, I reread Carver's famous story. Right off the bat, the author establishes a number of facts. By the end of the second sentence we learn that Mel McGinnis is a cardiologist, and in the following three sentences we discover the immediate setting of the story—Mel's kitchen—and the city in which the story takes place, Albuquerque, N.M. The other characters are introduced as well: Mel's second wife, Terri; the narrator, Nick; and Nick's wife, Laura. But that's not all. Carver also tells us that the four are drinking gin and that "sunlight filled the kitchen from the big window behind the sink." Because I live in Albuquerque, I know the quality of this sunlight, its clarity and brilliance. Those of you in Cleveland or Minneapolis or elsewhere don't have this advantage, but that's OK. The story's only a little less glorious for your not knowing the vivid blue of an Albuquerque sky.

So, what's the sky got to do with it? Actually, a lot more than you might think. In order to establish characters, Carver has to place them in a particular location, and the sooner the better. For Carver, it isn't enough to let us into Mel's kitchen, ice bucket and bottle of gin on the table. He also puts Mel's kitchen in a specific city, Albuquerque. In so doing, he allows readers to relax. We don't have to be casting about for clues to set up this scene. It's all there, in the first five sentences, which allows us to focus on the people, what they're saying and doing.

Early on, Nick, the narrator, gives us a clear physical description of his best friend: "Mel was 45 years old. He was tall and rangy with curly soft hair. His face and arms were brown from all the tennis he played. When he was sober, his gestures, all his movements, were precise, very careful." He also tells us a little something about Mel's past—that he spent five years in the seminary before going to medical school, which explains why he believes that real love is "nothing less than spiritual love."

Even sooner, in the middle of the first page, we get a description of Mel's wife, Terri: "She was a bone-thin woman with a pretty face, dark eyes, and brown hair that hung down her back. She liked necklaces made of turquoise, and long pendant earrings." Note that the details about Terri's jewelry reinforce our sense of place—New Mexico, where lots of women wear silver and turquoise.

Terri's description comes before Mel's because she's the first to speak, and the reader must visualize her first. What she says is a bit shocking: She regales those at the table with the story of her ex-lover, a man who beat her and dragged her around the room by her ankles. "What do you do with love like that?" she asks those at the table (and us). It's another rhetorical question, and one that provokes an argument. "My God, don't be silly. That's not love, and you know it," Mel responds. "I don't know what you'd call it, but I sure know you wouldn't call it love." Plenty of readers are sure to agree with him. They may even be relieved that someone in this story has his head on straight. (But keep in mind they haven't yet finished the story.)

"People are different, Mel," Terri replies. "Sure, sometimes he may have acted crazy. Okay. But he loved me. In his own way, maybe, but he loved me." And there we have it, the essential catalyst of fiction: conflict. It unfolds quite naturally in the first two pages—so naturally we hardly notice—and it deepens and darkens, like the light from the kitchen window as day gives way to night.

Like everything else that matters, love is in the details. Human beings believe they're loved because others *act* in loving ways. Words and words alone don't convince us, not for long, anyway. And it's the same in fiction. We believe in these people—Mel and Terri and, to a lesser degree, Nick and Laura—because

Carver has done the behind-the-scenes work. Either before he began writing, or else in successive drafts, he presented the relevant details that bring his characters to life: physical descriptions, personal histories, temperaments, quirks, and mannerisms. We note, for instance, that the newly marrieds repeatedly reach out to one another for reassurance; early on, Nick touches Laura's hand, then encircles her broad wrist with his fingers, holding her. Their body language alone speaks volumes.

To write convincingly, fiction writers must hold two complementary but seemingly opposing ideas in mind: People are both entirely similar and utterly different. We all walk, yes, but we all walk differently. Some of us skim along the surface of the sidewalk; others scuff, sidle, swagger, or schlump. A few of us make our way in wheelchairs, and if we're small enough or sick enough, we crawl. We all love, yes (well, all but sociopaths, my husband the psychologist would remind me), but we all love *differently*. Defending her ex-lover, Terri says, "It was love. Sure it was abnormal in most people's eyes. But he was willing to die for it." Mel scoffs at this notion. His preference is for chivalrous love, ethereal and everlasting. Late in the story, he admits that if he could be born in another day and time, he'd come back as a knight in shining armor. While our similarities bind us to the rest of humanity, our differences define us.

We writers have our theories on love. Southern writer Carson McCullers believed in what she called "the lover and the beloved." According to her, two people rarely have the good sense to love one another. Rather, she maintained that "love is a solitary thing," that we are destined to be either the lover or the beloved. My own theory has to do with childhood experience. As I see it, the way we make our way through this world is determined in large part by our pasts and, particularly, by what we experienced as children. Our definitions of love, our capacity for love—whom we love and why—are all strongly influenced by what we learned of love when we were young. Thus, I come to my characters through their childhoods. In developing them, I want to learn as much as possible about their formative experiences—for good and for ill.

> Since all of us are experts, then why is it so damned difficult to write a good love story?

Over the last seven years, I've written a novel called *Deep in the Heart*. Central to the story is a couple married 17 years, Carl and Hannah Solace. While composing the first few drafts, I took great pains to discover the childhood histories of the two. I knew, for instance, about the death of Hannah's mother and the aftermath of that death, which turns out to be critical to Hannah's decision not to have children. I also learned/discovered/made up all I could about Carl's early life in Terrell, Texas; about his mother's job at the state hospital; about his father's retreat to a fishing cabin at Lake Texoma; and about his bullying brother, Buddy.

I wrote whole chapters that have long since disappeared from the actual book. But the lost chapters were not a waste of time. Far from it. This sort of "research" is absolutely critical to my understanding of the characters' motivations. Because I did this work, I know that Carl yearns for unequivocal love, the sort that most of us get from our children. When he learns that his wife is pregnant for the first time, he is dumbstruck and overcome by an immense happiness he's desperate to convey to his miserable wife.

Needless to say, I felt fairly secure in my knowledge of these characters. It wasn't until after I sold the novel and made a trip to New York to meet my editors that I learned differently. During a two-hour meeting, I woke up to the limitations of my own process. Although I knew a great deal about some things, it turned out that I was entirely ignorant about others. "How did Hannah and Carl meet?" my editors asked. "How were the early years of their marriage? When did they stop being happy together?" I didn't have the faintest idea and had to admit it. A few days later, when the flush of embarrassment finally left me, I went over the notes of the meeting, then spent a month or so filling in the gaps. To do this, I turned to an exercise I've recommended to students over the years but had never completed myself.

It comes from "Chronology in the Short Story" in *The Passionate, Accurate Story* by Carol Bly. She brings up a story by Richard Brautigan, "The World War I Los Angeles Airplane," a three-page wonder that's nothing more than a list of 33 items from one man's life. Upon reading that story, I immediately saw Bly's point: "We can learn a chronology lesson from Brautigan," she writes. "It is that if a meaningful scene, no matter how short, is set next to another meaningful scene, feeling and value multiply."

I called my list "Story of a Marriage." It begins when Hannah and Carl met and concludes some 20 years later, after they divorce and remarry. In that way, I discovered what becomes of them in the years after the book ends, and this, too, has been useful because it has granted me a sort of omniscience. Once, I happened to mention Carl's remarriage to my editor, Carla Riccio. "He gets married again!" she exclaimed. "Oh, I'm so glad to hear that, Sharon!" Somewhere along the way, Carl had ceased to be a collection of characteristics and had become—for us, anyway—a real human being.

Perhaps you've heard the truism that the only people who can understand a marriage are the two living inside it. Accurate as this may be in real life, it's wrong when it comes to fiction. Writers interested in the vagaries of love must inhabit a relationship in the same way the couple does, from the inside out. Only then will they know enough to convince the rest of us to care.

At the end of "What We Talk About When We Talk About Love," Mel—thoroughly drunk and waxing nostalgic—says he wants to call his kids. Terri discourages him, pointing out that Mel's ex-wife, Marjorie, might answer. Terri knows all about Marjorie: "There isn't a day goes by that Mel doesn't say he wishes she'd get married again. Or else die," she explains. While some readers (and delicate little Laura) may be surprised by this harsh comment, Terri isn't and neither is Carver. Even knights in shining armor have their soft spots— even knights miss their children and grieve over their failures. Losing love, they may turn to hate. We begin to understand what Mel knows about love, and yes, *our hearts go out to him.*

Sharon Oard Warner of Albuquerque, N.M., is director of creative writing at the University of New Mexico and founding director of the school's Taos Summer Writers' Conference. This article is from *The Writer,* November 2002.

CHILDREN'S PICTURE BOOKS: BALANCING ART & TEXT

How the 2 elements of children's picture books work together

by Staton Rabin

Let's say that if you pasted your rejection slips end to end, they'd circle the globe more times than John Glenn. Is it time then to throw in the towel on getting your children's picture book published? Not necessarily. It depends on whether the problem is the quality of your manuscript, or some other aspect of it on which editors can legitimately disagree. You will need to be objective enough to tell the difference. Perhaps a recent experience of mine will be instructive.

My second published children's picture-book manuscript, *Casey Over There*, was rejected by 15 publishers before Harcourt, Inc., published it. The first four submissions were made by a top children's-book agency, and my agent quit representing me after that. But I persisted. Why?

I had enough experience as a writer of published magazine articles and short stories for children—as well as sufficient objectivity about my own work—to know that my manuscript was publishable. Not every book manuscript I write is, but I knew this one was. It was a story about a boy from Brooklyn who missed his older brother, who was away fighting in France during World War I. The book had a marketable subject (the "Great War") that had been virtually neglected in the children's-book field, a good format and structure, and educational value without the loss of entertainment value. It was also funny and affecting and aimed at the right age group. It met all the parameters of what picture-book editors require. So what was the problem?

Avoiding a common pitfall

I knew from the moment I wrote the manuscript that it would be tough to find a publisher for it. The text was very spare, and I knew it would take an unusual editor to understand what I was trying to do. I had noticed that too many children's-book authors write text that is redundant—the illustrations merely repeat what's in the text. Those writers, however, who illustrate their own manuscripts (something I don't recommend, but more about this later), write text that is appropriately spare and well-integrated with the pictures.

My goal was to write a picture-book text in the same way author-illustrators do: so that art and words would work together to enhance, not duplicate, each other. I would not, of course, illustrate my own book. But I approached the process as if I were only a part of the whole, not the sole "creator" of the book. The future illustrator of the book, selected by the publisher, would be an essential part of this collaborative process. He would, in a sense, be my co-author, without ever changing a word of the text.

Writers who create text only tend to overwrite. To sell their manuscript to a book editor, they write stories that are too wordy and don't need pictures to enhance them. This verbosity is almost necessary at the "selling" stage, to help children's-book editors visualize the final product. But once these books are acquired for publication, they are not edited down as they should be. As a result, when the manuscript is illustrated, in most cases the pictures are superfluous and the words just "explain" what's in the pictures.

I wanted to avoid this pitfall. My text would actually *require* pictures for the story to be complete. This doesn't mean that I drew pictures to illustrate my story, which would have been a terrible mistake. Nor does it mean that my story made no sense without the pictures. But what I did do was leave breathing room in my work for pictures, and write text that would work in concert with art to create an integrated whole.

The text included spaces for newspaper headlines announcing the Armistice, letters from a soldier to his brother, World War I posters ("Uncle Sam Wants You!"), etc. All of these were indicated in the text with a few words or a visual item or two literally pasted into the story. And these "illustrations" weren't merely embellishments, but necessary elements of the story.

For example, instead of writing, "World War I was over, we won and the soldiers came home and everyone was happy," I wrote, "And then, at the eleventh hour of the eleventh day of the eleventh month of 1918 . . ." and below this I drew a copy of the front page of *The New York Times* with its headline, "Armistice Signed, End of The War!" (In the pub-

Learning to write children's picture books is not easy. It is not a way to get started in publishing. It is not easier than writing for adults. It is, in most ways, exactly the same as writing for adults.

lished book, Greg Shed, the terrific artist I eventually was teamed with, painted that *Times* cover, added an American flag, and drew his own version of the famous photo of the victory parade in New York City.) The illustrations moved the story forward in time. Pictures and text worked together to tell a story, one incomplete without the other. And that's the way it should be.

I was walking a fine line by indicating some of the pictures—you should never try to illustrate a picture-book manuscript unless you're also a superb, professional-quality illustrator (which I most certainly am not). Children's-book editors do not want writers to illustrate their own stories unless they are extremely accomplished illustrators who are as good as the best in the business. Should your book be purchased, the publisher's art director will choose the right illustrator for your book by examining portfolios of professional illustrators. But I did use a simple notation or drawing here and there—or cut and pasted a small photocopy of a famous illustration (for example, the "Uncle Sam Wants You!" poster) right into my text—to indicate what was needed. This was done only when absolutely necessary to tell the story.

While I knew my book would be a tough sell because the writing was spare, I also knew it would "work" once it was illustrated, and that making it any less spare would ruin it. I also knew that because the book took place in two countries (the United States and France), it would require that kids understand I was "cutting away" to another location, as a movie does. Kids obviously understand movies, so I knew they'd have no trouble following my book. ("There was Casey, dipping his helmet into a muddy trench for water to shave with," and, on the facing page, "And there was Aubrey, playing kick the can on West 9th Street, wondering if Casey ever got the shaving soap.") But I didn't know if children's-book editors would give kids enough credit for intelligence, and trust in their ability to understand shifts in time and location.

My fears proved warranted. At least they did for those first 15 rejections. But I knew I shouldn't give up. And in a situation like this, neither should you. As a writer of children's books, you must have faith in children's intelligence, even when some editors and publishers may not. But if you write an "unusual" picture-book manuscript, as I did, you will have to follow the unwritten rules in every other respect if you hope to sell your work.

What you should know

Learning to write children's picture books is not easy. It is not a way to get started in publishing. It is not easier than writing for adults. It is, in most ways, exactly the same as writing for adults. There are some differences, however, just as there is a difference between writing a movie script and writing a novel. Here are some pointers about writing for children:

1. Don't believe anyone who tells you that children's books contain a special, limited vocabulary, drawn from lists. You can use any word you want in a picture book for young children, except profanity or sexually graphic material.

(And you can even use the latter if the book is nonfiction; if, for example, you're writing a science book about "how babies are made," it's perfectly appropriate to use the correct anatomical terms for human reproductive organs.) What determines whether a child can understand a book is the length and complexity of its sentences, not the difficulty of the words. Dr. Seuss did not shy away from using big or "strange" words, or even nonsense words. Children can understand words from context, or they will ask an adult what a puzzling word means. This is how they learn. Don't "protect" them from learning something new.

2. *Picture books should be about 1,000 words.* When published, they will be 32 pages, with illustrations on each page. Though there are a few exceptions to this, it is not wise to try to buck the system in that regard. Publishers' costs are affected by this restriction. If you write a book that is more than a hundred or so words over 1,000, you will find it very difficult to get it published. So aim for 1,000 words—about five pages, double-spaced.

Don't type your manuscript like a picture book. Just type it as you would any other manuscript, in continuous text with paragraph breaks. Don't make a "dummy"—an illustrated manuscript that is in the shape of a picture book. Don't indicate page breaks; that's up to the publisher. Don't indicate illustrations in any way unless it is absolutely necessary or you are a top-quality professional illustrator or photographer. (You should only provide an indication of an illustration if the text is incomprehensible without it. And don't attempt a serious drawing of it. If possible, indicate it in some other way, preferably with words, or by cutting out or reproducing an illustration from some published source, or—as a last resort—drawing stick figures.)

3. *Do not team up with an illustrator to create your picture-book manuscript.* Editors want to choose their own illustrators, and will do so if they accept your book for publication. If you submit a manuscript that includes someone else's pictures, this will greatly reduce your chances of getting your book published.

What if editors like the text but not the illustrations? They will reject the book, assuming you and the illustrator are a "complete package." In any case, chances are you don't know an illustrator who is good enough and experienced enough to illustrate children's picture books. If you do, they will probably be too busy with paid work to illustrate your book for free. Your editor will find an illustrator far better than one you could find.

4. *For the reasons stated above, do not attempt to illustrate your own book.* If you are truly a professionally trained artist and know how to illustrate children's books, then assemble a portfolio and bring it to a children's-book art director, after getting an appointment. The most successful children's-book authors are author-illustrators who illustrate their own books. Almost invariably, though, these people are primarily artists, their art is stronger than their writ-

ing, and all of them have enormous talent and experience as professional illustrators. These are some of the best artists in the nation. They are the people you'll be competing with if you choose to illustrate your own books.

5. *Your children's-book manuscript must have a tightly structured plot.* Read published children's picture books—dozens of them—to learn how to structure a story. Notice how the author indicates where the page turns will be, by using transitions of some sort ("The next day . . ."). But try to be subtle and inventive in how you move the story along.

6. *Start out by writing for children's magazines like* Cricket *or* Ranger Rick. Doing this will give you experience. Short stories, however, are not the same as children's books. First, they often are longer than picture books. Second, their plots needn't be as tightly constructed. More important, they don't require illustrations on every page. They are not "visual storytelling" to the extent picture books are.

Most important of all, children's picture books simply have to be of higher quality than magazine stories for children. Children's picture books are meant to be permanent fixtures in the home; they may be passed down from generation to generation. Their quality must reflect this fact. Picture-book manuscripts must be very unusual and special to get published.

7. *Especially in the wake of* Harry Potter, *children's-book publishers get tens of thousands of submissions each year—that's per publisher, not industrywide.* The competition is very intense.

8. *Don't write "cute" stories.* Don't write about bunnies, kitties, etc. Beatrix Potter's animals (*Peter Rabbit,* etc.) and Robert McCloskey's ducks (*Make Way for Ducklings*) were not "cute"—they were very realistic. Respect children's intelligence. Writing for children really isn't different from writing for adults. All the best children's books appeal to adults as much as they do to kids. Study great children's picture books, including *Make Way for Ducklings,* Maurice Sendak's *Little Bear,* Dr. Seuss' books, and others. *My Father's Dragon* (first published in the 1940s by Ruth Stiles Gannett) is for slightly older kids, and is the sort of book that would probably never find a publisher today. It has violence and cruelty, and it is a very unusual length for this age group. But it is a great book. Perhaps the success of *Harry Potter* will make children's-book publishers more open-minded about what is "appropriate" for children.

Keep in mind: The stories you've invented that delight your own children may not be good enough to delight other people's children.

9. *Learn about the differences between writing for toddlers, for picture-book-age kids, for "young readers," middle readers, etc., and the approximate number of words required for each.* You can learn this by reading published

books and noting what age group the publisher has chosen for them (this will be printed on the book jacket). Although these categories are becoming increasingly murky and there is considerable overlap among them, they are still a useful guide. Study the level of sophistication of writing for each age group. Notice that books for "young readers"—aimed roughly at ages 5 to 8—often use *less* complicated text than picture books, which are mostly intended for preschoolers and the lower end of that age range. Why? Because the younger age groups may not be reading the book themselves—it may be read to them by adults. And young children can understand what's read to them better than they can read. Decide what age group your style can be most easily adapted to, and write for that.

Writer's and Illustrator's Guide to Children's Book Publishers and Agents by Ellen R. Shapiro, published annually, lists the names and addresses of children's-book publishers and editors and what kinds of work they publish. When submitting your book manuscript to children's-book publishers, include a cover letter that lists your published writing credits, if any. Let them know your manuscript is a "simultaneous submission," and then submit your manuscript to more than one publisher at once. This is perfectly appropriate, no matter what some book editors or writing organizations may tell you. Some book publishers may take a year or more to reply. It is not fair to you as a writer, nor realistic, to make these submissions singly. If, as may occasionally happen, a children's-book publisher won't read a simultaneous submission, so be it. Accept this and move on.

After waiting three months or so, you can call a publisher to learn the status of your manuscript. If any publisher offers you a contract, call the others who are reading the manuscript (after the deal is closed) and let them know, politely and without gloating, that the manuscript has been bought, that you had notified them it was a simultaneous submission in your cover letter, and that you now must withdraw it from consideration.

Never negotiate your own book contract. If you get an offer, call a reputable literary agency and ask them to negotiate the deal for you. The agent should be a member of a legitimate agency organization, such as the Association of Authors' Representatives, and should not charge clients for reading manuscripts. Never work with agents who charge for reading or marketing manuscripts. If they negotiate a book contract for you, they should only charge you a commission of 10 or 15 percent. The money will be taken out of your advance and royalties.

Start out by writing for children's magazines like *Cricket* or *Ranger Rick*. Doing this will give you experience.

If an editor doesn't offer you a contract but requests a rewrite without one, should you do it? Probably not. A picture book is only 1,000 words. If the editor doesn't think you're capable of rewriting fewer than 1,000 words, how much confidence could she have in you or your manuscript? The manuscript is probably light years away from being something she'd accept. Let me emphasize: If you agree to rewrite it for free, the chances she will ultimately offer you a contract are slim. This is true even if you rewrite the manuscript repeatedly.

What you decide, however, really depends on how desperate you are to be published. If an editor asks you to rewrite a manuscript but doesn't offer a contract, try to determine how serious she is about it, how "close" she thinks it is to being acceptable, and how carefully she's thought about what needs to be done to fix it. If her written suggestions are detailed enough to convince you she is very serious about working with you, and the suggestions don't sound silly (such as: "Can you change the African-American kid to a Hispanic kid?"), you might consider doing one free rewrite, if you are an unpublished author. But if her request seems only a casual one, and you sense she hasn't thought through all the details of the rewrite, don't bother. You can reply (politely and with gratitude) that you would be happy to do it if she can offer you a contract before you start work on it.

Years ago, children's-book editors worked closely with new but promising writers to get their manuscripts in shape, and then offered a contract when the writer did what was asked. Today, this is seldom the case. Editors are busier and don't have time to do substantial editing on manuscripts, especially picture books. Most reputable editors will accept a manuscript only when they have confidence in it and can offer you a contract. That's good news, but it also means that they will not accept work that is merely "promising" or "shows talent." They want a manuscript that, like Mary Poppins, is "practically perfect." It's your job to write one. Good luck.

Staton Rabin of Irvington, N.Y., has sold many articles and stories to children's markets, and teaches screenwriting. Her novel *Betsy and the Emperor* is in development as a movie. This article is from *The Writer*, February 2003.

HOW TO EVALUATE YOUR PICTURE BOOK

There are times when, as an aspiring children's-book author, you need to give up on a manuscript. And there are times when you shouldn't. Here are some key questions to ask yourself:

• Is my picture book structurally similar to all other children's picture books and the right length?

• Does it have a strong plot?

• Is it appropriate for the age group it's aimed at?

• Is it incredibly "different" and original?

• Is it genuinely moving, very funny, or a combination of both?

• Does it have a beginning, a middle, and an end?

• Does it have moments or transitions that imply (not state) page turns?

• Can it be illustrated? Will the illustrations enhance it, but does the text make sense even without the illustrations? (And if not, have you indicated, *only where absolutely necessary*, what and where a picture must be?)

• Has your book manuscript been rejected only because it is very different and progressive in some way that children will find acceptable?

• Has your book been rejected 10 times by 10 publishers? Has at least one of those editors shown an enormous amount of enthusiasm for the book but rejected it due to some reason other than its quality?

If you can honestly say yes to all those questions, then perhaps you should persist in submitting your rejected book manuscript until it sells. But if you can't answer in the affirmative, perhaps you ought to retire the manuscript and start a new one, after analyzing what might be wrong with it. Reading rejection letters from children's-book editors can be helpful, or useless. Read every one carefully and see if their comments make sense. And of course, if they encourage you to send future submissions, save the letter and do so when you have a new manuscript, reminding them in your cover letter of their request. —*Staton Rabin*

WRITING A YOUNG-ADULT BIOGRAPHY

Bringing the Brontë family to life was a labor of love

by Karen Kenyon

When I began my book on the Brontë family, it was quite a departure for me. Previously, I had published hundreds of essays, articles, poems, and a personal narrative, *Sunshower* (Richard Marek, 1981). With the Brontës, though, I'd be writing in a new genre and for a new audience: a biography that was also a book for young adults (grades 6 through 12). It seemed worth the challenge, for there was no way I could turn my back on the extraordinary Brontës (sisters Charlotte, who wrote *Jane Eyre;* Emily, author of *Wuthering Heights;* and Anne, who penned *The Tenant of Wildfell Hall;* and their brother, Branwell, who also wrote poetry and started a novel (though his talents never reached fruition).

I had gone to England in 1992, as I had on previous occasions, to visit and possibly to write about the historic and literary sites—in fact, I'd felt drawn to return several times. I had visited other famous authors' homes—John Keats, Charles Dickens, Beatrix Potter. And though I enjoyed them all and wrote articles about them, none took hold of my heart and soul the way the Brontë family did. With the Brontës, what gripped me so was the combination of landscape and atmosphere and seeing the actual artifacts of the sisters' lives.

From the moment my son, daughter-in-law, and I stepped off the steam train at Haworth, in Yorkshire, I knew this would be a special adventure. I truly felt we had ridden back in time. We walked up the steep, narrow, cobblestone main street all the way to the two-story gray stone parsonage where they all had lived, and which is now the Brontë Parsonage Museum. All around us, the landscape was angled and dramatic. Inside, we found the home much as the Brontës had left it, with original furniture, paintings, and artifacts. Among them were a replica of the famous portrait of Charlotte by George Richmond;

a baby bonnet given to her by a villager; a cross-stitch sampler by Maria Brontë, the oldest child, who died at age 11 (Helen Burns of *Jane Eyre* is based on Maria's character); the comb Emily is said to have dropped by the fire on the day she died; a China tea service; a few of the tiny books Charlotte and Branwell wrote as children; and some of Branwells' paintings.

We went outside and took the little path to the moors, past the tombstones that fill the churchyard just in front of the house. Once out there, it was easy to believe the Brontës' spirits were out there, too, on this fine, wuthering day— breezy, sunny, and slightly cool. In fact, they might be coming just over one of the rises in this green shaken-blanket of a landscape.

Back home in San Diego, it seemed they were still with me. I *knew* I needed to write about them and my visit to the parsonage. And this I did, based on my observations, my notes, and the excellent guidebook I had purchased, which refreshed my mind about what was in which room.

Soon I was making trips to the nearby University of California, San Diego, library to read books about the Brontës from its extensive collection, which included Katherine Frank's *Emily Brontë* and Christine Alexander's *The Early Writings of Charlotte Brontë*. I made notes of interesting facts, quotes, and descriptions, and once I finished each book, I typed up those notes and labeled the pages with the title of the book and author. Most of the time, I noted the page numbers of my discoveries as well.

As the project grew, my plan to write about the Brontës also grew, and retelling their story for young people seemed the logical choice. An adult biography would mean I'd need to provide new information, or perhaps come across some new letters or diary writings, or offer information in a new way. So very many Brontë scholars had already chosen those paths. The young-adult level seemed perfect: This was, after all, the age when the Brontë novels are first read; moreover, *Jane Eyre* is still considered the coming-of-age story for girls, and both it and the passionate, powerful *Wuthering Heights* are on the core curriculum reading list in many states.

If this was to be a juvenile book, I felt, it should be written in a fairly straightforward, factual, and mostly chronological way. It seemed a natural approach to telling the story, and not unlike the journalism or feature writing I had done.

As I began to research, I came across conflicting facts. Each time I wrote the parsonage and received excellent, useful replies. "What color were Charlotte's eyes?" Turns out they were described as various colors—truly chameleon eyes. "What did they eat?" Beef, boiled potatoes, turnips, and apple pie. When I needed to know what color bilberries were (they picked them on the moors), I called around San Diego until I found a nurseryman who had a book about English plants.

As I progressed through 20 or 30 Brontë biographies, the urge to write ripened. I began with a scene from a book about the Brontës' Irish background. It told of the girls' father, the Rev. Patrick Brontë, and his habit of telling stories to his children (his father had been a storyteller in Ireland). The reverend evidently had a flair for drama, and he transfixed his young children, particularly Emily, and undoubtedly gave rise to his children's storytelling techniques.

From that scene, I then started at the beginning with the family's sojourn to Haworth, telling of the arrival of the family of six children (ranging from infant Anne to 7-year-old Maria) at the parsonage with their parents, Patrick and Maria; I told of the mother's death not long after their aunt had arrived to care for the children; the deaths from tuberculosis of the two older girls, Maria and Elizabeth, at the Clergy Daughters' School at Cowan Bridge; the creation of their childhood drawings and writings (their juvenilia); and on and on.

I studied the juvenile biography section at the local public library and found many excellent literary biographies for young people—of Walt Whitman, Emily Dickinson, Beatrix Potter, Charles Dickens, Robert Frost, Eleanor Roosevelt—but nothing on the Brontës. I noted which publishers seemed to do quality biographies, featuring good research, good writing, and historical photos—houses like Clarion Books, Henry Holt & Co., and Lerner Publications Co. In addition, I sent for catalogs to see the range of books each publisher was producing. Lerner especially caught my eye. Its recent book on Emily Dickinson had impressed me with its well-written narrative, quality photographs, attractive cover, source list, and bibliography.

Though perhaps illogical, my urge to write my Brontë book was greater than the desire to first find a publisher. If I write a second such biography, I'm sure I'll prefer to know *first* if there is interest. But with the Brontës, it was just a work of love. I needed to write it, and so I went ahead with the task.

Once finished, I realized my book was too long and wrote a second, shorter version. I began to send a letter describing the book, two or three sample chapters, and an outline to some of the publishers I'd considered.

While I do have an agent for adult books, the juvenile market is not her field, so it seemed best in this instance to try on my own. In fact, it is common for authors of juvenile books to find publishers on their own. (I did have my agent go over the contract, which is important for authors, unless they are especially business-savvy.)

Lerner was interested enough in my material to ask for the entire book a few months later, and eventually I received a call saying they would like to publish it.

This was the start of a fairly extensive editing process, with a change of editors midstream. I was asked to write another beginning that would precede the one I had already written—something to show the Brontës' success, some scene to gain the reader's interest and show in some small way where all this was going. I chose the scene where Charlotte and Anne travel to London to encounter Charlotte's publisher, George Smith, of Smith, Elder, and Co., for the first time. All three sisters were writing under male pen names, and Anne and Emily's unscrupulous publisher, T.C. Newby, was suggesting there was only one author, Currer Bell, Charlotte's pen name (since *Jane Eyre* was such a success). The scene is humorous as the two simply dressed country women approach George Smith and reveal their identities as authors.

In addition to the scene, the editor asked me to add more original quotes from the Brontës to give the story more immediacy; that way, the Brontës would also be telling the story. This task took on a life of its own. I reread several of the best Brontë biographies and scoured them for interesting quotes from letters and a few diaries. The richest vein was found in Charlotte's letters, where she poured her heart out.

I was fortunate during this time to be able to visit the Huntington Library in San Marino, Calif., where I was allowed (after three letters of recommendation) to read a number of Charlotte's original letters—a thrilling experience. As I looked at them and handled them, it was like reaching through time.

I loved finding the new quotes, and I found myself more in touch than ever with the emotional story I was telling. Each time I read again or rewrote the part where Charlotte dies, I found myself tearing up. She had become very real to me. Such is the power of personal letters. (In fact, my newfound appreciation of the letters led me later on to create a narrated reading of a selection of them.)

As I added the quotes, the book became too long and I had to cut it back. (Lerner has a set size for its "Long Biographies" of 129 pages). In addition, I had to make sure every quote was properly referenced in the end notes. In those cases where I had kept notes a little too casually, I paid for it. Eventually, I found the correct references down to the page number for each quote. But if there is one important word of advice I have for anyone writing a similar book, it is to very carefully note each quote at the start—book, author, publisher, city, date, page number.

In time, I received a final galley proof of my book for a final check of the text and historical photos. I found few errors and the book read well, yet some of my end notes and sources now failed to match up correctly with quotes. So I checked each one individually until I was satisfied all were correct. I questioned the authenticity of a few photos, feeling fairly confident that I had seen practically every genuine Brontë-related painting, drawing, and photo available, since I had read so many Brontë biographies and editions of the journal *Brontë Society Transactions* (now *Brontë Studies*). I wrote Ann Dinsdale, librarian at the Brontë Parsonage Museum, and sent photocopies of questionable images. She seconded my concern. For example, a purported sketch of Anne by Charlotte turned out to be "suspect." I relayed this to the editor and was gratified to know that the photo editor was able to make changes.

My part in the process was now over, and I had only to wait the nine months for publication. I had enjoyed my time with the Brontës and learned so much about their lives. I recalled how they had written their stories as children.

Often, when their characters died or were killed off, the children would use their powers of writing to bring them back to life at some later point in the story, calling it "making alive again." I suppose that in a way, I, too, was happy to have that power to bring these wonderful writers to life, so that they could be enjoyed and appreciated once more.

Karen Kenyon of San Diego is an author, journalist, and poet who teaches writing at local colleges. Her previous book is *Sunshower*. This article is from *The Writer*, March 2003.

TIPS ON WRITING A YOUNG-ADULT BIOGRAPHY

If you have an all-consuming interest or passion in a person, consider writing a young-adult biography. It's a fun, useful way to indulge yourself, while making a contribution to young people's knowledge of literature. Here are some do's and don'ts I learned along the way:

Do thorough research. Reading eight to 10 books plus visiting the site or area where your subject lived or worked is minimal. Also, explore magazine or journal articles and, if possible, original sources, such as letters, journals, or interviews with someone who knew the person.

Do take thorough notes—book or periodical, author, date, publisher, edition, year, page number.

Do look at several biographies published by the publisher you are contacting.

Do create a chapter outline and a few chapters you can send to the publisher.

Do write for catalogs from publishers of juvenile books.

Don't write the entire book before approaching a publisher, but rather only the outline and a few chapters.

Don't fictionalize. Only quotes that are verifiable may be used.

Don't take the easy way out—double- or triple-check your facts.

Don't give up. And lastly, *do* enjoy the process.

—*Karen Kenyon*

MAKING GOOD USE OF YOUR DOWN TIME

Once the final edits and proofing of a book are done, the months you spend waiting for publication and the months just after publication can be productive ones.

While waiting for publication of *The Brontë Family*, my favorite bookstore, The BookWorks, in Del Mar, Calif., said it could give me a book-signing party. So a date was chosen for late September 2002.

Then I began to work on writing a staged reading that would be a way to bring the letters of Charlotte Brontë (and others) to life. Although I was originally inspired to create the reading from love of the material rather than promotional value, the reading would be part of the book-signing party.

An actress who had been in the creative writing class I teach at a junior college agreed to participate. Then, at a party I met a young Englishman who also had trained as an actor. He, too, was interested in being involved. A friend who is a pianist for the San Diego Symphony agreed to play excerpts from selections in Emily Brontë's songbook (Mozart, Haydn, Bach) to help add drama to the reading.

The reading/book signing was a great success. At least 70 people attended, and more than half bought a copy of my book.

I also had postcards of my book cover printed (about $100 for 500). These were a way to let people know the book was coming out soon and to invite friends and others to the reading and signing. They're also useful at any book signings or talks a writer is involved in, and offer an option for people to pick up the card and order the book later. Also, when I speak in schools, young people especially like to have something to take away.

Once the book was published, I was happy to see the product of so much work, time, and yes, love. But the time spent with it wasn't over. Now it was time to try to talk about it, or bring it to the community in different ways.

I applied to the San Diego city schools' Gifted and Talented Education Department so that I could be listed in a catalog of speakers whom teachers can choose to give presentations to their students.

Last December, I spoke at a conference for the Greater San Diego Council of Teachers of English—another way for the author of a literary biography to get involved and let people (especially teachers) know about the book. In addition, I wrote a study guide for teachers to accompany my book, and offered to do presentations on the Brontës at my local library.

—K.K.

SCIENCE FOR KIDS

Capture young readers' attention
with a sense of wonder & fascinating facts

by Staton Rabin

Whether he was writing about the mysteries of the cosmos or the enigmas of the human brain, Carl Sagan made science a wonder—and wonderfully easy to understand. He knew that when it comes to the nonscientists among us, we are, in a sense, all children. If you are writing about science for children, you can find no better inspiration than this famous astronomer. He understood that the best scientists never lose their childlike sense of wonder.

The mysteries of scientific exploration and its special jargon are often baffling to laymen. We must have things explained to us, with clarity and without condescension, almost as if we are children--or aliens from another galaxy, setting foot on Earth for the first time.

Certainly, we live in a scientific age, and ideas and principles that once were the sole province of the educated strata of society—clergymen, physicians, scientists, and educators—have now trickled down to the masses. Today, many children are very sophisticated about science. Last winter, I presented my 5-year-old cousin Sloane with a windup toy dinosaur. "Oh," she said, examining it briefly before setting it aside, "stegosaurus." And she was right.

The average schoolchild today knows things about science that even Galileo, Sir Isaac Newton, or Louis Pasteur didn't know. A typical kid of the 21st century knows more about the germ theory of disease and preventing infection than did a Civil War surgeon amputating legs during the battle of Gettysburg. Many a time I have wondered what a difference the simple admonition "Wash your hands!" or a small vial of sulfa powder could have made to ease suffering and prevent needless deaths throughout history.

What would it be like to go back in time with a bottle of antibiotic pills, and perhaps save the life of President Garfield, dying a very slow and painful death after being felled by an assassin's bullet? Or to travel back to the 1860s with modern medicine that might have saved President Lincoln's 12-year-old son Willie, who died in the White House of what was thought to have been typhoid. Today, there are no living Abraham Lincoln descendants, though one of his sons, Robert, lived until 1926. Science might have changed all that.

This sort of imaginative conjecture comes as naturally to me as breathing, and it comes into play whenever I write about science for kids. If science at times seems as remote to children's present-day lives as Alpha Centauri, then take them on a flight of fancy. Bring their everyday existence into the world of science. Encourage them to imagine "What if?" Give them something familiar they can relate to, and use this as a pathway to the unknown. Write about something they know, and then relate it to an idea in science with which they may be less familiar. Ask them to imagine a world before a particular scientific discovery that we take for granted—such as the airplane or computer chip— was made.

Why is the study of dinosaurs so appealing to children? Because, unlike atoms, you can see them with the naked eye. They are monsters that don't move, that, ferociously posed, "threaten" to eat children—but never actually do. Like roller coasters, they are a "safe danger." They give children a sense of mastery over their world. In a sense, children are able to dominate the dinosaurs by walking by their massive skeletons, reading and learning about them, but never being eaten by them. "Dinosaurs" are really an everyday experience for children—kids are small creatures who live in a world of scary giants (adults). By learning to overcome their fear of dinosaurs, children gain a sense of their place and power in the world.

Never shy away from a topic because it seems too simple. Often, the simplest questions—like why the sky is blue or the grass is green—can make for the most interesting articles.

For example, as a child, I was so terrified of dinosaurs, my parents had to lead me through the dinosaur skeleton display rooms at New York City's American Museum of Natural History with my eyes shut. It wasn't until I was 8 and visiting the Smithsonian in Washington, D.C., that I opened my eyes long enough to look at a giant stuffed elephant in the lobby. From then on, I've been able to look at dinosaurs. I even write about them now—perhaps evidence of an ongoing effort to master my fears. For, truth be told, I am still afraid of walking through dinosaur exhibits by myself in the dark, as if the scary beasts could suddenly awaken from suspended animation at any time and attack me.

This fear of mine became the basis of one of my short stories, "Serenade," which has been published in numerous children's magazines. It is about a boy, the son of a museum employee, who wanders the halls of the creepy natural history museum alone at night and finds fossil dinosaur eggs that crack, hatching out baby, horn-tooting dinosaurs. He goes for help—but when he returns with his dad, the baby dinos are gone. Or, are they?

This story may be fantasy, but it contains plenty of fact. The information about dinosaurs in the story is accurate, and was checked by renowned paleontologist Robert T. Bakker, whose book *The Dinosaur Heresies* and theories about warm-blooded, horn-tooting dinosaurs caught my interest.

I have written about dinosaurs for children's publications such as *Ranger Rick*, *Cricket*, and Australia's *The School Magazine*. Some of these stories were nonfiction, and some a combination of fact and fantasy. But all of them have been as scientifically accurate as I can make them. I often have a scientist review the manuscript for accuracy before it is submitted or published.

Which brings me to one of the most important points you need to remember when writing about science for children. Always be sure your scientific foundation is accurate. If you do your job right, even if you are writing fiction, children will be able to tell which parts of the story are based on fact and which are imagined.

Also keep in mind that children like stories. Tell them stories from your own life or quote from stories others have written, as a way of capturing their attention and easing them into and personalizing the scientific material.

You can use interesting original quotations from scientists, as when the taciturn aviation pioneer Wilbur Wright was asked to give a speech and his entire oration was: "I know of only one bird, the parrot, that talks, and he can't fly very high."

Sometimes I tell the stories of scientists, providing anecdotes and ironies. I tell of their struggles, and give surprising glimpses of their lives, as when I wrote about the time the Wright brothers invited the press to watch a demonstration of their experimental plane (they knew it would work) and intentionally crashed it to put their competitors off the scent. I also wrote about how Apollo astronaut Neil Armstrong took to the moon a square of fabric from the Wrights' original airplane.

Often, I combine the personal with the objective. For example, in writing about the *Titanic*, I quoted an old song my brother used to sing to me when I was a child: "Oh, it was sad! It was sad! It was sad when the great ship went down . . . to the bottom of the sea . . . Husbands and wives, little children lost their lives. Oh, it was sad when the great ship went down!" And I wrote about the old, yellowing newspaper stuck in the bathroom window of the railroad station in the small town where I grew up. Its 1912 headline reported the sinking of the *Titanic* and the tragic loss of life.

From there, I discussed Robert Ballard's 1985 rediscovery and exploration of the *Titanic* via his *Argo*, a remote-controlled device that can be dragged along the ocean floor, using optical fiber technology to transmit "live" video images. I included some of Ballard's profound emotions on finding the *Titanic* at last and his solemn prayers for those souls lost on it, and what we know about why the ship sank.

History is always changing, as is science, and one must keep up-to-date. When I was in the midst of writing about the *Titanic*, the ship was found, and I had to rewrite my article. Even the theory about what sank the ship had changed (pockmarked damage to the ship's hull plates, with rivets sheared off as the "berg" grazed by—rather than one long gash inflicted by the ice).

Most of my articles or books begin with a story, anecdote or "scene" out of life or history. In writing about crocodiles for my science book *Monster Myths: The Truth About Water Monsters*, I told the story of Captain Hook in *Peter Pan*. Hook is chased by a murderous, man-eating crocodile that goes after him much the way Moby Dick went after Captain Ahab—with single-minded devotion. The croc had swallowed a clock, and whenever Hook heard the ominous sound of a ticking clock getting nearer and nearer, he knew the croc was after him again, and he would run for his life.

Why do I tell this story in my book? Because tales like this may already be familiar to children, so they give them a point of reference. The story illustrates myths, beliefs, and characteristics concerning crocodiles that can lead into scientific discussion. I simply separate fact from fiction, explaining which supposedly crocodile characteristics are true (crocs' stealth in hunting prey) and which aren't (chronically singling out a favorite victim, like Captain Hook, for special disfavor).

In *Monster Myths*, I also write about the octopus craze that hit Paris in the wake of Victor Hugo's popular novel *Toilers of the Sea*, and how piranhas got an undeserved reputation for being finger-chomping monsters that can turn a man into a skeleton in five minutes. This myth came about largely because of a lurid book President Teddy Roosevelt wrote after a trip to the Amazon; in it, he mentioned "the most ferocious fish in the world—the piranha or cannibal fish—that eats men when it can get the chance." I tell these stories—properly attributed to their authors, of course—because they often provide juicy quotes that children love.

Combining scientific information and entertaining storytelling makes science writing fun and rewarding. In addition to my advice that you always check your facts and tell compelling stories, here are more tips for bringing youngsters into the world of science.

• When writing about unfamiliar things, such as scientific ideas that kids may not know, compare them to what they already know. Think of things that are common to most children's everyday experience, and use analogies. For an article on dinosaur extinction, I compared the fiery, explosive cosmic event of a giant asteroid's collision with the Earth (which some theorize led to the dinos' demise) with something most kids know far more about: a scene out of *Star Wars*.

• Compare large numbers to something more easily understood. For example, saying a blue whale weighs an average of 120 tons may not compute, but if you say it weighs about as much as 96 Honda Accords, or that the whale's heart alone can weigh as much as a Volkswagen "bug," it registers.

When choosing topics to write about, choose what interests you, because then you will write about it with passion.

• Never shy away from a science topic because you think it is too complex or sophisticated to explain to children. There is always a way to make complicated topics easier to understand. Even string theory, human genome research, or neuroscience can be at your readers' level.

• The converse is also true. Never shy away from a topic because it seems too simple. Often, the simplest questions, like why is the sky blue, can make for the most interesting articles. I recently wrote an article for children about the science of belly buttons, which will be published by *The School Magazine*. This is a far more complex subject than meets the eye. It turned out that topics such as human gestation, stem cell research, religion, theoretical physics, and many other subjects came into play when I was writing about belly buttons.

• Even science fiction or science fantasy should be scientifically accurate in its details. If you are not a scientist, or what you're writing about is outside your area of expertise, consult a scientist in that field and have your work checked for accuracy before you submit it to publishers. Consider quoting scientists in your book.

• It almost goes without saying: Do thorough scientific research. The Internet can give you a good head start, provided you make sure the Web sites you use are written by recognized authorities in their field. Most universities have Web sites with faculty e-mail addresses. Many universities have lists of experts you can consult. Teachers and other scientific experts are usually happy to answer a quick, concise question or two by e-mail.

Your local zoo or aquarium's Web site also can put you in touch with helpful scientists. And don't forget about your friends who are scientists. How much research is enough? You should do just enough to make sure there are no errors in your work. You don't need to be an authority on an entire scientific field to write an article about one aspect of it.

• Don't shy away from using scientific terms where necessary, but don't get too bogged down in defining terms. Try to make your meaning clear from the context. If, for example, you write—"When geologists examine rocks from 65 million years ago, they find . . ."—you don't need to define "geologist," you've made this clear from the words surrounding it.

• You don't need to be a scientist to write about science for kids or adults; you just need a sense of curiosity, an ability to explain things simply, entertainingly, and clearly, and good research skills. Being a scientist can even be a handicap, as it may be hard for an expert to put herself in a "beginner's mind."
The key to teaching somebody a new skill or piece of information is to try to remember what it was like to know almost nothing about it—which is not easy to do once you're an expert. But just as important, never write down to children.

• Choose a topic nobody else is writing about. Provide ideas for safe experiments that children can try at home, when appropriate. And test your article out on children of the appropriate age to make sure they can understand it.

Good luck, earthlings!

Staton Rabin of Irvington, N.Y., has sold many articles and stories to children's markets, and teaches screenwriting. Her novel *Betsy and the Emperor* is in development as a movie. This article is from *The Writer,* June 2002.

10 SECRETS TO WRITING FANTASY

What you can learn from the masters of the genre

by Philip Martin

On the eve of the 21st century, an 11-year-old British lad named Harry Potter, with an odd lightning-bolt scar on his forehead, emerged from nowhere to enchant the world of fantasy.

Just four years and four books later, the Harry Potter series by J.K. Rowling had sold more than 100 million copies around the world. The titles dominated bestseller lists for adults and children alike, garnering prizes and breaking sales records everywhere.

The remarkable performance of the Harry Potter books has turned the heads of publishers, booksellers, librarians—and authors, who are looking closely at fantasy as a way to commercial and literary success.

Fantasy stories also are dominating movie and television screens, and not just in Disney's recycling of popular fairy tales and myths. The first Harry Potter movie and the live-action movie version of J.R.R. Tolkien's 1950s epic, *The Lord of the Rings*, both were released as blockbusters at the end of 2001. Other fantasy-based movies, from *Shrek* to Natalie Babbit's *Tuck Everlasting* have done well in film, while Marion Zimmer Bradley's *The Mists of Avalon* was produced for cable TV, and animated version of Brian Jacques' popular *Redwall* series has been popular on PBS channels.

Why this sudden surge in fantasy stories? Is this a short-lived trend? Or will fantasy's magic wand continue to wield its power for years into the future?

It isn't really a sudden phenomenon. Although nothing like the immense worldwide appeal of the Potter series has been seen before, fantasy's appeal is hardly new. *Watership Down* won widespread readership in the 1970s. British author Tolkien's *Lord of the Rings* trilogy first rose to popularity in America in the 1960s in popular paperback editions

Among fantasy's greatest hits are *The Wind in the Willows* (1908), *The Wonderful Wizard of Oz* (1900), and *Alice's Adventures in Wonderland* (1865), which were embraced by adults and children alike. Literary giants such as William Shakespeare, Charles Dickens, Rudyard Kipling, Oscar Wilde, and Mark Twain all wrote major works of fantasy.

Fantasy is now back in the literary mainstream. Major publishing houses such as HarperCollins, Penguin Putnam, and others are building or strengthening their fantasy lines, including the reissuing of classic backlist titles by award-winning authors such as Robin McKinley, Lloyd Alexander, and Susan Cooper.

Is there still a place in this field for yet another story? After centuries of great fantasy storytelling, haven't all the good tales been told?

Hardly. Fantasies are often recycled, reshaped tales, but that doesn't mean it's a snap to write one.

"So many writers think fantasy is easy," says Peter S. Beagle, whose *The Last Unicorn* is often included in lists of the top 10 fantasy novels of the 20th century. "All you have to do is rip off some elves, goblins, and a few other things from Tolkien and spend about 10 minutes making up imaginary words and another 10 minutes working up a rough idea of the country and a little local history and bingo, you're in business. You're a fantasist. It's not at all like that. What made Tolkien unique is that he spent 50 years building his world, and he built it from the inside out."

Rowling claims that the idea for her series came to her in a flash while she was on a long train ride. Harry Potter popped into her mind almost fully formed, scar and all, she has said in interviews. Yet getting an idea is one thing; writing a successful book is another.

In her case, she is committed to the daunting task of writing seven books, chronicling Harry's schooling as a wizard at the Hogwarts School for Witchcraft and Wizardry, and following his maturation from an 11-year-old boy to a young man.

To enter fantasy's magic door as a writer, you just need a fertile imagination, some solid fiction-writing skills, and knowledge of a few basic rules of fantasy writing. If you can tap into your inner child's sense of wonder, if you can dream of imaginary worlds where good triumphs over evil and magic can happen at any moment, you can write fantasy.

Before you start, remember: You need to write well. As Madeleine L'Engle, author of *A Wrinkle in Time*, wrote in an article for *The Writer* (June 1976), the rules of fiction are the same for Beatrix Potter as they are for Fyodor Dostoyevsky. You have to write good beginnings. You have to plan solid, page-turning plots. You need to create characters that readers care about. And you need to deliver satisfying endings.

If you carefully read and study the authors mentioned here, you can learn some of the secrets of good fantasy writing. Though there is no substitute for hard work and the ability to write well, there *are* a few things that, if done right, help to make a fantasy story work.

Here are 10 suggestions that will hold you in good stead.

1. Put new wine in old bottles.

Storytelling is the art of recycling. Pick an old form and refresh it. Play with it. Unleash your imagination—but stay true to its traditions.

The countless retellings of the Arthurian cycle of Britain are good examples of this. The legend of Camelot, King Arthur, and the Round Table has inspired writers from Nobel Prize-winner John Steinbeck, who retold the classic tale in *The Acts of King Arthur and His Noble Knights*, to spiritual guru Deepak Chopra, whose novel *The Return of Merlin* is a mix of modern mystery, Arthurian legend, and self-help philosophy.

Certainly, many ideas found in Rowling's novels are not original. Consider a tale of a young lad who has just turned 11, who has a bit of wizard's blood in him. He enters a school for fledgling magicians, held in a far-off castle that has odd rooms, doors, and passageways, with pictures on the wall that wink back at him. He starts as a First Year student, forms friendships with a girl and a boy in his class, messes up some early spells in classes like Curses and Transformations. Despite his unprepossessing appearance, everyone knows he is destined to play a key role in facing a threat from an evil lord who will threaten the school's very existence.

Harry Potter? No, it's young Thornmallow, from Jane Yolen's 1991 novel, *Wizard's Hall*.

Other elements in Harry Potter echo works of British authors Eva Ibbotsen and Diana Wynne Jones, whose humorous magical novels for children are considered as imaginative as Rowling's.

2. Learn the differences between archetypes, stereotypes, and good characters.

Archetypes are the originals from whom the mold was made. Merlin, heroes in Greek myths, and the witch in *Sleeping Beauty* are archetypes. Stereotypes, on the other hand, are shorthand knock-offs: the crone with a crooked nose who cackles. These are the mark of a lazy writer—or perhaps just of needing a minor character whom you don't have time to develop.

Good characters are richer. They may be based on archetypes, but they lead their own lives, follow their own passions, make mistakes, learn and grow. For a new vision of a witch, read Gregory Maguire's *Wicked: The Life and Times of the Wicked Witch of the West*. The evil witch is transformed into a complex, sensitive political outcast crusading for animal rights and free speech in an Oz oppressed by the iron fist of the Wizard and his minions.

For a delightful mock guide that skewers stereotypes, read Diana Wynne Jones' *Tough Guide to Fantasyland* (1996), with alphabetical entries, such as Dark Lord, Mystical Master, Quest Objects, and Zombie.

3. Use magic, but limit its powers.

And define its rules carefully. If magic has unlimited powers to cure or over-come, where is the tension in the story? Whoever possesses magic powers should not be able to solve all problems with a wand. Instead, magic should be mysterious, even to its own users. It may be debilitating, draining users of energy. It may need the cooperation of others to have its effect.

For young Harry Potter, magic is a fickle skill that takes a long time to master. Spells sometimes backfire, or there is a problem finding the correct spell to use.

How will characters use magic? How strong are their powers? What limits should be placed on its use? Therein lies much of the plot of many a fantasy story: finding just the right way to use the right magic.

4. Make your hero an orphan.

Harry Potter, Dorothy in Oz, and Taran in Lloyd Alexander's Prydain series are all orphans.

Sometimes a child is separated from his or her parents. Examples include Ged in Ursula Le Guin's Earthsea trilogy or young King Arthur, who is raised by Merlin.

In other stories, the parents are simply left conveniently behind for most of the story, as when the Darling children go off to Neverland, or when Alice falls down the rabbit hole, or when the children in C.S. Lewis' series go through the wardrobe into the land of Narnia.

The purpose of all the orphans in the fantasy world is to allow young protagonists to venture out entirely on their own, to discover the limits of their powers, and to overcome trials without parents to hold them back.

In Robin McKinley's *The Blue Sword*, the heroine is three-times removed: first orphaned, then sent to a far-off foreign land to live with strangers, and then kidnapped.

5. Take a trip.

As Tolkien noted, "To a storyteller, a journey is a marvelous device." His masterpieces, *The Hobbit* and *The Lord of the Rings*, involve quests, as small bands of heroes venture forth to see remarkable sights, overcome obstacles, and resolve problems. The sense of wonder in discovering new magical places is essential to a good story.

With his wry, understated humor, Tolkien chose for *The Hobbit* the subtitle *There and Back Again*. In fact, this phrase stands for the realm of fantasy itself. As readers, we go into the world of fantasy and then return to the real world. It is the quality of the journey that is the source of our satisfaction.

Sometimes the trip goes to a place that is nearby, but wondrous. Neil Gaiman's novel *Neverwhere* tells of a man whisked off into a magical world in the London underground, where he meets many odd characters—a modern, dark, urban version of *Alice in Wonderland*.

The Hero's Quest is a classic form of journey that pervades many fantasy stories. The hero leaves home, passes through a portal, has a series of trials and acquires wisdom, friends, and magical powers, and then returns home, changed forever. These strong patterns, wrote Natalie Babbit, "are immutable, and as writers we must follow them willy-nilly or suffer a plot come askew. It is annoying, but it is miraculous, too."

6. Sell the impossible with the "trick of particularity."

Dorothy L. Sayers used this phrase to describe the success of Dante's *Inferno*, because the author made his fantasy world seem real by using realistic details.

In Franny Billingsley's award-winning novel *The Folk Keeper*, she uses many real facts about the sea, seals, and manor houses to give her story based on old *selkie* (seal-people) legends a ring of truth. She says, "I try very hard to establish a world that seems real and solid, internally convincing. And then I overlay my element of magic." She put a lot of work into researching late 18th-century country houses and making sketches. "Then when I got to writing, I didn't use most of it. I just put in little details that I hoped would evoke the whole feeling of place."

7. Freely mix humor and fantasy.

With its new twists on human ways, fantasy is often ripe for a humorous treatment. Terry Pratchett's extended series of Discworld novels contains some of the brightest, most piercing blend of humor and social satire being written today. Pratchett's intelligent and side-splitting novels, which regularly top the British bestseller charts and have many fans in the United States, have been described as Mark Twain meets Matt Groenig (creator of *The Simpsons*). Even the gentle fantasies, from *Winnie-the-Pooh* to *The Hobbit* to the tales of Beatrix Potter, are full of delightful whimsy.

8. Withhold information to increase surprise, wonder, or tension.

Like all stories of discovery, many successful fantasy stories tell the tale from the point of view of the person who least understands what is going on—often from the perspective of a child or an outsider.

In *The Amber Spyglass*, Philip Pullman's final volume of his trilogy, *His Dark Materials*, the young Lyra and Will encounter a race of very tiny people, the Gallivespians. At one point, Lyra contemplates how the surface tension of a drop of water must seem like that of a fruit rind to the Gallivespians. To be able to imagine such newness is a key skill in fantasy, to approach even the simplest of objects, like a drop of water, with fresh vision.

A sense that anything could happen in a fantasy world heightens the reader's awareness. In suspenseful scenes, such as the Hobbit Bilbo's riddling exchange with the dragon Smaug, any piece of information is potentially dangerous or useful.

This kind of veiled exchange, as author Joan Aiken points out, is crucial to developing gripping supernatural stories. What we don't know (but imagine for ourselves) is more chilling sometimes than that which we do.

9. Remember: In fantasy, all images have meaning.

Fantasy writers draw heavily on the rich imagery of old legends and myths. These ancient tales are full of magic rings, enchanted swords, dragon's lairs, and other age-old symbols.

As Christian scholar Peter Kreeft says, the reason that authors like Tolkien and C.S. Lewis fascinate us so much is that, "For them, everything means something more than itself. Everything is not only a thing, but a sign, full of significance."

10. In the end, a heart of gold trumps all.

In fantasy stories, despite the power of magic, readers want the human qualities of your characters to carry the day. What matters are not magical powers but how and why your chief characters use them—what they care about enough to use magic to save and serve. These are things like friendships, kindness to strangers, trust, and goodness. Harry Potter is a young wizard, but he is also a boy—one who is unsure of himself at times, who wants to win at Quidditch and collects wizard trading cards. He stands up for his friends. Likewise, Tolkien's hobbits are stalwart and unpretentious. They slog on faithfully and persist, and through their humble efforts defeat great hordes of evil orcs and goblins.

Whenever possible, focus your story on those elements of love, faith, and deep convictions, and your readers will be willing to follow you through all sorts of magical conundrums and curses in the hope that human qualities will prevail.

If you follow these rules, you will be in good company. You may not sell 100 million copies of your story or make every bestseller list. But your words may lead your readers into a new world, one they have never imagined before but which, after reading your story, will be as real to them as the reaches of Middle-Earth or the halls of Hogwarts.

There will always be fantasy that calls to be written—as long as readers yearn for heroes, as long as there are dragons in the world to conquer, and as long as magic flows from the pens of imaginative authors.

Philip Martin of Shorewood, Wis., is acquisitions editor for The Writer Books and author of *The Writer's Guide to Fantasy Literature: From Dragon's Lair to Hero's Quest* (The Writer Books, 2002). A version of this article appeared in *The Writer,* November 2001.

WORDS OF WISDOM

by Madeleine L'Engle

[If we had such a designation, Madeleine L'Engle, now in her eighties, would surely be named a national treasure. She has written more than 60 books beloved by children and adults alike, including *A Swiftly Tilting Planet, Walking on Water,* and the classic *A Wrinkle in Time*—which won the Newbery Award in 1963.

Among the hundreds of thousands of writers who have attended her workshops, she is known for creating a spirit of community, intellectual rigor, and spiritual renewal, writes Carole F. Chase in her introduction to *Madeleine L'Engle {Herself}: Reflections on a Writing Life.*

"Madeleine does not teach writing. Instead, she creates a safe space for writers in which she midwifes the birth of latent talent. . . . Because she said we were writers, we could begin to believe that we were," writes Chase, who compiled this volume that reflects 50 years of writing wisdom gleaned from L'Engle's workshops and writings.

What follows are L'Engle's gems of practical and inspirational observations about writing and the writing life.]

Three recommendations

Read at least an hour a day. I try to read something I feel I ought to read for most of the time, and then for a little bit of the time I read something just for sheer fun. Fun reading is important, and I think we underestimate reading for fun. I have fun reading the Bible. Nobody told me I was supposed to take it as a moral trap, to be serious and long-faced about it.

Part of your technique of writing is built by writing, and with this you should also have some fun. I do think that keeping an honest, unpublishable journal is helpful. Include what you are thinking, what you are feeling, what you are responding to. Include what you are angry about that you heard on the news. Don't talk about the news in terms of politics but in terms of your own life. What does this mean to you? So these are my three recommendations: Read, keep an honest journal, and write every day.

Being a writer means writing

Being a writer does not necessarily mean being published. It's very nice to be published. It's what you want. When you have a vision, you want to share it. But being a writer means writing. It means building up a body of work. It means writing every day. You can hardly say that van Gogh was not a painter because he sold one painting during his lifetime, and that to his brother. Van Gogh was a painter because he painted, because he held true to his vision as he saw it.

Cooking up stories

When I start working on a book (and I'm usually thinking about several books over several years before I actually start to write one), I'm somewhat like a French peasant cook. There is a big black stove, several pots on the back of it. And the cook goes by and drops a carrot in one pot and a piece of potato in another and an onion and a piece of meat in another. At dinnertime, you look and see which pot smells best and pull it forward. The same thing is true with writing. There are several pots on my back burners.

An idea for a scene goes into one pot, a character into another, and a description of the tree in the fog in another. And when it comes time to write, I bring forward the pot that has the most in it—or more likely, this being a less literal world, the pot shoves itself out at me.

Now the dropping in of the ideas is sometimes quite conscious. I know I'm putting a carrot in this pot. But sometimes something has been added when I don't even realize it. And I look into the pot and say, "Oh, that's there, just what I need." I don't know when it got put in. When it comes time to write, I look at everything in the pot. I sort, I organize, I arrange, I discover, I think about character and storyline. And most of this part of the work is . . . a conscious act.

Reveal the invisible

Conrad says, "The novelist's first task is to make us see." To make us see not only the readily visible—the sunset over the Litchfield Hills, the snow falling, slanting in from the east. . . . But also to see the less readily visible—the anger couched in exquisite courtesy, the self-sacrifice given in such a way as to be hardly noticeable, the carefully hidden anguish in the eyes of someone who has been betrayed. The novelist helps us to see things we might not notice otherwise.

Mechanics

You have to know a lot of details when you begin a book but very often those details change. Joshua in *The Arm of the Starfish* is a very good example. *The Arm of the Starfish* is a novel of international intrigue. It takes place in Portugal, largely in Lisbon. The young hero gets involved in this intrigue. I had the book pretty intricately plotted. This is essential, because if you do not have a plot there is nothing to change.

So, as I had planned the story, Adam Eddington, the protagonist, has gone three nights without sleep, and he finally is allowed to go to sleep in the Ritz Hotel in Lisbon. In the morning when he wakes up after having slept probably 15 hours, there sitting and looking at him was a young man called Joshua. Now Adam was surprised to see Joshua. I was surprised to see Joshua. There had been no Joshua in my plot.

As a writer I had a choice. I could say, "Out, Joshua. I will not have you. You're going to make me rewrite 150 pages. I don't want to do that. I'm lazy like everybody else." Or I could say, "Okay. I'll rewrite 150 pages," which I did. I cannot imagine the book without Joshua. But where did he come from? And why did he come named Joshua? When he arrived, I had a strong suspicion that he would be dead before the end of the book. And, indeed, he was.

And that is how it goes. You must practice your techniques. You must have a strong plot, but then you must be willing to . . . let it alter itself.

When I start a book, I know what I want to say, where I want to go, what my theme is. I think about my characters, what they are like, inside and out. But, as creator of the book, I give my characters free will. They surprise me by saying things I didn't expect them to say, rather than what I had planned for them to say. They are frequently far better or far worse than I had thought they were going to be. Sometimes they make radical changes in the plot. But in the end the book is far more mine than if I had insisted on knowing everything ahead of time, keeping control of every little action.

Writing for children

A child is not afraid of new ideas, does not have to worry about the status quo or rocking the boat, is willing to sail into uncharted waters. Those tired old editors who had a hard time understanding *A Wrinkle in Time* assumed that children couldn't understand it, either. Even when Farrar, Straus and Giroux, a publisher to which I am devoted, decided to risk taking it, they warned me that they did not expect it to sell well, and they did not think it could possibly be read by anyone under high school age. This is the typical underestimation of the adult as to the capacity of children to understand philosophical, scientific, and theological concepts. But there is no idea that is too difficult for children as long as it underlies a good story.

The writer's life

Many people in walks of life that do not involve creation are completely unaware of the necessity of discipline. It is not only that few serious artists who live lives of debauchery produce a large body of work, but that few serious artists are able to live lives that are without interruption. We do not shed all obligations when the children leave home. I am working on this section of this manuscript while teaching an intensive four-and-a-half-week credit course, and neither may be skimped. Many writers work in the evenings after a nine-to-five job. And there are letters to be answered, the phone which constantly calls us. I travel a lot in order to give lectures, teach at writers' conferences. To write consistently, I must seize opportunities. I write in airports. I write on planes. I find airports and planes and hotel rooms excellent places in which to write, because while I am in them, I am not responsible for anything except my work. Once I have my seat assignment, I can write until the flight is called; when I am on the plane, the pilot is responsible for the flight; I am not; and so I can work on my manuscript. In a hotel room I do not have to think about the vacuum cleaner (though sometimes I would like to have one); domestic chores are not my responsibility; I am free to write.

No work is too small

If the work comes to the artist and says, "Here I am, serve me," then the job of the artist, great or small, is to serve. The amount of the artist's talent is not what it is about. Jean Rhys said in an interview in *The Paris Review*, "Listen to me. All of writing is a huge lake. There are great rivers that feed the lake, like Tolstoy and Dostoyevsky. And there are mere trickles, like Jean Rhys. All that matters is feeding the lake. I don't matter. The lake matters. You must keep feeding the lake."

Take a chance

Risk is essential. It's scary. Every time I sit down and start the first page of a novel I am risking failure. We are encouraged in this world not to fail. College students are often encouraged to take the courses they are going to get A's in so that they can get that nice grant to graduate school. And they are discouraged from taking courses that they may not get a good grade in but that fascinate them nevertheless. I think that is a bad thing that the world has done to us.

We are encouraged only to do that which we can be successful in. But things are accomplished only by our risk of failure. Writers will never do anything beyond the first thing unless they risk growing. I took a great risk when I wrote A *Wrinkle in Time*—and it almost didn't work.

With free will, we are able to try something new. Maybe it doesn't work, or we make mistakes and learn from them. We try something else. That doesn't work either. So we try yet something else again. When I study the working processes of the great artists I am awed at the hundreds and hundreds of sketches made before the painter begins to be ready to put anything on the canvas. It gives me fresh courage to know of the massive revision Dostoyevsky made of all his books—the hundreds of pages that got written and thrown out before one was kept. A performer must rehearse and rehearse and rehearse, making mistakes, discarding, and trying again and again.

Why we tell stories

Stories make us more alive, more human, more courageous, more loving. Why does anybody tell a story? It does indeed have something to do with faith, faith that the universe has meaning, that our little human lives are not irrelevant, that what we choose or say or do matters, matters cosmically. We look at the world around us, and it is a complex world, full of incomprehensible greed, irrationality, brutality, war, terrorism—but also self-sacrifice, honor, dignity—and in all of this we look for, and usually find, pattern, structure, meaning. Our truest response to the irrationality of the world is to paint or sing or write, for only in such response do we find truth.

7 ELEMENTS OF A GOOD MOVIE SCENE

Give every scene its own story line
and end up with a great script

by Rick Reichman

Scene structure is one of the most vital but least discussed aspects of film writing. If each scene in your script is written clearly and paces well, doesn't it make sense that the script itself will do the same? If each scene has a story line that engages the reader, advances the plot, and makes one want to turn the page, doesn't it follow that the script itself will be a winner? When you start by writing terrific scenes, you end by creating an excellent script.

What, then, is a scene? As I define it in my book, *Formatting Your Screenplay*, "A scene is a section of the script, generally three-and-one-half to seven pages, possessing a definitive beginning, middle, and end, and centering on a theme and/or action." In short, it is a mini story, a unit, a section that could stand alone—although it is influenced by what came before and it affects what will follow.

Every well-written scene, in my view, contains seven elements. These are Bridging In, Conflict, Set Up, Characterization, Exposition (Information), Reversal, and Bridging Out, and each of these elements must appear in *every scene* you write. What all this means is that you can't write a scene to give just information, conflict, or characterization. You need to include these essentials, certainly, but you must also include all the other elements listed above.

Bridging in

Bridging in is the opening of your scene. It includes the primary slug and the paragraph(s) that appear afterward. While it should be no more than 1 to 1½ inches on the page, it must accomplish several tasks: set time and place, introduce the reader to the type of scene it is (action, dramatic, comedic, etc.), introduce a place, a character, a setting, or even an object. Finally, bridging in needs to make the reader believe (falsely) that the scene is headed toward a predictable climax.

Following is the bridging in from a scene in *The Sixth Sense* (by M. Night Shyamalan, Blinding Edge Pictures, Inc., 1997). In this scene, 8-year-old Cole tells psychologist Dr. Malcolm Crowe that he, Cole, sees and communicates with dead people. Malcolm diagnoses Cole as suffering from schizophrenia. In a memo to himself, Malcolm recommends that Cole be put on medication and perhaps hospitalized.

INT. HOSPITAL ROOM — EVENING

Cole lies rigid in the hospital bed. His eyes fixed at the end of the room.

Malcolm quietly enters the room. Cole sees him and visibly relaxes.

Conflict

There must be *conflict* in every scene, preferably on every page. Without conflict, there is no drama. Two or more people getting along may be nice for those particular people, but harmony isn't what gets your script playing in a theater near you.

What, though, is conflict? Someone once described it as two dogs, one bone. Yeah, and how Kay retrieves the lost galaxy in *Men in Black,* or the uneasiness between brother and sister in *You Can Count on Me,* or the dark-humored ferocity of *The Mummy.*

Drama deals with three basic types of conflict: individual vs. self; individual vs. a nonhuman entity (nature, God, technology, monsters, etc.); and individual vs. other(s).

The conflict of individual vs. self is fine for writing prose or plays. In novels or short stories, it is easy to describe thoughts and images in a character's head. In plays, the character is allowed a soliloquy, but that device is rarely used in film. Of course, a skillful actor can dramatize this type of conflict, but a scriptwriter can never guarantee such casting. Individual vs. self is difficult, although not impossible, to represent visually, but it should almost never be the predominant type of conflict in a screenplay.

A conflict involving an individual and a nonhuman entity is easier to represent visually. From *2001: A Space Odyssey* to the recent *The Matrix,* the scriptwriter deals with the nature of reality against the insidious creep of artificial existences. In *Dogma, Castaway,* and the various versions of *Godzilla,* we encounter conflict with religion, nature, and monsters. In *The Sixth Sense,* we see dead people, and in *Independence Day,* aliens.

In many of these kinds of films, anthropomorphizing, or giving the nonhuman entity human attributes, is a popular device. Writers have been known to make just about anything human: cars, animals, agents. The field is wide open. And this segues nicely into the third kind of conflict.

Individual vs. other(s) is the conflict that is easiest to depict, the simplest to bring to the screen, and therefore the most used. Whether it is Rambo taking on armies of nations or George Bailey battling Mr. Potter in Bedford Falls, conflict with others allows the writer more access to the full range of visual and emotional discord. This type of conflict is the easiest way to transfer the characters' emotions to the reader and the audience.

To create a powerful scene, you must include at least one of the three types of conflict. If you can include two or all three types of conflicts, so much the better.

Set up

Set up has much the same function as a magician who focuses your attention here while executing an incredible stunt over there. Set up throws the reader and the audience the proverbial red herring.

If the cowboy rides into town seeking the "toughest guy" around, the reader is set for a fight. If there is a reunion of a close family, the reader expects to see the relatives sharing wonderful moments from the past. If character A chases character B, the reader anticipates a capture or a fight, sometime, somewhere.

You as a writer purposely provide these seemingly obvious clues. You let the readers believe that they have figured it out. You lead the readers to think they are one step ahead of you. But always remember: *You* are the magician. While you set up a direction, you also set up the ingredients for unanticipated shifts a little further down the road.

Characterization

In every scene in which a character appears, the reader should learn a little more about that character. Let's analyze both parts of this sentence. A character *appears* in a scene in many different ways. The most obvious is that the character is physically present. But a character also "appears" if:

• Others in the script discuss him or her.

• Someone or something in the scene represents him or her (the boss's henchman, a character's artwork).

• The character is on tape or film in the movie itself.

• There are various manifestations of the character (such as his or her image, ghost, or holograph).

What do I mean by saying the reader should learn *a little more* about a character? Many writers make the mistake of giving the character's entire resume as soon as he or she enters the story. If your character is a major one, you have over 100 pages to present, develop, and change him or her. But if your character is not as important, why do you need to tell the reader more than a few details?

Portraying character in a script is somewhat like eating an artichoke. You take one leaf at a time. You savor it. You take the next leaf, and so on. In each scene, give the reader a little something more about the character. Show something. Tell something. Peel back one of those leaves. Ultimately, you will reach the heart.

Exposition

Exposition is information that the reader must have in order to understand the scene. Like characterization, exposition is given a little at a time on a need-to-know basis. One way of presenting exposition is through situation. Situation is backstory, relationships, locales, and time. What are these things and how are they used?

Backstory is who, what, and why. Who are your characters? What are their reasons for being the type of people they are? Why and how did these characters find themselves in the circumstances they are in when the script opens? That is backstory.

Relationships provide more insight. Who are your character's friends and lovers? Who are his or her acquaintances, co-workers and family? How does your character deal with these people? The answers to these questions push the plot forward and help the reader discover the temperament and psyche of the people who inhabit your pages.

Locales impart the texture of the universe your characters inhabit. Washington, D.C., adds a slightly different flavor to your story than Los Angeles, Nashville, or New York City. The central city differs from the suburbs or countryside. The United States is different from elsewhere. While certain locales evoke certain expectations, these expectations do not mean that every story set in a particular area must or should center on the "industry" for which it is famous. Every Washington, D.C., script need not be about politics, nor every Nashville story about country music. Still, there should be a reason for your choice that has to do with the plot—as opposed to "that's where I wanted to set it." Remember that everything written in a film script is purposeful and interconnected.

Time, too, serves as a tool for scene exposition. Historical time clues the reader into the manners, mores, and sympathies of the moment. The hour and sometimes the season let the reader know about the lighting, the weather, and occasionally other nuances. Time rounds out the reader's view of the coming fantasy and allows him or her, and later the audience, to spend their time not trying to guess "when" they are.

Most of the information an audience receives in a movie, however, will be conveyed the old-fashioned way, by what is seen and heard. Let's imagine that

> Exposition is information that the reader must have in order to understand the scene. Like characterization, exposition is given a little at a time on a need-to-know basis.

your script has been sold for the first eight-figure deal in history and is presently on screen. What do we see? What do we hear? We see characters, costumes, settings, symbols, signs, props, titles, special effects, lighting, and yes, camera angles. (Some of these items, such as lighting and angles, the writer would not include in the script.) We hear dialogue, narration, voice-overs, sound effects, music, ambient noise.

Once a writer realizes what information he or she might include, the next question becomes: "How much information does the reader need to know, and when does the reader need to know it?"

A reader generally needs to know enough so that what the characters do and what happens in the scene are clear. The reader need not always be privy in each scene to the motivation, background, problems, reasons, or possible consequences of each character or his or her actions. Readers may be aware of all these aspects, but as long as they comprehend what is happening on the page, they can assume the rest will be revealed later.

Information is like good seasoning. It ought to be sprinkled in a little at a time. Without such seasoning, the food would be bland at best. And without the correct use of exposition, a screenplay will be either unintelligible or tiresome.

Reversal

A reversal is the scene's climax, a turning point, a change. A reversal is the magic. A reversal is the linchpin of the entire scene. A reversal surprises, lifts, and enlivens the scene. It is that point in a scene when the action and/or the emotion takes either a surprising twist or reaches an unexpected intensity. Picture a heart monitor. The monitor depicts a patient's heartbeat as a jagged line, which spurts to a peak at regular intervals. Reversals are those peaks in your screenplay. Without the surge (reversal) occurring at least every five to six pages, your feature will flat-line. A reversal assures that your scene has life and that your story maintains its momentum.

While placing a reversal in each scene is important, it is not always enough. To be effective, a reversal must accomplish three tasks: It must change the direction of the scene; change the emotions of the main characters in the scene and/or of the audience; and surprise the main characters in the scene and/or the audience. Let's consider each of these criteria.

Change the direction of the scene: Did the turning point change the audiences' and/or characters' expectations about where events were headed?

For instance, in *Raiders of the Lost Ark,* Indy finds Marion alive but bound and gagged in the Germans' tent. The audience and Marion expect Indy to set her free. Instead, Indy leaves Marion in the tent so the Germans will continue to believe that he, Indy, is dead.

In *Erin Brockovich,* Erin tries to leave the bar where she is getting coffee because a man—whom she has seen watching her in other places—is hitting on her and may even endanger her. But it turns out the man wants to talk to her because he has just the evidence Erin has been searching for.

Change the emotions of one or more of the main characters in the scene and/or the audience: A reversal should alter not only the direction but the mood of the scene.

Marion's joy at seeing Indy becomes protest and fear when he replaces the gag. On the other hand, the audience, worried whether Indy can release Marion before the Germans return, now laughs because of Indy's unexpected, but logical, action.

Erin's fear about the man in the bar (Charles Embry) turns to excitement and trepidation when she discovers where he has worked and what information he might have.

Surprise one of the main characters in the scene and/or the audience: In the scene from *Indiana Jones,* Indy, Marion, and the audience are surprised in different ways by what Indy does. In *Erin Brockovich,* the only one who isn't surprised is Charles Embry, as Erin and the audience perceive the entire situation differently from the way it really is.

Reversal is the glue that binds the scene together. It is the point of emotional change, the surprise, the energy, and the main factor in keeping your screenplay vibrant and marketable. To ensure that your script is always alive and kicking, make sure each scene has at least one reversal.

Bridging out

Bridging out is knowing when and how to exit the scene. That doesn't mean you simply type a "CUT TO:" or write another slug line. Linger too long in a scene and you will bore your reader; stop short and you will confuse him. In a sitcom, the rule is always to leave the scene on a joke. No corresponding convention applies to drama or even a film comedy. The best approach is to take your exit cue from the six elements you have planted. Let's review them:

Do you have a conflict? Is the conflict visual and emotional? Are characterizations and exposition provocative, clear, and not overdone? Does your bridging in and direction permit the reader a "guess" at what will happen next? Do you have a reversal—a climax, a turning point—that causes the audience and/or the characters in the scene to be surprised at what actually does happen next? Do you exit the scene before the power of the reversal is lost? If the answers are "Yes—absolutely," your scenes should sparkle, shine, and light the inside of movie theaters and living rooms for years to come.

Rick Reichman of Santa Fe, N.M., is the author of *Formatting Your Screenplay* and a veteran screenwriting teacher. This article is from *The Writer,* March 2003.

GREAT REVERSALS

There are millions of classic and clever scene reversals. One of the most famous is in *Casablanca*, when Rick (Humphrey Bogart) has shot Major Strasser and doesn't know whether Louie will tell the Germans. Finally, Louie tells the soldiers, "Round up the usual suspects." Another, more contemporary, reversal is from *A Beautiful Mind*, when Alicia learns that the Cambridge mansion where her husband, John, has been leaving supposedly secret documents has been abandoned and unused for years. Here are some more of my favorite reversals:

Butch Cassidy and the Sundance Kid
Harvey Logan challenges Butch to a knife fight. But Butch says they first have to get the rules straight. Harvey hesitates a moment to question the idea of rules in a knife fight. The moment he hesitates, "Butch delivers the most aesthetically exquisite kick in the [crotch] in the history of the modern American cinema," in the words of screenwriter William Goldman.

Raiders of the Lost Ark
When confronted by a sword-wielding man, Indy simply pulls his gun and shoots the swordsman.

Chinatown
Detective Jake Gittes, who is getting too close to discovering what is happening to Los Angeles' water supply, is captured by several men. To show Jake what happens to "nosy people," "the man with a knife" slices Jake's nose.

Time After Time
H.G. Wells believes that Jack the Ripper has killed Amy. But Amy has hidden and is safe, and we discover that the woman killed was a friend of Amy's.

Dead Poets Society
The painfully reticent Todd has not done his class assignment, which was to write a poem. Under gentle pressure from Mr. Keating, however, Todd is able to create a poem.

—*Rick Reichman*

SET THE RIGHT PACE

The right pacing will energize your writing

by Polly Campbell

Every school term, I hand students in my writing class a sheet titled "Elements of Good Writing." The page includes 24 techniques, which, when used properly and practiced, can create a piece of well-crafted prose, whether fiction or nonfiction. On that list are things like description and dialogue, voice and verbs, as well as something that is often overlooked: pace.

Proper pace—the speed at which a story moves—energizes the writing. It creates a rhythm readers remember. Instead of a blend of letters, words, and sentences strung across the page, the story transcends the structure and becomes lyrical.

If the story moves too fast, it weakens the drama and leaves the reader unsatisfied, unfulfilled. Too slow and the story lurches and lags, leaving readers feeling disconnected, uninterested, and worse, unmoved.

Pace is that combination of nearly intangible elements like timing, speed, space, and rhythm. But it requires concrete steps to create.

Here are six tips to help you write a story that's lyrical, not lagging.

1. Say it slowly.

Each article is a balance of facts, scenes, and actions. The way that information is presented alters the pacing.

Imagine if I had started this article with the following sentence: "To establish the proper pace in your story and connect with readers, you must clear the clutter, provide action, vary sentence length, use repetition, and manage the details by choosing only those elements that apply to your story focus."

Whoa. Too fast. Too much information. Instead, provide material slowly. Use a bit of detail to hook the reader in the lead, and provide some background. Then release pieces of new material that enhance the story's focus as you go. Don't hold all of the best material until the end.

And don't shy away from using a quick stream of strategically placed information to build intensity. Just avoid dishing it out all at once.

2. Give us action.

Even the smallest actions add intensity and movement to the story. Get your subjects moving, encountering obstacles, making choices.

In a profile I wrote about piano player Ida Colby, for example, I began with movement:

"Ida Colby, 80, steers her motorized scooter to the edge of the stage and pushes herself up until she's leaning against the banister, holding herself up on her hands. Then she drags her paralyzed legs over to the piano bench, at the top of the stairs."

I could start with Ida sitting at the piano, but I want readers to share in her struggle and become involved in the action.

In *How to Tell a Story: The Secrets of Writing Captivating Tales,* Peter Rubie and Gary Provost encourage writers to strengthen the pace of a story by using big and small actions to move the reader through a piece. But make sure each sentence, action, or movement of the story adds new information.

3. Dump the garbage.

Get rid of the prepositions, adverbs, phrases, modifiers, any chunk of prose that doesn't add to the story.

"Clutter is the laborious phrase which has pushed out the short word that means the same thing. These locutions are a drag on energy and momentum," says William Zinsser in *On Writing Well.*

Garbage in writing is like a speed bump on the avenue. The bump slows you down, jostles you around, and delays you for several seconds.

In your writing, garbage bumps your readers out of the moment, causing them to feel disoriented and disconnected. It disrupts patterns, hurts the flow, and depletes the energy of the piece. Choose strong words that can stand on their own and your pacing will improve.

4. Vary sentence length.

Long sentences build tension and infuse drama. Short sentences release energy. Both create momentum and pace in a story. So mix it up. Distribute the energy of your piece throughout the sentences. Pacing is a result of how the words and sentences play off each other.

Look at how I mixed it up in a newspaper feature I wrote on mental illness:

"Twice, she lost her son.

"The first time was in 1996 when Michele Grussmeyer's oldest child, Wade, sensitive and hardworking, turned irrational and hostile. During the next year, the Milwaukie [Ore.] High School graduate severed friendships, beat up his brother, lost jobs, and repeatedly ran away from home.

"His personality became unrecognizable."

To heighten the impact of the first five words, I changed the pace, and followed with a stream of straightforward information.

5. Repeat yourself.

Imagine if President Kennedy's famed inaugural speech of 1961 went like this: "Ask not what the country can do for you, but what you might be able to do for your neighborhood." It lacks impact and unity when compared to his original words: "Ask not what your country can do for you—ask what you can do for your country."

That speech, like so many delivered by powerful orators, relies on repetition and parallel structure to deliver drama, reinforce ideas, and create momentum. The repeated words or phrases gain significance while adding a lyrical quality to the language. The technique also works to unify ideas and patterns, stitching together main points to provide a thread for the reader to follow as well as a powerful pace.

6. Count the details.

A sentence that contains a few well-chosen details can enliven the writing and ignite readers' interest. Too many details take the reader away from the main focus. Pacing becomes sluggish. Choose only those details that provide insight into the story.

For example, in my profile of a 91-year-old inventor, I wrote: "With a rounded teaspoon of sugar in his right hand and a paring knife in his left, Allen Schlabach scrapes the top of the mound of sugar, dropping single particles onto Quaker Oats in the bowl below."

For this story, it was important to characterize this man as precise and unyielding. Describing how he put the sugar on his cereal establishes that precision and moves the reader closer to the subject. Auxiliary details, such as what he was wearing, who prepared the cereal, or who washed the dishes, would have muddled the meaning and slowed the pace of the piece.

Polly Campbell of Beaverton, Ore., writes human-interest features for newspapers and magazines and teaches writing workshops. Her articles have appeared in *Family Circle, American Profile, Arthritis Today,* and other publications. This article is from *The Writer,* March 2003.

BUILD ACTION WITH OBJECTS

Look to objects as catalysts for action that will enhance the pacing of your piece. Portland, Ore., teacher and writer Carolyn Altman calls it "loving your objects."

"The stories feel static, with everybody and everything sitting around in their own descriptions. I encourage my students to activate their prose—put their characters and objects into action," Altman says. "Sure, it's nice to have a vase on a mantel, but it is even better for a character to hide something in it, hit someone with it, or steal it, because it is the one thing that reminds him of his mother."

With Altman's words in mind, choose objects and actions that add something to the story. Don't introduce a vase if it doesn't reveal something new about the character. And don't overlook even the most mundane objects. For example, how a woman shuts a door or hangs up a telephone says a lot about her mood and character.

When you create action around the objects, Altman says, two things happen: You have more material to work with as a writer, and the reader gets a well-woven, well-paced, dramatic story.

—*Polly Campbell*

ON WRITING PERSONAL ESSAYS

by Barbara Abercrombie

We read personal essays to understand our lives, to find humor, to discover a new way of looking at the world. We write them for the same reasons. The short personal essay (about 500 to 1,200 words) is your journey through a specific experience, whether commonplace or one of life's milestones, and ranges from the personal to something more universal, something your readers can connect with.

You move to a new town, you go white-river rafting for the first time, your dog dies, you try to order something from a catalog, you get a divorce, you celebrate an anniversary, someone cuts in front of you in line. When you pay attention and reflect on your own world, from large events to small moments, the topics for essays are endless.

Unlike the formal essay, the personal essay is rooted in experience and emotion, and structured around a theme, not a thesis. Rather than proving a premise, you're writing about an experience you had, serious or ordinary, that led you to understanding and insight.

Though not adhering to the formal rules of the essays you wrote in English class, the personal essay is crafted and shaped; it has a beginning, a middle, and an ending. The opening must draw the reader in, set up expectations for what the essay is about. The essay's tone and subject are clear in the first paragraph.

In the middle of the essay, something happens: An anecdote illustrates your theme. The reader wants to go through the experience with you, not be told about it from a distance. Use the devices of fiction. Set the scene. What were your five senses picking up? What was said? Use dialogue if you can. Be specific in your details and descriptions of people and places.

The ending of your essay, the understanding and insight you gain, can be life-changing or simply a slight shift in awareness. The personal essay is not just for reflecting or remembering; there's a point to it. Through your flash of insight or your humorous take on something ordinary, the reader can connect to the essay and identify with either the experience you wrote about or the feelings you had. The essay has a theme and comes to a conclusion, like a satisfying story.

Sometimes, you start writing a personal piece not knowing where it's going, what the end will be, or even the theme. When this happens, be patient and keep writing. Write your way through the experience. Sometimes, you can find the point of your essay by going back to the first paragraphs.

When my mother died, I tried to write about our relationship, how we became friends at the end of her life, how she blossomed as a widow in her mid-80s, the lovely romance she was involved in, and her discipline in practicing the piano six hours a day. The first drafts I wrote were mired in me, unshaped and messy. Writing can be good therapy, but therapy is not always good writing. What tied these memories together? Yes, it was about our bumpy journey to understanding each other at the end of her life, the failed expectations we'd always had of each other, but what point was I trying to make? What were the connections beyond our relationship that a reader could identify with?

It took me six months to finish that 1,200-word essay. I'd take it out periodically, make notes and write another draft, but I couldn't figure out the point of it. Finally, I went back to what I'd written in the opening paragraphs, about wanting a mother more connected to the outside world, a mother who worked and wasn't so obsessed with her children and playing the piano. But in my family, professional women were thought of as "tough."

By going back to this beginning, the themes and point of my essay finally became clear to me. It was about the nature of work and also grief. When I realized this, I could write the ending:

> As this first year after her death wheels through the seasons, I grow, if not comfortable, at least familiar with grief. I've become accustomed to the way grief goes underground, gives you a respite, fools you into thinking you've recovered, only to ambush you with memory and hollow you out with pain at the sight of a carefully ironed napkin, the scent of White Linen, or the sound of a piano.
>
> I realize that I am the daughter of a woman who became independent in her 80s and surpassed all my expectations of the kind of mother I needed. A woman who bloomed and left me with inspiration for my own old age. A woman who never stopped working and was, in all the good ways, tough.

"The Mother I Really Wanted" was published in United Airlines' *Hemispheres,* which has a circulation of 500,000. Yet when I read it aloud to my students to illustrate the step-by-step process of writing this type of essay and the need for patience in searching for the point, I'm struck by how personal it is, how I'm revealing things to my class that only my family and close friends know. But when we write a personal essay, we are telling the truth—and we're telling it in the first person, without the mask of fiction or metaphor of poetry to hide behind.

"We are here on this island in the middle of the Pacific in lieu of filing for divorce," wrote Joan Didion in her classic essay "In the Islands," first published in *Life.* This was my introduction to the personal essay, and when I read that line, I was riveted by the honesty of the sentence, the elegance of the writing, and how the essay was rooted in the very personal while remaining controlled and connected to a wider world.

Writing honestly, writing the truth about the most private subjects, does not mean revealing everything. What you leave out can shape your essay as much as the truth that you put into it.

Finding the truth and meaning in an experience, turning it into an essay and getting it published, involves the following process:

Find the topic and explore it.

Find the tone for your essay and write everything that comes into your mind about the subject. If you're stuck on finding a subject, try making a list. (Lists are a good tool for writers. You don't have to feel inspired or creative to make one; a list doesn't carry the weight of commitment—it gives you space to flirt and fool around with ideas.) Spend five minutes listing all the issues and experiences, important and trivial, in your life right now. What frustrated you in the past month? What made you laugh or cry, or lose your temper? What was the worse thing that happened? The best? The most disturbing and weird?

Unlike the formal essay, the personal essay is rooted in experience and emotion, and structured around a theme, not a thesis.

Get it down.

Try free-writing: Keep your pen, or fingers on the keyboard, moving, and don't stop writing until 10 minutes are up. Don't judge, just write. If the subject you chose from your list runs dry on you, choose another. Word count doesn't matter at this point, nor does spelling or grammar. This is your sloppy first draft. Remember, no one will ever have to see it, so take chances with your writing; be free and adventurous, take risks.

After you have a first draft, you can let your critic out, that sharp-eyed, never-satisfied editor obsessed with perfection, and rewrite. Cut all the unnecessary words—the adjectives and adverbs that add no new information, the observations that are obvious, and any rambling passages. Cut the first paragraph if it doesn't go directly to the subject. Figure out the point of the essay. Check your spelling.

Editing and rewriting can only happen when you have something written, so accumulate pages before you try to edit. And leave time between drafts. Often, you'll discover that something you were critical of makes sense when you come back to it.

Study the market.

Go to the library and read magazines and newspapers on file, write away for guidelines, or check publication sites on the Internet. If you want to be published, knowing the market is as important as creating the article. You can write the most moving, insightful, beautifully crafted essay, but if it's not suited to the publications you've sent it to—subject, tone, or length—it will be rejected.

Always be on the lookout for new markets. If you're traveling, study in-flight magazines and local publications. Look up professional and vocational trade magazines in your field of work. Doctors' offices usually have a wide variety of publications, including baby and parenting magazines. Veterinarian offices have an array of animal magazines. Check reference books like *The Writer's Handbook* for market lists.

And what if you do your marketing homework, send your essay out with its cover letter and self-addressed stamped envelope—and it doesn't sell? Because rejection slips can be so painful and paralyzing, be prepared. Know where you'll send the essay next. If it comes back, read it over, ask yourself if it needs any rewriting, and then send it out again. And again and again.

The short personal essay is the most publishable of all genres of creative writing. Unlike the market for fiction or poetry, there is always a place to send a personal essay. If you write something true and honest from your heart (or funny bone), if there's a point to it, if the subject and word count is right for the market, it will eventually be published.

And maybe even more important than being published is the deep pleasure and satisfaction of turning something that happened to you, messy and chaotic as most experience is, into order and clarity, into shape and meaning.

Barbara Abercrombie of Santa Monica, Calif., has written personal essays and articles for numerous magazines and newspapers, including the *Los Angeles Times* and *The Christian Science Monitor*. The latest of her nine books is *Writing Out the Storm: Reading and Writing Your Way Through Serious Illness or Injury*. Her Web site is www. barbaraabercrombie.com. This article is from *The Writer*, January 2003.

7 SECRETS
OF GOOD PROSE

Ways to pare and polish your work as you revise

by Constance Hale

"One pearl is better than a whole necklace of potatoes," French mime Etienne Decroux used to remind his students. His dictum works equally well for students of writing. Each word we choose is—or should be—a pearl.

Whether you're a floodgates-open writer or a blocked writer, remember: The first draft is for just getting the ideas down. It's in the revising that we sift through our words, letting only the most perfect specimens adorn the thread of syntax. These "seven secrets of good prose" will help you banish the potatoes and burnish the pearls.

1. Use specific and concrete nouns and adjectives.

Well-chosen nouns and adjectives are critical in setting scenes, establishing character, and giving readers strong visual images. The best nouns are not just concrete (naming something that can be seen, touched, heard, tasted, or felt), but also highly specific; search for the most evocative and exact. Why choose "house" when the options include *cottage, Victorian, duplex, dacha, shack, bungalow,* and *bachelor's pad*? (Stay away from abstractions like *abode, dwelling, domicile,* or *residence.*)

Watch for clusters of abstract nouns. When a school principal wrote to parents urging a "communication facilitation skills development intervention," he should have tried harder to be clear: "We need to help students write better." Cross out groups of polysyllabic abstract nouns and start over with one or two simple, clear words.

Strong nouns help you cut adjectives. Novice writers make the mistake of gooing up their descriptions with a lot of lush adjectives. Resist. Make every adjective count. Why use "yellow" given the options: *bamboo, butter, jonquil, lemon, mimosa, saffron,* and *sauterne*? Diane Ackerman, in an article on golden lion tamarins, described the yellowish monkey as a "sunset-and-corn-silk-colored creature" with "sweet-potato-colored" legs, a "reddish" beard, and a chest and belly "the tawny gold of an autumn cornfield." Now that's exact!

Adjectives can do double duty, painting both physical *and* psychological detail. In his profile of a North Carolina revenue agent, Alec Wilkinson wrote that Garland Bunting has "eyes that are clear and close-set and steel blue." Those three adjectives convey Bunting's glare and capture his gritty personality.

2. Pick action-packed verbs.

All verbs are either static (*to be, to seem, to become*) or dynamic (*to whistle, to waffle, to wonder*). The static verbs are the ones that pour out naturally when we write or speak—"is" appears endlessly in most first drafts. But dynamic verbs give writing power and drama. Rephrase sentences with static verbs, filling them with action. And not just any action: To describe someone walking down the street, consider *gambol, shamble, lumber, lurch, sway, swagger,* and *sashay.*

Roger Angell packs his description of a baseball catcher with powerhouse verbs (italics are mine):

"He *whacks* his cap against his leg, *producing* a puff of dust, and *settles* it in place, its bill astern, with an oddly feminine gesture and then, *reversing* the movement, *pulls* on the mask and *firms* it with a soldierly downward tug. The hand *dips* between his thighs, *semaphoring* a plan. . . ."

Angell notes all the little movements as well as the grand ones, and in his search for the right verb, drafts nouns if necessary (a "semaphore" is a hand-held signal flag).

3. Avoid adverbs.

If you pick pointed verbs, you'll be able to forgo adverbs. Many adverbs merely prop up a ho-hum verb. Strike "speaks softly" and insert *murmurs.* Erase "eats quickly" in favor of *vacuums.*

Many adverbs are hauled in just to add emphasis—*very, definitely, really, quite.* But, oddly enough, in writing these actually subtract power. In lieu of "very pretty," write *fetching.* Forget "extremely good"; try *delicious.* Rather than "really nervous," use *trembling.*

4. Pare prepositional pileups.

Prepositions—words like *on, of, above, beyond, near,* and *next to*—are little words that act like connective tissue in sentences. If we say "Let's go to the store on the corner of my street," we've used two prepositional phrases: "on the corner" tells us which store and "of my street" tells us which corner. But isn't it cleaner just to say "the corner store"?

Prepositional pileups can be distracting. Clear the clutter! Convert prepositional phrases into single words:

- *now,* not "at this point in time" or "in this day and age"
- *for,* not "in the interest of"
- *neat,* not "neat in appearance"
- *to believe,* not "to be of the opinion that"
- *to consider,* not "to take into consideration."

5. Keep sentences lean and keep their parts parallel.

After picking the pearls, focus on how to string them onto the filament of the sentence. Start by tracking your subjects and verbs. After you've reviewed the verbs, making sure they are dynamic and specific, do a subject check. Can you identify the person or thing that is performing the action? By controlling the subjects of individual sentences, we control the *focus* of the entire piece.

The more you eliminate noun clutter, excessive adjectives, adverbs, and prepositional pileups, the closer your sentences will hew to these four basic sentence patterns:

- *subject + dynamic verb*
- *subject + dynamic verb + direct object*
- *subject + dynamic verb + indirect object + direct object*
- *subject + static verb + complement.*

Don't be afraid to keep your sentences stark. This lead from a newspaper story on California's tofu industry sticks to simple sentences and accomplishes both clarity and comedy: "It's white. It's weird. It wiggles on a plate." The writer keeps tofu as her subject and resists the urge to insert herself ("I've always thought tofu . . ."). Then she follows each subject immediately with a verb (is/is/wiggles).

In his heyday, Muhammad Ali was a master of the powerful punch, whether physical or verbal. This rap from 1974 shows he could keep sentence parts parallel: "Only last week, I *murdered a rock, injured a stone, hospitalized a brick.* I'm so mean, I *make medicine sick.*" Ali kept his subject steady and repeated the same construction as often as he did his jabs.

6. Play with sound and rhythm.

Ali also played with musicality, creating the unexpected rhyme of "brick" and "sick." Begin to experiment with elements like rhyme, alliteration, and onomatopoeia. Alliteration repeats the initial sounds in words: *seven secrets, content of their character, Walter Winchell wannabee.* Onomatopoeia allows the sound of a word to echo the sound of the thing: dishes *crash,* teeth *gnash,* and Saran Wrap *crinkles.*

Play also with rhythm. Choose short, single-syllable words to set up a staccato rhythm (Churchill's bracing "I have nothing to offer but blood, toil, tears, and sweat") or more mellifluous words for a more melodious flow (Lincoln's "Four score and seven years ago, our fathers brought forth on this continent a new nation, conceived in liberty and dedicated to the proposition that all men are created equal"). Vary the rhythm of sentences: Write a passage in short, crisp sentences. Write it again, letting phrases elongate. Mix long and short, noting how short sentences pack a punch and how longer ones soften your message.

7. Make metaphors.

Metaphor, the comparison of disparate things, adds surprise, freshness, and depth. Don't just repeat an old cliché ("tension so thick you could cut it with a knife"). Metaphors must be invented by the writer for the particular occasion. Theodore Roosevelt accused William McKinley of having "all the backbone of a chocolate éclair." Novelist James Salter used "the silence of a folded flag" to describe the quiet of an afternoon in provincial France.

And, of course, Etienne Decroux made a metaphor when he declared that "One pearl is better than a whole necklace of potatoes."

Constance Hale of Oakland, Calif., is a journalist and author of *Wired Style* and *Sin and Syntax*. This article appeared in *The Writer*, June 2002.

THE VALUE OF A PERSONAL CRITIC

A fresh set of eyes can spot things
in your manuscript you can't

by William G. Tapply

You've finally finished! You've written and rewritten, edited and re-edited. You've agonized over every word. Now your novel, that Thing that has clawed around in your head for one, two, or five years and haunted your waking and sleeping hours, is done. You can't change another word of it. It's perfect. Time to ship it off to an editor or a literary agent, right?

Wrong.

That little rodent of doubt persists in gnawing at your confidence. Maybe the characters don't ring true, or the suspense falls flat, or a scene is off, or there are contradictions in the plot. Maybe it's not scary, or funny, or sad the way you intended. Maybe it's not perfect, you think. Maybe it's flawed, but you just can't see it. Maybe you're too close to it.

Well, send it in anyway. That's why they have editors, right?

Wrong again.

Editors don't edit

Maxwell Perkins, the legendary editor at Scribner's, used to tell his writers: "Just get it down on paper, then we'll see what to do with it." Perkins argued, cajoled, and bullied Ernest Hemingway over every paragraph in his novels. He nurtured the brilliant but unreliable F. Scott Fitzgerald. He burrowed through cartons of Thomas Wolfe's manuscript pages and distilled them into elegant novels.

Unfortunately for today's writers, the Maxwell Perkinses of the world have all but disappeared. Nowadays, editors and literary agents are not looking for unknown writers with promise. Agents are swamped with submissions from aspiring authors like you. They're looking for a finished, polished product—something they can sell. Editors are too busy negotiating contracts and promoting their lists and working with their established writers to edit unestablished ones. Submit a flawed manuscript to an agent today—even one written by an author, like you, who has the promise of a Hemingway, Fitzgerald, or Wolfe—and you will receive his standard, noncommittally polite form rejection letter.

Acceptance or rejection: Unless you're a well-established author, you can't expect any more than that from an editor or agent nowadays.

Open your study door

So how can you maximize your chances of showing that agent something he thinks he can sell? How can you give an editor a novel he will want to publish?

The answer, of course, is to be sure that the manuscript you submit is not flawed. And since you, quite intelligently, know enough not to place all your trust in your own judgment, you've got to enlist some help.

Stephen King advises beginning writers to "take your story through at least two drafts: the one you do with the study door closed and the one you do with it open." So after you've taken your novel as far as you can go with it, open your study door and invite in your own personal critic, someone who can see your manuscript with fresh eyes and give you straightforward feedback that will help guide you through the vital process of revision. (The word "revision," remember, comes from the Latin roots meaning "to see again.")

Even well-established authors rely on others to help them see what they can't see for themselves. Few authors are better established than King, yet he never sends a manuscript off before getting feedback from his wife, Tabitha. In *On Writing*, King says of Tabby: "She has always been an extremely sympathetic and supportive first reader. . . . But she's also unflinching when she sees something she thinks is wrong. When she does, she lets me know loud and clear."

Sympathy and support, but unflinching honesty, too. That's what you want from a personal critic.

"Very few writers," says John Irving, "are really seeking advice when they give out their work to be read. They want someone to say, 'Good job!' "

Serious writers do seek advice. They welcome criticism. Serious writers want to hear "good job" only from a reader they trust to be unflinchingly honest.

Finding your own personal critic

Tabitha King happens to be a successful author in her own right. But you can find sympathy and support—and unflinching honesty—from anybody who loves to read the kind of stories you write, and has read many of them . . . provided they are absolutely convinced you don't just want them to say, "Good job."

Look first to your friends and relatives. Supportive, well-read spouses like Tabby King—and my wife, Vicki, who's also a professional writer—make excellent critics, whether or not they're writers themselves. They know you, they know you're serious, and they have a stake in your success. They don't want you to be rejected. They understand that supportiveness and candor go hand in hand, so they're not afraid to tell you what they think.

Willing readers can come from anywhere, but you might have to audition several of them before you find one who gives you the right combination of support and honesty.

If you can find two or three good critics, all the better. By comparing the responses of a few trusted readers, you should have all you need to revise with confidence.

Not everyone makes an effective critic. But with guidance, almost any well-intentioned book lover can give you useful feedback. Don't just give readers your manuscript and ask them to comment on it. Tell them specifically what you want:

• I don't expect you to be an editor. I just want you to respond to my book like a reader.

• Read my manuscript with a pen in your hand and "talk" to me in the margins. Don't censor yourself. Write down whatever comes into your head.

• The most useful feedback you can give me focuses on what doesn't work for you.

• Don't worry about hurting my feelings. I'm serious about this. I want candor, not kindness.

• I'm not asking for solutions. Fixing what's wrong is my responsibility.

• Of course, if you have ideas about how I could handle something differently, I'm all ears.

• Note your emotional responses to the story (both positive and negative) in the margins.

• I especially need to know anyplace you found yourself bored (just write "Ho, hum" in the margin) or confused (write "Huh?").

• Did you find yourself skipping parts? Where?

• Did anything in the story contradict itself or seem inconsistent?

• Was there anything—a character, a place, an event—that you didn't believe? Did the dialogue ring true?

• Did I seem to make any factual errors? Please note them, even if you're not sure. I'll double-check them myself.

• Put a circle around every word or phrase or punctuation mark that sounds "off" to you. Don't worry about whether you're right or not. That's my job.

How to handle criticism

Criticism is easier to give—and to take—in writing than in person. So after your readers have marked up your manuscript, ask them to write you a letter that points out and explains their most important observations and gives you their overall response to the story.

When they deliver their letters and your marked-up manuscript, tell them you might want to make a date for later, after you've had a chance to absorb their comments, to sit down and talk about it.

Give yourself at least a week to reread your manuscript and to review and digest your readers' responses in private. That way, if you feel like screaming in frustration or anger or disappointment, no one will hear you.

Get over it. Then consider your critics' comments objectively. Unless you find the comments utterly useless, arrange to get together with the readers individually.

Use face-to-face sessions to encourage clarification and elaboration and suggestions from each reader. You will probably disagree with some of their comments, but you should not dispute their observations or try to defend yourself. Remember: How you end up using their feedback is entirely up to you.

Whether or not you have found your critics' responses helpful, be sure that they know you appreciate their effort. Buy them presents. Send flowers. Take them to dinner.

And when your book is accepted for publication, don't forget to give them a great big thank-you on the acknowledgments page.

William G. Tapply of Hancock, N.H., has written 21 novels, including *A Fine Line* and 18 more novels in the Brady Coyne mystery series, and 10 nonfiction books, including *The Elements of Mystery Fiction* (The Writer Books). This article appeared in *The Writer*, April 2003.

WHAT I KNOW FOR SURE (I THINK)

A bestselling author offers words of wisdom

by Susan Elizabeth Phillips

Each month, Oprah ends her magazine with a column entitled, "This is what I know for sure." I love this column, as much for its generally wise content as for the fact that Oprah has the confidence to state that she knows anything for sure. After writing for 20-plus years, however, I've decided there are a few things I also know for sure. So, in no particular order, here they are:

Everybody won't like everything you write. Some people won't like anything you write. Get over it.

Writing is hard for everybody except fools.

Writing is sedentary. Without a regular exercise program, both your body and your creative brain will be in trouble. (Oh, stop whining. You know I'm right.)

There's no right and wrong way to write. Anyone who tries to tell you otherwise is feeling insecure. Be compassionate.

Some people love to write. Many are simply compelled. I wish I were one of the first group.

Fear goes hand-in-hand with artistic creation, and no amount of success will make the fear go away entirely.

I love whoever wrote this motivational quote: "I can fix a bad page, but I can't fix a blank one."

Being forced to write a synopsis before you've written the book is necessary for some of us and is eating away the artistic souls of others. Figure out which one you are.

Stay off an editor's "Life's too short to deal with this person" list. At the same time, don't be a wimp. Practice professionalism.

Anyone who's waiting for her or his in-basket to be empty before starting to write will never start to write.

E-mail creates the illusion that you're writing. You're not.

Don't get overly invested in awards and writing contests. Some of our most successful writers have won them, lost them, or simply bypassed them.

Nasty reviews of good books are a blessing. They remind us that no matter how hard we try, we can't please everyone. This gives us permission to write for ourselves.

People who write nasty reviews of any kind will come back in their next lives as eyeball-eating ants.

The writing process that works so beautifully for a talented friend won't work for you. Find your own way.

Figure out what depletes you creatively and get it out of your life. (This doesn't apply to spouse and kids.)

Give yourself permission to put garbage on the screen. A lot of days it's the only way you'll be able to keep going. You can clean it up later.

Put your kids first when they're young. You won't regret it.

Find time and space for yourself when your kids are young. If you don't, you'll empty out.

Don't tell yourself lies about either your strengths or your weaknesses as a person and a writer. Looking yourself in the face is the first step to creating great characters.

If you critique others, heed the wise words of the best critiquer I know, author Lindsay Longford, who says, "First, do no harm."

When you put your work out for critique, choose carefully.

Take joy in the writing journey. If you only take pleasure in the final product, most of your working life will suck.

Read widely.

Celebrate the success of others. High tide floats all ships.

Find your own voice, but don't worry about *how* you're going to find it. None of the rest of us have that figured out either.

Try to live with a generous heart. Doing anything else is too hard.

Susan Elizabeth Phillips is the only four-time recipient of the Romance Writers of America's Favorite Book of the Year award. Her latest book is *Breathing Room.* More information can be found at her Web site: www.susanelizabethphillips.com. This article, which appeared in *The Writer,* January 2003, originally appeared in *Romance Writers' Report,* September 2001, published by Romance Writers of America. It is reprinted here with permission of the author. © Susan Elizabeth Phillips.

WHAT IS A POEM?

by Jane Yolen

What is a poem?
Hard work.
A single great line.
What we see and hear the moment before sleep takes us.
The pause between heartbeats.
The first touch of the drumstick on the tight stretch of drum
and the slight burring after.
A word discovered after an afternoon of trying.
An emotion caught in the hand, in the mouth.
Two words that bump up against one another
and create something new.
Hard work.

What is a poem?
Hard work.
Literature's soul.
A touch of lemon swab on a parched mouth.
A son who smells of sweat instead of cigarettes.
A new word, like frass, which is what the caterpillar
leaves behind.
A story compressed to a paragraph,
a paragraph squeezed to a phrase,
a phrase pared to its essence.
Hard work.

What is a poem?
Hard work.
Emotion surprised.
Throwing a colored shadow.
A word that doubles back on itself, not once but twice.
The exact crunch of carrots.
Precise joys.
A prayer that sounds like a curse until it is said again.
Crows punctuating a field of snow.
Hard work.

What is a poem?
Hard work.
The space between a hummingbird's wingbeats.
A child's meddlefurs.
A whistle too high for a dog to hear.
One bloody word after another after another.
The graceful ellipse of memory.
The graceful collapse of memory.
The graceful lapse of memory.
The graceless lips of memory.
Hard work.

What is a poem?
Hard work.
Hard work.
Hard work.
Hard work.

Jane Yolen has been called America's Hans Christian Andersen (*Newsweek*) and a modern-day Aesop (*The New York Times*). Her books and stories have won many awards, including the Caldecott Medal (for *Owl Moon*, and an Honor Award for *The Emperor and the Kite*), the Christopher Medal, the World Fantasy Award, the Golden Kite Award, and many other honors. Her recent picture books include *How Do Dinosaurs Say Goodnight?* and *How Do Dinosaurs Get Well Soon?* This poem is from an essay on writing poetry in her recent book, *Take Joy: A Book for Writers* (The Writer Books, 2003), and is used by permission. Her website is www.janeyolen.com.

SECTION THREE

Professional Development

LOOK AGAIN AT LOCAL MARKETS

"Backyard" markets offer plenty of opportunities

by Bill Nelson

Sometimes it's easy to overlook the obvious. It took me almost a decade to realize that going for the gold—landing feature stories in the national "slicks"—isn't the only path to a satisfying freelance career. Writing for local and regional publications offers an alternative that can be just as rewarding.

Of course, it would be a thrill to have your work featured in the likes of *Ladies' Home Journal, The Atlantic Monthly,* and *The New York Times.* For most of us, that would fulfill a lifelong dream. But the road to the nationals is littered with the dashed hopes of writers who tried, failed, and grew so disillusioned that they abandoned the quest and sought out other callings.

Sadly, this happens to more than a few talented writers. But many others discover the countless number of smaller publications that are always on the lookout for meaningful, well-crafted freelance material. Have you made this discovery? If not, keep this in mind: What is it that writers, especially part-time freelancers like me, need most?

We need to have our efforts rewarded. In other words, to have our work published, stoking our fragile egos. Oh, the pay—modest as it often may be—is useful, and we never would turn down a publisher's check. But for many of us, the satisfaction of seeing our bylines, of having our work showcased and getting feedback on our articles, ranks even higher.

Selling locally and regionally also can serve as a springboard to higher-paying markets. Confidence is what writers need most to take shots at big-time outlets—a can-do feeling that stems mainly from published success. When spirits are high and anything seems possible, that's a good time to ship an essay to *Newsweek*'s "My Turn" or to send a diet success story to *Good Housekeeping.*

As a longtime Sunday-magazine writer and copy editor, I did my share of moonlighting and scored early on with bigger outlets—a piece on the Liars Club for *Reader's Digest,* a profile of motivational speaker and author Leo Buscaglia for *USA Today,* a feature on the National Railroad Museum for *The New York Times'* travel section.

As the years rolled on, and commitments to my family and job grew, the time I could devote to freelance writing waned. One evening at a writer's club meeting in Milwaukee, a friend casually asked, "How's it going?" My reply, "So much pain, so little pleasure," was meant as a joke, but my friend took it seriously.

Your problem, he said, is that "you have limited time, and you're ignoring a huge opportunity—dozens of 'backyard' publications—right at your doorstep. Most of them favor shorter articles, the kind of quick bursts you obviously enjoy. And you shouldn't forget the many regional markets out there, hungry for good material and a stable of skilled freelancers."

He had my interest now.

"I'm not recommending that you do *all* your work for smaller markets," he went on, "but don't restrict your efforts to strictly the nationals. Save them for your Very Best Work—articles with clout and lots of pizzazz that interest readers all over the country."

I hated to admit it, but he probably was right: I had been overlooking local and regional markets. The time had come to take a new tack.

> Your problem, a friend said, is that "you have limited time, and you're ignoring a huge opportunity— dozens of 'backyard' publications— right at your doorstep. Most of them favor shorter articles, the kind of quick bursts you obviously enjoy."

I made the local library a hangout, browsing through close-to-home newspapers and magazines. I sought out writer friends to ask about promising outlets. And instead of watching Jay Leno and David Letterman, I paged through market lists in *The Writer.*

One local outlet I discovered turned out to be a total surprise: ADAMM, the Automobile Dealers Association of Mega Milwaukee. In the weekend transportation section of the *Milwaukee Journal Sentinel,* ADAMM showcases state tourist sites, as well as profiles of auto dealers and car maintenance tips. I like travel and cars, and I was fortunate to make a connection with the editor. A simple query listing five potential topics got the ball rolling.

That connection has paid off handsomely, resulting in the sale of more than 40 articles in the last few years, with several more in the hopper. In my headier days of freelancing, I might have missed this market.

The *Chicago Tribune* was another pleasant discovery. The *Trib*'s Sunday travel section covers

Wisconsin extensively and is receptive to out-of-the-way attractions that sight-seers should know about. One such feature that clicked focused on the mid-winter "candlelight" skiing offered at many state parks. Another spotlighted the waysides and rest areas so helpful to travelers. I knew my connection was solid when an assignment came to compile a 150-year timeline for Wisconsin's sesquicentennial celebration.

So, for writers with limited time and a yen to publish regularly, here are nine suggestions.

Discover local and area markets. Visit your library. Study area newspapers, regional publications, and specialty magazines. Log on to the Internet and look at regional Web sites. Read writing magazines, pen in hand. Work up a marketing notebook as an on-the-spot reference, emphasizing smaller poten-tial outlets.

Check with fellow writers. You'll find them at local writing clubs, or you'll see their bylines. Consider inviting them for coffee or a drink, and talk marketing. You'll come away with ideas and outlets worth exploring.

Be a browser. Look through the free publications that are stacked near the entrances of your local supermarket and drugstore. You might find a gem. One rule of thumb: If you enjoy the contents of a publication and can visualize your byline in its table of contents, consider it fair game.

Make a quick follow-up. Once you've scored with a publication, go back again—and soon. Mention your published article, lest the editor forget, and offer two or three new ideas. It's a cliché, but what you're doing is striking while the iron is hot. You're creating a *relationship* with an editor. He or she will grow to trust you, and likely will give your work higher priority.

Ask for assignments. Make it clear that you're available for assignments as well as speculative work. Send queries. The day will come when an editor begins asking you to do selected stories. When that happens, you've made a good connection and your success ratio will soar.

Look for other opportunities. Keep your eyes open for multiple marketing opportunities. Look for other outlets for local pieces that could be used in non-competing markets, such as trade or specialty magazines.

Consider the nationals. For your finest material, revise it for a larger audi-ence and, yes, test the national outlets. Nothing ventured, nothing gained. Of course, some writers work the other way: They try the nationals first, then retool the story for regional or local markets. Either system can work. The mes-sage here: Be bold.

Look beyond the print media. Electronic publications are popping up daily. Take the time to browse the Internet for potential markets. Check out writer's groups and *The Writer* for counsel. There's an e-zine or another online venue waiting, ripe for discovery.

Try "fee-lancing." Be on the lookout, too, for writing opportunities with local businesses and industries: writing newsletters, fliers, brochures, and Web site copy. These fees often dwarf payments made by traditional media. A friend of mine seized such a business opportunity, doing an anniversary pamphlet for a railroad-theme restaurant.

The bottom line: Don't confine your freelance prospecting to distant gold fields. There are nuggets in your backyard, too—and you will find that they're easier to mine.

Bill Nelson of Elm Grove, Wis., is copy chief and special-projects writer for Morgan & Myers, a Milwaukee communications counseling firm. This article is from *The Writer*, November 2002.

GETTING STARTED

Do you have a story idea? Use this brief worksheet to organize your thoughts.

Topic: My article is about:

Working headline:

The key point I'd like to make:

The chief reason an editor would be interested:

"Backyard" markets to target:

Regional or national markets:

—Bill Nelson

10 GREAT PLACES TO FIND ARTICLE IDEAS

by Doug McPherson

Ideas to writers are like water to fish. And if you're having trouble finding ideas, your career as a writer might be flipping and flopping on dry land. Not a good place to be. Fortunately, ideas are everywhere—if you know where to look—and they can haul you back out to sea where you belong. Here are 10 places to get your writing life back in the swim of things:

1. "Snapshots"

(These are the little boxes in the lower left-hand corner of *USA Today*.) These blurbs can easily be rebuilt into fun articles for all kinds of publications. I saw one in 2001 that had a survey on how often office workers let all their calls go to voice mail. About half answered in the affirmative. Why not write a story on time management for the local business section and focus on the phone as both a tool and a hindrance?

Another, more recent survey in *USA Today* listed what employees thought were the keys to promotions. Thirty-nine percent of the respondents thought merit should yield promotions. Other keys mentioned were seniority, connections, and luck. With the help of some human-resource managers and bosses, why not try a story on the best steps employees should take to climb the corporate ladder?

These snapshots also list the source of the information, so you have a good starting point to build an article.

2. Personal experiences

A couple years ago I was getting my teeth cleaned and the dental hygienist began to talk to me about bad breath. (OK, so she caught me on a bad day.) But

I started thinking about doing an article on the real causes of bad breath and what cures work best. I thought it would make a salable piece—and so did an editor at the *Rocky Mountain News*. " 'Til Breath Do Us Part" ran a few weeks later and a $350 check landed in my mailbox.

Several months later, a family of raccoons moved into my chimney (without even offering to pay rent). The *Rocky Mountain News* liked my pitch on how to get rid of the unwelcome guests—add another $350 to my checking account. (While I'm at it, maybe I should do an article about giving in-laws the boot, too.)

3. Current and old newspaper and magazine articles

Hold on—I'm not supporting plagiarism. I'm just suggesting you look at articles differently. How many times have you seen an article and thought, "Why didn't I come up with that?" But if you think of articles as stepping stones, you'll appreciate that all of them contain ideas you can use to make money.

Make a pledge to yourself right now to start thinking of articles as contortionists. They can bend, stretch, spread out, flex, and curve. I'll even go so far as to say that every story in the news media can be reworked into at least one other article—and often, many articles.

Dig deeper into news articles. Pick up any newspaper, read any article, and ask yourself, "What's the practical application for people?" Last year, I read that a physical fitness organization unveiled exercise guidelines for children ages 5 and under. I immediately wondered what specific kinds of exercises children could do. My article on this topic, "Kids in Motion," ran in *The Denver Post* a few weeks later.

> Make a pledge to yourself right now to start thinking of articles as contortionists. They can bend, stretch, spread out, flex, and curve.

4. Tables of contents in nonfiction books

When you break them down, most books are just a series of articles. Look at the table of contents in books that interest you, then add a different spin to a chapter title that captures your imagination.

In his classic *The Affluent Society*, economist John Kenneth Galbraith has a chapter entitled "The American Mood." That's a phrase you often hear from news broadcasters. How do you capture the mood of an entire country? Pollsters have to be behind this somewhere. Why not write a story on the latest techniques of capturing the American mood? How is it done? Just how accurate are the measuring sticks? You can even use the book's author as a source in your article.

5. Word play with potential titles

Ever hear that the title is supposed to be the last part of a story? Not if you're a freelance writer trying to make a living. It works like this: Look through a book of clichés and do some word play. Turn "All's well that ends well" into "All's well that bends well" and you have a story on yoga. It's easy. Just substitute a rhyming word and then use the topic that comes from your new cliché as the start of a story idea.

Here's another one: "Two heads are better than one" could become "Two beds are better than one." The story? How couples have trouble sleeping together because of snoring, nightmares, twitching, or other bedtime ailments.

You'll need to buy a book of clichés and a rhyming dictionary, but that's a small investment. And if you let your mind wander, you'll be able to create hundreds of article ideas. And another benefit: You already have a good title.

6. Eavesdropping

This might sound a little mischievous, but you have to make a living, and there's no better way to learn what's on people's minds than to listen in on juicy conversations.

I once overhead a guy talking about two teens who started their own business selling chocolate over the Internet and cleared $200,000 in one year. I started asking the guy questions about that tasty morsel and ended up selling "The Sweet Taste of Success" to the *Denver Business Journal*.

7. College course catalogs

These catalogs are replete with fun courses that can easily be turned into interesting and informative nonfiction articles. I saw a course on memory improvement in a local community college catalog and sold "Honey, Have You Seen My Knowledge?"—about how much people forget over time- -to a magazine a few months later.

8. College Web sites

While I'm on colleges, I have to tell you that college Web sites are a gold mine of ideas. And most have several tunnels within those mines. Think of all the disciplines within universities: anthropology to zoology and every letter in between. And many of these sites share professors' findings on current and past research projects. Need I say more? When I found research on the University of Colorado's Web site related to lifelong learning, I pitched the idea of how people can stay mentally sharp as they age to the editor of the school's alumni magazine. She liked the idea because it fit her readership and tooted the school's horn.

9. A calendar

Get a calendar and look it over well. For each month, ask yourself what people think about and do during that time. Spring has arrived and people head outside. Why not an article about the most common injuries suffered in outdoor sports? Summertime means grilling out. Why not an article on safe grilling techniques? Fall can mean the start of the cold and flu season. How can you help prevent children from getting a cold? Interview a pediatrician to find out.

10. Trend reports

Everyone wants to know what the future holds, and there are a lot of people out there trying to predict what will happen with consumers, the economy, technology, and on and on. Grab a book on trends or seek out reports on the Internet about what trends are emerging. Practically any trend-related news is easy to write and easier to sell.

I learned, for example, about a travel trend called house-swapping. Travelers who find each other (usually via the Internet) coordinate vacations so they can stay in each other's homes instead of expensive hotel rooms. A travel editor jumped on it like an airplane's first-class seat.

Doug McPherson of Centennial, Colo., runs McPherson's Word Pub, a writing and editing business. His writing has appeared in a variety of publications including *The Denver Post* and the *Denver Business Journal*. This article is from *The Writer*, May 2003.

EXPLORING TECHNICAL WRITING

Earn lucrative fees in technical writing
by making the complex understandable

by Brad Manzo

Several years ago, a friend asked me if I wanted to earn $40 an hour as a free-lance technical writer. At the time, I was making about $30,000 a year, so my answer was an emphatic "yes!" His company was looking for someone who could write well and knew Microsoft Word. I was a little nervous because I was still learning about technical writing, but the income was a motivating factor.

I soon learned that technical writing is a lucrative field for freelancers. How many professions can you name in which two to three years' experience commands $40 per hour and five years' experience can command $60 per hour? My freelance work has ranged from $43 to $70 per hour.

The "technical" aspect of the field may sound intimidating. It needn't be. If you have good writing skills and a basic understanding of the markets, you can succeed in this field.

What is technical writing?

Technical writing is a broad term covering everything from product-user guides to highly technical manuals for engineers. "Breaking into Technical Writing," an article on the National Writers Union Web site (www.nwu.org), divides the field into three categories:

Technical education: "Writing about technology for a nontechnical audience." Examples include computer hardware and software manuals, articles about computers, computer peripherals, or other technology for general-interest publications, or writing technology-based reports, such as environmental impact statements. The NWU article says the job essentially "requires you to learn something and then to teach it to others through a written document, which may be printed on paper or displayed on the Web, or both."

A software package (for example, Microsoft Word or TurboTax) is only good if people understand how to use it. That's where the technical writer comes in. Well-written help files or manuals can be powerful assets to a user's experience with a product and can boost sales.

At one time, computer programmers and technicians were responsible for writing their own manuals, not always with good results. You've probably come across a manual or two filled with incomprehensible techno-speak.

Companies realized that user-friendly documentation helped customer satisfaction and sales. Documentation formats include online help services and the printed materials.

Traditional technical: The NWU describes this as "writing about technology for a technical audience. For example, repair and maintenance manuals, scientific papers, programmers manuals, research reports. . . ." Generally, you need a college degree in the field that is the subject of your writing, such as engineering.

Technology marketing (marcom): This field "consists of writing sales, promotional, and corporate communications materials for hi-tech companies and services," according to NWU.

As a freelancer (also referred to as a consultant or contractor), you enter into a contract with a company to provide technical writing services for a stated period of time. You may get the job through the company, a consulting firm, or an employment agency. Usually, though, you are contracted and paid by an agency or consulting firm specializing in technical writing—not by the company.

Over the last several years, I've worked as a technical writer on Wall Street and in New Jersey, Florida, and Connecticut. I've realized one thing: No matter the location or type of business, almost every company is producing documentation and has a need for a seasoned writer or a team of seasoned writers.

What skills do you need?

Documentation, such as a user manual or an installation guide, is something people generally don't want to read. They read it out of necessity. The technical writer's job is to make reading documentation as painless but as productive as possible. If you can write in a clear, concise manner and have the ability to produce instructions the reader can understand, you have the basics you need to write for a nontechnical audience. Since many of the assignments are computer-related, you have to know your way around computers, software, and the Internet. And you must be comfortable using e-mail.

Before you begin writing, get to know your audience. Does it consist of lay persons or members of a technical profession? Are you explaining equipment to users or to companies that sell the equipment?

You must be detail-oriented. Usually, you are telling someone how to perform something (for example, attaching a file to e-mail). If you incorrectly document one step or leave something out, the process will probably fail.

You need to be a motivated self-starter, as you'll have to find new assignments frequently. Freelance assignments generally last about three to six months (some longer, some shorter).

In addition, it's important to stay abreast of the latest technologies in your specific area. The more you know, the more marketable your skills will be.

Where do you find jobs?

I landed my first freelance assignment after I had worked about three years full time as a technical writer. I recommend this approach because it allows you to learn the craft of technical writing and build up your confidence, as well as your portfolio.

You can find both freelancing and full-time employment opportunities by posting your resume on Internet job sites and contacting local employment agencies. Technical writing jobs can be found in many different industries.

Most companies, regardless of the industry, are using computers to help run their businesses and can't function without them. I've worked on computer documentation for consulting companies, software development firms, investment banks, insurance companies, newspapers, and an automobile manufacturer. Employment agencies, however, frequently can take the legwork out of finding which industries are hiring. Check in your area for an agency that specializes in technical writing or communications.

Internet job sites such as Monster.com and Dice.com provide a place for job seekers to post their resumes and for employers and employment agencies to find talented people. I began posting my resume on Monster about five years ago (I update it every few months) and haven't been out of work for more than two weeks since. Sam Tabaziba, a freelance technical writer with over 10 years of experience, reports similar results. "Posting my resume on the Web has brought an enormous amount of exposure. Recruiters are always reaching out to check on my availability. It's a great way to network and stay abreast of the job market," he says.

Networking with other information technology professionals can be another invaluable resource. Brenda Petrizzi, a member of the Society for Technical Communicators (STC) since 1992, says, "The best resource for me has been my membership in the STC. I started my own business about seven years ago and about 60 to 70 percent of my work has come from other STC members. It has also provided a network of people I can call to find out about a company or see what the current pay rates are for a particular area or industry."

You should also keep an eye on the economy and hiring trends. If fewer companies are hiring, be negotiable on your hourly rate.

Freelance contracts generally do not provide any retirement or medical benefits or paid days off. This is a risk as well as a possible reward—you can invest your retirement money as you see fit. Your salary, of course, should offset your expenses, as well as provide you additional income. Before setting your rates, research the additional out-of-pocket expenses required to freelance; then factor these into the hourly fee you will charge.

If you're computer- and Internet-savvy and are excited about the prospect of finding new writing assignments every few months, freelance technical writing may be for you. It can be both challenging and financially rewarding.

Brad Manzo of Brooklyn, N.Y., is a technical and freelance writer whose work has appeared in *Tickled by Thunder*'s list of "The Year's Best Fiction." This article is from *The Writer,* November 2002.

Resources

The National Writers Union represents freelance writers. For more information about benefits and resources, go to www.nwu.org.

The Society for Technical Communication (www.stc.org) is an organization devoted to technical communication. Its members consist of technical writers, editors, illustrators, printers, publishers, and educators. Local chapters are listed on the Web site.

The Elements of Technical Writing by Gary Blake and Robert W. Bly (Macmillan). Covers the basics of technical writing.

The Handbook of Technical Writing by Gerald J. Alred, Walter E. Oliu, and Charles T. Brusaw (St. Martin's Press). A quick reference with 500 alphabetically arranged entries.

Microsoft Manual of Style for Technical Publications (Microsoft Press). An excellent reference source specifically written for technical writers.

Dice.com is an information technology (IT) job board. You can announce your availability to the IT industry and search for jobs. Its Career Links section lists resources such as *The Contract Employee's Handbook*—an excellent source for freelance workers.

Monster.com. The Monster job board is a place to post your resume and search for jobs. If you perform a search for "technical writer" or "documentation specialist," you'll quickly see why I'm rarely out of work.

Local colleges and universities. Many schools now offer certification programs or four-year undergraduate degree programs in technical writing.

RETOOL YOUR STORY FOR OTHER MARKETS

Maximize your mileage

by Kelly James-Enger

Want to make more money from the articles you write? It's easy—rather than taking a "one-story, one-market" approach, spin off related ideas to other markets and you'll get more out of your initial research.

I call these types of stories "reslants." Reslants are different than reprints. A reprint is a previously published piece that's offered verbatim to another market. A reslant is a whole new story—different angle, different approach, and possibly different experts, anecdotes, and research, as well. There's also a hybrid of sorts, what I call a "tweak." A tweak is a previously published piece that's modified slightly to fit a new market. While you may add some material, the majority of it has already been published, so I still consider this a reprint of sorts and market it accordingly.

To come up with reslants, take a look at your initial story idea and consider other angles and markets for it. If you're pitching a piece on aromatherapy, for example, you might write about using aromatherapy to reduce stress for a general-interest magazine or how certain scents can improve your athletic performance for a fitness magazine. Perhaps you can pitch a story on what scents consumers find most compelling for a small business magazine or a short piece on using scented oils for massage for a women's publication.

For example, I wrote a piece several years ago about how to determine your "money personality" for a bridal magazine. A few months later, I pitched and wrote a story on the same topic for a general-interest publication. I used the same expert, but interviewed her again for fresh quotes and found new "real people" anecdotes to use as examples. Because I had done most of my background research, however, the second story took less time to write.

Even if you can't come up with a slew of different angles at the outset, you may find unexpected story ideas popping up during the research process. Freelancer Kristin Baird Rattini of Reno, Nev., wrote a feature for *People* about a 25-year-old who had cleared 1 million pounds of trash from the Mississippi River, but the story didn't mention his "Adopt a Mississippi River Mile" program. Rattini pitched a story about that specific program to *Field & Stream,* and an editor there assigned the piece.

Rattini also writes for trade publications such as *IGA Grocergram.* During an interview on another topic, a grocery store owner said he was renovating a 100-year-old house into a bed and breakfast with the help of the local high school building trades class. She pitched a story on the project to *This Old House,* which bought it.

One idea, eight stories

The number of ideas you can spin off from one basic concept is as unlimited as your imagination—and the number of interested markets you can find. And the more you know about a particular subject, the easier it is to come up with different angles for it. Take the stories I've written about birth control. In 1998, I saw a press release about the "morning-after pill," also called emergency contraception. While it's been available for years, most women are unaware of it. I pitched an idea to *Fit,* which purchased a 1,500-word story on emergency contraception and how it works.

As I was researching the story for *Fit,* I pitched a related idea to *Marie Claire.* My editor there wanted to cover emergency contraception, but as part of a larger story on oral contraceptives. I wound up writing a 2,500-word feature on oral contraceptives that included sidebars on emergency contraception, the pros and cons of different birth control methods, and new birth control developments.

I then pitched a short piece on "the latest in birth control" to *Shape.* While researching the story for *Marie Claire,* I'd found some studies that suggested it might be healthier to take the pill continuously and avoid having monthly periods. That concept led to articles for two more magazines: I wrote "Cancer Prevention Breakthrough" for *Redbook* and "Your Monthly Period: Necessity or Nuisance?" for *Oxygen.*

And because I'd done so much background on different birth control methods for that sidebar for *Marie Claire,* I could query *Parents* with "Mom's Guide to Birth Control" and pitch *For the Bride by Demetrios* with the "Bride's Guide to Birth Control." I used a similar query, but wrote two different articles for the markets. A few months later, I revisited the latest in birth control for a story called "Contraceptive Breakthroughs" for *Complete Woman.* All told, these stories have netted me more than $12,000 worth of work—all from the same kernel of an idea.

While not every idea can be spun off for different markets, the key is to think creatively when pitching and researching stories. To query an idea, you come up with a specific angle on the idea. Ask yourself how many other angles you can find. A travel piece on Las Vegas could cover places to get married for a bridal magazine or ways to get the most for your money for a retirement magazine. Or showcase the city and nearby attractions as a family destination for a regional newspaper. Keep a running list of angles, and then look for publications that might be interested in those ideas and start querying.

As you research your current story, watch for possible spin-off ideas, especially if you don't plan to cover the material in the article you're writing. Again, look for other potential markets and pitch a new angle on the material to those publications.

Finally, even after the story is completed, look for other ways to rework your idea. Perhaps recent events have made your topic timely again, or maybe you can tie in new research with your original idea. By making the most of the information you already have—whether on your hard drive or in your story files— you can save time and make more from your initial idea and your research.

Kelly James-Enger is a freelance journalist, writing instructor, and Contributing Editor at *The Writer.* She is also author of the recent book, *Ready, Aim, Specialize!: Create Your Own Writing Speciality and Make More Money* (The Writer Books, 2003), with advice to freelance writers on how to increase their income by focusing on top niche markets. She may be reached at her Web site: www.kellyjamesenger.com. This article appeared in *The Writer,* February 2003.

Definitions

A reprint
A reprint is a previously published piece that's offered verbatim to another market.

A reslant
A reslant is a whole new story—different angle, different approach, and possibly different experts, anecdotes, and research, as well.

A tweak
A tweak is a previously published piece that's modified slightly to fit a new market.

BREAK INTO EDUCATIONAL MARKETS

Back to school for freelance success

by Colleen Madonna Flood Williams

Let's go back in time for a moment, back to your school days. Think about your old classrooms, which likely were full of textbooks, children's books, educational puzzles, lesson plans, study guides, games, flash cards, trivia cards, workbooks, and standardized tests. All of these study aids were items published by one educational publishing house or another—and a freelance writer, then as now, had to write these educational materials. Well, why can't that person be you?

Educational freelance markets include children's nonfiction books, nonfiction magazine articles aimed at specific grade levels or learning groups, tests, and test-preparation materials. Freelancers develop lesson plans, crossword puzzles, brain teasers, and textbooks, as well as how-to and self-help materials.

You do not necessarily need a teaching degree to succeed at educational freelancing. If you love to learn and write about a topic and to use your writing to teach, then this area has much to offer you. Not only do you get to work at being a lifelong learner and teacher, you also get paid for writing. What could be better?

I never dreamed that educational freelancing would be my field, but it is now. I had always dreamed of being a published author. I imagined being a famous novelist. I hoped my poetry would become part of the coursework in American literature classes. After receiving my fair share of rejection letters, however, I decided that if I was going to eat, I had better get a job.

I went to college and got my teaching degree in elementary education. I signed my first full-time teaching contract a few months after graduation. I had accepted, even warmed up to, the idea of writing lesson plans for the rest of my life. Unfortunately, I was then diagnosed with breast cancer.

I resigned from my teaching position and went through high-dose chemotherapy and radiation treatments. All the while, I assumed that I would find a teaching job when my days in and out of the hospital were over. No such luck. My doctors told me I needed to take a year off from teaching. Take a year off? I hadn't even started. I told my husband that I needed a computer and an Internet connection or I would go crazy.

That was the summer of 2000. By devoting a great deal of time and energy to finding markets suited to my particular strengths, and by honing my writing skills to fill the needs of those markets, I was able to develop a career as an educational freelance writer. I spent just as much time seeking out markets as I did polishing my writing skills. To date, I have written and sold six nonfiction children's books on Mexican and Native American topics, and am currently writing children's reference books about Surinam and Ecuador and a high school biography of Yasser Arafat. In addition, I have written one standardized test and many education-themed articles focusing mainly on the arts and parenting topics. (I also write regularly on tech topics for *Alaska Business Monthly Magazine*.)

While I have a teaching degree, I don't think that's what sold me to my editors and developed my portfolio of publications. I began my quest, during my recovery, by writing for small Internet Web sites that would pay me at least $25 to $50 an article. I kept searching for better markets and sending them writing samples and queries.

I quit thinking about writing the great American novel and focused on what I knew best. Given my teaching degree, I figured I should focus on writing articles that taught people how to do things. I wrote for parenting sites, art education sites, and a Seattle-based parenting newsletter. I wrote an art education column at Suite101.com that provided teachers and parents with lesson-plan ideas and art activities. I wrote a variety of how-to articles for Lifeserv.com, on topics ranging from how to exercise with your dog to choosing a preschool for your toddler. I wrote for WriteforCash.com, too, everything from "How to Smoke Salmon" to "Driving the Alcan Safely." I turned anything I had ever done into a teachable skill that could be used as the basis of an article. Then, all I had to do was find a market for that article and skill. The markets were out there; it just took a lot of determination to find them. These articles all formed the basis of my portfolio.

In the field of educational freelancing, I learned, write what you know. Doesn't every good English teacher tell his or her students that? It's great advice, though. If you are a math whiz, seek out markets that want math materials. Love the History Channel? Look for social studies markets. Are you an illustrator as well as writer? Look into companies that create art lessons. Can you tear a car apart? Write for shop teachers and students.

Traditionally, educational freelance writers are teachers, scholars, or other "subject-matter experts"—lingo for someone who has specialized in one area of learning—with at least a bachelor's degree. Nevertheless, if you write well, have found your niche, and have developed a decent portfolio, then whether you have a teaching degree or not, you can make it as an educational freelancer.

Let me warn you, though, that if you're seeking a get-rich-quick type of career, you've chosen the wrong one. Educational freelance writers can expect to make anywhere from 3 cents a word to $30 to $50 an hour on a per-project basis. Yearly incomes range from $10,000 to $70,000.

For more advice about the educational freelance market, here are some comments from two professionals in the field for whom I have worked. Mercedes Baltzell is production editor of Englefield & Arnold publishing, which specializes in test-preparation materials. Jim Gallagher is editor of OTTN Publishing in Stockton, N.J., a book packager that provides services to other publishing companies.

How can a writer break into the educational freelance market?
Baltzell: Look at a variety of postings: the Internet (freelance sites), educational magazines/journals, Web sites for various educational publishers, newspapers, etc. Network with individuals at local universities and/or school districts.

Gallagher: Persistence. Research companies in the market, then find out what kinds of books/series they publish. You can find that information on the Internet, or ask the publishers to send you their catalog. You can then approach publishers with suggested titles to add to their existing series, or you could suggest an idea for a book or series in an area they do not cover.

Even if they don't take you up on the suggestion, it can lead to other work. For example, one woman wrote to ask if my company would be interested in a book about a woman who had been a Civil War spy. Although we ultimately decided not to publish that book, we were in the process of developing a set of books on well-known figures of the Civil War era, and we offered her an opportunity to write one of the other books.

You do not have to have a teaching degree to succeed at educational freelancing.

Will you work with unpublished writers? Why do certain writers appeal to you?
Gallagher: I'll work with new writers if they can sell themselves—that is, if I feel they have the educational background and skills to get the job done well. You can learn a lot from a person's resume or cover letter—if a person cannot compose a letter, they probably will have trouble writing a book that holds together.

Baltzell: If a writer insists that he or she is perfect for a project, without clarification of the project's details—this is a good sign that a writer should be avoided. Experienced writers know they can't accurately do justice to every single writing project they come across. While writing ability is important, in the education market, equally important is familiarity with content. Many times I have heard, "I can write anything after a little research." I hire writers for their knowledge, not their research abilities.

For our purposes, knowledge coupled with writing talent is the ideal. Thus, a large portfolio isn't necessarily the only hiring factor. A knowledgeable writer will get a break over an experienced writer who is unfamiliar with our content requirements. Editors are very busy, and there is a plethora of writing talent available. Stick with what you know; I assure you, your editor will figure quickly out what you don't know, and this could impact your reputation. Keep in mind that with freelancing, reputation is essential.

Who's your ideal educational freelancer?
Gallagher: The ideal freelance writer can write a manuscript that's entertaining as well as informative, with good transitions between sentences, paragraphs, and chapters. Basic concepts or historical backgrounds will be explained in a way that adds to the story and isn't awkward or confusing. He should be able to work fairly fast.

Baltzell: My ideal writer has knowledge, experience, and exceptional writing skills.

Colleen Madonna Flood Williams of Homer, Alaska, is the author of six nonfiction children's books and the e-book *How to Break into Educational Freelancing,* available at www.DreamJobsToGo.com. This article is from *The Writer,* August 2002.

TAKE A SWING
AT SPORTSWRITING

Start with small markets and work your way
to the majors

by Steve Salerno

When my wife delivered our son, Graig, 25 years ago, I realized I had new responsibilities and a new tax deduction. What I didn't realize was that I now had a new sideline as well: freelance sportswriting.

It's true. Over the years, and to the eternal chagrin of The Anecdote Formerly Known As Graig, I've transformed our dysfunctional, on-field father-son relationship into an authentic cottage industry. I've sold a couple dozen articles about our various misadventures in football, baseball, basketball, and other sports. These tragicomic memoirs have appeared, among other places, in *Sports Illustrated*, the *Los Angeles Times Magazine*, *Men's Health*, *The Washington Post*, and *America West*. Not quite A to Z, but close. They've earned me, on average, about $1,750 apiece, and led to a slew of more ambitious assignments for some of these same publications.

Reflecting on my career in freelance sportswriting, I see definite lessons for those just starting out in arguably the most competitive writing specialty around. What's more, these lessons apply to freelanced sports stories in general—as opposed, say, to just stories about dealing with combative offspring.

I'd summarize my suggested game plan in the following three bits of whimsical wisdom:

1. Play for the farm teams.

2. Cut down on your swing. (Or if you prefer, go for the short yardage.)

3. Think outside the box score.

No. 1 means you probably need to postpone your assault on Gotham until you have some decent local clips to show. No. 2 means you shouldn't expect to be writing 5,000-word works of bellwether journalism that a publication, even a local one, is apt to put on its cover. At least not right away. And No. 3? The message here is that if your story is already as public as last night's box score, well, what the heck do editors need *you* for? There are plenty of writers in the average editor's Palm Pilot who've shown they can get the job done. You want to find subjects editors don't quite know or care about. That's your job: to *make* them care.

Sportswriting hopefuls must train themselves to think in the margins of the mega-stories, to hear the quiet local chords that harmonize with the thunderous national symphonies. If my early years taught me any one thing that prepared me for the success I've had, it's that I needed to pick my spots. I learned to distinguish between assignments I had a decent shot at landing, and assignments where I might as well drop the query in the SASE and mail it back to myself, because that's where it was headed anyway.

As a freelancer trying to enter this market, you want to write about the small things that symbolize, or help explain, the big things. No, they're not going to let an untested freelancer interview Bobby Knight or Serena Williams. But maybe there's a Little League or high school coach in your neighborhood who's a lot like Bob Knight, and can give readers an added insight into the Knight experience. Or maybe you know a winning coach who couldn't be more *unlike* Knight. Let readers see how everything worked out. Coax vivid, meaningful quotes from parents, players, fans.

Or, want to show how money is corrupting the sports world? Don't do it by asking to interview Major League Baseball Commissioner Bud Selig. You won't get that assignment either, and besides, fans already know what Bud has to say. Start from the other end: Find some 14-year-old high school phenom who's already being stalked by scouts. Use the kid as your lens into the larger story.

Which brings us to something else you need to remember, if you really want to go places in this genre, or just eat more often: Don't think *news;* think *context.* Anybody with an Associated Press stylebook can tell people what happened. What's going to put you in the starting lineup is your ability to show readers what it all *means.*

A few years ago, in an award-winning cover piece for *Sports Illustrated,* a superlative journalist named Gary Smith wrote about a high school basketball star for whom the powers-that-be continued to cut corners and open doors even after the player apparently committed a rape. Smith's lengthy tale didn't win awards just because it told a riveting yarn. It won them because it revealed the hypocrisy behind the high-minded rhetoric of scholastic sports. Smith introduced us to a cast of characters who talked about honor while they bent rules and made excuses for a felon they thought could help them win.

That's context. And by the way, Smith was also thinking *people.* You should, too. Who are the major players in the story? What makes them worth hearing from and about?

Or think *service.* This means you mine the experiences of successful athletes to show weekend warriors readers the right way to approach the net, the wrong way to approach the 7-10 split, the best way to throw a curve that actually curves. The benefit doesn't have to fall under the heading of technique. Readers also can learn a new way of thinking about the sport and a new way of dealing with crises that arise during competition. I like to think, for example, that my 1996 essay for *Sports Illustrated,* "Life with Father," taught readers something important about the father-son coaching experience. The piece was a harrowing portrait of my futile, decade-long attempt to enjoy coaching my son in Little League—a pursuit I recommend only to those with strong constitutions. It was also one of many personal essays that have been reprinted in various magazines, newspapers, and anthologies (thus vastly multiplying the bucks).

Depending on where you hope to publish, your service angle may be more or less overt. If you're writing for *Men's Health,* your story may consist of a breezy lead that makes a quick segue to the hard-core info. ("As you can see from the foregoing vignette, I was not exactly the world's best coach. How can you avoid a similar catastrophe? Here are the top 10 things to keep in mind . . .") If you're aiming at *Esquire's* front-of-the-book compilation of advice for men, the service element can be more creatively phrased, or even just implied.

Which brings us to something you might want to take into account before you start firing off queries: your target market. I drill my students in the various ways to recognize the "ethos" of a particular publication. Ask yourself: Who is my audience? Why do they buy this publication? How much background knowledge do I take as a given? Overall, *The New York Times Magazine* may be edited for a more sophisticated audience than *ESPN The Magazine,* but *ESPN* takes more for granted about its readership's sports IQ than the *Times. Forbes,* meanwhile, assumes its readers want to know far more about the financial underpinnings of sports than readers of *Men's Health.*

To maximize your chances with general-interest markets, keep an eye out for sports stories that are about more than sports. The *Los Angeles Times Magazine,* which seldom runs any straightforward sports coverage, nonetheless was happy to have my 1991 feature on athletes who moonlight as motivational speakers. And I was happy to have their $4,500 check.

Following are a few more things you should know before starting out:

Know your stuff.
Nothing can short-circuit a career faster than having to admit to your interview subject that he just mentioned something that's common knowledge to

everyone but you. Try it in front of a guy like, say, Mike Ditka. Call me from surgery and let me know how it went.

Know your limits.

Save your postage on omnibus proposals like "The 10 Best Sports Colleges in America." When a *Sports Illustrated* or the sports section of *USA Today* undertakes such complex roundup stories, it may commit more than half its staff to the effort. The end result includes sidebars, short Q&As, and other subordinate features. You can't handle such a project solo, and you shouldn't try. Also, leave the gritty, legally sensitive jobs to the seasoned pros for now.

Know the market.

Keep in mind that there are a few good specialty sport magazines that are open to freelancers, including *Bicycling, Outside, Golf Digest*, and *Field & Stream.*

You can also make something of a name for yourself writing sports pieces for newspapers—just not for the sports sections. Surprisingly enough, the greatest break-in opportunity here resides in the so-called "viewpoint," "commentary," or lifestyle sections of mid- to larger-sized newspapers. These sections frequently appear on Sundays only and bear many different names, some of which might seem to have nothing to do with sports. (In *The Washington Post,* for example, the section is called "Style.")

This is the place for short, thoughtful essays that connect sports to the larger world. My "Life with Father" piece, for example, easily could have run in many newspaper Sunday sections.

Know what's already "out there."

It's said that every baseball writer at some point produces a story that might be titled "Me and my dad." This phenomenon makes for some wonderfully evocative essays, which appear each spring along with the crocuses. It also makes for a *very* stiff cut, pitting you against some of the premier writers in America. My own success at selling such pieces is a by-product of knowing what's gone before. That knowledge enables me to spin my memoirs differently.

This is true of sports essays as a class. There will always be a place in journalism for a piece that just nails the spirit of this or that aspect of our national obsession with sports, so I don't want to discourage anyone with a truly original vision from running that vision by an editor—the operative phrase being *truly original.* You have no idea how many warmed-over riffs on "why I love baseball" the typical national magazine receives each year. This applies, also, to "why I love football" and "why I love basketball." I'm not sure about lacrosse.

The obvious implication here is that if you expect to write, *you'd better be prepared to read.* Among the worst sins you can commit is sending a magazine a pitch for a piece that happened to be their cover story last month. Those are the proposals that draw a tart response from the editor. Don't make them remember you for all the wrong reasons.

Last but never least is that familiar Shakespearean adage that brings us back to my experiences with my son:

Know thyself.

Those around thyself, too. And pay attention to the things that happen to thyself as thyself muddles through the day. The one thing common to most of us who like to write about sports is that we also like to play sports (or at least we used to, before our knees started making noises like an ancient Ford Pinto on a bumpy road in subzero weather). We've all experienced things that other sports nuts might identify with, want to read about, and above all, *profit from* somehow. Thing is, nobody can tell your story *but you*. You can't get scooped!

As you sit down to map out such articles, ask yourself these all-important questions: Am I telling a story likely to hold the reader's interest? Is there *action* at the heart of the piece, or is it just a lot of sermonizing? Sports readers don't usually want to know what you think. They want to *see* what happened to you.

Then ask yourself this: In the end, *of what use* is the piece I plan to write? Do readers learn anything they can apply? If the answer to either question is no, go back to the drawing board.

If the answer to both questions is yes . . . congratulations, you may already be a winner.

Steve Salerno of Macungie, Penn., is a veteran freelance writer and writer-in-residence at Muhlenberg College in Allentown, Penn. His articles have appeared in many top publications, including *Esquire*, *The New York Times Magazine*, and *Playboy*. This article appeared in *The Writer*, April 2003.

HARNESS THE POWER OF YOUR COMPUTER

Pump up your productivity with 6 proven strategies

by Samuel Greengard

As a writer, you make your living selling your words. But don't think for a second that technology doesn't matter. Would you shop at a convenience store that uses an abacus to add up orders? Would you set foot in a pharmacy that tracks its inventory with scribbles on a piece of paper? Didn't think so.

If you want to stand out from the crowd and ratchet up your productivity, think technology. With a well-equipped office and efficient work processes, you'll be able to handle more assignments—and thus earn more income—than you can now. What's more, you'll impress editors with your professionalism and emphasis on fast service. Skeptical? In 2000, I earned $275,000 freelancing. In 2001, in the depths of a recession in the publishing industry, I pulled down nearly $220,000. While I like to think of myself as a decent writer, I recognize that these days, success requires more than literary skills.

Here's the good part: You don't need a degree in computer science or have to feel a pinch in your wallet to cash in. Implement some simple, straightforward strategies and you'll immediately harness the power of your computer and the Internet to help you research and write far more efficiently. Ultimately, that means you can turn out more work in less time.

Here are six often-overlooked ways to boost your bottom line on the front lines of freelancing:

1. Think beyond a single file format.

These days, it seems as though there are more file formats than flavors of ice cream. Certain file types, however, including Acrobat (.pdf), Word (.doc), Excel (.xls), and PowerPoint (.ppt), are *de facto* standards. When a source sends you a PowerPoint presentation or an editor asks you to review the final layout of your article in Acrobat, don't plead ignorance. You need to view the file quickly—no ifs, ands, or buts. If you're easy to work with and turn around requests quickly, editors are likely to keep you busy with additional assignments.

Acrobat is a free download from Adobe (see Resources at end of article). If Word, Excel, and PowerPoint aren't already on your PC—and you don't want to shell out the money for these Microsoft programs—then consider a utility such as PowerDesk Pro ($29.95), which lets you view almost every major file format. When you click on a file, the text or graphics appear in a viewing window. In addition, Microsoft offers free file viewers for its key applications at its Web site, www.microsoft.com/office/000/viewers.asp.

2. Leverage your current applications.

Usability experts say 90 percent of all features in applications go unused. It's no wonder. Trying to decipher arcane menus and commands can tax anyone. Yet investing a few minutes to learn the basics of a program can pay huge dividends.

For example, editors increasingly expect writers to handle revisions electronically, using the revision feature in Word. To do so, click on the *TRK* icon at the bottom of Word or select *Track Revisions* from the Tools menu, and the program color-codes your changes and lets the recipient accept or reject them. Word also offers other simple but powerful tools, including bookmarks, bullets, and an electronic highlighter—all great timesavers.

Some e-mail programs also allow you to color-code incoming messages from known e-mail addresses. That way, e-mail from editors might appear in red, PR folks in green, and fellow writers in blue. The end result? You're less likely to lose a key message in the glut. Suffice it to say that spending 15 minutes clicking on different menu items in any given program will yield a bounty of "aha!" moments.

3. Mine your own data.

Most of us have a wealth of information—old transcripts, articles, notes, phone numbers, and a lot more—scattered across our computer's hard drive. The problem is locating tidbits when we need them or, worse, when we're on deadline. Instead of frittering away time conducting new research, tap into existing data.

PowerDesk Pro offers a high-octane search utility that can ferret out items based on keywords or types of files. Meanwhile, Enfish Personal and Enfish Find can search for keywords, names, phone numbers, and more—across dozens of programs and file formats on your PC—and serve up a list of files that match your criteria, including graphics and photos. You can then view them in an accompanying window or open the actual file. Finally, Micro Logic's Info Select lets you enter random notes into the program and then retrieve the notes that match words or text strings you type in. With these tools, the information you need will always be right at your fingertips.

4. Make connections fast.

Imagine plugging in your phone every time you intend to use it, and then unplugging it when you're finished with a conversation. If this sounds way too complicated, then ask yourself why you're dialing into your Internet service provider 10 or 20 times a day. A cable modem or DSL line will let you know when key messages arrive from editors, including assignments. It will also help you speed your research. Instead of waiting 30 seconds for a Web page to load, you can view it in a few seconds. Multiply that by hundreds of pages and you're talking about some real time.

If you think that it isn't worth the extra $25 per month for a high-speed connection, consider this: If you earn $50 an hour and save only an hour or so a month, you're at the break-even point (assuming your dial-up connection runs about $25 per month). If you save five hours a month, you've freed up your most important employee (you) to write more queries and handle more assignments. That's money in the bank.

5. Dial into better telecommunications.

While a personal computer might serve as the brain for the modern office, telecommunications is the heart and soul. And no device is as important as your telephone. It should include speed dialing, volume control, a hold button, a mute button, a speakerphone, and automated redialing. Some phones, particularly those designed for a small office, also provide advanced functionality—including jacks for recorders and headsets, Caller ID, distinctive line-ringing, and conference-calling capabilities. These features can help you save time and boost productivity.

Most long-distance companies also offer billing codes. If you subscribe to this service, typically available free or for a few dollars per month, you enter a three- or four-digit code when you dial a long-distance number. Later, when your bill arrives, the calls are all sorted by code. That makes it easier to track expenses and saves time when compiling an expense report.

6. Don't leave home without your data.

It's a sinking feeling when you need to call an editor and don't have her number. Or when an editor says he didn't receive the article you sent him last week and now you're out of town. The best remedy? Make sure you can access your data *anytime* and *anywhere*. A good starting point is to use a PDA, which stores contact information, notes, and a calendar electronically for quick reference. You can carry the device in your pocket and synchronize it with your PC.

Also, don't overlook various applications that can make your life simpler—or save it in a crunch. If you want to store articles, queries, whatever on the Web and access them from another computer—or share them with an editor—consider using My Docs Online or Xdrive Plus. If you're working at another computer, e-mail yourself a key file so that if the computer is damaged or lost, your file will be found.

With the right tech tools and a solid strategy, you can boost your output and efficiency and, in turn, unleash your creativity. In today's high-tech world, working faster, smarter, and better is a formula for success . . . and it's an approach that's always on the money.

Samuel Greengard of Burbank, Calif., is a freelance writer who has contributed to *Discover, Wired, Modern Maturity,* and many other magazines. He is a past president of the American Society of Journalists and Authors. This article appeared in *The Writer,* March 2003.

Resources

Adobe (www.adobe.com)
Acrobat

Enfish (www.enfish.com)
Enfish Personal, Enfish Find

Micro Logic (www.miclog.com)
InfoSelect

Microsoft (www.microsoft.com)
Excel, Outlook, PowerPoint, Word

My Docs Online (www.mydocsonline.com)
Offers Internet-based storage

V Communications (www.v-com.com)
PowerDesk Pro

Xdrive Technologies (www.xdrive.com)
Offers Internet-based storage

CONFERENCE SURVIVAL KIT

by Stephanie Dooley

It's no secret that writing conferences are important to a writer's development and career. But what you bring is as important as where you go. Don't be caught unprepared. The following suggestions will help ensure that your conference experience is a successful one.

Make a list of goals. This list will help you determine what activities are important and what you can skip. It will help you focus on why you're there. Nothing is worse than leaving a huge conference and feeling like you accomplished next to nothing.

Conferences are big investments, both of time and money. Put them to good use by knowing what you want out of the experience. This will also help you determine which conference is best for you. Not all conferences are created equal. Some will focus on instruction, others on networking. If you want to enhance your writing skills, find a brand of conference that offers many workshops and time for discussion. If your manuscript is ready to be published and you need to find an editor or agent, find a conference that offers appointments. This isn't to say you can't be flexible in your agenda. If an editor wants to take you to lunch to discuss book contract possibilities, skip the workshop you'd planned on attending.

Pass out business cards. They don't have to be fancy. Print 50 or so on your computer, or have a box done at an office supply store. Some can be purchased for less than $20. Information need only include your name, address, phone number, and e-mail address. If you want to include your genre or some other tidbit of writerly information, keep it simple. While business cards allow you to pass along your information, more importantly they encourage an exchange. In other words, once you pull out your card, the other person is likely to hand you theirs or at least give you the opportunity to ask for it. These cards are crucial to after-conference follow-up. Be sure you write the date and location you met the person on the back of the card. In case you don't contact the person right away, you'll have a record of when and where you met him or her.

Create a conference notebook. For those you meet who don't have cards, this is a good place to jot down their information. It's also a perfect place to record future article or book ideas, or brainstorm a new angle on marketing your manuscript. Many writers claim amazing inspirations from encounters with groups of other writers, workshops, and abundant networking opportunities. But like all brilliant inspirations, they're often fleeting. Jot them down as you go. Sort them out later.

Bring along examples of your writing. It's unlikely that editors and agents will look at your manuscript while at the conference, and they're less likely to take it with them. But you never know. Having the first three chapters, an outline, or just a synopsis on hand keeps you prepared. Plus, your new conference-going friends will be interested in your work and might ask to read something. You can get new perspectives on your theme, or insight into a plot problem. You might also get leads on where to market your work. Your new writing friend just may have an editor who has been looking for your exact writing style.

Promote your work. If you have a new book out, don't forget fliers or post cards announcing your upcoming book signing. If you provide writing services, promote what you do. Usually there is a handout table at which you may place material. Check with someone in charge to find out the policy on displaying promotional material. And make sure you have plenty of books on hand, or available at the conference bookstore. You might even set up a book signing at a nearby bookstore not involved with the conference. However you plan to promote, don't be shy. You've devoted time, energy, and funds to get the most out of your conference. Use this time to sell books!

Other items to bring might include plenty of bottled water, aspirin, and comfortable—but professional—clothes. Be prepared for long days and late nights, when some of the most interesting discussions take place. Conferences are intense and exhausting. It's easy to become worn down, even sick. Take extra care of your health. Don't miss opportunities because you're not feeling well.

Finally, you must attend the conference with an open mind. Even if you have a mission, be flexible about incorporating a new objective, or at least entertain new angles on your career. Not every writing career is built on a carefully laid-out agenda with no room for compromise. Listen to all that goes on. You never know what tidbits you'll pick up—advice, markets, or leads.

Stephanie Dooley is director of events for Author's Venue, an organization for aspiring and experienced writers (www.authorsvenue.com), which provides education and networking opportunities through its annual Journey Conference, sponsored by *The Writer*.

SECTION FOUR

Ideas & Inspiration

ELIZABETH BERG

A novelist who follows her own path

Interview by Ronald Kovach

In looking back at novelist Elizabeth Berg's now flourishing writing career, it is a little difficult to connect the dots. First, you begin with a college dropout with no writing degree or writing classes to her credit. Then she earns a *nursing* degree and works as an RN for 10 years, before quitting to spend more time with her children. Then she starts freelancing nonfiction articles. And last but not least, she manages—starting at age 44—to become the popular author of 10 novels, nearly all of them bestsellers like *Open House,* which gets picked by Oprah's Book Club.

It is a career trajectory, Berg admits, that "still seems miraculous to me, and I can't think about it too much because it just sort of makes me nuts. It makes me nervous."

Her unconventional journey has shaped a novelist who, perhaps unsurprisingly, has never gotten locked into rigid rules. If you want reassurance that writing should be as difficult and painful as a root canal, try someone else—for Berg, it's a good time, even fun. If you insist that a novel must be carefully plotted in advance, try someone else—sometimes Berg starts out with a feeling in her head and nothing else. If you think that your short story or novel *has* to be a certain way and *must* contain certain elements, don't ask Berg to back you up; she has a disdain for such "regulations." And if you're agonizing over how you might please a particular publisher, Berg has a basic message: Write "to please an audience of only one—you."

Her main strength as a novelist is an emotional directness and an ability to create characters and situations full of pain, tears, confusion, love, and growth that speak to many readers' lives. "Reading a book by Elizabeth Berg is like sitting down for a long chat with your best friend," said reviewer Judith Handschuh.

In Berg's first novel, *Durable Goods* (1993), a young girl, Katie, comes to terms with a difficult childhood and a villainous father. Two later novels take up Katie's story: *Joy School* and Berg's newest, *True to Form*. In *The Pull of the Moon,* Nan, a woman of 50, temporarily escapes a "pleasantly" suffocating marriage for a solo journey of spontaneity and rediscovery. In *Talk Before Sleep,* perhaps Berg's most popular novel, a group of women helps one of its own in her battle against breast cancer. *Open House* is a tale of a woman who divorces and must remake her life, while *Range of Motion* is about a young man left comatose by an accident, and his wife's persistence and love during the ordeal.

One reason for Berg's loyal following among women is that she so clearly appreciates them and their special camaraderie in her writing. In *Pull of the Moon,* for example, Nan writes to her husband, "It seems to me that the working minds and hearts of women are just so interesting, so full of color and life." Women are born with a "reservoir of sacred strength," says Ann in *Talk Before Sleep.* Berg's characters are ultra-domestic and careers are secondary, giving them a somewhat retro quality. But their open, searching good hearts give her women a broad appeal. So intense is their search, in fact, that they frequently need to escape for a while to sort it all out.

The men come off not nearly as well; indeed, Berg sometimes seems to stack the deck against the males in her tales, who so often are clueless and silent. (Two of Berg's men, however, get to speak their piece in "Martin's Letter to Nan" and "Take This Quiz," two stories from her recent collection, *Ordinary Life,* which contains some of her best writing.) She has drawn praise from male writers like Richard Bausch and Andre Dubus, but also was included in a snide reference by *Washington Post* critic Jonathan Yardley to "Oprah authors" as being "a lot stronger on squish than substance."

Gender issues aside, Berg's writing is spare and direct, and her passing observations can be dead on. In *Talk Before Sleep,* she has us watch a long-married couple at a restaurant, concluding: "All their lights were out." Her treatment of female sexuality can be quite frank. She can skillfully suggest a world of marital tension in a wife's simple statement, or capture the challenges of aging, and the weird thoughts and ironies of dying. Samantha, the estranged wife in *Open House,* watches her sleeping 11-year-old son, now past the point of being cuddled, and wishes she could have known that the last time she held him "was going to *be* the last time." Nan in *The Pull of the Moon* ruminates on being 50 ("the age of losses"): "It's been a while since I turned any heads . . . Now I am seen by men as a number in line, a bakery customer; some old gal who needs her sink fixed; the driver of the nice Mercedes passing through a road-construction site." Nan writes in her journal:

> I need a jump-start to have sex . . . I'll suddenly think of how we look, two middle-aged people, going at it. I'll feel like I'm floating above us looking at our

thickening middles and thinning hair and flabby asses and any desire I had will feel like it's draining out the soles of my feet. I'll think of what are we doing? Why are we doing this? Martin will be moving against me, moaning a little, and I'll be thinking, I need to clean that oven.

Berg grew up an "Army brat," living six years in Texas, six years in Germany, on a farm in Indiana, and in Oklahoma, Minnesota, and St. Louis. Her father, now retired as a major, was a career military man and her mother a homemaker. As a child, Berg did a lot of creative writing and even submitted a poem to *American Girl* at age 9. It was rejected. Young Elizabeth lay on her bed and wept—and didn't submit another thing for 25 years. She never envisioned a writing career. "I thought writers had to have an education abroad, and wear tweed, and be interestingly tormented," she once wrote.

After dropping out of the University of Minnesota, she took a variety of jobs, then earned her nursing degree. She worked in nursing for a decade, then quit to be a full-time mom, while finding time on the side to write for a small-town newspaper. She won an essay contest sponsored by *Parents* and started writing articles for that magazine and others, including the now-defunct *Special Reports*. The latter expanded into television, and for a time, Berg did video essays. A book developer's proposal led her to write a book on family traditions in 1992, but she kept writing fiction on the side. *Durable Goods,* her first novel, came out in 1993.

Berg was divorced in 1996 but is now happily engaged in a six-year-long relationship with Bill Young, an author escort and publicist she met on a book tour. In 2000, Berg relocated from Massachusetts to the Chicago area to be with Young, and they live in Oak Park. Berg was interviewed at her idyllic summer home in Wisconsin, as her 85-pound golden retriever, Toby, bounded about. Friendly and open, she spoke candidly about her life, the process of writing, and the importance of honoring your individuality.

There's a freshness about your writing, like you haven't had people pummeling you to do it this way or do it that way.
Well, basically I don't know what I'm doing and I don't want to know what I'm doing. It's very much driven by the subconscious, truly it is—when you're writing and you get into that zone. I think it must be like joggers feel when they reach that level [where the hormones kick in]—I don't feel like I'm writing any more; I feel as though the story is writing itself and I'm typing.

I often have the experience of not realizing I wrote something. When it comes off the printer I say, "Oh! I don't remember writing that at all." It's really akin to a trancelike state. I don't ever look under the hood, and I don't ever want to.

I get really worried sometimes when I do a reading or go to someone else's reading and the questions focus *so much* on: What is your practice—what do you write on, do you write a certain number of pages a day, do you write a certain number of words per day, how do you maintain your discipline, and all that stuff. There isn't a formula; I think it's so critical for writers, as well as artists of any kind, to ask what is unique about themselves. And that's really what I wanted to focus on in my book about writing—to just *please* lay attention to what *you* have. It might not be like what anyone else has done and that's great. But don't just think that there's a winning formula.

Just recently I did a reading in Wisconsin and someone was asking all these questions about agents and I said, "What have you done?" and she had barely [started her book]. People are worried about marketing and how they're going to ride in limousines before they write anything, and that's really putting the cart before the horse.

Where did the urge to write come from?
I think I was a very oversensitive and overly dramatic kid, and I think it needed to go somewhere. I would imagine things all the time; I would imagine stories. I'd say to my mother, "I'm bored, I'm bored," and she'd say, "Go out and count cars." Being the dutiful child that I was, I would go out and count cars, which is pretty boring. So I would make up stories to entertain myself in my head while I was counting cars. And really, very early on, teachers commented on my writing ability; that was always a strong source of support for me.

How is it that this future bestselling novelist became a nurse for 10 years, and did it influence your writing?
I was such a good girl in high school that when I got to college, I had to quick make up for all that, so I was a bad girl. I never went to class. Also, I didn't know what I wanted to do. And it occurred to me that if I wanted to be a humanities major, if I wanted to know about life, the last place to be was school, which was insulated from "real life." So I dropped out, and I got a series of jobs, and then it really came as a kind of epiphany: I decided that I wanted to be a nurse, in a kind of dramatic moment, and I wanted to hurry up and do it. I figured, I'll just go for 2 years and end up with an RN degree. So I did. And I really liked it.

It certainly informed my writing, oh my God. First of all, [many of my] characters are ex-nurses or, in fact, nurses. We were taught in nursing school to have what was called "unconditional positive regard" toward our patients, no matter who they were. And that's an amazing concept—I mean, try it for a day. It's really hard to do. Just accepting them for what they are. It makes you open your heart, and when you do that, people respond. So the relationships that you have in nursing are—it's an overused word—but they really are very special. When you see people so vulnerable and sick, they don't bullshit, you know. You are provided a unique kind of access into someone. That kind of emotional intensity and immediacy is something I prize, and that is in a lot of what I write.

It's certainly one of the central traits of your writing.
Yeah. I think it's only when you look back on your body of work that you begin

THE ELIZABETH BERG FILE

• Her favorite authors include Alice Munro, E.B. White, Richard Russo, and Jane Hamilton.

• She took a few writing classes only after she had some publishing experience. She was also in a writing group, off and on, for some nine or 10 years and speaks very positively of the experience.

• Among Berg's pre-writing jobs were: hotel clerk, receptionist, waitress, singer in a rock band, and chicken-washer in a cafeteria.

• She describes herself as very domestic. Her encouraging book on writing, *Escaping into the Open: The Art of Writing True*, reflects the author's love of food and cooking. As a reward for hard work at the keyboard, it offers 10 scrumptious-looking recipes, including Wickedly Delicious Chocolate Cake, Molasses Glazed Salmon on Mixed Greens with Black Mustard, and Nora Ephron's Sauce Segretto.

• Nearly all her novels have been optioned for film, and a dramatization of *Range of Motion* aired on Lifetime Television.

• Berg's oldest daughter, Julie, 26, works in advertising in Washington, D.C.; her youngest, Jennifer, 21, recently graduated from the University of Chicago with an art history degree.

• Among Berg's honors: the American Library Association Best Book of the Year award for both *Durable Goods* and *Joy School*; shortlisted for The American Bookseller's Book of the Year for *Talk Before Sleep*; and the New England Booksellers Association award for her body of work (1997).

• *Talk Before Sleep* won the AMC Cancer Research Center Illuminator Award for shedding light on breast cancer, resulting in increased public awareness.

to understand the pattern of what you're doing. I believe writers write the same thing over and over again, in different ways. There seems to be a central theme. When I look back on my own novels, it seems like I'm still nursing, like I'm still trying to heal, not only my issues, but characters who have issues who need to heal from that.

Somebody once said, "Your books ought to be in the self-help section," and it's true that, again looking back, I do pick issues. *Talk Before Sleep* was breast cancer, *Durable Goods* was coming to terms with an emotionally abusive father, *Range of Motion* was about understanding the extraordinariness of ordinary life no matter what befalls you—that's a book about a guy who's in a coma and his wife's unwavering belief she is not going to give in to what everybody else is telling her, that he's not going to make it. When I wrote it, I wanted to write a book that, no matter what happened—and I didn't know whether he was going to live or die—I knew that she would feel that she had come to this acute appreciation of her life. She was the kind of person who was a pretty happy person—*that* was hard to write! [Laughter.] A really happy person!

And a decent husband, too!
I *know*—everyone was so *shocked*. But I knew that I wanted to have her come to that place of deep appreciation regardless.

You're not really plotting or outlining in advance, but just starting with a feeling?
Yeah. *Range of Motion,* for example, was written because I wanted to write from the point of view of someone in a coma—*there's* a writing challenge. And I wanted to celebrate the extraordinariness of ordinary life; I wanted to make a big point about that. And I really like the 1940s, so I put in a ghost character from the '40s who lived in the house before the main character did. With *Never Change* [about a man with brain cancer and his nurse], the ending is the opposite of what I intended to do.
What We Keep is a book about a woman coming to terms with a mother who abandoned her and her sister 35 years ago. She's not seen her mother for 35 years and she goes back, and while she's on the plane, she reminisces. She goes back in time to that last summer with her mother. When I wrote that book, I just felt like writing the first scene. And it ended with, "That was the summer that Jasmine Johnson moved into town and changed our lives forever." I had *no idea* how that was going to happen or who this person was. I knew that after I wrote that scene, I wanted this *exotic* creature to move in next door to the most normal of 1950s families, and I wanted her to impact on every single member of that family in a different way. I wanted her to seduce every member in some way. And that's all I knew.

What would you tell developing writers about the issue of whether or not to plot or outline in advance?
I would tell them there are so many answers already inside them that they just need to pay attention to, and to try different things and do the thing that feels truest to them. Again, I think that people who look for a set of rules and regulations about how to write are missing the boat. It's magical. It's intuitive. It's creative. I mean, you can't put it in a box and parcel it out. You have to give

ELIZABETH BERG IN PRINT

Novels
True to Form (2002)
Never Change (2001)
Open House (2000)
Until the Real Thing Comes Along (1999)
What We Keep (1998)
Joy School (1997)
The Pull of the Moon (1996)
Range of Motion (1995)
Talk Before Sleep (1994)
Durable Goods (1993)

Short-story collection
Ordinary Life (2002)

Nonfiction
Escaping into the Open: The Art of Writing True (1999)
Family Traditions: Celebrations for Holidays and Everyday (1992)

yourself, I think, a lot of freedom. That having been said, other writers will tell you that they *do* plot, that they put things on index cards. So you have to honor your own way. And I think your way of doing things will tell you if you let it.

On the issue of whether you're a so-called "women's writer," do you write self-consciously at all for women?

No, I write for myself, but I happen to be a woman. I remember when that phrase was coined, in fact. It was after *Talk Before Sleep*, because in *Publishers Weekly* somebody said: "Berg may be creating a new form of fiction." And they called it "women's fiction," as separated from other things. It wasn't romance but it was "for women." And I think it was because *Talk Before Sleep* really did celebrate women's friendships, women's relationships. So then they started assigning that label to me.

One of the things I feel deeply grateful for is that when I get letters, when I go to readings, the audience for my books is predominantly women, but the age is from 8 to 80-something, literally. So the bulk of my readers tend to be women about my age—that is to say, in their 50s, 40s—but it's all across the board. And more men are coming on board. A lot of times the women make them [she laughs] read portions of my books, especially *Pull of the Moon,* for some reason.

Your fiction offers a rather bleak view of relationships. Are things that bleak between the sexes, between spouses?

Two answers, one yes and one no. I think that there are basic differences between men and women, and I think what we need to do is honor those differences rather than chafe against them. I don't think men try to make women be like them, but I think women try to make men be like them, a lot.

And also, what I write is reflective of the life I'm living; maybe there's no getting away from that. I had problems in my marriage, and I think it's reflected in my writing a lot. Since I'm in a relationship now where I feel more compatible and more comfortable, and also more heard, by Bill [Young], I notice that I have a gentler take.

A woman at a reading asked, "Are the men in your stories all obtuse?" I said, "No, they're not." In fact, in *Ordinary Lives* there's a story about a woman who just won't leave her husband alone—"Take This Quiz." She just won't leave him alone, until she breaks it. So she's the one who's obtuse in that situation. I just finished a novel from a man's point of view [*Say When,* due out next year].

You're very fond of writing in the first person. What does it offer you?

A kind of emotional immediacy. In fact, *Open House* I wrote originally third person past tense, and I just wasn't happy with it. I put it on the shelf for five years. I knew there were things in it that I liked, but I just didn't like the book as a whole. So all those years later I took it out again, rewrote it from the first person point of view.

I'm a really easy boss; if something emerges, I let it be; I feel there must be a reason for it. But most of the time I do write in first person. It's interesting, because I'm doing a novel now and I began it in first person present tense, and then I wrote a scene that was third person past tense, so now I'm debating, well, how do I want to do this? I think you have to be open to letting yourself grow and change as a writer.

> I think writing is really difficult compared to other arts. With a painter, you don't have an editor coming along and saying, "Move that blue a little bit over there."

Ordinary Life is your first collection of short stories. Can you compare the challenge of doing stories versus your novels?

I know that a lot of people say short stories are much harder. I don't find that to be true. I find them both easy and both difficult. The difficulty in doing a novel is sustaining it. I remember worrying, how am I going to remember what I said on page 1 when I'm on page 200? So keeping that level of intensity and interest up is the challenge for me in writing a novel.

Whereas in a short story, it's this *burst*—it's done. I write them very quickly, so I'll finish it in a day, typically, and then I'll go back and edit it. But I tend to write with economy anyway, which you have to do in a short story, so I find both forms really pleasurable and, in fact, would like to do more stories.

Do you keep a daily regimen?

No, not at all. But I love to write, and I usually do write. The normal routine is, I write in the mornings, Monday through Friday. But, for example, now, when I'm trying to [outfit my new summer home] and all I'm thinking of is fabric and wall coloring and furniture, [I let the writing ride for a while].

For me, I can tell if it's a really good writing day; it just happens immediately that the words come and the metaphors and all that stuff; it's just happening. And other times it's more labored. I've learned that if writing is labored for me, don't do it; it's not going to be the stuff that I want to keep anyway. It will be flat, lifeless.

One of the striking parts of your writing book is the idea that writing should be play, should be fun. That goes against the grain, because we're brought up thinking that nothing of substance is supposed to be easy. You take the opposite point of view.

I guess it's a little strong to say it should be fun. I want to make the point that it is fun for me. You hear a lot of talk from writer after writer that "this is really difficult, oh God, I've got to force myself, I've got to open a vein, blah, blah, blah." I just wanted to say a word against that and say, well, that may be true for them, but it certainly is not for me. So don't decide for yourself that, "Well, I might as well get used to it; it's going to be really hard." I think it's really joyful. And I've gotten letters from people who have read my book on writing who have said, "You know, I felt weird that I thought it was so much fun, but now I feel OK."

You gave them permission to not feel guilty about having fun.

Yes! And I mean, don't you want to just do a little dance when you write a good page or a good moment? There's *nothing* like it.

What would you advise writers about getting into that zone, that trance, where you become a "typist"?

For me, if I know that I have to leave in a while, I can't get there. The reason I try to schedule everything late in the afternoon is so it's not at the back of my mind that I have to do something. [But] I want to preface everything I say about other writers by saying you have to find your own way, and honor your own instincts. Some people get up at 5 in the morning and write before they go to work; that wouldn't work for me, because I'd be looking at the clock all the time.

I was listening to a Paul Simon song on the way up here and he talks about, "You want to be a writer? Find a quiet place and a humble pen." And I think that's it. I think it doesn't matter whether you write longhand or type or use a computer or use blood—just find a quiet place and something to write with and trust in what your self is trying to tell you it wants to do.

I think writing is really difficult compared to other arts. With a painter, you don't have an editor coming along and saying, "Move that blue a little bit over there." I mean, it's ridiculous! It's so fraught with shoulds and shouldn'ts and what a story is and what a story isn't. If you're going to write a short story it must have this, and if you're going to write a novel, it must have that. I don't believe that. I don't even think the people who say it believe it, because I think often times editors will tell you what they're looking for and then they get something completely different and say, "Oh, isn't it wonderful—it's *totally* unlike anything we've ever seen!" So how will that come about if people don't trust themselves to do something altogether different or uniquely their own?

Do you have any parting advice for developing writers?

It's helpful to remember if you're just starting writing that both magazine and book editors *really* want to find good material. I honestly believe that if you have some talent, you will get published. It's a matter of sticking to it and trying not to take rejections personally. Don't write for anyone but yourself, believe in yourself, and understand that this is a business: They need you as much or more than you need them. You wouldn't know it from the walls you run up against, but where are they going to be without new writers?

Ronald Kovach is senior editor of *The Writer*. This interview appeared in *The Writer*, September 2002.

ROBERT W. BLY

How I write

[He has been called "perhaps the most famous copywriter of them all." From his office in Dumont, N.J., Robert W. Bly, author of the popular guide *The Copywriter's Handbook,* has been a full-time freelance copywriter for 20 years. The job, often described as "selling with words," involves creating such products as ads, news releases, press kits, brochures, direct-mail letters, and Web sites. As a "side gig," Bly, in his forties, has also written or co-authored some 50 books, most on business topics (though his oeuvre includes such lighter fare as *Star Trek* quiz books). He has made a specialty of direct mail, he says, because it lets him write in a more personal voice and its success can be precisely measured. Copywriting novices, he reports, can earn $40,000 to $60,000 a year; savvy veterans, $75,000 to $150,000; and "superstars," $200,000 to $500,000 a year or more if they specialize in direct mail.

His credits as an author/co-author include: *Write More, Sell More, The Elements of Technical Writing, The Online Copywriter's Handbook,* and many other books.]

Why. It's an impulse bordering on addiction. I love it. I can't imagine doing anything else. I love words, writing, communication, ideas, information.

How. For a nonfiction book, I make a detailed outline of the chapters and subheads within each chapter, and then basically fill them in with text. For copywriting, my process is to gather and digest research, then write headlines that represent different concepts until I find one that works. Once I pick the concept and the client agrees, I do a rough outline, then a first draft, then polish until satisfied. Most work is done on a PC, though I do print out and read hard copies with a red pencil after each draft. Alternating between hard copy and PC for draft review helps keep me fresh.

Ideas. For copywriting, I continually study the market. By studying what others are mailing and taking note of which direct-mail packages are being mailed over and over again, you can find out what is working and adapt those winning techniques. A direct-mail package that is successful and is mailed repeatedly is called a "control." Studying controls is the best education you can get about what works and what doesn't in direct mail. For books, I tend to write about things I have learned about through practical experience and can therefore teach others about.

Research. The more, the better. You are not trying to be clever; you're trying to be relevant: Find out what about this particular product would make people want to buy it. You can never do too much research. (The preparation process I follow is on the Methodology page of www.bly.com.)

Success secret. In freelancing copywriting, the people who are busiest and most successful are those who are the best at marketing and promoting themselves, and at client service. Lots of people can write copy, but they don't know how to get clients.

Another secret. You don't want assignments; you want clients. Too many freelance writers fail to realize the profits are in repeat orders for the same client, and do not do nearly enough to cultivate good client relationships. Another tip: Specialize in an industry (e.g., health care) or format (e.g., annual reports, direct mail). Specialists are more in demand and get paid better than generalists.

Writer's block. I don't get it because I use a method I learned from Isaac Asimov: Work on many different projects at one time. If I get stuck on a direct-mail package, I can turn to my book project and write that until ideas for the direct-mail piece start to flow again. If I have to stop the book because I need more research, and don't have an idea for the direct mail yet, I turn to another project, like writing a Web site or ad. And so on.

Other advice. My book *Secrets of a Freelance Writer* shares everything I have learned about being a freelance copywriter. Others in the field have also written books (a recent one is *The Well-Fed Writer* by Peter Bowerman). Reading a book by someone in the field can shave years off your learning curve. Whatever you decide to write, make up your mind to be the best. It's the only edge you have over your competitors. Be a student of your craft and art.

How I Write is a monthly feature of *The Writer*. This piece appeared in the July 2002 issue.

RICK BRAGG

On the art of storytelling

Interview by Elfrieda Abbe

Writing about your family is a tricky endeavor. You constantly work under the shadow of a question that won't go away: Why would anyone outside my relatives and friends be interested in my life? With each word, you seek the courage to continue and the faith in yourself to tell a good story that will keep readers absorbed.

Writers of family histories and memoirs will find inspiration and instruction in Rick Bragg's beautifully written bestseller *All Over but the Shoutin'*, about his journey from a poverty-ridden childhood to Pulitzer Prize-winning *New York Times* reporter, and *Ava's Man*, the biography of his grandfather Charlie Bundrum, a man he never knew.

Bragg writes with emotional honesty, humor, and compassion. In *All Over but the Shoutin'* he pays tribute to his mother, Margaret Bragg, who toiled in the cotton fields so her sons could have a better life. *Ava's Man* is a celebration of a man who was so beloved his kin couldn't bear to talk about him after he died. With lyrical language and storytelling prowess, Bragg brings the reader to an understanding of what made this flawed man so special. "As far as just the sheer joy of telling a story, I never had more fun than I did with *Ava's Man*," he says.

All Over but the Shoutin' tells the darker story of his childhood in Jacksonville, Ala., with an absent alcoholic father, a strong, determined mother, and his own struggles. Some of it is so raw that the words sting.

In one segment he recalls his high school girlfriend breaking up with him because "we were too different . . . because I was poor and she was not." Coming to terms with himself and his humble beginnings is a theme in his memoir.

Bragg dropped out of college his first year at Jacksonville State University, but not before he learned from his feature-writing instructor, Mamie B. Herb, that he had "talent and promise." He was recruited from the college newspaper, where he was a sportswriter, by the *Jacksonville News*. By the time he was 20, he was working full time for the *Anniston Star,* which he describes as the "best small newspaper in Alabama and one of the best in the country." He later moved to *The Birmingham News*, the biggest newspaper in Alabama, where he wrote front-page stories that led to jobs at the *St. Petersburg* [Fla.] *Times* and then the *Los Angeles Times*. Based in New Orleans, he now is a national correspondent for *The New York Times*.

As he followed this path, he writes, "the chip I had carried on my shoulder for a lifetime grew . . . to the size of a concrete block." Just when he thought he had dropped this heavy load, it turned up again. In his memoir, Bragg writes about an incident that occurred when he was at Harvard on a Nieman Fellowship for journalists.

"I let my temper push through my paper-thin veneer of respectability . . . during a white-tablecloth dinner at the Harvard Faculty Club, sometime between the chateaubriand and the stirring speech by a Native American newspaper publisher."

Bragg had gotten into what he thought was a friendly argument with a fellow diner, an intellectual, until the diner took a swipe at Bragg's reasoning by saying, "You embarrass yourself." "I'll tell you what," Bragg said. "I'll drag you out of here and whip your ass." The silence that followed was unbearable. "I felt like I had dragged my sleeve through the peach cobbler or committed some other terrible faux pas," Bragg writes.

The Harvard story is more than an example of self-deprecating humor. Throughout his memoir, Bragg lays out his vulnerabilities along with his accomplishments. A reporter who had won many awards and would one day go on to win journalism's top prize, Bragg writes that he wondered if he was "as good, as smart, as clean as the people around me. Now this, this insult, hurt like salt flung in my eyes."

Writing about his own life was difficult, Bragg says, but writing about his maternal grandfather was a joy. For himself and his readers, Bragg brings Charlie Bundrum, who died before his grandson was born, to life. When Bragg was growing up, Bundrum was a mysterious figure, because no one in his family of two sons and five daughters would talk about him. "Talking about his life always led to thinking of his death, to a feeling like running your fingers through saw briers—and what good did that do?" But slowly he got his mother, aunts, uncles, and family friends to tell their Charlie stories. The result is a big-hearted portrait of a man who worked hard, sometimes drank too much, and got into fights but remained a hero to his family and community. Bragg's masterful use of descriptive details and colorful stories gives the reader a sense of what it was like to know Bundrum. Reading his passage about his grandfather's funeral, it's hard to believe that Bragg wasn't an eyewitness.

> Charlie Bundrum took giant steps in run-down boots. He grew up in hateful poverty, fought it all his life and died with nothing except a family that worshiped him and a name that gleams like new money. When he died, mourners packed Tredegar Congregational Holiness Church. Men in overalls and oil-stained jumpers and women with hands stung red from picking okra sat by men in dry-cleaned suits and women in dresses bought on Peachtree Street . . . even the preacher cried.

Writing about family is harder than writing about strangers, says Bragg, who has tackled more than his share of difficult assignments. In the introduction to an anthology of his feature stories, *Somebody Told Me*, he says he has written about everything from "bloody coups in Haiti to bloody courtyards in New Orleans, from soldiers in the Persian Gulf, waiting to risk their lives, to eighty-year-old prison inmates in Alabama, just waiting to die." No matter what the subject is, he gives it a human face.

Bragg says he learned storytelling "at the knees of some of the best storytellers—back-porch talkers." His writing simmers with down-home phrases: "His temper was as hot as bird's blood." "His daddy was just a name, but his momma was a bird flying." He thickens it with detail. Picnics on the grounds of the Protestant church are "where people sat on the springtime grass and ate potato salad and sipped sweet tea from an aluminum tub with a huge block of ice floating in it." He pulls you into his Alabama world where ". . . the foothills were not black, white, or gray. They were loud, and green, and often splashed with red, and smelled of manure and honey, and hot biscuit dough."

Writing may have taken Bragg out of poverty, but it's the working folks he still likes to write about the most.

"Every life deserves a certain amount of dignity, no matter how poor or damaged the shell that carries it," he writes in *All Over but the Shoutin'*. During our interview, he talked about his desire to honor his family and to tell their story straight and true. His mother calls that "telling God's sanction."

Bragg receives two or three calls and dozens of e-mails a day from readers who were inspired by his books to interview their parents, grandparents, brothers, sisters, aunts, uncles, and cousins and start writing down their own family stories.

"I wrote the book about my mom because I wanted to honor her. I wrote the book about my grandfather because I didn't know him, and I wanted to build myself a grandfather. To have it embraced in a broader sense is really great," he says. "Down here in Louisiana we call it *lagniappe*, a little something extra."

Why was writing about your family so important to you?
I made it a point in the introduction of *All Over but the Shoutin'* to say what momma had done was what a lot of mommas had done. They sacrifice for their children, they drag those cotton sacks over a million miles of dirt. A lot of

mommas do that. It might be a metaphorical cotton field; it might be diners where they wash dishes or wait on tables all day. Or they might take in laundry. I don't want anyone to think I thought we were anything special in that regard, but I did want to honor her for that.

What happened was that the book became this anthem not just for working people, but people who, if you scratched underneath the surface of their lives, would be just one generation removed from someone who had worked with their hands.

Ava's Man honored a man who worked hard for a living, a flawed, sometimes boozy man; but it honored him for the fact that for all the years he raised those children, he never once missed a day of work.

What advice do you give the people who call and want to write about their families? How can they keep their stories interesting?

I tell people to tell the stories the way they heard them told. It's hard to scratch a culture and not find a storyteller somewhere in it. Tell it with the flavor, the drama, the grace, and the wit that it's told to you. People say [my] language is so beautiful. Well, the language was stolen. I stole it from my people. It was their rhythms, their cadences, their beautiful communications that came through. I have some skill at it, but the truth is, I had it at hand.

How did you finally get your family to talk about your grandfather?

For *Ava's Man* I would just ask my aunts: "What happened that day?" They would tell stories the way they tell stories. Then they would get three-quarters of the way through the story, right to the good part, and one or another aunt would jump in and take it down a completely irrelevant trail. I would have to patiently, so patiently guide them back to the point. It would take forever, but I can't say I wasted one second of time, because often the trail they would go down would be information I did not have. I just let them talk.

> Every life deserves a certain amount of dignity, no matter how poor or damaged the shell that carries it.
>
> —from *All Over but the Shoutin'*

They would start talking about a dog and they'd be saying, "Daddy got the gun and pointed at the dog." Then one of them would say, "You know I think we had a dog like that." Right at the most dramatic moment, you're talking about an irrelevant dog that is not involved with the story and doesn't have anything to do with anything.

In families, each individual often has his or her own point of view concerning the same events. How did you verify elements of the stories they told?

You try to do the very best you can. There aren't any public records of any of this stuff. What you do is you talk to everybody you can and get each one to tell the same story. The most efficient way is one-on-one, but understand something, the best way to avoid [confusion] is to get them all in one place. I'm not saying the consensus is more accurate than one person's story, but it's at least the best you can do.

That's one of the problems of doing memoirs about blue-collar people. If you do a biography of Howard Taft or Lyndon B. Johnson, you've got evidence of their places on the planet. As I said in the first book, we didn't make the "historical registers" unless we knocked some rich man off his horse.

When you are ready to write, how do you sort through and organize all the material that you have gathered?

Organization is the hardest thing. I probably had a thousand pages of fairly orderly notes. By that I mean they filled big notebooks. They had dates and even some drawings. But I must have had another thousand scraps of paper—little bitty scraps of information that were just as valuable as the orderly story. I would come across somebody and didn't have anything to write on but a stub of an airline ticket. It was a logistical nightmare getting it all together.

I didn't tape-record my people, because I knew the tape recorder would turn them off. I never really like to use a tape recorder. I use a notebook. Most of my stories don't lend themselves to a long narrative.

You start Ava's Man *with the story of your grandmother, Ava, beating up Blackie Lee, a woman who had designs on Charlie. It's comical, but also shows your grandparents' flaws. Why did you decide to start with that particular episode?*

The Blackie Lee chapter was very important to me and to the story. I wanted to begin with a personal story. Frankly, I also wanted to begin with a story that would paint a picture of their relationship. I wanted people to see early that Ava was not a meek and timid person, and that Charlie was not perfect. He was not a pious man who carried a Bible in one hand and went out and did good deeds. I spent many chapters showing his good deeds and his heroism, but he could be flawed. I wanted to show that in the first chapter. Of all the stories they told me, it was the one I could most see in my mind's eye.

If you have a grand story that kind of sums things up—that would be your lead. It's just like newspaper writing. As a mechanical thing, it's just the right thing to do. Tell a great little story, get people's attention, make them stand up and take notice, then you can go with the pure chronology.

In *All Over but the Shoutin'*, it was the same way. I talked about my daddy in the first couple of chapters. You can paint that bright hot, strong, sweet, sad picture; then readers will care about your people. The introduction and the first chapter or two can do that for you.

What do you try to get across in your books' prologues?

I like a long introduction because it tells people what they are going to get, and you're not selling anybody a bill of goods. A long introduction helps you get the book straight in your mind and lets you be really personal. The introduction is your chance to tell people why you wrote the book and why it was important to you. You can tell how much you love your people without feeling self-conscious about it. It's the place where you can have this bone-naked love and then the narrative can even be a little stark as the book goes on because you've explained it. You've said, "I wrote about these people because I love them and this will show you how I love them and why I love them."

Did you ever get blocked while writing?

I pretty much flew through *Ava's Man* in that it was written in about a year. I got to the section where my grandfather has to die. It was like running into a wall. I just stood and looked at the wall. There was sadness in it I had not expected. I knew I would love my grandfather, because my aunts, whom I love very much, loved him, but I didn't expect there to be real pain. From being this picturesque figure to being family to being somebody I really had breathed life into—to have to kill him . . . I could have ended the book with him still alive. I could have ended the book with the sad and sweet story of the last few days of his life. If I could change anything at all in it, I might not do that. But there was so much story to tell and life to be lived that needed to be talked about after his death. I had to do it. It took me between two months and four months, but once that chapter was done, I was able to move on.

You've said that you wrote All Over but the Shoutin' *in honor of your mother. What did it mean in terms of writing about yourself? How did you know how much to leave in and take out?*

Writing is so subjective. I'm sure some people think [the memoir] was self-indulgent, but I think if it really had been self-indulgent, it would have never gotten the critical praise that it received. People said, "Wasn't that a difficult book to write?"

It should have been a lot easier because it was plucked from memory, but it was not. It was more personal and it was sadder. *Ava's Man* doesn't have the unrelenting sadness. It was more fun. The other one was more bitter, angry, and personal.

Could you have written Ava's Man *if you had not written* All Over but the Shoutin'?

I don't think I would have enjoyed it so much. One reason I wrote *Ava's Man* was so many people who read *All Over but the Shoutin'* wanted to know where my momma came from. Where do people get that much character and back-bone? They knew it was from her daddy and momma. My momma always said she wished she had her daddy's strength of character, and she does. She just has a meeker way of presenting it to the world.

THE RICK BRAGG FILE

• Rick Bragg was born in Piedmont, Ala., in 1959 and often writes about his Southern roots. "The South I was born in was eulogized by pay-as-you-pray TV preachers, enclosed in a coffin of light blue aluminum siding, and laid to rest in a polyester suit from Wal-Mart," he writes in his memoir *All Over but the Shoutin'*.

• He began his journalism career as a sportswriter for the *Jacksonville News* in Alabama. In a *JB Online* interview, he said of those days: "I got to sit in a room with Paul 'Bear' Bryant and listen to him mumble. I got to talk to Richard Petty, the Allison Brothers, and Buddy Baker. These weren't the kind of athletes who spoke through their sports agents. These were characters, individuals. The differences between them and sports figures today are unbridgeable."

• His journalism jobs have included working on the state desk at the *Anniston* [Ala.] *Star* and as the Miami bureau chief for the *St. Petersburg* [Fla.] *Times*. Bragg's feature writing includes stories about George Wallace's apology to civil rights marchers 30 years after the Selma-to-Montgomery march; the Oklahoma City bombing; the Susan Smith trial; the Elian Gonzalez conflict; schoolyard killings in Jonesboro, Ark.; gun fights in New York bodegas; and bloody uprisings in Haiti.

• He won the American Society of Newspaper Editors Distinguished Writing Award twice and the Pulitzer Prize in 1996.

• Bragg on journalism, from the *Harvard Gazette*: "We have a greater responsibility than ever not to let these things that are so important that we write about fade, bleach, lose their flesh and blood. A million mute statistics won't make anybody cry, but you paint them a picture and you can [make people cry]."

How did your experience as a reporter help you write?

Every word I ever wrote for every newspaper I worked for made me a better writer, gave me discipline and experience. Having discipline and experience is an advantage. I've written a lot about great sadness—bombings, violence in housing projects, and murder cases. It teaches you how to write about pain and suffering without being maudlin. That helped me a great deal in writing *All*

Over but the Shoutin'. Just doing it, just getting to write every day or every week, just writing and meeting deadlines helps.

How did you begin your journalism career?

I lucked into it. I was on the high school newspaper staff. I was only in college for about six months and was on the college newspaper staff. That turned into a little job at a local weekly paper for $50 a week. I went from the weekly to a daily, from a small daily to another small daily to a mid-size daily, and mid-size daily to the *St. Petersburg Times* to the *Los Angeles Times*, where I was only briefly employed, to *The New York Times*. I've really served at all stations of the cross. I've been pretty much everywhere. I don't think there's a difference between writing for a newspaper or magazine and doing a chapter in a book. People who think there is something pedestrian about journalism are just ignorant. The best writers who have put pen to paper have often had a journalism background. There are these boutique writers out there who think if they are not writing their novels sitting at a bistro with their laptops, then they're not real writers. That's ridiculous.

How do you find time to write books while you are traveling all over the world on assignments?

I steal time to write at the same computer I do my newspaper stories on. When I can, I write at night, write on weekends. When I have a couple weeks off, I use it to write. I have not had a vacation for seven years. I have been using that time to write books. For instance, I'll take my vacation time this fall and do the paperback book tour. I'll steal a little extra time if I can. Publicizing the books is just as time-consuming as writing them. I have to do it. I owe that to the publisher.

> Every word I ever wrote for every newspaper I worked for made me a better writer, gave me discipline and experience.

What's the tour experience like?

You get to meet and talk to the people who read your book, and if you don't enjoy it, there is something wrong with you. I don't mind the tour. I travel for a living anyway. If I travel for the paper, that means I fly to a city I've probably never been to, get off a plane, rent a car, drive out in bumper-to-bumper traffic heading for a little town that nobody knows the name of and can't give me directions to, and it's not on the map. When I get there, I try to get information in 15 minutes for a story I have to write in 45. I try to find a quiet place, or at least a place to sit down with my laptop. Then I have to find a working phone. I write until deadline and spend another hour haggling with the editor, and then go eat fast food. Not all the time, but often, I go back and go to sleep way too late.

If you are on a book tour, you fly somewhere, somebody picks you up holding a copy of your book, so you know at least one copy sold, and drives you to the talk. You talk to people who loved your book or at least came. Then somebody takes you to the hotel, and you go to sleep in a good bed. You wake up the next morning and do it all over again. Hell, that's easy.

What other writers have helped or influenced your writing?

I've had some people take a personal interest in my writing—Willie Morris, the great Mississippi writer. Pat Conroy has been very kind to me. Stephen King . . . because when I was a kid, I just ate up his phrases. I've continued to read him all these years. Some of the things he wrote were just so descriptive and so beautiful. Larry McMurtry writes about friendship and makes you care about people, makes you care if they live or die.

Robert Penn Warren's *All the King's Men* is one of my favorite books. I read a lot of Southern writers—Faulkner, Eudora Welty—and a lot of Dickens. It seems I stole something from everybody I ever read. I hope in a good way.

What has your relationship with editors been like?

I was lucky. The first editor I had was Linda Healey [at Pantheon Books] for *All Over but the Shoutin'*. I couldn't afford a [second] draft. I barely had the time to do the book as it was. We went over it chapter by chapter. She and I did a lot of pre-emptive editing. Every day we'd talk about a chapter.

At Knopf it was Jordan Pavlin. Jordon and I have such a good relationship. I can kind of guess what she's going to say before she says it and vice versa. Much of the editing she did on *Ava's Man* was in saying something like—"I think we made that point." She made it leaner. There were a lot of dangling participles. I'm not talking about the real dangling participles, but places where she just made it more pointed and more effective. I've never had an editor in the book business who didn't make it better.

It sounds like you spend your waking moments either getting ready to write or writing. What motivates you?

The truth is I wrote at first because it was the skill that I had and got paid for it. I love doing it, and I get to see a lot of interesting things. It went from being a means of survival to being a real delight. I love to tell a story. That's at the heart of it.

I have a real joy in doing a pretty newspaper story, but doing the books—there's real love in it.

Elfrieda Abbe is Editor of *The Writer*. This interview appeared in *The Writer*, December 2002.

LOIS LOWRY

How I write

[In her 1994 Newbery Award-winning novel *The Giver,* Lois Lowry describes a world where people don't suffer pain or unhappiness, but the price they pay for this utopia is their humanity. Lowry challenges her young readers to ask: Is living in a "perfect" world worth giving up individual freedom, memories, the right to make wrong choices? The author, who also won a Newbery in 1990 for *Number the Stars,* once said she wrote to "help adolescents answer their own questions about life, identity, and human relationships." With compassion and humor, her books often explore, rather than avoid, complex and difficult topics such as mental illness, death, and the Holocaust. Born in Hawaii, Lowry attended Brown University, married, and raised four children, then completed her degree at the University of Southern Maine. She lives in Cambridge, Mass., with her companion, Martin Small, and her dog, Bandit.

Her novels include *The Giver* (1993), *Number the Stars* (1989), *Rabble Starkey* (1987), *Anastasia Krupnik* (1979), *Find a Stranger, Say Goodbye* (1978), and *A Summer to Die* (1977). Awards include the Newbery Award (two times) and the Boston Globe-Horn Book Award (1987).]

Why. I used to work as a photographer, and I'm looking at a photograph I took years ago of my two oldest children when they were 1 and 2 years old. What's interesting to me is the way the light falls on these children. For me, writing is a very visual thing. I think part of the process is deciding what to illuminate, what to make the light fall on, and what to blur.

The process of deciding how to focus has to reflect itself in my writing as well. In most photographs, there are secrets hidden that you see only if you look carefully. I think that should be true in the writing—the writer puts in things that are almost hidden and hopes the reader will find them.

Ideas. Ideas come by being observant, which all writers are, keeping my eyes, ears, and mind open. That's something that comes to me quite naturally. I travel a lot, often alone. I might watch a family in a restaurant, and I'm interested in how they interact. I'm most interested in the hint that you sometimes get that something is awry in the interaction. You can read that in somebody's posture or a tone of voice. Then the people are gone, but the imagination takes over and begins to fill in the blank spaces. By then, it's become a story in my imagination.

How. I start each day by reading a poem. I have several poets who are my favorites, and I turn at random to a poem. That works so well for me because poetry, although I don't write it, reminds me of how precise and evocative a good selection of words can be, how words can become transcendent.

This morning, I turned to a poem by Mary Oliver, "Robert Schumann." A line from the poem—"Now I understand something so frightening and wonderful, how the mind clings to the road it knows"— set me off. That says so much to me and so precisely.

I work through a book chapter by chapter, revising as I go. When I have a collection of chapters that seem like a finished book, it often needs another complete revision. It's a matter of going back and making the connections of things more clear. That's the fun part for me. It's intriguing, like working on a puzzle.

Advice. I do think a writer needs to immerse her- or himself in good literature. If you never eat good food, you'll never be a good cook.

I get the most inspiration from—and this is soon to be an obsolete genre—collected letters. I have a huge shelf of collected letters. My favorites are Flannery O'Connor's and E.B. White's. The intimacy and the immediacy and the eloquence with which they write are reflected in those letters. It's reflected in their work as well. Of course, those collections are soon to be gone because we don't write letters any more. We send e-mail. I'm as guilty of that as the next guy.

How I Write is a monthly feature of *The Writer*. This piece appeared in the June 2002 issue.

JANET EVANOVICH

Writing crime in a comic vein

by Robert Allen Papinchak

Janet Evanovich says the reason she switched from writing romance novels to mysteries is because she ran out of sexual positions. The good news for readers of her highly successful Stephanie Plum series (which began with *One for the Money*) is that she's unlikely to run out of numbers. Although she's currently contracted through 10 titles (with *Hard Eight* her latest), her current plans don't include stopping there. She ought to be able to find enough compromising situations for her feisty former-discount-lingerie-buyer-turned-bumptious-bounty-hunter to compile a comfortable *Kamasutra* of comic mysteries.

Making murder funny is serious business. For Evanovich, finding her comic vein didn't come easily. Hers is another one of those long, "overnight" success stories that followed a slow, steady climb to the top of the bestseller lists.

Janet finished high school in South River, N.J., with designs on being a painter. She entered Douglass College (part of Rutgers) in Piscataway, N.J., as a fine arts major. Peter Evanovich, a doctoral candidate in mathematics at Rutgers, became part of her life between her junior and senior years. After college, she served a few short months as a secretary for a temp agency. She also did time as an insurance claims adjuster, worked in hospital supply sales, sold used cars, and was "the world's worst waitress." What followed was the well-known domestic routine of juggling marriage, motherhood, and a writing schedule jammed between school hours and bedtime.

There was more than a decade of rejected manuscripts. Evanovich says every agent in New York turned her down "at least four times." She finally sold her first romance novel, *Hero at Large*, in 1987 to the now-defunct imprint Second Chance at Love for $2,000. She wrote as Steffie Hall. Six years, 12 novels (mostly for Bantam Loveswept), and two pseudonyms later, Evanovich had grown bored with the romance genre format. She wanted to write bigger books with more action. Romance editors wouldn't hear of it.

When they neglected to give her the kind of contract she wanted, she abandoned the bodice-rippers forever. That's when the business of writing mysteries began in earnest. But it would be another two years before Stephanie Plum was born. During that time, Janet did some serious research and reading and watched a lot of movies. Her early dominant literary influences, she says, included comic book characters like Little Lulu and Betty and Veronica. She swears that Junie B. Jones (in the children's series written by Barbara Parks) "was me when I was little. Walt Disney also deserves marks. Uncle Scrooge had some pretty crazy adventures."

A movie also played a role in the formulation of Stephanie's character. Evanovich happened to see Martin Brest's 1988 action comedy *Midnight Run* on television. In the film, Robert De Niro plays former cop Jack Walsh, who works for a bondsman as a bounty hunter, bringing back clients who have tried to jump bail. The FBI, the Mafia, and a zany cross-country trip with an embezzling accountant add up to a comedy of errors. For Evanovich, it was "Eureka!" time. She decided her protagonist would be a bounty hunter.

But she still needed a model for the series itself. That came from what might seem an unlikely source—the world of TV sitcoms, specifically *Seinfeld*. "Stephanie is Seinfeld, the central character everybody revolves around," Evanovich says. The Plum novels would become a series of episodic mysteries with humor. They would be driven by a female character who was "always trying to fly off the garage roof." And she would be surrounded by a lovable group of south Jersey eccentrics.

Above everything else, humorous dialogue became the trademark of the Plum series. Evanovich says she "sucks at internal narrative" but her "trash mouth from Jersey" made her a natural for the snappy patter that makes readers roar with laughter. She perfected the fast-paced verbal exchanges by taking improvisational acting classes to learn about dialogue. Brisk and sassy became her hallmarks. Talking about vice cop Morelli, a regular character and romance interest, Stephanie says, "Morelli was many things. Cute wasn't one of them. Cocker spaniels were cute. Baby shoes were cute. Morelli wasn't cute. Morelli could look at water and make it boil." This is the guy to whom "half of all the women in New Jersey have sold their cannoli." Stephanie spends a lot of time getting in and out of costumes. Once, dressed as a hooker and wired for sound, she finds herself "talking to my crotch." Another time she shimmies into a "sports bra and Jockey bikinis. This wasn't going to be one of those silk and lace days. This was going to be a no-nonsense Jockey day all the way through."

For Evanovich, a strong central character, a sense that a series was in the making, a supporting cast of idiosyncratic crazies, and an environment that suited it all finally came together in the summer of 1994 with publication of *One for the Money*.

As fate would would have it, Stephanie's first assignment involves Morelli, who is to become the bane of her existence in the series even as the two strike up a relationship. He's now a former vice cop on the run from a murder charge. Thirty-year-old Stephanie, with no prior experience in criminal investigation, convinces her irascible cousin Vinnie, a bail bondsman, to give her a chance to live above the poverty level by chasing down bail jumpers.

Apart from her persuasive temperament, Stephanie's greatest asset on her short resume is that she knows her neighborhood. Setting is as important as character or plot in the Plum novels. Evanovich says she "works with a map of Trenton. I try never to use the name of a real business unless it's large and a landmark—like St. Francis Hospital or 7-Eleven. I also try not to infringe on anyone's privacy. So I fictionalize house locations and change street names."

One for the Money identifies the area as a "blue-collar chunk of Trenton called the burg. Houses were attached and narrow. Yards were small. Cars were American. The people were mostly of Italian descent, with enough Hungarians and Germans thrown in to offset inbreeding. It was a good place to buy calzone or play the numbers. And, if you had to live in Trenton anyway, it was an okay place to raise a family." It's the kind of south Jersey neighborhood Evanovich knows well.

Stephanie's immediate Hungarian-Italian family includes a mother who makes a mean Sunday pot roast dinner, a father who cares a lot about the cars Stephanie is driving, and 72-year-old Grandma Mazur, who shoots (literally) at some chicken on a plate ("I shot that sucker right in the gumpy," she says) and threatens to steal several of the novels in the series, especially when she becomes Stephanie's accomplice. "Most of the characters are relatives," Evanovich says, "so I have a jumping-off point that is based in reality."

For more than a decade, Evanovich's manuscripts were rejected. She says every agent in New York turned her down "at least four times."

Stephanie's extended family includes an accomplished fellow bounty hunter, Ranger, and a big, blonde, black hooker named Lula who, like Grandma, often threatens to steal the stage from Stephanie. One other character that can't be ignored is Stephanie's pet hamster, Rex. Stephanie "needed companionship," the author allows, "but it had to be a pet she could leave home all day and not worry about. Plus, she lives in an apartment, so a pet with small poop is important."

With all of these elements in place, *One for the Money* enjoyed the kind of success many writers dream of. In England, it won the Crime Writers Association award for best first novel, and, in the United States, the Dilys Award from the Independent Mystery Booksellers Association.

Movie rights were sold to Tri-Star Pictures for an as yet unproduced film.

As a result of the movie sale, Evanovich's life and the life of her family changed significantly. They had already moved from New Jersey to northern Virginia, where her husband worked for the Navy. Then they moved to New Hampshire, where they live now, a small business (Evanovich, Inc.) unto themselves. Their son, Peter, a Dartmouth graduate, handles all the financial matters. Their daughter, Alex, a film and photography school graduate, carries Janet's art genes and created a Web site, www.evanovich.com, which receives upwards of a million hits a month.

Evanovich's New Hampshire office is "tacked onto the end of my house. It's got lots of windows looking out over the Connecticut River Valley and I can look into Vermont and see the ski slopes of Killington." There, she has two desks, "one for writing and the other for answering mail and taking care of business."

She follows the progress of her novels with a "huge whiteboard on one wall, where I keep track of my book chapter by chapter." Her constant companions may not include a hamster, but a "big green parrot lives in my office and there's a bed for my golden retriever," she says, She also keeps a treadmill in the office "so I have no excuse for doing without exercise." When she finds her energy lagging, she eats Cheez Doodles.

Evanovich says she enjoys meeting fans and checks her Web site for constant feedback. She even involves her readers in an annual book-naming contest at her site, with the winner receiving a signed advance copy of the book and an acknowledgement.

She routinely puts in 50-hour weeks in front of her computer, and periodically makes lengthy book tours in the United States and abroad. At her readings, she often looks like a pixie in a beaded jacket. She knows her fan base well and rewards them with enough one-liners to fill several Plum novels.

Indeed, her humor garnered a Last Laugh Award from the British Crime Writers Association when her second Plum novel, *Two for the Dough,* came out in 1996. Grandma Mazur's shenanigans at one of the local funeral parlors (there are five in the burg) set up several mortuary moments that occasion a few howlers. Grandma uses the funeral parlors for social occasions. Caskets, body parts, and smuggled goods play a large role in the novel. There were "two good funeral parlors where I lived," Evanovich recalled in a *New York Times* article. "The ladies would visit my aunt and sit around reading the obituaries together and then decide what funerals to go to. I learned everything I knew about sex and medicine from those ladies."

In the next novel, *Three to Get Deadly* (1997), Stephanie and the neighborhood are in for a shock. The body count climbs quickly as Stephanie pursues a beloved penny candy and ice cream salesman. Grandma and Lula pitch in on a trail littered with dead drug dealers. The book won a Silver Dagger award from the British Crime Writers Association. The series was on a roll. A complicated series of clues involving blackmail and firebombs surfaced in the main plot of *Four to Score,* which appeared in 1998.

Evanovich would always "leave the ending of each novel a little open. So the reader knows that Stephanie's adventures aren't over yet." And since any series "always has some amount of repetition," she'd always have "Steph destroy at least one car, or it wouldn't be a Plum novel."

A high-water mark for Evanovich's series came with the publication of *High Five* in 1999: It was the first of the Plum novels to make it to the top of *The New York Times* bestseller list. *Hot Six* (2000) and *Seven Up* (2001) racked up similar numbers; both novels shot to the top of the national charts within about a week.

The fifth, sixth, and seventh Plum sagas share something more than topping the charts. The on-again, off-again romantic moments between Morelli vie with torrid possibilities involving Ranger. Evanovich wrote a passionate cliffhanger ending for *High Five.* "Authors have to have fun, too," she says, so she gave her fans something to think about. The fifth novel ends with Stephanie's apartment door opening, her slinky black dress coming off, but the identity of the dark-eyed, slow-breathing visitor kept a secret until the opening pages of *Hot Six.* At the end of *Hot Six,* it looks as though Stephanie and Morelli are on the edge of an engagement. But by the end of *Seven Up,* Ranger is in radar range and Stephanie's heart is headed toward the Jersey shore with the possibility of marriage.

Without revealing too much of *Hard Eight*'s plot, Evanovich says there's more "murder, mayhem, and sex in Trenton, New Jersey." Readers can also count on a few of the set pieces they've come to expect. There probably will be the requisite car smash-up; there probably will be some hamster tales; and there will be lots of fractious family dinners. Two other features are certain: Evanovich says she will never kill off Grandma Mazur or Rex.

Regardless of the plot, everyone comes out a winner with Evanovich. Her hard work pays off with some fun, easy reading. No matter what position you're in when you're reading.

Robert Allen Papinchak of Seattle has taught and written extensively about mystery writing; his critical essay on Dorothy L. Sayers and another on three forgotten female writers appear in the Edgar Award-winning *Mystery & Suspense Writers*. This interview appeared in *The Writer*, August 2002.

ROBERT B. PARKER

How I write

[Surely, a large part of the success of Robert B. Parker's 30-year-old Spenser series is that its male leads—the title character, who is a private detective, and his intimidating sidekick, Hawk—offer some of the best smart-ass humor around, "Spenser says the things you wish you'd said the next day, without a fear of repercussion," Parker says. "He doesn't care if he gets fired, he's not intimidated by force, not manipulatable by sex. I'm sure everyone would like to have the grand putdown that I thought up at my leisure." Parker's comfortable status as a bestseller in crime fiction is also due to his dependability: Buy a Parker novel and you're largely assured of a strong story line, tight writing, and sharp dialogue. A *New York Times* reviewer said of the Spenser books, "We are witnessing one of the great series in the history of the American detective story." Last year, Parker was named Grand Master by The Mystery Writers of America.

His credits include more than 40 books, including *Shrink Rap* (2002, the third Sunny Randall novel starring a female P.I.), and 29 titles in the Spenser series.]

Why. Well, the answer is, I don't know other than that this is something I can do. It allows me autonomy to make things and this is what I like to make. It gives me a good income and a certain amount of public celebration. In addition to being an English professor, I used to be a technical writer, an advertising writer, and an industrial editor. I never liked the work.

Where. At my home in Cambridge [Mass.], where I have an office. I write five pages a day, five days a week. After I'm done writing, I go do something else.

How. I work on a Macintosh. I do a finished draft as I go—what you read is what came out of my computer at the end of each day.

Ideas. I think them up. These are works of the imagination. I make this stuff up. It is probably the hardest thing for people who don't write fiction to understand that I don't get them from anywhere; I imagine them. I obviously imagine them out of the material of my own experience.

I don't know where I'm going. The first five pages lead to the second five and the next five grow out of the second. I have only the vaguest idea—with *Shrink Rap*, I knew Sunny would be hired to protect a woman on a book tour.

I've never taken a note in my life. I used to outline when I began, but that was for psychological support. After a while, you realize you can think this stuff up and people will buy it. The way I do it now allows for more serendipity.

Influences. Raymond Chandler, clearly. In the early days, I was blatantly trying to imitate Philip Marlowe [Chandler's most memorable character] with another name [Spenser] on the East Coast. I stopped doing that at some time.

Writer's block. Never. I've never not been able to work out what I'm trying to do. Some days it takes longer than others; some days it flows and you're through in an hour. Dutch [Elmore] Leonard will say, "Writer's block is another word for lazy."

Advice to writers. Sadly, I can only tell them [to] write it and send it to someone who can publish it. There's nothing else you can do. You can't rig it.

Writers write. Finish it. The idea isn't the trick; the execution is everything. Any story will do as long as you execute it well. So write it and send it in. And if you keep getting rejected, you might want to re-examine your professional goals.

Making characters so alive. I have no idea why I'm able to do that other than I'm able to do it. You want to tell your story through the actions of people. I'll quote Henry James: "What is plot but the dramatization of character; what is character but the determinant of plot," or something like that.

How I Write is a monthly feature of *The Writer*. This piece appeared in the January 2003 issue.

ANNE LAMOTT

Honest writing from a straight shooter

Interview by Ronald Kovach

It is a chilly November night at a temple in suburban Minneapolis and Anne Lamott, bestselling writer and unabashed Christian, rather incongruously is keeping a synagogue full of 900 listeners in the palm of her hand for nearly two hours. Self-assured and witty, with a fine sense of comedic timing and perfectly pitched sarcasm, this dreadlocked woman in blue jeans, sweater, and clogs speaks of things close to her heart, or just on her mind.

"The theme of my life," she says, "is the *insistence* on knowing what happened, and saying it out loud." She throws some darts at Republicans, tells of the wounds of a difficult childhood and her love for her friends, touches on her twin demons, alcohol and drug abuse. "Everything I've let go of," she says, "has claw marks on it." She describes the pleasures and challenges of her writing life, deplores society's insistence on quickie-grieving, does a riff on the American obsession with body image. "When you get to heaven and see what really matters," she says to laughter, "what your *butt* looks like is about number 180."

What makes Lamott's address so entertaining are the same qualities that explain her writing success: blunt honesty, a sometimes painful vulnerability, and no-holds-barred humor (though at the synagogue, she does clean up the profanity that can hilariously spew out in her writing). Other writers may wear their heart on their sleeve; Lamott sometimes puts her heart in your face.

At 48, she is riding a big wave as a bestselling author of both memoirs and novels; as the author of the hugely popular how-to book for writers, *Bird by Bird;* as a columnist for the online magazine *Salon,* whose first stint *Newsweek* voted "Best of the Web"; and as a speaker who commands lucrative lecture fees. And who can begrudge her her success? This is a determined woman, after all, who has only built herself up after coming from a long way down.

Indeed, Lamott's life pre-sobriety, pre-motherhood, and pre-religion is a checklist of emotional turmoil. Reflecting on her feeling of aloneness during pregnancy in *Operating Instructions: A Journal of My Son's First Year* (1993), Lamott sums up, "For the last twenty-some years I have tried everything in sometimes suicidally vast quantities—alcohol, drugs, work, food, excitement, good deeds, popularity, men, exercise, and just rampant compulsion and obsession—to avoid having to be in the same room with that sense of total aloneness." Her 20s and early 30s, she says, were "lost and debauched," full of sickness and anxiety; she used to snort cocaine "like an anteater." Add to this list Lamott's upbringing in an unstable bohemian family, a very trying mother, a beloved father who died young, and her rebirth as a devout Christian and loving mom, and you have the terrain of much of her writing.

She grew up in Tiburon, a suburban enclave in Northern California, in a time and place she depicts as Cheever country—a sun-kissed land of parties and cocktails and jazz and affairs. The counterculture arrived in full force, bringing with it considerable quantities of alcohol, drugs, and infidelity. Three children Lamott knew well died of drug overdoses.

Her father, Kenneth Lamott, the son of Presbyterian missionaries who raised their children in Japan, was a writer who despised Christianity. He died at age 56 of a brain tumor, and Lamott has written movingly about him in her essay "Dad." Her mother, Dorothy, whom Anne describes as destructively "needy, dependent, and angry," eventually divorced Kenneth and began the first women's law firm in Honolulu when she was nearly 50. She died of Alzheimer's disease in 2001. The profound ambivalence Lamott appears to feel about her mother she summed up in Minneapolis this way: "I've spent 16 years in therapy trying to exorcise her. . . . I loved her more than life itself."

Young Anne was, she tells her audience, "a terrified little kid." But even as a kid, she was a "movie camera" who noticed a lot and saw plenty. She was very insecure about her looks and her frizzy hair. She won poetry prizes as a young child, did well in school, and earned high state rankings as a tennis player from age 10 to 16. Against all odds, given the fashionable atheism of her environment, she clung to a religious faith. She attended Goucher College near Baltimore but dropped out after her sophomore year. "I really had The Bug. I *had* to write," Lamott says.

Her first novel, *Hard Laughter,* about a father's battle with brain cancer, was published in 1980, followed by *Rosie* (1983), a coming-of-age story; *Joe Jones* (1985), about a group of characters who gather at a cafe; *All New People* (1989), an unsentimental look at a family over two decades; and *Crooked Little Heart* (1997), a novel of family and adolescence in which the same Rosie is now 13 and a championship tennis player.

But it has been Lamott's nonfiction books that have proved most popular. Her first was *Operating Instructions,* a ruthlessly honest diary of her exhausting experience as a first-time mother and her son Sam's first year of life. For Lamott, motherhood came at age 35 and without the help of the father, who bolted after she became pregnant. (He has since become a part of Sam's life.) *Operating Instructions* was the debut of a vivid new voice in personal narrative—a crabby, funny, irreverent writer with edges and issues who seemed hell-bent on shredding Hallmark-card notions of life and family. If this was a born-again Christian, it wasn't one you had ever run into before. Here's one of Anne's really bad days in the parenting trenches:

> "I was just hating Sam there for a while. I'm so . . . tired, so burnt beyond recognition that I didn't know how I was going to get through to the morning. The baby was really colicky, kvetching, farting, weeping, and I couldn't get him back to sleep. Then the kitty starts in, choking like mad and barfing for a while and continuing to make retching sounds for a while longer, but curiously enough it all seemed to soothe Sam, who fell back to sleep."

Lamott's next foray into nonfiction, *Bird by Bird: Some Instructions on Writing and Life* (1994), has become a classic amid the mountain of books on writing. In it, she encourages developing writers to stop trying to scale a glacier and work instead from a one-inch picture frame—telling only a one-inch piece of their story at a time. *Bird by Bird*'s devoted fans also know the book's other mantras: Give yourself short assignments and write lousy first drafts.

Lamott's next nonfiction book, *Traveling Mercies: Some Thoughts on Faith* (1999), an adaptation of her columns for *Salon* describing her religious odyssey, was also a great success.

Her latest novel is the bestselling *Blue Shoe* (2002), a tale about a woman, Mattie, trying to keep her life and her children's lives together amid divorce, a mother in failing health, a rotting house, and her attraction to a married man. When a little blue shoe is discovered, it functions as both a key to unlocking family secrets and a pass-around symbol.

Lamott discussed the origins of *Blue Shoe* and much more during an interview in Minneapolis, where she appeared as part of the Pen Pals author-lecture series. More serious in person than she is before audiences and very passionate, she bore down hard on questions and took them for quite a spin.

You're very frank about all the turmoil you've been through in your life, including alcoholism, drugs, bulimia, family issues. Some of our writing audience might wonder, "If I have not been through all that, where does that leave me? Do I have enough to write about?"

I think that everybody has, if they've gotten to the age of reading your magazine, survived enough to write about for the rest of their lives. If they've survived childhood, they've got enough to write for the rest of their lives. I mean, the form of people's loss and pain and confusion and struggle has different biographical details, but I think we're all in the same boat.

I happen to have a very addictive personality, but other people have tried to cope in other ways, usually with a lot of mistakes made and a pretty high price paid for whatever wisdom or growth they've managed to eke out. So I don't think you have to have a lot of drama or outward destruction to have a lot to write about if you're trying to tell the truth, whether or not you're making up stories or relying a lot on your own life. But you need to have been paying attention, you need to probably have felt things very deeply. If people are funny and can just tell me stories about life or give me their version of things, and choose their words carefully, I'm in. I'm interested.

Developing writers might also wonder how they could ever be as revealing as Anne Lamott.

Well, there's no reason for other writers to be as "revealing," to use your word, as I have chosen to be. I happen to like really honest writing. I love it when people will tell me the truth and really take the lid off the soup pot and let me peer in. But by the same token, I don't talk about or write about the stuff that's really most intimate to me. The stuff that I talk about with my close friends is really much more intimate.

In Blue Shoe, *the little blue shoe and the paint-can opener are neat devices. How did the shoe find its way into the novel?*

The blue shoe was a real trinket from about 20 years ago that I found in a gumball machine in Tiburon. I was in my late 20s and I had had a much older friend. I was staying with her for a while and when things got really bad, we would just pass this shoe back and forth. So it had been a really incredibly touching symbol of friendship and of really being there for one another over the course of time.

I had actually started this book that I knew certain things about. I knew that it took place in Marin [Calif.], I knew it took place in the same years that I've taken place, I knew that it involved family secrets, because I grew up in a really great-looking family with a lot of secrets. I met the character of Mattie and I started to meet her children, I met Daniel, and they just sort of came to me in the way that your characters just sort of tug on your sleeve.

I started writing and amassing information, and then I was just taking a walk one day and I thought about this blue shoe, which I still have, this really dumb blue shoe. I thought, that would be a great way to tell the story of a friendship. [The shoe] wasn't the seed of the book, I don't think, because I'd already had a lot of the book in progress by the time I realized it would be a great device.

Did you use the Anne Lamott approach with this novel, following your own advice of terrible first drafts and short assignments?

Yes. I keep a one-inch picture frame on my desk. I can really only see a little bit. I'll get a lot of ideas all at once. I have huge sheets of graph paper on my

THE LAMOTT FILE

• Anne Lamott lives in Northern California with her son, Sam, now 13, about whom readers often ask. These days, she reports, Sam is tall, skinny, artistic, and funny, with "gigantic brown eyes."

"We're a baggy-jeans kind of family," she says. "Sam told me, 'We're the only family I know that doesn't display its china.' And I said, 'We don't *have* any china.'"

• She is an elder and runs the church school at St. Andrew Presbyterian Church in Marin City, Calif.

• Her favorite writers include Mary Oliver, Sharon Olds, Charles Portis, Alice Munro, Margaret Atwood, Laurie Colwin, Michael Cunningham, and Fran Leibowitz.

• She is the subject of a 1999 documentary by Academy Award-winning filmmaker Freida Mock titled *Bird by Bird with Annie*.

wall. I scribble notes to myself. I start to kind of mark out sort of a trajectory—I think of the plot as the path of lily pads across the pond—and I'll start to draw big circles from one end of the graph paper, which is most of a wall, to the other. So I'll sort of have a vague sense of how things are going to unfold, but it will just be revealing itself to me little by little. Or I'll just get one good idea. Or I'll be somewhere and I'll see something and realize I really want to write about it. I'll make a note to myself—I always have paper and pencil—and then I'll write about it, really just a one-inch picture frame, and I'll do a really [lousy] job of it. And then I'll move on.

And did you roughly know how this novel was going to end?
No. I had no idea.

Did the plot of Blue Shoe *grow out of your characters, as you put it in* Bird by Bird?
Yeah. It's also sort of peeling away the onion skin of the characters. I didn't know the details of Mattie's life when I started. I knew that her world was up

in flames, and it's autumn outside and the trees look like flames. I wanted everything that could be taken away from her to pretty much have been taken away, so that she has given up her husband, she's broke, her mother has just moved out of this house where she grew up. So she moves into the house and what you find is that everything about the house has been designed to cover up the rot and the mildew and the holes and the problems and the family's very poor solutions to its very human and universal problems. I just sort of knew who some of the people were, I knew enough about them to go on. I just took it one day at a time, and screwed up, you know. I believe in a lot of mistakes and false starts and messes.

This is your sixth novel. Has it gotten any easier?
I'm not sure it's easier. I think, like a pianist or something, you just definitely get better if you do it day after day and year after year. And I'm better at editing; I'm more willing to take stuff out now, and that's helpful. I finally got to the point where I asked somebody to do a real intense edit for me who wasn't my editor, because the world of New York publishing has changed so much and editors can't really edit the way they did even 10 or 15 years ago. So I had a friend doing really hands-on editing with me, really week-to-week work with me, and that made a huge difference.

But it doesn't get easier for me. I don't really enjoy it all that much. I would much rather watch CNN, or I hike almost every day up on the mountain where I live. I'd rather do almost anything than write. I really love the third and fourth drafts. The first and second drafts are what I don't like. I don't have the kind of confidence you might assume [after this many books]. The difference between me and a lot of people who would want to write is that I do it anyway. I do it with fear and loathing and trembling and a lot of really bad thoughts about how it's going to be received.

> I happen to like really honest writing. I love it when people will tell me the truth and really take the lid off the soup pot and let me peer in.

I have to ask you about the essay about your mother in Traveling Mercies. *In fact, the back-to-back punch of the essays on your mother and father just leaped out at me. Was it painful to write?*
It was painful to have my mother for a mother. It was really so excruciating to have such a needy, dependent, and angry mother that to write about it wasn't painful so much as it was so risky because she was still alive. I think I was probably 45 or 44 when I wrote it. I'd spent all of those years not writing about her because I was so desperate to make her happy, and to kind of rewrite history, which is why so many of my students have felt so stuck and voiceless,

because they don't want to hurt anyone's feelings. They had mothers or fathers who held their hands over flame to punish them; they had mothers and fathers who very, very routinely sent them out to the yard to select the switch with which they were then going to be hit—and they don't want to hurt these people's feelings.

So with my mom, who didn't do anything overtly violent but had a very, very destructive effect on my soul and my sense of self, I had always either not written about her or made the mother [in my fiction] so, *so* different. Or I'd sugar-coated it, like in *Operating Instructions,* so as to make my mom happy. And I finally got too tired—it wasn't making her happy, it was giving her a little hit. The hit was that we were all keeping the secret. And I finally decided I wasn't going to do it.

I didn't know how long she was going to live, and as it turns out, she died [in 2001]. And it was painful, because she read it and it hurt her, but I think a great deal more good came out of it, certainly for me as the daughter, and for all the daughters and many, many mothers out there. And my mother and I went through a bad patch for about a week and then it was, you know, good that I had written it, because it's good—it's a *miracle*, it's a *miracle*, for an old, black-belt codependent like me to tell the truth. . . And I think if you read the piece again, you would find that there's so much more love than you notice the first time, kind of radiant with tenderness. But it was hurtful, and I'd do it again in a hot second.

How many hours do you work in a day?

I work about four a day now. Before I had a kid, I obviously worked a lot more, and a lot more efficiently. I get to work at about 9 in the morning and most days I set aside four hours, which is to say I get about three hours of work done. But in a different way I'm working a lot of the time, and I've got notes with me and paper with me and notebooks with me and I print out all the time. And so I'm always reading it later, and I might just stretch out on the couch with that day's work later and think about it or grab just a chunk of material and see how it's holding together. Like a random urinalysis, you know—just grab 50 pages and start reading and see, without preparing myself, if it reads fairly fluidly.

Your nonfiction is written in a very conversational style.

That's the illusion. I write three and four and five drafts of everything. Most of the pieces in *Traveling Mercies* and many of the little pieces and bits in *Blue Shoe* were written at *Salon,* which has been a really great vehicle for me, because I'm comfortable writing five or six pages. So by the time I started putting them together for *Traveling Mercies,* for instance, I'd already written them three and four times for *Salon.* But then when I went to put it into the book, it still needed more rewriting, editing, taking stuff out, not agreeing with my editor about what should go in, what should stay, and a whole other rewrite. So if it comes out very conversational and fluid, it's because I've done it *so* many times.

Spirituality is a very big part of who you are and a big part of your writing, and you also don't pull any punches in the area of politics. Do you give any consideration to turning off some percentage of your readers?

No. I just can't think that way, or I'm going to start editing and censoring myself. I mean, I'm just a hard-core, born-to-die, left-wing activist, and I was raised by left-wing activists. I [actually] take out most of the diatribes, [but] I insist on the right to be who I am.

I think maybe the more interesting question is about religion and being a Christian. This friend Doug, who edited *Blue Shoe* for me, said, "A whole lot of people are gonna be turned off by the fact that Mattie is a Christian and that she is a believer and that when she's struggling, she prays, and when she's happy, she prays, and that she thinks in terms of her spiritual identity."

But I thought about it, because, God knows, I want people to read me. But most of the books I read don't even mention God or spirit or soul, but yet they're very, very much about soul and spirit. But they're mostly by other left-wing intellectuals, by well-known popular and sometimes slightly more esoteric writers. I read them, even though they don't talk about God and spirit, because they're great storytellers, and because I love how painstaking with language they are, and I don't hold it against *them*. So I thought, why am I going to censor myself so that I don't alienate people who don't care about God, since I read all their stuff when they don't write about the stuff I'm most passionate about? So I just can't think that way, I can't censor myself.

I think a lot more people care about God and goodness and good orderly direction—which is an acronym for God—and faith and soul and spirit than you would think. I mean, *Traveling Mercies* sold hundreds and hundreds of thousands of copies. The thing is, I'm not evangelical, I'm not trying to convert anyone. What I'm trying to do is sort of witness to the fact that I'm alive and I can just feel the miracle of my life.

> The third draft is the dental draft. You go paragraph by paragraph and you jiggle each section, each tooth, and you floss. You see what's healthy and strong.

In recent years, there's been a tide of memoir writing, which has taken some critical hits. There are certainly some potential pitfalls to this genre. Some writers might wonder, "How do I make my life interesting? And what makes my own life interesting anyway?"

Well, on the one hand, I think you probably shouldn't be reading the critics, because so many of them are just really angry, jealous people who haven't made it as writers. On the other hand, I think it's the pitfall of all writing. I *love* memoirs, and I just love personal essays—really, it's my favorite form of literature. I think you probably need somebody to work with [a reader] who can be strict but also very, very loving. I don't think writing about "me" or thinking about "me" or talking about "me-me-me" is the problem. I think bad writing is the problem, and going on way too long about stuff that should maybe just be a sentence or a paragraph instead of a whole chapter or passage.

I don't think there's anything more interesting than one human telling the truth in the clearest, truest possible way. If somebody has a sense of humor, it's so fantastic. Everybody has been through something that no one else has seen, and he or she alone can be the tour guide for that time, that place, that house, and that role in the family—I think it's all just inherently interesting.

You write a terrible draft, you get it all down. Like in *Bird by Bird,* it talks about the down draft. The first draft is the down draft—you just get it all down. The second draft is the up draft, and you clean it all up. The third draft is the dental draft. You go paragraph by paragraph and you jiggle each section, each tooth, and you floss. You see what's healthy and strong. You see if the gums are good and holding on and you see what needs to be pulled. You see what needs to be cleaned up. But it's OK to have people help you.

Anyone who has done any freelancing and reads Operating Instructions *knows it was a tough road for you.*

I didn't make more than $10,000 a year until the early '90s. I was always willing to be broke. I was always willing to make just enough money. I had half-time jobs. *Operating Instructions* came out in '93 and I made in the very low five figures and I didn't have any money, I didn't have any savings, I didn't have a car that worked with any efficiency. But I got to be a writer when I grew up. And so, it's only been the last five or six years that I've been making a really good living at it.

But I always just wanted to write and I thought, God, what a great gift to give your kid, to just say, "The money's not going to buy you much of anything that's going to hold up over time, and we're going to get by." It's pretty hard to feel any kind of self-pity when you get to be an artist, when you get to live out your artistic dream. You just don't care. I mean, I worked four hours a day making a living doing something, and I worked on my books four hours a day, you know, and I brought my kid to readings. I taught writing classes and I took my kid to these classes in a playpen with a big bag of Legos. We have just gotten my writing life to happen, because I wanted it so badly.

Ronald Kovach is senior editor of *The Writer.* This interview appeared in *The Writer,* April 2003.

M.J. ROSE

How I write

[M.J. Rose is an inspiration to writers who, after countless rejections, still pursue their dream of getting published. Once dubbed by *Time* the "poster girl of e-publishing," Rose never gave up on her first novel, *Lip Service* (about a woman who gets involved in the world of phone sex), even when she couldn't find a publisher. Taking the book's fate into her own hands, she published it in 1998 as an e-book. After she sold 2,500 copies online, the book was picked up by the Literary Guild/Doubleday Book Club. Pocket Books brought it out in paperback.

Rose describes her work as "a mix of psychological suspense, mystery, adventure, and erotica." *Booklist* compared her third novel, *Flesh Tones* (2002), set in the art world, to Ruth Rendell's psychological thrillers.

The author also wrote a column for *Wired*. She is a graduate of Syracuse University and lives in Connecticut with composer Doug Scofield and their dog, Winka.

Her credits include *Flesh Tones* (2002), *In Fidelity* (2001), *Lip Service* (1998).]

Why. When I was about 6 years old, I noticed my grandmother's wonderful IBM Selectric, and I was entranced by it. My mother said that if I came up with a story, she'd show me how to type it on the magical machine. Within a few days I had come up with a story about a very small man with very large feet, who was named Mr. Big.

Now, I simply feel as if I am doing the one thing that I was meant to do in the world. I suppose what keeps me going is the novel itself. I become obsessed with the unfolding of the story.

When and where. I swim every morning for an hour. While I am doing my laps, I'm thinking about what I'm going to write that day. Then I do errands and usually settle down to write in the late morning or early afternoon. I have a quota of five pages a day. And usually I stick to it—four to six hours a day, six days a week.

How. I don't even try to start a new novel until I've spent six to 12 weeks researching, outlining, and making a scrapbook for my main characters—in other words, procrastinating. I actually teach an outline class called "How to Procrastinate Your Way Into Writing."

I believe that you need to live with a story and its main characters for a long time and discover as much as you can about them and their world before you actually put fingers to the keyboard. Once I've done a good amount of gathering scrapbook items and making notes, I start to write.

I do a two-page outline [of the novel] with one line describing the main action in each chapter. No details. I see a book like a journey. I like knowing where I'm going to end up before I set forth. It changes like crazy in the writing, but the outline keeps me from getting stuck. Then, I revise like a madwoman. I love revising. If I didn't have a deadline on my contracts, I'd never finish.

My novels always start off with a "what if?" For *Flesh Tones,* I asked: What if a man asked the woman who loved him to help him die? Can you love someone enough to kill them? I carry the "what if?" around in my head, and if it has legs, the story tells itself to me. I literally see it all in my head, like a movie, and just write down what I see.

Hurdles. If I don't see anything, I stop for that day. That night, before I go to sleep, I concentrate on where I stopped. The next morning, before I get out of bed, I focus again on where I stopped. Then I go swimming, and while I'm doing my laps, I see what's next. I am very good friends with my subconscious—we work well together.

I'm not a wordsmith as much as I am a storyteller. I struggle with finding the perfect words, the right imagery. Plus, I'm dyslexic, so I write a lot of inverted sentences and have to go back and reorder the phrases.

Advice. There are so many obstacles in the writer's path to getting published, that you have to be totally committed in order to get through the tough times.

How I Write is a monthly feature of *The Writer.* This piece appeared in the February 2003 issue.

DENNIS LEHANE

How I write

[Being called (by *Publishers Weekly*) "the hippest heir" of crime fiction masters Dashiell Hammett and Raymond Chandler is a tough billing to live up to. But Dennis Lehane's six stylish novels have put him in such esteemed company, in the eyes of some critics. His latest, the bestselling *Mystic River*, his first stand-alone after five Patrick Kenzie/Angela Gennaro detective novels, is a haunting, impressively controlled tale of a traumatic childhood incident that plays itself out in adulthood. Lehane grew up the son of Irish immigrant parents in Boston, graduated from the writing program at Florida International University, and hit the ground running: *A Drink Before the War*, his first mystery, which he wrote for fun, won him the Shamus Award for best first novel.

His credits include *Mystic River* (2001); *Prayers for Rain* (1999, a *New York Times* Notable Book); *Gone, Baby, Gone* (1998); *Sacred* (1997); *Darkness, Take My Hand* (1996); and *A Drink Before the War* (1994).]

Why. Because I suck at everything else. I can't imagine working in corporate America—all those cubicles and Palm Pilots; I'd die. I have no head for math or science; I can't draw a passable stick figure; I'm too private to be an actor; can't sing worth a lick; and every comedian I've ever known is certifiably insane, so . . . I guess writing just works for me.

How. I write longhand and then try to input it into a computer within 24 hours. I need the flow of a pen across a page; something about a computer screen leaves me feeling self-conscious and boxed in. I plot loosely in advance—I usually know six or seven major structural movements—but I rarely outline unless I've jammed myself up in the middle of a manuscript and don't know how to move forward. I'm a revision fanatic; the early drafts are just pasta on the wall, trying to see what sticks. I find the book through a honing process, going back through the pages and making myself look a lot smarter than I am.

When and where. I write mostly in the mornings. I need the sense that the phone's not going to ring much. I have this dream office, but I still spend half my time at the dining room table. When I'm into a book, though, I could write from dead center on the 50-yard line at the Super Bowl.

Ideas. I get my ideas from sitting in a room, staring at the ceiling, and thinking stuff up. It's that simple. The genesis of the idea might have locked into my brain matter 20 years ago, as with *Mystic River,* but I can't get to it unless I sit in that chair, tilt back my head, and say to myself, "OK, tell me a story."

Writer's block. If I get it, it means I did something structurally wrong, something that will hurt me 150 pages down the line. And my subconscious picks up on it before I do and freezes me, and I can't move forward until I figure out what that thing is.

Influences. Richard Price had the biggest influence. I read *The Wanderers* when I was 14 and realized that it was OK to write about the kind of people I knew and wanted to write about because, hell, he did it. That was the single most important moment in my life as a writer. Up until then, I thought characters had to be rich or live in France under Louis XIV to be worthy of a book.

Advice. It's the hoariest cliché out there—but read, damn it. Unpublished writers who proudly declare how little they read just baffle me. There's an established canon of great literature and we all know some of the names— Shakespeare, Tolstoy, Joyce, Flannery O'Connor, Hemingway, Chekhov, Austen, Faulkner, etc. Read them. I don't care if you "get" them, or like them. But earn your right to dismiss them by understanding them first. And gradually you'll stumble on sneaky little threads that will lead you to other great writers who, for whatever reason, aren't considered part of the canon yet. If you like Conrad, try Greene, then DeLillo, and that might lead you to le Carré or Alan Furst. Hemingway leads to Elmore Leonard. Faulkner leads to García Márquez, Cormac McCarthy, James Crumley.

But if you don't steep yourself in what's out there, then you're just flying a kite without a string, dumbfounded that it somehow got away from you.

How I Write is a monthly feature of *The Writer*. This piece appeared in the August 2002 issue.

RAY BRADBURY

Bradbury's "theater of the morning":
when his characters talk to him, he listens

Interview by Beatrice Cassina

For Ray Bradbury, one of the most celebrated American authors of the last 50 years, the writing day starts in the morning when he's still in bed—"half conscious and half still in contact with my inner voices." Then, rather like an episode of *The Twilight Zone,* the visitation begins.

"At that point of the day," Bradbury explains, "all kinds of thoughts and stories come to my mind. Many of those are metaphors. It is like all my characters come to me and talk to me. What I have to do then is wake up and start writing what these voices are suggesting to me. I let them write the story! I call it the theater of the morning.

"You know, there are some characters that have been following me since I was a child. You know them but there is always something new to learn from them. In those moments, I just free all my thoughts and ideas. When two of those ideas meet and suddenly create a third one, well, that is the moment when I wake up and I start writing. I am done before noon.

"I do not plan," he adds. "Everything has to be written in that precise moment, when it comes to my mind. It is my instinct that takes care of everything. Otherwise, it means that I am not involved enough from an emotional point, and what I am writing is not that good."

Bradbury's instincts have carried him a very long way. In his early 20s, Bradbury, whose formal education never extended past high school, sold newspapers on street corners while reading fanatically and making his first attempts at writing. Today, still in love with life and with writing in his eighties, Bradbury has published more than 30 books, in addition to some 600 short stories, many poems and essays, and work for theater, television, and film. (Small wonder

Bradbury has said he literally has been writing every day of his life for 65 years.) In 2000, the National Book Foundation awarded him its Medal for Distinguished Contribution to American Letters.

Bradbury builds his stories on metaphors, and in his hands, a simple idea or question can be transformed into a wonderful, emotional novel. This is perhaps the reason why his books are so appreciated around the world.

His first book, *Dark Carnival*, was published in 1947, followed by *The Martian Chronicles* (1950), in which Martians become the victims of human colonization, and *The Illustrated Man* (1951), in which the exotic tattoos on a wanderer come alive to tell some chilling tales. His most famous novel is *Fahrenheit 451* (1953), a tale of censorship, defiance, and totalitarianism that has sold more than 5 million copies. The origins of *Fahrenheit 451* lay in a simple question: What would the world be like if people were no longer allowed to read? The novel describes a world in which firemen are supposed to burn books.

Bradbury's oeuvre also includes *Dandelion Wine* (1957), a semi-autobiographical recollection of a magical small-town summer in 1928; *Something Wicked This Way Comes* (1962), a nightmarish tale—which has been called "a masterpiece of Gothic literature"—about two boys and the darkness that grips their small town when an evil carnival arrives; and murder mysteries like *Death Is a Lonely Business* (1985) and *A Graveyard for Lunatics* (1990). He won an Emmy in 1993 for his teleplay of *The Halloween Tree* and wrote the screenplay for John Huston's classic film treatment of *Moby Dick* (1956). His latest books are a collection of stories called *One More for the Road* (2002) and a new mystery titled *Let's All Kill Constance*.

Bradbury's approach to so-called science fiction is rather unusual: In his writing we meet people like us; people who are not all that involved with futuristic machines; human beings who cry, love, and sometimes live in doubt. We read about people who are emotionally involved with their lives, and about places and times that everybody can, in some way, recognize and relate to.

In an article for the online magazine *Salon*, James Hibberd wrote of Bradbury: "By mocking the electronic shortcuts and distracting entertainment that replace human contact and active thinking, Bradbury shows his science-fiction label is misplaced. He cares little for science or its fictions . . . Bradbury is a consistent champion of things human and real.

"There is simply no ready label for a writer who mixes poetry and mythology with fantasy and technology to create literate tales of suspense and social criticism; no ideal bookstore section for the author whose stories of rockets and carnivals and Halloween capture the fascination of 12-year-olds, while also stunning adult readers with his powerful prose and knowing grasp of the human condition."

Hibberd's August 2001 article was headlined "Ray Bradbury is on fire" because, at the time, five films based on his work were all going into production.

I met Bradbury in Los Angeles, where he lives and where he was signing a new edition of *Fahrenheit 451.* Encountering his deep voice, shining eyes behind big glasses, and warm, energetic manner was a little like meeting an old friend you haven't seen in a long time. Earlier, we had talked by phone about his writing life.

What are you working on right now?
Many projects. Lately, I have been focusing on my third murder mystery. It is exciting! I want it to be perfect, perfect to me. [A later phone chat with Bradbury underscores his productivity: By then, he has finished the murder mystery, written two new plays, begun preparing a collection of his short stories, helped ready a new Los Angeles production of his stage version of *Fahrenheit 451,* and begun preparing for the L.A. opening of a ballet for which he has written the story.]

What do you mean by wanting something you have written to be "perfect to me"?
It means that when you write something, you do not really have to care about what other people think about it. Your voice is unique.
The best thing is writing what you need, what you feel, and doing it your own way. It's just you, only you, who can say if something is worthwhile. Basically, I think it is a huge mistake to write trying to please whoever's expectation. You just have to let yourself talk. There is no chance it can work if you are speaking with a phony voice. Anybody can tell it is not genuine.

> You know, when you write, everything you need to know is already inside of you and outside in the world. You just have to listen carefully to what your heart is telling you.

Are you also working on a science-fiction book?
Everybody has always considered my writing like science fiction. You know what? I do not feel like a science-fiction writer at all. I just write what I see, through a different lens, the lens of my heart. I have always written with the power that love and life give me every day. This is the only thing I need every morning when I sit down and I start my creation. Love is what you need in life and being in love [with what you do] is what all writers should need and start from.

Not a science-fiction writer? But you've also written about life on Mars . . .
Yes, but I do not really know anything about technology. I just try to imagine impossible things—of course, impossible in this given world we are living in!
Technology is a little depressing. I have never written about complicated tools, machines, things that an everyday man can't really use.

I have always focused, first of all, on feelings, passions, things that are available to everybody. It is like I want and need to tell stories that I see behind the curtains of what people in general see.

One short story I do still love is one I wrote many years ago. It tells about a dinosaur that falls in love with a lighthouse. He sees it at night, shining in the dark sky and he thinks that is just a beautiful lady-dinosaur. When he finds out that she is just made of stones, he cries, like anybody else could do. He was in love, you know.

Writers read a lot. What can you tell us about your own reading life?

My passion for reading, therefore for writing, has been with me since I was a kid.

From the age of 9 through 14, I was a voracious reader. I never went to college; I'm a library graduate. When you're that young, you eat everything in sight.

I used to read many comics at that time. Since I was 8, I started collecting those comics and I still have some of them. It was my introduction to writing. Some years ago, I had the pleasure to publish *The Ray Bradbury Comics* and *The Martian Chronicles Comics*. See? What you really love keeps coming back to you. You never forget anything. And I do think comics are the best way to bring children into the reading room and make them feel the wonderful power of words.

What do you think about contemporary writers?

I do read a lot, but not really any contemporary writer. I can go on and on with those I consider the classic writers. Alexander Pope, Loren Eiseley, all the great playwrights, all the writers of history. Once you can read Shakespeare, you can receive a lot just from that, maybe all you need. I learned from Steinbeck and Hemingway, from Melville, Edgar Allan Poe. I always learned from people in the past; there are no people alive today who I learn from.

Many contemporary writers tell stories about things we already know. Any time you turn on the TV, you can see sad stories happening all around the real world. So the reality is just out there, waiting to be seen on TV. I like writers who can tell stories from a very peculiar point of view, stories that are not written yet. I like reading stories that can open my mind to new perspectives on reality or make me dream of wonderful things like love. By loving fiction and reading intensely and writing and experimenting, I grew into becoming a writer of short stories and novels. Nothing's worth doing unless you love it. If you don't love school, get the hell out and do something else. If you don't like your job, get out and do something. But for christsake, stay in love.

What about contemporary science-fiction writers?

Those, most of all. I do not read those writers. [He laughs.] Well, first of all, I don't read them because when you're working on a novel, you are always a little worried that somebody else has already had that same idea. And then also because I can't really find any love and passion in what they write.

If you were a young writer today, what do you think you would do?

Probably the same things I did many years ago. The most important thing, to me, is never losing my personal passion and my inspiration. You see, too often publishers and people in the business try to teach you what you have to write and how. I just believe that if one is a good writer, he or she will [be published] some day. If you work on given rules, you lose yourself and everything you say is no longer sincere. Being a writer takes a lot of patience, a lot of strength. But the best you can do is not pretend to be different from what you really are.

I would start, again, with short novels, short stories. It is the simplest way to get in touch with your way to create. And the plot does not need to be too long, so you can have every part of your writing under control.

I think everybody knows what he or she needs to tell. Maybe it takes a little time, but constancy is the best way to go. Every day, every single day, a writer or a writer-to-be needs to spend some time on his creation. Just to keep in exercise, to be every day more confident in what one is doing.

This is not a lesson; this is just the way I have spent my entire life. Whatever fascinates you deserves to be told, always in your own way. Do not think about what people are expecting from you. Do it just because you love it.

So you write every day?

Oh yes, still. It is not that I have to. It is just that I feel I need to. Every day, every morning when I wake up. It is nice to be in the 21st century. It is like a new challenge. It is really a good and threatening new century to create for!

How were your very early days as a writer?

Well, my family wasn't rich. And I did not have enough money to go to college. So to make some money, I started selling newspapers on the corner of the street. When somebody asked me what I was doing there, I used to answer that I was becoming a writer. That job started at 4 p.m., and by 6 p.m. I was done. This way, I had the money to pay my bills—I got paid 10 dollars a week—and I had time to go back home and write my stories.

Besides novels, stories, and comics, you also write poetry, don't you?

It took me 40 years to learn to write poetry and now, after all this time, my big book of poetry has been published with 400 poems: *They Have Not Seen the Stars: The Collected Poetry of Ray Bradbury*.

Poetry is one of the most exciting arts. You can really tell your feelings, what really counts. You can evoke life in thousands of shades. This makes me recall simple but very important parts of my life. You know, when you write, everything you need to know is already inside of you and outside in the world. You

THE RAY BRADBURY FILE

• Born in Waukegan, Ill., in 1920, he soon moved to Los Angeles with his parents. He graduated from Los Angeles High School in 1938.

• Last April he received the 2,193rd star on the world-famous Hollywood Walk of Fame for his contributions to literature, science-fiction films, and television.

• In addition to his National Book Foundation Medal for Distinguished Contribution to American Letters (2000), Bradbury's many honors include the O. Henry Memorial Award, the World Fantasy Award for lifetime achievement, and the Grand Master Award from the Science Fiction Writers of America.

• His work was included in the *Best American Short Story* collections in 1946, 1948, and 1952.

• His work has been adapted for television in a number of series, including *The Twilight Zone, Night Gallery*, and *The Ray Bradbury Theater*.

• He lives with his wife, Marguerite, in Los Angeles. They have four daughters and eight grandchildren.

• He has been acclaimed in particular as a science-fiction writer, yet he doesn't know how to turn on a computer or drive a car.

• Singer Elton John's tune "Rocket Man" was based upon Bradbury's story of the same name, and an Apollo astronaut named a moon crater Dandelion in honor of Bradbury's book *Dandelion Wine*.

• A common writing problem and its solution, according to Bradbury: "People try to force things. It's disastrous. Just leave your mind alone; your intuition knows what it wants to write, so get out of the way." (From a 1990 interview with Robert Couteau.)

just have to listen carefully to what your heart is telling you. Nothing more, nothing less!

Everything you have been writing is based on a very sharp observation of the world, isn't it?

I'm not an observer; I'm a sponge that takes in what it's seen, and then later it all comes out. It's in my subconscious. I don't observe; I feel, without knowing it, and later these things become stories and books.

Can you offer an example of a metaphor that runs through one of your writings?

I was very young, 12 years old. One day I was in the car with my parents, coming back from a funeral, and I saw a carnival that had just arrived in town. I ran down and met a man named Mr. Electrico, and he told me to live forever and he introduced me to all the carnival freaks, including a man with tattoos. All of a sudden, I thought: What if these drawings, the images on his skin, would turn to life? Well, this was the reason why I then wrote, years later, *The Illustrated Man.*

See, you meet many things in your life. Sometimes you ask yourself many whys and hows. Sometimes you can find answers, your personal answers.

When you start a new novel, how do you work?

At the beginning, I just have a very vague idea. I start and keep going. Sometimes it happens that I do not really know what the hell I am writing. I just know that in what I am writing, I can find myself. And it is a lot. You have to be very brave to be one person.

How do you feel about your own writing life?

I am simply in love with it.

How do you judge your work?

It's simple. When you read what you wrote and can be emotionally touched from that, if you can cry reading it, well, then you know you actually did a good job. I have cried many times reading my writings.

I remember a very short story I wrote when I was very young, "The Lake." When I was a child, a little girl used to play with me at the lake where we used to spend our vacations. One day, the waves of the lake took her away and she never came back. I was deeply touched by it. When, years later, I wrote that story and read it afterwards, I started crying like a little child. At that point, I felt it was a good story.

Beatrice Cassina of Beverly Hills, Calif., is a freelance writer from Milan, Italy, who writes for a number of Italian magazines. This interview appeared in *The Writer*, January 2003.

CHRISTINA SCHWARZ

How I write

[It was a stunning piece of good fortune when Oprah picked as her book club selection Christina Schwarz's first novel, *Drowning Ruth*, an unsettling story of secrets that take their toll on a family. Schwarz knew she had written a good book. "But I didn't deserve that kind of luck," she says. The "idea that what you deserve and what you get don't necessarily match up" fascinates the author.

Her second book, *All Is Vanity*, a hilarious account of a blocked writer in New York City and her social-climbing friend in Los Angeles, tells a story in sharp contrast to her own. Schwarz, who proves to be a biting social commentator, doesn't spare her characters, who encounter one misfortune after another. While mild-mannered in person, she's wicked on the page.

The author, who has an M.A. in English from Yale and taught 12th-grade English before writing her first novel, is married to Benjamin Schwarz, literary editor at *Atlantic Monthly*. They live in New Hampshire with their son, Nicholas.]

Why: As a child, I was a big, big reader, one of those kids who would read the cereal boxes if there was nothing else. I remember at some point thinking, "Oh, if I wrote some books, I'd have more to read." I was always better at writing than I was at anything else, except reading. I wrote a lot of letters and thought in terms of stories.

Writing is a way to legitimize daydreaming because that's what you really get to do. You get to just dream up this world and live in it, like living inside a book. I really like that.

When and where: That's changed a lot. I have a 1-year-old son, and since he has gotten to a stage where I cannot take my eyes off him, I've hired a babysitter for three hours a day, four days a week. That is the only time I'm working now. It's unbelievable how much I can get done in three hours, especially compared to how little I used to get done in three hours when I had eight hours.

How: In a notebook, I often write something I could imagine someone saying, things that go into a character's motivations, history, what they do, what kind of coffee they drink, something that is a telling detail.

With *Drowning Ruth*, I just wrote any scene that came to mind. I didn't know how I was going to put them together. I didn't know what the plot was going to be. For years, I didn't know how to write a scene that I might need to stitch things together. I really taught myself how to write with that book. There was a key scene . . . where [two characters] get together. It wasn't coming to me like other things were. I figured it out, and I wrote it. It was a huge breakthrough. I felt like I had a lot more control.

Sometimes I just sketch out a scene. I make notes to myself in the scene. I'll often ask myself questions like, "Should there be more of this?" I like talking to myself on the paper. When I'm trying to get the scene down, I write sentences very slowly. I'm very aware, I hope, when it's flat. If it's not right, I'm not going to be able to get on to the next thing.

Obstacles: It took me a long, long time to write *Drowning Ruth*. I wanted to give up so, so often. Every other week I thought, "What are you doing? This is ridiculous. You're wasting your time. You're making a fool of yourself." Underneath all that doubt, I knew there was some story there, and if I could just get at it, it would be good.

The same was true for *All Is Vanity*. I had a lot of doubts, different ones than I had with the first [book]. But there was something about each of these stories that I knew would be a good novel, if I could just crack it.

Advice: Find someone you trust to read your work. You can't always tell if something is working. You have to find someone whose opinion you respect. They have to be a good reader and be able to be honest with you. My husband is my main reader. I would listen to his advice above all others'.

How I Write is a monthly feature of *The Writer*. This piece appeared in the March 2003 issue.

ALAN FURST

A master of intrigue meticulously creates an atmospheric world

Interview by Elfrieda Abbe

Alan Furst uses words the way a great filmmaker uses a camera. His sentences flow like tracking shots (Renoir comes to mind), taking in every detail without interrupting the movement forward. Once you start reading, the motion takes over. Every word is there for a reason; every sentence builds the scene.

Furst writes what he calls "historical spy novels," set between 1933 and 1945, covering the years of Hitler's rise to power and the first Stalinist purges in Moscow. Fascism looms and war in Europe engulfs the lives of his unwilling heroes. A few years ago, his thrillers (seven so far) were hard to find in bookstores. You'll have no trouble spotting them today. Furst is one of the preeminent spymasters, often compared to John le Carré.

His novels draw you into a labyrinth of spies and resistance fighters during World War II, but he never bogs you down with exposition. The events of the war come through the details and dialogue. He puts his heroes and the reader into the middle of the fray. Like his central characters, you discover what's going on in bits and pieces as it happens. A profile in *Time* cites the author's "vivid, precise evocation of mood, time, place, a letter-perfect re-creation of the quotidian details of World War II Europe."

In *Dark Star,* for example, it is the terrifying sound of thugs singing as they march to beat up Jews that alerts the main character, Szara, and his companion, Baumann, who are trapped inside a synagogue.

By now the words of the song were plainly audible; it was something they sang in the Rathskellers as they drank their beer:

259

Wenn's Judenblut vom Messer spritzt / Dann geht's nochmal so gut, dann geht's nochmal so gut. When Jewish blood squirts under knives / Then all is well, then all is well.

Baumann turned away from the door and the two men stared at each other, both frightened, uncertain what to do and, suddenly, perfect equals.

"Hide." Baumann spoke the word in a broken whisper, the voice of a terrified child.

Szara fought for control of himself. He had been through pogroms before—in Kishinev and Odessa. They always attacked the synagogue.

In another example, the hero and his lover find themselves stranded during a coup d'état in Bucharest (*Blood of Victory*) as they make their way across town in a *trasuri* (horse-drawn cab).

It was so quiet they did not speak. The cold night smelled good after the smoky cellar . . . for a time, there was only the squeak of the turning wheels and the steady trot of the horse on the snow-covered pavement. When the horse slowed abruptly, Serebin looked up to see where they were. . . . The horse went a little further, then stopped, its ears pricked up for a moment, then flattened back against its head. *Now what?* The cabman made a clicking sound but the horse didn't move, so he spoke to it, very gently, a question. Suddenly, Marie-Galante's hand went rigid on his arm, so tight he could feel her fingernails, and he smelled burning. In the distance, a muffled snap, then another, and a third.

Neither reader nor hero knows what's coming next. But with impeccably placed details—the singing, the tightening grip on the arm—he puts you in the moment. You are caught up in the confusion.

A master of show-don't-tell, Furst lets you know enough to keep your bearings. You discover the big picture in much the same way you would if you were there.

> The hardest part of writing is transition from one paragraph to the next— that's where people fail.

"In life you're ignorant an extraordinary amount of the time," he says. "What does this person think of me? What's going on with the news? What's going to happen next week? We live in a sea of unknowing. That's what makes human life what it is."

His heroes—including a Polish military cartographer, a French filmmaker, and a Soviet journalist—move with ease across borders and are comfortable in more than one language. They operate on the shadowy fringes of smoky cafés and intellectual salons; traveling by barge or train to Poland, Romania, Germany, and Paris, always Paris; often living in sparse rooms; never knowing if the next person they meet is friend or foe. They blend in and because they do, they are called upon to perform seemingly doomed heroic deeds. But they always have a choice—to lie low and survive as best they can or to endanger themselves for the greater good.

Against the backdrop of war, fascism, communism, and unspeakable evil, Furst writes about courage and character. In his novels, the struggle between good and evil takes place in shop fronts, pensions, and drawing rooms, in the decision to deliver a message or hide an acquaintance.

I first met Furst in New York City at a Marymount Manhattan College writing conference. In between his presentations, he stood apart, quietly observing. Like his characters, he didn't draw attention to himself. During a later interview while he was on tour to promote *Blood of Victory,* the author spoke intensely and passionately about his research and writing methods, his fascination with courage and heroism, and despite the dark nature of his novels, his unswerving optimism.

You begin Red Gold *and* Blood of Victory *with an intimate bedroom scene.* The Polish Officer *begins with a battle between Poles and Germans over control of the telephone exchange in Warsaw in 1939. In both you bring the reader into something that has already started, into the heat of the moment. How did you decide on these beginnings?*

I have a good sense of where to start. You must understand I'm a writer totally, absolutely tied to a calendar because I'm writing historical fiction, so it's not a big decision nor is it a very skillful decision. These are obvious decisions for me.

I had to start *The Polish Officer* somewhere between the 1st and 17th of September, 1939. I could have started it, I suppose, with the German secret operations that attempted to justify their attack on Poland, but I had no interest in writing about that. I knew I wanted to start this book with the telephone exchange in Warsaw. Always they fight over the telephone exchange, the radio station. It's conventional to World War II and really all kinds of wars that communications are crucial. Now we use all kinds of smart bombs and electronics, but in those days they used infantry, because airplanes were not precise enough to do the job.

What do you try to accomplish in the first few pages?

When I was 29 years old, a friend of mine, who was a writer, read my first book manuscript. "Well, one thing that's missing is the corpse on Page 1," he said. *"Oh, there's supposed to be a corpse on Page 1?"* "Of course," he said, as in "didn't you know that?"

I adapted that to my own work. You can't dawdle and fool around with readers. I believe you have to do several things and do them quickly. One of the things you have to do is engage the reader's attention in your main character, and you have to [make] the reader like that character, right away. I like to tell myself this story:

When I was in high school I was in the theater, I acted. I had a wonderful man, Fred Little, who was the director . . . a really good director. He had once directed a play about a king. A good king. And in one scene, the king had to play chess with his page. So the two of them were on stage with a chess board and chess pieces. At some point, the page left and the king sat there alone for a few minutes, perhaps he had a soliloquy. One night when the page got up and left, the actor playing the king noticed that one of the pieces was halfway on and halfway off one of the squares. So he reached out his hand, moved the piece, and destroyed the play, because from that moment the audience thought, "this king cheats." The whole character of the king was changed for the rest of the play, no matter what he did.

That's the story I use to remind myself that you can lose an audience immediately if you do the wrong thing with a main character. You don't have a long time to have the main character be liked by the reader; therefore, it's best to show him when he's at his best in a situation with some tension in it. Conflict or intimacy—those are the two areas where people experience tension, want to do their best.

How do you write that first scene and get everything you need in one or two pages?
I will write a first paragraph over 40 or 60 times. I change the words, the actions, what is described, how it's described, the mix. It's like building something out of many different kinds of blocks. There are all kinds of things that are happening. That's how I do paragraphs. I write books in paragraphs, and every paragraph has to pay off.

> If you're doing a historical novel, you need to have a macro picture, and you need to have that macro picture enter through the lead character.

What do you mean by pay off?
The hardest part of writing is transition from one paragraph to the next—that's where people fail. It's not easy. It takes a lot of work. When I said every paragraph has to pay off, I wasn't kidding. There has to be something good in every paragraph. It's not just a question of you needing to get Smith from 42nd to 50th Street. Either you start the next paragraph: "Smith is now on 50th Street," or you work something into the paragraph that pays off—a funny, dramatic, interesting phrase, an interesting characteristic, an observation. It can be anything, but it has to be something. You cannot have just an expository paragraph in a novel. (See "On writing a paragraph" sidebar on page 267.)

How do you keep the history part of the story on track without getting the reader bogged down?

It comes in a conversation, newspapers, radio, newsreels, which are the ways people learned things. The rules of the game for me are that it has to happen organically.

[In *Blood of Victory*], Serebin goes to a florist. I mention there are flowers in the window, and there are two nice young girls in the shop wearing smocks and being very nice to him. The theory being that girls like working in florist shops. He has a bouquet made—this is for clandestine reasons, mind you. We describe how the flowers are laid down and how some greenery is put in among the roses. He makes a very conventional choice, but he's like that. He asks for a dozen red roses. Despite the fact that it's a clandestine reason (the girl doesn't know that), she makes a little joke with him in Romanian—which he doesn't understand, but he knows what she's saying: "Oh, I wish somebody would bring me this bouquet." So normal life is continuing.

The next thing that happens is there's a radio in the shop, and the station goes off. Logically, that is a technical problem. One of them goes and hits the radio. What actually happens is that this is the first moment of a coup d'état. The radio station has gone off the air, and there's just a buzz on the radio, but they have no reason to believe that. I'm hoping the reader might know it at that point. If the reader knows, that's good. I'm very reserved as a writer. I don't have them saying, "Oh, I wonder if it's a coup d'état." You leave a lot out.

There's not much exposition in your books nor do you usually use an omniscient narrator.

I make sure that the reader is on board, knows what's happening, and has the macro picture. But then my characters are always characters who will be interested in the macro picture. And that's important.

If you're doing a historical novel, you need to have a macro picture, and you need to have that macro picture enter through the lead character. So the lead character has to be someone who will want to know or knows or is interested in just precisely that. It can't be somebody who doesn't care.

You pack so much historical detail into your novels. What are your research methods?

I'm a very eclectic researcher. I use every possible source. I don't do a lot of primary research. I read journalists' books. I read histories of the period. I read technical books, personal biographies, memoirs. Some contemporary histories of long-ago periods, some long-ago histories of a long-ago period, immediately thereafter-type histories, which are the best. I read everything. It comes from all over the place.

I take notes copiously to teach myself the history of this period. You cannot write about something until you understand it. For *Kingdom of Shadows,* I had to understand the history of Hungary from 1930 to 1940. I think I spent days writing stuff out until I understood precisely what had happened. By understanding, I mean you can sit down and tell someone else about it, which is, after all, what you're doing in a novel. That's my research technique. I have a prodigious memory. Once I've learned it, I remember it forever.

How do you decide what to use?

You don't get to put it all in. I have the most wonderful leftovers . . . good stuff. Do you end up using it? Rarely. You really have to be reserved. It's the cardinal sin of historical writing that people put things in because they are just too good to leave out. They don't lead to anything. They're just flapping around like something loose. It's awful. Readers hate it. I don't like it. You can't do it. Good historical writers never do it.

But, alas, you do spend time developing certain things, finding certain things historically, great lines. I have one thing I'm waiting to use. I've been waiting for two books. I can't get it in. The moment hasn't come to use this particular line.

What techniques do you use to create the atmosphere of an era without overdoing it?

When you read [works from] a period, that really transmits a sense of time and place. You have to absorb that in some kind of way and be able to fall back into it. There are a lot of ways I do that. Not just one way. I'm very careful with language. Nobody ever says "OK" in my books. They often say, "that's right."

The language is important, the setting is important. Even things like weather. You have to put those kinds of things into 1940s terminology. It's the same terminology that would be used now, but somehow it's a 1940s snowstorm. It's not quite like a [2003] snowstorm. I was reading a passage from *Blood of Victory*, where there was some snow on the streets, but what you really see is a horse-drawn cab, which is what they had. So the snow is different. I think so, at any rate.

When I'm writing, I'm in that year, and I can sort of project myself into that year.

They have a person who works on movies and [his] job is called continuity. That person's job is to make sure everything is right where it was the day before. And it's my job to make sure that everything is in the right place, and it's all the right stuff, that it's not out of date, and that it's not the wrong thing to be there at the time. The phone in the office of the phone company director in Warsaw is Bakelite. I do that every now and then; again, you can't do it too often. You can't make your book chockablock—a beginning writer will say, "Oh, what a great idea! I'll use these eight other terms for things." No you can't.

Do you create a backstory for your characters? And if you do, how much do you include?

I always work out all the backstories. I tend to take copious notes about them. Who is this person? Not every character. There are too many characters in the

THE ALAN FURST FILE

• Alan Furst grew up on Manhattan's Upper West Side. His father manufactured ladies' millinery, and his mother organized theater and film char-
ity events. Furst graduated from Oberlin College in Ohio. He lives with his
wife, Karen Olowinski, a landscape designer, in Sag Harbor, N.Y.

• *The New York Times* described Furst's first novels, *Your Day in the
Barrel* (1976), *The Paris Drop* (1980), and *The Caribbean Account* (1981),
as "comic novels about a Jewish marijuana dealer from Great Neck, N.Y."

• Furst's jobs have included clerical work at a textile firm, handling complaints for a company that made plastic wading pools, and running an arts
festival. He's written geopolitical travel pieces, essays, and book reviews for
Esquire, *The New York Times*, *The Wall Street Journal*, and *The
Washington Post*. He wrote a monthly column for the *International Herald
Tribune*. Furst also wrote *One Smart Cookie* (1987), an as-told-to autobiography of Debi Fields, founder of Mrs. Field's Cookies, to underwrite
travel to France, where he lived for several years.

• Among Furst's literary influences are Arthur Koestler (*Darkness at
Noon*), Eric Ambler (*A Coffin for Dimitrios*), Gregor von Rezzori
(*Memoirs of an Anti-Semite*), and Christopher Isherwood (*Goodbye to
Berlin*). He says British writer Anthony Powell (*A Dance to the Music of
Time*, 12 volumes) "taught me a lot about writing. He taught me a lot
about dialogue. It's very sparse, monosyllabic. The dialogue is always different, depending on who is talking. He comes from a British generation
that really knew how to write. Somerset Maugham, Evelyn Waugh,
Isherwood, George Orwell, Graham Greene. They are very precise about
what they say. The British, for whatever reason, believe it's important to
say precisely what you mean."

book to do that. Most of the characters—I want to know their history. I want
you to know their history.

It can be anything from a three-word history to a 10-paragraph history. It just
depends on how important, interesting, and appealing that history is. The
reader has to say, "Oh, isn't this great! I'm reading a terrific history of this person." You can't say, "The reader has to learn the history of this person even

though it's a boring, stupid history, so I'm just going to impinge upon, demand the reader's good graces for two pages here while I do this important thing." You can't do that.

Are some parts of writing a novel harder than others?

Here's something to say to all writers: Beware of the end of the middle. In a 350-page manuscript, along about page 240, even earlier, you are going to have a case of the miseries. Page 220, in there, that's suicide alley because you know what the end is, but it's too early to start ending. You're stretching the middle at that point. It's very uncomfortable.

Your material is getting short, and you're going to let plot take over for the run to the station. You can't avoid it. It's organic. It's a structural problem. Of necessity, at that point, you're running out of material, or you haven't written a good book.

If you figure the book in thirds, the first third is easy. Anybody can write the first third of a novel, and the last third is not hard because you're going somewhere. The middle is like the middle of anything, like the middle of the afternoon. What do you do with it? You have to do something, so you kind of go along with your story, you go along with your characters, and you go along with the development of the relationships between characters. All of this threatens to get boring at the end of the middle. At least, I begin to get very panicky at that point.

One theme in your work is the optimism that comes through in moments of pleasure and kindness between characters. The last paragraphs of The Polish Officer *really capture that. Here are these two characters who have just come through a horrendous journey, who don't know what will happen tomorrow, who stop to take some pleasure in the thought of hot coffee and the sound of dogs barking.*

It's the little things. At the end of the day, all of us live lives under difficulty. You won't find anyone to tell you life is perfect. They do one day at a time. Everybody comes back to that at the end. What small pleasure can I have? How am I going to deal with this problem? And then, tomorrow is another day.

I love the end of *The Polish Officer*. And the last line just blows me away. It goes, "a dog barked, another answered." In five words you have the essence about optimism, about life. I was very emotional when I wrote that ending. I was very moved by it, because it means that life is going to go on, as bad as it might be. As bad as it might be, these common daily notes of positiveness will be there. So, it's very hopeful.

I think given that period, given the terrible things that went on, it's very important for me as a writer to end in such a way. All the characters say, "I may not be here tomorrow." You know that they are there tomorrow, but you also know that they are the kind of people who accept the possibility that they won't be. Like we all have to. That's the deal.

ON WRITING A PARAGRAPH

"He came out of the theatre into swirling snow and white streets. Two women held on to each other, taking timid steps on the slippery pavement. Usually, the sidewalks were shoveled right away. But not tonight. On the other side of the avenue, Floristi Stefan, a light in the window shining on the flowers. He waited while an army truck rolled past, then crossed the street and entered the shop."

I had a character in *Blood of Victory* who comes out of a movie theater in Bucharest. He comes out in a snowstorm. It wasn't snowing when he went in. I liked the idea of what it feels like—and every reader knows this. I know they know what it feels like to go into a movie theater in the afternoon and come out when the weather has changed, and it's dark. That is a very particular feeling, not particularly nice, but everyone knows the feeling.

The last thing that came to me was that I had to put something there. He couldn't just walk out into the snow. There needed to be something that he saw. And P.S., if I really get technical about it, he couldn't come out in the snow and have an epiphany—that's shooting sitting ducks and won't work with readers. It had to be external to the character—whatever it was. But it couldn't be big and exciting, because big and exciting is coming up five or six paragraphs later—we're going to get there.

The way that whole moment pays off is that he sees two women in the street and they're doing something—it took me a long time to write this. I don't remember exactly how I did it, but . . . they are holding on to each other and taking tiny steps. Two women will sometimes, when the footing is bad and they don't have the right shoes on, cling to each other, trying to walk along snow or ice, and normally they will laugh. I've never seen two women being distressed as they do this. I don't know if they like doing it, but for whatever reason it makes them laugh.

I had the damnedest time trying to find the right verb for what that looked like. I had "baby steps," but I didn't like that, so I got rid of it and [used] the less strong but more general and more acceptable "timid steps." You don't want to stir up the reader. You don't want to divert the reader. Then, what you've done is florid writing, which is impossible to read for more than two pages, so I cut it back to timid steps and had the two women holding onto each other.

If you do that 800 or 1,000 times, you have a novel, something like that. I don't know how many paragraphs there are, but they're all like that.

— Alan Furst

I like optimistic fiction. I used to say to people (I don't say it so much any-more), "I'm in the business of consolation." That's a word you almost never hear, but I say it all the time because I think it's a very crucial and important one. The sub-theme of being in the business of consolation is to look at the world as a place where people do good things. It's a world where strong people take responsibility for those not as strong as themselves. That's the greatest human act there is. You see it again and again.

You address the idea of taking responsibility in Blood of Victory, *when Serebin's friend tells him, ". . . if you don't stand up to evil it eats you first and kills you later, but not soon enough." What does this passage mean to you?*

I put that passage in after 9/11 as a memorial. I did it absolutely on purpose. That was a late fix. At the end of the day after that experience, I thought, well, it's the truest thing I know to say. I'm not a public spokesman or anything like that, but I do write books and they are publicly read. That gives me the right to say something sometimes that's close to my heart. That's exactly what I did.

The world is a place where good struggles with evil. You can see it. Turn on the television. It's not far away from you. And that has been true in all history. When didn't you have terribly negative things going on, evil people, brutal things, catastrophes, predatory people? Then you have heroes who come along and try to save the day. To save is such an elemental part of humanity. When you see how 9/11 finally is playing itself out . . . we have chosen to think about it in terms of the fireman and policeman. That is the emotional final paragraph of 9/11. That's the hopeful thing [we] found in it—that there are people who are heroic.

What does it mean to be heroic? It means you try to save people when they need to be saved. My books are about that all of the time. None of these people have to do what they do. None of my heroes. I always give them an option.

Elfrieda Abbe is Editor of *The Writer*. This interview appeared in *The Writer*, May 2003.

CARL HIAASEN

How I write

[Bestselling novelist Carl Hiaasen acknowledges having an imagination twisted enough to deserve clinical research after he's gone, but also credits his native Florida—"a place just crawling with characters"—for his ideas. In nine comic mystery novels, Hiaasen has gained a devoted following for people and situations whose wackiness is matched only by his satirical bite, aimed most often at various despoilers of Florida.

Among his memorable creations are a Republicans-only hooker and Chemo, a hit man with a Weed Whacker attached to the stump of his arm. Hiaasen's latest book, a children's novel titled *Hoot*, won a 2003 Newbery Honor. An award-winning reporter at *The Miami Herald*, Hiaasen, 50, continues to write a weekly column for the newspaper. He lives in Islamorada, Fla.

His credits include novels *Sick Puppy* (1999) and *Strip Tease* (1993); three earlier novels as coauthor; and two collections of columns.]

Why: I know I wanted to do this from a very young age and I was lucky in that sense, that I knew early on that I enjoyed writing and getting a reaction. I think it's some sort of extension of being a class clown—that if you could write something and make somebody laugh, it was a good gig to have. I think there was an element of psychotherapy—it was a legal outlet for some of the ideas I was wanting to express as a kid.

When: I try to write in the mornings, starting by about 8:30 or 9. I may knock off at 2 if the weather's nice or I may write till 4 or 5 o'clock, depending on how it's going. I don't set a number of pages or words; if it's not going well, I see no point in writing a thousand mediocre words. If I'm not traveling, I write seven days a week.

Starting a novel: Both [the entertainment and political satire elements] are necessary. I've got to be interested in these characters and find them entertaining, and they have to be bent in a way that I can live with them for the next 18 months and not get bored at the same time. To even begin writing, I have to be ticked off about something; I have to have some sort of burr under my saddle before I can get rockin' and rollin' on these things. I have to be sustained by more than just an entertaining cast.

Technically, the way I start is usually with, one by one, a cast of characters I'm sort of fiddling with in the back of my head and then on paper—characters I'd like to get on stage and see what happens.

Outlining: When I got out of college, I promised myself I'd never outline anything again in my life. I consider an outline a handcuff. I want to be surprised by my characters; I want to be able to change direction; I want to be able to eliminate characters if they're boring me.

Having said this, I understand the value of an outline for a writer whose mind works that way. For some types of novels, it's probably essential.

I can be two-thirds of the way into the book and not know how it's going to end up. I can tell you when I start what the tone is going to be at the end, but in terms of the choreography of the ending or who exactly is left standing and who is in shreds at the end, that I'm not sure of.

Influences: Joseph Heller; Kurt Vonnegut; John Irving—some of his early books are amazing; John D. MacDonald—he was a revelation for me.

Keeping up his column: I continue writing the column because it's not just a privilege but an opportunity to make a difference in a place where I was born and raised. Florida is very much a character in my books, and it often plays a similar role in my columns.

On writing for children: In my case, it was simply being able to transport myself back into my own childhood and how I looked at the world when I was 10 or 12. Once I was able to do that, it went pretty smoothly.

One pitfall I could have easily fallen into is writing down to kids, but I had a terrific editor watching over me. I found myself aiming higher than I do for my adult audience.

In terms of content and message and characters, all of it has to be very finely tuned for kids; I found myself working just as hard, if not harder, on the structure and characters and everything.

How I Write is a monthly feature of *The Writer*. This piece appeared in the June 2003 issue.

NONFICTION MAGAZINES

NONFICTION MAGAZINES

The magazines in the following list are in the market for freelance articles in many categories. Unless listings state otherwise, a writer should submit a query first, including a brief description of the proposed article and any relevant qualifications or credits. A few editors want to see samples of published work, if available.

Submit photos or slides only if the editor has specifically requested them. A self-addressed envelope with postage sufficient to cover the return of the manuscript or the answer to a query should accompany all submissions.

All information in these lists comes from query responses from the editors, publishers, and directors and from their published guidelines, but personnel and addresses change, as do requirements. No published listing can give as clear a picture of editorial needs and tastes as a careful study of several issues of a magazine, and writers should never submit material without first thoroughly researching the prospective market. If a magazine is not available in the local library or on the newsstand, write directly to the editor for the price of a sample copy. Many companies also offer a formal set of writer's guidelines, available for an SASE (self-addressed, stamped envelope) upon request, or posted on its Web site.

While some of the more established markets may seem difficult to break into, especially for the beginner, there are thousands of lesser-known publications where editors will consider submissions from first-time freelancers.

All manuscripts must be typed double-space and submitted with self-addressed envelopes bearing postage sufficient for the return of the material. If a manuscript need not be returned, note this with the submission, and enclose an SASE or a self-addressed, stamped postcard for editorial reply. Use good white paper. Always keep a copy, since occasionally material is lost in the mail. Magazines may take several weeks, or longer, to read and report on submissions. If an editor has not reported on a manuscript after a reasonable length of time, write a brief, courteous letter of inquiry.

Some publishers will accept, and may in fact prefer, work submitted on computer disk, usually noting the procedure and type of disk in their guidelines.

ABILITIES

ABILITIES MAGAZINE
489 College St., Suite 501, Toronto, Ontario M6G 1A5 Canada. 416-923-1885.
E-mail: lisa@abilities.ca. Web site: www.abilities.ca. Quarterly. Lisa Bendall, Managing Editor. **Description:** For people with disabilities, their families, and professionals engaged in disabilities issues. Covers travel, health, sport, recreation, employment, education, housing, social policy, sexuality, movie/book reviews, profiles. **Nonfiction:** Articles, 500-2,000 words, $50-$400. **Columns, Departments:** News and updates (FYI); humor (The Lighter Side). **Queries:** Preferred. **Unsolicited mss:** Accepts. **Rights:** 1st print, non-exclusive electronic.

ABLE

P.O. Box 395, Old Bethpage, NY 11804-0395. 516-939-2253.
E-mail: ablenews@aol.com. Web site: www.ablenews.com. Monthly. $15/yr. Circ.:
35,000. Angela Miele Melledy, Editor. **Description:** "The Newspaper For, By, and
About the Disabled." Features news, events, and informative articles that are of inter-
est to people with disabilities, family and friends, and involved professionals.
Nonfiction: to 500 words; pays $40. **Art:** Color and B&W photos. **Queries:**
Required. **E-Queries:** No. **Unsolicited mss:** Accepts. **Freelance Content:** 40%.
Payment: On publication.

ACTIVE LIVING MAGAZINE

Disability Today Publishing Group
2276 Rosendene Rd., St. Ann's, Ontario L0R 1Y0 Canada. 905-957-6016.
E-mail: lfleming@softhome.net. Web site: www.activelivingmagazine.com.
Bimonthly. $19.97/yr. Circ.: Bimonthly. Liz Fleming, Managing Editor. **Description:**
Health, fitness, and recreation magazine for people with disabilities. **Nonfiction:**
Articles, 750-1,000 words, on improving fitness and mobility, accessible travel and
leisure, and new therapeutic and sporting activities; pays $.18/word. **Tips:** Avoid
labeling or condescending language. **Queries:** Preferred. **Payment:** On publication.

CAREERS & THE DISABLED

445 Broadhollow Rd., Suite 425, Melville, NY 11747-4803. 631-421-9421.
E-mail: jschneider@eop.com. Web site: www.eop.com. 3x/yr. $10/yr. Circ.: 10,500.
James Schneider, Editor. **Description:** *CAREERS & the disABLED* is a career guid-
ance publication for students and professionals with disabilities. Role-model profiles
and career guidance strategies; 1,000-1,500 words; $.10/word. **Queries:** Preferred.
E-Queries: Yes. **Unsolicited mss:** Accepts. **Response:** 2 weeks. **Freelance
Content:** 60%. **Rights:** FNAR. **Payment:** On publication.

CHALLENGE

Disabled Sports/USA
9406 N 107th St., Milwaukee, WI 53224-1106. 414-354-0200.
E-mail: patty@rspr.com. Web site: www.dsusa.org. 3x/yr. $25/yr. Circ.: 20,000. Patty
Johnson, Editor. **Description:** Non-profit publication that promotes adaptive sports
and recreation for children and adults with physical disabilities—from elite para-
lympic athletes to youngsters just entering competition. Also has emphasis on family
recreation, fitness training, and activities of DS/USA chapters nationwide.
Nonfiction: Articles should relate to regional, national, and international competitions. Also seeks features on adaptive recreation relating to winter and summer
sports. Offers by-line and photo credits only; does not offer monetary payment. **Art:**
Accepts color and B&W photos; hard copy or JPG. **Tips:** "Avoid 'gushing' when writing. Disabled athletes are extremely talented, train hard, and set world records close
to those of able-bodied contestants. These athletes do not want to be considered as
"inspirations" or otherwise presented in a patronizing manner. Use correct terminol-

ogy relating to disabilities." **Queries:** Required. **E-Queries:** Yes. **Unsolicited mss:** Accepts. **Freelance Content:** 10%. **Rights:** None.

CLOSING THE GAP
526 Main St., P.O. Box 68, Henderson, MN 56044. 507-248-3294. E-mail: info@closingthegap.com. Web site: www.closingthegap.com. Bimonthly. $32/yr. Circ.: 10,000. Megan Turek, Managing Editor. **Description:** Newspaper providing practical, up-to-date information on assistive technology products, procedures, and best practices. Feature articles cover how technology enhances the education, vocation, recreation, mobility, communication, etc. of individuals with disabilities. Non-product related articles also used. 800-1,000 words. **Tips:** Use "person first" wording (refer to the person first, followed by disability, e.g., "the boy with a disability"). Original, unpublished material only. No pure research or "one of a kind" product descriptions; interested only in easily replicated procedures or commercially available products. If commercial products covered within an article, include the price and contact information of producer. **E-Queries:** Yes. **Rights:** All.

DIALOGUE
P.O. Box 5181, Salem, OR 97304-0181. 503-581-4224, 800-860-4224. E-mail: blindskl@teleport.com. Web site: www.blindsklls.com. Quarterly. Carol McCarl, Editor. **Description:** Seeks to give readers an opportunity to learn about interesting and successful people who are visually impaired. Subject matter covers a variety of topics including independence, mobility, employment, technology, and health. Also spotlights short pieces of fiction in each issue. **Nonfiction:** Articles for youth and adults who are visually impaired. Career opportunities, educational skills, and recreational activities. 800-1,200 words; pay varies. **Queries:** Preferred. **Response:** SASE. **Payment:** On publication.

KALEIDOSCOPE
United Disability Services
701 S Main St., Akron, OH 44311-1019. 330-762-9755. E-mail: mshiplett@udsakron.org. Web site: www.udsakron.org. Semi-annual. Circ.: 1,000. Gail Willmott, Senior Editor. **Description:** Explores the experience of disability through literature and fine arts, from the perspective of individuals, families, health-care professionals, and society. Seeks to challenge and overcome stereotypical, patronizing, sentimental attitudes about disability. Pay $25 and 2 copies. **Fiction:** Character-centered stories, not action pieces. No romance. 5,000 words max. **Nonfiction:** Narratives and articles on experiences and issues of disability. 5,000 words max. **Poetry:** Free verse on disability or written by someone with a disability. Also, short nature poems and light humor. 1-5 poems. **Art:** 35mm color, B&W 8x10 glossy; up to $100. **Tips:** "Photos are a plus." **Queries:** Not necessary. **E-Queries:** Yes. **Unsolicited mss:** Accepts. **Response:** Queries 2 weeks, submissions 6 months, SASE required. **Freelance Content:** 60%. **Rights:** 1st serial rights. **Payment:** On publication. **Contact:** Mildred Shiplett, Editorial Director.

MINDPRINTS
See full listing in Literary Fiction & Poetry category.

WEMEDIA
130 William St., New York, NY 10038. 212-931-6700.
E-mail: editorial@wemedia.com. Web site: www.wemedia.com. Bimonthly. $12.95/yr.
Circ.: 150,000. Cary Fields, Publisher. **Description:** For people with disabilities,
their families and friends, focusing on news, sports, accessible and assistive technologies, politics and advocacy, shopping, employment, education, finance, and real estate
from a disability perspective. **Fiction:** 1,500-2,000 words. **Nonfiction:** Varying
lengths; pay varies. **Art:** Photos. **Tips:** Include a JPG photo of the author and a JPG
logo of the organization the author represents, plus a one- to two-line description that
states the author's role and organization. **Queries:** Preferred. **Payment:** On publication. **Contact:** Laura Silver, Editor.

AGRICULTURE & RURAL LIFE

ACRES USA
P.O. Box 91299, Austin, TX 78709-1299. 512-892-4400.
E-mail: editor@acresusa.com. Web site: www.acresusa.com. Monthly. $27/yr. Circ.:
11,500. Fred C. Walters, Publisher. **Description:** Articles offer ecological and economical advice for farmers who practice sustainable agriculture. Features hands-on
techniques and natural methods for growing crops and raising livestock. **Nonfiction:**
Emphasis on commercial production of quality food without use of toxic chemicals;
pays $.05/word. **Unsolicited mss:** Accepts. **Payment:** On publication.

AG JOURNAL
122 San Juan, P.O. Box 500, La Junta, CO 81050. 719-384-8121.
E-mail: ag-edit@centurytel.net. Web site: www.agjournalonline.com. Weekly. $32.
Circ.: 12,000. Jeanette Larson, Managing Editor. **Description:** Covers agriculture
news in the Western and Southwestern states. **Nonfiction:** On prominent people in
agriculture. Also covers ag market and pricing trends, latest industry news, grain and
forage production, equestrian happenings, and equipment for-sale listings; 250-2,000
words; $.04/word. **Art:** Color slides and negatives; TIF or JPG 200 dpi or higher;
$8/photo, $25 cover shot. **Queries:** Required. **E-Queries:** Yes. **Response:** 2 weeks.
Rights: All, no reprints. **Payment:** On publication.

AMERICAN BEE JOURNAL
51 S Second St., Hamilton, IL 62341-1398. 217-847-3324.
E-mail: abj@dadant.com. Web site: www.dadant.com. Monthly. $19.95/yr. Circ.:
13,000. Joe M. Graham, Editor. **Description:** Articles on beekeeping for both professionals and hobbyists. Offers how-to articles as well as scientific information on disease and treatments for bees. **Nonfiction:** Articles, pays $.75/column inch. **Art:**
Photos. **Queries:** Preferred. **Payment:** On publication.

BACKHOME MAGAZINE

P.O. Box 70, Hendersonville, NC 28793. 828-696-3838.
E-mail: backhome@ioa.com. Web site: www.backhomemagazine.com. Bimonthly.
$4.95/$21.97. Circ.: 29,000. Lorna K. Loveless, Editor. **Description:** Do-it-yourself
information on sustainable, self-reliant living. Offers information and resources on
rural land, mortgage-free building, solar/renewable energy, chemical-free gardening,
wholesome cooking, home business, home schooling, small livestock, vehicle and
workshop projects, family activities. **Nonfiction:** On self-sufficient, sustainable-living
practices, preferably first-person experiences; buying a used tractor, installing a door,
maintaining a pasture, etc.; 800-3,000 words; $35/printed page. **Tips:** "Focus not on
'dropping out,' but on becoming better citizens and caretakers of the planet. Avoid
essays." **Queries:** Not necessary. **E-Queries:** Accepts. **Unsolicited mss:** Accepts.
Response: 2-4 weeks, SASE. **Freelance Content:** 80%. **Payment:** On publication.

BEE CULTURE

623 W Liberty St., Medina, OH 44256-2225. 330-725-6677.
E-mail: kim@beeculture.com. Web site: www.beeculture.com. Monthly. $3.95/
$21.50. Circ.: 13,500. Mr. Kim Flottum, Editor. **Description:** Articles on beekeeping,
pollination, gardening with bees, nature, etc. **Nonfiction:** Basic how-to, some profiles
of commercial operations, 1,000-2,000 words; $100-$250. **Art:** Slides, B&W prints,
color, or electronic. **Tips:** "Writers must know bee and commercial beekeeping. Avoid
"How I got started in beekeeping" stories." **Queries:** Preferred. **E-Queries:** Yes.
Unsolicited mss: Accepts. **Response:** 1-3 months, SASE required. **Freelance
Content:** 25%. **Rights:** FNAR. **Payment:** On publication or negotiated.

BEEF

PRIMEDIA Business Magazines & Media
7900 International Dr., Suite 300, Minneapolis, MN 55425. 952-851-9329.
E-mail: beef@primediabusiness.com. Web site: www.beef-mag.com. Monthly. $35/yr.
Circ.: 101,000. Joe Roybal, Editor. **Description:** Informational articles for cattlemen
and cattle industry; covers production, animal health, nutrition, finance, and marketing issues. **Nonfiction:** Articles on feeding, cowherds, stock operations, cattle industry; up to $300. **Queries:** Required. **E-Queries:** Yes. **Unsolicited mss:** Does not
accept. **Payment:** On acceptance.

CAPPER'S

Ogden Publications, Inc., 1503 SW 42nd St., Topeka, KS 66609-1265. 785-274-4345.
E-mail: cappers@cjnetworks.com. Web site: www.cappers.com. Biweekly. $27.98/yr.
Circ.: 210,000. Ann Crahan, Editor. **Description:** Focuses on home and family, for
readers in the rural Midwest. **Fiction:** Query first, with brief description; $75-$300.
Nonfiction: Inspirational, nostalgic, family-oriented, travel, human-interest; 700
words max; $2.50/inch. **Poetry:** Easy to read, down-to-earth themes; 4-16 lines; $10-
$15. **Fillers:** Jokes (limit to batches of 5-6; no jokes returned); $2 gift certificate. **Art:**
color transparencies or sharp color prints; include captions; $10-$40. **Tips:** Does not
accept simultaneous submissions. **Queries:** Not necessary. **E-Queries:** No.

Unsolicited mss: Accepts. **Response:** Submissions 2-6 months. SASE required. **Freelance Content:** 25%. **Rights:** FNASR. **Payment:** On publication.

THE CATTLEMAN
Texas & Southwestern Cattle Raisers Assn.
1301 W Seventh St., Fort Worth, TX 76102-2604. 817-332-7064.
E-mail: lionel@thecattlemanmagazine.com.
Web site: www.thecattlemanmagazine.com. $25/yr. Circ.: 16,900. Lionel Chambers, Editor. **Description:** For ranchers who raise beef cattle. **Queries:** Preferred.

COUNTRY
Reiman Publications/Reader's Digest Assn.
5400 S 60th St., Greendale, WI 53129. 414-423-0100.
E-mail: editors@country-magazine.com. Web site: www.country-magazine.com. Bimonthly. $14.98/yr. Circ.: 1,400,000. Jerry Wiebel, Editor. **Description:** Articles and photographs describing the allure of country life today. Mostly reader-written. **Nonfiction:** First-person articles; 500-700 words; $75-$200. **Art:** Good candid color photos. **Tips:** No articles on farm production techniques. **Queries:** Not necessary. **Unsolicited mss:** Accepts. **Response:** 2 months. **Freelance Content:** 90%. **Payment:** On publication.

COUNTRY FOLK
HC 77 Box 608, Pittsburg, MO 65724-9717.
E-mail: salaki@countryfolkmag.com. Web site: www.countryfolkmag.com. Bimonthly. $3.24/$19.50. Circ.: 6,500. Susan Salaki, Editor. **Description:** True Ozark history stories, old rare recipes, historical photos, and interesting fillers. **Nonfiction:** Ozark history; 800-1,000 words; $5-$25. **Poetry:** Traditional, rhyming; 3 verses max; must be about Ozark region; complimentary copy. **Tips:** "All of our stories are true, complete with real names and places." **Freelance Content:** 99%.

COUNTRY WOMAN
Reiman Publications/Reader's Digest Assn.
5400 S 60th St., Greendale, WI 53129. 414-423-0100.
E-mail: editors@countrywomanmagazine.com.
Web site: www.countrywomanmagazine.com. Bimonthly. $3.99/issue. Circ.: 1,700,000. Kathy Pohl, Executive Editor. **Description:** For women living in the country or interested in country life. Recipes, craft projects, fiction and nostalgia stories, decorating, profiles of country woman, and poetry. **Fiction:** Wholesome fiction with country perspective or rural theme; 1,000 words; $90-$125. **Nonfiction:** Nostalgia pieces, essays on farm/country life, humorous stories, decorating features, inspirational articles; 750-1,000 words; $50-$75. **Poetry:** Good rhythm and rhyme, seasonal in nature; 12-24 lines; $10-$25. **Art:** Good candid color photos. **Queries:** Not necessary. **Unsolicited mss:** Accepts. **Response:** 2-3 months, SASE required. **Freelance Content:** 90%. **Payment:** On acceptance. **Contact:** Kathleen Anderson, Managing Editor.

DAIRY GOAT JOURNAL

P.O. Box 10, Lake Mills, WI 53551. 920-648-8285.
Web site: www.dairygoatjournal.com. 6x/yr. $2.50/$21. Circ.: 7,000. Dave Thompson, Editor. **Description:** Magazine for successful dairy-goat owners. Features interesting people and practical husbandry ideas. **Nonfiction:** 1,000-1,500 words; $75-$150. **Fillers:** $25-$75. **Art:** B&W prints, $25-$75. **Tips:** Needs practical stories about goats and their owners; about marketing goat cheese and dairy products. Readership in U.S. and over 70 foreign countries. **Queries:** Preferred. **E-Queries:** No. **Unsolicited mss:** Accepts. **Response:** 2 weeks, SASE. **Freelance Content:** 50%. **Rights:** All. **Payment:** On acceptance.

FARM AND RANCH LIVING

Reiman Publications/Reader's Digest Assn.
5400 S 60th St., Greendale, WI 53129. 414-423-0100.
E-mail: editors@farmandranchliving.com. Web site: www.farmandranchliving.com. Bimonthly. $3.99/issue, $17.98/year. Circ.: 350,000. Nick Pabst, Editor. **Description:** For U.S. and Canadian families that farm or ranch full-time. Focuses on people; includes diaries, humor, rural nostalgia, tractor talk, 4-H, events calendar. **Nonfiction:** Photo-illustrated stories about today's farmers and ranchers; 1,200 words; $75-$150. **Fillers:** Farm-related humor; 100 words; $25-$50. **Tips:** "Submit upbeat, positive stories." **Queries:** Not necessary. **E-Queries:** Yes. **Unsolicited mss:** Accepts. **Response:** 4 weeks, SASE required. **Freelance Content:** 30%. **Rights:** 1st, one-time. **Payment:** On publication.

FARM INDUSTRY NEWS

PRIMEDIA Business Magazines & Media
7900 International Dr., Suite 300, Minneapolis, MN 55425. 612-851-4609.
E-mail: kmcmahon@primediabusiness.com. Web site: www.farmindustrynews.com. 12x/yr. $25/yr. Circ.: 250,700. Karen McMahon, Editor. **Description:** Publication for farmers that covers new products, machinery, equipment, chemicals, and seeds. **Nonfiction:** Articles; pays $350-$500. **Queries:** Required. **Payment:** On acceptance.

FARM JOURNAL

610 Freedom Business Center, Suite 114, King of Prussia, PA 19406. 610-491-9800.
E-mail: feedback@agweb.com. Web site: www.agweb.com. Monthly. $19.50/yr. Circ.: 580,000. Sonja Hillgren, Editor. **Description:** On the business of farming. **Nonfiction:** Articles, 500-1,500 words, with photos; pays $.20-$.50/word. **Queries:** Preferred. **Payment:** On acceptance.

FLORIDA GROWER

1555 Howell Branch Rd., Suite C-204, Winter Park, FL 32789. 407-539-6552.
E-mail: flg_edit@meisternet.com. Monthly. Circ.: 13,400. Michael Allen, Managing Editor. **Description:** The voice of Florida agriculture. Covers all aspects of commercial fruit and vegetable industries. **Nonfiction:** On production or marketing Florida's agricultural products; 1,400 words; $300. **Queries:** Not necessary.

E-Queries: Yes. **Unsolicited mss:** Accepts. **Freelance Content:** 20%. **Rights:** All. **Payment:** On publication.

THE LAND

P.O. Box 3169, Mankato, MN 56002-3169. 507-345-4523.
E-mail: kschulz@the-land.com. Web site: www.the-land.com. Biweekly. $20/yr. Circ.: 40,000. Kevin Schulz, Editor. **Description:** Agricultural and rural-life magazine for Minnesota farm families. **Nonfiction:** On Minnesota agriculture and rural issues, production, how-tos; 500 words; $35-$60. **Queries:** Preferred. **E-Queries:** Yes. **Unsolicited mss:** Does not accept. **Response:** 1-4 weeks, SASE required. **Freelance Content:** 50%. **Rights:** FNAR. **Payment:** On acceptance.

THE MAINE ORGANIC FARMER & GARDENER

662 Slab City Rd., Lincolnville, ME 04849. 207-763-3043.
E-mail: jenglish@midcoast.com. Web site: www.mofga.org. Quarterly. $12/yr. Circ.: 5,000. Jean English. **Description:** Published by the Maine Organic Farmers and Gardeners Association. **Nonfiction:** Organic farming and gardening, environmental issues relating to food/health, consumer issues, book reviews; 250-2,000 words; $.08/word. **Fillers:** Gardening and farming tips; $.08/word. **Tips:** Avoid rehashing old material. No chemical fertilizers and no potato-flake recipes. Readers know organic methods, and they seek new ideas, new crops, and new cultivation techniques. **Queries:** Preferred. **E-Queries:** Yes. **Unsolicited mss:** Accepts. **Response:** 2-4 weeks, SASE required. **Freelance Content:** 50%. **Rights:** 1st, reprint. **Payment:** On publication.

NEW HOLLAND NEWS

P.O. Box 1895, New Holland, PA 17557-0903. 717-393-3821.
Web site: www.newholland.com/na. 8x/yr. Gary Martin, Editor. **Description:** Farm management, rural features for modern farm families. **Nonfiction:** People stories about farm life, ways to improve farm income, etc. 800-1,500 words; $600-$800. **Art:** Transparencies or prints; $500/cover. **Tips:** No farmer profiles. **Queries:** Preferred. **E-Queries:** No. **Unsolicited mss:** Accepts. **Response:** 2 months, SASE required. **Freelance Content:** 60%. **Rights:** FNAR. **Payment:** On acceptance.

PEANUT FARMER

5808 Faringdon Pl., Raleigh, NC 27609. 919-872-5040.
E-mail: editor@peanutfarmer.com. Web site: www.peanutfarmer.com. Monthly. $25. Circ.: 20,165. Mary Ann Rood, Editor. **Description:** Magazine for commercial peanut farmers. Articles on production practices, 500-2,000 words. **Queries:** Preferred. **E-Queries:** Yes. **Unsolicited mss:** Accepts. **Response:** 2 weeks, SASE required. **Freelance Content:** 10%. **Rights:** FNAR. **Payment:** On publication.

PROGRESSIVE FARMER

2100 Lakeshore Dr., Birmingham, AL 35209-6721. 205-877-6415.
E-mail: letters@progressivefarmer.com. Web site: www.progressivefarmer.com.

Monthly. $16/yr. Circ.: 600,000. Jack Odle, Editor. **Description:** For farmers. Covers new developments in agriculture; rural communities; personal business issues for farmstead and home office; relationships; worker safety; finances, taxes, and regulations. **Nonfiction:** Articles; to 5 double-spaced pages (3 pages preferred); pays $50-$400. **Queries:** Preferred. **Payment:** On publication.

RURAL HERITAGE
281 Dean Ridge Ln., Gainesboro, TN 38562-5039. 931-268-0655.
E-mail: editor@ruralheritage.com. Web site: www.ruralheritage.com. Bimonthly. $8/$26. Circ.: 6,700. Gail Damerow, Editor. Description: Covers modern farming and logging with horses, mules, and oxen. Articles on draft animal use, training, implements, etc.; 1,200 words; $.05/word. **Queries:** Preferred. **E-Queries:** Yes. **Unsolicited mss:** Accepts. **Response:** Queries 1 week, submissions 3 months. **Freelance Content:** 90%. **Rights:** FNASR. **Payment:** On publication.

RURALITE
P.O. Box 558, Forest Grove, OR 97116. 503-357-2105.
E-mail: curtisc@ruralite.org. Web site: www.ruralite.org. Monthly. $10/yr. Circ.: 287,600. Curtis Condon, Editor. **Description:** For rural electric cooperatives and public power districts in 7 western states, General interest and energy-related. **Nonfiction:** For rural/small-town audiences (Oregon, Washington, Idaho, Wyoming, Nevada, northern California, Alaska), on issues affecting rural electric cooperatives, rural living, people features, regional history, and celebrations, humorous photos; 400-2,000 words; $50-$400. **Art:** 35mm, 2¼; $25-$300. **Tips:** Readership 60% women, 50 years and older. **Queries:** Required. **E-Queries:** Yes. **Unsolicited mss:** Does not accept. **Response:** 1-2 months, SASE. **Freelance Content:** 80%. **Payment:** On acceptance.

SHEEP! MAGAZINE
P.O. Box 10, Lake Mills, WI 53551. 920-648-8285.
E-mail: csymag@tdsn.net. Web site: www.sheepmagazine.com. 6x/yr. $21/yr. Circ.: 12,000. Dave Thompson, Editor. **Description:** For sheep and wool farmers across the U.S. and Canada. How-tos, flock owner stories, and industry news. **Nonfiction:** Articles, to 1,500 words, on successful shepherds, woolcrafts, sheep raising, sheep dogs; 800-1,500 words; $80-$125. **Art:** Yes. **Tips:** "We are especially interested in people who raise sheep successfully as a sideline enterprise." **Queries:** Preferred. **E-Queries:** No. **Unsolicited mss:** Accepts. **Response:** 1 month, SASE. **Freelance Content:** 50%. **Payment:** On acceptance.

SMALL FARM TODAY
3903 W Ridge Trail Rd., Clark, MO 65243-9525. 573-687-3525.
E-mail: smallfarm@socket.net. Web site: www.smallfarmtoday.com. Bimonthly. $4.95/$23.95. Circ.: 12,000. Ron Macher, Editor. **Description:** A "how-to" magazine of alternative and traditional crops, livestock, and direct marketing, to help farmers make their operations profitable and sustainable. **Nonfiction:** Stories about a specific

crop, livestock, or marketing method, with how-to and budget information; 1,000-1,800 words; $.35/word. **Tips:** Readers prefer alternative sustainable methods over traditional chemical farming. Sample copy $3. **Queries:** Preferred. **E-Queries:** Yes. **Unsolicited mss:** Accepts. **Response:** Queries 2 months, submissions 4 months, SASE. **Freelance Content:** 40%. **Rights:** 1st. **Payment:** On publication.

SMALL FARMER'S JOURNAL

P.O. Box 1627, Sisters, OR 97759-1627. 541-549-2064.
E-mail: agrarian@smallfarmersjournal.com. Web site: www.smallfarmersjournal.com.
Quarterly. $8.50/$30 yr. Circ.: 18,000. Mr. Lynn R. Miller, Editor. **Description:** Covers practical farming for families who own small farms—natural farming, stock raising, alternative farm research, and research on horses and horsedrawn equipment sales. **Nonfiction:** How-tos, humor, practical work-horse information, livestock and produce marketing, gardening, and articles for the independent family farm. Pay varies. **Tips:** Write of your own farm experiences. Avoid use of chemicals. **Queries:** Not necessary. **E-Queries:** Yes. **Unsolicited mss:** Accepts. **Response:** 3 months, SASE. **Freelance Content:** 50%. **Rights:** 1st. **Payment:** On publication.

SUCCESSFUL FARMING

Meredith Corp., 1716 Locust St., Des Moines, IA 50309-3023. 515-284-2853.
Web site: www.agriculture.com. Monthly. $15/yr. Circ.: 475,000. Loren Kruse, Editor-in-Chief. **Description:** Magazine for farmers and ranchers. Articles focus on successful family farms/businesses (all sizes, all types) that illustrate positive aspects. **Art:** Color transparencies preferred; pay varies. **Tips:** "Provide ideas families can take right to the barn, shop, office, home, and heart to add value to their lives. Measure new practices and trends with dollar signs. Use examples and have multiple sources." **Queries:** Preferred. **E-Queries:** No. **Unsolicited mss:** Accepts. **Response:** 2-7 days, SASE required. **Freelance Content:** 20%. **Rights:** All. **Payment:** On acceptance. **Contact:** Gene Johnston, Managing Editor.

WALLACES FARMER

6200 Aurora Ave., Suite 609E, Urbandale, IA 50322. 515-278-7782.
E-mail: fholdmeyer@farmprogress.com. Web site: www.wallacesfarmer.com. 15 issues/year. Circ.: 60,000. Frank Holdmeyer, Editor. **Description:** Provides Iowa farmers with useful information that helps them profitably manage their farming operations. **Nonfiction:** Articles on methods and equipment; interviews; 600-700 words. **Queries:** Required. **E-Queries:** Yes. **Unsolicited mss:** Accepts. **Freelance Content:** 1%. **Payment:** On acceptance.

THE WESTERN PRODUCER

P.O. Box 2500, 2310 Millar Ave.
Saskatoon, Saskatchewan S7K 2C4 Canada. 306-665-3544.
E-mail: newsroom@producer.com. Web site: www.producer.com. Brenda Washburn.
Description: On agricultural and rural subjects, preferably Canadian slant. Articles 600 words or less; $.23/word. Color photos $60-$100. **Payment:** On publication.

ANIMALS & PETS

AKC GAZETTE
American Kennel Club, Inc.
260 Madison Ave., New York, NY 10016. 212-696-8321.
E-mail: gazette@akc.org. Web site: www.akc.org. Monthly. $29.93/yr. Circ.: 60,000.
Erika Mansourian, Features Editor. **Description:** Official journal for the sport of purebred dogs. Articles, 1,000-2,500 words, for serious breeders, exhibitors, and judges; pays $250-$600. **Queries:** Preferred. **Payment:** On acceptance.

AMERICAN FIELD
542 S Dearborn St., Suite 1350, Chicago, IL 60605. 312-663-9797.
E-mail: amfieldedit@att.net. Web site: www.americanfield.com. 50x/yr. $49/yr. Circ.: 8,000. B.J. Matthys, Managing Editor. **Description:** Short items and anecdotes on hunting dogs and field trials for bird dogs. Yarns on hunting trips, bird-shooting; articles, to 1,500 words, on dogs and field trials, emphasizing conservation of game resources. Pay varies. **Payment:** On acceptance.

ANIMAL PEOPLE
P.O. Box 960, Clinton, WA 98236, 360-579-2505.
E-mail: anmlpepl@whidbey.com. Web site: www.animalpeoplenews.org. 10x/yr. Circ.: 15,000. Merritt Clifton, Editor. **Description:** Leading independent newspaper providing original investigative coverage of animal protection worldwide. **Nonfiction:** Articles and profiles, of individuals of positive accomplishment, in any capacity that benefits animals or illustrates the intrinsic value of other species. **Tips:** No fiction or poetry. No stories about atrocities, essays on why animals have rights, or material that promotes animal abuse (hunting, fishing, trapping, and slaughter). **Queries:** Preferred. **Payment:** On acceptance.

ANIMALS
Massachusetts Society for the Prevention of Cruelty to Animals
350 S Huntington Ave., Boston, MA 02130. 617-522-7400.
Web site: www.mspca.org/animals. Quarterly. $15/year. Circ.: 50,000. Paula Abend, Editor. **Description:** Full-color publication with timely, reliable, provocative coverage of wildlife issues, pet-care topics, and animal protection concerns. **Nonfiction:** Informative, well-researched articles, to 2,500 words. **Columns, Departments:** Profiles, 800 words, on individuals who work to make life better for animals, wild or domestic, or to save habitat. Reviews, 300-500 words. **Tips:** "We do not accept personal accounts or favorite pet stories." **Queries:** Required. **E-Queries:** No. **Unsolicited mss:** Accepts. **Response:** 6 weeks, SASE required. **Freelance Content:** 90%. **Payment:** On acceptance.

APPALOOSA JOURNAL
2720 W Pullman Rd., Moscow, ID 83843.
E-mail: rhendrickson@appaloosa.com. Web site: www.appaloosajournal.com.

Description: Official publication of the Appaloosa Horse Club covering all aspects of the breed, from breeding and training to showing and racing. **Nonfiction:** Articles, 1,000-2,000 words, on breeders, trainers, specific training methods, influential horses, youth and non-pro competitors, breed history, trail riding, and artists using Appaloosas as subjects. Pay varies. **Payment:** On publication.

AQUARIUM FISH

Fancy Publications, Inc.
P.O. Box 6050, Mission Viejo, CA 92690. 949-855-8822.
E-mail: aquariumfish@fancypubs.com. Web site: www.animalnetwork.com/fish. Monthly. $24.97/yr. Circ.: 75,000. Russ Case, Editor. **Description:** On all types of freshwater, saltwater, and pond fish. **Nonfiction:** Articles (with or without color transparencies); 2,500 words; pay varies. **Tips:** No "pet fish" stories. Send SASE for photo or writer guidelines. **E-Queries:** Yes. **Payment:** On publication.

THE BACKSTRETCH

United Throroughbred Trainers of America
P.O. Box 7065, Louisville, KY 40257-0065. 502-893-0025.
E-mail: bstretch@infi.net. Web site: www.thebackstretch.com. Bimonthly. $25/yr. Circ.: 10,000. Amy Bramblette, Editor. **Description:** Publication for the thoroughbred industry. **Nonfiction:** Feature articles, with photos, on subjects related to thoroughbred horse racing. **Payment:** On publication.

THE BARK

2810 Eighth St., Berkeley, CA 94710.
E-mail: submissions@thebark.com. Web site: www.thebark.com. Quarterly. **Description:** "We pay homage to the age-old relationship between our two species. We seek to bring our readers a literate and entertaining approach to dog-centric articles and stories." Short stories, essays, and articles run 1,200 words; pay varies. **Tips:** Essay tributes to dogs that have died are discouraged with the exception of tribute section on Web site. **Response:** 8-12 months. **Payment:** On publication.

BIRD TALK

Fancy Publications, Inc.
P.O. Box 6050, Mission Viejo, CA 92690. 949-855-8822.
E-mail: birdtalk@fancypubs.com. Web site: www.animalnetwork.com/birds. Monthly. $29.79/yr. Circ.: 160,000. Melissa Kauffman, Editor. **Description:** Articles for pet bird owners (care and feeding, training, safety, outstanding personal adventures, exotic birds in their native countries, profiles of celebrities' pet birds, travel to bird parks or shows). **Nonfiction:** Good transparencies a plus; pays to $.10/word. **Queries:** Required. **Payment:** On publication.

CAT FANCY

Fancy Publications, Inc.
P.O. Box 6050, Mission Viejo, CA 92690. 949-855-8822.

Web site: www.catfancy.com. Monthly. $25.97/yr. Circ.: 303,000. Bridget C. Johnson, Editor. **Description:** Covers cat care, health, and culture. Articles, 1,200-1,500 words; $200-$400. **Queries:** Required. **Response:** SASE required. **Payment:** On publication.

DOG FANCY

Fancy Publications, Inc.

P.O. Box 6050, Mission Viejo, CA 92690-6050. 949-855-8822.

E-mail: dogfancy@fancypubs.com. Web site: www.animalnetwork.com/dogs. Monthly. $27.97/yr. Circ.: 286,000. Allen Reznik, Editor-in-Chief. **Description:** On the care and enjoyment of all dogs, purebreds and mixed breeds. Readers are college-educated, middle-class adults interested in dog training, health, behavior, activities, and general care. **Nonfiction:** Well-written, well-researched articles on dog care, health, grooming, breeds, activities, and events; 850-1,200 words; pay varies. **Art:** Quality color slides or photos. **Tips:** No poetry, fiction, or articles in which the dog speaks as if human. Avoid tributes to dogs that have died or to beloved family pets. **Queries:** Required. **Unsolicited mss:** Does not accept. **Freelance Content:** 80%. **Payment:** On publication.

DOG WORLD

Fancy Publications, Inc.

3 Burroughs, Irvine, CA 92618. 949-855-8822.

Web site: www.dogworldmag.com. Monthly. $28/yr. Circ.: 60,000. Allen Reznik, Editor. **Description:** For breeders, exhibitors, hobbyists, and professionals in kennel operations, veterinary medical research, grooming, legislation, show awards, training, and dog sports. **Nonfiction:** 1,500-5,000 words; pay varies. **Columns, Departments:** 1,000 words. **Tips:** Written for the serious enthusiast. Seeking in-depth science, training, and health stories. Only one human-interest piece per issue; no poetry or fiction. **Queries:** Preferred. **E-Queries:** Yes. **Unsolicited mss:** Accepts. **Response:** 4-6 months, SASE. **Freelance Content:** 25%. **Rights:** 1st. **Payment:** On publication.

EQUUS

PRIMEDIA Enthusiast Group

656 Quince Orchard Rd., Suite 600, Gaithersburg, MD 20878-1409. 301-977-3900. E-mail: equuslts@aol.com. Web site: www.equusmagazine.com. Monthly. $24/yr. Circ.: 148,000. Laurie Prinz, Editor. **Description:** On all breeds of horses, covering their health and care as well as the latest advances in equine medicine and research. Articles run 1,000-3,000 words; $100-$400. **Tips:** "Speak as one horseperson to another." **Payment:** On publication.

FERRETS

Fancy Publications, Inc.

P.O. Box 6050, Mission Viejo, CA 92690. 949-855-8822.

E-mail: ferrets@fancypubs.com. Web site: www.ferretsmagazine.com. Bimonthly.

Description: "The ultimate guide for today's ferret owner." Articles on ferret behavior, training, health care, nutrition, legal issues, and developments in the ferret community. **E-Queries:** Yes.

THE FLORIDA HORSE
Florida Thoroughbred Breeders and Owners Assn.
801 SW 60th Ave., Ocala, FL 34474. 352-732-8858.
Web site: www.thefloridahorse.com. Michael Compton, Editor-in-Chief. **Description:** On Florida thoroughbred breeding and racing. Also veterinary articles, financial articles, topics of general interest to horse owners and breeders. Articles run 1,500 words; $200-$300. **Queries:** Preferred. **Payment:** On publication.

FRESHWATER AND MARINE AQUARIUM
144 West Sierra Madre, P.O. Box 487, Sierra Madre, CA 91025-0487. 626-355-6415.
E-mail: dondewey@msn.com. Web site: www.mag-web.com. Monthly. $22.00/yr.
Circ.: 53,000. Don Dewey, Publisher/Editor. **Description:** For tropical-fish enthusiasts. **Nonfiction:** How-to articles, varying lengths, on basic, semi-technical, and technical aspects of freshwater and marine aquariology; pays $50-$350. **Fillers:** $25-$75.

GREYHOUND REVIEW
See full listing in Business category.

GUN DOG
PRIMEDIA Enthusiast Group
6420 Wilshire Blvd., Suite 14, Los Angeles, CA 90048-5502. 323-782-2316.
E-mail: gundog@primedia.com. Bimonthly. $24.97/yr. Circ.: 49,000. Rick Van Etten, Editor. **Description:** On bird hunting (how-tos, where-tos, dog training, canine medicine, breeding strategy). Some fiction, humor. **Nonfiction:** Features, 1,000-2,500 words, with photos; $250-$550. **Payment:** On acceptance.

HORSE ILLUSTRATED
Fancy Publications, Inc.
P.O. Box 6050, Mission Viejo, CA 92690. 949-855-8822.
E-mail: horseillustrated@fancypubs.com. Web site: www.animalnetwork.com/horses. Monthly. $3.50. Circ.: 200,000. Moira C. Harris, Editor. **Description:** For horse owners, covers all breeds, all disciplines. Also, medical care, training, grooming, how-to, and human interest. **Nonfiction:** How-to (horse care/owning horses), training (English and Western); to 2,000 words; $300-$400. **Fillers:** Humor, $50-$75. Cartoons and spot art, $40. **Art:** Illustrations, $100 and up. Photos (slides preferred), $60-$90, $200 for cover. **Tips:** "Our readers are mostly women, ages 18-40, who ride and show for pleasure and are concerned about well-being of their horses." **Queries:** Preferred. **E-Queries:** Yes. **Unsolicited mss:** Accepts. **Response:** 3-6 weeks, SASE required. **Freelance Content:** 15-20%. **Rights:** FNAR. **Payment:** On publication.

HORSE & RIDER
See full listing in Sports & Recreation/Outdoors category.

THE HORSEMEN'S YANKEE PEDLAR
83 Leicester St., North Oxford, MA 01537. 508-987-5886.
E-mail: editorial@pedlar.com. Web site: www.pedlar.com. Monthly. $18/yr. Circ.: 25,000. Molly Johns, Editor. **Description:** About horses and horsemen in the Northeast. **Nonfiction:** News and feature-length articles, with photos; $.06/word. **Payment:** On publication.

I LOVE CATS
16 Meadow Hill Ln., Armonk, NY 10504. 908-222-0990.
E-mail: yankee@izzy.net. Web site: www.iluvcats.com. Bimonthly. Circ.: 50,000. Lisa Allmendinger, Editor. **Description:** All about cats. **Fiction:** 500-1,000 words. **Nonfiction:** Features, to 1,000 words; pays $40-$125. **Art:** $300 for cover, $50 for inside shots. **Tips:** "We're always looking for interesting cat-related stories." **Queries:** Preferred. **Payment:** On publication.

MODERN FERRET
P.O. Box 1007, Smithtown, NY 11787. 516-781-5080.
E-mail: mary@modernferret.com. Web site: www.modernferret.com. Bimonthly. $27.95/yr. Mary R. Shefferman, Editor. **Description:** Articles for ferret owners, by ferret owners. **Columns, Departments:** Pet ferret care. Personal experience with ferrets, training and grooming tips, medical/health (by vets or vet technicians). Also some fiction and poetry. **Tips:** "We're open to everything on living with pet ferrets."

MUSHING
See full listing in Sports & Recreation/Outdoors category.

PERFORMANCE HORSE
2895 Chad Dr., P.O. Box 7426, Eugene, OR 97401. 541-341-6508.
E-mail: betsylynch@performancehorse.com. Web site: www.performancehorse.com. Monthly. $24.95/yr. Circ.: 15,000. Betsy Lynch, Editor. **Description:** Seeks to help high-level western performance horse breeders, owners, trainers, and competitors to excel in the sports of cutting, reining, and working cow-horses. **Nonfiction:** Training, breeding, management, competitive strategies, how-to; for reining, cutting, and working cow-horse competition; 500-3,000 words; to $500. **Art:** Photos to accompany feature stories and articles; 35mm or larger prints or slides; to $50. **Queries:** Preferred. **E-Queries:** Yes. **Unsolicited mss:** Accepts. **Response:** 4-6 weeks, SASE. **Freelance Content:** 80%. **Rights:** FNASR. **Payment:** On publication.

PET BUSINESS
See full listing in Business category.

PETLIFE
3451 Boston Ave., Fort Worth, TX 76116-6330. 817-560-6100.
E-mail: awilson@mmgweb.com. Web site: www.petlifeweb.com. Bimonthly. $3.95/$19.99. Circ.: 120,000. Alexis Wilson, Editor. **Description:** For pet owners and enthusiasts. **Nonfiction:** On pet health care and nutrition, training, interviews, products, humor, and general interest; 100-1,500 words; payment varies. **Columns, Departments:** Pet Health, Vet Perspective, Odd Pets, Celebrity Interviews; 100-1,000 words; payment varies. **Tips:** "The majority of our audience is women, and they are truly pet lovers. We keep our stories positive—we're animal advocates, but we stay away from political issues. We seek ways to better care for animal companions; heartwarming stories about human/animal bond." **Queries:** Required. **E-Queries:** Yes. **Unsolicited mss:** Does not accept. **Response:** 3-4 weeks. **Freelance Content:** 80%. **Rights:** Worldwide. **Payment:** On publication.

PRACTICAL HORSEMAN
See full listing in Sports & Recreation/Outdoors category.

THE RETRIEVER JOURNAL
2779 Aero Park Dr., P.O. Box 968, Traverse City, MI 49685. 231-946-3712.
E-mail: editor@villagepress.com. Web site: www.retrieverjournal.com. Bimonthly. $25.95/yr. Circ.: 16,000. Steve Smith, Editor. **Description:** On topics of interest to hunting retriever owners and breeders. **Nonfiction:** Articles, 1,500-2,200 words; pays $250 and up. **Queries:** Preferred.

TROPICAL FISH HOBBYIST
211 W Sylvania Ave., Neptune, NJ 07753. 732-988-8400.
E-mail: editor@tfh.com. Web site: www.tfh.com. Monthly. $3.95/issue. Circ.: 65,000. Mary Sweeney, Editor. **Description:** Covers tropical fish and aquariums. **Nonfiction:** For beginning and experienced tropical and marine fish enthusiasts; 2,500 words; $100-$250. **Fillers:** Cartoons (¼ page vertical); $25. **Queries:** Not necessary. **E-Queries:** Yes. **Unsolicited mss:** Accepts. **Response:** 60 days, SASE. **Freelance Content:** 50%. **Rights:** All. **Payment:** On acceptance.

THE WESTERN HORSEMAN
P.O. Box 7980, Colorado Springs, CO 80933-7980. 719-633-5524.
E-mail: edit@westernhorseman.com. Web site: www.westernhorseman.com. Monthly. $22/yr. Circ.: 230,000. A.J. Mangum, Editor. **Description:** On the care and training of horses; farm, ranch, and stable management; health care and veterinary medicine. Articles run 1,500 words, pays to $800. Include photos with submission. **Payment:** On acceptance.

YOUNG RIDER
See full listing in Juvenile category.

ARTS & ARCHITECTURE
(For music, dance, etc., see Performing Arts)

AIRBRUSH ACTION
See full listing in Hobbies, Crafts, Collecting category.

THE AMERICAN ART JOURNAL
730 Fifth Ave., New York, NY 10019-4105. 212-541-9600.
E-mail: aaj@kgny.com. Web site: www.kgny.com. Annual. $35.00/issue. Circ.: 2,000.
Jayne A. Kuchna, Editor-in-Chief. **Description:** American art of 17th through mid-20th centuries. **Nonfiction:** Scholarly articles; 2,000-10,000 words; $200-$500.
Payment: On acceptance.

AMERICAN INDIAN ART
7314 E Osborn Dr., Scottsdale, AZ 85251-6401. 480-994-5445.
Quarterly. $20/yr. Circ.: 25,000. Roanne P. Goldfein, Editorial Director.
Description: Detailed articles on American Indian arts: painting, carving, beadwork, basketry, textiles, ceramics, jewelry, etc. Articles run 6,000-7,000 words; pay varies.
Queries: Preferred. **Response:** 6 weeks. **Rights:** FNAR. **Payment:** On publication.

ARCHITECTURE
770 Broadway, New York, NY 10003-9522. 646-654-5766.
E-mail: info@architecturemag.com. Web site: www.architecturemag.com. Monthly.
$42/yr. Circ.: 67,000. Chris Sullivan, Editor-in-Chief. **Description:** On architectural design and culture. **Nonfiction:** Articles on architecture, building technology, professional practice; up to 2,000 words; $.50/word. **Queries:** Preferred.

ART & ANTIQUES
2100 Powers Ferry Rd., Atlanta, GA 30339. 770-955-5656.
E-mail: editor@artantiquesmag.com. Web site: www.artandantiques.net. 11x/yr.
$5/$39.95. Circ.: 170,000. Barbara S. Tapp, Editor. **Description:** For lovers of fine art and antiques. **Nonfiction:** Research articles, art and antiques in context (interiors), overviews, personal narratives; 150-1,200 words; $1/word. **Tips:** Query with resume and clips. **Queries:** Preferred. **E-Queries:** Yes. **Unsolicited mss:** Accepts.
Response: 1-2 months. **Freelance Content:** 90%. **Payment:** On acceptance.
Contact: Patti Verbanas, Managing Editor.

ART PAPERS
P.O. Box 5748, Atlanta, GA 31107-5748.
E-mail: editor@artpapers.org. Web site: www.artpapers.org. 6x/yr. $7/$35. Circ.:
20,000. Charles Reeve, Editor-in-Chief. **Description:** Southeastern review of regional, national, and international contemporary art. **Nonfiction:** In-depth analyses, readable by the general public, of recent art. Accepts discussions or profiles of individual artists, as well as observations of recent trends; 2,500-3,000 words; $200.
Also accepts exhibition reviews; 600-800 words; $40. **Columns, Departments:**

Artist profiles, career advice, collector profiles, book reviews, music news, etc. 1,100 words; $100. **Tips:** "Review section emphasizes (but is not limited to) important regional artists who have not found national/international audience." **Queries:** Preferred. **E-Queries:** Yes. **Unsolicited mss:** Accepts. **Response:** 1 month, SASE required. **Freelance Content:** 95%. **Payment:** 30 days after publication.

ART-TALK

P.O. Box 8508, Scottsdale, AZ 85252-8508. 480-948-1799.
E-mail: arttalked@hotmail.com. 9x/yr. $18. Circ.: 40,000. John Jarvis, Editor.
Description: A fine-art publication, for the collector. **Nonfiction:** Articles, fillers; pay varies. **Payment:** On acceptance.

THE ARTIST'S MAGAZINE

F&W Publications, Inc.
4700 E Galbraith Rd., Cincinnati, OH 45236. 513-531-2690.
E-mail: tamedit@fwpubs.com. Web site: www.artistsmagazine.com. Monthly. $3.99/$19.96. Circ.: 250,000. Sandra Carpenter, Editor. **Description:** Written by artists for artists. Offers instruction for professional success, on painting techniques, media and materials, design and composition, problem solving, special effects, marketing, and other business topics. **Nonfiction:** Specific art instruction (e.g., "Behind the Scenes," from start to finish: master the elements to improve your watercolor landscapes); 1,200-1,500 words; $300-$500. **Columns, Departments:** Color Corner (e.g., "Paint It Black," get those tubes of black paint out of the closet and use them to improve your paintings); 900-1,200 words; $200-$300. **Art:** Art-related cartoons; $65. **Tips:** "Best opportunities include: Artist's Life and Business columns. Writers must be able to write from the artist's viewpoint, using the language of art." **Queries:** Preferred. **E-Queries:** No. **Unsolicited mss:** Accepts. **Response:** 90 days, SASE required. **Freelance Content:** 80%. **Rights:** FNASR. **Payment:** On publication. **Contact:** Tom Zeit, Senior Editor.

BLACKLINES

2011 Newkirk Ave., Suite 7D, Brooklyn, NY 11226. 718-703-8000.
E-mail: kathleen@blacklines.net. Web site: www.blacklines.net. Quarterly. Scott Louis, Managing Editor. **Description:** Showcases black designers in architecture, interior design, construction, development, and the arts. Challenges traditional ideas and perceptions, offers context for design and means to exchange ideas and information. **Tips:** Send cover letter and resume, with 2-5 clips that show ability to interview diverse subjects. **Queries:** Preferred. **E-Queries:** Yes. **Unsolicited mss:** Accepts.

CAMERA ARTS

P.O. Box 2328, Corrales, NM 87048. 505-899-8054.
E-mail: camartsmag@aol.com. Web site: www.cameraarts.com. Bimonthly. $22/yr. Circ.: 18,000. Tim Anderson, Managing Editor. **Description:** The art and craft of photography in the 21st century. Articles run 1,000-2,000 words; $.25/word. **Tips:** "Before you write about a photographer, send us a query with samples of his/her art-

work first. If you are a new writer, please send us samples or clips of previous pieces you have written." **Queries:** Required. **E-Queries:** Yes. **Unsolicited mss:** Accepts. **Response:** 2-8 weeks, SASE required. **Freelance Content:** 80%. **Rights:** FNAR. **Payment:** On publication.

CLAY TIMES
15481 Second St., P.O. Box 365, Waterford, VA 20197. 540-882-3576. E-mail: claytimes@aol.com. Web site: www.claytimes.com. Bimonthly. $5.95/$26. Circ.: 20,000. Polly Beach, Editor. **Description:** Pottery information for students, teachers, professionals, and hobbyists. **Nonfiction:** Seeks features on wheel-throwing, handbuilding, glazing, firing, marketing, health/safety, artist profiles, and how-to articles with step-by-step instructions; 1,000-1,500 words; $75. **Art:** Submit high-quality artwork/photos with how-to articles. Photos should illustrate a series of steps. **Tips:** "All submissions should be targeted at clay artists of all levels. Assume the reader has no knowledge of the topic you are writing about." **Queries:** Preferred. **E-Queries:** Yes. **Unsolicited mss:** Accepts. **Response:** 1 month, SASE required. **Freelance Content:** 80%. **Rights:** Exclusive. **Payment:** On publication.

THE COMICS JOURNAL
Fantagraphics Books, Inc.
7563 Lake City Way NE, Seattle, WA 09115-4218. 206-524-1967. E-mail: milo@tcj.com. Web site: www.tcj.com. Monthly. $25/5 issues. Circ.: 9,000. Gary Groth, Editor. **Description:** Covers the comics medium as an art form. An eclectic mix of industry news, interviews, criticism, and reviews. Articles run 200-2,000 words; $.04/word. **Queries:** Preferred. **E-Queries:** Yes. **Unsolicited mss:** Accepts. **Response:** 1-2 months, SASE required. **Freelance Content:** 95%. **Payment:** On publication.

CONTEMPORARY STONE & TILE DESIGN
210 Route 4 East, Suite 311, Paramus, NJ 07652. 201-291-9001. E-mail: michael@stoneworld.com. Web site: www.stoneworld.com. Quarterly. $29.95/yr. Circ.: 15,000. Michael Reis, Editor Director/Associate Publisher. **Description:** On using stone in architecture and interior design. **Nonfiction:** Articles, 1,500 words; $6/column inch. **Art:** Photos or drawings. **Payment:** On publication.

DECORATIVE ARTIST'S WORKBOOK
See full listing in Hobbies, Crafts, Collecting category.

DOUBLETAKE
55 Davis Square, Somerville, MA 02144. 617-591-9389. E-mail: dtmag@doubletakemagazine.org. Web site: www.doubletakemagazine.org. Quarterly. $19/yr. Circ.: 40,000. Robert Coles, Editor. **Description:** Fiction, poetry, and photography devoted to revealing "extraordinary events and qualities found in everyday lives of Americans and others." **Fiction:** Realistic fiction in all its variety.

Nonfiction: Narrative reporting or personal essays distinguished by documentary, literary, aesthetic, or reportorial excellence. **Poetry:** Yes. **Art:** Photos. **Queries:** Not necessary. **E-Queries:** No. **Unsolicited mss:** Accepts. **Response:** 3 months, SASE. **Freelance Content:** 90%. **Rights:** 1st worldwide English-language serial. **Payment:** On publication.

FIBERARTS
See full listing in Hobbies, Crafts, Collecting category.

LOG HOME DESIGN IDEAS
See full listing in Home & Garden category.

PHOTO LIFE
One Dundas St. W, Suite 2500, Toronto, Ontario M5G 1Z3 Canada. 418-692-2110. E-mail: editor@photolife.com. Web site: www.photolife.com. 6x/yr. $3.95/$19.75. Circ.: 55,000. Darwin Wiggett, Anita Dammer, Editors. **Description:** The art, culture, and science of photography. **Nonfiction:** Photo techniques, trade information, new equipment, technology, etc. **Tips:** "Writers can break into our market by providing high-quality photography with articles. Our general theme is promoting photography as a universal language—a higher form of self-expression." **Queries:** Preferred. **E-Queries:** Yes. **Unsolicited mss:** Does not accept. **Response:** 1-2 months, SASE. **Freelance Content:** 100%. **Rights:** FNAR. **Payment:** On publication. **Contact:** Nicole Richard, Assistant Editor.

POPULAR PHOTOGRAPHY
Hachette Filipacchi Magazines
1633 Broadway, Fl. 43, New York, NY 10019. 212-767-6000.
E-mail: popeditor@aol.com. Web site: www.popphoto.com. Monthly. $19.94/yr. Circ.: 450,000. Jason Schneider, Editor. **Description:** For serious amateur photographers. **Nonfiction:** Illustrated how-to articles, 500-2,000 words. **Art:** With all photos, submit technical data (camera used, lens, film, shutter speed, aperture, lighting, etc.) to show how picture was made; Varies. **Tips:** "We're interested in new, unusual phases of photography not covered previously. No general articles." **Queries:** Required. **Payment:** On acceptance.

PROFESSIONAL PHOTOGRAPHER
Professional Photographers of America, Inc.
229 Peachtree St. NE, Suite 2200 International Tower
Atlanta, GA 30303. 404-522-8600.
E-mail: cbishopp@ppa.com. Web site: www.ppmag.com. Monthly. $27/yr. Circ.: 24,000. **Description:** Since 1907, for professional photographers engaged in all types of photography.

SCULPTURE
International Sculpture Center
1529 18th St. NW, Washington, DC 20036. 202-234-0555.
E-mail: sculpt@dgsys.com. Web site: www.sculpture.org. Monthly. $45/yr. Circ.: 25,000. Glenn Harper. **Description:** Published by International Sculpture Center. Articles on sculpture, sculptors, collections, books, criticism, technical processes, etc. **Nonfiction:** Pay varies. **Queries:** Preferred. **Unsolicited mss:** Accepts.

SOUTHWEST ART
5444 Westheimer, Suite 1440, Houston, TX 77056. 713-296-7900.
E-mail: southwestart@southwestart.com. Web site: www.southwestart.com. Monthly. $5.99/$32.00. Circ.: 65,000. Kristin Bucher, Editor. **Description:** For collectors of Western art (about the West or created, exhibited, or sold in the West). Provides artist profiles and gallery/museum events. **Nonfiction:** On artists, collectors, exhibitions, events, dealers, history, trends in Western American art. Most interested in representational or figurative arts. 1,400 words; $600. **Queries:** Preferred. **E-Queries:** No. **Unsolicited mss:** Accepts. **Response:** Queries/submissions 4 months, SASE. **Freelance Content:** 70%. **Rights:** Exclusive worldwide. **Payment:** On acceptance.

SUNSHINE ARTIST MAGAZINE
3210 Dade Ave., Orlando, FL 32804. 407-228-9772.
E-mail: editor@sunshineartist.com. Web site: www.sunshineartist.com. Monthly. $34.95/yr. Circ.: 20,000. Bill Sievert, Editor. **Description:** Covers national outdoor art shows, fairs, festivals. Business, education, and art-show focus. **Tips:** Sample issue $8. **E-Queries:** Yes.

U.S. ART
220 S Sixth St., Suite 500, Minneapolis, MN 55402. 612-339-7571.
E-mail: tmccormick@mspmag.com. 6x/yr. $32.95/yr. Circ.: 50,000. Tracy McCormick, Editor. **Description:** For collectors of reproductions, original prints, and paintings. **Nonfiction:** Features and artist profiles; 1,200 words; $300-$600. **Queries:** Required. **Payment:** On acceptance.

WATERCOLOR
770 Broadway, New York, NY 10003-9522. 646-654-5506.
E-mail: mail@myamericanartist.com. Web site: www.myamericanartist.com. Quarterly. $23.95/yr. Circ.: 80,000. M. Stephen Doherty, Editor. **Description:** Features and articles on watercolor and other water media (gouache, casein, acrylic, etc.). Length and pay varies. **Queries:** Preferred. **Payment:** On publication.

WEST ART
198 Hillmont Ave., P.O. Box 6868, Auburn, CA 95604-6868. 530-885-0969.
Semimonthly. $16/yr. Circ.: 4,000. Martha Garcia, Editor. **Description:** Tabloid

magazine featuring fine arts and crafts. **Nonfiction:** Features, 700-800 words. No hobbies; $.50/column inch. **Art:** Photos. **Queries:** Preferred. **Rights:** All. **Payment:** On publication.

ASSOCIATIONS

AOPA PILOT
See full listing in Aviation category.

CATHOLIC FORESTER
355 Shuman Blvd., P.O. Box 3012, Naperville, IL 60566-7012. 630-983-4900. E-mail: cofpr@aol.com. Web site: www.catholicforester.com. Quarterly. Circ.: 97,000. Mary Anne File, Editor. **Description:** Full-color, with organizational news, general interest, fiction, and some nonfiction articles for members. **Fiction:** Humor, children, inspirational; 500-1,500 words; $.30/word. **Nonfiction:** Health, fitness, parenting, financial; 500-1,500 words; $.30/word. **Poetry:** Inspirational, religious; 25-50 words; $.30/word. **Queries:** Does not accept. **Unsolicited mss:** Accepts. **Response:** 8 weeks, SASE required. **Freelance Content:** 20%. **Rights:** FNAR. **Payment:** On acceptance. **Contact:** Patricia Baron, Associate Editor.

COLUMBIA
One Columbus Plaza, New Haven, CT 06510. 203-772-2130. E-mail: tim.hickey@kofc-supreme.com. Web site: www.kofc.org. Monthly. $6/yr. Circ.: 1,600,000. Tim S. Hickey, Editor. **Description:** Published by the Knights of Columbus, the world's largest Catholic family fraternal service organization. Articles on current events, societal trends, parenting and family life, finances, and Catholic practice and teachings. **Nonfiction:** Articles on topics of interest to members, their families, and the Catholic layman. Topics include current events, religion, education, art, etc. 500-1,500 words; to $600. **Tips:** Sample copies and guidelines available. **Queries:** Required. **E-Queries:** Yes. **Response:** 2 weeks, SASE required. **Freelance Content:** 80%. **Payment:** On acceptance.

ELKS
425 West Diversey Parkway, Chicago, IL 60614. 773-755-4900. E-mail: elksmag@elks.org. Web site: www.elks.org/elksmag/. 10x/year. Circ.: 1,100,000. Fred D. Oakes, Editor. **Description:** General interest magazine published by the Elks fraternal organization. Typical reader is over 40 with an above-average income and living in a town of 500,000 or less. **Nonfiction:** Authoritative articles (please include sources) for lay person, varied topics: technology, science, sports, history, seasonal. Accepts material related to membership or lodge events; 1,500-2,500 words; $.20/word. **Art:** Cover art; slides, transparencies; $25 per photo. **Tips:** No fiction, travel, business, health, political, or religious material, humor, fillers, or poetry. Do not send queries or clips. **Queries:** Not necessary. **E-Queries:** No. **Unsolicited mss:** Accepts. **Response:** Queries 1 week, submissions 1-6 weeks, SASE required. **Freelance Content:** 30%. **Rights:** FNASR. **Payment:** On acceptance.

HARVARD MAGAZINE

7 Ware St., Cambridge, MA 02138-4037. 617-495-5746.
Web site: www.harvardmagazine.com. Bimonthly. $4.95/$30. Circ.: 225,000. John Rosenberg, Editor. **Description:** Articles and profiles on Harvard faculty, staff, students, and alumni. Also, features on research and teaching being conducted in this educational community. **Nonfiction:** Profiles and examples of work and research; 800-10,000 words; $300-$2,000. **Queries:** Required. **E-Queries:** Yes. **Unsolicited mss:** Accepts. **Response:** 1-2 weeks, SASE required. **Freelance Content:** 50%. **Rights:** One-time. **Payment:** On publication.

KIWANIS

3636 Woodview Trace, Indianapolis, IN 46268-3196. 317-875-8755.
E-mail: cjonak@kiwanis.org. Web site: www.kiwanis.org. 10x/yr. $2/issue. Circ.: 240,000. Chuck Jonak, Managing Editor. **Description:** Service organization that supports children and young adults around the world. **Nonfiction:** Articles focus on a variety of topics, including family life, small business, international issues, community concerns, health/fitness, and the needs of children (especially under age 6). Also feature pieces relating to personal finance, technology, religion, education, and consumer trends. No travel pieces, interviews, or profiles; 1,500-2,000 words; $400-$1,000. **Tips:** Read sample copy before submitting. "We consider submissions based on two criteria; 1) They should have an overall subject or scope, versus relating to a specific individual, place, or event. 2) They should be applicable to the lives of KIWANIS members and readers." **Queries:** Preferred. **E-Queries:** Yes. **Unsolicited mss:** Accepts. **Response:** Queries 3-4 weeks, submissions 2-4 weeks, SASE required. **Freelance Content:** 40%. **Rights:** First. **Payment:** On acceptance.

THE LION

300 W 22nd St., Oak Brook, IL 60523-8815. 630-571-5466.
E-mail: rkleinfe@lionsclub.org. Web site: www.lionsclubs.org. 10x/yr. $6/issue. Circ.: 510,000. Robert Kleinfelder, Senior Editor. **Description:** Published by Lions Clubs International, reflecting service activities for men and women interested in voluntary community service. **Nonfiction:** Primarily photo stories of Lion's service activities; 300-2,000 words; $300-$600. **Fillers:** Family-oriented humor; 500-1,000 words; $300-$500. **Tips:** No political, religious, or autobiographical topics. **Queries:** Preferred. **E-Queries:** Yes. **Unsolicited mss:** Accepts. **Response:** 1-3 weeks, SASE required. **Freelance Content:** 20%. **Rights:** All. **Payment:** On acceptance.

MODERN WOODMEN

1701 First Ave., P.O. Box 2005, Rock Island, IL 61204-2005. 309-786-6481.
E-mail: jweaver@modern-woodmen.org. Web site: www.modern-woodmen.org. Quarterly. Circ.: 400,000. Gloria Bergh, Editor. **Description:** Publication for members of Modern Woodmen of America, a fraternal financial services provider. **Fiction:** Stories that promote family, patriotism, and volunteerism; 1,000 words; $100-$500. **Nonfiction:** On positive family and community life, community service, patriotism, and financial well-being; 1,000 words; $100-$500. **Tips:** Readers mostly

middle-class, with children in the home. **Queries:** Not necessary. **E-Queries:** No. **Response:** 4-8 weeks. **Freelance Content:** less than 5%. **Rights:** One-time. **Payment:** On acceptance. **Contact:** Jill Weaver, Assistant Editor.

OPTIMIST
4494 Lindell Blvd., St. Louis, MO 63108. 314-371-6000.
E-mail: magazine@optimist.org. Web site: www.optimist.org. Dena Hull, Editor. **Description:** On activities of local Optimist Clubs, and techniques for personal and club success. **Nonfiction:** Articles, to 1,000 words; pays from $100. **Queries:** Preferred. **Payment:** On acceptance.

ROTARIAN
One Rotary Center, 1560 Sherman Ave., Evanston, IL 60201-3698. 847-866-3000.
E-mail: chamberjl@rotaryinc.org. Web site: www.rotary.org. Monthly. $12. Circ.: 500,000. Vince Aversano, Editor-in-Chief. **Description:** Personal and business interests for Rotary members (international understanding, goodwill and peace, vocational relationships, community life, human relationships). **Nonfiction:** Business, travel, health, education, environment, management and ethics, sciences, sports, and adventure. **Columns, Departments:** Executive Health, Book Review, Trends, Manager's Memo, Earth Diary. **Queries:** Preferred. **Unsolicited mss:** Accepts. **Contact:** Janice Chambers, Managing Editor.

SCOUTING
Boy Scouts of America
1325 W Walnut Hill Ln., P.O. Box 152079, Irving, TX 75015-2079. 972-580-2367.
Web site: www.scoutingmagazine.org. 6x/yr. **Description:** Covers successful program activities conducted by or for Cub Scout packs, Boy Scout troops, and Venturing crews. Also includes features on winning leadership techniques/styles, profiles of outstanding individual leaders, and first-person inspirational accounts of Scouting's impact on an individual, either as a youth or while serving as a volunteer adult leader. **Nonfiction:** Short features, 500-700 words, $300-$500; longer features, up to 1,200 words, $650-$800. **Tips:** "Most stories are staff-written or assigned to professional writers. We rely heavily on regional writers to cover an event or activity in a particular part of the country." No fiction or poetry. **Queries:** Required. **Unsolicited mss:** Does not accept. **Response:** 3 weeks, SASE required. **Rights:** FNAR. **Payment:** On acceptance.

THE TOASTMASTER
Toastmasters International
P.O. Box 9052, Mission Viejo, CA 92690-9052. 949-858-8255.
E-mail: tminfo@toastmasters.org. Web site: www.toastmasters.org. Monthly. Circ.: 180,000. Suzanne Frey, Editor. **Description:** On public speaking, leadership, and communication skills. **Nonfiction:** Articles on decision making, leadership, language, interpersonal and professional communication, humor, logical thinking, rhetorical devices, public speaking, profiles of great orators, etc. Payment negotiable upon

acceptance; 700-2,200 words. **Tips:** Do not send unsolicited manuscripts via e-mail. **Queries:** Preferred. **E-Queries:** Yes. **Unsolicited mss:** Accepts. **Response:** 3-4 months. **Rights:** All. **Payment:** On acceptance.

VFW
406 W 34th St., Kansas City, MO 64111. 816-756-3390.
E-mail: pbrown@vfw.org. Web site: www.vfw.org. Monthly. $15/yr. Circ.: 1,800,000. Richard K. Kolb, Editor. **Description:** Focuses on military history and issues relating to veterans and the military. **Nonfiction:** Articles on current foreign policy and defense, along with all veterans' issues; 1,000 words. **Tips:** Write with clarity and simplicity, concrete detail and short paragraphs. Use active voice, and avoid flowery prose and military jargon. **Queries:** Preferred. **Unsolicited mss:** Accepts. **Rights:** FNASR. **Payment:** On publication.

WOODMEN
1700 Farnam St., Omaha, NE 68102. 402-342-1890.
E-mail: wow@woodmen.com. Web site: www.woodmen.com. Scott J. Darling, Editor. **Description:** On history, insurance, family, health, science, fraternal lodge activities, etc. **Nonfiction:** Articles; pay is negotiable. **Art:** Photos. **Queries:** Preferred. **Payment:** On acceptance.

AUTOMOTIVE

AMERICAN MOTORCYCLIST
American Motorcyclist Assn.
13515 Yarmouth Dr., Pickerington, OH 43147. 614-856-1900.
E-mail: ama@ama-cycle.org. Web site: www.amadirectlink.com. Monthly. $10/yr. Circ.: 245,700. Bill Wood, Editor. **Description:** Articles and fiction, to 3,000 words, on motorcycling: news coverage, personalities, tours. **Nonfiction:** Pay varies. **Art:** Photos. **Queries:** Preferred. **Response:** SASE required. **Payment:** On publication.

AUTOMOBILE QUARTERLY
137 E Market St., New Albany, IN 47150.
E-mail: editor@autoquarterly.com. Web site: www.autoquarterly.com.
Quarterly. Tracy Powell, Managing Editor. **Description:** Journal of automotive history targeting serious enthusiasts and collectors. **Tips:** Prefers hard copy of query with clips. "Please study back issues for desired style and required depth before querying. AQ does not repeat specific marque treatments, so studying previous coverage is important." Sample copy $10. **Queries:** Required. **E-Queries:** Yes. **Freelance Content:** 85%.

AUTOMUNDO
2960 SW Eighth St., Fl. 2, Miami, FL 33135. 305-541-4198.
E-mail: editor@automundo.com. Web site: www.automundo.com. Monthly. $19.95.

Circ.: 50,000. Ernesto Lanata, Editor. **Description:** Spanish-language publication for auto fans. Articles on makes, models, scenic drives, the latest technology, and more.

CAR AND DRIVER
Hachette Filipacchi Media US, Inc.
2002 Hogback Rd., Ann Arbor, MI 48105-9795. 734-971-3600.
E-mail: editors@caranddriver.com; spence1cd@aol.com. Web site: www.caranddriver.com. Monthly. $21.94/yr. Circ.: 1,300,000. Csaba Csere, Editor-in-Chief.
Description: "Car and Driver is mostly staff-written, but we're always looking to develop feature writers for non-product pieces—profiles, weird events, little-known historical pieces on auto related subjects." **Nonfiction:** To 2,500 words. **Tips:** Query with 2 clips. **Queries:** Required. **E-Queries:** Yes. **Unsolicited mss:** Does not accept. **Freelance Content:** 5%. **Payment:** On acceptance. **Contact:** Steve Spence, Managing Editor.

CAR CRAFT
PRIMEDIA Enthusiast Group
6420 Wilshire Blvd. 9th Fl., Los Angeles, CA 90048-5502. 323-782-2000.
E-mail: carcraft@primediacmmg.com. Web site: www.carcraft.com. Monthly. $19.94/yr. Circ.: 375,186. Matt King, Editor-in-Chief. **Description:** Covers high-performance street machines, drag cars, and racing events. Also includes technical pieces and action photos. **Nonfiction:** Articles and photo-features; pays from $150/page. **Payment:** On publication.

CC MOTORCYCLE NEWS
P.O. Box 808, Nyack, NY 10960-0808. 845-353-6686.
E-mail: info@motorcyclenews.cc. Web site: www.motorcyclenews.cc. Monthly. $20/yr. Circ.: 60,000. Mark Kalan, Editor. **Description:** Motorcycles news, travel, technology, and entertainment. **Fiction:** About motorcycles or on sport of motorcycling, in a positive manner; 1,200 words; $10. **Nonfiction:** Motorcycle themes; up to 2,500 words; $50-$150. **Poetry:** Poems with a positive theme and tone; $10. **Fillers:** Humorous stories; $10. **Columns, Departments:** Technical on the sport of motorcycling; 800 words; $75-$100. **Tips:** Don't submit "I used to ride but . . ." stories. **E-Queries:** Yes. **Unsolicited mss:** Accepts. **Response:** 60 days, SASE. **Freelance Content:** 10%. **Rights:** All. **Payment:** On publication.

CYCLE WORLD
1499 Monrovia Ave., Newport Beach, CA 92663-2752. 949-720-5300.
E-mail: dedwards@hfmag.com. Web site: www.cycleworld.com. Monthly. $21.94/yr. Circ.: 312,000. David Edwards, Editor-in-Chief. **Description:** News items on the motorcycle industry, legislation, and trends. Technical and feature articles for motorcycle enthusiasts; 1,500-2,500 words; $100-$200/page. **Queries:** Preferred. **Payment:** On publication.

DRIVER
Volkswagen of America
Mail Code 3C03, 3800 Hamlin Rd., Auburn, MI 48326.
Web site: www.vw.com/owners/magazine. Marlene Goldsmith, Editor. **Description:** For Volkswagen owners: profiles of well-known personalities; inspirational or human-interest pieces; travel; humor; German travel. **Nonfiction:** Articles, 600-1,200 words; pays $300. **Fillers:** Anecdotes, to 100 words, about Volkswagen owners' experiences; humorous photos of current model Volkswagens. Pays $100. **Art:** Photos. **Queries:** Preferred. **Payment:** On acceptance.

EASYRIDERS
28210 Dorothy Dr., P.O. Box 3000, Agoura Hills, CA 91376-3000. 818-889-8740. Web site: www.easyriders.com. Monthly. $39.95. Circ.: 211,500. Dave Nichols, Editor. **Description:** Hard-hitting, rugged fiction, 1,200-2,000 words, that depicts bikers in a favorable light; humorous bent preferred. Pays $.10-$.25/word. **Payment:** On acceptance.

HOT BIKE
PRIMEDIA Enthusiast Group
2400 E Katella Ave. Suite 1100, Anaheim, CA 02806-5945. 714-939-2400. E-mail: hot.bike@primedia.com. Web site: www.hotbikeweb.com. Monthly. $20.95. Circ.: 49,732. Howard Kelly, Editor. **Description:** On Harley-Davidson motorcycles (contemporary and antique). Event coverage on high-performance street and track and sport touring motorcycles, with emphasis on Harley-Davidsons. Geographical motorcycle features. **Nonfiction:** Articles, 250-2,500 words, with photos; pays $50-$100/printed page. **Payment:** On publication.

HOT ROD
PRIMEDIA Enthusiast Group
6420 Wilshire Blvd., Los Angeles, CA 90048-5502. 323-782-2280.
E-mail: hotrod@primediacmmg.com. Web site: www.hotrod.com. Monthly. $3.99/$12. Circ.: 805,035. David Freiburger, Editor-in-Chief. **Description:** Publication for automotive enthusiasts. Articles on street machines, rods, customs, engine buildups, nostalgia, and recent trends. **Nonfiction:** How-tos and articles on auto mechanics, hot rods, track and drag racing. Photo-features on custom or per-formance-modified cars; $300-$500/page. **Tips:** "Our freelance content is limited. Writers need either a deep sense of automotive history or hands-on technical know-how." **Queries:** Required. **E-Queries:** Yes. **Unsolicited mss:** Accepts. **Response:** SASE required. **Freelance Content:** 10%. **Rights:** All.

MOTOR TREND
PRIMEDIA Enthusiast Group
6420 Wilshire Blvd., Los Angeles, CA 90048-5515. 323-782-2220.
E-mail: motortrend@primedia.com. Web site: www.motortrend.com. Monthly. $23.94/yr. Circ.: 1,285,000. Kevin Smith, Editor. **Description:** On autos, auto history,

racing, events, and profiles. **Nonfiction:** Articles, 250-2,000 words, photos required; pay varies. **Queries:** Preferred. **Payment:** On acceptance.

MOTORCYCLIST
PRIMEDIA Enthusiast Group
6420 Wilshire Blvd., Los Angeles, CA 90048. 323-782-2230.
E-mail: mcmail@primediacmmg.com. Monthly. $11.97. Circ.: 500,000. Mitch Boehm, Editor-in-Chief. **Description:** Features in-depth information for motorcycle enthusiasts. Includes technical how-to stories, riding tips, gear information, motorcycle tests, and useful bike-buying advice. Purpose is for readers to maximize their riding experience. **Nonfiction:** Articles with photos; 1,000-3,000 words; $150-$300/published page. **Payment:** On publication.

OLD CARS WEEKLY
Krause Publications, Inc.
700 E State St., Iola, WI 54990. 715-445-4612.
E-mail: vanbogarta@krause.com. Web site: www.oldcarsweekly.com. Weekly. $39.98/yr. Circ.: 76,700. Angelo Van Bogart, Associate Editor. **Description:** On the hobby of collectible cars and trucks (restoration, researching, company histories, collector profiles, toys, etc.). **Nonfiction:** Features, to 2,000 words; pays $.03/word. **Art:** Photos to accompany articles; $5/photo. **Queries:** Preferred.

OPEN WHEEL
3816 Industry Blvd., P.O. Box 7157, Lakeland, FL 33807-7157. 863-644-0449. Monthly. $31. Circ.: 165,000. Doug Auld, Editor. **Description:** On open-wheel drivers, races, and vehicles. **Nonfiction:** Articles, to 6,000 words; pays to $400. **Art:** Photos. **Payment:** On publication.

RIDER
2575 Vista Del Mar Dr., Ventura, CA 93001-3920. 805-667-4100.
Web site: www.ridermagazine.com. Monthly. $11.98/yr. Circ.: 140,000. Mark Tuttle Jr., Editor. **Description:** Covers travel, touring, commuting, and camping motorcyclists **Nonfiction:** to 2,000 words; $100-$750. **Art:** Color slides. **Tips:** Editorial guidelines available upon request. **Queries:** Required. **Response:** SASE. **Payment:** On publication.

STOCK CAR RACING MAGAZINE
PRIMEDIA Enthusiast Group
3816 Industry Blvd., Lakeland, FL 33811-1340. 863-644-0449.
E-mail: scrbackfire@primedia.com. Web site: www.stockcarracing.com. Monthly. $12. Circ.: 257,296. David Bourne, Editor. **Description:** For oval-track enthusiasts. **Nonfiction:** Technical automotive pieces, and profiles of interesting racing personalities. Articles on stock car drivers, races, and vehicles; up to 6,000 words; pay varies. **Payment:** On publication.

WOMAN RIDER MAGAZINE
6420 Sycamore Ln., Maple Grove, MN 55369. 513-932-5461.
E-mail: womanrider1@aol.com. Web site: www.riderreport.com. Quarterly. Circ.: 40,000. Genevieve Schmitt, Editor. **Description:** National motorcycle magazine aimed at women. Focus is on the lifestyle side of motorcycling from a female point of view. **Tips:** Seeks people who are motorcyclist journalists who can write a mostly third-person point of view. First-person stories are rarely used. Submit query with bio. **Queries:** Required.

AVIATION

AIR LINE PILOT
Air Line Pilots Assn.
P.O. Box 1169, Herndon, VA 20172-1169. 703-481-4460.
E-mail: magazine@alpa.org. Web site: www.alpa.org. 10x/yr. $32/yr. Circ.: 85,000.
J. Gary DiNunno, Editor-in-Chief. **Description:** For airline pilots, on industry news, air safety, technology, and other issues related to the piloting profession. **Nonfiction:** Technical articles for airline pilots. Popular topics are pilot training and health issues; 2,000-6,000 words; $200-$600. **Art:** Submit slides, prints, or negatives. Accepts hi-res digital images on CD (300 dpi) or low-res images via e-mail (for review only). Pays $100-$250 for inside photos; $450 for cover. "We try to show members at work on our covers." **Tips:** "Our readers are professional airline pilots and the magazine reflects their interests, concerns, and labor union policies. Therefore our editorial content requires accuracy, knowledge, and an extensive background in piloting." **Queries:** Preferred. **E-Queries:** Yes. **Unsolicited mss:** Accepts. **Response:** 1-2 weeks. **Freelance Content:** 20%. **Rights:** All. **Payment:** On acceptance.

AOPA PILOT
Aircraft Owners and Pilots Assn.
421 Aviation Way, Frederick, MD 21701. 301-695-2350.
E-mail: pilot@aopa.org. Web site: www.aopa.org. Monthly. $5.00/issue. Circ.: 390,000. Thomas B. Haines, Editor. **Description:** Nation's leading general aviation magazine. Department and features for private aircraft owners and pilots. Length varies, usually 1,000-1,500 words. **Tips:** Include telephone and/or fax numbers, and your AOPA membership number with all submissions. Do not send original art or manuscripts. "We're looking for articles relating to personal flight stories in which a lesson was learned, personal profiles of pilots, and pieces that depict an adventurous destination. Emphasis on aeronautical themes is preferred. Avoid subject matter relating to aviation history." **Queries:** Preferred. **E-Queries:** No. **Unsolicited mss:** Accepts. **Payment:** On publication.

AVIATION HISTORY
PRIMEDIA Enthusiast Group
741 Miller Dr. SE, Suite D-2, Leesburg, VA 20175-8994. 703-771-9400.

E-mail: aviationhistory@thehistorynet.com. Web site: www.thehistorynet.com/aviationhistory. Bimonthly. $23.95/yr. Circ.: 62,500. Arthur H. Sanfelici, Editor. **Description:** On aeronautical history. **Nonfiction:** Articles, 3,500-4,000 words, with 500-word sidebars and excellent illustrations. **Columns, Departments:** 2,000 words; pays $150-$300. **Queries:** Preferred. **Payment:** On publication.

BUSINESS & COMMERCIAL AVIATION
See full listing in Trade & Technical category.

GENERAL AVIATION NEWS
P.O. Box 39099, Lakewood, WA 98439-0099. 253-471-9888.
E-mail: janice@generalaviationnews.com. Web site: www.generalaviationnews.com. Biweekly. Circ.: 35,000. Janice Wood, Editor. **Description:** Of interest to "general aviation" pilots. **Nonfiction:** 500-2,500 words; to $3/column inch (about 40 words). **Art:** $10 for B&W photos; $50 for color photos. **Freelance Content:** 30%. **Payment:** Within 1 month of publication.

PLANE & PILOT
12121 Wilshire Blvd., Suite 1200, Los Angeles, CA 90025-1175. 310-820-1500.
E-mail: editors@planeandpilotmag.com. Web site: www.planeandpilotmag.com. Monthly. $16.95/yr. Circ.: 110,000. Lyn Freeman, Editor. **Description:** Aviation-related articles, for pilots of single-engine, piston-powered recreational airplanes. **Nonfiction:** Training, maintenance, travel, equipment, pilot reports. Occasional features on antique, classic, and kit- or home-built aircraft; 1,500-2,500 words; pay varies. **Queries:** Preferred. **Payment:** On publication.

PRIVATE PILOT
265 S Anita Dr., Suite 120, Orange, CA 92868-3310. 714-939-9991.
E-mail: bfedork@aol.com. Web site: www.privatepilotmag.com. Monthly. $3.99/issue $21.95/year. Circ.: 60,000. Bill Fedorko, Editorial Director. **Description:** General aviation, for pilots and owners of single and multi-engine aircraft, who want to read about places to go, aircraft, and ways to save money. **Nonfiction:** Fly-in destinations, hands-on, how-to, informative articles for pilots, aircraft owners, and aviation enthusiasts; 1,500-3,000 words; $400-$700. **Art:** $300 fee for photography assignments. **Queries:** Preferred. **E-Queries:** No. **Unsolicited mss:** Accepts. **Response:** 2-4 weeks, SASE. **Freelance Content:** 80%. **Rights:** FNAR. **Payment:** On publication.

BUSINESS

ACCESSORIES
185 Madison Avenue, Fl. 5, New York, NY 10016. 212-686-4412.
E-mail: irenka@busjour.com. Web site: www.busjour.com. Monthly. $35. Circ.: 20,229. Irenka Jakubiak, Editor-in-Chief. **Description:** Illustrated articles, for women's fash-

ion-accessories buyers and manufacturers. **Nonfiction:** Profiles of retailers, designers, manufacturers; articles on merchandising and marketing. Pays $75-$200 (short articles), $200-$500 (features). **Queries:** Preferred. **Payment:** On publication.

ACROSS THE BOARD
845 Third Ave., New York, NY 10022-6679. 212-339-0214.
E-mail: atb@conference-board.org. Web site: www.acrosstheboardmagazine.com.
6x/yr. $59/yr. Circ.: 35,000. A.J. Vogl, Editor. **Description:** Features in-depth articles on business-management and social-policy issues for senior managers of global companies. Presents fresh business ideas and sharp opinions from business management experts. **Nonfiction:** Articles are thought-provoking and cover the most recent topics in business and management; 1,000-3,500 words; pay varies. **Tips:** "Do not send highly technical pieces nor simple "how-to" pieces on business or market strategy. We prefer pieces that present new ideas that are applicable to real business." **Queries:** Preferred. **E-Queries:** Yes. **Unsolicited mss:** Accepts. **Response:** Queries 2-3 weeks. **Freelance Content:** 70%. **Rights:** FNAR. **Payment:** On acceptance. **Contact:** Vadim Liberman, Assistant Editor.

ALASKA BUSINESS MONTHLY
501 Northern Lights Blvd. Suite 100
P.O. Box 241288, Anchorage, AK 99524-1288. 907-276-4373.
E-mail: info@akbizmag.com. Web site: www.akbizmag.com. Monthly. $3.95/$21.95.
Circ.: 10,000. Debbie Cutler, Editor. **Description:** For Alaskans and other audiences interested in the business affairs of the 49th State. **Nonfiction:** Thorough, objective analysis of issues and trends affecting Alaskan businesses; 500-2,500 words; $100-$300. **Art:** 35mm photos; pay varies. **Tips:** Query first, Alaska business topics only. Avoid generalities, need to be specific for this market. **Queries:** Preferred. **E-Queries:** Yes. **Unsolicited mss:** Accepts. **Response:** 1 month. **Freelance Content:** 80%. **Rights:** All. **Payment:** On publication.

ALTERNATIVE ENERGY RETAILER
P.O. Box 2180, Waterbury, CT 06722-2180. 203-755-0158.
E-mail: griffin@aer-online.com. Web site: www.aer-online.com. Monthly. $36/yr.
Circ.: 14,000. Michael Griffin, Editor. **Description:** For retailers of hearth products (appliances that burn wood, coal, pellets, and gas, also accessories and services). **Nonfiction:** Articles address topics related to the hearth manufacturing and retail industry; 1,500 words. **Art:** Accepts charts, tables, and photographs to illustrate articles. **Tips:** "Articles should focus on the hearth industry, but should not mention the author's company." **Queries:** Preferred. **Payment:** On publication.

AMERICAN BANKER
One State St. Plaza, Fl. 26, New York, NY 10004. 212-803-8200.
E-mail: david.longobardi@tfn.com.Web site: www.americanbanker.com. Daily.
$795/yr. Circ.: 14,600. David Longobardi, Editor-in-Chief. **Description:** Articles,

1,000-3,000 words, on banking and financial services, technology in banking, consumer financial services, investment products. Pay varies. **Queries:** Preferred. **Payment:** On publication.

THE AMERICAN SALESMAN

320 Valley St., Burlington, IA 52601. 319-752-5415.
Monthly. $60.55/yr. Circ.: 1,500. Teresa Levinson, Editor. **Description:** For company sales reps. Articles on techniques to increase sales (case histories or public-relations articles). **Nonfiction:** Sales seminars, customer service, closing sales, competition, phone usage, managing territory, new sales concepts; 900-1,200 words. **Tips:** Freelance content limited. **Queries:** Preferred. **Unsolicited mss:** Does not accept.

ART BUSINESS NEWS

One Park Avenue, New York, NY 10016-5802. 212-951-6646.
Web site: www.artbusinessnews.com. 12x/yr. $43/yr. Circ.: 32,000. Julie Keller, Editor-in-Chief. **Description:** For art dealers and framers, on trends and events of national importance to the art and framing industry, and relevant business subjects. **Nonfiction:** Articles; 1,000 words; pay varies. **Queries:** Preferred. **Payment:** On publication.

BARRON'S

Dow Jones & Company, Inc.
200 Liberty St., New York, NY 10281-0099. 212-416-2700.
E-mail: editors@barrons.com. Web site: www.barrons.com. Weekly. $145/yr. Circ.: 290,955. Edwin A. Finn Jr., President/Editor. **Description:** Provides information on such topics as investments, financial portfolios, industrial developments, market analysis, and electronic investing. **Queries:** Preferred. **Contact:** Richard Rescigno, Managing Editor.

BARTENDER

P.O. Box 158, Liberty Corner, NJ 07938. 908-766-6006.
E-mail: barmag@aol.com. Web site: www.bartender.com. Quarterly. $25. Circ.: 148,225. Jaclyn W. Foley. **Description:** On liquor and bartending for bartenders, tavern owners, and owners of restaurants with full-service liquor licenses. **Nonfiction:** General interest, how-to pieces, new products or bartending techniques, interviews, descriptions of unique or interesting bars; 100-1,000 words; $50-$200. **Fillers:** Humor, news, anecdotes; 25-100 words; $5-$25. **Columns, Departments:** 200-1,000 words; $50-$200. **Art:** 8x10 color or B&W glossy prints. **Unsolicited mss:** Accepts. **Response:** 2 months. **Freelance Content:** 100%. **Rights:** FNAR. **Payment:** On publication.

BICYCLE RETAILER AND INDUSTRY NEWS

25431 Cabot Rd., Suite 204, Laguna Hills, CA 92653. 949-206-1677.
E-mail: msani@bicycleretailer.com. Web site: www.bicycleretailer.com. 18x/yr. $45.

Circ.: 13,000. Marc Sani, Publisher; Michael Gamstetter, Editor-in-Chief. **Description:** On employee management, employment strategies, and general business subjects for bicycle manufacturers, distributors, and retailers. Articles, to 1,200 words; pays $.20/word (higher rates by assignment). **Queries:** Preferred. **Payment:** On publication.

BLACK ENTERPRISE MAGAZINE
See full listing in Ethnic & Multicultural category.

BOATING INDUSTRY INTERNATIONAL
13 Century Hill Dr., Latham, NY 12110-2113. 518-783-1281.
E-mail: info@boating-industry.com. Web site: www.boating-industry.com. Bimonthly. $38/yr. Circ.: 23,700. Humphrey Tyler, Editor-in-Chief. **Description:** On recreational marine products, management, merchandising, and selling, for boat dealers and marina owners/operators. **Nonfiction:** Articles; 1,000-2,500 words; pay varies. **Art:** Photos. **Queries:** Preferred. **Payment:** On publication. **Contact:** Liz Walz, Executive Editor.

BOXOFFICE
155 S El Molino Ave., Suite 100, Pasadena, CA 91101, 626-396 0250.
E-mail: editorial@boxoffice.com. Web site: www.boxoffice.com. Monthly. $40/yr. Circ.: 8,000. Kim Williamson, Editor-in-Chief. **Description:** Business magazine for the movie theater industry. **Nonfiction:** Interviews, profiles, new products, technical information, and other topics in the movie theater industry; 800-2,500 words; $.10/word. **Columns, Departments:** Insights on business of movie theaters; 600 words. **Art:** Captions required; 8x10 B&W prints; $10 maximum. **Tips:** Do not submit pieces that cover gossip or celebrity news. Content must cover the real issues and trends facing this industry. Submit proposal with resume and clip samples. **Queries:** Preferred. **E-Queries:** Yes. **Unsolicited mss:** Accepts. **Response:** 1 month, SASE required. **Freelance Content:** 15%. **Rights:** All, including electronic. **Payment:** On publication. **Contact:** Christine James, Managing Editor.

BUSINESS START-UPS
2445 McCabe Way, Suite 400, Irvine, CA 92614.
E-mail: bsumag@entrepreneur.com. Web site: www.bizstartups.com. Karen E. Spaeder, Editor. **Description:** Entrepreneur's *BizStartUps*.com is an online magazine for Gen-X entrepreneurs who have started a business recently or plan to soon. **Nonfiction:** How-to, motivational/psychological, trend pieces, sales/marketing, technology, start-up money issues, management; 1,000 words; $400 and up. **Tips:** Send well-written queries with relevant clips. **Queries:** Required. **E-Queries:** Yes. **Unsolicited mss:** Does not accept. **Response:** 8-12 weeks, SASE or by e-mail. **Freelance Content:** 10%. **Rights:** FNASR. **Payment:** On acceptance.

BUSINESSWOMAN MAGAZINE

1900 M Street, Washington, DC 20036. 202-293-1100.
E-mail: businesswoman@bpwusa.org. Web site: www.bpwusa.org. Quarterly. $12/yr.
Circ.: 30,000. **Description:** Articles, varying lengths, of concern to working women.
Areas of interest: economic equity and security, business practices and management,
political activity, work life balance, and women in the workplace.

CHRISTIAN RETAILING

Strang Communications, Inc.
600 Rinehart Rd., Lake Mary, FL 32746. 407-333-0600.
E-mail: leech@strang.com. Web site: www.christianretailing.com. 20x/yr. $75/yr.
Circ.: 10,000. Larry J. Leech II, Editor. **Description:** Covers new products, trends
pertaining to books, music, video, children, and Spanish, and topics related to running
a profitable Christian retail store. **Nonfiction:** Features, 1,500-2,300 words; pays
$150-$400. **Payment:** On publication.

CLUB MANAGEMENT

107 W Pacific Ave., St. Louis, MO 63119-3776. 314-961-6644.
E-mail: avincent@finan.com. Web site: www.club-mgmt.com. Bimonthly. $21.95/yr.
Circ.: 16,702. Anne Marie Vincent, Editor. **Description:** For managers of private
clubs in U.S. and abroad. Provides information and resources for successful operations. **Nonfiction:** Construction/renovation profiles, insurance, technology, staffing
issues, golf-course design and maintenance, special events, maintenance, food/bever-
age trends, guest-room amenities, spa facilities, outsourcing; 1,500-2,000 words.
Columns, Departments: Sports, tax, law, management, membership marketing,
manager career perspectives, service, beverage/food trends, pools, entertainment;
1,200-1,600 words. **Tips:** "Must be targeted for the busy club manager, with informative, timely, relevant and challenging articles." **Queries:** Preferred. **E-Queries:** Yes.
Unsolicited mss: Accepts. **Response:** 2-3 weeks, SASE required. **Freelance
Content:** 40%. **Rights:** FNAR and electronic. **Payment:** On publication.

COLORADOBIZ

7009 S Potomac St., Suite 200, Englewood, CO 80112. 303-662-5283.
E-mail: rschwab@cobizmag.com. Web site: www.cobizmag.com. Monthly.
$3.95/$22.97. Circ.: 17,000. Robert Schwab, Editor. **Description:** Features articles
on business in Colorado. Readers are business owners and managers who work and
reside in Colorado. **Nonfiction:** Articles cover market analysis, economic trends,
forecasts, profiles, and individuals involved in business activities in Colorado; 650-
1,200 words; $50-$400. **Art:** Accepts original color transparencies, slides, and digital
art. Digital work should be scanned to 8x10, 300 dpi, CMYK in TIF format; pay
varies. **Tips:** Articles must target business in Colorado. Do not send general business
articles, book reviews, commentaries, syndicated work, humor, or poetry. **Queries:**
Required. **E-Queries:** Yes. **Payment:** On publication.

CONVENIENCE STORE NEWS
770 Broadway, New York, NY 10003-9522. 646-654-4500.
E-mail: jlofstock@csnews.com. Web site: www.csnews.com. 15x/yr. $72/yr. Circ.: 101,095. Claire Pumplin, Editor-in-Chief. **Description:** Articles cover the convenience store and petroleum marketing industry. Provides news, research, trends, and best-practice information to convenience store and petroleum chain executives, store owners and managers, suppliers, and distributors. **Nonfiction:** Features, news items. Pay negotiated; 750-1,200 words. **Art:** Photos; pay varies. **Queries:** Preferred. **Contact:** John Lofstock, Senior Editor.

CORPORATE GIFT REVIEW
815 Haines St., Jacksonville, FL 32206.
Quarterly. $19.95. Circ.: 5,000. Debra Paulk, Editor; Tonya Ringgold, Writer/Researcher, Editor. **Description:** Innovative tips and how-tos on sales, marketing, management, and operations. Focuses on business gifting. Hard data, stats and research requested. Readers are college-educated, successful business owners. **Tips:** "Avoid generalizations, basic content, and outdated theories." **Queries:** Not necessary. **E-Queries:** No. **Unsolicited mss:** Accepts. **Response:** 30 days, SASE required. **Freelance Content:** 50%. **Rights:** One-time. **Payment:** On publication.

COUNTRY BUSINESS
707 Kautz Rd., St. Charles, IL 60174. 630-377-8000.
E-mail: cbiz@sampler.emmis.com. Web site: www.country-business.com. Bimonthly. Circ.: 32,000. Susan Wagner, Editor. **Description:** For retailers of country gifts and accessories. Articles feature new products and trends in giftware markets and provide business and marketing advice. **Nonfiction:** Seeking business articles on small business management and retail (e.g. finance, legal, technology, marketing, management, etc); 800-1,800 words; pay varies. **Queries:** Preferred. **E-Queries:** Yes. **Unsolicited mss:** Accepts. **Response:** SASE required. **Freelance Content:** 60%. **Payment:** On acceptance.

CRAIN'S CHICAGO BUSINESS
360 N Michigan Ave., Chicago, IL 60601. 312-649-5411.
E-mail: editor@chicagobusiness.com. Web site: www.chicagobusiness.com. Weekly. Circ.: 50,500. Robert Reed, Editor. **Description:** Provides business owners, executives, professionals, and other consumers with articles covering the current news and analysis of the business community in the Chicago metro area.

CRAIN'S DETROIT BUSINESS
1400 Woodbridge Ave., Detroit, MI 48207. 313-446-0419.
E-mail: jmelton@crain.com. Web site: www.crainsdetroit.com. Weekly. $1.50/issue. Circ.: 38,000. Cindy Goodaker, Executive Editor. **Description:** Local business publication. **Columns, Departments:** Business articles about Detroit; 800 words. **Queries:** Required. **E-Queries:** Yes. **Payment:** On publication. **Contact:** James Melton, Assistant Managing Editor.

EMPLOYEE SERVICES MANAGEMENT

2211 York Rd., Suite 207, Oak Brook, IL 60523-2371. 630-368-1280.
E-mail: reneemula@esmassn.org. Web site: www.esmassn.org. 16x/yr. $52/yr. Circ.: 3,000. Renee Mula, Editor. **Description:** For human resource professionals, employee services professionals, and ESM members. Topics include recruitment and retention, becoming an employer of choice, work/life issues, employee services, wellness, management, and more. Articles run 1,200-2,500 words. **Tips:** Prefers to receive submissions via e-mail. **E-Queries:** Yes. **Payment:** In copies.

ENTREPRENEUR

2445 McCabe Way, Suite 400, Irvine, CA 92614. 949-261-2325.
E-mail: pbennett@entrepreneur.com. Web site: www.entrepreneur.com. Monthly. $15.97/yr. Peggy Bennett, Editor. **Description:** Features accurate, unbiased business information and innovative strategies for entrepreneurs. Covers all aspects of running and growing a successful business. **Nonfiction:** Articles and features should convey the voice of experience. Style should be informative, yet have an interesting flair. Primary purpose is to educate readers and include them in the business community. **Tips:** Read sample issues before submitting. Do not send complete manuscript. "If you're not a regular contributor, include a brief personal bio. Also include contact information so that readers may contact you. E-mail address is fine." **Queries:** Required. **Response:** 8 weeks. **Payment:** On acceptance.

ENTREPRENEUR.COM

2445 McCabe Way, Suite 400, Irvine, CA 92614. 949-261-2325.
E-mail: kspaeder@entrepreneur.com. Web site: www.entrepreneur.com. Karen Spaeder, Editor. **Description:** Online version *Entrepreneur* magazine. features accurate, unbiased business information and innovative strategies for entrepreneurs. Covers all aspects of starting, running, and growing a successful business. **Nonfiction:** Articles and features should convey the voice of experience. Style should be informative, yet have an interesting flair. Primary purpose is to educate readers and include them in the business community. 200-2,000 words. **Tips:** Read articles on the Web site before submitting. **Queries:** Required. **Response:** 8 weeks. **Payment:** On acceptance.

FLORIDA TREND

Trend Magazines, Inc., 490 First Ave. S, St. Petersburg, FL 33701. 727-821-5800.
E-mail: mhoward@floridatrend.com. Web site: www.floridatrend.com. Monthly. Mark R. Howard, Executive Editor. **Description:** Features articles and profiles on business, technology, the economy, etc., in the state of Florida. Targets businessmen and other professionals who work and reside in this region. **Queries:** Required. **Response:** SASE.

FLOWERS &

Teleflora, 11444 W Olympic Blvd., Los Angeles, CA 90064-1549. 310-966-3590.
E-mail: flowersand@teleflora.com. Monthly. $42. Circ.: 40,000. Bruce Wright,

Editor. **Description:** How-to information for retail florists. **Nonfiction:** Articles, 500-1,500 words; pays $.50/word. **Tips:** Send clips. **Queries:** Preferred. **Payment:** On acceptance.

GROWERTALKS

Ball Publishing, 335 N River St., P.O. Box 9, Batavia, IL 60510-0009. 630-208-9080. E-mail: beytes@growertalks.com. Web site: www.growertalks.com. Monthly. $29/yr. Circ.: 9,000. Chris Beytes, Editor. **Description:** Seeks to help commercial greenhouse growers (not florist/retailers or home gardeners) perform their jobs better. Covers trends, successes in new types of production, marketing, business management, new crops, and issues facing the industry. **Queries:** Preferred. **Payment:** On publication.

HARDWARE TRADE

PTS Marketing, Inc., P.O. Box 151, Hull, IA 51239-0151. 712-439-1962. E-mail: hdwtrade@hickorytech.net. Web site: www.hardwaretrade.com. Bimonthly. $24/yr. Circ.: 33,000. Russ Goold, Editor. **Description:** Magazine for hardware manufacturers, wholesalers, and dealers. The majority of readers are owners, but some are employed. Appreciates stories on unusual hardware and home center stores or promotions throughout the nation. Also features stories about people in the hardware business and general-interest stories on how readers might improve their businesses. **Nonfiction:** 800-1,000 words, no payment offered. **Queries:** Preferred.

HARVARD BUSINESS REVIEW

60 Harvard Way, Boston, MA 02163. 617-783-7410. E-mail: hbr_editorial@hbsp.harvard.edu. Web site: www.hbsp.harvard.edu. Monthly. Circ.: 249,000. Suzy Wetlaufer, Senior Executive Editor. **Description:** Articles cover a wide range of business-related topics such as leadership, strategy, manufacturing, and teamwork. Objective is to target senior-level managers or CEOs by offering innovative, strategic ideas for managing a large organization. **Nonfiction:** Articles are written by experts whose ideas and theories for business practice and management have been tested in the real world. **Tips:** Query should be a 3-4 page summary of proposed topic. Include your objective, intended audience, and credentials in proposal. Also describe the real-world application of your proposed idea. **Queries:** Required. **Response:** 6-8 weeks, SASE.

HEARTH & HOME

Village West Publishing, P.O. Box 1288, Laconia, NH 03247-2008. 603-528-4285. E-mail: mailbox@villagewest.com. Monthly. $36/yr. Circ.: 17,000. Richard Wright, Editor. **Description:** Profiles and interviews, with specialty retailers selling both casual furniture and hearth products (fireplaces, woodstoves, accessories, etc.). **Nonfiction:** 1,000-1,800 words; pays $150-$250. **Payment:** On acceptance.

HISPANIC BUSINESS

425 Pine Ave., Santa Barbara, CA 93117-3709.
E-mail: editorial@hbinc.com. Web site: www.hispanicbusiness.com. Monthly. $18/yr. Circ.: 250,000. Leslie Dinaberg, Managing Editor. **Description:** Features personalities, political agendas, and fascinating stories, with focus on technology and finance. Pays $350 (negotiable). **Tips:** "An ongoing need for experienced freelance writers with expertise and contacts in the Hispanic business market."

HISPANIC MARKET NEWS

13014 N Dale Mabry Hwy. #663, Tampa, FL 33618-2808. 813-264-0560.
Monthly. Circ.: 25,000. **Description:** For people involved with merchandising to Hispanic markets. Printed in both English and Spanish.

HOBBY MERCHANDISER

See full listing in Hobbies, Crafts, Collecting category.

HOMEBUSINESS JOURNAL

Steffen Publishing, 9584 Main St., Holland Patent, NY 13354. 800-756-8484.
E-mail: kim@homebusinessjournal.net. Web site: www.homebusinessjournal.net. Bimonthly. $18.96 (U.S.), $34 (Canada). Circ.: 50,000. Kim Lisi, Managing Editor. **Description:** National publication offering quality information and advice for readers in a home business, or those seriously interested in such work, to help them thrive and enjoy working at home. **Nonfiction:** Editorials pertaining to home-based business issues; financial, family, health, etc. 1,000 words; $75. **Tips:** Common mistake is to fail to note the difference in needs between small businesses and home businesses. Welcomes new writers. **Queries:** Required. **E-Queries:** Yes. **Unsolicited mss:** Accepts. **Response:** 4-6 weeks. **Rights:** FNASR. **Payment:** On publication.

HUMAN RESOURCE EXECUTIVE

LRP Publications Co.
747 Dresher Rd. Suite 500, P.O. Box 980, Horsham, PA 19044-0980. 215-784-0910.
E-mail: dshadovitz@lrp.com. Web site: www.hrexecutive.com. 16x/yr. David Shadovitz, Editor-in-Chief. **Description:** Profiles and case stories, for executives in the human-resource profession. Articles run 1,800-2,000 words; pay varies. **Queries:** Required. **Payment:** On acceptance.

INC.

Gruner + Jahr USA Publishing
38 Commercial Wharf, Boston, MA 02110. 617-248-8000.
E-mail: editors@inc.com. Web site: www.inc.com. 14x/yr. $5/$20. Circ.: 660,000. John Koten, Editor-in-Chief. **Description:** Business magazine focusing on small, rapidly growing, privately held companies. **Nonfiction:** Helpful how-to tips on how readers can grow and manage their companies; payment varies. **Tips:** "We look for stories that are not specific to only one industry. Don't write about products; write about managing the company." **Queries:** Preferred. **E-Queries:** No. **Unsolicited mss:** Accepts.

Response: 30 days; SASE required. **Freelance Content:** 3%. **Rights:** First serial. **Payment:** On publication.

INDUSTRY WEEK
The Penton Media Building, 1300 E Ninth St.
Cleveland, OH 44114-2543. 216-696-7000.
E-mail: tvinas@industryweek.com. Web site: www.industryweek.com. Monthly. Circ.: 233,000. Patricia Panchak, Editor-in-Chief. **Description:** Written for a senior-level management audience, on the challenges facing today's companies. **Nonfiction:** Articles on business, management, and executive leadership; 1,800-3,000 words; Pay varies. **Columns, Departments:** Executive Briefing, Emerging Technologies, Finance, Economic Trends. **Queries:** Required. **Rights:** All. **Payment:** On acceptance. **Contact:** Tonya Vinas, Managing Editor.

INSTANT & SMALL COMMERCIAL PRINTER
28100 North Ashley Circle, P.O. Box 7280, Libertyville, IL 60048. 847-816-7900.
E-mail: iscpmag@innespub.com. Web site: www.innespub.com. Monthly. Circ.: 47,787. Denise Lontz, Editor. **Description:** Covers small commercial and instant printing market. **Nonfiction:** Case histories, how-tos, technical pieces, small-business management; 1,000-5,000 words; pay negotiable. **Queries:** Preferred. **E-Queries:** Yes. **Unsolicited mss:** Accepts. **Response:** 1-6 months, SASE required. **Freelance Content:** 20%. **Payment:** On publication.

IQ MAGAZINE
170 W Tasman Dr., MS 8/2, San Jose, CA 95134.
E-mail: iq-editorial@cisco.com. Web site: www.cisco.com/go/iqmagazine. Bimonthly. Circ.: 83,000. Heather Alter, Editor-in-Chief. **Description:** Covers how Internet business strategies can help businesses be more successful: news, analysis, success stories, interviews, trends, resources, and more. **Tips:** "Review Web site for content, writing style, etc." **E-Queries:** Yes. **Unsolicited mss:** Does not accept.

LATIN TRADE
95 Merrick Way, Suite 600, Coral Gables, FL 33134. 305-358-8373.
E-mail: mzellner@latintrade-inc.com. Web site: www.latintrade.com. Monthly. Circ.: 110,000. Mike Zellner, Editor-in-Chief. **Description:** For business persons in Latin America. Covers a wide variety of topics relating to trade, markets, research, technology, and investments. Articles run 800-2,000 words; $200-$1,000. **Queries:** Required. **E-Queries:** Yes. **Unsolicited mss:** Does not accept. **Response:** Queries 2 weeks. **Freelance Content:** 55%. **Rights:** All. **Payment:** On publication.

LONG ISLAND BUSINESS NEWS
2150 Smithtown Ave., Ronkonkoma, NY 11779. 631-737-1700.
E-mail: carl.corry@libn.com. Web site: www.libn.com. Weekly. Circ.: 11,000. John Kominicki, Publisher. **Description:** Regional economic and business news, for the business and financial community of Nassau and Suffolk counties in New York.

Nonfiction: Finance, technology, health, travel, and the environment, for business professionals; $.20-$.30/word. **Tips:** Occasionally works with new writers. **Queries:** Preferred. **E-Queries:** Yes. **Response:** 2 weeks, SASE required. **Rights:** One-time. **Payment:** On publication. **Contact:** Peter Mantius, Editor.

MANAGE

National Management Assn.
2210 Arbor Blvd., Dayton, OH 45439-1580. 937-294-0421.
E-mail: nma@nma1.org. Web site: www.nma1.org. Quarterly. $5/issue. Circ.: 30,000. Doug Shaw, Editor-in-Chief. **Description:** Covers human resource development, team building, leadership skills, ethics in the workplace, law, compensation, and technology. **Nonfiction:** On management and supervision for first-line and middle managers; 600-1,000 words; $.05/word. **Fillers:** Business management/leadership related; 500-600 words. **Queries:** Not necessary. **E-Queries:** Yes. **Unsolicited mss:** Accepts. **Response:** Queries 3 months, SASE. **Freelance Content:** 60%. **Rights:** FNAR. **Payment:** On acceptance.

MARKETING NEWS

American Marketing Assn.
311 S Wacker Dr. Suite 5800, Chicago, IL 60606-6629. 312-542-9000.
E-mail: news@ama.org. Web site: www.marketingpower.com. Biweekly. $100/yr. Circ.: 30,000. Lisa M. Keefe, Editor. **Description:** Authoritative analysis of news, current trends, and application of developments in marketing profession; also, information on American Marketing Association. **Nonfiction:** Timely articles on advertising, sales promotion, direct marketing, telecommunications, consumer and business-to-business marketing, and market research; 800-1,200 words; $.80/word. **Tips:** Due to potential conflict of interest, no news stories written by marketing professionals. **Queries:** Preferred. **E-Queries:** Yes. **Unsolicited mss:** Does not accept. **Response:** Queries 6-8 weeks, submissions 2-4 months. **Freelance Content:** 30%. **Rights:** 1st, all media. **Payment:** On acceptance.

THE MEETING PROFESSIONAL

4455 LBJ Freeway, Suite 1200, Dallas, TX 75244-5903. 972-702-3000.
E-mail: publications@mpiweb.org. Web site: www.mpiweb.org. Monthly. $50 U.S., $69 outside U.S. Circ.: 30,000. **Description:** For meeting professionals. **Tips:** Works only with published writers familiar with the meetings industry. Submit query by e-mail; send resume and clips by mail (with SASE). **Queries:** Preferred. **E-Queries:** Yes. **Unsolicited mss:** Does not accept. **Response:** 2 weeks, SASE required. **Freelance Content:** 50%. **Rights:** All. **Payment:** On acceptance.

MODERN PHYSICIAN

Crain Communications, Inc.
360 N Michigan Ave., Fl. 5, Chicago, IL 60601. 312-649-5350.
E-mail: moddoc@crain.com. Web site: www.modernphysician.com. Monthly. $45/yr. Circ.: 31,500. Joseph Conn, Editor. **Description:** Covers business and management

news for physician executives. **Nonfiction:** Business stories about how medical practices are changing; 1,000-1,500 words; $.80-$1/word. **Tips:** No product or clinical stories. Welcomes new writers. Check online to see what has already been published. **Queries:** Required. **E-Queries:** Yes. **Unsolicited mss:** Accepts. **Response:** Varies, SASE required. **Freelance Content:** 30%. **Rights:** All. **Payment:** On acceptance.

MONEY

Time Life Building, Rockefeller Center, New York, NY 10020. 212-552-1212. E-mail: letters@mfmag.com. Web site: http://money.cnn.com. Monthly. $14.95. Circ.: 830,000. Norman Pearlstine, Editor-in-Chief. **Description:** Seeking writers experienced in covering mutual funds for the print media. Send resume and clips. **Queries:** Preferred.

NEEDLEWORK RETAILER

Yarn Tree Designs, P.O. Box 724, Ames, IA 50010. 515-232-3121. E-mail: info@yarntree.com. Web site: yarntree.com/nr.htm. Bimonthly. $12/yr. Circ.: 13,000. Megan Chriswisser, Editor. **Description:** For owners and managers of independent needlework retail stores. Covers new products, trends, and designs in the counted cross-stitch and needlework industry. Includes info on trade shows. **Nonfiction:** Profiles of shop owners; articles on a successful store event or promotion, 500-1,000 words; pay varies. **Payment:** On acceptance.

THE NETWORK JOURNAL

29 John St., Suite 1402, New York, NY 10038. 212-962-3791. E-mail: editors@tnj.com. Web site: www.tnj.com. Monthly. Circ.: 16,000. Rosalind McLymont, Editor. **Description:** Small-business, personal finance, and career management for African-American small-business owners and professionals. **Nonfiction:** Profiles of entrepreneurs; how-to pieces; articles on sales and marketing, managing a small business, and personal finance; 1,200-1,500 words; $150. **E-Queries:** Yes. **Freelance Content:** 25%. **Rights:** All. **Payment:** On publication.

NSGA RETAIL FOCUS

National Sporting Goods Assn.
1601 Feehanville Dr., Suite 300, Mt. Prospect, IL 60056-6035. 847-296-6742. E-mail: info@nsga.org. Web site: www.nsga.org. Bimonthly. Circ.: 2,500. Larry Weindruch, Editor. **Description:** Covers industry news, consumer trends, management, and store operations, and new product development for retailers, wholesalers, manufacturers. **Queries:** Required. **E-Queries:** Yes. **Unsolicited mss:** Does not accept. **Response:** Queries 1 week, SASE. **Freelance Content:** 15%. **Rights:** 1st and electronic. **Payment:** On publication.

PARTY & PAPER RETAILER

107 Mill Plain Rd., Suite 204, Danbury, CT 06811. 203-730-4090. E-mail: editor@partypaper.com. Web site: www.partypaper.com. Monthly. $39. Circ.: 20,000. Jacqueline Shanley, Editor-in-Chief. **Description:** Features retail success

stories, gives tips on creative display designs, and offers practical retail advice to party and stationary store owners. Articles cover employee management, marketing, advertising, promotion, finance, and legal matters. **Nonfiction:** Articles, factual, anecdotes appreciated; 800-1,800 words; pay varies. **Tips:** Send query with published clips. **Queries:** Preferred. **Response:** Queries 2 months. **Freelance Content:** 90%. **Rights:** FNAR. **Payment:** On publication.

PET BUSINESS
Macfadden Communications Group
333 Seventh Ave., Fl. 11, New York, NY 10001-5004. 212-979-4800.
E-mail: dlitwak@petbusiness.com. Web site: www.petbusiness.com. 14x/yr. $49.97/yr. Circ.: 24,500. David Litwak, Editor-in-Chief. **Description:** Covers animals and products found in pet stores. Offers research findings, legislative/regulatory actions, and business and marketing tips/trends. **Nonfiction:** Brief, well-documented articles; pays $.10/word, $20/photo. **Payment:** On publication.

PET PRODUCT NEWS
Fancy Publications, P.O. Box 6050, Mission Viejo, CA 92690. 949-855-8822.
E-mail: miturri@fancypubs.com. Web site: www.petproductnews.com. Monthly. $42/yr. Circ.: 30,000. Marilyn Iturri, Editor. **Description:** Audience is pet-store retailers and managers of such operations, large and small. Includes pet and pet-product merchandising, retailer tips, industry news and opinion. Submit articles with photos; 1,200-1,500 words; $250 and up. **Tips:** Do not send fiction or pet stories. Articles should target pet store owners, product suppliers/distributors, and product manufacturers. Sample copy available for $5 plus SASE. **Queries:** Required. **E-Queries:** Yes. **Unsolicited mss:** Does not accept. **Response:** Queries 2 weeks. **Freelance Content:** 70%. **Rights:** FNASR. **Payment:** On publication.

PHOTO MARKETING
Photo Marketing Assn. International
3000 Picture Place, Jackson, MI 49201-8898. 517-788-8100.
E-mail: bgretzner@pmai.org. Web site: www.photomarketing.com. Monthly. $30/yr. Circ.: 18,000. Bonnie Gretzner, Managing Editor. **Description:** For owners and managers of camera/video stores or photo processing labs. **Nonfiction:** Business articles, 1,000-2,000 words; pays $150-$500, extra for photos. **Queries:** Preferred. **Unsolicited mss:** Does not accept. **Payment:** On acceptance.

POOL & SPA NEWS
Hanley-Wood LLC
4160 Wilshire Blvd., Los Angeles, CA 90010. 323-801-4900.
E-mail: etaylor@hanley-wood.com. Web site: www.poolspanews.com. 2x/month. Circ.: 16,012. Erika Taylor, Editor. **Description:** Provides industry news and feature articles to builders, retailers, technicians, and other pool and spa professionals. Articles cover design, construction, renovation, equipment repair, merchandising, etc.

Also provides annual directory, product listings, and technical manuals. **Queries:** Preferred. **Freelance Content:** 15%. **Payment:** On publication.

PRO
Cygnus Business Media, P.O. Box 803, Fort Atkinson, WI 53538. 920-563-6388. E-mail: noel.brown@cygnuspub.com. Web site: www.promagazine.com. 9x/yr. Circ.: 50,000. Noel Brown, Editor-in-Chief. **Description:** On business management for owners of lawn-maintenance firms. **Nonfiction:** Articles, 1,000-1,500 words; pays $150-$250. **Queries:** Preferred. **Payment:** On publication.

QUICK PRINTING
445 Broad Hollow Rd., Melville, NY 11747-3669. 631-845-2700. E-mail: editor@quickprinting.com. Web site: www.quickprinting.com. Monthly. $66/yr. Circ.: 48,000. Gerald Walsh, Editor. **Description:** For owners and operators of quick print shops, copy shops, and small commercial printers. How to make their businesses more profitable (including photos and figures). Also, articles on using computers and peripherals in graphic arts applications. **Nonfiction:** Articles, 1,500-2,500 words; pays from $150. **Tips:** No generic business articles. Currently not buying much freelance material. **Payment:** On publication.

RETAIL SYSTEMS RESELLER
4 Middlebury Blvd., Randolph, NJ 07869. 973-252-0100. E-mail: dbreeman@edgellmail.com. Web site: www.retailsystemsreseller.com. Monthly. Circ.: 20,000. Daniel Breeman, Managing Editor. **Description:** Covers news, products, technology, and services for value-added resellers and system integrators selling into the retail channel. Focuses retail point-of-sale and payment processing, extending into backend systems and retail supply chain. **Nonfiction:** 600-1,500 words; $400-$800. **Tips:** Seeking writers who can write for this specific market and know how to dig as a reporter. No syndicated articles or general business ideas. **E-Queries:** Yes. **Unsolicited mss:** Accepts. **Response:** 60-90 days, SASE required. **Freelance Content:** 80%. **Rights:** FNAR. **Payment:** On publication.

SALES & MARKETING MANAGEMENT
770 Broadway, New York, NY 10003. 646-654-7606. E-mail: cgalea@salesandmarketing.com. Web site: www.salesandmarketing.com. Christine Galea, Managing Editor. **Description:** Provides useful information for sales and marketing executives. Articles focus on techniques for better job performance, networking with colleagues, the value of continued education, and the most recent research and marketing tools. **Nonfiction:** Features and short articles; pay varies. **Tips:** Seeks practical "news you can use." **Queries:** Preferred. **Payment:** On acceptance.

SAN FRANCISCO BUSINESS TIMES

275 Battery St., Suite 940, San Francisco, CA 94111. 415-989-2522.
E-mail: ssymanovich@bizjournals.com. Web site: www.bizjournals.com/sanfrancisco.
Steve Symanovich, Editor. **Description:** Features articles that focus on business,
commerce, and technology in the San Francisco Bay area. **Nonfiction:** Limited freelance market; pays $250-$350. **Queries:** Preferred. **Payment:** On publication.

SIGN BUILDER ILLUSTRATED

323 Clifton St. Suite #7, Greenville, NC 27858. 252-355-5806.
E-mail: jeff@signshop.com. Web site: www.signshop.com. Bimonthly. Jeff Wooten,
Editor. **Description:** On the sign industry. **Nonfiction:** How-to articles and editori-
als, 1,500-2,500 words; pays $300-$500. **Payment:** On acceptance.

SIGN BUSINESS

P.O. Box 1416, Broomfield, CO 80038-1416. 303-469-0424.
E-mail: ewieber@nbm.com. Web site: www.signbusinessmag.com. Monthly. $38/yr.
Circ.: 18,400. Edward Patrick Wieber, Editor. **Description:** For the sign business.
Prefers step-by-step, how-to features; pays $150-$300. **Payment:** On publication.

SMALL BUSINESS OPPORTUNITIES

1115 Broadway, Fl. 8, New York, NY 10010-3455. 212-462-9567.
E-mail: sr@harris-pub.com. Web site: www.sbomag.com. Bimonthly. $3.25/$14.95.
Circ.: 250,000. Susan Rakowski, Editor-in-Chief. **Description:** How-to magazine for
entrepreneurs. Articles run 900-1,000 words; $250-$400. **Tips:** Prefers e-queries.
"Avoid general articles on small businesses. Our readers look for specifics. Currently
we're looking for how-tos, trends, and round-ups." **Queries:** Preferred. **Freelance
Content:** 40%. **Payment:** On acceptance.

SOUVENIRS, GIFTS, AND NOVELTIES

10 E Athens Ave., Ardmore, PA 19003. 610-645-6940.
E-mail: souvnovmag@aol.com. Tony De Masi, Editor. **Description:** On retailing and
merchandising gifts, collectibles, and souvenirs for managers at zoos, museums,
hotels, airports, and souvenir stores. Articles run 1,500 words; $.12/word. **Payment:**
On publication.

TANNING TRENDS

3101 Page Ave., P.O. Box 1630, Jackson, MI 49204-1630. 517-784-1772.
E-mail: editor@smarttan.com. Web site: www.tanning-trends.com. Monthly. $60/yr.
Circ.: 23,000. Joseph Levy, Executive Editor. **Description:** On small businesses and
skin care for tanning-salon owners, to help owners move to the "next level" of small
business ownership. Focuses on business principles, public relations, and marketing.
Nonfiction: Scientific pro-tanning articles, "smart tanning" pieces. Query for profiles. Pay varies. **Payment:** On publication.

TEA & COFFEE TRADE JOURNAL

26 Broadway Fl. 9M, New York, NY 10004. 212-391-2060.
E-mail: editor@teaandcoffee.net. Web site: www.teaandcoffee.net. Monthly. $42/yr. Circ.: 10,000. Jane P. McCabe, Publisher/Editor. **Description:** On issues of importance to the tea and coffee industry. Articles, 3-5 pages; pays $.20/word. **Queries:** Preferred. **Payment:** On publication.

TEENPRENEUR

See full listing in Teens category.

TEXAS TECHNOLOGY

13490 TI Boulevard, Suite 100, Dallas, TX 75243. 972-690-6222.
E-mail: lkline@ttechnology.com. Web site: www.thetechmag.com. Monthly. $30. Circ.: 700,000. Laurie Kline, Editor. **Description:** Covers latest innovations in technology and how it affects our lives. Targets general consumers, also technology and computer professionals. **Nonfiction:** Technology trends, new products information, features on obtaining and retaining employees in high-tech sector; 1,200-3,500 words; $200-$400. **Tips:** "No company- or product-specific stories. Seeking stories on trends and general topics to appeal to both business and mainstream audience. Welcomes new writers! Read a sample issue first." **Queries:** Required. **E Queries:** Yes. **Unsolicited mss:** Accepts. **Response:** Queries 3 weeks, mss 2 months. **Freelance Content:** 95%. **Rights:** 1st print and electronic. **Payment:** On publication.

TEXTILE WORLD

2100 Powers Ferry Rd., Atlanta, GA 30339. 770-955-5656.
E-mail: editor@textileindustries.com. Web site: www.textileworld.com. Monthly. $60/yr. Circ.: 33,000. **Description:** Serves textile executives in their dual roles as technologists and managers. **Nonfiction:** Business and technical articles; 1,500 words; $200/page. **Art:** Slides, prints, electronic. **Queries:** Required. **E-Queries:** Yes. **Response:** 4 weeks. **Freelance Content:** 5%. **Rights:** All. **Payment:** On publication.

TREASURY & RISK MANAGEMENT

52 Vanderbilt Ave. Suite 514, New York, NY 10017. 212-557-7480.
E-mail: pwechsler@treasuryandrisk.com. Web site: www.treasuryandrisk.com. 9x/yr. $64/yr. Circ.: 46,000. Patricia Wechsler, Editor. **Description:** On management for corporate treasurers, CFOs, and vice presidents of finance. **Nonfiction:** Articles, 200-3,000 words; pays $.50-$1.00/word. **Tips:** Seeking freelance writers. **Queries:** Preferred. **Payment:** On acceptance.

VIRGINIA BUSINESS

P.O. Box 85333, Richmond, VA 23293-0001. 804-649-6999.
E-mail: jbacon@va-business.com. Web site: www.virginiabusiness.com. Monthly. $30/yr. Circ.: 32,000. James Bacon, Publisher/Editor-in-Chief. **Description:** Covers

the business scene in Virginia. **Nonfiction:** Articles, 1,000-2,500 words; pay varies. **Queries:** Required. **Payment:** On publication.

WALL STREET JOURNAL SUNDAY
Dow Jones & Co., Inc.
200 Liberty St., Fl. 9, New York, NY 10281-1003. 212-416-2000.
Web site: http://sunday.wsj.com. Weekly. Circ.: 5,000,000. **Description:** Sunday insert to more than 15 major-market newspapers.

WOMEN IN BUSINESS
American Business Women's Assn.
9100 Ward Parkway, P.O. Box 8728, Kansas City, MO 64114-0728. 816-361-6621.
E-mail: kisaacson@abwa.org. Web site: www.abwa.org. Bimonthly. $12/yr (members), $20/yr (others). Circ.: 50,000. Kathleen Isaacson, Editor. **Description:** Focuses on leadership, education, networking support, and national recognition. Helps business women of diverse occupations to grow personally and professionally. **Nonfiction:** How-to business features for working women, ages 35-55 (trends, small-business ownership, self-improvement, retirement issues). Profiles of ABWA members only; 500-1,000 words; $.20/word. **E-Queries:** Yes. **Unsolicited mss:** Accepts. **Freelance Content:** 2%. **Payment:** On publication.

CAREER & PROFESSIONAL DEVELOPMENT

AMERICAN CAREERS
6701 W 64th St., Overland Park, KS 66202. 913-362-7788.
Web site: www.carcom.com. 2x/yr. Circ.: 500,000. Mary Pitchford, Editor. **Description:** Classroom career-development magazines for elementary, middle, and high school students. Introduces varied careers in different industries that offer realistic opportunities. **Nonfiction:** Articles on resumes, interviews, developing marketable work skills, and making career decisions. Also provides information on a variety of occupations, salaries, and the education/training needed to obtain employment; 300-1,000 words; $100-$450. **Tips:** Send query letter with resume and writing samples. "We seek stories that reflect racial and gender equality. Some careers require a college degree and some require other backgrounds to enter into the career. We welcome stories that reflect this diversity." **Queries:** Required. **E-Queries:** No. **Unsolicited mss:** Does not accept. **Response:** 1 month, SASE not required. **Freelance Content:** 50%. **Rights:** All, work for hire. **Payment:** Within 30 days of acceptance.

THE BLACK COLLEGIAN
See full listing in Ethnic & Multicultural category.

CAMPUS.CA
5397 Eglinton Ave. W, Suite 101, Toronto, Ontario M9C 5K6 Canada. 416-928-2909.
E-mail: turnbull@campus.ca. Web site: www.campus.ca. Quarterly. Lesley Turnbull,

Editor. **Description:** Articles to inform, entertain, and educate the student community in Canada. **Nonfiction:** Pay varies. **Queries:** Preferred.

CAREER WORLD

900 Skokie Blvd., Suite 200, Northbrook, IL 60062-4028. 847-205-3000.
E-mail: crubenstein@glcomm.com. Web site: www.weeklyreader.com. 6x/yr. Circ.:
87,000. Carole Rubenstein, Editor. **Description:** Educational magazine aimed at
junior and senior high school students to help prepare them for college and making
career choices. **Nonfiction:** Gender-neutral articles about specific occupations,
career awareness, and development. Topics: evaluating interests, setting goals, career
planning, college and tech choices, getting hired, hot jobs, etc. **Tips:** Send query, with
resume and clips. Sample copies available. **Queries:** Required. **E-Queries:** Yes.
Unsolicited mss: Does not accept. **Response:** Queries 1-6 months. **Freelance
Content:** 80%. **Rights:** All. **Payment:** On publication.

CAREERS AND THE COLLEGE GRAD

170 High St., Waltham, MA 02454. 888-222-3678.
E-mail: diversity@brassring.com. Web site: www.brassringdiversity.com. Annual.
Kathleen Grimes, Publisher. **Description:** Career-related articles, for junior and
senior liberal arts students. No payment. Publishes a number of other specialty magazines for the college market. **Nonfiction:** 1,500-2,000 words. **Fillers:** Career-
related fillers, 500 words. **Art:** Line art, color prints. **Queries:** Preferred.

CAREERS & COLLEGES

P.O. Box 22, Keypoint, NJ 07735. 732-264-0460.
Web site: www.careersandcolleges.com. Quarterly. $6.95/issue. Circ.: 750,000. Paul
McKeefry, Publisher. **Description:** Guides high-school juniors and seniors through
college admissions process, financial aid, life skills, and career opportunities.
Nonfiction: Interesting, new takes on college admission, scholarships, financial aid,
work skills, and careers. 800-2,500 words; pay varies. **Queries:** Required.
E-Queries: No. **Unsolicited mss:** Does not accept. **Response:** 1 month, SASE
required. **Freelance Content:** 80%. **Rights:** FNAR. **Payment:** On publication.

CAREERS & THE DISABLED

See full listing in Abilities category.

CIRCLE K MAGAZINE

3636 Woodview Trace, Indianapolis, IN 46268-3196. 317-875-8755.
E-mail: ckimagazine@kiwanis.org. Web site: www.circlek.org/magazine. 5x/yr. $6/yr.
Circ.: 15,000. Shanna Mooney, Executive Editor. **Description:** Official publication
of Circle K International (world's largest collegiate service organization). Articles are
targeted to college students who are committed to community service and leadership
development. **Nonfiction:** Both serious and light nonfiction, on community leadership and service. Also, articles on college lifestyle (trends, music, health, travel, and
technology); 1,500-2,000 words; $150-$400. **Tips:** "Focus on interviews and research,

not personal insights. Use illustrative examples and expert quotes." **Queries:** Preferred. **E-Queries:** Yes. **Unsolicited mss:** Accepts. **Response:** 2 months. **Freelance Content:** 60%. **Rights:** FNASR. **Payment:** On acceptance.

DIRECT AIM
7300 W 110th St., Fl. 7, Overland Park, KS 66210-2330. 913-317-2888. E-mail: directaim@neli.net. Web site: www.neli.net. Quarterly. $9/yr. Circ.: 500,000. Michelle Paige, Editor. **Description:** Provides college and career information to Black and Hispanic students who attend colleges, universities, or technical/vocational institutions. **Fiction:** Stories that are historical, cultural, humorous, etc.; 500-2,000 words; pay varies. **Nonfiction:** Topics include career preparation, college profiles, financial-aid sources, and interviews with college students from across the U.S. Also accepts pieces on general interest, personal experience, travel, humor, or new products/trends for college students; 750-2,000 words; pay varies. **Fillers:** Humor, anecdotes, newsbreaks; 25-250 words; $25-$100. **Queries:** Required. **Response:** Queries 1 month. **Freelance Content:** 80%. **Rights:** Reprint, work-for-hire.

FINANCIAL WOMAN TODAY
200 N Glebe Rd., Suite 820, Arlington, VA 22203-3728. 703-807-2007. E-mail: publications@fwi.org. Web site: www.fwi.org. Quarterly. $24/yr. Circ.: 5,000. Kathleen Robeson, Executive Editor. **Description:** Written for women working in the financial services industry. Content covers banking, retirement, management, leadership, the glass ceiling, e-commerce, and workplace issues, and features articles designed to promote both personal and professional growth. Feature articles run 2,000-4,000 words, columns run 250-1,000 words; no payment offered. **Queries:** Not necessary. **E-Queries:** Yes. **Unsolicited mss:** Accepts. **Freelance Content:** 80%. **Rights:** None.

FLORIDA LEADER
412 NW 16th Ave., P.O. Box 14081, Gainesville, FL 32604-2081. 352-373-6907. E-mail: vince@studentleader.com. Web site: www.floridaleader.com. 3x/yr. Vincent Alex Brown, Editor. **Description:** Articles on leadership, college success, and career growth in Florida and the Southeast. Targets Florida high school and college students who participate in student government, academic societies, honor societies, community-service organizations, and other student activities. **Payment:** On publication.

HISPANIC TIMES MAGAZINE
P.O. Box 579, Winchester, CA 92596. 909-926-2119. E-mail: foxiekoji@aol.com. Web site: www.hispanictimescareers.com. 3x/yr. Circ.: 35,000. Gloria J. Davis, Editor. **Description:** Magazine for Hispanic professionals and college students. Focus is on careers, businesses, and employment opportunities.

LINK MAGAZINE
32 E 57th St., Fl. 11, New York, NY 10022. 212-980-6600. E-mail: editor@linkmag.com. Web site: www.linkmag.com. Elizabeth Kessler, Editor.

Description: News, lifestyle, and entertainment issues, for college students. **Nonfiction:** Well-researched, insightful, authoritative articles, 2,000-3,000 words; pays $.50/word. **Columns, Departments:** How-to and short features, 300-500 words, on education news, finances, academics, employment, lifestyles, trends, entertainment, sports, and culture. **Queries:** Preferred. **Payment:** On publication.

MINORITY ENGINEER

445 Broad Hollow Rd., Suite 425, Melville, NY 11747-4803. 631-421-9421. E-mail: jschneider@eop.com. Web site: www.eop.com. 3x/yr. Circ.: 17,000. James Schneider, Editor. **Description:** Targets engineering, computer-science, and information technology students and professionals who are Black, Hispanic, Native American, and Asian American. **Nonfiction:** Career opportunities, job-hunting techniques, new technologies, role-model profiles, and interviews; 1,000-2,000 words; $.10/word. **Queries:** Preferred. **E-Queries:** Yes. **Unsolicited mss:** Accepts. **Response:** 2 weeks, SASE required. **Freelance Content:** 60%. **Rights:** FNAR. **Payment:** On publication.

STUDENT LEADER

412 NW 16th Ave., P.O. Box 14081, Gainesville, FL 32604-2081. 352-373-6907. E-mail: john@studentleader.com. Web site: www.studentleader.com. 3x/yr. $18/yr. Circ.: 115,000. John Lamothe, Assoc. Editor. **Description:** Articles on leadership issues and career and college success for outstanding students involved in campus leadership activities. **Nonfiction:** Articles on leadership issues, demonstrating useful methods for running an organization effectively and ethically. Sample topics: promotion, raising money, recruiting volunteers, communicating with administration and the media, etc.; 800-1,000 words; $50-$100. **Tips:** Include quotes from faculty, corporate recruiters, current students, and recent alumni. **Queries:** Required. **Unsolicited mss:** Accepts. **Payment:** On publication.

SUCCEED

1200 South Ave., Suite 202, Staten Island, NY 10314. 718-761-4800. E-mail: editorial@collegebound.net. Web site: www.classesusa.com/succeedonline. Quarterly. $15/yr. Circ.: 155,000. Gina LaGuardia, Editor-in-Chief. **Description:** Articles appeal to readers interested in lifelong learning, recommitment to education, and career transition. Includes database of graduate programs and continuing education classes. **Columns, Departments:** On financial advice, career-related profiles, news, book and software reviews, continuing education resources; 400-600 words; $75-$100. **Tips:** Query with 3 writing clips. Manuscripts must be accompanied by a source list. Use attributable expert advice and real-life scenarios. Guidelines and sample issues available. **Queries:** Preferred. **E-Queries:** Yes. **Unsolicited mss:** Accepts. **Response:** 6-8 weeks, SASE required. **Freelance Content:** 70%. **Rights:** 1st, 2nd. **Payment:** 30 days upon publication.

UCLA

10920 Wilshire Blvd., Suite 1500, Los Angeles, CA 90024. Web site: www.ucla.edu. Quarterly. Circ.: 110,000. David Greenwald, Editor. **Description:** Focus on people and issues relevant to the university and its primarily alumni readership. Articles include research, profiles, and issue-oriented columns. **Queries:** Required. **Unsolicited mss:** Does not accept. **Response:** SASE not required. **Freelance Content:** 30%. **Rights:** FNAR. **Payment:** On acceptance.

UNIQUE OPPORTUNITIES

455 S Fourth Ave., Suite 1236, Louisville, KY 40202. 502-589-8250. E-mail: tellus@uoworks.com. Web site: www.uoworks.com. Bimonthly. $5/$25. Circ.: 80,000. Mollie V. Hudson, Editor; Bett Coffman, Associate Editor. **Description:** Offers guidance to physicians on career development by providing the economic, business, legal, and career-related issues involved in finding and running a practice. Topics include contract negotiation, practice types, financial/legal matters, practice management, etc.; 1,500-3,500 words; $.50-$.75/word. **Queries:** Required. **E-Queries:** Yes. **Unsolicited mss:** Accepts. **Response:** 2 months, SASE required. **Freelance Content:** 45%. **Rights:** FNASR. **Payment:** On acceptance.

COMPUTERS

C/C++ (USERS JOURNAL)

1601 W 23rd St., Suite 200, Lawrence, KS 66046-2700. 785-841-1631. E-mail: apettle@cmp.com. Web site: www.cuj.com. Monthly. $34.95/yr. Circ.: 43,000. Amy Pettle, Managing Editor. **Description:** Features articles and source code on C/C++ and Java programming for professional programmers. **Nonfiction:** Articles should be practical, "how-to" guides that provide sample source code. Algorithms, libraries, frameworks, class designs, book reviews, tutorials, and other special techniques that solve programming problems are also accepted; 800-2,500 words (80-300 lines of code). **Tips:** Send proposal with 1-2 paragraph abstract, 1-page outline, and brief bio. Prefers to receive proposals and mss via e-mail. Check Call For Papers for immediate story needs. **Queries:** Preferred. **E-Queries:** Yes. **Unsolicited mss:** Does not accept. **Response:** 2-4 weeks. **Payment:** On publication.

CLOSING THE GAP

See full listing in Abilities category.

COMPUTER GRAPHICS WORLD

98 Spit Brook Rd., Nashua, NH 03062-5737. E-mail: phill@pennwell.com. Web site: www.cgw.com. Monthly. $50/yr. Circ.: 67,000. Phil LoPiccolo, Editor-in-Chief. **Description:** On computer graphics technology and its use in science, engineering, architecture, film and broadcast, and interactive entertainment. Computer-generated images. **Nonfiction:** Articles, 800-3,000 words; pays $600-$1,200. **Queries:** Preferred. **Payment:** On acceptance.

COMPUTOREDGE MAGAZINE
3655 Ruffin Rd., Suite 100, P.O. Box 83026, San Diego, CA 92123. 858-573-0315. E-mail: editor@computoredge.com; submissions@computoredge.com. Weekly. $35. Circ.: 525,000. Patricia Smith, Editor. **Description:** ComputorEdge features non-technical, entertaining articles on computer hardware and software for both average users and experts. **Nonfiction:** Feature articles and columns cover a variety of topics including online systems, the Internet, Macintosh systems, common computer problems, etc.; 1,000-1,200 words. **Columns, Departments:** Beyond Personal Computing, Mac Madness, I Don't Do Windows; 800-1,000 words. **Tips:** Query with brief description of idea and writing credentials. **Queries:** Required. **E-Queries:** Yes. **Unsolicited mss:** Does not accept. **Response:** 1-3 months. **Freelance Content:** 80%. **Rights:** FNAR.

IEEE COMPUTER GRAPHICS AND APPLICATIONS
IEEE Computer Society
10662 Los Vaqueros Circle, Los Alamitos, CA 90720.
E-mail: kkelly@computer.org. Web site: www.computer.org/cga. Bimonthly. Circ.: 7,000. Kristine Kelly, Staff Editor. **Description:** Peer-reviewed publication that covers the field of computer graphics and applications. Accepting application department proposals that show how computer graphics solve real world problems; 3,200-5500 words; $400/page. **Tips:** New writers should submit resume and writing samples. **Response:** 1 week. **Rights:** All.

MACWORLD COMMUNICATIONS
501 Second St., Fl. 5, San Francisco, CA 94107-1469.
E-mail: macworld@macworld.com. Web site: www.macworld.com. Monthly. $34.97/yr. Circ.: 433,000. Rick LePage, Editor-in-Chief. **Description:** On all aspects of Macintosh computers. **Nonfiction:** Reviews, news, consumer, how-to articles, varying lengths, for Macintosh computers. Query with clips only. Pays $150-$3,500. **Queries:** Preferred. **Unsolicited mss:** Does not accept. **Payment:** On acceptance.

NETWORK WORLD
118 Turnpike Rd., Southborough, MA 01772-9108. 508-460-3333.
E-mail: jdix@nww.com. Web site: www.nwfusion.com. Weekly. $95/yr. Circ.: 151,000. John Dix, Editor-in-Chief. **Description:** About applications of communications technology for management level users of data, voice, and video communications systems. **Nonfiction:** Articles, to 2,500 words; pay varies. **Payment:** On acceptance.

PEI (PHOTO ELECTRONIC IMAGING)
Professional Photographers of America, Inc.
229 Peachtree St. NE, Suite 2200 International Tower
Atlanta, GA 30303. 404-522-8600.
Web site: www.peimag.com. Monthly. $20/yr. Circ.: 43,500. Cameron Bishopp, Executive Editor. **Description:** On electronic imaging, computer graphics, desktop publishing, pre-press and commercial printing, and multimedia. **Nonfiction:** Articles

on professional imaging trends and techniques, hardware/software reviews, and the latest advances in electronic imaging technology; 1,000-3,000 words; varies. **Tips:** Articles by assignment only. **Queries:** Required. **Payment:** On publication.

PEN COMPUTING

4045 Sunset Lane, Suite A, Shingle Springs, CA 95682-6800. 530-676-7878.
E-mail: biz@pencomputing.com. Web site: www.pencomputing.com. Bimonthly. $18/yr. Circ.: 76,000. Conrad Blickenstorfer, Editor-in-Chief. **Description:** "Seeks submissions relating to pen computing technology, PDAs and mobile and wireless computing. Submissions can be in the form of columns, reviews, opinions, or feature articles." Articles should be written for a technically knowledgeable audience; no "fluff" or rewritten product press releases. "Our readership shares a passion for new technology that will help them get their tasks completed better, faster, and more efficiently." Submission lengths should be negotiated with the editor. Payment runs $150-$450 for one-page columns and $100-$1,000 for full-length features.

SOFTWARE MAGAZINE

P.O. Box 135, East Walpole, MA 02032. 508-668-9928.
Web site: www.softwaremag.com. Quarterly. $30/yr. Circ.: 110,000. John P. Desmond, Publisher/Editorial Director. **Description:** For corporate systems managers and MIS personnel. **Nonfiction:** Features and information on latest software. **Tips:** E-mail abstract and brief bio to jdesmond@softwaremag.com. **E-Queries:** Yes. **Unsolicited mss:** Accepts.

TECHNOLOGY & LEARNING

See full listing in Education category.

TECHNOLOGY REVIEW

Massachusetts Institute of Technology
One Main St., Fl. 7, Cambridge, MA 02142. 617-475-8000.
Web site: www.technologyreview.com. Robert Buderi, Editor-in-Chief. **Description:** General-interest articles on technology and innovation. Pay varies. **Queries:** Preferred. **Payment:** On acceptance.

WIRED

See full listing in Lifestyle Magazines category.

CONSUMER & PERSONAL FINANCE

THE AMERICAN SPECTATOR

3220 N St. NW, PMB 175, Washington, DC 20007.
E-mail: editor@spectator.org. Web site: www.spectator.org. Monthly. Circ.: 130,000. R. Emmett Tyrrell, Jr., Editor. **Description:** Technical, political, and cultural guide for the investor in the new economy. **Nonfiction:** Pay varies. **Tips:** Query with arti-

cle clips. Sample copy $5.95. **Queries:** Required. **E-Queries:** No. **Unsolicited mss:** Does not accept. **Response:** 30 days. **Freelance Content:** 50%. **Rights:** All.

CONSUMER REPORTS
101 Truman Ave., Yonkers, NY 10703. 914-378-2000.
Web site: www.consumerreports.org. Monthly. $26/yr. Circ.: 4,100,000. Kimberly Kleman, Managing Editor. **Description:** Award-winning journalistic research on health, personal finance, and matters of public policy. Also, independent product-testing reports. **Tips:** "We're mostly staff-written, except for occasional back-of-book columns on health or personal finance. We only work with published writers." **Queries:** Required. **E-Queries:** Yes. **Unsolicited mss:** Accepts. **Response:** 1-3 weeks, SASE required. **Freelance Content:** 1%. **Rights:** All. **Payment:** On acceptance.

CONSUMER REPORTS FOR KIDS ONLINE
See full listing in Juvenile category.

KIPLINGER'S PERSONAL FINANCE
1729 II Street NW, Washington, DC 20006-3904. 202-887-6400.
E-mail: magazine@kiplinger.com. Web site: www.kiplinger.com. Monthly. $19.95/yr. Circ.: 1,018,000. Knight Kiplinger, Editor-in-Chief. **Description:** Provides practical advice to individual investors on personal finance issues. Topics include investments, mutual funds, buying insurance, taxes, retirement planning, college loans, etc. **Tips:** Primarily staff-written, but accepts some material from freelance authors. Be familiar with the publication before pitching story ideas. **Queries:** Required. **Response:** 1 month. **Freelance Content:** 10%. **Rights:** All. **Payment:** On acceptance.

THE MONEYPAPER
555 Theodore Fremd Ave., Suite B-103, Rye, NY 10580-1451. 914-925-0022.
E-mail: moneypaper@moneypaper.com. Web site: www.moneypaper.com. Monthly. $90/yr. Vita Nelson, Publisher/Editor. **Description:** Financial news and money-saving ideas. Brief, well-researched articles on personal finance, money management, saving, earning, investing, taxes, insurance, and related subjects. **Nonfiction:** Pays $75 for articles. **Tips:** Include resume and writing sample. Seeking information about companies with dividend reinvestment plans. **Queries:** Preferred. **Payment:** On publication. **Contact:** David Fish, Executive Editor.

CONTEMPORARY CULTURE

AMERICAN DEMOGRAPHICS
PRIMEDIA Business Magazines & Media
470 Park Ave. S, New York, NY 10020. 212-332-6300.
E-mail: editors@demographics.com. Web site: www.demographics.com. Monthly. Circ.: 22,400. Seema Nayyar, Editor. **Description:** Articles, 500-2,000 words, on four

key elements of a consumer market (size, needs and wants, ability to pay, and how it can be reached). With specific examples of how companies market to consumers. Readers include marketers, advertisers, and planners. **Queries:** Preferred.

AMERICAN VISIONS
See full listing in Ethnic & Multicultural category.

AMERICAN SCHOLAR
1606 New Hampshire Ave., NW, Washington, DC 20009. 202-265-3808. E-mail: scholar@pbk.org. Web site: www.pbk.org. Quarterly. $6.95/issue. Circ.: 25,000. Anne Fadiman, Editor. **Description:** For intelligent people who love the English language. **Nonfiction:** By experts, for general audience; 3,000-5,000 words; $500. **Poetry:** Highly original; to 33 lines; $50. **Queries:** Preferred. **E-Queries:** Yes. **Unsolicited mss:** Accepts. **Response:** 2-4 months, SASE required. **Freelance Content:** 100%. **Rights:** FNAR. **Payment:** On acceptance.

AMERICAS
Organization of American States
19th & Constitution Ave., NW #300, Washington, DC 20036. 202-458-6846. E-mail: americasmagazine@oas.org. Web site: www.oas.org. Bimonthly. $18. Circ.: 65,000. James Patrick Kiernan, Editorial Director. **Description:** Articles on a variety of topics (anthropology, the arts, travel, science, etc.) in relation to Latin America and the Caribbean. **Nonfiction:** Articles should be between 8-12 pages (3,000 words max). **Tips:** Prefers stories that can be well-illustrated. No political material. **Queries:** Required. **Rights:** One-time. **Payment:** On publication. **Contact:** Rebecca Medrano, Managing Editor.

BPM CULTURE MAGAZINE
8517 Santa Monica Blvd., Los Angeles, CA 90069-4107. 310-360-7170. E-mail: david@djmixed.com. Web site: www.djmixed.com. 10x/yr. $3.95/$15. Circ.: 70,000. David Ireland, Editor-in-Chief. **Description:** For young adults interested in electronic music, entertainment, video games, DVDs, Internet topics, and other high-tech gadgets. **Tips:** "Understand the culture that we cover—we are a youth culture magazine and are talking to the tastemakers (hip, cool, edgy). Writers should avoid topics geared towards mainstream or older people." **Queries:** Preferred. **Unsolicited mss:** Accepts. **Response:** 5-10 weeks, SASE. **Freelance Content:** 70%. **Rights:** One-time. **Payment:** On publication. **Contact:** Rob Simas.

BRICK
Box 537, Stn Q, Toronto, Ontario M4T 2M5 Canada. E-mail: info@brickmag.com. Web site: www.brickmag.com. **Description:** Literary journal for nonfiction. **Tips:** Do not query; prefers complete manuscript. Sample copy $12 (U.S.) plus $3 (U.S.) for shipping. **Queries:** Not necessary. **Response:** 3+ months.

CHRONICLES
The Rockford Institute, 928 N Main St., Rockford, IL 61103. 815-964-5054. E-mail: tri@rockfordinstitute.org. Web site: www.chroniclesmagazine.org. Monthly. $39/yr. Circ.: 14,000. Scott Richert, Executive Editor. **Description:** "A Magazine of American Culture." Articles and poetry that display craftsmanship and a sense of form.

COMMONWEAL
475 Riverside Dr., Room 405, New York, NY 10115. 212-662-4200. E-mail: editors@commonwealmagazine.org. Web site: www.commonwealmagazine.org. 22x/yr. $3/$47. Circ.: 20,000. Paul Baumann, Editor. **Description:** Review of public affairs, religion, literature, and the arts, published by Catholic lay people. **Nonfiction:** On political, religious, social, and literary subjects; 1,000-3,000 words; $100. **Poetry:** Submit 5 poems max (Oct.-May), serious, witty. $.75/line. **Columns, Departments:** Brief newsy facts, behind the headlines, reflective pieces; 750-1,000 words; $75. **Tips:** No simultaneous submissions. "Focus on religion, politics, and culture and how they intertwine." **Queries:** Not necessary. **E-Queries:** Yes. **Unsolicited mss:** Accepts. **Response:** 4-6 weeks, SASE required. **Freelance Content:** 20%. **Rights:** All. **Payment:** On publication.

FLAUNT MAGAZINE
1422 N Highland Ave., Los Angeles, CA 90028-7611. 323-836-1000. E-mail: mail@flauntmagazine.com. Monthly. $5.95. Circ.: 100,000. Dale Brasel, Features Editor. **Description:** Photography and writing, also coverage of arts, fashion, architecture, design, and music. Accepts fiction, nonfiction, and puzzles. **Tips:** Send published clips. **Queries:** Preferred. **E-Queries:** Yes. **Freelance Content:** 90%. **Rights:** One-time. **Payment:** On publication. **Contact:** Cheever Bahar.

GEIST
1014 Homer St., #103, Vancouver British Columbia V6B 2W9 Canada. 604-681-9161. E-mail: geist@geist.com. Web site: www.geist.com. Quarterly. **Description:** "Canadian Magazine of Ideas and Culture." **Nonfiction:** Creative nonfiction, 200-1,000 words; excerpts, 300-1,500 words, from works in progress; long essays and short stories, 2,000-5,000 words. Pay varies. **Tips:** Strongly prefers Canadian content. No e-mail submissions. Sample copy $5. **Queries:** Preferred. **Payment:** On publication.

LOLLIPOP
See full listing in Performing Arts category.

PARABOLA
See full listing in New Age/Spiritual category.

ROLLING STONE
See full listing in Performing Arts category.

RUMINATOR REVIEW

1648 Grand Ave., St. Paul, MN 55105-1804. 651-699-2610.
E-mail: review@ruminator.com. Web site: www.ruminator.com. $14/yr. Circ.: 25,000.
Margaret Todd Maitland, Editor. **Description:** Quarterly, thematic magazine of book reviews and essays. **Art:** B&W, digital, or CRC. **Tips:** "Very few unsolicited reviews are used. But if you've got solid, published clips, send them in with a list of styles and genres you're interested in. If it is a good match, it can lead to an assignment." **Queries:** Preferred. **E-Queries:** Yes. **Response:** 1-2 months, SASE. **Freelance Content:** 50%. **Rights:** 1st and 2nd serial.

THE SOUTHWEST REVIEW

Southern Methodist University
P.O. Box 750374, Dallas, TX 75275-0374. 214-768-1037.
E-mail: swr@mail.smu.edu. Web site: www.southwestreview.org. Quarterly. $6/issue.
Elizabeth Mills, Editor. **Description:** Wide-ranging, on contemporary affairs, history, folklore, fiction, poetry, literary criticism, art, music, theater. Prose pieces, 3,500-7,000 words; $100-$300. Submit 1 page for poetry, $50-$150. **Tips:** See Web site for guidelines. **Queries:** Not necessary. **E-Queries:** No. **Unsolicited mss:** Accepts. **Response:** 3 months, SASE required. **Rights:** FNAR. **Payment:** On publication.

THIRSTY EAR MAGAZINE

P.O. Box 29600, Santa Fe, NM 87592-9600. 505-473-5723.
E-mail: info@thirstyearmagazine.com. Web site: www.thirstyearmagazine.com. 5x/yr.
$15. Circ.: 50,000. Michael Koster, Editor. **Description:** On-line magazine, on music, art, and culture. **Fiction:** Short stories (music, arts, or American culture themes); up to 2,500 words; $75-$100. **Nonfiction:** Articles on "non-tuxedo" music; also reviews, 300-500 words. **Columns, Departments:** Opinion; 800-1,000 words; $100. **Queries:** Required. **E-Queries:** Yes. **Unsolicited mss:** Does not accept. **Freelance Content:** 80%. **Rights:** FNAR. **Payment:** On publication.

TROIKAMAGAZINE.COM

P.O. Box 1006, Weston, CT 06883. 203-319-0873. E-mail: eric@troikamagazine.com.
Web site: www.troikamagazine.com. Daily. Circ.: 400,000. Jonathan P. Atwood, Senior Editor. **Description:** Cutting-edge, online contemporary culture forum. Informs, entertains, and enlightens; a global voice in a rapidly globalizing world. **Fiction:** All types; varied length; $200 and up. **Nonfiction:** Features on arts, health, science, human interest, international interests, business, leisure, ethics. For educated, affluent baby-boomers, seeking to balance personal achievements, family commitments, and community involvement; varied length; $200 and up. **Poetry:** All types; varied length. **Queries:** Not necessary. **E-Queries:** Preferred. **Unsolicited mss:** Accepts. **Response:** Queries 10 days, submissions to 3 months, SASE. **Freelance Content:** 100%. **Rights:** All. **Payment:** 90 days from publication. **Contact:** submit@troikamagazine.com.

UTNE MAGAZINE
1624 Harmon Pl., Fawkes Bldg., Suite 330
Minneapolis, MN 55403-1906. 612-338-5040.
E-mail: editor@utne.com. Web site: www.utne.com. Bimonthly. $4.99/$19.97. Circ.: 232,000. Jay Waljasper, Editor. **Description:** Offers alternative ideas and culture, reprinting articles selected from over 2,000 alternative media sources. **Nonfiction:** Short pieces and reviews, 300-1,000 words. Provocative perspectives, analysis of art and media, down-to-earth news and resources, compelling people and issues. **Queries:** Preferred. **E-Queries:** Yes. **Unsolicited mss:** Accepts. **Response:** 4-6 weeks, SASE required. **Freelance Content:** 20%. **Rights:** Non-exclusive worldwide. **Payment:** On publication.

CURRENT EVENTS & POLITICS

AMERICAN EDUCATOR
See full listing in Education category.

THE AMERICAN LEGION MAGAZINE
P.O. Box 1055, Indianapolis, IN 46206-1055. 317-630-1200.
E-mail: magazine@legion.org. Web site: www.legion.org. Monthly. $15. Circ.: 2,670,000. John B. Raughter, Editor. **Description:** Covers current world affairs, public policy, and subjects of contemporary interest. **Nonfiction:** 750 to 2,000 words; pay negotiable. **Tips:** Sample copy $3.50. **Queries:** Preferred. **E-Queries:** Yes. **Payment:** On acceptance.

BRIARPATCH
2138 McIntyre St., Regina, Saskatchewan S4P 2R7 Canada. 306-525-2949.
E-mail: briarpatch.mag@sasktel.net. Web site: www.briarpatchmagazine.com. 10x/yr. $3/$24.61. Circ.: 5,000. Debra Brin, Managing Editor. **Description:** Progressive Canadian newsmagazine with a left-wing political slant. **Nonfiction:** Articles on politics, women's issues, environment, labor, international affairs for Canadian activists involved in social-change issues. Also, short reviews of recent books, CDs. **Tips:** Use journalistic style, with quotes from involved people. Looking for hard-hitting, thought-provoking stories. **Queries:** Preferred. **E-Queries:** Yes. **Unsolicited mss:** Accepts. **Response:** Immediately. **Freelance Content:** 100%. **Rights:** None. **Payment:** In copies.

CALIFORNIA JOURNAL
2101 K St., Sacramento, CA 95816. 916-444-2840.
E-mail: edit@statenet.com. Web site: www.californiajournal.com. Monthly. $39.95. Circ.: 8,000. David Lesher, Editor. **Description:** Features nonpartisan reports on California government and politics. Articles run 1,000-2,500 words; $300-$1,200.

Queries: Required. **E-Queries:** Yes. **Unsolicited mss:** Does not accept. **Response:** 1-2 weeks, SASE required. **Freelance Content:** 30%. **Rights:** All. **Payment:** On publication.

CAMPAIGNS & ELECTIONS

Congressional Quarterly, Inc.

1414 22nd St., NW, Washington, DC 20037-1001. 202-887-8529.

E-mail: rfaucheux@campaignline.com. Web site: www.campaignline.com. Monthly. $39.95/yr. Circ.: 30,400. Ron Faucheux, Editor-in-Chief. **Description:** On strategies, techniques, trends, and personalities of political campaigning. **Nonfiction:** Features, 700-4,000 words; campaign case-studies, 1,500-3,000 words; how-tos, 700-2,000 words, on aspects of campaigning; in-depth studies, 700-3,000 words, on public opinion, election results, and political trends. **Columns, Departments:** 100-800 words, for Inside Politics. **Payment:** In copies.

CHRISTIAN SOCIAL ACTION

See full listing in Religion category.

COLUMBIA JOURNALISM REVIEW

Columbia University

2950 Broadway #207 Journalism Bldg., New York, NY 10027-7004. 212-854-1881.

E-mail: cjr@columbia.edu. Web site: www.cjr.org. Bimonthly. $25.95/yr. Circ.: 28,000. Gloria Cooper, Deputy Executive Editor. **Description:** Amusing mistakes in news stories, headlines, photos, etc. (original clippings required), for "Lower Case." Pays $25. **Payment:** On publication.

COMMENTARY

See full listing in Religion category.

THE CRISIS

See full listing in Ethnic & Multicultural category.

FOREIGN SERVICE JOURNAL

American Foreign Service Assn.

2101 E Street NW, Washington, DC 20037. 202-338-4045.

E-mail: journal@afsa.org. Web site: www.afsa.org/fsj/index.html. Monthly. $3.50/issue. Circ.: 13,000. Steve Honley, Editor. **Description:** Covers foreign affairs and the U.S. Foreign Service. **Fiction:** Stories with overseas settings, for fiction issue (summer), submit by April 1; 3,000 words max; $250. **Nonfiction:** On foreign policy and international issues, for Foreign Service and diplomatic community; 2,000-3,000 words; payment negotiable. **Columns, Departments:** Short travel pieces about foreign scene, person, place, incident; 600-700 words; $100. **Tips:** "Knowledge of foreign service concerns essential." **Queries:** Not necessary. **Unsolicited mss:** Accepts. **Response:** 1 month. **Freelance Content:** 25%. **Payment:** On publication.

HARPER'S MAGAZINE
666 Broadway, Fl. 11, New York, NY 10012-2317. 212-420-5720.
E-mail: editorial@harpers.org. Web site: www.harpers.org. Monthly. $18/yr. Circ.: 213,000. Lewis H. Lapham, Editor. **Description:** On politics, literary, cultural, scientific issues. **Fiction:** Will consider unsolicited manuscripts; SASE required. **Nonfiction:** Very limited market; 2,000-5,000 words. **Queries:** Required. **Response:** SASE required.

THE HOMELESS REPORTER NEWS-SHEET
P.O. Box 1053, Dallas, TX 75221-1053. Bill Mason, Editor. **Description:** An insider's view and dialogue on solving homelessness. Articles and essays (300-1,500 words) on ways to solve the socioeconomic problems of homelessness and poverty. Also publishes human-interest love stories set in that context. **Queries:** Preferred. **E-Queries:** No. **Unsolicited mss:** Accepts. **Payment:** In copies.

IDEAS ON LIBERTY
The Foundation for Economic Education
30 S Broadway, Irvington, NY 10533. 914-591-7230.
E-mail: fee@fee.org; srichman@fee.org. Web site: www.fee.org. Sheldon Richman, Editor. **Description:** On economic, political, and moral benefits of private property, voluntary exchange, and individual choice. Articles to 3,000 words; $.10/ published word. **Payment:** On publication.

IN THESE TIMES
2040 N Milwaukee Ave., Fl. 2, Chicago, IL 60647. 773-772-0100.
E-mail: itt@inthesetimes.com. Web site: www.inthesetimes.com. Biweekly. $2.50/$36.95. Circ.: 20,000. Joel Bleifuss, Editor. **Description:** Seeks to inform and analyze popular movements for social, environmental, and economic justice in the U.S. and abroad. **Nonfiction:** News reporting, op-eds, and book reviews on left politics, the environment, human rights, labor, etc. 500-3,000 words; $.12/word. **Tips:** "Avoid excessive editorializing. We look for strong news reporting and writing skills." **Queries:** Preferred. **E-Queries:** Yes. **Unsolicited mss:** Accepts. **Response:** 6-8 weeks. **Freelance Content:** 90%. **Rights:** Reprint. **Payment:** On publication.

JUNIOR SCHOLASTIC
See full listing in Juvenile category.

LATINO LEADERS
See full listing in Ethnic & Multicultural category.

MIDSTREAM
633 Third Ave., Fl. 21, New York, NY 10017.
E-mail: info@midstream.org. Web site: www.midstream.org. 8x/yr. $3/$21/yr. Circ.: 8,000. Leo Haber, Editor. **Description:** Zionist publication with content on political U.S. and Israel culture, literature, book reviews, religion, and poetry. Varied points of

view presented. **Fiction:** Stories on Jewish themes; 1,500-4,000 words; $.05/word. **Nonfiction:** Jewish (Zionist) political, cultural, literary, religious themes; 1,500-6,000 words; $.05/word. **Poetry:** Jewish themes; 20 lines; $25/poem. **Tips:** Readers mostly scholarly, Israel-oriented professionals. **Queries:** Not necessary. **E-Queries:** No. **Unsolicited mss:** Accepts. **Response:** Up to 3 months, SASE. **Freelance Content:** 20%. **Rights:** 1st. **Payment:** On publication.

MIDWEST QUARTERLY
Pittsburg State University
Pittsburg, KS 66762. 316-235-4369.
E-mail: midwestq@pittstate.edu. Web site: www.pittstate.edu/engl/midwest.htm. Quarterly. $15. Circ.: 550. James B. M. Schick, Editor. **Description:** Scholarly articles on contemporary academic and public issues, 18-20 pages. Also accepts poetry, to 70 lines. **Tips:** No payment offered. **Queries:** Preferred. **E-Queries:** Yes. **Unsolicited mss:** Accepts. **Response:** Queries 1 week, submissions 4-6 months, SASE required.

MOTHER JONES
Foundation for National Progress
731 Market St., Suite 600, San Francisco, CA 94103. 415-665-6637.
E-mail: query@motherjones.com. Web site: www.motherjones.com. Bimonthly. $4.95/$24. Circ.: 190,000. Roger Cohn, Editor-in-Chief. **Description:** Independent journalism publication focusing on issues of social justice. **Nonfiction:** Features, 1,500-4,000 words, $1,500-$4,000. Short pieces, 100-800 words, $100-$500. Book, film, and music reviews. **Tips:** "We're looking for investigative reports exposing government cover-ups, corporate malfeasance, scientific myopia, institutional fraud or hypocrisy." **Queries:** Required. **E-Queries:** Yes. **Unsolicited mss:** Does not accept. **Response:** 2-3 months, SASE required. **Freelance Content:** 95%. **Payment:** On acceptance.

MS. MAGAZINE
See full listing in Women's Publications category.

THE NATION
33 Irving Place, Fl. 8, New York, NY 10003-2332. 212-209-5400.
E-mail: info@thenation.com. Web site: www.thenation.com. Weekly. $48/yr. Circ.: 100,000. Katrina vanden Heuvel, Editor. **Description:** Politics and culture from a liberal, left perspective, on national and international affairs. **Nonfiction:** Editorials and full-length pieces; 1,500-2,500 words; $75/printed page ($300 max). **Poetry:** Quality poems. **Columns, Departments:** Editorials; 750-1,000 words. **Tips:** "Looking for reporting, with fresh analysis and national significance, on U.S. civil liberties, civil rights, labor, economics, environmental, feminist issues, and role and future of Democratic Party." **Queries:** Required. **Unsolicited mss:** Accepts. **Response:** SASE. **Payment:** On publication.

NETWORK
See full listing in Seniors Magazines category.

NEW JERSEY REPORTER
See full listing in Regional & City Publications category.

THE NEW YORKER
4 Times Square, Fl. 20, New York, NY 10036. 212-286-5900.
E-mail: Fiction: fiction@newyorker.com; The Talk of the Town: talkofthetown@ newyorker.com; Shouts & Murmurs: shouts@newyorker.com; Poetry: poetry@ newyorker.com; Letters to the editor: themail@newyorker.com. Web site: www.newyorker.com. Weekly. $3.50/$49.95. Circ.: 851,000. David Remnick, Editor. **Description:** "We cover the vital stories of our time with intelligence, wit, stylish prose, and a keen eye." **Fiction:** Short stories, humor, and satire. **Nonfiction:** Amusing mistakes in newspapers, books, magazines, etc. Political/social essays; 1,000 words. **Poetry:** Quality poetry; up to 6 poems. **Columns, Departments:** Factual and biographical articles for Profiles, Reporter at Large, etc.; 1,000 words. **Tips:** Send submissions to the appropriate department in the body of an e-mail, not as an attachment. **Queries:** Not necessary. **E-Queries:** Yes. **Unsolicited mss:** Does not accept. **Response:** Up to 8 weeks. **Rights:** First. **Payment:** On publication.

THE OLDER AMERICAN
See full listing in Seniors Magazines category.

ON EARTH
See full listing in Environment & Conservation category.

POLICY REVIEW
Hoover Institution
818 Connecticut Ave. NW, Suite 601, Washington, DC 20006. 202-466-6730.
E-mail: polrev@hoover.stanford.edu. Web site: www.policyreview.org. Bimonthly. $6/issue. Circ.: 8,000. Tod Lindberg, Editor. **Description:** Book reviews and full-length articles on public policy; 1,000-5,000 words. **Tips:** Freelance content limited. **Queries:** Preferred. **E-Queries:** Yes. **Unsolicited mss:** Accepts. **Response:** 2-4 weeks, SASE required. **Freelance Content:** 5%. **Payment:** On publication. **Contact:** Steven Menashi.

THE PROGRESSIVE
409 E Main St., Madison, WI 53703. 608-257-4626.
E-mail: editorial@progressive.org. Web site: www.progressive.org. Monthly. $3.50/$32. Circ.: 53,000. Matthew Rothschild, Editor. **Description:** A leading voice for peace and social justice, with fresh and lively commentary on major issues. **Nonfiction:** Investigative reporting; coverage of elections, social movements, foreign policy; interviews, activism, book reviews; $500-$1,300. **Poetry:** On political

concerns; $150/poem. **Queries:** Preferred. **Unsolicited mss:** Accepts. **Freelance Content:** 30%. **Payment:** On publication.

REASON

3415 S Sepulveda Blvd., Suite 400, Los Angeles, CA 90034. 310-391-2245. E-mail: malissi@reason.com. Web site: www.reason.com. Monthly. $19.95/yr. Circ.: 55,000. Mike Alissi, Publisher. **Description:** "Free Minds and Free Markets." Looks at politics, economics, and culture from libertarian perspective. **Nonfiction:** Articles, 850-5,000 words; pay varies. **Queries:** Preferred. **Payment:** On acceptance.

ROLL CALL

50 F Street NW, Suite 700, Washington, DC 20001. 202-824-6800. E-mail: letters@rollcall.com. Web site: www.rollcall.com. Biweekly. $280/yr. Circ.: 18,500. Morton Kondracke, Executive Editor. **Description:** Covers Capitol Hill. Factual, breezy articles, political or Congressional angle (history, human-interest, political lore, opinion, commentary). **Queries:** Preferred. **Payment:** On publication. **Contact:** Tim Curran, Editor.

SOCIAL JUSTICE REVIEW

3835 Westminster Pl., St. Louis, MO 63108-3409. 314-371-1653. E-mail: centbur@juno.com. Web site: www.socialjusticereview.org. Bimonthly. $20. Circ.: 5,500. Rev. John H. Miller, C.S.C., Editor. **Description:** Focuses on social justice and related issues. Articles should be under 3,000 words; $.02/word. **Tips:** Submissions must be faithful to doctrine of the Catholic Church. **Queries:** Preferred. **E-Queries:** No. **Unsolicited mss:** Accepts. **Response:** Queries 2 weeks, SASE required. **Freelance Content:** 80%. **Rights:** FNAR. **Payment:** On publication.

TIKKUN

2342 Shattuck Ave., Suite 1200, Berkeley, CA 94704. 510-644-1200. E-mail: magazine@tikkun.org. Web site: www.tikkun.org. Bimonthly. $5.95/$29. Circ.: 20,000. Michael Lerner, Editor. **Description:** Progressive Jewish commentary on politics, culture, and society. Based on the Jewish principle of Tikkun Olam (healing the world), encourages writers to join spirituality to politics, for politics infused with compassion and meaning. **Fiction:** 3,000 words. **Nonfiction:** 1,600 words. **Poetry:** 20 lines. **Art:** Electronic (JPG, TIF); $50/photo. **Tips:** Avoid "My trip to Israel (or Eastern Europe/Auschwitz)," "My adult bar mitzvah," "How I became religious." **Queries:** Not necessary. **E-Queries:** No. **Unsolicited mss:** Accepts. **Response:** 3-4 months, SASE. **Freelance Content:** 20%. **Rights:** FNAR and electronic. **Payment:** In copies.

UTNE MAGAZINE

See full listing in Contemporary Culture category.

THE VILLAGE VOICE
36 Cooper Square, New York, NY 10003.
Web site: www.villagevoice.com. Donald H. Forst, Editor-in-Chief. **Description:** Alternative newspaper covering current and controversial topics in New York City. Features reports and criticism on local and national politics. Also reviews on art, music, dance, film, theater, and other arts. **Nonfiction:** Articles, 500-2,000 words; pays $100-$1,500. **Queries:** Preferred. **Response:** SASE required. **Payment:** On publication. **Contact:** Doug Simmons, Managing Editor.

THE WASHINGTON MONTHLY
733 15th St. NW, Suite 1000, Washington, DC 20005. 202-393-5155.
E-mail: editors@washingtonmonthly.com. Web site: www.washingtonmonthly.com. $5/issue. Paul Glastris, Editor. **Description:** Helpful, informative articles, 1,000-4,000 words, on DC-related topics, including politics, and government and popular culture. Pays $.10/word, on publication.

YES!
P.O. Box 10818, Bainbridge Island, WA 98110. 206-842-0216.
E-mail: editors@futurenet.org. Web site: www.futurenet.org. Quarterly. Circ.: 35,000. **Description:** "Journal of Positive Futures." Focuses on ways people are working to create a more just, sustainable, and compassionate world. **Tips:** Don't simply expose problems; highlight a practical solution. Honorarium. **Queries:** Required.

YOUTH TODAY
1200 17th St. NW, Fl. 4, Washington, DC 20036. 202-785-0764.
E-mail: info@youthtoday.org. Web site: www.youthtoday.org. 10x/yr. $18/yr. Circ.: 60,000. Patrick Boyle, Editor. **Description:** For people who work with kids (8 years old+), on the business of providing youth services. **Nonfiction:** Articles on funding, legislation, personal matters, and those that show evidence of "best practices" in serving youth; 1,500-2,000 words; $800-$2,000. **Tips:** "Read stories on our Web site first. Our readers are managers and frontline youth workers. The stories serve them, not parents and children. Avoid feel-good features." **Queries:** Required. **E-Queries:** Yes. **Unsolicited mss:** Does not accept. **Response:** 2 weeks, SASE. **Freelance Content:** 50%. **Rights:** FNAR. **Payment:** On publication.

EDUCATION

AMERICAN EDUCATOR
American Federation of Teachers
555 New Jersey Ave. NW, Washington, DC 20001. 202-879-4400.
E-mail: amered@aft.org. Web site: www.aft.org. Quarterly. Ruth Wattenberg, Editor.
Description: On trends in education; also well-researched news features on current problems in education, education law, professional ethics; "think" pieces and essays

that explore current social issues relevant to American society. **Nonfiction:** Articles, 500-2,500 words; pays from $300. **Queries:** Preferred. **Payment:** On publication.

AMERICAN JOURNAL OF HEALTH EDUCATION

1900 Association Dr., Reston, VA 20191. 703-476-3400.

Web site: www.aahperd.org/aahe.html. **Description:** For health education and promotion specialists in schools, agencies, business, hospitals, and professional preparation. **Tips:** "All articles undergo peer review. Please submit your manuscript to us online at www.journalsubmit.com or send us a query at ajhe@aahperd.org." Does not offer payment. **Queries:** Preferred.

AMERICAN SCHOOL BOARD JOURNAL

National School Boards Assn.

1680 Duke St., Alexandria, VA 22314-3455. 703-838-6722.

E-mail: submissions@asbj.com. Web site: www.asbj.com. Monthly. Circ.: 36,000. Sally Zakariya, Editor. **Description:** Publishes informative articles in a practical format regarding educational trends for school board members and administrators.

AMERICAN SCHOOL & UNIVERSITY

PRIMEDIA Business Magazines & Media

9800 Metcalf, P.O. Box 12901, Overland Park, KS 66212. 913-967-1960.

E-mail: asu@primediabusiness.com. Web site: www.asumag.com. Monthly. $50/yr. Circ.: 63,540. Joe Agron, Editor-in-Chief. **Description:** Articles and case studies, 1,200-1,500 words, on the design, construction, operation, and management of school and university facilities. **Queries:** Preferred.

BLACK ISSUES IN HIGHER EDUCATION

10520 Warwick Ave., Suite B-8, Fairfax, VA 22030-3136. 703-385-2981.

E-mail: hilary@cmabiccw.com. Web site: www.blackissues.com. Biweekly. $3.50/$26. Circ.: 12,000. Hilary L. Hurd, Editor. **Description:** News and features on blacks in post-secondary education and public policy. **Nonfiction:** On issues affecting minorities in higher education. **Fillers:** On education and public policy. **Columns, Departments:** Opinion pieces. **Queries:** Preferred. **E-Queries:** Yes. **Unsolicited mss:** Accepts. **Freelance Content:** 40%. **Payment:** On publication.

BOOK LINKS

American Library Assn., 50 E Huron St., Chicago, IL 60611. 312-280-5718.

E-mail: ltillotson@ala.org. Web site: www.ala.org/booklinks. Bimonthly. $28.95/yr. Circ.: 25,000. Laura Tillotson, Editor. **Description:** "Connecting Books, Libraries, and Classrooms." Professional journal for K-12 teachers, librarians, parents, and other educators who wish to connect children's and young adult literature into the curriculum. **Nonfiction:** Articles should demonstrate ways in which thematic literature can be integrated into curriculum for preschool to high school students. 2,000 words; $100. **Tips:** Query first or send draft as an attachment if it is written using Book Links style. **Queries:** Required. **E-Queries:** Yes. **Response:** 6-8 weeks. **Freelance Content:** 90%. **Rights:** All. **Payment:** On publication.

CABLE IN THE CLASSROOM
214 Lincoln St., Suite 112, Boston, MA 02134. 617-254-9481.
E-mail: edhazell@ccicrosby.com. Web site: www.ciconline.org. Monthly. $21.95/yr.
Circ.: 120,000. Al Race, Editor. **Description:** Lists commercial free, educational cable programming, plus online resources. Profiles educators who use programming and resources; offers tips for finding and using resources effectively. **Nonfiction:** Articles by or about K-12 teachers, librarians, and media specialists who use educational cable technology and programming to benefit students. By assignment, no unsolicited manuscripts; 500-1,000 words; $250-$500. **Columns, Departments:** Teacher-authored tips for using Cable in the Classroom resources to meet curriculum requirements. Query first; 100-150 words; $50. **Tips:** By assignment only. Don't pitch a story without identifying educators and the classroom cable connection. **Queries:** Required. **E-Queries:** Yes. **Unsolicited mss:** Does not accept. **Response:** Queries 1-3 months, SASE. **Freelance Content:** 50%. **Payment:** On acceptance.

CHURCH EDUCATOR
Educational Ministries, Inc., 165 Plaza Dr., Prescott, AZ 86303. 800-221-0910.
E-mail: edmin2@aol.com. Web site: www.educational ministries.com. Monthly. $28/year. Circ.: 3,000. Robert G. Davidson, Editor. **Description:** Resource for mainline Protestant Christian educators. Articles focus on programs used in mainline churches; 200-1,500 words; $.03/word. **Queries:** Not necessary. **E-Queries:** Yes. **Unsolicited mss:** Accepts. **Response:** Queries 1 week, submissions 3 months, SASE required. **Freelance Content:** 80%. **Rights:** One-time rights. **Payment:** On publication. **Contact:** Linda Davidson.

CLASS ACT
P.O. Box 802, Henderson, KY 42419.
E-mail: classact@lightpower.net. Web site: www.classactpress.com. 9x/yr. $25/yr.
Circ.: 300. Susan Thurman, Editor. **Description:** Newsletter for English and language arts teachers. Provides fun, ready-to-use lessons and units that help teachers make learning language, writing, and literature interesting to students. **Nonfiction:** Articles with ideas that teachers can use immediately. "What a Character" (developing characterization); "Writing Similes, Metaphors, and Extended Metaphors" 300-1,000 words; $10-$40. **Fillers:** English education related only; 1-2 pages; $10-$20. **Tips:** "Know how to write for teenagers. Humor helps. Avoid telling part of your life as a writer." Accepts e-mail submissions in body of text (no attachments). **Queries:** Not necessary. **E-Queries:** Yes. **Unsolicited mss:** Accepts. **Response:** 1 month, SASE. **Freelance Content:** 70%. **Rights:** All. **Payment:** On acceptance.

CLASSROOM NOTES PLUS

National Council of Teachers of English (NCTE)
1111 W Kenyon Rd., Urbana, IL 61801-1096. 217-278-3870.
E-mail: notesplus@ncte.org. Web site: www.ncte.org/notesplus. 4x/yr. $60/yr (includes membership). Circ.: 17,000. Editor: Felice A. Kaufmann. **Description:** Newsletter offering practical teaching ideas for the secondary classroom. Includes in-depth articles on literature, poetry, and writing. Also provides classroom management tips, recommended Web sites and resources, and advice for new teachers. **Nonfiction:** Articles must be original, previously unpublished, and identify any necessary sources. **Tips:** See Web site for specific submission guidelines.

COLLEGE COMPOSITION AND COMMUNICATION

National Council of Teachers of English (NCTE)
1111 W Kenyon Rd., Urbana, IL 61801-1096. 217-278-3870.
E-mail: mmcooper@mtu.edu. Web site: www.ncte.org/ccc. 4x/yr. $58/yr. Circ.: 9,500. Editor: Marilyn M. Cooper, Michigan Technological University, Houghton. **Description:** Research and scholarship in composition studies to help college teachers reflect on and improve their practices in teaching writing. **Nonfiction:** The field draws on research and theories from many humanistic disciplines (e.g. English, linguistics, cultural/racial studies, communication, sociology, etc.); so articles may present discussions within any of these fields, if clearly relevant to the work of college writing teachers. **Tips:** See Web site for submission guidelines.

COLLEGE ENGLISH

National Council of Teachers of English (NCTE)
1111 W Kenyon Rd., Urbana, IL 61801-1096. 217-278-3870.
E-mail: coleng@scu.edu. Web site: www.ncte.org/ce. 6x/yr. $65/yr (includes membership). Circ.: 10,000. Editor: Jean Gunner, Santa Clara University, California. **Description:** Provides a forum in which scholars working within any of the various subspecialties of the discipline can address a broad cross-section of the profession. Covers a wide spectrum of topics relevant to the discipline of English at the level of higher education. **Nonfiction:** Publishes articles on literature, composition, and other disciplinary concerns; open to all theoretical approaches and schools of thought. Does not accept practical articles on classroom practice. Readership is broad-based; therefore, seeks to insure that articles appeal to nonspecialists as well as specialists in particular areas. **Tips:** See Web site for specific guidelines.

COMMUNITY COLLEGE WEEK

10520 Warwick Ave., #B-8, Fairfax, VA 22030. 703-385-2981.
E-mail: scottc@cmabiccw.com. Web site: www.ccweek.com. Bi-weekly. $2.75/issue. Circ.: 10,000. Scott Cech, Editor. **Description:** A national newspaper covering community, technical, and junior-college issues. **Nonfiction:** Articles of interest to 2-year academia; 500-700 words; $.35/word. **Tips:** Use AP style. "Always query first by e-mail. Include your resume and a couple of clips when querying. Please visit our web site to see what kind of copy we print before you query." **Queries:** Required.

E-Queries: Yes. **Unsolicited mss:** Accepts. **Response:** 1-14 days, SASE required. **Freelance Content:** 95%. **Rights:** FNAR and electronic. **Payment:** On publication.

CURRENT HEALTH
900 Skokie Blvd., Suite 200, Northbrook, IL 60062-4028. 847-205-3000.
E-mail: crubenstein@glcomm.com. Web site: www.weeklyreader.com. 8x/yr. Carole Rubenstein, Editorial Director. **Description:** Magazine for classrooms covering physical and psychological health. Printed in two editions (for grades 4-7, and grades 7-12). **Nonfiction:** Articles on drug education, nutrition, diseases, fitness and exercise, first aid and safety, psychology, and relationships. By assignment only, no unsolicited manuscripts. Pay varies. **Tips:** Must write well for appropriate age level. Send query with resume and clips. Sample copies available. **Queries:** Required. **E-Queries:** Yes. **Unsolicited mss:** Does not accept. **Response:** 1-6 months. **Freelance Content:** 80%. **Rights:** All. **Payment:** On publication.

DRAMATICS MAGAZINE
See full listing in Performing Arts category.

EARLY CHILDHOOD NEWS
2 Lower Ragsdale, Suite 125, Monterey, CA 93940. 831-333-2000.
E-mail: mshaw@excelligencencomail.com. Web site: www.earlychildhoodnews.com. Bimonthly. Circ.: 50,000. Megan Shaw, Editor. **Description:** For teachers and parents of young children, infants to age 8, on developmentally appropriate activities, behavior, health, safety, and more. **Fiction:** Personal-experience stories from teacher's perspective; up to 500 words. **Nonfiction:** Research-based articles on child development, behavior, curriculum, health and safety; 500-2,000 words. **Poetry:** Related to young children (birth-age 6), teaching, educating, or family; 100 words. **Columns, Departments:** Ask the Expert, Problem-Solving Parent, newsletters for child care staff; 500-600 words. **Queries:** Preferred. **E-Queries:** Yes. **Unsolicited mss:** Accepts. **Response:** 6 weeks for queries, 2-3 months for submissions. **Freelance Content:** 75%. **Rights:** All. **Payment:** On publication.

EARLY CHILDHOOD TODAY
Scholastic, Inc., 555 Broadway, Fl. 5, New York, NY 10012-3919. 212-343-6100.
E-mail: ect@scholastic.com. Web site: www.earlychildhoodtoday.com. 8x/yr. Circ.: 55,000. Judsen Culbreth, Editor-in-Chief. **Description:** For teachers. Offers practical information, strategies, and tips on child development and education. Also personal stories and program spotlights. **Nonfiction:** Articles, 500-900 words; pay varies. **Queries:** Preferred. **Payment:** On publication. **Contact:** Article Submissions.

ENGLISH EDUCATION
National Council of Teachers of English (NCTE)
1111 W Kenyon Rd., Urbana, IL 61801-1096. 217-278-3870.
E-mail: engedu@gsu.edu. Web site: www.ncte.org/ee. 4x/yr. $55/yr (includes memberships). Circ.: 2,800. Editors: Dana L. Fox, Georgia State University, Atlanta, and

Cathy Fleischer, Eastern Michigan University, Ypsilanti. **Description:** Features articles that focus on issues related to the nature of the discipline and the education and development of teachers of English at all levels. **Tips:** See Web site for specific submission guidelines. **Response:** 3 months.

ENGLISH JOURNAL

National Council of Teachers of English (NCTE)
1111 W Kenyon Rd., Urbana, IL 61801-1096. 217-328-3870.
E-mail: louann.reid@colostate.edu. Web site: www.ncte.org/ej. 6x/yr. $65/yr (included membership). Circ.: 31,000. Editor: Louann Reid, Colorado State University. **Description:** Professional journal for middle, junior high, and high school teachers, supervisors, and teacher educators. **Nonfiction:** Manuscripts can focus on an upcoming theme or can be used in ongoing features that appear in each issue. **Tips:** See Web site for submission guidelines. **Queries:** Preferred.

ENGLISH LEADERSHIP QUARTERLY

National Council of Teachers of English (NTCE)
1111 W Kenyon Rd., Urbana, IL 61801-1096. 217-278-3870.
E-mail: jwilcox@toolcity.net. Web site: www.ncte.org/elq. 4x/yr. $58/yr (includes memberships). Circ.: 2,000. Editor: Bonita L. Wilcox, Duquesne University. **Description:** Seeks to help department chairs, K-12 supervisors, and other leaders in their role of improving the quality of English instruction. **Nonfiction:** Short articles on a variety of important issues. **Tips:** See Web site for specific guidelines.

GIFTED EDUCATION PRESS QUARTERLY

10201 Yuma Ct., Manassas, VA 20109. 703-369-5017.
E-mail: mfisher345@comcast.net. Web site: www.giftededpress.com. Quarterly. Circ.: 1,000. Maurice Fisher, Editor. **Description:** Covers problems and issues of identifying and educating gifted students. GEPQ is now issued through password codes on Web site. **Nonfiction:** Issues related to educating gifted students, including teaching science and humanities, home education, and more; 3,500-4,000 words. **Tips:** "We're looking for highly imaginative, knowledgeable authors to write about this field." **Queries:** Required. **E-Queries:** Yes. **Unsolicited mss:** Does not accept. **Response:** 1 month, SASE required. **Freelance Content:** 50%. **Payment:** In copies.

GREEN TEACHER

95 Robert St., Toronto, Ontario M5S 2K5 Canada. 416-960-1244.
E-mail: info@greenteachers.com. Web site: www.greenteacher.com. Quarterly. $6.95/$26. Circ.: 7,500. Tim Grant, Gail Littlejohn, Editors. **Description:** Teachers, parents, and educators look to this magazine for practical, ready-to-use strategies and activities that educate and promote environmental/global awareness in the classroom. **Nonfiction:** Schoolyard naturalization, green economics, energy education, climate change, rainforest studies, and sustainable food systems; 1,500-3,000 words. **Tips:** Most articles are written by K-12 teachers working in the field of

environmental/global education. Does not publish articles about environmental issues, but rather on how to teach about the environment. Submit 1-page outline or summary of article with drawings or photographs. **Queries:** Preferred. **E-Queries:** Yes. **Unsolicited mss:** Accepts. **Response:** Queries 2 weeks; submissions 2-3 months. **Rights:** None. **Payment:** In copies.

THE HISPANIC OUTLOOK IN HIGHER EDUCATION
210 E State Rt. 4, #310, Paramus, NJ 07652. 201-587-8800.
E-mail: sloutlook@aol.com. Web site: www.Hispanicoutlook@com. Biweekly. Circ.: 28,000. Adalyn Hixson, Editor. **Description:** On issues, concerns, and potential models to further academic results of Hispanics in higher education. Articles, 1,700-2,000 words; pay varies. **Tips:** Queries should be sent 3 months in advance of tentative submission. **Queries:** Required. **Payment:** On publication.

HOME EDUCATION
P.O. Box 1083, Tonasket, WA 98855-1083. 509-486-1351.
E-mail: hem@home-ed-magazine.com. Web site: www.home-edmagazine.com. Bimonthly. $6.50/issue, $32.50/yr. Circ.: 12,000. Helen Hegener, Managing Editor. **Description:** For families who homeschool their children. Seeking submissions from writers who are familiar with homeschooling and who can share the humorous side without being negative about the alternatives. **Nonfiction:** Articles on homeschooling, 1,000-2,000 words; $50-$150. **Tips:** Encourages submissions from homeschooling parents who love to write. Focus on practical experience, not textbook theories. **Queries:** Not necessary. **E-Queries:** Yes. **Unsolicited mss:** Accepts. **Response:** 1-2 months, SASE required. **Freelance Content:** 60%. **Rights:** FNASR. **Payment:** On acceptance.

INSTRUCTOR
Scholastic, Inc., 524 Broadway, New York, NY 10012. 212-343-6100.
Web site: www.scholastic.com/instructor. 8x/year. $14/yr. Circ.: 218,000. Jennifer Prescott, Managing Editor. **Description:** Prominent national magazine for K-8 teachers. **Nonfiction:** Topics for teachers (timely issues, classroom ideas, activities, ways to improve, etc); 800-2,000 words; $500-$1,200. **Fillers:** E-Activities (tech-based activities); also, short, ready-to-use activities by teachers, for teachers; 100-200 words; $50. **Columns, Departments:** End of the Day (revelatory or humorous pieces about your experience as a teacher); 400-500 words; $250. **Tips:** Keep in mind: Can a teacher take these ideas into the classroom immediately? **Queries:** Not necessary. **E-Queries:** Yes. **Unsolicited mss:** Accepts. **Response:** Queries 1 month, submissions 2 months, SASE. **Freelance Content:** 80%. **Rights:** All. **Payment:** On publication.

LANGUAGE ARTS
National Council of Teachers of English (NCTE)
1111 W Kenyon Rd., Urbana, IL 61801-1096. 217-278-3870.
E-mail: langarts@u.arizona.edu. Web site: www.ncte.org/la. 6x/yr. $65/yr (includes membership). Circ.: 13,500. Coeditors: Kathy G. Short, University of Arizona,

Tucson; Jean Schroeder, Gloria Kauffman, Sander Kaser, Tucson Unified School District, Arizona. **Description:** Professional journal for elementary and middle school teachers and teacher educators. Provides a forum for discussion on all aspects of language arts learning and teaching, primarily as they relate to children in pre-kindergarten through the eighth grade. Issues discuss both theory and classroom practice, highlight current research, and review children's and young adolescent literature, as well as classroom and professional materials of interest to language arts educators. **Nonfiction:** Original articles on all facets of language arts education. **Tips:** See Web site for specific guidelines.

MOMENTUM
National Catholic Educational Assn.
1077 30th St. NW, Suite 100, Washington, DC 20007-3852. 202-337-6232.
E-mail: momentum@ncea.org. Web site: www.ncea.org. Quarterly. $20/yr. Circ.: 26,000. Brian Gray, Editor. **Description:** Covers outstanding programs, issues, and research in education, with relevance to Catholic schools or religious education programs. 500-1,500 words; $50-$75. **Tips:** No simultaneous submissions. Prefers query via e-mail. **Queries:** Preferred. **E-Queries:** Yes. **Payment:** On publication.

RESEARCH IN THE TEACHING OF ENGLISH
National Council of Teachers of English (NCTE)
1111 W Kenyon Rd., Urbana, IL 61801-1096. 217-278-3870.
E-mail: melanie.sperling@ucr.edu. Web site: www.ncte.org/rte. 4x/yr. $60/yr (includes membership). Circ.: 4,500. Editors: Melanie Sperling, University of California, and Anne DiPardo, University of Iowa. **Description:** Multidisciplinary journal of original research and scholarly essays on the relationships between language teaching and learning at all levels, preschool through adult. **Tips:** See Web site for submission guidelines.

SCHOLASTIC DYNAMATH
Scholastic, Inc.
555 Broadway, New York, NY 10012-3999. 212-343-6100.
E-mail: dynamath@scholastic.com. Web site: www.scholastic.com. 8x/yr. Circ.: 200,000. David Goody, Editor-in-Chief. **Description:** Offer an engaging mix of humor, news, popular-culture references, and original activities to help readers enjoy learning, while reinforcing and applying key math curriculum concepts. Content must be acceptable for classroom use. **Nonfiction:** Fun math content, tied to current events, popular culture, cool real-life kids, or national holidays (i.e., Martin Luther King Day, President's Day, Thanksgiving); to 600 words; $350-$450/article. **Fillers:** $25-$50 puzzles, to 75 words. **Art:** $50-$400. **Tips:** Has dual goals of being entertaining and educational. Need to get style and mathematical grade level just right. Request a sample copy to familiarize yourself with unique approach. **Queries:** Preferred. **E-Queries:** Yes. **Unsolicited mss:** Accepts. **Response:** 2 months, SASE required. **Freelance Content:** 25%. **Rights:** All. **Payment:** On acceptance.

THE SCHOOL ADMINISTRATOR
American Assn. of School Administrators
1801 N Moore St., Arlington, VA 22209-1813.
E-mail: magazine@aasa.org. Web site: www.aasa.org. 11x/yr. Members only. Circ.:
23,000. Jay P. Goldman, Editor. **Description:** For school administrators (K-12), on
school system practices, policies, and programs with wide appeal. **Nonfiction:** 1,500-
3,000 words. **Fillers:** To 400 words. **Columns, Departments:** To 750 words.
Queries: Preferred. **E-Queries:** Yes. **Unsolicited mss:** Accepts. **Response:**
Queries 2 weeks, submissions 8-10 weeks. **Freelance Content:** 10%. **Rights:** All.
Payment: On publication.

SCHOOL ARTS
50 Portland St., Worcester, MA 01608. 508-754-7201.
E-mail: contactus@davis-art.com. Web site: www.davis-art.com. 9x/yr. $4/issue. Circ.:
25,000. Dr. Eldon Katter, Editor. **Description:** Covers the field of art education.
Articles, 600-1,400 words, on art education in the classroom: successful, meaningful
approaches to teaching, innovative projects, uncommon applications of techniques or
equipment, etc. Pays $30-$150. **Art:** Professional-quality photos showing lessons in
art; pay varies. **Queries:** Preferred. **E-Queries:** Yes. **Unsolicited mss:** Accepts.
Response: 3 months, SASE required. **Freelance Content:** 85%. **Rights:** All.
Payment: On publication.

SCIENCE & CHILDREN
National Science Teachers Assn.
1840 Wilson Blvd., Arlington, VA 22201-3000. 703-243-7100.
E-mail: s&c@nsta.org. Web site: www.nsta.org. 8x/yr. $60/yr. Circ.: 23,500. Joan
McShane, Editor. **Description:** Articles and activities, based on current approaches
to instruction and issues in science education. For Pre-K to 8th-grade science teachers. **Queries:** Preferred.

TALKING POINTS
National Council of Teachers of English (NCTE)
1111 W Kenyon Rd., Urbana, IL 61801-1096. 217-278-3870.
E-mail: pma8@mindspring.com; koshewa@lclark.edu. Web site: www.ncte.org/tp.
2x/yr. $55/yr (includes membership). Circ.: 1,700. Editors: Peggy Albers, Georgia
State University, Atlanta, and Allen Koshewa, Lewis and Clark College, Portland,
Oregon. **Description:** Helps promote literacy research and the use of whole language instruction in classrooms. Provides a forum for parents, classroom teachers,
and researchers to reflect about literacy and learning. **Tips:** See Web site for submission guidelines.

TEACHING ELEMENTARY PHYSICAL EDUCATION
Human Kinetics Publishers
P.O. Box 5076, Champaign, IL 61825-5076. 217-351-5076.
E-mail: marjorier@hkusa.com. Web site: www.humankinetics.com. Bimonthly. Circ.:

3,500. Marjorie Robinson, Managing Editor. **Description:** Resources and ideas on instructional and fun physical-education programs for K-8 physical education teachers. **Queries:** Preferred.

TEACHING ENGLISH IN THE TWO-YEAR COLLEGE

National Council of Teachers of English (NCTE)
1111 W Kenyon Rd., Urbana, IL 61801-1096. 217-278-3870.
E-mail: htinberg@bristol.mass.edu. 4x/yr. $60/yr (includes membership). Circ.: 4,500.
Editor: Howard Tinberg, Bristol Community College, Fall River, Massachusetts.
Description: For two-year college teachers and those teaching the first two years of English in four-year institutions; on all areas of composition (basic, first-year, and advanced); business, technical, and creative writing, teaching literature. Also, on staffing, assessment, technology, writing program administration, speech, journalism, reading, ESL, etc. **Columns, Departments:** Instructional Notes (short articles describing successful classroom practices); Readers Write (50-200 word comments on published articles or professional issues); What Works for Me (brief descriptions of successful classroom activities, 50-200 words); also reviews of books, software, and other nonprint materials. **Tips:** See Web site for submission guidelines.

TEACHING K-8

Subsidiary of Highlights for Children, Inc.
40 Richards Ave., Norwalk, CT 06854. 203-855-2650.
E-mail: teachingk-8@aol.com. Web site: www.teachingk-8.com. 8x/yr. $14.97/yr.
Circ.: 100,000. Patricia Broderick, Editor. **Description:** A classroom service magazine, with useful teaching ideas for teachers who work with grades K-8. **Nonfiction:** Articles, 1,000 words, on classroom-tested ideas, techniques, strategies for teaching students (K-8). **Queries:** Not necessary. **E-Queries:** No. **Unsolicited mss:** Accepts. **Response:** 1 month, SASE required. **Rights:** All. **Payment:** On publication.

TEACHING THEATRE

Educational Theatre Assn.
2343 Auburn Ave., Cincinnati, OH 45219. 513-421-3900.
E-mail: jpalmarini@edta.org. Web site: www.edta.org. Quarterly. James Palmarini, Editor. **Description:** Journal for middle and high school drama educators. Offers play suggestions, curriculum ideas, classroom exercises, and technical production. **Queries:** Preferred. **E-Queries:** Yes.

TEACHING TOLERANCE

Southern Poverty Law Center
400 Washington Ave., Montgomery, AL 36104.
Web site: www.teachingtolerance.org. Semi-annual. Free to educators. Circ.: 600,000. Jim Carnes. **Description:** Helps teachers promote interracial and intercultural understanding in the classroom and beyond. Example topics include: the role of white teachers in multicultural education, creating safe space for refugee students, inclusion for students with disabilities, gay students coming out at school, etc. Articles

run 500-3,500 words; $1.25/word. **Art:** Rarely uses stock images. Seeking photographer to travel on assignment, work well with school children and teachers/administrators, in varied locations; B&W, color, hand-tinted; $100-$800. **Tips:** Submit clear focused query. No rhetoric, scholarly analysis, or articles that reinvent the wheel on multicultural education. **Queries:** Preferred. **E-Queries:** Yes. **Unsolicited mss:** Accepts. **Response:** 3 months, SASE required. **Freelance Content:** 75%. **Rights:** All. **Payment:** On acceptance.

TECH DIRECTIONS

3970 Varsity Dr., Box 8623, Ann Arbor, MI 48107-8623. 734-975-2800.

E-mail: susanne@techdirections.com. Web site: www.techdirections.com. Susanne Peckham, Editor. **Description:** For teachers in science, technology, and vocational educational fields. Seeking classroom projects for students from upper elementary through community college levels. **Nonfiction:** Articles, 9-12 double-spaced typed pages; $50-$150. **Fillers:** Cartoons (pays $20); puzzles, brainteasers, humorous anecdotes, short classroom activities (pays $25); humorous anecdotes (pays $5). **Payment:** On publication.

TECHNOLOGY & LEARNING

600 Harrison St., San Francisco, CA 94107-1370. 415-947-6000.

E-mail: techlearning_editors@cmp.com. Web site: www.techlearning.com. Monthly. $29.95/yr. Circ.: 80,000. Susan McLester, Editor-in-Chief. **Description:** For K-12 teachers on uses of computers and related technology in the classroom: human-interest and philosophical articles, how-to pieces, software reviews, and hands-on ideas. **Nonfiction:** Articles should be of general interest to K-12 educators and should encourage them to try new approaches to teaching by using the latest technology in computers, peripherals, integrated learning systems, etc.; 1,200-2,500 words; $400. **Queries:** Not necessary. **E-Queries:** Yes. **Unsolicited mss:** Accepts. **Response:** 8 weeks; SASE required. **Payment:** On publication.

TODAY'S CATHOLIC TEACHER

2621 Dryden Rd., Dayton, OH 45439. 937-293-1415.

E-mail: mnoschang@peterli.com. Web site: www.catholicteacher.com. Bimonthly. $14.95/yr. Circ.: 50,000. Mary Noschang, Editor. **Description:** For K-12 educators concerned with private education and particularly Catholic education. **Nonfiction:** Curriculum, classroom management, other articles (religious and nonreligious) for classroom teachers in Catholic K-12 schools; 700-3,000 words; $150-$300. **Queries:** Not necessary. **E-Queries:** Yes. **Unsolicited mss:** Accepts. **Response:** 2 months, SASE. **Freelance Content:** 80%. **Rights:** FNAR. **Payment:** On publication.

VOICES FROM THE MIDDLE

National Council of Teachers of English (NCTE)

1111 W Kenyon Rd., Urbana, IL 61801-1096. 217-278-3870.

E-mail: cschanche@ncte.org. Web site: www.ncte.org/vm. 4x/yr. $60/yr (includes membership). Circ.: 10,500. Editor: Kylene Beers, University of Houston, Texas.

Description: Journal for teachers at the middle school level. Based on the premise that middle school teachers face a unique set of circumstances and challenges, this journal presents a variety of voices. Each issue is devoted to one topic or concept related to literacy and learning at the middle school level. **Nonfiction:** Each issue includes teachers' descriptions of authentic classroom practices, middle school students' reviews of adolescent literature, a technology column, and reviews of professional resources for teachers. Also explores the connections between the theory and practice of each issue's topic. **Tips:** See Web site for specific submission guidelines.

YOUTH AND CHRISTIAN EDUCATION LEADERSHIP
1080 Montgomery Ave. NE, P.O. Box 2250
Cleveland, TN 37320-2250. 423-478-7597.
E-mail: wandagriffith@pathwaypress.org. Web site: www.pathwaypress.org.
Quarterly. $8. Circ.: 14,000. Wanda Griffith, Editor. **Description:** For Christian education workers who teach God's word to kids, teens, and adults. Seeks articles that encourage, inform, and inspire those who teach the Bible in local churches; 500-1,000 words; $25-$45. **Queries:** Not necessary. **E-Queries:** Yes. **Unsolicited mss:** Accepts. **Response:** 6-9 weeks, SASE required. **Payment:** On publication.

ENVIRONMENT, CONSERVATION, NATURE
(See also Sports, Recreation, Outdoors)

ADIRONDACK LIFE
P.O. Box 410, Jay, NY 12941. 518-946-2191.
E-mail: gcrane@adirondacklife.com. Web site: www.adirondacklife.com. 8x/yr.
$21.95/yr. Circ.: 50,000. Elizabeth Folwell, Editor. **Description:** Covers outdoor and environmental activities, issues, arts, wilderness, and wildlife of the Adirondack Park region of New York State. **Fiction:** Excerpts of upcoming Adirondack and related books; to 4,000 words; $.25/word. **Nonfiction:** Contemporary and historical articles on employment, poverty, prison system, water quality, timber industry, etc.; to 5,000 words; $.25/word. **Columns, Departments:** Profiles of people and places, first-person travel/outdoor historical vignettes; to 2,200 words; $.25/word. **Art:** Color transparencies or B&W prints; $125/full page photo, $300/cover. **Queries:** Preferred. **E-Queries:** Yes. **Unsolicited mss:** Accepts. **Response:** 1 month, SASE required. **Freelance Content:** 80%. **Rights:** FNAR. **Payment:** On publication.

ALTERNATIVES JOURNAL
Faculty of Environmental Studies
University of Waterloo, Waterloo, Ontario N2L 3G1 Canada. 519-888-4442.
E-mail: editor@alternativesjournal.ca. Web site: www.alternativesjournal.ca.
Quarterly. Cheryl Lousley, Executive Editor. **Description:** Environmental thought, policy, and action. Canadian focus. **Nonfiction:** Feature articles, 4,000 words; notes, 200-500 words; and reports, 750-1,000 words. Pays small honoraria only.

AMERICAN FORESTS

910 17th St., Suite 600, Washington, DC 20006. 202-955-4500.
E-mail: mrobbins@amfor.org. Web site: www.americanforests.org. Quarterly. $3/$25.
Circ.: 25,000. Michelle Robbins, Editor. **Description:** For people, rural and urban,
who share a love for trees and forests. **Nonfiction:** Articles on trees, forests, issues
(worldwide); inspirational, educational; 150-2,000 words; $100-$1,200. **Columns,
Departments:** Communities (working together on problems); Woodswise (for
small-forest owners); Perspectives (current events); Earthkeepers (1-page profiles);
Clippings (news briefs). **Art:** 35mm or larger; B&W or color. $75-$400. **Tips:** No
straight travel pieces. No fiction. "Write for general audience, but on a slightly more
informed level. Tell specifics: issues, what's being done, how it has affected forests.
We're looking for skilled science writers for assignments documenting forest use,
enjoyment, and management." **Queries:** Required. **E-Queries:** Yes. **Unsolicited
mss:** Accepts. **Response:** Queries 2-3 months, submissions 2-3 months, SASE
required. **Freelance Content:** 75%. **Rights:** one-time. **Payment:** On acceptance.

ATLANTIC SALMON JOURNAL

P.O. Box 5200, St. Andrews, New Brunswick E5B 3S8 Canada. 506-529-4581.
E-mail: silverstone@nb.aibn.com. Web site: www.asf.ca. Quarterly. Circ.: 11,000.
Martin Silverstone, Editor. **Description:** Covers fishing, conservation, ecology,
travel, politics, biology, how-tos, and anecdotes. **Nonfiction:** Articles related to
Atlantic salmon; 1,500-3,000 words; $200-$600. **Fillers:** Salmon politics, conserva-
tion, and nature; 200-500 words; $100. **Tips:** Sample copy free on request. **Queries:**
Preferred. **E-Queries:** Yes. **Payment:** On publication.

AUDUBON

National Audubon Society
700 Broadway, Fl. 4, New York, NY 10003-9501.
E-mail: editor@audubon.org. Web site: www.audubon.org. Bimonthly. $20/yr. Circ.:
460,000. David Seideman, Editor-in-Chief. **Description:** Conservation and environmental issues, natural history, ecology, and related subjects. **Nonfiction:** Articles;
150-4,000 words; pay varies. **Tips:** Submit queries, with clips and SASE, to Editorial
Assistant. **Queries:** Required. **Payment:** On acceptance. **Contact:** Audrey Colyar,
Editorial Assistant.

BIRD WATCHER'S DIGEST

P.O. Box 110, Marietta, OH 45750-0110. 740-373-5285.
E-mail: editor@birdwatchersdigest.com. Web site: www.birdwatchersdigest.com.
Bimonthly. $19.99/yr. Circ.: 75,000. William H. Thompson III, Editor. **Description:**
Bird-watching experiences and expeditions; interesting backyard topics and how-tos.
Nonfiction: Articles for bird watchers: first-person accounts; profiles of bird species;
600-2,500 words; from $100. **Tips:** Write for guidelines. Submit complete manu-
script. **Queries:** Preferred. **Response:** 8 weeks, SASE required. **Payment:** On publication. **Contact:** Bill Thompson III, Editor.

BIRDER'S WORLD

Kalmbach Publishing Co.

21027 Crossroads Circle, Waukesha, WI 53187. 262-796-8776.

E-mail: mail@birdersworld.com. Web site: www.birdersworld.com. Bimonthly. $4.95/$22.50. Circ.: 64,000. Charles J. Hagner, Editor. **Description:** On all aspects of birds and birding. Offers tips on birding, attracting and feeding birds, gardening, and travel. **Nonfiction:** Feature articles, 1,600-2,000 words; $400-$500. **Columns, Departments:** Personal essays, 500-1,500 words. **Queries:** Preferred. **E-Queries:** Yes. **Unsolicited mss:** Accepts. **Response:** 3 months, SASE (if visuals are sent). **Freelance Content:** 75%. **Rights:** FNAR. **Payment:** On publication.

BUGLE

Rocky Mountain Elk Foundation

2291 W Broadway, Missoula, MT 59808. 406-523-4538.

E-mail: bugle@rmef.org. Web site: www.rmef.org. Bimonthly. $30/yr. Circ.: 132,000. Dan Crockett, Editor. **Description:** Journal of the Rocky Mountain Elk Foundation. Original, critical thinking about wildlife conservation, elk ecology, and hunting. **Fiction:** Thoughtful elk-hunting stories; human-interest stories; 1,500-4,500 words; $.20/word. **Nonfiction:** About conservation, elk ecology and natural history, elk hunting; 1,500-3,000 words; $.20/word. **Poetry:** 1 page; $100/poem. **Fillers:** Humor. **Columns, Departments:** Essays on hunting or conservation issues; 1,000-3,000 woods; $.20/word. **Tips:** Do not submit how-to pieces. All articles must have a connection to elk. **Queries:** Preferred. **E-Queries:** Yes. **Unsolicited mss:** Accepts. **Response:** 3 months, SASE required. **Freelance Content:** 80%. **Rights:** FNAR. **Payment:** On acceptance. **Contact:** Paul Queneau, Assistant Editor.

CALIFORNIA WILD

California Academy of Sciences

Golden Gate Park, San Francisco, CA 94118-4599. 415-750-7116.

E-mail: calwild@calacademy.org. Web site: www.calacademy.org. Quarterly. $4/$12.95. Circ.: 30,000. Kathleen Wong, Senior Editor. **Description:** Based at the research facility, natural-history museum, and aquarium in San Francisco's Golden Gate Park. **Nonfiction:** Well-researched articles on natural history and preservation of the environment; 1,000-2,500 words; $.30/word. **Columns, Departments:** Skywatcher; A Closer Look; Wild Lives; In Pursuit of Science. **Art:** Color, transparencies. **Tips:** Prefers queries with clips. **Unsolicited mss:** Accepts. **Rights:** FNAR. **Payment:** On publication.

CANADIAN GEOGRAPHIC

39 McArthur Ave., Ottawa, Ontario K1L 8L7 Canada. 613-745-4629.

E-mail: editorial@canadiangeographic.ca. Web site: www.canadiangeographic.ca. Bimonthly. $5.95/$29.95. Circ.: 240,000. Rick Boychuk, Editor. **Description:** Covers Canadian landscape, nature, wildlife, and people. Pay varies. **Queries:** Required. **E-Queries:** Yes. **Unsolicited mss:** Does not accept. **Response:** 3 months, SASE. **Rights:** FNAR. **Payment:** On publication.

CANADIAN WILDLIFE/BIOSPHERE
71 Barber Green Rd., Toronto, Ontario M3C 2A2 Canada. 416-445-0544.
E-mail: wild@tribute.ca. $25 (Canada), $37 (outside Canada). Circ.: 35,000. Kendra
Toby, Editor. **Description:** On national and international wildlife issues. Articles on
wild areas, nature-related research, endangered species, wildlife management, land-
use issues, character profiles, and science and politics of conservation. **Queries:**
Preferred. **Payment:** On publication.

THE CONSERVATIONIST
New York State Dept. of Environmental Conservation
625 Broadway, Fl. 2, Albany, NY 12233-4502. 518-402-8047.
E-mail: dhnleson@gw.dec.state.ny.us. Web site: www.dec.state.ny.us. Bimonthly.
$12. Circ.: 110,000. David H. Nelson, Editor. **Description:** Articles on environmen-
tal/conservation programs and policies of New York. Articles 1,500 words or more,
$100. Articles of fewer than 1,500 words, $50. **Columns, Departments:** Books, letters. **Art:** Original artwork, $50. Photography (color or B&W), $15. **Queries:**
Preferred. **Payment:** On publication.

THE COUNTRY CONNECTION
691 Pinecrest Rd., Boulter, Ontario K0L 1G0 Canada. 613-332-3651.
E-mail: magazine@pinecone.on.ca. Web site: www.pinecone.on.ca. 3x/yr. $3.95. Circ.:
10,000. Gus Zylstra, Editor. **Description:** Eco-friendly publication for Ontario.
Focuses on nature, heritage, history, nostalgia, environment, country living, the arts,
and "green" travel. **Tips:** Canadian material only. Please request writer's guidelines by
mail or online for specifications on length/payment of articles. Sample copy $4.55.
Queries: Not necessary. **E-Queries:** Yes. **Unsolicited mss:** Accepts. **Response:**
Queries 1 week, submissions to 6 months, SASE (Canadian postage). **Freelance
Content:** 75%. **Rights:** FNAR. **Payment:** On publication.

THE DOLPHIN LOG
Cousteau Society, Inc.
3612 E Tremont Ave., Bronx, NY 10465-2022. 718-409-3370.
E-mail: cousteau@cousteausociety.org. Web site: www.dolphinlog.org. Bimonthly.
$15/yr. Circ.: 80,000. Lisa Rao, Editor. **Description:** On a variety of topics related to
our global water system (marine biology, ecology, natural history, and water-related
subjects, for 7- to 13-year-olds). **Nonfiction:** Articles, 400-600 words; pays $50-$200.
Queries: Preferred. **Payment:** On publication.

E/THE ENVIRONMENTAL MAGAZINE
Earth Action Network
28 Knight St., Norwalk, CT 06851. 203-854-5559.
E-mail: info@emagazine.com. Web site: www.emagazine.com. Bimonthly. $3.95/$20.
Circ.: 50,000. Jim Motavalli, Editor. **Description:** Focuses on environmental concerns. **Nonfiction:** Features and short pieces, on environmental issues (community
gardens, mass transit, global warming, activism, trends, etc.). 400-4,200 words.

Columns, Departments: Your Health, Money Matters, Eating Right, Going Green, House and Home, Consumer News. 750-1,200 words. **Tips:** "Reporting must be objective. Include quoted sources and end-of-article contact information." Sample copy $5. **Queries:** Preferred. **E-Queries:** Yes. **Unsolicited mss:** Accepts. **Freelance Content:** 60%. **Rights:** FNAR. **Payment:** On publication.

ENVIRONMENT

1319 18th St. NW, Washington, DC 20036-1826. 202-296-6267.
E-mail: env@heldref.org. Web site: www.heldref.org. Monthly. $4.95/issue. Circ.: 5,800. Barbara T. Richman, Managing Editor. **Description:** Solid analysis of environmental science and policy issues. **Nonfiction:** On major scientific and policy issues of a significant topic; concise, objective, accurate, jargon-free; use graphics and sidebars for key points; 2,500-4,000 words. **Fillers:** Cartoons; $50. **Columns, Departments:** Education, energy, economics, public opinion; 1,000-1,700 words; $100. **Tips:** Avoid news and feature formats. **Queries:** Required. **E-Queries:** Yes. **Unsolicited mss:** Accepts. **Response:** 6-8 weeks. **Freelance Content:** 98%. **Rights:** FNAR. **Payment:** On publication.

FLORIDA WILDLIFE

Florida Fish & Wildlife Conservation Commission
620 S Meridian St., Tallahassee, FL 32399-1600. 850-488-5563.
Web site: www.floridawildlifemagazine.com. Bimonthly. Circ.: 18,000. Dick Sublette, Editor. **Description:** Articles, 800-1,200 words, that promote native flora and fauna, hunting, fishing in Florida's waters, outdoor ethics, and conservation of natural resources. Pays $55/page plus extra for published photos. Prefers color slides. **Freelance Content:** 50%. **Payment:** On publication.

GREEN TEACHER

See full listing in Education category.

HIGH COUNTRY NEWS

P.O. Box 1090, Paonia, CO 81428. 970-527-4898.
E-mail: editor@hcn.org. Web site: www.hcn.org. Biweekly. $32/yr. Circ.: 23,000. Greg Hanscom, Editor. **Description:** Environmental and cultural newspaper on the American West (from West Coast to Great Plains). Covers Western environmental and public lands issues, management, rural community, and natural resource issues, profiles of innovators, and Western politics. **Nonfiction:** Well-researched stories on any natural resource (including people, culture, and aesthetic values) or environmental topics; 4,000 words; $.25/word and up. **Columns, Departments:** Bulletin boards (book reviews, activist profiles, event announcements); 200 words. Hotlines (news briefs); 250 words. Roundups (topical stories); 800 words. Essays; to 1,000 words. Pays $.25/word and up. **Art:** Color or B&W prints (8x10 preferred); 35mm slides; JPG files, 300 dpi or higher; $35-$100. **Queries:** Preferred. **E-Queries:** Yes. **Unsolicited mss:** Accepts. **Freelance Content:** 90%. **Payment:** On publication.

THE ILLINOIS STEWARD
See full listing in History category.

INTERNATIONAL WILDLIFE
National Wildlife Federation
11100 Wildlife Center Dr., Reston, VA 20190-5362. 703-438-6510.
E-mail: pubs@nwf.org. Web site: www.nwf.org. Bimonthly. $26 (members). Circ.: 130,000. Jonathan Fisher, Editor. **Description:** Covers wildlife, conservation, and environmental issues outside the U.S. **Nonfiction:** Articles on nature, and human use and stewardship of it; buys species profiles and status reports, on-scene issue pieces, personality profiles, science stories; 1,200-2,000 words; $800-$2,200. **Art:** 35mm; $300 up. **Tips:** "Consider photo potential of all story ideas." **Queries:** Required. **E-Queries:** Yes. **Unsolicited mss:** Does not accept. **Response:** 4 weeks, SASE required. **Freelance Content:** 85%. **Rights:** Exclusive 1st-time worldwide rights; non-exclusive worldwide thereafter. **Payment:** On acceptance.

KEYSTONE OUTDOORS
P.O. Box 730, Camp Hill, PA 17011-2308. 717-730-6263.
E-mail: bille@celticmooninc.com. Quarterly. $14.95/yr. Circ.: 30,000. Sherry Yearick Ritchey, Publisher; Bill Einsig, Editor. **Description:** Wildlife and natural history magazine with a strong conservation and educational focus. Most articles have a tie to Pennsylvania and neighboring states. **Tips:** Guidelines available. **Queries:** Required. **E-Queries:** Yes. **Unsolicited mss:** Does not accept. **Response:** 4 weeks. **Freelance Content:** 80%. **Rights:** One-time. **Payment:** On publication.

MOTHER EARTH NEWS
See full listing in Lifestyle Magazines category.

NATIONAL GEOGRAPHIC KIDS
See full listing in Juvenile category.

NATIONAL GEOGRAPHIC MAGAZINE
National Geographic Society
1145 17th St. NW, Washington, DC 20036-4688. 202-857-7000.
E-mail: editor@nationalgeographic.com. Web site: www.nationalgeographic.com. Monthly. $3.95/$29. Circ.: 7,800,000. William Allen, Editor-in-Chief. **Description:** On geography, world cultures, and environmental conservation. **Nonfiction:** First-person, general-interest, heavily illustrated articles on science, natural history, exploration, and geographical regions. **Tips:** "We're 40% staff-written; the balance of our material is by published authors." **Queries:** Required. **E-Queries:** No. **Unsolicited mss:** Does not accept. **Response:** 4 weeks, SASE. **Freelance Content:** 70%. **Rights:** One-time worldwide serial, plus secondary NGS rights. **Payment:** On publication. **Contact:** Oliver Payne, Sr. Editor, Manuscripts.

NATIONAL PARKS

National Parks Conservation Assn.

1300 19th St., NW, Suite 300, Washington, DC 20036. 202-223-6722.

E-mail: npmag@npca.org. Web site: www.npca.org. Bimonthly. $2.95. Circ.: 350,000. Linda M. Rancourt, Editor-in-Chief. **Description:** Covers areas within the National Park System. **Nonfiction:** Articles, 1,200-1,500 words, on National Park areas, proposed new areas, threats to parks or wildlife, new trends in use, legislative issues, endangered species. **Tips:** "Write for a nonscientific, but well-educated audience. Be specific and include descriptive details and quotes. No "My Trip to . . ." stories." **Queries:** Required. **E-Queries:** Yes. **Unsolicited mss:** Does not accept. **Response:** 2 months, SASE required. **Freelance Content:** 60%. **Rights:** FNASR. **Payment:** On acceptance.

NATURE FRIEND

See full listing in Juvenile category.

ON EARTH

Natural Resources Defense Council

40 W 20th St., New York, NY 10011. 212-727-4412.

E-mail: onearth@nrdc.org. Web site: www.nrdc.org/onearth. Quarterly. $2.95/issue. Circ.: 140,000. **Description:** Journal of thought and opinion for the general public on environmental affairs, especially on policies of national and international significance. Strives to be a flagship of environmental thinking and covers critical emerging events and new ideas. **Nonfiction:** Investigative articles, profiles, book reviews, and essays; pay varies. **Poetry:** Conveying emotional and spiritual sources of environmental commitment; $50. **Tips:** "We're a national magazine—no stories with limited, localized perspective. We are less a nature magazine than we are a magazine about environmental issues (politics, policy, etc.)." **Queries:** Required. **Unsolicited mss:** Accepts. **Response:** 6-8 weeks, SASE required.

ORION

Orion Society

187 Main St., Great Barrington, MA 01230. 413-528-4422.

E-mail: orion@orionsociety.org. Web site: www.oriononline.org. Bimonthly. $7.50/issue. Circ.: 25,000. H. Emerson Blake, Executive Editor. **Description:** Explores the relationship between people and nature. Looks for compelling, reflective writing that connects readers to important issues by heightening awareness of the interconnections between humans and nature. **Nonfiction:** 750-4,000 words; manuscripts longer than 4,000 words may not be considered; $.10/word. **Columns, Departments:** Natural history, arts, poetry, book reviews; 750 words; $.10/word. **Tips:** "*Orion* is meant as a lively, personal, informative, and provocative dialogue. Review copies of submission guidelines before submitting. Contact for upcoming themes." **E-Queries:** No. **Unsolicited mss:** Accepts. **Response:** 10-12 weeks, SASE. **Freelance Content:** 20%. **Rights:** FNASR. **Payment:** On publication.

OUTDOOR AMERICA
Izaak Walton League of America
707 Conservation Ln., Gaithersburg, MD 20878-2983. 301-548-0150.
E-mail: oa@iwla.org. Web site: www.iwla.org. Quarterly. Circ.: 40,000. Jason McGarvey, Editor. **Description:** Publication of the Izaak Walton League of America. Covers national conservation issues that are top priorities of the league. **Nonfiction:** On endangered species, public lands management, and the protection of air quality, water quality, and water resources. Also, farm-related issues, wildlife and fisheries management controversies of national interest; 1,500-3,000 words; $.25-$.30/word. **Tips:** Send clips. **Queries:** Preferred. **Response:** SASE required.

RANGE MAGAZINE
106 E Adams, Suite 201, Carson City, NV 89706. 775-884-2200.
E-mail: bw@rangemagazine.com. Web site: www.rangemagazine.com. Quarterly. $3.95/$19.95. Circ.: 21,000. C.J. Hadley, Editor. **Description:** Features controversial issues and provides a forum for opposing viewpoints, seeking solutions to halt the depletion of a national resource: the American cowboy. Devoted to issues that threaten the West, its people, lifestyles, rangelands, and wildlife. **Nonfiction:** Feature articles, 1,500-1,800. **Columns, Departments:** Red Meat Survivors (500 words, interviews with oldtimers, including historic/current photos); $100-$150. **Art:** Original illustrations, slides, high quality prints; $40-$150. **Tips:** Submit concise, colorful pieces that address issues affecting those who live on and work the land. Avoid academic, overly technical material. **Queries:** Preferred. **E-Queries:** Yes. **Unsolicited mss:** Accepts. **Response:** Queries 6-8 weeks, submissions 8-10 weeks, SASE. **Freelance Content:** 90%. **Rights:** FNAR. **Payment:** On publication.

SIERRA
Sierra Club
85 Second St., Fl. 2, San Francisco, CA 94105-3441. 415-977-5656.
E-mail: sierra.letters@sierraclub.org. Web site: www.sierraclub.org. Bimonthly. $2.95/issue. Circ.: 710,000. Joan Hamilton, Editor. **Description:** Publication of the Sierra Club with a strong environmental emphasis. Provides outstanding nature photography and outdoor recreation and travel information. **Nonfiction:** Stories on nature and environmental issues; 100-4,000 words; $1/word. **Columns, Departments:** what you can do in your home to make the environment safer; visiting a wild place; environmental problems, policy, etc.; 750-1,500 words; $1/word. **Queries:** Required. **E-Queries:** Accepts. **Unsolicited mss:** Accepts. **Response:** 6 weeks. **Freelance Content:** 70%. **Rights:** FNASR and electronic. **Payment:** On acceptance.

TEXAS PARKS & WILDLIFE
Fountain Park Plaza, 3000 S Interstate Hwy. 35, Suite 120
Austin, TX 78704. 512-912-7000.
E-mail: magazine@tpwd.state.tx.us. Web site: www.tpwmagazine.com. Monthly. $15.95. Circ.: 153,000. Susan Ebert, Publisher/Editor. **Description:** Promotes con-

servation and enjoyment of Texas wildlife, parks, waters, and all outdoors. **Nonfiction:** Features on hunting, fishing, birding, camping, and the environment. Photos a plus.; 400-1,500 words; $.30-$.50/word. **Payment:** On acceptance.

VIRGINIA WILDLIFE
4010 West Broad St., Richmond, VA 23230. 804-367-1000.
E-mail: lwalker@dgif.state.va.us. Web site: www.dgif.state.va.us. **Description:** On fishing, hunting, wildlife management, outdoor safety and ethics, with Virginia tie-in. Articles run 500-1,200 words, $.18/word. Pays extra for color photos. **Queries:** Preferred. **Payment:** On publication.

WHOLE EARTH
Point Foundation, 1408 Mission Ave., San Rafael, CA 94901. 415-256-2800.
E-mail: editor@wholeearthmag.com. Web site: www.wholeearthmag.com. Quarterly. $24/yr. Circ.: 30,000. Peter Warshall, Editor. **Description:** Covers issues related to the environment and conservation, culture, social change, education, media, technology, medical self-care, and all aspects of creating a more interesting life in a sustainable society. **Nonfiction:** Articles, pay varies. Reviews of books and other tools, $50. **Tips:** Good article material can be found in passionate personal statements or descriptions of writer's activities. **Queries:** Preferred. **Payment:** On publication.

WILDLIFE CONSERVATION MAGAZINE
Wildlife Conservation Society
2300 Southern Blvd., Bronx, NY 10460-1090. 718-220-5121.
E-mail: magazine@wcs.org. Web site: www.wcs.org. Bimonthly. $19.95. Circ.: 154,000. Deborah Behler, Editor-in-Chief. **Description:** Popular natural history. First-person articles, based on authors' research and experience. **Nonfiction:** Include personal observations; weave in atmosphere, sights, sounds, smells, colors, weather; if pertinent, include your own feelings; 1,500-2,000 words; $1,500-$2,000. **Columns, Departments:** Wild places; 1,000 words; $750-$1,000 words. **Tips:** Contribute short news items for Conservation Hotline. **Queries:** Required. **E-Queries:** Yes. **Unsolicited mss:** Accepts. **Response:** 1 month, SASE. **Freelance Content:** 75%. **Rights:** FNAR. **Payment:** On acceptance.

WILD OUTDOOR WORLD (W.O.W.)
See full listing in Juvenile category.

WISCONSIN NATURAL RESOURCES
Wisconsin Dept. of Natural Resources
101 S Webster St., P.O. Box 7921, Madison, WI 53702-0005. 608-266-1510.
E-mail: david.sperling@dnr.state.wi.us. Web site: www.wnrmag.com. Bimonthly. $3.50/$8.97. Circ.: 130,000. David L. Sperling, Editor. **Description:** Covers outdoor and environmental issues. Also, keen outdoor observations, nature appreciation, and agency activities. **Nonfiction:** Discussions of emerging environmental issues such as PDBE contamination, arsenic in water, powers of observation, hunting ethics, etc.;

1,500-2,200 words. **Fillers:** Nature notes and monographs about individual species; 400-600 words. **Tips:** Does not offer payment to contributors. **Queries:** Preferred. **E-Queries:** Yes. **Unsolicited mss:** Accepts. **Response:** Queries 2 weeks; Submissions 2-3 months, SASE. **Freelance Content:** 20%. **Rights:** One-time.

ETHNIC & MULTICULTURAL

AFRICAN VOICES
See full listing in Literary Fiction & Poetry category.

AIM
P.O. Box 1174, Maywood, IL 60153. 708-344-4414.
E-mail: apiladoone@aol.com. Web site: www.aimmagazine.org. Quarterly. $5/issue. Circ.: 7,000. Myron Apilado, Editor. **Description:** America's intercultural magazine. Committed to fighting racism. **Fiction:** Short stories reflecting that people from different backgrounds are more alike than different; 3,500 words; $25-$100. **Nonfiction:** 1,000-1,500 words; $15-$25. **Poetry:** 20 lines; $3. **Fillers:** 30 words; $5. **Columns, Departments:** 1,500 words; $15. **Art:** Images promoting racial equality; $10. **Tips:** "Write about your experiences." **Queries:** Not necessary. **E-Queries:** No. **Unsolicited mss:** Accepts. **Response:** 1 month; SASE required. **Freelance Content:** 75%. **Rights:** First. **Payment:** On publication.

ALBERTA SWEETGRASS
Aboriginal Multi-Media Society of Alberta
13245 146th St., Edmonton, Alberta T5L 4S8 Canada. 780-455-2700
E-mail: edsweet@ammsa.com. Web site: www.ammsa.com. Monthly. Circ.: 7,500. Debora Steel, Editor. **Description:** Newspaper covering Aboriginal issues for communities in Alberta. **Nonfiction:** Articles, 300-900 words (prefers 500-800 words; briefs, 100-150 words): features, profiles, and community-based topics.

AMERICAN INDIAN ART
See full listing in Arts & Architecture category.

AMERICAN LEGACY
28 W 23rd St., New York, NY 10010. 212-620-2200.
E-mail: amlegacy@americanheritage.com.
Web site: www.americanlegacymagazine.com. Quarterly. $2.95/$9.95. Circ.: 500,000. Audrey Peterson, Editor. **Description:** Covers all aspects of Black history and culture. **Nonfiction:** Articles on people and events that have shaped history for African-Americans; up to 4,000 words; pay negotiable. **Tips:** No lifestyle articles or features on contemporary figures in the Black community unless they have a strong connection with history. Proposals should be 1 page only plus a 1 page cover letter. **Queries:** Required. **E-Queries:** Yes. **Unsolicited mss:** Accepts. **Response:** 2-4 months, SASE. **Freelance Content:** 95%. **Payment:** On acceptance.

AMERICAN VISIONS
1101 Pennsylvania Ave NW, Suite 820, Washington, DC 20004. 202-347-3820.
E-mail: editor@avs.americanvisions.com. Web site: www.americanvisions.com.
Bimonthly. Circ.: 125,000. Joanne Harris, Executive Editor. **Description:** Focuses
on African-American culture with special emphasis on the arts. **Nonfiction:** Articles
500-2,500 words; pays $100-$600. **Columns, Departments:** Columns; 1,000 words;
Varies. **Queries:** Required. **Freelance Content:** 75%. **Payment:** On publication.

AMERICAS
See full listing in Contemporary Culture category.

ASIAN PACIFIC AMERICAN JOURNAL
See full listing in Literary Fiction & Poetry category.

THE BLACK COLLEGIAN
909 Poydras St., Fl. 36, New Orleans, LA 70112. 504-523-0154.
E-mail: robert@black-collegiate.com. Web site: www.black-collegian.com.
Semiannual. $8/yr. Circ.: 122,000. Robert G. Miller, VP/Editor. **Description:**
Articles focus on the opportunities and experiences of African-American college students
and recent graduates in relation to careers and self-development. Provides
entry-level career opportunities and methods on preparing to enter the work force.
Also read by faculty, career counselors, and placement directors. **Nonfiction:** Most
pieces focus on professional life, but the culture and experiences of African-American
collegians is also explored by offering information on sports, personalities, history,
interviews/profiles, opinions, and current events. 900-1,900 words; $100-$500. **Tips:**
"Personalize your article—use "you" rather than the impersonal "college students."
Most of our articles are assigned, but we will consider ideas with a brief, detailed
query." **Queries:** Required. **E-Queries:** Yes. **Unsolicited mss:** Does not accept.
Response: 60 days. **Freelance Content:** 90%. **Rights:** FNAR. **Payment:** On
publication.

BLACK ENTERPRISE MAGAZINE
130 Fifth Ave., Fl. 10, New York, NY 10011-4306. 212-242-8000.
E-mail: edmonda@blackenterprise.com. Web site: www.blackenterprise.com.
Monthly. $19.95/yr. Circ.: 420,000. Alfred Edmond, Editor-in-Chief. **Description:**
Articles on money management, careers, political issues, entrepreneurship, high
technology, and lifestyles for black professionals. Also profiles and interviews with
successful black professionals. **Queries:** Preferred. **Payment:** On acceptance.

BLACK ISSUES IN HIGHER EDUCATION
See full listing in Education category.

BLACK ROMANCE/BRONZE THRILLS
Sterling/Macfadden Partnership
333 Seventh Ave., Fl. 11, New York, NY 10001-5004. 212-979-4800.

E-mail: info@sterlingmacfadden.com. Web site: www.sterlingmacfadden.com. Bimonthly. $19/yr. Circ.: 70,000. Lisa Finn, Editor. **Description:** Short romantic fiction for African-American women. **Fiction:** First-person, featuring African-American women; 19-21 pages; pay varies. **Nonfiction:** On relationships. **Columns, Departments:** On spicing up romance/sex lives for couples; tips on dating, beauty; 3 pages; $125. **Tips:** Avoid cultural stereotypes. Stories should be juicy (mild sex scenes), romantic, but not offensive. **Queries:** Not necessary. **E-Queries:** Yes. **Unsolicited mss:** Accepts. **Response:** 3-4 weeks, SASE. **Freelance Content:** 100%. **Rights:** All. **Payment:** On publication.

BLACK SECRETS
See full listing in Romance & Confession category.

BLACKLINES
See full listing in Arts & Architecture category.

BRAZZIL
2039 N Ave. 52, Los Angeles, CA 90042. 323-255-8062.
E-mail: brazzil@brazzil.com. Web site: www.brazzil.com. Monthly. $2/issue. Circ.: 12,000. Rodney Mello, Editor. **Description:** Publication printed in English that centers on the politics, way of life, economy, ecology, tourism, music, literature, and arts of Brazil. Some short stories printed in Portuguese. **Fiction:** 1,000-5,000 words. **Nonfiction:** 1,000-5,000 words. **Tips:** Liberal viewpoint; controversial material preferred. **Queries:** Not necessary. **E-Queries:** Yes. **Unsolicited mss:** Accepts. **Response:** 2 days, SASE required. **Freelance Content:** 60%. **Rights:** One-time. **Payment:** On publication.

CALLALOO
Dept. of English, Texas A&M University
4227 TAMU, College Station, TX 77843-4227. 979-458-3108.
E-mail: callaloo@tamu.edu. Web site: http://callaloo.tamu.edu. Quarterly. $10/$37. Circ.: 2,000. Charles H. Rowell, Editor. **Description:** African Diaspora literary journal, with original work by and critical studies of Black writers worldwide. **Fiction:** Fiction, drama; up to 10,000 words. **Nonfiction:** Academic and cultural criticism; up to 10,000 words. **Poetry:** Up to 10 poems. **Art:** Glossy prints or slides. **Tips:** Submit cover letter with titles of submitted works, and detailed contact information for author, with e-mail address if available. Submit three copies of each manuscript, without author's name or any other identifying information. **Queries:** Not necessary. **E-Queries:** No. **Unsolicited mss:** Accepts. **Response:** 6-8 months, SASE or e-mail required. **Freelance Content:** 100%. **Payment:** In copies.

CNEWA WORLD
Catholic Near East Welfare Assoc.
1011 First Ave., New York, NY 10022-4195. 212-826-1480.
E-mail: cnewa@cnewa.org. Web site: www.cnewa.org. Bimonthly. $2.50/$12.00.

Circ.: 90,000. Michael La Civita, Executive Editor. **Description:** Offers educational profiles of cultures, histories, religions, and social issues of the peoples of Eastern Europe, India, the Middle East, and Northeast Africa. **Nonfiction:** 1,500 words, $.20/word. **Art:** Slides, prints; $50 and up. **Tips:** "Writers and photographers in each Pontifical Mission city and in other CNEWA countries offer the most objective, accurate, sensitive portraits of their subjects." **Queries:** Preferred. **Unsolicited mss:** Accepts. **Response:** SASE required. **Freelance Content:** 50%. **Payment:** On publication. **Contact:** Eileen Reinhard, Assistant Editor.

THE CRISIS
7600 Georgia Ave. NW, Suite 405, Washington, DC 20012. 202-829-5700. E-mail: thecrisiseditorial@naacpnet.org. Web site: www.thecrisismagazine.com. Bimonthly. $12/yr. Circ.: 250,000. Victoria Valentine, Editor-in-Chief. **Description:** A journal of civil rights, politics, African-American history and culture. Articles range from short briefs to 3,000-word features. **Payment:** On acceptance.

DIRECT AIM
See full listing in Career & Professional Development category.

ESSENCE
See full listing in Women's Publications category.

FACES
See full listing in Juvenile category.

FILIPINAS
1486 Huntington Ave., Suite 300, South San Francisco, CA 94080. 650-872-8660. E-mail: myuchengco@filipinasmag.com. Web site: www.filipinasmag.com. Monthly. $2.95/$18. Circ.: 30,000. Mona Lisa Yuchengco, Editor. **Description:** For and about Filipinas and their communities in North America. **Nonfiction:** Profiles on successful Filipino Americans, human-interest stories, issues affecting the Filipino American community; 750-3,000 words; $50-$100. **Art:** Color photos, $25; B&W, $15. **Queries:** Required. **E-Queries:** Yes. **Unsolicited mss:** Accepts. **Response:** SASE required. **Freelance Content:** 70%. **Rights:** All. **Payment:** On publication.

FOOTSTEPS
See full listing in Juvenile category.

GERMAN LIFE
Zeitgeist Publishing, P.O. Box 3000, Denville, NJ 07834. 800-875-2997. E-mail: editor@germanlife.com. Web site: www.GermanLife.com. Bimonthly. Circ.: 40,000. Carolyn Cook, Editor. **Description:** German culture, its past and present, and how America has been influenced by its German immigrants: history, travel, people, the arts, and social and political issues. **Nonfiction:** Up to 2,000 words; $300-$500. **Fillers:** Up to $80. **Columns, Departments:** Book reviews and short articles;

250-800 words; $100-$130. **Art:** Photos and illustrations that capture and/or detail the diversity of German(-American) life and culture; everyday life, landscapes, people, architecture, art, festivals. **Queries:** Preferred. **Response:** 4-6 weeks. **Rights:** First English/German language serial rights. **Payment:** On publication.

GLOBAL CITY REVIEW
See full listing in Literary Fiction & Poetry category.

GOSPEL TODAY
See full listing in Religion category.

HEALTH QUEST
See full listing in Health category.

HEART & SOUL
315 Park Ave. S, Fl. 11, New York, NY 10010-3607. 646-654-4200.
E-mail: heartandsoul@vanguarde.com. Web site: www.heartandsoul.com. 10x/yr. $16.97. Circ.: 308,000. Corynne Corbett, Editor-in-Chief. **Description:** The African-American woman's ultimate guide to total well-being (body, mind, and spirit) **Nonfiction:** Health, spirituality, beauty, fitness, relationships, finance, and life issues for African-American women; 800-1,500 words; pay varies. **Queries:** Preferred. **Payment:** On acceptance.

THE HIGHLANDER
See full listing in History category.

HISPANIC
999 Ponce de Leon Blvd., Suite 600, Coral Gables, FL 33134-3037. 305-442-2462.
E-mail: editor@hispaniconline.com. Web site: www.hispaniconline.com. Monthly. Circ.: 250,000. Carlos Verdecia, Editor. **Description:** General-interest (career, business, politics, and culture). Confronts issues affecting the Hispanic community, emphasis on solutions rather than problems. English-language. **Nonfiction:** Features, 1,400-2,500 words; $450. **Columns, Departments:** Hispanic Journal, Portfolio; $75-$150. **Queries:** Preferred.

HISPANIC BUSINESS
See full listing in Business category.

HISPANIC MARKET NEWS
See full listing in Business category.

THE HISPANIC OUTLOOK IN HIGHER EDUCATION
See full listing in Education category.

HISPANIC TIMES MAGAZINE

See full listing in Career & Professional Development category.

HURRICANE ALICE

Rhode Island College, Dept. of English, Providence, RI 02908. 401-456-8377. E-mail: mreddy@ric.edu. Quarterly. $2.50/$12. Circ.: 1,000. Maureen Reddy, Editor. **Description:** Feminist exploration, from diverse perspectives, of all aspects of culture. Especially committed to work by women of color, lesbians, working-class women, and young women. **Fiction:** Fictional critiques of culture; 3,500 words max. **Nonfiction:** Articles, essays, interviews, and reviews; 3,500 words max. **Poetry:** Yes. **Art:** B&W (5x7 or 8x10). **Queries:** Not necessary. **E-Queries:** Yes. **Unsolicited mss:** Accepts. **Response:** Queries 30 days, submissions 6 months, SASE required. **Freelance Content:** 100%. **Rights:** FNASR. **Payment:** In copies.

INDIA CURRENTS

P.O. Box 21285, San Jose, CA 95151. 408-274-6966. E-mail: editor@indiacurrents.com. Web site: www.indiacurrents.com. 11x/yr. $19.95/yr. Circ.: 25,800. Vandana Kumar, Editor. **Description:** Explores the heritage and culture of India. **Fiction:** To 3,000 words; $50-$150. **Nonfiction:** On India culture, arts, and entertainment in the U.S. and Canada. Also, music/book reviews, commentary on events affecting the lives of Indians. Travel articles (first-person stories of trips to India or the subcontinent); to 3,000 words; $50-$150. **Queries:** Preferred. **E-Queries:** Yes. **Unsolicited mss:** Accepts. **Response:** 4 weeks, SASE. **Freelance Content:** 99%. **Rights:** One-time. **Payment:** On publication.

INDIAN LIFE

Box 3765, Redwood Post Office, Winnipeg, MB R2W 3R6 Canada. 204-661-9333. E-mail: viola.editor@indianlife.org. Web site: www.indianlife.org. Bimonthly. $10. Circ.: 29,000. Viola Fehr, Editor. **Description:** Presents news from across Native North America. **Fiction:** Stories which accurately portray Native Americans; 500-2,000 words; $20-$150. **Nonfiction:** News, first-person views, special features, interviews; 500-1,200 words; $20-$75. **Poetry:** To 100 words; $20-$40. **Fillers:** 50-200 words; $10-$25. **Art:** Photos and illustrations; JPG, 200 dpi; $25-$75. **Tips:** "Writers need to know Native Americans (historical and contemporary). No Native spirituality, politics, or land claims." **Queries:** Preferred. **E-Queries:** Yes. **Unsolicited mss:** Accepts. **Response:** 4 weeks for queries, 8 weeks for submissions; SASE required. U.S. contributors please send check for $2.00 with return envelope. **Freelance Content:** 20%. **Rights:** First or all. **Payment:** On publication.

IRISH AMERICA

875 Sixth Ave., Suite 2100, New York, NY 10001. 212-725-2993. E-mail: irishamag@aol.com. Web site: www.irishamerica.com. Bimonthly. $21.95. Circ.: 85,000. Patricia Harty, Editor-in-Chief. **Description:** For Irish-American audience; prefers history, sports, the arts, and politics. **Nonfiction:** Articles, 1,500-2,000 words; pays $.12/word. **Queries:** Preferred. **Payment:** On publication.

IRISH AMERICAN POST

301 N Water St., Milwaukee, WI 53202. 414-273-8132.
E-mail: editor@irishamericanpost.com. Web site: www.irishamericanpost.com.
Martin Hinz, Publisher. **Description:** Online publication for Irish and Irish
Americans. Profiles, business stories, sports, travel, politics; 800-1,200 words; $100.
Also considers short fiction pieces and poetry. **Tips:** No quaint photos or stories; no
"going back home" stories. **Queries:** Preferred.

THE IRISH EDITION

903 E Willow Grove Ave., Wyndmoor, PA 19038-7909. 215-836-4900.
Jane M. Duffin, Editor. **Description:** Short fiction, nonfiction, fillers, humor, and
puzzles, for Irish-American and Irish-born readers. Pay negotiable. **Queries:**
Preferred. **Payment:** On acceptance.

ITALIAN AMERICA

219 E Street NE, Washington, DC 20002-4922. 202-547-2900.
E-mail: italianamerica@osia.org. Web site: www.osia.org. Quarterly. $12/yr. Circ.:
65,000. Dr. Dona De Sanctis, Editor. **Description:** Published by the Order Sons of
Italy in America. Covers Italian-American news, history, personalities, culture, etc.
Articles on people, institutions, and events of interest to the Italian-American community. Also book reviews. 500-1,200 words; $50-$250. **Tips:** Avoid "My grandmother used to spend hours making her spaghetti sauce . . ." Focus on unique, interesting cultural facets. **Queries:** Preferred. **E-Queries:** Yes. **Unsolicited mss:** Does
not accept. **Response:** 2-3 months. **Freelance Content:** 20%. **Rights:** Worldwide
non-exclusive. **Payment:** On publication.

JOURNAL OF ASIAN MARTIAL ARTS

See full listing in Sports & Recreation/Outdoors category.

LA FACTORIA DE SONIDO

See full listing in Performing Arts category.

LATIN STYLE MAGAZINE

P.O. Box 2969, Venice, CA 90294-2969. 323-462-4409.
E-mail: info@latinstylemag.com. Web site: www.latinstylemag.com. Monthly. Circ.:
120,000. **Description:** Latin arts and entertainment magazine targeting English-
speaking Hispanic markets. Covers entertainment, music, fashion, art, and leisure.

LATIN TRADE

See full listing in Business category.

LATINA MAGAZINE

See full listing in Women's Publications category.

LATINO LEADERS

4229 Hunt Dr., Suite 3910, Carrollton, TX 75010. 888-528-4532.
E-mail: editor@latinoleaders.com. Web site: www.latinoleaders.com. Bimonthly.
$2.95/issue. Circ.: 100,000. Patrizia Rossi, Editor. **Description:** Profiles the lives of
successful Hispanic-American leaders through inspirational stories that reveal who
they really are and how they got to be where they are today. **Columns,
Departments:** Mundo Latino (news and events); Up and Coming (Hispanic event
guide); Leader of the Past; Leader of the Future; Gallery (photos); Shelf Life (book,
movie, music reviews). **E-Queries:** Yes. **Unsolicited mss:** Does not accept.
Response: Varies.

LILITH

See full listing in Women's Publications category.

LIVING BLUES

See full listing in Performing Arts category.

LSR

See full listing in Literary Fiction & Poetry category.

MOMENT

4710 41st St NW, Washington, DC 20016. 202-364-3300.
E-mail: editor@momentmag.com. Web site: www.momentmag.com. Bimonthly.
$4.50/issue. Circ.: 50,000. Hershel Shanks, Editor. **Description:** On Jewish culture,
politics, and religion. **Fiction:** 8,000 max. **Nonfiction:** Sophisticated articles on
Jewish culture, politics, religion, personalities. Pay negotiated; 100-3,500 words.
Poetry: 150-300 words. **Columns, Departments:** Shorts (250 words, on events,
people, and living); Olam/The Jewish World (colorful, first-person reports); Book
Reviews (to 400 words). **Tips:** Seeking fresh angles on Jewish themes. **Queries:**
Preferred. **E-Queries:** Yes. **Unsolicited mss:** Accepts. **Response:** 3-4 months,
SASE. **Freelance Content:** 90%. **Rights:** FNASR. **Payment:** On publication.

NA'AMAT WOMAN

See full listing in Women's Publications category.

NATIONAL GEOGRAPHIC MAGAZINE

See full listing in Environment & Conservation category.

NATIVE PEOPLES

5333 N Seventh St., Suite C-224, Phoenix, AZ 85014-2804. 602-265-4855.
E-mail: editorial@nativepeoples.com. Web site: www.nativepeoples.com. Bimonthly.
$4.95/issue. Circ.: 60,000. Daniel Gibson, Editor. **Description:** Dedicated to the
sensitive portrayal of arts and lifeways of the Native peoples of the Americas.
Nonfiction: Artist profiles (traditional and contemporary); issue-oriented pieces with

Native American angle; program/people profiles in education, health, politics; economic development; 1,000-3,000 words; $.25/word. **Columns, Departments:** Pathways (travels with Native site/culture/history focus; Viewpoint (open subject matter); 400-1,200 words; $.25/word. **Tips:** "Readership is both Native American and those interested in Native culture. Our stories need to appeal to both, serving as a bridge between cultures." **Queries:** Preferred. **E-Queries:** Yes. **Unsolicited mss:** Accepts. **Response:** 4 weeks, SASE required. **Freelance Content:** 80%. **Rights:** FNAR. **Payment:** On publication.

THE NETWORK JOURNAL
See full listing in Business category.

NEW YORK TREND
14 Bond St., Suite 176, Great Neck, NY 11021. 516-466-0028.
E-mail: nytrend@aol.com. Web site: www.nytrend.com. Biweekly. $1/$15. Circ.: 50,000. Felicia Persand, Editor. **Description:** Articles focus on the issues affecting Black and other minority communities in New York City and other regions across the United States. Topics include politics, business, entertainment, and other special features. **Columns, Departments:** Seeks material on politics, human rights, and hard news; 800 words; $30. **Art:** JPGs; $10/picture. **Tips:** "Avoid fluff writing. We have a strong interest in hard news and business features." **E-Queries:** Yes. **Unsolicited mss:** Accepts. **Response:** 1 week. **Freelance Content:** 50%. **Rights:** 1st print.

PAPYRUS
See full listing in Writing & Publishing category.

RUSSIAN LIFE
P.O. Box 567, Montpelier, VT 05601-0567. 802-223-4955.
E-mail: ruslife@rspubs.com. Web site: www.russian-life.com. Bimonthly. $29/yr. Circ.: 15,000. Mikhail Ivanov, Editor. **Description:** Russian culture, travel, history, politics, art, business, and society. Very visual; most stories include professional-quality photos. Articles run 1,000-3,000 words; $.07-$.10/word. **Tips:** "Submit solid, third-person American journalism (AP stylebook); frank, terse, and incisive. No stories about personal trips to Russia, editorials on developments in Russia, or articles promoting a specific company, organization, or government agency. We seek to provide coverage of Russia that is free of illusions (but not blemishes) and full of hope (but not ideology or agendas). Our job is to present a realistic, truthful, and independent view that balances these realities, providing enjoyable, insightful reading." **Queries:** Required. **E-Queries:** Yes. **Unsolicited mss:** Accepts. **Response:** 1 month, SASE required. **Freelance Content:** 75%. **Rights:** All. **Payment:** On publication.

SABOR MAGAZINE
557 E Cypress Ave., Suite E, Burbank, CA 91501. 818-841-2231.
E-mail: info@sabormagazine.com. Web site: www.sabormagazine.com. Monthly.

$26/yr. Circ.: 50,000. Kathy Diaz, Editor. **Description:** Features news and articles on Latin entertainment, including music, dance, night life, restaurants, and upcoming events. **Columns, Departments:** Human-interest pieces related to Latin culture; 400 words; $100. **Queries:** Not necessary. **E-Queries:** Yes. **Unsolicited mss:** Accepts. **Response:** 3 days. **Payment:** On acceptance.

SCANDINAVIAN REVIEW
American-Scandinavian Foundation
58 Park Ave., New York, NY 10016. 212-879-9779.
E-mail: rjlitell@amscan.org. Web site: www.amscan.org. 3x/yr. Circ.: 6,000. Richard J. Litell, Editor. **Description:** Presents the arts, sciences, business, politics, and culture of contemporary Denmark, Finland, Iceland, Norway, and Sweden to a lay audience with interest in Nordic countries. Accepts illustrated articles, essays, and poetry; 1,500-2,000 words; pays $300 honorarium. **Tips:** No original English-language poetry, only Nordic poetry in translation. **Queries:** Preferred. **E-Queries:** Yes. **Response:** 1 month, SASE. **Freelance Content:** 50%. **Rights:** One-time. **Payment:** On publication.

SELECTA
1717 N Bayshore Dr., Suite 113, Miami, FL 33132-1195. 305-579-0979.
E-mail: selectamag@aol.com. Web site: www.revistaselecta.com. Monthly. $36. Circ.: 30,000. Eva Hughes, Editor. **Description:** For upscale Hispanics in the U.S. and Latin America.

SOUTH AMERICAN EXPLORERS
See full listing in Travel Articles category.

TEACHING TOLERANCE
See full listing in Education category.

VISTA
999 Ponce de Leon Blvd., Suite 600, Coral Gables, FL 33134. 305-442-2462.
E-mail: ggodoy@hisp.com; editor@vistamagazine.com.
Web site: www.vistamagazine.com. Monthly. Circ.: 1,000,000. Gustavo Godoy, Publisher/Editor. **Description:** Covers news, events, and issues of interest to the Hispanic community throughout the U.S. **Nonfiction:** On job advancement, bilingualism, immigration, the media, fashion, education, medicine, sports, and food; to 1,500 words. **Columns, Departments:** Book reviews, and profiles of interesting, community-oriented Hispanics; 100 words. **Tips:** Sample copy and guidelines free on request. **Queries:** Required. **Unsolicited mss:** Does not accept. **Payment:** On publication.

FAMILY & PARENTING

ADOPTIVE FAMILIES

42 W 38th St., Suite 901, New York, NY 10018. 646-366-0830.
E-mail: beth@adoptivefam.com. Web site: www.adoptivefam.com. Bimonthly. $24.95/yr. Circ.: 25,000. Beth Kracklauer, Editor. **Description:** On parenting adoptive children and other adoption issues. **Nonfiction:** Middle-school and teen years, relatives and community, adoptive parent support groups, school, foster adoption, transracial adoption, domestic adoption, adoptive parents of color; 1,000-1,500 words; payment negotiable. **Columns, Departments:** The Waiting Game, Parenting the Child Who Waited, About Birthparents, Been There, Adoption & School, In My Opinion, At Home, Single Parent, Living with Diversity, Parent Exchange. **Tips:** Prefers queries by fax (646-366-0842) or e-mail. **Queries:** Preferred. **E-Queries:** Yes. **Response:** 6-8 weeks.

AMERICAN BABY

Meredith Corp.
125 Park Ave., Fl. 16, New York, NY 10017. 212-886-3600.
Web site: www.americanbaby.com. Monthly. $23.94/yr. Circ.: 2,000,000. Judith Nolte, Editor-in-Chief. **Description:** For new or expectant parents on prenatal and infant care. **Fiction:** No fantasy pieces or dreamy musings. **Nonfiction:** Features, 1,000-2,000 words; personal experience pieces (do not submit in diary format), 900-1,200 words; $800-$2,000. **Columns, Departments:** Crib Notes (news and feature topics); 50-350 words; $500. **Payment:** On acceptance.

ATLANTA PARENT

2346 Perimeter Park Dr., Suite 101, Atlanta, GA 30341. 770-454-7599.
E-mail: atlantaparent@atlantaparent.com. Web site: www.atlantaparent.com. Monthly. $15. Circ.: 85,000. Liz White, Editor. **Description:** For parents with children, birth to 18 years. **Nonfiction:** On family, child, and parent topics; 300-1,500 words; $15-$35. **Fillers:** Humor; 800-1,200 words. **Queries:** Preferred. **E-Queries:** Yes. **Unsolicited mss:** Accepts. **Response:** 3-6 months, SASE. **Freelance Content:** 50%. **Rights:** One-time. **Payment:** On publication. **Contact:** Amy Dusek.

BABY TALK

Time, Inc.
530 Fifth Ave., Fl. 4, New York, NY 10036-5101. 212-522-8989.
E-mail: letters@babytalk.com. Web site: www.parenting.com. 10x/yr. $19.50/yr. Circ.: 1,725,000. Susan Kane, Editor-in-Chief. **Description:** Pregnancy, babies, baby care, women's health, child development, work, and family. **Nonfiction:** Articles, by professional writers with expertise and experience; 1,000-3,000 words; pay varies. **Queries:** Required. **E-Queries:** No. **Response:** SASE required. **Payment:** On acceptance. **Contact:** Emily Hebert, Editorial Assistant.

BEST WISHES

37 Hanna Ave., Unit 1, Toronto, Ontario M6K 1W9 Canada. 416-537-2604.
E-mail: tracy@parentscanada.com. Web site: www.parentscanada.com. Semi-annual.
Circ.: 155,000. Tracy Cooper, Editor. **Description:** Publication for new parents written by Canadian health care professionals.

BIG APPLE PARENT

9 E 38th St., Fl. 4, New York, NY 10016. 212-889-6400.
E-mail: edit@parentsknow.com. Web site: www.parentsknow.com. Monthly. Free.
Circ.: 70,000. Helen Rosengren Freedman, Executive Editor. **Description:**
Newspaper for New York City parents, with separate editions for Queens and
Westchester County. Interviews, news, op-ed pieces; 750 words; $50. **Art:** Hard copy,
JPG; $20. **Tips:** "We are looking for news and controversy concerning New York City
parenting; we do not need travel, essays, humor, or general child-raising pieces."
Queries: Not necessary. **E-Queries:** Yes. **Unsolicited mss:** Accepts. **Response:** 1
week, SASE required. **Freelance Content:** 90%. **Rights:** FNAR. **Payment:** On
publication.

BRAIN CHILD

P.O. Box 1161, Harrisonburg, VA 22803-1161. 540-574-2379.
E-mail: editor@brainchildmag.com. Web site: www.brainchildmag.com. Quarterly.
$5/$18. Circ.: 15,000. Jennifer Niesslein, Stephanie Wilkinson, Co-Editors.
Description: "The Magazine for Thinking Mothers." Explores the personal transformation that motherhood brings. Spotlights women's own view of motherhood.
Fiction: Literary short stories on an aspect of motherhood; e.g., "The Life of the
Body," by Jane Smiley; 1,500-4,500 words; pay varies. **Nonfiction:** Personal essays,
features, book reviews, parodies, debate essays. **Tips:** "We're seeking smart, down-to-earth work that's sometimes funny, sometimes poignant." **Queries:** Preferred.
E-Queries: Yes. **Unsolicited mss:** Accepts. **Response:** 1-3 months, SASE.
Freelance Content: 90%. **Rights:** FNAR and electronic. **Payment:** On publication. **Contact:** Jennifer Niesslein.

CATHOLIC PARENT

200 Noll Plaza, Huntington, IN 46750. 219-356-8400.
E-mail: cparent@osv.com. Web site: www.osv.com. Woodeene Koenig-Bricker,
Editor. **Description:** For Catholic parents. Anecdotal and practical, with an emphasis on values and family life. **Nonfiction:** Features, how-tos, and general-interest articles; 800-1,000 words; pay varies. **Tips:** "Don't preach." **Payment:** On acceptance.

CENTRAL CALIFORNIA PARENT

7638 N Ingram Ave., Suite 101, Fresno, CA 93711-6201. 559-435-1409.
E-mail: ccparent@qnis.net. Web site: www.ccparent.com. Monthly. $15. Circ.:
35,000. Sally Cook, Publisher. **Description:** For parents. **Nonfiction:** Articles, 500-1,500 words; pay varies. **Queries:** Preferred. **Payment:** On publication. **Contact:**
Kristi Soss, Editor.

CENTRAL PENN PARENT
101 N Second St., Harrisburg, PA 17101-1402. 717-236-4300.
E-mail: karrenm@journalpub.com. Web site: www.journalpub.com. Monthly. $16.95.
Circ.: 35,000. Karren Miller, Editor. **Description:** On family and parenting issues
Nonfiction: 1,400 words; $125. **Columns, Departments:** 700 words; $50. **Art:**
Submit photos with article. **Tips:** Welcomes new writers. **Queries:** Required.
E-Queries: Yes. **Unsolicited mss:** Accepts. **Response:** 3 weeks, SASE required.
Freelance Content: 50%. **Rights:** 1st. **Payment:** On publication.

CHICAGO PARENT
141 S Oak Park Ave., Oak Park, IL 60302-2972. 708-386-5555.
Web site: www.chicagoparent.com. Monthly. Circ.: 125,000. **Description:** Magazine
for parents in the Chicago metro area.

CHILD
Gruner + Jahr USA Publishing
375 Lexington Ave., New York, NY 10017. 212-499-2000.
E-mail: mailcenter@child.com. Web site: www.child.com. 10x/yr. $13.97/yr. Circ.:
1,020,000. Miriam Arond, Editor-in-Chief. **Description:** A sophisticated lifestyle
magazine for today's young parents. **Columns, Departments:** Kids' Fashion, Mom's
Beauty, Fashion and Home, Pregnancy column, Baby Bytes column, and "What I
Wish Every Parent Knew" back-page essay. Also features lifestyle section, which
includes travel and home design. Fees vary. **Tips:** Prefers queries and manuscripts via
regular mail. "Offer news that parents need to know (e.g., options for products/serv-
ices, ways to preserve precious parenthood time) in a lively, stylish fashion." **Queries:**
Preferred. **E-Queries:** Yes. **Unsolicited mss:** Accepts. **Response:** 2 months, SASE
required. **Freelance Content:** 95%. **Rights:** FNAR. **Payment:** On acceptance.

CHRISTIAN PARENTING TODAY
Christianity Today, 465 Gundersen Dr., Carol Stream, IL 60188-2489. 630-260-6200.
E-mail: cptmag@aol.com. Bimonthly. Circ.: 90,000. Carla Barnhill, Editor.
Description: Serves the needs of today's families in a positive and practical format.
Nonfiction: Articles on real-life experiences and the truths of the Bible. **Queries:**
Required.

CHRISTIAN SINGLE
See full listing in Religion category.

CITY PARENT
467 Speers Rd., Oakville, Ontario L6K 3S4 Canada. 905-815-0017.
E-mail: cityparent@metroland.com. Web site: www.cityparent.com. Monthly. Circ.:
250,000. Jane Muller, Editor. **Description:** Offers stories, new-product information,
computer news, parenting advice, places to go and things to do with kids.
Nonfiction: Pays $75-$150. **Queries:** Required. **E-Queries:** Yes. **Unsolicited mss:**
Accepts. **Freelance Content:** 50%. **Rights:** All.

CLEVELAND/AKRON FAMILY

35475 Vine St., Suite 224, Eastlake, OH 44095. 440-510-2000.
E-mail: editor@tntpublications.com. Monthly. Circ.: 50,000. Francis Richards, Editor. **Description:** For parents in the Cleveland/Akron region. Seeks to encourage positive family interaction. Provides articles on general topics, area events, trends, and services for area families. Pays $30/article or column. **Queries:** Required. **E-Queries:** Yes. **Unsolicited mss:** Accepts. **Payment:** On publication.

THE COMPLEAT MOTHER

5703 Hillcrest, Richmond, IL 60071. 815-678-7531.
E-mail: greg@rsg.org. Web site: www.compleatmother.com. Quarterly. Circ.: 12,000. **Description:** For new moms and mom-to-be.

DALLAS FAMILY

1321 Valwood Parkway, Suite 530, Carrollton, TX 75006-8412. 972-488-3555.
E-mail: phwcomments@unitedad.com. Web site: www.parenthood.com. Monthly. $19.95. Circ.: 80,000. Bill Lindsay, Editor-in-Chief. **Description:** For parents in the Dallas metro area.

DOVETAIL

775 Simon Greenwell Lane, Boston, KY 40107. 502-549-5499.
E-mail: di-ifr@boardstown.com. Web site: www.dovetailinstitute.org. Bimonthly. $29.95/yr. Circ.: 1,000. Mary Helène Rosenbaum, Editor. **Description:** "A Journal by and for Jewish/Christian Families." Resources for dual-faith couples, and their families, friends, and professionals who serve them, from a non-denominational perspective. **Nonfiction:** Advice, anecdotes, and research on aspects of interfaith marriage; e.g., "Challah Baking: Thoughts of a Christian Cook," or "Intermarriage in Australia"; 800-1,000 words; $25. **Fillers:** Related cartoons, humor, and photos also used. **Tips:** "Have experience or knowledge in the field of intermarriage. Avoid broad generalizations, or strongly partisan religious creeds." **Queries:** Not necessary. **E-Queries:** Yes. **Unsolicited mss:** Accepts. **Response:** Queries 2-4 weeks, submissions 4-6 weeks, SASE required. **Freelance Content:** 80%. **Rights:** All. **Payment:** On publication.

EASTSIDE PARENT

123 NW 36th St., Suite 215, Seattle, WA 98107-4959. 206-441-0191.
E-mail: epnwpp@aol.com. Web site: www.parenthood.com. Monthly. $15/yr. Circ.: 30,000. Bill Lindsay, Editor-in-Chief. **Description:** For parents of children under 14. Readers tend to be professional, two-career families. Also publishes *Portland Parent, Seattle's Child,* etc. **Nonfiction:** Articles, 300-2,500 words; pays $50-$600. **Queries:** Preferred. **Payment:** On publication. **Contact:** Karen Matthee, Editor.

EP NEWS

National Assn. of Entrepreneurial Parents
P.O. Box 320722, Fairfield, CT 06432. 203-371-6212.

E-mail: epideas@en-parent.com. Web site: www.en-parent.com. Monthly. Lisa Roberts, Cofounder. **Description:** E-zine for entrepreneurial parents. Serves as a resource for parents who balance family and professional careers. Offers advice, serves as a support network, and addresses the needs of these parents from both the business and parenting perspectives.

EXPECTING

37 Hanna Ave., Unit 1, Toronto, Ontario M6K 1W9 Canada. 416-537-2604. E-mail: info@pregnancycanada.com. Web site: www.parentscanada.com. Semi-annual. Circ.: 292,000. Tracy Cooper, Editor. **Description:** For pregnant Canadian women.

FAITH & FAMILY

432 Washington Ave., North Haven, CT 06473. 203-230-3832. E-mail: editor@faithandfamilymag.com. Web site: www.faithandfamilymag.com. Bimonthly. $14.95/yr. Circ.: 30,000. Duncan Maxwell Anderson, Editor. **Description:** "The Magazine of Catholic Living." How-to articles and interviews of interest to Catholic families, with photos. **Nonfiction:** 1,000-2,000 words; pays $75-$300. **Columns, Departments:** Opinion or inspirational columns, 600-800 words, with strict attention to Catholic doctrine. **Queries:** Preferred. **Unsolicited mss:** Accepts. **Freelance Content:** 70%. **Rights:** 1st. **Payment:** On publication.

FAMILY

Military Force Features
51 Atlantic Ave., Suite 200, Floral Park, NY 11001. 516-616-1930. E-mail: hq1@familymedia.com. Web site: www.familymedia.com. Monthly. Circ.: 500,000. Don Hirst, Editor. **Description:** For military families. Covers topics of interest to women with children (military lifestyle, home decorating, travel, moving, food, personal finances, career, relationships, family, parenting, health and fitness). **Nonfiction:** Articles, 1,000-2,000 words; pays to $200. **Payment:** On publication.

FAMILY

Kids Monthly Publications
1122 US Highway 22 W, Mountainside, NJ 07092-2812. 908-232-2913. E-mail: ucfamily@aol.com. Monthly. $18/yr. Circ.: 120,000. Fam Dupre, Editor. **Description:** Parenting magazine for families in New Jersey. Offers information on education, child development, health, safety, and other parenting issues.

FLORIDA FAMILY MAGAZINE

1840 Glengary St., Sarasota, FL 34231-3604. 941-922-5437. E-mail: emily@floridafamilymagazine.com. Web site: www.floridafamilymagazine.com. Bimonthly. Circ.: 60,000. Emily Leinfuss, Executive Editor. **Description:** For families in and around Sarasota, central Florida, and Tampa.

FOCUS ON THE FAMILY

8605 Explorer Dr., Colorado Springs, CO 80920-1051. 719-531-3400.
E-mail: grahamsg@mm.fotf.org. Web site: www.family.org. Monthly. Circ.: 2,600,000.
Susan G. Graham, Editor. **Description:** Provides information for Christian families.

HOMELIFE

LifeWay Christian Resources
One LifeWay Plaza, Nashville, TN 37234-0175. 615-251-2860.
E-mail: homelife@lifeway.com. Monthly. Circ.: 400,000. **Description:** For Christian families about honoring God in their daily lives. **Nonfiction:** Articles consistent with the vision and doctrinal statements of LifeWay Christian Resources. **Tips:** All articles by assignment. Accepts queries, but not freelance submissions or simultaneous submissions. Purchases all rights; no reprints. Free sample copy on request. **E-Queries:** Yes. **Unsolicited mss:** Does not accept. **Response:** 8 weeks, SASE.

L.A. PARENT

443 E Irving Dr., Suite D, Burbank, CA 91504-2447. 818-846-0400.
Web site: www.parenthoodweb.com. Monthly. $14/yr. Circ.: 110,000. Bill Lindsay, Editor-in-Chief. **Description:** Articles on child development, health, nutrition, education, and local travel/activities for parents of children up to age 12. Also publishes *San Diego Parent, Parenting* (Orange Co.), and *Arizona Parenting*. **Nonfiction:** Articles, 1,000 words; pays $100-$350. **Queries:** Preferred. **Payment:** On acceptance.

LIVING WITH TEENAGERS

LifeWay Christian Resources
One LifeWay Plaza, Nashville, TN 37234-0174. 615-251-2226.
E-mail: lwt@lifeway.com. Web site: www.lifeway.com. Monthly. $18.95/yr. Circ.: 48,000. Sherrie Thomas, Editor. **Description:** Informs and educates parents of teenagers on how to best deal with typical issues and problems faced by teens. Provides strong Christian emphasis and biblical solutions.

METROKIDS

1080 N Delaware Ave., Suite 702, Philadelphia, PA 19125. 215-291-5560 x102.
E-mail: editor@metrokids.com. Web site: www.metrokids.com. Monthly. Circ.: 125,000. Tom Livingston, Executive Editor. **Description:** For Delaware Valley area parents with kids, ages 0-16. **Nonfiction:** Parenting subjects in the Philadelphia metro region; 800-1,500 words; $35-$50. **Columns, Departments:** Product reviews, books, music, video, software, health, safety, women's subjects, family finance, travel; 800 words; $35-$50. **Tips:** Prefers queries via e-mail; responds only if interested. **Queries:** Preferred. **E-Queries:** Yes. **Unsolicited mss:** Accepts. **Response:. Freelance Content:** 40%. **Rights:** One-time and electronic. **Payment:** On publication.

NEW BEGINNINGS

La Leche League International

P.O. Box 4079, Schaumburg, IL 60168-4079. 847-519-7730.

E-mail: editornb@llli.org. Web site: www.lalecheleague.org. Bimonthly. Circ.: 25,000. Kathleen Whitfield, Managing Editor. **Description:** Member publication of a non-profit organization. Provides articles and information for women who breast-feed. **Tips:** Does not offer payment for any material.

NEW PARENT

10 New King St., White Plains, NY 10604-1205. 914-949-4726.

E-mail: knenneker@newparent.com. Web site: www.newparent.com. Semi-annual. Circ.: 1,100,000. Kathy Nenneker, Editor. **Description:** For new parents and parents-to-be.

NEW YORK FAMILY

141 Halstead Ave., Mamaroneck, NY 10543-2607. 914-381-7474.

E-mail: hhart@unitedad.com. Web site: www.parenthoodweb.com. Monthly. $22/yr. Circ.: 58,000. Heather Hart, Editor-in-Chief. **Description:** Articles related to family life in New York City and general parenting topics. **Nonfiction:** Pays $50-$200. **Payment:** On publication.

NORTHWEST BABY & CHILD

15417 204th Ave. SE, Renton, WA 98059-9021. 425-235-6826.

E-mail: editor@nwbaby.com. Web site: www.nwbaby.com. Monthly. Circ.: 45,000. Betty Freeman, Editor. **Description:** For parents in Western Washington. **Tips:** Writer's guidelines and editorial calendar available on Web site. **E-Queries:** Yes.

NORTHWEST FAMILY NEWS

7907 212th St., Suite 201, Edmonds, WA 98026. 425-775-6546.

E-mail: nwfamily@earthlink.net. Web site: www.nwfamily.com. Monthly. $15/yr. Circ.: 50,000. Chris Hope, Editor. **Description:** Regional parenting and family publication for Western Washington. Nonfiction pieces, $25-$40. Humor, $25-$40. Photos, $5-$20. **Tips:** Send articles in e-mail (no attachments); include word count. **Queries:** Required. **E-Queries:** Yes. **Unsolicited mss:** Accepts. **Freelance Content:** 65%. **Rights:** One-time (print and electronic).

PARENT CONNECTION

P.O. Box 707, Setauket, NY 11733-0769. 631-751-0356.

E-mail: parent@tbrnewspapers.com. Web site: www.tbrnewspapers.com. Monthly. Circ.: 125,000. Leah Dunaief, Editor. **Description:** For parents in New York City and the surrounding area.

THE PARENT PAPER
1 Garret Mountain Plaza, West Paterson, NJ 07424-3320. 973-569-7720.
E-mail: info@parentpaper.com. Web site: www.parentpaper.com. Monthly. $25/yr.
Circ.: 50,000. Mary Vallo, Editor. **Description:** For parents in New Jersey.

PARENTGUIDE NEWS
419 Park Ave. S., Fl. 13, New York, NY 10016. 212-213-8840.
E-mail: annmarie@parentguidenews.com. Web site: www.parentguidenews.com.
Monthly. $19.95/yr. Circ.: 210,000. Annmarie Evola, Editor. **Description:** For parents with children under 12 years old. **Fiction:** 1,000 words. **Nonfiction:** Articles on families and parenting: health, education, child-rearing; 1,000 words. **Queries:** Preferred. **E-Queries:** Yes. **Unsolicited mss:** Accepts. **Response:** 1-2 weeks; SASE required. **Freelance Content:** 80%.

PARENTING
Time, Inc., 530 Fifth Ave., Fl. 4, New York, NY 10019. 212-522-8989.
E-mail: letters@parenting.com. Web site: www.parenting.com. 10x/yr. Circ.: 1,560,000. Janet Chan, Editor-in-Chief. **Description:** Seeks to make pregnancy and parenthood easier and less stressful by educating parents. Offers resources, tools, real-life wisdom, and solutions/strategies for effective parenting to moms and dads. **Nonfiction:** On education, health, fitness, nutrition, child development, psychology, and social issues for parents of young children; 500-3,000 words. **Queries:** Preferred. **E-Queries:** No. **Unsolicited mss:** Accepts. **Response:** 2 months, SASE.

PARENTING TODAY'S TEEN
P.O. Box 11864, Olympia, WA 98508.
E-mail: editor@parentingteens.com. Web site: www.parentingteens.com. Bimonthly.
Diana Kathrein, Publisher/Editor. **Description:** E-zine, written by parents and professionals, about the issues of parenting teenagers, including tough issues like drug/alcohol abuse, sex, AIDS, violence, and running away. **Nonfiction:** Pays $10-$25. **Queries:** Required. **E-Queries:** Yes. **Response:** 2-3 weeks. **Rights:** FNAR. **Contact:** Diana Kathrein.

PARENTLIFE
LifeWay Christian Resources
One LifeWay Plaza, MSN 172, Nashville, TN 37234-0172. 615-251-2000.
E-mail: parentlife@lifeway.com. Web site: www.lifeway.com. Monthly. Circ.: 105,000.
Mary Ann Bradberry, Editor-in-Chief. **Description:** Publication focusing on Christian parenting. **E-Queries:** Yes. **Contact:** William Summey.

PARENTS
Gruner + Jahr USA Publishing
375 Lexington Ave., New York, NY 10017-5514. 212-499-2000.
E-mail: mailbag@parentsmagazine.com. Web site: www.parents.com. Monthly.
$12.97/yr. Circ.: 2,153,000. Sally Lee, Editor-in-Chief. **Description:** Features arti-

cles on parenting and raising healthy, well-adjusted children. Topics include children's health/safety, behavior, new technology, family life, and travel.

PARENTS EXPRESS

290 Commerce Dr., Fort Washington, PA 19034-2400. 215-629-1774.
E-mail: parexpress@aol.com. Web site: www.parents-express.net. Monthly. $24.95/yr. Circ.: 80,000. Laura Winchester, Editor. **Description:** For parents in southeastern Pennsylvania and southern New Jersey. **Nonfiction:** Articles; pays $35-$150. **Payment:** On publication.

PARENTS' PRESS

1454 Sixth St., Berkeley, CA 94710-1431. 510-524-1602.
E-mail: parentsprs@aol.com. Web site: www.parentspress.com. Monthly. $15. Circ.: 75,000. Dixie Jordan, Editor. **Description:** Parenting newspaper for the Berkeley bay area. **Nonfiction:** Pays $50 and up. **E-Queries:** Yes. **Response:** SASE required. **Freelance Content:** 30%. **Rights:** varies.

PITTSBURGH PARENT

P.O. Box 374, Bakerstown, PA 15007-0374. 724-443-1891.
E-mail: pgparent@nauticom.net. Web site: www.pittsburghparent.com. Monthly. Circ.: 55,000. Patricia Poshard, Editor. **Description:** For parents in the Pittsburgh metro area.

PORTLAND PARENT

123 NW 36th St., Suite 215, Seattle, WA 98107-4959. 206-441-0191.
Web site: www.parenthoodweb.com. Monthly. $15. Circ.: 42,000. Bill Lindsay, Editor-in-Chief. **Description:** For parents in the Portland, Oregon, metro area.

QUEENS PARENT

9 E 38th St., Fl. 4, New York, NY 10016-0003. 212-889-6400.
E-mail: edit@parentsknow.com. Web site: www.parentsknow.com. Monthly. $28/yr. Circ.: 68,000. Helen Rosengren Freedman, Executive Editor. **Description:** For parents in the borough of Queens, NYC.

RAINY DAY CORNER

See full listing in Writing & Publishing category.

SACRAMENTO SIERRA PARENT MAGAZINE

457 Grass Valley Hwy, Suite 5, Auburn, CA 95603-3725. 530-888-0573. Monthly. Circ.: 55,000. **Description:** Provides articles and information to families with children and grandchildren of all ages in the greater Sacramento area. **Nonfiction:** Interested in articles that promote a developmentally appropriate, healthy, and peaceful environment for children. 300-500 words for short pieces; 700-1,000 words for feature articles.

SAN DIEGO FAMILY MAGAZINE

1475 Sixth Ave., Fl. 5, San Diego, CA 92101. 619-685-6970.
Web site: www.sandiegofamily.com. Monthly. Circ.: 120,000. Sharon Bay,
Publisher/Editor-in-Chief. **Description:** Family magazine for residents in the San
Diego area. Provides informative, educational articles on parenting with a distinct San
Diego focus. **Tips:** Does not accept phone or e-queries. Submit query by mail with
outline, clips, and SASE for response. See Web site for submission guidelines.
Queries: Required. **E-Queries:** No. **Freelance Content:** 50%. **Rights:** 1st & 2nd.
Contact: Claire Yezbak Fadden, Editor.

SEATTLE'S CHILD

123 NW 36th St., Suite 215, Seattle, WA 98107. 206-441-0191.
E-mail: scnwpp@aol.com. Web site: www.parenthood.com. Monthly. $15/yr. Circ.:
36,000. Karen Matthee, Editor. **Description:** For parents, educators, and childcare
providers in the Puget Sound region with children 14 and under. Investigative reports
and consumer tips on issues affecting families. **Nonfiction:** Articles, 400-2,500
words; pays $75-$600. **Queries:** Preferred. **Payment:** On publication.

SINGLE PARENT FAMILY

Focus on the Family
8605 Explorer Dr., Colorado Springs, CO 80920-1049. 719-531-3400.
E-mail: singleparent@family.org. Web site: www.singleparentfamily.org. Circ.:
30,000. Elsa Kok, Editor. **Description:** Information for the Christian single parent.
Addresses issues of divorce, grief, finances, and more. Pay varies. **Queries:**
Preferred. **E-Queries:** Yes. **Unsolicited mss:** Accepts. **Response:** SASE required.
Rights: FNAR. **Payment:** On acceptance.

SOUTH FLORIDA PARENTING

5555 Nob Hill Rd., Sunrise, FL 33351-4707. 954-747-3050.
E-mail: vmccash@sfparenting.com. Web site: www.sfparenting.com. Monthly. Circ.:
100,000. **Description:** For parents in south Florida.

TODAY'S FAMILY

280 N Main St., East Longmeadow, MA 01108. 413-525-6661.
E-mail: news@thereminder.com. Web site: www.thereminder.com. Bimonthly. $9.99.
Circ.: 20,000. Carla Valentine, Editor. **Description:** Parenting magazine for Western
Massachusetts. Focuses on local news, events, and activities for families. Columns on
family issues, health, day trips, etc. **Tips:** Writers must have expertise on the subject
and be from the region. Local content, advice by local experts. **Queries:** Required.
E-Queries: Yes. **Unsolicited mss:** Does not accept. **Response:** Queries 2 weeks;
SASE required. **Freelance Content:** 10%.

TODAY'S GRANDPARENT

See full listing in Seniors Magazines category.

TOLEDO AREA PARENT NEWS

1120 Adams St., Toledo, OH 43624. 419-244-9859.
E-mail: editor@toledoparent.com. Web site: www.toledoparent.com. Monthly.
$20/yr. Circ.: 50,000. Marcia Chambers, Editor. **Description:** For parents in
Northwest Ohio and Southern Michigan. **Nonfiction:** On parenting, child and family health, and other family topics. Writers must be from the region; 750-1,200 words;
$75-$200. **Queries:** Preferred. **Unsolicited mss:** Accepts.

TWINS

5350 S. Roslyn St., Suite 400, Englewood, CO 80111-2125. 303-290-8500.
E-mail: twins.editor@businessword.com. Web site: www.twinsmagazine.com.
Bimonthly. Circ.: 55,000. Sharon Withers, Editor. **Description:** Expert advice from
professionals and parents, about the needs of multiple-birth parents. **Nonfiction:**
Parenting issues specific to multiples; 1,200 words; $200-$250. **Fillers:** Practical tips
(for specific ages: birth-2, 3-4, 5-6); 125-150 words; $20. **Columns, Departments:**
Special Miracles (personal experiences); 500-600 words; $40. **Art:** Yes. **Queries:**
Preferred. **E-Queries:** Accepts. **Unsolicited mss:** Accepts. **Response:** 3 months.
Freelance Content: 60%. **Payment:** On publication.

WASHINGTON PARENT

4701 Sangamore Rd., #N270, Bethesda, MD 20816-2508. 301-320-2321.
E-mail: washpar@washingtonparent.com. Web site: www.washingtonparent.com.
Monthly. Circ.: 90,000. Margaret Hut, Editor. **Description:** For parents in and
around the Washington Metro area, Maryland, and Northern Virginia.

WESTCHESTER PARENT

9 E 38th St., Fl. 4, New York, NY 10016-0003. 212-889-6400.
E-mail: edit@parentsknow.com. Web site: www.parentsknow.com. Monthly. $28/yr.
Circ.: 70,000. Helen Rosengren Freedman, Executive Editor. **Description:** For par-
ents in Westchester County, New York.

ZELLERS FAMILY

269 Richmond St. W, Toronto, Ontario M5V 1X1 Canada. 416-596-8675.
4x/yr. Circ.: 1,200,000. Beth Thompson, Editor. **Description:** Magazine for Zellers
store customers. Focuses on fashion, decorating, cooking, etc.

FILM, TV, ENTERTAINMENT

AMERICAN CINEMATOGRAPHER

1782 N Orange Dr., Los Angeles, CA 90028-4307. 323-969-4333.
E-mail: stephen@theasc.com. Web site: www.cinematographer.com. Monthly. $40/yr.
Circ.: 42,700. Stephen Pizzello, Executive Editor. **Description:** Trade magazine for
the cinematography industry. Call for writer's guidelines.

BOMB

594 Broadway, Suite 905, New York, NY 10012. 212-431-3943.
E-mail: info@bombsite.com. Web site: www.bombsite.com. Quarterly. $4.96/$18. Circ.: 25,000. Betsy Sussler, Editor. **Description:** Interviews, varying lengths, on artists, musicians, writers, actors, and directors. Special section in each issue featuring new fiction and poetry. **Fiction:** 20 pages max; $100. **Poetry:** 10 pages; $100. **Queries:** Preferred. **E-Queries:** Yes. **Unsolicited mss:** Accepts. **Response:** Queries 4 months, submissions 4 months, SASE. **Freelance Content:** 5%. **Rights:** 1st serial. **Payment:** On publication. **Contact:** Susan Sherman, Associate Editor.

CINEASTE

304 Hudson St., Fl. 6, New York, NY 10013-1015. 212-366-5720.
E-mail: cineaste@cineaste.com. Web site: www.cineaste.com. Quarterly. $6/$20. Circ.: 11,000. Gary Crowdus, Editor-in-Chief. **Description:** Covers the art and politics of the cinema. Views, analyzes, and interprets films. **Nonfiction:** Articles should discuss a film, film genre, a career, a theory, a movement, or related topic, in depth. Interviews with people in filmmaking. 2,000-3,000 words; $75-$100. **Columns, Departments:** 1,000-1,500 words. **Tips:** "Our readers are intelligent general public, sophisticated about art and politics. No matter how complex the ideas or arguments, style must be readable." **Queries:** Preferred. **E-Queries:** Yes. **Unsolicited mss:** Accepts. **Response:** 2-3 months, SASE required. **Freelance Content:** 50%. **Rights:** FNAR. **Payment:** On publication.

EMMY

Academy of Television Arts and Sciences
5220 Lankershim Blvd., North Hollywood, CA 91601-2800. 818-754-2800.
E-mail: emmymag@emmys.org. Web site: www.emmys.tv. Bimonthy. $4.95/$28. Circ.: 15,000. Gail Polevoi, Editor. **Description:** Television industry magazine for TV professionals and enthusiasts. **Nonfiction:** Profiles and trend stories; 1,500-2,000 words; $900-$1,200. **Columns, Departments:** New writers can break in with Labors of Love or In the Mix filler items; 250-500 words; $200-$400. **Tips:** Should have TV business background. No academic, fan-magazine, or highly technical articles. **Queries:** Required. **E-Queries:** Yes. **Unsolicited mss:** Accepts. **Response:** 4-6 weeks, SASE required (unless by e-mail). **Freelance Content:** 80%. **Rights:** FNAR. **Payment:** On publication.

ENTERTAINMENT DESIGN

PRIMEDIA Business Magazines & Media
32 W 18th St., New York, NY 10011. 212-229-2965.
E-mail: jtien@primediabusiness.com. Web site: www.entertainmentdesignmag.com. Jacqueline Tien, Publisher. **Description:** Trade publication that centers on the art and technology of entertainment. Articles cover design, technical, and management aspects of theater, opera, dance, television, and film for those in performing arts and the entertainment trade. **Nonfiction:** Articles, 500-2,500 words. **Queries:** Preferred. **Payment:** On acceptance.

FANGORIA

475 Park Ave. S., Fl. 7, New York, NY 10016. 212-689-2830.
E-mail: tony@starloggroup.com. Web site: www.fangoria.com. 10x/yr. $7.99/$39.97.
Circ.: 260,000. Anthony Timpone, Editor. **Description:** Nonfiction articles and
interviews on horror films, TV series, books, and the artists who create this genre.
Emphasizes personalities and behind-the-scenes angles of horror film making.
Nonfiction: Movie, TV, and book previews; reviews; and interviews connected to
upcoming horror films; 2,000-3,000 words; $150-$250. **Tips:** A strong love of the
genre is essential. Readers are experts on horror who want to read about the latest
films and film makers. **Queries:** Required. **E-Queries:** No. **Unsolicited mss:** Does
not accept. **Response:** 6-8 weeks, SASE required. **Freelance Content:** 92%.
Rights: All. **Payment:** On publication.

FILM COMMENT

Film Society of Lincoln Center
70 Lincoln Center Plaza, New York, NY 10023-6595. 212-875-5610.
E-mail: filmcomment@filmlinc.com. Web site: www.filmlinc.com. Bimonthly.
$24.95/yr. Circ.: 45,000. Gavin Smith, Editor. **Description:** On films (new and old,
foreign and domestic), also performers, writers, cinematographers, studios, national
cinemas, genres. Opinion and historical pieces also used. **Nonfiction.** Articles, 1,000-
5,000 words; pays $.33/word. **Payment:** On publication.

FILM QUARTERLY

University of California Press
2000 Center St., Suite 303, Berkeley, CA 94704-1233. 510-643-7154.
E-mail: ann.martin@ucpress.ucop.edu. Web site: www.ucpress.edu/journals/fq.
Quarterly. $24/yr. Circ.: 7,600. Ann Martin, Editor. **Description:** Historical, analyti-
cal, and critical articles, to 6,000 words. Also, film reviews, book reviews. **Queries:**
Preferred.

HADLEY MEDIA

21 Melrose Ave., Norwalk, CT 06855.
Web site: www.univercity.com. 10x/yr. D. Patrick Hadley, Editor. **Description:**
Publisher of *Univercity* magazine and *Univercity.com*. Provides entertainment news,
fashion trends, celebrity interviews, and reviews of music, movies, and books for New
York City and Boston college students. **Queries:** Preferred.

HEROES FROM HACKLAND

1225 Evans, Arkadelphia, AR 71923. 870-246-6223.
3x/yr. $6.50/$18. Circ.: 150. Mike Grogan, Editor. **Description:** Takes a nostalgic,
popular-culture approach to the review of B-movies, cartoons, series books, radio, TV,
comic books, and newspaper comic strips. **Nonfiction:** Any fresh article casting light
on the popular culture of yesterday and its relation to today; 220-1,500 words; $5 and
copies. **Poetry:** Nostalgic with a bite, coherent imagery, no impenetrable college
quarterly stuff; to 40 lines; $5 and copies. **Fillers:** Vignettes about customs, little-

known facts about pop culture icons. **Art:** B&W only; $5/photo. **Tips:** Sample copy $5. **Queries:** Not necessary. **Unsolicited mss:** Accepts. **Response:** 10 days, SASE. **Freelance Content:** 75%. **Rights:** 1st. **Payment:** On publication.

ILLINOIS ENTERTAINER

124 W Polk, Suite 103, Chicago, IL 60605-1770. 312-922-9333.
E-mail: editors@illinoisentertainer.com. Web site: www.illinoisentertainer.com. Monthly. $35/yr. Circ.: 73,000. Althea Legaspi, Editor-in-Chief. **Description:** Covers entertainment and media, especially music. Open to non-music/band features, especially of odd, quixotic kind. **Nonfiction:** On local and national entertainment (especially alternative music) in greater Chicago area. Personality profiles, interviews, reviews; 500-1,500 words; $75. **Art:** By assignment; $30-200. **Tips:** "Send clips (via snail mail) and be patient." **Queries:** Not necessary. **E-Queries:** Yes. **Unsolicited mss:** Accepts. **Response:** Queries 30 days, submissions 30-90 days, SASE not required. **Freelance Content:** 70%. **Rights:** FNASR. **Payment:** On publication.

INDEPENDENT FILM AND VIDEO MONTHLY

304 Hudson St., Fl. 6, New York, NY 10013. 212-807-1400.
E-mail: editor@aivf.org. Web site: www.aivf.org. 10x/yr. $4.95/issue. Circ.: 15,000. Beth Pinsker, Editor-in-Chief. **Description:** For active mediamakers, on all aspects of independently-produced film and video (scripting, funding, production, technology, editing, film festivals, and distribution). **Nonfiction:** On production techniques; interviews with directors, producers, writers; book reviews; technology news, legal issues; media advocacy; 700-1,300 words. **Queries:** Required. **E-Queries:** Yes. **Unsolicited mss:** Accepts. **Response:** To 4 months, SASE. **Freelance Content:** 80%. **Rights:** FNAR and electronic. **Payment:** On publication.

KIDS TRIBUTE

See full listing in Juvenile category.

NEW ENGLAND ENTERTAINMENT DIGEST

P.O. Box 88, Burlington, MA 01803. 781-272-2066.
E-mail: jacneed@aol.com. Web site: www.jacneed.com. Monthly. $2/issue, $20/yr. Circ.: 5,000. JulieAnn Charest, editor. **Description:** Theater and entertainment news for residents in New England and New York. **Nonfiction:** On professional, regional, college, community, and children's theatre, dance, music, film, and video; length/payment varies. **Art:** Photographs, illustrations; electronic format; $5/print. **Queries:** Preferred. **E-Queries:** Yes. **Unsolicited mss:** Accepts. **Freelance Content:** 25%. **Payment:** On publication.

PERFORMING ARTS AND ENTERTAINMENT IN CANADA

104 Glenrose Ave., Toronto, Ontario M4T 1K8. 416-484-4534.
E-mail: kbell@interlog.ca. Quarterly. $8.56/issue. Circ.: 44,000. Karen Bell, Editor. **Description:** Canadian performing arts and entertainment, including theater,

music (especially classical, new, jazz, world, and folk), dance, film, TV and related fields. Also profiles, opinion, issues, etc. **Nonfiction:** Of national interest, but values submissions from smaller, out-of-the-way locations (not just downtown Montreal and Toronto). Especially interested in stories that reflect aspect of Canadian diversity. Publishes very few reviews; 600-1,500 words; $95-$170. **Art:** Prints; B&W, color. **Tips:** Welcomes new writers. Prefers stories with original ideas and opinions, or addressing issues of complexity or sophistication—not just profiles of people or companies. "Please be patient in awaiting a response on queries." **Queries:** Required. **E-Queries:** Yes. **Unsolicited mss:** Accepts. **Response:** Slow to respond, be patient, SASE required. **Rights:** 1st print and electronic. **Payment:** On publication.

PLAYBILL

525 Seventh Ave., Suite 1801, New York, NY 10018. 212-557-5757.
E-mail: jsamelson@playbill.com. Web site: www.playbill.com. Monthly. $24/yr. Circ.: 1,364,878. Judy Samelson, Editor. **Description:** Increases the understanding and enjoyment of each Broadway production, certain Lincoln Center and Off-Broadway productions, and regional attractions. Also, features about theatre personalities, fashion, entertainment, dining, etc. **Unsolicited mss:** Does not accept.

STAR MAGAZINE

5401 Broken Sound Blvd. NW, Boca Raton, FL 33487-3512. 561-997-7733.
E-mail: letters@starmagazine.com. Web site: www.starmagazine.com. Weekly. $47.76/yr. Circ.: 1,630,000. Candance Trunzo, Editor-in-Chief. **Description:** On show business and celebrities, health, fitness, parenting, and diet and food. **Nonfiction:** Topical articles, 50-800 words; pay varies.

TV GUIDE

1211 Avenue of the Americas, New York, NY 10036-8701. 212-852-7500.
Web site: www.tvguide.com. Weekly. $39.88. Circ.: 10,000,000. Steven Reddicliffe, Editor-in-Chief. **Description:** Short, light, brightly written pieces about humorous or offbeat angles of television and industry trends. Most personality pieces are staff-written. **Queries:** Required. **Payment:** On acceptance.

UNIVERCITY

Hadley Media, 21 Melrose Ave., Norwalk, CT 06855. 203-838-5303.
E-mail: katie@univercity.com. Web site: www.univercity.com. Patrick Hadley, Publisher. **Description:** An entertainment magazine for college students. Prints east-coast and west-coast editions. **Tips:** To submit, visit *UniverCity*'s Web site for details. Also interested in screenplays for their production company. "Everyone knows how difficult it is to 'break in,' with that in mind, we are committed to discovering new talent that we know exists out there but may not have an 'in.' " **Queries:** Preferred. **E-Queries:** Yes. **Unsolicited mss:** Accepts. **Contact:** Katherine Spafford, Managing Editor.

VIDEOMAKER
P.O. Box 4591, Chico, CA 95927. 530-891-8410.
E-mail: editor@videomaker.com. Web site: www.videomaker.com. Monthly. Circ.: 92,600. Stephen Muratore, Editor-in-Chief. **Description:** Covers consumer video production: camcorders, computers, tools, and techniques. For hobbyists and professional users. **Nonfiction:** Authoritative how-to articles, instructionals, editing, desktop video, audio/video production, innovative applications, tools and tips, industry developments, new products; to 1,500 words; $.10/word. **Queries:** Preferred. **E-Queries:** Yes. **Unsolicited mss:** Accepts. **Response:** 6-8 weeks, SASE. **Freelance Content:** 60%. **Rights:** All. **Payment:** On publication.

WRITTEN BY
7000 W Third St., Los Angeles, CA 90048-4329. 213-782-4522.
E-mail: writtenby@wga.org. Web site: www.wga.org. 9x/yr. $40/yr. Circ.: 12,500. Richard Slayton, Editor. **Description:** Official publication of the Writers Guild of America, by and for America's screen and television writers. **Nonfiction:** Feature articles (2,500 words), special reports (1,500-2,000 words), interviews, technical articles, and product reviews. **Tips:** Review previous issues before submitting queries or manuscripts. **Queries:** Required. **Unsolicited mss:** Accepts. **Response:** 8 weeks. **Freelance Content:** 80%. **Rights:** 1st world-wide and electronic. **Payment:** On acceptance.

FITNESS
(See also Health)

AMERICAN FITNESS
Aerobics and Fitness Assn. of America
15250 Ventura Blvd., Suite 200, Sherman Oaks, CA 91403-3297. 818-905-0040.
E-mail: americanfitness@afaa.com. Web site: www.afaa.com. Bimonthly. $48/yr. Circ.: 42,000. Meg Jordan, Editor. **Description:** Trade journal for fitness instructors. **Nonfiction:** Articles on exercise, health, trends in aerobic sports, research, nutrition, class instruction, alternative paths. No first-person stories. 1,200 words; $200/article. **Tips:** Needs research-oriented articles. **Queries:** Required. **E-Queries:** Yes. **Unsolicited mss:** Accepts. **Response:** 2 months, SASE required. **Freelance Content:** 90%. **Rights:** All. **Payment:** On publication.

AMERICAN HEALTH & FITNESS FOR MEN
5775 McLaughlin Rd., Mississauga, Ontario L5R 3P7 Canada. 905-507-3545.
E-mail: editorial@ahfmag.com. Web site: www.ahfmag.com. Kerrie-Lee Brown, Editor. **Description:** Men's lifestyle fitness magazine dealing with training, sports, gear, sex. **Nonfiction:** Sports commentary, instructional training, health and nutrition news, celebrity profiles, sexy women pictorials and bios; 1,200-1,500 words; pay varies. **Fillers:** Sex, women, gear, etc.; 500 words; pay varies. **Columns, Departments:** Sports commentary, instructional training, health and nutrition news;

800 words; pay varies. **Art:** Action, sports, couples, women, training, etc.; any format; pay varies. **Queries:** Not necessary. **E-Queries:** Yes. **Unsolicited mss:** Accepts. **Response:** SASE required. **Freelance Content:** 95%. **Rights:** All international. **Payment:** On acceptance.

ENERGY FOR WOMEN

555 Corporate Circle, Golden, CO 80401-5621. 303-384-0080.
E-mail: editorial@energyforwomen.com. Web site: www.energyforwomen.com. Bimonthly. $17.99/$4.99. Circ.: 125,000. Gretchen Ferraro, Editor-in-Chief. **Description:** Magazine for women ages 25-45 who are interested in leading a healthy lifestyle. Editorial provides ways for women to increase their energy and improve their lives by following a consistent nutrition and exercise program. **Nonfiction:** Well-researched, in-depth articles about health, fitness, nutrition, weight-training, cardio, supplementation, motivation, and mind/body issues; 800-2,000 words; $1/word. **Columns, Departments:** Short, catchy, well-researched pieces on training, nutrition, mind/body issues, and health; 300-1,000 words; $1/word. **Tips:** "Read the magazine before submitting. We're not about quick fixes, fad diets, or the latest celebrity trends. We are a magazine for real women who want to embrace fitness and health as a lifestyle." **Queries:** Required. **E-Queries:** Yes. **Unsolicited mss:** Does not accept. **Response:** 1 month. **Rights:** First NA.

FIT PREGNANCY

21100 Erwin St., Woodland Hills, CA 91367-3712. 818-884-6800.
E-mail: peg.moline@weiderpub.com. Web site: www.fitpregnancy.com. Bimonthly. $9.97/yr. Circ.: 378,000. Peg Moline, Editor-in-Chief. **Description:** Offers expert advice for the pregnant or postpartum woman and her newborn. Provides safe workouts, nutrition guidance, meal plans, medical news, baby gear, and more. **Nonfiction:** Articles, 500-2,000 words, on women's health (pregnant and postpartum), nutrition, and physical fitness. **Queries:** Preferred. **Unsolicited mss:** Accepts. **Payment:** On publication.

FITNESS

Gruner + Jahr USA Publishing
15 E 26th St., New York, NY 10010. 646-758-0430.
E-mail: kgreen@fitnessmagazine.com. Web site: www.fitnessmagazine.com. Monthly. $3/issue. Circ.: 1,000,000. Emily Listfield, Editor-in-Chief. **Description:** Features on health, exercise, nutrition, and general well-being. Targets women in their twenties and thirties. **Nonfiction:** Articles on exercise, nutrition, beauty, sex and relationships, stress, etc. Also includes features on new products, how-to pieces on exercise, and first-person profiles of individuals with healthy lifestyles; 1,500-2,500 words; $1,500-$2,500. **Queries:** Required. **Unsolicited mss:** Does not accept. **Response:** Queries 2 months. **Rights:** FNAR. **Payment:** On acceptance. **Contact:** Kathy Green, Managing Editor.

FITNESS PLUS
3402 E Kleindale Rd., Tucson, AZ 85716-1334. 520-881-6696.
E-mail: editor@fitplusmag.com. Monthly. $15/yr. Circ.: 90,000. Kari Redfield, Editor.
Description: On serious health and fitness training. Articles, 600 words; pay varies.
Queries: Required. **Payment:** On publication.

FITNESS RX FOR WOMEN
690 Rt. 25A, Setauket, NY 11733-1200. 631-751-9696.
E-mail: editor@musculardevelopment.com. Web site: www.fitnessrx.com. Monthly.
$3.99/$17.95. Circ.: 225,000. **Description:** For women featuring well-researched
articles on diet, fitness, health, cosmetic enhancement, and sexual fulfillment. Articles
run 1,000-2,500 words; pays $500-$1,500. **Queries:** Preferred. **Payment:** On
publication.

IDEA HEALTH & FITNESS SOURCE
6190 Cornerstone Ct. E, Suite 204, San Diego, CA 92121-3773. 858-535-8979.
E-mail: member@ideafit.com. Web site: www.ideafit.com. Monthly. Circ.: 23,000.
Patricia Ryan, Editorial Director. **Description:** For all levels of fitness professionals.
Nonfiction: Practical articles on new exercise programs, business management,
nutrition, health, motivation, sports medicine, group exercise, one-to-one training
techniques. Length, pay vary. **Tips:** "Gear articles for exercise studio owners/man-
agers, personal trainers, and fitness instructors. No consumer or general health
pieces." **Queries:** Preferred. **E-Queries:** Yes. **Unsolicited mss:** Accepts.
Response: 2-3 months. **Freelance Content:** 75%. **Rights:** All NA (print and electronic). **Payment:** On acceptance. **Contact:** Cynthia Roth, Editorial Assistant.

IDEA PERSONAL TRAINER
6190 Cornerstone Ct. E, Suite 204, San Diego, CA 92121-4701. 858-535-8979.
E-mail: member@ideafit.com. Web site: www.ideafit.com. Monthly. $36.70. Circ.:
13,000. Sandy Todd Webster, Executive Editor. **Description:** For the professional
personal trainer. **Nonfiction:** On exercise science; program design; profiles of successful trainers; business, legal, and marketing topics; tips for networking with other
trainers and with allied medical professionals; client counseling; and training tips. Pay
varies. **Columns, Departments:** What's New (industry news, products, research).
Queries: Preferred. **E-Queries:** Yes. **Unsolicited mss:** Accepts. **Response:** 1
month, SASE for mailed materials. **Payment:** On publication.

MEN'S FITNESS
21100 Erwin St., Woodland Hills, CA 91367-3712. 818-884-6800.
E-mail: mensfitness@weiderpub.com. Web site: www.mensfitness.com. Monthly.
$21.97/yr. Circ.: 607,000. Jerry Kindela, Editor-in-Chief. **Description:** On sports, fit-
ness, health, nutrition, and men's issues. **Nonfiction:** Authoritative, practical articles,
1,500-1,800 words; pays $500-$1,000. **Columns, Departments:** 1,200-1,500 words.
Tips: Send clips. **Queries:** Preferred. **Payment:** On acceptance.

MS. FITNESS

P.O. Box 2490, White City, OR 97503-0490. 541-830-0400.
E-mail: msfitness@aol.com. Web site: www.msfitness.com. 4x/yr. $3.99/$12. Circ.: 150,000. Greta Blackburn, Editor. **Description:** Created for the dedicated, fit woman of today. Covers all areas of interest including exercise, home equipment, nutrition, fashion, and competitions. **Queries:** Not necessary. **E-Queries:** Yes. **Response:** 60-90 days, SASE. **Freelance Content:** 50%. **Rights:** None.

MUSCLE & FITNESS

21100 Erwin St., Woodland Hills, CA 91367-3712. 818-884-6800.
E-mail: jkrumm@weiderpub.com. Web site: www.muscle-fitness.com. Monthly. $34.97. Circ.: 491,000. Bill Geiger, Executive Editor. **Description:** Bodybuilding and fitness publication for healthy, active men and women. **Nonfiction:** All areas of bodybuilding, health, fitness, injury prevention and treatment, and nutrition. Feature articles run 1,500-1,800 words; $400-$800. Short pieces and departments run 500-800 words; $360. **Tips:** All features and departments are written on assignment. Send 1 page query with potential sources, qualifications, and recent clips. **Queries:** Required. **Unsolicited mss:** Does not accept. **Rights:** FNAR. **Payment:** On acceptance. **Contact:** Jo Ellen Krumm, Managing Editor.

MUSCLE & FITNESS HERS

21100 Erwin St., Woodland Hills, CA 91367-3712. 818-884-6800.
E-mail: carey.rossi-walker@weiderpub.com. Web site: www.muscle-fitnesshers.com. Bimonthly. $5.95/$34.97. Circ.: 280,000. Carey Rossi Walker, Executive Editor. **Description:** Publication for healthy, active women interested in fitness. **Nonfiction:** Weight training, bodybuilding techniques, instructional fitness, health, injury prevention and treatment, and nutrition. Features run 1,500-2,000 words; $400-$800. Shorter pieces and departments run 750-1,000 words; $400. **Tips:** All features and departments are written on assignment. Send 1-page query with potential sources, qualifications, and recent clips. **Queries:** Required. **E-Queries:** No. **Unsolicited mss:** Does not accept. **Rights:** FNAR. **Payment:** On acceptance.

MUSCULAR DEVELOPMENT

690 Rt. 25A, Setauket, NY 11733-1200. 631-751-9696.
E-mail: editor@musculardevelopment.com.
Web site: www.musculardevelopment.com. Monthly. $6.99/$34.97. Circ.: 137,500. Steve Blechman, Editor-in-Chief. **Description:** For serious weight-training athletes, on any aspect of competitive body building, powerlifting, sports, and nutrition. **Nonfiction:** Articles, 1,000-2,500 words, photos; pays $500-$1,500. **Queries:** Preferred. **Payment:** On publication.

OXYGEN

5775 McLaughlin Rd., Mississauga, Ontario L5R 3P7 Canada. 905-507-3545.
E-mail: editorial@oxygenmag.com. Web site: www.emusclemag.com. Monthly. $22.50/yr. Circ.: 310,000. Nancy Lepatourel, Editor-in-Chief. **Description:**

Women's health and fitness magazine. **Nonfiction:** Training articles featuring fitness and competition; shorter articles on motivation; 1,000-2,000 words; $0.50/word. **Tips:** Submit query outlining your topic, the angle you wish to take, and a list of sources. Also include a small paragraph stating why you're qualified to write the article. **Queries:** Required. **E-Queries:** Yes. **Unsolicited mss:** Accepts. **Response:** Queries 2-4 weeks; submissions 1-2 weeks. **Freelance Content:** 60%. **Rights:** FNAR. **Payment:** On acceptance.

THE PHYSICIAN AND SPORTSMEDICINE MAGAZINE

McGraw-Hill, Inc., 4530 W 77th St., Minneapolis, MN 55435. 952-835-3222. Web site: www.physsportmed.com. Monthly. $48/yr. Circ.: 96.800. Gordon Matheson, Editor-in-Chief. **Description:** News articles, with sports-medicine angle. **Nonfiction:** Pays $300-$500. **Queries:** Preferred. **Payment:** On acceptance. **Contact:** Jim Wappes, Executive Editor.

SHAPE

21100 Erwin St., Woodland Hills, CA 91367-3772. 818-595-0593. Web site: www.shape.com. Monthly. $3.99/issue. Circ.: 1,600,000. Anne Russell, Editor-in-Chief. **Description:** Provides women with tools to create better lives and a deeper understanding of fitness. Uses only solid, well-respected experts in the fields of exercise, health, nutrition, sport, beauty, and psychology. **Nonfiction:** New and interesting ideas on physical and mental aspects of getting and staying in shape; 1,200-1,500 words; pay varies. **Tips:** "Readers have come to trust us for the final word on the issue most important to them, presented in a clear, challenging and visually beautiful fashion." **Queries:** Preferred. **Unsolicited mss:** Does not accept. **Freelance Content:** 70%. **Payment:** On acceptance.

SWEAT MAGAZINE

736 E Loyola Dr., Tempe, AZ 85282. 480-947-3900. E-mail: editor@sweatmagazine.com. Web site: www.sweatmagazine.com. Monthly. $18/yr. Circ.: 50,000. Joan Kay Westlake, Editor. **Description:** Covers amateur sports, outdoor activities, wellness, and fitness, with an Arizona angle. **Nonfiction:** Articles, 500-1,200 words. No self-indulgent or personal tales. Prefers investigative pieces, must relate to Arizona or Arizonans. Pays $35-$100. **Art:** Photos, $20-$100. **Queries:** Required. **Unsolicited mss:** Does not accept. **Payment:** Within 1 month of publication.

VIM & VIGOR

1010 E Missouri Ave., Phoenix, AZ 85014-2602. 602-395-5850. E-mail: careyj@mcmurry.com. Web site: www.vigormagazine.com. Quarterly. $2.95. Circ.: 1,100,000. Carey E. Jones, Editor. **Description:** A national health and fitness publication with 20 regional editions. **Nonfiction:** Positive articles, with medical facts, healthcare news, medical breakthroughs, exercise/fitness, health trends, wellness, general physical and emotional health, disease updates; written for a general reader. 900-1,500 words; $.80-$1.25/word. **Tips:** No healthcare product promotion, book reviews, personal accounts (unless to illustrate a topic), or unfounded medical claims for disease prevention and treatment. Style is serious, poignant, informative; with a slant that speaks to the reader as "you." Write for an educated reader, but remember to explain scientific terms and complex procedures. **E-Queries:** Yes. **Unsolicited mss:** Does not accept. **Rights:** FNAR, international, and electronic.

TEACHING ELEMENTARY PHYSICAL EDUCATION
See full listing in Education category.

WEIGHT WATCHERS MAGAZINE
See full listing in Health category.

FOOD & WINE

BON APPETIT
Condé Nast Publications, Inc.
6300 Wilshire Blvd., Fl. 10, Los Angeles, CA 90048-5204. 323-965-3600.
Web site: www.bonappetit.com. Monthly. $3.95/$20. Circ.: 1,283,375. Barbara Fairchild, Editor-in-Chief. **Description:** "America's Food and Entertaining Magazine." Covers food, entertainment, and travel. **Queries:** Required. **E-Queries:** No. **Unsolicited mss:** Does not accept. **Response:** 4-6 weeks, SASE required. **Rights:** All. **Payment:** On acceptance. **Contact:** Victoria von Biel, Exec. Editor.

BREW YOUR OWN
5053 Main St., Suite A, Manchester Center, VT 05255. 802-362-3981.
E-mail: edit@byo.com. Web site: www.byo.com. Monthly. Circ.: 40,000. Kathleen James Ring, Editor. **Description:** Practical information for homebrewers. **Queries:** Required. **Payment:** On publication.

CHEF
20 W Kinzie, Fl. 12, Chicago, IL 60610. 312-849-2220.
Web site: www.chefmagazine.com. Monthly. $24/yr. Circ.: 43,600. **Description:** "The Food Magazine for Professionals." Offers professionals in the foodservice business ideas for food marketing, preparation, and presentation. **Nonfiction:** Articles, 800-1,200 words; pays $250 to first-time writers, others $400. **Payment:** On publication. **Contact:** Melanie Wolkoff, Senior Editor.

CHOCOLATIER
45 W 34th St., Suite 600, New York, NY 10001-3073. 212-239-0855.
E-mail: chocmag@aol.com. Web site: www.godiva.com. Bimonthly. $21.95/yr. Circ.: 150,000. Michael Schneider, Publisher/Editor-in-Chief. **Description:** Articles cover chocolate and desserts, cooking/baking techniques, lifestyle, and travel. **Nonfiction:** Pay varies. **Queries:** Required. **Payment:** On acceptance.

COOK'S ILLUSTRATED
17 Station St., Brookline, MA 02445-7995. 617-232-1000.
E-mail: cooks@bcpress.com. Web site: www.cooksillustrated.com. Bimonthly.
$24.95/yr. Circ.: 470,000. Christopher Kimball, Editor. **Description:** Articles on
techniques of home cooking. Features master recipes based on careful testing, trial
and error. **Nonfiction:** Pay varies. **Art:** Hand-drawn illustrations. Send portfolio.
Queries: Required. **Payment:** On acceptance.

COOKING FOR PROFIT
P.O. Box 267, Fond du Lac, WI 54936-0267. 920-923-3700.
E-mail: comments@cookingforprofit.com. Web site: www.cookingforprofit.com.
Monthly. $24/yr. Circ.: 70,000. Colleen Phalen, Editor. **Description:** For foodservice
professionals. **Nonfiction:** Profiles of successful restaurants, chains, and franchises,
schools, hospitals, nursing homes, etc. Also, case studies on energy management in
foodservice environment. Business-to-business articles. Pay varies. **Payment:** On
publication.

FANCY FOOD & CULINARY PRODUCTS
20 W Kinzie, Fl. 12 Dr., Chicago, IL 60610. 312-849-2220.
E-mail: fancyfood@talcott.com. Web site: www.talcott.com. Monthly. $3.95/issue.
Circ.: 28,000. **Description:** Covers the business of specialty foods, coffee and tea,
natural foods, confections, and upscale housewares. **Nonfiction:** 1,200-1,500 words;
$300. **Art:** prints, transparencies, digital; $50. **Tips:** Readers are retailers, not customers. **Queries:** Required. **E-Queries:** Yes. **Unsolicited mss:** Accepts.
Response: 1 month. **Freelance Content:** 35%. **Rights:** FNASR. **Payment:** On
publication. **Contact:** John Saxtan, Editor.

FOOD & WINE
American Express Publishing Corp.
1120 Avenue of the Americas, Fl. 9, New York, NY 10036-6700. 212-382-5600.
E-mail: food&wine@amexpub.com. Web site: www.foodandwine.com. Monthly.
$26/yr. Circ.: 861,000. Dana Cowin, Editor-in-Chief. **Description: Queries:**
Required. **Unsolicited mss:** Does not accept. **Contact:** Mary Ellen Ward,
Managing Editor.

GOURMET
Condé Nast Publications, Inc.
4 Times Square, Fl. 5, New York, NY 10036-6563. 212-286-2860.
E-mail: ruth_reichl@gourmet.com. Web site: www.epicurious.com. Monthly. $15/yr.
Circ.: 946,000. Ruth Reichl, Editor-in-Chief. **Description:** "The magazine of good
living." **Queries:** Preferred. **Unsolicited mss:** Does not accept.

KASHRUS
P.O. Box 204, Brooklyn, NY 11204-0204. 718-336-8544.
E-mail: editorial@kashrusmagazine.com. Web site: www.kashrusmagazine.com. 5x/yr.

$3.75/$18. Circ.: 10,000. Yosef Wikler, Editor. **Description:** Provides up-to-date information to the kosher consumer on food, travel, catering, health issues, mislabeled food products, etc. **Nonfiction:** Articles on food technology, new kosher products, catering, new kitchens, and medicine; 250-1,500 words; $25-$200. **Fillers:** Accepts food-related humor and cartoons. **Art:** Color photos of food, dining, travel, and Israel. Submit on disk or hard copy. **Tips:** "We seek writers who can be sensitive to the feelings of Orthodox Jews." **Queries:** Preferred. **E-Queries:** No. **Unsolicited mss:** Accepts. **Response:** 2 days, SASE required. **Rights:** FNAR and reprint. **Payment:** On publication.

NORTHWEST PALATE

P.O. Box 10860, Portland, OR 97296-0860. 503-224-6039.
E-mail: editorial@nwpalate.com. Web site: www.nwpalate.com. $4.95/$21. Circ.: 45,000. Cameron Nagel, Publisher/Editor. **Description:** Covers food, wine, and travel in the Pacific Northwest (Oregon, Washington, Idaho, and British Columbia). Articles should be 100-2,000 words; $.25/word. **Tips:** "Writers should familiarize themselves with our content and style. Get a copy of our magazine and also visit our Web site's back issues to see what we've covered. Please do not submit articles that have no bearing on food, wine, or travel in the Pacific Northwest." **Queries:** Preferred. **E-Queries:** Yes. **Unsolicited mss:** Accepts. **Response:** 1-8 weeks. **Freelance Content:** 80%. **Rights:** FNAR. **Payment:** On publication. **Contact:** Angie Jabine, Managing Editor.

TEA: A MAGAZINE

P.O. Box 348, Scotland, CT 06264-0348. 860-456-1145.
E-mail: teamag@teamag.com. Web site: www.teamag.com. Quarterly. $5/$17. Circ.: 12,000. Pearl Dexter, Editor. **Description:** "Focus on tea, not only as a beverage, but as an influence on art, music, literature, history, design, and global societies." Features current trends in health research and tea's impact in relationships, families, and psychological well-being. **Tips:** Does not assign articles to writers and does not accept query letters. Send complete manuscript; fees are negotiable and may be discussed with the editor. **Queries:** Not necessary. **Unsolicited mss:** Accepts. **Response:** 30 days, SASE. **Freelance Content:** 75%. **Payment:** On publication.

VEGETARIAN TIMES

301 Concourse Blvd., Suite 350, Glen Allen, VA 23059. 203-328-7040.
E-mail: cdavis@sabot.net. Web site: www.vegetariantimes.com. Monthly. $19.90/yr. Circ.: 321,000. Carla Davis, Managing Editor. **Description:** Articles on vegetarian cooking, nutrition, health and fitness, travel and entertaining. Pay negotiable. **Columns, Departments:** Wellness, First Person, Lifestyle. **Queries:** Required. **Payment:** On acceptance.

VEGGIE LIFE

1041 Shary Circle, Concord, CA 94518. 925-671-9852.
E-mail: smasters@egw.com. Web site: www.veggielife.com. Quarterly. $15.96/yr.

Circ.: 189,000. Shanna Masters, Editor. **Description:** For people interested in low-fat, meatless cuisine and nutrition. **Nonfiction:** Food features (include 7-8 recipes); 1,500-2,000 words. **Columns, Departments:** 1,000-1,500 words. **Queries:** Preferred. **Payment:** On publication.

THE WINE NEWS

P.O. Box 142096, Coral Gables, FL 33143-5824. 305-740-7170.
E-mail: wineline@aol.com. Web site: www.thewinenews.com. Bimonthly. $5/$30. Circ.: 70,000. Kathy Sinnes, Managing Editor. **Description:** Upscale, with commentary, interviews, historical perspectives, and wine recommendations. Targets wine-savvy consumers seeking guidance and entertainment in all areas regarding wine. **Tips:** "Articles should demonstrate a depth of expertise and a distinctive and engaging writing style." **Queries:** Required. **E-Queries:** Yes. **Unsolicited mss:** Accepts. **Response:** 90 days. **Freelance Content:** 10%. **Rights:** One-time. **Payment:** On publication. **Contact:** Kathy Sinnes.

WINE SPECTATOR

387 Park Ave. S., New York, NY 10016. 212-684-4224.
Web site: www.winespectator.com. Thomas Matthews, Executive Editor.
Description: On news and people in the wine world, travel, food, and other lifestyle topics. **Nonfiction:** Features, 600-2,000 words, preferably with photos; pays from $400, extra for photos. **Queries:** Required. **Payment:** On publication.

WINE TIDINGS

5165 Sherbrooke St. W, Suite 414
Montreal, Quebec H4A 1T6 Canada. 514-481-5892.
E-mail: winetidings@majesticlaser.com. 8x/yr. $32/yr. Circ.: 13,000. Aldo Parise, Editor-in-Chief. **Description:** Accurate wine information, written for a Canadian audience. **Nonfiction:** Articles (1,000-1,500 words, $100-$300), and shorts (400-1,000 words, $30-$150). **Art:** B&W photos, $20-$50; color, $200-$400 (covers). **Queries:** Preferred. **Payment:** On publication.

WINEMAKER

5053 Main St., Suite A, Manchester Center, VT 05255. 802-362-3981.
E-mail: edit@winemakermag.com. Web site: www.winemakermag.com. Monthly. Circ.: 35,000. Kathleen James Ring, Editor. **Description:** Practical information for home winemakers. **Queries:** Required. **Payment:** On publication.

WINES & VINES

1800 Lincoln Ave., San Rafael, CA 94901. 415-453-9700.
E-mail: edit@winesandvines.com. Web site: www.winesandvines.com. Monthly. Tina Caputo, Managing Editor. **Description:** Trade journal for the grape and wine industry, emphasizing marketing, management, vineyard techniques, and production. Emphasizes technology with valuable, scientific winemaking articles. Articles, 2,000

words; pays $.15/word. **Tips:** No travel or consumer-oriented articles. Visit Web site for examples of style and coverage before querying. **Queries:** Required. **E-Queries:** Yes. **Unsolicited mss:** Does not accept. **Payment:** On acceptance.

ZYMURGY
American Homebrewers Assn.
736 Pearl St., Boulder, CO 80302-5006. 303-447-0816.
E-mail: info@aob.org. Web site: www.beertown.org. 6x/yr. $33/yr. Circ.: 24,000. Ray Daniels, Editor-in-Chief. **Description:** Articles appealing to beer lovers and home-brewers. **Queries:** Preferred. **Payment:** On publication.

GAMES & PASTIMES
(See also Hobbies, Crafts, Collecting)

BINGO BUGLE
Frontier Publications, Inc., P.O. Box 527, Vashon, WA 98070-0527. 206-463-5656.
E-mail: tara@bingobugle.com. Web site: www.bingobugle.com. Monthly. Circ.: 1,061,000. Tara Snowden, Managing Editor. **Description:** For bingo players.

THE BRIDGE BULLETIN
American Contract Bridge League
2990 Airways Blvd., Memphis, TN 38116-3847. 901-332-5586.
E-mail: editor@acbl.org. Web site: www.acbl.org. Monthly. $30/yr. Circ.: 150,000. Brent Manley, Editor. **Description:** Covers tournament/duplicate bridge. **Nonfiction:** Submit articles that teach or report on trends and issues related to the game. Seeks humor and human-interest pieces as they relate to bridge; $50/page. **Queries:** Required. **E-Queries:** Yes. **Unsolicited mss:** Accepts. **Freelance Content:** 10%. **Rights:** One-time. **Payment:** On publication.

CARD PLAYER
3140 S Polaris Ave., Suite 8, Las Vegas, NV 89102-0008. 702-871-1720.
E-mail: info@cardplayer.com. Web site: www.cardplayer.com. Biweekly. $59/yr. Circ.: 50,000. Jeff Shulman, Editor-in-Chief. **Description:** For competitive players, on poker events, personalities, legal issues, new casinos, tournaments, strategies, and psychology to improve poker play. **Nonfiction:** Any length; payment negotiable. **Fillers:** Humor. **Queries:** Preferred. **E-Queries:** No. **Unsolicited mss:** Accepts. **Response:** 1 month. **Freelance Content:** 1%. **Payment:** On publication. **Contact:** Steve Radulovich, Senior Executive Editor.

CASINO PLAYER
8025 Black Horse Pike, Suite 470, West Atlantic City, NJ 08232-2950. 609-484-8866.
E-mail: letters@casinocenter.com. Web site: www.casinocenter.com. Monthly. $24. Circ.: 700,000. Adam Fine, Editor-in-Chief. **Description:** For beginning to

intermediate gamblers, on slots, video poker, table games, and gaming lifestyle/travel. Articles, 1,000-2,000 words, with photos; pays from $250. **Tips:** No first-person or real-life gambling stories. **Payment:** On publication.

CHANCE: THE BEST OF GAMING
16 E 41st St., Fl. 2, New York, NY 10017-7213. 212-889-3467.
E-mail: letters@chancemag.com. Web site: www.chancemag.com. Bimonthly. $25/yr. Circ.: 190,000. Anthony C. Reilly, Editor-in-Chief. **Description:** "The Best of Gaming." For casino and betting individuals.

CHESS LIFE
United States Chess Federation
3054 US Route 9W, New Windsor, NY 12553-7698. 716-676-2402.
E-mail: magazines@uschess.org. Web site: www.uschess.org. Monthly. $3.75/$30. Circ.: 70,000. Peter Kurzdorfer, Editor. **Description:** Published by United States Chess Federation. Covers news of major chess events (U.S. and abroad), with emphasis on the triumphs and exploits of American players. **Nonfiction:** Articles on news, profiles, technical aspects. Features on history, humor, puzzles, etc.; 500-3,000 words; $105/page. **Art:** B&W glossies, color slides. $25-$25. **Tips:** Does not accept fiction. **Queries:** Preferred. **Unsolicited mss:** Accepts. **Payment:** On publication.

COMPUTER GAMES MAGAZINE
The Globe.com , 63 Millet St., Richmond, VT 05477-9492. 802-434-3060.
E-mail: editor@cdmag.com. Web site: www.cgonline.com. Monthly. $9.99. Circ.: 374,500. **Description:** Computer gaming information.

COMPUTER GAMING WORLD
50 Beale St., Suite 12, San Francisco, CA 94105-1813. 415-357-4900.
E-mail: cgwletter@zd.com. Web site: www.computergaming.com. Monthly. Circ.: 345,200. Jeff Green, Editor-in-Chief. **Description:** All aspects of computer gaming.

ELECTRONIC GAMING MONTHLY
P.O. Box 3338, Hinsdale, IL 60522-3338. 630-382-9000.
E-mail: egm@zd.com. Web site: www.videogames.com. Monthly. Circ.: 426,794. Dan Hsu, Editor-in-Chief. **Description:** Reports on home video console games.

GAMBLING TIMES
3883 W Century Blvd., Inglewood, CA 90303. 310-674-3365.
E-mail: editor@gamblingtimes.com. Web site: www.gamblingtimes.com. Monthly. $3.95/$24. Circ.: 125,000. John Hill, Editor. **Description:** For the gaming public, provides information on all forms of legal gambling worldwide. **Nonfiction:** 1,100-1,500 words; pays $250/article. **Tips:** "We are a pro-gambling publication, seeking to improve the expertise and knowledge of our readers. Writers must be experts in their fields." **Queries:** Preferred. **E-Queries:** Yes. **Unsolicited mss:** Does not accept.

Response: 30 days, SASE. **Freelance Content:** 10%. **Payment:** On publication. **Contact:** Stanley Sludikoff, Editorial Director.

GAMEPRO

501 Second St., Suite 114, San Francisco, CA 94107-4133. 415-979-9845. E-mail: letters@gamepro.com. Web site: www.gamepro.com. Monthly. Circ.: 500,000. Wes Nihei, Editor-in-Chief. **Description:** For computer and video gamers.

GAMES MAGAZINE

7002 W Butler Pike, Suite 210, Ambler, PA 19002. 215-643-6385. E-mail: gamespub@voicenet.com. 9x/yr. Circ.: 100,000. R. Wayne Schmittberger, Editor-in-Chief. **Description:** "For creative minds at play." **Nonfiction:** Features and short articles on games and playful, offbeat subjects. Visual and verbal puzzles, pop culture quizzes, brainteasers, contests, game reviews. **Tips:** Send SASE for guidelines (specify writer's, crosswords, variety puzzles, or brainteasers). **Freelance Content:** 50%. **Payment:** On publication.

JACKPOT!

6064 Apple Tree Dr., Suite 9, Memphis, TN 38115-0307. 901-360-0777. E-mail: jackpot@memphisonline.com. Web site: www.jackpotmagazine.com. Semimonthly. Circ.: 40,000. Lori Beth Sunderman, Executive Editor. **Description:** Covers all aspects of casino entertainment, gaming, and food.

POOL & BILLIARD

810 Travelers Blvd. Bldg. D, Summerville, SC 29485. 843-875-5115. E-mail: poolmag@poolmag.com. Web site: www.poolmag.com. Monthly. $34.95. Circ.: 20,000. Shari J. Stauch, Executive Editor. **Description:** Consumer and trade magazine for players and others interested in the pool industry. Articles must be relevant to the game of pool. Particular interest in instruction and tourney coverage; 600-2,500 words; $130/page. **Tips:** No fiction or poetry. **Response:** 5 days. **Freelance Content:** 10%.

STRICTLY SLOTS

5240 S Eastern Ave., Las Vegas, NV 89119. 702-736-8886. E-mail: mraimondi@casinocenter.com. Web site: www.casinocenter.com. Monthly. $24/yr. Circ.: 110,000. Melissa Raimond, Editor. **Description:** Everything there is to know about all the new slots, slot clubs, promotions, and property profiles. Nonfiction pieces, 1,000 words with photos pays $.25/word. **Payment:** On publication.

WINNING!

15115 S 76th E Ave., Bixby, OK 74008-4114. 918-366-6191. E-mail: editor@newslinc.com. Monthly. Circ.: 125,000. Jason Sowards, Managing Editor. **Description:** Articles on how to increase the odds of winning prizes and money in sweepstakes, lotteries, casino gaming, and contests.

GAY & LESBIAN

THE ADVOCATE
6922 Hollywood Boulevard, Suite 1000, Los Angeles, CA 90028. 323-871-1225. E-mail: bsteele@advocate.com. Web site: www.advocate.com. Biweekly. $3.99/$39.97. Circ.: 103,000. Judy Wieder, Editorial Director. **Description:** National news magazine for gay men and lesbians, with news, politics, entertainment, interviews, etc. **Nonfiction:** Should employ a specific angle to set the tone and grab the reader's attention; 1,000 words. **Columns, Departments:** My Perspective; 1 column each issue is written by freelancers; 700 words. **Tips:** No fiction or simultaneous submissions. E-mail info@advocate.com for guidelines. **Queries:** Required. **E-Queries:** Yes. **Unsolicited mss:** Does not accept. **Freelance Content:** 50%. **Rights:** FNAR. **Payment:** On publication. **Contact:** Bruce Steele, Editor-in-Chief.

ARISE MAGAZINE
1533 41st St., Sacramento, CA 95819. 916-454-2781. E-mail: arise@arisemag.com. Web site: www.arisemag.com. Monthly. $4/$35. Circ.: 50,000. MacArthur H. Flournoy, Editor-in-Chief. **Description:** Lifestyle magazine for lesbian, gay, bisexual, and transgender African-Americans. Articles cover health, finance, spirituality, music, travel, politics, and lifestyle issues. Also features poetry and book reviews. Articles run 1,500 words; poetry 500 words. Payment negotiable. **Queries:** Not necessary. **E-Queries:** Yes. **Unsolicited mss:** Does not accept. **Response:** 3 months, SASE. **Payment:** On publication.

ECHO MAGAZINE
P.O. Box 16630, Phoenix, AZ 85011. 602-266-0550. E-mail: editor@echomag.com. Web site: www.echomag.com. $55/yr. Circ.: 18,000. **Description:** Biweekly, for gay and lesbian readers in Phoenix metro area and across Arizona. Covers gay-relevant developments in news, health, entertainment, business, and more. **Nonfiction:** Feature stories, human interest, art features, and op-ed guest column; 800-1,500 words; $30/article. **Columns, Departments:** Book, CD, and movie reviews and op-ed pieces; most by regular contributors; 800-1,000 words; $30/article. **Art:** Accepts quality photo-essays of GLBT life in Phoenix; submit electronic files; fee negotiable. **Tips:** "We are a pro-gay advocacy publication dedicated to informing readers and helping them find valuable resources. You don't have to be gay to write for us, but you do have to support equality for GLBT persons and be very familiar with the gay community." **Queries:** Preferred. **E-Queries:** Yes. **Response:** 2-4 weeks. **Freelance Content:** 40-50%. **Rights:** All. **Payment:** On publication.

EMPIRE
230 W 17th St., Fl. 8, New York, NY 10011. 212-352-3535. E-mail: akrach@hx.com. Web site: www.empiremag.com. Quarterly. $12.95/yr. Circ.: 50,000. Aaron Krach, Editor. **Description:** For gay men who want the most out of life.

THE GAY & LESBIAN REVIEW

P.O. Box 180300, Boston, MA 02118. 617-421-0082.
E-mail: hglr@aol.com. Web site: www.glreview.com. $29.70. Circ.: 10,500. Richard Schneider, Editor. **Description:** Bimonthly, for the gay and lesbian community, on culture, politics, the arts, and history. Includes reviews of books, film, and art. Articles, 200-5,000 words; no payment offered. **Tips:** "Avoid memoirs and overly personal pieces. Articles should have a larger significance. We aim to have a lengthy 'shelf life' so articles need not have late-breaking news." **Queries:** Not necessary. **E-Queries:** Yes. **Unsolicited mss:** Accepts. **Freelance Content:** 100%.

GENRE

7080 Hollywood Blvd., Suite 818, Hollywood, CA 90028. 323-467-8300.
E-mail: genre@genremagazine.com. Web site: www.genremagazine.com. Monthly. $4.95/$24.95. Circ.: 60,000. Andy Towle, Editor-in-Chief. **Description:** Fashion, entertainment, travel, fiction, and reviews for gay men. **Fiction:** Gay themes. Pay varies; 2,000 words. **Nonfiction:** Travel, celebrity interviews, etc.; 300-1,500 words. **Art:** Slides, JPG. **Queries:** Preferred. **E-Queries:** Yes. **Unsolicited mss:** Accepts. **Response:** SASE required. **Freelance Content:** 60%. **Rights:** Print, electronic. **Payment:** On publication.

GLOBAL CITY REVIEW

See full listing in Literary Fiction & Poetry category.

HURRICANE ALICE

See full listing in Ethnic & Multicultural category.

INSTINCT MAGAZINE

15335 Morrison St., Suite 325, Sherman Oaks, CA 91403. 818-205-9033.
E-mail: editor@instinctmag.com. Web site: www.instinctmag.com. Monthly. $4.95/$19.95. Circ.: 60,000. Ben Rogers, Editor-in-Chief. **Description:** For gay men, with news, entertainment, celebrity profiles, and features on controversial topics. **Nonfiction:** Seeks gay men's lifestyle pieces, relevant news or investigative pieces, and articles on entertainment, fashion, fitness, and health; 1,500-2,400 words. **Tips:** "Become familiar with our trademark style. Avoid general themes such as dating or first-person columns. Prefers fresh takes on gay men's lifestyle issues, controversial or against-the-grain viewpoints, and the scoop on upcoming themes. Keep your writing conversational and grounded." **Queries:** Preferred. **E-Queries:** Yes. **Unsolicited mss:** Accepts. **Response:** 90 days, SASE. **Freelance Content:** 60%. **Rights:** All. **Payment:** On publication. **Contact:** Ben R. Rogers or Alexander Cho.

THE JAMES WHITE REVIEW

Lambda Literary Foundation
P.O. Box 73910, Washington, DC 20056-3910. 202-682-0952.
E-mail: jwr@lambdalit.org. Web site: www.lambdalit.org. Quarterly. $4.95/$17.50. Circ.: 3,000. Patrick Merla, Editor. **Description:** Gay men's literary magazine, with

fiction, poetry, photography, art, essays, and reviews. Welcomes both unpublished and established writers. **Fiction:** Seeking well-crafted literary fiction with strongly developed characters; gay themes; to 10,000 words; pay varies. **Poetry:** Submit up to 3 poems at a time. **Tips:** "Be patient—we're a small staff with a lot of submissions." **Queries:** Preferred. **E-Queries:** No. **Unsolicited mss:** Accepts. **Response:** Queries 3 weeks, submissions 3-6 months, SASE required. **Rights:** 1st. **Payment:** On publication. **Contact:** Jonathan Harper, Editorial Assistant.

LAMBDA BOOK REPORT
See full listing in Writing & Publishing category.

METROSOURCE MAGAZINE
180 Varick St., Fl. 5, New York, NY 10014-4606. 212-691-5127.
E-mail: rwalsh@metrosource.com. Web site: www.metrosource.com. 5x/yr. $4.95/issue. Circ.: 85,000. Richard Walsh, Editor. **Description:** Lifestyle magazine for gay and lesbian readers. **Nonfiction:** Articles on travel, entertainment, health/fitness, gay adoption, fashion, etc. Also runs profiles of significant people who are gay or lesbian. 1,500-2,000 words. **Queries:** Preferred. **E-Queries:** Yes. **Unsolicited mss:** Does not accept. **Response:** 1 month, SASE required. **Freelance Content:** 30%.

OUT MAGAZINE
80 Eighth Ave., Suite 315, New York, NY 10011. 212-242-8100.
E-mail: blemon@out.com. Web site: www.out.com. Monthly. $17.95/yr. Circ.: 136,000. Brendan Lemon, Editor-in-Chief. **Description:** Articles on arts, politics, fashion, finance, and other subjects for gay and lesbian readers. No fiction or poetry. Pay varies. **Queries:** Preferred. **Payment:** On publication.

GENERAL INTEREST

THE ATLANTIC MONTHLY
77 N Washington St., Boston, MA 02114. 617-854-7700.
E-mail: letters@theatlantic.com. Web site: www.theatlantic.com. Monthly. $3.95/issue. Circ.: 500,000. Cullen Murphy, Managing Editor. **Description:** At the leading edge of contemporary issues, plus offers the best in fiction, travel, food, and humor. **Fiction:** 2,000-6,000 words; up to $3,000. **Nonfiction:** 1,000-7,500 words; payment varies. **Poetry:** Accepts. **Fillers:** Humor. **Queries:** Preferred. **E-Queries:** No. **Unsolicited mss:** Accepts. **Response:** 2-4 weeks; SASE required. **Freelance Content:** 50%. **Rights:** FNAR. **Payment:** On acceptance.

BLACK BOOK
116 Prince St., Fl. 2, New York, NY 10012-3178. 212-334-1800.
E-mail: info@blackbookmag.com. Web site: www.blackbookmag.com. Bimonthly.

$18.95/yr. Circ.: 150,000. Anuj Desai, Editor-in-Chief. **Description:** General interest lifestyle magazine covering trends, entertainment, arts, beauty and fashion, news, and cutting-edge journalism. Also features some fiction. **Queries:** Preferred.

CHICAGO TRIBUNE MAGAZINE

Chicago Tribune, 435 N Michigan Ave., Chicago, IL 60611. 312-222-3232. Web site: www.chicagotribune.com. **Description:** Sunday magazine of the *Chicago Tribune.*

THE CHRISTIAN SCIENCE MONITOR

One Norway St., Boston, MA 02115. 617-450-2372.
E-mail: oped@csps.com. Web site: www.csmonitor.com. Daily. Circ.: 95,000. **Description:** Lifestyle trends, women's rights, family, community, and how-to. **Nonfiction:** Pieces on domestic and foreign affairs, economics, education, environment, law, media, politics, and cultural commentary. Retains all rights for 90 days after publication; 400-900 words; up to $400. **Poetry:** Finely crafted poems that explore and celebrate daily life. Short preferred; submit no more than 5 poems at a time. Seasonal material always needed. (No violence or sensuality; death or disease; helplessness or hopelessness.) **Columns, Departments:** Arts and Leisure, Learning, Ideas, Home Front, National, International, Work & Money; 800 words; pay varies. **Tips:** Call for writer's guidelines.

CHRONOGRAM

P.O. Box 459, New Paltz, NY 12561. 845-255-4711.
E-mail: info@chronogram.com. Web site: www.chronogram.com. Circ.: 15,000. Brian K. Mahoney, Editor. **Description:** Monthly, based in New York's Hudson Valley, on politics, arts and culture, health, the environment, and regional issues. Publishes short fiction, poetry, first-person pieces, memoirs, and political and cultural reportage. Pays $.10/word. **Tips:** Seeks to be "an alternative media source to the hulking conglomerates that spew lulling pablum into the general consciousness." Feature people, events, ideas, organizations, opinions, etc., which are sometimes unorthodox, with information not offered through mainstream sources. No humor or 'occasional' pieces. Query with a fresh article idea, strong writing; no first-time writers. **Queries:** Required. **Unsolicited mss:** Does not accept. **Response:** 4 weeks. **Freelance Content:** 30%. **Rights:** FNAR. **Payment:** On publication.

THE CLEVELAND PLAIN DEALER

1801 Superior Ave., Cleveland, OH 44114. 216-999-4147 or 216-999-4145.
E-mail: forum@plaind.com. Web site: www.cleveland.com. Daily. **Description:** On variety of subjects: domestic affairs, economics, education, environment, foreign affairs, humor, politics, and regional interest. **Nonfiction:** Op-ed pieces, to 700 words; pays $75. **Tips:** No room for historical pieces not tied to a recent event. **E-Queries:** Yes. **Response:** 2-5 days. **Freelance Content:** 10-15%. **Rights:** Non-exclusive worldwide. **Payment:** On publication.

CONVERSELY

PMB #121, 3053 Fillmore St., San Francisco, CA 94123.

E-mail: writers@conversely.com. Web site: www.conversely.com. Quarterly. **Description:** Online publication exploring all aspects of relationships between men and women. **Fiction:** Literary stories on male-female relationships; to 3,000 words; $50-$200. **Nonfiction:** Essays and personal stories (memoirs); 500-2,000 words; $50-$200. **Tips:** Submissions are only accepted online at Web site. Review guidelines before submitting. "We get much more fiction than we can handle, but we don't see enough personal and opinion essays." **Queries:** Not necessary. **E-Queries:** Yes. **Unsolicited mss:** Accepts. **Freelance Content:** 70%. **Rights:** 90-day exclusive electronic, non-exclusive thereafter; one-time, non-exclusive print anthology rights. **Payment:** On publication.

DETROIT FREE PRESS

600 W Fort St., Detroit, MI 48226. 313-222-6400.

E-mail: oped@freepress.com. Web site: www.freep.com. Daily. **Description:** Newspaper with op-ed page published 6 days/week. Accepts unsolicited manuscripts. **Tips:** Priority given to local writers. **Queries:** Preferred. **Payment:** On publication.

FRIENDLY EXCHANGE

P.O. Box 2120, Warren, MI 48090-2120. 586-558-3080.

Web site: www.friendlyexchange.com. Quarterly. Circ.: 5,500,000. Dan Grantham, Editor. **Description:** For policyholders of Farmers Insurance Group of Companies. **Nonfiction:** Articles with "news you can use," on home, health, personal finance, travel; 700-1,500 words; $400-$1,000. **Queries:** Required.

GLOBE

5401 Broken Sound Blvd. NW, Boca Raton, FL 33487-3589. 561-997-7733.

E-mail: newstips@globefl.com. Weekly. $$29.97. Circ.: 775,600. Tony Frost, Editor-in-Chief. **Description:** Exposés, celebrity interviews, consumer and human-interest pieces. **Nonfiction:** Articles, 500-1,000 words, with photos; pays $50-$1,500. **Contact:** Joe Mullins, Managing Editor.

GRIT

1503 SW 42nd St., Topeka, KS 66609-1265. 785-274-4300.

E-mail: gritmagazine@grit.com. Web site: www.grit.com. Biweekly. $1.95/$27.98. Circ.: 120,000. Ann Crahan, Editor-in-Chief. **Description:** On American life and traditions with stories about ordinary people doing extraordinary things. **Fiction:** Heartwarming stories with a message, upbeat storyline and ending; 1,000-10,000 words; $.10-.$15/word. **Nonfiction:** Features on places or events, unsung heroes, nostalgic remembrances of rural communities and small towns; 500-1,800 words. **Poetry:** Romance, relationships, nature, family interaction; up to 30 lines; $2/line. **Fillers:** Sayings, humor, funny sayings from children; up to 25 words; $5-$15. **Art:**

Photos must accompany features; $35-$50 ($100-$250 cover). **Tips:** Prefers full man-uscript with photos. **Queries:** Not necessary. **E-Queries:** No. **Unsolicited mss:** Accepts. **Freelance Content:** 90%. **Rights:** 1st. **Payment:** On publication.

HOPE

P.O. Box 160, Brooklin, ME 04616. 207-359-4651.
E-mail: info@hopemag.com. Web site: www.hopemag.com. Quarterly. Circ.: 22,000. Kimberly Ridley, Editor. **Description:** About people making a difference. Articles run 150-3,000 words; $75-$1,500. **Tips:** Query with clips. No nostalgia, sen-timental, political, opinion, or religious pieces. **Queries:** Required. **Payment:** On publication.

IDEALS

535 Metroplex Dr., Suite 250, Nashville, TN 37211. 615-333-0478.
Web site: www.idealsbooks.com. Bimonthly. $5.95/$19.95. Circ.: 200,000. Michelle Prater Burke, Editor. **Description:** Inspirational, seasonal poetry and prose, with art-work and photography, in turn on Easter, Mother's Day, Country, Friendship, Thanksgiving, and Christmas. **Fiction:** Holiday themes; 800-1,000 words; $.10/word. **Nonfiction:** On issue's theme; 800-1,000 words; $.10/word. **Poetry:** Light, nostalgic pieces; $10/poem. **Queries:** Not necessary. **E-Queries:** No. **Unsolicited mss:** Accepts. **Response:** Submissions 4-6 weeks, SASE required. **Rights:** One-time. **Payment:** On publication.

JOURNAL AMERICA

2019 Greenwood Lake Turnpike, Hewitt, NJ 07421-3027. 973-728-8355.
E-mail: journal@warick.net. Monthly. $19.95/yr. Circ.: 75,000. Glen Malmgren, Editor. **Description:** Covers varied subjects of interest to the American family. **Nonfiction:** On science, nature, or "true but strange stories." Also, articles on all aspects of today's demanding lifestyle, with a touch of humor; 200-1,000 words; pay varies. **Queries:** Preferred.

NATIONAL ENQUIRER

5401 Broken Sound Blvd, NW, Boca Raton, FL 33487-3512. 561-997-7733.
E-mail: letters@nationalenquirer.com. Web site: www.nationalenquirer.com. Weekly. $56.96/yr. Circ.: 2,075,000. Steve Plamann, Executive Editor. **Description:** Short, humorous or philosophical fillers, witticisms, anecdotes, jokes, tart comments. Original items only. Mass audience: topical news, celebrities, how-to, scientific discoveries, human drama, adventure, medical news, personalities. **Poetry:** Short, 8 lines or less, traditional rhyming verse (amusing, philosophical, or inspirational in nature). No obscure or artsy poetry. **Tips:** Submit seasonal/holiday material at least 3 months in advance. **Queries:** Preferred. **Response:** SASE. **Payment:** On publication.

THE NEW YORK TIMES MAGAZINE
229 W 43rd St., New York, NY 10036. 212-556-1234. Web site: www.nytimes.com. **Description:** On news items, trends, and culture. **Nonfiction:** Timely articles, up to 4,000 words; pays $1,000-$2,500. **Tips:** Send clips. **Queries:** Preferred. **Payment:** On acceptance.

NEWSWEEK
251 W 57th St., Fl. 17, New York, NY 10019-1802. 212-778-4000.
E-mail: letters@newsweek.com. Web site: www.newsweek.com. Weekly. $41.87/yr. Circ.: 3,144,000. Richard M. Smith, Editor-in-Chief. **Description:** Covers news throughout the world. Mostly staff-written. **Columns, Departments:** My Turn (original first-person opinion essays, must contain verifiable facts. Submit manuscript with SASE); 850-900 words; $1,000. **Queries:** Preferred. **Response:** 2 months, SASE. **Rights:** Non-exclusive worldwide. **Payment:** On publication. **Contact:** Kathleen Deveny, Assistant Managing Editor.

PARADE
711 Third Ave., New York, NY 10017. 212-450-7000.
Web site: www.parade.com. Weekly. Circ.: 76,000,000. Lee Kravitz, Editor. **Description:** National Sunday newspaper magazine. Subjects of national interest. **Nonfiction:** Factual and authoritative articles on social issues, common health concerns, sports, community problem-solving, and extraordinary achievements of ordinary people; 1,200 to 1,500 words; from $1,000. **Tips:** Query with two writing samples and SASE. "We seek unique angles on all topics." No fiction, poetry, cartoons, games, nostalgia, quotes, or puzzles. **Queries:** Required. **Unsolicited mss:** Does not accept. **Contact:** Steven J. Florio.

PEOPLE
Time, Inc.
1271 Avenue of the Americas, New York, NY 10020-1300. 212-522-1212.
E-mail: editor@people.com. Web site: www.people.com. Weekly. $93/yr. Circ.: 3,550,000. Carol Wallace, Managing Editor. **Description:** Mostly staff-written. Will consider article proposals, 3-4 paragraphs, on timely, entertaining, and topical personalities. **Payment:** On acceptance.

READER'S DIGEST
Box 100, Pleasantville, NY 10572. 914-238-1000.
E-mail: letters@rd.com. Web site: www.rd.com. Monthly. $2.99/issue. Circ.: 12,500,000. Jacqueline Leo, Editor-in-Chief. **Description:** Offers stories of broad interest. **Nonfiction:** Only general-interest articles already in print and well-developed story proposals will be considered. Send reprint or query to any editor on the masthead. **Fillers:** True, never-before-published stories for: Life in These United States; All in a Day's Work; Humor in Uniform; Virtual Hilarity. Previously published or original items for: Laughter, the Best Medicine; Quotable Quotes; short items used

at the end of articles; up to 100 words; $100-$300. **Tips:** Submissions are not acknowledged or returned. **Queries:** Preferred. **E-Queries:** No. **Unsolicited mss:** Accepts. **Contact:** Editorial Department.

READER'S DIGEST CANADA

1100 René-Lévesque Blvd. W, Montreal, Quebec H3B 5H5 Canada. 514-940-0751. E-mail: editor@readersdigest.ca. Web site: www.readersdigest.ca. Monthly. $29.97/yr. Circ.: 1,025,250. Murray Lewis, Editor-in-Chief. **Description:** Articles, essays, and human-interest pieces for a general audience. **Nonfiction:** Health/medicine, current events, real-life drama, humor, and anecdotes; 1,000-3,000 words; $1,500. **Fillers:** True, unpublished stories; to 300 words; $200. **Tips:** "We offer articles that are strong, sharp, fresh, and forceful. Our feature stories focus on the individual and his or her potential for greatness. Study our magazine and submit a detailed outline of your idea." **Queries:** Required. **E-Queries:** Yes. **Unsolicited mss:** Does not accept. **Response:** 3 weeks, SASE. **Freelance Content:** 40%. **Payment:** On acceptance.

THE SATURDAY EVENING POST

1100 Waterway Blvd., Indianapolis, IN 46202-2174. 317-634-1100. E-mail: satevepst@aol.com. Web site: www.satevepost.org. Bimonthly. $13.97. Circ.: 385,000. Cory J SerVaas, Editor-In-Chief. **Description:** Family-oriented publication. **Fiction:** Upbeat and humorous, stressing traditional relationships and family values. **Nonfiction:** Health and fitness, gardening, pet care, financial planning; 1,500-3,000 words; $25-$400. **Fillers:** Humor and anecdotes for "Post Scripts"; up to 100 words; $15. **Art:** Cartoons, illustrations, photos; $125 for cartoons; photos and illustrations vary. **Tips:** See Web site for guidelines. **Queries:** Preferred. **Unsolicited mss:** Accepts. **Response:** 3 weeks for queries, 6 weeks for mss; SASE required. **Rights:** All. **Payment:** On publication. **Contact:** Ted Kreiter, Executive Editor.

SELECCIONES DEL READER'S DIGEST

Readers Digest Assn.
Reader's Digest Rd., Pleasantville, NY 10570-7000. 914-238-1000. E-mail: conrad_kiechel@rd.com. Web site: www.rd.com. Monthly. Circ.: 352,000. Conrad Kiechel, Editor-in-Chief. **Description:** Spanish-language version of *Reader's Digest*.

SMITHSONIAN

MRC 951, P.O. Box 37012, Washington, DC 20013-7012. 202-275-2000. E-mail: articles@simag.si.edu. Web site: www.smithsonianmag.com. Monthly. $28. Circ.: 2,000,000. Carey Winfrey, Editor-in-Chief. **Description:** Offers wide-ranging coverage of history, art, natural history, physical science, profiles, etc. **Nonfiction:** History, art, natural history, physical science, profiles; 2,000-5,000 words; pay varies. **Columns, Departments:** "The Last Page"; humorous essays; 550-700 words. **Art:**

Photos or illustrations to accompany article, if available; 35mm color transparencies or B&W prints. **Tips:** See Web site for guidelines. **Queries:** Preferred. **E-Queries:** Yes. **Response:** 6-8 weeks; SASE required. **Rights:** FNASR. **Contact:** Marlane A. Liddell, Articles Editor.

STAR MAGAZINE
See full listing in Film, TV, Entertainment category.

THE SUN
107 N Roberson St., Chapel Hill, NC 27516. 919-942-5282.
E-mail: info@thesunmagazine.org. Web site: www.thesunmagazine.org. Monthly. $3.95/$34. Circ.: 55,000. Sy Safransky, Editor. **Description:** Essays, stories, interviews, and poetry in which people write of their struggles to understand their lives, often with surprising intimacy. Looking for writers willing to take risks and describe life honestly. **Fiction:** Fiction that feels like a lived experience; to 7,000 words; $300-$750. **Nonfiction:** Personal essays and interviews; to 7,000 words; $300-$1,250. **Poetry:** 1-2 pages; $50-$250. **Art:** B&W photographs only; $50-$200. **Tips:** No journalistic, academic, or opinion pieces. **Queries:** Not necessary. **E-Queries:** No. **Unsolicited mss:** Accepts. **Response:** 3 months, SASE required. **Freelance Content:** 80%. **Rights:** One-time. **Payment:** On publication.

USA WEEKEND
Gannett Newspapers
7950 Jones Branch Dr., McLean, VA 22107. 703-854-6445.
Web site: www.usaweekend.com. Weekly. Circ.: 23.7 million. **Description:** Sunday supplement to more than 590 newspapers.

THE WASHINGTON POST
1150 15th St. NW, Washington, DC 20071-0002. 202-334-6000.
E-mail: pgextra@washpost.com. Web site: www.washingtonpost.com. Daily. Leonard Downie, Executive Editor. **Description:** *Sunday Post* edition offers groundbreaking journalism, lifestyle features, and political and popular-culture commentary. **Nonfiction:** Length, pay varies. **Queries:** Preferred. **E-Queries:** Prefers hard copy. **Unsolicited mss:** Accepts. **Response:** 3 weeks. **Freelance Content:** 2%.

THE WORLD & I
The Washington Times Corp.
3600 New York Ave. NE, Washington, DC 20002. 202-635-4000.
E-mail: editor@worldandimag.com. Web site: www.worldandi.com. Monthly. $60. Circ.: 16,400. Michael Marshall, Executive Editor. **Description:** Current issues, arts, natural science, life, and culture. **Nonfiction:** Scholarly articles; 2,500 words; pay varies. **Tips:** Send SASE for guidelines. **Payment:** On publication.

HEALTH

ALTERNATIVE MEDICINE
1650 Tiburon Blvd., Tiburon, CA 94920. 415-789-1405.
E-mail: editor@alternativemedicine.com. Web site: www.alternativemedicine.com.
Bimonthly. $20/yr. Circ.: 140,000. Burton Goldberg, Founder/Publisher.
Description: Publication offering valuable information on effective, nontoxic options to traditional health care. Articles promote alternative methods for restoring and maintaining health. **Contact:** Tom Klaber, Editor.

AMERICAN HEALTH & FITNESS FOR MEN
See full listing in Fitness Magazines category.

AMERICAN JOURNAL OF HEALTH EDUCATION
See full listing in Education category.

AMERICAN JOURNAL OF NURSING
345 Hudson St., Fl. 16, New York, NY 10014. 212-886-1200.
E-mail: ajn@lww.com. Web site: www.ajnonline.com. Monthly. $29/yr. Circ.: 343,000.
Diana Mason, Editor-in-Chief. **Description:** Wide variety of clinical, policy, trends, and professional issues. Feature articles, 2,000-4,000 words; columns, 800-2,000 words. Photos/illustrations encouraged. **Tips:** See Web site for guidelines. **Queries:** Preferred. **Response:** 2-10 weeks.

AMERICAN MEDICAL NEWS
515 N State St., Chicago, IL 60610. 312-464-4429.
E-mail: kathryn_trombatore@ama-assn.org. Web site: www.amednews.com. Weekly.
Circ.: 250,000. Kathryn Trombatore, Editor. **Description:** Articles, on socioeconomic developments in health care, of interest to physicians across the country. Guidelines available. **Nonfiction:** Seeks well-researched, innovative pieces about health and science from physician's perspective; 900-1,500 words; pays $500-$1,500. **Queries:** Required. **Payment:** On acceptance.

ARTHRITIS TODAY
1330 W Peachtree St., Atlanta, GA 30309. 404-872-7100.
E-mail: writers@arthritis.org. Web site: www.arthritis.org. Bimonthly. $4.95/$20.
Circ.: 650,000. Marcy O'Koon Moss, Editor. **Description:** Comprehensive information about arthritis research, care, and treatment, offering help and hope to over 40 million Americans with an arthritis-related condition. **Nonfiction:** Features on research, care, treatment of arthritis; self-help, how-to, general interest, general health, lifestyle topics (very few inspirational articles); 200-1,000 words; $75-$1,000.
Tips: "We're looking for talented writers/reporters to execute staff-generated ideas. Send published clips." **Queries:** Preferred. **E-Queries:** Yes. **Unsolicited mss:** Accepts. **Response:** 4 weeks. **Freelance Content:** 50%. **Rights:** FNASR. **Payment:** On acceptance. **Contact:** Michele Taylor, Associate Editor.

ASTHMA MAGAZINE

11830 Westline Industrial Dr., St. Louis, MO 63146. 781-740-0221.
E-mail: rebutler@atti.com. Web site: www.mosby.com/asthma. Bimonthly. $21/yr.
Circ.: 65,000. Rachel Butler, Editor. **Description:** Focuses on ways to manage
asthma. **Nonfiction:** Articles on health and medical news, also human-interest sto-
ries about children, adults, and the elderly; to 1,200 words. **Queries:** Required.
Payment: On acceptance.

BABY TALK

See full listing in Family & Parenting category.

BALANCE MAGAZINE

See full listing in Lifestyle Magazines category.

BETTER HEALTH MAGAZINE

Saint Raphael Healthcare System
1450 Chapel St., New Haven, CT 06511-4405. 203-789-3972.
Web site: www.srhs.org/betterhealth.asp. Bimonthly. Circ.: 146,000. Cynthia Wolfe
Boynton, Editor. **Description:** Wellness and prevention magazine, published by
Hospital of Saint Raphael. **Nonfiction:** Upbeat articles to encourage healthier
lifestyle, with quotes and narrative from healthcare professionals at Saint Raphael's
and other local services. No first-person or personal-experience articles; 2,000-2,500
words; $700. **Tips:** Send $2.50 for sample copy and guidelines. **Queries:** Required.
E-Queries: No. **Payment:** On acceptance.

BODY & SOUL MAGAZINE

42 Pleasant St., Watertown, MA 02472. 617-926-0200.
Web site: www.bodyandsoulmag.com. **Description:** Features natural products,
holistic health, natural remedies, nutrition, spirituality, etc.

CONSCIOUS CHOICE

920 N Franklin, Suite 202, Chicago, IL 60610.
E-mail: rebecca@consiouschoice.com. Web site: www.consciouschoice.com.
Monthly. Circ.: 52,000. Rebecca Ephraim, Editor. **Description:** Covers issues and
information on natural health, natural foods, and the environment. Articles run 1,200-
2,200 words; $75-$150. **Tips:** Readers are mostly well-educated women with substantial income level. "Be familiar with content and style of the magazine. Note: 70%
of our editorial is local, so we mostly work with local writers." **Queries:** Preferred.
E-Queries: No. **Unsolicited mss:** Accepts. **Response:** 1-8 weeks. **Freelance
Content:** 90%. **Rights:** FNAR and electronic. **Payment:** On publication.

COPING WITH ALLERGIES & ASTHMA

P.O. Box 682268, Franklin, TN 37068-2268. 615-790-2400.
E-mail: copingmag@aol.com. Web site: www.copingmag.com. 5x/yr. $13.95/yr. Circ.:
30,000. Irene Wood, Editor. **Description:** Provides "knowledge, hope, and inspira-

tion to help readers learn to live with their conditions in the best ways possible." Seeks original manuscripts and photography. No payment. **Queries:** Not necessary.

COPING WITH CANCER

P.O. Box 682268, Franklin, TN 37068. 615-790-2400. E-mail: copingmag@aol.com. Web site: www.copingmag.com. 6x/yr. $19/yr. Circ.: 80,000. Kay Thomas, Editor. **Description:** Uplifting and practical articles for people living with cancer. Features medical news, lifestyle issues, and inspiring personal essays. No payment.

CURRENT HEALTH

See full listing in Education category.

DIABETES SELF-MANAGEMENT

150 W 22nd St., Suite 800, New York, NY 10011. 212-989-0200. E-mail: editor@diabetes-self-mgmt.com. Web site: www.diabetesselfmanagement.com. Bimonthly. $18/yr. Circ.: 465,000. James Hazlett, Editor. **Description:** For individuals who want to know more about controlling and managing their diabetes. **Nonfiction:** How-to articles on nutrition, pharmacology, exercise, medical advances, and self-help; 2,000-2,500 words; pay varies **Tips:** "Use plain English; avoid medical jargon, but explain technical terms in simple language. Writing style: upbeat, and leavened with tasteful humor where possible. Information should be accurate, up-to-date, and from reliable sources; references from lay publications not acceptable. No celebrity profiles or personal experiences." **Queries:** Required. **E-Queries:** Yes. **Unsolicited mss:** Accepts. **Response:** 3-4 weeks; SASE required. **Rights:** All. **Payment:** On publication. **Contact:** Ingrid Strauch, Managing Editor.

HEALTH PRODUCTS BUSINESS

445 Broad Hollow Rd., Suite 21, Melville, NY 11747. 631-845-2700 x288. E-mail: michael.schiavetta@cygnuspub.com. Web site: www.healthproductsbusiness.com. Monthly. Circ.: 18,500. Michael Schiavetta, Editor. **Description:** Helps retailers and manufacturers navigate the challenges of the health and nutrition industry. **Nonfiction:** Stories on health products (supplements, skin/body care, organic food and medicine, sports nutrition, etc.); 1,000-3,000 words; pay varies. **Tips:** Seeking writers in the industry with credentials and expert knowledge on health/nutrition products. **Queries:** Required. **E-Queries:** Yes. **Unsolicited mss:** Does not accept. **Response:** SASE. **Freelance Content:** 25%. **Rights:** All. **Payment:** On publication.

HEALTH PROGRESS

Catholic Health Assn., 4455 Woodson Rd., St. Louis, MO 63134-3701. 314-427-2500. E-mail: hpeditor@chausa.org. Web site: www.chausa.org. Bimonthly. $50. Circ.: 13,000. **Description:** On hospital/nursing-home management and administration, medical-moral questions, health care, public policy, technological developments and their effects, nursing, financial and human resource management for administrators, and innovative programs in hospitals and long-term care facilities. **Nonfiction:** Features, 2,000-4,000 words; pay negotiable. **Queries:** Preferred.

HEALTH QUEST

200 Highpoint Dr., Suite 215, Chalfont, PA 18914. 215-822-7935.
E-mail: editor@healthquestmag.com. Web site: www.healthquestmag.com. Bimonthly. Circ.: 500,000. Gerda Gallop-Goodman, Editor. **Description:** Health and wellness magazine on body, mind, and spirit for African-Americans. Covers traditional and alternative medicine. **Nonfiction:** Health articles. **Queries:** Preferred. **E-Queries:** No. **Unsolicited mss:** Accepts. **Freelance Content:** 20%. **Payment:** On publication.

HEART & SOUL

See full listing in Ethnic & Multicultural category.

HERBALGRAM

American Botanical Council
P.O. Box 144345, Austin, TX 78714-4345. 512-926-4900.
E-mail: herbcowboy@aol.com. Web site: www.herbalgram.org. Quarterly. $29/yr. Circ.: 50,000. Mark Blumenthal, Editor. **Description:** On herb and medicinal plant research, regulatory issues, market conditions, native plant conservation, and other aspects of herbal use. **Nonfiction:** Articles, 1,500-3,000 words. **Payment:** In copies.

HERBS FOR HEALTH

1504 SW 42nd St., Topeka, KS 66609. 785-274-4300.
Web site: www.discoverherbs.com. Bimonthly. $4.99/issue. Circ.: 160,000. **Description:** Offers sound information for general public on the wide range of benefits of herbs, including their role in various healing arts. **Nonfiction:** 500-2,000 words; $.33/word. **Columns, Departments:** 200-500 words. **Art:** 300 dpi (CMYK), slides. **Tips:** "List your sources, keep it short, and focus on reader benefit." **Queries:** Preferred. **E-Queries:** Yes. **Unsolicited mss:** Accepts. **Response:** 3 months, SASE required. **Freelance Content:** 90%. **Rights:** FNASR. **Payment:** On publication.

HOMECARE

PRIMEDIA, 6151 Powers Ferry Rd., Atlanta, GA 30339. 770-618-0460.
E-mail: ppatch@primediabusiness.com. Web site: www.homecaremag.com. Monthly. Paula Patch, Managing Editor. **Description:** Leading resource for the home medical equipment. Covers the business of renting and selling home care products and services (industry news, trend analysis, product segment features, stories with management and operational ideas). Pays up to $.50/word. **Tips:** Seeking writers with health industry experience. **Queries:** Required. **E-Queries:** Yes. **Unsolicited mss:** Accepts. **Response:** 2-8 weeks, SASE required. **Freelance Content:** 20%. **Payment:** On acceptance.

LET'S LIVE

11050 Santa Monica Blvd., Fl. 3, Los Angeles, CA 90025. 310-445-7500.
E-mail: info@letslivemag.com. Web site: www.letsliveonline.com. Monthly. Circ.: 1,700,000. Beth Salmon, Editor-in-Chief. **Description:** Preventive medicine and nutrition, alternative medicine, weight loss, vitamins, herbs, exercise, and anti-aging. Articles run 1,000-1,500 words; pays up to $1,000. **Queries:** Required. **Contact:** Nicole Brechka, Senior Editor; Ayn Niz, Copy Editor.

LISTEN

See full listing in Teens category.

MAMM

54 W 22nd St., Fl. 4, New York, NY 10010. 646-365-1350.
E-mail: elsieh@mamm.com. Web site: www.mamm.com. Monthly. $17.97/yr. Circ.: 100,000. Gwen Darien, Editor-in-Chief. **Description:** On cancer prevention, treatment, and survival, for women. **Nonfiction:** Articles on conventional and alternative treatment and medical news; survivor profiles; investigative features; essays; pay varies. **Queries:** Preferred. **Payment:** On acceptance. **Contact:** Elsie Hsieh, Assistant Editor.

MEN'S HEALTH

Rodale, Inc., 33 E Minor St., Emmaus, PA 18098. 610-967-5171.
Web site: www.menshealth.com. 10x/yr. $3.79/issue. Circ.: 1,625,000. David Zinczenko, Editor-in-Chief. **Description:** Covers fitness, health, sex, nutrition, relationships, lifestyle, sports, and travel. **Nonfiction:** Useful articles, for men ages 25-55; 1,000-2,000 words; $.50/word. **Queries:** Required. **E-Queries:** Yes. **Payment:** On acceptance.

MIDWIFERY TODAY

P.O. Box 2672-350, Eugene, OR 97402. 541-344-7438.
E-mail: editorial@midwiferytoday.com. Web site: www.midwiferytoday.com. **Description:** For birth practitioners, on pregnancy, natural childbirth, and breastfeeding. Promotes education and networking between families and midwife practitioners. Also features birth-related art, poetry, and humor. Does not offer payment.

THE NEW PHYSICIAN

American Medical Student Assn.
1902 Association Dr., Reston, VA 20191-1502. 703-620-6600.
E-mail: tnp@www.amsa.org. Web site: www.amsa.org. Monthly. $25/yr. Circ.: 38,000. Rebecca Sernett, Editor. **Description:** On medical issues of interest to medical students. **Nonfiction:** On social, ethical, and political issues in medical education. Recent articles: space medicine, dating in med school, history of surgeon general, etc.; to 3,500 words; pay varies. **Tips:** Readers are highly educated, generally in their 20s. **Queries:** Preferred. **Unsolicited mss:** Accepts. **Freelance Content:** 35%. **Rights:** FNAR. **Payment:** On publication.

NUTRITION HEALTH REVIEW
P.O. Box 406, Haverford, PA 19041. 610-896-1853.
Quarterly. $3/$24. Andrew Rifkin, Editor. **Description:** Vegetarian-oriented publication. **Nonfiction:** Articles on medical progress, nutritional therapy, genetics, psychiatry, behavior therapy, surgery, pharmacology, animal health; vignettes on health and nutrition. **Fillers:** Humor, cartoons, illustrations. **Tips:** "We do not accept material involving subjects that favor animal testing, animal foods, cruelty to animals, or recipes with animal products." Sample copy on request. **Queries:** Required. **Unsolicited mss:** Accepts. **Response:** SASE required. **Payment:** On publication.

PATIENT CARE
Thompson Medical Economics
5 Paragon Dr., Montvale, NJ 07645-1725.201-358-7421.
E-mail: patientcare@medec.com. Web site: www.patientcareonline.com. 12x/yr. $99/yr. Circ.: 135,000. Peter D'Epiro, Managing Editor. **Description:** On medical care, for primary-care physicians. **Tips:** All articles by assignment only. **Queries:** Required. **Unsolicited mss:** Does not accept. **Payment:** On acceptance.

THE PHOENIX
7152 Unity Ave. N, Brooklyn Center, MN 55429. 651-291-2691.
E-mail: psamples@infionline.net. Web site: www.phoenixrecovery.org. Monthly. Circ.: 40,000. Pat Samples, Editor. **Description:** For people working on their physical, mental, emotional, and spiritual well-being, seeking peace and serenity. Covers a broad spectrum of recovery, renewal, and growth information. Articles run 800-1,500 words. **Tips:** Contact for upcoming themes. **Queries:** Not necessary. **E-Queries:** Yes. **Unsolicited mss:** Accepts. **Response:** 1 month, SASE required. **Freelance Content:** 90%. **Rights:** FNAR. **Payment:** On publication.

PREVENTION
Rodale Press, Inc., 33 E Minor St., Emmaus, PA 18098. 610-967-5171.
E-mail: prevention@rodale.com. Web site: www.prevention.com. Monthly. $21.97/yr. Circ.: 3,008,000. Catherine Cassidy, Editor-in-Chief. **Description:** Leading magazine for preventative health research and practices. **Tips:** Freelance content limited. **Queries:** Required.

PSYCHOLOGY TODAY
49 E 21st St., Fl. 11, New York, NY 10010-6213. 212-260-7210.
E-mail: info@psychologytoday.com. Web site: www.psychologytoday.com. Bimonthly. $16/yr. Circ.: 323,000. Robert Epstein, Editor-in-Chief. **Description:** On general-interest psychological research. Timely subjects and news. Articles run 800-2,500 words; pay varies.

REMEDY

298 Fifth Ave., Fl. 2, New York, NY 10001-4522. 212-695-2223.
E-mail: info@medizine.com. Web site: www.medizine.com. Quarterly. $12/yr. Circ.: 2,236,700. Kalia Doner, Editor-in-Chief. **Description:** On health and medication issues, for readers 50 and over. **Nonfiction:** Articles, 600-2,500 words; pays $1.00-$1.25/word. **Columns, Departments:** Dispensary; Nutrition Prescription. **Queries:** Preferred. **Payment:** On acceptance.

SPIRITUALITY & HEALTH

See full listing in New Age/Spiritual category.

T'AI CHI

See full listing in Sports & Recreation/Outdoors category.

TOTAL HEALTH FOR LONGEVITY

165 N 100 E, Suite 2, St. George, UT 84770-2505. 435-673-1789.
E-mail: thm@infowest.com. Web site: www.totalhealthmagazine.com. Bimonthly. Circ.: 60,000. Lyle Hurd, Editor/Publisher. **Description:** On preventative health care, fitness, diet, and mental health. Articles run 1,200-1,400 words; pays $50-$75. **Art:** Color or B&W photos. **Queries:** Preferred. **Payment:** On publication.

TURTLE MAGAZINE

Children's Better Health Institute
1100 Waterway Blvd., P.O. Box 567, Indianapolis, IN 46206-0567. 317-636-8881.
E-mail: t.harshman@cbhi.org. Web site: www.turtlemag.org. 6x/yr. Circ.: 300,000. Ms. Terry Harshman, Editor. **Description:** Emphasis on health and nutrition for 2- to 5-year-olds. Only new material being accepted currently is short rebus stories (100-200 words), and short simple poems (4-8 lines). **Payment:** $.22/word. **Poetry:** from $25. **Tips:** Send SASE for guidelines. **Rights:** All. **Payment:** On publication.

VEGETARIAN TIMES

See full listing in Food & Wine category.

VEGETARIAN VOICE

P.O. Box 72, Dolgeville, NY 13329. 518-568-7970.
E-mail: navs@telenet.net. Web site: www.navs-online.org. Quarterly. $20/yr. Circ.: 8,000. Maribeth Abrams-McHenry, Managing Editor. **Description:** Consumer concerns, health, nutrition, animal rights, the environment, world hunger, etc. Total vegetarian philosophy; all recipes are vegan and we do not support the use of leather, wool, silk, etc. **Payment:** In copies.

VIBRANT LIFE

55 W Oak Ridge Dr., Hagerstown, MD 21740-7301. 301-393-4019.
E-mail: vibrantlife@rhpa.org. Web site: www.vibrantlife.com. Bimonthly. $18.95.

Circ.: 28,000. Larry Becker, Editor. **Description:** On health and fitness that combines the physical, mental, and spiritual aspects of a healthy lifestyle in a practical Christian approach. **Nonfiction:** Promotes a vegetarian lifestyle. 600-2,000 words; $80-$300. **Queries:** Preferred. **Unsolicited mss:** Accepts. **Freelance Content:** 80%. **Rights:** World Serial Rights and reprint rights. **Payment:** On acceptance.

VITALITY

356 Dupont St., Toronto, Ontario M5R 1V9 Canada. 416-964-0528.
E-mail: editorial@vitalitymagazine.com. 10x/yr. $32.10/yr. Circ.: 50,000. Julia Woodford, Editor. **Description:** Canadian natural health magazine and wellness journal. **Nonfiction:** Seeks success stories of people who have overcome a debilitating disease with natural medicine. Also articles on nutritional medicine, consumer information, and emotional wellness; 800-1,800 words; $.10/word (CDN). **Columns, Departments:** Earthwatch: (news of worthwhile environmental initiatives and solutions; 800-1,800 words; $.25/word (CDN). **Art:** Submit hard copy or electronic; fees negotiated. **Tips:** Submissions: double-spaced, one-inch margins, 14 pt. type. **Queries:** Preferred. **E-Queries:** No. **Unsolicited mss:** Accepts. **Response:** 6-8 weeks, SASE required. **Freelance Content:** 75%. **Payment:** On publication.

WEIGHT WATCHERS MAGAZINE

747 Third Ave., Fl. 24, New York, NY 10017-6547. 212-370-0644.
E-mail: wwmeditor@wwpublishinggroup.com. Web site: www.weightwatchers.com. 6x/yr. $24.95. Circ.: 350,000. Nancy Gagliardi, Editorial Director. **Description:** Health, nutrition, fitness, and weight-loss motivation and success. **Nonfiction:** Articles on fashion, beauty, food, health, nutrition, fitness, and weight-loss motivation and success; from $1/word. **Tips:** Query with clips required. Guidelines available. **Queries:** Required. **Payment:** On acceptance.

YOGA JOURNAL

2054 University Ave., Berkeley, CA 94704-1082. 510-841-9200.
E-mail: nisaacs@yogajournal.com. Web site: www.yogajournal.com. Monthly. Circ.: 215,000. Kathryn Arnold, Editor-in-Chief. **Description:** Serves the hatha yoga community. Holistic health, meditation, conscious living, spirituality, and yoga. Articles, 300-6,000 words; pays $75-$3,000. **Queries:** Preferred. **E-Queries:** Yes. **Unsolicited mss:** Accepts. **Response:** 8 weeks, SASE. **Freelance Content:** 10%. **Rights:** Non-exclusive worldwide, print and non-print. **Payment:** On acceptance. **Contact:** Nora Isaacs, Managing Editor.

HISTORY

AIR COMBAT

See full listing in Military category.

ALABAMA HERITAGE
University of Alabama
P.O. Box 870342, Tuscaloosa, AL 35487-0342. 205-348-7467.
Web site: www.alabamaheritage.com. Quarterly. $6/$18.95. Circ.: 6,500. Donna L. Cox, Editor. **Description:** Lively, well-researched, well-told, true stories of Alabama and Alabamians. **Nonfiction:** Interested in all aspects of Alabama's heritage/culture and of the contributions Alabamians have made to the larger world; 2,500-4,500 words; $200-$400. **Columns, Departments:** Southern Folkways (customs and traditions), Southern Architecture and Preservation, Recollections (history, as viewed by participants), Arts in the South, Alabama Album ("slice of life" photo), Alabama Treasures (artifacts, collections). 250-1,000 words; up to $50. **Tips:** "Excellent visual images (photos, maps, art) must be available to illustrate articles." **Queries:** Required. **E-Queries:** Yes. **Unsolicited mss:** Accepts. **Response:** Queries 4-6 weeks, submissions 6-8 weeks. **Freelance Content:** 90%. **Payment:** On publication.

AMERICA'S CIVIL WAR
PRIMEDIA History Group
741 Miller Dr. SE, Suite D2, Leesburg, VA 20175. 703-771-9400.
E-mail: americascivilwar@thehistorynet.com. Web site: www.historynet.com. Bimonthly. $4.99/issue. Circ.: 75,000. Dana B. Shoaf, Managing Editor. **Description:** Popular history for general readers and Civil War buffs, on strategy, tactics, history, narrative. **Nonfiction:** Strategy, tactics, personalities, arms, and equipment; 3,500-4,000 words, plus 500-word sidebar; $200-$400. **Columns, Departments:** Up to 2,000 words; $100-$200. **Art:** Cite known color or B&W illustrations, and sources (museums, historical societies, private collections, etc.). **Tips:** Readable style and historical accuracy imperative. Use action and quotes where possible. Attribute quotes, cite major sources. **Queries:** Required. **E-Queries:** Yes. **Unsolicited mss:** Accepts. **Response:** 6 months; SASE required. **Freelance Content:** 98%. **Payment:** Both on acceptance and on publication; kill fee offered.

AMERICAN HERITAGE
Forbes, Inc., 28 W 23rd St., New York, NY 10010-5204. 212-367-3100.
E-mail: mail@americanheritage.com. Web site: www.americanheritage.com. 8x/yr. $4.95/issue. Circ.: 310,000. Richard F. Snow, Editor. **Description:** Covers the American experience, from serious concerns to colorful sidelights, from powerful institutions to ordinary men and women, using the past to illuminate the present. **Nonfiction:** On the American experience. Annotate all quotations and factual statements; include brief biographical note about yourself; 1,500-6,000 words; pay varies. **Art:** B&W prints, color slides. **Tips:** No fiction or poetry. "We welcome freelancers, but we need detailed queries in advance. Also, consult indexes first." **Queries:** Preferred. **E-Queries:** No. **Unsolicited mss:** Accepts. **Response:** 8-10 weeks, SASE required. **Freelance Content:** 70%. **Payment:** On acceptance.

AMERICAN HERITAGE OF INVENTION & TECHNOLOGY
Forbes, Inc., 28 W 23rd St., New York, NY 10010. 212-367-3100.
E-mail: mail@americanheritage.com. Web site: www.americanheritage.com.
Quarterly. $15/yr. Circ.: 165,000. Frederick Allen, Editor. **Description:** Lively,
authoritative prose and illustrations (archival photos, rare paintings), on the history of
technology in America, for the sophisticated general reader. Articles run 2,000-5,000
words. **Queries:** Not necessary. **E-Queries:** Yes. **Payment:** On acceptance.

AMERICAN HISTORY
741 Miller Dr. SE, Suite D-2, Leesburg, VA 20175. 703-771-9400.
E-mail: americanhistory@thehistorynet.com. Web site: www.thehistorynet.com.
Bimonthly. $4.99/$23.95. Circ.: 95,000. Douglas G. Brinkley, Editor. **Description:**
Features the cultural, military, social, and political history of the United States for a
general audience. **Nonfiction:** Well-researched articles. General interest, not schol-
arly, with a good focus and strong anecdotal material. No travelogues, fiction, or puz-
zles. 2,000-4,000 words; $500-$600. **Tips:** "We seek tightly focused stories that show
an incident or short period of time in history." **Queries:** Preferred. **E-Queries:** Yes.
Unsolicited mss: Does not accept. **Response:** 10 weeks, SASE required.
Freelance Content: 60%. **Rights:** All worldwide. **Payment:** On publication.
Contact: Philip Brandt George, Associate Editor.

AMERICAN LEGACY
See full listing in Ethnic & Multicultural category.

AMERICAN OUTBACK JOURNAL
See full listing in Regional & City Publications category.

ANCESTRY
360 W 4800N, Provo, UT 84604. 801-705-7000.
E-mail: ameditor@ancestry.com. Web site: www.ancestry.com. Bimonthly. $24.95/yr.
Circ.: 60,000. Jennifer Utley, Managing Editor. **Description:** Family history/geneal-
ogy magazine for professional family historians and hobbyists interested in getting the
most out of their research. **Nonfiction:** Family articles, especially stories where novel
approaches are used to find information on the lives of ancestors; 2,000-2,500 words;
$500. **Fillers:** Humorous pieces about pursuit of the author's family history; 600
words; $200. **Art:** Interesting old photographs of ancestors. **Tips:** No typical family
histories, only interesting angles on family history, research methods, and specific case
studies. **Queries:** Preferred. **E-Queries:** Yes. **Unsolicited mss:** Accepts.
Response: Queries 3 months, submissions 3 months, SASE. **Freelance Content:**
20%. **Rights:** All. **Payment:** On publication. **Contact:** Jennifer Utley.

ANCIENT AMERICAN
P.O. Box 370, Colfax, WI 54730. 715-962-3299.
E-mail: articles@ancientamerican.com. Web site: www.ancientamerican.com.
Bimonthly. $5.50/$29.95. Circ.: 15,000. Frank Joseph, Editor. **Description:** On the

prehistory of the American Continent, regardless of presently fashionable beliefs. A forum for experts and nonprofessionals alike. **Nonfiction:** On prehistory, in clear, nontechnical language, with original color photographs/artwork; 2,000-3,000 words; $50-$150. **Art:** Adobe Photoshop, TIF. **Tips:** Translate complex research into accessible language with appealing format for ordinary readers. **Queries:** Not necessary. **E-Queries:** Yes. **Unsolicited mss:** Accepts. **Response:** SASE required. **Freelance Content:** 50%. **Payment:** On publication. **Contact:** Wayne May.

ARMOR
See full listing in Military category.

THE BEAVER
167 Lombard Ave., #478, Winnipeg, Manitoba R3B 0T6 Canada. 204-988-9300. E-mail: beaver@historysociety.ca. Web site: www.the beaver.ca. Bimonthly. $4.95/$27.50. Circ.: 45,000. Annalee Greenberg, Editor. **Description:** Canadian history for a general audience. **Nonfiction:** Canadian history subjects; 3,500 words max; $.30/word. **Tips:** "Combine impeccable research with good nonfiction story-writing skills." Full editorial guidelines on website. **Queries:** Required. **E-Queries:** No. **Unsolicited mss:** Accepts. **Response:** 6 weeks, SASE. **Freelance Content:** 50%. **Rights:** FNASR, electronic. **Payment:** On acceptance.

CALLIOPE
See full listing in Juvenile category.

CAROLOGUE
See full listing in Regional & City Publications category.

CIVIL WAR TIMES
6405 Flank Dr., Harrisburg, PA 17112. 717-657-9555. E-mail: civilwartimes.magazine@primedia.com. Web site: www.thehistorynet.com. 6x/yr. Circ.: 108,000. James Kushlan, Editor. **Description:** Relates the human experience of the American Civil War through lively, true stories. Relies heavily on primary sources and words of eyewitnesses. Articles run 2,500-3,000 words; $400-$650. **Tips:** Prefers gripping, quote-rich, well-documented accounts of battles, unusual events, eyewitness accounts (memoirs, diaries, letters), and common soldier photos. **Payment:** On acceptance.

COBBLESTONE
See full listing in Juvenile category.

COLUMBIA: THE MAGAZINE OF NORTHWEST HISTORY
Washington State Historical Society (WSHS) Research Center
315 N Stadium Way, Tacoma, WA 98403. 253-798-5918.
E-mail: cdubois@wshs.wa.gov. Web site: www.wshs.org. Quarterly. $7.50/issue. Circ.: 4,000. Christina Dubois, Managing Editor. **Description:** History publication for the

Pacific Northwest. Articles and commentary edited for the general reader. Submissions average 4,000 words. **Queries:** Preferred. **E-Queries:** Yes. **Unsolicited mss:** Accepts. **Response:** 2-4 weeks, SASE required. **Freelance Content:** 80%. **Rights:** FNAR.

FAMILY TREE
F&W Publications, Inc.
4700 E Galbraith Rd., Cincinnati, OH 45236. 513-531-2690.
E-mail: editor@familytreemagazine.com. Web site: www.familytreemagazine.com. Bimonthly. $27/yr. Circ.: 73,000. David Fryxell, Editor-in-Chief. **Description:** Articles on how to discover, preserve, and celebrate family history and traditions. **Queries:** Preferred.

GOLDENSEAL MAGAZINE
WV Division of Culture & History
The Cultural Center, 1900 Kanawha Blvd. E
Charleston, WV 25305-0300. 304-558-0220.
E-mail: goldenseal@wvculture.org. Web site: www.wvculture.org/goldenseal. Quarterly. $17/yr. Circ.: 20,000. John Lilly, Editor. **Description:** On traditional West Virginia culture and history. Oral histories, old and new B&W photos, research articles. Features, 3,000 words; shorter articles, 1,000 words. Pays $.10/word. **Payment:** On publication.

GOOD OLD DAYS
306 E Parr Rd., Berne, IN 46711. 260-589-4000.
E-mail: editor@goodolddaysonline.com. Web site: www.goodolddaysonline.com. Monthly. $2.50/issue. Circ.: 200,000. Ken Tate, Editor. **Description:** First-person nostalgia from the "Good Old Days" era (1900-1955), with particular attention to the period from the Great Depression to the end of World War II. **Nonfiction:** First-person nostalgia within this timeframe; 500-1,500 words; $.03-$.05/word. **Poetry:** Metered and rhymed; 8-24 lines; payment varies. **Columns, Departments:** Good Old Days in the Kitchen, Good Old Days on Wheels; 500-1,500 words; $.03-$.05/word. **Art:** Photos to accompany articles; prints; $5/photo. **Tips:** "Good photos are a key to acceptance. Readers are generally older, rather conservative. Keep a positive, pleasant tone. Pick out a particular memory and stick to it." **Queries:** Not necessary. **E-Queries:** Yes. **Unsolicited mss:** Accepts. **Response:** 2 months; SASE required. **Freelance Content:** 85%. **Rights:** All. **Payment:** On acceptance.

HERITAGE QUEST MAGAZINE
See full listing in Hobbies, Crafts, Collecting category.

THE HIGHLANDER
87 Highland Ave., Hull, MA 02045. 781-925-0600.
E-mail: info@highlandermagazine.com. Web site: www.highlandermagazine.com. 7x/yr. $17.50/yr. Circ.: 35,000. Neill Kennedy Ray, Editor. **Description:** Covers

Scottish heritage (history, clans, families), related to Scotland in the period 1300-1900 A.D. **Nonfiction:** 1,500-2,000 words; $185-$250. **Art:** Photos must accompany manuscripts; B&W, color transparencies, maps, line drawings. **Tips:** "We're not concerned with modern Scotland." **Queries:** Preferred. **E-Queries:** No. **Unsolicited mss:** Accepts. **Response:** Queries 6-8 weeks, submissions 1-2 months, SASE required. **Payment:** On acceptance.

THE ILLINOIS STEWARD
University of Illinois
1102 S Goodwin Ave., W503 Turner Hall, Urbana, IL 61801. 217-244-3896.
E-mail: karynk@uiuc.edu. Web site: http://ilsteward.nres.uiuc.edu. Karyn McDermaid, Managing Editor; Robert Reber, Managing Editor. **Description:** On Illinois history and heritage, with natural-resource stewardship theme. Articles run 1,700-1,800 words; no payment offered. **Tips:** Complimentary copy provided at no charge. **Queries:** Preferred. **E-Queries:** Yes.

MHQ: QUARTERLY JOURNAL OF MILITARY HISTORY
PRIMEDIA History Group
741 Miller Dr. SE, Suite D-2, Leesburg, VA 20175-8994. 703-771-9400.
E-mail: mhq@thehistorynet.com. Web site: www.historynet.com. Quarterly. $69.95/yr. Circ.: 45,000. Rod Paschall, Editor. **Description:** Offers an undistorted view of history, encourages understanding of events, personalities, and artifacts of the past. **Nonfiction:** Well-written military history; 5,000-6,000 words; $800. **Columns, Departments:** 1,500-2,500 words; $400. **Art:** Color, B&W illustrations. **Queries:** Preferred. **E-Queries:** Yes. **Unsolicited mss:** Accepts. **Response:** 4-8 weeks, SASE required. **Freelance Content:** 50%. **Payment:** On publication.

MILITARY
See full listing in Military category.

MONTANA
Montana Historical Society
225 N Roberts St., P.O. Box 201201, Helena, MT 59601. 406-444-4741.
E-mail: cwhitehorn@state.mt.us. Web site: www.montanahistoricalsociety.org. Quarterly. $8.50/$29 yr. Circ.: 10,000. W. Clark Whitehorn, Editor. **Description:** For members of state historical society and Western History Assn., covering history of Montana and the American and Canadian West. **Nonfiction:** Authentic articles on history of the region; new interpretative approaches to major developments in Western history. Must use footnotes or bibliography; 3,500-5,500 words. **Queries:** Preferred. **E-Queries:** Yes. **Unsolicited mss:** Accepts. **Response:** Queries 3 months, submissions 1 month, SASE. **Freelance Content:** 95%. **Rights:** All.

NAVAL HISTORY
291 Wood Rd., Annapolis, MD 21402. 410-295-1079.
E-mail: fschultz@usni.org. Web site: www.usni.org/navalhistory/nh.html.

Bimonthly. $5.99/issue. Circ.: 40,000. Fred L. Schultz, Editor-in-Chief. **Description:** On international naval and maritime history, published by U.S. Naval Institute. **Nonfiction:** Essays, book excerpts, interviews, profiles, personal experience, technical, photo feature; 1,000-3,000 words; pays $300-$500 (assigned articles); $75-$400 (unsolicited). **Fillers:** Inspirational humor; 50-100 words; $10-$50. **Tips:** "Write a good, concise story; support it with primary sources and good illustrations." **Queries:** Preferred. **E-Queries:** Yes. **Unsolicited mss:** Accepts. **Response:** 1-2 months, SASE required. **Freelance Content:** 90%. **Rights:** FNASR. **Payment:** On acceptance.

NEBRASKA HISTORY

P.O. Box 82554, Lincoln, NE 68501. 402-471-4748.
E-mail: publish@nebraskahistory.org. Web site: www.nebraskahistory.org. Quarterly. $30/yr. Circ.: 3,800. Donald B. Cunningham, Editor. **Description:** Seeks well-researched articles, edited documents, and other annotated primary materials on the history of Nebraska and the Great Plains. Articles run 3,000-7,000 words. **Art:** 8x10 B&W, 600 dpi scans. **Tips:** Rarely publishes family histories or reminiscence. Send submissions by regular mail only; no unsolicited e-mail attachments. Sample copy free on request. **Queries:** Preferred. **E-Queries:** Yes. **Unsolicited mss:** Accepts. **Response:** 1-8 weeks, SASE required. **Payment:** In copies.

OLD CALIFORNIA GAZETTE

2454 Heritage Park Row, San Diego, CA 92110. 619-491-0099.
E-mail: gazettes@cts.com. Annual. Circ.: 1,000,000. Karen Spring, Editor. **Description:** California history, 1800-1920s. **Nonfiction:** 500-750 words max; $.10/word. **Tips:** $25 bonus for front cover piece. $25 bonus if humorous. **Queries:** Preferred. **E-Queries:** Yes. **Unsolicited mss:** Accepts. **Response:** 1 month, SASE not needed. **Freelance Content:** 50%. **Rights:** 1st. **Payment:** On publication.

PENNSYLVANIA HERITAGE

Pennsylvania Heritage Society
300 North St., Harrisburg, PA 17120-0024. 717-787-2407.
E-mail: momalley@phmc.state.pa.us. Web site: www.paheritage.org. Quarterly. $20/yr. Circ.: 13,000. Michael J. O'Malley III, Editor. **Description:** On the state's rich culture and historic legacy. **Nonfiction:** Articles on Pennsylvania fine and decorative arts, architecture, archaeology, history, industry and technology, travel, and folklore, with ideas for possible illustration; 2,500-3,500 words; to $500. **Art:** Photos, drawings; photo essays; up to $100. **Tips:** "Seeks unusual, fresh angle to make history come to life, including pictorial or photo essays, interviews, travel/destination pieces. Submit complete manuscript." **Queries:** Preferred. **Payment:** On acceptance.

PERSIMMON HILL

1700 NE 63rd St., Oklahoma City, OK 73111. 405-478-6404.
E-mail: editor@nationalcowboymuseum.org. Web site: www/nationalcowboymuseum.org. Quarterly. $30/yr. Circ.: 15,000. M.J. Van Deventer, Editor. **Description:**

Historical and contemporary themes related to the American West, from Hollywood to cowboys. Honors those who have made positive contributions to the West, past or present. **Nonfiction:** On Western history and art, cowboys, ranching, rodeo, and nature; 1,000-1,500 words; $150-$350. **Columns, Departments:** Great hotels and lodgings; entrepreneurs; events, interesting places to visit, personalities; 750-1,000 words; $75-$150. **Art:** Slides, transparencies; up to $50/image. **Tips:** "No stories on western outlaws or 'bad guys' (Billy the Kid) stories." **Queries:** Required. **E-Queries:** Yes. **Unsolicited mss:** Accepts. **Response:** 6-8 weeks, SASE required. **Freelance Content:** 95%. **Rights:** One-time NA. **Payment:** On publication.

PRESERVATION
National Trust for Historic Preservation
1785 Massachusetts Ave. NW, Washington, DC 20036-2117. 202-588-6388.
E-mail: preservation@nthp.org. Web site: www.preservationonline.org. Bimonthly. $5/$20. Circ.: 200,000. Robert Wilson, Editor. **Description:** "Encourages a sense of place and passion for historic preservation." **Nonfiction:** Articles on the built environment, place, architecture, preservation issues, and people involved. Mostly freelance; 150-6,000 words; $.50-$1.00/word. **Queries:** Preferred. **E-Queries:** Yes. **Unsolicited mss:** Accepts. **Response:** Queries 2-3 weeks, submissions 6-8 weeks, SASE required. **Freelance Content:** 80%. **Rights:** FNAR. **Payment:** On acceptance.

REMINISCE
Reiman Publications/Reader's Digest Assn.
5400 S 60th St., Greendale, WI 53129.
E-mail: editors@reminisce.com. Web site: www.reminisce.com. Bimonthly. $17.98/yr. Circ.: 1,000,000. **Description:** "A stroll down memory lane." Vintage photographs and real-life, first-person stories recall the "good old days" (1960s and back). Articles should have an "I remember" element; 750 words. **Tips:** E-mail or send SASE for submission guidelines. **Queries:** Not necessary. **Unsolicited mss:** Accepts. **Response:** 2 months. **Freelance Content:** 90%. **Payment:** On publication.

RENAISSANCE
1450 Barnum Ave., Suite 207, Bridgeport, CT 06610. 800-232-2224.
E-mail: editor@renaissancemagazine.com. Web site: www.renaissancemagazine.com. Quarterly. Circ.: 30,000. Kim Guarnaccia, Editor/Publisher. **Description:** Renaissance and Medieval history, costuming, heraldry, reenactments, role-playing, and Renaissance faires. **Nonfiction:** Martial arts, travel, interviews, re-enactment groups, and reviews of books, music, movies, and games; 3,000 words; $.08/word. **Art:** Prefers electronic format for submissions. Pays $8/image. **Tips:** Send query with brief bio and sample article. **Queries:** Preferred. **E-Queries:** Yes. **Unsolicited mss:** Accepts. **Response:** 3-6 weeks, SASE. **Freelance Content:** 90%. **Rights:** FNAR. **Payment:** On publication.

SOUTH CAROLINA HISTORICAL MAGAZINE
South Carolina Historical Society
100 Meeting St., Charleston, SC 29401-2299. 843-723-3225.
E-mail: info@schistory.org. Web site: www.schistory.org. Eric Emerson, Editor.
Description: Scholarly articles, to 25 pages (with footnotes), on South Carolina history. Check previous issues to be aware of scholarship. **Payment:** In copies.

SOUTHERN OREGON HERITAGE TODAY
See full listing in Regional & City Publications category.

TIMELINE
1982 Velma Ave., Columbus, OH 43211-2497. 614-297-2360.
E-mail: timeline@ohiohistory.org. Bimonthly. $6/$30. Circ.: 15,000. Christopher S. Duckworth, Editor. **Description:** Covers fields of history, prehistory, and natural sciences, directed towards readers in the Midwest. **Nonfiction:** History, politics, economics, social, and natural history for lay readers in Ohio and the Midwest; 1,000-5,000 words. **Tips:** Writing style should be simple and direct; avoid jargon. **Queries:** Preferred. **E-Queries:** Yes. **Unsolicited mss:** Accepts. **Response:** 2 weeks, SASE required. **Freelance Content:** 90%. **Rights:** FNAR. **Payment:** On acceptance.

TRUE WEST
P.O. Box 8008, Cave Creek, AZ 85327. 888-587-1881.
E-mail: editor@truewestmagazine.com. Web site: www.truewestmagazine.com. 10x/yr. Circ.: 90,000. R.G. Robertson, Managing Editor. **Description:** Since 1953, *True West* Magazine has been celebrating the history of the American West. "From classic gunfights to Native Americans, it's all red, white, and true." **Tips:** "We recommend familiarity with our publication before submitting queries." Sample copy $5 plus $2 shipping. **Payment:** On publication.

VIETNAM
PRIMEDIA History Group
741 Miller Dr. SE, Suite D2, Leesburg, VA 20175-8994. 703-771-9400.
E-mail: vietnam@thehistorynet.com/vn. Web site: www.thehistorynet.com. Bimonthly. $4.99/$23.95. Circ.: 50,000. David T. Zabecki, Editor. **Description:** Popular military-history magazine. Seeks to record and document "the many truths about Vietnam." **Nonfiction:** First-person and third-person accounts of all historical aspects of the Vietnam War; strategy, tactics, personalities, arms, and equipment. 3,500-4,000 words; $300. **Columns, Departments:** Arsenal, Fighting Forces, Personality, Perspectives. 1,500-2,000 words; $150. **Tips:** Most readers are Vietnam veterans, current military personnel, military historians and enthusiasts. Does not publish fiction or war stories. **Queries:** Preferred. **E-Queries:** Accepts. **Rights:** All worldwide, reprint. **Payment:** On publication.

THE WESTERN HISTORICAL QUARTERLY

Utah State University, Logan, UT 84322-0740. 435-797-1301.
E-mail: whq@hass.usu.edu. Web site: www.usu.edu/history/whq. Quarterly. Circ.: 2,200. Anne M. Butler, Editor. **Description:** Covers the American West (United States, Canada, and Mexico). Focuses on occupation, settlement, and political, economic, social, cultural, and intellectual history. **Nonfiction:** Original articles about the American West, the Westward movement, 20th-century regional studies, Spanish borderlands, Canada, northern Mexico, Alaska, and Hawaii. To 10,000 words; no payment. **Tips:** Prefers descriptive, interpretive, and analytical essays on broad themes; use of primary sources and monographic literature. **Queries:** Not necessary. **E-Queries:** Yes. **Unsolicited mss:** Accepts. **Response:** 1 week, SASE required.

WILD WEST

PRIMEDIA History Group
741 Miller Dr. SE, Suite D-2, Leesburg, VA 20175-8920. 703-779-8302.
E-mail: wildwest@thehistorynet.com. Web site: www.thehistorynet.com./wildwest. Bimonthly. $23.95/yr. Circ.: 86,200. Gregory Lalire, Editor. **Description:** History of people, places, battles, and events that led to the taming of the great American frontier. **Nonfiction:** Articles, artwork, and picture essays on life and times of settlers, cowboys, Indians, gunmen, lawmen, all the fascinating characters and aspects of Western lore and culture; 3,500-4,000 words; $200-$400. **Queries:** Preferred. **E-Queries:** Yes. **Unsolicited mss:** Accepts. **Response:** 6 months, SASE required. **Payment:** On publication.

WORLD WAR II

PRIMEDIA History Group
741 Miller Dr. SE, Suite D-2, Leesburg, VA 20175-8994. 703-779-8302.
E-mail: mhaskew@cowles.com. Web site: www.thehistorynet.com. Bimonthly. $27.95. Circ.: 152,300. Chris Anderson, Editor. **Description:** Strategy, tactics, personalities, arms, and equipment. **Nonfiction:** Features, 3,500-4,00 words, plus 500-word sidebar; up to $200. **Art:** Cite any color or B&W illustrations, and sources. **Tips:** Readable style and historical accuracy imperative. **Queries:** Preferred. **Unsolicited mss:** Accepts. **Response:** 6 months, SASE. **Rights:** Exclusive worldwide. **Payment:** On publication.

HOBBIES, CRAFTS, COLLECTING

(See also Games & Pastimes)

AIRBRUSH ACTION

P.O. Box 438, 3209 Atlantic Ave., Allenwood, NJ 08720. 732-223-7878.
E-mail: editor@airbrushaction.com. Web site: www.airbrushaction.com. Bimonthly. $5.99/$26.95. Circ.: 60,000. Michael Duck, Editor. **Description:** Showcases innovative airbrush art. Profiles on notable artists, step-by-step "how-to" articles, columns on T-shirt painting, automotive airbrushing, fingernail design. Also, regular Buyer's

Guides with comparisons of airbrush art supplies. **Nonfiction:** Profiles of artists by request only; 1,000-2,000 words; $.15/word. **Queries:** Required. **E-Queries:** Yes. **Unsolicited mss:** Accepts. **Response:** 2 weeks, SASE required. **Freelance Content:** 50%. **Rights:** All. **Payment:** On publication.

ANCESTRY
See full listing in History category.

ANTIQUE SHOPPE
P.O. Box 2175, Keystone Heights, FL 32656. 352-475-1679.
E-mail: antshoppe@aol.com. Web site: www.antiqueshoppefl.com. Monthly. $17. Circ.: 20,000. Bruce G. Causey, Editor. **Description:** Serves the antique and collection industry. Articles on antiques, collectibles, communities with antique districts, historical locations, local auctions or shows; 1,000 words; $50. **Queries:** Preferred. **E-Queries:** Yes. **Unsolicited mss:** Accepts. **Freelance Content:** 60%. **Payment:** On publication.

ANTIQUE TRADER PUBLICATIONS
Krause Publications, Inc., 700 E State St., Iola, WI 54990. 715-445-2214.
E-mail: korbecks@krause.com. Web site: www.collect.com. Weekly. $37/yr. Circ.: 60,000. Sharon Korbeck, Editor. **Description:** Covers all types of antiques and collectibles. **Nonfiction:** Articles 500-1,200 words; $50-$250. **Rights:** Exclusive. **Payment:** On publication.

ANTIQUE WEEK
27 N Jefferson St., P.O. Box 90, Knightstown, IN 46148-1242. 765-345-5133.
E-mail: antiquewk@aol.com. Web site: www.antiqueweek.com. Weekly. $28.45/yr. Circ.: 64,000. Tom Hoepf, Editor. **Description:** Weekly antique, auction, and collectors' newspaper. Guidelines available. **Nonfiction:** Articles, 500-2,000 words, on antiques, collectibles, genealogy, auction and antique show reports; pays $40-$200 for in-depth articles. **Art:** Photos. **Queries:** Preferred. **Payment:** On publication. **Contact:** Connie Swaim, Managing Editor.

ANTIQUES & AUCTION NEWS
P.O. Box 500, Mount Joy, PA 17552-0500. 717-653-1833.
E-mail: antiquesnews@engleonline.com. Weekly. $15/yr. Circ.: 35,000. Denise Sater, Editor. **Description:** Factual articles, 600-1,500 words, on antiques, collectors, collections, and places of historic interest. **Nonfiction:** Pays $18-$40. **Art:** Photos. **Queries:** Required. **Payment:** On publication.

ARTS & CRAFTS
Krause Publications, Inc.
700 E State St., Iola, WI 54990-0001. 715-445-4612.
E-mail: reetza@krause.com. Web site: www.artsandcraftsmag.com. Bimonthly.

$19.99/yr. Circ.: 131,000. Althea Reetz, Editor. **Description:** Upscale magazine featuring intermediate to advanced level home decor, gift, and fashion ideas.

AUCTION EXCHANGE

929 Industrial Parkway, P.O. Box 57, Plainwell, MI 49080-0057. 616-685-1343.
E-mail: auctionexchange@wmis.net. Web site: www.eauctionexchange.com. Weekly.
$26.95/yr. Circ.: 13,000. Lars Svendsen, Editor. **Description:** For dealers and collectors, on auctions, antiques, and collectibles. Serves Michigan, Indiana, and Ohio.
Articles run 500 words. Pays $1.25/column, $3/photo. **Queries:** Not necessary.
E-Queries: Yes. **Unsolicited mss:** Accepts. **Freelance Content:** 70%. **Rights:**
FNAR. **Payment:** On publication.

AUTOGRAPH COLLECTOR

510A Corona Mall, Corona, CA 92879-1420. 909-371-7137.
E-mail: editorev@telus.net. Web site: www.autographcollector.com. Monthly. $38/yr.
Circ.: 20,000. Ev Phillips, Editor. **Description:** Covers all areas of autograph collecting (preservation, framing, and storage, specialty collections, documents and letters, collectors and dealers). **Nonfiction:** Articles; 1,000-2,000 words; pay varies.
Tips: Sample copy and guidelines free. **Queries:** Preferred.

BEAD & BUTTON

Kalmbach Publishing Co.
21027 Crossroads Circle, P.O. Box 1612, Waukesha, WI 53187-1612. 262-796-8776.
Web site: www.beadandbutton.com. 6x/yr. Circ.: 140,878. Alice Korach, Editor.
Description: Illustrated bead projects for enthusiasts: jewelry, home decor, clothing, and more. **Art:** Art is by authors; photo and illustration guidance is by authors; final photos and illustrations are done in-house. **Tips:** Articles are written by artisans in this hobby. **Queries:** Required. **E-Queries:** Yes. **Unsolicited mss:** Sometimes accepts.
Response: 3 months. **Rights:** All. **Payment:** On acceptance.

BEADSTYLE

Kalmbach Publishing Co.
21027 Crossroads Circle, P.O. Box 1612, Waukesha, WI 53187-1612. 262-796-8776.
Web site: www.beadstylemag.com. 6x/yr. Mindy Brooks, Editor. **Description:** Each issue of *BeadStyle* features 18+ beading projects that are fast, stylish, and offer simple techniques for beginning and seasoned beaders. **Tips:** Considers manuscript ideas from project designers only. Include photo or JPEG, brief introduction, list of materials, and step-by-step instructions. See website for specific guidelines. **Queries:** Not necessary. **E-queries:** No. **Unsolicited mss:** Accepts. **Rights:** All.

BECKETT BASKETBALL CARD MONTHLY

15850 Dallas Pkwy., Dallas, TX 75248-3308. 972-91-6657.
E-mail: jkelley@beckett.com. Web site: www.beckett.com. Monthly. $4.99/$27.99.
Circ.: 245,200. John Kelley, Managing Editor. **Description:** For hobbyists who col-

lect cards and memorabilia. (Also publishes *Beckett Sports Collectibles & Autographs, Football Card Monthly, Hockey Collector,* etc.) **Nonfiction:** Sports collectibles stories, with a trading card/basketball angle; 800-2,000 words. **Tips:** Promote the hobby in a positive, fun-loving way. **Queries:** Preferred. **E-Queries:** Yes. **Unsolicited mss:** Accepts. **Response:** 10 days, SASE not needed. **Freelance Content:** 30%. **Rights:** All. **Payment:** On publication.

BLADE MAGAZINE

Krause Publications, Inc., 700 E State St., Iola, WI 54945-5010. 715-445-2214. E-mail: blade@krause.com. Web site: www.blademag.com. Monthly. $4.95/$19.95. Circ.: 72,000. Steve Shackleford, Editor. **Description:** Information for knife makers, collectors, daily knife users, and enthusiasts. **Nonfiction:** Anything new and unusual about handmade and factory knives, historical pieces, interviews, celebrities, values on collectible knives and accessories, tips on use; 500-1,500 words. **Art:** Varied formats. **Queries:** Preferred. **E-Queries:** Yes. **Unsolicited mss:** Accepts. **Response:** Queries 1 month, submissions 2 months, SASE required. **Freelance Content:** 5%. **Rights:** All. **Payment:** On publication.

BREW YOUR OWN

See full listing in Food & Wine category.

CAROUSEL NEWS & TRADER

87 Park Ave. W, Suite 206, Mansfield, OH 44902-1612. 419-529-4999. E-mail: cnsam@aol.com. 10x/yr. $3.95/issue $35/year. Circ.: 3,500. Walter L. Loucks, Editor. **Description:** Covers all aspects of carousels (merry-go-rounds), including complete machines, individual animals, restoration, history, carving, buy-sell-trade. **Nonfiction:** On carousel history, profiles of operators and carvers, collectors, preservationists, restorationists; 500-1,000 words + photos; $50/printed page. **Art:** Photos. **Queries:** Preferred. **E-Queries:** Yes. **Unsolicited mss:** Accepts. **Response:** 4 weeks, SASE. **Payment:** On publication.

CLASSIC TOY TRAINS

Kalmbach Publishing Co.
21027 Crossroads Circle, Waukesha, WI 53187. 262-796-8776. E-mail: editor@classictoytrains.com. Web site: www.classictoytrains.com. 9x/yr. $5.50/$39.95. Circ.: 65,000. Neil Besougloff, Editor. **Description:** For enthusiasts of old and new toy trains produced by Lionel, American Flyer, and their competitors. **Nonfiction:** Articles, with photos, on toy train layouts and collections. Also toy train manufacturing history and repair/maintenance. Pays $75/printed page. **Queries:** Preferred. **E-Queries:** Yes. **Unsolicited mss:** Accepts. **Response:** Queries 15 days, submissions 30 days. **Freelance Content:** 60%. **Rights:** All. **Payment:** On acceptance.

CLASSIC TRAINS

Kalmbach Publishing Co.

21027 Crossroads Circle, Waukesha, WI 53187. 262-796-8776.

E-mail: rmcgonigal@classictrainsmag.com. Web site: www.classictrainsmag.com. Quarterly. $6.50/$21.95. Circ.: 61,528. Robert S. McGonigal, Editor. **Description:** *Classic Trains* is a celebration of the "Golden Years" of North American railroading, roughly 1920-1980. **Nonfiction:** First-person recollections of railroaders and railfans, studies of equipment or operations, and photo essays; 500-5,000 words; $.10-$.15/word. **Columns, Departments:** Essays on "fallen flag" (defunct) railroad companies; 1,300 words; $.10-$.15/word. **Art:** Prefers prints or transparencies; $30-$100, depending on use. **Tips:** "Our readership is mostly railroad enthusiasts so knowledge of railroading is essential. We do not cover any aspect of railroading today, only railroads in the past." **Queries:** Preferred. **E-Queries:** Yes. **Unsolicited mss:** Accepts. **Freelance Content:** 80%.

COLLECTOR EDITIONS

P.O. Box 1219, Old Chelsea Station, New York, NY 10113-1219. 212-989-8700.

Web site: www.collectoreditions.com. Bimonthly. $4.99/$29.90. Circ.: 50,000. Joan M. Pursley, Editor. **Description:** Covers limited and open-edition collectibles, figurines, plates, prints, crystal glass, porcelain, and other related items for individual collectors. **Nonfiction:** 250-1,000 words. Pays $100-$300. **Queries:** Required. **Unsolicited mss:** Does not accept. **Response:** Queries 30 days. **Freelance Content:** 10-15%. **Rights:** FNAR. **Payment:** Six weeks after acceptance.

COLLECTOR GLASS NEWS

P.O. Box 308, Slippery Rock, PA 16057. 724-946-2838.

E-mail: mark@glassnews.com. Web site: www.glassnews.com. Bimonthly. $3/issue. Circ.: 850. Dr. Mark E. Chase, Managing Editor. **Description:** For collectors of cartoon, promotional, sports, and fast-food glassware produced in past 70 years. **Nonfiction:** Well-researched pieces on specific promotions, glass sets, glass producers, or personalities; 100-500 words; $30-$50. **Tips:** "No general articles. Readers are advanced collectors looking for information on obscure sets or producers." **Queries:** Preferred. **E-Queries:** Yes. **Unsolicited mss:** Accepts. **Response:** 1-2 weeks, SASE required. **Freelance Content:** 30%. **Rights:** FNAR. **Payment:** On publication.

COLLECTORS NEWS

P.O. Box 306, 502 Second St., Grundy Center, IA 50638. 319-824-6981.

E-mail: collectors@collectors-news.com. Web site: www.collectors-news.com. Monthly. $4/$28. Circ.: 10,000. Linda Kruger, Editor. **Description:** Antiques and collectibles magazine for casual collectors and experienced dealers. Accurate information on wide variety of types, market trends, events, and collector interaction. **Nonfiction:** Background of collectibles; how to identify, care for, value items. 20th-century nostalgia, Americana, glass and china, music, furniture, transportation, timepieces, jewelry, farm-related items, and lamps; 900-1,200 words; $1.10/column inch

Art: Quality color or B&W photos. **Queries:** Preferred. **E-Queries:** Yes. **Response:** Queries 2 weeks, submissions 6 weeks, SASE required. **Freelance Content:** 30%. **Rights:** 1st serial, one-time. **Payment:** On publication.

CRAFTING TRADITIONS

Reiman Publications/Reader's Digest Assn.
5400 S 60th St., Greendale, WI 53129-091. 414-423-0100.
E-mail: editors@craftingtraditions.com. Web site: www.reimanpub.com. Bimonthly. $16.98/yr. Circ.: 50,000. Kathleen Anderson, Editor. **Description:** All types of craft designs (needlepoint, quilting, woodworking, etc.) with complete instructions and full-size patterns. **Nonfiction:** Pays $25-$250. **Rights:** All. **Payment:** On acceptance.

CRAFTS MAGAZINE

PRIMEDIA Enthusiast Group
14901 Heritagecrest Way, Bluffdale, UT 84065-4818. 801-984-2070.
E-mail: editor@craftsmag.com. Web site: www.craftsmag.com. Monthly. $21.98/yr. Circ.: 350,000. Valerie Pingree, Editor. **Description:** Project-based publication seeking writers who are professional craft designers and who can write detailed instructions for the creation of their crafts. **Nonfiction:** Interested in projects that include traditional and contemporary crafts: crochet, knitting, sewing, embroidery and needlework, decorative painting, beads, papercrafts, seasonal, kitchen crafts, etc. Seeks unique gifts and creative techniques for re-using second-hand items (but not household trash such as empty food containers). **Art:** Photos must illustrate steps in making the project/craft. **Tips:** Do not send projects. Submit written query or e-query with photos. Queries for seasonal projects must be submitted 7 months prior to publication. **Queries:** Required. **E-Queries:** Yes.

CRAFTS 'N THINGS

2400 Devon, Suite 375, Des Plaines, IL 60018-4618. 847-635-5800.
E-mail: bsunderlage@clapper.com. Web site: www.craftideas.com. 8x/yr. $4.99/issue. Circ.: 250,000. Barbara Sunderlage, Editor. **Description:** How-to articles on varied craft projects, with instructions. **Nonfiction:** Instructions, with photo of finished item. Pays $50-$250. **Tips:** Limited freelance content. **Queries:** Required. **Payment:** On acceptance.

THE CRAFTS REPORT

100 Rogers Rd., P.O. Box 1992, Wilmington, DE 19899-1992. 302-656-2209.
E-mail: editor@craftsreport.com. Web site: www.craftsreport.com. Monthly. $29/yr. Circ.: 48,000. Mary Petzak, Editor. **Description:** Focuses on the business side of the crafts industry; marketing, growing your craft business, time management, studio safety, retail relationships, features on other crafts professionals at all levels of the field, industry news, and more.

DECORATIVE ARTIST'S WORKBOOK

F&W Publications, 4700 E Galbraith Rd., Cincinnati, OH 45236. 513-531-2690.
E-mail: dawedit@fwpubs.com. Web site: www.decorativeartist.com. Bimonthly. Circ.:
90,000. Anne Hevener, Editor. **Description:** How-to articles on decorative painting.
Nonfiction: Step-by-step instructions on decorative painting subjects, including folk
art, stroke work, stenciling, fabric painting, and faux finishing methods; 1,000-2,000
words; $200-$300. **Queries:** Required. **Unsolicited mss:** Does not accept.
Response: 2 weeks to queries, SASE required. **Freelance Content:** 75%. **Rights:**
FNASR. **Payment:** On acceptance.

DOLLHOUSE MINIATURES

Kalmbach Publishing Co.
21027 Crossroads Circle, Waukesha, WI 53187. 262-796-8776.
Web site: www.dhminiatures.com. Monthly. $4.95/$39.95. Circ.: 35,000. Melanie
Buellesbach, Editor. **Description:** "America's leading miniatures magazine, for artisans, collectors, and hobbyists. We feature stories on artisans, exhibits, and collections
from around the world to inspire readers to try colorful, creative, and fun projects."
Nonfiction: How-to articles with easy-to-follow instructions, photos, and illustrations. Also features, profiles, and articles on collections, museums, and industry news.
Art: Color slides essential. Pay varies. **Tips:** "Focus on an artisan or collector, with
careful, specific story and professional visuals. Don't condescend; this is an art form
for high-end artisans." **Queries:** Preferred. **E-Queries:** Yes. **Unsolicited mss:**
Accepts. **Response:** Queries 2-4 months, submissions 3-6 months, SASE.
Freelance Content: 50%. **Rights:** All. **Payment:** On acceptance.

DOLLS

N7450 Aanstad Rd., P.O. Box 5000, Iola, WI 54945. 715-445-5000.
E-mail: jonespub@jonespublishing.com. Web site: www.jonespublishing.com. 10x/yr.
$26.95/yr. Circ.: 100,000. Nayda Rondon, Editor. **Description:** For knowledgeable
doll collectors. **Nonfiction:** Sharply focused, with strong collecting angle and concrete information (value, identification, restoration, etc.). Include quality slides or
transparencies; 500-1,500 words; $100-$350. **Queries:** Required. **Payment:** On
acceptance.

FIBERARTS

67 Broadway, Asheville, NC 28801. 828-253-0467.
E-mail: editor@fiberartsmagazine.com. Web site: www.fiberartsmagazine.com. 5x/yr.
$6/$24. Circ.: 25,000. Sunita Patterson, Editor. **Description:** Covers all fiber-arts:
weaving, quilting, embroidery, wearable art, 3-D work, basketry, and more. Readers
include professional artists, craftspeople, hobbyists, collectors, and curators.
Nonfiction: Articles and interviews (outstanding artists and craftspeople, trends and
issues, exhibitions, business concerns, historic and ethnic textiles); 250-2,000 words;
$65-$500. **Columns, Departments:** Profile (1 artist); Reviews (exhibits/books);
Commentary; Notable Events (conferences, exhibitions); Art & Technology; 250-500

words; $65-$125. **Art:** 35mm slides, transparencies; B&W glossies; electronic images (if 300 dpi or greater resolution). No color prints. **Tips:** "Good visuals are key to acceptance. Submit with synopsis, outline, and writing samples. Use accessible, not scholarly, writing tone." **Queries:** Preferred. **E-Queries:** No. **Unsolicited mss:** Accepts. **Response:** 1-2 months, SASE required. **Freelance Content:** 90%. **Rights:** FNAR. **Payment:** On publication.

FINE WOODWORKING

63 S Main St., P.O. Box 5506, Newtown, CT 06470-5506. 203-426-8171. E-mail: fw@taunton.com. Web site: www.taunton.com. Bimonthly. Circ.: 295,000. Timothy Schreiner, Publisher. **Description:** Covers high-quality worksmanship, thoughtful designs, and safe and proper procedures for outstanding results. **Nonfiction:** Articles on basics of tool use, stock preparation, and joinery; specialized techniques and finishing; shop-built tools, jigs, and fixtures; or any stage of design, construction, finishing, and installation of cabinetry and furniture; $150/page. **Columns, Departments:** Methods of Work, Q&A, Master Class, Finish Line, Tools & Materials, and Notes & Comment; $10. **Queries:** Required. **Payment:** On publication. **Contact:** Anatole Burkin, Executive Editor.

FINELINES

P.O. Box 8928, New Castle, PA 16107. 724-652-6259. E-mail: hngoffice@aol.com. Web site: www.historicneedlework.com. Quarterly. $6/issue. Circ.: 3,800. Deborah Novak Crain, Editor. **Description:** All about needlework. **Nonfiction:** Travel to historic places with significant needlework; museums; stitching (samplers, needlework tools, etc.); 500-1,500 words; pay varies. **Queries:** Not necessary. **E-Queries:** Yes. **Unsolicited mss:** Accepts. **Response:** SASE. **Freelance Content:** 35%. **Rights:** FNAR. **Payment:** On publication.

FINESCALE MODELER

Kalmbach Publishing Co.
21027 Crossroads Circle, Waukesha, WI 53187. 262-796-8776. E-mail: editor@finescale.com. Web site: www.finescale.com. 10x/yr. $4.95/$39.95. Circ.: 60,000. Mark Thompson, Editor. **Description:** Magazine for scale modelers, including builders of model aircraft, armor, ships, autos, and figures. **Nonfiction:** How-to articles for people who make non-operating models of aircraft, armored vehicles, automobiles, ships, and figures. Photos and drawings should accompany articles. Also, 1-page model-building hints and tips. Length and pay varies. **Art:** Prefers color slides, medium-format transparencies, or photo prints. Also accepts hi-res digital photos. **Tips:** Stories on scale-modeling hobby only. **Queries:** Preferred. **E-Queries:** Yes. **Unsolicited mss:** Accepts. **Response:** Queries 6 weeks, SASE required. **Freelance Content:** 80%. **Rights:** All. **Payment:** On acceptance.

GARDEN RAILWAYS

Kalmbach Publishing Co.
P.O. Box 460222, Denver, CO 80246. 303-377-7785.

E-mail: mhorovitz@gardenrailways.com. Web site: www.gardenrailways.com. Bimonthly. Circ.: 37,000. Marc Horovitz, Editor. **Description:** Covers all aspects of the garden-railroading hobby, including building, operating, and landscaping of garden railway trains. **Nonfiction:** Articles run 500-2,500 words; $45/page (including photos). **Tips:** Guidelines available on Web site or on request. **Queries:** Required. **E-Queries:** Yes. **Unsolicited mss:** Accepts. **Response:** 30 days. **Freelance Content:** 75%. **Rights:** All, one-time. **Payment:** On acceptance.

GOOD OLD BOAT

7340 Niagara Lane N, Maple Grove, MN 55311-2655. 763-420-8923.
E-mail: karen@goodoldboat.com. Web site: www.goodoldboat.com. Bimonthly. $39.95 in U.S./Canada, $63.95 other. Karen Larson, Editor. **Description:** On upgrading, maintaining, and restoring sailboats 10+ years old. Also profiles influential people who and companies which have helped shape this hobby. **Nonfiction:** Technical material relevant to older sailboats: in-depth, how-to articles on blister repair, deck delamination repair, tank repair, etc.; 3,000-5,000 words. Also short refit articles, 1,000-2,000 words, and "quick and easy" tips, 300-600 words. **Columns, Departments:** On boat owners and their boats, reflections, book reviews. **Art:** Prefers slides, but accepts color prints, B&W photos, and drawings/sketches. Accepts digital 300+ dpi. Pays $100 for covers, $200 for special photo spreads. **Tips:** Review products and services honestly. "Encourages pride of ownership and reminds sailors of why they do this work: the joy of sailing and the ability to own a sailboat without making a half-million-dollar investment." **E-Queries:** Yes. **Response:** 2-6 weeks, SASE required. **Rights:** FNAR. **Payment:** 60 days in advance of publication.

HERITAGE QUEST MAGAZINE

425 N 400 W, Suite 1A, North Salt Lake, UT 84054. 801-677-0048.
E-mail: leland@heritagequest.com. Web site: www.heritagequestmagazine.com. Bimonthly. $6.95/$28. Circ.: 21,000. Leland Meitzler, Managing Editor. **Description:** Offers help with genealogical research. **Nonfiction:** Genealogical how-to articles; 1,500-3,000 words; $75/printed page. **Tips:** Readers range from beginners to professionals. **Queries:** Preferred. **E-Queries:** Yes. **Unsolicited mss:** Accepts. **Response:** 90 days. **Freelance Content:** 90%. **Rights:** All. **Payment:** On publication.

HOBBY MERCHANDISER

225 Gordons Corner Rd., P.O. Box 420, Manalapan, NJ 07726-0420. 800-969-7176.
E-mail: editor@hobbymerchandiser.com. Web site: www.hobbymerchandiser.com. Monthly. $20/yr. Circ.: 9,000. Jeff Troy, Editor. **Description:** For the professional craft business; also general small-business advice. **Nonfiction:** Articles, 800-1,500 words; pays $75-$200. **Payment:** On publication.

INTERWEAVE KNITS

Interweave Press, Inc., 201 E 4th St., Loveland, CO 80537-5655. 970-669-7672.
E-mail: knits@interweave.com. Web site: www.interweave.com. Quarterly. $24/yr.

Circ.: 60,000. Pam Allen, Editor. **Description:** For those who love to knit. Presents beautifully finished projects, with clear step-by-step instruction. **Nonfiction:** Related to knitting; profiles of people who knit; pays $100/published page. **Queries:** Preferred. **Payment:** On publication.

KITPLANES

8745 Aero Dr., Suite 105, San Diego, CA 92123. 858-694-0491.
E-mail: editorial@kitplances.com. Web site: www.kitplanes.com. Monthly. $4.99/$29.95. Circ.: 70,000. Dave Martin, Editor. **Description:** For designers, builders, and pilots of home-built experimental aircraft. **Nonfiction:** On all aspects of design, construction, and performance for aircraft built from kits and plans by home craftsmen; 1,500-2,500 words; $70/page. **Tips:** Sample copy $6. **Queries:** Preferred. **E-Queries:** Yes. **Unsolicited mss:** Accepts. **Response:** Queries 2 days, submissions 2 weeks, SASE not required. **Freelance Content:** 80%. **Payment:** On publication.

KNIVES ILLUSTRATED

265 S Anita Dr., Suite 120, Orange, CA 92868-3310. 714-939-9991.
E-mail: knivesillustrated@yahoo.com. Web site: www.knivesillustrated.com. Bimonthly. $3.99/$16.95. Circ.: 97,000. Bruce Voyles, Editor. **Description:** A source for new knife information, from both factories and custom builders. Showcases quality color photos, well-known knife makers, new trends, news from shows, and articles from industry experts. **Nonfiction:** Knife tests, industry news, new trends, profiles of knife makers; 900-500 words; $200-$400. **Art:** Submit prints, slides, JPG, or TIF. **Tips:** "Our readership is very knowledgeable and vocal. Don't proclaim yourself an expert; our readers will know if you're not. Read a few copies of magazine before you query. Always seeking new talent, if you know your stuff." **Queries:** Required. **E-Queries:** Yes. **Unsolicited mss:** Accepts. **Response:** 2-6 weeks. **Freelance Content:** 85%. **Rights:** All. **Payment:** On publication.

LAPIDARY JOURNAL

PRIMEDIA Enthusiast Group
60 Chestnut Ave., Suite 201, Devon, PA 19333-1312. 610-964-6300.
E-mail: ljeditorial@primediamags.com. Web site: www.lapidaryjournal.com. Monthly. Circ.: 55,000. **Description:** All about amateur and professional jewelry making.

LOST TREASURE

Lee Harris, P.O. Box 451589, Grove, OK 74345. 918-786-2182.
E-mail: managingeditor@losttreasure.com. Web site: www.losttreasure.com. Monthly. $4.95/$29.95. Circ.: 50,000. Janet Warford-Perry, Managing Editor. **Description:** The treasure hunter's "magazine of choice." **Nonfiction:** How-tos, legends, folklore, stories of lost treasures; 500-1500 words; $.04/word. **Queries:** Not necessary. **E-Queries:** Yes. **Unsolicited mss:** Accepts. **Response:** Queries/submissions 1-2 weeks. **Freelance Content:** 35%. **Rights:** All. **Payment:** On publication.

MEMORY MAKERS

F&W Publications, Inc.

12365 Huron St., Suite 500, Denver, CO 80234-3438. 303-452-1968.

E-mail: editorial@memorymakersmagazine.com.

Web site: www.memorymakersmagazine.com. 6-7x/yr. $5.95/$30. Circ.: 260,000. Deborah Mock, Editor. **Description:** Magazine on scrapbooking, covering all aspects of the craft (including preservation issues and page ideas). Feature articles run 800-1,000 words. **Columns, Departments:** Departments cover safety issues of products, technology, beginner issues, writing help, and craft ideas; 400-700 words; $200-$350. **Tips:** "Break in by offering new and innovative ideas. Avoid basic scrapbook articles that do not show knowledge of the craft. View a recent issue to get an idea of the topics we cover." **Queries:** Not necessary. **E-Queries:** Yes. **Unsolicited mss:** Accepts. **Response:** 1 month. **Freelance Content:** 40%. **Rights:** 1st world rights. **Contact:** Copy Editor.

MIDATLANTIC ANTIQUES

P.O. Box 5040, Monroe, NC 28111. 704-289-1541.

E-mail: maeditor@theej.com. Monthly. $18/yr. Jennifer Benson, Editor. **Description:** Covers antique auctions, art and collectibles, news from Pennsylvania to Georgia. **Nonfiction:** Yes. **Fillers:** Unusual items; little-known tidbits. **Tips:** Color photos with stories helpful. **Queries:** Preferred. **E-Queries:** Yes. **Unsolicited mss:** Accepts. **Response:** Queries 2 months, SASE. **Payment:** On publication.

MINIATURE COLLECTOR

801 W Norton Ave., Suite 200, Muskegon, MI 49441-4155. 231-733-9382.

E-mail: contactus@scottpublications.com. Web site: www.scottpublications.com. Monthly. $37.95/yr. Circ.: 44,000. Barbara Aardema, Editor. **Description:** Showcases outstanding 1/12-scale and other scale (dollhouse) miniatures and the people who make and collect them. Features original, illustrated how-to projects for making miniatures. **Nonfiction:** Articles, 800-1,000 words, with photos; pay varies. **Tips:** Submit photos with queries. **Queries:** Preferred. **Payment:** On publication.

MODEL AIRPLANE NEWS

100 E Ridge Rd., Ridgefield, CT 06877-4623. 203-431-9000.

E-mail: man@airage.com. Web site: www.modelairplanenews.com.

Monthly. $34.95/yr. Circ.: 100,000. Debra D. Sharp, Executive Editor. **Description:** For enthusiasts of radio-controlled model airplanes. **Nonfiction:** Advice from experts in the radio-controlled aviation field; also pieces on design and construction of model airplanes, reviews of new products. Pay varies. **Queries:** Preferred.

MODEL RAILROADER

Kalmbach Publishing Co.

21027 Crossroads Circle, Waukesha, WI 53187. 262-796-8776.

E-mail: mrmag@mrmag.com. Web site: www.modelrailroader.com. Monthly. $4.95/$39.95. Circ.: 190,000. Terry Thompson, Editor. **Description:** Everything related to the hobby of model railroading. Covers hobby topics with expanded report-ing. **Nonfiction:** How-to stories on model railroading; $90/printed page. **Tips:** Authors must be model railroad hobbyists. **Queries:** Preferred. **E-Queries:** Yes. **Unsolicited mss:** Accepts. **Rights:** All. **Payment:** On acceptance.

MODEL RETAILER
Kalmbach Publishing Co.
21027 Crossroads Circle, Waukesha, WI 53187. 262-796-8776.
E-mail: msavage@modelretailer.com. Web site: www.modelretailer.com. Monthly. Mark Savage, Editor. **Description:** Trade publication for hobby store owners cover-ing the business of hobbies, from financial and shop management issues to industry trends and the latest in product releases. Provides hobby store entrepreneurs with the tools and information they need to be successful retailers. **Nonfiction:** Articles should provide tips or hints on how to be successful in this industry; 1,500 words. **Fillers:** Cartoons and hobby-related jokes; 500 words. **Queries:** Not necessary. **E-Queries:** Yes. **Unsolicited mss:** Accepts. **Response:** 4 weeks. **Freelance Content:** 5%. **Rights:** FNAR and electronic. **Payment:** On acceptance.

MODELER'S RESOURCE
4120 Douglas Blvd., #306-372, Granite Bay, CA 95746-5936. 916-784-9517.
E-mail: modres@surewest.net. Web site: www.modelersresource.com. Bimonthly. Fred DeRuvo, Executive Publisher. **Description:** Caters to builders of models, espe-cially sci-fi, fantasy, vehicular, and figures. Each issue includes previews, photos, reviews, and features on the latest genre kits. **Nonfiction:** Quality articles that delve into building and painting models, product reviews, interviews with the names behind the product, show coverage; 2,000-2,500 words. **Art:** Quality color photos or slides. Digital photos accepted if resolution is 300 dpi; no payment offered. **Tips:** Occasionally works with new writers. Seeking articles that go beyond the norm. Be clear and concise, yet allow your personal style to flow. "Often, new writers tend to not be instructive enough, or conversely, tend to go off on tangents." **E-Queries:** Yes. **Response:** 2-4 weeks, SASE required. **Freelance Content:** 10-15%. **Rights:** All. **Contact:** Managing Editor.

NEEDLEWORK RETAILER
See full listing in Business category.

NEW ENGLAND ANTIQUES JOURNAL
Turley Publications, 4 Church St., Ware, MA 01082. 800-432-3505.
E-mail: visit@antiquesjournal.com. Web site: www.antiquesjournal.com. Monthly. $3/$22.95. Circ.: 25,000. **Description:** Informative features for antiques profession-als and casual collectors. Includes event calendars, auction coverage, and more. Also publishes a glossy supplement magazine insert, *Living with Antiques*, with features on preserving and restoring antiques and historic properties. **Nonfiction:** On antiques, fine arts, and collectibles; 2,000 words; $200-$295. **Tips:** Submit well-

researched articles with at least 12 high-quality images. **Queries:** Preferred. **E-Queries:** Yes. **Unsolicited mss:** Accepts. **Response:** 1-2 months. **Freelance Content:** 50%. **Payment:** On publication.

PETERSEN'S PHOTOGRAPHIC MAGAZINE
PRIMEDIA Enthusiast Group
6420 Wilshire Blvd., Los Angeles, CA 90048-5502. 323-782-2200.
E-mail: photographic@primediacmmg.com. Web site: www.photographic.com. Monthly. $11.97. Circ.: 204,500. Ron Leach, Editor-in-Chief. **Description:** On all phases of still photography, for the amateur and advanced photographer. **Nonfiction:** How-tos; pays $125/printed page for articles, with photos. **Payment:** On publication.

PIECEWORK
Interweave Press, 201 E Fourth St., Loveland, CO 80537. 970-669-7672.
E-mail: piecework@interweave.com. Web site: www.interweave.com. Bimonthly. $5.95/$24. Circ.: 47,000. Jeanne Hutchins, Editor. **Description:** Features needlework and textile history. Presents stories and projects based on makers and techniques from needlework's rich past. **Nonfiction:** Well-researched articles on history of needlework techniques, motifs, and artists; 1,500-2,000 words; $100-$300. **Tips:** Prefers stories with needlework projects to demonstrate techniques covered in the article. Contact for upcoming editorial themes. **Queries:** Preferred. **E-Queries:** Yes. **Unsolicited mss:** Accepts. **Response:** Queries 1-2 weeks, submissions 1-4 months, SASE. **Freelance Content:** 80%. **Rights:** FNAR. **Payment:** On publication.

POPTRONICS
P.O. Box 11368, Hauppauge, NY 11788-0999. 631-592-6720.
E-mail: popeditor@gernsback.com. Web site: www.poptronics.com. Monthly. $24.99/yr. Circ.: 81,932. Larry Steckler, Editor. **Description:** For electronics hobbyists and experimenters. **Nonfiction:** Readers are science- and electronics-oriented, understand computer theory and operation, and like to build electronics projects; 2,000-3,500 words; $150-$500. **Payment:** On publication. **Contact:** Chris LaMorte, Managing Editor.

POPULAR MECHANICS
The Hearst Corp., 810 Seventh Ave., Fl. 6, New York, NY 10019-5818. 212-649-2000.
E-mail: popularmechanics@hearst.com; joldham@hearst.com.
Web site: www.popularmechanics.com. Monthly. $19.97/yr. Circ.: 1,200,000. Joseph Oldham, Editor-in-Chief. **Description:** Latest developments in mechanics, industry, science, telecommunications. **Nonfiction:** Features on hobbies with a mechanical slant; how-tos on home and shop projects; features on outdoor adventures, boating, and electronics. Photos and sketches a plus; 300-1,500 words; to $1,500 (to $500 for short pieces). **Rights:** All. **Payment:** On acceptance. **Contact:** Sarah Deem, Managing Editor.

POPULAR WOODWORKING

F&W Publications, Inc., 4700 E Galbraith Rd., Cincinnati, OH 45236. 513-531-2690. E-mail: popwood@fwpubs.com; kara.gebhart@fwpubs.com. Web site: www.popularwoodworking.com. Bimonthly. $23.97/yr. Circ.: 200,000. Steve Shanesy, Editor. **Description:** Technique articles, tool reviews, and projects for the home woodworker. Emphasis on practical techniques that have stood the test of time. **Nonfiction:** How-to (on woodworking projects, with plans), humor (woodworking anecdotes), technical (woodworking techniques); $150/page and up. **Tips:** Tool reviews written in-house. No profiles of woodworkers. Submissions should include materials list, complete diagrams (blueprints not necessary), and discussion of the step-by-step process. "Accepts only practical, attractive projects with quality construction." **Queries:** Preferred. **E-Queries:** Yes. **Unsolicited mss:** Accepts. **Response:** 3-4 months, SASE. **Freelance Content:** 30%. **Rights:** 1st worldwide, 2nd. **Payment:** On acceptance. **Contact:** Kara Gebhart, Assistant Editor.

QUICK & EASY CRAFTS

306 E Parr Rd., Berne, IN 46711-1138. 260-589-9741. Web site: www.quickandeasycrafts.com. Bimonthly. $15/yr. Circ.: 250,000. Beth Schwartz Wheeler, Editor. **Description:** How-to and instructional needlecrafts and other arts and crafts, book reviews, and tips. **Nonfiction:** Pay varies. **Art:** Photos. **Payment:** On acceptance.

QUILTING TODAY

2 Public Ave., Montrose, PA 18801-1220. 570-278-1984. E-mail: chritra@epix.net. Web site: www.quilttownusa.com. Bimonthly. $4.99/$19.95. Circ.: 68,000. Joyce Libal, Senior Editor. **Description:** Features colorful pictures, quilting-world news, and projects for traditional and original designs from teachers and talented quilters. **Nonfiction:** Features on quilt history, techniques, and tools. Quilt patterns (following magazine's established format). Book and product reviews; 750-1,500 words; $75 (800 words). **Art:** Professional-quality photos of quilts; 35mm glossy; pay varies. **Tips:** "We offer complete directions and diagrams for completing quilt projects, as well as interesting and instructional articles concerning all aspects of quilting. Articles should be informative to quilters, presenting new ideas or techniques." **Queries:** Not necessary. **E-Queries:** Accepts. **Unsolicited mss:** Accepts. **Response:** 4 weeks, SASE. **Payment:** On publication.

R/C MODELER

P.O. Box 487, Sierra Madre, CA 91025. 626-355-1476. E-mail: info@rcmmagazine.com. Web site: www.rcmmagazine.com. Monthly. $3.99/$25. Circ.: 165,000. Patricia E. Crews, Editor. **Description:** For the radio-control model aircraft enthusiast. **Nonfiction:** How-to, related to radio-control model aircraft, helicopters, boats, cars. Pays $50-$350 for features; $50-$250 for other articles. **Fillers:** $25-$75. **Queries:** Not necessary. **E-Queries:** Yes. **Response:** Queries 1 week, submissions 1-3 weeks, SASE. **Freelance Content:** 60%. **Rights:** 1st worldwide. **Payment:** On publication.

RADIO CONTROL CAR ACTION

100 E Ridge Rd., Ridgefield, CT 06877-4606. 203-431-9000.
E-mail: Web site: www.rccaraction.com. Monthly. $34.95/yr. Circ.: 95,127. Peter Vieira, Executive Editor. **Description:** Publishes articles on all aspects of R/C cars including product reviews, how-to articles, race coverage, home-builts, and more. Feature articles and columns present technical and general information on building electric and gas RC cars, modifications, modeling equipment, major competitive events, modeling personalities, and products. Also, "how-to" articles and in-depth, full-color product evaluations, with many articles for beginners. **Art:** 300 dpi Photoshop TIF or 35mm color slides. **Tips:** "Writers must have some sort of RC (radio control) experience. Send a writing sample first (using most current issue as a guide), with RC history." **Queries:** Not necessary. **E-Queries:** Yes. **Unsolicited mss:** Accepts. **Rights:** 1st serial publication rights. **Payment:** On publication.

RAILROAD MODEL CRAFTSMAN

P.O. Box 700, Newton, NJ 07860-0700. 973-383-3355.
E-mail: bills@rrmodelcraftsman.com. Web site: www.rrmodelcraftsman.com. Monthly. $34.95/yr. Circ.: 75,000. William C. Schaumburg, Editor. **Description:** How-to articles on scale model railroading; cars, operation, scenery, etc. **E-Queries:** Yes.

RUBBERSTAMPMADNESS

408 SW Monroe #210, Corvallis, OR 97330. 541-752-0075.
E-mail: rsm@rsmadness.com. Web site: www.rsmadness.com. Bimonthly. $5.95/$24.95. Circ.: 26,000. Roberta Sperling, Publisher/Editor. **Description:** Publication for rubber stamp artists and collectors. Articles and features explore the creative use of artistic rubber stamps. Issues include stories of artists, new product information, book reviews, convention calendars, a stamp news column, and basic, intermediate, and advanced stamping techniques. **Queries:** Required. **E-Queries:** Yes. **Unsolicited mss:** Does not accept.

RUG HOOKING

1300 Market St., Suite 202, Lemoyne, PA 17043. 717-234-5091.
E-mail: rughook@paonline.com. Web site: www.rughookingonline.com. 5x/yr. $6.95/$27.95. Wyatt R. Myers, Editor. **Description:** How-to features on rug hooking for beginners and advanced artists. **Nonfiction:** Instructional articles; also, profiles of fiber artists; 500-3,000 words; pay varies. **Queries:** Preferred. **E-Queries:** Yes. **Unsolicited mss:** Accepts. **Response:** 3 months, SASE. **Freelance Content:** 90%. **Payment:** On publication.

SCALE AUTO

Kalmbach Publishing Co.
21027 Crossroads Circle, Waukesha, WI 53187. 262-796-8776.
E-mail: editor@scaleautomag.com. Web site: www.scaleautomag.com. 8x/yr. $29.95/yr. Circ.: 30,000. Mark Thompson, Editor. **Description:** For the adult model

builder. Features how-to articles, modeling history, contest coverage, and kit and product news. **Nonfiction:** To 3,000 words, with photos; pays $60/page. **Tips:** "For how-to articles, the key is including many clean, crisp, step-by-step photos." **Queries:** Required. **E-Queries:** Yes. **Unsolicited mss:** Accepts. **Response:** 90 days. **Freelance Content:** 50%. **Rights:** All. **Payment:** On acceptance.

SEW NEWS

PRIMEDIA Consumer Media & Magazine Group
741 Corporate Circle, Suite A, Golden, CO 80401. 303-278-1010.
E-mail: sewnews@sewnews.com. Web site: www.sewnews.com. Monthly. $23.98/yr. Circ.: 173,700. Linda Turner Griepentrog, Editor. **Description:** Seeks articles that teach a specific technique, inspire a reader to try new sewing projects, or inform about an interesting person, company, or project related to sewing, textiles, or fashion. Emphasis on fashion (not craft) sewing. Articles, to 3,000 words; pays $25-$400. **Tips:** See Web site for guidelines. **Queries:** Preferred. **E-Queries:** Yes. **Unsolicited mss:** Does not accept. **Payment:** On acceptance.

SPORTS COLLECTORS DIGEST

Krause Publications, Inc., 700 E State St., Iola, WI 54990. 715-445-2214.
E-mail: kpsports@aol.com. Web site: www.krause.com. Weekly. Circ.: 30,000. T.S. O'Connell, Editor. **Description:** Sports memorabilia and collectibles. **Nonfiction:** Articles on old baseball card sets and other sports memorabilia; 750-2,000 words; $50-$100. **Columns, Departments:** Query; 600-3,000 words; $90-$150. **Art:** Unusual collectibles; B&W photos; $25-$150. **Tips:** Sample copy free. **Response:** Queries, 5 weeks; submissions 2 months. **Rights:** FNASR. **Payment:** On publication.

TEDDY BEAR AND FRIENDS

P.O. Box 10545, Lancaster, PA 17605-0545. 717-393-8371.
Web site: www.teddybearandfriends.com. Bimonthly. $17.95/yr. Circ.: 30,000. Mindy Kinsey, Managing Editor. **Description:** For adult collectors of teddy bears; profiles of artists and manufacturers. **Nonfiction:** Articles, 1,000-1,500 words; pays $.30-$.35/word. **Tips:** Now accepting some fiction or personal-experience stories. **Queries:** Preferred. **Payment:** On publication.

TEDDY BEAR REVIEW

N7450 Aanstad Rd., P.O. Box 5000, Iola, WI 54945-5000. 715-445-5000.
E-mail: editor@teddybearreview.com. Web site: www.teddybearreview.com. Bimonthly. $4.99/$24.95. Circ.: 45,000. Trina Laube, Editor. **Description:** For collectors, bearmakers, and teddy bear and soft sculpture enthusiasts. **Nonfiction:** On antique and contemporary teddy bears for makers, collectors, enthusiasts; 1,000-1,200 words; $200. **Tips:** Looking for articles on artists, manufacturers, and antique bears; prefers specialized topics. Submit photos of bears with queries. Readers treat teddy bears as art. No stories from the bear's point of view. **Queries:** Preferred. **E-Queries:** Yes. **Unsolicited mss:** Accepts. **Response:** 8-12 weeks, SASE required. **Freelance Content:** 70%. **Rights:** All. **Payment:** On acceptance.

THREADS

63 S Main St., P.O. Box 5506, Newtown, CT 06470. 203-426-8171.
E-mail: th@taunton.com. Web site: www.taunton.com. Bimonthly. Circ.: 160,000.
Carol Spier, Editor-in-Chief. **Description:** Garment construction and embellishment. **Nonfiction:** Technical pieces on garment construction and embellishment by writers who are expert sewers, quilters, embellishers, and other needle workers. Also covers sewing soft furnishings for home decor; $150/published page. **Payment:** On publication.

TRADITIONAL QUILTWORKS

Chitra Publications, 2 Public Ave., Montrose, PA 18801. 570-278-1984.
E-mail: chitraed@epix.net. Web site: www.quilttownusa.com.
Bimonthly. $4.99/$19.95. Circ.: 79,000. Joyce Libal, Senior Editor. **Description:** Pattern magazine with articles on quilt history, techniques, and tools. **Nonfiction:** Articles with 1-2 pages of text and quilts that illustrate the content; 750 words; pay varies. **Art:** 35mm color slides. **Queries:** Not necessary. **E-Queries:** No. **Unsolicited mss:** Accepts. **Response:** Queries 2 weeks, submissions 4 weeks, SASE. **Rights:** 1st. **Payment:** On publication.

TRAINS

Kalmbach Publishing Co.
21027 Crossroads Circle, Waukesha, WI 53187. 262-796-8776.
E-mail: editor@trainsmag.com. Web site: www.trainsmag.com. Monthly. $4.95. Circ.: 120,000. Mark W. Hemphill, Editor. **Description:** Railroad news, features, and stories. **Nonfiction:** History, business analysis, economics, technology, and operations studies of railroads in North America and elsewhere. Occasional first-person recollections; 600-8,000 words; $.10-$.15/word. **Art:** 35mm or medium-format slides; quality 8x10 or larger. Color and B&W prints; $30-$300. **Tips:** Avoid first-person travelogues or trip reports, unless historical. Writers require a good knowledge of industry and its technology. "We're a technically demanding publication for the railroad industry and knowledgeable railroad enthusiasts." **Queries:** Preferred. **E-queries:** Yes. **Unsolicited mss:** Accepts. **Response:** Queries 60 days, submissions 90 days, SASE. **Freelance Content:** 90%. **Rights:** All (manuscripts), one-time (art). **Payment:** On acceptance.

WATERCOLOR

See full listing in Arts & Architecture category.

WESTERN & EASTERN TREASURES

P.O. Box 219, San Anselmo, CA 94979. 415-454-3936.
E-mail: treasurenet@prodigy.net. Web site: www.treasurenet.com. Monthly. $4.95/$27.95. Circ.: 100,000. Rosemary Anderson, Editor. **Description:** For metal detectorists, covers all aspects of the hobby. Field-proven advice and instruction; entertaining presentation. **Nonfiction:** Articles new, true, and treasure-oriented, from all fields of responsible recreational metal detecting. 1,500 words; $.02-

$.04/word. **Art:** Color photo prints/35mm or 300 dpi TIF or JPG. $5-$7.50, $50-$100 (cover). **Queries:** Not necessary. **E-Queries:** No. **Unsolicited mss:** Accepts. **Response:** 1 month, SASE required. **Freelance Content:** 100%. **Rights:** All rights reserved. **Payment:** On publication.

WILDFOWL CARVING MAGAZINE

1300 Market St. Suite 202, Lemoyne, PA 17043-1420. 717-234-5091.
E-mail: wcc@paonline.com. Web site: wildfowl-carving.com. Quarterly. $29.95/yr. Circ.: 13,000. Candice Tennant, Editor-in-Chief. **Description:** Articles on bird carving and collecting antique and contemporary carvings. **Nonfiction:** How-to and reference articles, of varying lengths; pay varies. **Queries:** Preferred. **Payment:** On acceptance.

WOODWORK

Ross Periodicals, 42 Digital Dr., Suite 5, Novato, CA 94949. 415-382-0580.
E-mail: woodwork@rossperiodicals.com. Bimonthly. $4.99/$17.95. Circ.: 70,000. John Lavine, Editor. **Description:** Covers all aspects of woodworking. Assumes medium to advanced understanding in technical articles. Also, artist profiles, reviews. **Nonfiction:** Profiles, technical articles, projects, how-to; also shows, exhibition reviews, etc.; 1,000-4,000 words; $150-$200/printed page. **Queries:** Preferred. **E-Queries:** Yes. **Unsolicited mss:** Accepts. **Freelance Content:** 90%. **Rights:** FNAR. **Payment:** On publication.

YELLOWBACK LIBRARY

P.O. Box 36172, Des Moines, IA 50315. 515-287-0404.
Monthly. $36/yr. Circ.: 500. Gil O'Gara, Editor. **Description:** For collectors, dealers, enthusiasts, and researchers of children's series books such as Hardy Boys, Nancy Drew, Tom Swift. Dime novels and related juvenile literature also included. **Nonfiction:** Especially interested in interviews with, or articles by, past and present writers of juvenile series fiction; 300-3,000 words. **Tips:** No articles that ridicule the literature or try to fit it into a political, sexual, psychological, or religious context. Nostalgic reflections okay if interesting. **Queries:** Preferred. **E-Queries:** No. **Unsolicited mss:** Accepts. **Response:** 2-7 days. **Freelance Content:** 100%. **Payment:** In copies.

YESTERYEAR

P.O. Box 2, Princeton, WI 54968.
E-mail: yesteryear@vbe.com. Michael Jacobi, Editor. **Description:** Articles on antiques and collectibles for readers in Wisconsin, Illinois, Iowa, Minnesota, and surrounding states. Pays $20/article and up. **Tips:** Considers regular columns on collecting or antiques. **Payment:** On publication.

HOME & GARDEN
(See also Lifestyles)

AFRICAN VIOLET MAGAZINE
2375 North St., Beaumont, TX 77702. 409-839-4725.
E-mail: avsa@earthlink.net. Web site: www.avsa.org. Bimonthly. $$18/yr. Circ.:
15,000. Ruth Rumsey, Editor. **Description:** Offers techniques and methods for
growing African violets. No payment. **Nonfiction:** Articles, 700-1,400 words; history
and personal experience with African violets.

THE AMERICAN GARDENER
American Horticultural Society
7931 E Boulevard Dr., Alexandria, VA 22308-1300. 703-768-5700.
E-mail: editor@ahs.org. Web site: www.ahs.org. Bimonthly. $4.95. Circ.: 28,000.
David J. Ellis, Editor. **Description:** In-depth profiles of individual plant groups,
descriptions of innovative landscape design projects (especially involving regionally
native plants or naturalistic gardening), profiles of prominent American horticultur-
ists and gardeners, descriptions of historical developments in American gardening,
profiles of unusual public or private gardens, and descriptions of important plant
breeding and research programs tailored to a lay audience. Runs few how-to articles;
these should address relatively complex or unusual topics that most other gardening
magazines won't tackle—photography needs to be provided. 1,500-2,500 words;
$300-$500. **Columns, Departments:** Offshoots (personal essay), Natural
Connections, Conservationist's Notebook, Regional Happenings; 600-1,000 words;
$150-$200. **Tips:** Queries: describe topic and explain relevance to a national audience
of knowledgeable gardeners; outline major points to be covered. First-time authors:
send relevant writing samples and qualifications. **Queries:** Preferred. **E-Queries:**
No. **Unsolicited mss:** Accepts. **Response:** 90 days, SASE required. **Freelance
Content:** 75%. **Rights:** FNAR and electronic. **Payment:** On publication.

AMERICAN ROSE
P.O. Box 30000, Shreveport, LA 71130-0030. 318-938-5402.
E-mail: ars@ars-hq.org. Web site: www.ars.org. Monthly. $37/yr. Circ.: 24,500.
Michael C. Kromer, Editor. **Description:** Articles on home rose gardens (varieties,
products, helpful advice, rose care, etc.). **Queries:** Preferred.

ATLANTA HOMES AND LIFESTYLES
1100 Johnson Ferry Rd., Suite 595, Atlanta, GA 30342-1743. 404-252-6670.
E-mail: oblaise@atlantahomesmag.com. Web site: www.atlantahomesmag.com. 8x/yr.
$3.95/$24. Circ.: 33,000. Oma Blaise Ford, Editor-in-Chief. **Description:** On
upscale home and gardens. **Nonfiction:** Original stories with local angle (mostly by
assignment), on homes, gardening, food, wine, entertaining, and remodeling; 300-
1,200 words; $75-$500. **Columns, Departments:** Remodeling, shopping, profiles

(on assignment; 200-700 words; $75-$200). **Queries:** Required. **Unsolicited mss:** Does not accept. **Response:** 3 months, SASE. **Freelance Content:** 50%. **Payment:** On acceptance.

BETTER HOMES AND GARDENS

Meredith Corp., 1716 Locust St., Des Moines, IA 50309-3038. 515-284-3000. Web site: www.bhg.com. Monthly. $2.99/$19. Circ.: 7,600,000. Karol DeWulf Nickell, Editor-in-Chief. **Description:** Home and family magazine. Covers entertainment, building, decorating, food, gardening, money management, health, travel, pets, environment, and cars. **Tips:** "A freelancer's best chances are in travel, health, parenting, and education. No political subjects, poetry, beauty, or fiction." **Queries:** Preferred. **E-Queries:** No. **Unsolicited mss:** Does not accept. **Response:** 2-3 weeks, SASE required. **Freelance Content:** 15%. **Rights:** All. **Payment:** On acceptance. **Contact:** Lamont Olson, Managing Editor.

BIRDS AND BLOOMS

Reiman Publications/Reader's Digest Assn.
5400 S 60th St., Greendale, WI 53129. 414-423-0100.
E-mail: editors@birdsandblooms.com. Web site: www.birdsandblooms.com. Bimonthly. $19.98/yr. Circ.: 1,600,000. Jeff Nowak, Editor. **Description:** For people who love the beauty of their own backyard. Focuses on backyard birding and gardening. **Nonfiction:** First-person experiences from your own backyard; 200-900 words; $100-$200. **Fillers:** 50-300 words; $50-$75. **Art:** Slides or prints; $75-$300. **Tips:** Write conversationally, include tips to benefit readers, keep stories short and to the point. Submit photos. No bird rescue stories. Sample copy $2. **Queries:** Not necessary. **E-Queries:** Yes. **Unsolicited mss:** Accepts. **Response:** Queries 1-2 months, submissions 2-3 months, SASE. **Freelance Content:** 25%. **Rights:** FNAR. **Payment:** On publication.

CANADIAN GARDENING

340 Ferrier St., Suite 210, Markham, Ontario L3R 2Z5 Canada. 905-475-8440.
E-mail: letters@canadiangardening.com. Web site: www.canadiangardening.com. 8x/yr. $24.95/yr. Circ.: 152,000. Aldona Satterthwaite, Editor. **Description:** Canadian publication that features articles on gardening in Canada. Presents practical home gardening solutions and seeks to inspire readers with new ideas. Canadian angle imperative. **Nonfiction:** How-to pieces (to 1,000 words) on garden projects; include introduction and step-by-step instructions. Profiles of gardens (to 1,500 words). Pays $125 and up. **Columns, Departments:** 200-400 words. **Queries:** Preferred. **Payment:** On acceptance.

CAROLINA GARDENER

P.O. Box 4504, Greensboro, NC 27404-4504. 336-574-0087.
Web site: www.carolinagardener.com. Bimonthly. Circ.: 27,000. L.A. Jackson, Editor. **Description:** Specific to Southeast gardening (profiles of gardens in the region, new cultivars, "good ol' Southern heirlooms"). **Nonfiction:** 750-1,000 words; $175. **Art:**

Slides and illustrations essential to accompany articles. **Queries:** Required. **Payment:** On publication.

COASTAL LIVING

2100 Lakeshore Dr., Birmingham, AL 35209-6721.
E-mail: kay_fuston@timeinc.com. Web site: www.coastalliving.com. 7x/yr. $3.95/$18. Circ.: 550,000. Kay A. Fuston, Editor. **Description:** *"Coastal Living,* the magazine for people who love the coast, celebrates life along our shores. From the inviting homes that fill our pages to the relaxed destinations we discover for our readers and the interesting characters we meet along the way, the magazine reflects not only a lifestyle, but a state of mind." Articles run 800-1,000 words; $1/word. **Tips:** Writer's guidelines available. **Queries:** Required. **E-Queries:** No. **Unsolicited mss:** Does not accept. **Response:** 2-4 weeks. **Freelance Content:** 70%. **Rights:** 1st periodical and electronic.

COLORADO HOMES AND LIFESTYLES

7009 S Potomac St., Englewood, CO 80112. 303-397-7600.
E-mail: emcgraw@coloradohomesmag.com. Web site: www.coloradohomesmag.com. 9x/yr. $3.95/$19.97. Circ.: 35,000. Matthew Dakotah, Editor. **Description:** Features Colorado's finest design and architecture. **Nonfiction:** Articles, 1,300-1,500 words, on Colorado homes, design trends, lifestyles, and culture. **Queries:** Required. **E-Queries:** No. **Payment:** On acceptance. **Contact:** Kimberly Beekman, Associate Editor.

COUNTRY GARDENS

Meredith Corp., 1716 Locust St., Des Moines, IA 50309-3023. 515-284-3515.
E-mail: lbrandse@mdp.com. Web site: www.countryhomemagazine.com. Quarterly. $19.97/yr. Circ.: 350,000. LuAnn Brandsen, Editor. **Description:** Features gardens that are informal, lush, and old-fashioned. Stories emphasize both inspiration and information. **Nonfiction:** Garden-related how-tos and profiles of gardeners, 750-1,500 words; pays $500-1,500. **Columns, Departments:** 500-700 words, on garden-related travel, food, projects, decorating, entertaining; pays $450 and up. **Queries:** Required. **Payment:** On acceptance.

COUNTRY KITCHENS

1115 Broadway, Fl. 8, New York, NY 10010-2803. 212-462-9652.
Annual. Barbara Jacksier. **Description:** Articles offering bright, inviting, and afford-able decorating ideas. **Queries:** Preferred.

COUNTRY LIVING

The Hearst Corp., 224 W 57th St., New York, NY 10019. 212-649-3500.
E-mail: countryliving@hearst.com. Web site: www.countryliving.com. Monthly. $3.50/issue. Circ.: 1,700,000. Nancy Mernit Soriano, Editor-in-Chief. **Description:** Covers lifestyle, decorating, antiques, cooking, travel, home building, crafts, and gardens. **Nonfiction:** From 500 words; pay varies. **Tips:** Avoid grandmother stories.

Queries: Preferred. E-Queries: No. Unsolicited mss: Does not accept. Response: 8 weeks, SASE. Freelance Content: 30%. Rights: All, 1st serial. Payment: On acceptance. Contact: Marjorie E. Gage, Deputy Editor.

DECOR & STYLE MAGAZINE

337 S Cedros Ave., Suite A1, Solana Beach, CA 92075-1951. 858-755-4534. E-mail: editor@decorandstyle.com. Web site: www.decorandstyle.com. Monthly. $3.75/$21. Circ.: 53,347. M.B. Matthews, Editor. Description: Focuses on architecture, interior design, and an elegant style of living. Articles offer both cutting edge and classic designs. Nonfiction: Seeks articles on signature homes, pools and spas, remodeling ideas, home furnishings, art and antiques, home theater, lighting, wine, food, fashion, and entertaining. Feature stories should be 2,000-3,000 words; $100-$275. Short articles should be 1,000-2,000 words; $100-$200. Tips: "We seek material that speaks to affluent, sophisticated, well-traveled homeowners. Avoid "how-to" articles and 'do-it-yourself' projects." Queries: Preferred. E-Queries: Yes. Unsolicited mss: Accepts. Response: 2 months. Freelance Content: 40%. Rights: All rights, including electronic. Payment: On publication. Contact: Managing Editor.

EARLY AMERICAN LIFE

207 House Ave., Suite 103, Camp Hill, PA 17011. 717-730-6263. E-mail: ginnys@celticmooninc.com. Web site: www.earlyamericanlife.com. 7x/yr. $3.99/$19.97. Circ.: 94,800. Virginia P. Stimmel, Editor. Description: On early American past (traditions, antiques, architecture, history, period style). For people who are passionate about tangible aspects of the American past and aspire to incorporate them into their lifestyles and homes. Nonfiction: Detailed articles about American domestic past (1600-1850); travel, historic places, preservation, restoration, antiques, houses, textiles, furniture, decorative objects; 1,500-2,000 words; $500-$600. Columns, Departments: Eye on Antiques, Worth Seeing, Life in Early America, Side by Side; 800-1,500 words; $250-$600. Queries: Preferred. E-Queries: Yes. Unsolicited mss: Accepts. Response: 30 days, SASE required. Freelance Content: 10-20%. Rights: One-time worldwide. Payment: On publication.

ELLE DECOR

Hachette Filipacchi Media U.S., Inc. 1633 Broadway, Fl. 41, New York, NY 10019-6708. 212-767-5800. 8x/yr. $29. Circ.: 500,000. Margaret Russell, Editor-in-Chief. Description: On designers and craftspeople, and on houses and apartments with notable interior design and/or architecture. Articles run 300-800 words; $2/word. Tips: Query via regular mail; include photos of designers and their work. Queries: Preferred. E-Queries: No. Payment: On publication. Contact: Mitchell Owens, Interior Design Director.

FINE GARDENING

P.O. Box 5506, 63 S Main St, Newtown, CT 06470-5506. 203-426-8171. E-mail: fg@taunton.com. Web site: www.finegardening.com. Bimonthly. $29.95/yr.

Circ.: 200,000. Elizabeth Conklin, Editor-in-Chief. **Description:** For readers with a serious interest in gardening. Focuses on ornamental gardening and landscaping. **Nonfiction:** How-tos, garden design, as well as pieces on specific plants or garden tools. Picture possibilities are essential; 800-2,000 words; $300-$1,200. **Art:** Photos; $75-$500. **Queries:** Required. **Payment:** On acceptance.

FLOWER & GARDEN MAGAZINE

KC Publishing, Inc., 51 Kings Hwy. W, Haddenfield, NJ 08033. 856-354-5034.
E-mail: kcpublishing@earthlink.net. Web site: www.flowerandgardenmag.com.
Bimonthly. $3.99/issue, $19.95/yr. Circ.: 300,000. Jonathan Prebich, Editor.
Description: Offers ideas for outdoor environments, for home gardens.
Nonfiction: Practical how-to articles. Historical and background articles, if related to home gardening; 1,000 words max. **Art:** Yes. **Tips:** Provide well-researched material. **Queries:** Not necessary. **E-Queries:** Yes. **Unsolicited mss:** Accepts. **Response:** Queries 3 months, SASE required. **Freelance Content:** 75%. **Rights:** One-time (print and electronic).

GARDEN COMPASS

Streamopolis, 1450 Front St., San Diego, CA 92101. 619-239-2202.
E-mail: siri@gardencompass.com. Web site: www.gardencompass.com. Bimonthly.
$18.50/yr. Circ.: 112,000. Siri Kay Jostad, Editor. **Description:** For California gardening enthusiasts. Features, to 2,000 words. **E-Queries:** Yes. **Freelance Content:** 20%.

GARDEN DESIGN

460 N Orlando Ave., Winter Park, FL 32789. 407-628-4802.
E-mail: editor@gardendesignmag.com. Web site: www.gardendesignmag.com. Bill Marken, Editor-in-Chief. **Description:** On private, public, and community gardens; articles on art and history as they relate to gardens. **Nonfiction:** Features, 500-1,000 words, pays from $1/word. **Payment:** Within 30 days of contract.

GARDEN SHOWCASE

P.O. Box 23669, Portland, OR 97281-3669. 503-684-0153.
E-mail: gseditor@gardenshowcase.com. Web site: www.gardenshowcase.com. 4x/yr.
$9.95/yr. Circ.: 30,000. Lynn Lustberg, Editor. **Description:** Distributed in Oregon and Washington. Features regional plants, gardens, and nurseries, with gardening ideas and examples. **Nonfiction:** Articles on outstanding gardens, etc.; 800-1,000 words; $160. **Columns, Departments:** Gardening 101, Speaking Organically, Success with Vegetables; 380-400; $100. **Queries:** Preferred. **E-Queries:** Yes. **Unsolicited mss:** Accepts. **Response:** 1-3 months, SASE required. **Freelance Content:** 100%. **Rights:** FNAR. **Payment:** On publication.

GARDEN RAILWAYS

See full listing in Hobbies, Crafts, Collecting category.

THE GROWING EDGE

P.O. Box 1027, Corvallis, OR 97339-1027.
E-mail: editor@growingedge.com. Web site: www.growingedge.com.
6x/yr. $4.95/$26.95. Circ.: 20,000. Douglas J. Peckenpaugh, Editor. **Description:** News and information for indoor and outdoor growers. Covers hydroponic, aquaponic, and soilless greenhouse gardening. Targets both hobby and commercial growers. **Nonfiction:** 3,000 words; pays $.20/word. **Art:** Color prints or slides; high-res digital. Pays $25 for inside photo; $175 for cover. **Tips:** "Supply detailed queries first. Know our audience. We do not publish material on traditional, soil-based gardening." **Queries:** Preferred. **E-Queries:** Yes. **Unsolicited mss:** Accepts. **Response:** 1-2 months, SASE. **Freelance Content:** 60%. **Rights:** 1st world serial, 1st anthology, and non-exclusive electronic. **Payment:** On publication.

THE HERB COMPANION

1504 SW 42nd St., Topeka, KS 80537. 970-663-0831.
E-mail: herbcompanion@realhealthmedia.com. Web site: www.discoverherbs.com. Bimonthly. $4.99/issue. Circ.: 150,000. **Description:** For herb gardeners, cooks, crafters, and general enthusiasts. **Nonfiction:** Practical horticultural information, original recipes using herbs, well-researched historical insights, step-by-step instructions for herbal craft projects, book reviews; 500-2,000 words; $.33/word or negotiable. **Columns, Departments:** 200-500 words. **Art:** 300 dpi, slides; pay varies. **Tips:** "Technical accuracy essential. Strive for conciseness, clear organization; include subheads where appropriate, lists of similar information in chart form." **Queries:** Preferred. **E-Queries:** Yes. **Unsolicited mss:** Accepts. **Response:** 1-3 months, SASE. **Freelance Content:** 90%. **Payment:** On acceptance.

THE HERB QUARTERLY

1041 Shary Circle, Concord, CA 94518. 925-671-9852.
E-mail: jenniferbarrett@earthlink.net. Web site: www.herbquarterly.com. Quarterly. Circ.: 36,753. Jennifer Barrett, Editor. **Description:** Covers practical and professional aspects of herbs. **Nonfiction:** Practical uses, cultivation, gourmet cooking, landscaping, herb tradition, medicinal herbs, crafts ideas, unique garden designs, profiles of experts, and how-tos for the herb lover; 1,500-3,000 words. **E-Queries:** Yes. **Payment:** On publication.

HOME POOL & BAR-B-QUE

Hawks Media Group, Inc., P.O. Box 272, Cranford, NJ 07016-0272. 908-755-6138.
E-mail: jeanette@hawksmedia.com. Annual. $10. Circ.: 2,500. Jeanette Hawks, Editor. **Description:** For upscale owners of pools, hot tubs, and spas. **Nonfiction:** Pool experiences and recipes; 1,500; $40. **Art:** Photos of pools, spas, and barbecue grills (built-in especially); B&W, color, or digital photos; $10. **Queries:** Preferred. **E-Queries:** Yes. **Unsolicited mss:** Accepts. **Response:** 1 month, SASE. **Freelance Content:** 40%. **Rights:** All, may reassign. **Payment:** On publication.

HORTICULTURE, GARDENING AT ITS BEST

F&W Publications, 98 N Washington St., Boston, MA 02114-1922. 617-742-5600.
E-mail: edit@hortmag.com. Web site: www.hortmag.com. 6x/yr. $28. Circ.: 205,000.
Patricia Wesley Umbrell, Editor. **Description:** Covers all aspects of gardening.
Nonfiction: Authoritative, well-written articles on gardening; 500-2,500 words; pay
varies. **Queries:** Required. **Payment:** On publication.

HOUSE BEAUTIFUL

The Hearst Corp., 1700 Broadway, Fl. 29, New York, NY 10019-5905. 212-903-5084.
Web site: www.housebeautiful.com. Monthly. $19.97/yr. Circ.: 853,000. Mark
Mayfield, Editor-in-Chief. **Description:** Pieces on design, travel, and gardening.
Nonfiction: A literary, personal memoir, each month, 3,000 words, "Thoughts of
Home." Pays $1/word. **Tips:** Send detailed outline and SASE. **Queries:** Preferred.
Payment: On acceptance.

L.A. HOUSE & HOME

11470 Euclid Ave, #317, Cleveland, OH 44106. 216-320-9153.
E-mail: abillingsley@hearthmarketingandmedia.com. Monthly. $30/yr. Circ.: 35,000.
A. Billingsley, Editor. **Description:** A resource magazine for home decorating, reno-
vations, and landscaping. **Nonfiction:** All articles must focus on Los Angeles homes,
activities showcasing homes or decorating, or shopping for unique home items; $75
and up. **Tips:** "Our articles are mostly staff-written; however, we occasionally seek
shorter pieces for columns relating to Los Angeles' unique shopping areas or activities showcasing architecture, home tours, or decorating ideas." **Queries:** Preferred.
E-Queries: Yes. **Unsolicited mss:** Accepts. **Response:** 3-7 days. **Payment:** On
publication.

LANDSCAPE TRADES

See full listing in Trade & Technical category.

LOG HOME DESIGN IDEAS

1620 S Lawe St., Suite 2, Appleton, WI 54915-2411. 920-830-1701.
E-mail: editor@athenet.net. Web site: www.lhdi.com. 9x/yr. $23.95. Circ.: 150,000.
Teresa Hilgenberg, Editor. **Description:** For people interested in log homes.
Queries: Preferred.

LOG HOME LIVING

4125 Lafayette Center Dr., Suite 100, Chantilly, VA 20151-1208. 703-222-9411.
E-mail: editor@loghomeliving.com. Web site: www.loghomeliving.com. Monthly.
$19.95/yr. Circ.: 110,000. Kevin Ireland, Editor-in-Chief. **Description:** For people
who own or are planning to build contemporary log homes. Readers are mostly married couples, 30-45 years old, well-educated, do-it-yourselfers. **Nonfiction:** About
people who have built modern log homes from manufactured or handcrafted kits.
Conversational; describe home, tell how it came to be. Emphasize special elements:

intent, design, solutions to problems, features, furnishings, interior design, landscaping; 1,000-2,000 words; $350-$550/article. **Art:** If possible, please include color (professional quality) photos; floor plans, construction costs, schedules a plus. **Tips:** "We seek long-term relationships with contributors who deliver quality work." **Queries:** Preferred. **E-Queries:** Yes. **Response:** SASE. **Freelance Content:** 50%. **Rights:** FNASR. **Payment:** On acceptance.

METROPOLITAN HOME

Hachette Filipacchi Media
1633 Broadway, Fl. 41, New York, NY 10019-6708. 212-767-6041. Bimonthly. $19.94/yr. Circ.: 604,000. Donna Warner, Editor-in-Chief. **Description:** Interior design and home furnishing articles with emphasis on lifestyle. Service and informational articles on furniture and home products, gardening, food, collecting, trends, etc. **Tips:** Send clips. **Queries:** Preferred. **E-Queries:** No.

NATURAL HOME

201 E Fourth St., Loveland, CO 80537-5601. 970-669-7672.
E-mail: robynl@naturalhomemagazine.com.
Web site: www.naturalhomemagazine.com. Bimonthly. $24.95/yr. Circ.: 54,000. Robyn Griggs Lawrence, Editor-in-Chief. **Description:** Promotes earth-inspired living. Features "green," sustainable homes and lifestyles. **Nonfiction:** Pays $.33-$1.00/word; 300-2,000 words. **Tips:** "We need fresh, cutting-edge ideas on green living; also small, newsy items for front-of-the-book Journal section. Submit query or complete manuscript. Guidelines available for SASE or by e-mail." **Queries:** Preferred. **E-Queries:** Yes. **Unsolicited mss:** Accepts. **Rights:** FNAR.

NORTHWEST GARDEN NEWS

P.O. Box 18313, Seattle, WA 98118-1104. 206-725-2394.
E-mail: norwesgard@earthlink.net. 9x/yr. $20/yr. Circ.: 30,000. Mary Gutierrez, Editor-in-Chief. **Description:** Regional magazine with gardening information for gardeners west of the Cascade Mountains in Washington State. Geared toward zone 8 maritime climate. Nonfiction pieces run 100-500 words; $50-$100. **E-Queries:** Yes. **Unsolicited mss:** Accepts. **Response:** 3 months, SASE required. **Freelance Content:** 100%. **Payment:** On publication.

OLD HOUSE INTERIORS

108 East Main St., Gloucester, MA 01930. 978-283-3200.
E-mail: editorial@oldhouseinteriors.com. Web site: www.oldhouseinteriors.com. Bimonthly. Circ.: 125,000. Regina Cole, Senior Editor. **Description:** On architecture, decorative arts, and history. **Nonfiction:** Articles, 300-1,500 words; pays $1/word, or $200/page minimum. **Tips:** Most important thing is the art; when proposing an article, know how it should be illustrated. Professional photos not necessary. Query, with clips. **Payment:** On acceptance.

ORGANIC GARDENING MAGAZINE

Rodale, 33 E Minor St., Emmaus, PA 18098. 610-967-8926.
E-mail: og@rodale.com. Web site: www.organicgardening.com. 6x/yr. $3.99/$24.96.
Circ.: 300,000. Scott Meyer, Editor. **Description:** North America's only gardening magazine dedicated wholly to organic practices. **Nonfiction:** Gardening how-to, solid organic advice; profiles of organic gardens and gardeners; profiles of a vegetable, fruit, or flower. 1,000-1,800 words; $.60-$1.00/word. **Queries:** Preferred. **E-Queries:** Yes. **Unsolicited mss:** Accepts. **Response:** Queries 4 weeks, submissions 6 weeks, SASE required. **Freelance Content:** 40%. **Rights:** All. **Payment:** On acceptance.

SOUTHERN ACCENTS

2100 Lakeshore Dr., Birmingham, AL 35209. 205-445-6000.
E-mail: letters@southernaccents.com. Web site: www.southernaccents.com. Bimonthly. $28. Circ.: 375,000. Julie Goodwin, Managing Editor. **Description:** Celebrates southern style in interiors, gardens, art, antiques, and entertaining. Focuses on affluent homes and gardens in a 16-state region. Also features the homes of southerners living abroad and the travel destinations visited by upscale readership. **Nonfiction:** Query first with appropriate story ideas; 800-1,200 words; pay negotiable. **Queries:** Preferred. **Response:** SASE. **Payment:** On acceptance.

STYLE AT HOME

25 Sheppard Ave. W, Suite 100, Toronto, Ontario M2N 6S7 Canada. 416-733-7600.
E-mail: ghabs@styleathome.com. Web site: www.styleathome.com. 9x/yr. $28/yr. Circ.: 210,000. Gail Johnston Habs, Editor. **Description:** Profiles of Canadian homes, renovation, decoration, and gardening. Canadian content and locations only. **Nonfiction:** 300-800 words; $300-$800 (Canadian). **Tips:** Writer's guidelines available upon request. **Queries:** Preferred. **E-Queries:** Yes. **Payment:** On acceptance.

SU CASA

5931 Office Blvd. NE, Suite 2, Albuquerque, NM 87109-5838. 505-344-3294.
E-mail: cpoling@sucasamagazine.com. Web site: www.sucasmagazine.com. 4x/yr. $3.95/$18. Circ.: 35,000. Charles C. Poling, Editor. **Description:** Showcases the style and design of unique homes in the Southwest. **Nonfiction:** Articles on Southwestern architecture and design; profiles of builders, artisans, artists, and craftspeople; interior design; and other home-related topics; 800-2,000 words; $250-$500. **Art:** Submit 4x5 transparency, 35mm slides, or hi-res scans. **Tips:** "Our emphasis is New Mexico-based architecture and building. No how-to features or articles on generalized topics." **Queries:** Preferred. **E-Queries:** Yes. **Unsolicited mss:** Accepts. **Response:** 2 weeks, SASE required. **Freelance Content:** 95%.

SUNSET MAGAZINE

See full listing in Lifestyle Magazines category.

VICTORIAN HOMES

265 S Anita Dr., Suite 120, Orange, CA 92868. 714-939-9991.
E-mail: erika.kotite@prodigy.net. Web site: www.victorianhomesmag.com.
Bimonthly. $3.99/$19.95. Circ.: 80,000. Erika Kotite, Editor. **Description:** Covers the lifestyle of Victorian Revival. Articles explore decoration and architecture of 19th- and early 20th-century homes restored, decorated, and lived in by real people, also period museum houses. **Nonfiction:** On interior design, furnishings, gardens, florals, table settings, and decorative accessories. Also, kitchen or bathroom makeovers, whole-house restorations, renovation tips, paint colors/wall coverings, etc.; 1,000-1,500 words; $400-$500. **Columns, Departments:** Victorian furnishings, antiques, collectibles, lighting, flowers and food, for today's home. **Queries:** Preferred. **E-Queries:** Accepts. **Unsolicited mss:** Accepts. **Response:** 6-8 weeks. **Freelance Content:** 80%. **Rights:** All or FNAR. **Payment:** On acceptance.

WATER GARDENING

P.O. Box 607, St. John, IN 46373-0607. 219-374-9419.
E-mail: sue@watergardening.com. Web site: www.watergardening.com. Bimonthly. $4.99/$24.99. Circ.: 25,000. Susan Speichert, Editor-in-Chief. **Description:** Hobbyist magazine on how to build, design, landscape, and care for ponds and the plants and fish that live in them. **Nonfiction:** 1,200 words; $250. **Columns, Departments:** 500 words; $150. **Queries:** Preferred. **E-Queries:** Yes. **Unsolicited mss:** Accepts. **Response:** 6 months. **Rights:** FNAR. **Payment:** On publication.

WOMAN'S DAY GARDENING & DECK DESIGN

Hachette Filipacchi Magazines
1633 Broadway, Fl. 42, New York, NY 10019-6708. 212-767-6000.
E-mail: wdsip@hfmus.com. Web site: www.womanday.com/specials.
3x/yr. $4.50(U.S.);$4.99(Canada). Circ.: 450,000. Peter Walsh, Editor. **Description:** Offers gardening tips, designs, and solutions to common problems. Also features outdoor furniture, decks, and other outdoor accessories. **Tips:** Include resume and recent, related, published clips with all queries. No phone calls. **Queries:** Required. **E-Queries:** Yes. **Unsolicited mss:** Does not accept. **Response:** 2 months, SASE required. **Freelance Content:** 75%. **Rights:** All. **Payment:** On acceptance. **Contact:** Managing Editor.

HUMOR

THE FUNNY TIMES

2176 Lee Rd., Cleveland Heights, OH 44118. 216-371-8600.
E-mail: ft@funnytimes.com. Web site: www.funnytimes.com. Monthly. $2.95/$23. Circ.: 63,000. Ray Lesser, Editor. **Description:** Humor review. **Fiction:** Stories on anything relating to the general human condition: politics, news, relationships, food, technology, pets, work, death, environmental issues, business, religion, seasonal events, etc.; 500-700 words; $50. **Nonfiction:** Essays, interviews, book reviews; to

1,000 words. **Art:** Cartoons, 1-2 pages; $20-$30. **Queries:** Not necessary. **E-Queries:** No. **Unsolicited mss:** Accepts. **Response:** 4-6 weeks, SASE required. **Rights:** FNAR. **Payment:** On publication.

MAD MAGAZINE
1700 Broadway, Fl. 5, New York, NY 10019. 212-506-4850.
Web site: www.madmag.com. Monthly. **Description:** Humorous pieces on a wide variety of topics. **Fiction:** Humor; particularly interested in current trends; visual elements required; pay varies. **Art:** Cartoons, 2-8 panels (not necessary to include sketches with submission). **Tips:** Guidelines strongly recommended; must include SASE for response. **Queries:** Preferred. **E-Queries:** No. **Unsolicited mss:** Accepts. **Response:** 8-12 weeks; SASE required. **Payment:** On acceptance. **Contact:** Editorial Department.

STITCHES
See full listing in Trade & Technical category.

IN-FLIGHT MAGAZINES

ABOVE & BEYOND
First Air, P.O. Box 13142, Kanata, Ontario K2K 1X3 Canada. 613-599-4190.
E-mail: info@above-n-beyond.com. Web site: www.above-n-beyond.com. Bimonthly. $15.50. Circ.: 25,000. Season Osborne, Editor. **Description:** In-flight magazine for First Air Airlines (in the Canadian arctic).

ALASKA AIRLINES MAGAZINE
2701 First Ave., Suite 250, Seattle, WA 98121-1125. 206-441-5871.
E-mail: editorialaska@paradigmcg.com. Monthly. $50. Circ.: 50,000. Paul Frichtl, Editor. **Description:** On business, travel, and profiles of regional personalities for West Coast business travelers. **Nonfiction:** Articles, 250-2,500 words; pay varies. **Queries:** Preferred. **Payment:** On publication.

AMERICA WEST AIRLINES
4636 E Elwood St., Suite 5, Phoenix, AZ 85040-1963. 602-997-7200.
Web site: www.skyword.com. Monthly. $29/yr. Circ.: 135,000. Elizabeth Cullum, Managing Editor. **Description:** "We offer entertaining articles with an emphasis on first-rate reporting and compelling storytelling, including fiction, arts, and culture, and thoughtful essays." **Tips:** Sample copy $3. **Queries:** Required. **E-Queries:** No.

AMERICAN WAY
American Airlines Publishing
4255 Amon Carter Blvd., MD 4255, Fort Worth, TX 76155. 817-967-1804.
E-mail: editor@americanwaymag.com. Web site: www.americanwaymag.com. Biweekly. $72/yr. Circ.: 342,600. Sherri Burns, Editor. **Description:** Travel, business,

food and wine, health, technology, fitness, personality profiles, and more. **Nonfiction:** Features, 1,500-1,700 words. **Columns, Departments:** Travel, Lifestyle, Business; 600-800 words. **Queries:** Required. **Response:** SASE required. **Contact:** Jill Becker, Senior Editor; Richelle Thomson, Senior Editor; Tracy Staton, Senior Editor.

BOSTON AIRPORT JOURNAL
256 Marginal St., East Boston, MA 02128-2800. 617-561-4000.
Web site: www.travelpublications.net/baj.html. E-mail: travelnews@att.net.
Monthly. $55. Circ.: 30,000. Robert H. Weiss, Publisher/Editor. **Description:** Logan International Airport publication.

ENROUTE
355 Sainte Catherine W #400, Montreal, Quebec H3B 1A5 Canada. 514-844-2001.
E-mail: info@enroutemag.net. Monthly. $50/yr. Circ.: 200,000. Arjun Basu, Editor-in-Chief. **Description:** Air Canada in-flight magazine on travel and lifestyle.

FRONTIER
3983 S McCarran Blvd., Suite 434, Reno, NV 89502. 775-856-3532.
E-mail: laurah@adventuremedia.com. Web site: www.frontiermag.com. Monthly. Circ.: 20,000. Laura Hengstler, Editor-in-Chief. **Description:** In-flight magazine for Frontier Air Lines, serving northwest U.S. Nonfiction pieces run 50-2,000 words; $.25-$.50/word. **Queries:** Required. **E-Queries:** Yes. **Unsolicited mss:** Accepts. **Response:** 6 weeks. **Freelance Content:** 70%. **Rights:** FNASR. **Payment:** On publication.

HCP/ABOARD PUBLISHING
One Herald Plaza, Fl. 3, Miami, FL 33132. 305-376-5258.
E-mail: editorial@aboardpublishing.com. Web site: www.aboardpublishing.com. **Description:** Publishes custom publications in the travel/tourism industry including 4 inflight publications for Latin America and the Caribbean, and various hotel publications in Central America, the Caribbean, and the U.S. **Nonfiction:** Travel articles on specific Latin American and Caribbean destinations (also some U.S. destinations); general articles on health, business, cuisine; and celebrity interviews (particularly Latin celebrities). **Queries:** Not necessary. **E-Queries:** Yes. **Unsolicited mss:** Does not accept. **Response:** SASE required. **Freelance Content:** 70%. **Rights:** All Western Hemisphere. **Payment:** On publication. **Contact:** Abel Delgado (*Explore, Mundo del Sur, Aeropostal*); Rosa Rojas (*Latitudes*); Vanessa Molina (*Discover Charleston, Discover Bermuda, Cabo San Lucas*).

HEMISPHERES
Pace Communications, 1301 Carolina St., Greensboro, NC 27401. 336-378-6065.
E-mail: hemiedit@aol.com. Web site: www.hemispheresmagazine.com. Monthly. $50/yr. Circ.: 500,000. Randy Johnson, Editor. **Description:** In-flight magazine for

United Airlines. **Fiction:** 1,500-3,000 words; pay varies. **Nonfiction:** Articles on universal issues; 2,000-3,000 words; $.75+ per word. **Columns, Departments:** See writer guidelines; 1,500-1,800 words; $.50/word. **Tips:** "We offer a global perspective in a fresh, artful publication." **Queries:** Preferred. **E-Queries:** Yes. **Unsolicited mss:** Accepts. **Response:** 2 months, SASE. **Freelance Content:** 95%. **Rights:** 1st worldwide. **Payment:** On acceptance. **Contact:** Selby Bateman, Senior Editor.

HORIZON AIR

2701 First Ave., Suite 250, Seattle, WA 98121-1123. 206-441-5871.
Monthly. $45/yr. Circ.: 416,000. Michele Andrus Dill, Editor. **Description:** For travelers in the Northwest, Silicon Valley, California, Arizona, Southern British Columbia and Southern Alberta. **Nonfiction:** Business, travel, lifestyle, sports, and leisure; 500-2,500 words; pay varies. **Columns, Departments:** Personal essay on business, travel, life in Northwest; 500-1,500 words. **Art:** Transparencies, slides. **Tips:** Query with samples (photocopies preferred, not originals). **Queries:** Required. **E-Queries:** No. **Unsolicited mss:** Accepts. **Response:** 1-6 months, SASE. **Freelance Content:** 80%. **Rights:** FNASR. **Payment:** On publication.

MIDWEST AIRLINES MAGAZINES

2701 First Ave., Suite 250, Seattle, WA 98121. 206-441-5871.
Semi-monthly. Eric Lucas, Managing Editor. **Description:** Inflight magazine for Midwest Airlines. **Nonfiction:** Travel stories, business trends, and general features; 300-1,600 words. **Tips:** Keep queries concise. **Queries:** Required. **E-Queries:** No. **Unsolicited mss:** Does not accept. **Response:** 2 months, SASE required. **Freelance Content:** 60%. **Rights:** FNAR. **Payment:** On publication.

NORTHWEST AIRLINES WORLD TRAVELER

P.O. Box 4005, Beaverton, OR 97076-4005. 503-520-1955.
E-mail: editors@skies.com. Monthly. $50. Circ.: 350,000. Beverly Dirks, Editor. **Description:** For passengers of Northwest Airlines.

SKY

Pace Communications, 1301 Carolina St., Greensboro, NC 27401. 336-378-6065.
E-mail: editorial@delta-sky.com. Web site: www.delta-sky.com. Monthly. $50. Circ.: 500,000. Duncan Christy, Editorial Director. **Description:** Delta Air Lines inflight magazine. **Nonfiction:** Articles on business, lifestyle, high tech, sports, arts; pay varies. **Art:** Color slides. **Queries:** Preferred. **Response:** SASE required. **Payment:** On acceptance.

SOUTHWEST AIRLINES SPIRIT

4255 Amon Carter Blvd., Fort Worth, TX 76155. 817-967-1804.
E-mail: editors@spiritmag.com. Web site: www.spiritmag.com. Monthly. Circ.: 370,000. **Description:** Travel/lifestyle publication for passengers on Southwest Airlines.

SPIRIT OF ALOHA

707 Richards St., Suite 525, Honolulu, HI 96813. 808-524-7400.
E-mail: jotaguro@honpub.com. Web site: www.spiritofaloha.com. Janice Otaguro, Editor. **Description:** Magazine for Aloha Airlines with Hawaiian Island focus. **Queries:** Preferred. **E-Queries:** Yes.

US AIRWAYS ATTACHÉ

1301 Carolina St., Greensboro, NC 27401. 336-378-6065.
E-mail: attacheedit@attachemag.com. Web site: www.attachemag.com. Monthly. $50/yr. Circ.: 375,000. Lance Elko, Editor. **Description:** Entertaining articles for travelers. Ongoing departments, some features. 350-2,000 words; $1/word. **Columns, Departments:** Homefront; Sports; Things That Grow; Things That Go; Golf; Insider's Guide to . . . (destination piece). **Tips:** Include clips or list of past clients. **Queries:** Required. **E-Queries:** Yes. **Unsolicited mss:** Accepts. **Response:** 1 month, SASE required. **Freelance Content:** 60%. **Rights:** exclusive worldwide for 90 days. **Payment:** On acceptance.

JUVENILE

AMERICAN GIRL

Pleasant Company Publications
8400 Fairway Pl., Middleton, WI 53562. 608-836-4848.
E-mail: im_agmag_editor@pleasantco.com. Web site: www.americangirl.com. Bimonthly. $3.95/$19.95. Circ.: 650,000. Kristi Thom, Editor. **Description:** For girls ages 8 and up. **Fiction:** Protagonist should be a girl between 8 and 12. No science fiction, fantasy, or first romance stories. Good children's literature, with thoughtful plots and characters; 2,500 words; pay varies. **Nonfiction:** By assignment only; 150-1,000 words; $1/word. **Fillers:** Visual puzzles, mazes, math puzzles, word games, simple crosswords, cartoons; $50/item. **Columns, Departments:** Girls Express; short profiles of girls doing great, interesting things; 150 words; $1/word. **Tips:** "The girl must be the story's 'star,' told from her point of view. 'Girls Express' offers best chance to break in." **Queries:** Preferred. **E-Queries:** No. **Unsolicited mss:** Accepts. **Response:** 3 months, SASE required. **Freelance Content:** 5%. **Payment:** On acceptance.

APPLESEEDS

Carus Publishing Co., 140 E 83rd St., New York, NY 10028. 603-924-7209.
E-mail: swbuc@aol.com. Web site: www.cobblestonepub.com. 9 issues/yr. Barbara Burt, Susan Buckley, Editors. **Description:** For children ages 7-10; covers multidisciplinary social studies. **Fiction:** Short fiction, to 300 words. **Nonfiction:** Feature articles, profiles, how-to; 100-600 words; $50/page. **Fillers:** Games and activities; 100-300 words; $50/page. **Columns, Departments:** Reading Corner, Your Turn, Experts in Action, The Artist's Eye; 100-600 words; $50/page. **Tips:** All material must be theme-related; check Web site for coming themes. **Queries:** Required. **E-Queries:** No. **Rights:** All.

ASK

332 S Michigan Ave., Suite 100, Chicago, IL 60604-4416. 312-939-1500.
E-mail: lplecha@caruspub.com. 9x/yr. $4.95/$32.97. Circ.: 40,000. James L. Plecha, Editor. **Description:** Nonfiction science and discovery magazine for children ages 7-10. **Nonfiction:** Almost all articles commissioned for the theme of the issue; 400-600 words; pay varies. **Tips:** "Study the magazine and guidelines. Articles are clearly written and age appropriate, but do not talk down to children. We look for a lively style that explains the how and why of things. Raise questions and spark curiosity on important concepts." **Queries:** Not necessary. **Unsolicited mss:** Accepts. **Response:** 3-4 months, SASE required. **Freelance Content:** 5%. **Rights:** All. **Payment:** On publication.

BABYBUG

Carus Publishing Co.
315 Fifth St., P.O. Box 300, Peru, IL 61354-0300. 815-224-5803, ext. 656.
Web site: www.cricketmag.com. Monthly. $5/$35.97. Circ.: 48,000. Paula Morrow, Editor. **Description:** Offers simple rhymes and stories that parents will delight in reading to their infants and toddlers. **Fiction:** Very simple and concrete; read-aloud and picture stories for infants and toddlers; 4-6 short sentences; $25. **Nonfiction:** Very basic words and concepts; to 10 words; $25. **Poetry:** Rhythmic, rhyming. Humor or ending with mild surprise a plus; to 8 lines; $25. **Fillers:** Parent/child interactive activities; to 8 lines; $25. **Art:** Art by assignment only; no photos. Submit samples (tear sheets, photocopies) for consideration. Pays $250/page, $500/spread. **Queries:** Does not accept. **E-Queries:** No. **Unsolicited mss:** Accepts. **Response:** 12 weeks, SASE required. **Rights:** Vary. **Payment:** On publication.

BOYS' LIFE

Boy Scouts of America
P.O. Box 152079, Irving, TX 75015-2079. 972-580-2366.
Web site: www.boyslife.org. Monthly. $18/year. Circ.: 1,300,000. Michael Goldman, Senior Editor. **Description:** Magazine for boys ages 7-18. Covers broad range of interests (sports, hobbies, careers, crafts, and special interests of scouting). **Fiction:** 1-2 short stories per issue; featuring 1 or more boys; humor, mystery, science fiction, adventure; 1,000-1,500 words; $750 and up. **Nonfiction:** From professional sports to American history to how to pack a canoe, 500-1,500 words; $400-$1,500. Also science, nature, health, sports, aviation, cars, computers, entertainment, pets, history, music, and more; 300-750 words; $150-$400. **Art:** Quality photos only; most work by assignment. **Tips:** "Write for a boy you know who is 12. Use crisp, punchy writing; short, straightforward sentences." See Web site for guidelines. **Queries:** Required for nonfiction. **E-Queries:** Prefer mail. **Unsolicited mss:** Accepts fiction only. **Response:** 6-8 weeks, SASE required. **Freelance Content:** 75%. **Rights:** FNASR. **Payment:** On acceptance. **Contact:** W.E. Butterworth IV, Managing Editor.

BOYS' QUEST

P.O. Box 227, Bluffton, OH 45817-0227. 419-358-4610.
E-mail: hsbq@wcoil.com. Web site: www.boysquest.com. Bimonthly. $4.95/$17.95.
Circ.: 8,500. Marilyn Edwards, Editor. **Description:** Captures interests of all boys
with exciting, unique activities and fascinating articles. Each issue focuses on a theme.
Fiction: Stories on childhood interests, featuring young boys in wholesome childhood activities and pursuits; 350-600 words; $.05/word and up. **Nonfiction:** About
boys in activities, unusual and worthwhile. Photos with story essential. 500 words;
$.05/word minimum. **Poetry:** $10/poem. **Fillers:** Puzzles, jokes, riddles, games;
$10/puzzle minimum, varies for other fillers. **Art:** B&W photos, color slides, pen-and-
ink illustrations; $5-$35. **Tips:** Readers are boys, ages 8-10. Avoid Halloween, horror,
etc. Prefers traditional childhood themes. Buys 3 nonfiction articles for each 1 fiction
story. **Queries:** Not necessary. **E-Queries:** No. **Unsolicited mss:** Accepts.
Response: 4-6 weeks, SASE required. **Rights:** FNAR. **Payment:** On publication.

CALLIOPE

Cobblestone Publishing
30 Grove St., Suite C, Peterborough, NH 03458. 603-924-7209.
Web site: www.cobblestonepub.com. 9x/yr. $29.95/yr. Circ.: 11,000. Charles Baker,
Rosalie Baker, Editors. **Description:** "Exploring World History," for ages 8-14.
Issues are thematic, exciting, colorful, with maps, timelines, illustrations, and art from
major museums. **Fiction:** Authentic historical and biographical fiction, adventure,
retold legends, and plays; to 1,000 words; $.20-$.25/word. **Nonfiction:** In-depth non-
fiction, biographies; 1,000 words; $.20-$.25/word. **Fillers:** Puzzles and games; activi-
ties including crafts, recipes, and woodworking; to 700 words. **Columns,
Departments:** Supplemental nonfiction; 300-600 words; $.20-$.25/word. **Art:**
Photographs to accompany articles; $25-$100. **Tips:** Contact for upcoming themes.
Queries: Required. **E-Queries:** No. **Unsolicited mss:** Prefers not to accept.
Response: 2-4 months, SASE required. **Freelance Content:** 80%. **Rights:** All.
Payment: On publication.

CHILDREN'S DIGEST

Children's Better Health Institute
1100 Waterway Blvd., P.O. Box 567, Indianapolis, IN 46206-0567. 317-636-8881.
E-mail: cbhiseif@tcon.net. Web site: www.childrensdigestmag.org. 6x/yr. $21.95.
Circ.: 106,000. Penny Rasdall, Editor. **Description:** Health and fitness for ages 10-
12. **Fiction:** Stories with a message about health: exercise, sports, safety, nutrition,
hygiene, drug education; 500-1,500 words; up to $.12/word. **Nonfiction:** Profiles of
famous amateur and professional athletes, "average" athletes (especially children)
who have overcome obstacles to excel in their areas, new or unusual sports, exercise,
safety, nutrition, hygiene, drug education; 500-1,000 words; up to $.12/word. **Poetry:**
Poetry; $25 and up. **Fillers:** Healthy recipes that children can make, puzzles, games.
Queries: Not necessary. **Unsolicited mss:** Accepts. **Response:** 3 months; SASE
required. **Rights:** All.

CHILDREN'S PLAYMATE MAGAZINE

Children's Better Health Institute

1100 Waterway Blvd., P.O. Box 567, Indianapolis, IN 46206-0567. 317-636-8881. E-mail: customercare@cbhi.org. Web site: www.childrensplaymatemag.org. 6x/yr. $16.95/yr. Circ.: 114,000. Terry Harshman, Editor. **Description:** For 6- to 8-year-olds, emphasizing health, fitness, sports, safety, and nutrition. **Fiction:** Plays. **Nonfiction:** Articles, crafts, recipes, general-interest, and health-related short stories. Easy recipes and how-to crafts pieces with simple instructions; 500-600 words; to $.17/word. **Poetry:** Yes; from $30. **Fillers:** Puzzles, games, mazes. **Queries:** Preferred. **Rights:** All. **Payment:** On publication.

CLICK

Carus Publishing Co.

332 S Michigan Ave., Suite 1100, Chicago, IL 60604. 312-939-1500.

Web site: www.cricketmag.com. 9x/yr. $4.95/$32.97. Circ.: 50,000. James L. Plecha, Editor. **Description:** For children ages 3-7. Themes introduce ideas and concepts in natural, physical, or social sciences, the arts, technology, math, and history. **Fiction:** Stories that explain nonfiction concepts; 600-1,000 words; pay varies. **Nonfiction:** Articles that explain the how and why of something; 200-400 words; pay varies. **Tips:** See Web site for theme list and guidelines. **Queries:** Does not accept. **E-Queries:** No. **Unsolicited mss:** Accepts. **Response:** 3-4 months, SASE required. **Rights:** All. **Payment:** On publication.

CLUB CONNECTION

See full listing in Religion category.

CLUBHOUSE JR.

Focus on the Family, 8605 Explorer Dr., Colorado Springs, CO 80920. 719-531-3400. E-mail: mail@fotf.org. Web site: www.family.org. Monthly. $1.50/$15. Circ.: 96,000. Annette Bourland, Editor. **Description:** Inspires, entertains, and teaches Christian values to children ages 4-8. **Fiction:** Fresh, inviting, well-developed characters; fast-paced, interesting story. Stories not explicitly Christian but built on foundations of belief and family values; 250-750 words (for young readers); $125-$300. **Nonfiction:** Articles about real children with interesting experiences. Science and nature told from unique perspective. Use short-caption styled format; 500 words max; $125-$200. **Poetry:** Real-life experience of young children; humorous, descriptive; 250 words max; $50-$100. **Fillers:** Puzzles (no crosswords); fun crafts, parent/child together; repetition of images, concise wording, humorous or insightful ending; 1 page; $25-$45. **Art:** Send samples to Kathleen Gray-Ziegler, Designer. **Queries:** Does not accept. **E-Queries:** No. **Unsolicited mss:** Accepts. **Response:** 4-6 weeks, SASE required. **Freelance Content:** 25%. **Rights:** 1st. **Payment:** On acceptance.

CLUBHOUSE MAGAZINE

Focus on the Family, 8605 Explorer Dr., Colorado Springs, CO 80920. 719-531-3400. Web site: www.clubhousemagazine.org;www.family.org. Monthly. $18/yr. Circ.:

14,000. Jesse Florea, Editor. **Description:** Christian magazine for 8-12 year olds who desire to know more about God and the Bible. We accept stories (fiction and nonfiction), Bible stories, puzzles, crafts, recipes, and cartoons. **Fiction:** 500-1,500 words; $200+. **Nonfiction:** Action-oriented Christian stories about children who are wise, brave, funny, or kind; 500-1,500 words; $.15-$.25/word. **Fillers:** 50-100 words; $75. **Tips:** "Avoid poetry, contemporary middle-class family settings, and educational articles that are too technical or informative in nature. Right now our needs include historical fiction, holiday material, mystery stories, and humor with a point." **Response:** 8 weeks, SASE. **Freelance Content:** 25%. **Rights:** FNAR. **Payment:** On acceptance. **Contact:** Suzanne Hadley, Associate Editor.

COBBLESTONE
Carus Publishing Co.
30 Grove St., Suite C, Peterborough, NH 03458. 603-924-7209.
Web site: www.cobblestonepub.com. Monthly. $4.95/issue. Circ.: 30,000. Meg Chorlian, Editor. **Description:** American history for 8- to 14-year-olds; themed issues. **Fiction:** Authentic historical and biographical fiction, adventure, retold legends; up to 800 words; $.20-$.25/word. **Nonfiction:** In-depth nonfiction, plays, first-person accounts, and biographies.; 300-800 words; $.20-$.25/word. **Poetry:** Serious or light verse with clear, objective imagery; 30 lines; pay varies. **Fillers:** Crosswords, mazes, picture puzzles; pay varies. **Columns, Departments:** Activities such as crafts, recipes, and woodworking projects; pay varies. **Art:** Photographs related to theme; Color or B&W, transparencies or slides; $15-$100. **Queries:** Required. **E-Queries:** Yes. **Unsolicited mss:** Does not accept. **Response:** 6 months for queries, 2 months for submissions; SASE required. **Freelance Content:** 85%. **Rights:** All. **Payment:** On publication.

CONSUMER REPORTS FOR KIDS ONLINE
101 Truman Ave., Yonkers, NY 10703-1057. 914-378-2985.
Web site: www.zillions.org. **Description:** An online version of *Consumer Reports* for children, found at Zillions.org. For readers, ages 8-14, with Internet access.

CRICKET
Carus Publishing Co.
315 Fifth St., P.O. Box 300, Peru, IL 61354-0300. 815-224-5803, ext. 656.
E-mail: cricket@caruspub.com. Web site: www.cricketmag.com. Monthly. $5/$35.97. Circ.: 71,000. Marianne Carus, Editor-in-Chief. **Description:** Folk tales, fantasy, science fiction, history, poems, science, sports, and crafts, for young readers. **Fiction:** Any topic of interest to children; to 2,000 words; $.25/word. **Nonfiction:** Science, biography, history, nature; to 1,500 words; $.25/word. **Poetry:** Brief lyric poems; to 25 lines; $3/line. **Fillers:** Word or math puzzles, recipes, crafts, experiments; 150-200 words; $100. **Tips:** Include bibliography with nonfiction. **Queries:** Does not accept. **E-Queries:** No. **Unsolicited mss:** Accepts. **Response:** 12 weeks, SASE required. **Freelance Content:** 90%. **Rights:** All. **Payment:** On publication.

DIG MAGAZINE

Carus Publishing Co.

30 Grove St. #C, Peterborough, NH 03458-1438. 603-924-7209.
Web site: www.digonline.com. Bimonthly. $23.95/yr. Circ.: 20,000. Rosalie Baker, Editor. **Description:** For children ages 10-14 on archaeology. Nonfiction pieces, 400-1,000 words; $.20-$.25/word. **Tips:** "Query on a specific upcoming issue; include bibliography that shows understanding of proposed topic and lists key people in that field." **Queries:** Required. **Unsolicited mss:** Accepts. **Response:** 2-4 months, SASE required. **Freelance Content:** 80%. **Rights:** All. **Payment:** On publication.

DISCOVERIES

6401 The Paseo, Kansas City, MO 64131. 816-333-7000.
E-mail: jjsmith@aol.com. Weekly. Circ.: 22,000. Virginia Folsom, Editor. **Description:** Full-color take-home paper for 3rd and 4th graders connecting Evangelical Sunday School learning with daily growth. **Fiction:** Contemporary, true-to-life portrayals of 8-10 year olds; 500 words; $25. **Fillers:** Trivia, puzzles, miscellaneous areas of interest; $15. **Tips:** Illustrate character-building and scriptural application. Send for guidelines and upcoming themes. **Queries:** Preferred. **E-Queries:** Yes. **Unsolicited mss:** Accepts. **Response:** 6-8 weeks, SASE required. **Freelance Content:** 80%. **Rights:** Multi-use. **Payment:** On publication. **Contact:** Julie J. Smith, Editorial Assistant.

DISCOVERY TRAILS

1445 N Boonville Ave., Springfield, MO 65802-1894. 417-862-2781.
E-mail: rl-discoverytrails@gph.org. Web site: www.radiantlife.org. Quarterly. Circ.: 20,000. Sinda Zinn, Editor. **Description:** Take-home paper for children 10-11 years old, with fiction stories, activities, poems, articles, and puzzles to reinforce daily Christian living. **Fiction:** Stories that promote Christian living through application of biblical principles by the characters; 1000 words; $.07-$.10/word. **Nonfiction:** Articles about topics that show God's power, wisdom in creation, or correlation to a relationship with God; 300-500 words; $.07-$.10/word. **Tips:** No Santa, Easter Bunny, or Halloween stories. Accepts e-mail submissions, but not e-mail queries. **Queries:** Not necessary. **E-Queries:** No. **Unsolicited mss:** Accepts. **Response:** 2-4 weeks, SASE required. **Freelance Content:** 90%. **Payment:** On acceptance.

FACES

Cobblestone Publishing

30 Grove St., Suite C, Peterborough, NH 03458-1454. 603-924-7209.
E-mail: facesmag@yahoo.com. Web site: www.cobblestonepub.com. 9x/yr. $29.95/yr. Circ.: 11,000. Elizabeth Crooker Carpentiere, Editor. **Description:** "People, Places, and Cultures." Introduces young readers (ages 8-14) to different world cultures, religion, geography, government, and art. **Fiction:** Retold folktales, legends, plays; must relate to theme; to 800 words; $.20-$.25/word. **Nonfiction:** In-depth articles on aspect of featured culture; interviews and personal accounts; 600-800 words; $.20-$.25/word. **Fillers:** Activities (crafts, recipes, word puzzles); 100-600 words. **Art:**

35mm; $25-$100. **Tips:** "Avoid judgmental tone. Give our readers a clear image of life in other cultures. Check our Web site for upcoming themes." **Queries:** Required. **E-Queries:** Yes. **Unsolicited mss:** Accepts. **Response:** Queries, 4 weeks, submissions, 4 months, SASE required. **Freelance Content:** 80%. **Rights:** All. **Payment:** On publication.

FOOTSTEPS

Carus Publishing Co.

30 Grove St., Suite C, Peterborough, NH 03458. 603-924-7209.

E-mail: cfbaker@meganet.com. Web site: www.footstepsmagazine.com. 5x/yr. $23.95/yr. Circ.: 5,000. Charles F. Baker, Editor. **Description:** African-American history and heritage for students in grades 4-9. **Fiction:** Authentic retellings of historical and biographical events, adventure, and legends; 200-1,000 words; $.20-$.25/word. **Nonfiction:** On issue's theme; 200-1,000 words; $.20-$.25/word. **Fillers:** Activities, short articles, to 600 words. **Art:** Slides, transparencies, digital, prints; pay varies. **Tips:** Cultural sensitivity and historical accuracy required. Contact for upcoming themes. **Queries:** Required. **Unsolicited mss:** Accepts. **Response:** 2-6 months, SASE required. **Freelance Content:** 90%. **Rights:** All. **Payment:** On publication.

THE FRIEND

Church of Jesus Christ of Latter-day Saints

50 E North Temple, Fl. 24, Salt Lake City, UT 84150-3226. 801-240-2210.

Monthly. $8/yr. Circ.: 275,000. Vivian Paulsen, Managing Editor. **Description:** Nonfiction literary journal for children up to 12 years of age. **Nonfiction:** Articles and stories should be true, focus on character-building qualities and wholesome values without moralizing or preaching. Stories with universal settings, conflicts, and characters. No biographies of living people; 1,000 words; $.11/word. **Poetry:** Poems, uplifting and of substance. Picturable poems suitable for preschoolers of high interest. No nature poems or those with clever play on words; $25 and up. **Fillers:** How-to pieces on handicraft or homemaking projects. Also, cartoons, games, puzzles, recipes. **Tips:** No fiction. Send $1.50 and 9x12 SASE for sample copy. **Queries:** Not necessary. **E-Queries:** No. **Unsolicited mss:** Does not accept. **Response:** Submissions 8-12 weeks. **Rights:** All. **Payment:** On acceptance.

GIRLS' LIFE

4517 Harford Rd., Baltimore, MD 21214. 410-426-9600.

E-mail: kellygirl@girlslife.com. Web site: www.girlslife.com. Bimonthly. $3.50/$14.95. Circ.: 400,000. Karen Bokram, Publisher/Editor-in-Chief. **Description:** For girls, ages 10-15, with real information and advice on friends, parents, siblings, guys, school, puberty, and more. Includes profiles of real girls facing real challenges (e.g., young girl traveling through Nepal, young girl battling anorexia). Length and pay varies. **Tips:** Prefers e-queries; include SASE if sending by regular mail. No phone calls. Include resume, clips, and pitch letter or article. "Must be familiar with our editorial content, target audience, voice, and language. Read recent issues, and make sure pitch fits specific feature, column, or department." **Queries:** Required. **E-Queries:**

Yes. **Response:** 90 days. **Freelance Content:** 30%. **Rights:** All. **Payment:** On publication. **Contact:** Kelly White, Executive Editor (celebrity interviews, pop culture crafts, short profiles, newsworthy tidbits); Sarah Cordi, Senior Editor (service-oriented features, 1-page features, quizzes, "party" features, teen-targeted fiction).

GUIDEPOSTS FOR KIDS ON THE WEB

1050 Broadway, Suite 6, Chesterton, IN 46304. 219-929-4429.
E-mail: gp4k@guideposts.org. Web site: www.gp4k.com. Rosanne Tolin, Managing Editor. **Description:** E-zine for children, ages 7-12. Offers inspiring stories that focus on traditional values as well as other general-interest pieces on animals, school, sports, and more. Also has fun puzzles, arts and crafts, quizzes, trivia, animal stories, and interactive features such as a club, discussion boards, and monitored chats. **Fiction:** Stories by noted authors; 500-1,000 words; $100-$250. **Nonfiction:** Profiles of athletes and celebrities (150-500 words) and features that encourage kids to think (250-1,000 words); $100-$250. **Poetry:** 50-150 words; $25-$100. **Fillers:** $25-$150. **Tips:** "We do not consider ourselves a religious e-zine. No Bible-toting kids or preachy stories, please." Include bullets, links, sidebars, etc. **Queries:** Preferred. **E-Queries:** Yes. **Unsolicited mss:** Accepts. **Response:** 6 weeks, SASE required. **Freelance Content:** 80%. **Rights:** All. **Payment:** On acceptance.

HIGHLIGHTS FOR CHILDREN

803 Church St., Honesdale, PA 18431-1824. 570-253-1080.
Web site: www.highlights.com. Monthly. $29.64/yr. Circ.: 2,500,000. Christine French Clark, Editor. **Description:** "Fun with a purpose." The stories, hidden pictures, jokes, and activities bring engaging entertainment to children, ages 2-12, while developing learning skills. **Fiction:** Humor, mystery, sports, adventure, folktales, world cultures, urban stories. Engaging plot, strong characterization, lively language. To 800 words; $150 and up. **Nonfiction:** Biography, autobiography, arts, science, history, sports, world cultures, up to 800 words. If for younger readers (ages 3-7 years), 400 words or less. $150 and up. **Poetry:** 16 lines, $25 and up. **Fillers:** Crafts (3-7 numbered steps), $30 and up; include a sample; use common household items or inexpensive, easy-to-obtain materials. Holiday/religious/world cultures crafts welcome. **Tips:** "We prefer stories in which protagonist solves a dilemma through his/her own resources. Avoid stories that preach." **Queries:** Preferred. **E-Queries:** No. **Unsolicited mss:** Accepts. **Response:** 6-8 weeks, SASE required. **Rights:** All. **Payment:** On acceptance.

HOPSCOTCH

P.O. Box 164, Bluffton, OH 45817-0164. 419-358-4610.
Web site: www.hopscotchmagazine.com. Bimonthly. $4.95/$17.95. Circ.: 15,000. Marilyn Edwards, Editor. **Description:** Written for girls, without the emphasis on fads/fashion, boyfriends, and shopping. Focus is on educational activities and stories. Makes reading an adventure and problem-solving fun. **Fiction:** Features girls in wholesome childhood activities and pursuits; 500 words; $.05/word. **Nonfiction:** Features girls directly involved in an unusual and worthwhile activity; 500 words;

$.05/word. **Poetry:** $10/poem. **Fillers:** Puzzles, games, crafts, cartoons, recipes. **Art:** Photos are essential. B&W photos, color slides, and illustrations; $5-$35. **Tips:** "Nonfiction pieces make up 75% of our content. Please contact us for upcoming themes." **Queries:** Not necessary. **E-Queries:** No. **Unsolicited mss:** Accepts. **Response:** 4-6 weeks, SASE required. **Rights:** FNAR. **Payment:** On publication.

THE HORN BOOK MAGAZINE
See full listing in Writing & Publishing category.

HUMPTY DUMPTY'S MAGAZINE
Children's Better Health Institute
1100 Waterway Blvd., P.O. Box 567, Indianapolis, IN 46206-0567. 317-636-8881. Web site: www.humptydumptymag.org. 6x/yr. $25.95/yr. Circ.: 200,000. Nancy S. Axelrad, Editor. **Description:** Encourages children, ages 4-6, to strive for excellence, with focus on academics, health, personal fitness, medicine, and science. Fiction and nonfiction pieces run 350 words or less; $.22/word. Short verse and narratives, $25/piece. **Fillers:** Games, puzzles, crafts, simple science experiments, healthy and "no-cook" recipes (with minimum adult guidance). Include brief, clear instructions. **Tips:** "Stories should have good 'I can read' quality." **Unsolicited mss:** Accepts. **Response:** Submissions 3 months, SASE required. **Freelance Content:** 25-30%. **Rights:** All. **Payment:** On publication.

JACK AND JILL
Children's Better Health Institute
1100 Waterway Blvd., P.O. Box 567, Indianapolis, IN 46206-0567. 317-634-1100. Web site: www.jackandjillmag.org. 6x/yr. $21.95/yr. Circ.: 200,000. Daniel Lee, Editor. **Description:** For children, ages 7-10, offers health, fitness, science, and general-interest material. Encourages active, challenging lifestyles, and accomplishment and learning with a hearty helping of fun! **Fiction:** 700 words; $.17/word. **Nonfiction:** On history, biography, life in other countries, etc.; 500 words; $.17/word. **Poetry:** $15-$50. **Fillers:** Games, puzzles, projects, recipes. **Tips:** "Avoid usual topics (e.g., divorce, moving, new kid in school, etc.)." **Queries:** Not necessary. **E-Queries:** No. **Unsolicited mss:** Accepts. **Response:** Submissions 12 weeks, SASE required. **Freelance Content:** 50%. **Rights:** All. **Payment:** On publication.

JUNIOR SCHOLASTIC
Scholastic, Inc., 555 Broadway, New York, NY 10012. 212-343-6295. E-mail: junior@scholastic.com. Web site: www.juniorscholastic.com. 17x/yr. $7.75/yr. Circ.: 580,000. Lee Baier, Editor. **Description:** On-the-spot reports from countries in the news. **Queries:** Required. **Payment:** On acceptance.

KIDS TRIBUTE
71 Barber Greene Rd., Don Mills, Ontario M3C 2A2 Canada. 416-445-0544. Web site: www.tribute.ca. Quarterly. $12/yr. Circ.: 300,000. Sandra Stewart, Editor-in-Chief. **Description:** Features articles on movies and entertainment for young read-

ers, ages 8-13. **Nonfiction:** 350 words; pays $150-$200 (Canadian). **Queries:** Required. **Payment:** On acceptance.

LADYBUG

Carus Publishing Co.

315 Fifth St., P.O. Box 300, Peru, IL 61354-0300. 815-224-5803, ext. 656.

Web site: www.cricketmag.com. Monthly. $5/$35.97. Circ.: 131,000. Paula Morrow, Editor. **Description:** Stories, poems, songs, games, and adventures for young children, ages 3-6. Each page illustrated to delight parents and children alike. **Fiction:** Picture, read-aloud, and early reader stories with lively characters. Genres: adventure, humor, mild suspense, fairy tales, folktales, contemporary fiction; to 800 words; $.25/word, $25 minimum. **Nonfiction:** How-to, informational, and humorous pieces, on age-appropriate topics; to 300 words; $.25/word, $25 minimum. **Poetry:** Rhythmic, rhyming, serious, humorous, active; to 20 lines; $3/line, $25 minimum. **Fillers:** Rebus, learning activities, games, crafts, songs, finger games. **Tips:** "We're always looking for more activities." **Queries:** Does not accept. **E-Queries:** No. **Unsolicited mss:** Accepts. **Response:** 12 weeks, SASE required. **Freelance Content:** 70%. **Rights:** Vary. **Payment:** On publication.

MAD MAGAZINE

See full listing in Humor category.

MUSE

Carus Publishing Co.

332 S Michigan Ave., Suite 1100, Chicago, IL 60604. 312-939-1500.

E-mail: muse@caruspub.com. Web site: www.musemag.com. 10x/yr. Diana Lutz, Editor. **Description:** Focuses on problems connected with a discipline or area of practical knowledge, for children, ages 10-14. 1,000-2,500 words; $.50/word. **Tips:** No longer accepts unsolicited manuscripts or queries.

MY FRIEND

Pauline Books & Media

Daughters of St. Paul, 50 Saint Paul's Ave., Boston, MA 02130. 617-522-8911.

E-mail: myfriend@pauline.org. Web site: www.myfriendmagazine.org. Monthly. $2/issue. Circ.: 8,000. Sr. Maria Grace Dateno, Editor. **Description:** "The Catholic Magazine for Kids." Seeks to present "religious truth and positive values in an enjoyable and attractive way." **Fiction:** Stories with good dialogue, realistic character development, and current lingo; 800-1,100 words; $75-$150. **Nonfiction:** Fresh perspectives into a child's world: imaginative, unique, challenging, informative, fun; 800-1,100 words; $75-$150. **Tips:** "Also accept craft ideas. First send us your idea and if accepted, provide us with a well-made sample." Review sample copy ($2 plus 9x12 SASE) prior to submitting. See guidelines on Web site. **Queries:** Not necessary. **E-Queries:** No. **Unsolicited mss:** Accepts. **Response:** 3 months; SASE required. **Freelance Content:** 30% mostly fiction. **Rights:** FNAR. **Payment:** On acceptance.

NATIONAL GEOGRAPHIC KIDS

National Geographic Society
1145 17th St. NW, Washington, DC 20036-4688. 202-857-7000.
Web site: www.national geographic.com/ngkids. Monthly. $17.95/yr. Circ.: 900,000.
Melina Bellows, Editor-in-Chief. **Description:** For kids, ages 8-14, who dare to
explore. Seeks to increase geographic awareness by inspiring young readers' curiosity,
with big, bold photos and fun, fact-filled stories. **Nonfiction:** Adventure, outdoors,
sports, geography, history, archaeology, paleontology, human interest, natural history,
science, technology. 400-1,200 words; $.80-$1/word. **Tips:** "We work primarily
through assignments. We pick up few proposals or manuscripts. We do have submission guidelines and will send a sample copy. Send resume and relevant clips (hard
copy, no e-mail) that show ability to write for kids 8-14." **Queries:** Required.
E-Queries: No. **Unsolicited mss:** Does not accept. **Response:** 2 months, SASE
required. **Freelance Content:** 90%. **Rights:** All. **Payment:** On publication.
Contact: Julie Agnone, Executive Editor.

NATURE FRIEND

2673 Township Rd. 421, Sugarcreek, OH 44681. 330-852-1900.
Monthly. Circ.: 10,000. Marvin Wengerd, Editor. **Description:** Stories, puzzles,
activities, and experiments about nature for children. **Nonfiction:** Articles for children that teach them to be kind to animals, plants, and nature, increase their awareness of God, and illustrate spiritual lessons; 250-1,200 words; $.05/word. **Fillers:**
Games, puzzles, and activities concerning nature; 150-250 words; $15. **Art:** Photos to
accompany mss; transparencies, prints; $35-$50. **Tips:** Send complete manuscript (no
queries) via regular mail. Sample copies ($4) and guidelines available. **Response:** 4
months for submissions. **Freelance Content:** 80%. **Rights:** First or one-time.
Payment: On publication.

NEW MOON

34 E Superior St. #200, Duluth, MN 55802. 218-728-5507.
E-mail: girl@newmoon.org. Web site: www.newmoon.org. Bimonthly. $5.50/$29.
Circ.: 30,000. Deb Mylin, Managing Editor. **Description:** Celebrates girls—their
accomplishments and efforts to hold onto their voices, strengths, and dreams as they
move from being girls to becoming women. **Fiction:** Stories by female authors, with
girls as main characters. Fiction should fit theme (see Web site for upcoming list), for
girls ages 8-14; 900 words; $.06-$.10/word. **Nonfiction:** Women's work (profiles a
woman and her job, relates to theme); Herstory (profiles a woman from history);
Body Language (about puberty, body image, depression, menstruation, etc.); Girls on
the Go (by girl or woman adventurers); 600 words; $.06-$.10/word. **Tips:** Sample
copy $6.75. **Queries:** Not necessary. **E-Queries:** Accepts. **Unsolicited mss:**
Accepts. **Response:** 2 months, SASE. **Freelance Content:** 10%. **Rights:** All.
Payment: On publication.

NICK, JR.

1633 Broadway, Fl. 7, New York, NY 10019-6708. 212-654-6388.
E-mail: nickjr.editors@nick.com. Web site: www.nickjr.com. 8x/yr. $15.98/yr. Circ.: 1,000,000. Freddi Greenberg, Editor-in-Chief. **Description:** For parents and their children ages 2-11. Features do-together activities, games, stories, and expert parenting advice and information.

ON THE LINE

616 Walnut Ave., Scottdale, PA 15683. 724-887-8500.
E-mail: otl@mph.org. Web site: www.mph.org/otl. Monthly. $2.25/$27.25. Circ.: 5,000. Mary Clemens Meyer, Editor. **Description:** For youth, ages 9-14, to reinforce Christian values. Seeks to help upper elementary and junior high school kids understand God, the created world, themselves, and others. **Fiction:** Solving everyday problems, humor, holidays, Christian values; 1,000-1,800 words; $.03-$.05word. **Nonfiction:** Nature, history, health, how-to; 300-500 words; $.03-$.05/word. **Poetry:** Light verse, humor, nature, holidays; 3-24 lines; $10-$25. **Fillers:** Cartoons, crosswords, word finds, scrambled letters, mazes, codes, jokes, riddles, and recipes; $10-$20. **Tips:** "Let the story give the moral subtly; keep it fun." **Queries:** Not necessary. **E-Queries:** No. **Unsolicited mss:** Accepts. **Response:** 1 month, SASE required. **Freelance Content:** 85%. **Rights:** One-time. **Payment:** On acceptance.

OUR LITTLE FRIEND

P.O. Box 5353, Nampa, ID 83653. 208-465-2580.
E-mail: ailsox@pacificpress.com. Web site: www.pacificpress.com. Aileen Andres Sox, Editor. **Description:** Spiritually oriented magazine written for children who attend Seventh-day Adventist Sabbath School. **Nonfiction:** Stories must be from a Christian perspective and consistent with Seventh-day beliefs and practices. Use positive tone; 1-2 pages; $25-$50. **Tips:** "The best stories are those that help children develop a personal relationship with God. Please see detailed guidelines on our Web site." **Queries:** Not necessary. **Rights:** One-time. **Payment:** On acceptance.

PASSPORT

6401 The Paseo, Kansas City, MO 64131. 816-333-7000.
E-mail: jjsmith@nazarene.org. Circ.: 18,000. Emily Freeburg, Editor. **Description:** Full-color newspaper for preteens with resources for spiritual transformation and holy living. Corresponds with WordAction Sunday School materials (for 11-12 year olds). **Nonfiction:** Articles for grades 5-6 on hot topics and relevant issues; 400-600 words; $30 for main features. **Fillers:** $15 for cartoons and puzzles. **Queries:** Preferred. **E-Queries:** Yes. **Unsolicited mss:** Accepts. **Response:** 6-8 weeks, SASE required. **Freelance Content:** 30%. **Rights:** Multi-use. **Payment:** On publication. **Contact:** Julie J. Smith, Editorial Assistant.

POCKETS

1908 Grand Ave., P.O. Box 340004, Nashville, TN 37203-0004. 615-340-7333.
E-mail: pockets@upperroom.org. Web site: www.pockets.org. 11x/yr. $19.95/yr. Circ.:

90,000. Janet Knight, Editor. **Description:** Interdenominational publication seeking to promote the Gospel of Jesus Christ to children 6-11 and help them grow in their relationship with God. Readers include children of many cultures and ethnic backgrounds. These differences should be reflected in the stories (lifestyles, names, living environments, etc.) **Fiction:** Stories to help children deal with everyday life. Prefers real-life settings; no talking animals or inanimate objects; 600-1,400 words; $.14/word. **Nonfiction:** Theme for each issue. Profiles of persons whose lives reflect Christian commitment and values; articles about children involved in environmental, community, peace/justice issues; 400-1000 words; $.14/word. **Fillers:** Puzzles, games (on theme); $25 and up. **Columns, Departments:** Pocketsful of Love and Pocketsful of Prayer; $.14/word. **Tips:** Looking for puzzles and activities on themes (see Web site). Publishes 1 story in each issue for children 5-7 years. No more than 600 words. For sample copy send 9x12 SASE (4 first-class stamps). **E-Queries:** No. **Unsolicited mss:** Accepts. **Response:** SASE. **Freelance Content:** 90%. **Payment:** On acceptance. **Contact:** Lynn Gilliam, Associate Editor.

PRIMARY TREASURE
P.O. Box 5353, Nampa, ID 83653. 208-465-2580.
E-mail: ailsox@pacificpress.com. Web site: www.pacificpress.com. Aileen Andres Sox, Editor. **Description:** Spiritually oriented magazine written for children who attend Seventh-day Adventist Sabbath School. **Nonfiction:** Stories must be from a Christian perspective and consistent with Seventh-day beliefs and practices. Use positive tone; 4 pages; $25-$50. **Tips:** "The best stories are those that help children develop a personal relationship with God. Please see detailed guidelines on our Web site." **Queries:** Not necessary. **Rights:** One-time. **Payment:** On acceptance.

RANGER RICK
National Wildlife Federation
11100 Wildlife Center Dr., Reston, VA 20190. 703-438-6000.
Web site: www.nwf.org. Monthly. $17/yr. Circ.: 550,000. Gerald Bishop, Editor. **Description:** Write or e-mail for photo and art guidelines. No unsolicited queries or manuscripts.

SOCCER JR.
See full listing in Sports & Recreation/Outdoors category.

SCHOLASTIC CHOICES
555 Broadway, New York, NY 10012-3919. 212-343-6434.
E-mail: choicesmag@scholastic.com. Web site: www.scholastic.com. 8x/yr. $8.50/student with a minimum order of 10 copies per month. Circ.: 140,000. Bob Hugel, Editor. **Description:** Classroom magazine aimed at teen audience. Covers life skills, nutrition, health, substance abuse, family issues, peer relationships, careers, and consumer economics. Articles run 800-1,500 words; $600-$1,000. **Queries:** Preferred. **E-Queries:** No. **Unsolicited mss:** Does not accept. **Response:** 2 months, SASE. **Freelance Content:** 90%. **Rights:** All. **Payment:** On publication.

SHINE BRIGHTLY

P.O. Box 7259, Grand Rapids, MI 49510.
E-mail: sara@gemsgc.org. Web site: www.gospelcom.net/gems. Sara Lynne Hilton, Editor. **Description:** Upbeat fiction and features, 500-1,000 words, for Christian girls ages 8-14. Topics include personal life, nature, crafts, etc. Pays $.03/word, extra for photos. Also accepts puzzles; $10-$15. **Tips:** Send SASE for upcoming themes and writer's guidelines. **Queries:** Not necessary. **E-Queries:** No. **Unsolicited mss:** Accepts. **Payment:** On publication.

SKIPPING STONES

P.O. Box 3939, Eugene, OR 97403. 541-342-4956.
E-mail: editor@skippingstones.org. Web site: www.skippingstones.org. 5x/yr. $25/yr. Circ.: 2,500. Arun N. Toké, Executive Editor. **Description:** Original writing, art, and photography. Encourages cooperation, creativity, celebration of cultural diversity, and nature awareness. **Fiction:** Social awareness, interpersonal relationships; to 750 words. **Nonfiction:** Nature awareness, multicultural education, social responsibility, travelogues, journal entries; to 750 words. **Poetry:** By authors under age 19 only; on nature, social issues, reflections; to 30 lines. **Fillers:** Multicultural, nature; 150 words. **Art:** Original B&W or color prints with captions or photo essays. **Tips:** Include personal information in cover letter (i.e., cultural background, languages you speak, source of inspiration for submission) "We invite writing and art that promote multicultural awareness and/or ecological understanding, sustainable living, creative problem solving, peace, and justice. Send for guidelines." **Queries:** Not necessary. **E-Queries:** Accepts. **Unsolicited mss:** Accepts. **Response:** Queries to 1 month, submissions to 3 months, SASE. **Freelance Content:** 80%. **Rights:** 1st serial, non-exclusive reprint. **Payment:** In copies.

SPIDER

Carus Publishing Co.
315 Fifth St., P.O. Box 300, Peru, IL 61354-0300. 815-224-5803, ext. 656.
Web site: www.cricketmag.com. Monthly. $5/$35.97. Circ.: 76,000. Heather Delabre, Associate Editor. **Description:** Stories, articles, poems, and activities for children. Original artwork fills each issue. **Fiction:** Easy-to-read, realistic stories (fantasy, myths, fairy tales, fables, and science fiction). **Nonfiction:** Interviews, profiles, and how-to articles on science, animals, nature, technology, etc. **Art:** Art (especially children, animals, action, scenes from a story); photography (photo essays or article illustrations), color preferred, B&W considered. **Tips:** Looking for more fiction submissions, also activity ideas, puzzles, and jokes. **Queries:** Does not accept. **E-Queries:** No. **Unsolicited mss:** Accepts. **Response:** 12 weeks, SASE required. **Freelance Content:** 95%. **Rights:** Vary. **Payment:** On publication.

SPORTS ILLUSTRATED FOR KIDS

Time, Inc., 135 W 50th St., New York, NY 10020-1201. 212-522-1212.
E-mail: kidletters@sikids.com. Web site: www.sikids.com. Monthly. $2.99/$29.95. Circ.: 1,002,000. Neil Cohen, Managing Editor. **Description:** On the excitement,

joy, and challenge of sports, for boys and girls, ages 8-14. Action photos, interactive stories, profiles, puzzles, playing tips. Also, drawings and writing by kids. **Nonfiction:** Current, biographical, sports-related pieces; 500-700 words; $500-1,250. **Columns, Departments:** 300-500 words. **Art:** Photos, illustrations (submit non-returnable portfolio). **Queries:** Required. **E-Queries:** Yes. **Unsolicited mss:** Accepts. **Response:** 4-6 weeks, SASE required. **Rights:** Exclusive. **Payment:** 40% on acceptance, 60% on publication. **Contact:** Sean Nicholls.

STONE SOUP

P.O. Box 83, Santa Cruz, CA 95063-0083. 831-426-5557.
E-mail: editor@stonesoup.com. Web site: www.stonesoup.com.
Bimonthly. $5.50/$33. Circ.: 20,000. Gerry Mandel, Editor. **Description:** Stories, poems, book reviews, and art by young writers and artists, ages 8-13. **Fiction:** Personal narratives, arrival stories, family histories, sport stories, science fiction; 2,500 words; $40. **Nonfiction:** Book reviews by children under 14. Prefers writing based on real-life experiences. **Poetry:** Free-verse only; $40. **Art:** Work by kids ages 8-13 only; send 2-3 samples (photocopies OK). **Tips:** Do not send SASE w/ manuscript; will respond if interested. Sample copy $4. **Queries:** Not necessary. **E-Queries:** No. **Unsolicited mss:** Accepts. **Response:** Queries 2-3 weeks, submissions 4 weeks. **Freelance Content:** 100%. **Rights:** All. **Payment:** On publication.

STORY FRIENDS

Faith and Life Press/Mennonite Publishing House
616 Walnut Ave, Scottdale, PA 15683. 724-887-8500.
Monthly. Circ.: 6,000. Susan Reith Swan, Editor. **Description:** For ages 4-9, a general-interest magazine that promotes and reinforces traditional values taught by Christian families. **Fiction:** Realistic stories that empower children to face fears, resolve conflicts, creatively solve problems, and help them enjoy and care for things in nature; 300-800 words; $.03/word. **Nonfiction:** About animals, unusual nature facts, children in action, crosscultural experiences; 100-300 words; $.03/word. **Poetry:** Seasonal, humorous, active poems about ordinary things and events in children's lives; 6-12 lines; $10/poem. **Fillers:** Short and simple crafts and activities, age-appropriate puzzles. **Tips:** Humor and unique treatment of problem helps to break into this market. Avoid talking animals, "naughty children" stories, and preachiness. Avoid stories where adults provide the solution or explanation, respect younger characters' strength and ingenuity. Also, many parents of these readers have lived in third-world countries and value cross-cultural understanding. **Queries:** Not necessary. **E-Queries:** No. **Unsolicited mss:** Accepts. **Response:** SASE. **Freelance Content:** 70%. **Rights:** 1st, one-time. **Payment:** On acceptance.

TURTLE MAGAZINE

See full listing in Health category.

U MAGAZINE

9800 Fredericksburg Rd., San Antonio, TX 78288. 800-531-8013.
E-mail: umag@usaa.com. Circ.: 400,000. Julie Finlay, Editor. **Description:**
Quarterly, on topics of general interest to 9-12 year old dependents of USAA members. Past themes: citizenship, relationships, saving/managing money, and family business. Articles, 100-300 words; pay varies. **Tips:** "Know the children's market, including trends among the audience. Be aware, however, that our magazine is not about fashion and doesn't bank on fads or pop culture." **Queries:** Preferred. **E-Queries:**
Yes. **Unsolicited mss:** Does not accept. **Response:** 6 weeks, SASE. **Freelance Content:** 10%. **Rights:** All. **Payment:** On publication.

U.S. KIDS: A WEEKLY READER MAGAZINE

Children's Better Health Institute
1100 Waterway Blvd., P.O. Box 567, Indianapolis, IN 46206-0567. 317-634-1100.
E-mail: d.lee@cbhi.org. Web site: www.uskids.com. 6x/yr. $21.95/yr. Circ.: 250,000.
Daniel Lee, Editor. **Description:** For kids, ages 6-10. True-life stories, science/nature features, health/fitness, kids in the news, color photos, and lots of fun games, activities, and contests. **Fiction:** Science fiction, nature, etc.; 700 words; $.17/word. **Nonfiction:** Looking for profiles on interesting, regular kids (no celebrities), ages 5-10, involved in unusual pursuits (sports, adventures, science); 500-600 words; pay varies. **Tips:** Avoid counter culture, irony/sarcasm, depressing topics. Stay upbeat and wholesome. **Queries:** Preferred. **E-Queries:** Yes. **Unsolicited mss:**
Accepts. **Response:** 12 weeks, SASE required. **Freelance Content:** 20%. **Rights:**
All. **Payment:** On publication.

WILD OUTDOOR WORLD (W.O.W.)

P.O. Box 1329, Helena, MT 59624-1329. 406-449-1335.
E-mail: wowgirl@qwest.net. Web site: www.wowmag.com. 5x/yr. $14.95. Circ.:
200,000. Carolyn Underwood, Editorial Director. **Description:** North American wildlife, habitat, recycling, outdoor adventure for readers ages 8-12. **Nonfiction:**
Articles, 600-700 words; pays $50-$200. **Tips:** Used as a science supplement in many classrooms. Seeks stories that encourage environmental ethics, respect for wildlife, appreciation for importance of habitat protection. Especially interested in kids "making a difference" for the environment, whether large-scale or backyard project.
Queries: Preferred. **E-Queries:** Yes. **Rights:** FNAR and electronic. **Payment:** On acceptance.

YES MAG

3968 Long Gun Place, Victoria, British Columbia V8N 3A9 Canada. 250-477-5543.
E-mail: editor@yesmag.ca. Web site: www.yesmag.ca. Bimonthly. $3.50/$19.95
(Canadian). Circ.: 18,000. Shannon Hunt, Editor. **Description:** Canadian children's science magazine. Makes science accessible, interesting, and exciting, for children ages 8-14. Covers science and technology news, do-at-home projects, science-related book and software reviews, profiles of Canadian students and scientists. **Nonfiction:**
Science, technology, engineering, and math articles for kids, ages 8-14; 250-1,250

words; $.20/word. **Tips:** Seeking imaginative, fun, well-researched pieces. Be specific in query; ideally send an outline of the article, indicating how you will approach the topic. **Queries:** Preferred. **E-Queries:** Yes. **Unsolicited mss:** Accepts. **Response:** 6 weeks, SASE required. **Freelance Content:** 60%. **Rights:** One-time. **Payment:** On publication.

YOUNG RIDER
Fancy Publications
496 Southland Dr., Lexington, KY 40503. 859-260-9800.
E-mail: lward@fancypubs.com. Web site: www.youngrider.com. Bimonthly. $15/yr. Circ.: 41,000. Lesley Ward, Editor. **Description:** About horses and children. **Nonfiction:** Horse health, grooming tips, interesting breeds and famous horses, show-ring secrets, how to improve their riding skills, celebrity rider interviews; 1,200 words; $140. **Art:** Photos. **Tips:** Query or send manuscript. **Queries:** Not necessary. **Unsolicited mss:** Accepts. **Payment:** On publication.

LIFESTYLES

BALANCE MAGAZINE
P.O. Box 8608, Ft. Lauderdale, FL 33310-8608. 954-382-4325.
E-mail: publisher@balancemagazine.com.
Web site: www.balancemagazine.com. Quarterly. $20/yr. Circ.: 40,000. Susie Levan, Editor. **Description:** *Balance Magazine: Personal Growth for Women* is a "health, wealth, and happiness" magazine. Strives to provide straightforward, expert, and motivational solutions to pressing issues facing baby boomers. **Nonfiction:** Short articles on self-development and personal growth; 750-1,500 words; **Tips:** Send submissions in an e-mail attachment. Send 15-word bio. **Queries:** Preferred. **E-Queries:** Yes. **Unsolicited mss:** Accepts.

BLUE MAGAZINE
611 Broadway, New York, NY 10012. 212-777-0024.
E-mail: editorial@bluemagazine.com. Web site: www.bluemagazine.com. Bimonthly. $19.95. Circ.: 100,000. Claire Hochachka, Executive Editor. **Description:** Explores the world through travel and adventure sports. Described by one reviewer as *"National Geographic* with a rock-and-roll soundtrack." **Nonfiction:** Features in 3 categories: Blue Planet, Blue Nation, and Blue Asphalt. Exploration is key, whether a profile of coal miners of Bolivia, or inline skating through Central Park. **Tips:** "A well-written query is a good start. Convey your idea in a 500-word pitch; include any appropriate writing samples. We rely on freelance contributions and we're seeking new writers stationed in exotic locales with great stories to tell—who feel that life is, well, an adventure." **Queries:** Preferred. **E-Queries:** Yes. **Unsolicited mss:** Accepts. **Freelance Content:** 100%.

BUDGET LIVING

317 Madison Ave., New York, NY 10017-5204. 212-687-6060.
E-mail: editorial@budgetlivingmedia.com. Web site: www.budgetlivingmedia.com.
Bimonthly. $14.95/yr. Circ.: 300,000. Alex Bhattacharji, Editor. **Description:**
Lifestyle magazine for 25-40 year olds. Features travel, fashion, entertaining, finance,
home decorating. **Nonfiction:** Quirky, funny, off-the-beaten trail, personality-driven
creative ways of living cheaply (or people who do), also personal essays.

DIVERSION

The Hearst Corp., 1790 Broadway, Fl. 6, New York, NY 10019. 212-969-7517.
E-mail: ewetschler@hearst.com. Web site: www.diversion.com. Monthly. $60/yr.
Circ.: 185,000. Ed Wetschler, Editor-in-Chief. **Description:** Lifestyle magazine for
physicians. Does not accept articles on health-related subjects, but does accept features and profiles of doctors who excel at nonmedical pursuits and who do volunteer
medical work. **Nonfiction:** Sports, books, electronic gear, gardening, photography,
art, music, film, television, travel, food, and humor; 1,800 words; $1,000. **Columns,
Departments:** 1,100 words; $650. **Art:** Do not send originals or slides. **Tips:** Query
first with brief proposal explaining story focus and include credentials/clips of published work. **Queries:** Required. **E-Queries:** No. **Unsolicited mss:** Accepts.
Response: SASE required. **Payment:** On acceptance.

FIFTY PLUS

1510 Willow Lawn Dr., Suite 203, Richmond, VA 23230-3429. 508-752-2512.
E-mail: rpmag@aol.com. Web site: www.fiftyplusadvocates.com. Monthly. $15/yr. Circ.:
30,000. Sandra Shapiro, Editor. **Description:** Reflects and enhances 50-plus lifestyles
in Virginia region, with reader dialogue and input. **Queries:** Required. **E-Queries:**
Yes. **Response:** 2-4 weeks, SASE. **Rights:** 1st (regional). **Payment:** On publication.

INMOTION

Amputee Coalition of America
900 E Hill Ave., Suite 285, Knoxville, TN 37915. 865-524-8772.
E-mail: editor@amputee-coalition.org. Web site: www.amputee-coalition.org.
Bimonthly. $30/yr. Circ.: 40,000. Nancy Carroll, Editor. **Description:** Covers topics
of interest to amputees such as new technology, inspirational profiles, etc. Articles, to
2,000 words; $.25/word. **Payment:** On publication.

INSIDE MAGAZINE

2100 Arch St., Philadelphia, PA 19102-3392. 215-832-0797.
E-mail: mledger@insidemagazine.com. Quarterly. $3.50$10.95. Circ.: 60,000. Robert
Leiter, Editor. **Description:** Focuses on Jewish lifestyle. Covers ethnic interest, as
well as lifestyle subjects (fashion, home, health, finance, travel, dining). **Fiction:** 2,000
words; $350. **Nonfiction:** On Jewish issues, health, finance, and the arts; 2,000-3,000
words; $500. **Art:** $250, illustrations. **Tips:** "Write gracefully for upscale readers.
Teach something useful." **Queries:** Preferred. **E-Queries:** Yes. **Unsolicited mss:**
Accepts. **Freelance Content:** 80%. **Rights:** 1st only. **Payment:** On publication.

LIVING ABOARD

P.O. Box 91299, Austin, TX 78709-1299. 512-892-4446.
E-mail: editor@livingaboard.com. Web site: www.livingaboard.com. Bimonthly.
$18/yr. Circ.: 10,000. Linda Ridihalgh, Editor. **Description:** Lifestyle magazine for
those who live or dream of living on their boats. **Nonfiction:** Articles, 1,000-2,000,
on personal experience or practical information about living aboard; pays $.05/word.
Tips: Send complete manuscript with bio and credits; e-mail or disk submissions preferred. **Payment:** On publication.

LIVING WEST

5444 Westheimer, Suite 1440, Houston, TX 77056. 713-296-7900.
E-mail: livingwest@southwestart.com. Web site: www.livingwestmag.com. Margaret
Brown Pickworth, Editor. **Description:** Lifestyle magazine for those who live in the
Western region of the U.S. Features articles on architecture, home decor, gardening,
fashion, cuisine, and art.

MOTHER EARTH NEWS

1503 SW 42nd St., Topeka, KS 66609-1265.
E-mail: letters@motherearthnews.com. Web site: www.motherearthnews.com.
Bimonthly. $18/yr. Circ.: 320,000. Cheryl Long, Editor. **Description:** Publication
that emphasizes resourceful living and country skills for rural residents and urbanites
who aspire to a more independent lifestyle. **Nonfiction:** Articles on do-it-yourself
living, gardening, home building and repair, natural health, cooking, hobbies, and outdoor living; 300-3,000 words; $.30/word. **Tips:** Submit seasonal material 5 months in
advance. Review magazine before submitting material. **Queries:** Required.
E-Queries: Yes. **Response:** 6 months. **Payment:** On acceptance.

MOTORHOME

See full listing in Travel Articles category.

MOUNTAIN LIVING

7009 S Potomac St., Englewood, CO 80112-4037. 303-662-5211.
E-mail: irawlings@mountainliving.com. Web site: www.mountainliving.com. 6x/yr.
$3.95/issue. Circ.: 38,000. Irene Rawlings, Editor. **Description:** Features lifestyle
pieces for people who live in the mountains or who dream of living there. Articles on
home, garden, travel, architecture, art, and cuisine. **Tips:** Make sure your query
reflects the content of the magazine. Preview magazine or visit Web site to see the
kind of material that is published. "Our magazine is very specialized; writers cannot
break in without having a sense of the kinds of things we publish. Read the magazine.
Avoid clichés." **Queries:** Required. **E-Queries:** Yes. **Unsolicited mss:** Accepts.
Response: 4 weeks. **Freelance Content:** 50%. **Rights:** FNASR. **Payment:** On
acceptance.

NATURAL HOME

See full listing in Home & Garden category.

POSITIVE THINKING

66 E Main St., Pawling, NY 12564. 845-855-5000.
E-mail: azaengle@guideposts.org. 10x/yr. Circ.: 400,000. Patricia M. Planeta, Editor. **Description:** Magazine with inspirational messages. **Nonfiction:** First-person stories, an emphasis on faith or positive thinking. Practical how-to pieces; to 2,300 words; pay varies. **Tips:** Send SASE for sample copy or writer's guidelines. **Queries:** Preferred. **E-Queries:** Yes. **Unsolicited mss:** Accepts. **Rights:** One-time. **Payment:** On publication. **Contact:** Ann Zaengle.

REUNIONS MAGAZINE

P.O. Box 11727, Milwaukee, WI 53211-0727. 414-263-4567.
E-mail: reunions@execpc.com. Web site: www.reunionsmag.com. Bimonthly. $6/$24. Circ.: 12,000. Edith Wagner, Editor. **Description:** For persons who are organizing and making decisions for their family, class, military, or other reunions. Features, 1,000-1,500 words. **Nonfiction:** Reunion tips and techniques (e.g. how to make a memory book sparkle, how to cook for 150 people, and where to go/what to do when you get there). **Fillers:** Brief tips/hints; Clippings (about reunions); funny reunion material; reunion puzzles (appropriate for reunions). Examples: photo preservation, should you invite teachers?, time capsules, hot ideas, etc.; 500 words or less; $5-$10. **Tips:** "We use more short material than long. Subject must be reunions —don't bother with anything else. No fiction, unless it's reunion stories for children." **Queries:** Not necessary. **E-Queries:** Yes. **Response:** over 2 years at present, SASE. **Freelance Content:** 70%. **Rights:** FNAR. **Payment:** On publication.

ROBB REPORT

1 Acton Pl., Acton, MA 01720. 978-264-7500.
Web site: www.robbreport.com. Monthly. $65. Circ.: 100, 000. Larry Bean, Editor. **Description:** Consumer magazine for high-end luxury market. Lifestyles, home interiors, boats, travel, investment opportunities, exotic automobiles, business, technology, etc. **Nonfiction:** Geared to affluent lifestyles (travel, fashion, automobiles, etc.); 150-1,500 words. **Queries:** Required. **E-Queries:** No. **Unsolicited mss:** Accepts. **Response:** 1-3 months, SASE. **Freelance Content:** 75%. **Rights:** All. **Payment:** On acceptance.

7X7 MAGAZINE

59 Grant, Fl. 4, San Francisco, CA 94108. 415-362-7797.
E-mail: edit@7x7mag.com. Web site: www.7x7mag.com. 10x/yr. $3.50/$10. Richard Perez-Feria, Editor-in-Chief. **Description:** San Francisco lifestyle magazine with focus on food/wine, travel, fashion design, and local celebrities. **Queries:** Preferred. **E-Queries:** Yes. **Unsolicited mss:** Accepts. **Freelance Content:** 5%. **Rights:** FNAR. **Payment:** On publication. **Contact:** Editorial Department.

SOUTHERN ACCENTS

See full listing in Home & Garden category.

SUNSET MAGAZINE

80 Willow Rd., Menlo Park, CA 94025. 650-321-3600.
E-mail: openhouse@sunset.com. Web site: www.sunset.com. Monthly. $4.50. Circ.: 1,400,000. Katie Tamony, Editor. **Description:** Regional magazine for Western America, covering travel and recreation; garden and outdoor living; food and entertaining; building, design, and crafts. **Nonfiction:** Looking for well-written stories and Travel Guide items offering satisfying travel experiences accomplished in a day or weekend, or as part of a vacation, in American West, also parts of Canada and Mexico. 4 month lead-time. 300-1,000 words; $1/word. **Queries:** Preferred. **E-Queries:** No. **Unsolicited mss:** Does not accept. **Response:** 1-3 months, SASE required. **Freelance Content:** 5%. **Payment:** On acceptance.

TOWN & COUNTRY

The Hearst Corp., 1700 Broadway, New York, NY 10019-5905. 212-903-5000.
E-mail: tnc@hearst.com. Web site: www.tncweddings.com. Monthly. $24/yr. Circ.: 436,000. Pamela Fiori, Editor. **Description:** Articles for upscale market covering travel, beauty, fashion, individuals, and the arts. **Tips:** Considers 1-page proposals; include clips and resume. **Queries:** Required. **Unsolicited mss:** Does not accept. **Freelance Content:** 40%. **Payment:** On acceptance.

TRAILER LIFE

2575 Vista Del Mar, Ventura, CA 93001. 805-667-4100.
E-mail: bleonard@affinitygroup.com. Web site: www.trailerlife.com. Monthly. $3.99. Circ.: 280,000. Barbara Leonard, Editor. **Description:** New product information and vehicle tests, do-it-yourself articles, plus exciting travel and lifestyle features for RVers. **Nonfiction:** Features on trailers, motorhomes, truck campers used by active adventurous travelers, interesting destinations and on-the-road hobbies. 200-2,000 words; $100-$600. **Fillers:** 50-1,000 words; $75-$400. **Art:** 35mm, 2¼; $75-$250; $500-$700 (cover). **Tips:** Supply good 35mm slides and submit a complete package. **Queries:** Required. **E-Queries:** No. **Response:** 2-3 weeks, SASE required. **Freelance Content:** 45%. **Rights:** FNAR and electronic. **Payment:** On acceptance.

WHOLE LIFE TIMES

21225 Pacific Coast Hwy, Suite B, P.O. Box 1187, Malibu, CA 90265. 310-317-4200.
E-mail: editor@wholelifetimes.com. Web site: www.wholelifetimes.com. Monthly. Free. Circ.: 58,000. Abigail Lewis, Editor-in-Chief. **Description:** Covers issues of concern to "Cultural Creatives." Articles on alternative health/healing, environment, food/nutrition, personal growth, spirituality, and progressive social change. Prefers pieces dealing with the Southern California area. **Nonfiction:** To 2,000 words; pays $75-$750 depending on length and scope of story. **Tips:** Understand the holistic mindset. Readers are fairly sophisticated; avoid "Yoga 101." **Queries:** Not necessary. **E-Queries:** Yes. **Unsolicited mss:** Accepts. **Response:** 1 month-1 year, SASE. **Freelance Content:** 75%. **Rights:** FNAR. **Payment:** 30 days after publication. **Contact:** Kerri Hikida, Associate Editor.

WIRED

Condé Nast Publications
520 Third St., Fl. 3, San Francisco, CA 94107-1815. 415-276-5000.
E-mail: editor@wiredmag.com. Web site: www.wired.com/wired. Monthly. $39.95/yr.
Circ.: 500,000. Chris Anderson, Editor-in-Chief. **Description:** Lifestyle magazine
for the "digital generation." Discusses the meaning and context of digital technology
in today's world. **Nonfiction:** Articles, essays, profiles, etc.; pay varies. **Payment:** On
acceptance.

MEN'S

ADAM

4517 Harford Rd., Baltimore, MD 21214. 410-254-9200.
E-mail: adameditor@aol.com. Web site: adam-mag.com. Bimonthly. $9.97/yr. Tom
Dworetzky, Editor. **Description:** For men, ages 21-35. Offers creative nonfiction,
opinion, personal experience, informational and self-help articles, profiles, and interviews. **Nonfiction:** Articles on history, video, audio, music, relationships, electronics,
computers, sports, and entertainment; 1,500-2,000 words; $350-$400. **Columns,
Departments:** 500-800 words; $300. **Tips:** Avoid first-person, and use quotes from
experts. **Queries:** Preferred. **E-Queries.** Yes. **Response:** 2-4 weeks, SASE
required. **Freelance Content:** 50%. **Rights:** 1st. **Payment:** On publication.

BLACK MEN

210 E State Rt. 4, Suite 211, Paramus, NJ 07652-5103. 201-843-4004.
Bimonthly. $4.50/$18. Circ.: 150,000. Kate Ferguson, Editor-in-Chief. **Description:**
Lifestyle magazine aimed at African-American men, age 18-49. Editorial focus is on
sex/dating, health/fitness, sports, current events, business, personal finance, community affairs, arts, entertainment, and fashion. **Columns, Departments:** Accepts freelance work for "Sista Speak" department which features issue-oriented essays from
women concerning love, sex, relationships, and other matters of importance to
African-American men; 750 words. **Tips:** "Avoid submitting/querying articles which
don't fit in our format. Writers should submit queries in July and August because
September is the month we produce our editorial calendar for the upcoming year. An
interesting idea could be picked up and result in an assignment for a writer at this
time." **Queries:** Preferred. **E-Queries:** No. **Unsolicited mss:** Accepts. **Rights:**
FNAR. **Payment:** On publication.

ESQUIRE

The Hearst Corp.
250 W 55th St., New York, NY 10019-5201. 212-649-4020.
E-mail: esquire@hearst.com. Web site: www.esquire.com. Monthly. $15.94/yr. Circ.:
679,000. David Granger, Editor-in-Chief. **Description:** For intelligent adult male
readers. **Fiction:** Short stories; submit only 1 at a time. No pornography, science

fiction, poetry, or "true romance." Pay varies. **Nonfiction:** 2,500-6,500 words; Pay varies. **Tips:** Query with clips; unpublished writers, send complete manuscripts. **Queries:** Required. **Payment:** On publication.

GQ: GENTLEMEN'S QUARTERLY

Condé Nast Publications, Inc.
4 Times Square, New York, NY 10036-6518. 212-286-2860.
E-mail: gqmag@aol.com. Web site: www.gq.com. Monthly. $19.97. Circ.: 898,508. Arthur Cooper, Editor-in-Chief. **Description:** General-interest magazine on the life of the man. Covers politics, personalities, lifestyles, trends, grooming, sports, travel, business, and fashion. **Nonfiction:** 1,500-4,000 words. **Columns, Departments:** Private Lives (essays by men on life); Games (sports); Guy Food (food with recipes); Health; Humor; also on fitness, nutrition, investments, and music. 1,000-2,500 words. **Tips:** Send clips. **Queries:** Required. **Unsolicited mss:** Does not accept.

HEARTLAND U.S.A.

100 W Putnam Ave. Greenwich, CT 06830-5342. 203-622-3456.
E-mail: husaedit@ustnet.com. Bimonthly. $10/yr. Circ.: 1,200,000. Brad Pearson, Editor. **Description:** General-interest lifestyle magazine edited specifically for the active adult male interested in the outdoors. Seeks to address readers' traditional American lifestyles, interests, and values by providing compelling stories and covering a diverse range of topics such as sports, fishing, hunting, automotive, Western/rodeo, and human interest. Articles run 1,200 words; pays $.25-$1/word. **Art:** Send 35mm or larger format. Fee negotiable. **Tips:** "We are currently overstocked, so we aren't very aggressive in looking for new contributors. We offer a free sample to freelancers and encourage all prospective contributors to review it thoroughly for voice and style." **E-Queries:** Yes. **Response:** 1 month, SASE required. **Freelance Content:** 95%. **Rights:** FNAR. **Payment:** On acceptance.

MEN'S JOURNAL

1290 Avenue of the Americas, New York, NY 10104-0298. 212-484-1616.
E-mail: letters@mensjournal.com. Web site: www.mensjournal.com. 12x/year. $14.97/yr. Circ.: 635,000. Sid Evans, Editor. **Description:** Lifestyle magazine for active men, ages 25-49. **Nonfiction:** Articles and profiles on travel, fitness, health, adventure, and participatory sports; 2,000-7,000 words; good rates. **Columns, Departments:** Equipment, Fitness; 400-1,800 words. **Queries:** Required. **Payment:** On acceptance.

PENTHOUSE

11 Penn Plaza, Fl. 12, New York, NY 10001. 212-702-6000.
Web site: www.penthousemag.com. Monthly. $46. Circ.: 980,000. Bob Guccione, Editor-in-Chief. **Description:** Essays, sociological studies, travel, humor, food, and fashion, for the sophisticated male. **Fiction:** No unsolicited fiction. **Nonfiction:** General-interest profiles, interviews (with introduction), and investigative or contro-

versial pieces; to 5,000 words; to $1/word. **Queries:** Preferred. **Contact:** Peter Bloch, Editor.

PLAYBOY

9320 Wilshire Blvd., Suite 302, Beverly Hills, CA 90212. 310-786-7400. E-mail: articles@playboy.com. Monthly. Circ.: 3,125,000. Stephen Randall, Executive Editor. **Description:** Magazine for urban men. **Fiction:** Sophisticated fiction, 1,000-10,000 words (5,000 preferred). Pays $2,000 for short-shorts. Barbara Wellis, Fiction Editor. **Nonfiction:** Articles; 3,500-6,000 words; pays to $5,000. **Queries:** Required. **E-Queries:** No. **Unsolicited mss:** Does not accept. **Response:** 1 month, SASE. **Rights:** FNASR. **Payment:** On acceptance.

MEN'S FITNESS

See full listing in Fitness Magazines category.

MEN'S HEALTH

See full listing in Health category.

MILITARY

AIR COMBAT

230 Dale Place, Fullerton, CA 92833. 714-522-7590. Web site: www.aircombatusa.com. Bimonthly. Michael O'Leary, Editor. **Description:** Articles on latest warplanes and the men who fly them, recent air battles, and America's aerial involvement in Vietnam. **Tips:** Send for guidelines. **Queries:** Preferred.

AMERICA'S CIVIL WAR

See full listing in History category.

ARMOR

Bldg. 1109 A Sixth Ave., Room 371, Fort Knox, KY 40121-2103. 502-624-2249. Bimonthly. $20/yr. Circ.: 12,500. Christy Bourgeois, Managing Editor. **Description:** Professional magazine of the Armor Branch for military units and agencies responsible for direct-fire ground combat. **Nonfiction:** Military history; research and development of armaments; tactical benefits and strategies, logistics, and related topics. **Art:** Write captions on paper and tape to the back of the photos (don't write on photo backs). Indicate if you want the photos returned. **Tips:** Does not offer payment. **Response:** 2 weeks.

ARMY MAGAZINE

2425 Wilson Blvd., Arlington, VA 22201-3385. 703-841-4300. E-mail: armymag@ausa.org. Web site: www.ausa.org. Monthly. Circ.: 85,000. Mary Blake French, Editor-in-Chief. **Description:** Military subjects, essays, humor, history (especially Korea and World War II), news reports, first-person anecdotes. **Nonfiction:** 1,500 words; $.12-$.18/word. **Fillers:** Cartoons, strong military slant; $35-$50. **Columns, Departments:** Military news, books, commentary. **Art:** 35mm slides, 8x10 B&W; 8x10 color glossy prints; pay varies. **Queries:** Not necessary. **E-Queries:** No. **Unsolicited mss:** Accepts. **Freelance Content:** 70%. **Rights:** All. **Payment:** On publication.

ARMY RESERVE

2400 Army Pentagon, Washington, DC 20310-2400. 703-601-0854.
E-mail: usarmag@ocar.army.pentagon.mil. Quarterly. Circ.: 450,000. **Description:** Publication emphasizing the training and employment of Army Reservists. **Art:** Uses 80-120 photos/issue. Seeks photos related to the mission or function of the U.S. Army Reserve; 5x7 color prints; 35mm transparencies; high resolution digital photos. **Tips:** Seeks well-written articles accompanied by high-quality photos.

LEATHERNECK MAGAZINE

P.O. Box 1775, Quantico, VA 22134-0776. 703-640-6161.
E-mail: leatherneck@mca-marines.org. Web site: www.mca-marines.org. Monthly. $19/yr. Circ.: 96,800. Walter G. Ford, Editor. **Description:** On U.S. Marines. **Nonfiction:** Articles, to 2,500 words, with photos; pays $75/printed page. **Queries:** Preferred. **Payment:** On publication.

MARINE CORPS GAZETTE

P.O. Box 1775, Quantico, VA 22134. 703-640-6161.
E-mail: gazette@mca-marines.org.
Web site: http://mca-marines.org/Gazette/gaz.html. Monthly. $3.50/$29. Circ.: 29,000. Jack Glasgow, Editor. **Description:** Professional journal of U.S. Marines, oriented toward officers and senior enlisted personnel; provides a forum for open discussion and a free exchange of ideas relating to the U.S. Marine Corps and military capabilities. Articles run 750-1,500 words. **Tips:** Does not offer payment. **Queries:** Preferred. **E-Queries:** Yes. **Unsolicited mss:** Accepts. **Response:** 2-4 weeks. **Freelance Content:** 80%. **Rights:** All.

MHQ: QUARTERLY JOURNAL OF MILITARY HISTORY

See full listing in History category.

MILITARY

2122 28th St., Sacramento, CA 95818. 916-457-8990.
E-mail: generalinfo@milmag.com. Web site: www.milmag.com. Monthly. $16/yr. Circ.: 20,000. Armond Noble, Publisher/Editor. **Description:** Military history (WWII, Korea, Vietnam, and today). A conservative publication, prided in printing the truth, dedicated to all who served in the armed forces. **Nonfiction:** Personal war experiences; 4,000 words or less. **Fillers:** Humor in uniform, military humor; 1,000 words or less. **Art:** 200 dpi or better. **Tips:** No payment offered. Sample copy available for no charge. **Queries:** Preferred. **E-Queries:** Yes. **Unsolicited mss:** Accepts.

MILITARY OFFICER
See full listing in Seniors Magazines category.

NATIONAL GUARD
National Guard Assn.
One Massachusetts Ave. NW, Washington, DC 20001-1402. 202-789-0031.
E-mail: magazine@ngaus.org. Web site: www.ngaus.org. Monthly. $20. Circ.: 45,000.
Richard Alexander, Publisher. **Description:** Articles on national defense.
Nonfiction: Pay varies. **Queries:** Preferred. **Payment:** On publication.

SIGNAL
4400 Fair Lakes Court, Fairfax, VA 22033-3899. 703-631-6100.
E-mail: signal@afcea.org. Web site: www.afcea.org/signal. Monthly. $56. Circ.: 30,000.
Maryann Lawlor, Senior Editor. **Description:** Focuses on communications, electronics in the information systems arena. Readers include military, industry, and government leadership. **Nonfiction:** Communications/electronics issues within military, industry, and government; 1,400-2,500 words; $650 for 1,800 words. **Art:** Must include art with submission. **Tips:** Only works with published writers. **Queries:** Required. **E-Queries:** Yes. **Unsolicited mss:** Accepts. **Response:** 1-4 months, SASE required. **Freelance Content:** 10%. **Rights:** FNAR. **Payment:** On publication.

TIMES NEWS SERVICE
Army Times Publishing Co.
Springfield, VA 22159. 703-750-7479.
E-mail: gwillis@atpco.com. Web site: www.militarycity.com. Weekly. $2.25/$52. Circ.: 300,000. G.E. Willis, Features Editor. **Description:** Publishes *Air Force Times, Army Times, Navy Times* (Gannett weeklies serving the military community, covering breaking developments that affect the careers of readers). **Nonfiction:** Features on contemporary home and family life in the military. Recreation, finances, parenting, etc.; up to 1,500 words; up to $500. **Columns, Departments:** Fitness for young and athletic people; personal finance for moderate incomes; 500 words; $200. **Art:** color slides, electronic (high-res JPG); $75/image. **Tips:** Pitch an original story, interesting and entertaining, with a military connection, preferably with military people in the story. **Queries:** Required. **E-Queries:** Yes. **Unsolicited mss:** Does not accept. **Response:** Queries 2-8 weeks, submissions 1-3 weeks, SASE. **Freelance Content:** 75%. **Payment:** On acceptance.

VFW
See full listing in Associations category.

VIETNAM
See full listing in History category.

WORLD WAR II
See full listing in History category.

NEW AGE & SPIRITUAL

ALIVE NOW

P.O. Box 340004, Nashville, TN 37203-0004. 615-340-7218.
E-mail: alivenow@upperroom.org. Web site: www.alivenow.org. Bimonthly.
$3.50/$14.95. Circ.: 70,000. Melissa Tidwell, Editor. **Description:** For people who
are hungry for a sacred way of living. Each issue focuses on contemporary topic,
explored through prayers, personal experiences, poetry, photographs, and art.
Nonfiction: Personal experiences of how contemporary issues affect spiritual life,
meditations on scripture, prayers, and litanies; 350-600 words; $40-$150. **Poetry:** On
the issue's theme; 40 lines or less; $25-$100. **Tips:** "See Web site for coming themes.
Material unrelated to themes is not considered. Use inclusive language and personal
approach. Readership is clergy and lay, across denominations and theological spectrum." **Queries:** Not necessary. **E-Queries:** Yes. **Unsolicited mss:** Accepts.
Freelance Content: 30%. **Rights:** Serial (print and electronic). **Payment:** On
acceptance.

AQUARIUS

1035 Green St., Roswell, GA 30075. 770-641-9055.
E-mail: aquarius-editor@mindspring.com. Web site: www.aquarius-atlanta.com.
Monthly. Free at newsstands; $30/year. Circ.: 50,000. Kathryn Sargent, Editor.
Description: Seeks to expand awareness and support all those seeking spiritual
growth. **Nonfiction:** On astrology, divination, alternative spirituality, energy healing,
genetically engineered foods, intentional communities, meditation, yoga, herbs,
aromatherapy, etc.; 850 words. **Poetry:** Up to 850 words. **Fillers:** Cartoons, puzzles.
Art: Cover art, full color, light tones; JPGs, transparencies. **Tips:** Avoid spaceships,
aliens, channeled communications, lots of biblical quotations. **Queries:** Preferred.
E-Queries: Yes. **Unsolicited mss:** Accepts. **Response:** 1 month for queries, varies
for submissions; SASE required. **Freelance Content:** 90%.

BODY & SOUL

42 Pleasant St., Watertown, MA 02472. 617-926-0200.
E-mail: editor@newage.com. Web site: www.bodyandsoulmag.com. Bimonthly.
$4.95/$14.95. Circ.: 225,000. **Description:** Serves as a guide for all those who want
to live healthier, more balanced lives **Nonfiction:** Alternative medicine, natural
foods, self-help psychology, spirituality, mind/body connection, right livelihood, and
green politics; 1,500-3,500 words; up to $1,500. **Fillers:** Short news items; 50-250
words; $50. **Columns, Departments:** Holistic Health, Food/Nutrition, Spirit,
Home, Community, Travel, Life Lessons; 600-1,300 words. Book and music reviews;
200-750 words. **Art:** Photographs to accompany articles. **Tips:** Include recent clips
and resume. **Queries:** Preferred. **E-Queries:** No. **Unsolicited mss:** Accepts.
Response: 8 weeks; SASE required. **Freelance Content:** 90%. **Rights:** FNASR
and electronic. **Payment:** On acceptance. **Contact:** Christine Richmond, Editorial
Assistant.

FATE

P.O. Box 460, Lakeville, MN 55044. 800-728-2730.
E-mail: fate@fatemag.com. Web site: www.fatemag.com. Monthly. $4.95/$29.95. Circ.: 35,000. Phyllis Galde, Editor. **Description:** Covers the strange and unknown, for people willing to believe that unexplainable things happen. **Nonfiction:** True reports of the strange and unknown; 1,500-5,000 words; $.10/word. **Fillers:** Briefs on unusual events, odd folklore; up to 1,500 words; $.10/word. **Columns, Departments:** My Proof of Survival (true personal accounts of survival after death); True Mystic Experiences (personal accounts of unexplained happenings); up to 1,000 words; $25. **Tips:** "Much of our content contributed by readers." **Queries:** Preferred. **E-Queries:** Yes. **Response:** Queries 6 weeks, submissions 3 months, SASE required. **Freelance Content:** 80%. **Rights:** All. **Payment:** On publication.

MAGICAL BLEND

133-1/2 Broadway St., Chico, CA 95928-5317. 888-296-2442.
E-mail: editor@magicalblend.com. Web site: www.magicalblend.com. Bimonthly. $19.95/yr. Circ.: 105,000. Michael Langevin, Editor. **Description:** Offers an entertaining and unique look at modern spiritual lifestyles. **Nonfiction:** Positive, uplifting articles on spiritual exploration, alternative health, social change, self improvement, stimulating creativity, lifestyles, and interviews; 2000 words max. **Art:** Hard or digital copies (233-3,000 dpi). **Tips:** "No preaching." **Queries:** Not necessary. **E-Queries:** Yes. **Unsolicited mss:** Accepts. **Response:** Queries 1-3 months, submissions 1-6 months. **Freelance Content:** 90%. **Payment:** On publication.

THE MOUNTAIN ASTROLOGER

P.O. Box 970, Cedar Ridge, CA 95924.
E-mail: editorial@mountainastrologer.com. Web site: www.mountainastrologer.com. Bimonthly. $7/issue; $36/year. Circ.: 55,000. Nan Geary, editor. **Description:** Astrology magazine. **Nonfiction:** Articles, book reviews, humor, and astrological forecasts. **Columns, Departments:** Article Particles (only area which does not require a query): short anecdotal material, chart interpretation tips, poetry, humorous pieces, and cartoons. **Art:** Charts and illustrations to accompany articles. **Queries:** Required. **E-Queries:** Yes. **Unsolicited mss:** Does not accept. **Response:** 30-45 days. **Rights:** One-time.

MYSTERIES MAGAZINE

13 Appleton Rd., Nantucket, MA 02554. 603-352-1645.
E-mail: editor@mysteriesmagazine.com. Web site: www.mysteriesmagazine.com. Quarterly. Circ.: 6,000. Kim Guarnaccia, Editor/Publisher. **Description:** Articles on historical mysteries, the paranormal, conspiracies, archaeology, the occult, and scientific discoveries. **Nonfiction:** Feature articles (3,000-5,000 words) and book reviews (500 words). Pays $.05/word. **Art:** Prefers electronic format for submissions. Pays $5/image. **Tips:** "Inquire first, preferably by e-mail, with article ideas." **Queries:** Preferred. **E-Queries:** Yes. **Response:** 3-5 weeks, SASE. **Freelance Content:** 60%. **Rights:** FNAR. **Payment:** On publication.

PANGAIA

P.O. Box 641, Point Arena, CA 95468-0641. 707-882-2052.
E-mail: editor@pangaia.com. Web site: www.pangaia.com. Quarterly. Circ.: 7,000. Anne Newkirk Niven, Publisher. **Description:** Explores Pagan and Gaian Earth-based spirituality. Features essays, poetry, rituals, plays, interviews, articles, and art-work. **Nonfiction:** Activism, ecology, legends, magic, mythology, prayer, rituals, shamanism. 500-5,000 words; $.01/word. **Columns, Departments:** Toe to Toe, Scientific Mysticism, Pathfinders, and Sacred Space. **Tips:** Query for guidelines. **Queries:** Preferred. **Contact:** Elizabeth Barrette, Managing Editor.

PARABOLA

Society for Study of Myth & Tradition
656 Broadway, New York, NY 10012-2317. 212-505-9037.
E-mail: editors@parabola.org. Web site: www.parabola.org. Quarterly. $24/yr. Circ.: 40,000. Natalie Baan, Managing Editor. **Description:** "The magazine of myth and tradition." Thematic issues present essays and retellings of traditional myths and fairy tales. **Nonfiction:** Articles on myth, symbol, and spiritual teachings; to 3,000 words. Retellings of traditional stories; to 1,500 words. Pay varies. **Tips:** Contact for upcoming themes and guidelines. Seeks a balance between scholarly and accessible writing, on the ideas of myth and tradition. **Queries:** Preferred.

SAGEWOMAN

P.O. Box 469, Point Arena, CA 95468. 707-882-2052.
E-mail: editor@sagewoman.com. Web site: www.sagewoman.com. Quarterly. $6.95/$21. Circ.: 25,000. Anne Newkirk Niven, Editor. **Description:** Publishes articles that help women explore spiritual, emotional, and mundane lives and respect all people, creatures, and Earth. "Celebrates the Goddess in every woman." **Nonfiction:** On women's spiritual experience; focuses on issues of concern to pagan and other spiritually minded women; 1,000-5,000 words. **Tips:** "We prefer inquiries and submissions by e-mail. Please read a copy before submitting; features must be written to an upcoming theme." **Queries:** Not necessary. **E-Queries:** Yes. **Unsolicited mss:** Accepts. **Response:** 1-3 months, SASE required. **Freelance Content:** 80%. **Rights:** First worldwide serial. **Payment:** On publication.

SCIENCE OF MIND

3251 W Sixth St., P.O. Box 75127, Los Angeles, CA 90075-0127. 213-388-2181.
E-mail: edit@scienceofmind.com. Web site: www.scienceofmind.com. Monthly. Circ.: 68,000. Randall Friesen, Editor/Publisher; Amanda Pisani, Editor. **Description:** Thoughtful perspective on how to experience greater self-acceptance, empowerment, and a meaningful life. **Nonfiction:** Inspiring first-person pieces, 1,000-2,000 words. Interviews with notable spiritual leaders, 3,500 words.

SPIRITUALITY & HEALTH

74 Trinity Pl., New York, NY 10006.
E-mail: editor@spiritualityhealth.com. Web site: www.spiritualityhealth.com. Betsy

Robinson, Associate Editor. **Description:** Covers the people, practices, and ideas of the spiritual renaissance in contemporary society and their impact on personal and community well-being. Short department pieces, 100-600 words; features, 1,000-2,500 words. Fees negotiated, based on length, complexity, author experience, etc. **Tips:** "We look for articles that are useful, educational, rich in information, full of news. Read writer's guidelines and be familiar with our magazine." **E-Queries:** Yes.

VENTURE INWARD
215 67th Ave., Virginia Beach, VA 23451. 757-428-3588.
E-mail: letters@edgarcayce.org. Web site: www.edgarcayce.org. Bimonthly. Circ.: 35,000. Kevin J. Todeschi, Editor-in-Chief. **Description:** Membership magazine for Edgar Cayce organizations (A.R.E., Edgar Cayce Fdn., Atlantic Univ.), on holistic health, spiritual development, mystical experiences, and Cayce philosophy (reincarnation, etc.). **Nonfiction:** Personal mystical or holistic health experiences; to 3,000 words; $300-$400. **Columns, Departments:** Guest Column (opinion, to 800 words); Turning Point (a personal turning-point experience, to 800 words); The Mystical Way (a personal paranormal experience, to 1,500 words); Holistic Health (brief accounts of success using Edgar Cayce remedies); book reviews, to 500 words. Pays $50-$400. **Queries:** Required. **E-Queries:** Yes. **Unsolicited mss:** Does not accept. **Response:** 2-4 weeks, SASE required. **Freelance Content:** 75%. **Payment:** On publication.

WHOLE LIFE TIMES
See full listing in Lifestyle Magazines category.

PERFORMING ARTS

ACOUSTIC GUITAR
P.O. Box 767, San Anselmo, CA 94979. 415-485-6946.
E-mail: editors.ag@stringletter.com. Web site: www.acousticguitar.com. Monthly. $29.95/yr. Circ.: 54,600. Simone Solondz, Editor. **Description:** For players and makers of acoustic guitars. **Tips:** Prefers to receive material from musicians. **Queries:** Preferred.

AMERICAN SQUARE DANCE MAGAZINE
P.O. Box 777, North Scituate, RI 02857-0751. 401-647-9688.
E-mail: asd@squaredance.ws. Web site: www.squaredance.ws. Monthly. $25/yr. Circ.: 12,000. Ed & Pat Juaire, Editors. **Description:** Articles and fiction, 1,000-1,500 words, related to square dancing. Pays $1.50/column inch. **Fillers:** to 100 words.

BACK STAGE
770 Broadway, New York, NY 10003. 646-654-5500.
E-mail: seaker@backstage.com. Web site: www.backstage.com. Sherry Eaker, Editor in Chief. **Description:** "The Performing Arts Weekly." Service features on learning

one's craft, dealing with succeeding in the business, interviews with actors, directors, and playwrights, and industry news/trends. **Nonfiction:** Pay varies. **Queries:** Preferred. **Payment:** On publication.

BLUEGRASS UNLIMITED

P.O. Box 771, Warrenton, VA 20186. 540-349-8181.
E-mail: editor@bluegrassmusic.com. Web site: www.bluegrassmusic.com. Monthly. $24/yr. Circ.: 27,000. Peter V. Kuykendall, Editor. **Description:** Covers bluegrass and traditional country music. **Nonfiction:** Articles; to 3,000 words; pays $.08-$.10/word. **Art:** Photos. **Queries:** Preferred.

CHART

41 Britain St., Suite 200, Toronto, Ontario M5A 1R7 Canada. 416-363-3101.
E-mail: chart@chartattack.com. Web site: www.chartattack.com. Monthly. $3.95/$19.95. Circ.: 40,000. Nada Laskovski, Editor. **Description:** Covers Canada's music and pop culture, with slant to the cutting edge. **Queries:** Preferred.

CLAVIER

The Instrumentalist, 200 Northfield Rd., Northfield, IL 60093. 847-446-5000.
Web site: www.clavier.com. 10x/yr. $19/yr. Circ.: 16,000. Judy Nelson, Editor. **Description:** Professional journal for piano teachers at all levels. **Nonfiction:** Interview/profiles on artists, teachers, composers; teaching articles, music discussion, master classes, and humor pieces for performers and teachers; 8-10 page mss; $80-$100/printed page. **Art:** Color prints, $100/full page. **Tips:** Writers should have music degrees. **Queries:** Preferred. **E-Queries:** No. **Unsolicited mss:** Accepts. **Response:** 4-6 weeks, SASE required. **Freelance Content:** 75%. **Rights:** All. **Payment:** On publication.

COUNTRY WEEKLY

118 16th Ave. S, Suite 230, Nashville, TN 37203. 615-259-1111.
Web site: www.countryweekly.com. 26x/yr. $29.95. Circ.: 388,000. Neil Pond, Editor. **Description:** Features on the country music and entertainment industry, with industry news and profiles of musicians and other personalities in the field. **Art:** Clear, sharp, color transparencies. Varies. **Queries:** Required. **E-Queries:** Yes. **Rights:** All. **Payment:** On publication.

DANCE MAGAZINE

111 Myrtle St., Suite 203, Oakland, CA 94607-2535. 510-839-6060.
E-mail: editorial@dancemagazine.com. Web site: www.dancemagazine.com. Monthly. $34.95/yr. Circ.: 55,000. K.C. Patrick, Editor-in-Chief. **Description:** Covers all aspects of the world of dance. **Nonfiction:** On dancers, companies, history, professional concerns, health, news events. **Tips:** Freelance content limited. One sample copy available at no charge. **Queries:** Preferred. **E-Queries:** Yes.

DANCE SPIRIT

250 W 57th St., Suite 420, New York, NY 10107. 212-265-8890.
E-mail: editor@dancespirit.com; sjarrett@lifestyleventures.com.
Web site: www.dancespirit.com. Monthly. Circ.: 100,000. Caitlin Sims, Editorial Director. **Description:** For dancers of all disciplines. Articles on training, instruction and technique, choreography, dance styles, and profiles of dancers; pay varies. **Payment:** On publication. **Contact:** Sara Jarrett.

DANCE TEACHER

250 W 57th St., Suite 420, New York, NY 10107-0499. 212-265-8890.
E-mail: csims@lifestyleventures.com. Web site: www.dance-teacher.com. Monthly. $29.95/yr. Circ.: 20,000. Caitlin Sims, Editor. **Description:** For dance professionals. **Nonfiction:** For educators, students, and professionals; practical information on economic/business issues. Profiles of schools, methods, and people. 500-1,500 words; $100-$300. Photos helpful. **Tips:** All articles must be thoroughly researched. **Queries:** Preferred. **E-Queries:** Yes. **Unsolicited mss:** Accepts. **Freelance Content:** 70%.

DRAMATICS MAGAZINE

Educational Theatre Assn.
2343 Auburn Ave., Cincinnati, OH 45219-2815. 513-421 3900.
E-mail: dcorathers@edta.org. Web site: www.edta.org. Monthly September-May. $20/yr. Circ.: 37,000. Don Corathers, Editor. **Description:** Magazine for high school theatre students. **Fiction:** One-act and full-length plays for high school production; $100-$400. **Nonfiction:** Articles on acting, directing, playwriting, and technical subjects. Also interviews and book reviews. Pays $25-$400. **Tips:** Does not publish didactic scripts or musicals. Be aware of the script's production demands. Readers are active theatre students and teachers. **Queries:** Not necessary. **Unsolicited mss:** Accepts. **Freelance Content:** 70%. **Rights:** FNASR. **Payment:** On acceptance.

ELECTRONIC MUSICIAN

PRIMEDIA Business Magazines & Media
P.O. Box 1929, Marion, OH 43306. 510 653-3307.
E-mail: emeditorial@primediabusiness.com. Web site: www.emusician.com. Monthly. $36/yr. Circ.: 71,000. Steve Oppenheimer, Editor-in-Chief. **Description:** On audio recording, live sound engineering, technical applications, and product reviews. **Nonfiction:** Articles, 1,500-3,500 words; pays $350-$750. **Payment:** On acceptance.

FLUTE TALK

200 Northfield Rd., Northfield, IL 60093. 847-446-5000.
Monthly. $2. Circ.: 13,000. Victoria Jicha, Editor. **Description:** For flute teachers or performers. **Nonfiction:** Interviews with players, teachers, composers; other articles on flute playing; 3-5 pages; $90-$100/printed page. **Art:** Slides, color prints. **Queries:**

Preferred. **E-Queries:** No. **Unsolicited mss:** Accepts. **Response:** Queries 1 week, submissions 1 month, SASE required. **Payment:** On publication.

GLORY SONGS

One LifeWay Plaza, Nashville, TN 37234. 800-458-2772.
E-mail: don.schlosser@lifeway.com. Don Schlosser, Editor. **Description:** Choral music, for volunteer and part-time music directors and members of church choirs. Very easy music and accompaniments designed specifically for the small church (4-6 songs per issue). **Queries:** Preferred. **Payment:** On acceptance.

GUITAR PLAYER

2800 Campus Dr., San Mateo, CA 94403. 650-513-4300.
E-mail: guitplyr@musicplayer.com. Web site: www.guitarplayer.com. Monthly. $24/yr. Circ.: 143,000. Michael Molenda, Editor. **Description:** On guitars and related subjects. Articles run from 200 words, $100-$600. **Rights:** All. **Payment:** On acceptance. **Contact:** Emily Fasten, Managing Editor.

GUITAR ONE

6 E 32nd St., Fl. 6, New York, NY 10016.
E-mail: editors@guitaronemag.com. Web site: www.guitaronemag.com. Monthly. $19.95/yr. Circ.: 137,000. Chris O'Byrne, Associate Editor. **Description:** For serious guitarists. **Queries:** Preferred.

INTERNATIONAL MUSICIAN

American Federation of Musicians
120 Walton St., Syracuse, NY 13202-1179. 315-422-0900.
E-mail: afollett@afm.org. Web site: www.afm.org. Monthly. $25. Circ.: 110,000. Antoinette Follett, Managing Editor. **Description:** Official publication of AFM. Targets professional musicians. **Queries:** Required. **Payment:** On acceptance.

JAZZIZ

2650 N Military Trail, Suite 140, Boca Raton, FL 33431-6339. 561-893-6868.
E-mail: mkoretkzy@jazziz.com; dhogerty@jazziz.com. Web site: www.jazziz.com. Monthly. $69.95. Circ.: 172,000. Michael Fagien, Editor-in-Chief. **Description:** Jazz-lifestyle music publication. Features, interviews, profiles, and concept pieces on contemporary smooth jazz, adult alternative, world-Brazilian, Afro-Cuban, Latin, traditional, and straight ahead genres of jazz. Pay varies. **Columns, Departments:** Reviews of varied music genres, radio, and video; mostly new releases. Pay varies. **Tips:** Send resume with manuscript. **E-Queries:** Yes. **Freelance Content:** 80%. **Payment:** On acceptance. **Contact:** Mike Koretzky, Assignment Editor; Dave Hogerty, Creative Director.

KEYBOARD MAGAZINE

2800 Campus Dr., San Mateo, CA 94403-2506. 650-513-4300.
E-mail: keyboard@musicplayer.com. Web site: www.keyboardonline.com. Monthly.

Circ.: 72,000. Greg Rule, Editor-in-Chief. **Description:** On keyboard instruments, MIDI and computer technology, and players. **Nonfiction:** Articles, 300-5,000 words, photos; pays $200-$600. **Queries:** Preferred. **Payment:** On acceptance.

LA FACTORIA DE SONIDO

Barrera Publishing, 43 W 38th St., Fl. 5, New York, NY 10018-5515. 212-840-0227. E-mail: sonidocd@aol.com. Web site: www.lafactoriadesonido.com. Bimonthly. $15/yr. Circ.: 120,000. Jennifer Barrera, Executive Editor. **Description:** Hispanic music and art publication. Music events, reviews, interviews, fashion, and clubs focusing on Hispanic music of all kinds.

LIVING BLUES

University of Mississippi, Hill Hall, Room 301, University, MS 38677. 662-915-5742. E-mail: lblues@olemiss.edu. Web site: www.livingblues.com. Bimonthly. $23.95/yr. Circ.: 25,000. Scott Barretta, Editor. **Description:** About living African-American blues artists. **Nonfiction:** Interviews, some retrospective, historical articles, or investigative pieces; 1,500-10,000 words; pays $75-$200. **Art:** Photos. $25-$50. **Queries:** Preferred. **Payment:** On publication.

LOLLIPOP

P.O. Box 441493, Boston, MA 02144-0034. 617-623-5319. E-mail: scott@lollipop.com. Web site: www.lollipop.com. Quarterly. Circ.: 20,000. Scott Hefflon, Editor. **Description:** On music and youth culture. Fiction, essays, and "edgy" commentary. Reviews and interviews related to underground culture. **Nonfiction:** To 2,000 words; pays $25 (for anything over 1,000 words). **Art:** Photos, drawings; $25; **Queries:** Preferred.

MIX

PRIMEDIA Business Magazines & Media
6400 Hollis St., Suite 12, Emeryville, CA 94608. 510-653-3307. E-mail: mixeditorial@primediabusiness.com. Web site: www.mixonline.com. Monthly. $46/yr. Circ.: 53,000. George Peterson, Editorial Director. **Description:** For professionals, on audio, audio post-production, sound production, live sound, and music entertainment technology. **Nonfiction:** Articles, varying lengths; pay varies. **Queries:** Preferred. **Payment:** On publication.

MODERN DRUMMER

12 Old Bridge Rd., Cedar Grove, NJ 07009. 209-239-4140. E-mail: mdinfo@moderndrummer.com. Web site: www.moderndrummer.com. Monthly. $34.97/yr. Circ.: 102,000. Ronald L. Spagnardi, Editor-in-Chief. **Description:** Features drumming how-tos, interviews, and more. Articles run 500-2,000 words; $50-$500. **Payment:** On publication.

OPERA NEWS

The Metropolitan Opera Guild, Inc.

70 Lincoln Ctr. Plaza, New York, NY 10023-6548. 212-769-7080.

E-mail: info@operanews.com. Web site: www.operanews.com. Monthly. $30/yr. Circ.: 100,000. Rudolph S. Rauch, Publisher/Editor. **Description:** On all aspects of opera. Articles run 600-2,500 words; pay varies. **Queries:** Preferred. **Payment:** On publication.

PERFORMING ARTS AND ENTERTAINMENT IN CANADA

See full listing in Film, TV, Entertainment category.

PLAYS

Kalmbach Publishing Co., P.O. Box 600160, Newton, MA 02460. 617-332-4063.

E-mail: lpreston@playsmag.com. Web site: www.playsmag.com. Elizabeth Preston, Editor. **Description:** "The drama magazine for young people." Publishes one-act plays, for production by people ages 7-17. Comedies, dramas, farces, skits, holiday plays. Also adaptations of classics, biographies, puppet plays, creative dramatics. No religious themes. Cast: at least 8 characters. Sets should be within the capabilities of amateur set designers (school teachers, students, volunteers). **Tips:** Spec sheet available; send SASE to Kalmbach Publishing Co., P.O. Box 1612, Waukesha, WI, 53187-1612. "Read a copy of magazine to get a feel for the kinds of plays we publish. Plays should be entertaining, even if there is a moral message." **Queries:** Required. **E-Queries:** Yes. **Response:** 1-2 weeks, SASE required. **Freelance Content:** 100%.

ROLLING STONE

1290 Avenue of the Americas, Fl. 2, New York, NY 10104. 212-484-1616.

E-mail: letters@rollingstone.com. Web site: www.rollingstone.com. Biweekly. $17.95/yr. Circ.: 1,254,000. Jann S. Wenner, Editor-in-Chief. **Description:** Magazine of American music, culture, and politics. **Tips:** Rarely accepts freelance material. Read the editorial calendar before pitching. No fiction. **Queries:** Required. **Unsolicited mss:** Does not accept.

SHEET MUSIC MAGAZINE

333 Adams St., Bedford Hills, NY 10507-2001. 914-244-8500.

E-mail: editor@sheetmusicmagazine.com. Web site: www.sheetmusicmagazine.com. Bimonthly. $3.95/$18.97. Circ.: 75,000. Edward J. Shanaphy, Editor-in-Chief. **Description:** For amateur and professional musicians. Most content is the actual reproduction of popular songs (words and music). **Fiction:** On golden era of popular music, 1900-1950; 2,000 words; pay varies. **Nonfiction:** Pieces for pianists, organists, and singers; on musicians, composers, music education, pedagogy; also reviews (to 500 words); no hard rock or heavy metal; 2,000 words; pay varies. **Fillers:** Cartoons on golden era, 1900-1950; $10-$50. **Columns, Departments:** On golden era; keyboard and guitar; how-to; 1,000 words max. **Art:** Hard copy, digital. **Tips:** Avoid modern rock era subjects. **Queries:** Preferred. **E-Queries:** Yes. **Unsolicited mss:** Accepts. **Response:** 2 months, SASE. **Freelance Content:** 50%. **Rights:** Reprint.

STAGE DIRECTIONS

250 W 57th St., Suite 420, New York, NY 10107. 212-265-8890.
E-mail: idorbian@lifestyleventures.com. Web site: www.stage-directions.com. 12x/yr.
$26/yr. Circ.: 7,000. Iris Dorbian, Editor-in-Chief. **Description:** On acting, directing,
costuming, makeup, lighting, set design and decoration, props, special effects,
fundraising, and audience development, for readers active in all aspects of community, regional, academic, or youth theater. Submit how-to articles, to 2,000 words;
$.10/word. **Tips:** "Short pieces, 700-800 words, are a good way to approach us first."
Payment: On publication.

STORYTELLING

101 Courthouse Square, Jonesborough, TN 37659. 423-913-8201.
E-mail: nsn@storynet.org. Web site: www.storynet.org. Bimonthly. $4.95. Circ.:
5,000. Grace Hawthorne, Editor. **Description:** For the professional storyteller;
focuses on the oral tradition. **Nonfiction:** On the oral tradition. 1,000-2,000 words.
Columns, Departments: Unusual events or applications; 200-400 words. **Queries:**
Required. **E-Queries:** Yes. **Unsolicited mss:** Accepts. **Response:** 2 weeks.
Payment: In copies.

SYMPHONY

33 W 60th St., Fl. 5, New York, NY 10023. 212-262-5161.
E-mail: editor@symphony.org. Web site: www.symphony.org. Bimonthly. $35. Circ.:
20,000. Melinda Whiting, Editor-in-Chief. **Description:** Discusses issues critical to
the orchestra community. Communicates to the public the value and importance of
orchestras and their music. **Columns, Departments:** Book and CD reviews; profiles of musicians, orchestras, and conductors; 1,000-3,000 words; $500-$800. **Tips:**
Welcomes new writers. Prefers queries with ideas that can be shaped to match readers' interests. Serves the orchestral industry; while general-interest classical-music
subjects may be of interest, look first for specific orchestral connection before querying. **Queries:** Preferred. **E-Queries:** Yes. **Unsolicited mss:** Accepts. **Response:**
1-90 days, SASE required. **Freelance Content:** 30-50%. **Rights:** FNAR. **Payment:**
On acceptance. **Contact:** Chester Lane, Senior Editor.

TEACHING THEATRE

See full listing in Education category.

THIRSTY EAR MAGAZINE

See full listing in Contemporary Culture category.

URB

2410 Hyperion Ave., Los Angeles, CA 90027. 323-993-0291.
E-mail: word2urb@urb.com. Web site: www.urb.com. 10x/yr. $4.95/$15.95. Circ.:
70,000. Scott Sterling, Editor. **Description:** Covers future music culture: electronic
dance music, independent hip-hop and DJ culture. **Nonfiction:** Features, on dance
and underground hip-hop music (profiles of emerging musicians, singers, and

groups); pays $.10/word. **Tips:** Send published clips. **Queries:** Required. **E-Queries:** Yes. **Response:** 1 month. **Freelance Content:** 80%. **Payment:** On publication.

REGIONAL & CITY

(see also: Business, Environment & Conservation, Family & Parenting,
History, Home & Garden, Seniors,
Sports & Recreation, and Travel
for many regional publications)

ALASKA MAGAZINE

301 Arctic Slope Blvd., Suite 300, Anchorage, AK 99518. 907-275-2100.
E-mail: donnarae@alaskamagazine.com. Web site: www.alaskamagazine.com. Monthly. $30/yr. Circ.: 185,000. Andy Hall, Editor. **Description:** All aspects of life in Alaska. **Nonfiction:** Articles on well-researched, interesting topics. Travel, historical, interview/profile, personal experience, destination pieces, etc.; 1,000-2,500 words; $380-$950. **Tips:** Send SASE for guidelines. **Queries:** Preferred. **Freelance Content:** 70%. **Payment:** On publication. **Contact:** Donna Rae Thompson, Editorial Assistant.

ALBEMARLE

375 Greenbrier Dr., Suite 100, Charlottesville, VA 22901. 804-817-2000.
E-mail: rhart@cjp.com. Web site: www.cjp.com. Bimonthly. Circ.: 10,000. Ruth Hart, Editor. **Description:** Lifestyle magazine highlighting the news and events of Virginia. **Nonfiction:** Topics include health and medicine, the arts, home architecture, interior design, and gardening; pay varies. **Tips:** Write for complete guidelines.

AMERICAN OUTBACK JOURNAL

111 W Telegraph St., Suite 202, Carson City, NV 89703. 775-888-9330.
E-mail: curt@americanoutback.com. Web site: www.americanoutback.com. Curtis Pendergraft, Editor. **Description:** Online publication on the American West. Articles on lore, history, culture, ecology, politics, humor, and travel to offbeat Western destinations. **Queries:** Preferred.

ARIZONA HIGHWAYS

Arizona Dept. of Transportation
2039 W Lewis Ave., Phoenix, AZ 85009. 602-712-2024.
E-mail: queryeditor@arizonahighways.com. Web site: www.arizonahighways.com. Monthly. $3.99/$24 (US),$31 (Canada). Circ.: 325,000. Robert J. Early, Editor. **Description:** Covers travel in Arizona. Pieces on adventure, humor, lifestyles, nostalgia, history, archaeology, Indian culture/crafts, nature, etc. Some Arizona-based fiction on occasion. **Fiction:** Preferably frontier-oriented, upbeat and wholesome (for December and April issues); 1,800-2,500 words; $.55-$1.00/word. **Nonfiction:**

Travel-adventure, travel-history, travel-destination; personal-experience pieces. Insightful and third-person; 800-1,800 words; $.55-$1.00/word. **Fillers:** Jokes (humor page); 200 words or less; $50. **Columns, Departments:** Focus on Nature, Along the Way, Back Road Adventures, Hiking, Destination, Humor. Insightful or nostalgic viewpoint; 800 words; $440-$450. **Art:** 4x5 preferred; landscapes, also images to illustrate a story; pay varies. **Tips:** "To break in, submit short items to our Off-ramp department. Use active verbs. No stories on religion, government, or politics." **E-Queries:** Yes. **Unsolicited mss:** Does not accept. **Response:** 30 days or less, SASE required. **Freelance Content:** 100%. **Rights:** print (online for extra fee). **Payment:** On acceptance.

ARIZONA TRENDS OF THE SOUTHWEST

P.O. Box 8508, Scottsdale, AZ 85252-8508. 480-948-1799.
10x/yr. Circ.: 34,000. Marnie McGann, Editor. **Description:** Features on fashion, health and beauty, special events, dining, the performing arts, and book reviews. **Queries:** Preferred.

ARKANSAS TIMES

201 E Markham, Suite 200, P.O. Box 34010, Little Rock, AR 72203. 501-375-2985. E-mail: arktimes@arktimes.com. Web site: www.arktimes.com. Weekly. $24/yr. Circ.: 32,700. Max Brantley, Editor. **Description:** On Arkansas history, people, travel, politics. **Nonfiction:** Articles, strong Arkansas orientation; to 6,000 words; pays to $500. **Payment:** On acceptance.

ASPEN MAGAZINE

720 E Durant Ave., #E-8, Aspen, CO 81611-2071. 970-920-4040. E-mail: edit@aspenmagazine.com. Web site: www.aspenmagazine.com. Bimonthly. $4.95. Circ.: 18,500. Janet O'Grady, Editor-in-Chief. **Description:** City and regional news about Aspen, Colorado. **Nonfiction:** Lifestyle articles on Aspen, Snowmass, and the Roaring Fork Valley; outdoor sports, arts, profiles, food and wine, environment news, and photos essays related to Aspen and surrounding area. **Tips:** Sample copy $4.95 plus SASE. **Queries:** Required. **E-Queries:** Yes. **Unsolicited mss:** Does not accept. **Response:** 4 weeks, SASE required. **Freelance Content:** 30%. **Payment:** 60 days from publication. **Contact:** Dana R. Butler, Managing Editor.

ATLANTA MAGAZINE

1330 W Peachtree St., Suite 450, Atlanta, GA 30309-3214. 404-872-3100. E-mail: rburns@atlantamag.com. Web site: www.atlantamagazine.com. Monthly. $19.95/yr. Circ.: 65,000. Rebecca Burns, Editor-in-Chief. **Description:** Atlanta subjects or personalities. Articles run 1,500-5,000 words; $300-$2,000. **Queries:** Required. **Payment:** On acceptance.

AVANCE HISPANO

4230 Mission St., San Francisco, CA 94112-1520. 415-585-1080.
Monthly. Circ.: 30,000. **Description:** Spanish-language publication for people in the San Francisco Bay area.

BACK HOME IN KENTUCKY

295 Old Forge Mill Rd., P.O. Box 710, Clay City, KY 40312-0710. 606-663-1011.
6x/yr. $3/$20. Circ.: 8,000. Jerlene Rose, Editor/Publisher. **Description:** Focuses on Kentucky destinations, profiles, personal memories, county spotlights, natural history, and nostalgia. **Nonfiction:** 400-1,000 words; $25 and up. **Columns, Departments:** Chronicles (Kentucky history, 400-1,000 words); $25-$100. **Art:** Slides, photos; $25 and up. **Queries:** Not necessary. **E-Queries:** Yes. **Unsolicited mss:** Accepts. **Response:** 60 days. **Freelance Content:** 75%. **Payment:** On publication.

BALTIMORE MAGAZINE

1000 Lancaster St., Suite 400, Baltimore, MD 21202-4632. 410-752-4200.
E-mail: iken@baltimoremag.com. Web site: www.baltimoremagazine.net. Monthly. $3.50/$15. Circ.: 52,000. Ken Iglehart, Managing Editor. **Description:** Covers Baltimore metro area: local people, events, trends, and ideas. **Nonfiction:** Consumer advice, investigative, lifestyle, profiles, humor, personal experience; 250-4,000 words; $125 and up. **Columns, Departments:** News You Can Use; 800-2,000 words; $200 and up. **Tips:** Consider short articles for departments; send query letter and clips. **Queries:** Required. **E-Queries:** Yes. **Unsolicited mss:** Accepts. **Response:** 1 month for queries, 2 months for submissions; SASE required. **Freelance Content:** 60%. **Rights:** First serial; reprint. **Payment:** On publication.

BIG SKY JOURNAL

P.O. Box 1069, Bozeman, MT 59771-1069. 406-586-2712.
E-mail: bsj@bigskyjournal.com. Web site: www.bigskyjournal.com. Bimonthly. $30/yr. Circ.: 20,000. Michelle A. Steven-Orton, Editor. **Description:** On Montana art and architecture, hunting and fishing, ranching and recreation. **Fiction:** to 4,000 words; **Nonfiction:** Articles, to 2,500 words; pay varies. **Queries:** Preferred. **Payment:** On publication.

BIRMINGHAM

P.O. Box 10127, Birmingham, AL 35202-0127. 205-250-7653.
E-mail: jodonnell@bhammag.com. Web site: www.bhammag.com. Monthly. $12/yr. Circ.: 12,000. Joe O'Donnell, Editor. **Description:** Spotlights events, people, and activities in and around Birmingham. **Nonfiction:** Profiles, business articles, and nostalgia pieces, with local focus. Also, business features, dining, fashion, and general-interest; up to 2,500 words; $50-$175. **Response:** SASE required. **Payment:** On publication.

BLUE RIDGE COUNTRY

P.O. Box 21535, Roanoke, VA 24018. 540-989-6138.
E-mail: krheinheimer@leisurepublishing.com. Web site: www.blueridgecountry.com.
Bimonthly. $3.95/$17.95. Circ.: 90,000. Kurt Rheinheimer, Editor. **Description:**
Embraces the feel and spirit of the Blue Ridge region. **Nonfiction:** On the people,
places, history, and legends of the region; 750-2,500 words; $25-$250. **Art:**
Transparencies; color prints; B&W prints considered; $25-$100 for photo features.
Queries: Preferred. **Response:** 1-2 months, SASE. **Freelance Content:** 70%.
Rights: FNASR. **Payment:** On publication.

BOCA RATON

Amtec Ctr., Suite 100, 6413 Congress Ave., Boca Raton, FL 33487. 561-997-8683.
E-mail: magazine@bocamag.com. Web site: www.bocamag.com. Bimonthly. $20/yr.
Circ.: 20,000. Lisa Ocker, Editor. **Description:** Focuses on southern Florida.
Regional issues, lifestyle trends, relationships, cuisine, travel, fashion, and profiles of
local residents and celebrities. **Nonfiction:** Articles on Florida topics, personalities,
and travel; 800-3,000 words; $350-$1,000. **Tips:** Send query with clips. Guidelines
available. **Queries:** Required. **Response:** SASE required. **Payment:** On acceptance.

THE BOSTON GLOBE MAGAZINE

P.O. Box 2378, 135 Morrissey Blvd., Boston, MA 02107-2378. 617-929-2000.
Web site: www.boston.com/globe/magazine. Weekly. Circ.: 727,000. Nick King,
Editor-in-Chief. **Description:** Covers arts, entertainment, shopping, and news in the
Boston area. **Nonfiction:** 2,500-5,000 words. **Tips:** Send query first. **Queries:**
Preferred. **Unsolicited mss:** Accepts. **Response:** 3 weeks, SASE required.
Freelance Content: Varies. **Rights:** FNAR. **Payment:** On publication.

BOSTON MAGAZINE

300 Massachusetts Ave., Boston, MA 02115. 617-262-9700.
E-mail: editor@bostonmagazine.com. Web site: www.bostonmagazine.com. Monthly.
$9/yr. Circ.: 125,000. Jon Marcus, Editor. **Description:** Offers expository features,
narratives, and articles on Boston-area personalities, institutions, and phenomena. No
fiction. 500-700 words, pays $1/word. **Queries:** Required. **Payment:** On publication.

BOSTONIA

Boston University, 10 Lenox St., Brookline, MA 02446-4042. 617-353-3081.
E-mail: bostonia@bu.edu. Web site: www.bu.edu/alumni/bostonia/index.html.
Quarterly. Circ.: 230,000. Natalie Jacobsone McCracken, Editor-in-Chief.
Description: "The magazine of culture and ideas." General-interest magazine for
alumni covering politics, literature, music, art, science, and education, especially from
a Boston angle. Articles run to 3,000 words; $150-$2,500. **Queries:** Required.

BUFFALO SPREE

5678 Main St., Williamsville, NY 14221. 716-634-0820.
E-mail: info@buffalospree.com. Web site: www.buffalospree.com. Bimonthly. $12/yr.

Circ.: 25,000. Elizabeth Licata, Editor. **Description:** City/regional magazine for western New York. **Nonfiction:** Articles of local interest; to 1,800 words; $125-$150. **Tips:** Unsoliced articles discouraged. **Queries:** Preferred. **Unsolicited mss:** Does not accept. **Freelance Content:** 90%. **Payment:** On publication.

CAPE COD LIFE

4 Barlow Landings Rd., Unit 14, P.O. Box 1385, Pocasset, MA 02559-1385. 508-564-4466. E-mail: jrohlf@capecodlife.com. Web site: www.capecodlife.com. 7x/yr. $19.75/yr. Circ.: 40,000. Brian Shortsleeve, Editor. **Description:** About life on Cape Cod, Martha's Vineyard, and Nantucket (past, present, and future). **Nonfiction:** On events, business, art, history, gardening, lifestyle of region; 800-2,500 words; $.20-$.25/word. **Art:** Transparencies. **Queries:** Preferred. **E-Queries:** Yes. **Unsolicited mss:** Accepts. **Response:** 1-2 months, SASE required. **Freelance Content:** 90%. **Rights:** All. **Payment:** On publication. **Contact:** Janice Randall Rohlf, Managing Editor.

CAROLOGUE

South Carolina Historical Society
100 Meeting St., Charleston, SC 29401-2299. 843-723-3225.
E-mail: info@schistory.org. Web site: www.schistory.org. Quarterly. $50/yr. Circ.: 5,000. Eric Emerson, Editor. **Description:** On South Carolina history. **Nonfiction:** General-interest articles, to 10 pages. **Queries:** Preferred. **Payment:** In copies.

CENTRAL PA

P.O. Box 2954, Harrisburg, PA 17105-2954. 717-221-2800.
E-mail: centralpa@centralpa.org. Web site: www.centralpa.org. Monthly. $45. Circ.: 40,000. Gail Huganir, Managing Editor. **Description:** Topics of interest to central Pennsylvania, including profiles of notable central Pennsylvanians, and broadly based articles of social interest that "enlighten and inform." Articles, 1,500-3,500 words; pays $.10/word. **Tips:** "Strong Central PA connection and excellent writing essential." **Payment:** On publication.

CHARLESTON

P.O. Box 1794, Mt. Pleasant, SC 29465-1794. 843-971-9811.
E-mail: dshankland@charlestonmag.com. Web site: www.charlestonmag.com. Bimonthly. Circ.: 22,000. Darcy Shankland, Editor. **Description:** Nonfiction articles on local topics. **Nonfiction:** Past articles have ranged from winter getaways and holiday gift ideas to social issues like homeless shelters. **Columns, Departments:** In Good Taste, Top of the Shelf, Cityscape, Insight, Doing Business, Native Talent, Chef at Home, On the Road. **Tips:** Send SASE for guidelines. **Queries:** Preferred. **Payment:** 30 days from publication.

CHARLOTTE

Abarta Media Group
127 W Worthington Ave., Suite 208, Charlotte, NC 28203-4474. 704-335-7181.

E-mail: editor@charlottemag.com. Web site: www.charlottemag.com. Monthly. Circ.: 30,000. Richard Thurmond, Editorial Director. **Description:** Covers social, economic, and cultural life of Charlotte and surrounding area. **Nonfiction:** Politics, business, art and entertainment, education, sports, travel, society; pay varies.

CHICAGO MAGAZINE
Tribune Company
500 N Dearborn, Suite 1200, Chicago, IL 60610-4901. 312-222-8999.
E-mail: stritsch@chicagomag.com. Web site: www.chicagomag.com. Monthly. $19.90/yr. Circ.: 181,000. Richard Babcock, Editor. **Description:** Covers topics related to Chicago. Articles run 500-7,000 words; pay varies. **Tips:** Sample copy $6.45. **Queries:** Required. **E-Queries:** Yes. **Payment:** On acceptance. **Contact:** Shane Tritsch, Managing Editor.

CHICAGO READER
11 E Illinois St., Chicago, IL 60611. 312-828-0350.
E-mail: mail@chicagoreader.com. Web site: www.chicagoreader.com.
Description: Free weekly, for residents in the Chicago area. **Fiction:** Accepts. **Nonfiction:** News, commentary, opinion, arts and entertainment criticism; 4,000 words and up. Places to go, things to do, profiles of local people; 400-800 words; $100-$1,000. **Poetry:** Accepts. **Fillers:** Lists, charts, short humor; $75. **Columns, Departments:** First Person, Cityscape, Reading, Neighborhood News; 1,500-2,500 words. **Art:** Photos, cartoons, illustrations; $10-$300. **Queries:** Not necessary. **E-Queries:** Yes. **Unsolicited mss:** Accepts. **Response:** 3-4 weeks. **Rights:** First serial. **Payment:** On publication.

CINCINNATI MAGAZINE
One Centennial Plaza, 705 Central Ave.
Suite 175, Cincinnati, OH 45202-1900. 513-421-4300.
E-mail: editor@cintimag.emmis.com. Monthly. $18.95/yr. Circ.: 32,000. Kitty Morgan, Editor. **Description:** Cincinnati people and issues. **Nonfiction:** 500-3,500 words; $50-$500. **Tips:** Query with writing sample.

CITY AZ DESERT LIVING
342 E Thomas Rd., Phoenix, AZ 85012. 602-667-9798.
E-mail: info@cityaz.com. Web site: www.cityaz.com. Bimonthly. Circ.: 40,000. Leigh Flayton, Executive Editor. **Description:** For Phoenix area professionals, artists, and architecture/design afficionados. Covers food, fashion, travel, etc.; local and national profiles. **Tips:** Send for complete guidelines. **Queries:** Required.

CITY & SHORE
The Sun-Sentinel
200 E Las Olas Blvd., Fort Lauderdale, FL 33301-2293. 954-356-4685.
Web site: www.cityandshore.com. Bimonthly. $25.88. Circ.: 35,000. Mark Gauert, Editor. **Description:** Lifestyle magazine of the *Sun-Sentinel*. **Nonfiction:** Articles

on topics of interest to south Floridians; 1,000-3,000 words; pay varies. **Queries:** Preferred. **Payment:** On acceptance.

COMMON GROUND
P.O. Box 99, 6 W John St., McVeytown, PA 17051-0099. 717-899-6133.
E-mail: commonground@acsworld.net. Quarterly. $3.50/$12.95. Circ.: 9,000. Ruth Dunmire, Pam Brumbaugh, Editors. **Description:** Focuses on Pennsylvania's Juniata River Valley. Nonfiction pieces on hiking destinations, local history, personality profiles; $40/printed page. Also accepts short poetry; $5-$25. **Art:** Prints; $15-$25. **Tips:** Send complete manuscript with illustrations on spec. Read magazine for upcoming themes. **Queries:** Does not accept. **E-Queries:** No. **Unsolicited mss:** Accepts. **Response:** 1 month, SASE required. **Freelance Content:** 90%. **Rights:** FNAR. **Payment:** On publication.

COMMONWEALTH
18 Tremont St., Suite 1120, Boston, MA 02108. 617-742-6800.
E-mail: editor@massinc.org. Web site: www.massinc.org. Quarterly. $5/issue. Circ.: 8,000. Robert Keough, Editor. **Description:** Politics, ideas, and civic life in Massachusetts. Pays $.35-$.50/word **Nonfiction:** On politics, public policy; 3,000 words and up. **Columns, Departments:** Reflective essays on civic life; 800-1,500 words. **Queries:** Preferred. **E-Queries:** Yes. **Unsolicited mss:** Accepts. **Rights:** FNASR. **Payment:** On acceptance.

CONNECTICUT MAGAZINE
Journal Register Company
35 Nutmeg Dr., Trumbull, CT 06611. 203-380-6600.
Web site: www.connecticutmag.com. Monthly. $18/yr. Circ.: 86,675. Charles Monagan, Editor. **Description:** Connecticut topics, issues, people, and lifestyles. **Nonfiction:** 1,500-3,500 words; $500-$1,200. **Payment:** On acceptance.

COUNTY FAMILIES MAGAZINE
P.O. Box 29, Merritt, MI 49667.
E-mail: editor@countyfamilies.com. Web site: www.countyfamilies.com. **Description:** A parenting resource for parents in Crawford, Kalkaska, Missaukee, Ogemaw, Roscommon, and Wexford counties. **Nonfiction:** On positive parenting and supporting parents in their ongoing endeavor to become better parents; 1,200-1,800 words; $50. **Columns, Departments:** Travelin', Laugh Lines, Parent Talk, Teen Scene. **Queries:** Required. **E-Queries:** Yes. **Unsolicited mss:** Does not accept. **Response:** 6 weeks for queries, 8 weeks for submissions; SASE required. **Payment:** 30 days after publication.

DALLASCHILD
4275 Kellway Cir., Suite 146, Addison, TX 75001. 972-447-9188.
E-mail: editorial@dallaschild.com. Web site: www.dallaschild.com. Monthly. **Description:** Addresses the concerns and needs of families, with a special focus on

children from prenatal through adolescence; seeks to inform, educate, entertain, and inspire and provide a provocative discussion forum among parents, the community, and professionals who work with children. **Nonfiction:** Well-informed, local perspectives on issues affecting families. **Queries:** Not necessary. **E-Queries:** Yes. **Unsolicited mss:** Accepts.

DELAWARE TODAY

P.O. Box 2800, Wilmington, DE 19805-0800. 302-656-1809.
E-mail: editors@delawaretoday.com. Web site: www.delawaretoday.com. Monthly. $11.97/yr. Circ.: 25,000. Marsha Mah, Editor. **Description:** On topics of local interest. **Nonfiction:** Service articles, profiles, news, etc. Pays $150 for department pieces, $200-$500 for features. **Tips:** Queries with clips required. **Payment:** On publication.

DURANGO MAGAZINE

P.O. Box 3408, Durango, CO 81302. (p) 970-385-4030, (f) 970-385-4436.
E-mail: drgomag@animas.net. Web site: www.durangomagazine.com. 2x/yr. **Description:** For people who love Durango. **Nonfiction:** Area attractions, history, people, places, events, and culture.

EMERALD COAST

1932 Miccosokee Rd., P.O. Box 1837, Tallahassee, FL 32302-1837. 850-878-0554.
E-mail: editorial@rowlandinc.com. Web site: www.rowlandinc.com. Quarterly. $2.95/$16.95. Circ.: 17,300. **Description:** Lifestyle magazine celebrating life on Florida's Emerald Coast. **Columns, Departments:** Travel, People Profile, What's New (business section), Dining Guide, Sporting Life. **Queries:** Not necessary. **E-Queries:** Yes. **Unsolicited mss:** Accepts. **Response:** 1 week, SASE required. **Freelance Content:** 15%. **Payment:** On publication.

FLORIDA

Orlando Sentinel, 633 N Orange Ave., Orlando, FL 32801. 407-420-5000.
E-mail: mdame@tribune.com. Web site: www.orlandosentinel.com. Mike Dame, Executive Producer. **Description:** Online service of *Orlando Sentinel* newspaper.

FLORIDA MONTHLY

102 Drennen Road, Suite C-5, Orlando, FL 32806. 407-816-9596.
E-mail: editorial@floridamagazine.com. Web site: www.floridamagazine.com. Monthly. $2.99/$21.95. Circ.: 225,000. Jessica Baldwin, Assistant Editor. **Description:** Statewide lifestyle magazine. Articles and columns; 700-2,000 words; pays $.25/word. **Art:** Transparencies; $50 and up. **Queries:** Preferred. **E-Queries:** Yes. **Unsolicited mss:** Accepts. **Response:** 4 weeks, SASE required. **Freelance Content:** 50%. **Rights:** FNAR. **Payment:** On publication.

FREDERICK

6 East St., Suite 301, Frederick, MD 21701.
E-mail: dpatrell@fredmag.com. Web site: www.fredmag.com. Monthly. $2.95/$19.95.

Circ.: 18,000. Dan Patrell, Editor. **Description:** Covers lifestyles and issues in and around Frederick County, Maryland. **Nonfiction:** Articles with a direct link to Frederick County; 800-3,000 words; $100-$300. **Art:** Electronic, transparencies, slides; $25-$300. **Tips:** "Writers have to know Frederick or Frederick County, know the subject about which they are writing and how it directly affects Frederick/Frederick County." **Queries:** Required. **E-Queries:** Yes. **Unsolicited mss:** Does not accept. **Response:** 1-3 months. **Freelance Content:** 90%. **Rights:** FNASR. **Payment:** On publication.

GEORGIA BACKROADS
P.O. Box 127, Roswell, GA 30077. 770-642-5569.
E-mail: info@georgiahistory.ws. Web site: www.georgiahistory.ws. Quarterly. $4.98/$24. Circ.: 18,000. Olin Jackson, Editor. **Description:** For travelers in Georgia, offering travel destinations, leisure lifestyles, and history. **Nonfiction:** Travel, lifestyles, history, and historic real estate; 1,500-3,000 words; $.08-$.15/word. **Columns, Departments:** 1,200 words; $.08-$.15/word. **Art:** 35mm slides; $10/inside use, $150/cover. **Queries:** Required. **E-Queries:** Yes. **Unsolicited mss:** Accepts. **Response:** 2-4 weeks, SASE required. **Freelance Content:** 65%. **Rights:** All. **Payment:** On publication.

GO MAGAZINE
6600 AAA Dr., Charlotte, NC 28212-8250. 704-569-7733.
E-mail: trcrosby@aaaqa.com. Web site: www.aaa.com. 7x/year. for members. Circ.: 750,000. Tom Crosby. **Description:** For AAA members in North and South Carolina. Features on automotive, finance, insurance, and travel. **Columns, Departments:** Travel, auto safety; 750-1,000 words; $.15 /word. **Queries:** Preferred. **E-Queries:** No. **Unsolicited mss:** Accepts. **Response:** 1-3 weeks, SASE. **Freelance Content:** 15%. **Payment:** On publication. **Contact:** Jacquie Hughett, Associate Editor.

GRAND RAPIDS
549 Ottawa NW, Grand Rapids, MI 49503-1444. 616-459-4545.
E-mail: cvalade@geminipub.com. Web site: www.geminipub.com. Monthly. $15/yr. Circ.: 20,000. Carole R. Valade, Editor. **Description:** Covers local area. **Nonfiction:** Service articles (dining guide, travel, personal finance, humor) and issue-oriented pieces. Pays $35-$200. **Queries:** Preferred. **E-Queries:** Yes. **Unsolicited mss:** Accepts. **Payment:** On publication.

GULFSHORE LIFE
9051 Tamiami Trail N, Suite 202, Naples, FL 34108-2520. 941-594-9980.
E-mail: info@gulfshorelifemag.com. Web site: www.gulfshorelifemag.com. Monthly. $25. Circ.: 30,000. Pam Daniel, Editorial Director. **Description:** On Southwest Florida personalities, travel, sports, business, interior design, arts, history, and nature. Articles run 800-3,000 words; $200. **Queries:** Preferred.

HAWAII

1210 Auahi St, Suite 231, Honolulu, HI 96814. 808-589-1515.
E-mail: hawaii@fancypubs.com. Web site: www.hawaiimagazine.com. Bimonthly.
$27.97/yr. Circ.: 75,000. June Kikuchi, Editor. **Description:** Written for both residents and visitors, this magazine covers the culture and lifestyle of Hawaii. Articles feature information on Polynesian heritage and history, current events, restaurants, accommodations, music, festivals, and other activities. **Nonfiction:** Articles, 1,000-2,500 words; pays $.10/word. **Tips:** Accepts very little freelance material. **Queries:** Preferred. **E-Queries:** No. **Payment:** On publication.

HONOLULU MAGAZINE

1000 Bishop St., Suite 405, Honolulu, HI 96813. 808-537-9500.
E-mail: honpub@aloha.net. Web site: www.honolulumagazine.com. Monthly. $15/yr. Circ.: 30,000. John Heckathorn, Editor. **Description:** Regional magazine highlighting contemporary life in the Hawaiian Islands with particular emphasis on the area in and around Honolulu. **Nonfiction:** Feature stories on politics, sports, history, people, arts, and events; $500-$900. **Columns, Departments:** $100-$300. **Tips:** Include 2-3 published clips with query letter explaining your topic and listing your qualifications. "We are not a travel magazine and our readers know the Islands well. We are not a good market for writers whose knowledge of Hawai'i is superficial." **Queries:** Required. **Rights:** All. **Payment:** On publication. **Contact:** A. Kam Napier, Managing Editor.

HUDSON VALLEY

40 Garden St., Fl. 2, Poughkeepsie, NY 12601. 845-485-7844.
E-mail: rsparling@hvmag.com. Web site: www.hudsonvalleymagazine.com.
Description: Covers Albany, Columbia, Dutchess, Greene, Orange, Putnam, Rensselaer, Rockland, Ulster, and Westchester counties in New York state. Features explore the social, cultural, and business issues that most affect Valley residents; 1,500 words; $400. **Tips:** Send query with clips. "We guide the reader to great getaways, fascinating people, and the best in arts and entertainment." **Queries:** Required. **Rights:** All. **Payment:** On publication.

ILLINOIS ENTERTAINER

See full listing in Film, TV, Entertainment category.

IMAGEN

P.O. Box 7487, Albuquerque, NM 87194-7487. 505-889-4088.
Web site: www.imagenmag.com. Monthly. **Description:** "Reflections of Today's Latino." News and profiles of interesting people in the Latino community in New Mexico.

INDIANAPOLIS MONTHLY

One Emmis Plaza, 40 Monument Circle,
Suite 100 NE, Indianapolis, IN 46204-3019. 317-237-9288.

E-mail: contact@indymonthly.emmis.com. Web site: www.indianapolismonthly.com. Monthly. $19.95. Circ.: 45,000. Deborah Way, Editor-in-Chief. **Description:** All material must have an Indianapolis/Indiana focus. **Nonfiction:** Profiles, sports, business, travel, crime, controversy, service, first-person essays, book excerpts; 2,500-4,000 words, $400-$500. **Columns, Departments:** IndyScene (trendy "quick hits"), to 200 words, $50; departments, 1,500-2,500 words, $250-$350. **Payment:** On publication.

THE IOWAN

218 Sixth Ave., Suite 610, Des Moines, IA 50309. 515-282-8220. E-mail: kroberson@iowan.com. Web site: iowan@iowan.com. Bimonthly. $19.95/yr. Circ.: 25,000. Kelly Roberson, Editor. **Description:** Covers history, culture, people, places, and events of Iowa. **Fiction:** Short stories; to 5,000 words; $.30/word. **Nonfiction:** Articles on life in Iowa; to 5,000 words; $.30/word. **Queries:** Not necessary. **E-Queries:** Yes. **Unsolicited mss:** Accepts. **Response:** 24 weeks, SASE required. **Freelance Content:** 80%. **Rights:** One-time NA. **Payment:** On acceptance.

JACKSONVILLE

1032 Hendricks Ave., Jacksonville, FL 32207-8308. 904-396-8666. E-mail: mail@jacksonvillemag.com. Web site: www.jacksonvillemag.com. Monthly. $19.90/yr. Circ.: 25,000. Joseph White, Editor. **Description:** Issues and personalities of interest to readers in the greater Jacksonville area. **Nonfiction:** Home and garden articles on local homeowners, interior designers, remodelers, gardeners, craftsmen, etc.; 1,500-2,500 words; $200-$500. **Columns, Departments:** Business, health, travel, personal finance, real estate, arts and entertainment, sports, dining out, food; 1,200-1,500 words. **Queries:** Required. **Payment:** On publication.

KANSAS CITY

118 Southwest Blvd., Kansas City, MO 64108. 816-421-4111. E-mail: lelmore@abartapub.com. Web site: www.kcmag.com. 12x/yr. $3.50/$9.98. Circ.: 27,000. Leigh Elmore, Editor. **Description:** Celebrates life in Kansas City. **Nonfiction:** Serious piece on local issues, personality profiles, and fun features (Weekend Getaways, etc.); 1,000-3,000 words; $700-$1,000/features. **Columns, Departments:** Excursions (regional travel); Arts (local scene); 1,200 words; $200-$400. **Art:** Prints, transparencies, B&W, JPG. **Tips:** Avoid generic "fit any market" features. **Queries:** Preferred. **E-Queries:** Yes. **Unsolicited mss:** Accepts. **Response:** Queries 2 weeks, submissions 4 weeks. **Freelance Content:** 90%. **Rights:** 1st. **Payment:** On acceptance.

KANSAS! MAGAZINE

Kansas Dept. of Commerce and Housing
1000 SW Jackson St., Suite 100, Topeka, KS 66612-1324. 785-296-3479. E-mail: ksmagazine@kdoch.state.ks.us. Web site: www.travelks.com. Quarterly. $4/$15. Circ.: 45,000. Nancy Nowick Ramberg, Editor. **Description:** Magazine devoted to the state of Kansas. "Our aim is to encourage people to travel through

Kansas to experience its rich history, scenic landscape, exciting attractions, and Midwestern hospitality." **Nonfiction:** Length, pay varies. **Tips:** Avoid politics, religion, sex, and other topics unrelated to travel. **Queries:** Preferred. **E-Queries:** Yes. **Unsolicited mss:** Does not accept. **Freelance Content:** 100%. **Payment:** On acceptance. **Contact:** Shonda Titsworth.

KENTUCKY LIVING

P.O. Box 32170, Louisville, KY 40232. 502-451-2430.
E-mail: e-mail@kentuckyliving.com. Web site: www.kentuckyliving.com. Monthly. $15/year. Circ.: 480,000. Paul Wesslund, Editor. **Description:** On the character and culture of Kentucky. **Nonfiction:** On personalities, history, biography, recreation, travel, and leisure; 1,000 words; $450. **Queries:** Preferred. **E-Queries:** Yes. **Unsolicited mss:** Accepts. **Response:** Queries and submissions 4-6 weeks, SASE required. **Freelance Content:** 75%. **Payment:** On acceptance.

KENTUCKY MONTHLY

213 Saint Clair St., Frankfort, KY 40601. 502-227-0053.
E-mail: membry@kentuckymonthly.com. Web site: www.kentuckymonthly.com. Monthly. $2.95/issue. Circ.: 40,000. Michael Embry, Editor; Stephen M. Vest, Publisher. **Description:** General-interest magazine with focus on the Bluegrass State. **Fiction:** Stories by Kentucky authors or with Kentucky storyline. Has previously published fiction by Sue Grafton, Gwyn Hyman Rubio, and Wendell Berry; 1,000-3,000 words; $50. **Nonfiction:** Profiles of famous Kentuckians, travel, the arts, history, sports, lifestyle, medicine, cooking, gardening, and education. Also features music and book reviews; 300-3,000 words; $25-$300. **Poetry:** Accepts poetry of moderate length; pays in copies. **Art:** Accepts digital photos, prints, and slides; $25/image. **Tips:** "Make sure the story will appeal to all areas of the state." **Queries:** Preferred. **E-Queries:** Yes. **Unsolicited mss:** Accepts. **Response:** 6 weeks, SASE. **Freelance Content:** 75%. **Rights:** FNAR. **Payment:** On publication.

LAKE MICHIGAN TRAVEL GUIDE

P.O. Box 317, 1131 Mills St., Black Earth, WI 53515. 608-767-8000.
E-mail: nwood@wistrails.com. Web site: www.lakemichigantravelguide.com. Annual. $5.95/issue. Circ.: 60,000. Nick Wood, Editor. **Description:** Focused on unique travel opportunities and interesting destinations in the Lake Michigan region of Wisconsin, Michigan, Illinois, Indiana. Publishes regional features as well as brief sketches on culture, events, nature, adventure, dining, lodging, and family fun. 50-3,000 words; $.30/word. **Queries:** Required. **E-Queries:** Yes. **Unsolicited mss:** Does not accept. **Response:** 3-5 months, SASE required. **Freelance Content:** 100%. **Rights:** FNAR. **Payment:** On publication.

LAKE SUPERIOR

P.O. Box 16417, Duluth, MN 55816-0417. 218-727-2765.
E-mail: edit@lakesuprior.com. Web site: www.lakesuperior.com. Bimonthly. $21.95/yr. Circ.: 20,000. Konnie LeMay, Editor. **Description:** Focuses on Lake

Superior region (U.S. and Canada) and its peoples. **Nonfiction:** People, events, and places; 1,000-2,000 words; $100-$600. **Fillers:** Short pieces on Lake life; to 600 words; $50-$125. **Columns, Departments:** Science, history, humor, reminiscences; 600-1,500 words; $50-$225. **Art:** Varied formats; $50 B&W, $40 color, $150 cover. **Tips:** Lake Superior regional topics only. **Queries:** Preferred. **E-Queries:** No. **Unsolicited mss:** Accepts. **Response:** 3-6 months, SASE required. **Freelance Content:** 80%. **Rights:** FNASR. **Payment:** On publication.

LONG ISLAND WOMAN

Box 176, Malverne, NY 11565. 516-897-8900.
E-mail: editor@liwomanonline.com. Web site: www.liwomanonline.com. Monthly. Circ.: 37,000. A. Nadboy, Managing Editor. **Description:** For educated, active women of the Long Island, New York, region. Service-oriented pieces, preferably not first-person. 500-1,500 words; $35-$150. **Tips:** Does not accept submissions over 1,500 words. No phone calls. See Web site for guidelines. **Queries:** Required. **E-Queries:** Yes. **Unsolicited mss:** Accepts. **Freelance Content:** 40%. **Rights:** FNAR. **Payment:** On publication.

THE LOOK

P.O. Box 272, Cranford, NJ 07016-0272. 908-755-6138.
E-mail: jrhawks@thelookmag.com. Web site: www.thelookmag.com. Monthly. Free. Circ.: 3,500. John R. Hawks, Editor. **Description:** New Jersey entertainment magazine. **Nonfiction:** Articles and profiles on fashion, student life, employment, and relationships for readers ages 16-26. Also, beach stories about the New Jersey shore; 1,500-3,000 words; $30-$200. **Fillers:** Puzzles, trivia, and quizzes about area people, places, and events. **Queries:** Preferred. **E-Queries:** Yes. **Unsolicited mss:** Accepts. **Response:** Queries 30-60 days. **Freelance Content:** 50%. **Rights:** All, may reassign. **Payment:** On publication.

LOS ANGELES

5900 Wilshire Blvd., Fl. 10, Los Angeles, CA 90025. 323-801-0100.
E-mail: letters@lamag.com. Web site: www.lamag.com. Monthly. $3.50/$9.95. Circ.: 184,000. Kit Rachlis, Editor. **Description:** The diary of a great city for those enthralled by what the city has to offer and those overwhelmed by it. An essential guide. **Nonfiction:** On politics, business, film, sports, style, events, places; 400-5,000 words; Pay varies. **Tips:** Read the magazine before submitting story ideas. **Queries:** Required. **E-Queries:** Yes. **Unsolicited mss:** Accepts. **Response:** 3-4 weeks, SASE. **Freelance Content:** 50%. **Rights:** FNAR. **Payment:** On acceptance.

LOUISVILLE

137 W Muhammad Ali Blvd., Suite 101, Louisville, KY 40202. 502-625-0100.
Web site: www.louisville.com/loumag.html. Monthly. $3.75. Circ.: 28,000. Bruce Allar, Editor. **Description:** City magazine. **Nonfiction:** Articles on community issues, personalities, and entertainment in the Louisville area; 500-4,000 words; $150-$600.

Queries: Required. E-Queries: Yes. Unsolicited mss: Accepts. Response: 60 days, SASE. Freelance Content: 60%. Rights: FNASR. Payment: On acceptance.

MEMPHIS
P.O. Box 1738, Memphis, TN 38101-1738. 901-521-9000. E-mail: memmag@memphismagazine.com. Web site: www.memphismagazine.com. Monthly. $15/yr. Circ.: 21,000. James Roper, Editor. **Description:** Topics related to Memphis and the Mid-South region: politics, education, sports, business, history, etc. **Nonfiction:** Articles on a variety of subjects. Profiles; investigative pieces; 1,500-4,000 words; $50-$500. **Tips:** SASE for guidelines. **Queries:** Required. **Payment:** On publication.

MICHIGAN LIVING
Automobile Club of Michigan
1 Auto Club Dr., Dearborn, MI 48126-4213. 248-816-9265. E-mail: michliving@aol.com. Web site: www.aaamich.com. Bimonthly. $9/yr. Circ.: 1,030,200. Ron Garbinski, Editor. **Description:** Michigan topics, also area and Canadian tourist attractions and recreational opportunities; 300-2,000 words; $55-$500. No foreign destinations. Query by e-mail only. **Payment:** On publication.

MIDWEST LIVING
Meredith Corp.
1716 Locust St., Des Moines, IA 50309-3038. 515-284-2662. E-mail: mwl@mdp.com. Web site: www.midwestliving.com. Bimonthly. $19.97/yr. Circ.: 822,000. Dan Kaercher, Editor-in-Chief. **Description:** Lifestyle articles relating to any or all of the 12 Midwest states. **Nonfiction:** Town, neighborhood, and personality profiles. Humorous essays occasionally used. Pay varies. **Rights:** All. **Payment:** On acceptance. **Contact:** Greg Philby, Executive Editor.

MILWAUKEE MAGAZINE
417 E Chicago St., Milwaukee, WI 53202. 414-273-1101. E-mail: milmag@qg.com. Web site: www.milwaukeemagazine.com. Monthly. $3/$18. Circ.: 40,000. John Fennell, Editor. **Description:** Offers in-depth reporting and analysis of issues affecting the Milwaukee metro area by providing service features, stories, and essays. **Nonfiction:** Must be specific to Milwaukee area, solid research and reporting; 2,000-5,000 words; $500-$1,000. **Columns, Departments:** Issue-oriented commentary; 900-1200 words; $300-$600. **Queries:** Required. **E-Queries:** Yes. **Unsolicited mss:** Accepts. **Response:** Queries 6 weeks, submission 6 weeks if unsolicited, SASE. **Freelance Content:** 50%. **Rights:** 1st. **Payment:** On publication.

MINNESOTA MONTHLY
730 Second Ave. S, Minneapolis, MN 55402. 612-371-5800. E-mail: phnettleton@mnmo.com. Web site: www.mnmo.com. Monthly. $17.95/issue. Circ.: 80,000. Pamela Hill Nettleton, Editor. **Description:** People, places, events,

and issues in or about Minnesota. Articles, to 2,000 words; $150-$2,000. **Tips:** "Before querying, please see writer's guidelines on Web site for appropriate editor. All stories must have strong Minnesota connection of some kind." Contact Tammy Mitchell (tmitchell@mnmo.com) for sample copy. **Queries:** Required. **E-Queries:** Yes. **Payment:** On acceptance.

MISSOURI LIFE
P.O. Box 421, Fayette, MO 65248. 660-248-3489.
E-mail: info@missourilife.com. Web site: www.missourilife.com. Bimonthly. $4.50/$21.99. Circ.: 20,000. Danita Allen, Editor. **Description:** Explores Missouri and its diverse people and places, past and present. History, weekend getaways and day-trips, interesting people and events. **Nonfiction:** Regular features: Our Town, History, Roundups, People; 1,000-2,000 words; $.20/word. **Fillers:** Best of Missouri; to 300 words; $50. **Columns, Departments:** Missouri Artist, Made in Missouri, Historic Homes, Missouri Memory; 500 words. **Art:** Color slides, photos; $50-$150. **Queries:** Required. **E-Queries:** Yes. **Unsolicited mss:** Accepts. **Response:** Queries 2 weeks, submissions 6 months, SASE required. **Freelance Content:** 40%. **Payment:** On acceptance.

MONTANA MAGAZINE
P.O. Box 5630, Helena, MT 59604. 406-443-2842.
E-mail: editor@montanamagazine.com. Web site: www.montanamagazine.com. Bimonthly. $4.95. Circ.: 40,000. Beverly R. Magley, Editor. **Description:** Full-color photography and articles reflecting the grandeur and personality of Montana. **Nonfiction:** Articles on Montana's culture, history, outdoor recreation, communities, and people. Contemporary issues, places and events, ecology and conservation; 1,500-2,000 words; $.15/word. **Art:** Slides, transparencies, no digital. **Queries:** Required. **E-Queries:** Yes. **Unsolicited mss:** Accepts. **Response:** 4 months, SASE. **Freelance Content:** 90%. **Rights:** one-time. **Payment:** On publication.

MPLS.ST. PAUL
220 S Sixth St., Suite 500, Minneapolis, MN 55402-4507. 612-339-7571.
E-mail: edit@mspcommunications.com. Web site: www.mspmag.com. Monthly. $3.99/issue. Circ.: 72,000. Brian E. Anderson, Editor. **Description:** Covers what is new, exciting, newsworthy in the Twin Cities. **Nonfiction:** Timely local issues, dining/arts/entertainment, home decorating, profiles, etc. **Columns, Departments:** City Limits (news/gossip); About Town (arts and entertainment sidebars). **Queries:** Preferred. **E-Queries:** Yes. **Unsolicited mss:** Accepts. **Response:** 6-8 weeks, SASE required. **Payment:** On acceptance.

NEVADA
401 N Carson St., Suite 100, Carson City, NV 89701-4291. 775-687-5416.
E-mail: editor@nevadamagazine.com. Web site: www.nevadamagazine.com. Bimonthly. $18.95/yr. Circ.: 80,000. David Moore, Editor. **Description:** Covers top-

ics related to Nevada such as travel, history, recreation, profiles, humor, and attractions. **Nonfiction:** 500-1,800 words; pay varies. **Art:** Photos. **Payment:** On publication.

NEW HAMPSHIRE MAGAZINE

150 Dow St., Manchester, NH 03101. 603-624-1442.
E-mail: editor@nh.com. Web site: www.nhmagazine.com. Monthly. $3.95/$20. Circ.: 26,000. Rick Broussard, Editor. **Description:** Covers people, places, issues, and lifestyles of New Hampshire as revealed by the state's best writers, photographers, and artists. **Nonfiction:** Lifestyle, business, and history articles with New Hampshire angle, sources from all regions of the state; 400-2,000 words; $50-$200. **Art:** Prints, slides, negatives, or digital. $25-$300. **Queries:** Preferred. **E-Queries:** Yes. **Unsolicited mss:** Accepts. **Response:** 1 month, SASE required. **Freelance Content:** 30%. **Rights:** 1st serial and online reprint. **Payment:** On publication.

NEW JERSEY MONTHLY

55 Park Place, P.O. Box 920, Morristown, NJ 07963-0920. 973-539-8230.
E-mail: editor@njmonthly.com. Web site: www.njmonthly.com. Monthly. $12/yr. Circ.: 94,000. Kate S. Tomlinson, Editor-in-Chief. **Description:** Publication covering events and news in New Jersey. **Nonfiction:** Well-organized, well-written, thoughtful articles, profiles, and service pieces on a topic that is well-grounded in New Jersey; 200-3,000 words; $150-$2,500. **Columns, Departments:** Health, business, education, travel (within New Jersey), sports, local politics, arts, humor; $400-$1,000. **Tips:** Send query with clips to Christopher Hann, Senior Editor. **Queries:** Preferred. **Contact:** David Chmiel, Editor.

NEW JERSEY REPORTER

Public Policy Center of New Jersey
36 W Lafayette St., Trenton, NJ 08608. 609-392-2003.
E-mail: editor@publicpolicynj.org. Web site: www.njreporter.org. Bimonthly. Circ.: 3,200. Mark Magyar, Editor. **Description:** New Jersey politics and public affairs. In-depth articles 1,000-4,000 words; $175-$800. **Queries:** Required. **Payment:** On publication.

NEW MEXICO

Lew Wallace Bldg., 495 Old Santa Fe Trail, Santa Fe, NM 87501. 505-827-7447.
E-mail: submissions@nmmagazine.com. Web site: www.nmmagazine.com. Monthly. $3.95/$23.95. Circ.: 118,000. Emily Drabanski, Editor-in-Chief. **Description:** About everything New Mexican (products, places, style, history, books, food, recreation, archaeology, Native American culture and ranch life). **Nonfiction:** Regional interest only; 2,000 words max; $.30/word. **Fillers:** Out-of-the way cafes and ranch life. **Art:** Slides, transparencies; pay varies. Send c/o Steve Larese, photo editor. **Tips:** "We work about a year in advance. We rarely repeat topics, except for a new, exciting angle. Send in a story idea off the beaten path. We receive too many queries on Santa Fe. We would like to see three writing samples with a well-developed proposal."

Queries: Required. **E-Queries:** No. **Unsolicited mss:** Accepts. **Response:** Queries 1-3 months submissions 3-6 months, SASE. **Freelance Content:** 20%. **Rights:** FNAR. **Payment:** On acceptance.

NEW MEXICO JOURNEY

3333 Fairview Rd., A-327, Costa Mesa, CA 92626. 714-885-2380. Web site: www.aaa-newmexico.com. Bimonthly. Circ.: 80,000. Annette Winter, Editor. **Description:** For AAA members. Covers travel and people of New Mexico and surrounding states. **Nonfiction:** 1,000-2,000 words; $1/word. **Columns, Departments:** AutoNews, TravelNews; 75-200 words; $1/word. **Tips:** Seeks stories about offbeat and established destinations. **Queries:** Required. **E-Queries:** No. **Unsolicited mss:** Does not accept. **Response:** 8 weeks. **Freelance Content:** 80%. **Rights:** FNAR. **Payment:** On acceptance.

NEW ORLEANS MAGAZINE

111 Veterans Blvd., Metairie, LA 70005. 504-832-3555. E-mail: info@mcmediallc.com. Web site: www.neworleansmagazine.com. Monthly. $19.95/yr. Circ.: 37,700. Errol Laborde, Editor. **Description:** On New Orleans area people and issues. **Nonfiction:** Articles, 3-15 triple-spaced pages; pays $15-$500, extra for photos; **Queries:** Preferred. **Payment:** On publication.

NEWPORT LIFE

221 Third St., Newport, RI 02840. 401-841-0200. E-mail: info@newportlifemagazine.com. Web site: www.newportlifemagazine.com. Bimonthly. Circ.: 12,000. Lynne Tungett, Publisher/Editor. **Description:** On people, places, and attractions of Newport County. **Nonfiction:** General-interest, historical, profiles, international celebrities, and social and political issues; 500-2,500 words. **Columns, Departments:** Sailing, dining, food and wine, home and garden, arts, in Newport County; 200-750 words. **Art:** Photos needed for all articles. **Queries:** Preferred. **Response:** SASE required.

NORTH DAKOTA HORIZONS

P.O. Box 2639, Bismarck, ND 58502. 701-222-0929. E-mail: lyle_halvorson@gnda.com. Web site: www.ndhorizons.com. Quarterly. $5/$15. Circ.: 12,000. Lyle Halvorson, Editor. **Description:** Showcases North Dakota people, places, and events. **Nonfiction:** 1,000-3,000 words; $100-$300. **Art:** All formats; $10-$150/image. **Queries:** Preferred. **E-Queries:** Yes. **Unsolicited mss:** Accepts. **Response:** Queries/submissions up to 1 month, SASE. **Freelance Content:** 90%. **Rights:** One-time. **Payment:** On publication.

NORTHEAST MAGAZINE

Hartford Courant, 285 Broad St., Hartford, CT 06115. 860-241-3700. E-mail: northeast@courant.com. Weekly (Sunday only). Circ.: 316,000. Larry Bloom, Editor. **Description:** Sunday magazine for the major daily newspaper for Connecticut. **Nonfiction:** Articles spun off the news and compelling personal stories; 750-3,000 words; $250-$1,000. **Queries:** Preferred. **E-Queries:** No. **Unsolicited mss:** Accepts. **Response:** 2-3 months, SASE required. **Freelance Content:** 2%. **Rights:** One-time. **Payment:** On acceptance. **Contact:** Jane Bronfonan, Editorial Assistant.

NOW & THEN
P.O. Box 70556, Johnson City, TN 37614-1707. 423-439-5348. E-mail: woodsidj@mail.etsu.edu. Web site: www.cass.etsu.edu/n&t. 3x/yr. $25. Circ.: 1,500. Jane Harris Woodside, Editor. **Description:** Each issue focuses on one aspect of life in Appalachian region (from Northern Mississippi to Southern New York). Previous themes: paying tribute, first person Appalachia, Appalachia and the world, and natural resources. **Fiction:** Must relate to theme of issue and the Appalachian region; 1,500-3,000 words. **Nonfiction:** Articles, interviews, essays, memoirs; 1,000-2,500 words. Also book reviews; 750 words. **Poetry:** Up to 5 poems. **Tips:** Topics can be contemporary or historical. Accepts e-mail submissions for all material except poetry. Sample copy $5. **Queries:** Preferred. **E-Queries:** Yes. **Unsolicited mss:** Accepts. **Response:** SASE required.

OHIO
1422 Euclid Ave., Suite 730, Cleveland, OH 44115. E-mail: editorial@ohiomagazine.com. Web site: www.ohiomagazine.com. Monthly. Circ.: 90,000. Richard Osborne, Editorial Director. **Description:** On everything in Ohio—from people and places to food and entertainment. **Nonfiction:** On travel around Ohio with profiles of people, cities, towns, historic sites, tourist attractions, and little-known spots; 1,000-1,200 words. **Tips:** "We seek fresh stories with a decisively different Ohio angle." **Queries:** Preferred. **E-Queries:** Yes. **Unsolicited mss:** Accepts. **Response:** 6 weeks, SASE required. **Freelance Content:** 25%. **Payment:** On acceptance.

OKLAHOMA TODAY
P.O. Box 53384, Oklahoma City, OK 73102. 405-521-2496. E-mail: editorial@oklahomatoday.com. Web site: www.oklahomatoday.com. 7 x/yr. $3.95/$16.95. Circ.: 43,000. Louisa McCune, Editor. **Description:** Explores the people, places, history, and culture of Oklahoma. **Nonfiction:** Travel, history, nature, personality profiles; 250-3,000 words; $25-$750. **Fillers:** $25-$50. **Columns, Departments:** $75 and up. **Art:** Must evoke a sense of place; Color transparencies, slides, B&W prints; $50-$100/B&W, $50-$750/color. **Tips:** Query with biography and published clips. **Queries:** Preferred. **E-Queries:** Yes. **Unsolicited mss:** Accepts. **Response:** 4 months for queries, 6 months for submissions; SASE required. **Freelance Content:** 80%. **Rights:** First serial worldwide. **Payment:** On publication.

ORANGE COAST MAGAZINE
3701 Birch St., #100, Newport Beach, CA 92660-2618. 949-862-1133. E-mail: dgeorge@orangecoastmagazine.com. Web site: www.orangecoastmagazine.com. Monthly. $3.50/$9.98. Circ.: 50,000. Tina Borgatta, Editor. **Description:** Covers Orange County, California, for educated,

sophisticated readers. **Nonfiction:** Local trends, people, and news stories; workplace and family issues; 1,500-3,000 words; $250-$700. **Columns, Departments:** Escape (weekend travel), $250; Short Cuts (local items, 200 words), $50-$100. **Tips:** Query with cover letter, published clips, and SASE. **Queries:** Required. **E-Queries:** No. **Unsolicited mss:** Accepts. **Response:** 1-2 months. **Freelance Content:** 85%. **Rights:** FNASR; non-exclusive Web. **Payment:** On publication. **Contact:** DeAnna George, Managing Editor.

OREGON COAST

4969 Highway 101, #2, Florence, OR 97439. 541-997-8401.
E-mail: theresa@ohwy.com. Web site: www.northwestmagazine.com. $5/issue. Circ.: 50,000. Stephani Blair, Editor; Theresa Baer, Managing Editor. **Description:** Covers communities, businesses, people, events, activities, and the natural wonders that make up the Oregon coast. **Nonfiction:** First-person experiences, 500-1,500 words, with details in sidebars, with slides preferred. On travel, history, town/city profiles, outdoor activities, events, and nature; 800-1,200 words; $65-$250/feature. **Art:** Some stand-alone photos (verticals); also 2 calendars/yr; slides and transparencies; $25-75, $325 (cover). **Tips:** Accepts e-queries, but prefers hard copy. Back issues available for $3.75. **Queries:** Preferred. **E-Queries:** Yes. **Unsolicited mss:** Accepts. **Response:** 2-3 months, SASE required. **Freelance Content:** 60%. **Rights:** FNAR. **Payment:** On publication.

ORLANDO MAGAZINE

225 S Westmonte Dr., Suite 1100, Altamonte Springs, FL 32714. 407-767-8338.
E-mail: jclark@abartapub.com. Web site: www.orlandomag.com. Circ.: 30,000. James C. Clark, Editor. **Description:** Locally based articles for residents of Central Florida. Covers news, personalities, health, fashion, and technology. **Tips:** Send clips with query. **Queries:** Preferred.

OUR STATE

P.O. Box 4552, Greensboro, NC 27404. 336-286-0600.
E-mail: editorial@ourstate.com. Monthly. $3.95/$21.95. Circ.: 97,000. Vicky Jarrett, Editor. **Description:** "Down Home in North Carolina." Covers culture, events, travel, food, and folklore in the state; 1,500 words; $125-$500. **Columns, Departments:** North Carolina memories (holidays, summer, family). **Art:** 35mm slides; $75-$300; **Tips:** Most readers are over 50. **Queries:** Preferred. **E-Queries:** Yes. **Unsolicited mss:** Accepts. **Response:** 4-12 weeks, SASE required. **Freelance Content:** 80%. **Rights:** FNAR. **Payment:** On publication.

OVER THE BACK FENCE

14 S Paint St., Suite 69, P.O. Box 756, Chillicothe, OH 45601. 740-772-2165.
E-mail: backfenc@bright.net. Web site: www.backfence.com. Quarterly. **Description:** Serves counties in Southern Ohio. **Nonfiction:** Equated to a friendly and informative conversation with a neighbor about interesting people, places, and

events; 1,000-1,200 words; $.10/word, $25 minimum. **Art:** Photos or illustrations to accompany articles. **Queries:** Required. **Unsolicited mss:** Accepts. **Response:** SASE required. **Rights:** One-time. **Payment:** On publication.

PALM SPRINGS LIFE
303 N Indian Canyon Dr., Palm Springs, CA 92262. 760-325-2333.
E-mail: stewart@palmspringslife.com. Web site: www.palmspringslife.com. Monthly. $3.95/$38. Circ.: 20,000. Stewart Weiner, Editor. **Description:** Looks at upscale lifestyle of desert residents. Features celebrity profiles and articles on architecture, fashion, desert ecology, art, interior design, and history. **Nonfiction:** 1,500-2,500 words; $250-$500. **Columns, Departments:** On ecology, people, humor, desert sports, politics; 750; $250-$300. **Queries:** Required. **E-Queries:** Yes. **Unsolicited mss:** Accepts. **Response:** Queries 1 month, submissions 2 months, SASE. **Freelance Content:** 80%. **Rights:** All. **Payment:** On publication.

PENNSYLVANIA MAGAZINE
P.O. Box 755, Camp Hill, PA 17001. 717-697-4660.
E-mail: pamag@aol.com. Bimonthly. $3.50/$19.97. Circ.: 30,000. Matthew Holliday, Editor. **Description:** Profiles events, people, and history of Pennsylvania. **Nonfiction:** General-interest features; 1,000-2,500 words; $.10-$.12/word. **Columns, Departments:** 400-600 words; $.10-$.12/word. **Art:** To accompany articles; $20-$25/photo. **Tips:** No sports, poetry, hunting, or political. **Queries:** Preferred. **E-Queries:** Yes. **Unsolicited mss:** Accepts. **Response:** 4-6 weeks; SASE required. **Freelance Content:** 95%. **Rights:** One-time. **Payment:** On acceptance.

PHILADELPHIA
1818 Market St., Fl. 36, Philadelphia, PA 19103. 215-564-7700.
E-mail: duane@phillymag.com. Web site: www.phillymag.com. Monthly. $15/yr. Circ.: 138,000. Loren Feldman, Editor. **Description:** Covers events and topics in Philadelphia. **Nonfiction:** Articles for a sophisticated audience on the Philadelphia area; 1,000-5,000 words. **Queries:** Preferred. **Payment:** On acceptance. **Contact:** Duane Swierczynski, Senior Editor.

PHOENIX
8501 E Princess Dr., Suite 190, Scottsdale, AZ 85255. 480-664-3960.
E-mail: phxmag@citieswestpub.com. Monthly. $3.95. Circ.: 60,000. Robert Stieve, Editor. **Description:** Covers the Phoenix metro area. Issues relating to Phoenix and surrounding metro area. Service pieces (where to go, what to do) in the city; 50-2,000 words; pay varies. **Tips:** "Think small; short, timely pieces and profiles are always needed. No personal essays, please. Our travel stories are staff-written." **Queries:** Required. **E-Queries:** Yes. **Unsolicited mss:** Does not accept. **Response:** 2-6 weeks, SASE required. **Freelance Content:** 80%. **Rights:** FNAR. **Payment:** On publication. **Contact:** Kathy Montgomery, Managing Editor.

PITTSBURGH MAGAZINE

4802 Fifth Ave., Pittsburgh, PA 15213-2957.

E-mail: editor@wqed.org. Web site: www.wqed.org. Monthly. $3.50/$17.95. Circ.: 75,000. Betsy Benson, Publisher/Editor. **Description:** Covers Pittsburgh and surrounding region. Examines issues and strives to encourage a better understanding of the community. **Nonfiction:** News, features, service pieces, local celebrity profiles, regional lifestyles; must have a Pittsburgh region focus. 500-4,000 words. Pay negotiable. **Tips:** News, business, and service pieces needed. Sample copy $2. **Queries:** Required. **E-Queries:** No. **Unsolicited mss:** Does not accept. **Response:** 2 months, SASE. **Freelance Content:** 60%. **Rights:** FNASR. **Payment:** On publication. **Contact:** Michelle Pilecki, Executive Editor.

PORTLAND

722 Congress St., Portland, ME 04012. 207-775-4339.

E-mail: staff@portlandmagazine.com. Web site: www.portlandmagazine.com. 10x/yr. $29/yr. Circ.: 100,000. Colin Sargent, Editor. **Description:** Celebrates the Portland, Maine, region by providing profiles of businesses and people, columns about life on the waterfront, and features on arts, getaways, maritime history, geography, and cuisine. **Fiction:** Fiction, to 750 words. **Nonfiction:** Articles on local people, legends, culture, trends, etc. **Queries:** Required. **E-Queries:** Yes. **Unsolicited mss:** Accepts.

PROVINCETOWN ARTS

650 Commercial St., Provincetown, MA 02657. 508-487-3167.

E-mail: cbusa@attbi.com. Web site: www.provincetownarts.org. Annual. Circ.: 8,000. Christopher Busa, Editor. **Description:** Focuses on Cape Cod's artists, performers, and writers; covers the cultural life of the nation's oldest continuous art colony. **Fiction:** 500-5,000 words; $50-$150. **Nonfiction:** Essays, interviews, journals, performance pieces, profiles, reviews, and visual features. 500-5,000 words; $50-$150. **Poetry:** Up to 3 poems; $25-$100. **Queries:** Not necessary. **E-Queries:** No. **Unsolicited mss:** Accepts. **Response:** Queries 3 weeks, submissions 4 months, SASE required. **Freelance Content:** 90%. **Payment:** On publication.

RECREATION NEWS

Indiana Printing and Publishing Co.

7339 D Hanover Parkway, Greenbelt, MD 20770-3645. 301-474-4600.

E-mail: editor@recreationnews.com. Web site: www.recreationnews.com. Monthly. $12/yr. Circ.: 100,000. Francis X. Orphe, Editor. **Description:** Official publication of ESM Association of the Capital Region. Covers regional recreational activities, historical sites, fishing, parks, video reviews, food column, weekend getaways, day-off trips, etc. **Nonfiction:** On recreation and travel around the mid-Atlantic region for government and private-sector workers in the Washington, D.C., area. Conversational tone, lean and brisk; 900-2,200 words; $50 reprints, $300 cover features. **Queries:** Preferred. **Unsolicited mss:** Accepts. **Freelance Content:** 85%. **Payment:** On publication.

RHODE ISLAND MONTHLY

280 Kinsley Ave., Providence, RI 02903-1017. 401-277-8200.
E-mail: sfrancis@rimonthly.com. Web site: www.rimonthly.com. Monthly. $18/yr. Circ.: 41,000. Paula M. Bodah, Editor. **Description:** Features on Rhode Island and southeastern Massachusetts—places, customs, people, and events. **Nonfiction:** Features, from investigative reporting and in-depth profiles to service pieces and visual stories, seasonal material; 2,000-3,000 words; $250-$1,000. **Fillers:** On Rhode Island places, customs, people, events, products, and services; 150-500 words; $50-$150. **Tips:** Send clips with query. Sample copy for $3.50 plus postage. **Queries:** Required. **E-Queries:** Yes. **Payment:** On acceptance. **Contact:** Sarah Francis, Managing Editor.

SACRAMENTO MAGAZINE

706 56th St., Suite 210, Sacramento, CA 95819. 916-452-6200.
E-mail: krista@sacmag.com. Web site: www.sacmag.com. Monthly. Circ.: 29,000. Krista Minard, Editor. **Description:** Interesting and unusual people, places, and behind-the-scenes news items. **Nonfiction:** Articles, 1,000-1,500 words, on destinations within a 6-hour drive of Sacramento. Features, 2,500 words, on broad range of topics related to the region. Pay varies. **Columns, Departments:** City Lights, 400 words, $50-$300. **Queries:** Required. **Payment:** On publication.

SAN FRANCISCO MAGAZINE

243 Vallejo St., San Francisco, CA 94111-1511. 415-398-2800.
E-mail: letters@sanfran.com. Web site: www.sanfran.com. Monthly. $19. Circ.: 135,000. Bruce Kelley, Editor-in-Chief. **Description:** Exploring and celebrating San Francisco and bay area. Insightful analysis, investigative reporting, and eye-catching coverage of local food, culture, design, travel, and politics. **Nonfiction:** Service features, profiles, investigative pieces, 2,500-3,000 words. News items, 250-800 words, from business to arts to politics. Pay varies. **Queries:** Preferred. **Unsolicited mss:** Accepts. **Payment:** On acceptance. **Contact:** Lisa Trottier, Managing Editor.

SAVANNAH

P.O. Box 1088, Savannah, GA 31402. 912-652-0293.
E-mail: lindaw@savannahnow.com. Web site: www.savannahmagazine.com. Bimonthly. $3.95/$15.95. Circ.: 11,000. Linda Wittish, Editor. **Description:** On lifestyles of residents from coastal Georgia and South Carolina low country. **Nonfiction:** On local people, travel destinations (in a day's drive), local history, restaurants, business; 500-2,500 words; $100-$350. **Columns, Departments:** Travel Business; 1,000-1,500; $200-$300. **Queries:** Preferred. **E-Queries:** Yes. **Unsolicited mss:** Accepts. **Response:** Queries 2-3 weeks, submissions 3-4 weeks, SASE. **Freelance Content:** 100%. **Rights:** FNAR. **Payment:** On acceptance.

SEATTLE

423 Third Ave. W, Seattle, WA 98119. 206-284-1750.
E-mail: editor@seattlemag.com. Web site: www.seattlemag.com. 10x/yr. $3.95/issue.

Circ.: 45,000. Rachel Hart, Editor. **Description:** To help people live better in Seattle. **Nonfiction:** City, local issues, home, lifestyle articles on greater Seattle area; 50-2,500 words; $50-$1,200. **Queries:** Required. **E-Queries:** Yes. **Unsolicited mss:** Accepts. **Response:** 3 months, SASE required. **Freelance Content:** 70%. **Rights:** Exclusive 60 days. **Payment:** 30 days after publication.

SEATTLE WEEKLY

1008 Western, Suite 300, Seattle, WA 98104. 206-623-0500.
E-mail: info@seattleweekly.com. Web site: www.seattleweekly.com. Audrey Van Buskirk, Editor. **Description:** Newsmagazine offering investigative journalism, political commentary, arts/culture, and other articles and features on the community life and news of the Seattle metro region. **Nonfiction:** Articles, 600-4,000 words. **Queries:** Preferred. **Response:** 2-6 weeks, SASE. **Payment:** On publication. **Contact:** Editorial Assistant.

SOUTHERN EXPOSURE

Institute for Southern Studies
P.O. Box 531, Durham, NC 27702-0531. 919-419-8311.
E-mail: info@i4south.org. Web site: www.southernstudies.org. Quarterly. $24. Circ.: 5,000. Chris Kromm, Editor. **Description:** Forum on "Southern politics and culture." **Nonfiction:** Essays, investigative journalism, oral histories, and personal narratives; 500-3,600 words; $25-$250. **Queries:** Preferred. **Payment:** On publication.

SOUTHERN HUMANITIES REVIEW

See full listing in Literary Fiction & Poetry category.

SOUTHERN OREGON HERITAGE TODAY

Southern Oregon Historical Society
106 N Central Ave., Medford, OR 97501-5926. 541-773-6536.
E-mail: communications@sohs.org. Web site: www.sohs.org. Monthly. $20/yr. Cynthia Wicklund, Editorial Coordinator. **Description:** On the history of the southern Oregon region (people, places, buildings, and events). Articles run 700-3,500 words; $50-$250. **Tips:** "Make sure there is a storyline, not just a reiteration of facts." **Payment:** On publication.

SPRINGFIELD

P.O. Box 4749, Springfield, MO 65808. 417-831-1600.
E-mail: jim_hamilton@sgfmag.com. Monthly. $16.99/yr. Jim Hamilton, Managing Editor. **Description:** About local people, places, events, and issues. **Nonfiction:** Articles must have a clear link to Springfield, Missouri. Historical/nostalgic pieces and book reviews. **Tips:** Seeking features on Springfield couples at present. **Queries:** Preferred. **E-Queries:** Yes. **Unsolicited mss:** Accepts. **Response:** 2-3 weeks. **Freelance Content:** 85%. **Rights:** 1st serial. **Payment:** On publication.

SWEAT MAGAZINE
See full listing in Fitness Magazines category.

TALLAHASSEE
1932 Miccosokee Rd., P.O. Box 1837, Tallahassee, FL 32302-1837. 850-878-0554.
E-mail: jbettinger@rowlandinc.com. Web site: www.rowlandinc.com. Bimonthly.
$2.95/$16.95. Circ.: 17,300. Julie Strauss Bettinger, Editor. **Description:** Lifestyle
magazine celebrating life in Florida's Capital Region. **Nonfiction:** Feature stories on
local personalities and current events. Creative nonfiction style of writing preferred;
1,500-3,000 words; pay varies. **Columns, Departments:** Work Day, The Sporting
Life, Humor; 850 words; pay varies. **Queries:** Not necessary. **E-Queries:** Yes.
Unsolicited mss: Accepts. **Response:** 4-6 weeks, SASE required. **Freelance
Content:** 15%. **Payment:** On publication.

TEXAS MAGAZINE
801 Texas Ave., Houston, TX 77002. 713-220-7501.
E-mail: ken.hammond@chron.com. Web site: www.houstonchronicle.com. Kenneth
Hammond, Editor. **Description:** Sunday magazine of the *Houston Chronicle*.

TEXAS HIGHWAYS
P.O. Box 141009, Austin, TX 78714 1000. 512-486-5858.
E-mail: editors@texashighways.com. Web site: www.texashighways.com. Monthly.
Circ.: 300,000. Jack Lowry, Editor. **Description:** Articles and features on Texas his-
tory, travel, and scenery. **Nonfiction:** Travel, historical, cultural, scenic features on
Texas; 200-1,800 words; $.40-$.50/word. **Art:** Photos, $60-$550. **Queries:** Required.

TEXAS JOURNEY
3333 S Fairview Rd., A-327, Costa Mesa, CA 92626. 714-885-2380.
Bimonthly. Circ.: 580,000. Annette Winter, Editor. **Description:** Publication for
AAA Texas members. Features travel, people, and auto news in Texas and surround-
ing states. **Nonfiction:** Cultural travel, consumer travel, the outdoors, personality
profiles; 1,000-2,000 words; $1/word. **Columns, Departments:** Travel News, Auto
News; 75-200 words. **Tips:** Prefers published writers. Seeks stories about offbeat and
established destinations. **Queries:** Required. **E-Queries:** No. **Unsolicited mss:**
Does not accept. **Response:** 8 weeks; SASE required. **Freelance Content:** 80%.
Rights: FNASR. **Payment:** On acceptance. **Contact:** Nina Elder, Editor.

TEXAS MONTHLY
P.O. Box 1569, Austin, TX 78767-1569. 512-320-6900.
Web site: www.texasmonthly.com. Monthly. $18/yr. Circ.: 301,000. Evan Smith,
Editor. **Description:** Covers issues of public concern in Texas. **Nonfiction:** Features
on art, architecture, food, education, business, politics, etc. Articles must appeal to an
educated Texas audience and have well-researched reporting on issues (offbeat and
previously unreported topics, or with novel approach to familiar topics). 2,500-5,000

words; pay varies. **Tips:** No fiction, poetry, or cartoons. **Queries:** Required. **E-Queries:** No. **Unsolicited mss:** Accepts. **Response:** 6-8 weeks, SASE required. **Payment:** On acceptance.

TORONTO LIFE

59 Front St. E, Fl. 3, Toronto, Ontario M5E 1B3 Canada. 416-364-3333. E-mail: editorial@torontolife.com. Web site: www.torontolife.com. Monthly. $34. Circ.: 94,000. John Macfarlane, Editor. **Description:** Covers the urban scene. **Nonfiction:** Articles on Toronto; 1,500-4,500 words. **Queries:** Required. **Payment:** On acceptance.

TUCSON LIFESTYLE

7000 E Tanque Verde, Tucson, AZ 85715. 520-721-2929. E-mail: tucsonlife@aol.com. Monthly. $2.95. Circ.: 33,000. Sue Giles, Editor-In-Chief. **Description:** Covers subjects on Southern Arizona. Articles on businesses, lifestyles, the arts, homes, and gardens. 1,000-4,000 words; $125-$500. **Tips:** Base your article on interviews and research. No travel pieces or anecdotes as articles. **Queries:** Required. **E-Queries:** Yes. **Unsolicited mss:** Accepts. **Response:** 2 weeks, SASE required. **Freelance Content:** 80%. **Rights:** FNAR. **Payment:** On acceptance. **Contact:** Scott Barker, Executive Editor.

VANCOUVER

500-2608 Granville St., Vancouver
British Columbia V6H 3V3 Canada. 604-877-7732. E-mail: mail@vancouvermagazine.com. Web site: vancouvermagazine.com. 10x/yr. $3.50. Circ.: 65,000. Matthew Mallon, Editor. **Description:** City magazine with a focus on urban life (restaurants, fashion, shopping, and nightlife). **Nonfiction:** Seeking articles, varying lengths, including front-of-book pieces; 400-4,000 words; $.50/word. **Columns, Departments:** Sports, civics, social affairs, business, politics, media; 1,500-2,000 words; $.50/word. **Tips:** "Because we're a general-interest magazine, just about anything goes. But keep in mind that you're writing for an affluent, well-educated readership with strong opinions about the city." **Queries:** Preferred. **E-Queries:** Yes. **Unsolicited mss:** Accepts. **Response:** 2 weeks minimum. **Freelance Content:** 70%. **Rights:** FNASR. **Payment:** On acceptance.

VERMONT LIFE

6 Baldwin St., Montpelier, VT 05602. 802-828-3241. Web site: www.vtlife.com. Quarterly. $3.95/$14.95. Circ.: 85,000. Tom Slayton, Editor. **Description:** Explores and celebrates Vermont today by providing quality photographs and articles. **Nonfiction:** Articles about people, places, history, and issues; 200-2,000 words; $100-$700. **Art:** Send slides or transparencies, no prints; $75-$500. **Tips:** No "my recent trip to Vermont" or old jokes, rural homilies. Submit articles that shed light on and accurately reflect Vermont experience today. **Queries:** Preferred. **E-Queries:** Yes. **Unsolicited mss:** Accepts. **Response:** 2-4 weeks, SASE. **Freelance Content:** 90%. **Rights:** FNAR. **Payment:** On acceptance.

VERMONT MAGAZINE
31 John Graham Ct., Suite A, P.O. Box 800, Middlebury, VT 05753. 802-388-8480.
E-mail: vtmag@sover.net. Web site: www.vermontmagazine.com. Bimonthly.
$16.95/yr. Circ.: 40,000. Sally West Johnson, Editor. **Description:** On all aspects of
contemporary Vermont (its people, culture, politics, and special places). **Nonfiction:**
Articles; pays $150-$600. **Queries:** Preferred. **Payment:** On publication.

VERSION
P.O. Box 132024, Houston, TX 77219-2024. 713-228-2220.
E-mail: david.key@versionmag.com. Web site: www.versionmag.com. David Key,
Creative Director. **Description:** Lifestyle magazine covering the music, dining,
nightlife, art, and culture in Houston. Articles examine popular trends and stereo-
types. **Tips:** "Looking for writers with a fresh, unique, and grabbing style."

WASHINGTON FLYER
Metropolitan Washington Airports Authority
1707 L Street NW, Suite 800, Washington, DC 20036. 202-331-9393.
E-mail: readers@thcmagazinegroup.com. Web site: www.fly2dc.com. Bimonthly.
Michael McCarthy, Editor-in-Chief. **Description:** For upscale Washington residents
and visitors. Dining, entertainment, events in the D.C. area. **Nonfiction:** Briefs and
features; 350-1,500 words; $150-$800. **Tips:** Prefers queries via e-mail. **Queries:**
Preferred. **E-Queries:** Yes. **Payment:** On publication.

THE WASHINGTONIAN
1828 L St. NW, Suite 200, Washington, DC 20036. 202-296-3600.
E-mail: editorial@washingtonian.com. Web site: www.washingtonian.com. Monthly.
$2.95/$24. Circ.: 160,000. John Limpert, Editor. **Description:** Covers Washington,
D.C., topics. **Queries:** Preferred. **E-Queries:** Yes. **Unsolicited mss:** Accepts.
Response: 2-8 weeks, SASE required. **Freelance Content:** 50%. **Rights:** FNASR.
Payment: On publication.

WISCONSIN MEETINGS MAGAZINE
P.O. Box 317, 1131 Mills St., Black Earth, WI 53515. 608-767-8000.
E-mail: nwood@wistrails.com. Web site: www.lakemichigantravelguide.com.
Biannual. Circ.: 10,000. Nick Wood, Editor. **Description:** Provides corporate and
association meeting planners with informative features and columns about the meeting industry in Wisconsin. **Nonfiction:** Profiles of Wisconsin's big 4 convention centers. Destination pieces on Lake Geneva, Wisconsin Dells, etc. 500-2,000 words;
$.25/word. **Columns, Departments:** Industry trends, outings, team-building pro-
grams, etc. 750 words; $.25/word. **Queries:** Preferred. **E-Queries:** Yes. **Unsolicited
mss:** Does not accept. **Response:** 2-3 months, SASE required. **Freelance
Content:** 75%. **Rights:** FNAR. **Payment:** On publication.

WISCONSIN TRAILS

P.O. Box 317, 1131 Mills St., Black Earth, WI 53515. 608-767-8000.
E-mail: kbast@wistrails.com. Web site: www.wistrails.com. Bimonthly. $4.95/$24.95.
Circ.: 50,000. Kate Bast, Editor. **Description:** On Wisconsin people, history, nature,
travel/adventure, lifestyle, arts, theater, sports, recreation, home/garden, and business. **Nonfiction:** On the joys and experiences of living in the Badger state (history,
wildlife, natural history, environment, travel, profiles, culture). 200-3,000 words;
$.25/word. **Fillers:** Quirky Wisconsin news items, crossword puzzles; 50-300 words;
$.25/word. **Columns, Departments:** My WI (essays); Discover (events), State Talk
(short, quirky news), Profile (noteworthy people), Gone for the Weekend (travel destination), Home & Garden. 50-1,000 words, $.25/word. **Art:** Color transparencies,
slides, illustrations (8x11 inches largest); pay varies. **Tips:** Most readers are in their
40s and 50s, well-educated, active, and love history/travel. New authors must submit
resume, letter of introduction, and 3 relevant clips, nonreturnable. Send SASE or see
Web site for guidelines. **Queries:** Required. **E-Queries:** Yes. **Unsolicited mss:**
Accepts. **Response:** 3-5 months, SASE. **Freelance Content:** 40%. **Rights:** FNAR.
Payment: On publication.

WISCONSIN WEST

2905 Seymour Rd., Eau Claire, WI 54703. 715-835-3800.
E-mail: mci@charter.net. Bimonthly. $2.50. Circ.: 5,000. **Description:** Covers
Western Wisconsin. **Nonfiction:** Restaurants, weekend leisure activities and get-
aways, famous people of western Wisconsin, history, short humor; to 3,000 words;
$75-$150; **Art:** Slides, photos; $100-$150. **Tips:** Sample copy for $2.50. **Queries:**
Preferred. **E-Queries:** Yes. **Unsolicited mss:** Accepts. **Freelance Content:** 100%.
Rights: FNAR. **Payment:** On publication.

YANKEE

P.O. Box 520, Dublin, NH 03444. 603-563-8111.
E-mail: queries@yankeepub.com. Web site: www.newengland.com. 10x/yr.
$3.50/issue. Circ.: 500,000. Judson D. Hale, Sr., Editor-in-Chief. **Description:** On
travel and life in New England. **Nonfiction:** Narrative journalism, home and garden,
travel, food, etc.; 150-3,000 words. **Queries:** Preferred. **E-Queries:** Yes.
Unsolicited mss: Accepts. **Response:** 8 weeks, SASE. **Freelance Content:** 80%.
Rights: All. **Payment:** On acceptance.

RELIGION

AMERICA

106 W 56th St., New York, NY 10019-3803. 212-581-4640.
E-mail: articles@americamagazine.org. Web site: www.americamagazine.org. Weekly.
$2.75/issue. Circ.: 46,000. Thomas J. Reese, Editor. **Description:** For thinking
Catholics and those interested in what Catholics are thinking. Emphasis on social jus-
tice and religious/ethical perspectives on current issues facing the church and the

world. **Nonfiction:** Features on contemporary issues from a religious and ethical perspective; 1,500-2,000 words. **Poetry:** Serious poetry in contemporary prose idiom, free or formal verse. Submit 2-3 poems, 20-35 lines; $2-$3/line. **Tips:** "No sermons or speeches. Address educated audience who are not experts in your topic." **Queries:** Not necessary. **Unsolicited mss:** Accepts. **Response:** 1-3 weeks, SASE required. **Freelance Content:** 50%. **Rights:** All. **Payment:** On acceptance.

AMIT
Americans for Israel and Torah
817 Broadway, New York, NY 10003-4761. 212-477-4720.
E-mail: amitmag@amitchildren.org. Web site: www.amitchildren.org. Quarterly. $35/yr (with membership). Circ.: 39,000. Debra Stahl, Managing Editor. **Description:** Published by a nonprofit, Modern Orthodox Jewish organization which sponsors a network of schools helping over 16,000 underprivileged Israeli youths. **Nonfiction:** Articles of interest to Jewish women (education, the Middle East, Israel, history, holidays, travel, and culture); 2,500 words; $250-$500. **Columns, Departments:** Subject matter includes Israel, Zionism, parenting, and the Torah. Also, interviews with AMIT students in Israel, book reviews, and features on innovators in education, art, and music. 700 words; $100. **Tips:** "Avoid politics and religion. Focus on innovations in education, and on AMIT students in Israel." **Queries:** Preferred. **E-Queries:** Yes. **Unsolicited mss:** Accepts. **Response:** 2 weeks, SASE required. **Freelance Content:** 50%. **Payment:** On acceptance.

ANGLICAN JOURNAL
600 Jarvis St., Toronto, Ontario M4Y 2J6 Canada. 416-924-9192.
E-mail: editor@national.anglican.ca. Web site: www.anglicanjournal.com. 10x/yr. $10/yr. Circ.: 245,000. Leanne Larmondin, Editor. **Description:** Newspaper of the Anglican Church of Canada. Provides news and features of the Anglican Church, articles on social and ethical issues, and human-interest pieces. Articles to 1,000 words; $.23/word. **Queries:** Required. **E-Queries:** Yes. **Unsolicited mss:** Does not accept. **Freelance Content:** 15%. **Rights:** FNAR. **Payment:** On publication.

THE ANNALS OF ST. ANNE DE BEAUPRÉ
P.O. Box 1000, St. Anne de Beaupré, Quebec G0A 3C0 Canada. 418-827-4538.
Monthly. Circ.: 45,000. Father Bernard Mercier, CSs.R., Editor. **Description:** Articles, 500-1,500 words, that promote devotion to St. Anne and Christian family values. Pays $.03-$.04/word. **Tips:** No poetry. "We look for work that is inspirational, educational, objective, and uplifting." **Response:** 1 month to queries. **Freelance Content:** 80%. **Rights:** FNAR. **Payment:** On acceptance. **Contact:** Father Roch Achard, Managing Editor.

THE B'NAI B'RITH IJM
B'nai B'rith International
1640 Rhode Island Ave. NW, Washington, DC 20036. 202-857-6646.
E-mail: ijm@bnaibrith.org. Web site: www.bnaibrith.org. 4x/yr. Circ.: 160,000. Eric

Rozenman, Executive Editor. **Description:** Published by B'nai B'rith, with general-interest stories. **Nonfiction:** Profiles, stories of interest to Jewish communities in U.S. and abroad, politics, arts, Middle East; 1,500-2,000 words; $450-$700. **Queries:** Preferred.

THE BANNER

2850 Kalamazoo Ave. SE, Grand Rapids, MI 49560-0001. 616-224-0732. E-mail: editorial@thebanner.org. Web site: www.thebanner.org. Biweekly. Circ.: 32,000. John D. Suk, Editor. **Description:** For members of Christian Reformed Church in North America. **Fiction:** to 2,500 words. **Nonfiction:** to 1,800 words; pays $125-$200. **Poetry:** to 50 lines; $40. **Queries:** Preferred. **Payment:** On acceptance.

BIBLE ADVOCATE

P.O. Box 33677, Denver, CO 80233. 303-452-7973. E-mail: bibleadvocate@cog7.org. Web site: www.cog7.org/ba. 10x/yr. Circ.: 13,500. Calvin Burrell, Editor. **Description:** Helps Christians understand and obey the Bible. **Nonfiction:** On Bible doctrine, current social and religious issues, everyday-living Bible topics, textual or Biblical book studies, prophecy and personal experience; 1,500 words; $25-$55. **Poetry:** Free verse, blank verse, and traditional; 5-20 lines; $20. **Fillers:** Facts, inspirational pieces, anecdotes; 100-400 words; $20. **Columns, Departments:** Viewpoint, opinion pieces; 650 words. **Art:** Mac-compatible TIF or JPG files, 300 dpi; $10-$35/inside use, $25-$50/cover. **Tips:** No articles on Christmas or Easter. Theme list available. **Queries:** Not necessary. **E-Queries:** Yes. **Unsolicited mss:** Accepts. **Response:** 4-8 weeks; SASE required. **Freelance Content:** 10-20%. **Rights:** First, reprint, electronic. **Payment:** On publication.

BOOKS & CULTURE: A CHRISTIAN REVIEW

See full listing in Writing & Publishing category.

BREAD FOR GOD'S CHILDREN

P.O. Box 1017, Arcadia, FL 34265-1017. E-mail: bread@sunline.net. 8x/yr. Circ.: 10,000. Judith M. Gibbs, Editor. **Description:** Christian family magazine with Bible study, stories, teen pages, parent news, ideas, and more. **Nonfiction:** Articles or craft ideas based on Christian principles or activities; how to implement Christian ways into daily living; 600-800 words; $20-$30. **Tips:** Stories must be from a child's point of view, with story itself getting message across; no preaching or moralizing, no tag endings. No stories with speaking animals, occult, fantasy, or romance. "Our purpose is to help Christian families learn to apply God's word in everyday living. We are looking for writers with a solid knowledge of Biblical principles and who are concerned with the youth of today living according to these principles." **Queries:** Not necessary. **E-Queries:** No. **Unsolicited mss:** Accepts. **Response:** Submissions 1-6 months, SASE. **Freelance Content:** 20%. **Rights:** 1st. **Payment:** On publication.

Get published
with *The Writer*

When you subscribe to *The Writer*, you are investing in the future of your work!

Every issue brings you:

- Useful and up-to-date market news, special markets, and market listings
- Advice on running a successful writing business
- The latest tips from agents and editors
- Current trends and news from the publishing industry
- What you need to know about copyrights and contracts
- Advice from professionals like David McCullough, Sue Grafton, Janet Evanovich, and more
- Tips and techniques to help you get published
- And much, much more!

Subscribe Today!

☑ YES! Please send me one year (12 issues) of *The Writer* for only $19.95. I'll save **66% off** the annual newsstand rate!

Name _____

Address _____

City_____ State _____ Zip_____

☐ Payment enclosed   ☐ Please bill me later

Canadian price $30.00 (GST included, payable in U.S. funds). Foreign price $39.00 (payable in U.S.funds, checks must be drawn on a U.S. bank). Make checks payable to Kalmbach Publishing Co. New Subscribers only.

the Writer

Your satisfaction is guaranteed!

If you're ever dissatisfied—for any reason—you may receive a refund on any unmailed issues.

Since 1887, this highly respected magazine has helped writers at all levels improve their writing, get published, launch careers, and stay inspired.

The Writer covers every genre of writing including fiction, poetry, freelance articles, scripts, children's books, profiles, memoirs and more!

Mail this card today!

CAMPUS LIFE
See full listing in Teens category.

CATECHIST
2621 Dryden Rd., Dayton, OH 45449. 937-847-5900. Web site: www.catechist.com. 7x/yr. $19.95/yr. Circ.: 50,000. Patricia Fischer, Editor. **Description:** For Catholic teachers, coordinators, and administrators in religious education programs. **Nonfiction:** Informational and how-to articles; 1,200-1,500 words; $25-$100. **Payment:** On publication.

CATHOLIC DIGEST
P.O. Box 6001, Mystic, CT 06355. 860-536-2611, ext. 174.
E-mail: rreece@bayardpubs.com. Web site: www.catholicdigest.org. Monthly. $2.25/$19.95. Circ.: 400,000. Richard J. Reece, Editor. **Description:** For adult Roman Catholic readers, with general-interest topics on family life, religion, science, health, good works, and relationships. **Nonfiction:** Humor, profiles, how-to, personal experiences; 1,000-3,000 words; $100-$400. **Fillers:** Up to 500 words; $2/line. **Columns, Departments:** True incidents about good works, parish life, conversion to Catholicism; 100-500 words; $2/line. **Tips:** "We're interested in articles about the family and career concerns of baby boomers who have a stake in being Catholic. Illustrate topic with a series of true-life, interconnected vignettes." **E-Queries:** No. **Response:** 6-8 weeks, SASE required. **Freelance Content:** 30%. **Rights:** One-time. **Payment:** On acceptance.

CATHOLIC PARENT
See full listing in Family & Parenting category.

THE CHRISTIAN CENTURY
104 S Michigan Ave., Suite 700, Chicago, IL 60603. 312-263-7510.
E-mail: main@christiancentury.org. Web site: www.christiancentury.org. Biweekly. $49/yr. Circ.: 30,000. John M. Buchanan, Editor. **Description:** Shows how Christian faith calls people to a profound engagement with the world and how people of faith address issues of poverty, international relations, and popular culture. **Nonfiction:** Religious angle on political/social issues, international affairs, culture, the arts, and challenges in everyday lives; 1,500-3,000 words; $75-$200. **Poetry:** Free verse, traditional, haiku. No sentimental or didactic poems; 20 lines; $50. **Art:** Photos, $25-$100. **Tips:** "Many of our readers are ministers or teachers of religion." **Queries:** Preferred. **E-Queries:** Yes. **Response:** Queries 1 week, submissions 2 months, SASE required. **Freelance Content:** 90%. **Rights:** One-time. **Payment:** On publication.

CHRISTIAN HOME & SCHOOL
3350 E Paris Ave. SE, Grand Rapids, MI 49512. 616-957-1070.
E-mail: rogers@csionline.org. Web site: www.csionline.org/chs. Bimonthly. Circ.: 69,000. Gordon L. Bordewyk, Executive Editor. **Description:** For parents in Canada and U.S. who send their children to Christian schools and are concerned about chal-

lenges facing families today. Pays $175-$250. **Tips:** Send 9x12 envelope with 4 first-class stamps for sample copy and guidelines. **Queries:** Preferred. **Payment:** On publication. **Contact:** Roger W. Schmurr, Senior Editor.

CHRISTIAN PARENTING TODAY
See full listing in Family & Parenting category.

CHRISTIAN SINGLE
One LifeWay Plaza, Nashville, TN 37234-0175.
Description: For single adults on leisure activities, issues related to single parenting, and life from a Christian perspective. Also offers inspiring personal experiences and humor. **Nonfiction:** Articles, 600-1,200 words; pay varies. **Queries:** Preferred. **Payment:** On acceptance.

CHRISTIAN SOCIAL ACTION
100 Maryland Ave. NE, Washington, DC 20002. 202-488-5600.
E-mail: ealsgaard@umc-gbcs.org. Web site: www.umc-gbcs.org. Bimonthly. Circ.: 50,000. Gretchen Hakola, Editor. **Description:** For United Methodist clergy and lay people interested in the role and involvement of the church in social issues. **Nonfiction:** Stories that educate, analyze, and motivate people to Christian social action on justice and advocacy issues; 1,500-2,000 words; $125-$175. **Art:** Hard copy, electronic. **Queries:** Preferred. **E-Queries:** Yes. **Unsolicited mss:** Does not accept. **Response:** Queries 4-6 weeks, SASE required. **Freelance Content:** 30%. **Rights:** 1st. **Payment:** On publication.

CHRISTIANITY TODAY
465 Gundersen Dr., Carol Stream, IL 60188. 630-260-6200.
E-mail: cteditor@christianitytoday.com. Web site: www.christianitytoday.com. 14x/yr. $3.95/issue. Circ.: 150,000. David Neff, Editor. **Description:** Evangelical Christian publication covering Christian doctrines, current events, news, trends, and issues. **Nonfiction:** Doctrinal social issues and interpretive essays, 1,500-3,000 words, from evangelical Protestant perspective. Pays $200-$500. **Tips:** "We're seeking Internet-related stories with human interest." **Queries:** Preferred. **E-Queries:** Yes. **Unsolicited mss:** Accepts. **Response:** 3 months, SASE required. **Freelance Content:** 80%. **Rights:** One-time. **Payment:** On acceptance. **Contact:** Mark Galli, Managing Editor.

CHURCH EDUCATOR
See full listing in Education category.

CLUB CONNECTION
1445 N Boonville Ave., Springfield, MO 65802. 417-862-2781 ext. 4067.
E-mail: clubconnection@ag.org. Web site: www.missionettes.ag.org. Quarterly. $6.50/yr. Circ.: 13,000. Debby Seler, Editor. **Description:** For Missionettes (girls, ages 6-12). Focuses on message of salvation. **Fiction:** Short stories; to 700 words;

$25-$40. **Nonfiction:** Articles on friends, school, God, family, music, nature, and fun activities; to 700 words; $25-$40. **Poetry:** Leadership/devotional; to 700 words; $25-$40. **Fillers:** Crafts, games, puzzles, snack recipes, etc.; pays $10. **Tips:** For leaders of Missionettes clubs; Leader's Connection provides ideas and resources, discipleship materials, etc. **Queries:** Preferred. **E-Queries:** Yes. **Unsolicited mss:** Accepts. **Freelance Content:** 35%. **Rights:** FNAR. **Payment:** On acceptance. **Contact:** Ranee Carter, Assistant Editor.

CLUBHOUSE JR.
See full listing in Juvenile category.

CLUBHOUSE MAGAZINE
See full listing in Juvenile category.

CNEWA WORLD
See full listing in Ethnic & Multicultural category.

COMMENTARY
American Jewish Committee
165 E 56th St., New York, NY 10022. 212-891-1400.
E-mail: editorial@commentarymagazine.com.
Web site: www.commentarymagazine.com. Monthly. $45/yr. Circ.: 25,000. Neal Kozodoy, Editor. **Description:** Fiction, of literary quality, on contemporary social or Jewish issues, from 5,000-7,000 words. Articles, 5,000-7,000 words, on contemporary issues, Jewish affairs, social sciences, religious thought, and culture. Serious fiction; book reviews. **Payment:** On publication.

COMMONWEAL
See full listing in Contemporary Culture category.

THE COVENANT COMPANION
5101 N Francisco Ave., Chicago, IL 60625-3611. 773-784-3000.
E-mail: communication@covoffice.org. Web site: www.covchurch.org. Monthly. $19.95. Circ.: 18,000. Jane Swanson-Nystrom, Managing Editor. **Description:** Publication of Evangelical Covenant Church. Discusses issues of faith, spirituality, social justice, local ministry, and the life of the church. **Nonfiction:** Biographical profiles, local church ministries, current issues, and interviews with authors; 1,200-1,800 words; $35-$100. **Tips:** No "rants" about the culture or political agendas. Prefers human-interest pieces or articles on practical spirituality. **Queries:** Not necessary. **E-Queries:** Yes. **Unsolicited mss:** Accepts. **Response:** 4-6 weeks, SASE required. **Freelance Content:** 40%. **Rights:** FNAR. **Payment:** On publication.

CRUSADER
P.O. Box 7259, Grand Rapids, MI 49510. 616-241-5616.
Web site: www.calvinistcadets.org. 7x/yr. Circ.: 10,000. G. Richard Broene, Editor.

Description: Christian-oriented magazine for boys, ages 9-14, especially to members of Calvinist Cadet Corps. Purpose: "to show how God is at work in the lives of boys and in the world around them." **Fiction:** Fast-moving stories that appeal to a boy's sense of adventure and humor; 900-1,500 words; pay varies. **Tips:** Send 9x12 SASE for free sample copy and/or upcoming themes. Themes also available on Web site. **Queries:** Not necessary. **Unsolicited mss:** Accepts. **Payment:** On acceptance.

DAILY MEDITATION

P.O. Box 2710, San Antonio, TX 78299. 210-735-5247.
Semi-annual. $16/yr. Circ.: 761. Emilia Devno, Editor. **Description:** Offers inspirational, nonsectarian religious articles that show the way to self-improvement and greater spiritual growth. **Nonfiction:** 300-1,600 words. Pays $.02/word. **Poetry:** To 350 words; $.14/line. **Tips:** No fiction, handwritten material, meditations, photographs, or dated material. **Queries:** Not necessary. **E-Queries:** No. **Unsolicited mss:** Accepts. **Response:** SASE required. **Rights:** FNASR. **Payment:** On acceptance.

DECISION

Billy Graham Evangelistic Assn.
Two Parkway Plaza, Suite 200, 4828 Parkway Plaza Blvd., Charlotte, NC 28217.
E-mail: submissions@bgea.org. Web site: www.decisionmag.org. 12x/yr. $12/yr. Circ.: 1,200,000. Bob Paulson, Managing Editor. **Description:** Offers religious inspirational, personal experience, and how-to articles. **Nonfiction:** Personal conversion testimonies, personal experience articles on how God has intervened in a person's daily life; how Scripture was applied to solve a problem; 400-1,500 words; $30-$260. **Poetry:** Free verse and rhymed; 4-16 lines; $.60/word. **Columns, Departments:** Finding Jesus (Stories of people who have become Christians through Billy Graham ministries). 500-600 words; $85. **Tips:** All articles must have some connection with a Billy Graham or Franklin Graham ministry. Send 8.5x11 SASE for sample copy. **Queries:** Not necessary. **E-Queries:** Yes. **Unsolicited mss:** Accepts. **Response:** Queries, 3 months, submissions 10 months, SASE required. **Freelance Content:** 10%. **Rights:** FNAR. **Payment:** On publication.

DISCIPLESHIP JOURNAL

P.O. Box 35004, Colorado Springs, CO 80935. 719-531-3514.
E-mail: djwriters@navpress.com. Web site: www.disciplejournal.com. Bimonthly. $4.95/$23.97. Circ.: 130,000. Sue Kline, Editor. **Description:** Articles on Christian growth and practical application of Scripture. **Nonfiction:** Teaching based on Scripture (e.g., what Bible says on forgiveness); how-tos (to deepen devotional life; to reach out in community); 1,000-3,000 words; $.25/word. **Columns, Departments:** On the Home Front (Q&A on family issues); Getting into God's word (devotional or Bible study); DJ+ (up to 500 words, on practical ministry, leading small groups, evangelism, etc.); 750-950 words; $.25/word. **Tips:** First-time writers encouraged to write non-theme articles, on any aspect of living as a disciple of Christ. Seeking articles encouraging involvement in world missions, personal evangelism, and Christian leadership. No testimonials, devotionals, book reviews, or news. **Queries:** Required.

E-Queries: Yes. **Unsolicited mss:** Does not accept. **Response:** 6 weeks, SASE required. **Freelance Content:** 80%. **Rights:** 1st, electronic, anthology. **Payment:** On acceptance.

DISCOVERIES
See full listing in Juvenile category.

DISCOVERY TRAILS
See full listing in Juvenile category.

DOVETAIL
See full listing in Family & Parenting category.

ENRICHMENT
1445 N Boonville Ave., Springfield, MO 65802-1894. 417-862-2781.
E-mail: enrichment@ag.org. Quarterly. $22/yr. Circ.: 33,000. Gary Allen, Editor. **Description:** Resources to assist Pentecostal ministers in effective ministry. **Nonfiction:** Articles and features on wide range of ministry-related topics; 1,200-2,100; to $.10/word. **Tips:** Intended readership is Pentecostal/charismatic ministers and church leaders. **Queries:** Not necessary. **E-Queries:** Yes. **Unsolicited mss:** Accepts. **Response:** 1 week, SASE required. **Freelance Content:** less than 10%. **Rights:** FNAR. **Payment:** On publication. **Contact:** Rich Knoth.

EVANGEL
P.O. Box 535002, Indianapolis, IN 46253-5002. 317-244-3660.
Quarterly. $2.25/issue. Circ.: 12,000. Julie Innes, Editor. **Description:** "Devotional in nature, our publication seeks to increase reader's understanding of the nature and character of God and the nature of life lived under the lordship of Christ." **Fiction:** Solving problems through faith; to 1,200 words; $.04/word. **Nonfiction:** Free Methodist. Personal experience articles; short devotional items, 300-500 words (1,200 max); $.04/word. **Poetry:** Devotional or nature; 8-16 lines. **Fillers:** Crypto puzzles, cartoons; $.10-$.20. **Tips:** Send SASE for sample copy and guidelines. **Queries:** Not necessary. **E-Queries:** No. **Unsolicited mss:** Accepts. **Response:** Queries 2 weeks, submissions 6-8 weeks, SASE required. **Freelance Content:** 100%. **Rights:** One-time. **Payment:** On publication.

EVANGELICAL BEACON
901 E 78th St., Minneapolis, MN 55420. 952-854-1300.
Web site: www.efc.org/beacon.html. Diane McDougall, Editor. **Description:** Published by Evangelical Free Church. **Nonfiction:** Articles that fit editorial themes; 500-2,000 words; $.20/word. **Payment:** On publication.

FAITH & FAMILY
See full listing in Family & Parenting category.

FAITH TODAY

Evangelical Fellowship of Canada, P.O. Box 3745, Markham Industrial Park
Markham, Ontario L3R OY4 Canada. 905-479-5885.
E-mail: fteditor@efc-canada.com. Web site: www.faithtoday.ca. Bimonthly. Circ.:
18,000. Gail Reid, Managing Editor. **Description:** Seeks to inform, equip, and inspire
Christians across Canada. News stories and features on social trends and church
trends in Canada. Also, short, quirky items, with photo, on Christianity in Canada;
400-3,000 words; $.20-$.30/word (CDN). **Tips:** No devotionals or generic Christian-
living material. Sample copy free on request. **Queries:** Required. **E-Queries:** Yes.
Unsolicited mss: Does not accept. **Response:** 3 weeks, SASE required (IRCs).
Freelance Content: 75%. **Rights:** FNASR. **Payment:** On publication.

THE FAMILY DIGEST

P.O. Box 40137, Fort Wayne, IN 46804.
Bimonthly. Circ.: 150,000. Corine B. Erlandson, Manuscript Editor.
Description: Dedicated to the joy and fulfillment of Catholic family and parish life.
Especially looking for upbeat articles which affirm the simple ways in which the Catholic
faith is expressed in daily life. **Nonfiction:** Seeking articles on family life, parish life, spiritual life, saint's lives, prayer, how-to, and seasonal (seasonal articles should be submitted
7 months prior to issue date); 650-1,250 words; $40-$60. **Fillers:** Funny and unusual stories drawn from personal, real-life experience; 10-100 words; $25. **Tips:** Writing must
have a Catholic theme. Prefers original articles, but will consider reprints of pieces that
have appeared in non-competing markets. **Queries:** Not necessary. **E-Queries:** No.
Unsolicited mss: Accepts. **Response:** 4-8 weeks, SASE required. **Freelance
Content:** 90%. **Rights:** FNAR. **Payment:** 4-8 weeks following acceptance.

FELLOWSHIP

P.O. Box 271, Nyack, NY 10960-0271. 845-358-4601.
E-mail: editor@forusa.org. Web site: www.forusa.org. Bimonthly. $4.50/issue. Circ.:
8,000. Richard Deats, Editor. **Description:** Magazine of peace, justice, and nonvio-
lence. Published by the Fellowship of Reconciliation, an interfaith, pacifist organiza-
tion. **Nonfiction:** Articles for a just and peaceful world community; 750-2,500 words.
Art: B&W photo-essays on active nonviolence, peace and justice, opposition to war.
E-Queries: Yes. **Unsolicited mss:** Accepts. **Freelance Content:** 25%. **Payment:**
In copies.

FIRST THINGS

Institute on Religion & Public Life
156 Fifth Ave., #400, New York, NY 10010-7002. 212-627-1985.
E-mail: ft@firstthings.com. Web site: www.firstthings.com. 10x/yr. Circ.: 32,000.
James Nuechterlein, Editor. **Description:** General social commentary for academ-
ics, clergy, and general-educated readership on the role of religion in public life.
Nonfiction: Essays and features; 1,500-6,000 words; $400-$1,000. **Poetry:** 4-40
lines. **Tips:** Sample copy free upon request. **Queries:** Required. **E-Queries:** Yes.
Payment: On publication.

FOURSQUARE WORLD ADVANCE
1910 W Sunset Blvd., Suite 200, P.O. Box 26902, Los Angeles, CA 90026.
E-mail: comm@foursquare.org. Web site: www.foursquare.org. Ronald D. Williams, Editor. **Description:** Published by the International Church of the Foursquare Gospel. Religious fiction and nonfiction, 1,000-1,200 words, and religious poetry. Pays $75. Guidelines available. **Payment:** On publication.

THE FRIEND
See full listing in Juvenile category.

FRIENDS JOURNAL
1216 Arch St., 2A, Philadelphia, PA 19107. 215-563-5629.
E-mail: info@friendsjournal.org. Web site: www.friendsjournal.org. Monthly. $35/yr. Circ.: 8,000. Susan Corson-Finnerty, Publisher/Executive Editor. **Description:** Reflects Quaker life today by offering commentary on social issues, spiritual reflection, experiential articles, Quaker history, and world affairs. **Nonfiction:** With awareness of Friend's concerns and ways; fresh, nonacademic style; use language that clearly includes both sexes; to 2,500 words. **Poetry:** To 25 lines. **Fillers:** Quaker-related humor, games, and puzzles. **Tips:** Articles with positive approach to problems and spiritual seeking preferred. **Queries:** Not necessary. **E-Queries:** Yes. **Unsolicited mss:** Accepts. **Response:** 3-16 weeks, SASE required. **Freelance Content:** 70%. **Payment:** None.

THE GEM
Churches of God General Conference
P.O. Box 926, Findlay, OH 45839-0926.
E-mail: communications@cggc.org. Rachel Foreman, Editor. **Description:** Magazine offering true experiences of God's help, healed relationships, and maturing in faith; for adolescents to senior citizens. **Fiction:** 1,000-1,600 words; $15. **Nonfiction:** 300-1,600 words, $15. **Fillers:** $5-$10. **Tips:** Sample copy free on request with SASE.

GOSPEL TODAY
286 Highway 314, Suite C, Fayetteville, GA 37027-4519. 770-719-4825.
E-mail: gospeltodaymag@aol.com. Web site: www.gospeltoday.com. 8x/yr. $3/$20. Circ.: 50,000. Teresa Hairston, Publisher/Editor. **Description:** "America's leading gospel lifestyle magazine," aimed at African-American Christians. **Nonfiction:** Human-interest stories on Christian personalities, events. Book reviews welcome; 1,500-2,000 words; $150-$250. **Columns, Departments:** $50-$75. **Tips:** No opinions or poetry. **Queries:** Required. **E-Queries:** Yes. **Unsolicited mss:** Does not accept. **Response:** 6 weeks, SASE required. **Freelance Content:** 60%. **Rights:** All. **Payment:** On publication.

GROUP MAGAZINE

P.O.Box 481, Loveland, CO 80539. 970-669-3836.
E-mail: greditor@grouppublishing.com. Web site: www.groupmag.com; www.youthministry.com. $29.95. Circ.: 55,000. Rick Lawrence, Executive Editor. **Description:** Interdenominational Youth Ministry magazine for leaders of Christian youth. Provides ideas, practical help, inspiration, and training. **Nonfiction:** 500-2,000 words, $125-$350. **Columns, Departments:** Try This One (short ideas for groups: games, fundraisers, Bible study); Hands on Help (tips for leaders). **Tips:** "Use real-life examples, personal experience. Include practical tips, self-quizzes, checklists. Use Scripture. For guidelines and copy of magazine, send $2 with 9x12 SASE." **Queries:** Not necessary. **Unsolicited mss:** Accepts. **Response:** 6-8 weeks, SASE required. **Freelance Content:** 70%. **Rights:** All. **Payment:** On publication.

GUIDE

55 W Oak Ridge Dr., Hagerstown, MD 21740. 301-393-4038.
E-mail: guide@rhpa.org. Web site: www.guidemagazine.org. Weekly (52x/yr). $43.95/yr. Circ.: 33,000. Randy Fishell, Editor. **Description:** Christian publication for young people, ages 10-14. Adventure, personal growth, Christian humor, inspiration, biography, nature; with spiritual emphasis; 800-1,200 words. **Tips:** "Set forth a clearly evident Christian principle without being preachy." Encourages e-mail submissions (attached file or pasted into message). **Queries:** Not necessary. **Unsolicited mss:** Accepts. **Response:** 4-6 weeks, SASE required. **Freelance Content:** 95%. **Rights:** 1st, or one-time reprint. **Payment:** On acceptance.

GUIDEPOSTS

16 E 34th St., New York, NY 10016. 212-251-8100.
Web site: www.guideposts.com. Monthly. $12.97/yr. Circ.: 3,200,000. Edward Grinnan, Editor. **Description:** First-person inspirational magazine about people overcoming challenges through faith. **Nonfiction:** First-person true stories of people who face challenges, fears, illnesses through faith; 500 words and up; $100-$400. **Fillers:** Spiritual quotes; $25. **Columns, Departments:** What Prayer Can Do (power of prayer); Pass It On (people helping people) His Mysterious Ways (more than coincidence). 50-500 words; $25-$100. **Tips:** "Don't tell an entire life story; pick your specific "take-away" message." **E-Queries:** No. **Unsolicited mss:** Accepts. **Response:** 3 months, SASE required. **Freelance Content:** 75%. **Rights:** All. **Payment:** On publication.

GUIDEPOSTS FOR TEENS

See full listing in Teens category.

HADASSAH

Women's Zionist Organization of America
50 W 58th St., New York, NY 10019-2505. 212-355-7900.
E-mail: zshluker@aol.com. Web site: www.hadassah.org. Monthly. $25/yr. Circ.:

309,000. Zelda Shluker, Senior Editor. **Description:** General-interest Jewish feature and literary magazine; challenges, inspires, and informs while reinforcing the commitment of its readers to Judaism, Zionism, and Israel. **Nonfiction:** On issues important to Jewish life. **Queries:** Preferred.

INSIGHT

See full listing in Teens category.

JEWISH CURRENTS

22 E 17th St., #601, New York, NY 10003. 212-924-5740.
E-mail: babush@ulster.net. 6x/yr. $30. Circ.: 2,100. Lawrence Bush, Editor. **Description:** Articles, reviews, fiction and poetry on Jewish subjects. Seeks to present a progressive Jewish point of view on an issue. **Fiction:** Jewish angle, humor, contemporary flavor; to 2,500 words. **Nonfiction:** Jewish history, politics, culture, Yiddish language and literature (in English); to 3,500 words. **Tips:** "Our readers are secular, politically liberal." **Queries:** Not necessary. **E-Queries:** Yes. **Unsolicited mss:** Accepts. **Response:** Queries/submissions 1 month, SASE. **Payment:** In copies.

THE JEWISH JOURNAL

3580 Wilshire Blvd., Suite 1510, Los Angeles, CA 90010. 213-368-1661.
E-mail: editorial@jewishjournal.com. Web site: www.jewishjournal.com. **Description:** A nonprofit community weekly serving the Jewish community of greater Los Angeles. It welcomes unsolicited mss, and offers $100 per story for articles of up to 1,200 words, paying on publication. Submit by e-mail or surface mail to The Jewish Journal of Greater Los Angeles.

JOURNAL OF CHRISTIAN NURSING

Nurses Christian Fellowship
P.O. Box 7895, Madison, WI 53707-7895. 608-846-8560.
E-mail: jcn.me@ivcf.org. Web site: www.ncf-jcn.org. Quarterly. $22.95. Circ.: 7,000. Judith Allen, Editor. **Description:** Practical, biblically based articles to help nurses grow spiritually, meet patient's spiritual needs, and face ethical dilemmas. **Nonfiction:** Articles should help readers view nursing practice through the eyes of faith: spiritual care, ethics, values, healing and wholeness, psychology and religion, personal and professional growth, etc. Priority to nurse authors; work by others considered. 8-12 pages; $25-$80. **Poetry:** 1 page or less; $25. **Tips:** Avoid academic style. Prefers e-mail submissions sent as an attachment in MS Word. **Queries:** Not necessary. **E-Queries:** Yes. **Unsolicited mss:** Accepts. **Response:** 2-4 weeks, SASE required. **Rights:** 1st time, some reprint. **Payment:** On acceptance.

LEADERSHIP

Christianity Today International
465 Gundersen Dr., Carol Stream, IL 60188. 630-260-6200.
E-mail: ljeditor@leadershipjournal.net. Web site: www.leadershipjournal.net.

Quarterly. $24.95/yr. Circ.: 65,000. Marshall Shelley, Editor. **Description:** Provides first-person accounts of real-life experiences in the ministry for church leaders. **Nonfiction:** First-person stories of life in ministry; situation faced, solutions found. Articles must offer practical help (how-to format) for problems church leaders face; 2,000 words; $.15/word. **Tips:** "Avoid essays expounding, editorials arguing, or homilies explaining." **Queries:** Preferred. **E-Queries:** Yes. **Unsolicited mss:** Accepts. **Response:** Queries 3 weeks, submissions 6 weeks, SASE. **Freelance Content:** 30%. **Payment:** On acceptance.

LIBERTY

12501 Old Columbia Pike, Silver Spring, MD 20904-1608. 301-680-6690.
E-mail: steeli@nad.adventist.org. Web site: www.liberty magazine.org. Bimonthly. $6.95/issue. Circ.: 200,000. Lincoln Steed, Editor. **Description:** Focuses on religious freedom and church-state relations. Readers are legislators at every level, judges, lawyers, and other leaders. **Nonfiction:** Articles on religious freedom and 1st amendment rights; 1,000-2,500 words; $250 and up. **Tips:** Submit resume and clips. **Queries:** Preferred. **E-Queries:** Yes. **Unsolicited mss:** Does not accept. **Response:** Queries 1-3 months, submissions 30 days, SASE. **Freelance Content:** 95%. **Rights:** FNAR. **Payment:** On acceptance.

LIGHT AND LIFE MAGAZINE

P.O. Box 535002, Indianapolis, IN 46253-5002. 317-244-3660.
E-mail: llmauthors@fmcna.org. Web site: www.freemethodistchurch.org/Magazine. Bimonthly. $16/yr. Circ.: 18,000. Doug Newton, Editor. **Description:** Social and cultural analysis from evangelical perspective. **Fiction:** Short stories; 800-2,000 words. **Nonfiction:** Thoughtful articles about practical Christian living; 800-2,000 words. **Queries:** Not necessary. **E-Queries:** Yes. **Unsolicited mss:** Accepts. **Response:** Queries/submissions 8-10 weeks, SASE. **Rights:** FNAR. **Payment:** On publication.

LIGUORIAN

One Liguori Dr., Liguori, MO 63057. 636-464-2500.
E-mail: liguorianeditor@liguori.org. Web site: www.liguori.org. 10x/yr. Circ.: 230,000. William Parker, Editor. **Description:** Faithful to the charisma of St. Alphonsus, seeks to help readers develop a personal call to holiness. **Fiction:** Short stories with Catholic content; 1,700-1,900 words; $.12/word. **Nonfiction:** On Catholic Christian values in modern life; 1,700-1,900 words; $.12/word. **Queries:** Preferred. **E-Queries:** Yes. **Unsolicited mss:** Accepts. **Response:** 1-8 weeks, SASE required. **Freelance Content:** 20-30%. **Payment:** On acceptance.

THE LIVING LIGHT

U.S. Catholic Conference of Bishops, Dept. of Ed., Caldwell 345
Catholic University of America, Washington, DC 20064. 202-319-6660.
E-mail: bridoyle@aol.com. Quarterly. $39.95/yr. Circ.: 5,000. Berard Marthaler, Editor. **Description:** Catechetical educational journal sponsored by the U.S. Catholic Conference of Bishops. **Nonfiction:** Theoretical and practical articles, 1,500-4,000

words, on religious education, catechesis, and pastoral ministry. **Queries:** Preferred. **E-Queries:** No. **Unsolicited mss:** Does not accept. **Payment:** On publication.

LIVING LIGHT NEWS
Living Light Ministries
#200, 5306-89 St., Edmonton, Alberta T6E 5P9 Canada.780-468-6397.
E-mail: shine@livinglightnews.org; jeff@livinglightnews.org.
Web site: www.livinglightnews.org. 7x/yr. $2.50/$19.95. Circ.: 34,000. Jeff Caporale, Editor. **Description:** Family-oriented, contemporary Christian newspaper written primarily for non-Christians as a way of sharing the gospel. **Fiction:** Uses fiction for Christmas issue only. Send Christmas-related material that focuses on the true meaning of Christmas (the birth of Christ) and the values it brings. Seeks stories with humor; 300-1,000 words; $.08/word. **Nonfiction:** Powerful testimonials of well-known Christians in music, sports, and entertainment; 300-1,000 words; $.08/word. **Columns, Departments:** Helpful, informative family-related articles; 600-650 words. **Tips:** "Visit Web site to view our writer's guidelines and to grasp our editorial vision. We like writers who write with pizzazz!" **Queries:** Preferred. **E-Queries:** Yes. **Unsolicited mss:** Accepts. **Response:** 2-4 weeks, SASE required with Canadian postage or IRCs. **Freelance Content:** 80%. **Rights:** All. **Payment:** On publication.

LIVING WITH TEENAGERS
See full listing in Family & Parenting category.

THE LOOKOUT
8121 Hamilton Ave., Cincinnati, OH 45231. 513-931-4050.
E-mail: lookout@standardpub.com. Web site: www.standardpub.com. Weekly. $29.99/yr. Circ.: 100,000. Shawn McMullen, Editor. **Description:** Focuses on spiritual growth, family issues, people overcoming problems, and applying Christian faith to current issues. Articles run 500-1,800 words; $.05-$.12/word. **Queries:** Preferred. **E-Queries:** Yes. **Unsolicited mss:** Accepts. **Response:** 6-10 weeks, SASE required. **Rights:** First or reprint. **Payment:** On acceptance.

THE LUTHERAN
Evangelical Lutheran Church in America
8765 W Higgins Rd., Chicago, IL 60631-4183. 773-380-2540.
E-mail: lutheran@elca.org. Web site: www.thelutheran.org. Monthly. $15.95. Circ.: 600,000. David L. Miller, Editor. **Description:** Christian ideology, personal religious experiences, social and ethical issues, family life, church, and community of Evangelical Lutheran Church in America. **Nonfiction:** Articles on spirituality and Christian living; describing the unique life, service, challenges, and problems of ELCA congregations; describing the life and work of the ELCA and of its institutions, colleges, and seminaries; 400-1,400 words; $75-$600. **Columns, Departments:** My View; opinions on a current societal event or issue in the life of this church; up to 400 words. **Queries:** Required. **E-Queries:** Yes. **Response:** 1 month. **Rights:** One-time. **Payment:** On acceptance.

MARRIAGE PARTNERSHIP

Christianity Today International
465 Gundersen Dr., Carol Stream, IL 60188. 630-260-6200.
E-mail: mp@marriagepartnership.com. Web site: www.marriagepartnership.com.
Quarterly. $19.95/yr. Circ.: 57,000. Ginger Kolbaba, Managing Editor. **Description:**
Offers realistic, practical, and expert advice for Christian married couples.
Nonfiction: Related to marriage for men and women who wish to fortify their rela-
tionships; 1,000-2,000 words; $.15/word. **Fillers:** Humor welcomed; 1200 words.
Tips: No simultaneous submissions. **Queries:** Required. **E-Queries:** Yes.
Unsolicited mss: Does not accept. **Response:** Queries 8 weeks, SASE. **Freelance
Content:** 25%. **Rights:** FNAR. **Payment:** On acceptance.

MARYKNOLL MAGAZINE

Catholic Foreign Mission Society of America
P.O. Box 311, Maryknoll, NY 10545-0308. 914-941-7590, ext. 2490.
E-mail: mklmag@maryknoll.org. Web site: www.maryknoll.org. 11x/yr. $10/yr. Circ.:
600,000. Frank Maurovich, Editor. **Description:** Published by the Maryknoll
Fathers and Brothers. Christian-oriented publication focusing on articles concerning
the work of missioners overseas. **Nonfiction:** Articles relating to missions or mis-
sioners overseas; 1,500-2,000 words; $150. **Art:** Prints or slides; $50. **Queries:**
Required. **E-Queries:** Yes. **Unsolicited mss:** Does not accept. **Response:** SASE.
Freelance Content: 5%. **Payment:** On publication.

THE MENNONITE

1700 S Main St., Goshen, IN 46526-4794. 574-535-6051.
E-mail: editor@themennonite.org. Web site: www.themennonite.org. Twice Monthly.
$1.50. Circ.: 15,000. Everett Thomas, Editor. **Description:** For members of the
Mennonite Church USA. **Nonfiction:** Stories, faith perspectives emphasizing
Christian theme; 1,400 words; $.07/word. **Poetry:** 2 pages or less; $50-$75/poem.
Art: Electronic preferred. $35-$50. **Queries:** Not necessary. **E-Queries:** Yes.
Unsolicited mss: Accepts. **Response:** 2 weeks, SASE. **Freelance Content:** 20%.
Rights: One-time and web. **Payment:** On publication. **Contact:** Everett Thomas.

MESSENGER OF THE SACRED HEART

661 Greenwood Ave., Toronto, Ontario M4J 4B3 Canada. 416-466-1195.
Monthly. Circ.: 11,000. F.J. Power, S.J., Editor. **Description:** For American and
Canadian Catholics. Fiction and nonfiction pieces should run about 1,500 words;
$.06/word and up. **Payment:** On acceptance.

MIDSTREAM

See full listing in Current Events, Politics category.

MINISTRY & LITURGY

160 E Virginia St., Suite 290, San Jose, CA 95112. 408-286-8505.
E-mail: mleditor@rpinet.com. Web site: www.rpinet.com/ml. 10x/yr. $50/yr. Circ.:

10,000. Williams Burns, Publisher. **Description:** Practical, imaginative how-to help for Roman Catholic liturgy planners. **Tips:** Sample copy free on request. **Queries:** Required. **E-Queries:** Yes. **Contact:** Donna Cole, Managing Editor.

THE MIRACULOUS MEDAL
475 E Chelten Ave., Philadelphia, PA 19144-5785. 215-848-1010.
Quarterly. James O. Kiernan, C.M., Editor. **Description:** Religious literary journal focusing on the Catholic Church. **Fiction:** Any subject matter which does not not contradict teachings of Roman Catholic Church; 1,000-2,400; $.02/word. **Poetry:** Religious, preferably about Blessed Virgin Mary. 20 lines; $.50/line. **Tips:** Original material only. **Queries:** Preferred. **E-Queries:** No. **Response:** 6 months, SASE required. **Freelance Content:** 25%. **Rights:** FNAR. **Payment:** On acceptance.

MOMENT
See full listing in Ethnic & Multicultural category.

MY FRIEND
See full listing in Juvenile category.

NEW WORLD OUTLOOK
The United Methodist Church
475 Riverside Dr., Rm. 1476, New York, NY 10115-0122. 212-870-3765.
E-mail: nwo@gbgm-umc.org. Web site: http://gbgm-umc.org/nwo. Bimonthly. $15/yr. Circ.: 24,000. Christie R. House, Editor. **Description:** On United Methodist missions and Methodist-related programs and ministries. Focus on national, global, and women's and children's issues, and on men and youth in missions. **Nonfiction:** Articles, 500-2,000 words, illustrated with color photos. **Queries:** Preferred. **Payment:** On publication.

OBLATES
9480 N De Mazenod Dr., Belleville, IL 62223-1160. 618-398-4848.
Web site: www.oblatesusa.org. Bimonthly. Circ.: 450,000. Christine Portell, Editor. **Description:** Published by the Missionary Association of Mary Immaculate. **Nonfiction:** Articles, to 500 words, that inspire, uplift, and motivate through positive Christian values in everyday life; $150. **Poetry:** Perceptive, inspirational verse. Avoid obscure imagery, allusions, irreverent humor. Make rhyme and rhythm flow. 12 lines max; $50. **Tips:** "Try first-person approach. No preachy, psychological, theological, or spiritual journey pieces. Christian slant or Gospel message should be apparent, but subtle." **Queries:** Not necessary. **E-Queries:** No. **Unsolicited mss:** Accepts. **Response:** 4-6 weeks, SASE required. **Freelance Content:** 15%. **Rights:** FNASR. **Payment:** On acceptance. **Contact:** Mary Mohrman.

ON THE LINE
See full listing in Juvenile category.

OUR LITTLE FRIEND
See full listing in Juvenile category.

OUR SUNDAY VISITOR
200 Noll Plaza, Huntington, IN 46750.
E-mail: oursunvis@osv.com. Web site: www.osv.com. Weekly. $2/$37.95. Circ.: 66,000. Gerald Korson, Editor. **Description:** Reports on national and international news for Catholics, from a sound Catholic perspective. **Tips:** Query by mail or e-mail. Place "query" or "manuscript" in subject line. No phone calls. **Queries:** Preferred. **E-Queries:** Yes. **Unsolicited mss:** Accepts. **Response:** 6 weeks, SASE. **Freelance Content:** 10%. **Rights:** FNAR. **Payment:** On acceptance.

PASSPORT
See full listing in Juvenile category.

PASTORAL LIFE
Society of St. Paul
P.O. Box 595, Canfield, OH 44406-0595. 330-533-5503.
E-mail: plmagazine@hotmail.com. Web site: www.albahouse.org. Monthly. $17/yr. Circ.: 1,200. Rev. Matthew Roehrig, SSP, Editor. **Description:** Addresses the issues of Catholic pastoral ministry. Articles run 1,000-2,500 words; $.04/word. **Tips:** Prefers query by e-mail. Writer's guidelines available. **Queries:** Preferred. **E-Queries:** Yes. **Unsolicited mss:** Accepts. **Payment:** On publication.

THE PENTECOSTAL MESSENGER
P.O. Box 850, Joplin, MO 64802. 417-624-7050.
E-mail: johnm@pcg.org. Web site: www.pcg.org. Monthly. Circ.: 6,000. John Mallinak, Editor. **Description:** Covers issues of Christian commitment. Topics include social and religious issues and the Bible. Provides articles, human interest features, inspirational stories, and seasonal material. Edited for those in leadership. **Nonfiction:** Articles, 500-2,000 words; pays $.02/word. **Freelance Content:** 10%. **Payment:** On publication.

POCKETS
See full listing in Juvenile category.

PREACHING MAGAZINE
P.O. Box 681868, Franklin, TN 37068-1868. 615-599-9889.
E-mail: editor@preaching.com. Web site: www.preaching.com. Bimontlhy. Michael Duduit, Editor. **Description:** For professional ministers. Each issue contains model sermons which reflect the best of preaching today. Interdenominational, rooted in evangelical convictions. **Nonfiction:** Features (guidance on preaching and worship leadership), 1,750-2,000 words, $50. Sermons, 1,250-1,500 words, $35. **Fillers:** Abridged sermons, 600 words, $20. Children's sermons, 250-300, $10. **Tips:** Virtually all material written by active/retired pastors or seminary faculty; articles by non-

ministers rarely accepted. **Queries:** Preferred. **E-Queries:** Yes. **Payment:** On publication. **Contact:** Jonathan Kever, Managing Editor.

PRESBYTERIAN RECORD

50 Wynford Dr., Toronto, Ontario M3C 1J7 Canada. 416-441-1111.
E-mail: pcrecord@presbyterian.ca. Web site: www.presbyterian.ca/record. 11x/yr.
$20/yr. (U.S. & Foreign). Circ.: 50,000. David Harres, Editor. **Description:**
Published by The Presbyterian Church in Canada. **Fiction:** Stories of faith in action
that are contemporary and often controversial in nature; 1,000 words; $100.
Nonfiction: On children and youth ministries, lay ministries, etc. 750 words; $100.
Columns, Departments: Opinion, Meditation, Spirituality; pay varies. **Art:** Prefers
prints. **Queries:** Preferred. **E-Queries:** Yes. **Unsolicited mss:** Accepts. **Response:**
1-2 weeks, SASE required. **Freelance Content:** 30%. **Rights:** One-time.
Payment: On publication.

PRESBYTERIANS TODAY

Presbyterian Church U.S.A.
100 Witherspoon, Louisville, KY 40202-1396. 502-569-5637.
E-mail: today@pcusa.org. Web site: www.pcusa.org/today. 10x/yr. $15.95. Circ.:
60,000. Eva Stimson, Editor. **Description:** General-interest magazine for members
of the Presbyterian church (U.S.). **Nonfiction:** About Presbyterian people and
churches; guidance for daily living; current issues; 1,200-1,500 words; $300. **Fillers:**
Humorous anecdotes; 100 words or less; no payment. **Queries:** Preferred.
E-Queries: Yes. **Unsolicited mss:** Accepts. **Response:** 2-6 weeks, SASE required.
Freelance Content: 30%. **Rights:** FNAR. **Payment:** On acceptance.

THE PRIEST

Our Sunday Visitor, Inc.
200 Noll Plaza, Huntington, IN 46750-4304. 260-356-8400.
E-mail: tpriest@osv.com. Web site: www.osv.com. Monthly. $5/$39.95. Circ.: 6,500.
Owen F. Campion, Editor. **Description:** Assists priests, deacons, and seminarians in
day-to-day ministry. Items on spirituality, counseling, administration, theology, personalities, the saints, etc. **Nonfiction:** Historical/nostalgic, humor, inspirational,
interview/profile, opinion, personal experience, religious; relating to priests and
church; 1,500-2,500 words; $175-$250. **Queries:** Preferred. **E-Queries:** Yes.
Unsolicited mss: Accepts. **Response:** 5-12 weeks, SASE required. **Freelance
Content:** 25%. **Rights:** FNASR. **Payment:** On acceptance. **Contact:** Murray
Hubley, Associate Editor

PRIMARY TREASURE

See full listing in Juvenile category.

PURPOSE

616 Walnut Ave., Scottdale, PA 15683-1999. 724-887-8500.
E-mail: horsch@mph.org. Web site: www.mph.org. $20.95/yr. Circ.: 11,000. James E.

Horsch, Editor. **Description:** Publication for committed Christians who want to apply their faith in daily life. Suggests ways to resolve life's issues consistent with biblical principles. **Fiction:** Christian themes to nurture the desire for world peace and provide tools for peaceful living. Stories introducing children to many cultures; 750 words; up to $.05/word. **Nonfiction:** Articles to help others grow toward commitment to Christ and the church; 750 words; up to $.05/word. **Poetry:** Positive expression of love and caring; up to 16 lines; up to $20. **Queries:** Not necessary. **E-Queries:** Yes. **Unsolicited mss:** Accepts. **Response:** Up to 3 months, SASE required. **Freelance Content:** 90%. **Rights:** One-time. **Payment:** On acceptance.

QUAKER LIFE
Friends United Meeting
101 Quaker Hill Dr., Richmond, IN 47374-1980. 765-962-7573.
E-mail: quakerlife@fum.org. Web site: www.fum.org/ql. 10x/yr. $24/yr. Circ.: 7,000. Trish Edwards-Konic, Editor. **Description:** For members of Friends United Meeting, other Friends (Quakers), evangelical Christians, religious pacifists, and those who aspire to live a simple lifestyle. **Nonfiction:** Inspirational, first-person articles on the Bible applied to daily living, news and analysis, devotional and study articles, and personal testimonies; 750-1,500 words. **Poetry:** Evangelical in nature. **Tips:** Sample copy $2. **Queries:** Not necessary. **E-Queries:** Yes. **Unsolicited mss:** Accepts. **Response:** 2-8 weeks, SASE required. **Freelance Content:** 80%. **Rights:** 1st and multimedia. **Payment:** 3 copies.

QUEEN OF ALL HEARTS
26 S Saxon Ave., Bay Shore, NY 11706-8993. 631-665-0726.
Web site: www.montfortmissionaries.com. Bimonthly. Reverend Roger Charest, S.S.M., Managing Editor. **Description:** Publication that covers Marian doctrine and devotion. Particular focus is on St. Louis de Montfort's Trinitarian and Christocentric approach to Mary in spiritual lives. **Fiction:** 1,500-2,000 words; $40-$60. **Nonfiction:** Essays, inspirational, personal experience; 750-2,000 words; $40-$60. **Poetry:** Free verse; 2 poems max. **Queries:** Preferred. **Unsolicited mss:** Accepts. **Rights:** One-time. **Payment:** On publication.

RECONSTRUCTIONISM TODAY
30 Old Whitfield Rd., Accord, NY 12404. 845-626-2427.
E-mail: babush@ulster.net. Web site: www.jrf.org. Quarterly. $20/yr. Circ.: 14,000. Lawrence Bush, Editor. **Description:** For the Reconstructionist synagogue movement, with emphasis on creative Jewish living. **Nonfiction:** Personal Jewish journey, with a Reconstructionist connection; 1,000-2,500 words. **Art:** Photographs, illustrations; TIF, EPS, prints. **Queries:** Preferred. **E-Queries:** Yes. **Unsolicited mss:** Accepts. **Response:** 1-2 months, SASE required. **Freelance Content:** 25%. **Rights:** FNAR.

REFORM JUDAISM
Union of American Hebrew Congregations
633 Third Ave., Fl. 6, New York, NY 10017. 212-650-4240.
Web site: http://uahc.org/rjmag. Quarterly. $3.50/issue. Circ.: 310,000. Aron Hirt-Manheimer, Editor. **Description:** Published by the Union of American Hebrew Congregations to convey the creativity, diversity, and dynamism of Reform Judaism. **Fiction:** Thought-provoking, contemporary Jewish fiction; 1,200-2,000 words; $.30/word. **Nonfiction:** 1,200-3,500 words; $.30/word. **Tips:** "Read and understand this publication thoroughly before sending manuscripts. Many freelance submissions are clearly inappropriate." **Queries:** Not necessary. **E-Queries:** No. **Unsolicited mss:** Accepts. **Response:** 6-8 weeks, SASE or postage-paid postcard. **Freelance Content:** 25%. **Rights:** FNASR. **Payment:** On publication. **Contact:** Joy Weinberg, Managing Editor.

REVIEW FOR RELIGIOUS
3601 Lindell Blvd., St. Louis, MO 63108. 314-977-7363.
E-mail: review@slu.edu. Quarterly. David L. Fleming, S.J., Editor. **Description:** Catholic spirituality tradition stemming from Catholic religious communities. **Nonfiction:** Informative, practical, or inspirational articles; 1,500-5,000 words; $6/page. **Queries:** Preferred. **Payment:** On publication.

SACRED JOURNEY
291 Witherspoon St., Princeton, NJ 08542. 609-924-6863.
E-mail: editorial@sacredjourney.org. Web site: www.sacredjourney.org. Bimonthly. $18. Circ.: 5,000. Rebecca Laird, Editor. **Description:** Journal of Fellowship in Prayer. Focuses on spiritual practice, prayer, meditation, and service issues. Articles about spiritual life practiced by men and women of all faith traditions; to 1,500 words. **Art:** B&W prints; $40. **Tips:** Use inclusive language where possible. Guidelines available. **Queries:** Not necessary. **E-Queries:** Yes. **Unsolicited mss:** Accepts. **Response:** 2 months, SASE required. **Freelance Content:** 75%. **Rights:** FNAR. **Payment:** In copies.

ST. ANTHONY MESSENGER
28 W Liberty St., Cincinnati, OH 45210-1298. 513-241-5615.
E-mail: stanthony@americancatholic.org. Web site: www.americancatholic.org. Pat McCloskey, O.F.M. Editor. **Description:** A Catholic family magazine which aims to help readers lead more fully human and Christian lives by: reporting and putting into context the major events and movements in a changing Church and world; commenting on matters of significance from the perspective of Christian faith and values; expanding awareness, tolerance and understanding by presenting the views and achievements of others through interviews, personality profiles, and opinion articles; enriching, entertaining, and informing with fiction, columns, and features. **Tips:** Readers are people living in families or the family-like situations of Church and community. **Contact:** Amy Luken or Monna Younger, Editorial Assistants.

SEEK

8121 Hamilton Ave., Cincinnati, OH 45231. 513-931-4050.
E-mail: ewilmoth@standardpub.com. Web site: www.standardpub.com. Weekly.
Circ.: 34,000. Eileen H. Wilmoth, Senior Editor. **Description:** Relates faith in action
or Christian living, through inspirational or controversial topics, timely religious
issues, and testimonials. Articles run 400-1,200 words; $.05/word. **Tips:** No poetry or
simultaneous submissions. Send SASE for guidelines. **Queries:** Not necessary.
E-Queries: No. **Unsolicited mss:** Accepts. **Response:** 3-6 months, SASE.
Freelance Content: 95%. **Rights:** 1st and reprint. **Payment:** On acceptance.

SHARING THE VICTORY

See full listing in Sports & Recreation/Outdoors category.

SIGNS OF THE TIMES

P.O. Box 5353, Nampa, ID 83653-5353. 208-465-2577.
E-mail: signs@pacificpress.com. Web site: www.pacificpress.com/signs. Monthly.
$18.95. Circ.: 200,000. Marvin Moore, Editor. **Description:** For the public, showing
the way to Jesus, based on the beliefs of the Seventh-day Adventist church.
Nonfiction: Articles, 600-1,500 words, on Christians who have performed community services; first-person experiences, to 1,000 words; health, home, marriage,
human-interest pieces; inspirational articles; $.10-$.20/word. **Queries:** Not necessary. **E-Queries:** Yes. **Unsolicited mss:** Accepts. **Response:** Queries 2 weeks, submission 6 weeks, SASE required. **Freelance Content:** 20%. **Rights:** First.
Payment: On acceptance.

SPIRITUAL LIFE

2131 Lincoln Rd. NE, Washington, DC 20002-1151. 202-832-8489.
E-mail: editor@spiritual-life.org. Web site: www.spiritual-life.org. Quarterly.
$4.75/$18. Circ.: 11,000. Edward O'Donnell, O.C.D., Editor. **Description:** A professional religious journal, with essays on Christian spirituality with a pastoral application to everyday life. Articles run 5,000-8,000 words; $50/page. **Art:** B&W cover;
$100-$200. **Queries:** Not necessary. **E-Queries:** Yes. **Unsolicited mss:** Accepts.
Response: 8-10 weeks, SASE required. **Freelance Content:** 90%. **Rights:**
FNASR. **Payment:** On acceptance.

STANDARD

6401 The Paseo, Kansas City, MO 64131. 816-333-7000.
E-mail: evlead@nazarene.org. Web site: www.nazarene.org. Weekly. $9.95. Circ.:
150,000. Dr. Everett Leadingham, Editor. **Description:** Denominational Sunday
School take-home paper with leisure reading for adults (generally older adults with
conservative Holiness church background). **Fiction:** Inspirational stories,
Christianity in action; 1,200 words; $.035/word (1st); $.02/ word (reprint).
Nonfiction: Helpful articles; 1,200 words. **Poetry:** Christian themes; 25 lines max;
$.25/line (minimum $5). **Fillers:** Inspirational; 300-500 words. **Art:** B&W preferred;

pay varies. **Tips:** New writers welcome. Prefers short fiction; avoid fictionalized Bible stories. **Queries:** Not necessary. **Unsolicited mss:** Accepts. **Response:** 3 months. **Freelance Content:** 100%. **Rights:** One-time. **Payment:** On acceptance.

STORY FRIENDS
See full listing in Juvenile category.

TEACHERS INTERACTION
Concordia Publishing House
3558 S Jefferson Ave., St. Louis, MO 63118. 314-268-1083.
E-mail: tom.nummela@cph.org. Quarterly. $3.95/$12.95. Circ.: 14,000. Tom Nummela, Editor. **Description:** Builds up volunteer teachers of the faith, and church professionals who support them, in the ministry of sharing ideas, inspirational stories, and education. **Nonfiction:** Practical assistance for volunteer Christian teachers, especially Sunday school. Each issue on a central theme; inquire about upcoming themes; 1,000-1,200 words; $110. **Fillers:** Teachers Interchange (short activities, ideas for Sunday school classes, creative and practical); 150-200 words; $20-$40. **Columns, Departments:** 9 regular columns; 400-500 words; $55. **Art:** Color photos of children, all ages, in Christian educational settings other than day school; seeks to include children with disabilities and children of various ethnic backgrounds; $50-$100. **Queries:** Preferred. **E-Queries:** Yes. **Unsolicited mss:** Accepts. **Response:** 10-30 days, SASE. **Freelance Content:** 30%. **Rights:** All. **Payment:** On acceptance.

TEAM NYI
NYI Ministries, 6401 The Paseo, Kansas City, MO 64131. 816-333-7000.
E-mail: teamnyi@nazarene.com. Quarterly. Circ.: 10,000. Jeff Edmondson, Editor. **Description:** On the business and philosophy of youth ministry. **Nonfiction:** On youth ministry for both professional and volunteers. Must have solid Christian, biblical foundation and conform to Nazarene theology; 500-1,000 words; $50-$100. **Tips:** "Avoid ideas from the '70s and '80s; 21st-century teens are different. Need a good handle on postmodern mindset and millennial generation. Send e-mail query, or cover letter with attached article. Don't send fiction, poetry, historical articles, or exposés." **Queries:** Preferred. **E-Queries:** Yes. **Unsolicited mss:** Accepts. **Response:** 4 weeks, SASE. **Freelance Content:** 60%. **Rights:** FNAR, reprints, some work-for-hire assignments. **Payment:** On acceptance.

TIKKUN
See full listing in Current Events, Politics category.

TODAY'S CATHOLIC TEACHER
See full listing in Education category.

TODAY'S CHRISTIAN WOMAN
See full listing in Women's Publications category.

TODAY'S PENTECOSTAL EVANGEL

1445 N Boonville Ave., Springfield, MO 65802. 417-862-2781.
E-mail: pe@ag.org. Web site: www.pe.ag.org. Weekly. $28.99/yr. Circ.: 260,000. Hal Donaldson, Editor. **Description:** For Assembly of God members and potential members. Provides biblical and practical articles to inspire believers. **Nonfiction:** Religious, personal experience, devotional; 800-1,000 words; $.08/word. **Tips:** No queries; send complete manuscript only. **Queries:** Not necessary. **E-Queries:** No. **Unsolicited mss:** Accepts. **Response:** Queries 2 weeks, submissions 6 weeks, SASE. **Freelance Content:** 5%. **Rights:** 1st and electronic. **Payment:** On acceptance.

TRICYCLE: THE BUDDHIST REVIEW

92 Vandam St., New York, NY 10013. 212-645-1143.
E-mail: editorial@tricycle.com. Web site: www.tricycle.com. Quarterly. **Description:** Non-profit. Explores the nature of Buddhism in America. Looks at changes when exposed to American traditions, expressions in literature and the arts, and how it can illuminate possibilities facing people today. **Nonfiction:** All submissions must relate to Buddhism. Prefers shorter pieces (3,000 words or less). **Tips:** Prefers to review query before reading manuscript. Send query letter outlining idea, bio information (stating familiarity with subject matter), clips/writing samples, and SASE. **Queries:** Preferred. **E-Queries:** Yes. **Unsolicited mss:** Accepts.

TURNING WHEEL

P.O. Box 4650, Berkeley, CA 94704. 510-655-6169.
E-mail: turningwheel@bpf.org. Web site: www.bpf.org/bpf. Quarterly. $20/$45. Circ.: 8,000. Susan Moon, Editor. **Description:** Journal of socially engaged Buddhism. Covers issues of social justice and environment from a Buddhist perspective. **Nonfiction:** Themes for each issue (e.g., reconciliation, death penalty; medical ethics); 1,800-3,500 words. **Poetry:** Related to issue's theme. **Columns, Departments:** Reviews of books and films on social/spiritual issues; 450-850 words. **Tips:** "Avoid academic prose and new-age mushiness. Submit compelling personal experience, with analytical commentary. Contact us for upcoming themes." Also offers $500 Young Writers' Award for one essay in each issue. E-mail for guidelines. **Queries:** Preferred. **E-Queries:** Yes. **Unsolicited mss:** Accepts. **Response:** Queries 1 month, submissions 2 months, SASE required. **Freelance Content:** 40%. **Rights:** One-time. **Payment:** In copies.

U.S. CATHOLIC

205 W. Monroe St., Chicago, IL 60606. 312-236-7782.
E-mail: editors@uscatholic.org. Monthly. $22/yr. Circ.: 50,000. Rev. John Molyneaux, C.M.F., Editor. **Description:** Celebrates vibrancy and diversity of contemporary Catholicism. Promotes a positive vision of the Catholic faith today. Combines tradition with sense of humor and firm beliefs. **Fiction:** With strong characters that cause readers to stop and consider their relationships with others, the world, and/or God. Overtly religious themes not required; 2,000-4,000 words; $500. **Poetry:** All forms and themes; no light verse; submit 3-5 original poems; up to 50 lines; $75/poem. **Tips:**

"We combine tradition with sense of humor and a firm belief that the Catholic faith, well lived, responds to our deepest longings and aspirations." **Queries:** Not necessary. **E-Queries:** Yes. **Unsolicited mss:** Accepts. **Response:** 8-10 weeks, SASE required. **Freelance Content:** 10%. **Rights:** First North American. **Payment:** On acceptance. **Contact:** Maureen Abood.

THE UNITED CHURCH OBSERVER
478 Huron St., Toronto, Ontario M5R 2R3 Canada. 416-960-8500.
Web site: www.ucobserver.org. 11x/yr. **Description:** On religious trends, human problems, and social issues. **Nonfiction:** Factual articles, 1,500-2,500 words. **Tips:** No poetry. **Queries:** Preferred. **Payment:** On publication.

UNITED SYNAGOGUE REVIEW
155 Fifth Ave., New York, NY 10010. 212-533-7800.
E-mail: info@uscj.org. Web site: www.uscj.org. 2x/yr. Circ.: 250,000. Ms. Lois Goldrich, Editor. **Description:** Publication of the Conservative Movement, with features related to synagogues, Jewish law, and that organization. **Nonfiction:** Stories about congregational programs or developments in Conservative Judaism; 1,500 words. **Art:** Photographic prints; $200 (cover photo). **Tips:** No payment, but wide exposure to 1 million readers. "Writing should be crisp but not edgy or overly familiar. Our mission is to educate Conservative Jews as to development in their movement. We need a willingness to write stories as directed." **Queries:** Not necessary. **E-Queries:** Yes. **Unsolicited mss:** Accepts. **Response:** Queries immediate, submissions 1-3 months. **Freelance Content:** 25%.

THE WAR CRY
The Salvation Army
615 Slaters Lane, Alexandria, VA 22314. 703-684-5500.
Web site: www.thewarcry.com. Bi-weekly. $26.50/yr. Circ.: 400,000. Lt. Col. Marlene Chase, Editor-in-Chief. **Description:** Evangelist periodical used to spread the Word of God. **Nonfiction:** Must relate to modern life, and offer inspiration, information, or evangelization; essays with insightful perspective on living the Christian life; 800-1,500 words; $.10-$.20/word. **Art:** 5x7 or 8x10 color prints, transparencies; $50, $250 (cover). **Queries:** Not necessary. **Response:** 4-5 weeks, SASE. **Freelance Content:** 10%. **Payment:** On acceptance.

WITH
See full listing in Teens category.

WOMAN'S TOUCH
See full listing in Women's Publications category.

WONDER TIME
6401 The Paseo, Kansas City, MO 64131. 816-333-7000 Ext. 2244.
Weekly. None. Circ.: 14,000. Pamela Smits, Editor. **Description:** For children, ages

5-7. Emphasis on the religious instruction of children and parents. Issues are thematic. **Fiction:** A Christian emphasis to correlate with Sunday School curriculum. **Poetry:** Free verse or rhyming; 6-12 lines; $.25/word. **Columns, Departments:** Parent or family fun; 25-50 words; $15/activity. **Queries:** Preferred. **E-Queries:** No. **Unsolicited mss:** Does not accept. **Response:** 1-2 months, SASE. **Freelance Content:** 50%. **Rights:** All. **Payment:** On publication.

YOUNG SALVATIONIST
See full listing in Teens category.

YOUR CHURCH
Christianity Today International,
465 Gundersen Dr., Carol Stream, IL 60188. 630-260-6200.
E-mail: yceditor@yourchurch.net. Web site: www.yourchurch.net. Bimonthly. Circ.: 150,000. Michael J. Schreiter, Managing Editor. **Description:** Trade publication to help church leaders with the business side of ministry. **Nonfiction:** Articles on music/audio, lighting/video, management/administration, church furnishings/ buildings/transportation, and finance/law. **Tips:** "Almost all our articles are assigned. Send writing samples and manuscript suggestions via e-mail. Many articles involve interviewing business people, so interview skills are a plus." Sample copy free. **Queries:** Preferred. **Unsolicited mss:** Accepts. **Response:** Queries 1-2 months. **Freelance Content:** 10%. **Rights:** 1st . **Payment:** On acceptance.

YOUTH AND CHRISTIAN EDUCATION LEADERSHIP
See full listing in Education category.

YOUTHWALK
6401 The Paseo, Kansas City, MO 64131. 816-333-7000.
E-mail: youthwalk@wordaction.com. Web site: www.wordaction.com. Bimonthly. $1.95/issue. Circ.: 24,000. Andrew J. Lauer, Editor. **Description:** About theology, devotional classics, spiritual disciplines, and the Christian calendar, in language that speaks to today's students. **Nonfiction:** Articles about teens demonstrating Christian principles in real-life situations; 300-600 words; $30. **Columns, Departments:** Christian themes; 300-600 words; $30. **Tips:** Articles should come from working with teenagers. **Queries:** Required. **E-Queries:** Yes. **Unsolicited mss:** Does not accept. **Response:** 1-2 months, SASE required. **Freelance Content:** 20%. **Rights:** All. **Payment:** On publication.

SCIENCE

AD ASTRA
National Space Society
600 Pennsylvania Ave. SE, Suite 201, Washington, DC 20003-4316. 202-543-1900.
E-mail: adastraed@nss.org. Web site: www.nss.org. Bimonthly. $38/yr. Circ.: 25,000.
Frank Sietzen, Jr., Editor-in-Chief. **Description:** Lively, semi-technical features, on
all aspects of international space exploration. Not interested in material on astronomy.
Articles run 1,500-3,000 words; $350-$450. **Tips:** Prefers queries by e-mail. **Queries:**
Preferred. **E-Queries:** Yes. **Freelance Content:** 80%. **Payment:** On publication.

AIR & SPACE SMITHSONIAN
Smithsonian Institution
P.O. Box 37012, MRC 951, Washington, DC 20013-7012. 202-275-1230.
E-mail: editors@airspacemag.com. Web site: www.airspacemag.com. Bimonthly.
$3.99. Circ.: 225,000. George C. Larson, Editor. **Description:** Original articles on
aerospace topics for a lay audience. **Nonfiction:** Feature stories with original reporting, research, and quotes. General-interest articles on aerospace experience, past,
present, and future; 2,000-5,000 words; $2,000-$3,500. **Columns, Departments:**
Book reviews, soft news pieces, first-person recollections, and essays; 500-1,500
words; $350-$1,500. **Tips:** "Avoid sentimentalities (the majesty of flight, etc.). Don't
rehash—original research only. Send 1-2 page proposal detailing sources and interview list with published clips. Emphasize fresh angle." **Queries:** Required.
E-Queries: Yes. **Unsolicited mss:** Accepts. **Response:** 4-8 weeks, SASE required.
Freelance Content: 90%. **Rights:** FNASR. **Payment:** On acceptance.

AMERICAN ARCHAEOLOGY
Archaeological Conservancy
5301 Central Ave. NE #902, Albuquerque, NM 87108-1517. 505-266-9668.
E-mail: tacmag@nm.net. Web site: www.americanarchaeology.org. Quarterly.
$3.95/issue. Circ.: 32,000. Michael Bawaya, Editor. **Description:** Articles on all
aspects of archaeology in North America. **Nonfiction:** Nonfiction pieces on excava-
tions and technological advances; 1,500-3,000 words; $600-$2,000. **Art:** Slides or digital photos. Pays $200-$900. **Tips:** "Read an issue of the magazine. Though we're a
popular magazine, we have to be sophisticated about archaeology. No personal essays
about visits to archaeological sites." **Queries:** Required. **E-Queries:** Yes.
Unsolicited mss: Does not accept. **Response:** 3 weeks, SASE required. **Freelance
Content:** 60%. **Rights:** FNAR. **Payment:** On acceptance.

AMERICAN HERITAGE OF INVENTION & TECHNOLOGY
See full listing in History category.

ANNALS OF IMPROBABLE RESEARCH
P.O. Box 380853, Cambridge, MA 02238. 617-491-4437.
E-mail: air@improbable.com. Web site: www.improbable.com. Bimonthly. $29/yr.

Marc Abrahams, Editor. **Description:** Presents the mischievous, funny, and icono-clastic side of science. **Nonfiction:** Science reports/analysis and humor; 1-4 pages. **Poetry:** Brief science-related poetry. **Art:** B&W. **Queries:** Preferred. **E-Queries:** Yes. **Unsolicited mss:** Accepts. **Response:** SASE required.

ARCHAEOLOGY
Archaeological Institute of America
3636 33rd St., Long Island City, NY 11106. 718-472-3050.
E-mail: editorial@archaeology.org. Web site: www.archaeology.org. Bimonthly. $4.95/$20. Circ.: 225,000. Peter A. Young, Editor-in-Chief. **Description:** News mag-azine about archaeology worldwide. Written for lay people by professionals or writers with a solid knowledge of this field. **Nonfiction:** Profiles, excavation reports, discov-eries, photo essays; 500-2,500 words; $500-$1,500. **Columns, Departments:** Multimedia, museum news, book reviews; 500 words; $250-$500. **Queries:** Required. **E-Queries:** Yes. **Unsolicited mss:** Accepts. **Response:** 1 month, SASE required. **Freelance Content:** 70%. **Payment:** On acceptance.

ASTRONOMY
Kalmbach Publishing Co.
21027 Crossroads Circle, Waukesha, WI 53187. 262-796-8776.
E-mail: editor@astronomy.com. Web site: www.astronomy.com. Monthly. $4.95/$39.95. Circ.: 160,000. David J. Eicher, Editor. **Description:** Astronomical sci-ence and hobby activities, covering our solar system, Milky Way galaxy, black holes, deep-space observing, personality profiles, astronomical travel, etc. **Nonfiction:** Science stories on astronomy, astrophysics, space programs, recent discoveries. Hobby stories on equipment and celestial events; short news items. Features run 2,000-3,000 words; $200-$1,000. **Art:** Photos of astronomical phenomena and other affiliated subjects relating to stories; digital, slides, prints; $25/use. **Queries:** Preferred. **E-Queries:** Yes. **Unsolicited mss:** Accepts. **Rights:** 1st serial, all. **Payment:** On acceptance.

ENVIRONMENT
See full listing in Environment & Conservation category.

NATURAL HISTORY MAGAZINE
American Museum of Natural History
Central Park W at 79th St., New York, NY 10024. 212-769-5500.
E-mail: nhmag@amnh.org. Web site: www.naturalhistory.com. 10x/yr. $30/yr. Circ.: 225,000. Peter Brown, Editor. **Description:** Published by American Museum of National History. Articles mostly by scientists, on biological sciences, cultural and physical anthropology, archaeology, earth sciences, astronomy, vertebrates and inver-tebrates. **Nonfiction:** Informative articles; 800-2,500 words; $500-$2,500. **Art:** $350 (full page), $500 (Natural Moment section photo). **Tips:** "Read our magazine first, and research recent articles before sending your query." **Queries:** Preferred.

E-Queries: No. **Unsolicited mss:** Accepts. **Response:** Queries 4-6 months. **Freelance Content:** 30%. **Rights:** 1st. **Payment:** On publication.

ODYSSEY

See full listing in Teens category.

POPULAR SCIENCE

2 Park Ave., New York, NY 10016-5604. 212-779-5000.
E-mail: jenny.everett@time4.com. Web site: www.popsci.com. Monthly. $13.94/yr. Circ.: 1,572,500. Scott Mowbray, Editor-in-Chief. **Description:** On developments in science and technology. **Nonfiction:** Short illustrated articles on new inventions and products; photo-essays, book excerpts; with photos and/or illustrations; pay varies. **Payment:** On acceptance. **Contact:** Jenny Everett, Assistant Editor.

QUEST

University of North Dakota Space Studies Dept.
P.O. Box 5752, Bethesda, MD 20824-5752. 703-524-2766.
E-mail: quest@spacebusiness.com; sjohnson@aero.und.edu.
Web site: www.spacebusiness.com/quest. $30/yr. Circ.: 1,100. Stephen Johnson, Editor. **Description:** "The History of Spaceflight Quarterly." Journal on the history of spaceflight; the stories behind the space industry's triumphs and failures; includes articles and interviews with key people in the field. **Nonfiction:** Peer-reviewed articles written at the level of professional space historians. Interviews from transcribed excerpts from oral interviews also welcome. 5,000-10,000 words. **Columns, Departments:** Seeks shorter pieces by students and scholars. Also accepts short "encyclopedia style" reference pieces. Departments: Human Flight & Robotic Exploration; Military; International; Technology; Business; and Museums & Archives. 750-3,000 words. **Tips:** No payment offered for published articles. Prefers e-mail queries. **Queries:** Not necessary. **E-Queries:** Yes. **Unsolicited mss:** Accepts. **Freelance Content:** 100%.

SCIENCE & CHILDREN

See full listing in Education category.

SCIENCE WORLD

Scholastic, Inc., 555 Broadway, Fl. 3, New York, NY 10012-3919. 212-343-6100.
E-mail: scienceworld@scholastic.com. Web site: www.scholastic.com. Biweekly. $7.50. Circ.: 404,600. Mark Bregman, Editor. **Description:** On life science, earth science, physical science, environmental science, or health science, for 7th-10th graders, ages 12-15. **Nonfiction:** Science articles, 750 words; $200-$650. **Columns, Departments:** Science news, 200 words; pays $100-$125. **Tips:** Submit well-researched proposal, with anticipated sources, 2-3 clips of your work, and SASE. Writing should be lively, with an understanding of teens' perspectives and interests.

SCIENTIFIC AMERICAN
415 Madison Ave., New York, NY 10017. 212-754-0550.
E-mail: editors@sciam.com. Web site: www.sciam.com. Monthly. $34.97/yr. Circ.: 696,000. John Rennie, Editor-in-Chief. **Description:** Addresses all aspects of American scientific endeavor. **Queries:** Preferred.

SKY & TELESCOPE
49 Bay State Rd., Cambridge, MA 02138-1203. 617-864-7360.
E-mail: editors@skyandtelescope.com. Web site: www.skyandtelescope.com. Monthly. $39.95/yr. Circ.: 119,000. Bud Sadler, Managing Editor. **Description:** For amateur and professional astronomers worldwide. **Nonfiction:** Articles, mention availability of diagrams and other illustrations. $.25/word. **Columns, Departments:** Amateur Astronomers, Computers in Astronomy, Telescope Techniques, Astro Imaging, Observer's Log, Gallery. Also, 800-word opinion pieces, for Focal Point. **Queries:** Required. **Payment:** On publication.

TECHNOLOGY REVIEW
See full listing in Computers category.

TIMELINE
See full listing in History category.

21ST CENTURY: SCIENCE AND TECHNOLOGY
P.O. Box 16285, Washington, DC 20041. 703-777-7473.
E-mail: tcs@mediasoft.net. Web site: www.21stcenturysciencetech.com. Quarterly. $3.50/$25. Circ.: 19,500. Laurence Hecht, Editor-in-Chief. **Description:** Dedicated to the promotion of unending scientific progress, all directed to serve the proper common aims of mankind. **Tips:** "We challenge the assumptions of modern scientific dogma, including quantum mechanics, relativity theory, biological reductionism, and the formalization and separation of mathematics from physics. We demand a science based on constructible (intelligible) representation of concepts, but shun the simple empiricist or sense-certainty methods associated with the Newton-Galileo paradigm." **Queries:** Required. **E-Queries:** Yes. **Unsolicited mss:** Does not accept. **Response:** Varies, SASE required. **Rights:** One-time. **Payment:** On publication. **Contact:** Marjorie Mazel Hecht, Managing Editor.

UPDATE
2 E 63rd St., New York, NY 10021. 212-838-0230.
E-mail: update@nyas.org. Web site: www.nyas.org. Dan Van Atta, Editor. **Description:** Magazine for members of the New York Academy of Sciences. On all scientific disciplines. **Nonfiction:** Essays and features, 1,000-2,000 words. **Columns, Departments:** Book reviews. **Queries:** Preferred. **Payment:** Honorarium, on publication.

WEATHERWISE
1319 18th St. NW, Washington, DC 20036. 202-296-6267.
E-mail: ww@heldref.org. Web site: www.weatherwise.org. 6x/yr. Circ.: 11,000. Doyle Rice, Managing Editor. **Description:** Magazine covering a variety of issues on weather. Explores weather history, reviews new books, software, Web sites, and other media, and answers readers' questions. **Nonfiction:** 1,500-2,000 words; pays $200-$500. **Columns, Departments:** 300-1,000 words; pays to $200. **Queries:** Required. **E-Queries:** Yes. **Unsolicited mss:** Accepts. **Response:** 2 months. **Freelance Content:** 50%. **Rights:** All.

YES MAG
See full listing in Juvenile category.

SENIORS

AARP BULLETIN
601 E Street NW, Washington, DC 20049-0001. 202-434-2277.
E-mail: bulletin@aarp.org. Web site: www.aarp.org. Monthly. $10. Circ.: 21,068,000. Elliot Carlson, Editor. **Description:** Publication of American Association of Retired Persons. **Nonfiction:** Pay varies. **Queries:** Required. **Payment:** On acceptance.

AARP MAGAZINE
AARP Publications
780 Third Ave., Fl. 41, New York, NY 10017-2024. 646-521-2500.
Web site: www.aarpmagazine.org. Bimonthly. Circ.: 21.5 million. Hugh Delehanty, Editor-in-Chief. **Description:** General-interest membership magazine for members of AARP.

FOREVER YOUNG
467 Speers Rd., Oakville, Ontario L6K 3S4 Canada. 905-815-0017.
E-mail: don.wall@metroland.com. Web site: www.haltonsearch.com. Monthly. $20. Circ.: 482,500. Don Wall, Editor. **Description:** Multi-province Canadian publication, for senior citizens. **Queries:** Preferred.

GOOD TIMES
25 Sheppard Ave., Suite 100, Toronto, Ontario M2N 6S7 Canada. 416-733-7600.
E-mail: goodtimes@transcontinental.ca. 11x/yr. $21.95/yr. Judy Brandow, Editor. **Description:** Canadian lifestyle magazine for retired individuals. **Nonfiction:** Celebrity profiles, also practical articles on health, beauty, cuisine, hobbies, fashion, leisure activities, travel, taxes, legal rights, consumer protection. 1,300-1,500 words; $.40/word. **Poetry:** Features some poetry; no payment. **Columns, Departments:** Health, relationship, travel stories; 1,500-2,000 words; $.40/word. **Tips:** Canadian content only. **Queries:** Required. **E-Queries:** No. **Freelance Content:** 100%. **Rights:** 1st Canadian. **Payment:** On acceptance.

LIFE LINES
Lincoln Area Agency on Aging
1001 O St., Suite 101, Lincoln, NE 68508-3610. 402-441-7022.
E-mail: lifelines@ci.lincoln.ne.us. Bimonthly. $10/yr. Circ.: 42,000. Dena Rust Zimmer, Editor. **Description:** Magazine for seniors. Features short stories (to 450 words), poetry (to 40 lines), humor, and regular columns (Sports/Hobbies, Remember When . . ., Travels With . . ., Perspectives on Aging). **Tips:** Does not offer payment.

MATURE LIFESTYLES
P.O. Box 44327, Madison, WI 53744. 608-274-5200.
E-mail: anitaj@execpc.com. Monthly. $10/yr. Circ.: 43,000. Anita J. Martin, Editor. **Description:** Newspaper for the active, 50-plus population who reside in south central Wisconsin. **Tips:** Fax 1-page inquiries to 608-274-5492. Do not send materials through the mail or electronically. **E-Queries:** No.

MATURE LIFESTYLES
220 W Brandon Blvd., Suite 203, Brandon, FL 33511.
E-mail: srconnect@aol.com. Web site: www.srconnect.com. **Description:** For readers over 50, in Florida. **Nonfiction:** Articles, 500-700 words. **Tips:** No fiction or poetry. Florida angle required. **Payment:** On publication.

MATURE LIVING
Lifeway Christian Resources
One LifeWay Plaza, Nashville, TN 37234-1001. 615-251-2485.
E-mail: matureliving@lifeway.com. Web site: www.lifewayonline.com/mags. Monthly. $19.95/yr. Circ.: 330,000. David T. Seay, Editor-in-Chief. **Description:** A leisure reading magazine focusing on the personal and spiritual needs of senior adults to encourage growth, hope, and fulfillment in Christian living. **Queries:** Not necessary. **Unsolicited mss:** Accepts.

MATURE LIVING
255 N El Cielo Rd., #452, Palm Springs, CA 92262-6974. 760-320-2221.
E-mail: desertbiz1@aol.com. Monthly. $18. Circ.: 30,000. Carson Parlan, Editor. **Description:** For older adults in and around Palm Springs, California.

MATURE YEARS
United Methodist Publishing House
201 Eighth Ave. S, Nashville, TN 37202. 615-749-6292.
E-mail: matureyears@umpublishing.org. Quarterly. $18. Circ.: 50,000. Marvin W. Cropsey, Editor. **Description:** Seeks to help individuals in and near retirement years to understand the appropriate resources of the Christian faith that can assist them with the specific problems and opportunities of aging. **Fiction:** Stories with older adult characters in older adult situations; to 2,000 words. **Nonfiction:** Religious and inspirational articles; also, older adults in active lifestyles; 2,000 words; $.05/word.

Fillers: Bible puzzles. **Columns, Departments:** Health and fitness, personal finance, travel, poetry, fiction. **Art:** Photos. **Tips:** Welcomes new writers. **Queries:** Preferred. **E-Queries:** Yes. **Unsolicited mss:** Accepts. **Response:** 4-8 weeks, SASE required. **Rights:** One-time NA. **Payment:** On acceptance.

MILESTONES
Philadelphia Corporation for Aging
642 N Broad St., Philadelphia, PA 19103-3424. 215-765-9000.
Web site: www.pcaphl.org. Monthly. Circ.: 60,000. Don Harrison, Editor. **Description:** For seniors in the greater Philadelphia area.

MILITARY OFFICER
Military Officers Assn. of America
201 N Washington St., Alexandria, VA 22314-2539. 703-838-8115.
E-mail: editor@moaa.org. Web site: www.moaa.org/magazine. Monthly. $20/yr. Circ.: 386,000. Warren S. Lacy, Editor. **Description:** For active duty, reserve/national guard, retired and soon-to-be-retired members of the army, marine corps, navy, air force, coast guard, public health service, or NOAA and their surviving spouses. **Nonfiction:** Current military/political affairs, recent history (especially Vietnam and Korea), retirement topics, and general interest. Original only, no reprints. 1,400-2,500 words; $1,000-$1,800. **Tips:** Active voice, nontechnical, with direct quotes. Optimistic, upbeat themes. **Queries:** Required. **E-Queries:** Yes. **Unsolicited mss:** Does not accept. **Response:** 90 days. **Rights:** 1st, also Internet and reprint. **Payment:** On acceptance. **Contact:** Molly Wyman, Managing Editor.

NETWORK
Gray Panthers
733 15th St. NW, #437, Washington, DC 20005-2112. 202-737-6637.
E-mail: info@graypanthers.org. Web site: www.graypanthers.org. 6x/yr. Circ.: 30,000. George Neighbors, Editor. **Description:** National advocacy magazine for older adults.

NJ BOOMER X
1830 Rt. 9, Toms River, NJ 08755. 732-505-9700.
E-mail: pjasin@comcast.net. Web site: www.maturemarketnet.com. Monthly. Circ.: 250,000. Pat Jasin, Editor. **Description:** For active adults aged 45-65, in New Jersey. Upbeat articles on travel, sex, computers, dating, health/fitness, and books. **Queries:** Required. **E-Queries:** Yes. **Unsolicited mss:** Does not accept. **Response:** 2 months. **Freelance Content:** 10%. **Rights:** FNAR. **Payment:** In copies.

THE OLDER AMERICAN
Massachusetts Assn. of Older Americans
108 Arlington St., Boston, MA 02116-5302. 617-426-0804.
E-mail: bostonsrs1@aol.com. Web site: www.maoa-inc.org. Quarterly. $50. Circ.:

10,000. Phyllis Galante, Editor. **Description:** Local, state, and national advocacy and current affairs magazine for older adults.

PITTSBURGH SENIOR NEWS
3345 Evergreen Rd., Pittsburgh, PA 15237-2650. 412-367-2522.
Monthly. Circ.: 40,000. Teresa K. Flatley, Editor. **Description:** Topics of interest to older adults in the Pittsburgh area.

PLUS
823 Via Esteban., San Luis Obispo, CA 93401. 805-544-8711.
E-mail: gbrand@plusmagazine.net. Web site: www.seniormagazine.com. Monthly. Circ.: 60,000. George Brand, Editor. **Description:** Features entertainment and informative articles for readers ages 50 and up. **Nonfiction:** Book reviews, profiles, travel, business, sports, movies, television, and health; 600-1,200 words. **Queries:** Preferred. **E-Queries:** No. **Unsolicited mss:** Accepts. **Response:** Queries 1 week, submission 2 weeks, SASE. **Freelance Content:** 60%. **Rights:** 1st. **Payment:** On publication.

PRIME TIMES
P.O. Box 707, East Setauket, NY 11733-0769. 631-751-0356.
Monthly. Circ.: 50,000. Ann Fossan, Editor. **Description:** For older adults on Long Island, New York.

RETIREMENT LIFE
National Assn. of Retired Federal Employees
606 N Washington St., Alexandria, VA 22314. 703-838-7760.
Web site: www.narfe.org. Monthly. Circ.: 385,000. Margaret M. Carter, Editor. **Description:** Issues of interest to retired federal employees.

SECURE RETIREMENT
National Committee to Preserve Social Security and Medicare
10 G St. NE, Suite 600, Washington, DC 20002-4215. 202-216-0420.
E-mail: jbouley@imaginpub.com. Web site: www.ncpssm.org. Bimonthly. Circ.: 1.000,000. Jeffrey Bouley, Editor. **Description:** Advocates health and retirement issues for members of NCPSSM. **Nonfiction:** Policy and lifestyle features on age-related and retirement issues; 500-1,500 words; payment varies. **Queries:** Preferred. **E-Queries:** Yes. **Unsolicited mss:** Accepts. **Response:** 2-6 weeks; SASE required. **Freelance Content:** 70%. **Payment:** On publication. **Contact:** Jeffrey Bouley.

SENIOR CONNECTION
220 W Brandon Blvd., Suite 203, Brandon, FL 33511. 813-653-1988.
E-mail: srconnect@aol.com. Web site: www.srconnect.com. Monthly. $15/yr. Circ.: 130,000. Kathy Beck, Editor. **Description:** General-interest articles, for senior citizens in the west central and Tampa areas of Florida.

SENIOR CONNECTION

P.O. Box 38, Dundee, IL 60118. 847-428-0205.
Monthly. $18.95/yr. Circ.: 190,000. Peter Rubino, Editor-in-Chief. **Description:** For Catholics, ages 50-plus, with connections to northern Illinois parishes.

THE SENIOR TIMES

435 King St., Littleton, MA 01460. 978-742-9171.
E-mail: theseniortimes@aol.com. Monthly. Free newsstand/$18 subscription. Circ.: 28,000. Jane Jackson, Editor. **Description:** Features art and entertainment news for the active, over age 50 reader. **Nonfiction:** Articles on travel, entertainment, health, finance, senior advocacy issues, opinions, and local interviews. **Art:** Photos; 8x10 B&W; subjects from the greater Boston area (people, places, art); pay negotiable. **Queries:** Not necessary. **E-Queries:** Yes. **Unsolicited mss:** Does not accept. **Response:** SASE. **Payment:** On publication.

SENIOR TIMES

P.O. Box 30965, Columbus, OH 43230-0965. 614-337-2055.
E-mail: seniortimes@insight.rr.com. Monthly. $15.95/yr. Circ.: 60,000. Judith P. Franklin, Editor. **Description:** Ohio's newsmagazine for people over 55.

SENIOR TIMES

P.O. Box 142020, Spokane, WA 99214-2020. 500-024-2440.
E-mail: vnh@iea.com. Monthly. $24/yr. Circ.: 60,000. Mike Huffman, Editor. **Description:** For senior citizens in Washington State.

TODAY'S GRANDPARENT

Today's Parent Group
269 Richmond St. W, Toronto, Ontario M5V 1X1 Canada. 416-596-8680.
Web site: www.todaysparent.com. Quarterly. Circ.: 200,000. Laura Bickle, Editor. **Description:** For grandparents of all ages.

WHERE TO RETIRE

1502 Augusta Dr., Suite 415, Houston, TX 77057. 713-974-6903.
Web site: www.wheretoretire.com. 5x/yr. $11.95. Circ.: 20,000. R. Alan Fox, Publisher/Editor. **Description:** For anyone seeking retirement locale advice.

SPORTS, RECREATION, OUTDOORS

ADVENTURE CYCLIST

P.O. Box 8308, Missoula, MT 59807. 406-721-1776.
E-mail: mdeme@adventurecyling.org. Web site: www.adventurecycling.org. 9x/yr. $30/yr. Circ.: 41,000. Michael Deme, Editor. **Description:** Covers bicycle adventure travel; 1,500-3,000 words; $450-$1,200. **Queries:** Not necessary. **E-Queries:** Yes.

Unsolicited mss: Accepts. **Response:** 3 weeks, SASE required. **Freelance Content:** 80%. **Rights:** 1st. **Payment:** On publication.

AMERICAN FIELD
See full listing in Animals & Pets category.

AMERICAN HANDGUNNER
591 Camino de la Reina, Suite 200, San Diego, CA 92108. 619-297-5352.
E-mail: ed@americanhandgunner.com. Web site: www.americanhandgunner.com. Bimonthly. $16.95/yr. Circ.: 171,000. Roy Huntington, Editor. **Description:** Semi-technical articles on shooting sports, custom handguns, gun repair and alteration, handgun matches and tournaments, for lay readers. **Nonfiction:** Pays $100-$500. **Queries:** Required. **Payment:** On publication.

AMERICAN HUNTER
National Rifle Assn. of America
11250 Waples Mill Rd., Fairfax, VA 22030-9400. 703-267-1300.
E-mail: publications@nrahq.org. Web site: www.nra.org. Monthly. Membership. Circ.: 1,070,000. John Zent, Editor. **Description:** On all aspects of hunting and related activities (techniques, equipment, top places to hunt, legislation and current issues, and role of hunting in wildlife management). Safety and sportsmanship emphasized. **Nonfiction:** Features on deer, upland birds, waterfowl, big game, and varmints/small game. Includes how-to, where-to; general-interest pieces; humor; personal narratives and semi-technical articles on firearms, wildlife management, or hunting; 1,800-2,000 words; up to $800. **Columns, Departments:** Hunting Guns, Public Hunting Grounds; 1,000-1,200 words; $300-$450. **Art:** Color slides; pay varies, $450-$600 (cover). **Tips:** Judges submissions on story angle, quality of writing, and quality/quantity of photos." **Queries:** Preferred. **E-Queries:** Yes. **Unsolicited mss:** Accepts. **Response:** 2 months or more, SASE required. **Freelance Content:** 50%. **Rights:** FNASR, reprint in NRA publication. **Payment:** On acceptance.

AMERICAN RIFLEMAN
National Rifle Assn. of America
11250 Waples Mill Rd., Suite 4, Fairfax, VA 22030-7400. 703-267-1336.
E-mail: mkeefe@nrahq.org. Web site: www.publications.nrhq.org. Monthly. $35. Circ.: 1,366,000. Mark Keefe, Executive Editor. **Description:** Articles on use and enjoyment of sporting firearms. **Payment:** On acceptance.

AQUA-FIELD
P.O. Box 575, Navesink, NJ 07752.
17x/yr. **Description:** Recreation/outdoors publication with how-to features on hunting, fishing, fly-fishing, and outdoor adventure. Interested in new approaches to activities or improvements on tried-and-true methods. Articles run 1,500-3,000 words. **Art:** Color slides or B&W prints. **Queries:** Preferred.

BACKPACKER
Rodale Press, Inc., 33 E Minor St., Emmaus, PA 18098. 610-967-8296.
E-mail: editor@backpacker.com. Web site: www.backpacker.com. 9x/yr. $19.97/yr.
Circ.: 285,500. Jonathan Dorn, Executive Editor. **Description:** On self-propelled
backcountry travel (backpacking, kayaking/canoeing, mountaineering; technique,
nordic skiing, health, natural science). **Nonfiction:** Articles; 250-3,000 words; pay
varies. **Art:** Photos. **Queries:** Preferred.

BACKWOODSMAN
P.O. Box 627, Westcliffe, CO 81252. 719-783-9028.
E-mail: bwmmag@ris.net. Web site: www.backwoodsmanmag@.com. Bimonthly.
$4/issue. Circ.: 40,000. Charlie Richie, Editor. **Description:** On muzzleloaders,
19th-century woods lore, early cartridge guns, primitive survival, craft items,
American history, gardening, leather crafting, homesteading, log cabin construction,
mountain men, Indians, building primitive weapons. **Nonfiction:** Historical and
how-to articles for the 20th-century frontiersman. **Queries:** Preferred. **E-Queries:**
Yes. **Unsolicited mss:** Accepts. **Response:** 3 days, SASE required. **Freelance
Content:** 50%. **Payment:** In copies.

BALLOON LIFE
2336 47th Ave. SW, Seattle, WA 98116-2331. 206-935-3649.
E-mail: tom@balloonlife.com. Web site: www.balloonlife.com. Monthly. $30/yr. Circ.:
2,500. Tom Hamilton, Editor-in-Chief. **Description:** Magazine for those involved in
the sport of hot air ballooning. **Nonfiction:** Balloon events/rallies; safety seminars;
balloon clubs/organizations; and general-interest stories with interviews or biographies of people who have made a contribution to the sport. Most pieces run 1,000-
1,500 words, some shorter articles 300-500 words. Pays $20-$50. **Columns,
Departments:** "Crew Quarters" (column on crewing; 900 words. **Art:** Photos:
35mm color transparencies. Also accepts B&W. Pays $50 for cover photos, $15 for
inside color or B&W. **Queries:** Preferred. **E-Queries:** Yes. **Unsolicited mss:**
Accepts. **Response:** 2 weeks, SASE required. **Freelance Content:** 80%. **Rights:**
One-time, non-exclusive.

BASSIN'
15115 S 76th E Ave., Bixby, OK 74008-4114. 918-366-6191.
Web site: www.ebassin.com. 7x/yr. $15.95/yr. Circ.: 165,000. Jason Sowards, Editor.
Description: How and where to bass fish, for the amateur fisherman. **Nonfiction:**
Articles; 1,200-1,400 words; pays $350-$500. **Queries:** Preferred. **Payment:** On
acceptance.

BAY & DELTA YACHTSMAN
4090 S McCarran Blvd., Suite E, Reno, NV 89502-7529. 775-353-5100.
E-mail: christina@renotahoeshowtime.com. Web site: www.yachtsforsale.com.
Monthly. $17.60/yr. Circ.: 30,000. Don Abbott, Publisher. **Description:** Cruising sto-
ries and features, how-tos, with northern California focus. **Nonfiction:** Boating

experiences, anecdotes, around San Francisco Bay and Delta; 2,000 words; pay varies. **Columns, Departments:** Boating stories, boat maintenance; 4,000 words. **Art:** TIF or JPG (300 dpi). **Queries:** Preferred. **E-Queries:** Yes. **Unsolicited mss:** Accepts. **Response:** 1 week, SASE required. **Freelance Content:** 0%. **Payment:** On publication. **Contact:** Christina Montroy, Editor.

BICYCLING

Rodale Press, Inc., 135 N Sixth St., Emmaus, PA 18098-0001. 610-967-5171. E-mail: bicycling@rodale.com. Web site: www.bicycling.com. Monthly. $19.97/yr. Circ.: 286,800. Steve Madden, Editor. **Description:** For cyclists, on recreational riding, fitness training, nutrition, bike maintenance, equipment, and racing. Covers all aspects of sport (road, mountain biking, leisure, etc.). **Nonfiction:** Articles; 500-2,500 words; pays $50-$2,000. **Art:** Photos, illustrations. **Tips:** "We prefer queries instead of manuscripts. We're currently looking for interesting cycling personalities and adventure stories." **Queries:** Preferred. **Payment:** On acceptance. **Contact:** Doug Donaldson, Associate Editor.

BIRD WATCHER'S DIGEST

See full listing in Environment & Conservation category.

BIRDER'S WORLD

See full listing in Environment & Conservation category.

BLACK BELT

24900 Anza Dr., Unit E, Valencia, CA 91355. 661-257-4066. E-mail: byoung@sabot.net. Web site: www.blackbeltmag.com. Monthly. $32/yr. Circ.: 85,000. Robert Young, Executive Editor. **Description:** Articles on self-defense (how-tos on fitness/technique; historical, travel, philosophy); $100-$300.

THE BOUNDARY WATERS JOURNAL

9396 Rocky Ledge Rd., Ely, MN 55731. 218-365-6184. E-mail: bwjournal@boundarywatersjournal.com. Web site: www.boundarywatersjournal.com. Quarterly. $4.95/$18. Circ.: 32,000. Stuart Osthoff, Publisher. **Description:** In-depth outdoor guide covering Boundary Waters Canoe Area Wilderness, Quetico Provincial Park, and surrounding Superior National Forest. **Fiction:** Must relate to coverage area; $100-$400. **Nonfiction:** Canoe routes, camping, fishing, resort vacations, hiking, hunting, photography, wildlife, ecology, outdoor cooking, area history, regional personalities; must relate to coverage area; 1-5 pages; $100-$400. **Poetry:** Up to 1 page; must relate to coverage area; $50-$100. **Art:** Color slides; B&W photos and artwork; $50/half page, $100/full page, $150/cover. **Tips:** Often needs winter stories. **Queries:** Not necessary. **E-Queries:** Yes. **Unsolicited mss:** Accepts. **Response:** 1-2 weeks for queries, 1-3 months for submissions; SASE required. **Freelance Content:** 50%. **Rights:** FNAR. **Payment:** On publication. **Contact:** Laurie Antonson, Editor.

BOW & ARROW HUNTING

265 S Anita Dr., Suite 120, Orange, CA 92868. 714-939-9991.
E-mail: editorial@bowandarrowhunting.com.
Web site: www.bowandarrowhunting.com. 9x/yr. $20/yr. Circ.: 90,673. Joe Bell,
Editor. **Description:** On bowhunting (profiles and technical pieces), primarily on
deer hunting. **Nonfiction:** Articles 1,200-2,500 words, with color slides, B&W, or
color photos; pays $250-$500. **Payment:** On publication.

BOWHUNTER

PRIMEDIA Enthusiast Group
6405 Flank Dr., Harrisburg, PA 17112. 717-657-9555.
E-mail: bowhunter_magazine@primediamags.com. Web site: www.bowhunter.com.
9x/yr. $3.50/$23.94. Circ.: 180,250. Dwight Schuh, Editor-in-Chief. **Description:**
Information for bowhunters, on all aspects of the sport, to entertain and inform
readers, making them better bowhunters. **Nonfiction:** General interest, how-to,
interview/profile, opinion, personal experience, photo features; 250-2,000 words;
$100-$400. **Art:** 35mm slides, 5x7 or 8x10 prints; $75-$250. **Tips:** "Anticipate all
questions, then answer them in article or sidebar." **Queries:** Preferred. **E-Queries:**
Yes. **Unsolicited mss:** Accepts. **Response:** Queries 1 month, submissions 5 weeks,
SASE required. **Freelance Content:** 100%. **Rights:** FNASR, one-time. **Payment:**
On acceptance. **Contact:** Jeff S. Waring, Managing Editor.

BOWHUNTING WORLD

6420 Sycamore Lane N #100, Maple Grove, MN 55305. 612-476-2200.
E-mail: bowhuntwor@aol.com. Web site: www.bowhuntingworld.com. Bimonthly.
$20/yr. Circ.: 130,000. Mike Strandlund, Editor. **Description:** Covers all aspects of
bowhunting and competitive archery equipment, with photos. **Nonfiction:** Seeking
how-to articles on bowhunting techniques, feature articles on hunting and the
mechanics of archery gear (traditional to high-tech); 1,800-3,000 words. **Columns,
Departments:** Mini-features; 1,000-1,600 words. **Tips:** Outline no more than 6 article ideas per query. **Queries:** Preferred. **E-Queries:** Yes. **Unsolicited mss:** Accepts.
Response: Queries 3 week, submission 6 weeks, SASE required. **Freelance
Content:** 50%. **Rights:** 1st. **Payment:** On acceptance.

BOWLERS JOURNAL INTERNATIONAL

122 S. Michigan Ave., Ste. 1506, Chicago, IL 60603-6194. 312-341-1110.
E-mail: jimd@lubypublishing.com. Web site: www.bowlersjournal.com. Monthly.
$24. Circ.: 22,300. Jim Dressel, Editor. **Description:** Covers the bowling industry
with features on trends, new products, and management. **Nonfiction:** Trade and
consumer articles; 1,200-2,200 words; $75-$250. **Art:** Photos to accompany articles.
Queries: Required. **E-Queries:** Yes. **Unsolicited mss:** Does not accept. **Payment:**
On acceptance.

BOYS' LIFE

See full listing in Juvenile category.

BUCKMASTERS WHITETAIL MAGAZINE

P.O. Box 244022, Montgomery, AL 36124-4022. 334-215-3337.
E-mail: rthornberry@buckmasters.com. Web site: www.buckmasters.com. 6x/yr.
$26/yr. Circ.: 330,000. Russell Thornberry, Executive Editor. **Description:** For serious sportsmen. **Nonfiction:** Articles, to 2,500 words. "Big Buck Adventures" capture details and adventure of the hunt of a newly discovered trophy. Fresh, new whitetail hunting how-tos; new useful biological information about whitetail deer. Pays $250-$400. **Columns, Departments:** Entertaining deer stories. **Art:** Photos helpful. **Queries:** Preferred.

CANOE & KAYAK MAGAZINE

PRIMEDIA Enthusiast Group
P.O. Box 3146, Kirkland, WA 98083-3146 . 425-827-6363.
E-mail: mike@canoekayak.com. Web site: www.canoekayak.com. Bimonthly.
$17.95/yr. Circ.: 67,300. Ross Prather, Editor-in-Chief. **Description:** Articles and features on canoeing and kayaking adventures, destinations, boat and equipment reviews, techniques and how-tos, short essays, camping, environment, safety, humor, health, and history. **Nonfiction:** Features (1,500-2,000 words); department pieces (500-1,200 words); $.15/word. **Queries:** Preferred. **Payment:** On publication.

CASCADES EAST

716 NE Fourth St., PO Box 5784, Bend, OR 97708-5784. 541-382-0127. E-mail: sunpub@sun-pub.com. Web site: www.sun-pub.com. Quarterly. $16/yr. Circ.: 10,000. Geoff Hill, Publisher/Editor. **Description:** Outdoor activities (fishing, hunting, golfing, backpacking, rafting, skiing, snowmobiling, etc.), history, special events, and scenic tours in central Oregon Cascades. **Nonfiction:** 1,000-2,000 words; $.05-$.15/word. **Fillers:** Travel, history, and recreation in central Oregon; $.05-.$15/word. **Art:** Photos; pays extra. **Queries:** Preferred. **Payment:** On publication.

CHESAPEAKE BAY MAGAZINE

1819 Bay Ridge Ave., Annapolis, MD 21403. 410-263-2662.
E-mail: editor@cbmmag.net. Web site: www.cbmmag.net. Monthly. $4.50/issue. Circ.: 46,000. T.F. Sayles, Editor. **Description:** For recreational boaters on the Chesapeake Bay. Boating, fishing, destinations, people, history, and traditions of the Chesapeake Bay; to 3,000 words; $75-$800. **Tips:** "Writers need to be familiar with the Chesapeake Bay region and boating. Our readers are well-educated and well-traveled." **Queries:** Preferred. **E-Queries:** Yes. **Unsolicited mss:** Accepts. **Response:** 1-4 weeks, SASE required. **Freelance Content:** 30%. **Rights:** FNASR. **Payment:** On acceptance. **Contact:** Jane Meneely, Managing Editor.

CROSS COUNTRY SKIER

P.O. Box 550, Cable, WI 54821-0550. 715-798-5500.
E-mail: lou@crosscountryskier.com. Web site: www.crosscountryskier.com. 4x/yr.
$12.97/yr. Circ.: 30,000. Lou Dzierzak, Executive Editor. **Description:** Publishes

articles on all aspects of cross-country skiing. **Nonfiction:** Destination articles; to 2,000 words; $200-$400. **Columns, Departments:** Pieces on ski lifestyle, techniques, health/fitness, etc. 1,000-1,500 words; $100-$250. **Tips:** Published October-January. **Queries:** Preferred. **Payment:** On publication.

DAKOTA OUTDOORS
P.O. Box 669, 333 W Dakota Ave., Pierre, SD 57501. 605-224-7301.
Monthly. $2.25/$10. Circ.: 8,000. Kevin Hipple, Editor. **Description:** Articles on hunting and fishing for outdoorsman in the Dakotas. Fiction and nonfiction pieces run 1,000-1,500 words; $5-$50. **Queries:** Not necessary. **E-Queries:** No. **Unsolicited mss:** Accepts. **Response:** 2 weeks, SASE required. **Freelance Content:** 75%. **Rights:** One-time. **Payment:** On publication.

DIVER MAGAZINE
P.O. Box 1312, Delta, British Columbia V4M 3Y8 Canada. 604-948-9937.
E-mail: divermag@axion.net. Web site: www.divermag.com. 9x/yr. $18/yr. Circ.: 7,000. Peter Vassilopoulos, Editor. **Description:** On scuba diving, ocean science and technology for well-educated, outdoor enthusiasts. **Nonfiction:** Illustrated articles on Canadian and North American dive destinations, interviews, personal experiences; 500-1,000 words; $2.50/column inch. **Art:** To accompany articles; original slides, color prints, maps, drawings; C$15 and up. **Tips:** Does not offer payment for travel articles. **Queries:** Not necessary. **E-Queries:** Yes. **Unsolicited mss:** Accepts. **Response:** SASE required. **Freelance Content:** 30%. **Rights:** FNAR. **Payment:** On publication. **Contact:** Barb Roy, Assistant Editor.

ELYSIAN FIELDS QUARTERLY
P.O. Box 14385, St. Paul, MN 55114-0385. 651-644-8558.
E-mail: info@efqreview.com. Web site: www.efqreview.com. Quarterly. $5.95/$22.50. Circ.: 2,500. Tom Goldstein, Editor. **Description:** "The Baseball Review." Literary review for baseball, with essays, poetry, commentary, drama, book reviews, and humor ("anything about baseball is fair game"). 400-4,500 words. **Tips:** Must have a passion and appreciation for baseball, and be able to write well. "This is not a journal about hero-worship and nostalgia. Sentimental, ill-conceived, formulaic writing from would-be writers or those looking to publish a 'baseball' story get tossed quickly." **Queries:** Not necessary. **E-Queries:** Yes. **Unsolicited mss:** Accepts. **Response:** 6-9 months (fiction/poetry), 3-4 months (other), SASE. **Freelance Content:** 75%. **Rights:** One-time, anthology. **Payment:** In copies.

EXPLORE: CANADA'S OUTDOOR ADVENTURE MAGAZINE
54 Saint Patrick St., Toronto, Ontario M5T 1V1 Canada. 416-599-2000.
E-mail: explore@explore-mag.com. Web site: www.explore-mag.com. 6x/yr. Circ.: 30,700. James Little, Editor. **Description:** For Canada's active outdoor enthusiasts. Covers adventure travel, hiking, mountain biking, climbing, paddling, winter sports, and more. **Nonfiction:** Features (profiles, adventure stories, destinations).

Columns, Departments: Explorata (people & outdoor events in the news); The Lowdown (outdoor gear); Techniques; Places to Go; Backcountry (humor). **Queries:** Required. **E-Queries:** Yes.

FIELD & STREAM
2 Park Ave., New York, NY 10016-5604. 212-779-5286.
E-mail: fsmagazine@aol.com. Web site: www.fieldandstream.com. Monthly. $3.99/$15.97. Circ.: 1,500,000. Sid Evans, Editor-in-Chief. **Description:** The nation's largest hunting and fishing magazine. **Fiction:** On aspects of hunting and fishing. **Nonfiction:** On aspects of hunting and fishing: tactics/techniques, nostalgia, conversation essays, profiles, humor. Pay, length vary. **Fillers:** Cartoons, small fillers (how-to); $100-$250. **Queries:** Preferred. **E-Queries:** Yes. **Unsolicited mss:** Accepts. **Response:** 2-4 weeks, SASE required. **Freelance Content:** 85%. **Rights:** FNAR. **Payment:** On acceptance.

FISHING FACTS
111 Shore Dr., Burr Ridge, IL 60527. 630-887-7722.
E-mail: info@midwestoutdoors.com. Web site: www.fishingfacts.com. Bimonthly. $23.95. Gene Laulunen, Publisher/Editor. **Description:** For the angler who wants to improve skills and maximize success. In-depth articles on fish behavior, techniques for taking fish from all kinds of structure, the latest in fishing products and technology, and simple tips from experts. **Nonfiction:** Seeking cutting-edge information on latest fishing techniques and tips; 750-1,500 words; $30. **Art:** Submit quality, full-color prints with each article. **Tips:** No elementary fishing techniques or everyday fishing stories. **Queries:** Required. **E-Queries:** Yes. **Unsolicited mss:** Accepts. **Response:** 10 days, SASE required. **Rights:** 1st. **Payment:** On publication.

FLIGHT JOURNAL
100 E Ridge Rd., Ridgefield, CT 06877-4606. 203-431-9000.
E-mail: flightjournal@airage.com. Web site: www.flightjournal.com. Bimonthly. $19.95/yr. Circ.: 76,000. Tom Atwood, Editorial Director. **Description:** Covers "the history, the hardware, and the human heart of aviation." **Nonfiction:** Articles, 2,500-3,000 words; pays $600. **Tips:** Submit 1-page outline. **Contact:** Roger Post, Editor.

FLY FISHERMAN MAGAZINE
PRIMEDIA Enthusiast Group
6405 Flank Dr., Harrisburg, PA 17112-2750. 717-657-9555.
E-mail: john@cowles.com. Web site: www.flyshop.com. 6x/yr. $24/yr. Circ.: 122,500. John Randolph, Editor. **Description: Queries:** Required.

FLY ROD & REEL
P.O. Box 370, Camden, ME 04843. 207-594-9544.
E-mail: pguernsey@flyrodreel.com. Web site: www.flyrodreel.com. Paul Guernsey, Editor. **Description:** Articles and features on fly-fishing and the culture/history of

areas being fished; occasional fiction. 2,000-2,500 words; pay varies. **Queries:** Preferred. **Payment:** On acceptance.

FOOTBALL DIGEST
990 Grove St., Evanston, IL 60201-6510. 847-491-6440.
E-mail: fb@centurysports.net. Web site: www.centurysports.net. Monthly. $23.94/yr. Circ.: 180,000. William Wagner, Editor-in-Chief. **Description:** For the hard-core football fan. Profiles of pro and college stars, nostalgia, trends in the sport. **Nonfiction:** Articles, 1,500-2,500 words. **Queries:** Preferred. **Payment:** On publication.

FUR-FISH-GAME
2878 E Main St., Columbus, OH 43209. 614-231-9585.
Monthly. $3.99/issue. Circ.: 107,000. Mitch Cox, Editor. **Description:** For serious outdoorsmen of all ages. Covers hunting, trapping, freshwater fishing, predator calling, camping, boating, woodcrafting, conservation, and related topics. **Nonfiction:** Seeking short how-to, humor, and human-interest articles; 2,000-3,000 words; $100-$250. **Art:** Varied photos (close-ups, overall scenes); color slides, B&W, color prints; $25. **Queries:** Required. **E-Queries:** Yes. **Unsolicited mss:** Accepts. **Freelance Content:** 75%. **Rights:** FNAR. **Payment:** On acceptance.

GAME AND FISH PUBLICATIONS
P.O. Box 741, Marietta, GA 30061. 770-953-9222.
Ken Dunwoody, Editorial Department. **Description:** Publishes 30 monthly outdoor magazines for 48 states. **Nonfiction:** Articles, 1,500-2,500 words, on hunting and fishing (how-tos, where-tos, and adventure). Profiles of successful hunters and fishermen. No hiking, canoeing, camping, or backpacking pieces. Pays $125-$175 for state-specific articles, $200-$250 for multi-state articles. **Art:** Photos; pays $25-$75 (interior), $250 (covers). **Payment:** On acceptance.

GOLF COURSE NEWS
106 Lafayette St., P.O. Box 997, Yarmouth, ME 04096. 207-846-0600.
E-mail: aoverbeck@golfcoursenews.com. Web site: www.golfcoursenews.com. Andrew Overbeck, Editor. **Description:** News articles and analyses, 500-1,000 words, on all aspects of golf course maintenance, design, building, and management. Pays $200, on publication.

GOLF DIGEST
5520 Park Ave., Trumbull, CT 06611. 203-373-7000.
E-mail: editor@golfdigest.com. Web site: www.golfdigest.com. Monthly. $3.99. Circ.: 1,550,000. Jerry Tarde, Editor. **Description:** Covers golf instruction, equipment, and travel. **Tips:** Freelance content limited. **Queries:** Required.

GOLF FOR WOMEN
4 Times Square, New York, NY 10036. 212-286-3906.
E-mail: editors@golfforwomen.com. Susan K. Reed, Editor-in-Chief. **Description:**
Golf lifestyle magazine for avid women golfers. Includes travel, instruction, fashion,
equipment, news. Query with clips.

GOLF JOURNAL
77 Liberty Corner Road, Far Hills, NJ 07931-0708. 908-234-2300.
E-mail: golfjournal@usga.org. Web site: www.golfjournal.org. 9x/year. Membership
publication. Circ.: 800,000. Brett Avery, Editor. **Description:** Published by United
States Golf Assn., general interest, on contemporary issues and history as seen in the
game, people, and values. **Fiction:** On humor, values; 500 words and up; $1/word.
Nonfiction: On golf history, lore, rules, equipment, general information. Focus is on
amateur golf. No jokes, instruction, or travel pieces. Accepts poignant, humorous stories and essays; 500 words and up; $1/word. **Queries:** Not necessary. **E-Queries:**
Yes. **Unsolicited mss:** Accepts. **Response:** 4 weeks, SASE required. **Freelance
Content:** 35-40%. **Payment:** On publication.

GOLF MAGAZINE
2 Park Ave., New York, NY 10016-5675. 212-779-5000.
E-mail: golfletters@golfonline.com. Web site: www.golfonline.com. Monthly. $19.94.
Circ.: 1,403,000. James Frank, Editor. **Description:** Articles, 1,000 words with photos, on golf history and travel (places to play around the world); profiles of professional tour players. Shorts, to 500 words. Pays $.75 a word, on acceptance. Queries
preferred.

GOLF TIPS
12121 Wilshire Blvd., #1200, Los Angeles, CA 90025-1123. 310-820-1500.
E-mail: editors@golftipsmag.com. Web site: www.golftipsmag.com. 9x/yr. $17.94.
Circ.: 292,500. Dave DeNunzio, Editor. **Description:** For serious golfers.
Nonfiction: Articles, 500-1,500 words, unique golf instruction, golf products, inter-
views with pro players; pays $200-$600. **Fillers:** Short "shotmaking" instruction tips.
Queries: Preferred. **Payment:** On publication.

GOLF TODAY
204 Industrial Rd., San Carlos, CA 94070. 650-802-8165.
E-mail: bob@golftodaymagazine.com. Web site: www.golftodaymagazine.com.
Monthly. $22/yr. Circ.: 151,000. Bob Koczor, Editor. **Description:** Golf magazine for
players in California, Nevada, Arizona, and Utah. **Nonfiction:** Travel stories, golf tips,
product reviews, and guest columns; $5-$15/page. **Tips:** Works with new writers.
Queries: Not necessary. **E-Queries:** Yes. **Unsolicited mss:** Accepts. **Response:** 1
day. **Freelance Content:** 25%. **Rights:** FNAR. **Payment:** On acceptance.

GUN DIGEST
Krause Publications, Inc., 700 E State St., Iola, WI 54990. 888-457-2873.
E-mail: ramagek@krause.com. Web site: www.krause.com. Ken Ramage, Editor.
Description: On guns and shooting, equipment, etc. **Nonfiction:** Well-researched
articles, to 5,000 words; pays to $.10/word. **Queries:** Preferred. **E-Queries:** Yes.
Payment: On acceptance.

GUN DOG
See full listing in Animals & Pets category.

GUNGAMES MAGAZINE
421 Coeur d'Alene Ave., Coeur d'Alene, ID 83814-2862. 208-765-8062.
E-mail: managingeditor@gungames.com. Web site: www.gungames.com. Bimonthly.
$16.95/yr. Circ.: 80,000. Jocelyn Stott, Managing Editor. **Description:** Articles and
fiction, 1,200-1,500 words, about "the fun side of guns and shooting." No self-defense
articles. Pays $150-$250. **Payment:** On publication.

GUNS & AMMO
PRIMEDIA Enthusiast Group
6420 Wilshire Blvd., Fl. 14, Los Angeles, CA 90048-5502. 323-782-2000.
E-mail: gunsandammo@primediacmmg.com.
Web site: www.gunsandammomag.com. Monthly. $23.94/yr. Circ.: 607,000. Lee
Hoots, Editor. **Description:** On guns, ammunition, and target shooting. **Nonfiction:**
Technical and general articles, 800-2,500 words; pays from $150. **Art:** Photos.
Payment: On acceptance.

HANG GLIDING & PARAGLIDING
U.S. Hang Gliding Assn., P.O. Box 1537, Puyallup, WA 98371. 949-888-7363.
E-mail: editor@ushga.org. Web site: www.ushga.org. Monthly. $26/yr. Circ.: 11,500.
Dan A. Nelson, Editor-in-Chief. **Description:** Explores all areas of hang gliding,
paragliding, and the free flight lifestyle. Articles run 2-3 pages; pays $50. **Queries:**
Preferred. **Payment:** On publication.

HORSE & RIDER
PRIMEDIA Enthusiast Group
P.O. Box 4101, 741 Corporate Circle, Suite A, Golden, CO 80401. 720-836-1257.
E-mail: horse&rider@primediamags.com. Web site: www.equisearch.com. Monthly.
$3.99/$19.95. Circ.: 165,000. René Riley, Managing Editor. **Description:** Educates,
informs, and entertains competitive and recreational Western riders with training
articles, practical stable management techniques, hands-on health care, safe trail riding practices, and coverage of major Western events. **Nonfiction:** Personality profiles, consumer buying advice, and how-tos (training, horse care/horsekeeping); 150-
2,000 words; $150-$1,000. **Fillers:** Humorous experiences; 150-1,000 words; $150-
$1,000. **Columns, Departments:** Real-life horse stories, trail-riding tips, training

tips; 150-1,000 words; $0-$1,000. **Art:** Send query before submitting. Include SASE and photo spec sheet outlining the details of your work; photos. **Tips:** "Please be familiar with our subject matter and style before sending manuscript or query." **Queries:** Preferred. **E-Queries:** No. **Unsolicited mss:** Accepts. **Response:** 3 months; SASE required. **Freelance Content:** 5%. **Rights:** FNAR. **Payment:** On acceptance.

HOT BOAT

8484 Wilshire Blvd., Suite 900, Beverly Hills, CA 90211-3221. 323-651-5400.
E-mail: hbmail@aol.com. Web site: www.hotboat.net. Monthly. $23.95. Circ.: 40,000. Brett Bayne, Editor. **Description:** On motorized water sport events and personalities: general-interest, how-to, and technical features. **Nonfiction:** Family-oriented articles, 600-1,000 words; pays $85-$300. **Queries:** Preferred. **Payment:** On publication.

THE IN-FISHERMAN

PRIMEDIA Enthusiast Group
2 In-Fisherman Dr., Brainerd, MN 56425-8098. 218-829-1648.
Web site: www.in-fisherman.com. 8x/yr. $16/yr. Circ.: 300,000. Doug Stange, Editor-in-Chief. **Description:** On all aspects of freshwater fishing. **Nonfiction:** How-to articles, 1,500-4,500 words; pays $250-$1,000. **Columns, Departments:** Reflections (humorous or nostalgic looks at fishing), 1,000-1,500 words. **Payment:** On acceptance.

INSIDE TEXAS RUNNING

P.O. Box 19909, Houston, TX 77224. 281-759-0555.
E-mail: rtnews@ix.netcom.com. Web site: www.insidetexasrunning.com. 10x/yr. $12. Circ.: 8,000. Joanne Schmidt, Editor. **Description:** Tabloid newspaper, for runners in Texas. **Nonfiction:** Travel pieces for runners attending out-of-town races; unusual runners (not just fast runners); race write-ups; 300-1,500 words; $300-$1,500. **Columns, Departments:** "Texas Roundup (news items, 2-5 paragraphs max.). **Art:** $10-$25. **Tips:** Avoid "How I ran the marathon" articles or subject matter on other sports. Use quotes. Welcomes new writers with appropriate expertise. **Queries:** Required. **E-Queries:** Yes. **Unsolicited mss:** Accepts. **Response:** 4 weeks, SASE required. **Freelance Content:** 30%. **Rights:** One-time. **Payment:** On publication.

JOURNAL OF ASIAN MARTIAL ARTS

821 W 24th St., Erie, PA 16502. 814-455-9517.
E-mail: info@goviamedia.com. Web site: www.goviamedia.com. Quarterly. Michael A. DeMarco, Editor. **Description:** On martial arts and Asian culture: interviews (with scholars, master practitioners, etc.) and scholarly articles based on primary research in key disciplines (cultural anthropology, comparative religion, etc.). **Nonfiction:** Articles, 2,000-10,000 words; pays $150-$500. **Columns, Departments:** Reviews, 1,000 words, of books and audiovisual material; pays in copies. **Response:** 2-8 weeks. **Freelance Content:** 90%. **Rights:** 1st world and reprint. **Payment:** On publication.

JUNIOR BASEBALL

P.O. Box 9099, Canoga Park, CA 91309-0099. 818-710-1234.
E-mail: dave@juniorbaseball.com. Web site: www.juniorbaseball.com. Bimonthly.
$3.95/$17.70. Circ.: 50,000. Dave Destler, Editor. **Description:** "America's youth
baseball magazine." Targets youth and high school baseball players, coaches, and parents. Articles run 500-2,500 words; pay varies. **Tips:** "Read a few issues to familiarize
yourself with our topics, focus, and editorial environment. Writers must know baseball very well! No "my kid is the next Barry Bonds" articles. No fiction, poems, or tributes." **Queries:** Preferred. **E-Queries:** Yes. **Unsolicited mss:** Accepts. **Response:**
2 weeks, SASE required. **Freelance Content:** 50%. **Rights:** All. **Payment:** On
publication.

KEYSTONE SPORTSMAN

P.O. Box 739, Camp Hill, PA 17011-2308. 717-730-6263.
E-mail: bille@celticmooninc.com. Web site: www.keystonesportsman.com.
Bimonthly. $9.95/yr. Circ.: 30,000. Bill Einsig, Editor. **Description:** Covers hunting
and fishing in Pennsylvania and neighboring states. **Tips:** Guidelines available.
Queries: Required. **E-Queries:** Yes. **Unsolicited mss:** Does not accept.
Response: 4 weeks. **Freelance Content:** 80%. **Rights:** One-time. **Payment:** On
publication.

KITPLANES

See full listing in Hobbies, Crafts, Collecting category.

LAKELAND BOATING

500 Davis St., Suite 1000, Evanston, IL 60201-4643. 847-869-5400.
E-mail: lb@omeara-brown.com. Web site: www.lakelandboating.com. Monthly.
$21.95. Circ.: 38,200. Matthew Wright, Editor. **Description:** On boating in the
Great Lakes and surrounding areas. **Nonfiction:** Cruising features, boating and
Great Lakes information. also, newsy bits, maintenance tips (100 words up); 800-
2,500 words; $50-$600. **Columns, Departments:** Cruising, Port O' Call,
Weekender, Historical Subjects, Environment, Bosun's Locker, Antique and Classic
Boats, Profiles; 800-2,500 words; $50-$600. **Tips:** "We're looking for freelance writers who are also skilled photographers." **Queries:** Required. **E-Queries:** Yes.
Unsolicited mss: Accepts. **Response:** 2-4 weeks, SASE. **Rights:** FNASR and electronic. **Payment:** On publication.

MICHIGAN OUT-OF-DOORS

Michigan United Conservation Clubs, Inc.
P.O. Box 30235, Lansing, MI 48909. 517-371-1041.
E-mail: magazine@mucc.org. Web site: www.mucc.org. Monthly. $3.50/$25. Circ.:
90,000. Dennis Knickerbocker, Editor. **Description:** On Michigan's natural environment and outdoor recreation, with emphasis on hunting, fishing, and nature study.
Nonfiction: Informative, entertaining features for sportsmen/women, and all who
enjoy the out-of-doors; how-to, investigative, personal adventure, nature lore;

1,000-1,500 words; $90-$200. **Fillers:** Cartoons and line drawings; $30. **Columns, Departments:** By assignment; 700-800 words; $75-$100. **Art:** B&W and color photos; slides, transparencies, prints; $20-$175. **Queries:** Preferred. **E-Queries:** No. **Unsolicited mss:** Accepts. **Response:** 1 month for queries, 3-4 months for submissions; SASE required. **Freelance Content:** 75%. **Payment:** On acceptance.

MIDWEST OUTDOORS

111 Shore Dr., Burr Ridge, IL 60521-5885. 638-887-7722.
E-mail: info@midwestoutdoors.com. Web site: www.midwestoutdoors.com. Monthly. $2.99/$14.95. Circ.: 36,000. Gene Laulunen, Publisher/Editor. **Description:** Hunting, fishing, and outdoor recreation in the Midwest. **Nonfiction:** Where, when, why, how-to articles about the Midwest; 1,500 words; $30. **Tips:** Avoid first-time experience stories. **E-Queries:** Yes. **Unsolicited mss:** Accepts. **Freelance Content:** 95%. **Rights:** One-time and web. **Payment:** On publication.

MOUNTAIN BIKE

Rodale Press, Inc., 135 N Sixth St., Emmaus, PA 18049-2441. 610-967-5171.
E-mail: mbcrank@mountainbike.com. Web site: www.mountainbike.com. 11x/yr. $19.97/yr. Circ.: 150,300. Zapata Espinoza, Executive Editor. **Description:** On mountain-bike touring; major off-road cycling events; political, sport, or land-access issues; riding techniques; fitness and training tips. **Nonfiction:** Articles, 500-2,000 words; pays $100-$650. **Columns, Departments:** Descriptions, detailing routes of off-road rides, to 500 words; pays $75. **Queries:** Preferred. **Payment:** On publication.

MUSHING

P.O. Box 149, Ester, AK 99725-0149. 907-479-0454.
E-mail: editor@mushing.com. Web site: www.mushing.com. Bimonthly. $24/yr. Circ.: 6,000. Todd Hoener, Editor-in-Chief. **Description:** Dog-driving how-tos, innovations, history, profiles, interviews, and features related to sled dogs. International audience. **Nonfiction:** 1,000-2,500 words. **Columns, Departments:** Competitive and recreational dog drivers; weight pullers, dog packers, and skijorers; 500-1,000 words. **Art:** 50-80% B&W; $20-$250. **Tips:** "Send your qualifications and clips of previous published work. Also include a short biography. We will work with new and unpublished authors." **Queries:** Preferred. **E-Queries:** Yes. **Unsolicited mss:** Accepts. **Rights:** FNAR. **Payment:** On publication. **Contact:** Deirdre Helfferich, Managing Editor.

MUZZLE BLASTS

P.O. Box 67, Friendship, IN 47021-0067. 812-667-5131.
E-mail: mblastdop@seidata.com. Web site: www.nmlra.org. Monthly. $40/yr (members). Circ.: 22,000. Eric A. Bye, Editor. **Description:** Published by the National Muzzle Loading Rifle Association. **Nonfiction:** Articles on antique muzzleloading guns, gunmakers, events in America's past; how-tos on crafts related to muzzleloaders (gunbuilding, making powder horns, engraving, etc.), safe handling, loading, etc. 1,500-2,000 words; $150-$250. **Art:** Photos, illustrations; must reflect highest stan-

dard of safety. **Tips:** Must know muzzleloaders (preferably traditional) and safety. Avoid modern topics. **Queries:** Preferred. **E-Queries:** Yes. **Unsolicited mss:** Accepts. **Response:** 2-6 weeks. **Freelance Content:** 70%. **Rights:** FNAR. **Payment:** On publication.

NEW HAMPSHIRE WILDLIFE
54 Portsmouth St., Concord, NH 63301. 603-224-5953.
E-mail: nhwf@aol.com. Web site: www.nhwf.org. Bimonthly. Circ.: 7,000. Margaret Lane, Editor. **Description:** First-person experiences (400-1,500 words) on hunting, fishing, trapping, and other active outdoor pursuits in New Hampshire. No payment offered. **Queries:** Not necessary. **Unsolicited mss:** Accepts.

NORTHEAST OUTDOORS
2575 Vista Del Mar, Ventura, CA 93001. 805-667-4100.
E-mail: editor@woodallpub.com. Web site: www.woodalls.com. Monthly. $20/yr. Circ.: 15,000. Jennifer Detweiler, Editor. **Description:** On camping and recreational vehicle (RV) touring in northeast U.S. **Nonfiction:** Prefers how-to, where-to (camp cookery, recreational vehicle hints). Articles, 1,000-2,000 words, preferably with B&W photos; pay varies. **Contact:** Melinda Baccanari, Senior Managing Editor.

OFFSHORE
500 Victory Rd., Marina Bay, Quincy, MA 02171. 617-221-1400.
E-mail: editors@offshoremag.net. Web site: www.offshoremag.net. Monthly. $4.50/$19.95. Circ.: 32,000. Betsy Frawley Haggerty, Editor. **Description:** Northeast powerboaters and sailboaters (East Coast from Maine to New Jersey). **Nonfiction:** Destinations (seaports in New England, New York, New Jersey); things to do, places to see, navigation guidelines. First-hand accounts of boating adventures and mishaps. Also, fishing pieces. 1,500-3,000 words; $350-$1,000. **Columns, Departments:** Marina profiles (detail on Northeast marinas); Boater's Workshop (tips and techniques on boat care). 200-1,500 words; $100-$350. **Art:** 35mm color slides; $75-$400/image. **Queries:** Required. **E-Queries:** Yes. **Unsolicited mss:** Accepts. **Response:** 6 weeks, SASE required. **Freelance Content:** 80%. **Rights:** FNAR. **Payment:** On acceptance.

OUTDOOR CANADA
340 Ferrier St., Suite 210, Markham, Ontario L3R 2Z5 Canada. 905-475-8440.
E-mail: walsh@outdooorcanada.ca. 8x/year. Circ.: 80,000. Patrick Walsh, Editor-in-Chief. **Description:** Articles on fishing, hunting, and conservation. **Nonfiction:** 100-4,000 words. Payment depends on length and complexity of article; $.50/word and up. **Payment:** On acceptance.

OUTSIDE
400 Market St., Santa Fe, NM 87501-7300. 505-989-7100.
E-mail: letters@outsidemag.com. Web site: www.outsidemag.com. Monthly. $4.95/$18. Circ.: 650,000. Hal Epsen, Editor. **Description:** Magazine for people

with active lifestyles. Covers outdoor sports, adventure travel, the environment, and outdoor equipment. **Nonfiction:** On the environment, outdoor sports, how-to, personal experience, reviews of equipment, etc. 1,500-4,000 words. **Columns, Departments:** Dispatches (news events); Destinations (places to explore). **Tips:** "Departments are best areas for new writers to break in." **Queries:** Preferred. **Unsolicited mss:** Does not accept. **Response:** 2 months, SASE. **Freelance Content:** 90%. **Rights:** FNASR.

PADDLER

P.O. Box 775450, Steamboat Springs, CO 80477. 970-879-1450.
Web site: www.paddlermagazine.com. Eugene Buchanan, Editor. **Description:** On canoeing, kayaking, rafting, and sea kayaking. Pays $.15-$.25/word. **Tips:** "The best way to break in is to target a specific department such as Hotlines or Paddle People." **Queries:** Preferred. **Payment:** On publication. **Contact:** Frederick Reimers.

PEDAL MAGAZINE

703-317 Adelaide St. W, Toronto, Ontario M5V 1P9 Canada. 416-977-2100.
E-mail: pedal@passport.ca. Web site: www.pedalmag.com. 6x/yr. $19.95/yr. Circ.: 18,000. Benjamin Sadavoy, Editor. **Description:** Covers all aspects of cycling from mountain bike and road bike adventure touring to recreational cycling and destinations across Canada and abroad. Also features coverage of events, profiles of Canada's top cyclists, product reviews, complete bike tests, maintenance tips, and a calendar of Canadian events. **Tips:** "Our editor is extremely busy. You're chances are better if your query is attention-grabbing and to the point." **Queries:** Preferred. **E-Queries:** Yes. **Unsolicited mss:** Accepts. **Freelance Content:** 100%.

PENNSYLVANIA ANGLER & BOATER

P.O. Box 67000, Harrisburg, PA 17106-7000. 717-705-7835.
E-mail: amichaels@state.pa.us. Web site: www.fish.state.pa.us. Bimonthly. $9/yr. Circ.: 28,000. Art Michaels, Editor. **Description:** On freshwater fishing and boating in Pennsylvania. Articles, 500-3,000 words, with photos; pays $50-$300. **Queries:** Preferred. **Response:** SASE required. **Payment:** On acceptance.

PENNSYLVANIA GAME NEWS

Game Commission, 2001 Elmerton Ave., Harrisburg, PA 17110-9797. 717-787-3745.
Monthly. $1.50/issue. Circ.: 120,000. Bob Mitchell, Editor. **Description:** Published by the state Game Commission, to promote wildlife programs, hunting and trapping in the state. **Nonfiction:** On hunting or wildlife, with Pennsylvania interest; 2,000 words; $.08/word. **Tips:** No controversial issues, or technical subjects by freelancers. Avoid "first deer" stories. **Queries:** Not necessary. **E-Queries:** No. **Unsolicited mss:** Accepts. **Response:** 4-6 weeks, SASE. **Freelance Content:** 40%. **Rights:** 1st. **Payment:** On acceptance.

PETERSEN'S BOWHUNTING

6420 Wilshire Blvd., Los Angeles, CA 90048-5515. 323-782-2721.
E-mail: bowhunting@primedia.com. Web site: www.bowhuntingmag.com. 9x/yr.
$3.99/11.97. Circ.: 192,000. Jay Michael Strangis, Editor. **Description:** How-to help
for bowhunter enthusiasts. Also, interesting stories about bowhunting. **Nonfiction:**
Bowhunting adventure stories. How-to and technical (equipment, products) articles;
2,000 words; $150-$400. **Art:** Photos must accompany all manuscripts; B&W or color
prints; $100-$600. **Queries:** Preferred. **E-Queries:** Yes. **Unsolicited mss:** Accepts.
Response: Queries 3-4 days, submissions 6-7 days, SASE. **Freelance Content:**
40%. **Rights:** All, 1st (photos). **Payment:** On acceptance.

PGA MAGAZINE

122 Sycamore Dr., Jupiter, FL 33485-2860. 561-776-0069.
Web site: www.pga.com. Monthly. $29.95. Circ.: 30,500. Matt Marsom, Editorial
Director. **Description:** On golf-related subjects. **Nonfiction:** Articles, 1,500-2,500
words; pays $300-$500. **Queries:** Preferred. **Payment:** On acceptance.

POWER AND MOTORYACHT

PRIMEDIA Enthusiast Group
260 Madison Ave., Fl. 8, New York, NY 10016. 917-256-2276.
E-mail: diane_byrne@primediamags.com. Web site: www.powerandmotoryacht,com
Monthly. Circ.: 157,179. Richard Thiel, Editor. **Description:** For affluent, experienced owners of powerboats, mostly 35 feet and larger. Reaches almost every U.S.
owner of a large powerboat, with advice on how to choose, operate, and maintain
their boats. Also provides information on where to cruise and how to get the most
enjoyment of the lifestyle. **Nonfiction:** Clear, concise, authoritative articles. Include
personal experience and information from marine industry experts where appropriate; 800-1,400 words; $500-$1,200. **Tips:** No stories on trailer boats or sailboats of any
length. Sample copy and guidelines free with SASE. **Queries:** Required.
E-Queries: Yes. **Unsolicited mss:** Do not accept. **Response:** Queries 1 month,
SASE required. **Freelance Content:** 20-25%. **Rights:** All. **Payment:** On acceptance. **Contact:** Diane Byrne, Executive Editor.

POWERBOAT

1691 Spinnaker Dr., Suite 206, Ventura, CA 93001. 805-639-2222.
E-mail: edit-dept@powerboatmag.com. Web site: www.powerboatmag.com. 11x/yr.
$4.95/$29 yr. Circ.: 41,000. Brett Becker, Editor. **Description:** Covers all types of
powerboats, from tournament inboards to offshore boats. **Nonfiction:** For high-
performance powerboat owners, on achievements, water-skiing, competitions; technical articles on hull and engine developments; how-to. 500-3,000 words; pay negotiable. **Art:** 35mm or larger formats; $50-$400. **Queries:** Required. **E-Queries:** Yes.
Unsolicited mss: Accepts. **Response:** 3 weeks, SASE required. **Freelance
Content:** 25%. **Payment:** On publication.

PRACTICAL HORSEMAN
PRIMEDIA Enthusiast Group
P.O. Box 589, Unionville, PA 19375. 610-380-8977.
E-mail: prachorse@aol.com. Monthly. $33/yr. Circ.: 80,000. Mandy Lorraine, Editor.
Description: How-to articles conveying leading experts' advice on English riding, training, and horse care. **Tips:** Send clips. **Queries:** Preferred. **Payment:** On acceptance.

REAL SPORTS
P.O. Box 8204, San Jose, CA 95155-8204. 408-924-7434.
E-mail: freelance@real-sports.com. Web site: www.real-sports.com. Quarterly. $9.95/$29.99. Circ.: 150,000. Brian Styers, Editor. **Description:** Authoritative coverage of women's sports. Girls' and women's sports, team sports, professional, collegiate, and amateur. Uses action-oriented photographs to show drama of competition. **Nonfiction:** Women's sports coverage; 500-2,000 words; $.50/word. **Art:** Slides; pay varies. **Tips:** Submit original, insightful, realistic portraits of women's sports. **Queries:** Required. **E-Queries:** Yes. **Unsolicited mss:** Does not accept. **Response:** 2 weeks, SASE. **Freelance Content:** 70%. **Rights:** 1st. **Payment:** On publication.

ROCK & ICE
1101 Village Rd., UL-4D, Carbondale, CO 81623. 970-704-1442.
E-mail: editorial@rockandice.com. Web site: www.rockandice.com. Bimonthly. $24.95/yr. Circ.: 38,000. Duane Raleigh, Publisher/Editor-in-Chief. **Description:** For technical rock and ice climbers (sport climbers, mountaineers, alpinists, and other adventurers). **Nonfiction:** Articles, 500-4,000 words; pays $300/published page. **Art:** Slides, B&W photos considered. **Queries:** Preferred.

RUNNER TRIATHLETE NEWS
14201 Memorial Dr., Suite 204, Houston, TX 77079-6731. 281-759-0555.
E-mail: rtnews@ix.netcom.com. Web site: www.runnertriathletenews.com. Monthly. $15/yr. Circ.: 13,500. Lance Phegley, Editor. **Description:** Covers running, cycling, triathlons, and duathlons in a 5-state area: Texas, Louisiana, Arkansas, Oklahoma, New Mexico. Articles on running for road racing, and multi-sport enthusiasts. Pay varies. **Queries:** Preferred. **E-Queries:** Yes. **Unsolicited mss:** Accepts. **Response:** 1-7 days. **Freelance Content:** 40%. **Payment:** On publication.

RUNNER'S WORLD
Rodale Press, Inc., 33 E Minor St., Emmaus, PA 18098. 610-967-5171.
E-mail: rwedit@rodale.com. Web site: www.runnersworld.com. Monthly. $18/yr. Circ.: 550,000. Amby Burfoot, Editor. **Description:** For recreational runners who train for and race in long-distance events. **Nonfiction:** To 3,000 words. Payment varies. **Tips:** No first-time marathon stories. **Queries:** Required. **E-Queries:** Yes. **Unsolicited mss:** Accepts. **Response:** 2 weeks; SASE required. **Freelance Content:** 25%. **Rights:** Worldwide. **Payment:** On acceptance. **Contact:** Adam Bean, Managing Editor.

RUNNING TIMES

213 Danbury Rd., Wilson, CT 06897-4006. 203-761-1113.
E-mail: editor@runningtimes.com. Web site: www.runningtimes.com. 10x/year.
$3.99/$24.97. Circ.: 70,000. Jonathan Beverly, Editor. **Description:** For the experienced running participant and fan. **Fiction:** Running related, any genre; 1,500-3,000 words; $100-$500. **Nonfiction:** Book excerpts, essays, historical/nostalgic, how-to, humor, inspirational, interview/profile, new product, opinion, personal experience, photo feature, travel, news, reports; 1,500-3,000 words; $100-$500. **Columns, Departments:** Training (short topics on enhancing performance, 1,000 words); Sports-Med (applying medical knowledge, 1,000 words); Nutrition, 1,000 words); Cool Down (lighter essay on aspect of the running life), 400 words. 400-1,000 words; $50-$200. **Tips:** Get to know runners and running culture, at participant and professional, elite level. No basic, beginner's how-to, generic fitness/nutrition or generic first-person stories. **Queries:** Preferred. **E-Queries:** Yes. **Unsolicited mss:** Accepts. **Response:** Queries 2-4 weeks, submissions 4-6 weeks, SASE. **Freelance Content:** 50%. **Rights:** FNAR and electronic. **Payment:** On publication.

SAFARI

4800 W Gates Pass Rd., Tucson, AZ 85745. 520-620-1220.
E-mail: sskinner@safariclub.org. Web site: www.safariclub.org. William Quimby, Editor. **Description:** On worldwide big game hunting and/or conservation projects of Safari Club International's local chapters. **Nonfiction:** Articles, 2,000 words; pays $200, extra for photos. **Payment:** On publication.

SAIL

98 N Washington St., Fl. 2, Boston, MA 02114. 617-720-8600.
Web site: www.sailingmag.com. Peter Nielsen, Editor. **Description:** On sailboats, equipment, racing, and cruising. How-to articles on navigation, sail trim, etc. **Nonfiction:** Articles, 1,000-2,500 words, with photos; pays $75-$1,000. **Payment:** On publication. **Contact:** Amy Ullrich.

SAILING MAGAZINE

125 F. Main St., P.O. Box 249, Port Washington, WI 53074-1915. 262-284-3494.
E-mail: general@sailingmagazine.net. Web site: sailingonline.com. Monthly.
$3.99/issue. Circ.: 43,000. Greta Schanen, Managing Editor. **Description:** Illustrated, for the experienced sailor. Covers cruises, races, boat tests, gear and book reviews, personality profiles; also regular columns. **Nonfiction:** No cruising stories that are just logbooks. No "my first sail" stories. Must be familiar with sailing, provide good photos, and write for readers who are also genuine sailors; 200-4,000 words; $125-$600. **Art:** 35mm transparencies; $50-$600. **Tips:** "Suggest a story not done in the past four years, include good photographs, and you're in!" **Queries:** Preferred. **E-Queries:** Yes. **Unsolicited mss:** Accepts. **Response:** 2-4 weeks. **Freelance Content:** 60%. **Payment:** On publication.

SALT WATER SPORTSMAN

263 Summer St., Boston, MA 02210. 617-303-3660.
E-mail: barryg@saltwatersportsman.com. Web site: www.saltwatersportsman.com.
Monthly. $4.99/$22.95. Circ.: 161,000. Barry Gibson, Editor. **Description:** Covers
marine sport fishing along the coasts of the United States, Canada, the Caribbean,
Central America, Bermuda, occasionally South America and other overseas locations.
Fiction: Fishing stories, humor, mood, and nostalgia; 1,500-2,000 words; $1,000.
Nonfiction: How-to and where-to articles; 1,200-1,500 words; $500-$750.
Columns, Departments: Sportsman's Tips: short how-to-make-it; tackle, rigs, boat
equipment; 100-300 words; $150. **Art:** Color slides and prints; $100-$500/inside use,
$1,500/cover. **Tips:** No blood and thunder, no romantic "remember when." **Queries:**
Preferred. **E-Queries:** Yes. **Unsolicited mss:** Accepts. **Response:** 2 weeks, SASE
required. **Freelance Content:** 50%. **Rights:** FNASR. **Payment:** On acceptance.

SCORE GOLF

Canadian Controlled Media Communications
5397 Eglinton Ave. W, Suite 101, Toronto, Ontario M9C 5K6 Canada. 416-928-2909.
Web site: www.scoregolf.com. 6x/yr. $18/yr. Circ.: 120,000. Robert Weeks, Editor.
Description: On travel, golf equipment, golf history, personalities, and prominent
professionals. Canadian content only. **Nonfiction:** By assignment; 800-2,000 words;
$125-$600. **Fillers:** On Canadian golf scene. Rarely uses humor or poems; 50-100
words; $10-$25. **Tips:** Query with SASE (IRC); send published clips. **Queries:**
Required. **Payment:** On publication.

SEA KAYAKER

P.O. Box 17170, Seattle, WA 17029. 206-789-9536.
E-mail: editorial@seakayakermag.com. Web site: www.seakayakermag.com.
Bimonthly. $23.95/yr. Circ.: 25,000. Christopher Cunningham, Editor. **Description:**
For serious paddlers. Guides sea kayakers through coastal and island waters and gives
readers both entertainment and information. **Fiction:** Short stories on ocean kayaking; 1,000-3,000 words; pays $.12/word. **Nonfiction:** Articles, 1,500-4,000 words, on
ocean kayaking (technical, personal experience, profile, new product). Pays $.12-
$.15/word; $.18-$.20/word (by assignment). **Art:** Send photos with submission. **Tips:**
Combine personal narrative with a sense of place. **Queries:** Preferred. **E-Queries:**
Yes. **Unsolicited mss:** Accepts. **Response:** 2 months, SASE. **Freelance Content:**
95%. **Rights:** FNASR or second serial. **Payment:** On publication. **Contact:** Karin
Redmond, Executive Editor.

SEA MAGAZINE

17782 Cowan, Irvine, CA 92614. 949-660-6150.
E-mail: editorial@goboatingamerica.com. Web site: www.goboatingamerica.com.
Monthly. $3.99/$19.97. Circ.: 50,000. Duncan McIntosh Jr., Publisher/Editor.
Description: For active West Coast boat owners. Readers are power boaters and
sportfishing enthusiasts, Alaska to Mexico, across the Pacific to Hawaii. **Nonfiction:**
West Coast boating destination stories, new trends in power boat design, late-season

maintenance secrets, how to finance a new boat; 1,200-1,600 words; $250-$400. **Columns, Departments:** Hands-On Boater (do-it-yourself boat maintenance tips); 500-1,200 words; $100-$200. **Art:** 35mm color transparencies or hi-res digital (300 dpi+); $50, $250 (cover). **Tips:** No articles on sailboats, cruise ships, commercial sportfishing party boats, accidents, historic vessels, or chartering. **Queries:** Not necessary. **E-Queries:** Yes. **Unsolicited mss:** Accepts. **Response:** 6 weeks. **Freelance Content:** 60%. **Rights:** FNAR, reprint (print and electronic). **Payment:** On publication. **Contact:** Eston Ellis, Managing Editor.

SHARING THE VICTORY

Fellowship of Christian Athletes
8701 Leeds Rd., Kansas City, MO 64129. 816-921-0909.
E-mail: stv@fca.org; fca@fca.org. Web site: www.fca.org. 9x/yr. $2.50/issue. Circ.: 90,000. David Smale, Editor. **Description:** Offers spiritual support and advice to coaches and athletes, and those whom they influence. Also profiles of Christian athletes. Articles run 1,200-1,500 words; $150-$400. **Tips:** All material must present Christian inspiration. Send SASE for guidelines. **Unsolicited mss:** Does not accept. **Freelance Content:** 50%. **Payment:** On publication.

SHOTGUN SPORTS

P.O. Box 6810, Auburn, CA 95604-6810. 530-889-2220.
E-mail: shotgun@shotgunsportsmagazine.com.
Web site: www.shotgunsportsmagazine.com. Monthly. $31/yr. Circ.: 155,000. Frank Kodl, Publisher/Editor. **Description:** On trap and skeet shooting, sporting clays, hunting with shotguns, reloading, gun tests, and instructional shooting. Nonfiction pieces with photos $25-$200. **Freelance Content:** 100%. **Rights:** FNAR. **Payment:** On publication.

SILENT SPORTS

717 Tenth St., P.O. Box 152, Waupaca, WI 54981-9990. 715-258-5546.
E-mail: info@silentsports.net. Web site: www.silentsports.net. **Description:** On bicycling, cross country skiing, running, canoeing, hiking, backpacking, and other "silent" sports. Must have regional (upper Midwest) focus. **Nonfiction:** Articles, 1,000-2,000 words; pays $50-$100 for features; $20-$50 for fillers. **Queries:** Preferred. **Payment:** On publication.

SKATING

20 First St., Colorado Springs, CO 80906. 719-635-5200.
E-mail: lfawcett@usfsa.org. Web site: www.usfsa.org. 10x/year. $25 (U.S.), $35 (Canada). Circ.: 48,000. Laura Fawcett, Director of Publications/Editor. **Description:** Official publication of the U.S. Figure Skating Association. Communicates information about the sport to USFSA members and figure-skating fans. Promotes USFSA programs, personalities, and trends that affect the sport. **Nonfiction:** Feature articles profiling interesting USFSA members: athletes, judges, etc. Looking for what makes these people unique besides their skating; 1,500 words

and up; $75- $150. **Art:** Photos, discussed when story is assigned, usually must be included. Pay negotiable. **E-Queries:** Yes. **Unsolicited mss:** Accepts. **Response:** 1-3 months, SASE required. **Freelance Content:** 75%. **Rights:** 1st serial. **Payment:** On publication.

SKI MAGAZINE

929 Pearl St., Suite 200, Boulder, Co 80302-5108. 303-448-7600.
E-mail: editor@skimag.com. Web site: www.skimag.com. 8x/yr. $13.94. Circ.: 430,000. Kendall Hamilton, Editor-in-Chief. **Description:** For experienced skiers: profiles, and destination articles. Articles run 1,300-2,500 words; $.50-$1/word. **Columns, Departments:** Ski Life (news items, 100-300 words). **Tips:** Send clips. **Queries:** Preferred. **Payment:** On acceptance.

SKI RACING INTERNATIONAL

6971 Main St., Suite No. 1, Waitsfield, VT 05673-6023. 802-496-7700.
E-mail: sracing@skiracing.com. Web site: www.skiracing.com. Weekly. $29.95/yr. Circ.: 30,000. Tim Etchells, Editor. **Description:** On race techniques and conditioning secrets. Coverage of World Cup, pro, collegiate, and junior ski, and snowboard competition. **Nonfiction:** Articles by experts, with photos; pay varies.

SKIING MAGAZINE

929 Pearl St., Boulder, CO 80302-5108. 303-448-7600.
E-mail: editor@skiingmag.com. Web site: www.skiingmag.com. 7x/yr. $13.94. Circ.: 404,000. Perkins Miller, Editor-in-Chief. **Description:** For the active skier, with destination ideas and instructional tips. Departments include health, fitness, latest trends in skiing industry. Also, profiles of regional runs and their users. **Nonfiction:** Personal adventures on skis, from 2,500 words (no "first time on skis" stories); profiles and interviews, 50-300 words. Pays $150-$300/printed page. **Fillers:** Humorous vignettes, skiing oddities; $.15/word and up. **Tips:** "We're looking for ski adventures that are new, undiscovered, and close to home for most people. Write in first-person." **Queries:** Preferred. **E-Queries:** Yes. **Unsolicited mss:** Accepts. **Freelance Content:** 10%. **Contact:** Helen Olsson, Executive Editor.

SKIN DIVER

PRIMEDIA Enthusiast Group
6420 Wilshire Blvd., Los Angeles, CA 90048-5502. 323-782-2960.
E-mail: skindiver@primedia.com. Web site: www.skin-diver.com. Monthly. $19.94/yr. Circ.: 230,000. Daryl Carson, Editor. **Description:** On scuba diving activities, equipment, and dive sites. **Nonfiction:** Illustrated articles, 500-1,000 words; pays $50/ published page. **Payment:** On publication.

SKITRAX

703-317 Adelaide St. W, Toronto, Ontario M5V 1P9 Canada. 416-977-2100.
E-mail: skitrax@passport.ca. Web site: www.skitrax.com. 4x/yr. $3.95/$12.95 CND. Circ.: 30,000. Benjamin Sadavoy, Editor. **Description:** Official publication of Cross

Country Canada and the United States Ski Association. Offers destination and adventure articles. Also features competition coverage of North American and international events, product reviews, a calendar of events, and columns on training, technique, telemarking, masters, waxing, and ski jumping. **Tips:** "Our editor is extremely busy. Your chances are better if your query is attention-grabbing and to the point." **Queries:** Preferred. **E-Queries:** Yes. **Unsolicited mss:** Accepts. **Freelance Content:** 100%.

SKYDIVING MAGAZINE

1725 N Lexington Ave., DeLand, FL 32724-2148. 386-736-4793.
E-mail: editor@skydivingmagazine.com. Web site: www.skydivingmagazine.com. Monthly. $4/$20. Circ.: 14,000. Sue Clifton, Editor. **Description:** Techniques, equipment, places, people, and events of sport parachuting, written by jumpers for jumpers. **Nonfiction:** Timely news articles on sport and military parachuting; $1/per column inch. **Tips:** Send short bio that shows skydiving experience. **Queries:** Preferred. **E-Queries:** Yes. **Unsolicited mss:** Accepts. **Response:** 2 weeks. **Freelance Content:** 40%. **Rights:** All. **Payment:** On publication.

SNOWBOARDER

PRIMEDIA Enthusiast Group
P.O. Box 1028, Dana Point, CA 92629-5028. 949-496-5922.
E-mail: snwbrdrmag@primedia.com. Web site: www.snowboardermag.com. Bimonthly. $9.99. Circ.: 137,800. Mark Sullivan, Editor. **Description:** On snowboarding personalities, techniques, and adventure. **Nonfiction:** Articles, with color transparencies or B&W prints; 1,000-1,500 words; pays $150-$800. **Payment:** On publication.

SNOWEST

360 B Street, Idaho Falls, ID 83402. 208-524-7000.
E-mail: lindstrm@snowest.com. Web site: www.snowest.com. Monthly. $2.95. Circ.: 160,000. Lane Lindstrom, Editor. **Description:** *SnoWest* is a family-oriented, snowmobile publication for winter recreationists across the U.S. and parts of Canada. **Nonfiction:** Manufacturer reviews, test reports, travel destinations, new product reviews, land use issues, events, technical information, anything related to winter motorized recreation. Also, fillers (500-1,500 words). Query first; 2,000 word max; $100-$300 (with photos). **Art:** Color transparencies (Kodachrome or FujiChrome). **Tips:** Submit 10-15 photos to illustrate a feature, with people involved in every photo; show action; use dawn/dusk for dramatic lighting. **Queries:** Preferred. **Unsolicited mss:** Accepts. **Rights:** FNASR. **Payment:** On publication.

SOCCER AMERICA

P.O. Box 23704, Oakland, CA 94623. 510-528-5000.
E-mail: mike@socceramerica.com. Web site: www.socceramerica.com. Mike Woitalla, Editor. **Description:** Soccer news and profiles.

SOCCER JR.

Scholastic, Inc., 555 Broadway, New York, NY 10012-3919. 212-343-6830. E-mail: dearsj@scholastic.com. Web site: www.soccerjr.com. 6x/yr. $16.97/yr. Circ.: 150,000. Mark Wright, Editor. **Description:** Fiction and fillers about soccer for readers ages 8-14. Pays $450 for feature or story; $250 for shorter pieces. **Queries:** Preferred. **Payment:** On acceptance.

SOUTH CAROLINA WILDLIFE

P.O. Box 167, Columbia, SC 29202-0167. 803-734-3972. Web site: www.scwildlife.com. Bimonthly. $10/yr. Circ.: 60,000. **Description:** Published by Dept. of Natural Resources, for readers interested in the outdoors. **Nonfiction:** South Carolina focus, on outdoor interests; 1,500 words; $.15-$.20/word. **Art:** 35mm or large transparencies; pay varies. **Tips:** Avoid first-person accounts. **Queries:** Preferred. **E-Queries:** Yes. **Unsolicited mss:** Accepts. **Response:** 3-6 weeks, SASE. **Freelance Content:** 75%. **Rights:** FNASR. **Payment:** On acceptance. **Contact:** Caroline Foster, Managing Editor.

SPORTS ILLUSTRATED

Time, Inc., 135 W 50th St., New York, NY 10020-1201. 212-522-1212. E-mail: letters@si.timeinc.com. Web site: www.cnnsi.com. Weekly. $80.46. Circ.: 3,205,000. Norman Pearlstine, Editor-in-Chief. **Description:** Sports news magazine. Articles run 800-1,200 words; pay varies. **Tips:** Limited market; query by mail with clips before submitting. **Queries:** Required. **E-Queries:** No. **Unsolicited mss:** Accepts. **Response:** 4 weeks, SASE required. **Freelance Content:** less than 5%. **Rights:** All. **Payment:** On acceptance. **Contact:** Terry McDonell, Managing Editor.

SPORTS ILLUSTRATED FOR KIDS

See full listing in Juvenile category.

SPORTSFAN MAGAZINE

4948 St. Elmo Ave., Suite 208, Bethesda, MD 20814. 301-986-7901. E-mail: rose@sportsfanmagazine.com. Web site: www.sportsfanmagazine.com. Bimonthly. $19.95/yr;$24.95/yr (Canada). Circ.: 80,000. James J. Patterson, Editor-in-Chief. **Description:** For and by sports lovers whose mission is to chronicle the life and times of America's sports fans. **Poetry:** Regular poetry and prose department with sports-related material. **Fillers:** Accepts sports-related puzzles, humor, illustrations, etc. **Columns, Departments:** "Visitor's Locker" features an outside writer; 1,200-1,300 words. **Tips:** All articles should be fan-focused. **Queries:** Preferred. **E-Queries:** Yes. **Unsolicited mss:** Accepts. **Freelance Content:** 50%. **Rights:** FNAR. **Payment:** On publication. **Contact:** Rose Solari, Senior Editor.

SURFER MAGAZINE

PRIMEDIA Enthusiast Group
P.O. Box 1028, Dana Point, CA 92629. 949-496-5922. E-mail: surfermag@primediacmmg.com. Web site: www.surfermag.com. Monthly.

Circ.: 111,855. Sam George, Editor-in-Chief. **Description:** On surfing and surfers. **Nonfiction:** Articles, 500-5,000 words, photos; pays $.20-$.30/word, $10-$600 for photos. **Payment:** On publication.

SURFING

PRIMEDIA Enthusiast Group
P.O. Box 3010, San Clemente, CA 92674-3010. 949-492-7873.
E-mail: surfing@mcmullenargus.com. Web site: www.surfingthemag.com. Monthly. $21.95. Circ.: 108,000. Scooter Leonard, Managing Editor. **Description:** Short newsy and humorous articles, 200-500 words. Pay varies. **Tips:** No first-person travel articles. **Payment:** On publication.

T'AI CHI

P.O. Box 39938, Los Angeles, CA 90039. 323-665-7773.
E-mail: taichi@tai-chi.com. Web site: www.tai-chi.com. Bimonthly. $20/yr. Circ.: 50,000. Marvin Smalheiser, Editor. **Description:** For persons interested in T'ai Chi Ch'uan (Taijiquan), Qigong, and other internal martial arts, and in similar Chinese disciplines which contribute to fitness, health, and a balanced sense of well being. **Nonfiction:** Articles about different internal styles, self-defense techniques, martial arts principles and philosophy, training methods, weapons, case histories of benefits, new or unusual uses for T'ai Chi Ch'uan, interviews; 100-4,500 words; $75-500, **Art:** 4x6 or 5x7 glossy B&W prints. **Tips:** Readers' abilities range from beginners to serious students and teachers. **Queries:** Required. **E-Queries:** Yes. **Unsolicited mss:** Does not accept. **Response:** 2-3 weeks, SASE required. **Freelance Content:** 85%. **Rights:** FNAR. **Payment:** On publication.

TENNIS WEEK

15 Elm Place, Rye, NY 10580. 914-967-4890.
E-mail: tennisweek@tennisweek.com. Web site: www.tennisweek.com. 12x/yr. $4/$40. Circ.: 97,000. Andre Christopher, Managing Editor. **Description:** Covers the ATP and WTA (men's and women's professional tours), the tennis industry, major tournaments, new products, retail stores, schedules, scores, rankings, and earnings. **Nonfiction:** In-depth, researched articles on current issues and personalities; 1,500-2,000 words; pay varies. **Queries:** Required. **E-Queries:** No. **Unsolicited mss:** Does not accept. **Response:** SASE. **Rights:** FNAR. **Payment:** On publication.

TEXAS GOLFER

5 Briar Dale Ct., Houston, TX 77027-2904. 713-680-1680.
E-mail: info@golfermagazines.com. Web site: www.texasgolfermagazine.com. Monthly. $22. Circ.: 55,000. Doug Mitchell, Editor. **Description:** For Texas golfers, with golf-course and tournament information, golf tips, and news. **Nonfiction:** Articles, 800-1,500 words, for north Texas golfers. **Tips:** "Most freelance work is by assignment." **Queries:** Required. **E-Queries:** Yes. **Unsolicited mss:** Accepts. **Response:** 2-4 Weeks, SASE. **Freelance Content:** 20%. **Rights:** All. **Payment:** On publication.

TRAIL RUNNER

1101 Village Rd., UL-4D, Carbondale, CO 81623. 970-704-1442.
E-mail: mbenge@bigstonepub.com. Web site: www.trailrunnermag.com. Bimonthly.
$16.95/yr. Circ.: 27,000. Michael Benge, Editor. **Description:** Feature articles and
news on off-road running. **Queries:** Preferred. **Freelance Content:** 65%.

TRAILER BOATS

20700 Belshaw Ave., Carson, CA 90746-3510. 310-537-6322.
E-mail: editors@trailerboats.com. Web site: www.trailerboats.com. Monthly.
$4.99/$16.97. Circ.: 98,000. Jim Hendricks, Editor. **Description:** Magazine on trailer
boating. Covers boat, trailer, and tow-vehicle maintenance and operation, skiing, fishing, cruising, and lifestyle. **Nonfiction:** Technical and how-to articles. Also fillers and
humor. 500-2,000 words; $100-$700. **Art:** Photos, slides, transparencies. **Queries:**
Preferred. **Unsolicited mss:** Accepts. **Response:** Queries 6 weeks, SASE.
Freelance Content: 51%. **Payment:** On acceptance.

TRIATHLETE

2037 San Elijo Ave., Cardiff, CA 92007-1726. 760-634-4100.
Web site: www.triathletemag.com. Monthly. $29.95/yr. Circ.: 43,000. Christina
Gandolfo, Editor. **Description:** Covers the sport of triathlon. **Nonfiction:** Articles,
varying lengths, with color slides; pays $.20/word. **Tips:** No "my first triathlon" sto-
ries. **Payment:** On publication.

USA CYCLING

One Olympic Plaza, Colorado Springs, CO 80909-5775. 719-578-4581.
E-mail: media@usacycling.org. Web site: www.usacycling.org. Bimonthly. $25/yr
(nonmembers). Circ.: 49,500. Patrice Quintero, Communications Director.
Description: On bicycle racing; contains U.S. cycling news, race coverage and
results, features, race information, information on training and coaching.
Nonfiction: Articles on bicycle racing and racers. **Queries:** Preferred.

USA GYMNASTICS

Pan American Plaza, 201 S Capitol Ave., Suite 300
Indianapolis, IN 46225. 317-237-5050.
E-mail: publications@usa-gymnastics.org. Web site: www.usa-gymnastics.org.
Bimonthly. $15. Circ.: 95,000. Luan Peszek, Editor. **Description:** Covers gymnastics,
including men's artistic and women's artistic, rhythmic, trampoline, tumbling, and
sports acrobatics. Coverage of national and international competitions leading up to
Olympic Games. In-depth features on athletes and coaches, provides coaching tips.
Nonfiction: Gymnastics-related articles; fee negotiable. **Tips:** Query or call first to
discuss article and interest level. Welcomes new writers. **Queries:** Preferred.
E-Queries: Yes. **Unsolicited mss:** Accepts. **Response:** 4-6 weeks, SASE required.
Freelance Content: 10%. **Rights:** 1st. **Payment:** On publication.

VELONEWS

1830 N 55th St., Boulder, CO 80301. 303-440-0601.
E-mail: vnedit@7dogs.com. Web site: www.velonews.com. 20x/yr. Circ.: 48,000. Kip Mikler, Editor. **Description:** Journal of record for North American bicycle racing, and the world's largest competitive cycling publication. **Nonfiction:** On competitive cycling, training, nutrition; profiles, interviews. No how-to or touring articles; 500-1,500 words; pay varies. **Tips:** Focus on elite, competitive aspect of the sport. **Queries:** Required. **E-Queries:** Yes. **Response:** Queries 1 month, SASE. **Freelance Content:** 20%. **Payment:** On publication.

THE WATER SKIER

1251 Holy Cow Rd., Polk City, FL 33868-8200. 863-324-4341.
E-mail: satkinson@usawaterski.org. Web site: www.usawaterski.org. 9x/yr. $3.50/issue. Circ.: 35,000. Scott Atkinson, Editor. **Description:** Published by USA Water Ski, national governing body for competitive water skiing in the U.S. **Nonfiction:** On water skiing (interviews, profiles must be assigned), new products, equipment for boating and water skiing; 1,500-3,000 words; pays $100-$150 (for assigned features). **Art:** Color slides. **Tips:** Submit articles about people involved in the competitive sport. **Queries:** Preferred. **E-Queries:** No. **Unsolicited mss:** Does not accept. **Response:** Queries 24 hours, submissions 1 week, SASE. **Freelance Content:** 10%. **Rights:** All. **Payment:** On publication.

WATERSKI MAGAZINE

460 N Orlando Ave., Winter Park, FL 32789. 407-628-5662.
E-mail: editor@waterskimag.com. Web site: www.waterskimag.com. 9x/yr. Circ.: 105,000. **Description:** Waterskiing, wakeboarding, and towed water sports. **Nonfiction:** Instructional features, 1,350 words, including sidebars; $125-$500. **Fillers:** Quick tips, 350 words; $35-$125. **Tips:** Travel pieces and profiles by assignment only. **Queries:** Preferred. **Freelance Content:** 25%. **Payment:** On acceptance. **Contact:** Jim Frye, Managing Editor.

WESTERN OUTDOORS

3197-E Airport Loop, Costa Mesa, CA 92626. 714-546-4370.
E-mail: lew@wonews.com. 9x/yr. $3.50/$14.95. Circ.: 100,000. Lew Carpenter, Editor. **Description:** On western saltwater and freshwater fishing techniques, tackle, and destinations. Includes the states of California, Oregon, and Washington. Also Alaska, Baja California, and British Columbia. **Nonfiction:** On saltwater or freshwater fishing in the West; facts and comments must be attributed to recognized authorities in their fields; 1,500 words; $450-$600. **Art:** Quality photos and artwork to illustrate articles; $50-$300. **Tips:** Present seasonal materials 6 months in advance. Best time to query is June. **Queries:** Required. **E-Queries:** Yes. **Unsolicited mss:** Accepts. **Response:** 4-6 weeks, SASE. **Freelance Content:** 75%. **Rights:** FNASR. **Payment:** On acceptance.

WESTERN SPORTSMAN

1080 Howe St., Suite 900
Vancouver, British Columbia V6Z 2T1 Canada. 604-606-4644.
E-mail: editor@westernsportsman.com. Web site: www.oppublishing.com.
Bimonthly. $23.95/yr. Circ.: 23,600. Tracey Ellis, Editor. **Description:** On hunting
and fishing in British Columbia, Alberta, Saskatchewan, and Manitoba. **Nonfiction:**
Informative, how-tos, to 2,000 words. **Art:** Photos. **Payment:** On publication.

WILDFOWL

PRIMEDIA Enthusiast Group
6420 Wilshire Blvd., Fl. 14, Los Angeles, CA 90048-5502. 323-782-2173.
Bimonthly. $24.97/yr. Circ.: 42,000. Diana Rupp, Editor. **Description:** Occasional
fiction, humor, related to duck hunters and wildfowl. Pays $400. **Payment:** On
acceptance.

WINDSURFING

460 N Orlando Ave., Suite 200, Winter Park, FL 32703. 407-628-4802.
E-mail: editor@windsurfingmag.com. Web site: www.windsuringmag.com. 7x/yr.
$19.97/yr. Circ.: 68,000. David Combe, Editor. **Description:** For experienced board-
sailors. **Nonfiction:** Features and instructional pieces ($250-$300), tips ($50-$75),
extra for photos. **Art:** Fast action photos. **Response:** SASE required.

WINDY CITY SPORTS

1450 W Randolph, Chicago, IL 60607. 312-421-1551.
E-mail: jason@windycitysports.com. Web site: www.windycitysports.com. Monthly.
Free. Circ.: 110,000. Jason Effmann, Editor. **Description:** Covers amateur sports in
Chicago and surrounding area. **Nonfiction:** Up to 1,200 words. **Art:** Hard copies,
electronic (300 dpi or more). **Tips:** Need to be knowledgeable in sport covered.
Queries: Preferred. **E-Queries:** Yes. **Unsolicited mss:** Accepts. **Response:** 2
weeks, SASE. **Freelance Content:** 25%. **Rights:** 1st. **Payment:** On publication.

WOODENBOAT

P.O. Box 78, Brooklin, ME 04616. 207-359-4651.
Web site: www.woodenboat.com. Bimonthly. $5.99/$29.95. Circ.: 110,000. Matthew
Murphy, Editor. **Description:** For wooden boat owners, builders, and designers.
Covers design, construction, and maintenance. **Nonfiction:** How-to and technical
articles on construction, repair, and maintenance; design, history, and use; profiles of
outstanding builders, designers; wooden boat lore. 1,000-5,000 words; $.30/word.
Queries: Required. **Unsolicited mss:** Accepts. **Response:** 3 months, SASE
required. **Freelance Content:** 70%. **Rights:** 1st worldwide serial. **Payment:** On
publication.

YACHTING

18 Marshall St., Suite 114, So. Norwalk, CT 06854. 203-299-5900.
Web site: www.yachtingnet.com. Annual. $5/issue. Circ.: 137,000. Kenny Wooton,

Editor-in-Chief. **Description:** Covers news and trends in boating (power, sail, and charter) for the seasoned, upscale boating enthusiast. **Nonfiction:** Articles on upscale, recreational boating—both power and sail; 1,500 words. **Art:** Photos; $350-$1,000. **Tips:** No "how-to" articles. **Queries:** Preferred. **E-Queries:** No. **Unsolicited mss:** Accepts. **Response:** 1-3 months. **Freelance Content:** 15-25%. **Rights:** All. **Payment:** On publication. **Contact:** Kim Kavin, Executive Editor.

TEENS

BREAKAWAY
Focus on the Family
8605 Explorer Dr., Colorado Springs, CO 80920. 719-531-3400.
Web site: www.breakawaymag.com. Monthly. $15/yr. Circ.: 100,000. Michael Ross, Editor. **Description:** Readers are Christian boys, ages 12-18. **Fiction:** Stories with male slant; to 1,800 words. **Nonfiction:** Real-life adventure articles; to 1,500 words; $.12-$.15/word. **Fillers:** Humor and interesting facts; 500-800 words. **Tips:** No e-mail submissions. Writer's guidelines with #10 SASE. Sample copy with 8.5x11 SASE and $1.50 check. **Payment:** On acceptance.

BRIO
Focus on the Family
8605 Explorer Dr., Colorado Springs, CO 80920. 719-531-3400.
E-mail: briomag@macmail.fotf.org. Web site: www.briomag.com. Monthly. $15/yr. Circ.: 165,000. Susie Shellenberger, Editor. **Description:** For Christian teen girls (profiles, how-to pieces, adventures that show the fun Christian teens can have together). **Fiction:** Fiction with realistic character development, good dialogue, and a plot that teen girls will be drawn to. May contain a spiritual slant but should not be preachy; to 2,000 words. **Nonfiction:** Articles; pays $.08-$.12/word. **Fillers:** Short humorous pieces. **Payment:** On acceptance.

CAMPUS LIFE
Christianity Today International
465 Gundersen Dr., Carol Stream, IL 60188. 630-260-6200.
E-mail: clmag@campuslife.net. Web site: www.campuslife.net. 9x/yr. $19.95/yr. Circ.: 100,000. Chris Lutes, Editor. **Description:** Advice on love, sex, self-image, popularity, and other issues of relevance to high school students, with dramatic stories about teens radically changed by their relationship with Jesus Christ. Also, in-depth profiles of Christian musicians. **Fiction:** A "life lesson" with a Christian worldview, by experienced writers. 2,000 words max; $.20-$.25/word. **Nonfiction:** First-person stories presenting the lives of teenagers, ordinary or dramatic. 2,000 words max; $.20-$.25/word. **Tips:** "Avoid religious clichés, misuse of religious language, lack of respect or empathy for teenagers." Sample copy $3. **Queries:** Required. **E-Queries:** Accepts. **Unsolicited mss:** Does not accept. **Response:** 4-6 weeks, SASE required. **Freelance Content:** 10%. **Rights:** FNAR. **Payment:** On acceptance.

COLLEGE BOUND MAGAZINE

1200 South Ave., Suite 202, Staten Island, NY 10314. 718-761-4800.
E-mail: editorial@collegebound.net. Web site: www.collegeboundmag.com. $15/year.
Circ.: 755,000. Gina LaGuardia, Editor-in-Chief. **Description:** Provides high school students with an insider's look at all aspects of college life. **Nonfiction:** Real-life student experiences and expert voices dealing with dorm life, choosing the right college, joining a fraternity/sorority, college dating, campus events, scholarship strategies, etc.; 600-1,000 words; $75-$100. **Columns, Departments:** Straight Up Strategies, Cash Crunch, Personal Statement, Debate Team; 300-600 words; $50-$75. **Tips:** Send 2-3 clips or samples of your work (from college newspaper, journalism class, etc.) **Queries:** Preferred. **E-Queries:** Yes. **Unsolicited mss:** Accepts. **Response:** 6-8 weeks for queries, 8-10 weeks for manuscripts, SASE required. **Freelance Content:** 75%. **Rights:** First. **Payment:** 30 days upon publication.

COSMOGIRL!

The Hearst Corp., 224 W 57th St., Fl. 3, New York, NY 10019-3212. 212-649-3000.
E-mail: inbox@cosmogirl.com. Web site: www.cosmogirl.com. Monthly. $14.90. Circ.: 1,054,600. Atoosa Rubenstein, Editor-in-Chief. **Description:** Teen version of *Cosmopolitan*, for girls 12-17. Snappy, teen-friendly style. **Nonfiction:** Articles, 900 words, about outstanding young women; first-person narratives of interesting or unusual happenings in the lives of young women; pay varies. **Fillers:** Fillers, 150 words, on ways readers can get involved in social issues. **Queries:** Preferred. **Payment:** On publication. **Contact:** Kim St. Clair Bodden, Editorial Director.

ENCOUNTER

8121 Hamilton Ave., Cincinnati, OH 45231. 513-931-4050.
E-mail: kcarr@standardpub.com. Quarterly. $13. Circ.: 25,000. Kelly Carr, Editor. **Description:** Weekly magazine published quarterly that is focused on encouraging teens in their relationship with Jesus. Read by teens in grades 6-12. Features fiction, nonfiction, and daily devotion. **Fiction:** Contemporary teens, uplifting and character-building, conflicts resolved realistically, with moral message; 500-1,100 words; $.08/word (1st), $.06/word (reprint). **Nonfiction:** Current issues from Christian perspective. Also, teen profiles. Topics: school, family, recreation, friends, part-time jobs, dating, music; 500-1,100; $.08/word (1st), $.06/word (reprint). **Poetry:** Poems by teens only; $20/poem. **Tips:** "Writers can request our quarterly theme list, which is the best way to be considered. Send seasonal material 9-12 months in advance." **Queries:** Not necessary. **E-Queries:** Yes. **Unsolicited mss:** Accepts. **Response:** Queries 1-3 weeks, submissions 8-15 weeks, SASE. **Freelance Content:** 40%. **Rights:** FNAR. **Payment:** On acceptance.

GUIDEPOSTS FOR TEENS

1050 Broadway, Suite 6, Chesterton, IN 46304. 219-929-4429.
E-mail: gp4t@guideposts.org. Web site: www.gp4teens.com. Bimonthly. Circ.: 250,000. Betsy Kohn, Editor. **Description:** Interfaith, for teens (ages 12-18). True stories with adventure and inspiration. Also, quizzes, how-tos, advice, music reviews,

Q&As, and profiles of role models (celebrity and "real" teens). **Nonfiction:** True first-person dangerous, miraculous, or inspirational stories; ghostwritten for (or written by) teens. Protagonist must change in course of the story; must deliver clear inspirational takeaway. **Fillers:** Quizzes (Are you a winner or a whiner? Are you dating a dud?); How-tos (how to find a good job, how to get along with your parents); Celebrity Q&As, interviews. "Soul Food," short 250 word miraculous stories or "A-Ha" moments, written in first person by teens. **Tips:** No preachy, overtly religious stories. **Queries:** Preferred. **E-Queries:** Yes. **Unsolicited mss:** Accepts. **Response:** Queries 4 weeks, submissions 6 weeks, SASE. **Freelance Content:** 80%. **Rights:** All. **Payment:** On acceptance. **Contact:** Allison Payne, Assistant Editor.

GUMBO
1818 N Dr. Martin Luther King Dr., Milwaukee, WI 53212. 414-374-3511.
E-mail: amy@mygumbo.com. Web site: www.mygumbo.com. Bimonthly. $15/yr. Circ.: 25,000. Amy Muchlbauer, Managing Editor. **Description:** Multicultural magazine written, edited, and designed for teens by teens. Mission is to teach journalism and design skills to young adults by having them work with adult mentors who are professionals in journalism, graphic design, and photography. Editorial content reflects diversity in a range of subjects such as careers, sports, health, fashion, news, and entertainment. **Tips:** "We do not offer payment as we are published by a non-profit organization. All work is written and edited by teens and is a learning process. Contact the managing editor directly if you are interested in working for *Gumbo*. Do not send unsolicited material; only assigned articles are published." **Queries:** Required. **E-Queries:** Yes. **Unsolicited mss:** Does not accept. **Response:** 2 weeks. **Rights:** None.

HECKLER
1915 21st St., Sacramento, CA 95814-6813. 916-456-2300.
E-mail: lance@heckler.com. Web site: www.heckler.com. Monthly. $3.99/$6.99. Circ.: 60,000. Lance Dalgart, Executive Editor. **Description:** Magazine on the culture of skateboarding, snowboarding, and music. Features, essays, and reviews; to 3,000 words; $15-$75. **Tips:** "We are looking for great interviews with pro skateboarders, snowboarders, or about-to-break bands. Be patient, but be persistent." **Queries:** Preferred. **E-Queries:** Yes. **Unsolicited mss:** Accepts. **Response:** 7 days. **Freelance Content:** 40%. **Rights:** None. **Payment:** On publication.

INSIGHT
55 W Oak Ridge Dr., Hagerstown, MD 21740-7301. 301-393-4038.
E-mail: insight@rhpa.org. Web site: www.insightmagazine.org. Weekly. $46.95/yr. Circ.: 20,000. Dwain Neilson Esmond, Editor. **Description:** Magazine for high school and college students on growing in their relationship with God. Articles address typical issues these students face in today's changing society. **Tips:** Accepts poems, stories, and articles written by students in high school/college.

KEYNOTER
Key Club International
3636 Woodview Trace, Indianapolis, IN 46268. 317-875-8755.
E-mail: keynoter@kiwanis.org. Web site: www.keyclub.org. 7x/yr. $4/yr. Circ.: 200,000. Amy L. Wiser, Executive Editor. **Description:** For teens, ages 13-18, offering informative, entertaining articles on self-help, school, and community issues. **Nonfiction:** For service-minded high-school students; well-researched, with expert references, interviews with respected sources; 1,200 words; $200-$400. **Tips:** No first-person accounts, fiction, or articles for younger readers. **Queries:** Preferred. **E-Queries:** Yes. **Unsolicited mss:** Accepts. **Response:** Queries 1-4 months, submissions 1 week, SASE required. **Freelance Content:** 65%. **Rights:** FNASR. **Payment:** On acceptance.

LISTEN
55 W Oak Ridge Dr., Hagerstown, MD 21740. 301-393-4019.
E-mail: listen@healthconnection.org. Web site: www.listenmagazine.org. Monthly. $26.95/yr. Circ.: 50,000. Anita Jacobs, Editor. **Description:** Provides teens with vigorous, positive, educational approach to problems arising from use of tobacco, alcohol, and other drugs. **Fiction:** True-to-life stories; 1,000-1,200 words; $.05-$.10/word. **Nonfiction:** For teenagers, on problems of alcohol and drug abuse; personality profiles; self-improvement; drug-free activities; 1,000-1,200 words; $.05-$.10/word. **Poetry:** Open to poems by high-school students only. **Tips:** "Use upbeat approach." Sample copy and guidelines available for $2 with 9x12 envelope with 2 first-class stamps. **Queries:** Preferred. **E-Queries:** Yes. **Unsolicited mss:** Accepts. **Response:** 2 weeks queries, 3 months submissions; SASE. **Rights:** FNASR. **Payment:** On acceptance.

MERLYN'S PEN
See full listing in Fiction for Teens category.

THE NEW YORK TIMES UPFRONT
The New York Times/Scholastic Inc.
557 Broadway, New York, NY 10012-3999. 212-343-6100.
E-mail: pyoung@scholastic.com. Web site: www.upfrontmagazine.com. Biweekly. Peter S. Young, Editor. **Description:** News magazine for teenagers. **Nonfiction:** News articles, 500-1,500 words; pays $150 and up. **Queries:** Preferred. **Payment:** On acceptance.

ODYSSEY
Cobblestone Publishing
30 Grove St., Suite C, Peterborough, NH 03458. 603-924-7209.
E-mail: bethlindstrom2000@hotmail.com. Web site: www.cobblestonepub.com. 9x/year. Circ.: 21,000. Elizabeth Lindstrom, Editor. **Description:** Features, 750-1,000 words, on science and technology, for readers, ages 10-16. Science-related fiction, myths, legends, and science-fiction stories. Activities. Pays $.20-$.25/word.

Fiction: Science-related stories, poems, science fiction, retold legends, etc., relating to theme; up to 1,000 words; $.20-$.25/word. **Nonfiction:** Subjects directly and indirectly related to theme; with little-known information (but don't overlook the obvious); 720-950 words; $.20-$.25/word. **Fillers:** Critical-thinking activities, experiments, models, science fair projects, etc., for children alone, with adult supervision, or in classroom setting. **Columns, Departments:** Far Out; Places, Media, People to Discover; Fantastic Journeys; 400-650 words. **Art:** Transparencies, slides, color prints; $15-$100 (B&W); $25-$100 (color). **Tips:** Material must relate to specific theme; contact for upcoming list. Scientific accuracy, lively approach, and inclusion of primary research are crucial to being accepted. **Payment:** On publication.

SCHOLASTIC SCOPE

Scholastic, Inc., 555 Broadway, New York, NY 10012-3999. 212-343-6100. E-mail: scopemag@scholastic.com. Web site: www.scholastic.com. 18x/yr. $7.50. Circ.: 750,000. Diane Webber, Editor. **Description:** Fiction for 15- to 18-year-olds, with 4th-6th grade reading ability. Short stories, 400-1,200 words, on teenage interests and relationships; family, job, and school situations. Plays to 5,000 words. Pays good rates. **Payment:** On acceptance.

SCIENCE WORLD

See full listing in Science category.

SEVENTEEN

1440 Broadway, Fl. 13, New York, NY 10018. 212-204-4300. Web site: www.seventeen.com. Monthly. $3.99/$12. Circ.: 2,400,000. Sabrina Weill, Editor-in-Chief. **Description:** Popular beauty/fashion magazine, written for young women ages 13-21. **Fiction:** "Stories with issues important and familiar to our readers, that also challenge them and make them think." **Nonfiction:** Feature stories unique and relevant to teenage girls; 1,000-2,000 words; $1/word. **Columns, Departments:** Features, Guys, Voice, Real Life, To Your Health, College, Quizzes; 350-500 words. **Tips:** "Story ideas should spring from a teenage viewpoint and sensibility, not that of parent, teacher, or other adult." **Queries:** Required. **Response:** 4-8 weeks, SASE required. **Freelance Content:** 30%. **Rights:** FNAR. **Payment:** On publication. **Note:** The Hearst Corp. has agreed to purchase *Seventeen* in the summer of 2003.

SPANK! YOUTH CULTURE ONLINE

Ububik, #505, 300 Meredith Rd., Calgary, Alberta T2E 7A8 Canada. 403-217-0468. E-mail: happyrandom@spankmag.com. Web site: www.spankmag.com. Stephen R. Cassady, Editor. **Description:** E-zine written by youth for youth, for ages 14 to 24. Only accepts submissions from youth.

SÚPERONDA

425 Pine Ave., Santa Barbara, CA 93117-3709. 805-964-4554. E-mail: editorial@hbinc.com. Web site: www.superonda.com. 5x/yr. $12/yr. Circ.:

100,000. Jesus Chavarria, Editor. **Description:** English-language magazine for U.S. Hispanics in college/college-bound, ages 18-24. Features, 600-1,800 words; columns, 600 words; pays to $.75/word. **Queries:** Required. **E-Queries:** Yes. **Unsolicited mss:** Does not accept. **Response:** 30-60 days. **Freelance Content:** 80%. **Rights:** All. **Payment:** On publication. **Contact:** Leslie Dinaberg, Managing Editor.

TEEN

PRIMEDIA Consumer Media & Magazine Group
6420 Wilshire Blvd., Los Angeles, CA 90048-5502. 323-782-2000.
E-mail: teenedit@primediacmmg.com. Web site: www.teenmag.com. Quarterly. Circ.: 600,000. Jane Fort, Editor-in-Chief. **Description:** Established in 1955, *Teen* is now the little-sister publication to *Seventeen* magazine, appealing to young teens interested in fashion, beauty, body image, and empowerment. Nonfiction and some fiction; pay varies. **Queries:** Preferred. **Payment:** On publication.

TEEN VOICES

Women Express, Inc., 80 Summer St., Boston, MA 02110. 617-426-5505.
E-mail: womenexp@teenvoices.com. Web site: www.teenvoices.com. Quarterly. $2.95/$19.95. Circ.: 25,000. Celina DeLeon, Editor. **Description:** Written by, for, and about teenaged and young-adult women. Offers a place to share thoughts with others the same age. **Fiction:** Short stories, any subject and length. **Nonfiction:** About any important issue or experience. **Poetry:** "Your feelings, thoughts, etc." **Columns, Departments:** Opinions/editorial pieces. **Art:** Digital file (TIF or EPS), or hardcopy. **Tips:** Be honest and candid. Appreciates material that promotes feminism, equality, and self-esteem, "You're more than just a pretty face." **Queries:** Not necessary. **E-Queries:** Yes. **Unsolicited mss:** Accepts. **Response:** 3-5 days, SASE not required. **Rights:** FNAR. **Payment:** In copies.

TEENPRENEUR

130 Fifth Ave., Fl. 10, New York, NY 10011. 212-242-8000. 6x/year. Circ.: 4,000.
Description: For African-American teens interested in business.

TWIST

270 Sylvan Ave., Englewood Cliffs, NJ 07632-2521. 201-569-6699.
E-mail: twistmail@aol.com. Web site: www.twistmag.com. Monthly. $9.97. Circ.: 366,300. Richard Spencer, Editor-in-Chief. **Description:** On relationships, entertainment, fitness, fashion, and other topics, for today's young women. **Nonfiction:** Articles, 1,500 words. **Tips:** Mostly staff-written; queries with clips required.

WHAT MAGAZINE

108-93 Lombard Ave., Winnipeg, Manitoba R3B 3B1 Canada. 204-985-8160.
E-mail: what@whatmagnet.com. Web site: www.whatmagnet.com. Bimonthly. $14. Circ.: 250,000. Barbara Chabai, Editor. **Description:** Canadian teen pop-culture magazine (including music, movie and TV interviews, typical issues and themes affecting readers, ages 13-19). **Nonfiction:** Charged, edgy, unconventional, from pop cul-

ture to social issues; 450 words and up; pay negotiable. **Tips:** Query with working story title, 1-sentence explanation of angle, justification and proposed treatment, potential contacts, proposed length. Welcomes new writers. **Queries:** Required. **E-Queries:** Yes. **Unsolicited mss:** Does not accept. **Response:** 1-2 months, SASE required. **Freelance Content:** 60%. **Rights:** 1st Canadian. **Payment:** On publication.

WITH

722 Main St., P.O. Box 347, Newton, KS 67114. 316-283-5100.
Web site: www.withonline.org. Bimonthly. $26.95/yr. Circ.: 5,000. Carol Duerksen, Editor. **Description:** "The Magazine for Radical Christian Youth." Seeks to "empower teens to be radically committed to Jesus Christ, peace, justice, and sharing God's good news through words and action." **Fiction:** First-person stories; 1,500 words; $100. **Nonfiction:** Creative, "inside the life of a teen," first-person preferred. Avoid preaching. Themes: sex/dating, Who is God?, Christmas, and service/mission; 1,500 words; pay varies. **Fillers:** Wholesome humor and poetry. **Art:** 8x10 B&W. **Queries:** Not necessary. **E-Queries:** Yes. **Unsolicited mss:** Accepts. **Response:** 1 month, SASE required. **Freelance Content:** 20%. **Rights:** FNAR and electronic. **Payment:** On acceptance.

YM

Gruner + Jahr, 15 E 26th St., Fl. 14, New York, NY 10010-1505. 646-758-0555.
Web site: www.ym.com. 11x/yr. $2.99/issue. Circ.: 2,262,000. Christian Kelly, Editor-in-Chief. **Description:** Fashion, beauty, boys, advice, and features for girls, ages 12-24. **Queries:** Required. **Unsolicited mss:** Accepts. **Response:** Queries 1-2 months. **Freelance Content:** 40%. **Payment:** On publication.

YOUNG AND ALIVE

P.O. Box 6097, Lincoln, NE 68506.
E-mail: info@christianrecord.org. Quarterly. Circ.: 25,000. Gaylena Gibson, Editor. **Description:** Publication for young adults who are blind or visually impaired. Presents material from a non-denominational, Christian viewpoint and features articles on adventure, biography, camping, careers, health, history, hobbies, holidays, marriage, nature, practical Christianity, sports, and travel. Features run 800-1,400 words; pay varies. **Art:** Slides or prints; $10/photo. **Queries:** Not necessary. **E-Queries:** No. **Unsolicited mss:** Accepts. **Response:** 12 months, SASE required. **Freelance Content:** 90%. **Rights:** One-time. **Payment:** On acceptance.

YOUNG SALVATIONIST

The Salvation Army, P.O. Box 269, Alexandria, VA 22313-0269. 703-684-5500.
E-mail: ys@usn.salvationarmy.org. 10x/yr. Circ.: 48,000. Laura Ezzell, Managing Editor. **Description:** For teenagers, seeks to teach Christian view of everyday living. **Fiction:** Uses some fiction; 500-1,200 words; $.15/word. **Nonfiction:** Articles (to 1,000-1,500 words); short-shorts, first-person testimonies (600-800 words). Pays $.15/word ($.10/word for reprints). **Tips:** Write for theme list or sample issue. **Response:** SASE required. **Freelance Content:** 80%. **Payment:** On acceptance.

YOUTH UPDATE
St. Anthony Messenger Press
28 W Liberty St., Cincinnati, OH 45202-6498. 513-241-5615.
Web site: www.americancatholic.org. Monthly. Circ.: 15,000. Carol Ann Morrow, Editor. **Description:** Newsletter that supports the growth of Catholic teens, ages 14-18, in a life of faith. **Nonfiction:** Biblical books, personal growth, doctrinal truths, issues of peace and justice; 2,300 words; $.16/word. **Queries:** Required. **E-Queries:** Yes. **Response:** 9-12 weeks. **Freelance Content:** 80%. **Payment:** On acceptance.

TRADE & TECHNICAL

AMERICAN CITY & COUNTY
PRIMEDIA Business Magazines & Media, Inc.
6151 Powers Ferry Rd. NW, Suite 200, Atlanta, GA 30339. 770-618-0112.
E-mail: bwolpin@primediabusiness.com.
Web site: www.americancityandcounty.com. Bill Wolpin, Editorial Director.
Description: On local government issues (wastewater, water, solid waste, financial management, information technology, etc.). Articles run 600-2,500 words. **Tips:** Readers are elected and appointed local government officials.

AMERICAN COIN-OP
500 N Dearborn St., Suite 1000, Chicago, IL 60610-4964. 312-337-7700.
E-mail: ppartyka@crain.com. Web site: www.crain.com. Monthly. $35/yr. Circ.: 17,000. Paul Partika, Editor. **Description:** Articles on successful coin-operated laundries (management, promotion, decor, maintenance). SASE for guidelines. **Nonfiction:** To 2,500 words; pays from $.08/word. **Art:** B&W photos; pays $8/each. **Queries:** Preferred.

AMERICAN DEMOGRAPHICS
See full listing in Contemporary Culture category.

AMERICAN LAUNDRY NEWS
500 N Dearborn St., Suite 1000, Chicago, IL 60610. 312-337-7700.
E-mail: laundrynews@crain.com;bbeggs@crain.com. Monthly. $39/yr. Circ.: 16,000. Bruce Beggs, Editor. **Description:** Laundry and linen management, including institutional, commercial, and industrial laundries, and uniform rental and linen supply companies. **Nonfiction:** New technology, industry news and trends, profiles; 1,000-2,000 words; to $.22/word. **Art:** Color prints; $25-$50. **Tips:** "We do not cover the drycleaning or coin-operated laundry segments of our industry." Sample copy for $6 and 10x13 SASE. **Queries:** Preferred. **E-Queries:** Yes. **Unsolicited mss:** Accepts. **Response:** 1 month for queries, 2 months for submissions; SASE required. **Freelance Content:** 10%. **Rights:** All. **Payment:** On publication.

AREA DEVELOPMENT
400 Post Ave., Westbury, NY 11590-2289. 516-338-0900.
E-mail: gerri@area-development.com. Web site: www.areadevelopment.com.
Monthly. Circ.: 45,500. Geraldine Gambale, Editor. **Description:** On site-selection
and facility-planning issues for executives at industrial companies (site selection, real
estate, taxes, labor, energy, environment, government regulations, etc.); 2,000 words;
$.30-$.40/word. **Tips:** No promotional material about particular areas or communities. **Queries:** Preferred. **E-Queries:** Yes. **Unsolicited mss:** Accepts. **Freelance
Content:** 90%. **Payment:** On publication.

BUILDER
One Thomas Cir. NW, Suite 600, Washington, DC 20005-5802. 202-452-0800.
Web site: www.builderonline.com. 16x/yr. $29.95/yr. Circ.: 138,000. Boyce
Thompson, Editor-in-Chief. **Description:** On trends and news in home building
(design, marketing, new products, etc.). **Nonfiction:** Articles; to 1,500 words; pay
negotiable. **Queries:** Preferred. **Payment:** On acceptance.

BUSINESS & COMMERCIAL AVIATION
4 International Dr., Suite 260, Rye Brook, NY 10573-1065. 914-933-7600.
E-mail: feedback@aviationnow.com. Web site: www.aviationnow.com/bca. Monthly.
$60/yr. Circ.: 47,000. William Garvey, Editor-in-Chief. **Description:** For pilots, on
use of private aircraft for business transportation. **Nonfiction:** Articles; 2,500 words,
with photos; pays $100-$500. **Queries:** Preferred. **Payment:** On acceptance.

CALIFORNIA LAWYER
1145 Market St., Fl. 8, San Francisco, CA 94103. 415-252-0500.
E-mail: tema_goodwin@dailyjournal.com. Web site: www.dailyjournal.com. Monthly.
$5/$75. Circ.: 140,000. Peter Allen, Editor. **Description:** General-interest magazine
on legal issues. Combines hard-hitting legal news, case commentary and technology
coverage. **Nonfiction:** Features, 1,500-2,000 words; $500-$2,500. **Columns,
Departments:** News, commentary, features, essays, technology, legal advice, technology, book reviews; 500-1,500 words; $50-$500. **Tips:** "Break in with something
small in news section." **Queries:** Preferred. **E-Queries:** Yes. **Unsolicited mss:**
Accepts. **Response:** 1-6 weeks. **Freelance Content:** 80%. **Rights:** FNAR and electronic. **Payment:** On acceptance. **Contact:** Tema Goodwin, Managing Editor.

CLEANING & MAINTENANCE MANAGEMENT
13 Century Hill Dr., Latham, NY 12110-2197. 518-783-1281.
Web site: www.cmmonline.com. Monthly. $45/yr. Circ.: 40,000. Michael McCagg,
Managing Editor. **Description:** Features articles on managing efficient cleaning and
custodial/maintenance operations. Also provides technical/mechanical how-to articles. **Nonfiction:** Articles, 500-1,200 words; pays to $300 for commissioned features.
Art: Photos. **Queries:** Preferred. **Payment:** On publication.

THE CONSTRUCTION SPECIFIER
289 Elmwood Ave., Suite 226, Buffalo, NY 14222-2201. 866-572-5633.
E-mail: editor@constructionspecifier.com. Web site: www.constructionspecifier.com.
Monthly. $40. Circ.: 18,000. Anthony Capkun, Editor. **Description:** Articles, 2,000-
3,000 words, on the "nuts and bolts" of nonresidential construction, for owners/
facility managers, architects, engineers, specifiers, contractors, and manufacturers.

COOKING FOR PROFIT
See full listing in Food & Wine category.

DAIRY FOODS
1050 Illinois Route 83, Suite 200, Bensenville, IL 60106-1096. 630-694-4341.
E-mail: phillipsd@bnp.com. Web site: www.dairyfoods.com. Monthly. $100/yr. Circ.:
18,000. David Phillips, Editor. **Description:** On innovative dairies, processing operations, marketing, new products for milk handlers, and makers of dairy products.
Articles run 2,500 words. No payment offered.

DEALERSCOPE
401 N Broad St., Philadelphia, PA 19108-1080. 215-238-5300.
Web site: www.dealerscope.com. Monthly. Circ.: 22,000. Grant Clauser, Editor-in-
Chief. **Description:** On new consumer electronics, computer and electronics prod-
ucts, and new technologies. **Nonfiction:** Articles, to 1,000 words, pay varies. **Tips:**
Query with clips and resume. **Payment:** On publication.

DENTAL ECONOMICS
Penwell, P.O. Box 3408, Tulsa, OK 74101-3408. 918-835-3161.
Web site: www.dentaleconomics.com. Monthly. $78. Circ.: 102,000. Joseph A. Blaes,
DDS, Editor. **Description:** On business side of dental practice, patient and staff
communication, personal investments. **Nonfiction:** Articles, 1,200-3,500 words; pays
$100-$400. **Payment:** On acceptance.

DISPLAY & DESIGN IDEAS
1115 Northmeadow Pkwy, Roswell, GA 30076-3857. 770-569-1540.
E-mail: jclark@ddimagazine.com. Web site: www.ddimagazine.com. Monthly. Circ.:
19,500. RoxAnna Sway, Editor. **Description:** For visual merchandisers and store
planners/designers (new retail store design, design trends, merchandising strategies,
and product information). **Nonfiction:** Stories on cutting-edge store design, with
special attention to visual merchandising, fixtures, flooring, lighting, and ceiling and
wall treatments. 1,000 words; fees negotiable. **Art:** Submit at least 2-3 high-quality,
color photos with each article. **Tips:** Articles should quote at least 3 different sources.
Queries: Required. **E-Queries:** Yes. **Unsolicited mss:** Does not accept.
Response: 1-2 weeks. **Freelance Content:** 30%. **Rights:** Unlimited. **Payment:**
On publication. **Contact:** Julie Clark, Senior Editor.

DRUG TOPICS

Thompson Medical Economics, 5 Paragon Dr., Montvale, NJ 07645. 201-358-7258. E-mail: drug.topics@medec.com. Web site: www.drugtopics.com. Semi-monthly. $61/yr. Circ.: 112,000. Harold E. Cohen, Editor. **Description:** Covers pharmacy news, issues, trends, products marketing for pharmacists, buyers, wholesalers, academia, and others. **Nonfiction:** News stories, trends in pharmacy, editorials; 750-2,000 words. **Tips:** Payment is offered for commissioned articles only. **Queries:** Required. **Rights:** First. **Payment:** On acceptance.

ELECTRONIC INFORMATION REPORT

Simba Information, P.O. Box 4234, Stamford, CT 06907-0234. 203-358-4100. E-mail: eir@simbanet.com. Web site: www.simbanet.com. Weekly. Linda Kopp, Executive Editor. **Description:** Covers all aspects of the marketing of electronic information.

ENGINEERED SYSTEMS

P.O. Box 4270, Troy, MI 48099-4270. 248-362-3700. E-mail: beverlyr@bnp.com. Web site: www.esmagazine.com. Monthly. $58/yr. Circ.: 57,500. Robert C. Beverly, Editor. **Description:** Articles, case histories, news, and product information related to engineered HVAC systems in commercial, industrial, or institutional buildings. **Tips:** "Prefers e-mail inquiries. See Web site for style and content." **Queries:** Preferred. **E-Queries:** Yes. **Payment:** On publication.

THE ENGRAVERS JOURNAL

P.O. Box 318, Brighton, MI 48116. 810-229-5725. E-mail: editor@engraversjournal.com. Web site: www.engraversjournal.com. Monthly. Sonja Davis, Publisher. **Description:** Trade magazine for engravers featuring articles on small business operations. Pays $75-$300. **Queries:** Preferred. **E-Queries:** No. **Unsolicited mss:** Accepts. **Freelance Content:** 60%. **Rights:** Varies. **Payment:** On acceptance.

ENTERTAINMENT DESIGN

See full listing in Film, TV, Entertainment category.

FIRE CHIEF

PRIMEDIA Business Magazines & Media
330 N Wabash, Suite 2300, Chicago, IL 60611. E-mail: jwilmoth@primediabusiness.com. Web site: www.firechief.com. Monthly. $54/yr. Circ.: 52,600. Janet Wilmoth, Editor. **Description:** For fire officers. **Nonfiction:** Training, safety and health, communications, fire investigation, finance and budgeting, professional development, incident command, hazmat response, vehicle maintenance; 1,000-5,000 words; to $.30/word. **Columns, Departments:** Training Perspectives, EMS Viewpoint, Sound Off; 1,000-1,800 words. **Queries:** Preferred. **Response:** SASE. **Payment:** On publication.

FIREHOUSE
Cygnus Business Media
445 Broad Hollow Rd., Suite 21, Melville, NY 11747. 631-845-2700.
E-mail: harvey.eisner@cygnuspub.com. Web site: www.firehouse.com. Monthly.
$29/yr. Circ.: 100,000. Harvey Eisner, Editor-in-Chief. **Description:** For firefighters and fire buffs; to educate, inform, and entertain. **Nonfiction:** On major fires and disasters, apparatus and equipment, communications, training, law, safety, EMS, etc.; 500-2,000 words. **Art:** Prefers color photos, illustrations, charts, and diagrams. **Queries:** Required. **E-Queries:** Yes. **Rights:** FNAR. **Payment:** On publication.

FOOD MANAGEMENT
1300 E Ninth St., Cleveland, OH 44114-1503. 216-696-7000.
E-mail: fmeditor@aol.com. Web site: www.penton.com. Monthly. Circ.: 47,895. John Lawn, Editor-in-Chief. **Description:** On food service in hospitals, nursing homes, schools, colleges, prisons, businesses, and industrial sites. **Nonfiction:** Trends, legislative issues, how-tos, management, and retail-oriented food service pieces. **Queries:** Required.

FOUNDATION NEWS & COMMENTARY
1828 L Street NW, Washington, DC 20036. 202-467-0467.
E-mail: curtj@cof.org. Web site: www.foundationnews.org. Bimonthly. $48/year. Circ.: 10,000. Jody Curtis, Editor. **Description:** Covers the world of grant making, for professional grant makers, volunteer trustees, and grant seekers. **Nonfiction:** 1,200-3,000 words; pay varies. **Tips:** Avoid fundraising topics. **Queries:** Required. **E-Queries:** Yes. **Unsolicited mss:** Accepts. **Response:** Varies. **Freelance Content:** 25%. **Rights:** All. **Payment:** On acceptance.

GLASS DIGEST
18 E 41st St., Fl. 20, New York, NY 10017-6222. 212-376-7722.
E-mail: glass@ashlee.com. Web site: www.ashlee.com. Monthly. $40/yr. Circ.: 11,730. Alec Bradford, Editor. **Description:** On building projects and glass/metal dealers, distributors, storefront and glazing contractors. **Nonfiction:** Articles, 1,200-1,500 words. **Payment:** On publication. **Contact:** Joel Bruinooge, Editorial Director.

GOVERNMENT EXECUTIVE
1501 M St. NW, Suite 300, Washington, DC 20005-1700. 202-739-8500.
E-mail: govexec@govexec.com. Web site: www.govexec.com. Monthly. $48/yr. Circ.: 60,000. Timothy Clark, President/Editor. **Description:** Articles, 1,500-3,000 words, for civilian and military government workers at the management level.

GREENHOUSE MANAGEMENT & PRODUCTION
P.O. Box 1868, Fort Worth, TX 76101-1868.
David Kuack, Editor. **Description:** For professional greenhouse growers. **Nonfiction:** How-tos, innovative production or marketing techniques; 500-1,800

words. **Art:** Color slides or electronic images; $50-$300. **Queries:** Preferred. **Unsolicited mss:** Accepts. **Payment:** On acceptance.

HEATING/PIPING/AIR CONDITIONING/ENGINEERING
1300 E Ninth St., Cleveland, OH 44114-1501. 216-696-7000.
E-mail: hpac@penton.com. Web site: www.hpac.com. Monthly. $65. Circ.: 31,000. Michael G. Ivanovich, Editor. **Description:** On heating, piping, and air conditioning systems and related issues (indoor air quality, energy efficiency), for industrial plants and large buildings only. **Nonfiction:** Articles, to 3,500 words; pays $70/printed page. **Queries:** Preferred. **Payment:** On publication.

HOME SHOP MACHINIST
2779 Aero Park Dr., Traverse City, MI 49686. 231-946-3712.
E-mail: nknopf@villagepress.com. Web site: www.homeshopmachinist.com. Bimonthly. $5.95. Circ.: 36,000. Neil A. Knopf, Editor. **Description:** Publishes how-to articles for serious machinists and hobbyists. **Nonfiction:** Machine how-to projects. Photos, drawings, and text required. No people profiles. $40/page. **Art:** $9/photo. **Tips:** Write in first-person only; accuracy and detail essential. **Queries:** Preferred. **E-Queries:** Yes. **Unsolicited mss:** Accepts. **Response:** Queries 1 week, submissions 1 month, SASE required. **Freelance Content:** 95%. **Rights:** FNASR. **Payment:** On publication.

HOSPITALS & HEALTH NETWORKS
One N Franklin St., Fl. 29, Chicago, IL 60606. 312-893-6800.
E-mail: bsantamour@healthforum.com. Web site: www.hhnmag.com.
Bill Santamour, Managing Editor. **Description:** Publication for health-care executives and hospital administrators on financing, staffing, coordinating, and providing facilities for health-care services. **Nonfiction:** Articles, 250-1,800 words. Pay varies. **Unsolicited mss:** Does not accept. **Payment:** On publication.

IDEA HEALTH & FITNESS SOURCE
See full listing in Fitness Magazines category.

JD JUNGLE
632 Broadway, Fl. 7, New York, NY 10012-2614. 212-352-0840.
E-mail: editors@jdjungle.com. Web site: www.jdjungle.com. Monthly. $12. Circ.: 132,000. Jon Gluck, Editor-in-Chief. **Description:** For law students. Seeks to provide professionals with the tools they need to be successful. Online and print versions. **Queries:** Preferred. **Unsolicited mss:** Accepts. **Response:** SASE required.

JOURNAL OF EMERGENCY MEDICAL SERVICES (JEMS)
525 B Street, Suite 1900, Carlsbad, CA 92101. 800-266-5367.
Web site: www.jems.com. Monthly. $27.97. Circ.: 40,000. A.J. Heightman, Editor-in-Chief. **Description:** A leading voice in emergency medicine and prehospital care.

Readers include EMTs, paramedics, nurses, physicians, EMS managers, administrators, and educators. **Nonfiction:** On provider health and professional development; innovative applications of EMS; interviews/profiles, new equipment and technology; industry news and commentary; $200-$400. **Columns, Departments:** $150-$200/department; $25/new items. **Art:** Only real-life EMS action shots; completed model release form must accompany photos when appropriate. $150-$400 (cover). **Queries:** Preferred. **E-Queries:** Yes. **Unsolicited mss:** Accepts. **Response:** 3 months. **Freelance Content:** 70%. **Payment:** On publication.

LANDSCAPE TRADES
Landscape Ontario Horticulture Trades Assn.
7856 Fifth Line S., RR4, Milton, Ontario L9T 2X8 Canada. 905-875-1805.
E-mail: linerskine@landscapeontario.com. Web site: www.landscapetrades.com.
9x/yr. $45. Circ.: 8,000. Sarah Willis, Editorial Director. **Description:** Articles on landscape design, construction, and maintenance. Also, pieces on retail and wholesale nursery industries. **Queries:** Required. **Unsolicited mss:** Does not accept. **Response:** 2-3 weeks. **Freelance Content:** 50%. **Rights:** FNAR. **Payment:** On publication. **Contact:** Linda Erskine.

LP-GAS
7500 Old Oak Blvd., Cleveland, OH 44130. 440-891-2616.
E-mail: phyland@advanstar.com. Web site: www.lpgasmagazine.com. $30/yr. Circ.: 14,500. Patrick Hyland, Editor. **Description:** On LP-gas dealer operations: marketing, management, etc. **Nonfiction:** Articles, 1,500-2,500 words, with photos; pays flat fee schedule. **Queries:** Preferred. **Payment:** On acceptance.

MACHINE DESIGN
Penton Media Bldg., 1300 E Ninth St., Cleveland, OH 44114-1503. 216-696-7000.
E-mail: mdeditor@penton.com. Web site: www.machinedesign.com. Semi-monthly. $105/yr. Circ.: 185,000. Ronald Khol, Editor. **Description:** On mechanical and electromechanical design topics for engineers. **Nonfiction:** Articles, to 10 typed pages; pay varies. **Queries:** Preferred. **Payment:** On publication.

MAINTENANCE TECHNOLOGY
1300 S Grove Ave., Suite 105, Barrington, IL 60010-5246. 847-382-8100.
E-mail: editors@mt-online.com. Web site: www.mt-online.com. Monthly. Circ.: 54,000. Robert C. Baldwin, Editor. **Description:** Technical articles with how-to information to increase reliability and maintainability of electrical and mechanical systems and equipment. For managers, supervisors, and engineers in all industries and facilities. **Nonfiction:** Pay varies. **Queries:** Preferred. **Payment:** On acceptance.

NAILPRO
7628 Densmore Ave., Van Nuys, CA 91406-2042. 818-782-7328.
E-mail: nailpro@creativeage.com. Web site: www.nailpro.com. Monthly. $24/yr.

Circ.: 60,000. Jodi Mills, Editor. **Description:** For nail professionals, on new products, techniques, business ideas, and other beauty industry news. **Tips:** "Writers must have a knowledge of the beauty industry and specifically the nailcare industry." **Queries:** Preferred. **E-Queries:** Yes. **Unsolicited mss:** Accepts. **Response:** 2 weeks. **Freelance Content:** 80%. **Rights:** All. **Payment:** On acceptance.

NATIONAL FISHERMAN
121 Free St., Portland, ME 04101-3919. 207-842-5606.
E-mail: editor@nationalfisherman.com. Web site: www.nationalfisherman.com. Monthly. $22.95/yr. Circ.: 38,000. Jerry Fraser, Editor-in-Chief. **Description:** For commercial fishermen and boat builders. **Nonfiction:** Articles; 200-2,000 words; $4-$6/inch. **Art:** Photos. **Queries:** Preferred. **Payment:** On publication.

9-1-1 MAGAZINE
18201 Weston Pl., Tustin, CA 92780. 714-544-7776.
E-mail: info@9-1-1magazine.com. Web site: www.9-1-1magazine.com. Randall D. Larson, Editor. **Description:** Managing emergency communications for PSAPs, dispatch and field communications for EMS, fire, law enforcement, and emergency/disaster management. Product-related technical, operational, and coverage of skills, training, and equipment. Features on provocative issues and major incidents. Features, $.10-$.20/word. Columns, $50/piece. **Tips:** "Rarely accepts work that has been published elsewhere. **Rights:** FNAR. **Payment:** On publication.

THE NORTHERN LOGGER AND TIMBER PROCESSOR
P.O. Box 69, Old Forge, NY 13420-0069. 315-369-3078.
E-mail: nela@telnet.net. Monthly. $12. Circ.: 13,200. Eric A. Johnson, Editor. **Description:** Covers the forest-product industry. **Nonfiction:** Features, 1,000-2,000 words; pays $.15/word. **Art:** Photos. **Queries:** Preferred. **Payment:** On publication.

PI MAGAZINE
870 Pompton Ave., Suite B2, Cedar Grove, NJ 07009-1252. 973-571-0400.
E-mail: info@pimagazine.com. Web site: www.pimagazine.com. Bimontly. $39/yr. Circ.: 10,000. Jimmie Mesis, Publisher/Editor. **Description:** Journal for professional investigators. Profiles of PIs, with true accounts of their most difficult cases. Pays $100-$200. **Tips:** No fiction. **Payment:** On publication.

PIZZA TODAY
P.O. Box 1347, New Albany, IN 47151-1347. 812-949-0909.
E-mail: jwhite@pizzatoday.com. Web site: www.pizzatoday.com. Monthly. $29.95/yr. Circ.: 41,000. Jeremy White, Executive Editor. **Description:** On pizza business management for entrepreneurs. **Nonfiction:** On food preparation, marketing strategies, business management, hiring and training, etc.; 500-1,500 words; $.50/word. **Tips:** Send query by e-mail, fax, or mail. **Queries:** Preferred. **Payment:** On acceptance.

POLICE AND SECURITY NEWS
1208 Juniper St., Quakertown, PA 18951. 215-538-1240.
E-mail: jdevery@policeandsecuritynews.com.
Web site: www.policeandsecuritynews.com. Bimonthly. $18/yr. Circ.: 22,000. James
Devery, Editor. **Description:** For public and private law-enforcement and security
industries. **Nonfiction:** Law enforcement and security related articles, for middle
and upper management. Written for experts in a manner which non-experts can comprehend. 500-3,000 words; $.10/word. **Tips:** Submit query, cover letter, complete
manuscript, bio, and SASE. **Queries:** Preferred. **E-Queries:** Yes. **Unsolicited mss:**
Accepts. **Response:** 1-2 weeks. **Freelance Content:** 50%. **Rights:** FNAR.
Payment: On publication.

POOL & BILLIARD
See full listing in Games & Pastimes category.

PUBLISH
462 Boston St., Topsfield, MA 01983-1200. 978-887-7900.
E-mail: edit@publish.com. Web site: www.publish.com. Bimonthly. Circ.: 96,000.
Melissa Reyen, Executive Editor. **Description:** On all aspects of enterprise communication and publishing technology. **Nonfiction:** Features (1,500-2,000 words);
reviews (400-800 words); pay varies. **Payment:** On acceptance.

REMODELING
One Thomas Cir. NW, Suite 600, Washington, DC 20005. 202-452-0390.
E-mail: salfano@hanley-wood.com; chartman@hanley-wood.com.
Web site: www.remodelingmagazine.com. Monthly. Circ.: 80,000. Sal Alfano, Editor;
Christine Hartman, Managing Editor. **Description:** For full-service remodeling con-
tractors. **Nonfiction:** Articles (by assignment only) on industry news for residential
and light commercial remodelers; 250-1,700 words. **Queries:** Required. **E-Queries:**
Yes. **Unsolicited mss:** Does not accept. **Response:** 1 month. **Freelance Content:**
10%. **Payment:** On acceptance.

RV BUSINESS
2575 Vista Del Mar Dr., Ventura, CA 93001. 800-765-1912.
E-mail: rvb@tl.com. Web site: www.rvbusiness.com. Monthly. Circ.: 21,000. John
Sullaway, Editor. **Description:** Publication for the RV industry offering news and
product-related features. Also covers legislative matters affecting the industry.
Nonfiction: Articles, to 1,500 words; pay varies. **Tips:** No generic business features.

SOUTHERN LUMBERMAN
P.O. Box 681629, Franklin, TN 37068-1629. 615-791-1961.
E-mail: ngregg@southernlumberman.com. Web site: www.southernlumberman.com.
Monthly. $23/yr. Circ.: 15,500. Nanci P. Gregg, Editor. **Description:** For owners and
operators of small- to medium-sized sawmills. **Nonfiction:** Ideal: a feature on a
sawmill with description of equipment and tips from owner/manager on how to work

efficiently, save and make money; 500-2,500 words; $100-$300. **Queries:** Preferred. **E-Queries:** No. **Unsolicited mss:** Accepts. **Response:** 4-6 weeks, SASE. **Freelance Content:** 45%. **Rights:** FNASR. **Payment:** On publication.

STITCHES

16787 Warden Ave., RR #3, Newmarket, Ontario L3Y 4W1 Canada. 905-853-1884. E-mail: simon@stitchesmagazine.com. Web site: www.stitchesmagazine.com. Monthly. $40/yr (Canada), $45 (U.S.). Circ.: 39,000. Peter Cocker, Publisher. **Description:** "The Journal of Medical Humor." Specializes in humor and lifestyle pieces for physicians. **Fiction:** To 2,000 words; $.35/word (Canada), $.25/word (U.S.). **Nonfiction:** To 2,000 words. **Poetry:** Shorter; $.50/word (Canada), $.40/word (U.S.). **Art:** Cartoons only. $50 (Canada), $40 (U.S.). **Queries:** Not necessary. **E-Queries:** Yes. **Unsolicited mss:** Accepts. **Freelance Content:** 95%. **Rights:** FNASR. **Payment:** On publication. **Contact:** Simon Hally, Editor.

STONE WORLD

210 Route 4 E, Suite 311, Paramus, NJ 07652. 201-291-9001. E-mail: michael@stoneworld.com. Web site: www.stoneworld.com. Michael Reis, Editor/Associate Publisher. **Description:** On new trends in installing and designing with stone. For architects, interior designers, design professionals, and stone fabricators and dealers. **Nonfiction:** Articles, 750-1,500 words, pays $6/column inch. **Queries:** Preferred. **Payment:** On publication.

TECHNICAL COMMUNICATION

See full listing in Writing & Publishing category.

TODAY'S FACILITY MANAGER

P.O. Box 2060, Red Bank, NJ 07701. 732-842-7433. Web site: www.todaysfacilitymanager.com. Circ.: 50,000. Jill Korot, New Products Editor. **Description:** News and new-product information for in-house, on-site facility professionals. Articles run 1,000-1,500 words; pays flat fee. **Tips:** Welcomes new writers. Requires solid research and reporting skills. **Queries:** Preferred. **E-Queries:** Yes. **Unsolicited mss:** Accepts. **Response:** Varies, SASE required. **Freelance Content:** 10%. **Payment:** 30 day after publication.

TOURIST ATTRACTIONS AND PARKS

10 E Athen Ave., Suite 208, Ardmore, PA 19003. 610-645-6940. E-mail: tapmag@aol.com. Web site: www.touristattractionparks.com. Scott C. Borowsky, Executive Editor. **Description:** On successful management of parks, entertainment centers, zoos, museums, arcades, fairs, arenas, and leisure attractions. Articles run 1,500 words; $.12/word. **Queries:** Preferred. **Payment:** On publication.

WOODSHOP NEWS

35 Pratt St., Essex, CT 06426. 860-767-8227. E-mail: editorial@woodshopnews.com. Web site: www.woodshopnews.com. Monthly.

$3.95/$21.95. A.J. Hamler, Editor. **Description:** Business stories, profiles, and news for people who work with wood. **Nonfiction:** Advice for professional woodworkers; profiles of shops with unique businesses, furniture lines, or stories; economics and marketing techniques applicable to small and medium size woodworking shops; trends in equipment, new technology, and construction techniques; to 1,400 words; $150-$500. **Columns, Departments:** Pro Shop, Profiles, Jigs & Tips. **Tips:** Need profiles of woodworkers outside the Northeast region. **Queries:** Preferred. **Unsolicited mss:** Accepts. **Payment:** On publication.

TRAVEL

AAA GOING PLACES
1515 N Westshore Blvd., Tampa, FL 33607. 813-289-1391.
E-mail: sklim@aaasouth.com. Web site: aaagoingplaces.com. Bimonthly. Circ.: 4,000,000. Sandy Klim, Editor. **Description:** On domestic travel and lifestyle, for AAA Members. **Nonfiction:** Well-researched domestic and international travel, automotive, lifestyle. Third-person preferred; 800-1,200 words; $200-$400. **Art:** Color photos. **Tips:** Prefers general, rather than niche, travel stories to a destination, with an angle; e.g., Washington D.C., "The Monuments," rather than the annual art exhibit at Lincoln Memorial. Weekend or week-long vacation ideas for seniors and families. Fun vacation stops, a little unusual but with lots to offer ("Hershey, PA: something for everyone"). **Queries:** Not necessary. **E-Queries:** Yes. **Unsolicited mss:** Accepts. **Response:** Queries 6 months, submissions 3 months, SASE. **Freelance Content:** 50%. **Rights:** 1st, Web, and reprint rights, some reprints from local markets. **Payment:** On acceptance.

ARIZONA HIGHWAYS
See full listing in Regional & City Publications category.

BRITISH HERITAGE
PRIMEDIA Enthusiast Group
6405 Flank Dr., Harrisburg, PA 17112-2750. 717-657-9555.
E-mail: britishheritage_magazine@primediamags.com.
Web site: www.britishheritage.com. Bimonthly. $25.90/yr. Circ.: 100,000. Bruce Heydt, Managing Editor. **Description:** Travel articles on places to visit in the British Isles. **Nonfiction:** Include detailed historical information in a "For the Visitor" sidebar; 800-1,500 words; $100-$200. **Payment:** On acceptance.

CARIBBEAN TRAVEL AND LIFE
460 N Orlando Ave., Winter Park, FL 32789. 407-628-4802.
E-mail: editor@caribbeantravelmag.com. Web site: www.caribbeantravelmag.com. 9x/yr. $23.95/yr. Circ.: 150,000. Bob Friel, Executive Editor. Description: For the upscale traveler, on travel, recreation, leisure, and culture in the Caribbean, the Bahamas, and Bermuda. **Nonfiction:** Topics include shopping, dining, arts and

entertainment, and sightseeing suggestions; 500-3,000 words; pays $75-$750. **Tips:** Send published clips. **Queries:** Preferred. **Payment:** On publication.

COAST TO COAST
2575 Vista del Mar Dr., Ventura, CA 93001. 805-667-4100.
E-mail: vlaw@affinitygroup.com. Web site: www.rv.net. 8x/yr. $4/$28. Circ.: 200,000. Valerie Law, Editor. **Description:** Membership magazine for a network of upscale RV resorts across North America. Focuses on travel and outdoor recreation. **Nonfiction:** Essays on travel, recreation, and good times. Destination features on a North American city or region. Activity/recreation features introduce a sport, hobby, or other diversion. Also, features on RV lifestyle; 1,200-3,000 words; $300-$600. **Art:** Slides, digital images, prints; $75-$600. **Queries:** Not necessary. **E-Queries:** Yes. **Unsolicited mss:** Accepts. **Response:** SASE. **Freelance Content:** 75%. **Rights:** FNAR. **Payment:** On acceptance.

CRUISE TRAVEL
990 Grove St., Evanston, IL 60201. 847-491-6440.
E-mail: cs@centurysports.net. Web site: www.cruisetravelmag.com. Bimonthly. $29.95/yr. Circ.: 172,000. Robert Meyers, Editor-in-Chief. **Description:** Ship-, port-, and cruise-of-the-month features, 800-2,000 words; cruise guides; cruise roundups; cruise company profiles; travel suggestions for one-day port stops. Photo features strongly recommended; pay varies. **Tips:** Query by mail only, with sample color photos. **Queries:** Preferred. **Payment:** On publication.

ENDLESS VACATION
9998 N Michigan Rd., Carmel, IN 46032-9640. 317-805-8120.
E-mail: julie.woodard@rci.com. Web site: www.rci.com. Bimonthly. $84/yr. Circ.: 1,200,000. Jackson Mahaney, Managing Editor. **Description:** Magazine for families with features on where to go and what to do on vacation, and why. **Nonfiction:** Focus is primarily on domestic vacation travel, with some mainstream international vacation articles. Features should cover new and interesting vacation options, with a solid angle; 1,000-2,000 words; $500-$1,200. **Columns, Departments:** Weekend travel destinations, health and safety on the road, short travel news-oriented and service pieces, hot news tips and travel trends; 800-1,200; $300-$800. **Art:** Travel-oriented photos (landscapes, scenics, people, activities, etc.); slides, originals. **Tips:** "Write for doers, not dreamers. Describe activities in which readers can participate." **Queries:** Preferred. **E-Queries:** No. **Response:** 4-8 weeks. **Freelance Content:** 90%. **Rights:** FNAR. **Payment:** On acceptance.

EPICUREAN TRAVELER
740 Stetson St., Moss Beach, CA 94038. 650-728-5389.
E-mail: editor@epicurean-traveler.com. Web site: www.epicurean-traveler.com. 8x/yr. $28/yr. Circ.: 25,000. Scott Clemens, Publisher. **Description:** E-zine on luxury travel with a special emphasis on food and wine. **Tips:** Editorial calendar is currently full, but will consider queries. All articles must have a connection to the local food/wine of

a particular region or area. **Queries:** Required. **E-Queries:** Yes. **Response:** 6 weeks. **Freelance Content:** 75%. **Rights:** 1st electronic. **Payment:** On publication.

FAMILY MOTOR COACHING
8291 Clough Pike, Cincinnati, OH 45244-2796. 513-474-3622.
E-mail: magazine@fmca.com. Web site: www.fmca.com. Monthly. $3.99/$27. Circ.: 140,000. Robbin Gould, Editor. **Description:** Offers articles on motorhome travel for members of the Family Motor Coach Association. **Nonfiction:** Travel articles keyed to noteworthy sites, attractions, and events that are accessible by motorhome, as well as personality profiles of travelers who have interesting uses for their motorhomes. Also technical articles relating to motorhome maintenance, do-it-yourself projects, etc. 1,200-2,000 words; $50-$500. **Art:** Articles with photos preferred. Prefers transparencies, but accepts 4x6 digital with 300+ dpi. Drawings, sketches, or photos should accompany technical articles. **Queries:** Preferred. **E-Queries:** Yes. **Unsolicited mss:** Accepts. **Response:** 4-12 weeks, SASE. **Rights:** FNASR and electronic. **Payment:** On acceptance.

HIGHWAYS
2575 Vista Del Mar Dr., P.O. Box 8545, Ventura, CA 93001. 805-667-4100.
E-mail: kwinters@affinitygroup.com. Web site: www.goodsamclub.com. 11x/yr. $25/yr (includes membership). Circ.: 1,000,000. Kimberley Winters, Managing Editor. **Description:** Published for Good Sam Club, world's largest recreation vehicle owner's organization. Articles on outdoor recreation and RV industry news, travel destination and technical features; $300 and up. **Art:** Travel features should include at least 15 color transparencies (originals). **Tips:** Does not accept unsolicited manuscripts via e-mail. "Study recent issues before sending queries. Conduct research to understand the RV market. We're different from most travel magazines, and we're not an automotive publication." **Queries:** Required. **E-Queries:** Yes. **Unsolicited mss:** Does not accept. **Response:** 4-8 weeks, SASE required. **Freelance Content:** 40%. **Rights:** FNAR and electronic. **Payment:** On acceptance.

HILL COUNTRY SUN
P.O. Box 1482, Wimberley, TX 78676. 512-847-5162.
E-mail: allan@hillcountrysun.com. Web site: www.hillcountrysun.com. Monthly. Allan C. Kimball, Editor. **Description:** Tourist-oriented magazine covering the Central Texas Hill Country. **Nonfiction:** On interesting things to do in the region, places to visit, or interesting people. Include logistical information (where, what, when, how to get there, etc.) and photos with all submissions. 500-700 words; $40-$50. **Tips:** Query first with 3-4 ideas. No first-person accounts, fiction, or poetry. **Queries:** Required. **Unsolicited mss:** Does not accept.

THE INTERNATIONAL RAILWAY TRAVELER
P.O. Box 3747, San Diego, CA 92163. 619-260-1332.
E-mail: irteditor@aol.com. Web site: www.irtsociety.com. Monthly. $65/U.S., $70/Canada. Circ.: 5,000. Gena Holle, Editor. **Description:** Train-travel stories from

around the world, written with verve and wit, that show writer's love of train travel as the most environmentally friendly, adventurous, and exciting mode of travel. **Nonfiction:** Anything involving trains, from luxury to seat-of-the-pants trips. Hotels with a rail history, sightseeing by tram or metro. Articles must be factually sound, with ample logistical detail so readers can easily replicate the author's trip. 300-1,400 words; $.03/word. **Art:** "We always need good photos of trains to go with stories." B&W glossies, transparencies, or color prints; $10 inside stories, $20 for cover. **Tips:** "Your travel stories need not be written chronologically. Try building your story around a few key points or impressions from your trip. Read our publication. Our most valued writers know our readers well, write with verve and wit, are scrupulously accurate, and have a love of and genuine interest in rail travel in all its forms." **Queries:** Preferred. **E-Queries:** Yes. **Unsolicited mss:** Accepts. **Response:** 2 months, SASE required. **Freelance Content:** 80%. **Rights:** FNASR, electronic. **Payment:** On publication.

INTERVAL WORLD

Interval International, Inc., 6262 Sunset Dr., Miami, FL 33143-4843.
E-mail: intervaleditors@interval-intl.com. Web site: www.intervalworld.com. Quarterly. Circ.: 1,000,035. Lisa Willard, Editor-in-Chief. **Description:** For time-share vacationers. **Tips:** No phone calls or faxes.

ISLANDS

6309 Carpinteria Ave., Carpinteria, CA 93013. 805-745-7100.
E-mail: islands@islands.com. Web site: www.islands.com. 8x/yr. $4.95/$24.95. Circ.: 280,000. James Badham, Editor-in-Chief. **Description:** "*Islands* covers islands around the world in stories that get at the essence of the place covered. Photos and narratives take readers to warm popular islands like Bora-Bora and Hawaii, cold places like Aleutians and Iceland, and off-the-beaten track islands everywhere." **Nonfiction:** Illuminate what makes a place tick through strong narrative-based writing. Profiles of unforgettable people; 850-3,500 words; $.50/word and up. **Columns, Departments:** Horizons (short, quicky island-related items); 50-250 words. **Tips:** Break in by writing for Horizons, Crossroads (essays), IslandWise (500-word quick-hit profiles of places). Does not assign major features to unfamiliar writers. Do not query by phone. **Queries:** Preferred. **E-Queries:** Yes. **Unsolicited mss:** Accepts. **Response:** 3 months, SASE required. **Freelance Content:** 90%. **Rights:** All. **Payment:** On acceptance.

LONG WEEKENDS

1422 Euclid Ave., Cleveland, OH 44115. 216-771-2833.
E-mail: mcarey@long-weekends.com. Web site: www.long-weekends.com. 2x/yr. Circ.: 200,000. Miriam Carey, Editor. **Description:** Travel magazine covering unusual destinations in 8 states—New York, Pennsylvania, West Virginia, Ohio, Indiana, Kentucky, Illinois, Michigan. Looking for off-the-beaten-path destinations, privately owned inns, and unusual B&Bs. **Tips:** "We look for good, solid queries backed up by 3 clips from regional publications. Avoid pitching anything "main-

stream." Visit our Web site for writers' guidelines and to search past articles." **Queries:** Required. **Unsolicited mss:** Does not accept. **Response:** 3 months. **Freelance Content:** 80%. **Rights:** FNAR. **Payment:** On publication.

MICHIGAN LIVING
See full listing in Regional & City Publications category.

THE MIDWEST TRAVELER
12901 N Forty Dr., St. Louis, MO 63141. 314-523-7350.
E-mail: mright@aaamissouri.com. Web site: www.aaatravelermags.com. Bimonthly. $3/yr. Circ.: 435,000. Michael J. Right, Editor. **Description:** For AAA members in Missouri and parts of Illinois, Indiana, and Kansas. **Nonfiction:** Lively writing to encourage readers to take the trip they've just read about. Include useful information (travel tips). AAA properties preferred. 1,200-1,500 words; $150-$350. **Art:** Slides (color), prints, or digital; $75-$150. **Tips:** Request editorial calendar. **Queries:** Preferred. **E-Queries:** No. **Unsolicited mss:** Accepts. **Response:** 4-6 weeks, SASE required. **Freelance Content:** 80%. **Rights:** FNAR, reprint, and electronic. **Payment:** On acceptance.

MOTION SICKNESS
See full listing in Literary Fiction & Poetry category.

MOTORHOME
2575 Vista Del Mar, Ventura, CA 93001.805-667-4100.
E-mail: smcbride@affinitygroup.com. Web site: www.motorhomemagazine.com. Monthly. $26/yr. Circ.: 146,000. Sherry McBride, Senior Managing Editor. **Description:** Covers destinations for RV travelers. Also, activities, hobbies, how-tos, motorhome tests, RV product evaluations, technical theory features, legislative updates, special events, and profiles of celebrities who own motorhomes. 150-2,000 words; $100-$600. **Columns, Departments:** Crossroads (varied topics: unique motorhomes, great cafes, museums, festivals; with 1-2 good color transparencies); Quick Tips (do-it-yourself ideas for motorhomes; no photo, just a sketch if necessary; 150 words; $100). **Art:** 35mm slides; $25-$500. **Tips:** "Departments are best way to break in. Readers are active travelers; most retirees, but more baby boomers entering the RV lifestyle, so some articles for novices and families. No diaries or product tests." **Queries:** Preferred. **E-Queries:** No. **Unsolicited mss:** Accepts. **Response:** 3-4 weeks, SASE required. **Freelance Content:** 65%. **Payment:** On acceptance.

NATIONAL GEOGRAPHIC ADVENTURE
National Geographic Society
104 W 40th St., Fl. 19, New York, NY 10018. 212-790-9020.
E-mail: adventure@ngs.org. Web site: www.nationalgeographic.com/adventure. 10x/yr. $9.97/yr. Circ.: 400,000. Mark Jannot, Executive Editor. **Description:** Covers adventure and general travel (adventure as travel designed to push the envelope on experience and, to some degree, comfort). Destinations are divided evenly between

U.S. and international. **Nonfiction:** Features, 4,000-8,000 words, on well-known adventures, expeditions, and scientific exploration; unknown historical tales. E.g., diving near Australia's Ningaloo Reef; paddling on New England's Merrimack River. **Columns, Departments:** Profiles, opinions, commentaries (2,000-3,000 words); Trips (500-2,000 words, how readers can bring adventure into their own lives). **Tips:** Helps to have written for other travel magazines. Carefully target query and make it compelling. Readers aged 20-55. "The driving force is compelling writing that inspires travelers to go places and do things, while entertaining readers who don't travel." **Queries:** Preferred. **Unsolicited mss:** Accepts. **Freelance Content:** 90%.

NATIONAL GEOGRAPHIC TRAVELER

National Geographic Society
1145 17th St. NW, Washington, DC 20036. 202-857-7000.
E-mail: traveler@nationalgeographic.com.
Web site: nationalgeographic.com/traveler. 8x/yr. $17.95/yr. Circ.: 738,900. Keith Bellows, Editor. **Description:** Most articles by assignment only; query first with 1-2 page proposal, resume, and published clips required. **Nonfiction:** Articles 1,500-4,000 words; pays $1/word. **Payment:** On acceptance.

NATIONAL MOTORIST

National Automobile Club
1151 E Hillsdale Blvd., Foster City, CA 94404-1609. 650-294-7000.
E-mail: contact@nationalautoclub.com.
Web site: www.nationalautoclub.com/html/national_motorist.html. Quarterly. $2/issue. Circ.: 100,000. Jane Offers, Editor. **Description:** Publishes articles for California travelers on motoring in the West, domestic and international travel, car care, roads, news, transportation, personalities, places, etc. **Nonfiction:** Illustrated articles, 500-1,100 words; pays from $.20/word, extra for photos. **Art:** Color slides or digital images. **Queries:** Preferred. **Response:** SASE required. **Payment:** On acceptance.

NAVIGATOR

1301 Carolina St., Greensboro, NC 27401-1090. 336-378-6065.
E-mail: navedit@paceco.com. Bimonthly. Circ.: 400,000. Brian Cook, Editor-in-Chief. **Description:** General-interest magazine distributed at Holiday Inn Express Hotels. Articles on sports, entertainment, and food. Photo essays, news on traveling trends, gear, and information. **Tips:** SASE for guidelines.

NORTHWEST TRAVEL

4969 Highway 101, #2, Florence, OR 97439. 800-348-8401.
E-mail: judy@ohwy.com. Web site: www.ohwy.com. Bimonthly. Circ.: 50,000. Stefani Blair, Stefanie Griesi, Judy Fleagle, Editors. **Description:** Where to go and what to see in Oregon, Washington, Idaho, British Columbia, Western Montana, sometimes Alaska. Every article has a travel connection; each issue has detailed drive guide to one area. **Nonfiction:** First-person experience. Put details in sidebars; 500-1,500

words; $65-$350/features. **Fillers:** Worth a Stop; $50. **Art:** Seeking terrific slides of wildlife, artsy or dramatic scenery shots. Also does 2 annual calendars; slides, transparencies; $25-75 ($325 cover). **Tips:** "Be flexible, appear eager, try not to tell us what we need. Be willing to follow our suggestions on rewriting and resubmitting." **Queries:** Preferred. **Unsolicited mss:** Accepts. **Response:** Queries 3 months, submissions 2-3 months, SASE. **Freelance Content:** 60%. **Rights:** FNAR. **Payment:** On publication.

OUTPOST
474 Adelaide St. E, Toronto, Ontario M5A 1N6 Canada. 416-972-6635.
E-mail: editor@outpostmagazine.com. Web site: www.outpostmagazine.com. Bimonthly. $14/yr. Circ.: 22,000. Kisha Ferguson, Editor. **Description:** Adventurous and realistic look at the world and how people travel through it. **Nonfiction:** Features, 2,800-4,200 words. **Columns, Departments:** Tripping (100-1,200 words), useful travel info, serious and funny short news bits from around the world, human interest, environmental, dispatches. Health (1,800-2,000 words). Culture (300-1,500 words), reviews of books, movies, food, and profiles. Global Citizens (must include snapshot of person), see magazine for desired format. **Art:** Photos, do not submit originals unless requested. **Tips:** "We seek stories in an honest, sometimes irreverent voice." **Queries:** Required. **E-Queries:** Yes. **Unsolicited mss:** Does not accept.

RIDER
See full listing in Automotive category.

ROMANTIC DESTINATIONS
6254 Poplar Ave., Suite 200, Memphis, TN 38119-4723. 901-761-1505.
E-mail: smeyers@southernbride.com. Web site: www.southernbride.com. 2x/yr. $4.95/issue. Circ.: 140,000. Sherra Meyers, Editor. **Description:** Romantic travel magazine focusing on places for romantic getaways, honeymoons, and wedding destinations. **Nonfiction:** Stories from brides and/or grooms sharing their experiences of wedding planning and honeymoon planning. 500-1,000 words; $.75/word or flat fee. **Columns, Departments:** 200-400 words, flat fee. **Queries:** Preferred. **Unsolicited mss:** Accepts. **Freelance Content:** 50%. **Payment:** On publication.

ROUTE 66 MAGAZINE
401 W Railroad Ave., Williams, AZ 86046. 928-635-4322.
E-mail: info@route66magazine.com. Web site: www.route66magazine.com. Quarterly. $16/yr. Circ.: 35,000. Paul Taylor, Publisher/Executive Editor. **Description:** Features articles on travel and life along Route 66 between Chicago and Los Angeles. **Nonfiction:** Articles, 1,500-2,000 words; pays $20/column. **Art:** Accepts B&W and color photos. **Queries:** Preferred. **Payment:** On publication.

RV JOURNAL
P.O. Box 7675, Laguna Niguel, CA 92607. 949-489-7729.
E-mail: editor@rvjournal.com. Web site: www.rvjournal.com. Quarterly. **Description:**

Features destinations for RV travelers in New Mexico, Arizona, Nevada, Utah, California, Oregon, and Washington. **Nonfiction:** Travel and destination articles, 800-1,000 words. **Tips:** Submit query with bio and samples of previously published work. Priority is given to articles that accompany high-quality, color photographs. **Queries:** Required. **Unsolicited mss:** Accepts. **Rights:** FNAR.

SOUTH AMERICAN EXPLORERS
South American Explorers Club
126 Indian Creek Rd., Ithaca, NY 14850-1310. 607-277-0488.
E-mail: don@saexplorers.org. Web site: www.saexplorers.org. Quarterly. $22/yr. Circ.: 8,600. Don Montague, Editor. **Description:** Feature articles on scientific studies, travel, historical personalities, archeology, exploration, social sciences, peoples and culture, etc. **Nonfiction:** Length varies from 1,200-10,000 words; $50-$250. **Art:** Photos, sketches, maps. **Tips:** Write or e-mail for guidelines and sample issue. **Queries:** Preferred. **E-Queries:** Yes. **Unsolicited mss:** Accepts. **Payment:** On publication.

SPECIALTY TRAVEL INDEX
305 San Anselmo Ave., #309, San Anselmo, CA 94960. 800-442-4922.
E-mail: info@specialtytravel.com. Web site: www.specialtytravel.com. Biannual. $6/issue. Circ.: 45,000. Risa Weinreb, Editor. **Description:** Travel directory listing 350 worldwide operators. Also provides travel articles for consumers and travel agents. **Nonfiction:** Stories on special interest, adventure-type travel, from soft adventures (e.g., cycling through French wine country) to daring exploits (an exploratory river-rafting run in Pakistan). Varied styles okay (first-person, descriptive); in general, not written in the present tense, but with a lively immediacy; 1,250 words; $300. **Art:** Slides, EPS digital, pay varies. **Tips:** Seeking off-the-beaten-path perspectives. Send published clips. **Queries:** Preferred. **E-Queries:** Yes. **Unsolicited mss:** Accepts. **Response:** 3-6 months, SASE required. **Freelance Content:** 80%. **Payment:** On acceptance. **Contact:** Susan Kostrzewa, Managing Editor.

TRAILER LIFE
See full listing in Lifestyle Magazines category.

TRANSITIONS ABROAD
P.O. Box 1300, Amherst, MA 01004-1300. 413-256-3414.
E-mail: info@transitionsabroad.com Web site: www.transitionsabroad.com. Bimonthly. $4.95/$28. Circ.: 25,000. Clay Hubbs, Editor. **Description:** Founded in 1977, *Transitions Abroad* is for overseas travelers of all ages who seek information on enriching, in-depth experiences of different cultures. Includes features with practical focus on work, study, travel, and living abroad. **Nonfiction:** Practical how-to travel articles; 800-1,000 words; $2/column inch. **Columns, Departments:** Info exchange letters (200-300 words, free subscription); Itineraries (up to 500 words, $25-$50). **Art:** B&W, JPG; $25-$50, $150 (cover). **Tips:** Eager for new writers with information not usually found in guidebooks. Also seeking special expertise on cultural travel

opportunities for specific groups: seniors, students, families, etc. No journal writing; no U.S. travel. Send all material electronically. Sample copies $6.45. **Queries:** Not necessary. **E-Queries:** Yes. **Unsolicited mss:** Accepts. **Response:** SASE. **Freelance Content:** 65%. **Rights:** FNAR. **Payment:** On publication.

TRAVEL AMERICA

990 Grove St., Evanston, IL 60201-4370. 847-491-6440.
E-mail: rmink@centurysports.net. Web site: www.travelamerica.com. Bimonthly. $5.99/$23.94. Circ.: 241,000. Robert Meyers, Editor-in-Chief. **Description:** Consumer travel magazine, exclusively U.S. destinations. **Nonfiction:** General destination stories; 1,000 words; $300. **Columns, Departments:** If You Only Have a Day (in any city); 500-600 words; $150-$175. **Art:** Slides, usually with text package; individual photos $25-$35. **Tips:** Submit short 1-page stories on narrow topics. Sample copy $5 with SASE. **Queries:** Not necessary. **E-Queries:** No. **Unsolicited mss:** Accepts. **Response:** 2-6 weeks, SASE. **Freelance Content:** 80%. **Rights:** FNAR. **Payment:** On publication. **Contact:** Randy Mink, Managing Editor.

TRAVEL + LEISURE

American Express Publishing Corp.
1120 Avenue of the Americas, New York, NY 10036. 212-382-5600.
E-mail: tlquery@amexpub.com. Web site: www.travelandleisure.com. Monthly. $4.50/$39. Circ.: 1,000,000. Nancy Novogrod, Editor-in-Chief. **Description:** Provides practical advice for leisure travelers and information on international travel destinations, luxury lodgings, and travel-related fashion and products. **Nonfiction:** Travel-related stories on shopping, trends, new hotels, products, nightlife, art, architecture; 1,000-4,000 words; $1,000-$5,000. **Columns, Departments:** Next; Update. **Tips:** Departments are best chances for new writers. Writers should have same sophistication and travel experience as readers. **Queries:** Required. **E-Queries:** Yes. **Unsolicited mss:** Does not accept. **Response:** Queries 4 weeks, submissions 2 weeks, SASE. **Freelance Content:** 80%. **Rights:** 1st. **Payment:** On acceptance.

TRAVEL SMART

P.O. Box 397, Dobbs Ferry, NY 10522-3098. 800-327-3633.
E-mail: travel.now@aol.com. Web site: www.travelsmartnewsletter.com. Nancy Dunnan, Publisher/Editor. **Description:** Covers interesting, unusual, or economical destinations. Offers useful travel-related tips and practical information for vacation or business travel. **Nonfiction:** Short pieces, 250-1,000 words; $50-$150. **Tips:** Give specific details on hotels, restaurants, transportation (e.g., costs, telephone numbers, and Web sites). Query for longer pieces. **Payment:** On publication.

WEEKEND ADVENTURES

P.O. Box 1895, Cumberland,, MD 21501.
E-mail: ideas@wamonline.com. Web site: www.wamonline.com. **Description:** Quarterly travel publication focusing on vacation destinations in Western Maryland, the Potomac Highlands of West Virginia, and the Laurel Highlands of Pennsylvania.

"Articles include outdoor adventures, historical places, dining out, getaways, day trips, equipment, attractions, etc. We try to help our readers understand the outdoors better, to help our readers relax, and live better, and to make our mountain communities a better place to live." Pays $50 for features of 1,000 words or more, on publication, for FNASR and Web site rights. E-mail queries preferred. Contact the editor, *Weekend Adventures* Magazine, P.O. Box 1895, Cumberland, MD 21501.

WESTWAYS
Automobile Club of Southern California
P.O. Box 25222, Santa Ana, CA 92799-5222. 714-885-2376.
E-mail: westways@aaa-calif.com. Web site: www.aaa-calif.com. Bimonthly. Circ.: 3,000,000. John Lehrer, Editor-in-Chief. **Description:** Travel articles, on southern California, the West, greater U.S., and foreign destinations. **Nonfiction:** 1,000-2,500 words; pays $1/word. **Queries:** Preferred. **Payment:** On acceptance.

YANKEE MAGAZINE'S TRAVEL GUIDE TO NEW ENGLAND
Yankee Publishing, P.O. Box 520, Dublin, NH 03444. 603-563-8111.
E-mail: travel@yankeepub.com. Web site: www.newengland.com. Annual. $4.99. Circ.: 100,000. Judson D. Hale, Sr., Editor-in-Chief. **Description:** Features and travel information for residents and tourists in New England. **Nonfiction:** 500-1,500 words; $1/word. **Art:** Photos. **Tips:** Looking for fresh ideas. **Queries:** Required. **E-Queries:** Yes. **Freelance Content:** 70%. **Payment:** On acceptance.

WOMEN

BBW: BIG BEAUTIFUL WOMAN
P.O. Box 1297, Elk Grove, CA 95759. 916-684-7904.
E-mail: sesmith@bbwmagazine.com. Web site: www.bbwmagazine.com. Bimonthly. $14.95/yr. Circ.: 100,000. Sally E. Smith, Editor-in-Chief. **Description:** For women ages 25-45, especially plus-size women, including interviews with successful plus-size women. **Nonfiction:** Articles; 800-3,000 words; pay varies. **Queries:** Preferred. **Payment:** On publication.

BRIDAL GUIDE
3 E 54th St., Fl. 15, New York, NY 10022. 212-838-7733.
Web site: www.bridalguide.com. Bimonthly. $5.99/$6.99. Circ.: 250,000. Diane Forden, Editor-in-Chief. **Description:** Covers wedding topics, wedding fashions, home design, travel, and marriage/relationship issues. Accepts queries for articles on marriage/relationships/sexuality, wedding planning, budgeting, and travel; 1,000-2,000 words; $.50/word.

BRIDE AGAIN
1240 N Jefferson Ave., Suite G, Anaheim, CA 92807. 714-632-7000.
E-mail: beth@brideagain.com. Web site: www.brideagain.com. Quarterly. Beth Reed

Ramirez, Editor. **Description:** Online publication for "encore" brides (women who are planning to remarry). **Nonfiction:** Helpful, positive, upbeat articles; no first-person. Topics: remarriage, blending families/religions, etiquette, finances, legal issues, honeymoon locations, book reviews. 600 words; $.25/word. **Tips:** Articles should be specific to second-time brides. **Queries:** Not necessary. **E-Queries:** No. **Unsolicited mss:** Accepts. **Response:** 2 months, SASE required. **Freelance Content:** 70%. **Rights:** FNAR. **Payment:** On publication.

BRIDE & GROOM

415 Boston Turnpike, Suite 104, Shrewsbury, MA 01545.
E-mail: bgeditor@townisp.com. Web site: www.originalweddingexpo.com. 3x/yr. Circ.: 50,000. Lisa Dayne, Editor. **Description:** Provides comprehensive planning information to Central Massachusetts' engaged couples. **Nonfiction:** Articles that focus on the various aspects of wedding planning; 500-1,000 words; $100-$200. **Queries:** Preferred. **E-Queries:** Yes. **Unsolicited mss:** Accepts. **Response:** 2-4 weeks, SASE required. **Freelance Content:** 50%. **Rights:** First and reprint. **Payment:** On publication.

BRIDE'S

Condé Nast Publications, 4 Times Square, New York, NY 10036. 212-286-7528.
E-mail: letters@brides.com. Web site: www.brides.com. Bimonthly. $18. Circ.: 450,000. Millie Martini Bratten, Editor-in-Chief. **Description:** For engaged couples or newlyweds on wedding planning, relationships, communication, sex, decorating, finances, careers, health, birth control, religion, and in-laws. **Nonfiction:** Articles, 800-3,000 words, for newlyweds; pays $.50/word. **Queries:** Preferred. **Unsolicited mss:** Accepts. **Payment:** On acceptance. **Contact:** Sally Kilbridge, Managing Editor.

BUSINESSWOMAN MAGAZINE

See full listing in Business category.

CHATELAINE

One Mount Pleasant Rd., Toronto, Ontario M4Y 2Y5 Canada. 416-764-1888.
E-mail: editors@chatelaine.com. Web site: www.chatelaine.com. Monthly. $3.50/issue (Canadian). Circ.: 800,000. Rona Maynard, Editor. **Description:** Empowers Canada's busiest women to create the lives they want. Speaks to the strength of the inner woman—her passion, purpose, and sense of possibility. **Nonfiction:** Articles of interest to Canadian women, on all aspects of Canadian life. A written proposal is essential. 500-3,000 words; $500 and up. **Columns, Departments:** Upfront (relationships, health, balance). **Queries:** Required. **E-Queries:** No. **Unsolicited mss:** Accepts. **Response:** 6 weeks, SASE required. **Freelance Content:** 75%. **Rights:** FNAR. **Payment:** On acceptance.

CITY WOMAN

1250 Main St., P.O. Box 85022, Ottawa, Ontario K2S 1X6 Canada. 613-831-0980.
E-mail: editor@citywomanmagazine.com. Web site: www.citywomanmagazine.com.

Quarterly. $12.95/yr. Circ.: 30,000. Patricia den Boer, Editor-in-Chief. **Description:** Written for the professional Canadian woman, this magazine focuses on ways to balance career, family, and personal life. Each issue profiles an outstanding woman from this region. **Nonfiction:** Health/nutrition, travel, finance, and wellness.

COMPLETE WOMAN

875 N Michigan Ave., Suite 3434, Chicago, IL 60611. 312-266-8680. Bimonthly. $3.99/issue. Circ.: 500,000. Bonnie L. Krueger, Editor. **Description:** Practical advice for women on love, sex, careers, health, and personal relationships. **Nonfiction:** Articles (include how-to sidebars) with practical advice for women; 1,000-2,000 words. **Tips:** Send query with clips. **Queries:** Required. **E-Queries:** No. **Unsolicited mss:** Accepts. **Response:** 90 days. **Freelance Content:** 90%. **Rights:** One-time, all rights. **Payment:** On acceptance. **Contact:** Lora Wintz, Executive Editor.

COSMOPOLITAN

The Hearst Corp., 224 W 57th St., New York, NY 10018. 212-649-3570. E-mail: cosmo_letters@hearst.com. Web site: www.cosmopolitan.com. Monthly. $24.97/yr. Circ.: 2,592,887. Kate White, Editor-in-Chief. **Description:** On issues affecting young career women, with emphasis on beauty, health, fitness, career, relationships, and personal life. **Fiction:** On male-female relationships (only publishes fiction excerpted from a forthcoming novel). **Nonfiction:** Articles, to 3,000 words; features, 500-2,000 words. **Tips:** Submissions must be sent by a publisher or agent.

COUNTRY WOMAN

See full listing in Agriculture & Rural Life category.

ELLE CANADA

25 Sheppard Ave. W, Suite 100, Toronto, Ontario M2N 6S7 Canada. 416-227-8212. E-mail: rsilvan@ellecanada.com. Web site: www.ellecanada.com. Monthly. $3.50/$12. Circ.: 100,000. Rita Silvan, Editor-in-Chief. **Description:** Women's magazine featuring fashion, beauty, and trends. Targets a young, single, female audience. **Nonfiction:** Seeks articles on hard-to-get items, unique stories, and interviews with celebrities or designers; 500-1,500 words; pay varies. **Tips:** "A good idea is always considered even from a first-time writer. Make sure there's a point and tell us why our readers would take an interest in your topic. Make sure you convey what they can get out of the story for themselves." **Queries:** Preferred. **E-Queries:** Yes. **Unsolicited mss:** Accepts. **Response:** 1-2 months, SASE. **Freelance Content:** 80%. **Rights:** Exclusive. **Payment:** On acceptance.

ESSENCE

1500 Broadway, Fl. 6, New York, NY 10036. 212-642-0600. E-mail: info@essence.com. Web site: www.essence.com. Monthly. $20/yr. Circ.: 1,200,000. Diane Weathers, Editor-in-Chief. **Description:** The first national magazine for African-American women. **Nonfiction:** Provocative articles on personal development, relationships, wealth building, work-related issues, parenting, health, political and social issues, travel, art. Cover stories on African-American celebrities. Departments: 400 words and up. Features: 1,200 words and up. Pay varies ($1/word minimum). **Queries:** Required.

FAMILY CIRCLE
Gruner + Jahr USA Publishing
375 Lexington Ave., New York, NY 10017-5514. 212-499-2000.
E-mail: fcfeedback@gjusa.com. Web site: www.familycircle.com. 15x/yr. $2.50/issue. Circ.: 4,500,000. Susan Ungaro, Editor-in-Chief. **Description:** Covers women who have made a difference. Also marriage, family, childcare/eldercare issues, consumer affairs, psychology, and humor. **Nonfiction:** Useful articles for all phases of a woman's life; true life, dramatic narratives; 1,000-2,000 words; $1/word. **Fillers:** Humor about family life; 750 words. **Columns, Departments:** Full Circle (current issues affecting families); 750 words. **Tips:** Often uses new writers in "Women Who Make A Difference" column. **Queries:** Required. **E-Queries:** No. **Unsolicited mss:** Accepts. **Response:** 4 weeks; SASE not required. **Freelance Content:** 80%. **Rights:** One-time, electronic. **Payment:** On acceptance.

FINANCIAL WOMAN TODAY
See full listing in Career & Professional Development category.

FIRST FOR WOMEN
270 Sylvan Ave., Englewood Cliffs, NJ 07632-2521. 201-569-6699.
E-mail: editor@firstforwomen.com. Web site: www.firstforwomen.com. 17x/yr. $34/yr. Circ.: 1,542,000. Carol Brooks, Editor-in-Chief. **Description:** Reflects concerns of contemporary women. **Nonfiction:** Articles,1,500-2,500 words; pay varies. **Queries:** Preferred. **E-Queries:** Yes. **Response:** 2 months. **Payment:** On acceptance.

GLAMOUR
Condé Nast Publications, 4 Times Square, New York, NY 10036. 212-286-2860.
E-mail: letters@glamour.com. Web site: www.glamour.com. Monthly. $18/yr. Circ.: 2,147,000. Cynthia Leive, Editor-in-Chief. **Description:** On careers, health, psychology, politics, current events, interpersonal relationships, for women, ages 18-35. **Nonfiction:** Articles, from 1,000 words; pays from $500. **Columns, Departments:** Hear Me Out (opinion page), 1,000 words. **Tips:** Fashion, entertainment, travel, food, and beauty pieces are staff-written. **Queries:** Required. **Payment:** On acceptance. **Contact:** Ellen Payne, Managing Editor.

GOLF FOR WOMEN
See full listing in Sports & Recreation/Outdoors category.

GOOD HOUSEKEEPING
The Hearst Corp., 959 Eighth Ave., New York, NY 10019. 212-649-2200.
E-mail: ghkletters@hearst.com. Web site: www.goodhousekeeping.com. Monthly.

$2.50/issue. Circ.: 2,400,000. Ellen Levine, Editor-in-Chief. **Description:** Expert advice on marriage and family, finances, health issues, and more. **Nonfiction:** Better Way (consumer pieces), 300-500 words. Profiles (on people involved in inspiring, heroic, fascinating pursuits), 400-600 words. My Story (first-person or as-told-to, in which a woman (using her real name) tells how she overcame a difficult problem. **Queries:** Required. **E-Queries:** No. **Unsolicited mss:** Accepts. **Response:** 2-3 months, SASE required.

HARPER'S BAZAAR

The Hearst Corp., 1700 Broadway, Fl. 37, New York, NY 10019-5905. 212-903-5000. E-mail: bazaar@hearst.com. Web site: www.harpersbazaar.com. Monthly. $19.97/yr. Circ.: 721,000. Glenda Bailey, Editor-in-Chief. **Description:** For active, sophisticated women. **Nonfiction:** Arts, world affairs, travel, families, education, careers, health, sexuality; 1,500-2,500 words; pay varies. **Tips:** Send query with proposal of 1-2 paragraphs; include clips. **Queries:** Required. **Unsolicited mss:** Does not accept. **Response:** SASE required. **Payment:** On acceptance.

LADIES' HOME JOURNAL

Meredith Corp., 125 Park Ave., Fl. 20, New York, NY 10017-5516. 212-557-6600. E-mail: lhj@mdp.com. Web site: www.lhj.com. Monthly. $2.49/issue. Circ.: 4,100,000. Diane Salvator, Editor-in-Chief. **Description:** Information on topics of interest to today's woman. Most readers are in their 30s, married, and working at least part-time. **Fiction:** Fiction, only through agents. **Nonfiction:** Articles on health, psychology, human-interest stories, etc.; 1,000-3,000 words; Pay varies. **Columns, Departments:** Parenting, health, and first-person drama; 150-1,500 words. **Tips:** "We seek human-interest pieces, shorter items, and new twists on established themes." **Queries:** Preferred. **E-Queries:** No. **Unsolicited mss:** Accepts. **Response:** Queries 8 weeks, submissions 4 weeks, SASE required. **Freelance Content:** 70%. **Rights:** All. **Payment:** On acceptance. **Contact:** Sarah Mohoney, Editor.

LATINA MAGAZINE

1500 Broadway, New York, NY 10036-4015. 212-642-0200. E-mail: editor@latina.com. Web site: www.latina.com. 11x/yr. $20. Circ.: 239,000. Sylvia Martinez, Editor-in-Chief. **Description:** Bilingual lifestyle magazine for Hispanic women in the U.S. Features articles on Latino fashion, beauty, culture, and food. Also runs celebrity profiles and interviews.

LATINA STYLE

1730 Rhode Island Ave. NW, Suite 1207
Washington, DC 20036-3109. 202-955-7930. E-mail: info@latinastyle.com. Web site: www.latinastyle.com. 5x/yr. Circ.: 150,000. Robert Bard, Editor. **Description:** For the contemporary Latina woman, showcases Latina achievements in business, science, civic affairs, education, entertainment, sports, arts and culture. Also, covers career opportunities, technology, travel, book

and film reviews. **Nonfiction:** 300-2,000 words; pay varies. **Art:** TIF, EPS, JPG, PDF; 300 dpi. **Queries:** Preferred. **E-Queries:** No. **Unsolicited mss:** Accepts. **Response:** 2 months, SASE optional. **Freelance Content:** 20%. **Rights:** FNAR. **Payment:** On publication.

LILITH

250 W 57th St., #2432, New York, NY 10107. 212-757-0818.
E-mail: lilithmag@aol.com. Web site: www.lilithmag.com. Quarterly. $6/$21. Circ.: 10,000. Susan Weidman Schneider, Editor-in-Chief. **Description:** Showcases Jewish women writers, educators, and artists; illuminates Jewish women's lives in their religious, ethnic, sexual, and social-class diversity. **Fiction:** On the lives of Jewish women; 1,000-2,000 words. **Nonfiction:** Autobiographies, interviews, social analysis, sociological research, oral history, new rituals, reviews, investigative reporting, opinion pieces. Also news briefs (500 words) and lists of resources, projects, events. 1,000-2,000 words. **Tips:** Welcomes new writers. **Queries:** Not necessary. **E-Queries:** Yes. **Unsolicited mss:** Accepts. **Response:** 12-16 weeks, SASE required. **Rights:** FNAR and electronic. **Payment:** On publication.

MAMM

See full listing in Health category.

MODERN BRIDE

Condé Nast Publications, 4 Times Square, Fl. 6, New York, NY 10036. 212-286-2860
E-mail: readermail@modernbride.com. Web site: www.modernbride.com. Bimonthly. $11.97/yr. Circ.: 406,000. Antonia Van der Meer, Editor-in-Chief. **Description:** For bride and groom, on wedding planning, financial planning, juggling career and home, etc. **Nonfiction:** Articles, 1,500-2,000 words, pays $600-$1,200. **Fillers:** Humorous pieces, 500-1,000 words, for brides. **Payment:** On acceptance.

MORE

Meredith Corp., 125 Park Ave., New York, NY 10017. 212-455-1190.
E-mail: more@mdp.com. Web site: www.moremag.com. 10x/yr. Circ.: 850,000. Susan Crandell, Editor. **Description:** Sophisticate and upscale editorial for women of the baby-boomer generation. Features essay, interviews, etc.; little service/how-to pieces. **Queries:** Preferred. **E-Queries:** No. **Unsolicited mss:** Accepts. **Response:** to 3 months, SASE. **Rights:** All. **Payment:** On acceptance.

MOTHERING

P.O. Box 1690, Santa Fe, NM 87504-1690. 505-984-8116.
E-mail: ashisha@mothering.com. Web site: www.mothering.com. Bimonthly. Circ.: 70,000. Ashisha, Senior Editor. **Description:** On natural family living, covering topics such as pregnancy, birthing, parenting, etc. **Nonfiction:** Articles, to 2,000 words; pays $200-$500. **Poetry:** 3-20 lines. **Queries:** Preferred. **Payment:** On publication.

MS. MAGAZINE

433 S Beverly Dr., Beverly Hills, CA 90212. 310-556-2515.
E-mail: info@msmagazine.com. Web site: www.msmagazine.com. Quarterly. $35/yr.
Circ.: 200,000. Elaine Lafferty, Editor-in-Chief. **Description:** On feminism,
women's roles, and social change. Nonfiction articles and essays on national and international news reporting, profiles, theory, and analysis. Also accepts short fiction and
poetry. **Tips:** Query with resume, published clips, and SASE. **Queries:** Required.
Response: 12 weeks. **Contact:** Manuscripts Editor.

NA'AMAT WOMAN

350 Fifth Ave., Suite 4700, New York, NY 10118. 212-563-5222.
E-mail: judith@naamat.org. Web site: www.naamat.org. Quarterly. $25 members, $10
non-members. Circ.: 20,000. Judith A. Sokoloff, Editor. **Description:** For Jewish
communities, covering varied topics: aspects of life in Israel, Jewish women's issues,
social issues, Jewish art and literature. **Fiction:** 2,000-3,000 words; $.10/word.
Nonfiction: 2,000-3,000 words; $.10-$.12/word. **Columns, Departments:** Book
reviews (ca. 800 words); Personal essays (ca. 1,200-1,500 words); $.10/word. **Art:**
B&W (hard copy or electronic); $25-$100. **Tips:** "Avoid trite Jewish humor, maudlin
fiction, and war stories." **Queries:** Preferred. **Unsolicited mss:** Accepts. **Response:**
1-3 months, SASE required. **Freelance Content:** 75%. **Rights:** FNAR. **Payment:**
On publication.

PLAYGIRL

801 Second Ave., Fl. 9, New York, NY 10017. 212-661-7878.
Monthly. $4.99. Circ.: 500,000. Michele Zipp, Editor-in-Chief. **Description:**
Women's magazine focusing on sex, relationships, and women's health. **Fiction:**
Erotic first-person fiction. Female perspective for Fantasy Forum section; 1,200-
1,500 words. **Nonfiction:** Articles, 750-3,000 words, on women's issues, sexuality,
relationships, and celebrities, for women ages 18 and up. **Fillers:** Quizzes. **Tips:**
"Easiest way to break in is to write for Fantasy Forum." **Queries:** Preferred.
E-Queries: No. **Unsolicited mss:** Accepts. **Response:** 1 month. **Freelance
Content:** 20%. **Payment:** On publication.

PRIMAVERA

Box 37-7547, Chicago, IL 60637.
Annual. $10. Circ.: 1,000. **Description:** Original fiction (to 25 pages) and poetry that
reflects the experience of women of different ages, races, sexual orientations, social
classes. **Tips:** Encourages new writers. No material that is confessional, formulaic, or
scholarly. **Queries:** Not necessary. **E-Queries:** No. **Unsolicited mss:** Accepts.
Response: Queries 2 weeks, submissions 1-6 months, SASE required. **Freelance
Content:** 100%. **Rights:** FNAR. **Payment:** In copies.

REDBOOK

The Hearst Corp., 224 W 57th St., Fl. 6, New York, NY 10019-3212. 212-649-3450.
E-mail: redbook@hearst.com. Web site: www.redbookmag.com. Monthly. $15.97/yr.

Circ.: 2,269,000. Ellen Kunes, Editor-in-Chief. **Description:** On subjects related to relationships, marriage, sex, current social issues, crime, human interest, health, psychology, and parenting. **Fiction:** Fresh, distinctive short stories, of interest to women. No unsolicited poetry, novellas, or novels; query first. Pays from $1,500 for short stories (to 25 pages). **Nonfiction:** Articles, 1,000-2,500 words; dramatic inspirational narratives, 1,000-2,000 words; pay varies. **Tips:** Send published clips, writing samples. **Queries:** Preferred. **Response:** Allow 12 weeks, SASE required. **Payment:** On acceptance.

ROOM OF ONE'S OWN

See full listing in Literary Fiction & Poetry category.

SAGEWOMAN

See full listing in New Age/Spiritual category.

SELF

Condé Nast Publications, 4 Times Square, New York, NY 10036-6522. 212-286-2860. E-mail: comments@self.com. Web site: www.self.com. Monthly. $2.99/$12. Circ.: 1,300,000. Lucy Danziger, Editor-in-Chief. **Description:** Covers all aspects of healthy lifestyle, with latest information on health, fitness, nutrition, mental wellness, beauty, and style. **Nonfiction:** Reports, features, stories, personal essays; on topics related to women's health and well-being; to 4,000 words. **Columns, Departments:** Health, nutrition, fitness, beauty, style, psychology. **Tips:** Pitch stories with a news hook. Send queries via regular mail. **Queries:** Preferred. **E-Queries:** No. **Unsolicited mss:** Accepts. **Response:** 1 month, SASE. **Freelance Content:** 75%. **Rights:** FNAR. **Payment:** On acceptance. **Contact:** Dana Points, Executive Editor.

SNAP

Box 130, 2137 33rd Ave. SW, Calgary, Alberta T2T 1Z7 Canada. 403-243-1769. E-mail: editorial@snapmagazine.com. Web site: www.snapmagazine.com. 5x/yr. $2.95/$6 (CND). Circ.: 40,000. Carolyn Fleming, Editor-in-Chief. **Description:** For professional women; covers new business developments, technology, and developments in design and culture. Also, profiles of people making an impact in these areas, and articles on music, books, and art. **Tips:** "Write about what is really new, what no one else has covered yet. If you can spot what is hot now, you might have a story for us. Send brief, concise story ideas describing intended focus, and whom you intend to interview. Back up with facts and figures and give information on your writing experience." **Queries:** Required. **E-Queries:** Yes. **Unsolicited mss:** Does not accept. **Response:** 4 weeks. **Rights:** FNAR.

SO TO SPEAK

See full listing in Literary Fiction & Poetry category.

SOUTHERN BRIDE

6254 Poplar Ave., Suite 200, Memphis, TN 38119-4723. 901-761-1505.
E-mail: smeyers@southernbride.com. Web site: www.southernbride.com. 2x/yr.
$4.95/issue. Circ.: 140,000. Sherra Meyers, Editor. **Description:** Bridal publication
primarily circulated throughout the Southeast that shows the trends and traditions of
the South. **Nonfiction:** Stories from brides and/or grooms sharing their experience of
wedding nuptials and honeymoon planning. 500-1,000 words; $.75/word or flat fee.
Columns, Departments: 200-400 words, flat fee. **Queries:** Preferred. **Unsolicited
mss:** Accepts. **Freelance Content:** 50%. **Rights:** FNAR. **Payment:** On publication.

TODAY'S CHRISTIAN WOMAN

Christianity Today International
465 Gundersen Dr., Carol Stream, IL 60188. 630-260-6200.
E-mail: tcwedit@christianitytoday.com. Bimonthly. Circ.: 250,000. Jane Johnson
Struck, Editor. **Description:** For women, ages 20-40, on contemporary issues and
hot topics that impact their lives. Articles provide depth, balance, and biblical perspective to women's daily relationships. **Nonfiction:** Articles to help women grow in
their relationship to God, and to provide practical help on family/parenting, friendship, marriage, health, single life, finances, and work; 1,000-1,800 words. **Tips:** No
poetry, fiction, or Bible studies. Looking for humor, issues/hot topics, and "My Story"
articles. Sample copy $5. **Queries:** Required. **E-Queries:** Yes. **Unsolicited mss:**
Accepts. **Response:** 8 weeks, SASE. **Rights:** 1st. **Payment:** On acceptance.
Contact: Corrie Cutrer, Assistant Editor.

TRUE CONFESSIONS

Sterling/Macfadden
333 Seventh Ave., Fl. 11, New York, NY 10001-5004. 212-979-4800.
E-mail: trueconfessions@sterlingmacfadden.com; trueconfessionstales@yahoo.com.
Web site: www.truestorymail.com. Monthly. Pat Byrdsong, Editor. **Description:**
First-person, true-to-life stories that reflect the lives of working class families.
Romance, mystery, modern social problems, etc. Stories run 1,000-7,000 words.
Confessions: Emotionally charged stories with a strong emphasis on characterization
and well-defined plots are preferred. Stories should be intriguing, suspenseful,
humorous, romantic, or tragic. Pays $.03/word. **Tips:** Seeks 3,000-4,000 word stories
and stories about African-, Latina-, and Asian-Americans. Sample copy $3.99.
Unsolicited mss: Accepts. **Response:** 90 days. **Freelance Content:** 95%. **Rights:**
All. **Payment:** One month after publication.

TRUE LOVE

Sterling/Macfadden
333 Seventh Ave., Fl. 11, New York, NY 10001-5004. 212-979-4800.
E-mail: away@sterlingmacfadden.com. Web site: www.truestorymail.com. Monthly.
$10.97. Circ.: 225,000. Alison Way, Editor. **Description:** Fresh, young, true-to-life
stories, on love and topics of current interest. Pays $.03/word. **Tips:** Must use past
tense and first-person style. **Payment:** On publication.

VOGUE
Condé Nast Publications, 4 Times Square, New York, NY 10036-6518. 212-286-2860. E-mail: voguemail@aol.com. Web site: www.vogue.com. Monthly. $28/yr. Circ.: 1,174,000. Anna Wintour, Editor-in-Chief. **Description:** General features for the contemporary woman. **Nonfiction:** Articles, to 1,500 words, on women, entertainment and arts, travel, medicine, and health. **Queries:** Preferred. **Contact:** Laurie Jones, Managing Editor.

WAHM.COM
P.O. Box 366, Folsom, CA 95763. 916-985-2078.
E-mail: cheryl@wahm.com. Web site: www.wahm.com. Weekly. Cheryl Demas, Editor. **Description:** E-zine for work-at-home moms.

WEDDINGBELLS
34 King St. E, Suite 1200, Toronto, Ontario M5C 2X8 Canada. 416-363-1574.
E-mail: info@weddingbells.com. Web site: www.weddingbells.com. Semiannual. Circ.: 325,000. Crys Stewart, Editor. **Description:** Offers pre- and post-wedding lifestyle and service journalism to bridal couples. By assignment only. **Tips:** Send resume and copies of published work. **Queries:** Not necessary. **Unsolicited mss:** Does not accept. **Contact:** Michael Killingsworth, Managing Editor.

WISCONSIN WOMAN
P.O. Box 230, Hartland, WI 53029. 262-367-5303.
E-mail: 50plus@pitnet.net. Monthly. $14.95/yr. Circ.: 30,000. Michele Hein, Editor-in-Chief. **Description:** Publication featuring news about women in the four-county Metro Milwaukee area.

WOMAN'S DAY
Hachette Filipacchi Magazines
1633 Broadway, Fl. 42, New York, NY 10019. 212-767-6000.
E-mail: womansday@hfmus.com; sabarbanel@hfmus.com.
Web site: www.womansday.com. 17x/yr. $8.99/yr. Circ.: 4,168,000. Jane Chesnutt, Editor-in-Chief. **Description:** Covers marriage, child-rearing, health, careers, relationships, money management, etc. **Nonfiction:** Human-interest or service-oriented articles, 750-1,600 words. Dramatic first-person narratives of medical miracles, rescues, women's experiences, etc. Pays standard rates. **Contact:** Stephanie Abarbanel, Senior Editor.

WOMAN'S OWN
1115 Broadway, Fl. 8, New York, NY 10010-2803. 212-807-7100.
E-mail: editor@womansown.com. Web site: www.womansown.com. Bimonthly. $11.97. Circ.: 253,000. Lynn Varacalli, Editor-in-Chief. **Description:** Inspirational, practical advice on relationships, career, and lifestyle choices for women, ages 25-35. Topics: staying together, second marriages, working women, asserting yourself, meeting new men, sex, etc. **Nonfiction:** Articles, 1,500-2,000 words; pays $50-$500.

Fillers: Woman in the News (profiles, 250-500 words, women who have overcome great odds); fun, in-depth quizzes; Let's Put Our Heads Together (short pieces on trends and breakthroughs). **Columns, Departments:** Suddenly Single, Moving Up, Round-Up, Mindpower, Dieter's Notes, Fashion Advisor, Financial Advisor; 800 words. **Queries:** Preferred. **Payment:** On acceptance.

WOMAN'S TOUCH

1445 Boonville, Springfield, MO 65802-1894.
E-mail: womanstouch@ag.org. Web site: www.womanstouch.ag.org. 6x/yr. $9.95/issue. Circ.: 12,000. Darla Knoth, Managing Editor. **Description:** Inspirational ministry magazine for Christian women. **Nonfiction:** About triumph in times of trouble, celebrity interviews with women leaders, cooking, reaching the unchurched, testimonies, unique activities for women's groups or mature singles; 800 words; $20-$40. **Tips:** Seeking articles with fresh themes. Publishes some book excerpts. **Queries:** Required. **E-Queries:** Yes. **Unsolicited mss:** Does not accept. **Response:** 12 weeks. **Freelance Content:** 20%. **Rights:** One-time. **Payment:** On publication.

WOMAN'S WORLD

270 Sylvan Ave., Englewood Cliffs, NJ 07632-2521. 201-569-6699.
E-mail: dearww@aol.com. Weekly. $59.80/yr. Circ.: 1,604,000. Stephanie Saible, Editor-in-Chief. **Description:** For middle-income women, ages 18-60, on love, romance, careers, medicine, health, psychology, family life, travel; dramatic stories of adventure or crisis, investigative reports. **Fiction:** Fast-moving short stories, 1,000 words, with light romantic theme; prefers dialogue-driven to propel the story. (Specify "short story" on outside of envelope.) Mini-mysteries, 1,200 words, with "whodunit" or "howdunit" theme. No science fiction, fantasy, horror, ghost stories, or gratuitous violence. Pays $1,000 for short stories; $500 for mini-mysteries. **Nonfiction:** Articles (query first), 600-1,800 words; pays $300-$900. **Payment:** On acceptance.

WOMEN IN BUSINESS

See full listing in Business category.

WORKING MOTHER

260 Madison Ave., Fl. 3, New York, NY 10016. 212-351-6400.
E-mail: editors@workingmother.com. Web site: www.workingmother.com. Monthly. Circ.: 750,000. Jill Kirshenbaum, Editor-in-Chief. **Description:** Features articles that help working women balance their professional life, family life, and inner life. Offers solutions to the stress that comes with juggling both family and career. **Nonfiction:** Articles focus on time management, money management, family relationships, and other job-related issues; 700-1,500 words. **Tips:** Send queries first. Enclose clips of previously published work. "Its best to be familiar with the tone and content of our publication before sending us your query." **Queries:** Required. **E-Queries:** No. **Response:** 3 months. **Rights:** All. **Contact:** Christine L. Ford, Managing Editor.

WRITING & PUBLISHING

AMERICAN JOURNALISM REVIEW
University of Maryland
1117 Journalism Bldg., Suite 2116, College Park, MD 20742-0001. 301-405-8803.
E-mail: editor@ajr.umd.edu. Web site: www.ajr.org. Monthly. $24. Circ.: 25,000. Rem Rieder, Editor. **Description:** Covers print, broadcast, and online journalism. Articles, 500-5,000 words, on trends, ethics, and coverage that falls short. Pay varies. **Queries:** Required. **E-Queries:** Yes. **Unsolicited mss:** Accepts. **Freelance Content:** 70%. **Rights:** Print and electronic. **Payment:** On publication.

AUTHORSHIP
National Writers Assn.
3140 S Peoria St., #295, Aurora, CO 80014-3178. 303-841-0246.
E-mail: authorship@nationalwriters.com. Web site: www.nationalwriters.com. Quarterly. $2.95/$18. Circ.: 6,200. Kathe Gustafson, Editor. **Description:** In-house publication for writers at all levels and all areas of interest. **Nonfiction:** How-to articles for writers; 800-1,200 words; $10. **Poetry:** Poems on writing and the writing process; to 40 lines; $10. **Fillers:** On writing and writers; 2-4 lines; $10 for bundles of 5. **Tips:** "Avoid 'How I Became a Success' stories. We seek short (800 words) author interviews, humor, and well-written how-to pieces. Sidebars with story are appreciated." **Queries:** Preferred. **E-Queries:** Yes. **Unsolicited mss:** Accepts. **Response:** Queries 2-4 weeks, submissions 2-4 months, SASE required. **Freelance Content:** 75%. **Rights:** FNAR. **Payment:** On publication. **Contact:** Sandy Whelchel.

BLOOMSBURY REVIEW
1553 Platte St., Suite 206, Denver, CO 80202. 303-455-3123.
E-mail: bloomsb@aol.com. Bimonthly. $3. Circ.: 50,000. Tom Auer, Editor. **Description:** Book reviews, literary features, interviews, essays, and poetry. **Nonfiction:** Essays, features, and interviews; 600 words or more; $10-$40. **Poetry:** Yes; $5-$15/poem. **Queries:** Preferred. **E-Queries:** Yes. **Unsolicited mss:** Accepts. **Response:** Queries 2 weeks, submissions 2 months, SASE required. **Freelance Content:** 25%. **Rights:** 1st. **Payment:** On publication.

BOOK
252 W 37th St., Fl. 5, New York, NY 10018. 212-659-7070.
E-mail: jkramer@bookmagazine.com. Web site: www.bookmagazine.com. 10x/yr. $20/yr. Circ.: 525,000. Jerome V. Kramer, Editor-in-Chief. **Description:** Publication covering the book industry. Provides information on authors, publishing news/trends, bookstores, technology affecting books, and book reviews. Targets book lovers. **Tips:** Send query letter with clips or writing samples. **Queries:** Preferred. **Unsolicited mss:** Does not accept.

BOOK LINKS
See full listing in Education category.

BOOKPAGE

2143 Belcourt Ave., Nashville, TN 37212. 615-292-8926.
E-mail: lynn@bookpage.com. Web site: www.bookpage.com. Monthly. Circ.: 500,000.
Lynn Green, Editor. **Description:** Consumer-oriented tabloid used by booksellers
and libraries to promote new titles and authors. Provides book reviews, 400 words.
$20/review. **Tips:** Query with writing samples and areas of interest; editor will make
assignments for reviews. **Queries:** Required. **Freelance Content:** 90%.

BOOKS & CULTURE: A CHRISTIAN REVIEW

Christianity Today International
465 Gundersen Dr., Carol Stream, IL 60188-2415. 630-260-6200.
E-mail: bcedit@aol.com. Web site: www.christianity.net. Bimonthly. $17.95. Circ.:
20,000. Michael Maudlin, Executive Editor. **Description:** Looks at Christian books,
culture, and religion.

BYLINE

P.O. Box 5240, Edmond, OK 73083-5240. 405-348-5591.
E-mail: mpreston@bylinemag.com. Web site: www.bylinemag.com. Monthly. $22/yr.
Circ.: 3,500. Marcia Preston, Editor. **Description:** Publication for writers. **Fiction:**
Genre, mainstream, literary, humor; 2,000-4,000 words; $100. **Nonfiction:** Articles
on the craft and business of writing; 1,500-1,800 words; $75. **Poetry:** About writing
or the creative process; 30 lines max; $10. **Columns, Departments:** End Piece,
humorous or motivational (700 words, $35); First $ale (250-300 words, $20); Great
American Bookstores! (500-600 words, $35-$40); Only When I Laugh, writing-
related humor (50-400 words, $15-$25). **Tips:** "Queries preferred for feature articles
only. Include practical information that can help writers succeed." Accepts queries via
e-mail (but not submissions). **Queries:** Preferred. **E-Queries:** Yes. **Unsolicited
mss:** Accepts. **Response:** 1-6 weeks for queries, 1 month for submissions; SASE
required. **Freelance Content:** 80%. **Rights:** FNAR. **Payment:** On acceptance.

C/OASIS

491 Moraga Way, Orinda, CA 94563.
E-mail: eide491@earthlink.net. Web site: www.sunoasis.com/oasis.html. Monthly.
David Eide, Editor; Vicki Colker, Poetry Editor. **Description:** Original stories,
poetry, essays, as well as insightful articles about electronic publishing, legal aspects
to writing, and job markets for writers. **Nonfiction:** 700-3,000 words, pays $10-20.
Tips: See website for guidelines. Send poetry submissions to poetmuse@swbell.net
c/o Vicki Colker. **Unsolicited mss:** Accepts.

CANADIAN WRITER'S JOURNAL

Box 5180, New Liskeard, Ontario POJ 1PO. 705-647-5424.
E-mail: cwj@cwj.ca. Web site: www.cwj.ca. Bimonthly. Circ.: 350. Deborah
Ranchuk, Managing Editor. **Description:** Digest-sized magazine emphasizing short
"how-to" articles targeted for the Canadian writer. **Nonfiction:** Any subject related
to writing, from generating ideas to marketing and publishing; 400-2,000 words;

$7.50/page. Book reviews, 250-500 words, on books about writing or books published in Canada. **Tips:** Prefers electronic submissions. "Be specific and concise. Use your personal experience and achievements. Avoid overworked subjects (overcoming writer's block, handling rejection, finding time to write, etc.)." See guidelines on Web site. **Queries:** Not necessary. **E-Queries:** Yes. **Unsolicited mss:** Accepts. **Response:** 2 months, SASE required (use IRCs). **Freelance Content:** 75%. **Payment:** On publication.

CATHOLIC LIBRARY WORLD

Catholic Library Assn.

100 North St., Suite 224, Pittsfield, MA 01201-5109. 413-443-2CLA.

E-mail: cla@cathla.org. Web site: www.cathla.org. Quarterly. $60/yr. Mary E. Gallagher, SSJ, General Editor. **Description:** Articles, reviews, and association news for school, academic, and institutional librarians/archivists. **Tips:** No payment offered. **Queries:** Not necessary. **E-Queries:** Yes. **Unsolicited mss:** Accepts. **Contact:** Jean R. Bostley, SSJ.

CHILDREN'S BOOK INSIDER

901 Columbia Rd., Ft. Collins, CO 80525-1838. 800-807-1916.

E-mail: mail@write4kids.com;laura@write4kids.com. Web site: www.write4kids.com. Monthly. Jon Bard, Managing Editor. **Description:** "The Newsletter for Children's Writers." Provides the "inside scoop" on publishing books for children. Accepts queries for how-to articles on writing children's books. **Tips:** Send SASE with $.60 postage for sample copy. **E-Queries:** Yes. **Contact:** Laura Backes.

CHILDREN'S WRITER

Institute of Children's Literature

93 Long Ridge Rd., West Redding, CT 06896-1124. 800-443-6078.

Web site: www.childrenswriter.com. Monthly. $24/yr. Susan M. Tierney, Editor. **Description:** 12-page newsletter reporting on the marketplace for children's writing. **Nonfiction:** 850-2,000 words; pays $200-$300 for very tightly written articles. **Queries:** Preferred. **Response:** 1 month, SASE required. **Rights:** FNAR.

COLLEGE COMPOSITION AND COMMUNICATION

See full listing in Education category.

EDITOR & PUBLISHER

770 Broadway, Fl. 7, New York, NY 10003. 646-654-5270.

E-mail: edpub@editorandpublisher.com. Web site: www.editorandpublisher.com. Weekly. $79/yr. Circ.: 17,000. Sid Holt, Editor-in-Chief. **Description:** Articles on the newspaper industry. Newspaper Web sites, features, how-tos, opinion pieces, etc. **Nonfiction:** News articles, 900 words; pay varies. **Tips:** Send complete manuscripts. **Payment:** On publication.

THE EDITORIAL EYE

66 Canal Center Plz, Suite 200, Alexandria, VA 22314-5507. 703-683-0683.
E-mail: eye@eeicommunications.com. Web site: www.eeicommunications.com/eye.
Monthly. Circ.: 2,000. Linda Jorgensen, Editor. **Description:** Resource for editors,
writers, managers, journalists, and educators on publications standards, practices, and
trends. Focuses on clear writing, intelligent editing, project management, changing
grammar/usage rules and conventions, and quality control priorities.

FOLIO

470 Park Ave., Fl. 7, New York, NY 10016-6820. 212-545-3600.
E-mail: folioedit@inside.com. Web site: www.foliomag.com. 16x/yr. $96/yr. Cable
Neuhaus, Editor-in-Chief. **Description:** For the magazine publishing executive.

FOREWORD

129 1/2 Front St., Traverse City, MI 49684-2508. 231-933-3699.
E-mail: alex@forewordmagazine.com. Web site: www.forewordmagazine.com. 6x/yr.
$10/$40. Circ.: 20,000. Alex Moore, Managing Editor. **Description:** Trade journal
reviewing new titles from independent publishers and university presses. Audience:
librarians and booksellers. **Tips:** Sample copy available for $10 plus $2 for shipping.
Queries: Required. **E-Queries:** Yes. **Unsolicited mss:** Accepts.

THE HORN BOOK MAGAZINE

56 Roland St., Suite 200, Boston, MA 02129. 617-628-0225.
E-mail: info@hbook.com. Web site: www.hbook.com. Bimonthly. $9.75/$48. Circ.:
18,500. Roger Sutton, Editor. **Description:** A critical review of introductory
children's/YA books. Also, editorials, columns, and articles about children's literature.
Nonfiction: Critical essays on children's literature and related subjects for librarians,
teachers, parents; to 280 words. **Queries:** Not necessary. **E-Queries:** Yes.
Unsolicited mss: Accepts. **Response:** 4-6 months, SASE required. **Payment:** On
publication.

INTERCOM

Society for Technical Information
901 N Stuart St., Suite 904, Arlington, VA 22203. 703-522-4114.
E-mail: intercom@stc.org. Web site: www.stc.org. 10x/yr. Circ.: 20,000. Maurice
Martin, Editor. **Description:** Industry information for technical writers, publishers,
and editors.

THE INTERNET WRITING JOURNAL

Writers Write, Inc., 8214 Westchester, Suite 500, Dallas, TX 75225.
E-mail: journal@writerswrite.com. Web site: www.writerswrite.com. Claire E.
White, Editor-in-Chief. **Description:** Articles on all aspects of writing, in all gen-
res. No payment, offers byline and link to author's Web site. **Nonfiction:** Seeks

original articles on writing skills, the publishing industry, journalism, songwriting, screenwriting, business writing, songwriting, and writing markets; 1,500-1,700 words. **Tips:** Accepts queries by e-mail only. **E-Queries:** Yes. **Rights:** 1st worldwide electronic.

IPI GLOBAL JOURNALIST
132 A Neff Annex, Columbia, MO 65211. 573-884-1599.
E-mail: globaljournalist@missouri.edu. Web site: www.globaljournalist.org. Quarterly. $19.95/yr. Circ.: 4,500. Prof. Stuart H. Loory, Editor. **Description:** International journalism publication for working journalists, students, and the general public. **Nonfiction:** Articles on international news and events; interviews with journalists in the field; survey articles on international press freedom concerns; 500-1,200 words; $350. **Queries:** Required. **E-Queries:** Yes. **Unsolicited mss:** Does not accept. **Response:** 1-2 weeks. **Freelance Content:** 70%. **Rights:** 1st. **Payment:** On publication. **Contact:** Pat Kelly.

LAMBDA BOOK REPORT
Lambda Literary Foundation
P.O. Box 73910, Washington, DC 20056-3910. 202-462-7924.
E-mail: lbreditor@lamdalit.org. Web site: www.lambdalit.org. Monthly. $34.95/yr. Circ.: 8,000. Jim Marks, Editor. **Description:** Reviews and features on gay and lesbian books. Articles run 250-1,500 words; $10-$75. **Queries:** Preferred. **Payment:** On publication.

LITERARY TRAVELER
P.O. Box 400272, North Cambridge, MA 02140-0003. 617-628-3504.
E-mail: francis@literarytraveler.com. Web site: www.literarytraveler.com. Linda McGovern, Editor. **Description:** Online publication featuring articles about writers or places that have literary significance. Pays $5-$25. **Tips:** See Web site for guidelines. **Queries:** Preferred. **E-Queries:** Yes. **Unsolicited mss:** Accepts.

LOCUS
P.O. Box 13305, Oakland, CA 94661. 510-339-9196.
E-mail: locus@locusmag.com. Web site: www.locusmag.com. Monthly. Circ.: 8,000. Jennifer A. Hall, Executive Editor. **Description:** Covers industry news for professional writers and publishers of science fiction and fantasy. **Tips:** Sample copy $5.95 plus $2 shipping/handling. **E-Queries:** No.

NEWSLETTER ON NEWSLETTERS
P.O. Box 348, Rhinebeck, NY 12572. 845-876-5222.
Web site: www.newsletterbiz.com. Semi-monthly. Paul Swift, Publisher/Editor. **Description:** For professionals involved in publishing newsletters and specialized information, both in print and online.

OHIO WRITER

2200 Fairhill Rd., Townhouse 3-A, Cleveland, OH 44120. 216-421-0403.
E-mail: pwlgc@msn.com. 6x/yr. Circ.: 1,000. Gail Bellamy, Stephen Bellamy, Editors.
Description: Features, interviews, how-tos, and articles relevant to writing in Ohio.
Tips: Sample copy $3. **Queries:** Required. **Response:** 3 months. **Freelance Content:** 5%. **Rights:** revert to author after publication. **Payment:** On publication.

ONCE UPON A TIME

553 Winston Ct., St. Paul, MN 55118. 651-457-6223.
E-mail: audreyouat@aol.com. Web site: http://www.members.aol.com/ouatmag.
Quarterly. $25. Circ.: 1,000. Audrey B. Baird, Editor. **Description:** Support magazine that provides wisdom and advice for those who write and illustrate for children.
Nonfiction: Writing and/or illustrating how-tos (plotting, character development, revising, dialogue, how you work, handle rejections, the story behind your book, etc.; 100-900 words. **Poetry:** On related topics; 30 lines. **Art:** Illustrations, black ink on white paper only. **Tips:** Use friendly style, with tips and information that really work. **E-Queries:** No. **Unsolicited mss:** Accepts. **Response:** Submissions 1 month, SASE. **Freelance Content:** 50%. **Rights:** One-time. **Payment:** In copies.

PAPYRUS

P.O. Box 270797, West Hartford, CT 06127-0797.
E-mail: ple.papyrus@eudoramail.com. $2.20/issue. Ginger Whitaker, Editor.
Description: "The writer's craftletter featuring the black experience." **Tips:** All writers welcome, submit material with a black audience in mind.

POETS & WRITERS

72 Spring St., New York, NY 10012-4019. 212-226-3586.
E-mail: editor@pw.org. Web site: www.pw.org/mag. $4.95/$17.95. Circ.: 70,000.
Therese Eiben, Editor. **Description:** Bimonthly trade magazine for writers of poetry, fiction, and creative nonfiction. **Nonfiction:** Profiles of contemporary authors, essays on the creative process of writing, and articles with practical applications for both emerging and established writers; 500-3,500 words. **Tips:** Does not cover genre fiction, children's literature, or screenwriting/playwriting. **Queries:** Preferred. **E-Queries:** Yes. **Unsolicited mss:** Accepts. **Response:** 4-6 weeks, SASE. **Freelance Content:** 95%. **Rights:** FNASR. **Payment:** On publication.

PRESSTIME

1921 Gallows Rd., Suite 600, Vienna, VA 22182. 703-902-1600.
Web site: www.naa.org/ptime. Monthly. Circ.: 17,846. **Description:** Published by the Newspaper Association of America.

PUBLISHERS WEEKLY

360 Park Ave. S, New York, NY 10010-1710. 646-746-6400.
Web site: www.publishersweekly.com. Weekly. $139. Circ.: 34,400. Nora Rawlinson, Editor-in-Chief. **Description:** Seeking essays, 900 words, on current issue or prob-

lem facing publishing and bookselling for "My Say" column. Articles for "Booksellers' Forum" may be somewhat longer. Pay varies. **Contact:** Daisy Maryles, Executive Editor.

QUILL & QUIRE
70 The Esplanade #210, Toronto, Ontario M5E 1R2 Canada. 416-360-0044.
E-mail: info@quillandquire.com. Web site: www.quillandquire.com. Quarterly. $59.95/yr (Canadian), $95/yr (non-Canadian). Circ.: 6,000. Scott Anderson, Editor. **Description:** Trade publication for the Canadian publishing industry. Offers books news, author interviews, and reviews of Canadian books. Written for writers, publishers, editors, librarians, and booksellers. **Queries:** Required. **E-Queries:** Yes. **Unsolicited mss:** Does not accept. **Payment:** On acceptance.

RAINY DAY CORNER
5806 Jackson Rd., Fredericksburg, VA 22407.
E-mail: ldupie@rainydaycorner.com. Web site: www.rainydaycorner.com. Monthly. Linda S. Dupie, Editor. **Description:** Online publication, with information and tips for the writing family. Short articles on how to get children and parents interested in writing, on topic such as journaling, online and print newsletters, letter writing, family history; to 1,200 words; $10-$20/article. **Tips:** "Write at the comprehension level of children 8-18 years without talking down to them. Keep articles conversational, but factual. Open to new and unpublished writers. See guidelines on Web site." **Queries:** Preferred. **E-Queries:** Yes. **Unsolicited mss:** Accepts. **Response:** 2-4 weeks, SASE required. **Rights:** Non-exclusive, electronic. **Payment:** On publication.

ROMANTIC TIMES
55 Bergen St., Brooklyn, NY 11201. 718-237-1097.
E-mail: kfalk@romantictimes.com. Web site: www.romantictimes.com. Monthly. $42/yr. Circ.: 150,000. Kathryn Falk, Founder/CEO. **Description:** Topics on the romance-fiction publishing industry.

RUMINATOR REVIEW
See full listing in Contemporary Culture category.

SMALL PRESS REVIEW
Dustbooks, P.O. Box 100, Paradise, CA 95967. 530-877-6110.
E-mail: dustbooks@dcsi.net. Web site: www.dustbooks.com. Bimonthly. $25/yr. Circ.: 2,500. Len Fulton, Editor. **Description:** Features reviews and news about small presses and magazines. **Nonfiction:** Reviews and essays on small-press literary books, publishers, and small-circulation magazines; 200 words. **Tips:** Sample copy free on request. **Queries:** Preferred. **E-Queries:** Yes.

SOCIETY OF CHILDREN'S BOOK WRITERS & ILLUSTRATORS
8271 Beverly Blvd., Los Angeles, CA 90048. 323-782-1010.
E-mail: scbwi@scbwi.org. Web site: www.scbwi.org. Monthly. **Description:**

Articles pertinent to writers and/or illustrators of children's books. Pays $50/article. **Art:** Pays $10 for line drawings; $25 for B&W cover photo. **Queries:** Required. **Rights:** FNAR.

TECHNICAL COMMUNICATION

Society for Technical Communication
194 Aberdeen Dr., Aiken, SC 29803. 803-642-2156.
E-mail: george@ghayhoe.com. Web site: www.stc.org. Quarterly. Membership publication. Circ.: 25,000. George Hayhoe, Editor. **Description:** Industry information for technical writers, publishers, and editors. **Nonfiction:** Research results, technical communication theory, case studies, tutorials related to new laws, standards, requirements, techniques, or technologies, reviews of research, bibliographies, and bibliographic essays on technical communication. **Queries:** Not necessary. **E-Queries:** Yes. **Unsolicited mss:** Accepts.

VERBATIM

4907 N Washtenaw Ave., Chicago, IL 60625. 773-275-1516.
E-mail: editor@verbatimmag.com. Web site: www.verbatimmag.com. Quarterly. $7/$25. Circ.: 1,500. Erin McKean, Editor. **Description:** "The Language Quarterly." On language and linguistics, written for a general audience. **Nonfiction:** Seeks interesting, well-written articles on language. Topics include spelling reform, palindromes, puns, names, and citation finding. To 2,500 words; $75-$400. **Poetry:** Light verse only, specifically about language; to 30 lines; $75. **Fillers:** Cryptic crosswords only; $25-$100. **Tips:** "Avoid lamentations about declining language standards. Also, no puns, homonyms, or Shakespeare. Humor always a plus!" **Queries:** Required. **E-Queries:** Yes. **Unsolicited mss:** Accepts. **Response:** 1-3 months. **Freelance Content:** 80%. **Rights:** All. **Payment:** On publication.

THE WIN-INFORMER

Professional Assn. for Christian Writers
P.O. Box 11337, Bainbridge Island, WA 98110. 206-842-9103.
E-mail: writersinfonetwork@juno.com. Web site: www.bluejaypub.com/win. Bimonthly. $5/issue. Circ.: 1,000. Elaine Wright Colvin, Editor. **Description:** Professional development in writing and marketing for Christian writers. **Nonfiction:** Updates on markets; CBA industry news and trends; how-to advice; ethics; contracts; author/editor relations; book reviews; info on clubs, groups, and conferences; 50-500 words; $20-$50 and/or subscription. **Tips:** Submit articles pasted in body of e-mail; do not send attachments or printed version. Include bio with publishing credits. Sample copy: for $5 with SASE. **Queries:** Not necessary. **E-Queries:** Yes. **Freelance Content:** 30%. **Rights:** FNAR. **Payment:** On acceptance.

THE WRITER

Kalmbach Publishing Co.
21027 Crossroads Circle, Waukesha, WI 53187. 262-796-8776.
E-mail: queries@writermag.com. Web site: www.writermag.com. Monthly. Circ.:

40,000. Elfrieda Abbe, Editor. **Description:** Founded in 1887, the magazine uses articles and interviews that focus on the process of writing. **Nonfiction:** Articles, to 2,500 words. How-to, marketing ideas, publishing trends, profiles, and book reviews. Payment depends on length and complexity of article. $50-$75 for reviews; $150-$600 for features and columns. **Tips:** "We prefer submissions through the mail, but include your e-mail address and be sure your name is on every page; list your experience, but do not send clips." Sample copies $4.95, plus tax, S/H.

WRITER'S BLOCK MAGAZINE

300-30 Murray St., Ottawa, Ontario K1N 5M4 Canada.
E-mail: dgoldberger@niva.com. Web site: www.writersblock.ca. Circ.: 5,000. Dalya Goldberger, Managing Editor. **Description:** *"Writer's Block* is the only Canadian web magazine that explores ideas that matter most to Canadians in the writing trade. Each quarterly issue offers information, insight, and opinions that help define the environment in which we work, learn, and create." Aimed at established and aspiring Canadian writers. Fiction and poetry also accepted. 2,500 words max; offers byline.

THE WRITER'S CHRONICLE

Associated Writing Programs
MSN 1E3, George Mason University, Fairfax, VA 22030.
E-mail: awpchron@mason.gmu.edu. Web site: www.awpwriter.org/magazine. 6x/yr. Circ.: 20,000. **Description:** Publication featuring essays, articles, and news on writing. Designed to inform and entertain writers, students, editors, and teachers. **Nonfiction:** Information on grants, awards, fellowships, articles, news, and reviews. Pays $7 per 100 words, or as negotiated. **Queries:** Preferred. **E-Queries:** Yes.

WRITERS' JOURNAL

P.O. Box 394, Perham, MN 56573-0394. 218-346-7921.
E-mail: writersjournal@lakesplus.com. Web site: www.writersjournal.com. Bimonthly. $4.99/$19.97. Circ.: 26,000. Leon Ogroske, Editor. **Description:** For writers: professional communicators, independent/self-publishers, freelancers, screenwriters, desktop publishers, authors, editors, teachers, and poets. **Nonfiction:** The business side of writing, all types of publishing (traditional, self, electronic, POD), writing skills/composition; 1,000-2,000 words. **Poetry:** Light verse about writing. Also buys a few serious pieces, any subject/style, with strong imagery and impact; 25 lines max.; $5. **Tips:** Submit articles with positive, practical advice. Also offers fiction and poetry contests. Send SASE for guidelines or visit Web site. **E-Queries:** Yes. **Unsolicited mss:** Accepts. **Response:** Queries 6 weeks, submissions 5 months, SASE required. **Rights:** One-time. **Payment:** On publication.

FICTION & POETRY
MAGAZINES

FICTION & POETRY MAGAZINES

The following section presents a list of magazines whose primary focus in most cases is publishing fiction and poetry. The fiction usually appears in the form of short stories; however, some magazines also publish excerpts from novels and longer works.

The list is divided into markets for specific genres of fiction. These include: Fiction for Young Writers, Literary Magazines, Mystery & Detective, Romance & Confession, and Science Fiction & Fantasy.

The largest number of magazines are found in the Literary Magazine portion. These independent and college journals often publish not only fiction and poetry but also a potent range of creative nonfiction essays on varied cultural topics, as well as book reviews and interviews with authors and artists.

Although payment from these relatively small magazines, which range in circulation from 300 to 10,000, is modest (often in copies only), publication can begin to establish a writer's serious literary credentials and often will help bring the work of a beginning writer to the attention of editors at larger magazines. Notably, some of America's leading authors still contribute work to the smaller literary magazines. Together with emerging new voices, they form a community of writers whose only criteria are excellence and the elevation of stimulating thought in literary discourse.

These literary journals, little magazines, and college quarterlies welcome work from novices and pros alike; editors are always interested in seeing traditional and experimental fiction, poetry, essays, reviews, short articles, criticism, and satire. As long as the material is well-written, the fact that a writer has not yet been widely published doesn't adversely affect his or her chances for acceptance.

Most of these literary publications have small budgets and staffs, so they may be slow in their reporting time; several months is not unusual. In addition, some (particularly the college-based magazines) do not read manuscripts during the summer.

Publication may also lead to having one's work chosen for reprinting in one of the prestigious annual collections of work from the little magazines.

For a complete list of the thousands of literary publications and little magazines in existence, writers may wish to consult such comprehensive reference works as *The International Directory of Little Magazines and Small Presses*, published annually by Dustbooks (P.O. Box 100, Paradise, CA 95967) and available at many public libraries.

FICTION FOR YOUNG WRITERS

CICADA

Carus Publishing Co.

315 Fifth St., P.O. Box 300, Peru, IL 61354-0300. 812-224-5803, ext. 656.

Web site: www.cricketmag.com. Bimonthly. $7.95/$35.97. Circ.: 16,000. Marianne Carus, Editor-in-Chief. **Description:** For teens, fiction and poetry that is thought-provoking, yet entertaining, often humorous. Also publishes stories by teens reflecting their own unique perspective. **Fiction:** Literary and genre fiction (realistic, humorous, historical fiction, adventure, science fiction, and fantasy); to 15, 000 words; $.25/word. **Nonfiction:** First-person experiences that are relevant or interesting to teenagers; to 5,000 words; $.25/word. **Poetry:** To 25 lines; $3/line. **Queries:** Does not accept. **E-Queries:** No. **Unsolicited mss:** Accepts. **Response:** 12 weeks, SASE required. **Freelance Content:** 90%. **Rights:** Vary. **Payment:** On publication. **Contact:** Deborah Vetter.

CLAREMONT REVIEW

4980 Wesley Rd., Victoria, British Columbia V84 1Y9 Canada. 250-658-5221. E-mail: editor@theclaremontreview.com. Web site: www.theclaremontreview.com. Semi-annual. $8/$15. Circ.: 500. Susan Field, Business Editor. **Description:** Fiction (500-3,000 words) and poetry (to 1 page) by young writers in the English-speaking world, ages 13-19. **Tips:** "We seek fiction with a strong voice and poetry that stirs the heart." No science fiction/fantasy. **Queries:** Not necessary. **Unsolicited mss:** Accepts. **Response:** 6 weeks, SASE. **Freelance Content:** 100%.

GUMBO

1818 N Dr. Martin Luther King Dr., Milwaukee, WI 53212. 414-374-3511. E-mail: amy@mygumbo.com. Web site: www.mygumbo.com. Bimonthly. $15/yr. Circ.: 25,000. Amy Muehlbauer, Managing Editor. **Description:** Multicultural magazine written, edited, and designed for teens by teens. Mission is to teach journalism and design skills to young adults by having them work with adult mentors who are professionals in journalism, graphic design, and photography. Editorial content reflects diversity in a range of subjects such as careers, sports, health, fashion, news, and entertainment. **Tips:** "We do not offer payment as we are published by a non-profit organization. All work is written and edited by teens and is a learning process. Contact the managing editor directly if you are interested in working for *Gumbo*. Do not send unsolicited material; only assigned articles are published." **Queries:** Required. **E-Queries:** Yes. **Unsolicited mss:** Does not accept. **Response:** 2 weeks. **Rights:** None.

MERLYN'S PEN

P.O. Box 910, East Greenwich, RI 02818. 401-885-5175. Web site: www.merlynspen.org. Annual. $29.95. Circ.: 5,000. R. James Stahl, Editor. **Description:** Fiction, essays, and poems by America's teens. **Fiction:** Realistic fiction about contemporary teen life; also science fiction, fantasy, adventure, historical fiction; to 8,500 words; $20-$200. **Nonfiction:** Personal essays, memoirs, autobiographies, humorous or descriptive essays; 500-5,000 words. **Poetry:** Free verse, metric verse; $20-$50. **Art:** B&W illustrations; by assignment, submit samples. **Tips:** "Looking for new voices—teen writers who have something to say and say it with eloquence, honesty, and distinctiveness." **Queries:** Required. **E-Queries:** No. **Unsolicited mss:** Accepts. **Response:** 10-12 weeks, SASE required. **Freelance Content:** 100%. **Rights:** All. **Payment:** On publication.

NEW MOON
34 E Superior St. #200, Duluth, MN 55802. 218-728-5507.
E-mail: girl@newmoon.org. Web site: www.newmoon.org. Bimonthly. $5.50/$29.
Circ.: 30,000. Deb Mylin, Managing Editor. **Description:** Celebrates girls—their
accomplishments and efforts to hold onto their voices, strengths, and dreams. *New
Moon* is completely edited by a Girls Editorial Board (16 girls, ages 8-14). They want
to know what's on your mind? What are your dreams? What makes you happy? What
drives you crazy? See Web site for guidelines for young writers, regular departments
(letters, opinions, reviews, essays, poetry, favorite quotes), and coming themes.
Fiction: Share your short stories, especially those with strong characters and creative
subjects that we haven't written about before. Fiction should fit theme (see Web site
for upcoming list); 900 words; $.06-$.10/word. **Nonfiction:** Profiles (of a woman and
her job, relates to theme); Herstory (profiles a woman from history); and more; 600
words; $.06-$.10/word. **Tips:** Sample copy $6.75. **Queries:** Not necessary. **E-
Queries:** Accepts. **Unsolicited mss:** Accepts. **Response:** 2 months, SASE.
Freelance Content: 10%. **Rights:** All. **Payment:** On publication.

SKIPPING STONES
P.O. Box 3939, Eugene, OR 97403. 541-342-4956.
E-mail: editor@skippingstones.org. Web site: www.skippingstones.org. 5x/yr. $25/yr.
Circ.: 2,500. Arun N. Toké, Executive Editor. **Description:** Original writing, art, and
photography. Encourages cooperation, creativity, celebration of cultural diversity, and
nature awareness. **Fiction:** Social awareness, interpersonal relationships; to 750
words. **Nonfiction:** Nature awareness, multicultural education, social responsibility,
travelogues, journal entries; to 750 words. **Poetry:** By authors under age 19 only; on
nature, social issues, reflections; to 30 lines. **Tips:** Include personal information in
cover letter (i.e., cultural background, languages you speak, source of inspiration for
submission). "We invite writing and art that promote multicultural awareness and/or
ecological understanding, sustainable living, creative problem solving, peace, and justice. Send for guidelines." **Queries:** Not necessary. **E-Queries:** Accepts.
Unsolicited mss: Accepts. **Response:** Submissions, to 3 months, SASE. **Freelance
Content:** 80%. **Rights:** 1st serial, non-exclusive reprint. **Payment:** In copies.

SPANK! YOUTH CULTURE ONLINE
Ububik, #505, 300 Meredith Rd., Calgary, Alberta T2E 7A8 Canada. 403-217-0468.
E-mail: happyrandom@spankmag.com. Web site: www.spankmag.com. Stephen R.
Cassady, Editor. **Description:** E-zine written by youth for youth, for ages 14 to 24.
Only accepts submissions from youth.

STONE SOUP
P.O. Box 83, Santa Cruz, CA 95063-0083. 831-426-5557.
E-mail: editor@stonesoup.com. Web site: www.stonesoup.com.
Bimonthly. $5.50/$33. Circ.: 20,000. Gerry Mandel, Editor. **Description:** Stories,
poems, book reviews, and art by young writers and artists, ages 8-13. **Fiction:**

Personal narratives, arrival stories, family histories, sport stories, science fiction; 2,500 words; $40. **Nonfiction:** Book reviews by children under 14. Prefers writing based on real-life experiences. **Poetry:** Free-verse only; $40. **Art:** Work by kids ages 8-13 only; send 2-3 samples (photocopies OK). **Tips:** Do not send SASE w/ manuscript; will respond if interested. Sample copy $4. **Queries:** Not necessary. **E-Queries:** No. **Unsolicited mss:** Accepts. **Response:** Queries 2-3 weeks, submissions 4 weeks. **Freelance Content:** 100%. **Rights:** All. **Payment:** On publication.

STORYWORKS

Scholastic, Inc., 557 Broadway, New York, NY 10012. 212-343-6100. E-mail: storyworks@scholastic.com. Web site: www.scholastic.com/storyworks. Bimonthly. Circ.: 270,000. Lauren Tarshis, Editor. **Description:** Language Arts magazine for kids ages 8-12. **Queries:** Required. **Unsolicited mss:** Does not accept.

TEEN INK

Young Author's Foundation
P.O. Box 30, Newton, MA 02461. 617-964-6800.
E-mail: editor@teenink.com. Web site: www.teenink.com. 10x/yr. Circ.: 150,000. Kate Dunlop Seamans, Editor. **Description:** Magazine written by teens for teens. Features fiction, nonfiction, poetry, and art. Receives 40,000 submissions/year. **Tips:** "Our magazine is written entirely by teenagers, ages 13-19." Does not offer payment. **Queries:** Not necessary. **E-Queries:** Yes. **Unsolicited mss:** Accepts. **Freelance Content:** 100%.

TEEN VOICES

Women Express, Inc., 80 Summer St., Boston, MA 02110. 617-426-5505. E-mail: womenexp@teenvoices.com. Web site: www.teenvoices.com. Quarterly. $2.95/$19.95. Circ.: 25,000. Celina DeLeon, Editor. **Description:** Written by, for, and about teenaged and young-adult women. Offers a place to share thoughts with others the same age. **Fiction:** Short stories, any subject and length. **Nonfiction:** About any important issue or experience. **Poetry:** "Your feelings, thoughts, etc." **Columns, Departments:** Opinions/editorial pieces. **Art:** Digital file (TIF or EPS), or hardcopy. **Tips:** Be honest and candid. Appreciates material that promotes feminism, equality, and self-esteem, "You're more than just a pretty face." **Queries:** Not necessary. **E-Queries:** Yes. **Unsolicited mss:** Accepts. **Response:** 3-5 days, SASE not required. **Rights:** FNAR. **Payment:** In copies.

LITERARY MAGAZINES

AFRICAN VOICES

270 W 96th St., New York, NY 10025. 212-865-2982.
E-mail: africanvoices@aol.com. Web site: www.africanvoices.com. Quarterly. $3/$12. Circ.: 20,000. Carolyn A. Butts, Editor. **Description:** Fiction, nonfiction, poetry, and visual arts by people of color. **Fiction:** Humorous, erotic, and dramatic fiction by eth-

nic writers. All themes, subjects, and styles, emphasis on style and technique; 500-2,000 words. **Nonfiction:** Investigative articles, artist profiles, essays, book reviews, and first-person narratives; 500-2,500 words. **Poetry:** All styles; avant-garde, free verse, haiku, light verse, traditional. Submit up to 5 poems; 3 pages max. **Columns, Departments:** Book reviews; 500-1,200 words. **Art:** B&W photos. **Queries:** Preferred. **E-Queries:** Accepts. **Unsolicited mss:** Accepts. **Response:** Queries 6 weeks, submissions 6-12 weeks, SASE. **Freelance Content:** 80%. **Rights:** 1st American. **Payment:** In copies. **Contact:** Kim Horne, fiction; Layding Kalbia, poetry; Debbie Officer, book reviews.

AFRO-HISPANIC REVIEW

University of Missouri, Dept. of Romance Languages
143 Arts & Science Building, Columbia, MO 65211. 573-882-5040.
E-mail: lewism@missouri.edu. 2x/yr. $15/yr. Circ.: 310. Marvin A. Lewis, Editor.
Description: Literary fiction, poetry, and essays that focus on the literature and culture of Afro-Latin America. Emphasis on literary analysis and criticism of works by African diasporan authors living in the Spanish Caribbean, Central America, and South America. **Fiction:** Stories that deal with the Black experience in Spanish America; 1-20 pages. **Nonfiction:** Book reviews and scholarly articles treating literary works by Black writers of Spanish expression in the Americas; 20 pages. **Poetry:** Poems that deal with the Black experience in Spanish America. **Tips:** Does not offer payment for work published. Academic audience. **Queries:** Preferred. **E-Queries:** No. **Unsolicited mss:** Accepts.

AGNI

Boston University, Creative Writing Program
236 Bay State Rd., Boston, MA 02215. 617-353-7135.
E-mail: agni@bu.edu. Web site: www.bu.edu/agni. Semi-annual. $9.95/$17. Circ.: 4,000. Suen Birkerts, Editor. **Description:** Contemporary literature by established and new writers, on literary and political subjects, to engage readers in a broad cultural conversation. Accepts fiction, poetry, and nonfiction pieces on a group of books (not reviews of single books) or broader cultural or literary issues. Length varies. Pays $20-150 ($10/page). **Tips:** Reviews submissions between October 1-February 15. **Queries:** Not necessary. **E-Queries:** No. **Unsolicited mss:** Accepts. **Response:** 2-4 months, SASE required. **Freelance Content:** 15%. **Rights:** FNASR, anthology. **Payment:** On publication.

AGNIESZKA'S DOWRY

5445 N Sheridan, #3003, Chicago, IL 60640-7477.
E-mail: marek@enteract.com; ketzle@ketzle.net. Web site: www.asgp.org. $6/issue. Marek Lugowski, katrina grace craig (no caps), Editors. **Description:** Poetry community publishing online literary journal (permanently) and as chapbooks (being kept in print indefinitely). **Tips:** Submit material via e-mail only, to both editors. Does not accept hard copy. Follow guidelines posted on Web site. **Payment:** In copies.

ALASKA QUARTERLY REVIEW

University of Alaska-Anchorage

3211 Providence Dr., Anchorage, AK 99508. 907-786-6916.

E-mail: ayaqr@uaa.alaska.edu. Web site: www.uaa.alaska.edu/aqr. Semi-annual. $6.95/$10. Circ.: 2,500. Ronald Spatz, Editor. **Description:** "One of the nation's best literary magazines" (*Washington Post Book World*). **Fiction:** Experimental and traditional literary forms. No romance, children's, or inspirational/religious; up to 20,000 words. **Nonfiction:** Literary nonfiction, essays, and memoirs; 20,000 words. **Poetry:** Avant-garde, free verse, traditional. No light verse; 10 poems max. **Tips:** Send manuscript via regular mail. Sample copy $6. **Queries:** Not necessary. **Unsolicited mss:** Accepts. **Response:** SASE required. **Freelance Content:** 95%. **Rights:** FNAR. **Payment:** In copies.

ALLIGATOR JUNIPER

Prescott College, 220 Grove Ave., Prescott, AZ 86301. 928-778-2090.

E-mail: aj@prescott.edu. Web site: www.prescott.edu/highlights/aj.html. Annual. $7.50/$12. Circ.: 600. Miles Waggere, Managing Editor. **Description:** Literary journal that seeks to create a bridge between the arts and the environment. Features B&W photography, fiction, creative nonfiction, and poetry. **Fiction:** 30 pages max; pays $10/story. **Nonfiction:** 30 pages max; pays $10/story. **Poetry:** 5 poems or 5 pages; pays $10 per 5 poems or pages. **Tips:** "We select work based on merit. Occasional theme issues. Read guidelines before submitting." **Queries:** Not necessary. **E-Queries:** No. **Unsolicited mss:** Accepts. **Response:** Submissions 3-6 months. **Freelance Content:** 100%. **Rights:** FNAR. **Payment:** On acceptance.

AMERICAN BOOK REVIEW

Illinois State University

Unit for Contemporary Literature, Campus Box 4241, Normal, IL 61790-4241.

E-mail: rakaise@ilstu.edu. Web site: www.litline.org/abr. Bimonthly. $4/issue. Circ.: 5,000. Ron Sukenick, Editor. **Description:** Literary book reviews and essays on literature; 750-1,250 words; $50. **Tips:** Sample copy $4. **Queries:** Preferred. **E-Queries:** Yes. **Response:** Queries 1-4 weeks; submissions, 4 weeks, SASE required. **Freelance Content:** 20%. **Payment:** On publication. **Contact:** Rebecca Kaiser.

AMERICAN LITERARY REVIEW

University of North Texas

P.O. Box 311307, English Dept., Denton, TX 76203-1307. 940-565-2755.

E-mail: americanliteraryreview@yahoo.com. Web site: www.engl.univ.edu/alr. Bi-annual. $5/$10. Circ.: 500. Corey Marks, Editor. **Description:** Literary journal with fiction, creative nonfiction, and poetry. Both in print and online. **Tips:** Sample copy $6. **Queries:** Not necessary. **Unsolicited mss:** Accepts. **Response:** 3 months, SASE required. **Freelance Content:** 90%. **Rights:** FNASR. **Payment:** In copies.

AMERICAN SCHOLAR
See full listing in Contemporary Culture category.

AMERICAN POETRY REVIEW
117 S 17th St., Suite 910, Philadelphia, PA 19103. 215-496-0439.
E-mail: dbonanno@aprweb.org. Web site: www.aprweb.org. Bimonthly. $3.95. Circ.:
17,000. Stephen Berg, David Bonanno, Arthur Vogelsang, Editors. **Description:**
Premier forum for contemporary poetry, since 1972. Submit up to 4 poems, any
length; $1.60/line. **Tips:** Do not send manuscript by fax or e-mail. **Queries:** Not nec-
essary. **E-Queries:** No. **Unsolicited mss:** Accepts. **Response:** 8-10 weeks, SASE
required. **Rights:** FNASR. **Payment:** On publication.

ANOTHER CHICAGO MAGAZINE
3709 N Kenmore, Chicago, IL 60613-2905.
E-mail: editors@anotherchicagomag.com. Web site: www.anotherchicagomag.com.
Semiannual. $14.95. Circ.: 2,000. Barry Silesky, Editor. **Description:** Literary publi-
cation featuring poetry, fiction, and commentary. Also, issues feature an occasional
interview with a noted writer, translations, reviews of current literature, and an 8-page
center photography folio. **Fiction:** Quality literary fiction that is urgent, new, or
worldly; to 25 pages. **Columns, Departments:** Reviews of current fiction and
poetry, 500 words. **Art:** B&W photography; 8 photos (from a single artist) in each
issue. **Tips:** Reviews work from February 1-August 31. "We seek unusual, engaged
work of highest quality only." **Queries:** Not necessary. **E-Queries:** No. **Unsolicited
mss:** Accepts. **Response:** Submissions 10 weeks or longer, SASE required.
Freelance Content: 10%. **Rights:** FNASR. **Payment:** On publication.

ANTHOLOGY, INC.
P.O. Box 4411, Mesa, AZ 85211-4411. 480-461-8200.
E-mail: info@anthology.org. Web site: www.anthology.org. 6x/yr. $3.95/$20. Circ.:
1,500. **Description:** Poetry, prose, and art from new and upcoming writers and
artists from around the world. **Fiction:** Any genre; 5,000 words. **Nonfiction:** Any
genre; 5,000 words. **Poetry:** Any style; up to 100 lines. **Tips:** No graphic horror or
pornography. Avoid cliché and trick endings. **Queries:** Not necessary. **E-Queries:**
No. **Unsolicited mss:** Accepts. **Response:** 60-90 days, SASE required. **Freelance
Content:** 90%. **Rights:** FNAR. **Payment:** In copies. **Contact:** Sharon Skinner,
Executive Editor; Elissa Harris, Prose Editor; Trish Justrish, Poetry Editor.

ANTIETAM REVIEW
Washington County Arts Council
41 S Potomac St., Hagerstown, MD 21740. 301-791-3132. Annual. $8.40/issue.
Description: Publishes quality short fiction, poetry, and B&W photos (not previously
published). **Fiction:** Well-crafted, any subject. Prefers short stories; will consider
novel excerpt if it works as an independent piece; to 5,000 words; $100/story plus 2
copies. **Nonfiction:** Creative nonfiction. **Poetry:** Submit up to 3 poems, to 30 lines;
$25/poem plus 2 copies. **Tips:** Accepts material September 1- February 1. **Queries:**

Not necessary. **E-Queries:** No. **Unsolicited mss:** Accepts. **Response:** 3-6 months, SASE required. **Freelance Content:** 90%. **Rights:** FNAR. **Payment:** On publication. **Contact:** Winnie Wagaman, Exec. Editor, or Paul Grant, Poetry Editor.

THE ANTIGONISH REVIEW

St. Francis Xavier University
P.O. Box 5000, Antigonish, Nova Scotia B2G 2W5 Canada. 902-867-3962.
E-mail: tar@stfx.ca. Web site: www.antigonishreview.com. Quarterly. $24/yr. Circ.: 800. B. Allan Quigley, Editor. **Description:** Poetry, short stories, essays, book reviews. **Fiction:** 2,000-5,000 words; $50. **Nonfiction:** 2,000-5,000 words; $50-$150. **Poetry:** Any subject, any point of view. **Tips:** Considers stories from anywhere, original or translations, but encourages Atlantic Canadians and Canadian writers, and new and young writers. No submissions accepted by e-mail. **Queries:** Preferred. **Unsolicited mss:** Accepts. **Response:** 4-6 months, SASE required (IRCs). **Freelance Content:** 100%. **Payment:** On publication.

ANTIOCH REVIEW

P.O. Box 148, Yellow Springs, OH 45387. 937-769-1365.
Web site: www.antioch.edu/review. Quarterly. $35/yr. Circ.: 5,100. Robert S. Fogarty, Editor. **Description:** Fiction, essays, and poetry from emerging and established authors. **Fiction:** Intelligent, compelling stories written with distinction; to 8,000 words; $10/page. **Nonfiction:** Social sciences, humanities, literary journalism; to 8,000 words; $10/page. **Poetry:** 3-6 poems; $10/page. **Tips:** "Read an issue of magazine to obtain a good idea of subjects, treatment, and lengths." **Queries:** Not necessary. **E-Queries:** No. **Unsolicited mss:** Accepts. **Response:** 12-14 weeks, SASE required. **Freelance Content:** 100%. **Payment:** On publication.

APALACHEE REVIEW

P.O. Box 10469, Tallahassee, FL 32302.
2x/yr. **Description:** Literary journal for poetry, fiction, and creative nonfiction. **Tips:** Accepts simultaneous submissions. No e-mail submissions. Sample copy $5. **Unsolicited mss:** Accepts. **Response:** SASE required.

ARACHNE

2363 Page Rd., Kennedy, NY 14747-9717.
E-mail: litteacher199@yahoo.com. Semiannual. $10/year. Circ.: 500. Susan L. Leach, Editor. **Description:** Magazine with rural themes. Focus is on America's grassroots authors. **Fiction:** 1,500 words. **Poetry:** Submit up to 7 poems. **Tips:** No simultaneous submissions. **Queries:** Preferred. **E-Queries:** No. **Unsolicited mss:** Accepts. **Response:** Queries 1-2 weeks, submissions up to 5 months, SASE required. **Freelance Content:** 100%. **Rights:** 1st. **Payment:** In copies.

ARKANSAS REVIEW: A JOURNAL OF DELTA STUDIES

Arkansas State University; P.O. Box 1890, State University, AR 72467. 870-972-3043.
E-mail: delta@astate.edu. Web site: www.clt.astate.edu/arkreview. 3x/yr. $7.50/$20.

Circ.: 500. William M. Clements, General Editor. **Description:** Regional studies journal focusing on 7-state Mississippi River Delta. Publishes academic articles, interviews, reviews, fiction, poetry, and B&W visual art. **Tips:** "We have an interdisciplinary academic audience. All material must have regional focus." **Queries:** Not necessary. **E-Queries:** Yes. **Unsolicited mss:** Accepts. **Freelance Content:** 50%. **Rights:** FNAR. **Payment:** In copies.

ART TIMES
P.O. Box 730, Mt. Marion, NY 12456. 845-246-6944.
E-mail: info@arttimesjournal.com. Web site: www.arttimesjournal.com. 11x/year. Circ.: 24,000. Raymond J. Steiner, Editor. **Description:** Commentary resource on fine and performing arts. **Fiction:** No excessive sex, violence, racist themes; 1,500 words; $25 and subscription. **Nonfiction:** Feature essays are staff-written. **Poetry:** All forms; 20 lines; pays in copies. **Queries:** Not necessary. **E-Queries:** No. **Unsolicited mss:** Accepts. **Response:** Submission 6 months, SASE. **Freelance Content:** 100%. **Rights:** FNAR. **Payment:** On publication.

ASCENT
Concordia College
901 Eighth St. S, English Dept., Moorhead, MN 56562. 218-299-4000.
Web site: www4.cord.edu/english/ascent. 3x/yr. W. Scott Olsen, Editor. **Description:** Literary magazine with fiction, essays, and poetry. No reviews or editorial articles. Submit complete manuscripts with SASE. **Tips:** Review copy of magazine before submitting. **E-Queries:** No. **Payment:** In copies.

ASIAN PACIFIC AMERICAN JOURNAL
Asian American Writers' Workshop
16 W 32nd St., Suite 10A, New York, NY 10001. 212-494-0061.
E-mail: apaj@aaww.org. Web site: www.aaww.org. Hanya Yanagihara, Editor. **Description:** Short stories, also excerpts from longer fiction works by emerging or established Asian American writers. **Poetry:** Submit up to 10 poems. **Tips:** Send 4 copies of each piece submitted, in all genres. **Queries:** Preferred. **Payment:** In copies.

THE ATLANTIC MONTHLY
See full listing in General Interest category.

AURA LITERARY ARTS REVIEW
University of Alabama-Birmingham
1400 University Blvd., Suite 135, Birmingham, AL 35294-1150. 205-934-3216.
Semi-annual (Spring and Fall issues). $6/$25. Christopher Giganti, Editor-in-Chief. **Description:** Student-produced magazine for written and visual art. **Fiction:** Up to 10,000 words. **Nonfiction:** Up to 10,000 words. **Poetry:** Up to 10 pages. **Art:** Visual art. **Queries:** Not necessary. **E-Queries:** No. **Unsolicited mss:** Accepts. **Response:** SASE required. **Payment:** In copies.

BARROW STREET

Old Chelsea Station, P.O. Box 2017, New York, NY 10113-2017.
E-mail: info@barrowstreet.org. Web site: www.barrowstreet.org. **Description:** Literary journal publishing poetry. Send 3-5 poems (no more than 7 pages) with cover letter. Pays 2 copies. **Poetry:** 3-5 poems; up to 7 pages. **Tips:** Does not accept electronic submissions. Simultaneous submissions accepted with notice. **E-Queries:** No. **Response:** 3-5 months; SASE required. **Payment:** In copies.

BEACON STREET REVIEW

Emerson College, WLP Dept., 120 Boylston St., Boston, MA 02116.
E-mail: beaconstreetreview@hotmail.com. Semiannual. $6/$10. Circ.: 1,000.
Description: New fiction, creative nonfiction, and poetry. Send up to 5 poems for poetry, up to 25 pages for prose. **Tips:** No e-mail submissions or queries. Send SASE or e-mail for guidelines. Annual Editor's Choice Awards chosen from published works. **Queries:** Not necessary. **E-Queries:** No. **Unsolicited mss:** Accepts. **Rights:** FNAR. **Payment:** On publication.

THE BEAR DELUXE

P.O. Box 10342, Portland, OR 97296. 503-242-1047.
E-mail: bear@orlo.org. Web site: www.orlo.org. Biannual. $16/4 issues. Circ.: 19,000.
Tom Webb, Editor. **Description:** Explores environmental issues through the creative arts. **Fiction:** Environmental themes; 750-4,000 words; $.05/word. **Nonfiction:** News, reporting, interviews; seeks cultural connections to environmental issues; 200-4,000 words; $.05/word. **Poetry:** 3-5 poems, up to 50 lines; $10. **Fillers:** First-person opinion pieces, short news pieces, cartoons; 100-750 words; $.05/word, $10/cartoon. **Columns, Departments:** Portrait of an Artist, Technology, Reporter's Notebook; 100-1,500 words; $.05/word. **Art:** B&W and color photos, illustrations, cartoons, paintings, etc.; $30. **Queries:** Preferred. **E-Queries:** Yes. **Unsolicited mss:** Accepts. **Response:** Queries 1-2 months, submissions 3-6 months, SASE required. **Freelance Content:** 50%. **Rights:** FNAR. **Payment:** On publication.

BELLINGHAM REVIEW

Western Washington University, MS-9053, Bellingham, WA 98225. 360-650-4863.
E-mail: bhreview@cc.wwu.edu. Web site: www.wwu.edu/~bhreview. Semiannual. Brenda Miller, Editor-in-Chief. **Description:** Journal for fiction, poetry, and creative nonfiction. **Queries:** Does not accept. **E-Queries:** No. **Unsolicited mss:** Accepts. **Response:** 3 months, SASE required. **Freelance Content:** 100%. **Rights:** FNAR. **Payment:** On publication.

BELLOWING ARK

P.O. Box 55564, Shoreline, WA 98155. 206-440-0791.
E-mail: bellowingark@comcast.net (inquiries only). Bimonthly. $4/$18. Circ.: 850.
Robert R. Ward, Editor. **Description:** Literary magazine following the Romantic tradition. **Fiction:** Short fiction, portraying life as positive and meaningful; length varies. **Poetry:** Any style or length. **Queries:** Not necessary. **E-Queries:** Yes. **Unsolicited**

mss: Accepts. **Response:** 2-4 months; SASE required. **Freelance Content:** 95%. **Rights:** First, reprint. **Payment:** In copies.

BELOIT FICTION JOURNAL
Beloit College, Box 11, 700 College St, Beloit, WI 53511. 608-363-2577. E-mail: mccownc@beloit.edu. Web site: www.beloit.edu/~english/bfjournal.htm. Annual. $15/issue. Clint McCown, Editor. **Description:** Literary fiction. Interested in new and established writers. **Fiction:** Literary fiction, any theme (no genre fiction). Stories, 1-40 pages long (ave. 15 pages). **Tips:** Submit work during August 1-December 1. "Submit with a great opening line, original language, strong forward movement. No pornography, political propaganda, or religious dogma." **Queries:** Not necessary. **E-Queries:** No. **Unsolicited mss:** Accepts. **Response:** 2-4 weeks, SASE required. **Payment:** In copies. **Contact:** Heather Skyler, Managing Editor.

BELOIT POETRY JOURNAL
P.O. Box 151, Farmington, ME 04938. 207-778-0020. E-mail: sharkey@maine.edu. Web site: www.bpj.org. Quarterly. $5/$18. Circ.: 1,300. Lee Sharkey, John Rosenwald, Editors. **Description:** Publishes the best poems received, without bias for length, form, subject, or tradition. Looking to discover new voices. **Tips:** "Avoid lineated journal entries, clichés, self-absorbed 'how I feel' verse. A strong poem needs fresh insight and a distinctive music." **Queries:** Not necessary. **E-Queries:** No. **Unsolicited mss:** Accepts. **Response:** 4 months, SASE required. **Payment:** In copies.

BIGNEWS
302 E 45th St., New York, NY 10017. 212-883-0680. E-mail: bignewsmag@aol.com. Web site: www.mainchance.org/bignews. Monthly. $1/$25. Circ.: 25,000. Ron Grunberg, Editor. **Description:** Literary magazine featuring fiction, nonfiction, and artwork. Typical article runs 1,000-5,000 words; $50/article. **Tips:** "Please read our content online to get an idea of what we are looking for. We focus on the outcast or outsider point of view." **Queries:** Not necessary. **E-Queries:** Yes. **Unsolicited mss:** Accepts. **Response:** Queries 2 days, submissions 2 weeks. **Freelance Content:** 75%. **Rights:** FNAR and electronic. **Payment:** On publication.

BITTER OLEANDER
4983 Tall Oaks Dr., Fayetteville, NY 13066-9776. 315-637-3047. E-mail: info@bitteroleander.com. Web site: www.bitteroleander.com. Bi-annual. $8/$15. Circ.: 1,200. Paul B. Roth, Editor. **Description:** Imaginative poetry, fiction, interviews with known and new writers whose work is featured. **Fiction:** Original, imaginative, aware of language as possibility instead of slave. 2,500 words. **Poetry:** Imaginative, concentration on "deep image," the concrete particular. **Tips:** Seeking more contemporary poetry in translation. No confessional storytelling, overly abstract poetry. **Queries:** Not necessary. **E-Queries:** Yes. **Unsolicited mss:** Accepts. **Response:** 1-4 weeks, SASE required. **Freelance Content:** 80%. **Rights:** All, revert back to author. **Payment:** In copies.

BLACK BEAR REVIEW

1916 Lincoln St., Croydon, PA 19021-8026.
E-mail: editor@blackbearreview.com. Web site: www.blackbearreview.com.
Biannual. $12.00. Circ.: 750. Ave Jeanne, Editor. **Description:** Literary magazine for the concerned poet and artist. **Tips:** Prefers poems on social and environmental concerns. Avoid traditional forms. Submissions by e-mail only. **Queries:** Not necessary. **E-Queries:** Yes. **Unsolicited mss:** Does not accept. **Response:** 1 week, SASE not required. **Freelance Content:** 100%. **Rights:** FNASR. **Payment:** In copies.

BLACK WARRIOR REVIEW

P.O. Box 862936, Tuscaloosa, AL 35486-0027. 205-348-4518.
E-mail: bwr@ua.edu. Web site: http://webdelsol.com/bwr. Bi-annual. $14/yr. Circ.: 2,000. Dan Kaplan, Editor. **Description:** Contemporary fiction, poetry, nonfiction, art, interviews, reviews, and photography. Seeks work from emerging and established writers. "Send only your best work." **Tips:** Accepts queries via e-mail, but not submissions. See Web site for guidelines. **Queries:** Not necessary. **E-Queries:** Yes. **Unsolicited mss:** Accepts. **Response:** 2-5 months; SASE required.

BLOOMSBURY REVIEW

See full listing in Writing & Publishing category.

BLUE UNICORN

22 Avon Rd., Kensington, CA 94707. 510-526-8439.
3x/yr. $5/$14. Circ.: 500. Ruth G. Iodice, Editor. **Description:** Has published many of the nation's best poets over the past 25 years. **Poetry:** Well-crafted poems, in form or free verse, also expert translations. Shorter is better. **Tips:** "Study great poets, but develop your own voice; avoid copying whatever is popular. The sound of a poem helps make it memorable." **Queries:** Preferred. **E-Queries:** No. **Unsolicited mss:** Accepts. **Response:** Queries as possible, submissions 4-6 months, SASE required. **Freelance Content:** 100%. **Rights:** 1st. **Payment:** In copies.

BLUELINE

State University of New York, English Dept., Potsdam, NY 13676. 315-267-2043.
E-mail: blueline@potsdam.edu. Web site: www.potsdam.edu/engl/blueline. Annual. $10/yr. Circ.: 600. Rick Henry, Editor. **Description:** Poems, stories, and essays on the Adirondack and regions similar in geography and spirit, or on the shaping influence of nature. **Fiction:** To 3,500 words. **Nonfiction:** On Adirondack region or similar areas; to 3,500 words. **Poetry:** Submit up to 5 poems; to 75 lines. **Tips:** Accepts submissions from September 1-December 1 only. **Queries:** Not necessary. **E-Queries:** Yes. **Unsolicited mss:** Accepts. **Rights:** FNASR. **Payment:** In copies.

BOSTON REVIEW

30 Wadsworth St., E53, Room 407, Cambridge, MA 02139. 617-253-3642.
E-mail: chasman@mit.edu. Web site: http://bostonreview.mit.edu. Bimonthly. Circ.: 20,000. Deborah Chasman, Josh Cohen, Editors. **Description:** Nonfiction pieces on

politics, literature, art, music, film, photography, and culture. Also publishes short fiction (1,200-5,000 words) and poetry. **Queries:** Preferred. **Rights:** FNASR. **Contact:** Dan Ochsner, Managing Editor.

BOULEVARD

6614 Clayton Rd. #325, Richmond Heights, MO 63117. 314-862-2643.
Web site: www.richardburgin.com. 3x/yr. $8/$15. Circ.: 4,000. Richard Burgin, Editor. **Description:** Publishes established writers and new writers with exceptional promise. Recent authors: Joyce Carol Oates, Stephen Dixon, Ha Jin, Alice Hoffman, and Alice Adams. **Fiction:** Well-constructed, moving stories, in an original voice; to 30 typed pages; $50-$350. **Nonfiction:** Literary, film, music, criticism, travel pieces, memoirs, philosophical or social issues. **Poetry:** No light verse. Submit up to 5 poems of up to 200 lines; $25-$250/poem. **Tips:** No science fiction, erotica, westerns, horror, romance, or children's stories. **Queries:** Not necessary. **E-Queries:** No. **Unsolicited mss:** Accepts. **Response:** Queries 1 week, submissions 2-4 months, SASE required. **Freelance Content:** 85%. **Rights:** 1st. **Payment:** On publication.

BRIAR CLIFF REVIEW

Briar Cliff University, 3303 Rebecca St., Sioux City, IA 51104.
E-mail: currans@briarcliff.edu. Web site: www.briarcliff.edu/bcreview. Tricia Currans-Sheehan, Editor. **Description:** Eclectic literary/cultural magazine on Siouxland writers and subjects. **Fiction:** Yes. **Nonfiction:** To 5,000 words: humor/satire, regional history, essays. **Poetry:** Yes. **Columns, Departments:** Book reviews. **Tips:** Manuscripts read August-October. **Payment:** In copies.

BRICK

See full listing in Contemporary Culture category.

BRIDGE

119 N Peoria, 3D, Chicago, IL 60607.
E-mail: submissions@bridgemagazine.org. Web site: www.bridgemagazine.org. **Description:** A magazine based on "the simple belief that separate fields of inquiry can and should be thought of as having shared horizons." **Fiction:** Realistic fiction; 2,000-5,000 words. **Nonfiction:** Critical nonfiction; 2,000-5,000 words. **Queries:** Preferred. **Response:** SASE required.

BYLINE

See full listing in Writing & Publishing category.

CAIRN

St. Andrews College, 1700 Dogwood Mile, Laurinburg, NC 28352. 910-277-5310.
E-mail: cairn@sapc.edu. Web site: www.sapc.edu. Annual. $8/issue. Circ.: 1,000. April Link, Matt Phelps, Editors. **Description:** Fiction, nonfiction, and poetry. Recent contributors include Dana Gioia, Robert Creeley, Richard Blanco, Ted Enslin, and Jean Monahan. **Tips:** "We read manuscripts from September to December."

Queries: Not necessary. **E-Queries:** No. **Unsolicited mss:** Accepts. **Response:** 4 months, SASE required. **Payment:** In copies. **Contact:** Editorial Department.

CALIFORNIA QUARTERLY

California State Poetry Society
P.O. Box 7126, Orange, CA 92863. 949-854-8024.
E-mail: jipalley@aol.com. Web site: www.chapman.edu/comm/english/csps.
Quarterly. $5/$20. Circ.: 250. Julian Palley, Editorial Board. **Description:** "California State Poetry Quarterly." Submit up to 6 poems, to 40 lines on any subject or style. **Queries:** Not necessary. **Unsolicited mss:** Accepts. **Response:** 5-6 months, SASE required. **Freelance Content:** 100%. **Payment:** 1 copy/poem.

CALLALOO

See full listing in Ethnic & Multicultural category.

CALYX

P.O. Box B, Corvallis, OR 97339. 541-753-9384.
E-mail: calyx@proaxis.com. Web site: www.proaxis.com/~calyx. Biannual. $9.50/issue.
Circ.: 5,000. Veverly McFarland, Senior Editor. **Description:** Journal of art and literature by women, with poetry, prose, art, and book reviews. Presents wide spectrum of women's experience, especially work by unheard voices (new writers, women of color, working-class, older women). **Fiction:** 5,000 words. **Nonfiction:** 5,000 words. **Poetry:** 6 poems max. **Art:** Color cover, plus 16 pages of B&W art. **Tips:** Submit prose and poetry October 1-December 31. Art submissions accepted anytime. Send query for book reviews only. **Queries:** Not necessary. **Unsolicited mss:** Accepts. **Response:** Submissions 6-8 months, SASE required. **Payment:** In copies.

THE CAPE ROCK

Southeast Missouri State University
Dept. of English, Cape Girardeau, MO 63701. 573-651-2500.
E-mail: hhecht@semo.edu. Bi-annual. $5/$7. Circ.: 500. Harvey E. Hecht, Editor. **Description:** Poetry journal, with photography. **Poetry:** To 70 lines; pays $200 for "Best in issue." **Art:** A series of 12-15 B&W photos, featuring a sense of place; $100. **Tips:** Manuscripts read August-April. **Queries:** Not necessary. **E-Queries:** Yes. **Unsolicited mss:** Accepts. **Response:** Queries 1-2 weeks, submissions 2-4 months, SASE required. **Rights:** All. **Payment:** In copies.

THE CAPILANO REVIEW

2055 Purcell Way, N. Vancouver, British Columbia V7J 3H5 Canada. 604-984-1712.
E-mail: tcr@capcollege.bc.ca. Web site: www.capcollege.bc.ca/dept/TCR. 3x/yr.
$9/$25. Circ.: 900. Sharon Theson, Editor. **Description:** Innovative poetry, fiction, drama, and word in the visual media, in a cross-disciplinary format. **Fiction:** To 6,000 words (drama, to 10,000 words); $50-$200 (Canadian). **Poetry:** 5-6 poems; $50-$200 (Canadian). **Tips:** "We look for work pushing beyond the boundaries of traditional art

and writing." **Queries:** Not necessary. **E-Queries:** No. **Unsolicited mss:** Accepts. **Response:** 4 months, SASE with Canadian postage or IRCs required. **Rights:** FNASR. **Payment:** On publication. **Contact:** Carol L. Hamshaw, Managing Editor.

THE CARIBBEAN WRITER
University of the Virgin Islands
RR02, Box 10,000, Kingshill St. Croix, Virgin Islands 00850. 340-692-4152.
E-mail: qmars@uvi.edu. Web site: www.thecaribbeanwriter.com. Annual. $12/issue; $20/ 2 yr. individual subscription; $40/ 2 yr. institutional subscription. Circ.: 1,200. Marvin E. Williams, Editor. **Description:** Literary anthology with Caribbean focus. **Fiction:** Personal essays, also one-act plays (3,500 words or 10 pages max.), or up to 2 short stories (15 pages or less); Caribbean experience or heritage central. **Poetry:** Caribbean focus; submit up to 5 poems. **Tips:** Original, unpublished work only (if self-published, give details). Blind submissions policy: print only the title on your manuscript; give your name, address, and title on a separate sheet. **Queries:** Not necessary. **E-Queries:** Yes. **Unsolicited mss:** Accepts. **Response:** SASE required. **Freelance Content:** 80%. **Rights:** One-time. **Payment:** In copies. **Contact:** Ms. Quilin Mars.

CAROLINA QUARTERLY
University of North Carolina-Chapel Hill
English Dept., CB#3520 Greenlaw Hall, Chapel Hill, NC 27599-3520.
E-mail: cquarter@unc.edu. Web site: www.unc.edu/depts/cqonline. Tara Powell, Editor. **Description:** Features poetry, fiction, nonfiction, and graphic art by new and established writers. **Fiction:** Short stories, novel excerpts; up to 25 pages. **Nonfiction:** Personal essays, memoirs, book reviews. **Poetry:** Up to 6 poems. **Art:** Photos, illustrations, cartoons. **Tips:** Manuscripts not read May-July. Accepts queries via e-mail, but not submissions. Sample copy $5. **Queries:** Not necessary. **E-Queries:** Yes. **Unsolicited mss:** Accepts. **Response:** 4-6 months; SASE required.

CHARITON REVIEW
Truman State University, Kirksville, MO 63501-9915. 660-785-4499.
Semiannual. Circ.: 1,800. Jim Barnes, Editor. **Description:** Quality poetry and fiction and contemporary translations. To 6,000 words; $5/printed page. **Tips:** "The only guideline is excellence."

THE CHATTAHOOCHEE REVIEW
Georgia Perimeter College, 2101 Womack Rd., Dunwoody, GA 30338-4497.
E-mail: gpccr@gpc.edu. Web site: www.chattahoochee-review.org. Quarterly. $6/$16. Lawrence Hetrick, Editor. **Description:** Promotes fresh writing by emerging and established voices. **Fiction:** To 5,000 words; $20/page. **Nonfiction:** $15/page, reviews $50. **Poetry:** $30/poem. **Tips:** Also hosts annual Lamar York Prize for Nonfiction. See Web site for details. **Queries:** Not necessary. **Response:** 1-16 weeks, SASE required. **Freelance Content:** 80%. **Rights:** FNAR. **Payment:** On publication.

CHELSEA

P.O. Box 773, Cooper Station, New York, NY 10276.
Semiannual. $8/$13. Circ.: 1,800. Alfredo de Palchi, Editor. **Description:** New and established voices in literature. Eclectic, lively, with accent on translations, art, and cross-cultural exchange. Pays $15/page, plus copies. **Fiction:** Mainstream, literary; to 25 pages. **Nonfiction:** Essays; to 25 pages. **Poetry:** Traditional, avant-garde; 3-6 poems. **Columns, Departments:** Book reviews (by assignment only). **Art:** Submit slides; color (cover), B&W inside. **Tips:** Interested in avant-garde: original ideas and use of language. **Queries:** Not necessary. **E-Queries:** No. **Unsolicited mss:** Accepts. **Response:** 3-6 months, SASE required. **Rights:** FNAR. **Payment:** On publication.

CHIRON REVIEW

702 N Prairie, St. John, KS 67576-1516. 620-786-4955.
E-mail: chironreview@hotmail.com. Web site: www.geocities.com/soho/nook/1748/.
Quarterly. $5/$15. Circ.: 2,000. Michael Hathaway, Publisher/Editor. **Description:** A wide range of contemporary writing (fiction and nonfiction, traditional and offbeat) including artwork and photography of featured writers. Also provides news and literary reviews. **Fiction:** Contemporary; 700-3,000 words. **Nonfiction:** Essays, interviews, and reviews of literary books and magazines; 500-1,000 words. **Poetry:** Send 5 poems. **Tips:** All submissions welcome. Does not accept e-mail, simultaneous or previously published submissions. **Queries:** Not necessary. **Unsolicited mss:** Accepts. **Response:** 2-6 weeks, SASE required. **Freelance Content:** 100%. **Rights:** One-time. **Payment:** 1 copy.

CIA-CITIZEN IN AMERICA, INC

30 Ford St., Glen Cove, NY 11542. 516-759-8718.
E-mail: ciamc@webtv.net. 9x/year. John J. Maddox, Magazine Coordinator. **Description:** Fiction and nonfiction, to 2,000 words. Poetry to 100 words. Prefers self photos to be published with articles. Fillers accepted. Pays $40-$100. **Queries:** Required.

CIMARRON REVIEW

Oklahoma State University, 205 Morrill Hall, Stillwater, OK 74078-4069.
E-mail: cimarronreview@yahoo.com. Web site: http://cimarronreview.okstate.edu.
Quarterly. Circ.: 600. E.P. Walkiewicz, Editor. **Description:** Poetry, fiction, and essays. Seeks work with individual, innovative style and contemporary themes. **Fiction:** 300-800 words; pays 2 contributor's copies and a year's subscription. **Tips:** "We're open to anything fresh, exciting, savvy." No simultaneous submissions. Read a sample copy ($7) before submitting. **Queries:** Not necessary. **E-Queries:** No. **Unsolicited mss:** Accepts. **Response:** 1-6 months, SASE required. **Rights:** FNASR. **Payment:** In copies.

COLORADO REVIEW

Colorado State University, English Dept., Fort Collins, CO 80523. 970-491-5449.
E-mail: creview@colostate.edu. Web site: www.coloradoreview.com. 3x/yr. $9.50/$24.

Circ.: 1,300. David Milofsky, Editor. **Description:** Fiction, poetry, and personal essays by new and established writers; work that is vital, imaginative, highly realized, and avoids mere mannerism to embody human concern. Fiction and nonfiction to 20 pages. Poetry: length varies. Pays $5/page. **Art:** Slides, $100 (cover). **Tips:** No simultaneous submissions. Reading period, September-April only; submissions sent outside this period are returned unread. **Queries:** Not necessary. **E-Queries:** No. **Unsolicited mss:** Accepts. **Response:** Queries 2-4 weeks, submissions 4-6 weeks, SASE required. **Rights:** FNAR. **Payment:** On publication.

THE COLUMBIA REVIEW

Columbia University, 415 Dodge Hall, New York, NY 10027. 212-854-4216. E-mail: columbiajournal@columbia.edu. Web site: www.columbia.edu/~tnf12. Annual. $8/$15. Circ.: 2,200. Tiffany Fung, Editor-in-Chief. **Description:** Literary journal, with contemporary poetry, fiction, and creative nonfiction from established and emerging voices. **Fiction:** No restrictions (avoid children's stories or genre pieces). Open to experimental writing, mainstream narratives, work that takes risk; 25 pages or less. **Nonfiction:** Same as fiction (no reviews or academic criticism); 20 pages or less. **Poetry:** Wide range of forms and styles; 4 poems max. **Tips:** Accepts queries via e-mail, but not submissions. **Queries:** Not necessary. **E-Queries:** Yes. **Unsolicited mss:** Accepts. **Response:** Queries 2 weeks, submissions 3 months, SASE required. **Freelance Content:** 65%. **Rights:** 1st U.S. **Payment:** In copies.

COMBAT

P.O. Box 3, Circleville, WV 26804. E-mail: majordomo@combatmagazine.ws. Web site: www.combatmagazine.ws. Quarterly. **Description:** The literary expression of battlefield touchstones; wartime insights and experiences. **Fiction:** 3,000 words. **Nonfiction:** 3,000 words. **Poetry:** 300 words. **Tips:** Read submission guidelines. **Queries:** Not necessary. **E-Queries:** Yes. **Response:** SASE. **Freelance Content:** 90%. **Rights:** FNASR.

COMMENTARY

See full listing in Religion category.

CONDUIT

510 Eighth Ave. NE, Minneapolis, MN 55413. 612-326-0995. E-mail: info@conduit.org. Web site: www.conduit.org. 2x/yr. $8/$15. Circ.: 1,000. William D. Waltz, Editor. **Description:** Seeks previously unpublished poetry, prose, artwork, and B&W photography. Submit 3-5 poems or 1 prose piece (up to 3,500 words). **Tips:** "Feature innovative work by emerging and established writers. We dedicated 75% of our pages to poetry." **Queries:** Not necessary. **E-Queries:** Yes. **Unsolicited mss:** Accepts. **Response:** 6 weeks to 6 months, SASE. **Freelance Content:** 75%. **Rights:** FNAR.

CONFLUENCE

P.O. Box 336, Belpre, OH 45714-0336.
E-mail: wilmaacree@charter.net; confluence1989@yahoo.com. Annual. $5/issue. Circ.: 1,000. Wilma Acree, Editor. **Description:** Presents the work of emerging and established authors. **Fiction:** Literary fiction; to 5,000 words. **Nonfiction:** Interviews, essays; to 5,000 words. **Poetry:** Lyric, narrative poetry with fresh images. No rhymed poetry unless of exceptional quality; to 60 lines. **Tips:** No previously published work. Cover letter with short bio and complete contact info required. **Queries:** Not necessary. **E-Queries:** Yes. **Unsolicited mss:** Accepts. **Response:** Queries 1 month, submissions 1-5 months, SASE. **Freelance Content:** 80%. **Rights:** FNAR. **Payment:** In copies.

CONFRONTATION

Long Island University
C.W. Post Campus of L.I.U., Dept. of English, Brookville, NY 11548. 516-299-2720.
E-mail: mtucker@liu.edu. Semiannual. $10. Circ.: 2,000. Martin Tucker, Editor. **Description:** Poetry, fiction, essays, and memoir material. Also, original work by famous and emerging writers. **Fiction:** To 30 pages; $25-$150. **Nonfiction:** Mostly memoirs. Other nonfiction, including reviews, by assignment; $25-$150. **Poetry:** Pays $15-$100. **Tips:** Send query for nonfiction material only. Manuscripts read September-May only. **Queries:** Preferred. **E-Queries:** No. **Unsolicited mss:** Accepts. **Response:** Queries 2-4 weeks, submissions 6-8 weeks, SASE required. **Freelance Content:** 75%. **Rights:** FNASR. **Payment:** On publication.

THE CONNECTICUT POETRY REVIEW

P.O. Box 818, Stonington, CT 06378.
J. Claire White, Harley More, Editors. **Description:** Poetry, 5-20 lines; pays $5/poem. Reviews, 700 words; pays $10. **Tips:** Manuscripts read September-January, and April-June. **Payment:** On acceptance.

CONNECTICUT RIVER REVIEW

Connecticut Poetry Society
P.O. Box 4053, Waterbury, CT 06704-0053. 203-753-7815.
E-mail: editorcrr@yahoo.com (for queries only). Biannual. $7/$14. Circ.: 500. **Description:** National journal of poetry, est. 1978. Poetry accepted from professionals and new writers. Submit up to 3 poems (any form/subject, 40 lines max) between October 1-April 15. Upon notification of acceptance, poems must be submitted electronically. Include contact information and SASE. Accepts simultaneous submissions with notice. **Tips:** "To 'make the cut,' use fresh language!" **Payment:** In copies.

COTTONWOOD

University of Kansas, Box J, 400 Kansas Union, Lawrence, KS 66045.
2x/yr. **Description:** New and well-known writers. No rhymed poetry. Kansas and midwestern focus. Photos, graphics, and book reviews (midwest presses) also accepted. **Fiction:** Work from experience; no contrived or slick fiction. Submit only

1 story at a time; 1,500-8,000 words. **Poetry:** Submit up to 5 poems; 10-80 lines. **Art:** Photos, other graphic arts. **E-Queries:** No. **Response:** 3-6 months, SASE required. **Rights:** FNAR. **Payment:** In copies.

THE CREAM CITY REVIEW
University of Wisconsin-Milwaukee
English Dept., P.O. Box 413, Milwaukee, WI 53201. 414-229-4708.
E-mail: creamcity@uwm.edu. Web site: www.uwm.edu/dept/english/ccr. Semi-annual. $8/$15. Circ.: 700. Erica Wiest, Editor. **Description:** Fiction, nonfiction, poetry, interviews, and book reviews. **Queries:** Not necessary. **E-Queries:** No. **Unsolicited mss:** Accepts. **Response:** Queries 2 weeks, submissions 3-8 months, SASE required. **Freelance Content:** 100%. **Rights:** FNAR. **Payment:** 1-year subscription.

CREATIVE NONFICTION
5501 Walnut, Suite 202, Pittsburgh, PA 15232. 412-688-0304.
E-mail: creative.nonfiction@verizon.net. Web site: www.creativenonfiction.org. 3x/yr. $10/$29.95. Circ.: 4,000. Lee Gutkind, Editor. **Description:** Devoted exclusively to nonfiction. Personal essays, memoirs, literary journalism, profiles of creative nonfiction authors, book reviews. **Nonfiction:** Prose, rich with detail and distinctive voice on any subject; seeking essays based on research; $10/page. **Tips:** Material can be personal but must reach out universally in some way. **Queries:** Not necessary. **E-Queries:** Yes. **Unsolicited mss:** Accepts. **Response:** Submissions 3 months, SASE. **Freelance Content:** 95%. **Rights:** 1st serial and reprint. **Payment:** On publication.

CUTBANK
University of Montana, English Dept., Missoula, MT 59812. 406-243-6156.
E-mail: cutbank@selway.umt.edu. Web site: www.umt.edu/cutbank. Biannual. $6.95/$12. Circ.: 1,000. **Description:** Fiction, poetry, and artwork. **Tips:** "Request a sample copy to see what we publish." **Queries:** Not necessary. **E-Queries:** No. **Unsolicited mss:** Accepts. **Response:** 3-4 months, SASE required. **Freelance Content:** 90%. **Payment:** In copies.

DESCANT
Texas Christian University, Box 297270, Fort Worth, TX 76129. 817-257-6537.
E-mail: d.kuhne@tcu.edu. Web site: www.eng.tcu.edu/journals/descant/index.html. Quarterly. $12. Circ.: 750. Dave Kuhne, Editor; Lynn Risser, Editor, Editor. **Description:** Seeks quality work in traditional or innovative form. **Fiction:** No restrictions; most stories under 5,000 words. **Poetry:** Fewer than 60 lines. **Tips:** Submit September-April only. Also offers 4 cash awards. **Queries:** Not necessary. **E-Queries:** No. **Unsolicited mss:** Accepts. **Response:** 6-8 weeks, SASE required. **Freelance Content:** 100%. **Rights:** FNAR. **Payment:** In copies.

DESCANT
P.O. Box 314, Station P, Toronto, Ontario M5S 2S8 Canada. 416-593-2557.
E-mail: descant@web.net. Web site: www.descant.on.ca. Quarterly. Circ.: 2,000.

Karen Mulhallen, Editor. **Description:** New and established writers and artists from Canada and around the globe. Considers original, unpublished submissions of poetry, short stories, essays, plays, interviews, musical scores, novel excerpts, and visual arts. **Tips:** Does not accept simultaneous submissions. Send hard copy; does not accept electronic submissions. **Response:** SASE required.

THE DISTILLERY
Motlow State Community College
P.O. Box 8500, Lynchburg, TN 37352-8500. 931-393-1700.
Web site: www.mscc.cc.tn.vs/distillery/. Semiannual. $9/$15. Circ.: 750. Dawn Copeland, Editor. **Description:** Poetry, fiction, nonfiction, art, and photography. **Fiction:** Literary, emphasis on style, character, voice; 4,000 words. **Nonfiction:** Creative nonfiction, with a sense of style. Critical and personal essays; 4,000 words. **Poetry:** Voice, style, and image; any length. **Art:** Slides. **Tips:** Avoid warmed-over exercises in K-mart realism. **Queries:** Not necessary. **E-Queries:** No. **Unsolicited mss:** Accepts. **Response:** Submissions 2-4 months, SASE. **Rights:** FNAR. **Payment:** In copies.

DOUBLE DEALER REDUX
The Pirate's Alley Faulkner Society
Faulkner House, 624 Pirate's Alley, New Orleans, LA 70116. 504-586-1609.
E-mail: faulkhouse@aol.com. Web site: www.wordsandmusic.org. Annual. Circ.: 7,500. Rosemary James, Supervising Editor. **Description:** Poems, short stories, essays, and critical reviews, also portions of novels/novellas. **Tips:** Has published entire novellas. **Queries:** Preferred. **Unsolicited mss:** Does not accept. **Payment:** In copies.

DOUBLETAKE
See full listing in Arts & Architecture category.

ELEMENTS
3534 Chimira Ln., Houston, TX 77051. 713-614-8389.
E-mail: bernard_washington@hotmail.com. Bimonthly. $25/yr. Circ.: 500. Bernard Washington, Publisher/Editor. **Description:** A fresh perspective on current events, literature and the arts. Short stories, poetry, and nonfiction pieces on sports, current events, and music. **Fiction:** 1,500 words max. **Nonfiction:** 1,500 words max. **Poetry:** 500 words. **Fillers:** 200 words. **Tips:** "Write well; be entertaining. All writing should stand out for its clarity and style." **Queries:** Not necessary. **E-Queries:** No. **Unsolicited mss:** Accepts. **Response:** 1 month, SASE. **Freelance Content:** 100%. **Rights:** FNAR.

ELYSIAN FIELDS QUARTERLY
See full listing in Sports & Recreation/Outdoors category.

EPOCH

Cornell University, 251 Goldwin Smith Hall, Ithaca, NY 14853-3201. 607-255-3385. Tri-annual. $6.50/$11. Circ.: 1,000. Michael Koch, Editor. **Description:** Serious fiction, poetry, and personal essays. Pays $5-$10/page. **Queries:** Not necessary. **E-Queries:** No. **Unsolicited mss:** Accepts. **Response:** 4-6 weeks, SASE required. **Freelance Content:** 100%. **Rights:** FNAR. **Payment:** On publication.

EUREKA LITERARY MAGAZINE

Eureka College, 300 E College Ave., Eureka, IL 61530. 309-467-6336. E-mail: llogsdon@eureka.com. Biannual. $7.50/issue. Circ.: 500. Loren Logsdon, Editor. **Description:** Well-written, thought-provoking stories (2-28 pages) and poetry (any length). **Queries:** Not necessary. **E-Queries:** Yes. **Unsolicited mss:** Accepts. **Response:** Queries 2-3 weeks, submissions 4-5 months, SASE required. **Freelance Content:** 100%. **Rights:** One-time. **Payment:** In copies.

EVENT

Douglas College

P.O. Box 2503, New Westminster, British Columbia V3L 5B2 Canada. 604-527-5293. E-mail: event@douglas.bc.ca. Web site: http://event/douglas.bc.ca. 3x/yr. $8/$22. Circ.: 1,250. Cathy Stonehouse, Editor. **Description:** Fiction, poetry, and creative nonfiction. **Fiction:** Readable, stylish, with well-handled characters and strong point of view; submit up to 2 short stories, 5,000 words max; $22/page ($500 max). **Nonfiction:** Personal essays, memoirs, travel accounts, literary; 5,000 words max; $22/page ($500 max). **Poetry:** Appreciate strong narrative, sometimes confessional modes. Eclectic, open to content that invites involvement; submit 3-8 poems. **Art:** For cover only; $150. **Tips:** Accepts e-mail queries, but does not accept e-mail submissions. **Queries:** Not necessary. **E-Queries:** Yes. **Unsolicited mss:** Accepts. **Response:** 1-6 months, SASE required (IRCs). **Freelance Content:** 85%. **Rights:** FNASR. **Payment:** On publication.

EXQUISITE CORPSE

P.O. Box 25051, Baton Rouge, LA 70802. E-mail: submissions@corpse.org. Web site: www.corpse.org. Andrei Codrescu, Editor. **Description:** Fiction, nonfiction, and poetry for "a journal of letters and life." B&W photos and drawings. Read the magazine before submitting. **Tips:** Send all material via e-mail. Does not accept hard copy. See Web site for updated submission guidelines. **Queries:** Required.

FICTION

The City College of New York

English Dept., Convent Ave. at 138th St., New York, NY 10031. 212-650-6319. E-mail: fictionmagazine@yahoo.com. Web site: www.fictioninc.com. 2-3x/yr. $10/issue, $38/4 issues. Circ.: 1,700. Mark Jay Mirsky, Editor. **Description:** Short fiction from new and published authors. Seeks material that is new and experimental. **Tips:** Manuscripts not accepted May 15-September 1. **Queries:** Not necessary.

E-Queries: No. **Unsolicited mss:** Accepts. **Response:** Queries to 1 month, submissions 4-6 months, SASE. **Freelance Content:** 100%. **Rights:** All.

FIELD
Oberlin College Press, 10 N Professor St., Oberlin, OH 44074. 440-775-8124.
E-mail: oc.press@oberlin.edu. Web site: www.oberlin.edu/~ocpress. Bi-annual. $14/yr. Circ.: 1,250. David Young, David Walker, Martha Collins, Pamela Alexander, Editors. **Description:** Contemporary poetry, poetics, and translations. Seeks to be at forefront of what is happening in poetry. Fall issue features symposium on a famous writer. **Poetry:** Varied formats, length. Submit 3-5 poems; pays $15/page, plus copies and subscription. **Tips:** Accepts queries via e-mail, but not submissions. **E-Queries:** Yes. **Unsolicited mss:** Does not accept. **Response:** 1-6 weeks, SASE required. **Payment:** On publication. **Contact:** Linda Slocum, Managing Editor.

FINE MADNESS
P.O. Box 31138, Seattle, WA 98103-1138.
E-mail: beastly@oz.net. Web site: www.finemadness.org. Annual. $5/$9. Circ.: 1,000. **Description:** International poetry by writers, well-known and new, highly original in language and content. **Poetry:** Form open, strong sense of language, original imagery. **Tips:** No simultaneous submissions. "Avoid concrete poetry, light verse, topical poetry, or over-dependence on form. We prefer lyrical poems that use language in thoughtful and thought-provoking ways." **Queries:** Preferred. **E-Queries:** Yes. **Unsolicited mss:** Accepts. **Response:** Queries 1-2 months, submissions 3-4 months, SASE required. **Freelance Content:** 100%.

FIRST INTENSITY
P.O. Box 665, Lawrence, KS 66044-0665. 785-479-1501.
E-mail: leechapman@aol.com. Ms. Lee Chapman, Editor. **Description:** Poetry, short fiction, prose poetry, book reviews, interviews. Essays on poetics, writing, writers, visual artists. **Fiction:** 10 pages max. **Poetry:** 10 pages max. **Tips:** Seeking serious, experimental work, nothing "mainstream." **Queries:** Not necessary. **E-Queries:** Yes. **Unsolicited mss:** Accepts. **Response:** Queries 2 weeks, submissions 8-10 weeks, SASE required. **Freelance Content:** 50%. **Payment:** In copies.

THE FIRST LINE
P.O. Box 0382, Plano, TX 75025.
E-mail: submission@thefirstline.com. Web site: www.thefirstline.com. Quarterly. $3/$10. Circ.: 250. David LaBounty, Jeff Adams, Editors. **Description:** Celebrates the first line. **Fiction:** All stories stem from the same first line (see Web Site); 300-1,500 words. **Nonfiction:** Essays about a first line from book/story; 300-1,000 words. **Queries:** Not necessary. **E-Queries:** Yes. **Unsolicited mss:** Accepts. **Response:** 2-6 weeks; SASE required. **Freelance Content:** 100%. **Rights:** FNAR, first electronic, first anthology. **Payment:** $5/story and 1 copy. **Contact:** Robin LaBounty.

FIVE POINTS

Georgia State University

MSC 8R0318, 33 Gilmer St. SE, Unit 8, Atlanta, GA 30303-3083.

Web site: www.webdelsol.com/Five_Points. 3x/yr. $7/$20. Circ.: 2,000. David Bottoms, Editor. **Description:** Quality fiction, poetry, essays, and interviews. Writing must have original voice, substance, and significance. **Fiction:** 7,500 words; $15/page, $250 max. **Nonfiction:** Personal essays, literary essays, and creative nonfiction; 7,500 words; $15/page, $250 max. **Poetry:** 100 lines max per poem; $50/poem. **Art:** Photos (slides or prints) only. Paintings/illustrations sometimes considered. Pay varies. **Tips:** "No limitations on style or contents. Our only criterion is excellence. Publishes distinctive, intelligent writing that has something to say and maintains our attention." Reading period between September 1-April 30. **Queries:** Not necessary. **E-Queries:** No. **Unsolicited mss:** Accepts. **Response:** 2-3 months, SASE required. **Freelance Content:** 10%. **Rights:** FNAR. **Payment:** On publication.

FLINT HILLS REVIEW

Bluestem Press, Emporia State University

Dept. of English, Box 4019, Emporia, KS 66801-5087. 316-341-5216.

E-mail: webbamy@emporia.edu. Web site: www.emporia.edu/fhr. Annual. $5.50/issue. Circ.: 500. Amy Sage Webb, Philip Heldrich, Editors. **Description:** Writing from and about Kansas and the Great Plains region, with a strong sense of place. **Fiction:** Place-focused writing about or set in the region. **Nonfiction:** Interviews, essays. **Poetry:** Strong imagery. **Tips:** No genre fiction, religious writing. For critical essays or interviews, query first. **Queries:** Not necessary. **E-Queries:** Yes. **Unsolicited mss:** Accepts. **Response:** 2 months queries, 6 months submissions, SASE. **Freelance Content:** 5%. **Rights:** 1st. **Payment:** In copies.

FLYWAY LITERARY REVIEW

Iowa State University, 206 Ross Hall, Ames, IA 50011.

E-mail: flyway@iastate.edu.

Web site: www.engl.iastate.edu/publications/flyway/homepage.html. Tri-annual. $18/yr. Circ.: 500. Stephen Pett, Editor. **Description:** Poetry, nonfiction, and fiction by new and established writers. **Fiction:** Literary fiction; up to 20 pages. **Nonfiction:** Personal essays; up to 20 pages. **Poetry:** Ambitious; "open to all poetry that takes its experience seriously, including humorous poems." **Queries:** Not necessary. **E-Queries:** No. **Unsolicited mss:** Accepts. **Response:** 2 weeks, SASE. **Freelance Content:** 90%. **Rights:** One-time. **Payment:** In copies.

THE FOLIATE OAK

University of Arkansas, Arts and Humanities, Monticello, AR 71656. 870-460-1247. E-mail: foliateoak@uamont.edu. Web site: www.uamont.edu/foliateoak/. Monthly. Diane Payne, Faculty Advisor. **Description:** For new and established writers. Accepts submissions electronically, September-May. **Fiction:** No genre, racist, homophobic, maudlin writing; to 3,500 words. **Nonfiction:** Creative nonfiction to

3,500 words. **Poetry:** Submit up to 5 poems. **E-Queries:** Yes. **Response:** 1 month. **Payment:** In copies.

FOLIO
American University, Dept. of Literature, Washington, DC 20016. Bi-annual. $12/yr. Circ.: 500. **Description:** Quality fiction, creative nonfiction, memoirs, poetry, and B&W photos. Prose to 3,500 words, poetry to 5 poems. **Tips:** Submissions read September 1-March 1. **Queries:** Not necessary. **E-Queries:** No. **Unsolicited mss:** Accepts. **Response:** 2-6 months, SASE required. **Freelance Content:** 90%. **Payment:** In copies.

THE FORMALIST
320 Hunter Dr., Evansville, IN 47711. $7.50/$14 (2 issues). William Baer, Editor. **Description:** Well-crafted poetry in contemporary idiom which uses meter and traditional poetic conventions in vigorous and interesting ways. Especially interested in sonnets, couplets, tercets, ballads, the French forms, etc. Also, metrical translations of major, formalist, non-English poets. Does not accept haiku, sestinas, or syllabic verse. No erotica, blasphemy, vulgarity, or racism. No simultaneous submissions, previously published work, or disk submissions. Submit 3-5 poems at one time with SASE. **Tips:** Offers Howard Nemerov Sonnet Award, $1,000. **Queries:** Not necessary. **Response:** 8 weeks, SASE required. **Payment:** In copies.

FOURTEEN HILLS
San Francisco State University, Creative Writing Dept. 1600 Holloway Ave., San Francisco, CA 94132-1722. 415-338-3083. E-mail: hills@sfsu.edu. Biannual. $7/issue, $12/yr. Circ.: 600. Julian Kudritzki, Editor-in-Chief. **Description:** Innovative fiction, poetry, drama, and interviews. Seeking matter or styles overlooked by traditional journals. **Fiction:** Up to 5,000 words. **Poetry:** Submit up to 5 poems. **Queries:** Not necessary. **E-Queries:** No. **Unsolicited mss:** Accepts. **Response:** Queries 2 weeks, submissions up to 10 months. **Rights:** FNAR. **Payment:** In copies.

FROGPOND
Haiku Society of America, P.O. Box 2461, Winchester, VA 22604-1661. 540-722-2156. E-mail: redmoon@shentel.net; ithacan@earthlink.net. Web site: www.hsa-haiku.org. 3x/yr. $28/yr (US). Circ.: 1,000. Jim Kacian, Editor. **Description:** Features haiku and related forms; $1/poem. Also articles, essays, and reviews. **Tips:** Know what is current in contemporary haiku. "The largest Haiku journal outside of Japan." **E-Queries:** Yes. **Unsolicited mss:** Accepts. **Response:** 2-3 weeks, SASE required. **Freelance Content:** 95%. **Rights:** FNAR. **Payment:** On acceptance.

FUGUE
University of Idaho
English Dept., Brink Hall, Room 200, Moscow, ID 83844-1102.

E-mail: ronmcf@uidaho.edu. Web site: www.uidaho.edu/ls/eng/fugue. Semiannual. $6/$10. Circ.: 300. Scott McEachern, Managing Editor. **Description:** New voices and quality writing. **Fiction:** Well-written, traditional or experimental; up to 6,000 words; $20. **Nonfiction:** Creative nonfiction; up to 6,000 words; $20. **Poetry:** Any length and topic; submit up to 4 poems at a time; $10. **Art:** Seeking cover art; $50. **Tips:** "Don't send more than one genre together." **Queries:** Not necessary. **E-Queries:** No. **Unsolicited mss:** Accepts. **Response:** Queries 2 weeks, submissions 2-4 months, SASE required. **Freelance Content:** 20%. **Rights:** One-time, reverts with credit. **Payment:** On publication.

FUTURES MYSTERIOUS ANTHOLOGY
3039 38th Ave. S, Minneapolis, MN 55406-2140. 612-724-4023.
E-mail: babs@suspenseunlimited.net. Web site: www.fmam.biz. Quarterly. Circ.: 3,500. **Description:** Short fiction, primarily mystery, also horror, sci-fi, some literary, poetry, and games. Most stories run 500-12,000 words. **Art:** Illustrations and cartoons. **Tips:** "We seek writers and artists with the fire to fly!" Read sample issue; check guidelines before submitting. **Queries:** Not necessary. **Freelance Content:** 99%. **Contact:** Barbara (Babs) Lakey, Publisher; RC Hildebrandt, Poetry Editor; Earl Staggs, Senior Fiction Editor.

THE GEORGIA REVIEW
University of Georgia, Athens, GA 30602-9009. 706-542-3481.
E-mail: garev@uga.edu. Web site: www.uga.edu/garev. Quarterly. $9/issue. Circ.: 5,500. T.R. Hummer, Editor. **Description:** An eclectic blend of essays, fiction, poetry, book reviews, and visual art. **Fiction:** Short stories, no novel excerpts; $40/page. **Nonfiction:** Essays, no book chapters; $40/page. **Poetry:** $3/line. **Art:** Cover plus 8-page interior portfolio, each issue; $450 for the 9 images. **Tips:** Accepts material between August 16-May 14 only. Query for book reviews, send complete manuscript for all else. **E-Queries:** No. **Response:** Queries 1-2 weeks, submissions 1-3 months, SASE required. **Freelance Content:** 80%. **Payment:** On publication.

GETTYSBURG REVIEW
Gettysburg College, Gettysburg, PA 17325. 717-337-6770.
Web site: www.gettysburgreview.com. Quarterly. $6/$24. Circ.: 3,500. Peter Stitt, Editor. **Description:** Quality poetry, fiction, essays, essay reviews, and graphics by new and established writers and artists. **Fiction:** Literary fiction, fresh and surprising, including novel excerpts; 1,000-20,000 words; $25/printed page. **Nonfiction:** Varied (memoir, literary criticism, creative nonfiction, other); 3,000-7,000 words; $25/printed page. **Poetry:** All styles and forms; $2/line. **Tips:** Mss read Sept.-May. **Queries:** Not necessary. **E-Queries:** No. **Unsolicited mss:** Accepts. **Response:** 2-3 weeks for queries, 3-6 months for submissions; SASE required. **Freelance Content:** 100%. **Rights:** FNASR. **Payment:** On publication. **Contact:** Mark Drew, Assistant Editor.

GLIMMER TRAIN STORIES

710 SW Madison St., Suite 504, Portland, OR 97205. 503-221-0836.
E-mail: info@glimmertrain.com. Web site: www.glimmertrain.com. Quarterly.
$9.95/$32. Circ.: 18,000. Linda Burmeister Davies, Editor. **Description:** Short stories by established and emerging writers —"a feast of fiction." **Fiction:** Literary short stories; 1,200-8,000 words; $500/story. **Tips:** All stories must be submitted online; see Web site for submission guidelines. **Queries:** Not necessary. **E-Queries:** No. **Unsolicited mss:** Accepts. **Response:** 3 months, SASE required. **Freelance Content:** 100%. **Rights:** First publication. **Payment:** On acceptance.

GLOBAL CITY REVIEW

Simon H. Rifkind Center for the Humanities, The City College of New York
138th St. & Convent Ave., New York, NY 10031. 212-650-7382.
E-mail: globalcityreview@aol.com. Web site: http://webdelsol.com/globalcityreview.
Biannual. Linsey Abrams, Editor. **Description:** Intellectual literary forum for women, lesbian, and gay, and other culturally diverse writers; writers of color, international writers, activist writers. Thematic issues. Fiction, nonfiction, and poetry on issues of race, gender, and women's experience. **Tips:** No queries; see Web site for guidelines. **Payment:** In copies.

GRAIN

Saskatchewan Writers Guild
P.O. Box 67, Saskatoon, Saskatchewan S7K 3K1 Canada. 306-244-2828.
E-mail: grain@sasktel.net. Web site: www.grainmagazine.com. Quarterly.
$9.95/$26.95. Circ.: 1,500. Elizabeth Philips, Editor. **Description:** Canadian literary magazine; original work only (no reprints). New, emerging writers and established writers from Canada and around the world. **Fiction:** Literary fiction, any style, well-crafted stories; to 30 pages. No mainstream romance, historical fiction. **Nonfiction:** Creative nonfiction; to 30 pages. **Poetry:** Submit up to 8 poems. Avoid avant garde, but can push boundaries. Favors thoughtful work that takes risks. **Tips:** "We prefer imaginative fiction, even quirky. Common flaws: a lack of understanding of and attention to a story's subtext; expository writing; a lack of deftness with language and form." **Queries:** Not necessary. **Unsolicited mss:** Accepts. **Response:** 3 months, include SASE or e-mail address for reply. **Freelance Content:** 100%. **Rights:** 1st Canadian serial. **Payment:** On publication.

GRAND STREET

214 Sullivan St., 6C, New York, NY 10012. 212-533-2944.
E-mail: info@grandstreet.com. Web site: www.grandstreet.com. Quarterly. Jean Stein, Editor. **Description:** Art, fiction, nonfiction, and poetry. **Poetry:** Any length; $3/line. **Queries:** Not necessary. **E-Queries:** No. **Unsolicited mss:** Does not accept. **Response:** Queries 7 days, submissions 12-16 weeks, SASE. **Payment:** On publication.

GRASSLANDS REVIEW

P.O. Box 626, Berea, OH 44017.
E-mail: grasslandsreview@aol.com. Web site: http://grasslandsreview.blogspot.com.
Semiannual. $12/yr. Laura Kennelly, Editor. **Description:** Encourages new writers.
Seeks "imagination without sloppiness, ideas without lectures, and delight in language." Short stories 1,000-3,500 words. Poetry any length. **Tips:** Accepts manuscripts postmarked March or October only. **Queries:** Not necessary. **Response:**
SASE. **Payment:** In copies.

GREEN MOUNTAINS REVIEW

Johnson State College, Johnson, VT 05656. 802-635-1350.
E-mail: gmr@badger.jsc.vsc.edu. Biannual. $7/$14. Circ.: 1,700. **Description:**
Poems, stories, and creative nonfiction by well-known and promising new authors.
Also, interviews, literary criticism, and book reviews. **Fiction:** Wide range of styles
and subjects; to 30 pages. **Nonfiction:** Interviews with writers and literary essays; to
30 pages. **Poetry:** Any type. **Art:** B&W photos. **Tips:** Publishes 2% of submissions.
Occasionally features special-theme issues. **Queries:** Not necessary. **E-Queries:** No.
Unsolicited mss: Accepts. **Response:** 3-6 months, SASE required. **Freelance
Content:** 80%. **Rights:** FNASR. **Payment:** In copies. **Contact:** Neil Shepard,
Poetry Editor; Tony Whedon, Fiction Editor.

THE GREENSBORO REVIEW

University of North Carolina at Greensboro, MFA Writing Program
Dept. of English, 134 McIver Bldg., P.O. Box 26170, Greensboro, NC 27402-6170.
E-mail: jlclark@uncg.edu. Web site: www.uncg.edu/eng/mfa/review/review.htm.
Semi-annual. $5/$10. Circ.: 800. Jim Clark, Editor. **Description:** Quality fiction (any
theme/subject/style, to 7,500 words) and poetry (style and length varies). **Tips:**
Original work only; no multiple submissions. **Queries:** Not necessary. **E-Queries:**
No. **Unsolicited mss:** Accepts. **Rights:** FNASR. **Payment:** In copies.

GULF COAST

University of Houston, English Dept., Houston, TX 77204. 713-743-3223.
E-mail: editors@gulfcoastmag.org. Web site: www.gulfcoastmag.org. Biannual.
$7/issue. Circ.: 1,000. Pablo Peschiera, Editor. **Description:** A journal of literary fiction, nonfiction, poetry, and fine art. **Queries:** Not necessary. **E-Queries:** Yes.
Unsolicited mss: Accepts. **Response:** 3-6 months, SASE required.

HARP-STRINGS

P.O. Box 640387, Beverly Hills, FL 34464.
E-mail: verdure@digitalusa.net. Quarterly. $3.50/$12. Circ.: 105. Madelyn Eastlund,
Editor. **Description:** Seeks **Poetry:** narrative, lyrics, ballads, sestinas, rondeau
redoubles, blank verse, villanelles, sonnets, prose poems, etc. 14-80 lines. **Tips:** No
trite, broken prose masquerading as poetry; no confessions or raw-guts poems. No
simultaneous submissions. Reads only in February, May, July, and November.

Queries: Not necessary. **E-Queries:** Yes. **Unsolicited mss:** Accepts. **Freelance Content:** 100%. **Rights:** One-time and electronic. **Payment:** In copies.

HAWAI'I REVIEW

University of Hawaii
Dept. of English, 1733 Donaggho Rd., Honolulu, HI 96822. 808-956-3030.
E-mail: hi-review@hawaii.edu. Web site: www.hawaii.edu/bop/hr.html. Bi-annual. $10/issue. Circ.: 1,000. Michael Pulelua, Editor. **Description:** Literary poetry, fiction, nonfiction, and reviews. **Fiction:** Up to 20 pages. **Nonfiction:** Up to 20 pages. **Tips:** Submissions accepted year-round. **Queries:** Not necessary. **E-Queries:** Yes. **Unsolicited mss:** Accepts. **Response:** Queries 2-3 weeks submissions 3-6 months, SASE required. **Rights:** FNAR.

HAYDEN'S FERRY REVIEW

Arizona State University, P.O. Box 871502, Tempe, AZ 85287-1502. 480-965-1243.
E-mail: hfr@asu.edu. Web site: www.haydensferryreview.com. Biannual. $5/$10. Circ.: 1,300. **Description:** Art, poetry, fiction, and creative nonfiction by new and established artists and writers. Pays $25/page ($100 max). Submit no more than 6 poems. **Tips:** Accepts queries via e-mail, but not submissions. **Queries:** Not necessary. **E-Queries:** Yes. **Unsolicited mss:** Accepts. **Response:** Queries 1 week, submissions 8-12 weeks, SASE required. **Freelance Content:** 80%. **Rights:** NA serial. **Payment:** On publication. **Contact:** Poetry or Fiction Editor.

HEAVEN BONE

P.O. Box 486, Chester, NY 10918.
E-mail: heavenbone@aol.com. Annual. $10/issue. Circ.: 2,500. Steve Hirsch, Editor. **Description:** Poetry, fiction, reviews, and artwork with emphasis on surreal, beat, experimental, and Buddhist concerns. **Fiction:** 2,500-10,000 words. **Nonfiction:** Essays on creativity, philosophy, and consciousness studies, relating to writing; 7,500 words. **Poetry:** Surreal, experimental, visual, neo-beat, and Buddhist imagery and themes. **Art:** Any digital or traditional format. **Tips:** "Despite 'Heaven' in title, we are not a religious publication." **Queries:** Preferred. **E-Queries:** Yes. **Unsolicited mss:** Accepts. **Response:** 3 weeks for queries, up to 1 year for submissions; SASE required. **Rights:** FNASR. **Payment:** In copies.

THE HOLLINS CRITIC

Hollins University, P.O. Box 9538, Roanoke, VA 24020. 540-362-6275.
E-mail: acockrell@hollins.edu. Web site: www.hollins.edu. 5x/yr. $6/issue. Circ.: 500. R.H.W. Dillard, Editor. **Description:** Features an essay on a contemporary fiction writer, poet, or dramatist (cover sketch, brief biography, and book list). Also book reviews and poetry. Reviews poetry submissions from September-May only. Does accept unsolicited reviews. $25/poem, no pay for book reviews. **Tips:** Sample copy $1.50. **Queries:** Not necessary. **E-Queries:** No. **Unsolicited mss:** Accepts. **Response:** 2 months, SASE required. **Freelance Content:** 100%. **Rights:** FNAR. **Payment:** On publication.

HUDSON REVIEW

684 Park Ave., New York, NY 10021. 212-650-0020.
Web site: www.hudsonreview.com. Quarterly. $8/$28. Circ.: 5,000. Paula Deitz, Editor. **Description:** Fiction, poetry, essays, book reviews; criticism of literature, art, theatre, dance, film, and music; and articles on contemporary culture. **Tips:** Sample copy $8. **Queries:** Preferred. **E-Queries:** No. **Unsolicited mss:** Accepts. **Response:** 3 months, SASE required. **Payment:** On publication.

HURRICANE ALICE

See full listing in Ethnic & Multicultural category.

THE ICONOCLAST

1675 Amazon Rd., Mohegan Lake, NY 10547-1804.
Bimonthly. $2.50/$15. Circ.: 700. Phil Wagner, Editor. **Description:** Original work bypassed by corporate and institutional publications. **Fiction:** Literary stories, plots, and ideas with active characters engaged with the world; 100-3,500 words; $.01/word. **Nonfiction:** Nothing topical, fashionable, political, or academic; 100-3,500 words, $.01/word. **Poetry:** Well-crafted, with something to say; send 2-5 poems; to 2 pages; $2-$5/poem. **Fillers:** Humor (nothing silly, self-consciously zany); 20-2,000 words; $.01/word. **Art:** Line drawings. **Tips:** "Write well, be sincere, act professionally. No manuscripts mass-mailed to other publications at the same time." **Queries:** Not necessary. **E-Queries:** No. **Unsolicited mss:** Accepts. **Response:** Queries 1 week, submissions 1 month, SASE required. **Freelance Content:** 90%. **Rights:** FNASR. **Payment:** On acceptance.

INDIANA REVIEW

Indiana University
Ballantine Hall 465, 1020 E Kirkwood Ave., Bloomington, IN 47405. 812-855-3439.
Web site: www.indiana.edu/~inreview. Semi-annual. $8/$14. Circ.: 2,000. Danit Brown, Editor. **Description:** For emerging and established writers; quality writing within a wide aesthetic. **Fiction:** Daring stories which integrate theme, language, character, and form, with consequence beyond the world of its narrator; up to 40 pages. **Nonfiction:** Lively essays on engaging topics. Interviews with established writers and book reviews; to 30 pages; $5/page and copies. **Poetry:** Intelligent form and language, with risk, ambition, and scope. **Queries:** Not necessary. **E-Queries:** Yes. **Unsolicited mss:** Accepts. **Response:** 1 week to queries, submissions 2-3 months, SASE required. **Freelance Content:** 90%. **Rights:** FNASR. **Payment:** On publication. **Contact:** Poetry or Fiction Editor.

INTERIM

University of Nevada, Dept. of English, Las Vegas, NV 89154-5034.
Annual. Claudia Keelan, Editor. **Description:** Poetry, fiction, essays, and book reviews. **Fiction:** To 7,500 words. **Poetry:** Any form or length. **Response:** 3 weeks. **Payment:** In copies.

INTERNATIONAL POETRY REVIEW

University of North Carolina

Dept. of Romance Languages, Greensboro, NC 27402-6170.

Biannually. Circ.: 200. Kathleen Koestler, Editor. **Description:** Work that crosses language barriers to present the voices of poets in different countries. **Nonfiction:** Book reviews, interviews, and short essays; to 1,500 words. **Poetry:** Original English poems and contemporary translations from other languages. **Tips:** Prefers material with cross-cultural or international dimension. **Queries:** Preferred. **Unsolicited mss:** Accepts. **Payment:** In copies.

IOWA REVIEW

University of Iowa, 308 EPB, Iowa City, IA 52242. 319-335-0462.

E-mail: iowa-review@uiowa.edu. Web site: www.uiowa.edu/~iareview. Tri-annual. $7.95/$20. Circ.: 3,000. David Hamilton, Editor. **Description:** Essays, poems, stories, and reviews. Material can be any length. Pays $25 for first page and $15 for each additional page. **Tips:** "We strive to discover new writers; to be local but not provincial; experimental at times, but not without a respect for tradition." **Queries:** Not necessary. **E-Queries:** Accepts. **Unsolicited mss:** Accepts. **Response:** 1-4 months, SASE required. **Freelance Content:** 98%. **Rights:** FNASR. **Payment:** On publication.

THE IRISH EDITION

See full listing in Ethnic & Multicultural category.

THE JAMES WHITE REVIEW

See full listing in Gay & Lesbian category.

JOURNAL OF NEW JERSEY POETS

The Center for Teaching Excellence, County College of Morris

214 Center Grove Rd., Randolph, NJ 07869-2086. 973-328-5471.

E-mail: szulauf@ccm.edu.

Web site: www.ccm.edu/humanities/humanities/journal/html.

Annual. $10/issue. Circ.: 900. Sander Zulauf, Editor. **Description:** The works of poets and artists who live or have lived in New Jersey. **Nonfiction:** Essays on poetry; book reviews on new work by New Jersey poets; to 1,500 words. **Poetry:** Send up to 3 poems at a time (no epics). **Tips:** New Jersey not required as subject matter. "We seek mature, accomplished work appealing to a large audience." **Queries:** Not necessary. **E-Queries:** No. **Unsolicited mss:** Accepts. **Response:** Queries 2 weeks, submissions 6-12 months, SASE required. **Freelance Content:** 100%. **Rights:** FNASR. **Payment:** In copies.

JUBILAT

University of Massachusetts

Dept. of English, Bartlett 482, Amherst, MA 01003-0515.

Web site: www.jubilat.org. $6/issue. Robert N. Casper, Publisher. **Description:** Poetry, art, and short nonfiction. No short stories. Send one prose piece and/or 3-5 poems; please mail genres separately. **Nonfiction:** On poetry or other subjects. **Poetry:** 3-5 poems. **Art:** Slide, disk. **Tips:** Read a sample copy before submitting. No electronic submissions. **Unsolicited mss:** Accepts. **Response:** 3-5 months; SASE required.

KALEIDOSCOPE

See full listing in Abilities category.

KALLIOPE

Florida Community College at Jacksonville
11901 Beach Blvd., Jacksonville, FL 32246. 904-646-2081.
Web site: www.fccj.org/kalliope. Semiannual. $16/yr. Circ.: 1,600. Mary Sue Koeppel, Editor. **Description:** Women's literature and art with poetry, short fiction, interviews, reviews, and visual art by women. **Fiction:** Well-constructed literary work; 2,000 words. **Nonfiction:** Interviews with writers and/or artists; 200-2,000 words. **Poetry:** 3-4 pages. **Art:** Fine art, slides, or glossies. **Queries:** Not necessary. **E-Queries:** No. **Unsolicited mss:** Accepts. **Response:** Queries 1-3 weeks, submissions 3-6 months, SASE. **Freelance Content:** 100%. **Rights:** 1st. **Payment:** In copies.

KARAMU

Eastern Illinois University
English Dept., Charleston, IL 61920. 217-581-6297.
Annual. $7.50. Circ.: 500. Olga Abella, Editor. **Description:** Poetry, fiction, and creative nonfiction. **Fiction:** Stories that capture something essential about life, beyond the superficial, and develop genuine voices; 3,500 words. **Nonfiction:** Any subject except religion and politics; 3,500 words. **Poetry:** Yes. **Tips:** Avoid rhyming poetry or didactic prose. Recent sample copies available for $7.50; back issues 2 for $6. **Queries:** Preferred. **E-Queries:** No. **Unsolicited mss:** Accepts. **Response:** Queries 2-3 days, submissions 4-6 months, SASE required. **Freelance Content:** 100%. **Rights:** One-time. **Payment:** In copies.

KELSEY REVIEW

Mercer County Community College
P.O. Box B, Trenton, NJ 08690. 609-586-4800 x3326.
E-mail: kelsey.review@mccc.edu. Web site: www.mccc.edu. Annual. Circ.: 2,000. Robin Schore, Editor. **Description:** Literary journal exclusively for writers living or working in Mercer Country, New Jersey. Features fiction, essays, poetry, and B&W line art. Submit prose up to 2,000 words, poetry up to 6 poems. **Queries:** Not necessary. **Unsolicited mss:** Accepts. **Response:** Deadline May 1. Responds by June 30. **Freelance Content:** 100%. **Rights:** None. **Payment:** In copies.

THE KENYON REVIEW

104 College Dr., Gambier, OH 43022-9623. 740-427-5208.
E-mail: kenyonreview@kenyon.edu. Web site: www.kenyonreview.org. 3x/yr. $8/issue; $12 for double summer/fall issue. Circ.: 5,000. Meg Galipault, Managing Editor.

Description: New writing from emerging and established writers. Short fiction and essays: to 7,500 words; $10/page. **Poetry:** to 10 pages; $15/page. Plays: to 35 pages; $10/page. Excerpts: to 35 pages from larger works; $10/page. Translations of poetry and short prose; $10/page. **Tips:** "Due to editorial sabbatical, work received after March 31, 2003, will not be read until September 1, 2004." **Queries:** Not necessary. **E-Queries:** No. **Response:** 1-4 months, SASE required. **Freelance Content:** 90%. **Rights:** First. **Payment:** On publication. **Contact:** David H. Lynn, Editor.

THE KIT-CAT REVIEW
244 Halstead Ave., Harrison, NY 10528. 914-835-4833.
Quarterly. $7/$25. Circ.: 500. Claudia Fletcher, Editor. **Description:** Seeks excellence and originality, fiction and nonfiction, poetry. **Tips:** Avoid O. Henry-type endings. Sample copy $7. **Queries:** Not necessary. **E-Queries:** No. **Unsolicited mss:** Accepts. **Response:** 2-4 week, SASE required. **Freelance Content:** 100%. **Rights:** 1st, one-time. **Payment:** On acceptance.

THE LAUREL REVIEW
Greentower Press, Northwest Missouri State University
Dept. of English, Maryville, MO 64468. 816-562-1265.
Semiannual. Circ.: 900. Nancy Mayer, Co-editor. **Description:** Features poetry, fiction, and creative nonfiction. Reads between September-May. **Response:** 1 week-4 months. **Payment:** In copies.

THE LEDGE
78-44 80th St., Glendale, NY 11385.
Annual. $8.95/issue. Circ.: 1,200. Timothy Monaghan, Editor. **Description:** Seeks exceptional contemporary poetry. No restrictions on style or form. **Poetry:** Up to 80 lines; pay in copies. **Queries:** Not necessary. **E-Queries:** No. **Unsolicited mss:** Accepts. **Response:** Queries 2-3 weeks, submissions 3 months, SASE. **Freelance Content:** 100%. **Rights:** FNASR. **Payment:** On publication.

LIGHT
P.O. Box 7500, Chicago, IL 60680. 847-853-1028.
Web site: www.lightquarterly.com. Quarterly. $6/$20. Circ.: 1,000. John Mella, Editor. **Description:** Devoted exclusively to light verse. Also features some reviews and essays. **Tips:** "Think James Thurber, E.B.White, Ogden Nash, etc. If it has wit, point, edge, or barb, it has a home here." See Web site for submission guidelines. **Queries:** Preferred. **E-Queries:** No. **Unsolicited mss:** Accepts. **Response:** Queries 1-4 months. **Payment:** In copies.

LITERAL LATTE
61 E Eighth St., Suite 240, New York, NY 10003.
E-mail: litlatte@aol.com. Web site: www.literal-latte.com. Bimonthly. $3/$11. Circ.: 25,000. Jenine Gordon Bockman, Editor. **Description:** Mind-stimulating literary

journal brimming with stories, poetry, essays, and art. **Fiction:** Varied styles; the word is as important as the tale; 6,000 words. **Nonfiction:** Personal essays, all topics; thematic book reviews done as personal essays; 6,000 words. **Poetry:** All styles; 2,000 word max. **Fillers:** Intelligent literary cartoons. **Art:** Photocopies or slides (of photos, drawings, paintings, B&W or color). Open to styles, abstraction to photorealism. **Tips:** Looking for new talent. **Queries:** Not necessary. **E-Queries:** Accepts. **Unsolicited mss:** Accepts. **Rights:** FNASR. **Payment:** On publication.

THE LITERARY REVIEW

Fairleigh Dickinson University, Mail Code M-GH2-01
285 Madison Ave., Madison, NJ 07940. 973-443-8564.
E-mail: tlr@fdu.edu. Web site: www.theliteraryreview.org. Quarterly. $7/issue. Circ.: 2,000. Rene Steinke, Editor. **Description:** International journal of poetry, fiction, essays, and contemporary reviews. Prose any length, poetry up to 5 poems. **Tips:** Submissions read between September 1 and May 31 only. **Queries:** Not necessary. **E-Queries:** Yes. **Unsolicited mss:** Accepts. **Response:** Queries 1 week, submissions 12-16 weeks, SASE required. **Rights:** FNAR. **Payment:** In copies.

LONG SHOT

P.O. Box 6238, Hoboken, NJ 07030.
Web site: www.longshot.org. Semiannual. $8/issue, $24/2 yr. (4 issues). Circ.: 1,500. Editorial Board. **Description:** Raw, graphic, exuberant poetry devoid of pretense. **Fiction:** To 10 pages. **Nonfiction:** To 10 pages. **Poetry:** To 8 pages. **Art:** B&W photos, drawings. **Queries:** Not necessary. **E-Queries:** No. **Unsolicited mss:** Accepts. **Response:** 8-12 weeks, SASE. **Freelance Content:** 20%. **Payment:** In copies.

THE LONG STORY

18 Eaton St., Lawrence, MA 01843. 978-686-7638.
E-mail: rpburnham@mac.com. Web site: www.longstorymagazine.com. $6/issue. Circ.: 1,000. R.P. Burnham, Editor. **Description:** Stories with a moral/thematic core, particularly about poor and working-class people. 8,000-12,000 words (occasionally to 20,000). **Queries:** Not necessary. **E-Queries:** No. **Unsolicited mss:** Accepts. **Response:** 2 months, SASE required. **Freelance Content:** 95%. **Rights:** FNAR. **Payment:** In copies.

LSR

P.O. Box 440195, Miami, FL 33144. 305-447-3780.
E-mail: ejc@lspress.net. 2x/yr. $6. Circ.: 3,000. Nilda Cepero, Editor/Publisher. **Description:** Poetry, book reviews, interviews, and line art. (Formerly known as *Latino Stuff Review*.) **Nonfiction:** Book reviews or interviews, to 750 words. **Poetry:** Submit up to 4 poems, 5-45 lines each. Style, subject matter, and content open, prefers contemporary with meaning and message. No pornographic, religious, or surreal poetry. **Art:** Line artwork; submit up to 5 illustrations on 3.5-inch disk (to be printed 6 x 6 inches on cover, 8 x 10 on full-page inside). **Tips:** Cover letter required,

include SASE and bio. **Queries:** Not necessary. **E-Queries:** No. **Unsolicited mss:** Accepts. **Response:** 9 months, SASE required. **Freelance Content:** 100%. **Rights:** 1st. **Payment:** 2 copies.

LYNX EYE

Scribblefest Literary Group
542 Mitchell Dr., Los Osos, CA 93402. 805-528-8146.
E-mail: pamccully@aol.com. Quarterly. $7.95/$25. Circ.: 500. Pam McCully, Editor.
Description: Stories, poetry, essays, and B&W artwork in familiar and experimental formats. **Fiction:** Short stories, vignettes, novel excerpts, one-act plays, belles lettres, and satires; 500-5,000 words; $10/piece and copies. **Nonfiction:** Essays only; 500-5,000 words. **Poetry:** 30 lines. **Art:** B&W drawings only. **Queries:** Not necessary. **E-Queries:** No. **Unsolicited mss:** Accepts. **Response:** 12 weeks, SASE required. **Freelance Content:** 100%. **Rights:** FNASR. **Payment:** On acceptance.

MALAHAT REVIEW

University of Victoria
P.O. Box 1700, Stn CSC, Victoria, British Columbia V8W 2Y2 Canada. 250-721-8524.
E-mail: malahat@uvic.ca. Web site: www.malahatreview.com. Quarterly. $10/$30, Canadian. Circ.: 1,000. Marlene Cookshaw, Editor. **Description:** Short fiction, non-fiction, poetry, and reviews of Canadian fiction or books of poetry. Seeks balance of views and styles by established and new writers. Pays $30/page. **Queries:** Not necessary. **E-Queries:** Yes. **Unsolicited mss:** Accepts. **Response:** Up to 3 months, SASE. **Freelance Content:** 100%. **Rights:** 1st worldwide. **Payment:** On acceptance.

MANOA

University of Hawaii Press
English Dept., 1733 Donaghho Rd, Honolulu, HI 96822. 808-956-3070.
E-mail: fstewart@hawaii.edu. Web site: www.hawaii.edu/mjournal. Semiannual. Circ.: 2,500. Frank Stewart, Editor. **Description:** *"A Pacific Journal of International Writing."* Fiction, poetry, translations, essays, interviews, and artwork. **Fiction:** To 30 pages; $20-$25/page. **Nonfiction:** Essays, to 25 pages; book reviews (4-5 pages, pays $50). **Poetry:** Submit 4-6 poems; $50. **Tips:** "Contains a high proportion of international writers; definitely not for beginners." No e-mail submissions. **Queries:** Preferred. **E-Queries:** No. **Payment:** On publication.

MANY MOUNTAINS MOVING

420 22nd St., Boulder, CO 80302. 303-545-9942.
E-mail: mmm@mmminc.org. Web site: www.mmminc.org. 6x/yr. $4/$18. Circ.: 1,500. Naomi Horii, Editor. **Description:** Diverse contemporary voices, from varied cultural backgrounds. Fiction and nonfiction to 20,000 words. Poetry any length, 3-10 poems. No payment offered. **Tips:** Seeking excellent quality work. Accepts unsolicited material May-August only. Contact for upcoming themes. Sample copy $7.50. **Queries:** Not necessary. **E-Queries:** No. **Unsolicited mss:** Accepts. **Response:** Submissions 4 months, SASE. **Freelance Content:** 100%. **Rights:** FNAR.

THE MARLBORO REVIEW

P.O. Box 243, Marlboro, VT 05344.
Web site: www.marlbororeview.com. Biannual. Ellen Dudley, Editor. **Description:** Poetry, fiction, essays, translations, reviews, and interviews. **Fiction:** To 30 pages. **Nonfiction:** Literary/personal essays only; to 30 pages. **Poetry:** Any length. **Art:** For cover; film or camera-ready. **Tips:** Interested in cultural, philosophical, and scientific issues as seen from the writer's perspective. **Queries:** Not necessary. **E-Queries:** Yes. **Unsolicited mss:** Accepts. **Response:** Queries 1 month, submissions to 3 months, SASE. **Freelance Content:** 80%. **Rights:** 1st. **Payment:** In copies.

THE MASSACHUSETTS REVIEW

University of Massachusetts
South College, Amherst, MA 01003-9934. 413-545-2689.
E-mail: massrev@external.umass.edu. Web site: www.massreview.org. Quarterly. **Description:** Fiction, nonfiction, and poetry. **Fiction:** Short fiction; 15-25 pages; $50. **Nonfiction:** Essays, translations, interviews; $50. **Poetry:** $.35/line ($10 minimum). **Tips:** Reviews material October 1-June 1. **Payment:** On publication.

MICHIGAN QUARTERLY REVIEW

University of Michigan
3574 Rackham Bldg., 915 E Washington St., Ann Arbor, MI 48109-1070.
E-mail: mqr@umich.edu. Web site: www.umich.edu/~mqr. Laurence Goldstein, Editor. **Description:** Contemporary fiction, scholarly essays, creative nonfiction, and poetry. Pays $8-$10/page. **Tips:** Send $5 plus 2 first-class stamps for sample copy. **Queries:** Not necessary. **E-Queries:** No. **Unsolicited mss:** Accepts. **Response:** 6 weeks, SASE required. **Payment:** On publication.

MID-AMERICA POETRY REVIEW

P.O. Box 575, Warrensburg, MO 64093-0575. 660-747-4602.
3x/yr. $6/$15. Robert C. Jones, Editor. **Description:** Free verse, lyrical, and narrative poetry. "Many poems focus on pastoral/rural themes or our relationship to the natural world." **Tips:** Send SASE for response only; unaccepted submissions recycled. **Queries:** Not necessary. **E-Queries:** No. **Unsolicited mss:** Accepts. **Response:** 2-4 weeks. **Freelance Content:** 100%. **Rights:** FNAR. **Payment:** 2 copies plus $5 per accepted poem.

MID-AMERICAN REVIEW

Bowling Green State University
Dept. of English, Bowling Green, OH 43403. 419-372-2725.
E-mail: mikeczy@bgnet.bgsu.edu. Web site: www.bgsu.edu/midamericanreview.
2x/yr. Circ.: 2,000. Mike Czyzniejewski, Editor. **Description:** High-quality fiction, 10-20 pages, poetry, articles, translations, reviews of contemporary writing. Fiction, to 5,000 words; pays to $50. Review/articles, 500-2,500 words. **Tips:** Manuscripts read September-May. Query for longer works. **Response:** 1-4 months. **Payment:** In copies.

MINDPRINTS

Allan Hancock College, Learning Assistance Program
800 South College Dr., Santa Maria, CA 93454-6399. 805-922-6966 ext. 3274.
E-mail: pafahey@hancock.cc.ca.us. Annual. $6. Circ.: 500. Paul Fahey, Editor. **Description:** Short fiction, memoirs, poetry, and art for writers and artists with disabilities and those with an interest in this field. Showcases a variety of talent from this diverse population. **Fiction:** Short-short fiction, flash fiction; 250-750 words. **Nonfiction:** Short memoir, creative nonfiction (often disability-related); 250-750 words. **Poetry:** Rhymed and prose; to 35 lines. **Art:** B&W photos and artwork. **Tips:** Accepts simultaneous submissions and reprints. Must include cover letter with the author's reason for submitting to *Mindprints,* a 1-paragraph bio, and list of previous publications (if applicable). Looks for "short pieces with a strong voice, a narrowness of focus and rich detail—works that are brief, profound, and surprising." **Queries:** Not necessary. **E-Queries:** Yes. **Unsolicited mss:** Accepts. **Response:** Queries 1 week, submissions 3 months, SASE. **Rights:** One-time rights. **Payment:** In copies.

THE MINNESOTA REVIEW

University of Missouri
Dept. of English, 110 Tate Hall, Columbia, MO 65211. 573-882-3059.
E-mail: williamsjeff@missouri.edu. Semiannual. $30/2 yr. Circ.: 1,300. Jeffrey Williams, Editor. **Description:** A journal of committed writing, progressive in nature, committed to socialist and feminist writing. (Note: does not have a Minnesota focus; was founded there, but later moved and kept name.) **Fiction:** Political, experimental; to 5,000 words. **Nonfiction:** Essays and reviews. **Poetry:** Political; 1-10 pages. **Tips:** "Many of our issues are organized around a special topic." Sample copy $12. **Queries:** Not necessary. **E-Queries:** No. **Unsolicited mss:** Accepts. **Response:** Queries 2-4 weeks, submissions 4-6 weeks, SASE required. **Freelance Content:** 100%. **Rights:** FNASR. **Payment:** In copies.

THE MIRACULOUS MEDAL

See full listing in Religion category.

MISSISSIPPI REVIEW

Center for Writers, University of Southern Mississippi
Southern Sta., Box 5144, Hattiesburg, MS 39406-5144. 601-266-4321.
E-mail: rief@netdoor.com. Web site: www.mississippireview.com. Frederick Barthelme, Editor. **Description:** Literary journal, poetry and fiction. **Tips:** Annual fiction/poetry competition; deadline, May 31, $1,000 prize.

THE MISSOURI REVIEW

University of Missouri-Columbia
1507 Hillcrest Hall, Columbia, MO 65211. 573-882-4474.
Web site: www.missourireview.org. Tri-annual. $7.95/$22. Circ.: 6,000. Speer Morgan, Editor. **Description:** Contemporary fiction, poetry, interviews, book reviews, and personal essays. **Poetry:** 6-14 pages of poetry by 3-5 poets each issue;

pays $30/page. **Queries:** Not necessary. **E-Queries:** No. **Response:** Submissions 6-8 weeks, SASE. **Freelance Content:** 90%. **Rights:** All; revert to author. **Payment:** On publication.

MODERN HAIKU
Box 68, Lincoln, IL 62656.
Web site: www.modernhaiku.org. 3x/yr. $21/yr. Circ.: 780. Lee Gurga, Editor. **Description:** International journal of English-language haiku and translations, book reviews, articles, and essays. **Nonfiction:** Articles and essays related to haiku; $5/page. **Poetry:** Haiku and senryu; $1/poem. **Tips:** "No sentimental, pretty-pretty, or pseudo-Japanese work. Write about what you actually experience, not about an exotic, imaginary place. Juxtaposition of disparate perceptions that form a harmony is desirable." **Queries:** Not necessary. **E-Queries:** No. **Unsolicited mss:** Accepts. **Response:** 2 weeks, SASE required. **Freelance Content:** 90%. **Rights:** FNAR.

MOTION SICKNESS
4117 SE Division St. #417, Portland, OR 97202.
E-mail: editor@motionsickmag.com. Web site: www.motionsickmag.com. Steve Wilson, Editor. **Description:** Quarterly, with slant towards travel and tourism. Articles, essays, fiction, poetry, and narratives. Also, book reviews, media criticism, art, and cartoons. No destination articles. Features, 500-5,000 words. Pays $.10/word. **Tips:** "Seeks material that addresses the effect tourism has on a region, the change in economy, environment, language, morals, etc. Address travel from the standpoint of immigrants, bus drivers, guest-house employees. We want cultural reportage about the travel and tourism, stories of bad trips, humorous looks at disaster, narratives that experiment with form and style, and accounts of the travels of people from other cultures. Open to different styles and genres, but lean toward the satirical and literary." **Queries:** Not necessary. **Unsolicited mss:** Accepts. **Rights:** FNAR.

MUDLARK
University of North Florida
Dept. of English, 4567 St. Johns Bluff Rd. S, Jacksonville, FL 32224-2645.
E-mail: mudlark@unf.edu. Web site: http://www.unf.edu/mudlark. William Slaughter, Editor. **Description:** Online journal, poetry and nonfiction essays on poetry. "An Electronic Journal of Poetry & Poetics," considers accomplished work anywhere on the spectrum of contemporary practice." **Tips:** Considers simultaneous submissions with notice. No previously published work. "Acceptance rate is low; rejection rate high. The work of hobbyists and lobbyists is not for us. The poem is the thing at Mudlark, and the essay about it." **Queries:** Not necessary. **E-Queries:** Yes. **Unsolicited mss:** Accepts. **Response:** 1-30 days. **Freelance Content:** 100%.

NATURAL BRIDGE
University of Missouri-St. Louis/Dept. of English
8001 Natural Bridge Rd., St. Louis, MO 63121-4499. 314-516-5517.
E-mail: natural@jinx.umsl.edu. Web site: www.umsl.edu/~natural. Biannual. $8/issue.

Ryan Stone, Editor. **Description:** Literary short fiction, personal essays, poetry, and poetry translations. **Tips:** Submission periods are July 1-August 31, and November 1-December 31. Simultaneous submissions accepted. **E-Queries:** No. **Payment:** In copies.

NEBRASKA REVIEW

University of Nebraska-Omaha
Writer's Workshop, FAB 212, Omaha, NE 68182-0324. 402-554-3159.
E-mail: jreed@unomaha.edu. Bi-annual. $8/$15. Circ.: 1,000. James Reed, Editor.
Description: Contemporary fiction, poetry, and creative nonfiction. **Fiction:** Literary mainstream; 7,500 words. **Nonfiction:** Creative nonfiction and personal essays; 7,500 words. **Poetry:** Contemporary, literary; 5-6 pages max. **Tips:** "Eclectic tastes, professional, non-dogmatic; in fiction, we seek strong voices." General inquiries accepted via e-mail, but not submissions. Sample copy $4.50. **Queries:** Not necessary. **E-Queries:** Yes. **Unsolicited mss:** Accepts. **Response:** Submissions 3-6 months, SASE. **Freelance Content:** 100%. **Rights:** FNAR. **Payment:** In copies.

NEW AUTHOR'S JOURNAL

1542 Tibbits Ave., Troy, NY 12180. 518-274-2648.
Quarterly. $4/issue. Mario V. Farina, Editor. **Description:** Short stories and poetry for new authors previously unpublished. **Fiction:** Short stories, up to 2,000 words. **Nonfiction:** Topical nonfiction, up to 2,000 words. **Tips:** Manuscripts read year-round. **Queries:** Not necessary. **Unsolicited mss:** Accepts. **Response:** SASE required. **Rights:** None. **Payment:** In copies.

NEW DELTA REVIEW

Louisiana State University
15 Allen Hall, Dept. of English, Baton Rouge, LA 70803. 225-578-4079.
Web site: http://english.lsu.edu/journals/ndr. Semiannual. $7/$12. Circ.: 500. Brock Hamlin, Ronlyn Domingue, Editors. **Description:** The work of new and established writers. **Fiction:** Short stories; 6,000 words. **Nonfiction:** Creative nonfiction, interviews, reviews (no academic essays); 5,000 words. **Poetry:** Submit up to 4 poems, any length; also translations. **Queries:** Not necessary. **E-Queries:** No. **Unsolicited mss:** Accepts. **Response:** Queries 1 week, submissions 3 months, SASE required. **Freelance Content:** 95%. **Rights:** FNAR and electronic. **Payment:** In copies.

NEW ENGLAND REVIEW

Middlebury College, Middlebury, VT 05753. 802-443-5075.
E-mail: nereview@middlebury.edu. Web site: www.middlebury.edu/~nereview. Quarterly. $8/issue. Circ.: 2,000. Stephen Donadio, Editor. **Description:** Short stories, short-shorts, novellas, and excerpts from novels. Also, long and short poems, interpretive and personal essays, book reviews, critical reassessments, and letters from abroad. **Fiction:** 10,000 words; $10/page. **Nonfiction:** Exploration of all forms of contemporary cultural expression; 10,000 words; $10/page. **Poetry:** Submit up to

6 poems, any length; $10/page, $20 minimum. **Queries:** Not necessary. **E-Queries:** No. **Unsolicited mss:** Accepts. **Response:** Queries 2 weeks, submissions 12 weeks, SASE. **Payment:** On publication.

NEW ENGLAND WRITERS NETWORK
P.O. Box 483, Hudson, MA 01749-0483.
E-mail: newnmag@aol.com. Web site: www.newnmag.net. $20/yr. Glenda Baker, Editor-in-Chief. **Description:** Fiction, nonfiction, and poetry. **Fiction:** Short stories, novel excerpts, to 2,000 words. All genres; pays $10. **Nonfiction:** Personal, humorous essays, to 1,000 words; pays $5. **Poetry:** Upbeat, positive, to 32 lines; pays $5. **Tips:** June-August reading period. **Queries:** Not necessary. **E-Queries:** No. **Unsolicited mss:** Accepts. **Payment:** On publication.

NEW LETTERS
University of Missouri-Kansas City
University House, 5101 Rockhill Rd., Kansas City, MO 64110-2499. 816-235-1168.
E-mail: newletters@umkc.edu. Web site: www.newletters.org. Quarterly. $5/$17.
Circ.: 6,000. Robert Stewart, Editor-in-Chief. **Description:** "Poetry, fiction, art, and essays with fresh, sophisticated writing, by people who have read widely and who have lived interesting lives." **Fiction:** Any style, subject, or genre; to 5,000 words. **Nonfiction:** Essays, profiles; to 5,000 words. **Poetry:** Submit 3-6 poems. **Tips:** Also offers annual contests for poetry, fiction, and creative nonfiction. **Queries:** Not necessary. **E-Queries:** No. **Unsolicited mss:** Accepts. **Response:** 3 months, SASE required. **Freelance Content:** 50%. **Rights:** FNAR. **Payment:** On publication. **Contact:** Aleatha Ezra, Assistant Managing Editor.

NEW YORK STORIES
LaGuardia Community College
English Dept., E-103, 31-10 Thompson Ave., Long Island City, NY 11101.
E-mail: nystories@lagcc.cuny.edu. Web site: www.newyorkstories.org. 3x/yr.
$5.95/issue. Circ.: 1,500. Daniel Caplice Lynch, Editor-in-Chief. **Description:** Short stories (6-8 per issue), also nonfiction pieces about New York City. **Fiction:** Experimental or mainstream fiction; no genre fiction. Stories can be set anywhere; to 6,000 words; $100-$500. **Nonfiction:** Creative nonfiction, set in NYC or with NYC theme; to 6,000 words; $100-$500. **Art:** B&W artwork, NYC theme; to $200. **Tips:** "NYC-centered nonfiction gets a close look since we get surprisingly few submissions in that category. Stories that touch NYC's diversity, off-beat situations, and humor are always welcome." **Queries:** Not necessary. **Unsolicited mss:** Accepts. **Response:** Queries 1 week, submissions 3 months, SASE required. **Freelance Content:** 100%. **Rights:** FNASR. **Payment:** On publication.

THE NEW YORKER
See full listing in Current Events, Politics category.

NIMROD INTERNATIONAL JOURNAL OF POETRY AND PROSE

University of Tulsa, 600 S College Ave., Tulsa, OK 74104-3189. 918-631-3080.
E-mail: nimrod@utulsa.edu. Web site: www.utulsa.edu/nimrod. Semi-annual.
$17.50/yr. Circ.: 3,000. Dr. Francine Ringold, Editor. **Description:** Prose and fiction
by emerging writers of contemporary literature. **Fiction:** Quality fiction (no genre
fiction), vigorous writing with believable characters and dialogue; 7,500 words max.
Nonfiction: Vivid essays related to annual theme; 7,500 words max. **Poetry:** 1,900
words max. **Queries:** Not necessary. **E-Queries:** Yes. **Unsolicited mss:** Accepts.
Response: 6-8 weeks, SASE required. **Freelance Content:** 100%. **Rights:** FNAR.
Payment: In copies.

96 INC.

P.O. Box 15559, Boston, MA 02215. 617-267-0543.
E-mail: to96inc@ici.net. Annual. $5/issue; $15/membership. Circ.: 3,000. Gold,
Anderson, Mehegan, Editors. **Description:** New voices; established and novice writ-
ers. **Fiction:** All types. No restrictions on style or subject; up to 3,000 words.
Nonfiction: Stories with useful information for other writers (new publishers, etc.);
2,500 words. **Queries:** Preferred. **E-Queries:** No. **Unsolicited mss:** Accepts.
Response: 6 months-1 year, SASE. **Rights:** One-time. **Payment:** In copies.
Contact: Vera Gold.

THE NORTH AMERICAN REVIEW

University of Northern Iowa
1222 W 27th St., Cedar Falls, IA 50614-0516. 319-273-6455.
E-mail: nar@uni.edu. Web site: webdelsol.com/NorthAmReview/NAR/. Bimonthly.
$22/yr. Vince Gotera, Editor. **Description:** Poetry, fiction, nonfiction, and art on con-
temporary North American concerns and issues, especially environment, gender,
race, ethnicity, and class. **Fiction:** Literary realism, multicultural, or experimental; up
to 12,000 words; $20-$100. **Nonfiction:** Creative nonfiction, journals and diaries, letters, memoirs, profiles; nature, travel, and science writing; also literary journalism and
essays; up to 12,000 words; $20-$100. **Poetry:** Traditional or experimental, formal or
free verse (closed or open form); length varies; $20-$100. **Tips:** "We like stories with
strong narrative arc and sense of humor, where characters act on the world, are
responsible for their decisions, make mistakes." **Queries:** Not necessary. **E-Queries:**
Yes. **Unsolicited mss:** Accepts. **Response:** 3 months submissions, SASE.
Freelance Content: 80%. **Rights:** FNASR. **Payment:** On publication.

NORTH CAROLINA LITERARY REVIEW

East Carolina University
Bate Building, English Dept., Greenville, NC 27858-4353. 252-328-1537.
E-mail: bauerm@mail.edu.edu. Web site: www.ecu.edu/nclr. Annual. Circ.: 750.
Description: By and about North Carolina writers. Covers North Carolina history,
culture, and literature. Mostly nonfiction, accepts some poetry and fiction by North
Carolina writers. Pays $50/story or illustration. **Tips:** Sample copy $15. **Queries:** Not
necessary. **Response:** 3 months. **Rights:** FNAR. **Payment:** On publication.

NORTH DAKOTA QUARTERLY

University of North Dakota
Grand Forks, ND 58202-7209. 701-777-3322.
E-mail: ndq@sage.und.nodak.edu. Web site: www.und.nodak.edu/org/ndq/.
Quarterly. $8/sample, $12/special issue. Circ.: 700. Robert W. Lewis, Editor.
Description: Fiction, nonfiction, poetry, reviews, and criticism, often from unique
perspective of the Northern Plains. **Tips:** Authors published in journal include Louise
Erdrich, Larry Woiwode, Kathleen Norris, Roland Flint, Linda Hasselstrom, Adrian
C. Louis, Garrison Keillor, and Thomas McGrath. **Queries:** Not necessary.
E-Queries: Yes. **Unsolicited mss:** Accepts. **Response:** Queries 2-4 weeks, submis-
sions 2-4 months, SASE required. **Freelance Content:** 75%. **Rights:** FNASR.
Payment: In copies.

NORTHWEST REVIEW

University of Oregon, 369 PLC, Eugene, OR 97403. 541-346-3957.
E-mail: jwitte@oregon.uoregon.edu. Web site: www.darkwing.uoregon.edu. 3x/yr.
$8/$22. Circ.: 1,000. John Witte, Editor. **Description:** "The oldest literary journal
west of the Mississippi." Offers a forum for talented emerging young writers. **Fiction:**
All lengths. **Nonfiction:** Eclectic commentary and essays. **Poetry:** All lengths.
Queries: Not necessary. **E-Queries:** No. **Unsolicited mss:** Accepts. **Response:**
Queries immediately, submissions 8-10 weeks, SASE required. **Freelance Content:**
100%. **Rights:** FNASR. **Payment:** In copies.

NOTRE DAME REVIEW

University of Notre Dame
English Dept./Creative Writing Program, Notre Dame, IN 46556.
Web site: www.nd.edu/nndr/review.htm. Bi-annual. $8/$15. Circ.: 2,000. Steve
Tomasula, Senior Editor. **Description:** Fiction and poetry, any length. Also runs long
and short reviews, by assignment. **Tips:** Send query for reviews, complete manuscript
for all else. **E-Queries:** No. **Unsolicited mss:** Accepts. **Response:** Queries 1
month, submissions 3-5 months, SASE. **Freelance Content:** 60%. **Rights:** FNASR.
Payment: On publication.

OFFERINGS

P.O. Box 1667, Lebanon, MO 65536.
Quarterly. $5/$16. Circ.: 75. Velvet Fackeldey, Editor. **Description:** Quality poetry,
all forms; 30 lines max. **Tips:** Overstocked with nature poetry. Sample copy $3.
Queries: Not necessary. **E-Queries:** No. **Unsolicited mss:** Accepts. **Response:**
4-6 weeks, SASE. **Freelance Content:** 100%. **Rights:** 1st. **Payment:** No payment.

THE OLD RED KIMONO

Floyd College, Humanities Div., P.O. Box 1864, Rome, GA 30162.
E-mail: napplega@mail.fc.peachnet.edu. Annual. $5. Circ.: 1,400. La Neile Daneil,
Nancy Applegate, Editors. **Description:** Poems and short stories, all types. Fiction,
1,500 words or less. **Tips:** Local writers constitute 50% of journal. Annual Paris Lake

Poetry Contest. **Queries:** Not necessary. **E-Queries:** Yes. **Unsolicited mss:** Accepts. **Response:** 8 weeks, SASE. **Freelance Content:** 100%. **Rights:** 1st. **Payment:** On publication. Pays 2 copies.

OREGON EAST

Hoke #304 EOU, One University Blvd., La Grande, OR 97850. 541-962-3787. Annual. $5. Circ.: 1,000. Alyx Lyons, Editor. **Description:** Short fiction, nonfiction, one-act plays, poetry, and graphics. **Fiction:** Any subject; 3,000 words. **Poetry:** Any form. No "greeting card" verse; 60 lines. **Art:** Photos of original graphics should be B&W glossies, 4x5 or 5x7, high contrast; include titles or captions. **Queries:** Not necessary. **E-Queries:** No. **Unsolicited mss:** Accepts. **Response:** 2-3 months, SASE. **Freelance Content:** 100%. **Rights:** FNAR. **Payment:** In copies.

OSIRIS

P.O. Box 297, Deerfield, MA 01342. 413-774-4027. Semiannual. $7.50/issue. Circ.: 1,000. Andrea Moorhead, Editor. **Description:** A multilingual poetry journal. Contemporary foreign poetry in original language (English and French are principle languages). Other works appear in original language, with facing-page translation in English. Length varies. **Tips:** "We seek poetry that is well-crafted, non-narrative, and lyrical. Translators need to secure permission of both poet and publisher. Ask for a sample copy." **Queries:** Not necessary. **E-Queries:** No. **Unsolicited mss:** Accepts. **Response:** 4-8 weeks, SASE required. **Freelance Content:** 30%. **Payment:** In copies.

OTHER VOICES

University of Illinois-Chicago
Dept. of English (M/C 162), 601 S Morgan St., Chicago, IL 60607. 312-413-2209. E-mail: othervoices@listserv.uic.edu. Web site: www.othervoicesmagazine.org. Semiannual. $7/issue. Circ.: 1,500. Gina Frangello, Editor. **Description:** Literary journal. **Fiction:** Literary short stories, novel excerpts, one-act plays; traditional or experimental; no genre fiction; to 7,500 words. **Nonfiction:** Book reviews, interviews with esteemed fiction writers. **Tips:** Accepts manuscripts between October 1-April 1 only. **Queries:** Not necessary. **E-Queries:** No. **Unsolicited mss:** Accepts. **Response:** 3 months; SASE required. **Freelance Content:** 100%. **Rights:** First serial. **Payment:** In copies.

THE OXFORD AMERICAN

303 President Clinton Ave., Little Rock, AR 72201. 501-907-6418. Web site: www.oxfordamericanmag.com. $29.95. Circ.: 45,000. Marc Smirnoff, Editor. **Description:** "The Southern Magazine of Good Writing." General-interest magazine that explores the American South. Features fiction, nonfiction, and poetry. **Poetry:** 3-5 poems, any length; $125/poem. **Tips:** "Writers should always learn a little bit about the homes where their writing ends up—and should only send their beloved work to magazines to which they feel a special kinship." **Queries:** Not nec-

essary. **E-Queries:** No. **Unsolicited mss:** Accepts. **Response:** Queries varies, submissions up to 3 months, SASE. **Freelance Content:** 50%. **Rights:** FNASR. **Payment:** On publication.

OYSTER BOY REVIEW

P.O. Box 77842, San Francisco, CA 94107-0842.
E-mail: editors@oysterboyreview.com; fiction@oysterboyreview.com.
Web site: www.oysterboyreview.com. Quarterly. Damon Sauve, Publisher.
Description: In print and online, features "the underrated, ignored, misunderstood, and varietal." See Web site for guidelines. **Tips:** No previously published work. **Queries:** Not necessary. **E-Queries:** Yes. **Unsolicited mss:** Accepts. **Response:** 3-6 months, SASE required. **Rights:** FNASR. **Payment:** In copies.

PAINTBRUSH

Truman State University
Language & Literature Division, Kirksville, MO 63501. 660-785-4185.
Web site: www.paintbrush.org. Annual. $15/yr. Circ.: 500. Ben Bennani, Editor.
Description: Journal of poetry and translation. **Poetry:** Serious, original, highly imaginative work. Submit 3-5 poems with cover letter. **Queries:** Preferred. **E-Queries:** Yes. **Unsolicited mss:** Accepts. **Response:** 10 weeks, SASE required. **Freelance Content:** 60%. **Rights:** FNAR. **Payment:** In copies.

PAINTED BRIDE QUARTERLY

Rutgers University, English Dept., Armitage Hall, Camden, NJ 08102. 856-225-6129.
E-mail: pbq@camden.rutgers.edu. Web site: www.webdelsol.com/pbq
or www.pbq.rutgers.edu. Annual anthology. $15/yr. Circ.: 1,500. Marion Wrenn, Editor. **Description:** Fiction and poetry, in print and online. **Fiction:** Any genre; up to 5,000 words. **Nonfiction:** Essays, reviews; up to 3,000 words. **Poetry:** Up to 5 poems; length varies. **Art:** Photos, etchings, lithographs, line drawings; B&W. **Queries:** Not necessary. **E-Queries:** Yes. **Unsolicited mss:** Accepts. **Response:** 3 months; SASE required. **Freelance Content:** 100%. **Rights:** First. **Payment:** On publication.

PALO ALTO REVIEW

Palo Alto College, 1400 W Villaret, San Antonio, TX 78224-2499. 210-921-5017.
E-mail: paloaltoreview@aol.com. Semi-annual. $5.00. Circ.: 500. Ellen Shull, Editor.
Description: Articles, essays, memoirs, plus some poems and short fiction on varied historical, geographical, scientific, mathematical, artistic, political, and social topics. **Fiction:** No experimental or excessively avant-garde fiction. **Nonfiction:** Original, unpublished articles and interviews. **Poetry:** Submit 3-5 poems, to 50 lines. **Columns, Departments:** Food for Thought (200-word think pieces); reviews, to 500 words, of books, films, videos, or software. **Art:** Photo essays welcome. **Tips:** This is a "journal of ideas." Send SASE for upcoming themes. **Payment:** In copies.

PANGOLIN PAPERS

P.O. Box 241, Nordland, WA 98358. 360-385-3626.
E-mail: trtlbluf@olympus.net. Tri-annual. $7.95/$20. Circ.: 400. Pat Britt, Editor. **Description:** Literary short stories, to 8,000 words. **Tips:** No poetry, genre fiction, or essays. **Queries:** Not necessary. **E-Queries:** No. **Unsolicited mss:** Accepts. **Response:** 3 months, SASE required. **Rights:** FNAR. **Payment:** In copies.

THE PARIS REVIEW

541 E 72nd St., New York, NY 10021. 212-861-0016.
E-mail: queries@theparisreview.com. Web site: www.parisreview.com. Quarterly. $12/$40. Circ.: 12,000. George Plimpton, Editor. **Description:** International literary magazine featuring fiction, poetry, interviews, and essays from established and emerging writers and artists. **Fiction:** High literary quality. **Poetry:** Varied formats. **Fillers:** Humor. **Art:** Slides, drawings, copies. **Tips:** Annual prizes, in several categories, up to $1,000. **Queries:** Not necessary. **E-Queries:** Yes. **Unsolicited mss:** Accepts. **Response:** Queries 2-3 weeks, submissions 3-4 months, SASE. **Freelance Content:** 75%. **Rights:** FNAR. **Payment:** On publication.

PARNASSUS: POETRY IN REVIEW

205 W 89th St., Apt. 8F, New York, NY 10024-1835. 212-362-3492.
E-mail: parnew@aol.com. Web site: www.parnassuspoetry.com. Semi-annual. $12-$15. Circ.: 2,500. Herbert Leibowitz, Editor. **Description:** In-depth analysis of contemporary books of poetry. **Nonfiction:** Critical essays and reviews on contemporary poetry. No academic or theoretical work, looks for criticism that is colorful, idiosyncratic, well-written; 20 pages; $150. **Poetry:** Mostly by request; $25/page. **Queries:** Not necessary. **E-Queries:** Yes. **Unsolicited mss:** Accepts. **Response:** 2 months, SASE required. **Freelance Content:** 100%. **Rights:** All, reverts to author. **Payment:** On publication.

PARTISAN REVIEW

Boston University, 236 Bay State Rd., Boston, MA 02215. 617-353-4260.
E-mail: partisan@bu.edu. Web site: www.partisanreview.org. Quarterly. $7/$25. Circ.: 8,000. William Phillips, Editor-in-Chief. **Description:** Influential American literary and cultural journal, home to many fine writers. **Fiction:** Yes. **Poetry:** Yes. **Queries:** Preferred. **E-Queries:** No. **Unsolicited mss:** Accepts. **Response:** 4-8 weeks, SASE. **Payment:** On publication.

PASSAGES NORTH

Northern Michigan University, Dept. of English
Gries Hall, 1401 Presque Isle Ave., Marquette, MI 49855. 906-227-1203.
E-mail: passages@nmu.edu. Web site: http://myweb.nmu.edu/passages. Annual. $13. Circ.: 1,000. Kate Hanson, Editor. **Description:** Fiction, poetry, and nonfiction, for established and emerging writers. **Fiction:** Short stories; no genre fiction; up to 5,000 words. **Nonfiction:** Interviews, essays, literary nonfiction; up to 5,000 words. **Poetry:**

Up to 6 poems; up to 100 lines. **Tips:** Submissions read only from September 1 to May 1. **Queries:** Not necessary. **E-Queries:** No. **Unsolicited mss:** Accepts. **Response:** 6-8 weeks; SASE required. **Freelance Content:** 95%. **Rights:** FNAR. **Payment:** In copies.

PATERSON LITERARY REVIEW

Poetry Center at Passaic County Community College

1 College Blvd., Paterson, NJ 07505-1179. 973-684-6555.

E-mail: mgillan@pccc.cc.nj.us. Web site: www.pccc.cc.nj.us/poetry. Annual. $10. Circ.: 1,000. Maria Mazziotti Gillan, Editor. **Description:** Poetry, fiction, book reviews, articles, artwork. **Fiction:** 1,500 words. **Nonfiction:** 1,000 words. **Poetry:** 100-line limit. **Queries:** Not necessary. **E-Queries:** No. **Unsolicited mss:** Accepts. **Response:** Submissions 6 months, SASE required. **Freelance Content:** 100%. **Rights:** FNAR.

PEARL

3030 E Second St., Long Beach, CA 90803. 562-434-4523.

E-mail: pearlmag@aol.com. Web site: www.pearlmag.com. Bi-annual. $8/$18. Circ.: 700. Marilyn Johnson, Joan Jobe Smith, Editors. **Description:** Contemporary poetry and short fiction. **Fiction:** Accessible humanistic fiction, related to real life. Ironic, serious, and intense, humor and wit welcome; 1,200 words. **Poetry:** Humanistic; to 40 lines. **Art:** Camera-ready B&W. **Queries:** Not necessary. **E-Queries:** Yes. **Unsolicited mss:** Accepts. **Response:** Queries 1 week, submissions 6-8 weeks, SASE required. **Freelance Content:** 100%. **Rights:** FNAR. **Payment:** In copies.

PEDESTAL MAGAZINE

6815 Honors Court, Charlotte, NC 28210. 704-643-0244.

E-mail: pedestalmagazine@aol.com. Web site: www.thepedestalmagazine.com. Bimonthly. Circ.: 10,000. John Amen, Editor. **Description:** Online, new and estab-lished visual artists and writers of poetry, fiction, and nonfiction. Each issue includes an in-depth interview with a featured writer and visual artist, with examples of their work. **Fiction:** All types, including literary, experimental, science fiction, and fantasy. Prefers pieces that cross genres and do not fall into one specific category; to 6,000 words; $.05/word. **Nonfiction:** Accepts academic/scholarly pieces, also those on issues of aesthetics, psychology, philosophy, and religion; to 6,000 words; $.05/word. **Poetry:** Open to a wide variety, from highly experimental to traditionally formal; $30-$60/poem. **Art:** Artists should query before sending work. **Tips:** "We are looking for freshness, clarity, poignance. Avoid clichés, sentimentality, or inflated drama." **Queries:** Not necessary. **E-Queries:** Yes. **Unsolicited mss:** Accepts. **Response:** queries 1 week, submissions 6-8 weeks. **Freelance Content:** 100%. **Payment:** 30 days after publication.

PEREGRINE

P.O. Box 1076, Amherst, MA 01004. 413-253-3307.
E-mail: awapress@aol.com. Web site: www.amherstwriters.com. Annual. $12. Circ.: 1,000. Pat Schneider, Editor. **Description:** Poetry, fiction, and personal essays. **Fiction:** All styles, forms, and subjects; 3,000 words. **Nonfiction:** Short personal essays; to 1,200 words. **Poetry:** No greeting-card verse; 70 lines (3-5 poems). **Tips:** "A forum for national and international writers, committed to finding exceptional work by new as well as established writers. We seek work that is unpretentious and memorable, reflecting diversity of voice." **Queries:** Not necessary. **E-Queries:** No. **Unsolicited mss:** Accepts. **Response:** Submissions 2-3 months, SASE. **Payment:** On publication. **Contact:** Nancy Rose, Managing Editor.

PERMAFROST

University of Alaska–Fairbanks
English Dept., P.O. Box 75720, Fairbanks, AK 99775-0640. 907-474-5398.
Web site: www.uaf.edu/english/permafrost. Annual. $8/issue. **Description:** Literary journal for the arts. Fiction, nonfiction, poetry, and artwork of emerging and established writers and artists. **Fiction:** To 30 pages; avoid genre fiction (horror, sci-fi, fantasy). **Nonfiction:** To 30 pages. **Poetry:** To 5 poems. **Tips:** Alaskan themes discouraged. Reading period is September 1-March 1. **Queries:** Not necessary. **E-Queries:** No. **Unsolicited mss:** Accepts. **Response:** 3 months, SASE. **Rights:** FNAR. **Payment:** In copies.

PHANTASMAGORIA

Century College
English Dept., 3300 Century Ave. N, White Bear Lake, MN 55110. 651-779-3410.
E-mail: allenabigail@hotmail.com. Semiannual. $9/$15. Circ.: 1,000. Abigail Allen, Editor. **Description:** Previously unpublished short stories or poems of literary merit. **Fiction:** Short stories to 4,000 words. Submit only one story at a time. **Poetry:** 100 lines or fewer. Submit no more than six poems at a time. **Tips:** Send SASE for reply; faxed or e-mailed submissions will not be read. **Queries:** Not necessary. **E-Queries:** No. **Unsolicited mss:** Accepts. **Freelance Content:** 98%. **Rights:** FNAR. **Payment:** In copies.

THE PIKEVILLE REVIEW

Pikeville College
Humanities Division, 147 Sycamore St., Pikeville, KY 41501. 606-218-5002.
E-mail: eward@pc.edu. Web site: www.pc.edu. Annual. $4/issue. Circ.: 500. Elgin M. Ward, Editor. **Description:** Contemporary fiction, poetry, creative essays, and book reviews, for Kentucky writers and others. **Tips:** Open to new and unpublished writers. **Queries:** Not necessary. **E-Queries:** Yes. **Unsolicited mss:** Accepts. **Response:** Queries 2 weeks, submissions 30-60 days, SASE. **Payment:** On publication.

PINDELDYBOZ

21-17 25th Rd., Astoria, NY 11102. 516-510-7921.
E-mail: submissions@pindeldyboz.com. Web site: www.pindeldyboz.com. 2x/yr.
$12/$20. Jeff Boison, Editor. **Description:** Literary fiction, previously unpublished,
from established and up-and-coming authors. **Queries:** Not necessary. **E-Queries:**
Yes. **Unsolicited mss:** Accepts. **Freelance Content:** 100%. **Rights:** FNASR.
Payment: In copies.

PLEIADES

Central Missouri State University
Dept. of English, Warrensburg, MO 64093. 660-543-8106.
E-mail: kdp8106@cmsu2.cmsu.edu.
Web site: www.cmsu.edu/englphil/pleiades.html. 2x/yr. $6/$12. Circ.: 3,000. Kevin
Prufer, Editor. **Description:** Traditional and experimental poetry, fiction, criticism,
translations, and reviews. Cross-genre especially welcome. **Fiction:** Up to 10,000
words. **Nonfiction:** Up to 10,000 words; $10 and subscription. **Poetry:** Any length;
pays $3 or copies. **Tips:** Considers simultaneous submissions. "We are interested in a
very wide range of styles, genres, themes and writers." **E-Queries:** No. **Unsolicited
mss:** Accepts. **Response:** 1-2 months, SASE required. **Freelance Content:** 85%.
Rights: 1st serial, reprint online and in anthology. **Payment:** On publication.

PLOUGHSHARES

Emerson College, 120 Boylston St., Boston, MA 02116-4624. 617-824-8753.
E-mail: pshares@emerson.edu. Web site: www.pshares.org. 3x/yr. $10.95/issue. Circ.:
6,000. Don Lee, Editor. **Description:** Compelling fiction and poetry. Each issue is
guest-edited by a prominent writer. **Fiction:** To 30 pages; pays $25/printed page ($50
minimum, $250 maximum). **Poetry:** Send 1-3 poems; $25/printed page. **Tips:** No
genre work, unsolicited book reviews, or criticism. Reviews submissions postmarked
August 1-March 31 only. Submissions received April-July are returned unread.
Queries: Not necessary. **E-Queries:** No. **Unsolicited mss:** Accepts. **Response:** 3-
5 months, SASE required. **Rights:** FNASR. **Payment:** On publication.

POEM

University of Alabama-Huntsville
English Dept., Huntsville, AL 35899. 256-824-2379.
Semi-annual. $20. Circ.: 400. Nancy Frey Dillard, Editor. **Description:** Serious lyric
poetry. **Poetry:** Well-crafted, free verse. No light verse; "prose" poems; "visual" or
"conceptual" poetry; or other avant-garde verse. Submit 3-5 poems. **Tips:** "Submit
brief lyric poems only, with verbal and dramatic tension, that transpire from the particular to the universal." **Queries:** Preferred. **E-Queries:** No. **Unsolicited mss:**
Accepts. **Response:** Queries 1 week, submissions 1 month, SASE. **Rights:** 1st.
Payment: In copies.

POETRY MAGAZINE

Modern Poetry Assn., 60 W Walton St., Chicago, IL 60610. 303-255-3703.
E-mail: poetry@poetrymagazine.org. Web site: www.poetrymagazine.org. Monthly.
$3.75/issue. Circ.: 10,000. Joseph Parisi, Editor. **Description:** Literary journal of
poetry, by poets famous and new. **Poetry:** Any length; $2/line. **Queries:** Not neces-
sary. **E-Queries:** No. **Unsolicited mss:** Accepts. **Response:** 4 months, SASE.
Freelance Content: 100%. **Payment:** On publication.

PORTLAND REVIEW

Portland State University
P.O. Box 347, Portland, OR 97207.
Web site: www.portlandreview.org. Tri-annual. $7/issue. **Description:** Short fiction,
poetry, reviews, interviews, and art by both celebrated and unknown contributors.
Queries: Not necessary. **Unsolicited mss:** Accepts.

POTOMAC REVIEW

Montgomery College, Paul Peck Humanities Institute
51 Mannakee St., Rockville, MD 20850. 301-251-7417.
Web site: www.meral.com/potomac. Semi-annual. $10/$15. Circ.: 1,500. Eli Flam,
Editor. **Description:** Regionally rooted, with a conscience, a lurking sense of humor,
and a strong environmental/nature bent. **Fiction:** Vivid, with ethical depth and, in
Flannery O'Connor's words, "the vision to go with it"; 3,000 words. **Nonfiction:** 3,000
words. **Poetry:** That educates, challenges, or diverts in fresh ways; up to 3 poems, 5
pages. **Tips:** Contact for upcoming themes. **Queries:** Not necessary. **E-Queries:**
No. **Unsolicited mss:** Accepts. **Response:** Submissions 2-3 months, SASE.
Freelance Content: 75%. **Rights:** FNAR. **Payment:** In copies.

POTPOURRI

P.O. Box 8278, Prairie Village, KS 66208. 913-642-1503.
E-mail: editor@potpourri.org. Web site: www.potpourri.org. Quarterly. $6.95/$16.
Circ.: 3,000. Polly W. Swafford, Editor. **Description:** A modern literary journal, falls
between serious academic journals and glitzy commercial publications. **Fiction:**
Broad genres; no racist, sexist material; 3,500 words. **Nonfiction:** Essays with liter-
ary theme. Travel with a cultural theme; 2,500 words. **Poetry:** 75 lines. **Fillers:**
Light, humorous stories with fully developed plots. **Tips:** Seeks to promote work
reflecting a culturally diverse society. Sample copy $5.95 with 9x12 SASE. **Queries:**
Not necessary. **E-Queries:** Yes. **Unsolicited mss:** Accepts. **Response:** Queries 3
weeks, submissions 3 months, SASE. **Freelance Content:** 80%. **Rights:** FNAR.
Payment: In copies.

THE PRAIRIE JOURNAL OF CANADIAN LITERATURE

P.O. Box 61203, Brentwood Post Office, Calgary, AB T2L 2K6 Canada.
E-mail: prairiejournal@yahoo.com. Web site: www.geocities.com/prairiejournal/.
Semiannual. $4/issue. Circ.: 600. A. Burke, Editor. **Description:** Devoted to new,
previously unpublished writing. **Fiction:** Literary; any length, pay varies.

Nonfiction: Essays, reviews, and interviews on Canadian subjects. **Poetry:** Any length. **Art:** B&W photos. **Tips:** No simultaneous submissions. Accepts general inquiries via e-mail, but not submissions. Sample copy $6. **Queries:** Not necessary. **E-Queries:** Yes. **Unsolicited mss:** Accepts. **Response:** 2-3 months, SASE (IRCs). **Freelance Content:** 100%. **Payment:** On publication.

PRAIRIE SCHOONER
University of Nebraska
P.O. Box 880334, 201 Andrews Hall, Lincoln, NE 68588-0334. 402-472-0911.
E-mail: kgrey2@unl.edu. Web site: www.unl.edu/schooner/psmain.htm. Quarterly. $9/$26. Circ.: 3,000. Hilda Raz, Editor. **Description:** Contemporary poetry, fiction, essay, and reviews. **Fiction:** Short stories; 18-25 pages. **Nonfiction:** Essays, book reviews, translations; 15-25 pages. **Poetry:** Submit 5-7 poems at a time. **Queries:** Not necessary. **E-Queries:** No. **Unsolicited mss:** Accepts. **Response:** Queries 3 weeks, submissions 3-4 months, SASE required. **Rights:** All, electronic, can revert to author. **Payment:** In copies. **Contact:** Kelly Grey.

PRIMAVERA
See full listing in Women's Publications category.

PUDDING MAGAZINE
60 N Main St., Johnstown, OH 43031. 740-967-6060.
E-mail: pudding@johnstown.net. Web site: www.puddinghouse.com. Irregular. $7.95 or 3/$22. Circ.: 1,000. Jennifer Bosveld, Editor. **Description:** Mostly poetry, also features short-short stories, essays, writing exercises, and reviews. **Nonfiction:** Articles/essays on poetry and intentional living, social concerns, poetry applied to the times of our lives; 500-2,500 words. **Poetry:** On popular culture, social concerns, personal struggle, and wide open. **Columns, Departments:** Reviews of poetry books. **Tips:** Featured poet in each issue receives $10 and 4 copies. **E-Queries:** No. **Unsolicited mss:** Accepts. **Response:** 1 day, SASE required. **Freelance Content:** 98%. **Payment:** In copies.

PUERTO DEL SOL
New Mexico State University
Dept. of English, MSC 3E, Box 30001, Las Cruces, NM 88003-8001. 505-646-2345.
E-mail: puerto@nmsu.edu. Web site: www.nmsu.edu/~puerto/welcome.html. Kevin McIlvoy, Editor. **Description:** Poetry, short stories, personal essays, novel excerpts, book reviews, photo-essays, translations, and other artwork. Short stories and personal essays (to 30 pages); excerpts (to 65 pages). **Tips:** Manuscripts read September through December. **Response:** 3-5 months, SASE. **Payment:** In copies.

QUARTER AFTER EIGHT
Ohio University, 102 Ellis Hall, Athens, OH 45701. 740-593-2827.
E-mail: quartereight@hotmail.com. Web site: www.quartereight.org. Annual. $10. Circ.: 1,000. Hayley Haugen, Editor-in-Chief. **Description:** Literary

publication. **Fiction:** Experimental fiction, sudden fiction; 10,000 words max. **Nonfiction:** Commentary, but not scholarly work; novel excerpts, essays, criticism, investigations, interviews; 10,000 words max. **Poetry:** Submit 3-5 pieces; no traditional lined poetry. **Art:** B&W photos only. **Queries:** Not necessary. **E-Queries:** No. **Unsolicited mss:** Accepts. **Response:** 12-16 weeks, SASE required. **Rights:** FNAR. **Payment:** On publication.

QUARTERLY WEST
University of Utah
200 S Central Campus Dr., Rm 317, Salt Lake City, UT 84112-9109. 801-581-3938. E-mail: lynnkilpatrick@m.cc.utah.edu. Web site: www.utah.edu/quarterlywest. Semi-annual. $7.50/issue, $12/yr. Circ.: 1,600. David Hawkins, Editor. **Description:** For new writers and established authors. **Fiction:** Shorts and longer fiction, that play with form and language, not bound by convention; 500-6,000 words; pay varies. **Nonfiction:** Memoir, books reviews, essays; 500-6,000 words. **Poetry:** Up to 5 pages, 3 poems. **Tips:** No "Western" themes or religious verse. **Queries:** Not necessary. **E-Queries:** No. **Unsolicited mss:** Accepts. **Response:** 6-8 months, SASE. **Freelance Content:** 75%. **Payment:** On publication.

QUEEN'S QUARTERLY
Queens University
144 Barrie St., Kingston, Ontario K7L 3N6 Canada. 613-533-2667. E-mail: qquarter@post.queensu.ca. Web site: http://info.queensu.ca/quarterly. Quarterly. $20/yr. Circ.: 2,700. Boris Castel, Editor. **Description:** Nonfiction (covering a wide range of topics) and fiction. **Fiction:** In English and French; to 5,000 words; to $300. **Nonfiction:** To 5,000 words; to $400. **Poetry:** Send up to 6 poems; to $400. **Art:** B&W art; to $400. **E-Queries:** Yes. **Payment:** On publication.

RAMBUNCTIOUS REVIEW
1221 W Pratt Blvd., Chicago, IL 60626.
Annual. $4/issue. Circ.: 500. **Description:** Features new and established writers of poetry and fiction. **Queries:** Not necessary. **E-Queries:** No. **Unsolicited mss:** Accepts. **Freelance Content:** 100%. **Rights:** FNASR. **Payment:** In copies. **Contact:** Editorial Board.

RATTAPALLAX
532 La Guardia, Suite 353, New York, NY 10012. 212-560-7459. E-mail: info@rattapallax.com. Web site: www.rattapallax.com. 2x/yr. $7.95/issue. Circ.: 2,000. Martin Mitchell, Alan Cheuse, Editors. **Description:** Modern poetry and prose. Each issue comes with a CD, with selected poets reading their work. **Queries:** Not necessary. **E-Queries:** No. **Unsolicited mss:** Accepts. **Response:** 3-6 months, SASE required. **Freelance Content:** 5%. **Rights:** FNAR. **Payment:** In copies.

RATTLE

12411 Ventura Blvd., Studio City, CA 91604. 818-986-3274.
E-mail: stellasuel@aol.com. Web site: www.rattle.com. 2x/yr. $8/issue. **Description:** Poetry, translations, reviews, essays, and interviews. **Nonfiction:** Essays on any subject that pertains to writing; to 2,000 words. Reviews on poetry books; to 400 words. **Poetry:** Open to any type or form of contemporary poetry. Prefers shorter poems, but will read and consider everything. **Tips:** Send cover letter, bio, and SASE with submission. No previously published work or simultaneous submissions. **Queries:** Not necessary. **E-Queries:** Yes. **Unsolicited mss:** Accepts. **Payment:** In copies. **Contact:** Alan Fox, Editor; Stellasue Lee, Poetry Editor.

REAL

Stephen F. Austin State University
P.O. Box 13007, SFA Sta., Nacogdoches, TX 75962. 936-468-2059.
E-mail: real@sfasu.edu. Semi-annual. $15. Circ.: 400, W. Dale Hearell, Editor. **Description:** Short fiction, poetry, and criticism. **Fiction:** Realistic portrayal of human situations; to 5,000 words. **Nonfiction:** Well-written, scholarly articles; to 5,000 words. **Poetry:** Imagistic verse, not just reformatted prose; to 100 lines. **Art:** B&W line drawings. **Queries:** Not necessary. **E-Queries:** No. **Unsolicited mss:** Accepts. **Response:** Queries 1 week, submissions 3-6 weeks, SASE. **Freelance Content:** 100%. **Payment:** In copies.

RED CEDAR REVIEW

Michigan State University
Dept. of English, 17-C Morrill Hall, E. Lansing, MI 48824-1036. 517-355-1707.
E-mail: rcreview@msu.edu. Web site: www.msu.edu/~rcreview. Biannual. $5/$6. Meg Sparling, Editor. **Description:** Poetry, fiction, and creative nonfiction of all genres by both published and unpublished authors. **Fiction:** 5,000 words max; **Nonfiction:** Creative nonfiction; 5,000 words max. **Poetry:** Submit up to 5 poems; **Queries:** Preferred. **E-Queries:** Yes. **Unsolicited mss:** Accepts. **Response:** Queries 3 weeks, submissions 3 months, SASE. **Payment:** In copies.

RED ROCK REVIEW

Community College of Southern Nevada, English Dept. 12A
3200 E Cheyenne Ave., North Las Vegas, NV 89030. 702-651-4094.
E-mail: richard_logsdm@ccsn.nevada.edu. Semiannual. $5.50/$10. Circ.: 1,000. Dr. Richard Logsdon, Editor. **Description:** Work by new and well-established writers. **Fiction:** Mainstream; 5,000 words. **Nonfiction:** Book reviews (recent poetry and fiction); interviews with literary artists; 2,000 words. **Poetry:** up to 60 lines. **Tips:** Does not accept e-mail submissions. **Queries:** Not necessary. **E-Queries:** Yes. **Unsolicited mss:** Accepts. **Response:** Queries 2 weeks (e-mail responses sooner), submissions 3 months, SASE. **Freelance Content:** 60%. **Rights:** FNAR. **Payment:** In copies.

RED WHEELBARROW

De Anza College, 21250 Stevens Creek Blvd., Cupertino, CA 95014. 408-864-8600. E-mail: splitterrandolph@fhda.edu. Annual. $7.50/issue. Circ.: 500. Randolph Splitter, Editor. **Description:** Fiction, poetry, creative nonfiction, photography, comics, and drawings. **Fiction:** Short stories; to 4,000 words. **Nonfiction:** Creative nonfiction; to 4,000 words. **Poetry:** 5 poems max. **Tips:** Accepts work in September-January only. Diverse voices welcome. Note: not affiliated with Red Wheelbarrow Press or any other similarly named publication. **Queries:** Not necessary. **E-Queries:** No. **Unsolicited mss:** Accepts. **Response:** Submissions 2-6 months, SASE required for reply. **Freelance Content:** 95%.

RIVER CITY

University of Memphis, Dept. of English, Memphis, TN 38152. 901-678-4591. E-mail: rivercity@memphis.edu. Web site: www.people.memphis.edu/~rivercity. Semiannual. $7/$12. Circ.: 1,200. Dr. Marg Bryce Leader, Editor. **Description:** Original short stories, nonfiction, and poetry. **Art:** Photos, B&W or color; illustrations, B&W. **Tips:** "Avoid sentimentality, push the limits of the language." Now publishing non-thematic issues. **Queries:** Not necessary. **E-Queries:** Yes. **Unsolicited mss:** Accepts. **Response:** 1-3 months, SASE required. **Rights:** One-time.

RIVER OAK REVIEW

P.O. Box 3127, Oak Park, IL 60303. E-mail: info@riveroakarts.org. Web site: www.riveroakarts.org. Semiannual. Marylee MacDonald, Editor. **Description:** Fiction, poetry, and creative nonfiction. Limit prose to 20 pages; poetry to batches of no more than 4. **Tips:** No criticism, reviews, or translations. **Payment:** In copies.

RIVER STYX

634 N Grand Blvd., Fl. 12, St. Louis, MO 63103. 314-533-4541. Web site: www.riverstyx.org. Tri-annual. $7/$20. Circ.: 1,500. Richard Newman, Editor. **Description:** International, multicultural literary journal. Fiction, poetry, essays, and art by emerging and established writers and artists. Fiction and nonfiction should run 30 pages or less, poetry format is open. **Queries:** Not necessary. **E-Queries:** No. **Unsolicited mss:** Accepts. **Response:** 3-5 months, SASE required. **Rights:** FNAR. **Payment:** On publication.

ROOM OF ONE'S OWN

P.O. Box 46160, Sta. D, Vancouver, British Columbia V6J 5G5 Canada. E-mail: contactus@roommagazine.com. Web site: www.roommagazine.com. Quarterly. $22/yr (Can.), $25 (U.S.). **Description:** Short stories, poems, art, and reviews by, for, and about women. **Fiction:** To 5,000 words. **Nonfiction:** Creative nonfiction and essays; to 5,000 words. **Poetry:** Prefers groups of poems, rather than single poems. **Columns, Departments:** Book reviews; to 700 words. **Art:** Seeking original art and photography (by female artists) on the female experience; slides, photos, photocopies. **Tips:** Payment is $35 CDN, 1-year subscription, and two copies; or payment all in copies, plus 1-year subscription. **E-Queries:** No. **Unsolicited mss:** Accepts. **Response:** SASE (Canadian postage or IRC). **Rights:** FNASR. **Contact:** Editorial Collective.

SANSKRIT LITERARY-ARTS

University of North Carolina-Charlotte

Cone University Center, Charlotte, NC 28223. 704-687-2326.

E-mail: sanskrit@email.uncc.edu. Web site: www.uncc.edu/life/sanskrit. Annual. $10. Circ.: 3,500. Sarah Heinman, Literary Editor. **Description:** Literary-Arts magazine. Features short fiction and short-shorts (to 3,500 words), and poetry of all forms (prefers free form, modern, with concert imagery). **Art:** 35mm slides (no glass covered) labeled with last name, medium, size, and value. **Tips:** Annual deadline, first Friday in November. Send cover letter and 30-70 word bio with submission. **Queries:** Not necessary. **E-Queries:** Yes. **Unsolicited mss:** Accepts. **Response:** SASE. **Freelance Content:** 100%. **Rights:** FNAR and electronic.

THE SEATTLE REVIEW

University of Washington, Padelford Hall, Box 354330, Seattle, WA 98105.

E-mail: seaview@english.washington.edu.

Web site: http://depts.washington.edu/engl/seaview1.html. Colleen J. McElroy, Editor. **Description:** Stories, to 20 pages; poetry; essays on the craft of writing; art; and interviews with Northwest writers. **Tips:** Manuscripts read October 1 through May 31. **Payment:** In copies.

SENECA REVIEW

Hobart & William Smith Colleges, Geneva, NY 14456. 315-781-3392.

E-mail: senecareview@hws.edu. Web site: www.hws.edu/senecareview. Bi-annual. $7/$11. Circ.: 1,000. Deborah Tall, Editor. **Description:** A journal of poetry and lyric essays. Special interest in translations. **Queries:** Not necessary. **E-Queries:** No. **Unsolicited mss:** Accepts. **Response:** 2-3 months, SASE required. **Freelance Content:** 100%. **Rights:** FNAR. **Payment:** In copies and 2-year subscription.

THE SEWANEE REVIEW

University of the South, 735 University Ave., Sewanee, TN 37383-1000.

Web site: www.sewanee.edu/sreview/home.html. Quarterly. $8.50/$24. Bob Jones, Editor. **Description:** Literary publication. Considers unpublished original work only. Query for essays (7,500 words or less) and reviews; submit complete manuscript for fiction (3,500-7,500 words) and poetry (6 poems, 40 lines or less). SASE required for reply and return of manuscript. **Tips:** Do not submit between June 1-August 31. No simultaneous or electronic submissions. **E-Queries:** No. **Response:** 4-6 weeks.

SHENANDOAH

The Washington and Lee University Review

Troubadour Theater, Fl. 2, Lexington, VA 24450-0303. 540-463-8765.

Web site: http://shenandoah.wlu.edu. Quarterly. $22/yr. Circ.: 1,800. R.T. Smith, Editor. **Description:** Poems, essays, and reviews which display "passionate understanding, formal accomplishment, and serious mischief." **Fiction:** $25/page. **Nonfiction:** Criticism, essays, interviews; $25/page. **Poetry:** $2.50/line. **Tips:** Submissions accepted September 1-May 30. Sample copy $5. **Queries:** Not necessary. **E-Queries:** No. **Unsolicited mss:** Accepts. **Response:** Submissions 8 weeks, SASE. **Freelance Content:** 80%. **Rights:** FNASR. **Payment:** On publication.

SKYLARK
Purdue University Calumet, Dept. of English & Philosophy
2200 169th St., Hammond, IN 46323. 219-989-2273.
Annual. $8. Circ.: 1,000. **Description:** Publishes work (literary and visual) by children and mature adult artists, side-by-side. Interested in new and emerging artists and writers (of any age). **Fiction:** Well-plotted, well-characterized stories, realistic dialogue and action. Central character must be three-dimensional; 4,000 words. **Nonfiction:** Essays that reflect life in Northwest Indiana; interviews with artists, writers, poets; 3,000 words. **Poetry:** Concise wording, rich imagery, honest emotional impact; up to 30 lines. **Art:** Accepts work by either adults or children; original in design, unpublished, and original artwork (for four-color processing); B&W, color. **Tips:** "No erotic or religious material. Images should not be vague or trite." **Queries:** Not necessary. **E-Queries:** Yes. **Unsolicited mss:** Accepts. **Response:** 3 months. **Freelance Content:** 90%. **Rights:** 1st. **Payment:** In copies.

SLIPSTREAM
P.O. Box 2071, Niagara Falls, NY 14301. 716-282-2616.
E-mail: editors@slipstreampress.org. Web site: www.slipstreampress.org. Annual. $20. Circ.: 1,000. Robert Borgatti, Dan Sicoli, Livio Farallo, Editors. **Description:** Poetry, short fiction, and graphics not normally found in mainstream publications. Seeking contemporary urban themes and poetry with a strong voice. Prose up to 15 pages, poetry 1-6 pages. **Art:** Send photocopies of B&W photos/graphics. **Tips:** No rhyming, religious, or trite verse. **Queries:** Not necessary. **Unsolicited mss:** Accepts. **Response:** 1-6 weeks, SASE required. **Freelance Content:** 100%. **Rights:** FNAR. **Payment:** In copies. **Contact:** Dan Sicoli.

SNAKE NATION REVIEW
110 West Force St., Valdosta, GA 31601. 229-244-0752.
E-mail: jeana@snakenationpress.org. Web site: www.snakenationpress.org. 3x/year. $6/$20. Circ.: 2,000. Jean Arambula, Editor. **Description:** General-interest literary magazine, for unpublished/underpublished writers. Open to new and experimental writing. Submissions accepted year round. Send SASE for guidelines. Editor's choice for each category (poetry, fiction, art, or photos) receives $100, all others are paid in copies. **Queries:** Not necessary. **E-Queries:** Yes. **Unsolicited mss:** Accepts. **Response:** 3-6 months. **Freelance Content:** 100%. **Rights:** One-time.

SNOWY EGRET
P.O. Box 29, Terre Haute, IN 47808.
Bi-annual. $15/$25. Circ.: 400. Philip Repp, Editor. **Description:** "Oldest independent U.S. journal of nature writing." On natural history and human beings in relation to nature, from literary, artistic, philosophical, psychological, and historical perspectives. Pays $2/printed page. **Fiction:** Characters who relate strongly to nature; 500-10,000 words. **Nonfiction:** Essays on the natural world and humans' relationship to it, with detailed observations from author's own experience; 500-10,000 words. **Poetry:** Nature-oriented poems. **Columns, Departments:** "Woodnotes," first-hand experiences with landscape or wildlife encounters; 250-2,000 words. **Tips:** "Submit freshly observed material, with plenty of description and/or dialogue." Sample copy $8. **Queries:** Not necessary. **E-Queries:** No. **Response:** 2-8 weeks, SASE required. **Freelance Content:** 95%. **Rights:** FNAR. **Payment:** On publication.

SO TO SPEAK
George Mason University
4400 University Dr., MS2D6, Fairfax, VA 22030-4444. 703-993-3625.
E-mail: sts@gmu.edu. Web site: www.gmu.edu/org/sts. Bi-annual. $6/$11. Circ.: 1,300. Kirsten Hilgeford, Editor. **Description:** Feminist journal of language and arts, concerned with the history of women, of feminists, and looking to see the future through art. Includes fiction, poetry, nonfiction, reviews, visual arts (B&W). **Fiction:** Literary, feminist; to 5,000 words. **Nonfiction:** Literary, lyrical, critical; reviews (feminist books and hypertext); to 4,000 words. **Poetry:** Literary, experimental, lyrical, narrative. **Art:** B&W art, seeking color cover art. **Tips:** "A feminist journal. Ours is a vision of memory and prophesy." **Queries:** Not necessary. **E-Queries:** No. **Unsolicited mss:** Accepts. **Response:** 3-4 months, SASE required. **Payment:** In copies.

SONORA REVIEW
University of Arizona, Dept. of English, Tucson, AZ 85721. 520-321-7759.
E-mail: sonora@u.arizona.edu. Web site: www.coh.arizona.edu/sonora. Frank Montesonti, Editor-in-Chief. **Description:** Stories, poems, memoirs, personal essays, and creative nonfiction. Avoid genre work (mystery, romance, etc.). Send complete manuscript. Fiction and nonfiction, 8,000 words max. Poetry, 12 pages max. Accepts simultaneous submissions. **Tips:** Manuscripts read year-round. **Queries:** Not necessary. **Unsolicited mss:** Accepts. **Response:** 2-3 months, SASE required. **Rights:** FNAR. **Payment:** 2 copies.

SOUTH CAROLINA REVIEW
Clemson University, Dept. of English
Clemson, SC 29634-0523. 864-656-5399.
E-mail: cwayne@clemson.edu.
Web site: www.hubcap.clemson.edu/aah/engl/screview.htm. Semiannual. Circ.: 450. Wayne Chapman, Editor. **Description:** Fiction, essays, reviews, interviews, and poems. **Fiction:** 1,000-6,000 words. **Queries:** Preferred. **E-Queries:** No.

Response: Queries 1-2 weeks, submissions 1-2 months, SASE required. **Freelance Content:** 90%. **Rights:** World. **Payment:** In copies.

SOUTH DAKOTA REVIEW

University of South Dakota
English Dept., 414 E Clark St., Vermillion, SD 57069-2390. 605-677-5966.
E-mail: bbedard@usd.edu. Web site: www.usd.edu/sdreview. Quarterly. $7/$25. Brian Bedard, Editor. **Description:** Fiction, creative nonfiction, and poetry. Slight bias to works with western regional focus. For fiction and nonfiction, send only one piece at a time (1,500-6,000 words); for poetry, send 3-5 poems. Include short cover letter, bio, and SASE. **Tips:** "For a well-educated audience, many with a special interest in contemporary writing about the Great Plains and the American West. We look for substantial storyline, convincing characterization, authentic sense of place in fiction, and creative use of language in poetry." **Queries:** Not necessary. **E-Queries:** Yes. **Unsolicited mss:** Accepts. **Response:** Queries 4-10 weeks, submissions 4-8 weeks. **Freelance Content:** 90%. **Rights:** FNASR. **Payment:** In copies.

SOUTHERN EXPOSURE

See full listing in Regional & City Publications category.

SOUTHERN HUMANITIES REVIEW

9088 Haley Center, Auburn University, Auburn, AL 36849.
E-mail: shrengl@auburn.edu. Quarterly. $5/$15. Circ.: 700. Dan R. Latimer, Virginia M. Kouidis, Co-editors. **Description:** Scholarly, literary magazine. **Fiction:** Short stories; 3,500-15,000 words. **Nonfiction:** Essays, criticism; 3,500-15,000 words. **Poetry:** 2 pages. **Tips:** Sample copy $5. **Queries:** Not necessary. **E-Queries:** Yes. **Unsolicited mss:** Accepts. **Response:** Queries 1-2 weeks, submissions 1-3 months, SASE. **Freelance Content:** 70%. **Rights:** 1st, reverts to author. **Payment:** In copies.

SOUTHERN POETRY REVIEW

11935 Abercorn St., Savannah, GA 31419.
Armstrong Atlantic State University, Dept. of Languages, Literature, & Philosophy Semi-annual. $10. Circ.: 1,000. Robert Parham, Editor. **Description:** Literary journal featuring poetry. **Poetry:** Any style, length, content. **Tips:** Use strong, clear imagery. Avoid sentimental or "proselytizing" content. **Queries:** Not necessary. **E-Queries:** Yes. **Unsolicited mss:** Accepts. **Freelance Content:** 100%. **Rights:** 1st, reverts to writer. **Payment:** On publication.

THE SOUTHERN REVIEW

Louisiana State University
43 Allen Hall, Baton Rouge, LA 70803. 225-578-5108.
Web site: www.lsu.edu/thesouthernreview. Quarterly. Circ.: 3,100. John Easterly, Associate Editor. **Description:** Contemporary literature, with special interest in Southern culture and history. **Fiction:** 4,000-8,000 words; $12/page. **Nonfiction:**

Essays; 4,000-10,000 words; $12/page. **Poetry:** To 4 pages; $20/page. **Tips:** "We seek craftsmanship, technique, and seriousness of subject matter." **Queries:** Preferred. **Response:** 2 months, SASE required. **Rights:** 1st serial. **Payment:** On publication.

THE SOUTHWEST REVIEW
See full listing in Contemporary Culture category.

SOW'S EAR POETRY REVIEW
19535 Pleasant View Dr., Abingdon, VA 24211-6827. 276-628-2651.
E-mail: owens017@bama.ua.edu; richman@preferred.com. Quarterly. $5/$10. Circ.: 600. James Owen, Editor; Larry K. Richman, Managing Editor. **Description:** Poetry, artwork, and nonfiction. **Nonfiction:** Essays, reviews. **Poetry:** Contemporary, any style or length; up to 5 poems. **Art:** To complement poetry; B&W prints, drawings. **Tips:** Seeking poems that make the strange familiar or the familiar strange, that connect the little story of the text and the big story of the human situation. **Queries:** Not necessary. **E-Queries:** Yes. **Unsolicited mss:** Accepts. **Response:** 1 week for queries, 3-6 months for submissions; SASE required. **Freelance Content:** 100%. **Rights:** FNASR. **Payment:** In copies.

SPECTACLE
Pachanga Press
101 Middlesex Turnpike, Suite 6, PMB 155, Burlington, MA 01803-4914.
E-mail: spectaclejournal@hotmail.com. Semi-annual. $7. Circ.: 1,500. Richard Aguilar, Editor. **Description:** Essays, articles, reportage, and fiction on broad spectrum of lively, unconventional themes. **Fiction:** Relevant to issue's theme; up to 5,000 words; $30 and 2 copies. **Nonfiction:** Essays, memoirs, articles, reportage, interviews, and satire; 2,000-5,000 words; $30 and 2 copies. **Tips:** Contact for coming themes. **Queries:** Not necessary. **E-Queries:** Yes. **Unsolicited mss:** Accepts. **Response:** Queries 2 weeks, submissions 6-8 weeks, SASE. **Freelance Content:** 90%. **Rights:** FNASR. **Payment:** On publication.

SPINNING JENNY
P.O. Box 1373, New York, NY 10276.
E-mail: info@blackdresspress.com. Web site: www.blackdresspress.com. Annual. $8/issue. Circ.: 1,000. C.E. Harrison, Editor. **Description:** An open forum for poetry, fiction, and drama. **Tips:** No simultaneous submissions. **Queries:** Not necessary. **E-Queries:** No. **Unsolicited mss:** Accepts. **Response:** 8 weeks, SASE. **Payment:** In copies.

THE SPOON RIVER POETRY REVIEW
Illinois State University
4240 Dept. of English, Publications Unit, Normal, IL 61790-4241. 309-438-7906.
E-mail: rapicke@ilstu.edu. Web site: www.litline.org/spoon. 2x/yr. $10/$15. Circ.: 1,200. Dr. Lucia Getsi, Editor. **Description:** Poetry (original and translations) from

established and emerging poets. **Tips:** "As an international poetry journal, we accept only 1% of all submissions." **Queries:** Does not accept. **Unsolicited mss:** Accepts. **Response:** 2 months, SASE required. **Payment:** In copies. **Contact:** Rob Pickett.

STAND
Virginia Commonwealth University
Dept of English, Box 2005, Richmond, VA 23284-2005. 804-828-1331.
Web site: www.saturn.vcu.edu/~dlatane/stand.html. Quarterly. $12/$49.50. Circ.: 7,500. **Description:** Fiction (to 10,000 words) and poetry (to 250 lines). No genre writing. **Tips:** "Probably not the right market for new writers." **Queries:** Not necessary. **E-Queries:** Yes. **Unsolicited mss:** Accepts. **Response:** 1-3 months, SASE required. **Freelance Content:** 60%. **Payment:** On publication. **Contact:** Matthew Welton, John Whale, David Latané.

STORYHOUSE.COM
4019 SE Hawthorne Blvd., Portland, OR 97214. 503-233-1144.
E-mail: submissions@storyhouse.com. Web site: www.storyhouse.com. Todd Cowing, Esther Cowing, Editors. **Description:** Online retailer of roasted coffee in the Pacific Northwest, seeks original stories, poems, letters, and essays for coffee-can labels. Prefers short-short/flash fiction, especially romance, serialized, and mysteries. Also well-argued essays or academic pieces. **Tips:** Submit via e-mail. See Web site for guidelines, word count, pay rates. **Queries:** Preferred. **E-Queries:** Yes. **Unsolicited mss:** Accepts. **Rights:** Author retains copyright. **Payment:** On acceptance.

STORYQUARTERLY
431 Sheridan Rd., Kenilworth, IL 60043. 847-256-6998.
E-mail: storyquarterly@yahoo.com. Web site: www.storyquarterly.com. Annual. $10/issue. Circ.: 4,500. M.M.M. Hayes, Editor/Publisher; Dan Gutstein, Assoc. Editor; Katherine Hughes, Assoc. Editor. **Description:** Anthology of short stories, publishes contemporary American and foreign literature, full range of styles and forms. **Fiction:** Short stories, short-shorts, novel excerpts; 100-10,000 words. No genre. **Art:** B&W photographs, illustrations. **Tips:** Online submissions only. Go to Web site and click on "submissions." Individuals who do not have access to Internet/ e-mail, may submit hard copy with SASE. Reads submissions October-March. **Queries:** Not necessary. **E-Queries:** Yes. **Unsolicited mss:** Accepts. **Response:** 2-4 months. **Rights:** One-time. **Payment:** In copies.

STORYTELLER
858 Wingate Dr., Ottawa, Ontario K1G 1S5 Canada.
Description: General fiction magazine (humor, adventure, mystery, drama, suspense, horror, science fiction, and fantasy), 2,000-6,000 words. Do not submit material that falls too far within any one of these genres. **Tips:** Read a sample issue before submitting material. No simultaneous submissions. **Rights:** FNAR.

SUB-TERRAIN

P.O. Box 3008 MPO, Vancouver, British Columbia V6B 3X5 Canada. 604-876-8710. E-mail: subter@portal.ca. Web site: www.subterrain.ca. 3x/yr. $3.95 (U.S.) $4.95 (Canada). Circ.: 5,000. Brian Kaufman, Editor. **Description:** "Strong words for a polite nation—a progressive, stimulating fusion of fiction, poetry, photography and graphics from uprising Canadian, U.S., and international writers and artists." **Fiction:** 3,000 words max. **Poetry:** 3-4 pages max. **Art:** 5x7 B&W. **Tips:** "Seeks work with a point of view and some passion, on issues of pressing importance (especially with urban slant). Challenge conventional notions of what poetry is and do so with a social conscience. An eclectic fusion of fiction, poetry, and commentary aimed at an educated, curious reader." **Queries:** Preferred. **E-Queries:** Yes. **Unsolicited mss:** Accepts. **Response:** Queries 1-2 weeks, submissions 2-4 months, SASE required (IRCs). **Freelance Content:** 85%. **Rights:** FNAR. **Payment:** On publication.

THE SUN

See full listing in General Interest category.

SYCAMORE REVIEW

Purdue University
Dept. of English, 500 Oval Dr., West Lafayette, IN 47907-2038. 765-494-3783. E-mail: sycamore@purdue.edu. Web site: www.sla.purdue.edu/sycamore. Bi-annual. $7.00/$12.00. Circ.: 700. Paul D. Reich, Editor. **Description:** Fiction, poetry, essays, interviews, and translations. **Queries:** Not necessary. **Unsolicited mss:** Accepts. **Response:** Queries 1-2 weeks, submissions 3-4 months, SASE required.

TALKING RIVER REVIEW

Lewis-Clark State College, 500 Eighth Ave., Lewiston, ID 83501. 208-799-2307. Biannual. $7/$14. Circ.: 500. **Description:** Work from established and first-time writers. **Fiction:** Short stories; up to 25 pages. **Nonfiction:** Literary essays; up to 25 pages. **Poetry:** Any style; 1-5 pages. **Tips:** Send only your best work. Reads manuscripts September 1-March 1. **Queries:** Not necessary. **E-Queries:** No. **Unsolicited mss:** Accepts. **Response:** No queries, submissions 3-4 months, SASE. **Freelance Content:** 100%. **Rights:** 1st. **Payment:** In copies.

TAR RIVER POETRY

East Carolina University
Dept. of English, Greenville, NC 27858-4353. 252-328-6046. Bi-annual. $10/yr.,$18/2 years. Circ.: 650. Peter Makuck, Editor. **Description:** Formal and open form poetry, reviews, and interviews. **Poetry:** Strong imagery, figurative language; to 6 pages. **Tips:** No sentimental, flat poetry. Emphasize the visual. **Queries:** Not necessary. **E-Queries:** No. **Unsolicited mss:** Accepts. **Response:** Queries 1 week, submissions 4-6 weeks, SASE. **Freelance Content:** 100%. **Payment:** In copies.

TERRA INCOGNITA

P.O. Box 150585, Brooklyn, NY 11215-0585. 718-492-3508.
E-mail: terraincognitamagazine@yahoo.com. Web site: www.terra-incognita.com.
Annual. $7.51/issue. Circ.: 500. **Description:** Online and print journal that publishes poetry, fiction, essays, articles, and interviews in English and Spanish. Also features art and photography. **Nonfiction:** Articles, essays, interviews; 3,500-5,000 words. **Poetry:** Submit up to 7 poems. **Tips:** "Writers should submit work that they believe in deeply, that they've worked on carefully, and that has a unique voice." **Queries:** Preferred. **Unsolicited mss:** Accepts. **Response:** 1-3 months, SASE required. **Freelance Content:** 75%. **Rights:** FNASR. **Payment:** In copies. **Contact:** Alexandra Van de Kamp, Poetry Editor; William Glenn, Prose Editor.

THE TEXAS REVIEW

Sam Houston State University
English Dept., P.O. Box 2146, Huntsville, TX 77341-2146. 936-294-1992.
E-mail: eng_pdr@shsu.edu. Web site: www.shsu.edu/~www_trp. Semi-annual.
$20/yr. Circ.: 1,200. Paul Ruffin, Editor. **Description:** Poetry, fiction, and nonfiction. **Tips:** "We do not read manuscripts between May 1-September 1. **Queries:** Not necessary. **E-Queries:** Yes. **Unsolicited mss:** Does not accept. **Response:** Queries 1 week, submissions 6-8 weeks, SASE required. **Rights:** 1st.

THIRD COAST

Western Michigan University, Dept. of English, Kalamazoo, MI 49008-5092.
Biannually. $6/$11. Circ.: 500. Glenn Deutsch, Editor. **Description:** For contemporary writers and readers; fiction, creative nonfiction, and poetry. **Tips:** Address submissions to appropriate editor (fiction, creative nonfiction, or poetry). Accepts simultaneous submissions with notice. Sample copy $6, guidelines free with SASE. **Queries:** Not necessary. **E-Queries:** No. **Unsolicited mss:** Accepts. **Response:** SASE. **Freelance Content:** 80%. **Rights:** FNASR. **Payment:** On publication.

13TH MOON

University of Albany, SUNY
Dept. of English, HU 378, Albany, NY 12222. 518-442-5593.
E-mail: moon13@albany.edu. Web site: www.albany.edu/13thmoon. Annual.
$10/issue. Circ.: 500. Judith Emlyn Johnson, Editor. **Description:** Feminist literary journal, with literature and graphic arts by contemporary women. Seeks to draw attention to neglected categories of women artists. **Fiction:** 5 pages. **Nonfiction:** Feminist nonfiction on women's issues; 5 pages. **Poetry:** Women's reflections on global issues; 3-5 poems. **Tips:** Themed issues; accepts submissions September through May. "A historical and ongoing commitment to publishing the work of minority women, lesbians, and women of color." **Queries:** Preferred. **E-Queries:** No. **Unsolicited mss:** Accepts. **Response:** SASE required. **Freelance Content:** 100%. **Rights:** One-time. **Payment:** In copies.

THOUGHTS FOR ALL SEASONS
478 NE 56th St., Miami, FL 33137.
$6. Circ.: 1,000. Prof. Michael P. Richard, Editor. **Description:** Irregular serial publication that celebrates the epigram, of 2-4 lines, as a literary form. Includes humor and satire. **Poetry:** Rhyming, quatrains, limericks, nonsense verse with good imagery; to 1 page. **Columns, Departments:** Thematic by issue; to 10 pages. **Queries:** Not necessary. **E-Queries:** No. **Response:** 21 days, SASE required. **Freelance Content:** 60%. **Payment:** In copies.

THE THREEPENNY REVIEW
P.O. Box 9131, Berkeley, CA 94709. 510-849-4545.
Web site: www.threepennyreview.com. Quarterly. $25/yr. Circ.: 9,000. Wendy Lesser, Editor. **Description:** "Literary and immensely readable" (*Publishers Weekly*). Offers reviews of the arts. Features new poetry, short stories, memoirs, and essays. **Fiction:** To 5,000 words; pays up to $200. **Nonfiction:** Essays on books, theater, film, dance, music, art, television, and politics; 1,500-3,000 words; pays up to $200. **Poetry:** To 100 lines; pays $100. **Tips:** Manuscripts read September-May. **Queries:** Preferred. **Response:** 2 months, SASE. **Payment:** On publication.

TRIQUARTERLY
Northwestern University, 2020 Ridge Ave., Evanston, IL 60208-4302. 847-491-3490. Web site: www.triquarterly.org. 3x/yr. $11.95. Circ.: 4,000. Susan Firestone Hahn, Editor. **Description:** Fiction, poetry, and critical commentary, from authors of diverse heritage, backgrounds, and styles. **Fiction:** Literary fiction (not genre); $5/page. **Nonfiction:** Query first; $5/page. **Poetry:** Serious, aesthetically informed, inventive; $.50/line. **Queries:** Not necessary. **E-Queries:** No. **Unsolicited mss:** Accepts. **Response:** Queries 2 months, submissions 3 months, SASE. **Freelance Content:** 70%. **Rights:** FNASR. **Payment:** On publication.

TWO RIVERS REVIEW
P.O. Box 158, Clinton, NY 13323.
E-mail: tworiversreview@juno.com.
Web site: http://trrpoetry.tripod.com/tworiversreview/index.html. Bi-annual. $6/$12. Circ.: 400. Philip Memmer, Editor. **Description:** Poetry with strong craft and clear language. Original work only; all varieties. Submit up to 4 poems at a time (no more than 3 times/calendar year). **Tips:** No e-mail submissions. Manuscripts without SASE are discarded. **Queries:** Not necessary. **E-Queries:** Yes. **Unsolicited mss:** Accepts. **Response:** 2-8 weeks, SASE required. **Freelance Content:** 80%. **Rights:** FNAR. **Payment:** In copies.

VERMONT INK
P.O. Box 3297, Burlington, VT 05401-3297.
E-mail: vermontink@aol.com. Web site: www.vermontink.com. Donna Leach, Editor. **Description:** Quarterly, short stories and poetry. **Fiction:** Well-written, entertaining, G-rated stories (adventure, historical, humor, mainstream, mystery and suspense,

regional interest, romance, science fiction, westerns); 1,000-3,000 words; ¼ to ½ cent/word. **Poetry:** Upbeat and humorous; 4-20 lines; $5. **Tips:** Send complete manuscript, cover letter, short bio, and SASE. Sample copy $4. **Queries:** Not necessary.

VERSE
University of Georgia, English Dept., Athens, GA 30602.
3x/yr. $8/$18. Circ.: 1,000. Brian Henry, Andrew Zawacki, Editors. **Description:** Poetry, criticism, and interviews with poets. Focus is international and eclectic, and favors the innovative over the staid. **Nonfiction:** Essays on poetry, interviews, and reviews. **Poetry:** Up to 5 poems. **Queries:** Not necessary. **Unsolicited mss:** Accepts. **Response:** Queries 2 months, submissions 1-4 months, SASE. **Freelance Content:** 75%. **Rights:** FNAR. **Payment:** 2 copies and a one-year subscription.

VESTAL REVIEW
2609 Dartmouth Dr., Vestal, NY 13850.
E-mail: editor@stny.rr.com. Web site: www.vestalreview.net. Quarterly. Circ.: 2,000. Mark Budman, Sue O'Neill, Editors. **Description:** Flash fiction, any genre; under 500 words; $.03-$.10/word. **Tips:** Seeking literary stories; no children's stories or syrupy romance. E-mail submissions only. See Web site for details. Sample copy $4.50. **Queries:** Not necessary. **E-Queries:** Yes. **Unsolicited mss:** Accepts. **Response:** 2 months. **Freelance Content:** 100%. **Rights:** 1st electronic.

THE VIRGINIA QUARTERLY REVIEW
One W Range, P.O. Box 400223, Charlottesville, VA 22904-4223. 434-924-3124.
Web site: www.virginia.edu/vqr. Quarterly. $5/$18. Circ.: 4,000. Staige D. Blackford, Editor. **Description:** A journal of literature and discussion. **Fiction:** Quality fiction; $10/page. **Nonfiction:** Serious essays, articles on literature, science, politics, economics, etc.; 3,000-6,000 words; $10/page. **Poetry:** $1/line. **Queries:** Preferred. **Unsolicited mss:** Accepts. **Payment:** On publication.

WEBER STUDIES
Weber State University, 1214 University Circle, Ogden, UT 84408-1214. 626-6616.
E-mail: weberstudies@weber.edu. Web site: www.weberstudies.weber.edu. Triquarterly. Circ.: 1,000. Brad L. Roghaar, Editor. **Description:** Narratives, critical commentary/opinion, fiction, and poetry, on the environment and culture of the contemporary American west. **Fiction:** 5,000 words; $100-$150. **Nonfiction:** 5,000 words; $100-$150. **Poetry:** Submit multiple poems, up to 6 poems or 200 lines; $25-$70. **Queries:** Not necessary. **Unsolicited mss:** Accepts. **Response:** Queries 1 week, submissions 3-4 months, SASE required. **Freelance Content:** 80%. **Rights:** 1st and Web archive. **Payment:** On publication.

WEST BRANCH
Bucknell University, Bucknell Hall, Lewisburg, PA 17837-2029. 570-577-1853.
E-mail: westbranch@bucknell.edu. Web site: www.bucknell.edu/westbranch. Semiannual. $6/$10. Circ.: 700. Paula Closson Buck, Editor. **Description:** Original,

unpublished poetry, fiction, literary nonfiction, and book reviews. Pays $10/page ($20 minimum/$100 maximum). **Fiction:** Realistic and avant-garde. **Nonfiction:** Format open. **Poetry:** No confessional verse. **Tips:** Query for book reviews only; send complete mss for all else. Sample copy $3. **Queries:** Not necessary. **E-Queries:** Yes. **Unsolicited mss:** Accepts. **Response:** 1 month, SASE. **Freelance Content:** 90%. **Rights:** FNAR.

WESTERN HUMANITIES REVIEW

University of Utah
255 S Central Campus Dr., Room 3500, Salt Lake City, UT 84112. 801-581-6070.
E-mail: whr@mail.hum.utah.edu. Web site: www.hum.utah.edu/whr. Biannually. $16/yr. Barry Weller, Editor. **Description:** Fiction, nonfiction, and poetry for educated readers. Pays $5/page, dependent on funding. **Fiction:** Literary fiction, exciting and original (no genre fiction). **Nonfiction:** On humanities issues. **Tips:** Reviews submissions September-May; all other submissions returned unread. **Queries:** Not necessary. **E-Queries:** No. **Unsolicited mss:** Accepts. **Response:** 2-10 weeks, SASE required. **Rights:** FNAR. **Payment:** On publication.

WHETSTONE

Barrington Area Arts Council
P.O. Box 1266, Barrington, IL 60011. 847-382-5626.
E-mail: baacouncil@aol.com. Annual. $7. Circ.: 850. Dale Griffith, Editor-in-Chief. **Description:** Poetry, short fiction, novel excerpts, and creative fiction, from established and emerging artists across the country. **Fiction:** Character-driven prose that tells truth in detail; 5,000 words; pay varies. **Poetry:** Concrete rather than abstract; submit up to 5 poems. **E-Queries:** Yes. **Unsolicited mss:** Accepts. **Response:** Queries 2 weeks, submissions 5 months, SASE required. **Freelance Content:** 100%.

WILLOW SPRINGS

MS-1, Eastern Washington University
705 W First, Spokane, WA 99204. 509-623-4349.
Biannual. $6/$11.50. Circ.: 1,200. Jennifer Davis, Editor. **Description:** Poetry, short fiction, and nonfiction, of literary merit. **Tips:** No simultaneous submissions. Submit prose and poetry in separate envelopes. Manuscripts read September 15-May 15. **Queries:** Not necessary. **E-Queries:** No. **Unsolicited mss:** Accepts. **Response:** 4-8 weeks, SASE required. **Freelance Content:** 100%. **Rights:** FNAR. **Payment:** In copies.

WIND

P.O. Box 24548, Lexington, KY 40524.
E-mail: wind@wind.org. Web site: www.wind.wind.org. 3x/yr. $15/yr. Circ.: 500. Chris Green, Editor; Arwen Donahue, Fiction Editor; Rebecca Howell, Poetry Editor. **Description:** Short stories, poems, and essays. Also, reviews of books (small presses), literary news of interest . **Fiction:** Any style, genre, or subject matter; to 3,000 words. **Nonfiction:** Essays on any topic; to 3,000 words. **Poetry:** Varied subject matter,

style, poetic form, etc.; 3-5 poems. **Tips:** "We operate on the metaphor of neighborly conversation between writers about the differing worlds in which they live. Perhaps the most important thing to do is to listen to the conversation first!" **Queries:** Required. **E-Queries:** No. **Unsolicited mss:** Accepts. **Freelance Content:** 80%. **Rights:** FNASR. **Payment:** In copies.

WINDSOR REVIEW
University of Windsor
Dept. of English, Windsor, Ontario N9B 3P4 Canada. 519-253-3000.
E-mail: uwrevu@uwindsor.ca. Web site: www.windsorreview.com. Biannual. $15/issue. Circ.: 500. Marty Gervais, Editor. **Description:** Literary fiction and poetry. **Fiction:** Literary fiction; up to 5,000 words; $25/story plus 1-year subscription. **Nonfiction:** Interviews with well-known writers; 3,000-7,000 words; $50. **Poetry:** All types; experimental, concrete, or traditional; $10/poem plus 1-year subscription. **Art:** B&W preferred; $100-$200. **Tips:** Does not accept e-mail submissions, but will accept e-queries regarding submission status, etc. **Queries:** Not necessary. **E-Queries:** Yes. **Unsolicited mss:** Accepts. **Response:** Submissions 1-3 months, SASE. **Freelance Content:** 90%. **Rights:** FNAR. **Payment:** On publication.

WITNESS
Oakland Community College
27055 Orchard Lake Rd., Farmington Hills, MI 48334. 734-996-5732.
E-mail: stinepj@umich.edu. Web site: www.webdelsol.com/witness. Semi-annual. Peter Stine, Editor. **Description:** Literary journal featuring fiction, poetry, essays, memoirs, and artwork. **Fiction:** Fiction, 5-20 pages; pays $6/page. **Nonfiction:** Essays, 5-20 pages; pays $6/page. **Poetry:** Submit up to 3 at a time; pays $10/page. **Tips:** Accepts simultaneous submissions. Do not submit material electronically. **Payment:** On publication.

THE WORCESTER REVIEW
6 Chatham St., Worcester, MA 01609.
Web site: www.geocities.com/paris/leftbank/6433. Annual. $20. Rodger Martin, Editor. **Description:** Fiction, poetry, and critical nonfiction essays on poetry with New England connection. Submit fiction and nonfiction pieces of 4,000 words or less, and no more than 5 poems. **Tips:** Sample copy $6. **Queries:** Not necessary. **E-Queries:** No. **Unsolicited mss:** Accepts. **Response:** 6 months, SASE required. **Rights:** FNAR. **Payment:** In copies.

XAVIER REVIEW
Xavier Review Press, Box 110-C, Xavier University
1 Drexel Dr., New Orleans, LA 70125-1098. 504-483-7303.
E-mail: rskinner@xula.edu. 2/yr. $5/$10. Richard Collins, Editor. **Description:** Fiction, poetry, short drama, and nonfiction essays and criticism on African-American studies, the Deep South, and the Caribbean. Submit fiction and nonfiction pieces up to 4,000 words. For poetry, send 2-3 short poems, or 1 long poem (up to 3 pages).

Tips: "Read back issues, and don't send material obviously not within our stated interests. No sci-fi, romance, westerns, or other genre material." **Queries:** Not necessary. **E-Queries:** Yes. **Unsolicited mss:** Accepts. **Response:** Queries 30 days, submissions 60 days. **Freelance Content:** 90%. **Rights:** FNAR. **Payment:** In copies.

YALE REVIEW

Yale University, P.O. Box 208243, New Haven, CT 06520-8243. 203-432-0499. Web site: www.yale.edu/yalereview. Quarterly. $28/yr. Circ.: 6,000. J.D. McClatchy, Editor. **Description:** Fiction, nonfiction, and poetry. **Fiction:** $400/story. **Nonfiction:** $500. **Poetry:** Serious poetry; pay varies. **Queries:** Not necessary. **E-Queries:** No. **Unsolicited mss:** Accepts. **Response:** Queries 1 month, submissions 2 months, SASE. **Freelance Content:** 30%. **Rights:** 1st serial. **Payment:** On publication.

YEMASSEE

University of South Carolina
Dept. of English, Columbia, SC 29208. 803-777-2085.
Web site. www.cla.sc.edu/engl/index.html. Biannual. $15 ($7 student). Circ.: 500. Carl Johnson, Jill Carroll, Editors. **Description:** Poetry, short fiction, one-act plays, brief essays, and interviews. **Fiction:** Short, smart, accessible, character-driven; to 5,000 words. **Nonfiction:** Literary reviews, interviews with literary figures; to 3,000 words. **Poetry:** No fixed length; prefers poems under 3 pages. **Tips:** Offers $200 award for fiction and poetry in each issue. "Committed to publishing the work of emerging writers as well as established writers. Try us!" **Queries:** Not necessary. **E-Queries:** No. **Unsolicited mss:** Accepts. **Response:** 2 months after each deadline, SASE required. **Freelance Content:** 100%. **Rights:** 1st.

ZOETROPE: ALL STORY

916 Kearny St., San Francisco, CA 94133. 415-788-7500.
E-mail: info@all-story.com. Web site: www.all-story.com. Quarterly. Circ.: 20,000. Francis Ford Coppola, Publisher. **Description:** Stories and one-act plays, no longer than 7,000 words. **Tips:** No submissions accepted from June 1-August 31. **Queries:** Preferred. **E-Queries:** No. **Unsolicited mss:** Accepts. **Response:** 5 months, SASE required. **Rights:** FNASR. **Payment:** On acceptance.

ZYZZYVA

P.O. Box 590069, San Francisco, CA 94159-0069. 415-752-4393.
E-mail: editor@zyzzyva.org. Web site: www.zyzzyva.org. 3x/yr. $11/$24. Circ.: 4,000. Howard Junker, Editor. **Description:** West Coast writers and artists; fiction (no novel excerpts), nonfiction essays, and poetry. Pays $50/piece. **Tips:** Accepts material only from current West Coast (California, Oregon, Washington, Hawaii, Alaska) residents. **Queries:** Not necessary. **E-Queries:** No. **Unsolicited mss:** Accepts. **Response:** 1 month, SASE required. **Freelance Content:** 85%. **Rights:** FNASR. **Payment:** On publication.

MYSTERY & DETECTIVE

COZY DETECTIVE MYSTERY
686 Jakes Ct., McMinnville, OR 97128-2546.
E-mail: detectivemag@onlinemac.com.
Web site: www.angelfire.com/ms/COZYDETECTIVE. 3-5x/yr. $4.95/issue. Tom Youngblood, Editor. **Description:** Mystery stories by new authors breaking into the genre. Stories must be heavy on character and mystery content. **Tips:** No stories over 6,000 words. Also seeks cartoons, poems, and reviews. **Queries:** Preferred. **E-Queries:** Yes. **Unsolicited mss:** Accepts. **Response:** 6 weeks, SASE. **Rights:** FNASR. **Payment:** In copies.

ELLERY QUEEN'S MYSTERY MAGAZINE
475 Park Ave. S, Fl. 11, New York, NY 10016.
Web site: www.themysteryplace.com. 11x/yr. $3.50/$39.97. Circ.: 300,000. Janet Hutchings, Editor. **Description:** A short story mystery magazine. **Fiction:** Mystery and crime fiction: police procedurals, private-eye stories, tales of suspense, traditional whodunits, cozies; 250-20,000 words (usually 2,500-8,000 words); $.05-$.08/word. **Tips:** Interested in new authors. Seeks private-eye stories (avoid sex, sadism, sensationalism for its own sake). "We are always in the market for the best detective, crime, and mystery stories being written today." Sample copy for $5. **Queries:** Not necessary. **E-Queries:** No. **Unsolicited mss:** Accepts. **Response:** 3 months; SASE required. **Freelance Content:** 95%. **Rights:** 1st serial. **Payment:** On acceptance.

FANTASTIC STORIES OF THE IMAGINATION
See full listing in Science Fiction & Fantasy category.

HARDBOILED
P.O. Box 209, Brooklyn, NY 11228-0209.
Web site: www.gryphonbooks.com. Gary Lovisi, Editor. **Description:** "We seek hard-hitting crime fiction by new masters. Mind-blasting nonfiction and riveting private eye and crime stories." **Fiction:** Cutting-edge crime fiction, with impact; to 3,000 words. **Tips:** Sample copy $8. New double issue: 200+ pages, $20. **Queries:** Preferred. **E-Queries:** No. **Unsolicited mss:** Accepts. **Response:** Queries 2 weeks, submissions 6 weeks, SASE. **Freelance Content:** 35%. **Rights:** FNAR.

ALFRED HITCHCOCK'S MYSTERY MAGAZINE
475 Park Ave. S, Fl. 11, New York, NY 10016.
Web site: www.themysteryplace.com. 11x/yr. $3.50/issue. **Description:** Original mystery short stories. **Fiction:** Well-plotted, plausible mystery, suspense, detection, and crime stories. Ghost stories, humor, futuristic, or atmospheric tales considered if they include a crime (or the suggestion of one); to 12,000 words, pay varies. **Tips:** Submissions by new writers strongly encouraged. No reprints. **Queries:** Not necessary. **E-Queries:** No. **Unsolicited mss:** Accepts. **Response:** 3 months, SASE

required. **Freelance Content:** 100%. **Rights:** Anthology, foreign serial. **Payment:** On acceptance.

THE MYSTERY REVIEW

P.O. Box 233, Colborne, Ontario K0K 1S0 Canada. 613-475-4440. E-mail: mystrev@reach.net. Web site: www.themysteryreview.com. Quarterly. $25/yr. Circ.: 5,000. Barbara Davey, Editor. **Description:** Reviews, interviews, word games, and puzzles related to mystery titles and authors. No fiction. Pays honorarium. **Nonfiction:** True crime, interviews with authors or others related to the mystery genre; 2,000-5,000 words. **Fillers:** Short filler articles, puzzles, and word games related to the mystery/suspense genre. **Columns, Departments:** Book Reviews, Book Shop Beat; 500-700 words. **Tips:** Sample copy $7.50. **Queries:** Required. **E-Queries:** Yes. **Unsolicited mss:** Does not accept. **Freelance Content:** 90%. **Rights:** FNAR. **Payment:** On publication.

NEW MYSTERY MAGAZINE

101 W 23rd St., New York, NY 10011-2490. 212-353-3495. E-mail: editorial@newmystery.com. Web site: www.equisearch.com. Quarterly. $37.77/yr. Circ.: 100,000. Charles Raisch, Editor. **Description:** Mystery, crime, detection, and suspense short stories. **Fiction:** Prefers sympathetic characters in trouble, visual scenes; 2,000-6,000 words; pays to $500. **Columns, Departments:** Book reviews, 250-2,000 words, of upcoming or recent novels. **Tips:** No true-crime stories accepted. Send $8 with 9x12 SASE for contributor's packet and sample copy. **Payment:** On publication.

OVER MY DEAD BODY!

P.O. Box 1778, Auburn, WA 98071-1778. E-mail: omdb@worldnet.att.net. Web site: www.overmydeadbody.com. Quarterly. $5.95/$20. Circ.: 1,000. Cherie Jung, Editor. **Description:** Mystery, suspense, and crime fiction and nonfiction. **Fiction:** Mystery or crime-related fiction, from cozy to hardboiled, including suspense, and cross-over mysteries; 750-4,000 words; $.01/word. **Nonfiction:** Author profiles/interviews, mystery-related travel articles; 500 words and up; $10-$25. **Art:** Photographs to accompany mss. **Queries:** Required. **E-Queries:** Yes. **Unsolicited mss:** Accepts. **Response:** 4-6 weeks, SASE. **Freelance Content:** 100%. **Rights:** FNASR. **Payment:** On acceptance. **Contact:** Fiction Editor or Feature Editor.

THE STRAND

P.O. Box 1418, Birmingham, MI 48012-1418. 248-788-5948. E-mail: strandmag@worldnet.att.net. Web site: www.strandmag.com. Quarterly. $24.95/yr. Circ.: 16,000. Andrew Gulli, Editor. **Description:** Featured pieces are modeled after the writing styles of Sir Arthur Conan Doyle, Daphne du Maurier, and Robert Louis Stevenson. **Fiction:** 3,000-5,000 words; $50-$150. **Tips:** Send SASE for guidelines. **Payment:** On publication.

ROMANCE & CONFESSION

BLACK ROMANCE/BRONZE THRILLS
See full listing in Ethnic & Multicultural category.

BLACK SECRETS
Sterling/MacFadden
333 Seventh Ave., Fl. 11, New York, NY 10001-5004. 212-780-4800.
E-mail: tpowell@sterlingmacfadden.com. Web site: www.sterlingmacfadden.com.
Monthly. $11/yr. Circ.: 70,000. Takesha Powell, Editor. **Description:** For African-
American women. **Fiction:** Erotic, short, romantic fiction; $100. **Columns,
Departments:** $125. **Queries:** Required. **E-Queries:** Yes. **Unsolicited mss:**
Accepts. **Response:** SASE required. **Freelance Content:** 100%. **Rights:** All.
Payment: On publication.

INTIMACY
Sterling/Macfadden
333 Seventh Ave., Fl. 11, New York, NY 10001. 212-780-3500.
E-mail: tpowell@sterlingmacfadden.com. Web site: www.sterlingmacfadden.com.
Bimonthly. $2.99/issue. Circ.: 50,000. Takesha D. Powell, Editor. **Description:**
Short, first-person romantic fiction for African-American women. **Fiction:** For black
women, ages 18-45. Must have contemporary plot with two romantic/intimate love
scenes; 19-21 pages. **Tips:** "Avoid clichés, profanity, and stereotypes." **Queries:** Not
necessary. **E-Queries:** Yes. **Unsolicited mss:** Accepts. **Response:** 3-4 weeks, SASE
required. **Freelance Content:** 100%. **Rights:** All. **Payment:** On publication.

ROMANCE AND BEYOND
3527 Ambassador Caffery Pkwy., PMB 9, Lafayette, LA 70503-5130. 337-991-9095.
E-mail: rbeyond@aol.com. Web site: www.romanceandbeyond.com. Annual.
Softcover anthology $9.99. Mary Tarver, Editor. **Description:** Speculative romantic
short stories and poetry, combining elements of romance with science fiction, fantasy,
and the paranormal. **Fiction:** Up to 10,000 words; $.005/word. **Poetry:** Length
varies; pays in copies. **Tips:** Reading period February-May. Annual contest: October-
January. "Internal conflict created by attraction between hero and heroine. Tone can
be dark to humorous, but story must be a romance with happy ending. Sources of
external conflict left to your imagination, the more original the better." **Queries:** Not
necessary. **E-Queries:** No. **Unsolicited mss:** Accepts. **Response:** Submission 4
months, SASE. **Freelance Content:** 100%. **Rights:** One-time. **Payment:** On
acceptance.

ROMANTIC TIMES
See full listing in Writing & Publishing category.

TRUE ROMANCE

Sterling/Macfadden

333 Seventh Ave., Fl. 11, New York, NY 10001. 212-979-4800.

E-mail: pvitucci@sterlingmacfadden.com. Monthly. $2.99/issue. Circ.: 225,000. Pat Vitucci, Editor. **Description:** Dramatic stories of personal redemption, romance, family relationships, humor, women's issues. **Fiction:** Topical stories based on news events; intriguing subjects; 5,000-10,000 words; $.03/word. **Poetry:** Up to 24 lines; $10-$30. **Columns, Departments:** Cupid's Corner (photo and 1,000 words), $50; Passages (to 2,000 words), $50-$100; The Way I Lived It, first- or third-person fiction (2,000-4,000 words), $100-$150. **Tips:** "Our readers must sympathize with the narrator. Stories are to be first-person narrative. Please read an issue or two before submitting." **Queries:** Preferred. **E-Queries:** Yes. **Unsolicited mss:** Accepts. **Response:** 8-12 months, SASE required. **Freelance Content:** 100%. **Payment:** On publication.

WOMAN'S WORLD

See full listing in Women's Publications category.

SCIENCE FICTION & FANTASY

ABSOLUTE MAGNITUDE

P.O. Box 2988, Radford, VA 24143. 540-763-2925.

E-mail: absolutemagnitude@dnapublications.com.

Web site: www.dnapublications.com. Quarterly. Warren Lapine, Publisher/Editor/Art Director. **Description:** Full-size quarterly that features character-driven, technical science fiction. **Fiction:** No fantasy, horror, satire, or funny science fiction. Seeks tightly plotted stories with well-developed characters. Characters should be the driving force behind the main action in the story; 1,000-25,000 words (3,000-8,000 words preferred); $.02-$.06/word. **Tips:** Do not submit material via e-mail. See Web site for specific submission guidelines. **Queries:** Not necessary. **Rights:** FNASR. **Payment:** On publication.

ANALOG SCIENCE FICTION AND FACT

475 Park Ave. S, New York, NY 10016. 212-686-7188.

E-mail: analog@dellmagazines.com. Web site: www.analogsf.com. 11x/yr. $3.50/$39.97. Circ.: 50,000. Stanley Schmidt, Editor. **Description:** Science fiction, with strong characters in believable future or alien settings. Home to many of science fiction's foremost writers, with long tradition of discovering and cultivating new talent. **Fiction:** Short stories, 2,000-7,500 words; novelettes, 10,000-20,000 words; serials, to 80,000 words. Pays $.04-$.08/word. **Nonfiction:** Future-related articles; 4,000 words; $.06/word. **Poetry:** $1/line. **Tips:** Queries required for serials and nonfiction only. **Queries:** Preferred. **E-Queries:** No. **Unsolicited mss:** Accepts. **Response:** 1 month, SASE required. **Freelance Content:** 100%. **Rights:** FNASR, nonexclusive foreign serial. **Payment:** On acceptance.

ASIMOV'S SCIENCE FICTION MAGAZINE

475 Park Ave. S, Fl. 11, New York, NY 10016. 212-686-7188.
E-mail: asimovs@dellmagazines.com. Web site: www.asimovs.com. 11x/yr. Circ.:
40,000. Gardner Dozois, Editor. **Description:** Short, character-oriented science fiction and fantasy. **Fiction:** Stories in which characters, rather than science, provide main focus for reader's interest. Mostly serious, thoughtful fiction, some humorous; to 30,000 words; $.06-$.08/word. **Poetry:** Up to 40 lines; $1/line. **Tips:** "Borderline fantasy is fine, but no sword and/or sorcery. No explicit sex or violence." **Queries:** Does not accept. **E-Queries:** No. **Unsolicited mss:** Accepts. **Response:** 2-3 months, SASE required. **Freelance Content:** 90%. **Rights:** First English Rights, nonexclusive reprint rights. **Payment:** On acceptance.

CENTURY MAGAZINE

P.O. Box 336, Hastings-on-Hudson, NY 10706.
E-mail: editor@centurymag.com. Web site: www.centurymag.com. Robert K.J. Killheffer. **Description:** Literary science fiction, fantasy, and magic realism. **Fiction:** Speculative; 1,000-20,000 words; $.04/word. **Queries:** Not necessary. **E-Queries:** No. **Unsolicited mss:** Accepts. **Response:** 4-6 weeks; SASE required. **Rights:** First. **Payment:** On acceptance.

DRAGON

3245 146th Place SE, Suite 110, Bellevue, WA 98007. 425-289-0060.
E-mail: dragon@wizards.com. Web site: www.paizopublishing.com. Monthly. $37.95. Circ.: 45,000. Jesse Decker, Editor. **Description:** On fantasy and science fiction role-playing games. **Fiction:** Sword and sorcery short stories, humor, horror; up to 5,000 words; $.05/word. **Nonfiction:** Idea generators, new rules; up to 4,000 words; $.05/word. **Tips:** All submissions must include a disclosure form. **Queries:** Required. **E-Queries:** Yes. **Unsolicited mss:** Accepts. **Response:** 12 weeks, SASE required. **Rights:** First worldwide or all. **Payment:** On acceptance.

DREAMS OF DECADENCE

P.O. Box 2988, Radford, VA 24143-2988. 540-763-2925.
E-mail: dreamsofdecadence@dnapublications.com.
Web site: www.dnapublications.com. Angela Kessler, Editor/Art Director. **Description:** Quarterly digest devoted to vampire poetry and fiction. **Fiction:** Original, well-written short stories. Emphasis is on dark fantasy rather than horror. Seeks unique ideas, original story concepts, and well-developed characters. Do not send stories with over-used plots or themes; 1,000-15,000 words; $.01-$.05/word. **Poetry:** Seeks all forms of poetry relating to vampires. Poems should be not be horrific in nature, but should be explicitly vampiric; up to 2 pages; $3-$20/poem. **Tips:** Do not submit material via e-mail. Sample copy available for $5; see Web site for writers' guidelines. **Queries:** Not necessary. **Rights:** FNASR. **Payment:** On publication.

FANTASTIC STORIES OF THE IMAGINATION

P.O. Box 329, Brightwaters, NY 11718-0329.
E-mail: fantasticstories@dnapublications.com. Web site: www.dnapublications.com.
Edward J. McFadden, Editor/Art Director. **Description:** Quarterly fantasy and science fiction magazine. Stories, poetry, interviews, and art. **Fiction:** Stories must be well-written and entertaining. Mixing of other genres within stories acceptable, so long as basic science fiction and fantasy elements are present; 2,000-15,000 words (4,000-5,000 average); $.01-$.05/word. **Nonfiction:** Interviews. **Poetry:** Accepts all forms and styles; 3-20 lines; up to $1/line. **Tips:** Do not submit material via e-mail. Sample copy available for $5. See Web site for guidelines. **Queries:** Not necessary. **E-Queries:** No. **Unsolicited mss:** Accepts. **Response:** 1-2 months, SASE. **Rights:** FNASR.

FLESH AND BLOOD

121 Joseph St., Bayville, NJ 08721.
E-mail: horrorjack@aol.com. Web site: www.fleshandbloodpress.com. 4x/yr. Circ.: 500. Jack Fisher, Editor-in-Chief; Robert Swartwood, Senior Editor; Teri A. Jacobs, Assistant Editor. **Description:** Dark fantasy, bizarre, and supernatural stories. Despite name, prefers work that is subtle, magic realism, bizarre eccentric, avant-garde, or any mix thereof. **Fiction:** Currently seeking horror/dark fantasy work. Should have one or more following elements: darkly fantastic, surreal, supernatural, bizarre, offbeat. 6,000 words max; $.04-$.05/word. **Tips:** Don't exceed max. word count. Stories should be unique, entertaining, and imaginative. The more descriptive and dark, the better. Avoid stories with insane main characters; stories not set in the modern day; over-used vampire, werewolf stories; tales about evil gods and their followers; based solely on monsters; excessive gore, blood, sex, etc. Include SASE and brief letter with previous publication credits. **Queries:** Not necessary. **E-Queries:** Yes. **Unsolicited mss:** Accepts. **Response:** 2-3 months, SASE required. **Rights:** FNASR, reprints. **Payment:** On publication.

HADROSAUR TALES

P.O. Box 8468, Las Cruces, NM 88006.
E-mail: hadrosaur.productions@verizon.net. Web site: www.hadrosaur.com. 3x/yr. $6.95/$15. Circ.: 150. David Summers, Editor. **Description:** Short stories and poetry. **Fiction:** Literary science fiction and fantasy. Contemporary or historical fiction welcome if it includes a mythic or science-fictional element. Psychological or character-oriented horror considered if it does not present any graphic violence; to 6,000 words; $6/story. **Poetry:** Poems with science fiction/fantasy imagery and themes; to 50 lines; $2. **Art:** Pen-and-ink line drawings (cover); pay negotiable. **Tips:** Avoid cliché-fantasy (e.g., lone knight goes off to slay the evil dragon). **Queries:** Not necessary. **E-Queries:** Yes. **Unsolicited mss:** Accepts. **Response:** 1-6 weeks, SASE required. **Freelance Content:** 100%. **Rights:** One-time. **Payment:** On acceptance.

THE LEADING EDGE

3146 JKHB, Provo, UT 84604.
E-mail: leading-edge@email.byu.edu. Semiannual. $12 (3 issues). Circ.: 500. Kristina Kugler, Editor. **Description:** Science fiction and fantasy. Publishes many new writers. **Fiction:** To 17,000 words; $.01/word ($10-$100). **Nonfiction:** On science fiction, fantasy, or author interviews; to 10,000 words; pays in copies. **Poetry:** Length varies; $10/poem. **Columns, Departments:** Book reviews; to 2,000 words; pays in copies. **Tips:** Does not accept submissions by e-mail. Sample copy for $4.95. "Avoid rehashed plots, poor mechanics, poor plot resolution. No sex, graphic violence, or strong language." **Queries:** Not necessary. **E-Queries:** No. **Unsolicited mss:** Accepts. **Response:** Submissions 4-6 months, SASE. **Freelance Content:** 100%. **Rights:** FNASR. **Payment:** On publication.

MAGAZINE OF FANTASY & SCIENCE FICTION

P.O. Box 3447, Hoboken, NJ 07030.
E-mail: fandsf@aol.com. Web site: www.fsfmag.com. Monthly. $3.99/issue (U.S.), $4.99/issue (Canada). Circ.: 40,000. Gordon Van Gelder, Editor. **Description:** Digest-sized, devoted to speculative fiction. **Fiction:** Prefers character-oriented stories. Science fiction element may be slight, but present; to 25,000 words; $.05-$.08/word. **Tips:** "We receive a lot of fantasy submissions, but we're looking for more science fiction and humor." **Queries:** Does not accept. **E-Queries:** No. **Unsolicited mss:** Accepts. **Response:** 8 weeks, SASE. **Rights:** worldwide serial, and option on anthology. **Payment:** On acceptance.

MYTHIC DELIRIUM

P.O. Box 13511, Roanoke, VA 24034-3511.
E-mail: mythicdelirium@dnapublications.com. Web site: www.dnapublications.com. Quarterly. Mike Allen, Editor/Art Director. **Description:** Seeks science fiction, fantasy, horror, and cross-genre poetry. Particular interest in poetry that employs well use of rhyme or traditional form. Prefers material that is under 40 lines. Pays $5 for poems under 40 lines; $10 for poems over 40 lines. **Tips:** Do not submit material via e-mail. See Web site for specific guidelines. **Payment:** 30 days after publication.

NIGHT TERRORS

1202 W Market St., Orrville, OH 44667-1710. 330-683-0338.
E-mail: dedavidson@night-terrors-publications.com.
Web site: www.night-terrors-publications.com. Annual. $6/issue. Circ.: 1,000. Mr. D.E. Davidson, Editor. **Description:** Short stories of psychological horror, the supernatural, or occult. Emphasis on "continuing terror"; stories should have beginning, middle, and end, but in the end, the terror/threat should not be resolved. **Fiction:** 2,000-5,000 words; pay in copies or by arrangement. **Tips:** "We prefer stories which make the reader think and grow edgy, not those which make them flinch or grow nauseous. No horror in which women or children are abused; no stories with child as point-of-view character." **Queries:** Not necessary. **E-Queries:** Yes. **Unsolicited**

mss: Accepts. **Response:** Queries 1 week, submissions 12 weeks, SASE. **Freelance Content:** 95%. **Rights:** FNASR. **Payment:** On publication.

ON SPEC

P.O. Box 4727, Edmonton, AB T6E 5G6 Canada. 780-413-0215.
E-mail: onspec@canada.com. Web site: www.onspec.ca. Quarterly. $22/yr. Circ.: 1,500. Diane Walton, Editor. **Description:** Seeks original, unpublished speculative fiction and poetry by Canadian authors. **Fiction:** Science fiction, fantasy, horror, ghost stories, fairy stories, magic realism, speculative fiction; to 6,000 words; C$50-C$180. **Nonfiction:** By assignment only. **Poetry:** Science fiction, fantasy themes; blank, free verse, discursive prose; to 100 lines; C$20. **Fillers:** Science fiction, fantasy, horror, ghost stories, fairy stories, magic realism, speculative fiction; to 1,000 words; C$50. **Art:** Illustrations by assignment; B&W photos; $50/inside use, $200/cover. **Tips:** Does not consider e-mailed or faxed submissions. Welcomes non-Canadian authors, but content must remain 80% Canadian. Sample copy $7. **Queries:** Not necessary. **E-Queries:** Yes. **Unsolicited mss:** Accepts. **Response:** 2-3 months, SASE required. **Rights:** FNASR. **Payment:** On acceptance.

OUTER DARKNESS

1312 N Delaware Pl., Tulsa, OK 74110. 918-832-1246.
Quarterly. $2.95 (by mail, $3.95). Circ.: 500. Dennis Kirk, Editor. **Description:** "Where Nightmares Roam Unleashed," horror and science fiction. Also poetry, cartoons, and interviews. **Fiction:** Traditional horror and science fiction; to 5,000 words; **Nonfiction:** Interviews with authors, artists, editors; to 1,500 words. **Poetry:** Some free verse, prefers traditional rhyming; to 30 lines. **Art:** All stories illustrated, submit sample work. **Queries:** Not necessary. **E-Queries:** No. **Response:** Queries 2 weeks, submissions 8-10 weeks, SASE required. **Freelance Content:** 25%. **Rights:** FNAR. **Payment:** In copies.

REALMS OF FANTASY

P.O. Box 527, Rumson, NJ 07760.
Web site: www.rofmagazine.com. Bimonthly. Shawna McCarthy, Editor. **Description:** Fantastic short fiction, in all styles (heroic, contemporary, traditional feminists, dark, light, etc.), no longer than 10,000 words. Rates begin at $.05/word ($.03/word for stories over 7,500 words). **Tips:** No standard science-fiction stories (alien worlds, technology-driven, etc.). **Queries:** Not necessary. **Unsolicited mss:** Accepts.

THE SILVER WEB

P.O. Box 38190, Tallahassee, FL 32315. 850-385-8948.
E-mail: buzzcity@yourvillage.com. Ann Kennedy, Editor. **Description:** Fantastical fiction, including science fiction, dark fantasy, etc. **Tips:** Currently not accepting unsolicited submissions. **Queries:** Preferred.

SPACE AND TIME

138 W 70 St. 4B, New York, NY 10023-4468.
Web site: www.cith.org/space&time.html. Biannual. $5/issue. Circ.: 2,000. Gordon Linzner, Editor. **Description:** Science fiction, fantasy, horror, and things that fall between the cracks. Also, a healthy selection of poetry (same genre), along with the occasion short feature. **Fiction:** Science fiction, fantasy, horror; to 10,000 words; $.01/word. **Poetry:** All styles and forms (rhymed, unrhymed, etc.). **Art:** B&W artwork assigned, to illustrate specific stories. Send photocopied samples; $10. **Tips:** Avoid clichés. No media fiction. Appreciates material that deserves to be in print, but which other magazines don't quite know what to do with. **Queries:** Not necessary. **E-Queries:** No. **Unsolicited mss:** Accepts. **Response:** 1-4 months. **Freelance Content:** 99%. **Rights:** FNASR. **Payment:** on publication.

SPELLBOUND

Eggplant Productions, 135 Shady Lane, Bolingbrook, IL 60440.
E-mail: spellbound@eggplant-productions.com.
Web site: www.eggplant-productions.com. Quarterly. Rachael Henderson Moon, Editor. **Description:** Features fantasy short stories and poems for ages 9 to 13. **Fiction:** Stories with the elements of magic, myth, adventure, legend, etc. **Fillers:** Poetry, games, puzzles, recipes, and riddles. **Tips:** No stories with gore or adult content. Accepts submissions by e-mail only. **Rights:** 1st. **Payment:** $5 plus 2 copies.

STRANGE HORIZONS

P.O. Box 1693, Dubuque, IA 52004-1693.
E-mail: editor@strangehorizons.com. Web site: www.strangehorizons.com. Weekly. Mary Anne Mohanraj, Editor-in-Chief. **Description:** E-zine of speculative and science fiction. Features art, articles, fiction, poetry, and reviews. **Fiction:** To 9,000 words; pays $.04/word. **Nonfiction:** Articles, 1,000-5,000 words; pays $40/article; **Poetry:** To 100 lines; pays $20/poem. **Columns, Departments:** Art and book reviews, 750-1,000 words; pays $20/review. **Tips:** No simultaneous submissions accepted. Submit all material via e-mail (see Web site for specific guidelines). **E-Queries:** Yes. **Rights:** 1st, worldwide (exclusive for 2 months, then reverts to author).

TALEBONES

5203 Quincy Ave. SE, Auburn, WA 98092.
E-mail: talebones@fairwoodpress.com. Web site: www.fairwoodpress.com. Quarterly. $6/$20. Circ.: 1,000. Patrick Swenson, Honna Swenson, Editors. **Description:** Science fiction and dark fantasy. **Fiction:** Sci-fi and dark fantasy stories with a punch, often slanted toward darker fiction; 6,000 words; $.01-$.02/word. **Poetry:** All suitable forms and themes; $10. **Fillers:** Cartoons; $10. **Art:** Most formats; $15-50. **Tips:** "Send us your cover letter, but keep it to the point." **Queries:** Not necessary. **E-Queries:** Yes. **Unsolicited mss:** Accepts. **Response:** 1-8 weeks, SASE required. **Rights:** FNASR. **Payment:** On acceptance.

THE URBANITE

P.O. Box 4737, Davenport, IA 52808.
Web site: http://theurbanite.tripod.com. 3x/year. Circ.: 1,000. Mark McLaughlin, Editor. **Description:** Dark fantasy, horror (no gore), surrealism, reviews, and social commentary. **Fiction:** To 3,000 words; pays $.02-$.03/word. **Poetry:** Free-verse, to 2 pages, $10. **Tips:** Query for coming themes. **Payment:** On acceptance.

WEIRD TALES

123 Crooked Ln., King of Prussia, PA 19406-2570. 610-275-4463.
E-mail: weirdtales@comcast.net. Web site: www.weird-tales.com. Quarterly. $4.95/$16. Circ.: 10,000. George Scithers, Darrel Schweitzer, Editors/Art Directors. **Description:** Seeks short stories and poetry in fantasy-based horror, heroic fantasy, and exotic mood pieces. Rarely buys material that does not present fantasy elements. **Tips:** Send hard copy of manuscript; do not send via e-mail. E-mail or send SASE for guidelines. **Queries:** Not necessary. **Unsolicited mss:** Accepts. **Response:** Queries 1 week, submissions 1-3 months, SASE required. **Freelance Content:** 90%. **Rights:** FNASR. **Payment:** On publication.

BOOK PUBLISHERS

GENERAL ADULT BOOKS

This and the two following sections feature publishers, in turn, of general adult books, juvenile books, and religious books. These lists include a wide range of options, from some of the largest trade publishers to a selected list of many smaller presses and university presses.

Many publishers are willing to consider either unsolicited queries or manuscripts, but an increasing number have a policy of only reading submissions sent to them via literary agents. Since finding an agent willing to take on a new writer's work is not always an easy task, many writers still choose to present their manuscripts directly to publishers on their own.

Before even considering submitting a complete manuscript to an editor, it is always advisable to send a brief query letter describing the proposed book, and an SASE. The letter should also include information about the author's special qualifications for dealing with the particular topic covered, as well as any previous publication credits. An outline of the book (or a synopsis for fiction) and a sample chapter may also be included.

While it is common courtesy to submit a book manuscript to only one publisher at a time, it is often acceptable to submit the same query or proposal in advance to more than one editor simultaneously, as it takes an editor less time to review a query and respond with some indication of further interest. When sending simultaneous queries, however, always state clearly in your letter that you are doing this.

With any submission of manuscript materials to a publisher, be sure to enclose sufficient postage for the manuscript's return.

Royalty rates for hardcover books usually start at 10% of the retail price of the book and increase after a certain number of copies have been sold. Paperbacks generally have a somewhat lower rate, about 5% to 8%. Smaller presses and university presses sometimes base their royalty on net receipts (i.e., what they get after discounts), rather than the retail price (the "list price" printed on the book). It is customary for the publishing company to pay the author a cash advance against royalties when the book contract is signed or when the finished manuscript is received. Some publishers pay on a flat-fee basis.

Writers seeking publication of book-length poetry manuscripts are encouraged to consider contests that offer publication as the prize (see Prizes, in Other Markets & Resources).

A CAPPELLA BOOKS
Chicago Review Press
814 N Franklin St., Chicago, IL 60610. 312-337-0747.
Description: Nonfiction titles on music, performing arts, and film. **Books Statistics:** 8 titles/yr; 30-40% by first-time authors; 50% unagented. **Proposal Process:** Submit query, 2 sample chapters, and SASE. Responds in 1 month to queries. **Payment:** Royalty.

A.R.E. PRESS

Edgar Cayce's Assn. for Research & Enlightenment
215 67th St., Virginia Beach, VA 23451-2061.
E-mail: arepress@edgarcayce.org. Web site: www.edgarcayce.org. Ken Skidmore, Senior Editor. **Description:** Publishes materials that center on spirituality and self-help. **Books Statistics:** 12 titles/yr. **Sample Titles:** *God at the Speed of Light* by T. Lee Baumann, M.D.; *12 Positive Habits of Spiritually Centered People* by Mark Thurston and Sarah Thurston.

ABINGDON PRESS

The United Methodist Publishing House
201 Eighth Ave. S, P.O. Box 801, Nashville, TN 37203. 615-749-6301.
Web site: www.abingdon.org. Joseph A. Crowe, Editor. **Description:** General-interest books: mainline, social issues, marriage/family, self-help, exceptional people, etc. **Proposal Process:** Query with outline and 1-2 sample chapters. Guidelines available. **Sample Titles:** *Preaching Biblical Wisdom in a Self-Help Society* by Alyce McKenzie; *El Misterio Revelado* by Samuel Pagan.

HENRY N. ABRAMS, INC.

La Martiniere Groupe, 100 Fifth Ave., New York, NY 10011. 212-206-7715.
E-mail: submissions@abramsbooks.com. Web site: www.abramsbooks.com. Mark McGowan, Publisher. **Description:** Illustrated art books on a variety of subjects including art history, fine art, folk art, photography, history, performing arts, comics, architecture, food/wine, nature, jewelry/fashion, interior design, museum collections, pop culture, science, and sports. Also publishes art books for children, calendars, and journals. **Books Statistics:** 200 titles/yr. **Proposal Process:** Submit outline, sample chapters, and illustrations. **Payment:** Royalty. **Sample Titles:** *The Comics: Since 1945* by Brian Walker; *New York from the Air: An Architectural Heritage* by John Tauranac; **Contact:** Eric Himmel, Editor-in-Chief.

ACADEMIC PRESS

A Harcourt Science and Technology Company/Elsevier Science
525 B St., Suite 1900, San Diego, CA 92101-4495. 619-231-0926.
E-mail: ap@acad.com. Web site: www.academicpress.com. **Description:** Scientific/technical books, journals, textbooks, and other reference materials for research scientists, students, and professionals who work in the fields of life sciences, physical sciences, engineering, mathematics, computer sciences, and social/behavioral sciences. **Proposal Process:** Submit 1-2 page prospectus summarizing the topic and approach of manuscript; detailed chapter outline; description of audience and competing titles; and curriculum vitae. **Sample Titles:** *Origins of Life on the Earth and in the Cosmos* by Geoffrey Zubay; *Electronics and Communications for Scientists and Engineers* by Martin Plonus. **Contact:** Books Editorial Department.

ACADEMY CHICAGO PUBLISHERS

363 W Erie St., Chicago, IL 60610. 312-751-7300.
E-mail: info@academychicago.com. Web site: www.academychicago.com. Anita Miller, Senior Editor. **Description:** General-adult fiction (classic mysteries, Victorian classics) and nonfiction (history, biography, travel, film/video, Celtic, and Arthurian). Special interest in books by and about women. No how-to, explicit sex, grotesque violence, sci-fi, or horror. **Books Statistics:** 11 titles/yr. **Proposal Process:** Query with 4 sample chapters and SASE. **Sample Titles:** (Nonfiction) *Looking Backward: Stories from Chicago's Jewish Past* by Walter Roth. (Fiction) *Letters in the Attic* by Bonnie Shimko. **Contact:** Jordan Miller, Vice President/Publicity.

ADAMS MEDIA CORPORATION

57 Littlefield St., Avon, MA 02322. 508-427-7100.
Web site: www.adamsmedia.com. Gary M. Krebs, Director of Publishing. **Description:** Nonfiction trade paperbacks in the categories of self-help, how-to, relationships, parenting, inspiration, popular reference, business, small business, careers, and personal finance. **Books Statistics:** 150 titles/yr. **Proposal Process:** Query with outline, sample chapters, and SASE. Accepts simultaneous queries, but not e-queries. Hard copy only. Responds in 1 month. **Payment:** Advance/royalty or work-for-hire.

ADAMS-BLAKE PUBLISHING

8041 Sierra St., Suite 102, Fair Oaks, CA 95628. 916-962-9296.
E-mail: information@adams-blake.com. Web site: www.adams-blake.com. Monica Blane, Senior Editor. **Description:** Technical subjects for the corporate market. Books on business, careers, and technology. **Books Statistics:** 5 titles/yr (100 submissions); 90% by first-time authors; 100% unagented. **Proposal Process:** Query with outline. Accepts simultaneous queries, but not e-queries. Responds in 4 weeks. **Payment:** Royalty, 10-15% net. **Tips:** Limited market.

ADAMS-HALL PUBLISHING

P.O. Box 491002, Los Angeles, CA 90049. 800-888-4452.
Sue Ann Bacon, Editorial Director. **Description:** Business and personal finance books with wide market appeal. **Proposal Process:** Query with proposed book idea, list of current competitive titles, author qualifications, description of why your book is unique, and SASE. Does not accept complete manuscript. **Payment:** Royalty.

ADDICUS BOOKS, INC.

P.O. Box 45327, Omaha, NE 68145. 402-330-7493.
E-mail: info@addicusbooks.com. Web site: www.addicusbooks.com. Rod Colvin, Publisher. **Description:** Independent press publishing nonfiction titles on economics, investing, business, self-help, health, how-to, and regional topics. **Books Statistics:** 5-10 titles/yr; 70% by first-time authors; 60% unagented. **Proposal Process:** Submit 1-page overview, chapter outline, 2-3 sample chapters, description of intended audience, estimated word/photo count, and resume/bio. Also accepts 1-page e-queries (no attachments). **Payment:** Royalty. **Sample Titles:**

A Simple Guide to Thyroid Disorders by Paul Ruggieri, M.D.; *Understanding Lumpetctomy: A Guide to Breast Cancer Treatment* by Rosalind Benedet, N.P. **Contact:** Susan Adams, Managing Editor.

AEGIS PUBLISHING GROUP LTD

796 Aquidneck Ave., Newport, RI 02842-7246. 401-849-4200.
E-mail: aegis@aegisbooks.com. Web site: www.aegisbooks.com. Robert Mastin, Publisher. **Description:** Books on telecommunications and data networking, for both industry professionals and general consumers. **Sample Titles:** *Telecom Made Easy* by June Langhoff; *The Cell Phone Buyer's Guide* by Penelope Stetz.

AFRICA WORLD PRESS, INC.

541 W Ingham Ave., Suite B, Trenton, NJ 08638. 609-695-3200.
E-mail: awprsp@africanworld.com. Web site: www.africanworld.com. Kassahun Checole, Publisher. **Description:** Publisher of nonfiction and poetry. Material focuses on African, African-American, Caribbean, and Latin-American issues. **Proposal Process:** Query. **Payment:** Royalty. **Sample Titles:** *The Challenges of History and Leadership in Africa: The Essays of Bethwell Allan Ogot* edited by Toyin Falola and Atieno Odhiambo; *The African Renaissance: History, Significance, and Strategy* by Washington A.J. Okumu.

AFRICAN AMERICAN IMAGES

1909 W 95th St., Chicago, IL 60643. 773-445-0322.
E-mail: aaf@africanamericanimages.com.
Web site: www.africanamericanimages.com. **Description:** Publishes adult and children's nonfiction Africentric books. **Books Statistics:** 6 title/yr (100 submissions); 50% by first-time authors; 80% unagented. **Proposal Process:** Query with complete manuscript. Considers simultaneous queries. Prefers hard copy. Guidelines available. **Payment:** Royalty (10% net). **Tips:** "Write to promote self-esteem, collective values, liberation, and skill development." **Contact:** Editorial Department.

ALASKA NORTHWEST BOOKS

Graphic Arts Center Publishing Co.
P.O. Box 10306, Portland, OR 97296-0306. 503-226-2402.
E-mail: tricia@gacpc.com. Web site: www.gacpc.com. Tricia Brown, Acquisitions Editor. **Description:** Regional nonfiction about Alaska for a general audience. Specializes in history, natural history, biography, travel, Native heritage, cooking, guidebooks, factbooks, and children's books by Alaskans and about Alaska. **Books Statistics:** 6-8 titles/yr (250 submissions); 10% by first-time authors; 90% unagented. **Proposal Process:** Send cover letter, complete outline with ideas for photos/illustrations, TOC, author bio with examples of previous publications, market analysis, photocopies or slides of artwork, and SASE. Responds in 6 months. **Payment:** Pays royalty (10-12% net). **Sample Titles:** *A Place Beyond: Finding Home in Arctic Alaska* by Nick Jans; *Alaska's Natural Wonders: A Guide to the Phenomena of the Far North* by Robert Armstrong and Marge Hermans; *Baked Alaska: Recipes for Sweet Comforts*

from the North Country by Sarah Eppenbach. **Tips:** "Avoid poetry, adult fiction, and native 'legend' written by non-Native Americans. Children's book authors should avoid partnering with an illustrator before submission has been accepted."

ALBION PRESS
4532 W Kennedy Blvd., Suite 233, Tampa, FL 33609. 813-805-2665.
E-mail: mcgregpub@aol.com. Dave Rosenbaum, Acquisitions. **Description:** Nonfiction titles, emphasis on sports and true crime. No fiction. **Books Statistics:** 12 titles/yr (300 submissions); 50% by first-time authors; 50% unagented. **Proposal Process:** Query with outline, sample chapters, and SASE. Accepts simultaneous and electronic queries. Prefers hard copy. Responds in 2 months. **Payment:** Royalty.

ALGONQUIN BOOKS OF CHAPEL HILL
A Division of Workman Publishing Co.
P.O. Box 2225, Chapel Hill, NC 27515-2225. 919-967-0108.
E-mail: dialogue@algonquin.com. Web site: www.algonquin.com. Dana Stamey, Managing Editor. **Description:** Trade books, literary fiction and nonfiction, for adults. **Proposal Process:** Send query for fiction and book proposal for nonfiction. Responds in 6 weeks. **Sample Titles:** *The Last Girls* by Lee Smith; *Hollow Ground* by Stephen Marion.

ALLWORTH PRESS
10 E 23rd St., Suite 510, New York, NY 10010-4402. 212-777-8395.
E-mail: pub@allworth.com. Web site: www.allworth.com. Nicole Potter, Editor. **Description:** Nonfiction titles on business and self-help that target artists, designers, photographers, writers, and film/TV/performing artists. Also publishes books on business, money, and law for the general public. **Books Statistics:** 42 titles/yr. **Proposal Process:** Query with outline and sample chapters. **Payment:** Royalty. **Sample Titles:** *Creative Careers in Hollywood* by Laurie Scheer; *Design Humor: The Art of Graphic Wit* by Steven Heller.

ALPINE PUBLICATIONS, INC.
P.O. Box 7027, Loveland, CO 80537. 970-667-9317.
E-mail: alpinepubl@aol.com. Web site: www.alpinepub.com. B.J. McKinney, Publisher. **Description:** Nonfiction books on dogs and horses. Topics include breeding, care, training, health, management, etc. No fiction, poetry, humor, personal experience, or photo essays. **Books Statistics:** 4 titles/yr (50 submissions); 50% by first-time authors; 100% unagented. **Proposal Process:** Submit outline with 3 sample chapters (or complete manuscript) and SASE. Accepts simultaneous queries and e-queries. Hard copy preferred. Responds in 12 weeks. **Payment:** Royalty. **Sample Titles:** *Almost a Whisper: A Holistic Approach to Working with Your Horse* by Sam Powell; *The Alaskan Malamute* by Barbara A. Brooks and Sherry E. Wallis. **Tips:** Accepts queries via e-mail, but not submissions.

ALYSON PUBLICATIONS

6922 Hollywood Blvd., Suite 1000, Los Angeles, CA 90028. 323-860-6074.
E-mail: mail@alyson.com. Web site: www.alyson.com. Angela Brown, Editor-in-Chief. **Description:** Gay, lesbian, bisexual, and transgender fiction (novels, mysteries, erotica) and nonfiction (biography/memoir, history, humor, self-help, politics/queer theory, relationships). Also publishes children's and YA titles with gay/lesbian themes. **Proposal Process:** Send query with summary, chapter outline, and SASE. Do not send sample chapters or complete manuscript. Accepts simultaneous queries with notice. Responds in 2-4 months. **Payment:** Royalty. **Sample Titles:** (Nonfiction) *The Power of a Partner: Creating and Maintaining Healthy Gay and Lesbian Relationships* by Dr. Richard Pimental-Habib, Ph.D. (Children's) *Heather Has Two Mommies* by Lesléa Newman. **Tips:** See Web site for guidelines.

AMACOM BOOKS

American Management Assn.
1601 Broadway, Fl. 9, New York, NY 10019. 212-903-8391.
Web site: www.amacombooks.org. Adrienne Hickey, Editorial Director.
Description: Solution-oriented nonfiction on a variety of business issues including finance/accounting, computers/technology, human resources, communication, international relations, marketing, advertising, small business, sales, project management, and customer service. **Proposal Process:** Send formal proposal outlining content, approach, intended audience, and competing titles. Also include TOC, sample chapters, and resume/curriculum vitae. **Sample Titles:** *Creating a Total Rewards Strategy* by Todd M. Manus; *Delivering Knock Your Socks Off Service* by Ron Zemke. **Tips:** See Web site for specific guidelines.

AMADEUS PRESS

133 SW Second Avenue, Suite 450, Portland, OR 97204. 503-227-2878.
E-mail: eve@amadeuspress.com. Web site: www.amadeuspress.com. Eve S. Goodman, Editorial Director. **Description:** Trade books and textbooks on music (classical and traditional) and opera. **Sample Titles:** Send proposal with letter describing purpose and audience, TOC, 1-2 sample chapters, sample illustrations, bio/resume, and schedule for completing manuscript. Responds in 8-12 weeks.

AMBER BOOKS

1334 E Chandler Blvd., Suite 5-D67, Phoenix, AZ 85048. 480-460-1660.
E-mail: amberbk@aol.com. Web site: www.amberbooks.com. Tony Rose, Publisher.
Description: Publishes African-American self-help books, career-guide books, and biographies on successful entertainment personalities. Aims to publish materials that help African-Americans earn an income, obtain education, and find the empowerment to succeed. **Sample Titles:** *Wake Up and Smell the Dollars! Whose Inner City is this Anyway?* by Dorothy Pitman Hughes; *Beautiful Black Hair* by Shamboosie; *The African-American Teenager's Guide to Personal Growth, Health, Safety, Sex, & Survival* by Debrah Harris-Johnson.

AMERICAN PARADISE PUBLISHING

P.O. Box 781, St. John, USVI 00831. 304-779-4257.
E-mail: info@americanparadisepublishing.com.
Web site: www.americanparadisepublishing.com. Pamela Gaffin, Editor. **Description:** Nonfiction on the U.S. Virgin Islands aimed at Caribbean readers and tourists. Guidebooks, cookbooks, how-to, and books on sailing, yacht cruising, hiking, snorkeling, sportfishing, local history, and West Indian culture. **Proposal Process:** Query with outline and sample chapters. **Payment:** Royalty. **Tips:** "We seek useful, practical books that help our Virgin Island readers lead better and more enjoyable lives."

AMERICAN PSYCHIATRIC PUBLISHING, INC.

American Psychiatric Assn.
1000 Wilson Blvd., Suite 1825, Arlington, VA 22209. 703-907-7322.
Web site: www.appi.org. Robert E. Hales, M.D., M.B.A., Editor-in-Chief. **Description:** Books (professional, reference, trade, and academic), journals, and other media related to psychiatry, mental health, behavioral and social sciences, and medicine. **Proposal Process:** Submit completed author questionnaire, detailed chapter outline, curriculum vitae, and brief prospectus stating why APPI should publish the book. **Payment:** Royalty. **Sample Titles:** *Manual of Clinical Psychopharmacology, Fourth Edition* by Alan F. Schatzberg, M.D. **Contact:** John McDuffie, Editorial Director (703-907-7892).

ANDREWS MCMEEL PUBLISHING

4520 Main St., Kansas City, MO 64111. 816-932-6700.
Web site: www.amuniversal.com/amp. **Description:** Publisher of best-sellers, humor collections, general nonfiction trade, gift books, and calendars. **Proposal Process:** No unsolicited manuscripts. All material must be submitted through an agent. **Sample Titles:** *Dear Mom* by Bradley Taylor Greive; *Pure* by Anne Geddes.

ANDROS BOOK PUBLISHING

P.O. Box 12080, Prescott, AZ 86304. 520-778-4491.
E-mail: androsbks@aol.com. Web site: www.hometown.aol.com/androsbks. Susanne Bain, Publisher. **Description:** Small publishing house specializing in home schooling, school choice, and parental involvement in education. **Proposal Process:** Send proposal letter, two sample chapters and TOC, and SASE. **Tips:** "We currently seek uplifting material about home school and positive parental involvement in children's education or school choice issues. Looking less for feel-good works than for 'how-to or how we do it.' Looking for personal experience."

ANHINGA PRESS

P.O. Box 10595, Tallahassee, FL 32302-0595. 850-521-9920.
E-mail: info@anhinga.org. Web site: www.anhinga.org. Rick Campbell, Editorial Director. **Description:** Publishes books of contemporary poetry. **Books Statistics:** 4 titles/yr (750 submissions); 50% by first-time authors; 99% unagented. **Proposal**

Process: Query or send complete manuscripts with SASE. Accepts simultaneous queries, but not e-queries. Responds in 6 weeks. **Payment:** Royalty or flat fee.

THE ANONYMOUS PRESS

332 Bleecker St., #631, New York, NY 10014.
Gil Bonner, Acquisitions. **Description:** Adult nonfiction in the categories of history, military, memoirs, reference, self-help, religion, personal finance, and economics. **Books Statistics:** 1-3 titles/yr (500 submissions); 100% by first-time authors. **Proposal Process:** Send query via regular mail. **Payment:** Royalty, 10-20%.

ANTHROPOSOPHIC PRESS INC.

P.O. Box 799, Great Barrington, MA 10230. 413-528-8233.
E-mail: service@anthropress.org. Web site: www.anthropress.org. **Description:** Publisher of Rudolf Steiner's works on anthroposophy. Also publishes materials on spirituality, religion, philosophy, and psychology.

ANVIL PRESS

6 W 17th Ave., Vancouver, British Columbia V5Y 1Z4 Canada. 604-876-8710.
E-mail: info@anvilpress.com. Web site: www.anvilpress.com. Brian Kaufman, Editorial Director. **Description:** Fiction, poetry, creative nonfiction, some contemporary nonfiction, and progressive literature. **Books Statistics:** 8-10 titles/yr (200 submissions); 80% by first-time authors; 100% unagented. **Proposal Process:** Query with outline and sample chapters. Considers simultaneous queries and e-queries (no attachments). Responds in 4-6 months. **Payment:** Royalty, 10-15% net. Flat fee advance, $200-$500. **Sample Titles:** *Intensive Care* by Alan Twigg; *The Beautiful Dead End* by Clint Hutzulak; *Socket* by David Zimmerman. **Tips:** Canadian authors only. "We're looking for originality in style and voice, contemporary modern."

APA BOOKS

American Psychological Assn.
750 First St. NE, Washington, DC 20002-4242. 202-336-5500.
Web site: www.apa.org. **Description:** Nonfiction titles reflecting current research and discovery in the field of psychology. Materials have scholarly, professional focus. Also publishes children's books under the Magination Press imprint and adult self-help titles under the APA LifeTools imprint. **Proposal Process:** Submit prospectus with curriculum vitae. Prospectus should include the TOC, purpose, audience, market analysis, anticipated length, proposed schedule, and the theories or ideas that will be explored in the book. **Sample Titles:** (APA Books) *Behavioral Genetics in the Postgenomic Era* by Robert Plomin, Ph.D., et al.; (Magination Press) *Jenny is Scared! When Something Sad Happens in the World* by Carol Shurman, Ph.D.; (APA LifeTools) *Forgiveness Is a Choice: A Step by Step Process for Resolving Anger and Restoring Hope* by Robert D. Enright, Ph.D.

APERTURE
20 East 23rd St., New York, NY 10010. 212-505-5555.
E-mail: editorial@aperture.org. Web site: www.aperture.org. Ray K. Metzker.
Description: Photography books. **Proposal Process:** Submit 1 page synopsis; hard copy only. Include delivery memo that describes work, format, and the number of images, SASE. Allow 6-8 weeks for response.

APPALACHIAN MOUNTAIN CLUB BOOKS
5 Joy St., Boston, MA 02108. 617-523-0655.
Web site: www.outdoors.org. Beth Krusi, Publisher/Editor. **Description:** Regional (New England) and national nonfiction titles, 175-350 pages, for adults, juveniles, and young adults. Topics include guidebooks on non-motorized backcountry recreation, nature, outdoor recreation skills (how-to books), mountain history/biography, search and rescue, conservation, and environmental management. **Books Statistics:** 12 titles/yr (40 submissions); 75% by first-time authors. **Proposal Process:** Query with outline and sample chapters. Accepts simultaneous queries. Responds in 3 months. **Payment:** Royalty. **Sample Titles:** *Women on High: Pioneers of Mountaineering* by Rebecca A. Brown; *River Days: Exploring the Connecticut River from Source to Sea* by Michael Tougias. **Tips:** See Web site for submission guidelines.

APPLAUSE THEATRE & CINEMA BOOKS
Hal Leonard Corp, 151 W 46th St., Fl. 8, New York, NY 10036. 212-575-9265.
Web site: www.applausepub.com. Glenn Young, Publisher; John Cerullo, Chief Executive Officer. **Description:** Publishes biographies, reference materials, and guide books in the fields of stage, cinema, and entertainment. Topics include acting, music/literature, memoir, humor, biography, television, playwriting and screenwriting, Shakespeare, etc. **Sample Titles:** *At This Theatre: 100 Years of Broadway Shows, Stories, and Stars* by Louis Botto with Robert Viagas; *Ridiculous! The Theatrical Life and Times of Charles Ludlam* by David Kaufman.

APPLEWOOD BOOKS, INC.
128 The Great Rd., P.O. Box 365, Bedford, MA 01730. 781-271-0055.
E-mail: applewood@awb.com. Web site: www.awb.com. **Description:** Adult nonfiction on culture, nostalgia, history, literature, cooking, travel, sports, self-help, biography, etc. **Books Statistics:** 40 titles/yr.

AQUAQUEST PUBLICATIONS, INC.
P.O. Box 700, Locust Valley, NY 11560. 516-759-0476.
E-mail: editorial@aquaquest.com. Web site: www.aquaquest.com. **Description:** Nonfiction titles on underwater adventures and scuba diving. Books cover a range of underwater and marine topics such as travel, diving, shipwrecks, marine life, historical, technical, photography, and fiction. **Sample Titles:** *Diving Micronesia* by Eric Hanauer; *Solo Diving, 2nd Ed: The Art of Underwater Self-sufficiency* by Robert Von Maier.

ARCADE PUBLISHING, INC.

141 Fifth Ave., New York, NY 10010. 212-475-2633.
E-mail: arcadeinfo@arcadepub.com. Web site: www.arcadepub.com. Richard Seaver, President/Editor-in-Chief. **Description:** Adult nonfiction in the areas of business, travel, history, art, biography, African-American studies, women's studies, religion, philosophy, science, technology, and true crime. Also publishes fiction, poetry, and literature/essays. **Sample Titles:** *Lovesong: Becoming a Jew* by Julius Lester; *Race Manners* by Bruce A. Jacobs; *The Women Who Wrote the War* by Nancy Caldwell Sorel; *Hitler's Gift: The True Story of the Scientists Expelled by the Nazi Regime* by Jean Medaway and David Pyke. **Tips:** Does not accept unsolicited submissions. **Contact:** Greg Comer, Darcy Falkenhagen.

ARCADIA PUBLISHING

Tempus Publishing, 2 Cumberland St., Charleston, SC 29401. 843-853-2070.
Web site: www.arcadiapublishing.com. **Description:** Nonfiction regional history titles. Publishes Images of America and Making of America series. Other topics include Native America, the Civil War, sports, college history, postcard history, aviation, and motoring. **Books Statistics:** 800 titles/yr; 85% by first-time authors; 95% unagented. **Proposal Process:** Query with SASE. See Web site for list of regional acquisition editors. **Sample Titles:** *Irish Chicago* by John Gerard McLaughlin; *McDonough County Historic Sites* by John E. Hallwas.

ARSENAL PULP PRESS

103-1014 Homer St., Vancouver, British Columbia V6B2W9 Canada. 604-687-4233.
E-mail: contact@arsenalpulp.com. Web site: www.arsenalpulp.com. **Description:** Literary fiction and nonfiction in the areas of gay/lesbian, cultural studies, pop culture, cooking, visual art, humor, politics, and regional topics (particularly British Columbia). No genre fiction or children's books. **Proposal Process:** Send cover letter with synopsis, writing sample (50-60 pages), and SASE. No submissions by fax or e-mail. Considers proposals from Canadian authors only with the exception of anthologies. Responds in 3 months. **Sample Titles:** *Out/Lines: Underground Gay Graphics from Before Stonewall* by Thomas Waugh; *Montreal: The Unknown City* by Kristian Gravenor and John David Gravenor. **Tips:** Currently seeking short fiction for anthologies. Currently not accepting poetry.

ARTE PUBLICO PRESS

University of Houston, 4800 Calhoun, Houston, TX 77204-2174. 713-743-2843.
E-mail: carpen@mail.uh.edu. Web site: www.artepublicopress.com. Dr. Nicolas Kanellos, Founder/Director. **Description:** Contemporary and recovered literature by U.S. Hispanics, in both Spanish and English, with a focus on children's, women's, and civil rights literature. "Pinata Books." Novels, short stories, poetry, drama, nonfiction, and autobiographies. **Books Statistics:** 30 titles/yr (200 submissions); 80% by first-time authors; 20% unagented. **Proposal Process:** Query with outline, sample chapters, and SASE. No simultaneous or electronic queries. Hard copy only. Responds in 6 months. **Payment:** Royalty. **Sample Titles:** (Adult Fiction) *Close to*

the Heart by Diane Gonzales; (Children's) La Tierra de las Adivinanzas/ The Land of the Riddles by Cesar Villareal Elisondo. **Tips:** Looking for work by and about Hispanics in the U.S.

ARTECH HOUSE PUBLISHERS

685 Canton St., Norwood, MA 02062. 781-769-9750.

Web site: www.artechhouse.com. Mark Walsh, Senior Acquisitions Editor. **Description:** Professional-level books on telecommunications, wireless, microwave, radar, computer security, and software engineering. **Sample Titles:** *Running the Successful Hi-Tech Project Office* by Eduardo Miranda; *Centrex or PBX: The Impact of IP* by John R. Abrahams.

ARTISAN

Division of Workman Publishing Co.

708 Broadway, New York, NY 10003-9555. 212-254-5900.

E-mail: artisaninfo@workman.com. Web site: www.artisanbooks.com. **Description:** Illustrated nonfiction on art/architecture, biography/memoir, cooking, food/wine, crafts, gardening, film/TV, music, history, pets, sports, and travel. **Proposal Process:** Prefers to see as much of completed project as possible. Send copies of photos or illustrations (no originals). Does not accept submissions via e-mail, fax, or disk. Include SASE. **Sample Titles:** *Melons for the Passionate Grower* by Amy Goldman; *The French Laundry Cookbook* by Thomas Keller. **Contact:** Editorial Department.

AUGSBURG FORTRESS, PUBLISHERS

100 S Fifth St., Suite 700, P.O. Box 1209

Minneapolis, MN 55440-1209. 612-330-3300.

E-mail: booksub@augsburgfortress.org. Web site: www.augsburgbooks.com. **Description:** Books that focus on faith in daily life, biblical studies, history of Christianity, theology, ethics, religious studies, etc. **Tips:** See Web site for specific guidelines.

AVALON BOOKS

Thomas Bouregy & Co., Inc.

160 Madison Ave., New York, NY 10016. 212-598-0222.

E-mail: avalon@avalonbooks.com. Web site: www.avalonbooks.com. Erin Cartwright, Editor. **Description:** Hardcover secular romances, mysteries, and westerns for the library market. **Books Statistics:** 60 titles/yr. Receives 2,000 queries and 1,200 mss/yr. 65% first-time authors; 80% unagented. **Proposal Process:** Query with first 3 chapters and outline. Responds in 1 month to queries; 4 months to mss. Send SASE for guidelines. **Payment:** Royalty 5-15%. **Sample Titles:** *Hometown Reunion* by Cynthia Scott; *Labor of Love* by Carol Costa; *Violet's Wish* by Carolyn Brown; *Fontana* by Art Isberg. **Tips:** "No old-fashioned, predictable, formulaic books. Avoid graphic or premarital sex or sexual tension in your writing."

AVALON TRAVEL PUBLISHING

1400 65th St., Suite 250, Emeryville, CA 94608. 510-595-3664.
E-mail: acquisitions@avalonpub.com; info@travelmatters.com.
Web site: www.travelmatters.com. Rebecca Browning, Acquisitions Editor.
Description: Travel guides, 200-1,000 pages. Most titles fit into one of the following series: Adapter Kit, The Dog Lover's Companion, Foghorn Outdoors, Moon Handbooks, Moon Metro, Rick Steves, and Road Trip USA. No fiction, children's books, or travelogues/travel diaries. **Proposal Process:** Submit detailed query. Considers simultaneous submissions. **Payment:** Royalty.

AVANT-GUIDE TRAVEL BOOKS

350 Fifth Ave., Empire State Bldg., Suite 7815-78th Fl., New York, NY 10118.
212-563-1003. E-mail: editor@aventguide.com. Web site: www.avantguide.com. Dan Levine, Editor; Marilyn Wood, Editor. **Description:** Travel guidebooks. **Books Statistics:** 16 titles/yr (50 submissions); 50% by first-time authors; 100% unagented. **Proposal Process:** Query by e-mail. Considers simultaneous queries. Responds in 1 week to e-queries, 3 months to material sent by regular mail. **Payment:** Flat fee, $10,000-$20,000. **Tips:** "Please send only manuscripts that are travel guidebooks. We'll consider guides of other types if they are style-driven and fit into our publishing program. No phone calls please."

AVERY

Penguin Group (USA), 375 Hudson St., Fl. 4, New York, NY 10014. 212-366-2744.
Web site: www.penguin.com. John Duff, Publisher; Eileen Bertelli, Associate Publisher. **Description:** Trade books in alternative health, health, fitness, nutrition, and self-help. **Books Statistics:** 25 titles/yr; 75% by first-time authors; 50% unagented. **Proposal Process:** Query with outline or sample chapters. **Payment:** Royalty. **Sample Titles:** *Natural Highs* by Hyla Cass, M.D. and Patrick Holford. **Contact:** Dara Stewart, Editor.

BAEN BOOKS

P.O. Box 1403, Riverdale, NY 10471-0671. 718-548-3100.
Web site: www.baen.com. Jim Baen, Editor-in-Chief. **Description:** Strongly plotted science fiction; innovative fantasy. **Books Statistics:** 120 titles/yr (5,000 submissions); 5% by first-time authors; 50% unagented. **Proposal Process:** Query with synopsis and manuscript. **Payment:** Advance and royalty. **Sample Titles:** *War of Honor* by David Weber. **Tips:** Send SASE or check Web site for guidelines.

BALLANTINE BOOKS

The Ballantine Publishing Group/Random House, Inc.
1540 Broadway, New York, NY 10036. 212-782-9000.
Web site: www.randomhouse.com/bb. Leona Nevler, Editor. **Description:** General fiction and nonfiction. **Proposal Process:** Accepts material only through agents.

BANTAM DELL PUBLISHING GROUP

Random House, Inc.

1540 Broadway, New York, NY 10036. 212-782-9000.

Web site: www.bantamdell.com. **Description:** Executive Vice President and Deputy Publisher: Nita Taublib. Acquisitions: Toni Burbank (nonfiction: self-help, health/medicine, nature, spirituality, philosophy); Jackie Cantor (fiction: general commercial, literary, women's fiction, memoir); Tracy Devine (fiction and nonfiction: narrative nonfiction, history, adventure, military, science, general upscale commercial fiction, women's fiction, suspense); Anne Groell (fiction: fantasy, science fiction); Ann Harris (fiction and nonfiction: general commercial, literary, science, medicine, politics); Susan Kamil (The Dial Press, literary fiction and nonfiction); Robin Michaelson (nonfiction: health, women's health, child care/parenting, psychology, self-help); Bill Massey (fiction and nonfiction: thrillers, suspense, historical, military, nature/ outdoors, adventure, popular science); Kate Miciak (fiction: mystery, suspense, historical fiction); Wendy McCurdy (fiction: romance, women's fiction); Danielle Perez (fiction and nonfiction: suspense/thrillers, women's fiction, inspiration/spirituality, self-help, personal development, health, animals); Beth Rashbaum (nonfiction: health, psychology, self-help, women's issues, Judaica, history, memoir. Imprints: Bantam, Dell, Delacorte Press, Delta, The Dial Press. **Sample Titles:** *The Cottage* by Danielle Steel (Delacorte, fiction); *A Painted House* by John Grisham (Dell, fiction); *Body of Lies* by Iris Johansen (Bantam, fiction); *Love, Greg and Lauren* by Greg Manning (Bantam, nonfiction); *Safe Harbor* by Luanne Rice (Bantam, fiction); *The Wisdom of Menopause* by Christiane Northup, M.D. (Bantam, nonfiction); *Inside Delta Force* by Eric Haney (Delacorte, nonfiction); *American Chica* by Marie Arana (The Dial Press, fiction).

BARBOUR PUBLISHING: HEARTSONG PRESENTS

P.O. Box 719, Uhrichsville, OH 44683. 740-922-6045.

E-mail: info@heartsongpresents.com. Web site: www.barbourbooks.com or www.heartsongpresents.com. Rebecca Germany, Acquisitions Editor. **Description:** Adult mass-market inspirational romance (contemporary and historical). **Books Statistics:** 52 titles/yr (300 submissions), 15% first-time authors, 90% unagented. **Proposal Process:** Query with outline (1-2 pages), 2-3 sample chapters. Accepts simultaneous queries. No electronic queries. Response time: 3-4 months. Prefer hard-copy format. **Payment:** Royalty (8% net). **Tips:** SASE for guidelines.

BARD PRESS

2974 Hardman Ct. NE, Atlanta, GA 30305-3425. 800-927-1488.

E-mail: ray@bardpress.com. Web site: www.bardpress.com. **Description:** High-quality business and self-help books. **Books Statistics:** 3-4 titles/yr. **Proposal Process:** Submit short query with title, subject, and market. **Sample Titles:** *Owners Manual for the Personality at Work* by Pierce J. Howard, Ph.D. and Jane Mitchell Howard, M.A.; *Masters of Networking* by Ivan R. Misner, Ph.D. and Don Morgan, M.A.

BARNES & NOBLE PUBLISHING

122 Fifth Ave., New York, NY 10011. 212-633-3300.
Nathaniel Marunas, Editorial Director. **Description:** Nonfiction titles on music, gardening, food, history, sports, art/architecture, nature, interior decorating, and weddings. **Tips:** No unsolicited manuscripts.

BARRICADE BOOKS, INC.

185 Bridge Plaza N, Suite 308-A, Fort Lee, NJ 07024. 201-944-7600.
E-mail: cstuart@barricadebooks.com. Web site: www.barricadebooks.com. Carole
Stuart, Publisher. **Description:** Nonfiction on arts and entertainment, self-help,
biography, humor, natural science, New Age, health, sexuality, religion, psychology,
current events, and politics. Seeks material of a controversial nature; does not publish
fiction, poetry, or children's books. **Books Statistics:** 20 titles/yr (200 submissions);
25% by first-time authors; 60% unagented. **Proposal Process:** Submit query, outline, 1-2 sample chapters, and SASE. Hard copy format preferred. Responds in 3-4
weeks. **Payment:** Royalty with nominal advance. **Sample Titles:** *My Face for the
World to See* by Liz Renay; *Murder at the Conspiracy Convention* by Paul Krassner;
I Escaped from Auschwitz by Rudolf Vrba; *Surviving Terrorism* by Rainer Stahlberg.
Tips: "We're looking for unique, controversial nonfiction. Avoid subjects widely covered in the press or in other books. Writing should be short with easy-to-understand
sentences."

BARRON'S EDUCATIONAL SERIES, INC.

250 Wireless Blvd., Hauppauge, NY 11788. 631-434-3311.
E-mail: info@barronseduc.com. Web site: www.barronseduc.com. Wayne Barr,
Director of Acquisitions. **Description:** Publishes juvenile nonfiction (science,
nature, history, hobbies, and how-to), fiction for middle-grade students and teens, and
picture books for ages 3-6. Also publishes adult nonfiction (test preparation, business,
pet care, childcare, cookbooks, foreign languages). **Proposal Process:** Query with
SASE. See guidelines.

WILLIAM L. BAUHAN, PUBLISHER

P.O.Box 443, Dublin, NH 03444. 877-832-3738.
E-mail: info@bauhanpublishing.com. Web site: www.bauhanpublishing.com. William
L. Bauhan, Editor. **Description:** Publishes biographies, fine arts, gardening, architecture, and history books, with an emphasis on New England. **Proposal Process:**
Submit query with outline and sample chapter. **Sample Titles:** *Once: As It Was* by
Griselda Jackson Ohannessian; *An Historical Guide to Rhode Island Stained Glass*
by Paul Norton; *Some Sense of Transcendence* by Douglas Worth.

BAY SOMA PUBLISHING

444 De Haro St., Suite 130, San Francisco, CA 94107. 415-252-4350.
E-mail: info@baybooks.com. Web site: www.baybooks.com. Floyd Yearout, Editor.
Description: Publishes hardcover, trade paperback, coffee table, and full-color illustrated books. Topics include gardening, interior design, and cookbooks. Also pub-

lishes companion books to television shows and other media programming. **Books Statistics:** 15 titles/yr (100 queries); 10% by first-time authors. **Payment:** Royalties vary substantially. Offers $0-$25,000 in advance. **Sample Titles:** *Compact Living* by Jane Graining; *Party! Food* by Lorna Wing; *Color in the Garden* by Nori and Sandra Pope. **Tips:** "Authors should submit ideas or outlines with biographical information and a rationale as to why the book will sell."

BAYLOR UNIVERSITY PRESS
P.O. Box 97363, Waco, TX 76798-7363. 254-710-3164.
E-mail: carey_newman@baylor.edu. Web site: www.baylorpress.com. Carey C. Newman, Editor. **Description:** Scholarly nonfiction, especially religion, history, and church-state issues. **Proposal Process:** Query with outline. **Payment:** Royalty.

BEACON PRESS
25 Beacon St., Boston, MA 02108-2892. 617-742-2110.
Web site: www.beacon.org. Helene Atwan, Director. **Description:** General nonfiction and fiction. Subject matter includes world affairs, women's studies, anthropology, history, philosophy, religion, gay and lesbian studies, nature writing, African-American studies, Latino studies, Asian-American studies, and Native-American studies. **Proposal Process:** Send query letter, book proposal, and curriculum vitae. Do not send entire manuscript and do not submit via e-mail or fax. Prefers agented submissions. **Sample Titles:** *Choosing Naia: A Family's Journey* by Mitchell Zuckoff; *Free for All: Defending Liberty in America Today* by Wendy Kaminer; *Flying Colors: The Story of a Remarkable Group of Artists and the Transcendent Power of Art* by Tim Lefens.

BEHRMAN HOUSE INC.
11 Edison Place, Springfield, NJ 07081. 973-379-7200.
Web site: www.behrmanhouse.com. David Behrman, Acquisitions. **Description:** Hebrew language and Judaica textbooks for children. Adult Jewish nonfiction. **Books Statistics:** 20 titles/yr (200 submissions); 20% by first-time authors; 95% unagented. **Proposal Process:** Query with outline and sample chapters. **Payment:** Flat fee or royalty.

BELLWETHER-CROSS PUBLISHING
18319 Highway 20 W, East Dubuque, IL 61025. 815-747-6255.
E-mail: jsheldon@bellwethercross.com. Web site: www.bellwethercross.com. Jana Sheldon, Acquisitions Editor. **Description:** College textbooks and lab manuals related to environmental science, biology, botany, astronomy, oceanography, business, etc. Also computer software related to the publishing industry. **Books Statistics:** 55 titles/yr (600 submissions); 100% by first-time authors; 100% unagented. **Proposal Process:** For educational materials, query with proposed book idea, list of current competitive books, and bio. For trade nonfiction, query with outline and sample chapters. Send SASE for return of all materials. Prefers electronic format. Accepts simultaneous queries. Responds within 2 weeks. **Payment:** Royalty. **Sample Titles:**

Daring to Be Different by James A. Hatherley; *Palaces Under the Sea* by Joe Strykowski and Rena Bonem, Ph.D.; *Experiences in Environmental Science* by Barbara Krumhardt, Ph.D., and Danielle Wirth, Ph.D.

BENJAMIN CUMMINGS

1301 Sansome St., San Francisco, CA 94111. 415-402-2500.
Web site: www.aw.com/bc. Frank Ruggirello, VP/Editorial Director. **Description:** Educational nonfiction. Publishes textbooks and other materials on chemistry, health/kinesiology, life science, physics, and astronomy. **Proposal Process:** Send formal prospectus, TOC, sample chapters, and curriculum vitae to the appropriate editor. See Web site for detailed guidelines and staff listings.

THE BERKLEY PUBLISHING GROUP

Penguin Putnam Inc.
375 Hudson St., New York, NY 10014. 726-282-5074.
E-mail: online@penguinputnam.com. Web site: www.penguinputnam.com. Denise Silvestro, Senior Editor. **Description:** General-interest fiction and nonfiction; science fiction, suspense, mystery, and romance. Publishes both reprints and originals. Paperback books, except for some hardcover mysteries and science fiction. Imprints include Ace Books, Diamond, Jam, Jove, Perige, and Riverhead Books. **Books Statistics:** 800 titles/yr. **Proposal Process:** Submit through agent only. **Payment:** Royalty.

BERKSHIRE HOUSE PUBLISHERS

480 Pleasant St., Suite 5, Lee, MA 02138. 413-243-0303.
E-mail: info@berkshirehouse.com. Web site: www.berkshirehouse.com. Philip Rich, Editorial Director. **Description:** Publishes a series of regional travel guides and books on specific destinations of unusual charm and cultural importance in the Berkshires and New England. Also publishes regional cookbooks and books on country inns and country living. **Books Statistics:** 8-10 titles/yr (300 submissions); 10% by first-time authors; 97% unagented. **Proposal Process:** Send query letter, outline, prospectus, and sample chapter. Considers simultaneous and electronic queries. Responds in 4 weeks. **Payment:** Royalty. **Sample Titles:** *The Berkshire Book: A Complete Guide* by Lauren Stevens; *New England Cooking: Seasons and Celebrations* by Claire Hopley. **Tips:** "Avoid submitting general cookbooks (i.e. those not related to travel, etc.), memoirs, autobiographies, and biographies and history titles that are unrelated to New England. We do not accept children's books, poetry or fiction (with the possible exception of a novel related to this region)."

BERRETT-KOEHLER PUBLISHERS INC.

235 Montgomery St., Suite 650, San Francisco, CA 94104. 415-288-0260.
E-mail: bkpub@bkpub.com. Web site: www.bkconnection.com. Jeevan Sivasubramaniam, Managing Editor. **Description:** Books on the workplace, business, and organizations. Seeks to publish work that inspires a more humane, ethical, and globally conscious world. **Proposal Process:** Send proposal, outline, and 2-4

sample chapters. Make sure proposal states the need for your topic, the intended audience, your knowledge base and credentials, suggested marketing ideas, and an estimated timetable for completing the work. **Sample Titles:** *Change Is Everybody's Business* by Pat McLagan; *Repacking Your Bags* by Richard J. Leider and David A. Shapiro.

THE BESS PRESS
3565 Harding Ave., Honolulu, HI 96816. 808-734-7159.
E-mail: editor@besspress.com. Web site: www.besspress.com. Revé Shapard, Editor. **Description:** Nonfiction books about Hawaii and the Pacific for adults, children, and young adults. **Proposal Process:** Send query with outline. Hard copy. **Payment:** Royalty.

BEYOND WORDS PUBLISHING, INC.
20827 NW Cornell Rd., Suite 500, Hillsboro, OR 97124. 503-531-8700.
E-mail: info@beyondword.com. Web site: www.beyondword.com. Jenefer Angel, Adult Acquisitions Editor. **Description:** Photography, children's books, and books on personal growth, women, and spirituality. **Books Statistics:** 25 titles/yr (4,000 submissions); 90% by first-time authors; 75% unagented. **Proposal Process:** Submit outline and sample chapters for adult titles; complete manuscript for juvenile titles. Include SASE. Accepts simultaneous queries, but not e-queries. Prefers hard copy format. Responds in 3 months. **Payment:** Royalty. **Sample Titles:** (Adult nonfiction) *Spiritual Writing: From Inspiration to Publication* by Deborah Levine Herman; *The Letter Box: A Story of Enduring Love* by Mark and Diane Button. (Children's) *It's Your Rite: Girls Coming of Age Stories*; *Generation FIX: Young Ideas for a Better World.* **Tips:** No adult fiction, poetry, or fiction stories by children. Looking for original and creative children's stories. **Contact:** Barbara Mann, Children's Managing Editor.

BICK PUBLISHING HOUSE
307 Neck Rd., Madison, CT 06443. 203-245-0073.
E-mail: bickpubhse@aol.com. Web site: www.bickpubhouse.com. Dale Carlson, President. **Description:** Books, 64-250 pages, for teens and adults on science, philosophy, psychology, wildlife rehabilitation, and special needs/disabilities. **Proposal Process:** Submit outline and sample chapters. **Payment:** Royalty.

BILINGUAL REVIEW PRESS
Hispanic Research Center, Arizona State University
P.O. Box 872702, Tempe, AZ 85287-2702. 480-965-3867.
E-mail: brp@asu.edu. Web site: www.asu.edu/brp. **Description:** Publishes high-quality fiction, nonfiction, and poetry. Titles are by or about U.S. Hispanics. Publishes both established and emerging writers. **Books Statistics:** 8-10 titles/yr. **Sample Titles:** *Moving Target: A Memoir of Pursuit* by Ron Arias; *Sofias Saints* by Diana Lopez; *Contemporary Chicano and Chicana Art: Artists, Works, Cultura, and Education*, edited by Gary D. Keller, et al.

BINFORD & MORT PUBLISHING

5245 NE Elam Young Pkwy., Suite C, Hillsboro, OR 97124. 503-844-4960.
E-mail: polly@binfordandmort.com. Web site: www.binfordandmort.com. Pam
Henningsen, Publisher. **Description:** Nonfiction books about the Pacific Northwest.
Books Statistics: 10 titles/yr (200 submissions); 5% by first-time authors; 90% un-
agented. **Proposal Process:** Send query. Accepts simultaneous queries, but not
e-queries. Responds in 3 months. **Payment:** Pays royalty, typically 5-10% range.
Tips: No children's stories or poetry.

JOHN F. BLAIR, PUBLISHER

1406 Plaza Dr., Winston-Salem, NC 27103-1470. 336-768-1374.
E-mail: blairpub@blairpub.com. Web site: www.blairpub.com. Carolyn Sakowski,
Editor. **Description:** Biography, history, folklore, travel, and books with
Southeastern focus. **Proposal Process:** Send query via regular mail. Does not accept
electronic submissions. **Payment:** Royalty. **Sample Titles:** *Romantic Virginia* by
Andrea Sutcliffe; *Voices from the Trail of Tears* edited by Vicki Rozema.

BLOOMBERG PRESS

100 Business Park Dr., P.O. Box 888, Princeton, NJ 08542-0888. 609-750-5070.
E-mail: press@bloomberg.com. Web site: www.bloomberg.com/books. Kathleen
Peterson, Senior Acquisitions Editor. **Description:** Nonfiction, varying lengths, on
topics such as investing, finance, and business. **Proposal Process:** Query with outline
and sample chapter or send complete manuscript. Include SASE. **Payment:** Royalty.

BLOOMSBURY USA

175 Fifth Ave., Suite 300, New York, NY 10010.
E-mail: info@bloomsburyusa.com. Web site: www.bloomsbury.com/usa.
Description: High-quality publisher of fiction and nonfiction. **Sample Titles:** *City
of Masks* by Daniel Hecht; *Rough Amusements* by Ben Neilhart. **Tips:** See Web site
for detailed guidelines.

BLUEFISH RIVER PRESS

P.O. Box 1398, Duxbury, MA 02332. 781-934-5564.
E-mail: info@bluefishriverpress.com. Web site: www.bluefishriverpress.com.
Description: Serious fiction and books on sports with particular emphasis on baseball.
Books Statistics: 5 titles/yr (100 submissions); 50% by first-time authors; 50% una-
gented. **Proposal Process:** Submit query via e-mail. Accepts simultaneous queries.
Responds in 1 week. **Payment:** Royalty 7-15%. **Contact:** David Pallai, President.

BONUS BOOKS

160 E Illinois St., Chicago, IL 60611. 312-467-0580.
E-mail: bb@bonus-books.com. Web site: www.bonus-books.com. Erin Kahl,
Acquisitions Editor. **Description:** Nonfiction trade books, both paperback and hardcover. Subjects include automotive, biography, current events, journalism, business,
cooking, education, games/gambling, health, personal finance, regional and local

topics, and sports. **Books Statistics:** 20-30 titles/yr (600-800 submissions); 20% first-time authors; 97% unagented. **Proposal Process:** Query with complete manuscript and SASE. Simultaneous and e-queries accepted. Prefers hard copy format. **Payment:** Royalty. **Sample Titles:** (Journalism) *Best Newspaper Writing 2002* edited by Keith Woods; (Cooking) *Star Grazing* by Harry Schwartz; (Gaming) *Get the Edge at Roulette* by Christopher Pawlicki; (Regional) *Chicago the Beautiful* by Kenan Heise. **Tips:** No fiction or poetry.

BOOK PUBLISHING CO.
415 Farm Rd., P.O. Box 99, Summertown, TN 38483. 931-964-3571. E-mail: info@bookpubco.com. Web site: www.bookpubco.com. **Description:** Books on vegetarian nutrition and cooking, alternative health, and Native American history and culture. **Sample Titles:** *Plants of Power* by Alfred Savinelli; *Apple Cider Vinegar for Weight Loss and Good Health* by Cynthia Holzapfel.

BOWTIE PRESS
Fancy Publications, Inc.
P.O. Box 6050, Mission Viejo, CA 92690. 949-855-8822. E-mail: bowtiepress@fancypubs.com. Web site: www.bowtiepress.com. **Description:** Nonfiction books on pets, motorcycles, and horses. **Books Statistics:** 20 titles/yr. **Proposal Process:** Send summary of manuscript with outline, descriptions of illustrations and appendices, market analysis, bio/resume listing expertise and previous publishing credits, and SASE. Does not accept electronic submissions. **Sample Titles:** *Racing Through the Century* by Mary Simon; *Cat Blessings: A Collection of Poems, Quotes, Facts & Myths* by Bob Lovka. **Contact:** Acquisitions Editor.

BRANDEN PUBLISHING COMPANY
P.O. Box 812094, Wellesley, MA 02482. 781-235-3634. E-mail: branden@branden.com. Web site: www.branden.com. Adolfo Caso, Editorial Department. **Description:** Trade publisher of fiction, children's books/YA, and nonfiction on sports, crime/law, military, international/political studies, Italian American studies, health/medicine, and reference. **Sample Titles:** *Hillary!* by Michael Bowery; *Quilt of America* by Carol J. Gariepy; *The Wisdom of Angels: Unearthing My Italian Roots* by Martha T. Cummings; *The Scalp Hunters* by Alfred Kayworth.

BRASSEY'S, INC.
22841 Quicksilver Dr., Dulles, VA 20166. 703-661-1548. E-mail: don@booksintl.com. Web site: www.brasseysinc.com. Don McKeon, Publisher. **Description:** Nonfiction, 35,000-200,000 words, on history (especially military history), national and international affairs, foreign policy, intelligence, defense, aviation, biography, and sports. **Books Statistics:** 80 titles/yr (900 submissions); 10% by first-time authors; 80% unagented. **Proposal Process:** Send query with synopsis, author bio, outline, 2 sample chapters, and SASE. Accepts e-queries, but prefers hard copy. Responds in 1-2 months. **Payment:** Advance and royalty. **Sample Titles:** *Nerve Center: Inside the White House Situation Room* by Michael

K. Bohn; *Mickey Mantle: America's Prodigal Son* by Tony Castro. **Contact:** Donald Jacobs, Senior Assistant Editor.

GEORGE BRAZILLER, PUBLISHER
171 Madison Ave., New York, NY 10016. 212-889-0909. George Braziller, Publisher. **Description:** Fiction, nonfiction, international literature, art, architecture. **Proposal Process:** Send proposal with sample chapters and CV to editor's attention.

BREAKAWAY BOOKS
P.O. Box 24, Halcottsville, NY 12438. 212-898-0408.
E-mail: garth@breakawaybooks.com. Web site: www.breakawaybooks.com. Garth Battista, Publisher. **Description:** Fiction and essays on sports, specifically on the experience of being an athlete. Also illustrated storybooks for kids ages 3-8, all dealing with sports (running, cycling, swimming, triathlon, canoeing, kayaking, and sailing). **Books Statistics:** 8 titles/yr; 80% by first-time authors; 80% unagented. **Proposal Process:** Query (preferably by e-mail) with outline and sample chapters. Include SASE if submitting by mail. Accepts simultaneous queries. **Payment:** Royalty. **Tips:** Literary writing of the highest quality. No genre stories, how-tos, or celebrity bios. "Our goal is to bring to light literary writing on the athletic experience."

BRICK TOWER PRESS
1230 Park Ave., New York, NY 10128. 212-427-7139.
Web site: www.bricktowerpress.com. **Description:** Cookery, gardening, autobiography, military and maritime history. **Sample Titles:** (Cooking) *Fresh Bread Companion* by Liz Clark; (Maritime) *Return of the Coffin Ships: The Derbyshire Enigma* by Bernard Edwards; (Biography) *Reflexions* by Richard Olney.

BRIDGE WORKS
P.O. Box 1798, Bridgehampton, NY 11932. 631-537-3418.
E-mail: bap@hamptons.com. Barbara Phillips, Editorial Director. **Description:** Small press specializing in quality fiction and nonfiction. No family memoirs, cookbooks, sci-fi, supernatural, or romances. Biographies and mysteries are welcome. **Books Statistics:** 6-10 titles/yr (2,000 submissions/queries); 50% by first-time authors; 50% unagented. **Proposal Process:** Query with outline, sample chapters, and SASE. Accepts e-queries, but prefers hard copy. No simultaneous queries. Responds in 1 month. **Payment:** Royalty. **Tips:** "First-time fiction writers should have their manuscript vetted by a freelance editor before submitting."

BRISTOL PUBLISHING ENTERPRISES
2714 McCone Ave., Hayward, CA 94545. 800-346-4889.
Web site: www.bristolcookbooks.com. Aidan Wylde, Editor. **Description:** Cookbooks, craftbooks, health, and pet care. **Books Statistics:** 12-20 titles/year (300 submissions), 18% first-time authors, 100% unagented. **Proposal Process:** Query with outline, sample chapters, and SASE. Accepts simultaneous queries, but not e-queries. Prefers hard copy format. **Payment:** Royalty. **Sample Titles:** *Home Cooking*

Volume 5 by Lauren Groveman; *Quick and Easy Pasta Recipes* by Coleen and Bob Simmons. **Tips:** See Web site for guidelines.

BROADWAY BOOKS
Doubleday Broadway Publishing Group/Random House, Inc.
1540 Broadway, New York, NY 10036. 212-782-9000.
Web site: www.randomhouse/broadway. **Description:** Adult nonfiction; small and very selective fiction list. **Proposal Process:** No unsolicited submissions. Query first.

BUCKNELL UNIVERSITY PRESS
Bucknell University, Lewisburg, PA 17837. 570-577-3674.
Web site: www.departments.bucknell.edu/univ_press. Greg Clingham, Director.
Description: Scholarship and criticism in English, American and comparative literature, theory and cultural studies, history, philosophy, modern languages (especially Hispanic and Latin American studies), anthropology, political science, classics, cultural geography, or any combination of the above. **Books Statistics:** 38 titles/yr (500 submissions); 50% by first-time authors; 99% unagented. **Proposal Process:** Query with outline and sample chapters. No simultaneous or electronic queries. Hard copy only. Responds in 1 month to proposals, 3-4 months to manuscripts. **Payment:** Royalty, 10% net. **Sample Titles:** *The Politics of Philology: Alfonso Reyes and the Invention of the Latin American Literary Tradition* by Robert T. Conn; *Modes of Discipline: Women, Conservatism, and the Novel After the French Revolution* by Lisa Wood. **Tips:** "Excellent scholarship in the humanities and related social sciences; no 'popular' material."

BUILDERBOOKS
National Assn. of Home Builders
1201 15th St. NW, Washington, DC 20005-2800. 800-368-5242.
E-mail: publishing@nahb.com. Web site: www.builderbooks.com. **Description:** BuilderBooks(TM) publishes educational books and electronic products for builders, remodelers, developers, sales/marketing professionals, and consumers in the residential construction industry. **Books Statistics:** 24 titles/yr; 99% unagented. **Proposal Process:** Query with outline and sample chapter. Responds in 1-2 months. **Payment:** Royalty. **Sample Titles:** *Pro Builder: Business Planning* by Steve Maltzman and Mike Benshoof; *Decorating with Architectural Trimwork* by Jay Silber. **Tips:** Writers must be experts. **Contact:** Eric Johnson, Publisher (ejohnson@nahb.com); Doris M. Tennyson, Senior Acquisitions Editor (dtennyson@nahb.com); Theresa Minch, Acquisitions Editor (tminch@nahb.com).

BULFINCH PRESS
AOL Time Warner Book Group
1271 Avenue of the Americas, New York, NY 02108. 212-522-8700.
Web site: www.bulfinchpress.com. Michael L. Sand, Executive Managing Editor.
Description: Illustrated fine art and photography books, coffeetable books, and books on photojournalism, painting, and design. **Books Statistics:** 70 titles/yr.

Proposal Process: Query with outline or proposal, sample artwork and text (no originals), author/artist bio, and SASE. Accepts simultaneous queries, but not e-queries. Responds in 1-4 weeks. **Sample Titles:** *Stanley Kubrick: A Life in Pictures* by Christiane Kubrick; *The Breathing Field: Yoga as Art* by Wyatt Townley. **Tips:** "Visual material is crucial." **Contact:** Emily Martin, Department Assistant.

BULL PUBLISHING

P.O. Box 1377, Boulder, CO 94025-2865. 800-676-2855.
E-mail: jim.bullpublishing@attbi.com. Web site: www.bullpub.com. Jim Bull, Publisher. **Description:** Books on health, child care, nutrition, and self-help. **Sample Titles:** *Habits Not Diets: The Secret to Lifetime Weight Control* by James M. Ferguson, M.D.; *Hormonal Balance: Understanding Hormones, Weight, and Your Metabolism* by Scott Isaacs, M.D.

BURFORD BOOKS

32 Morris Ave., Springfield, NJ 07081. 973-258-0960.
Web site: www.burfordbooks.com. Peter Burford, Acquisitions Editor. **Description:** Publishes books on sports, the outdoors, military history, food, and wine. **Books Statistics:** 25 titles/yr (250 submissions); 50% by first-time authors; 50% unagented. **Proposal Process:** Query with outline. Considers simultaneous queries. Prefers hard-copy format. Responds in 3 weeks. **Payment:** Royalty. **Sample Titles:** *Everything You Need to Know About Wine* by Jonathan Ray; *The Joy of Family Camping* by Herb Gordon. **Tips:** Seeking well-written books on practically anything that can be done outside.

BURNHAM PUBLISHERS

111 N Canal St., Suite 955, Chicago, IL 60606. 312-930-9446.
Richard Meade, Senior Editor. **Description:** College textbooks in the fields of political science, archaeology, psychology, sociology, and mass communications. **Books Statistics:** 30 titles/yr (200 queries); 90% unagented. **Proposal Process:** Submit query, 2 sample chapters, curriculum vitae, and SASE. Responds in 1 month to queries. **Sample Titles:** *Living Off Crime* by Ken Tunnell; *History of Nazi Germany* by Joseph Bendersky. **Tips:** Welcomes new submissions; virtually all manuscripts are written by college professors.

BUTTE PUBLICATIONS, INC.

P.O. Box 1328, Hillsboro, OR 97123-1328. 503-648-9791.
Web site: www.buttepublications.com. **Description:** Publishes material related to deafness and education, especially for teachers of PreK-12 students. Also publishes college textbooks and resources for parents and professionals. Concentration is on the reading and writing aspects of teaching children who are deaf.

C&T PUBLISHING

1651 Challenge Dr., Concord, CA 94520.
E-mail: ctinfo@ctpub.com. Web site: www.ctpub.com. Darra Williamson, Editor-in-

Chief. **Description:** Quilting books, 48-200 finished pages. Focus is how-to, although will consider picture, inspirational, or history books on quilting. **Proposal Process:** Query with outline or sample chapters. Considers simultaneous queries. **Payment:** Royalty. **Sample Titles:** *Q Is for Quilt* by Diana McClun and Laura Nownes; *15 Two-Block Quilts* by Claudia Olson.

CAMBRIDGE UNIVERSITY PRESS
40 W 20th St., New York, NY 10011-4211. 212-924-3900.
Web site: www.cup.org. Richard Ziemacki, Director. **Description:** Scholarly books and college textbooks. Subjects include the behavioral, biological, physical, and social sciences. Also computer science and technology, as well as the humanities such as literature, music, and religion. **Sample Titles:** *Life at the Limits: Organisms in Extreme Environments* by David A. Wharton.

CAREER PRESS/NEW PAGE BOOKS
3 Tice Rd., Franklin Lakes, NJ 07417. 201-848-0310.
E-mail: mlewis@nisusa.net. Web site: www.careerpress.com. Michael Lewis, Acquisitions Editor. **Description:** Adult nonfiction books on business, career, education, personal finance, and reference. Seeks high-quality work that will help improve the lives of readers. **Proposal Process:** Prefers complete manuscript; will consider proposals. Include TOC, est. book length, two complete sample chapters, author bio, market analysis, and previously published clips. Responds within 30 days.

CARROLL AND GRAF PUBLISHERS, INC.
Avalon Publishing Group
161 William St., Fl. 16, New York, NY 10038. 646-375-2570.
Web site: www.avalonpub.com. Tina Pohlman, Senior Editor. **Description:** General fiction and nonfiction. **Books Statistics:** 120 titles/yr; 10% by first-time authors. **Proposal Process:** No unagented submissions.

CARSON-DELLOSA PUBLISHING CO., INC.
Subsidiary of Cinar Films
P.O. Box 35665, Greensboro, NC 27425. 336-632-0084.
Web site: www.carsondellosa.com. Wolfgang D. Hoelscher, Acquisitions Editor. **Description:** Supplemental educational materials and resources for elementary and middle school teachers. **Books Statistics:** 90 titles/yr. **Tips:** No trade fiction or nonfiction.

CASSANDRA PRESS
P.O. Box 150868, San Rafael, CA 94915. 415-382-8507.
E-mail: starvibe@indra.com. Fred Rubenfeld, President. **Description:** New age, holistic health, metaphysical, and psychological books. **Books Statistics:** 2-3 titles/yr; 50% by first-time authors; 50% unagented. **Proposal Process:** Query with outline and sample chapters, or complete manuscript. Include SASE. Accepts simultaneous

queries, but not e-queries. Prefers hard copy format. **Payment:** Royalty, 6-8%. **Contact:** Editorial Department.

THE CATHOLIC UNIVERSITY OF AMERICA PRESS

240 Leahy Hall, 620 Michigan Ave. NE, Washington, DC 20064. 202-319-5052. E-mail: cua-press@cua.edu. Web site: www.cuapress.cua.edu. David J. McGonagle, Director. **Description:** Scholarly works related to the humanities, namely ecclesiastical and secular history, literature, political theory, philosophy, social studies, and theology. **Books Statistics:** 25 titles/yr; 50% by first-time authors; 100% unagented. **Proposal Process:** Submit abstract or TOC, resume, and list of previous publications. **Sample Titles:** *The Orphans of Byzantium* by Timothy S. Miller; *Fiction, Intuition, and Creativity* by Angela Hague.

CCLS PUBLISHING HOUSE

Cultural Center for Language Studies
3191 Coral Way, Suite 114, Miami, FL 33145. 305-529-8563.
E-mail: info@cclscorp.com. Web site: www.cclscorp.com. Luiz Goncalves, President. **Description:** Language school and publishing house whose focus is to teach and create both multimedia and print language-instruction materials for students learning English or Spanish.

CHAMPION PRESS, LTD.

8689 N Port Washington Rd., Suite 329, Milwaukee, WI 53217.
Web site: www.championpress.com. **Description:** Fiction, poetry, and nonfiction in the categories of lifestyle, parenting, relationships, homeschooling/education, self-help, and cooking. **Proposal Process:** Submit proposal with overview, market analysis, outline, author bio, first 3 sample chapters, and SASE. No phone or e-queries. Responds in 3 months. **Sample Titles:** (Fiction) *Enoch's Portal* by A.W. Hill; (Nonfiction) *The Frantic Family Cookbook* by Leanne Ely, C.N.C.; *The Single Parent Resource* by Brook Noel. **Tips:** Must follow submission guidelines for consideration. **Contact:** Editorial Department.

CHARLES RIVER MEDIA

10 Downer Ave., Hingham, MA 02043. 781-740-0400.
Web site: www.charlesriver.com. **Description:** Books on computers, programming, networking, game development, and graphics.

CHECKMARK BOOKS

Facts On File, Inc.
132 W 31st St., New York, NY 10001-2006. 212-967-8800.
E-mail: jchambers@factsonfile.com. Web site: www.factsonfile.com. James Chambers, Editor-in-Chief. **Description:** Focuses on careers, education, health, popular history and culture, fashion, and fitness. Looking for materials that fit a particular market niche that are high-quality, with a strong reference component.

Proposal Process: Query with sample chapters or outline. **Payment:** Advance against royalty. **Tips:** Does not publish memoirs, autobiographies, or fiction.

CHELSEA GREEN PUBLISHING CO.

P.O. Box 428, Gates-Briggs Building, Suite 205
White River Junction, VT 05001. 802-295-6300.
E-mail: watson@chelseagreen.com. Web site: www.chelseagreen.com. Ben Watson, Acquisitions Editor. **Description:** Independent publisher specializing in nonfiction books on environmental issues. Also publishes cookbooks, biographies, and reference titles. **Books Statistics:** 15-20 titles/yr; 30% by first-time authors; 85% unagented. **Proposal Process:** Submit brief proposal, TOC, sample chapter, list of previously published works and SASE. **Sample Titles:** *This Organic Life* by Joan Dye Gussow; *The Solar House: Passive Heating and Cooling* by Dan Chiras. **Tips:** "We are an environmental publisher of titles with a strong, practical orientation. Topics include organic agriculture and food, shelter, renewable energy, and right livelihood."

CHICAGO REVIEW PRESS

814 N Franklin St., Chicago, IL 60610. 312-337-0747.
E-mail: publish@ipgbook.com Web site. www.ipgbook.com. Cynthia Sherry, Editor. **Description:** Nonfiction: activity books for children, general nonfiction, parenting, how-to, and regional gardening and other regional topics. **Proposal Process:** Query with outline and sample chapters.

CHRONICLE BOOKS

85 Second St., Fl. 6, San Francisco, CA 94105. 415-537-3730.
E-mail: frontdesk@chroniclebooks.com. Web site: www.chroniclebooks.com. **Description:** Fiction, children's books, giftbooks, and nonfiction titles on art, photography, architecture, design, travel, nature, and food. **Proposal Process:** Send proposal (complete manuscript for fiction) with SASE. Proposal should include cover letter with brief description of project, outline, introduction, sample text/chapters, sample illustrations/photographs (duplicates, not originals), market analysis, and brief bio. **Tips:** Does not publish romances, science fiction, fantasy, westerns, or other genre fiction. **Contact:** Editorial Department.

CLARKSON POTTER/PUBLISHERS

Crown Publishing Group/Random House, Inc.
201 E 50th St., New York, NY 10022. 212-751-2600.
Web site: www.randomhouse.com. Lauren Shakely, Senior Vice President/Editorial Director. **Description:** Illustrated trade books about such topics as cooking, gardening, and decorating. **Proposal Process:** Submissions accepted through agents only. **Sample Titles:** *Eden on Their Minds: American Gardeners with Bold Visions* by Starr Ockenga; *The Art of Expecting* by Veronique Vienne.

CLEAR LIGHT PUBLISHERS

823 Don Diego, Santa Fe, NM 87501-4224. 800-253-2747.
E-mail: clpublish@aol.com. Web site: www.clearlightbooks.com. Harmon Houghton, Publisher. **Description:** Focuses on Southwestern themes, especially Native American cultures. Publishes nonfiction, fiction, picture books, and young adult books. Fiction includes: multicultural, historical, inspirational, and regional. Seeking nonfiction mss on history, multicultural, ethnic issues, nature, religion, biographies of Native Americans. **Proposal Process:** Query with SASE.

CLEIS PRESS, INC.

P.O. Box 14684, San Francisco, CA 94114-0684. 415-575-4700.
Web site: www.cleispress.com. Frédérique Delacoste, Acquisitions Editor. **Description:** Lesbian and gay studies, literature by women, human rights, sexuality, and travel. Fiction and nonfiction, 200 pages. No poetry. **Payment:** Royalty. **Tips:** Enclose return postage with all submissions for return of materials.

CLOVER PARK PRESS

P.O. Box 5067-T, Santa Monica, CA 90409-5067. 310-452-7657.
E-mail: cloverparkpr@earthlink.net.
Web site: http://home.earthlink.net/~cloverparkpr. Martha Grant, Acquisitions Editor. **Description:** Nonfiction adult books on California (history, natural history, travel, culture, or the arts), biography of extraordinary women, nature, travel, exploration, scientific/medical discovery, travel, adventure. **Proposal Process:** Query with outline, sample chapter, author bio, and SASE.

COFFEE HOUSE PRESS

27 N Fourth St., Suite 400, Minneapolis, MN 55401. 612-338-0125.
Web site: www.coffeehousepress.org. Allan Kornblum, Publisher. **Description:** Publishes literary novels, full-length short story collections, poetry, essays, memoir, and anthologies. **Books Statistics:** 14 titles/yr (5,000 submissions); 15% by first-time authors; 10% unagented. **Proposal Process:** Query with sample chapters (20-30 pages) and SASE. Considers simultaneous queries. Send hard copy only; do not send via e-mail or fax. Responds in 4-6 weeks to queries, 4-5 months to manuscripts. **Payment:** Royalty. **Sample Titles:** *The Impossibly* by Laird Hunt; *That Kind of Sleep* by Susan Atefat-Peckman; *Circle K Cycles* by Karen Tei Yamashita. **Tips:** No genre fiction (mystery, romances, western, science fiction) or books for children.

COLLECTOR BOOKS

A Division of Schroeder Publishing Co.
P.O. Box 3009, Paducah, KY 42002-3009. 270-898-6211.
E-mail: editor@collectorbooks.com. Web site: www.collectorbooks.com. Gail Ashburn, Editor. **Description:** Publishes books for dealers and collectors on items such as dolls, toys, antiques, Depression glass, pottery and porcelain, china and dinnerware, quilts, jewelry, furniture, and other memorabilia. **Books Statistics:** 50 titles/yr (400 submissions); 50% by first-time authors. **Proposal Process:** Submit

proposal with resume or brief bio, outline, fully developed introduction, and at least one fully developed chapter accompanied by sample photos. For value guide proposals, please include a sample price guide for every item pictured with explanation of how you arrived at those prices. Responds in 3 weeks. **Payment:** Royalty 5% of retail price. **Sample Titles:** *Collector's Encyclopedia of Depression Glass* by Gene Florence; *Star Wars Super Collector's Wish Book* by Geoffrey Carlton.

COLLECTORS PRESS, INC.

P.O. Box 230986, Portland, OR 97281. 503-684-3030.
E-mail: info@collectorspress.com. Web site: www.collectorspress.com. Richard Perry, Publisher. **Description:** "We are an award-winning publisher of nostalgic art and retro cooking books. We do not publish fiction or children's books." **Books Statistics:** 20 titles/yr; 50% by first-time authors; 80% unagented. **Proposal Process:** Send proposal, include SASE for return of manuscript. **Payment:** Flat fee or royalty. **Sample Titles:** *Come Fly with Us! A Global History of the Airline Hostess* by Johanna Omelia and Michael Waldock; *Road Trip America* by Andrew Wood.

CONARI PRESS

Imprint of Red Wheel/Weiser, LLC
368 Congress St., Boston, MA 02210. 617-542-1324.
Web site: www.redwheelweiser.com. Ms. Pat Bryce, Editor. **Description:** Publishes books on health, personal growth, spirituality, women's issues, and relationships. **Proposal Process:** Submit outline, sample chapters, and 6½ x 9½-inch SASE. Hard copy only. Accepts simultaneous queries, but not e-queries. Responds in 3-6 months. **Payment:** Royalty. **Tips:** "Please visit our Web site for detailed submission guidelines. Before submitting any materials, please study our books in a bookstore, library, or publisher's catalog."

CONFLUENCE PRESS

Lewis-Clark State College
500 Eighth Ave., Lewiston, ID 83501-2698. 208-792-2336.
E-mail: conpress@lcsc.edu. Web site: www.confluencepress.com. James R. Hepworth, Editor. **Description:** Trade poetry, fiction, novels, essays, literary criticism, photography, art, science, and folklore. Special interest in the literature of the contemporary and American West. **Books Statistics:** 2 titles/yr (1,000 submissions); 50% by first-time authors; 75% unagented. **Proposal Process:** Send query with formal cover letter and SASE. Accepts simultaneous queries. Prefers hard copy. Responds in 6 weeks. **Payment:** Royalty. **Sample Titles:** (Fiction) *The Wild Awake* by Paulann Petersen; (Song Lyrics) *Earth & Sky: The Laurie Lewis Songbook* by Laurie Lewis; (Poetry) *Even in Quiet Places* by William Stafford. **Tips:** "We are currently seeking writing about the contemporary American Northwest."

CONTEMPORARY BOOKS

Imprint of McGraw-Hill Professional
Prudential Plaza, 130 E Randolph St., Suite 900, Chicago, IL 60601. 312-233-6520.

Description: Nonfiction trade books with a strong focus on sports and fitness, parenting, self-help, general reference, health, careers, foreign language, and dictionaries. **Books Statistics:** 400 titles/yr (600 submissions); 10% by first-time authors; 20% unagented. **Proposal Process:** Query with outline. Prefers hard copy. Considers simultaneous queries. **Payment:** Royalty 7.5% list paper, 10-15% list cloth or flat fee—typical range is $1,000-$4,000. **Sample Titles:** *Mindgames: Phil Jackson's Long Strange Journey* by Roland Lazenby; *Successful Direct Marketing Methods* by Bob Stone.

CONTINUUM INTERNATIONAL PUBLISHING GROUP

370 Lexington Ave., Suite 1700, New York, NY 10017. 212-953-5858.
Web site: www.continuumbooks.com. **Description:** General-interest trade titles, scholarly titles, and reference materials in the areas of literature, the arts, history, religion, philosophy, and social issues. **Proposal Process:** Query with SASE. **Sample Titles:** *All About Oscar* by Emanuel Levy; *Truly Our Sister: A Theology of Mary in the Communion of Saints* by Elizabeth A. Johnson. **Contact:** Evander Lomke, Vice President/Senior Editor; Frank Oveis, Vice President/Senior Editor.

COPPER CANYON PRESS

P.O. Box 271, Port Townsend, WA 98368. 360-385-4925.
E-mail: poetry@coppercanyonpress.org. Web site: www.coppercanyonpress.org. Sam Hamill, Editor. **Description:** Poetry publisher. **Books Statistics:** 18 titles/yr (1,000 submissions); 10% by first time authors; 95% unagented. **Proposal Process:** No unsolicited manuscripts. **Payment:** Royalty. **Sample Titles:** *Cool, Calm & Collected* by Carolyn Kizer; *Spring Essence: The Poetry of Ho Xuan Huong* translated by John Balaban. **Tips:** Currently not accepting unsolicited manuscripts; check Web site for updates. Also offers annual Hayden Carruth Award for first, second, and third books. **Contact:** Michael Wiegers.

COUNCIL OAK BOOKS

1615 S Baltimore, Suite 3, Tulsa, OK 74119. 918-587-6454.
E-mail: pmillichap@gigplanet.com. Web site: www.counciloakbooks.com. Paulette Millichap, Editor. **Description:** Distinguished nonfiction books based in personal, intimate history (letters, diaries, memoir, and first-person adventure/travel); Native American history and spiritual teachings; small inspirational gift books; unique vintage photo books and Americana. **Books Statistics:** 10 titles/yr (300 submissions); 25% by first-time authors; 75% unagented. **Proposal Process:** Query with outline and SASE. Do not send complete manuscript. Accepts simultaneous and electronic queries. Prefers hard copy. **Payment:** Royalty. **Sample Titles:** *The Blessing: A Memoir* by Gregory Orr. **Tips:** No fiction, poetry, or children's books. "We're looking for unique, elegant voices whose history, teachings, and experiences illuminate our lives."

COUNTERPOINT PRESS

Member of the Perseus Book Group
387 Park Ave. S, New York, NY 10016. 212-340-8138.

Web site: www.counterpointpress.com. **Description:** Serious literary works in the areas of history, philosophy, art, nature, science, poetry, and fiction. **Proposal Process:** Currently not accepting submissions. **Sample Titles:** *Deus Lo Volt* by Evan S. Connell; *Appetites* by Caroline Knapp. **Contact:** Acquisitions Editor.

THE COUNTRYMAN PRESS, INC.

W.W. Norton & Co., P.O. Box 748, Woodstock, VT 05091. 802-457-4826. Web site: www.countrymanpress.com. **Description:** Publishes nonfiction material on New England history and culture. Topics include country living, gardening, nature and the environment, and travel. Also publishes regional guidebooks on hiking, walking, canoeing, kayaking, bicycling, mountain biking, cross-country skiing, and flyfishing for all parts of the U.S. **Proposal Process:** Submit query or outline, 3 sample chapters, and SASE. **Payment:** Royalty.

CRAFTSMAN BOOK COMPANY

6058 Corte del Cedro, P.O. Box 6500, Carlsbad, CA 92018. 760-438-7828. E-mail: jacobs@costbook.com. Web site: www.craftsman-book.com. Laurence D. Jacobs, Editor. **Description:** Construction manuals for the professional builder and contractor. **Books Statistics:** 12 titles/yr (30 submissions); 90% by first-time authors; 100% unagented. **Proposal Process:** Query with outline and SASE. Simultaneous and electronic queries accepted. Prefers hardy copy format. **Payment:** Royalty. **Sample Titles:** *Cabinetmaking: From Design to Finish* by Byron W. Maguire; *Basic Concrete Engineering for Builders* by Max Schwartz; *Inspecting a House* by Rex Cauldwell. **Tips:** "We're looking for simple, practical hands-on text written in the second person. Only material for the professional builder. No handyman or do-it-yourself material."

CRANE HILL PUBLISHERS

3608 Clairmont Ave., Birmingham, AL 35222. 205-714-3007. E-mail: cranies@cranehill.com. Web site: www.cranehill.com. **Description:** History, biography/memoir, folklore, cookbooks, art, photography, humor, travel, and mind/body/spirit. "We search for quality books that reflect the history, perceptions, experience, and customs of people in regional locales around the U.S." **Payment:** Royalty. **Sample Titles:** *A Morning Cup of Yoga* by Jane Trechsel; *Whistlestop Cafe Cookbook* by Mary Jo Smith McMichael.

CREATIVE HOMEOWNER

24 Park Way, P.O. Box 38, Upper Saddle River, NJ 07458-0038. 201-934-7100. E-mail: sharon.ranftle@creativehomeowner.com. Web site: www.creativehomeowner.com. Timothy O. Bakke, Editorial Director. **Description:** Books on lifestyle for the home and garden. Topics include interior design/decorating, gardening/landscaping, and home improvement/repair. **Books Statistics:** 12-16 titles/yr (20-30 submissions); 70% by first-time authors; 98% unagented. **Proposal Process:** Query. Accepts simultaneous and electronic queries. Prefers hard copy. Responds in 2-4 months. **Payment:** Royalty or flat fee. **Sample**

Titles: *Decorating with Architectural Trimwork* by Jay Silber. **Tips:** Avoid passive voice. Prefers straightforward, expository, instructional text in clear language. **Contact:** Sharon Ranftle.

CREATIVE PUBLISHING INTERNATIONAL
18705 Lake Drive E, Chanhassen, MN 55317. 952-936-4700.
Web site: www.creativepub.com. **Description:** Worldwide publisher of how-to books, as well as a premier publisher of nature, photography, and wildlife books for children and adults under the NorthWord Press imprint. Also offers multilingual educational, nonfiction books and multimedia products for children, teachers, and parents under the Two-Can imprint.

CROSS CULTURAL PUBLICATIONS, INC.
P.O. Box 506, Notre Dame, IN 46556. 219-273-6526.
E-mail: crosscult@aol.com. Web site: crossculturalpub.com. Cyriac K. Pullapilly, General Editor. **Description:** All academic disciplines, also general-interest books. Special interest in intercultural and interfaith issues. Prefers books that push the boundaries of knowledge and existing systems of religion, philosophy, politics, economics, ethics, justice, and arts (whether through fiction, nonfiction, or poetry). **Books Statistics:** 30 titles/yr (5,000 submissions); 30% by first-time authors; 90% unagented. **Proposal Process:** Send proposal with TOC, resume, and SASE. Considers simultaneous and electronic queries. Prefers hard copy. **Payment:** Royalty. **Tips:** "Our primary concern is subject matter, then organization, clarity of argument, literary style. No superficially argued books."

THE CROSSING PRESS
1201 Shaffer Rd., Suite B, Santa Cruz, CA 95060. 408-722-0711.
E-mail: elaine@crossingpress.com. Web site: www.crossingpress.com. Elaine Goldman Gill, Publisher. **Description:** Publisher of books, videos, and audios on natural and alternative health, spirituality, personal growth, self-help, empowerment, and cookbooks. **Proposal Process:** Submit proposal with outline, market analysis, sample chapters, and author bio. Responds in 8 weeks. **Payment:** Royalty. **Sample Titles:** *Pocket Herbal Reference Guide* by Debra St. Claire; *Natural Healing for Dogs & Cats* by Diane Stein; *A Magical Guide to Love & Sex* by Cassandra Eason; *Wicca: The Complete Craft* by D.J. Conway. **Tips:** No longer accepts fiction, poetry, or calendars. **Contact:** Acquisitions Editor.

THE CROSSROAD PUBLISHING CO.
481 Eighth Ave., Suite 1550, New York, NY 10001. 212-868-1801.
E-mail: ask@crossroadpublishing.com. Web site: www.crossroadpublishing.com. **Description:** Publisher of spiritual and religious titles. **Books Statistics:** 55 titles/yr **Proposal Process:** Query with brief description, TOC, approximate word count, estimated timetable, intended audience, resume or curriculum vitae, and writing sample (no more than 2 chapters). **Sample Titles:** *Awake in the Spirit* by M. Basil

Pennington; *Faith That Makes Sense* by Robert J. Cormier; *Prayer & the Quest for Healing* by Barbara Fiand.

CUMBERLAND HOUSE PUBLISHING
431 Harding Industrial Dr., Nashville, TN 37211. 615-832-1171.
E-mail: info@cumberlandhouse.com. Web site: www.cumberlandhouse.com. Tilly Katz, Acquisitions Editor. **Description:** Nonfiction titles in history, sports, and cooking. Also publishes some mystery titles and Christian titles. **Books Statistics:** 60 titles/yr (1,300 submissions); 50% by first-time authors; 75% unagented. **Proposal Process:** Query with outline. No simultaneous or electronic queries. Hard copy only. Responds in 3-6 months. **Payment:** Royalty. **Sample Titles:** *Stonewall Jackson's Book of Maxims* by James Robertson Jr.; *Goodnight John-Boy* by Earl Hamner and Ralph E. Giffin. **Tips:** No poetry or westerns. Considers fiction, but stronger interest in nonfiction.

CURBSTONE PRESS
321 Jackson St., Willimantic, CT 06226. 860-423-5110.
E-mail: info@curbstone.org. Web site: www.curbstone.org Judith Doyle, Alexander Taylor, Co-Directors. **Description:** Fiction, creative nonfiction, poetry books, and picture books that reflect a commitment to social change, with an emphasis on contemporary writing from Latin America and Latino communities in the U.S. **Proposal Process:** Query with 10-20 sample pages. Does not accept complete manuscripts. Hard copy only. **Payment:** Royalty. **Sample Titles:** *My Mother's Island* by Marnie Mueller; *Maroon* by Danielle Legros Georges. **Contact:** Alexander Taylor, Co-Director.

DA CAPO PRESS
Perseus Books Group, 11 Cambridge Center, Cambridge, MA 02142. 617-252-5200.
Web site: www.dacapopress.com. **Description:** General nonfiction on film, dance, theatre, history, literature, art, sports, and African-American studies. **Books Statistics:** 60 titles/yr (250 submissions). **Proposal Process:** Query with outline and sample chapters. Accepts simultaneous queries, but not e-queries. Hard copy only. Responds in 3-6 months. **Payment:** Royalty. **Tips:** "We do fairly serious nonfiction with backlist potential; we're not right for very commercial front-list-only titles." **Contact:** Editorial Director.

DALKEY ARCHIVE PRESS
The Center for Book Culture
ISU Campus Box 8905, Normal, IL 61790-8905. 309-438-7555.
E-mail: contact@dalkeyarchive.com. Web site: www.dalkeyarchive.com. John O'Brien, Founder/Publisher. **Description:** Mostly publishes reprints of literary works and translations from the past 100 years. Publishes some original, avant-garde, experimental fiction. **Books Statistics:** 2-4 original titles/yr. **Proposal Process:** Query with SASE via regular mail. No unsolicited manuscripts. Responds in 2-4 months. **Contact:** Submissions Editor.

JONATHAN DAVID PUBLISHERS, INC.

68-22 Eliot Ave., Middle Village, NY 11379. 718-456-8611.

E-mail: info@jdbooks.com. Web site: www.jdbooks.com. Alfred J. Kolatch, Editor-in-Chief. **Description:** Nonfiction titles on sports, reference, and biography. Area of specialization is popular Judaica. **Books Statistics:** 25 titles/yr; 25% by first-time authors; 90% unagented. **Proposal Process:** Query with brief synopsis, TOC, sample chapter, resume, and SASE. No simultaneous queries. Accepts e-queries, but prefers hard copy. **Payment:** Royalty or outright purchase. **Sample Titles:** (Sports) *New York Yankees: Seasons of Glory* by William Hageman and Warren Wilbert; (Biography) *Great African-American Women* by Darryl Lyman; (Judaica) *Greatest Jewish Stories* by David Patterson.

DAVIES-BLACK PUBLISHING

Division of Consulting Psychologists Press, Inc.

3803 E Bayshore Rd., Palo Alto, CA 94303. 650-969-8901.

E-mail: clk@starband.net. Web site: www.cpp-db.com. Connie Kallback, Acquisitions Editor. **Description:** Professional and trade titles in business and careers with a focus on leadership and management, organization development, human resource development, career management, and professional improvement. **Sample Titles:** *What's Your Type of Career?* by Donna Dunning; *Successful Woman's Guide to Working Smart* by Caitlin Williams.

DAVIS PUBLICATIONS, INC.

50 Portland St., Worcester, MA 01608. 508-754-7201.

Web site: www.davis-art.com. Claire M. Golding, Editor-in-Chief. **Description:** Books, 100-300 manuscript pages, for the art education market. Most titles are for teachers of art, grades K-12. Must have an educational component. **Proposal Process:** Query with outline and sample chapters c/o Claire M. Golding.

DAW BOOKS, INC.

The Penguin Group/Penguin Putnam Inc.

375 Hudson St., Fl. 3, New York, NY 10014-3658. 212-366-2096.

E-mail: daw@penguinputnam.com. Web site: www.dawbooks.com. Elizabeth R. Wollheim, Publisher. **Description:** Specializes in science fiction and fantasy. Most books are targeted to an adult audience; however, some are appropriate for young adults as well. **Proposal Process:** Send complete manuscript with SASE. Responds in 3 months. **Sample Titles:** *The Saga of the Renunciates* by Marion Zimmer Bradley; *The Lost Dragons of Barakhai* by Mickey Zucker Reichert. **Tips:** Does not accept short stories, novellas, or poetry. **Contact:** Submissions Editor.

DEARBORN TRADE PUBLISHING, INC.

155 N Wacker Dr., Chicago, IL 60606-1719. 312-836-4400.

E-mail: hull@dearborn.com. Web site: www.dearborntrade.com. Don Hull, Editorial Director. **Description:** Professional and consumer books on investing, real estate, sales and marketing, general management, and business. **Proposal Process:** Query with outline and sample chapters. **Payment:** Royalty and flat fee.

IVAN R. DEE, PUBLISHER
Member of the Rowman & Littlefield Publishing Group
1332 N Halsted St., Chicago, IL 60622-2637. 312-787-6262.
E-mail: editorial@ivanrdee.com. Web site: www.ivanrdee.com. Ivan R. Dee, President/Publisher. **Description:** Serious nonfiction for general readers, in hardcover and paperback. Topics include history, biography, politics, literature, and theater. Imprints: New Amsterdam Books and J.S. Sanders & Co. **Books Statistics:** 60 titles/yr (1,000 submissions). **Proposal Process:** Query with outline, sample chapters, and SASE. Accepts simultaneous and electronic queries. Prefers hard copy. **Payment:** Royalty. **Sample Titles:** *Good Morning Mr. Zip Zip Zip: Movies, Memory, and World War II* by Richard Schickel; *The Rise of the New Woman: The Women's Movement in America, 1875-1930* by Jean V. Matthews.

DEL REY BOOKS
The Ballantine Publishing Group/Random House, Inc.
1540 Broadway, Fl. 11, New York, NY 10036. 212-782-8393.
E-mail: delrey@randomhouse.com. Web site: www.randomhouse.com/delrey/. Betsy Mitchell, Editor-in-Chief. **Description:** Science fiction and fantasy, 60,000- 120,000 words, average. **Books Statistics:** 75 titles/yr; 10% by first-time authors; 0% unagented. **Proposal Process:** No unsolicited manuscripts; accepts agented submissions only. **Payment:** Royalty. **Sample Titles:** *The Amber Spyglass* by Philip Pullman; *Redemption of Althalus* by David and Leigh Eddings. **Contact:** Editors: Steve Saffell, Chris Schluep, Kathleen David.

DELACORTE PRESS
Bantam Dell Publishing Group/Random House, Inc.
1540 Broadway, New York, NY 10036. 212-782-9140.
Web site: www.bantamdell.com. Leslie Schnur, Editor-in-Chief. **Description:** Imprint of The Bantam Dell Publishing Group. Commercial fiction (romance, historical, mystery) and nonfiction (politics/current affairs, psychology, parenting, self-help, and true crime). **Proposal Process:** Accepts material from literary agents only. **Sample Titles:** (Fiction) *Sometimes I Dream in Italian* by Rita Ciresi; *The Thief-Taker* by T.F. Banks; (Nonfiction) *For the Bride* by Colin Cowie; *How to Think Like Leonardo Da Vinci* by Michael Gelb.

DELMAR LEARNING
Division of Thompson Learning
5 Maxwell Dr., Clifton Park, NY 12065. 800-998-7498.
E-mail: info@delmar.com. Web site: www.delmar.com. **Description:** Technical nonfiction textbooks for post-secondary learning institutions. Topics include agriscience, electronics, graphic design, nursing, allied health, cosmetology, travel/tourism, etc. **Proposal Process:** Author guidelines available in PDF format on Web site.

DELTA BOOKS
Bantam Dell Publishing Group/Random House, Inc.
1540 Broadway, New York, NY 10036. 212-782-9140.
Web site: www.bantamdell.com. **Description:** Imprint of The Bantam Dell Publishing Group. Biography/memoir, literary fiction, short story collections, and women's fiction. **Proposal Process:** Accepts material from literary agents only. **Sample Titles:** *Shopaholic Ties the Knot* by Sophie Kinsella; *Paradise Park* by Allegra Goodman.

THE DERRYDALE PRESS
Rowman & Littlefield Publishing Group
4501 Fobes Blvd., Lanham, MD 20706. 301-459-3366.
Web site: www.derrydalepress.com. **Description:** Primarily nonfiction on travel, hunting, fishing, food/wine, nature, archery, golf, and games/hobbies. Also publishes some fiction with themes on hunting/fishing. **Proposal Process:** Submit description (outlining your qualifications, competing titles, target audience, and length), TOC, 1-2 sample chapters, and introduction or overview if available. Simultaneous submissions accepted with notice. **Sample Titles:** *True North: Reflections on Fishing and a Life Well Lived* by Jack Kulpa; *Tigers of the Sea* by Colonel Hugh D. Wise. **Contact:** Bethany Perry.

DEVIN-ADAIR PUBLISHERS, INC.
P.O. Box A, Old Greenwich, CT 06870. 203-622-1010.
J. Andrassi, Editor. **Description:** Books on conservative affairs, Irish topics, photography, Americana, self-help, health, gardening, cooking, and ecology. **Proposal Process:** Send outline, sample chapters, and SASE. **Payment:** Royalty.

THE DIAL PRESS
Bantam Dell Publishing Group/Random House, Inc.
1540 Broadway, New York, NY 10036. 212-782-9000.
Web site: www.bantamdell.com. Susan Kamil, VP/Editorial Director. **Description:** Imprint of The Bantam Dell Publishing Group. Quality literary fiction and nonfiction, on subjects that include biography, Americana, contemporary culture, government/politics, history, memoirs, psychology, women's issues/studies. **Books Statistics:** 6-12 titles/yr; 75% by first-time authors. **Proposal Process:** Accepts material from literary agents only. **Sample Titles:** *American Chica* by Marie Arana; *Franklin Flyer* by Nicholas Christopher.

THE DONNING COMPANY
184 Business Park, Suite 206, Virginia Beach, VA 23462. 757-497-1789.
E-mail: info@donning.com. Web site: www.donning.com. Scott Rule, Marketing Director. **Description:** Publishes coffee-table pictorial histories of local communities, colleges, businesses, and regional heritage. **Proposal Process:** Query with outline and sample chapters. **Payment:** Royalty. **Sample Titles:** *The History of*

Wilmington Country Club: Its First 100 Years by Dr. Joseph B. Dietz Jr.; *Our Time: Celebrating 75 Years of Learning and Leading* by Wendy Adair and Oscal Gutierrez.

DORLING KINDERSLEY

Pearson Plc, 375 Hudson St., New York, NY 10014. 212-213-4800. Web site: www.dk.com. **Description:** Picture books and fiction for middle-grade and older readers. Also, illustrated reference books for both adults and children. **Proposal Process:** Send outline and sample chapter. **Payment:** Royalty or flat fee.

DOUBLEDAY

Doubleday Broadway Publishing Group/Random House, Inc. 1540 Broadway, New York, NY 10036. 212-782-8911. Web site: www.randomhouse.com. William Thomas, VP/Editor-in-Chief. **Description:** Publishes high-quality fiction and non-fiction. Publishes hardcover and trade paperback originals and reprints. **Tips:** Does not respond to unsolicited submissions or queries.

DOWN THERE PRESS

938 Howard St., Suite 101, San Francisco, CA 94103. 415-974-8985. E-mail: downtherepress@excite.com. Web site: www.goodvibes.com/dtp/dtp. **Description:** Nonfiction titles for both children and adults addressing self-awareness and sexual health issues. Also publishes collections of erotic fiction. **Proposal Process:** Send cover letter, TOC, sample chapters and SASE. **Sample Titles:** *A Kid's First Book About Sex* by Joani Blank.

THOMAS DUNNE BOOKS

St. Martin's Press 175 Fifth Ave., New York, NY 10010. 212-674-5151. Thomas L. Dunne, Publisher. **Description:** Adult fiction (mysteries, trade, etc.) and nonfiction (history, biographies, science, politics, humor, etc.). **Proposal Process:** No unsolicited manuscripts. Agented queries only. **Payment:** Royalty.

DUQUESNE UNIVERSITY PRESS

600 Forbes Ave., Pittsburgh, PA 15282. 412-396-6610. Web site: www.dupress.duq.edu. Susan Wadsworth-Booth, Director. **Description:** Scholarly publications in the humanities and social sciences; creative nonfiction (book-length only) by emerging writers.

DURBAN HOUSE PUBLISHING

7502 Greenville Ave., Suite 500, Dallas, TX 75231. 214-890-4050. E-mail: info@durbanhouse.com. Web site: www.durbanhouse.com. Robert Middlemiss, Editor-in-Chief. **Description:** Quality fiction (suspense/thriller, mystery, historical, mainstream/contemporary, literary) and nonfiction (self-help, how-to, women's issues, memoirs, contemporary, true crime). **Books Statistics:** 10-20 titles/yr. **Proposal Process:** Fiction: query with 3 sample chapters, synopsis, and brief bio. Nonfiction: query with proposal, sample chapters, brief bio, and details of marketing platform. **Sample Titles:** (Fiction) *Secrets Are Anonymous* by Frederick L. Cullen; (Nonfiction) *Fish Heads, Rice, Rice Wine & War: A Vietnam Paradox* by Lt. Col. Thomas G. Smith.

EAKIN PRESS
P.O. Box 90159, Austin, TX 78709-0159. 512-288-1771.
Web site: www.eakinpress.com. **Description:** Regional publisher of both adult and children's titles on the history and culture of the Southwest. Particular emphasis on Texas and Oklahoma. **Books Statistics:** 65 titles/yr (1,200 submissions); 40% by first-time authors; 1% unagented. **Proposal Process:** Query with synopsis, brief bio, and publishing credits. Does not accept material electronically. Responds in 3 months. See Web site for detailed guidelines. **Payment:** Royalty. **Sample Titles:** *The Last Cowboy* by Davis L. Ford. **Contact:** Angela Buckley, Associate Editor.

EASTERN WASHINGTON UNIVERSITY PRESS
705 W First Ave., Spokane, WA 99201. 509-623-4286.
E-mail: ewupress@ewu.edu. Web site: www.ewu.edu/dcesso/press/. Chris Howell, Director. **Description:** Poetry, poetry translations, fiction, and nonfiction. **Books Statistics:** 6 titles/yr (75 submissions). **Proposal Process:** Query with complete manuscript and outline. Prefers hard copy. Accepts simultaneous queries. Responds in 4-6 months. **Payment:** Royalty. **Sample Titles:** *If Rock & Roll Were a Machine* by Terry Davis; *The Prince and the Salmon People* by Claire Rudolf Murphy.

ECLIPSE PRESS
1736 Alexandria Dr., Lexington, KY 40504. 859-278-2361.
E-mail: info@eclipsepress.com. Web site: www.eclipsepress.com. Jacqueline Duke, Editor. **Description:** Books on equine and equine-related subjects, including Thoroughbred racing, breeding, handicapping, English sport horses and disciplines, Western sport horses and disciplines, horse health care, and individuals interested in horses. **Proposal Process:** Send brief synopsis, resume or bio, outline/TOC, sample chapters, list of similar titles currently on the market, and SASE. Do not submit material via e-mail. **Sample Titles:** *Racing to the Table: A Culinary Tour of Sporting America* by Margaret Guthrie; *Secretariat: Thoroughbred Legends* by Tim Capps.

ECW PRESS
2120 Queen St. E, Suite 200, Toronto, Ontario M4E 1E2 Canada. 416-694-3348.
E-mail: info@ecwpress.com. Web site: www.ecwpress.com. Jack David, Publisher. **Description:** Trade books on poetry, fiction, pop culture, sports, travel, and celebrity bio. **Books Statistics:** 40 titles/yr (1,000 submissions). **Proposal Process:** Query first. See Web site for specific guidelines. **Sample Titles:** *Hawksley Burns for Isadora* by Hawksley Workman; *From Someplace Else: A Memoir* by Ralph Osborne.

Tips: Unsolicited manuscripts accepted. **Contact:** Michael Holmes, Poetry/Fiction Editor; Jennifer Hale, Nonfiction/Pop Culture Editor.

ENTREPRENEUR PRESS

2445 McCabe Way, Fl. 4, Irvine, CA 92614. 949-261-2325.
E-mail: jcalmes@entrepreneur.com. Web site: www.entrepreneur.com. Mike Drew, Marketing Director. **Description:** Nonfiction general and small business trade books. Areas include: business skills, motivational as well as how-to; and general business, including leadership, marketing, accounting, finance, new economy and business growth and start-ups, customer relations, innovation, stock market and online trading. **Books Statistics:** 15-20 titles/yr (600 submissions); 30% by first-time authors. **Proposal Process:** Query with outline, sample chapters, and SASE. Accepts simultaneous and electronic queries. Responds in 2 weeks. **Payment:** Royalty, 5-15%. **Contact:** Jere L. Calmes, Editorial Director.

EPIC PUBLISHING COMPANY

2101 S Pioneer Way, Las Vegas, NV 89117-2944. 702-248-7263.
E-mail: info@epicpublishing.com. Web site: www.epicpublishing.com. **Description:** Fiction, nonfiction, poetry, children's books, and biographies.

EPICENTER PRESS, INC.

P.O. Box 82368, Kenmore, WA 98028. 425-485-6822.
E-mail: info@epicenterpress.com. Web site: www.epicenterpress.com. Kent Sturgis, Publisher. **Description:** Quality nonfiction trade books emphasizing Alaska. Regional press whose interests include but are not limited to the arts, history, environment, and diverse cultures and lifestyles of the North Pacific and high latitudes.

PAUL S. ERIKSSON, PUBLISHER

P.O. Box 125, Forest Dale, VT 05745. 802-247-4210.
Description: Publishes general nonfiction and some fiction. **Proposal Process:** Send outline and cover letter and 3 chapters, SASE required. **Payment:** Royalty. **Contact:** Editorial Department.

M. EVANS & CO., INC.

216 E 49th St., New York, NY 10017. 212-688-2810.
E-mail: editorial@mevans.com. Web site: www.mevans.com. **Description:** Small commercial publisher of general nonfiction with an emphasis on health, cooking, history, relationships, current affairs, how-to, crime. Also publishes small list of adult commercial fiction. No poetry or belles lettres. **Books Statistics:** 30 titles/yr (500 submissions); 10-20% by first-time authors; 10% unagented. **Proposal Process:** Query with outline, sample chapters, and SASE. Accepts simultaneous and electronic queries. Prefers hard copy. **Payment:** Royalty. **Sample Titles:** *Hidden Agenda: How the Duke of Windsor Betrayed the Allies* by Martin Allen; *Amazingly Simple Lessons We Learned After Fifty* by William B. Toulouse. **Tips:** "Open to adult books for which we can identify a market." **Contact:** P.J. Dempsey or Marc Baller.

EXCALIBUR PUBLICATIONS

P.O. Box 35369, Tucson, AZ 85740-5369. 520-575-9057.

E-mail: excalibureditor@earthlink.net. Alan M. Petrillo, Editor. **Description:** Publishes work on military history, strategy and tactics, history of battles, military and historical personalities, firearms, arms and armor. **Books Statistics:** 6 titles/yr; 75% by first-time authors; 95% unagented. **Proposal Process:** Query with outline or synopsis, first 2 chapters, and SASE. If artwork is part of package, include samples. Accepts simultaneous queries, but not e-queries. Responds in 4-6 weeks. **Payment:** Royalty/flat fee. **Tips:** Seeking well researched and documented work. Unpublished writers are welcome and strongly encouraged.

FACTS ON FILE, INC.

132 W 31st St., Fl. 17, New York, NY 10001. 212-967-8800.

E-mail: llikoff@factsonfile.com. Web site: www.factsonfile.com. Laurie Likoff, Editorial Director. **Description:** Reference books on science, health, literature, language, history, the performing arts, ethnic studies, popular culture, and sports, etc. **Books Statistics:** 100-150 titles/yr (200-250 submissions); 10% by first-time authors; 30% unagented. **Proposal Process:** Query with outline, sample chapter, and SASE. Unsolicited synopses welcome. Accepts simultaneous queries and e-queries. Responds in 4-6 weeks. **Payment:** Royalty. **Sample Titles:** *Encyclopedia of American War Heroes*; *Encyclopedia of Ancient Egypt*. **Tips:** Strictly a reference and information publisher. (No fiction, poetry, computer/technical books, or cookbooks.)

FAIR WINDS PRESS

33 Commercial St., Gloucester, MA 01930-5089. 978-282-9590.

Web site: www.fairwindspress.com. **Description:** Publishes material on New Age, spirituality, and health. **Sample Titles:** *Earl Mindell's Diet Bible* by Earl Mindell, R.Ph., Ph.D.; *Yoga Burns Fat* by Jan Maddern; *Pilates Back Book* by Tia Stanmore.

FAIRVIEW PRESS

2450 Riverside Ave., Minneapolis, MN 55454. 800-544-8207.

E-mail: press@fairview.org. Web site: www.fairviewpress.org. Lane Stiles, Director. **Description:** Grief/bereavement, aging/seniors, caregiving, palliative and end-of-life care, and health/medicine (including complementary medicine). Also topics of interest to families, including childcare/parenting, psychology, self-help/inspirational, and spirituality. **Books Statistics:** 10-20 titles/yr (2,500 submissions); 50% by first-time authors; 70% unagented. **Proposal Process:** Query with sample chapters or complete manuscript, include SASE. Accepts simultaneous queries, but not e-queries. Hard copy only. **Tips:** No fiction, children's picture books, or adult memoirs.

FALCON PUBLISHING

The Globe Pequot Press, 246 Goose Ln., Guilford, CT 06437. 203-458-4500.

Web site: www.falcon.com. Scott Adams, Senior Acquisitions Editor. **Description:** Nonfiction titles on nature, outdoor recreation, travel, cooking, regional history, and Western Americana. **Books Statistics:** 130 titles/yr. **Proposal Process:** Send brief synopsis, TOC, sample chapter, description of target audience and competing titles, bio/resume, and SASE. Address material to: Submissions Editor [+ category]. Responds in 6-8 weeks.

FARRAR, STRAUS & GIROUX, INC.

19 Union Square W, New York, NY 10003. 212-741-6900.

E-mail: fsg.editorial@fsgee.com. Web site: www.fsgbooks.com. **Description:** Literary fiction, nonfiction, poetry, and children's books. **Books Statistics:** 175 titles/yr. **Proposal Process:** Query with cover letter, outline, sample chapters, resume or CV, and SASE. Responds in 2-3 months. **Sample Titles:** *The Time of Our Singing* by Richard Powers; *Second Founding: New York City and the Reconstruction of American Democracy* by David Quigley.

FAWCETT/IVY BOOKS

The Ballantine Publishing Group/Random House, Inc.

201 E 50th St., Fl. 9, New York, NY 10022.

Description: Adult mysteries, regencies, and historical romances, 75,000-120,000 words. **Proposal Process:** Acquisitions through agents. Query with outline and sample chapters. Responds in 3-6 months. **Payment:** Royalty.

FREDERICK FELL PUBLISHERS, INC.

2131 Hollywood Blvd., Suite 305, Hollywood, FL 33020. 954-925-5242.

E-mail: info@fellpub.com. Web site: www.fellpub.com. Barbara Newman, Acquisitions Editor. **Description:** New Age, self help, how-to, business, hobbies, and inspirational. **Books Statistics:** 40 titles/yr (2,000 submissions); 50% by first-time authors; 90% unagented. **Proposal Process:** Query with sample chapters and SASE. Accepts simultaneous queries, but not e-queries. Prefers hard copy. Responds in 2 months. **Payment:** Royalty. **Sample Titles:** *The Greatest Salesman in the World* by Og Mandino; *The Tiniest Acorn* by Marsha T. Danzig. **Tips:** "Seeking experts in all genres to help to make 'Fell's Official Know-It-All Guides' series grow." **Contact:** Lori Horton, Assistant Editor.

THE FEMINIST PRESS

The Graduate Center, CUNY, 365 Fifth Ave., Suite 5406

New York, NY 10016. 212-817-7920.

Web site: www.feministpress.org. Jean Casella, Publisher. **Description:** Educational press publishing books by and about multicultural women. Strives to resurrect the voices of women that have been repressed and silent. Publishes reprints of significant "lost" fiction, original memoirs, autobiographies, biographies, multicultural anthologies, nonfiction, and educational resources. **Tips:** Particular interest in international literature. Accepts no original fiction by U.S. authors; reprints and imports only. Accepts only e-mail queries of 200 words. See Web site for submission guidelines.

FERGUSON PUBLISHING CO.

200 W Jackson Blvd., Fl. 7, Chicago, IL 60606. 312-692-1000.
Web site: www.fergpubco.com. Andrew Morkes, Managing Editor. **Description:**
Nonfiction for the juvenile, young adult and college markets relating to career preparation and reference.

FINDHORN PRESS LTD.

305A The Park, Findhorn, Forres IV36 3TE Scotland, UK. 0144-1309-690582.
E-mail: info@findhornpress.com. Web site: www.findhornpress.com. Terry Bogliolo,
Publisher. **Description:** Nonfiction on self-help, health/healing, spirituality, music,
and dance. **Books Statistics:** 18 titles/yr **Proposal Process:** Send short synopsis via
e-mail. Does not accept unsolicited manuscripts. **Sample Titles:** *In Search of the
Magic Findhorn* by Karin Bogliolo; *Flight into Freedom and Beyond* by Eileen Caddy.

FIREBRAND BOOKS

2232 S Main St., Ann Arbor, MI 48103. 248-738-8202.
Web site: www.firebrandbooks.com. Karen Oosterhous, Publisher. **Description:**
Fiction, nonfiction, poetry, and cartoons—all with emphasis on feminist and/or lesbian themes. **Payment:** Royalty. **Sample Titles:** (Nonfiction) *Out in the World:
International Lesbian Organizing* by Shelley Anderson; (Poetry) *Presenting . . .
Sister Noblues* by Hattie Gossett.

FITZROY DEARBORN PUBLISHERS

919 N Michigan Ave., Suite 760, Chicago, IL 60611-1427. 312-587-0131.
Web site: www.fitzroydearborn.com. **Description:** Library reference books on a variety of academic subjects including the arts, humanities, business, and science.

FODOR'S TRAVEL PUBLICATIONS

Random House Information Group/Random House, Inc.
1745 Broadway, New York, NY 10019. 212-572-8702. E-mail: kcure@fodors.com.
Web site: www.fodors.com. Karen Cure, Editorial Director. **Description:** Publishes
fact-packed travel guidebook series, covering destinations around the world. Every
book is highly detailed. Both foreign and U.S. destinations. **Books Statistics:** 40
titles/yr (100 submissions); 100% unagented. **Proposal Process:** Query first, then
send an outline and writing sample. Accepts simultaneous queries, but not e-queries.
Prefers hard copy. Responds in 2-10 weeks. **Payment:** Flat fee, depending on the
work performed. **Sample Titles:** *Fodor's Paris 2003* by Fodor's; *Escape to Northern
New England* by Fodor's; *Compass Manhattan, 4th edition* by Gil Reavill. **Tips:**
"Avoid pitching general-interest guidebooks to destinations we already cover. Avoid
travel literature and other personal narratives."

FORDHAM UNIVERSITY PRESS

University Box L, 2546 Belmont Ave., Bronx, NY 10458-5172. 718-817-4795.
E-mail: manuscripts@fordhampress.com. Web site: www.fordhampress.com. Saverio
Procario, Director. **Description:** Scholarly nonfiction in the humanities, social sci-

ences, philosophy, theology, history, communications, economics, sociology, business, political science, law, literature, and the fine arts. Also publishes regional material on metro New York and books of interest to the general public. **Sample Titles:** *From First to Last: The Life of William B. Franklin* by Mark A. Snell; *The State of the Union: New York and the Civil War* edited by Harold Holzer. **Contact:** Anthony Chiffolo, Acquisitions Editor.

FORGE BOOKS

Tom Doherty Associates, LLC, 175 Fifth Ave., New York, NY 10010. 212-388-0100. E-mail: inquiries@tor.com. Web site: www.tor.com. Melissa Ann Singer, Senior Editor. **Description:** General fiction and limited nonfiction. From 80,000 words. **Proposal Process:** Send cover letter, complete synopsis, first 3 chapters, and SASE. Responds in 6-9 months. **Payment:** Advance and royalties. **Tips:** "For a complete listing of submission guidelines, please see our Web site."

WALTER FOSTER PUBLISHING, INC.

23062 La Cadena Dr., Laguna Hills, CA 92653. 949-380-7510. E-mail: info@walterfoster.com Web site. www.walterfoster.com. **Description:** How-to art and craft instruction books for artists of all ages and all skill levels.

FOUR WALLS EIGHT WINDOWS

39 W 14th, #503, New York, NY 10011. 212-206-8965. E-mail: edit@4w8w.com. Web site: www.4w8w.com. **Description:** Popular science, history, biography, and politics. **Books Statistics:** 30 titles/yr (5,000 submissions); 15% by first-time authors; 10% unagented. **Proposal Process:** Query with outline and SASE. Accepts simultaneous queries. Accepts queries via e-mail, but not submissions. Prefers hard copy. Responds in 2 months. **Payment:** Royalty. **Tips:** "Visit our Web site for complete submission guidelines. Please note that we do not accept poetry or any commercial fiction such as romance, mysteries, thrillers, etc."

FOUR WAY BOOKS

P.O. Box 535, Village Station, New York, NY 10014. 212-619-1105. E-mail: four_way_editors@yahoo.com. Web site: www.fourwaybooks.com. Martha Rhodes, Director/Founding Editor. **Description:** Nonprofit literary press accepting unsolicited poetry, short fiction, and novellas during the month of June. **Books Statistics:** 6-8 titles/yr. **Proposal Process:** Send complete manuscript via regular mail; does not accept e-mail or faxed submissions. Include SASE for notification. **Sample Titles:** *New Messiahs* by Henry Israeli; *Six Small Fires* by Paul Jenkins; *The Little Bat Trainer* by Gwen Ebert. **Tips:** Also offers the annual Levis Poetry Prize. Send SASE for guidelines or check Web site.

OLIN FREDERICK, INC.

P.O. Box 547, Dunkirk, NY 14048. 716-672-6176. E-mail: magwynne@olinfrederick.com. Web site: www.olinfrederick.com. **Description:** Political nonfiction as well as biography; history; economics; health and medicine; business; and other subjects; political fiction; and poetry, all focused on "revealing the truth about issues in the government." **Proposal Process:** Query with outline, synopsis, author bio, and SASE. Do not send sample chapters unless requested. **Payment:** Royalty. **Sample Titles:** *A Woman's Odyssey* by Erika Hansen; *Flag Mischief* by Douglas Campbell; *Secret Players* by Carl A. Nelson. **Contact:** Editorial Director.

W.H. FREEMAN & COMPANY PUBLISHERS
41 Madison Ave., Fl. 37, New York, NY 10010. 212-576-9400.
Web site: www.whfreeman.com. John Michael, Executive Editor. **Description:** Textbooks and educational materials with strong emphasis in the sciences and mathematics. Also publishes serious nonfiction for the general reader on topics such as nature/environment, astronomy, current events, anthropology, health, and psychology. Imprints: Computer Science Press and Scientific American Books. **Proposal Process:** Query with formal proposal and credentials. **Sample Titles:** *Universe: Stars and Galaxies* by Roger Freedman and William Kaufmann; *Physical Chemistry* by Peter Atkin and Julio DePaula; *The Basics of Abstract Algebra* by Paul Bland.

FULCRUM PUBLISHING, INC.
16100 Table Mountain Parkway, Suite 300, Golden, CO 80403. 303-277-1623.
E-mail: fulcrum@fulcrum-books.com. Web site: www.fulcrum-books.com. Daniel Forrest-Bank, Managing Editor. **Description:** Adult trade nonfiction with focus on western regional topics (gardening, travel, nature, history, education, Native American culture). **Proposal Process:** Send cover letter, sample chapters, TOC, author credentials, and market analysis. **Payment:** Royalty. **Sample Titles:** *Our Stories Remember: American History, Culture, and Values Through Storytelling* by Joseph Bruchac; *Wild Women of the Old West* by Richard W. Etulain and Glenda Riley.

GALLOPADE INTERNATIONAL
665 Highway 74 S, Suite 600, Peachtree City, GA 30269. 770-631-4222.
E-mail: info@gallopade.com. Web site: www.gallopade.com. **Description:** Full-color pocket guide, activity books, maps, stickers, etc.

GEMSTONE PRESS
Sunset Farm Offices, P.O. Box 237, Woodstock, VT 05091-0237. 802-457-4000.
Web site: www.gemstonepress.com. **Description:** Nonfiction titles on jewelry, gems, gemology. **Proposal Process:** Send cover letter, TOC, introduction, 2 sample chapters, and SASE. Hard copy only. Responds in 3 months. **Tips:** "Books are designed to help consumers and those who work in the gem trade increase their understanding, appreciation, and enjoyment of jewelry, gems, and gemology. Our books are easy to read, easy to use." **Contact:** Submissions Editor.

GLENBRIDGE PUBLISHING LTD.

19923 E Long Ave., Centennial, CO 80016. 720-870-8381.
E-mail: glenbr@eazy.net. Web site: www.glenbridgepublishing.com. James A. Keene, Editor. **Description:** Nonfiction titles on self-help, business, education, food, history, music, medical studies, and the environment. Also publishes a small list of suspense/thriller novels. **Books Statistics:** 4-6 titles/yr (15,000 submissions); 85% first-time authors; 98% unagented. **Proposal Process:** Query with sample chapter and SASE. Accepts simultaneous queries. Responds in 1 month. **Payment:** Royalty. **Sample Titles:** (Self-Help) *Three Minute Therapy: Change Your Thinking, Change Your Life* by Dr. Michael Edelstein with David R. Steele. (Food) *Ice Cream: The Whole Scoop* by Gail Damerow. (Fiction) *The Chaos Chip* by Gil Howard. **Contact:** Mary B. Keene, President.

THE GLOBE PEQUOT PRESS

246 Goose Ln., Guilford, CT 06437. 203-458-4500.
E-mail: info@globe-pequot.com. Web site: www.globe-pequot.com. Shelley Wolf, Submissions Editor. **Description:** Nonfiction with national and regional focus. Topics include travel, outdoor recreation, home-based businesses, etc. **Proposal Process:** Query with sample chapter, table of contents, 1-page synopsis, and SASE. **Payment:** Royalty or flat fee. **Sample Titles:** *The Fitness Factor* by Lisa Callahan, M.D.; *100 Best All-Inclusive Resorts of the World* by Jay Paris and Carmi Zona-Paris.

DAVID R. GODINE PUBLISHER

9 Hamilton Place, Boston, MA 02108. 617-451-9600.
E-mail: info@godine.com. Web site: www.godine.com. **Description:** Fiction, nonfiction, poetry, photography, children's books, cookbooks, and translations. **Books Statistics:** 20 titles/yr (800-1,000 submissions). **Proposal Process:** No unsolicited manuscripts. Accepts material from literary agents only.

GOLDEN WEST PUBLISHERS

4113 N Longview, Phoenix, AZ 85014. 602-265-4392.
E-mail: goldwest1@mindspring.com. Web site: www.goldenwestpublishers.com. Hal Mitchell, Editor. **Description:** Cookbooks, nonfiction Western history titles, and travel books. Currently seeking writers for state and regional cookbooks. **Proposal Process:** Query. **Payment:** Royalty or flat fee.

GOOD BOOKS

P.O. Box 419, Intercourse, PA 17534-0419. 717-768-7171.
Web site: www.goodbks.com. Merle Good, Publisher. **Description:** General nonfiction on crafts, how-to, family/parenting, cooking, Americana, children's, and inspirational topics. **Sample Titles:** *Awash with Color: Watercolor Wall Quilts* by Judy Turner; *Fix-It and Forget-It: Recipes for Entertaining* by Phyllis Pellman Good and Dawn J. Ranck. **Contact:** Phyllis Pellman Good, Senior Editor.

GRAYWOLF PRESS

2402 University Ave., Suite 203, St. Paul, MN 55114. 651-641-0077.
Web site: www.graywolfpress.org. Fiona McCrae, Publisher. **Description:** Literary fiction (short story collections and novels), poetry, and essays. **Books Statistics:** 16 titles/yr (2,500 submissions); 20% by first-time authors; 50% unagented. **Proposal Process:** Send SASE for guidelines. Responds in 3 months to queries. **Payment:** Royalty; offers advance.

GREAT QUOTATIONS PUBLISHING

8102 Lemont Rd., Suite 300, Woodridge, IL 60517. 630-390-3586.
E-mail: greatquotations@yahoo.com. Ringo Suek, Editor. **Description:** Gift books with humorous, inspiration, and business categories. 100-150 pages with short sentences. **Books Statistics:** 50 titles/yr (250 manuscripts); 50% by first-time authors; 70% unagented. **Proposal Process:** Query with outline and sample chapters or send complete manuscript, include SASE. **Payment:** Royalty and flat fee. **Sample Titles:** *The Secret Language of Women: A Humorous Guide to Understanding Women* by Sherrie Weaver.

GREENHAVEN PRESS

The Gale Group, 10911 Technology Place, San Diego, CA 92127.
Web site: www.gale.com/greenhaven. **Description:** Series publisher of anthologies for high school and college-level readers, most notably the Opposing Viewpoints series. Anthologies cover current events and controversies, historical events, and geo-political issues. **Proposal Process:** Seeks freelance writers to research, edit, and write on work-for-hire basis. Grad students, professors, and professional researchers preferred. Send query letter and resume/curriculum vitae. No unsolicited manuscripts. **Payment:** Flat fee. **Contact:** Chandra Howard, Senior Acquisitions Editor.

GREENLINE PUBLICATIONS

P.O. Box 590780, San Francisco, CA 94159-0780. 415-386-8646.
E-mail: info@greenlinepub.com. Web site: www.greenlinepub.com. **Description:** Publisher of *The Fun Also Rises Travel Guides* and *Greenline's Historic Travel Guides*. **Sample Titles:** *The Fun Seeker's North America* by Alan Davis; *The 25 Best World War II Sites, Pacific Theater: The Ultimate Traveler's Guide to the Battlefields, Monuments, and Museums* by Chuck Thompson.

GREENWOOD PUBLISHING GROUP

88 Post Rd W, Westport, CT 06881. 203-226-3571 ext. 3390.
Web site: www.greenwood.com. **Description:** Professional and scholarly nonfiction reference titles/textbooks on business, economics, natural science, law, the humanities, and the social sciences. **Tips:** See Web site for specific submission guidelines. Submit book proposal to one editor only.

GREYSTONE BOOKS
Douglas & McIntyre Publishing Group
2323 Quebec St., Suite 201, Vancouver
British Columbia V5T 4S7 Canada. 604-254-7191.
E-mail: dm@douglas-mcintyre.com. Web site: www.greystonebooks.com.
Description: Nonfiction on natural history, natural science and environmental issues, popular culture, health, and sports. **Books Statistics:** 30 titles/yr **Sample Titles:** *Sacred Balance* by David Suzuki; *Gordie: A Hockey Legend* by Roy MacSkimming.

GRIFFIN PUBLISHING GROUP
18022 Cowan, Suite 202, Cowan, CA 92614. 949-263-3733.
E-mail: griffinbooks@griffinpublishing.com. Web site: www.griffinpublishing.com.
Robin Howland. **Description:** Books on business/finance, education, the Olympics, sports/fitness, health/nutrition, and general trade. **Sample Titles:** *Journey of the Olympic Flame* by U.S. Olympic Committee; *How to Get Kids to Eat Great and Love It!* by Christine Wood.

GROVE/ATLANTIC, INC.
841 Broadway, New York, NY 10003. 212-353-7960.
Joan Bingham, Executive Editor. **Description:** Distinguished fiction and nonfiction. **Books Statistics:** 60 titles/yr. 10-15% of books by first-time authors. **Proposal Process:** Query. No unsolicited manuscripts. **Payment:** Royalty.

GRYPHON HOUSE, INC.
P.O. Box 207, Beltsville, MD 20704. 301-595-9500.
E-mail: kathyc@ghbooks.com. Web site: www.gryphonhouse.com. Kathy Charner, Editor-in-Chief. **Description:** Early childhood learning and activity books for teachers and parents.

HANCOCK HOUSE PUBLISHERS
1431 Harrison Ave., Blaine, WA 98230-5005. 604-538-1114.
E-mail: david@hancockhouse.com. Web site: www.hancockhouse.com. **Description:** Adult nonfiction: guidebooks, biographies, natural history, popular science, conservation, animal husbandry, and falconry. **Proposal Process:** Query with outline and sample chapters or send complete manuscript. Simultaneous queries considered. **Payment:** Royalty.

HARBOR PRESS, INC./HARBOR HEALTH
P.O. Box 1656, Gig Harbor, WA 98335. 253-851-5190.
E-mail: submissions@harborhealth.com. Web site: www.harborpress.com. Debby Young, Senior Editor. **Description:** Books on health, diet, psychology, parenting, self-improvement, etc. **Proposal Process:** Query with TOC, 2 sample chapters, and bio/resume. Send all submissions c/o Debby Young, Senior Editor, at 5 Glen Dr.,

Plainview, NY 11803. See Web site for specific guidelines. **Sample Titles:** *Smart Buys Drug-Wise* by Lee Haak and Rick Melcher; *Healing Back Pain Naturally* by Art Brownstein, M.D.

HARCOURT INC.
15 E 26th St., New York, NY 10010. 212-592-1045.
Web site: www.harcourtbooks.com. Lori Benton, VP/Publisher. **Description:** General trade adult and children's books. **Books Statistics:** 120 titles/yr; 5% by first-time authors. **Proposal Process:** No unsolicited manuscripts, queries, or illustrations. Accepts work from agents only. **Payment:** Royalty.

HARLEQUIN ENTERPRISES, LTD.
225 Duncan Mill Rd., Don Mills, Ontario M3B 3K9 Canada. 416-445-5860.
Web site: www.eharlequin.com. Donna Hayes, President/Publisher; Isabel Swift, VP Editorial. **Description:** Women's fiction (romance, action adventure, mystery). **Proposal Process:** Query appropriate editor, include SASE. **Sample Titles:** (Silhouette Books) *The Courage to Dream* by Margaret Daley; (Red Dress Ink) *Fashionistas* Lynn Messina; (Mira Books) *Home Before Dark* by Susan Wiggs. **Contact:** Randall Toye, Gold Eagle Books (series action adventure fiction) and Worldwide Mystery (contemporary mystery fiction). Tara Gavin, Harlequin Books (contemporary and historical series romance), Red Dress Ink (20's something fiction), Silhouette Books (contemporary romance series), and Steeple Hill (contemporary inspirational romance series). Dianne Moggy, Mira Books (women's fiction, contemporary/historical drama, family sagas, romantic suspense, and relationship novels).

HARPERCOLLINS PUBLISHERS
10 E 53rd St., New York, NY 10022-5299. 212-207-7000.
Web site: www.harpercollins.com. **Description:** High-quality book publisher with many imprints. **Proposal Process:** Adult trade books, send to Managing Editor for Fiction, Nonfiction (biography, history, etc.). For reference books: submissions from agents only. For college texts: address queries to College Department (no unsolicited manuscripts; query first).

HARVARD BUSINESS SCHOOL PRESS
60 Harvard Way, Boston, MA 02163. 617-783-7500.
Web site: www.hbsp.harvard.edu. Hollis Heimbouch, Editorial Director. **Description:** Professional nonfiction titles on business and management. **Sample Titles:** *The Company of the Future: How the Communications Revolution is Changing Management* by Frances Cairncross; *Marketing Moves: A New Approach to Profits, Growth, and Renewal* by Philip Kotler.

HARVARD COMMON PRESS
535 Albany St., Boston, MA 02118-2500. 617-423-5803.
E-mail: bshaw@harvardcommonpress.com.
Web site: www.harvardcommonpress.com. Bruce Shaw, Publisher. **Description:**

Adult nonfiction on childcare/parenting, health, gardening, and cooking. **Books Statistics:** 15 titles/yr; 25% by first-time authors; 40% unagented. **Proposal Process:** Send outline, analysis of competing books, and sample chapters or complete manuscript with SASE. **Payment:** Royalty. **Sample Titles:** *The Ultimate Rotisserie Cookbook* by Diane Phillips; *The Wild Vegetarian Cookbook* by Steve Brill; *The Birth Partner* by Penny Simkin, P.T.; *The Hummingbird Garden* by Matthew Tekulsky. **Contact:** Pamela Hoenig, Executive Editor.

HARVARD UNIVERSITY PRESS

79 Garden St., Cambridge, MA 02138-1499. 617-495-2600.
Web site: www.hup.harvard.edu. Mary Ann Lane, Managing Editor. **Description:** Scholarly books and serious works of general interest in the humanities, the social and behavioral sciences, the natural sciences, and medicine. Does not normally publish poetry, fiction, festschriften, memoirs, symposia, or unrevised doctoral dissertations.

HATHERLEIGH PRESS

5-22 46 Ave., Suite 200, Long Island, NY 11101. 212-832-1584.
E-mail: lori@hatherleigh.com. Web site: www.hatherleighpress.com. Lori Baird, Editorial Director. **Description:** Nonfiction titles on health, fitness, diet, exercise, and cooking. Publishes "Living With" series of chronic illness books. **Books Statistics:** 25 titles/yr (100 submissions); 20% by first-time authors; 90% unagented. **Proposal Process:** Query with sample chapter, TOC, and SASE. Considers simultaneous and electronic queries. Prefers hard copy. Responds in 3-6 months. **Payment:** Royalty or flat fee. **Sample Titles:** *The Body Sculpting Bible for Men/Women* by James Villepigue and Hugo Rivera; *Ski Flex* by Paul Frediani and Harald Harb. **Tips:** "No first-person accounts, e.g., "How I survived this illness." It helps if you can bring a celebrity draw to the project. Experts in the fields of health and fitness who can write are very desirable."

HAWORTH PRESS, INC.

10 Alice St., Binghamton, NY 13904-1580. 607-722-5857.
Web site: www.haworthpressinc.com. Bill Palmer, Managing Editor. **Description:** Scholarly press interested in research-based adult nonfiction. Topics include psychology, social work, gay and lesbian studies, women's studies, and family/marital relations. Also covers some subject matter related to recreation and entertainment. **Proposal Process:** Send outline with sample chapters or complete manuscript. **Payment:** Royalty.

HAY HOUSE, INC.

P.O. Box 5100, Carlsbad, CA 92018-5100. 760-431-7695.
E-mail: slittrell@hayhouse.com. Web site: www.hayhouse.com. Shannon Littrell, Submissions Editor. **Description:** Publishes books that center on the topics of self-help, New Age, transformational, and alternative health. **Books Statistics:** 45 titles/yr (2,000 submissions); 2% by first-time authors; 10% unagented. **Proposal Process:** "As of January 2004 (not before, please), you may query with outline, a few

sample chapters, and SASE." Accepts simultaneous queries, but not e-queries. Hard copy only. Responds in 3 weeks. **Payment:** Royalty. **Tips:** "Audience is concerned with the planet, the healing properties of love, and self-help principles. Research the market thoroughly to make sure that there aren't too many books already on the subject." No poetry, children's books, books of quotations.

HAZELDEN PUBLISHING

15245 Pleasant Valley Rd., P.O. Box 176, Center City, MN 55012-0176. 651-213-4000. E-mail: info@hazelden.org. Web site: www.hazelden.org. **Description:** Self-help books, curricula, videos, audios, and pamphlets relating to addiction, recovery, spirituality, mental health, chronic illness, and family issues. **Proposal Process:** Query with outline and sample chapters. Considers simultaneous queries. **Payment:** Royalty.

HEALTH COMMUNICATIONS, INC.

3201 SW 15th St., Deerfield Beach, FL 33442. 954-360-0909. E-mail: editorial@hcibooks.com. Web site: www.hcibooks.com. Christine Belleris, Editorial Director. **Description:** Books, 250 pages, on self-help, recovery, inspiration, and personal growth for adults. **Proposal Process:** Query with outline, 2 sample chapters, and SASE. **Payment:** Royalty.

HEALTH INFORMATION PRESS

Practice Management Information Corporation
4727 Wilshire Blvd., #300, Los Angeles, CA 90010. 323-954-0224. Web site: www.medicalbookstore.com. Kathryn Swanson, Acquisitions Editor. **Description:** Nonfiction titles on health/medicine for a general audience. **Proposal Process:** Query with outline and sample chapters. Manuscripts average 250 pages. **Payment:** Royalty. **Tips:** "Simplify complicated health and medical issues so that consumers can make informed decisions about their health and medical care."

HEALTH PRESS

P.O. Box 37470, Albuquerque, NM 87176-7470. 505-888-1394. E-mail: goodbooks@healthpress.com. Web site: www.healthpress.com. K. Frazier, Editor. **Description:** Health-related adult and children's books, 100-300 pages. "We're seeking cutting-edge, original manuscripts that will excite, educate, and help readers." Author must have credentials, or preface/intro must be written by M.D., Ph.D., etc. Controversial topics are desired; must be well researched and documented. **Proposal Process:** Submit outline, TOC, first chapter, and SASE. **Payment:** Royalty.

HEARST BOOKS

The Hearst Corp., 959 Eighth Ave., New York, NY 10019. 212-649-2000. E-mail: hearstbooks@hearst.com. Web site: www.hearstbooks.com. Jacqueline Deval, Vice President/Publisher. **Description:** Publishes general trade nonfiction titles in conjunction with Hearst magazines. Subject matter includes how-to, cooking, decorating/interior design, crafts, gardening, lifestyle, etc. **Books Statistics:** 30 titles/yr.

HEBREW UNION COLLEGE PRESS

3101 Clifton Ave., Cincinnati, OH 45220. 513-221-1875 ext. 293. E-mail: hucpress@phuc.edu. Barbara Selya, Acquisitions Editor. **Description:** Scholarly Jewish publisher on very specific topics in Judaic studies. Target audience is mainly rabbis and professors. **Books Statistics:** 4 titles/yr (15 submissions); 100% unagented authors. **Proposal Process:** Query with outline and sample chapters. Prefers hard copy. Responds in 1 week. **Tips:** No Holocaust memoirs or fiction.

HEIAN INTERNATIONAL, INC.

400 W Artesia Blvd., Suite 301, Compton, CA 90220. 310-782-6268. E-mail: heianemail@earthlink.net. Web site: www.heian.com. Diane Ooka, Editor. **Description:** Nonfiction titles on the Asian culture. Topics include art, literature, language, cultural studies, cooking, astrology, Feng Shui, Buddhism, origami, travel, health, and nature. Also publishes children's books with Asian themes. **Sample Titles:** *Otedama: Traditional Japanese Juggling Toys and Games* by Denichiro Onishi; *Welcome Home Swallows* by Marlene Shigekawa.

HEIMBURGER HOUSE PUBLISHING CO.

7236 Madison St., Forest Park, IL 60130-1765. 708-366-1973. E-mail: heimbrgrhouse@aol.com. Web site: www.heimburgerhouse.com. **Description:** Model and prototype railroad books. Also publishes magazines, maps, cookbooks, books on California and Colorado history, and historical hobby books. **Sample Titles:** *The American Streamliner, Postwar Years* by Donald J. Heimburger and Carl R. Byron; *The Milwaukee Road 1928-1985* by Jim Scribbins.

HEINEMANN

Reed Elsevier USA, Inc.
361 Hanover St., Portsmouth, NH 03801. 603-431-7894. Web site: www.heinemann.com. **Description:** Practical theatre, drama education, professional education, K-12, and literacy education. **Books Statistics:** 80-100 titles/yr; 50% by first-time authors; 75% unagented. **Proposal Process:** Submit cover letter, statement of objectives, TOC, sample chapters, resume or curriculum vitae, and SASE. **Tips:** Welcomes first-time authors. See website for specific guidelines.

HEMINGWAY WESTERN STUDIES SERIES

Boise State University, 1910 University Dr., Boise, ID 83725. 208-426-1999. Web site: www.boisestate.edu/hemingway/series.htm. Tom Trusky, Editor. **Description:** Publishes work relating to Rocky Mountain environment, race, religion, gender, and other public issues.

HENRY HOLT AND COMPANY

115 W 18th St., New York, NY 10011-4113. 212-886-9200.
E-mail: info@hholt.com. Web site: www.henryholt.com. Sara Bershtel, Acquisitions.
Description: Distinguished works of biography, history, fiction, current events, and natural history. **Proposal Process:** Prefers submissions from literary agents.

HERITAGE HOUSE PUBLISHING CO. LTD.

#301-3555 Outrigger Rd., Nanoose Bay
British Columbia V9P 9K1 Canada. 250-468-5328.
E-mail: editorial@heritagehouse.ca. Web site: www.heritagehouse.ca. Vivian Sinclair, Managing Editor. **Description:** Publisher of recreation guides, nature books, and special-interest titles. Dedicated to publishing nonfiction by Canadian authors. **Books Statistics:** 10-15 titles/yr; 50% by first-time authors; 100% unagented. **Proposal Process:** Submit introduction, TOC, 2-3 sample chapters, and SASE. **Sample Titles:** *Fort Steele: Gold Rush to Boom Town* by Naomi Miller; *Magnificently Unrepentant: The Story of Merve Wilkinson and Wildwood* by Goody Niosi. **Tips:** See Web site for specific submission guidelines.

HEYDAY BOOKS

P.O. Box 9145, Berkeley, CA 94709. 510-549-3564.
E-mail: heyday@heydaybooks.com. Web site: www.heydaybooks.com. Malcolm Margolin, Publisher. **Description:** Titles on California history, culture, natural history, literature, poetry, California Native American life, and other regional topics. **Books Statistics:** 15 titles/yr. **Sample Titles:** *The Ohlone Way: Indian Life in the San Francisco-Monterey Bay Area* by Malcolm Margolin; *The Dirt Is Red Here: Art and Poetry from Native California* edited by Margaret Dubin. **Contact:** Jeannine Gendar, Editorial Director.

HIGGINSON BOOK COMPANY

148 Washington St., Salem, MA 01970. 978-745-7170.
E-mail: acquisitions@higginsonbooks.com. Web site: www.higginsonbooks.com. Laura Bjorklund, Editor. **Description:** Nonfiction genealogy and local history only, 20-1,000 pages. Specializes in reprints. **Proposal Process:** Query with outline, sample chapters, and SASE. Accepts simultaneous queries. Prefers e-queries. Responds in 1 month. **Payment:** Royalty.

HILL STREET PRESS

191 E Broad St., Suite 209, Athens, GA 30601-2848.
E-mail: editorial@hillstreetpress.com. Web site: www.hillstreetpress.com. Judy Long, Editor-in-Chief. **Description:** Nonfiction titles in history, music, pop culture, cooking/food, gardening, sports, business, journalism, gay/lesbian, gender studies, memoir, and biography. Many titles have regional or international focus. Also publishes some literary fiction from previously published authors. **Books Statistics:** 20 titles/yr (500 submissions); 10% by first-time authors; 10% unagented. Most manu-

scripts range from 50,000-85,000 words. **Proposal Process:** Submit query, 1-page synopsis, 3 sample chapters, complete author bio with resume, and SASE. Do not send complete manuscript. Do not send material electronically; hard copy only. Responds in 3-6 months. **Payment:** Annual royalty (8-10%). **Tips:** Not accepting fiction submissions at this time. No poetry, children's books, science fiction, horror, or romance. See guidelines on Web site before submitting.

HIPPOCRENE BOOKS

171 Madison Ave., New York, NY 10016. 212-685-4371.
E-mail: hippocrene.books@verizone.net. Web site: www.hippocrenebooks.com.
Description: Foreign language dictionaries and learning guides; trade nonfiction, including bilingual anthologies of classic poetry, proverbs, and short stories; international cookbooks; history, military history, WWII and Holocaust studies; Polish-interest titles, and Judaic interest titles. **Books Statistics:** 50 titles/yr (200-300 submissions); 80% by first-time authors; 90% unagented. **Proposal Process:** Send query describing project and its marketability, with projected TOC. Accepts simultaneous queries. Prefers hard copy. Responds in 1-2 months. **Payment:** Royalty, typically 6-10%. Flat Fee $500-$1,500. **Sample Titles:** (Cooking) *Flavors of Burma: Cuisine and Culture from the Land of Golden Pagodas* by Susan Chan; (Language) *Beginner's Swedish* by Scott Mellor; (History) *Romania: An Illustrated History* by Nicolae Klepper. **Contact:** Anne E. McBride (cooking, travel, biography, history), Nicholas Williams (foreign language/dictionaries), Anne Kemper (illustrated histories).

HOHM PRESS

P.O. Box 2501, Prescott, AZ 86302. 928-778-9189.
Web site: www.hohmpress.com. Regina Sara Ryan, Senior Editor. **Description:** Nutrition, natural health, transpersonal psychology, religious studies, enneagrams, parenting, children, women's studies, and music. No children's books. **Proposal Process:** Submit cover letter with summary, outline, sample chapter, and SASE.

HOLLOWAY HOUSE PUBLISHING CO

8060 Melrose Ave., Los Angeles, CA 90046-7082. 323-653-8060.
Web site: www.hollowayhousebooks.com. **Description:** Black American, American Indian, and gambling fiction and nonfiction. **Books Statistics:** 16 titles/yr. **Sample Titles:** *The New Book of the Navajo* by R.F. Locke; *Dorothy Dandridge* by Earl Mills.

HOME PLANNERS

3275 W Ina Rd., Suite 220, Tucson, AZ 85741. 520-297-8200.
E-mail: lballamy@homeplanners.com. Web site: www.eplans.com. Linda Bellamy, Executive Editor. **Description:** How-to reference materials on planning and design for homes, landscapes, and outdoor projects. **Books Statistics:** 12-15 titles/yr. **Proposal Process:** Query with SASE or submit a proposal with outline, sample chapters, and photocopies of artwork.

HOMESTEAD PUBLISHING

4030 West Lake Creek Dr., Jackson, WY 83001. 307-733-6248.
Carl Schreier, Publisher. **Description:** Fiction, guidebooks, art, history, natural history, and biography. **Payment:** Royalty.

HONOR BOOKS

Imprint of Cook Communication Ministries
4050 Lee Vance View, Colorado Springs, CO 80918.
Web site: www.cookministries.com/proposals. **Description:** Inspirational, devotional, and motivational books/materials. **Proposal Process:** All submissions must be submitted online at Web site. **Sample Titles:** *A Simple Book of Prayers* by Kenneth and Karen Boa.

HOUGHTON MIFFLIN CO.

222 Berkeley St., Boston, MA 02116-3764. 617-351-5100.
Web site: www.hmco.com. Janet Silver, VP/Publisher, Adult Trade. **Description:** Trade literary fiction, nonfiction, biography, history, science, gardening, nature books, cookbooks. Adult fiction/nonfiction to 100,000 words. **Books Statistics:** 100 original titles/yr. **Proposal Process:** No unsolicited manuscripts. Considers material from literary agents only. **Tips:** Unsolicited manuscripts are generally rejected.

HOWELL PRESS

1713-2D Allied Ln., Charlottesville, VA 22903. 434-977-4006.
E-mail: rhowell@howellpress.com. Web site: www.howellpress.com. Ross A. Howell, Jr., Editorial Director. **Description:** Illustrated books and gift books on history, transportation, aviation, cooking, wine appreciation, quilts and crafts, and topics of regional interest. **Books Statistics:** 10-12 titles/yr (300 submissions); 60% first-time authors; 95% unagented. **Proposal Process:** Query with outline and sample chapters. Considers simultaneous and electronic queries. Prefers hard copy. **Payment:** Royalty. **Tips:** "We seek 'novelty' cooking and gift books."

HP BOOKS

The Putnam Berkley Group/Penguin Putnam, Inc.
375 Hudson St., New York, NY 10014.
E-mail: online@penguinputnam.com. Web site: www.penguinputnam.com. **Description:** How-tos on cooking, automotive topics. **Proposal Process:** Query with SASE. **Contact:** Editorial Department.

HUMAN KINETICS PUBLISHERS, INC.

P.O. Box 5076, Champaign, IL 61825-5076. 217-351-5076.
E-mail: hk@hkusa.com. Web site: www.humankinetics.com. Rainer Martens, Publisher. **Description:** Nonfiction reference, self-help, and textbooks on health, medicine, recreation, and sports. **Books Statistics:** 120 titles/yr; 30% by first-time authors; 90% unagented. **Proposal Process:** Submit outline with sample chapters and artwork.

HUNTER HOUSE PUBLISHERS

P.O. Box 2914, 1515 1/2 Park St., Alameda, CA 94501-0914. 510-865-5282. E-mail: acquisitions@hunterhouse.com. Web site: www.hunterhouse.com. Jeanne Brondino, Acquisitions Editor. **Description:** Nonfiction materials for families and communities. Topics include health, self-help/personal growth, sexuality/relationships, violence intervention/prevention, activity books for teachers, and counseling resources. **Books Statistics:** 21 titles/yr (300 submissions); 5% by first time authors; 80% unagented. **Proposal Process:** Query for guidelines, then submit complete proposal. Accepts simultaneous and electronic queries. Prefers hard copy. Responds in 2-3 months. **Payment:** Royalty, 12% of net. **Sample Titles:** *Women Living with Fibromyalgia* by Mari Skelly; *Men's Cancers* by Pamela J. Haylock, R.N. **Tips:** No fiction, autobiographies/memoirs, or personal stories.

HUNTER PUBLISHING, INC.

239 S Beach Route, Hobe Sound, FL 33455. 772-546-7986. E-mail: hunterp@bellsouth.net. Web site: www.hunterpublishing.com. Michael Hunter, Acquisitions Department. **Description:** Travel guides to destinations around the world. **Books Statistics:** 70 titles/yr (300 submissions); 40% by first-time authors; 90% unagented. **Proposal Process:** Query with outline and SASE. Accepts simultaneous and electronic queries. Responds in 2 weeks. **Payment:** Royalty. **Tips:** "No travelogs. We publish practical guidebooks to various destinations."

IDEA GROUP PUBLISHING

1331 East Chocolate Ave., Hershey, PA 17033-1117. 717-533-8845. Web site: www.idea-group.com. **Description:** Journals and books on information science, education, technology, and management. **Proposal Process:** Submit 2-4 page proposal with suggested titles (3-5), introduction, list of objectives, target audience, current competitors, TOC, and timetable. **Contact:** Senior Academic Editor.

IMPACT PUBLISHERS, INC.

P.O. Box 6016, Atascadero, CA 93423-6016. 805-466-5917. E-mail: editor@impactpublishers.com. Web site: www.impactpublishers.com. Melissa Froehner, Publisher. **Description:** Popular and professional psychology books, from 200 pages. Titles on personal growth, relationships, families, communities, and health for adults. Nonfiction children's books for "Little Imp" series on issues of self-esteem. **Proposal Process:** Query with outline and sample chapters. **Payment:** Royalty. **Tips:** "Writers must have advanced degrees and professional experience in human-service fields."

INDIANA UNIVERSITY PRESS

601 N Morton St., Bloomington, IN 47404-3797. 812-855-8817. E-mail: iupress@indiana.edu. Web site: www.indiana.edu/~iupress. Jane Lyle, Managing Editor. **Description:** Scholarly nonfiction, especially Jewish studies, literary criticism, music, history, women's studies, African-American studies, science, philosophy, African studies, Middle East studies, Russian studies, anthropology, regional, etc.

Proposal Process: Query with outline and sample chapters. **Payment:** Royalty. **Sample Titles:** *Seizing the New Day: African Americans in Post-Civil War Charleston* by Wilbert L. Jenkins.

INDO US BOOKS
37-46 74th St., Jackson Heights, NY 11372. 718-899-5590.
Web site: www.indousbooks.com. **Description:** Books and journals on philosophy, health, herbals, music, beauty care, and religion. Seeks to bring the culture of India closer to those living in the United States.

INNER OCEAN PUBLISHING INC.
1037 Makawao Ave., P.O. Box 1239, Makawao, HI 96768. 808-573-8000.
Web site: www.innerocean.com. John Elder, Publisher. **Description:** Publishes nonfiction titles in self-help, personal growth, inspirational, and alternative medicine genres.

INNER TRADITIONS INTERNATIONAL
One Park St., P.O. Box 388, Rochester, VT 05767. 802-767-3174.
E-mail: info@innertraditions.com. Web site: www.innertraditions.com. Jon Graham, Acquisitions Editor. **Description:** Nonfiction titles on indigenous cultures, perennial philosophy, visionary art, spiritual traditions of the East and West, holistic health/healing, sexuality, and self-development. Seeks to "help transform our culture philosophically, environmentally, and spiritually." **Books Statistics:** 60 titles/yr (1,000 submissions); 30% by first-time authors; 65% unagented. **Proposal Process:** Query with outline, sample chapters, and SASE. Accepts simultaneous and electronic queries. Prefers hard copy. Responds in 6-12 weeks. **Payment:** Royalty. **Contact:** Jeanie Levitan.

INNISFREE PRESS, INC.
136 Roumfort Rd., Philadelphia, PA 19119-1632. 215-247-4085.
E-mail: innisfreep@aol.com. Web site: www.innisfreepress.com. Marcia Broucek, Publisher. **Description:** Adult nonfiction, 40,000-60,000 words, on spiritual issues. No novels, poetry, or children's books. **Proposal Process:** Query with outline and sample chapters. Accepts simultaneous queries. **Payment:** Royalty.

INTERLINK PUBLISHING
46 Crosby St., Northampton, MA 01060. 413-582-7054.
E-mail: info@interlinkbooks.com. Web site: www.interlinkbooks.com. Pam Thompson, Acquisitions Editor. **Description:** Independent publisher specializing in world travel, literature, history, and translated fiction. Uses 3 imprints: Crocodile Books, Interlink Books, Olive Branch Press. **Books Statistics:** 50 titles/yr (2,000 submissions); 5% by first-time authors; 50% unagented. **Proposal Process:** Query with outline, 2 sample chapters, and SASE. No e-queries; hard copy only. Responds in 4-6

months. **Payment:** Royalty, 5-10%. **Sample Titles:** *The Arabs in Israel* by Azmi Bishara; *Paris by Bistro* by Christine Graf and Dennis Graf; *The Great Terror War* by Richard Falk. **Tips:** "Please study our list carefully before sending your submission."

INTERNATIONAL MARINE

The McGraw-Hill Companies
P.O. Box 220, Camden, ME 04843-0220. 207-236-4838.
E-mail: alex_barnett@mcgraw-hill.com. Web site: www.internationalmarine.com. Jonathan Eaton, Editorial Director. **Description:** Nonfiction titles on boating (sailing and power). **Sample Titles:** *The Voyager's Handbook: The Essential Guide to Bluewater Cruising* by Beth A. Leonard; *One Minute Guide to the Nautical Rules of the Road* by Charlie Wing. **Contact:** Alex Barnett, Acquisitions Editor.

ISI BOOKS

Imprint of the Intercollegiate Studies Institute
3901 Centerville Rd., P.O. Box 4431, Wilmington, DE 19807-0431. 302-652-4600. E-mail: booklist@isi.org. Web site: www.isibooks.org. **Description:** Interdisciplinary nonfiction titles in the humanities and social sciences that explore current political, economic, and social issues.

JAI PRESS, INC.

Elsevier Science, Ltd.
655 Avenue of the Americas, New York, NY 10010-5107. 203-323-9606. E-mail: jai@jaipress.com. Web site: www.jaipress.com. Roger A. Dunn, Managing Director. **Description:** Research and technical reference books on such subjects as business, economics, management, sociology, political science, computer science, life sciences, and chemistry. **Proposal Process:** Query or send complete manuscript. **Payment:** Royalty.

JALMAR PRESS

24426 S Main St., Suite 702, Carson, CA 90745. 310-816-3085. E-mail: jalmarpress@att.net. Web site: www.jalmarpress.com. Susanna Palomones, Editor. **Description:** Activity-driven books that help kids develop their social, emotional, ethical, and moral skills that lead to academic achievement and lifelong learning. **Books Statistics:** 10 titles/yr (200 submissions); 1-2% by first-time authors; 100% unagented. **Proposal Process:** Query with complete manuscript, include SASE. Accepts simultaneous and electronic queries. Prefers hard copy. Responds in 4-6 weeks. **Payment:** Royalty. **Tips:** Does not publish children's story books. Market is teachers and school counselors.

JEWISH LIGHTS PUBLISHING

Sunset Farm Offices, Route 4, P.O. Box 237, Woodstock, VT 05091. 802-457-4000. E-mail: submissions@jewishlights.com. Web site: www.jewishlights.com. **Description:**

Nonfiction in the areas of spirituality, Jewish life cycle, theology, philosophy, healing/recovery, gardening, cooking, history, and travel. Also publishes reference materials and resources for Jewish pastoral leaders and books for children and youth. **Proposal Process:** For adult nonfiction, send cover letter, TOC, introduction, 2 sample chapters, and SASE. For children's books under 40 pages, send entire text. No electronic submissions; hard copy only. Responds in 3 months. **Sample Titles:** *The Jewish Family Fun Book* by Danielle Dardashti and Roni Sarig; *The Rituals & Practices of a Jewish Life: A Handbook for Personal Spiritual Renewal* by Rabbi Kerry M. Olitzky and Rabbi Daniel Judson. **Contact:** Submissions Editor.

JIST PUBLISHING
8902 Otis Ave., Indianapolis, IN 46216-1033. 317-613-4200.
E-mail: info@jist.com. Web site: www.jist.com. **Description:** Nonfiction books and materials in the areas of career, job search, business, and families in crisis. **Books Statistics:** 35 titles/yr (60+ submissions). **Proposal Process:** Query with outline and sample chapters. No simultaneous or electronic queries. Prefers hard copy. Responds in 14-16 weeks. **Payment:** Royalty or flat fee basis. **Sample Titles:** *300 Best Jobs Without a Four-Year Degree* by Michael Farr and LaVerne L. Ludden, Ed.D.; *Self-Employment: From Dream to Reality! 2nd Ed.* by Linda Gilkerson and Theresia Paauwe. **Tips:** See Web site for guidelines. **Contact:** Lori Cates Hand (Trade Editor), Susan Pines (Reference Books Editor), Randy Haubner (Workbook Editor).

THE JOHNS HOPKINS UNIVERSITY PRESS
2715 N Charles St., Baltimore, MD 21218. 410-516-6900.
Trevor Lipscombe, Editor-in-Chief. **Description:** Scholarly nonfiction in the following areas: ancient studies, history of science/medicine/technology, history, literary criticism, political science, religious studies, and science. **Proposal Process:** Unsolicited queries and proposals are accepted, but no unsolicited poetry or fiction. No e-mail submissions. Hard copy only. Include resume, description of the project, sample text and descriptive TOC.

JOHNSON BOOKS
1880 S 57th Ct., Boulder, CO 80301. 303-443-9766.
E-mail: books@jpcolorado.com. Steve Topping, Editorial Director. **Description:** Nonfiction titles on environmental subjects, archaeology, geology, natural history, astronomy, travel guides, outdoor guidebooks, fly fishing, and regional topics. **Proposal Process:** Send proposal. **Payment:** Royalty.

JONA BOOKS
P.O. Box 336, Bedford, IN 47421. 812-278-9512.
E-mail: jonabook@kiva.net. Web site: www.kiva.net/~jonabook. Marina Guba, Editor. **Description:** Sci-fi, mystery, historical fiction, horror, true crime, law enforcement, old West and military history. 50,000 word minimum. **Books Statistics:** 50 titles/yr (800 submissions); 50% by first-time authors; 80% unagented. **Proposal Process:** Query with outline, sample chapters, and SASE. Accepts simultaneous and electronic

queries. Prefers hard copy. **Payment:** Royalty. **Tips:** "We're looking for more true crime, stories of individual soldiers, and true stories from the old West. Fiction should be based on historical events." Are now accepting a few nonfiction projects.

THE JOSEPH HENRY PRESS

National Academies Press, 500 Fifth St. NW, Washington, DC 20001. 202-334-3336. E-mail: smautner@nas.edu. Web site: www.nap.edu. Stephen Mautner, Executive Editor. **Description:** Publishes general trade nonfiction titles that address topics in science, technology, and health. **Books Statistics:** 12-15 titles/yr. **Proposal Process:** Send initial inquiry via e-mail. **Tips:** Extremely selective; most acquisitions are either commissioned or come through agents.

JOVE BOOKS

Putnam Berkley Group/Penguin Putnam, Inc.
375 Hudson St., New York, NY 10014.
E-mail: online@penguinputnam.com. Web site: www.penguinputnam.com. **Description:** Fiction and nonfiction. **Proposal Process:** No unsolicited manuscripts. Query first.

KALMBACH PUBLISHING CO.

21027 Crossroads Circle, Waukesha, WI 53187. 262-796-8776.
E-mail: books@kalmbach.com. Web site: www.kalmbachbooks.com. Candice St. Jacques, Editor-in-Chief. **Description:** Reference materials and how-to books for serious hobbyists in the railfan, model railroading, plastic modeling, toy train collecting/operating hobbies. Also publishes books on the craft and business of creative and freelance writing. **Books Statistics:** 20 titles/yr (100 submissions); 50% by first-time authors; 80% unagented. **Proposal Process:** Query first. Upon approval, follow with detailed outline and complete sample chapter with photos, drawings, and how-to text. Include SASE. Accepts simultaneous and electronic queries. Prefers hard copy. Responds in 2 months. **Payment:** Royalty, 10% on net price. **Sample Titles:** (Hobby) *Tourist Trains 2003: Guide to Tourist Railroads and Museums; Basic Model Railroad Benchwork* by Jeff Wilson. (Writing) *How to Become a Fulltime Freelancer* by Michael Banks; *Take Joy: A Book for Writers* by Jane Yolen. **Tips:** "Our hobby books are about half text and half illustrations. Authors must be able to furnish good photographs and rough drawings. Telephone inquiries welcomed to save time, misconceptions, and wasted work." **Contact:** Kent Johnson, Senior Acquisitions Editor (hobbies); Philip Martin, Acquisitions Editor (writing).

KAR-BEN PUBLISHING

Division of Lerner Publishing Group
6800 Tildenwood Ln., Rockville, MD 20852. 800-452-7236.
E-mail: karben@aol.com. Web site: www.karben.com. Judyth Groner, Madeline Wikler, Editorial Directors. **Description:** Picture books, fiction, and nonfiction on Jewish themes for preschool and elementary children (to age 9). **Books Statistics:** 10-12 titles/yr (50-100 queries and 300-400 mss/yr); 5% by first-time authors; 100%

unagented. **Proposal Process:** Send complete manuscript with SASE. **Payment:** Flat fee or royalty. **Sample Titles:** *The Mouse in the Matzah Factory* by Francine Medoff; *The Sounds of My Jewish Year* by Marji Gold-Vukson.

KENSINGTON PUBLISHING CORP.

850 Third Ave., New York, NY 10022. 212-407-1518.
Web site: www.kensingtonbooks.com. Michaela Hamilton, Editor-in-Chief.
Description: Fiction: historical romance, erotica, women's contemporary, mysteries/ thrillers, horror, westerns, mainstream. Nonfiction: narrative, traditional health, alternative health, pets, New Age/occult, spirituality, self-help, psychology, sex/relationships, pop culture, film/entertainment, gambling, true crime, current events/politics, military, business, sports, women's issues, cooking, biography, Judaica. Also both fiction and nonfiction in gay/lesbian, Asian, and African-American studies. Imprints: BET/Sepia, Arabesque, Dafina, Regency Romance, Brava, Strapless, Zebra, Pinnacle, Kensington, Citadel, and Lyle Stuart. **Books Statistics:** 600 titles/yr. **Proposal Process:** Prefers to receive submissions through literary agents. Considers unsolicited manuscripts for Arabesque and Regency Romance imprints only. **Sample Titles:** *About Face* by Fern Michaels; *Cry Me a River* by Ernest Hill.

KENT STATE UNIVERSITY PRESS

P.O. Box 5190, 307 Lowry Hall, Terrace Dr., Kent, OH 44242-0001. 330-672-7913.
E-mail: ksupress@kent.edu. Web site: www.kentstateuniversitypress.com. Joanna Hildebrand Craig, Editor-in-Chief. **Description:** Interested in high-quality, scholarly works in history and literary criticism, American studies, regional topics for Ohio, biographies, the arts, and general nonfiction. **Proposal Process:** Submit letter of inquiry. No faxes, phone calls, or e-mail submissions. **Sample Titles:** *Blood & Ink: An International Guide to Fact-Based Crime Literature* by Albert Borowitz; *Not All Politics is Local: Reflections of a Former County Chairman* by William D. Angel Jr.

KEY PORTER BOOKS

70 The Esplanade, Toronto, Ontario M5E 1R2 Canada. 416-862-7777.
E-mail: cmclieon@keyporter.com. Web site: www.keyporter.com. **Description:** General-interest nonfiction in the areas of natural history, self-help, health, environment, food and wine, gardening, business, sports, biography/memoir, and children's books. Does not accept unsolicited materials. **Sample Titles:** (Sports) *Gold on Ice: The Sale and Pelletier Story* by Beverly Smith; (Nature) *Beluga Cafe: My Strange Adventure with Art, Music, and Whales in the Far North* by Jim Nollman.

KIPLINGER BOOKS

1729 H St. NW, Washington, DC 20006. 202-887-6680.
E-mail: dharrison@kiplinger.com. Web site: www.kiplinger.com/books. **Description:** Publishes material on personal finance and business management. **Sample Titles:** *Kiplinger's Practical Guide to Your Money* by Ted Miller; *Switching Careers* by Robert K. Otterbourgh; *Making Money in Real Estate* by Carolyn Janik.

ALFRED A. KNOPF, INC.

The Knopf Publishing Group/Random House, Inc.
1745 Broadway, New York, NY 10019. 212-782-9000.
Web site: www.randomhouse.com/knopf. **Description:** Distinguished adult fiction and general nonfiction (biography/memoir, nature, history, travel, food/wine). **Proposal Process:** Query for nonfiction. **Sample Titles:** *Mark Twain: An Illustrated Biography* by Geoffrey C. Ward; *Paperboy: Confessions of a Future Engineer* by Henry Petroski. **Contact:** Editorial Board.

KRAUSE PUBLICATIONS, INC.

700 E State St., Iola, WI 54990-0001. 715-445-2214.
Web site: www.krause.com. Deb Faupel, Editor. **Description:** Nonfiction how-to books, hobby books, and price guides. Topics include antiques and collectibles, sewing and crafts, automotive, numismatics, sports, philatelics, outdoors, guns and knives, toys, records, and comics. **Books Statistics:** 150 titles/yr; 5-10% by first-time authors; 90% unagented. **Sample Titles:** *100 Years of Vintage Watches: A Collector's Identification & Price Guide* by Dean Judy; *Granny Quilts: Vintage Quilts of the '30s Made New for Today* by Darlene Zimmerman. **Contact:** Acquisitions Editor.

LANGENSCHEIDT PUBLISHING GROUP

46-35 54th Rd., Maspeth, NY 11378. 718-784-0055.
E-mail: feedback@langenscheidt.com. Web site: www.langenscheidt.com. Sue Pohja, Acquisitions Editor. **Description:** Travel guides, phrasebooks, foreign language dictionaries, travel reference titles, and language audio. Imprints: Berlitz Publishing, Hammond World Atlas, Insight Guides, American Map, Hagstrom Map, ADC Map, Arrow Map. **Sample Titles:** *Hawaii Insight Guide* by Scott Rutherford.

LANTERN BOOKS

1 Union Square W, Suite 201, New York, NY 10003. 212-414-2275.
E-mail: info@booklightinc.com. Web site: www.lanternbooks.com. **Description:** Books on spirituality, health and healing, animal advocacy, religion, social thought, and vegetarianism.

LARK BOOKS

Sterling Publishing, 67 Broadway, Asheville, NC 28801. 828-253-0467.
E-mail: nicole@larkbooks.com. Web site: www.larkbooks.com. Nicole Tuggle, Acquisitions Editor. **Description:** Distinctive books for creative people in crafts, how-to, leisure activities, and gardening. **Proposal Process:** Query with outline. **Payment:** Royalty.

LAST GASP OF SAN FRANCISCO

777 Florida St., San Francisco, CA 94110. 415-824-6636.
E-mail: gasp@lastgasp.com. Web site: www.lastgasp.com. **Description:** Publisher and distributor of books, comics, and magazines that reflect an eclectic mix of topics.

Subject matter includes pop culture, fashion, horticulture, occultism, literature, erotica, art, and humor. **Sample Titles:** *Mini-Mod Sixties Book* by Samantha Bleikorn.

LAWRENCE HILL BOOKS

814 N Franklin, Chicago, IL 60610. 312-337-0747.
E-mail: frontdesk@ipgbook.com. Web site: www.ipgbook.com. Linda Matthews, Publisher. **Description:** Publishes titles on Black and African-American topics and interests.

LECTORUM PUBLICATIONS, INC.

Scholastic, Inc., 524 Broadway, New York, NY 10012-3999. 212-965-7466.
E-mail: crivera@scholastic.com. Web site: www.lectorum.com. **Description:** Publisher and distributor of children's books written or translated in Spanish. **Sample Titles:** *La Historia de Johnny Appleseed* translated by Teresa Mlawer; *Calor: A Story of Warmth for All Ages* by Amado Pena.

LEISURE BOOKS

Dorchester Publishing Co., Inc.
276 Fifth Ave., Suite 1008, New York, NY 10001. 212-725-8811.
E-mail: dorchesterpub@dorchesterpub.com. Web site: www.dorchesterpub.com. Alicia Condon, VP/Editorial Director. **Description:** Mass-market paperback in the categories of historical fiction, historical romance, paranormal romance, futuristic romance, horror, thrillers, and Westerns. **Books Statistics:** 170 titles/yr (2,500 submissions); 10% by first-time authors; 30% unagented. **Proposal Process:** Submit query or synopsis with first 3 chapters and SASE. Manuscripts range from 70,000-100,000 words depending on genre. Responds in 8 months. **Payment:** Royalty. **Sample Titles:** *Savage Love* by Cassie Edwards; *Red* by Jack Ketchum; *The Tombstone Conspiracy* by Tim Champlin **Tips:** Check guidelines on Web site for specific submission guidelines for each genre. **Contact:** Ashley Kuehl, Editorial Assistant.

LIBRA PUBLISHERS, INC.

3089C Clairemont Dr., Suite 383, San Diego, CA 92117. 858-571-1414.
William Kroll, Editorial Director. **Description:** Nonfiction titles on behavioral and social sciences, medical topics, and general-interest. Also publishes fiction, poetry, and professional journals.

LITTLE, BROWN AND COMPANY

AOL Time Warner Book Group
1271 Avenue of the Americas, New York, NY 10020. 212-522-8700.
Web site: www.twbookmark.com. Michael Pietsch, Senior VP/Publisher.
Description: Fiction and nonfiction in the areas of biography/memoir, history, current affairs, art/photography, health/fitness, reference, science, sports, self-help/inspirational. **Proposal Process:** No unsolicited manuscripts. Accepts agented queries only. **Sample Titles:** *The Lovely Bones* by Alice Sebold; *An Unfinished Life* by Robert Dallek; *All He Ever Wanted* by Anita Shreve.

LITTLE, BROWN AND COMPANY CHILDREN'S PUBLISHING

AOL Time Warner Book Group

1271 Avenue of the Americas, New York, NY 10020. 212-522-8700.

Web site: www.twbookmark.com. Megan Tingley, Editor-in-Chief. **Description:** Picture books, chapter books, and general YA fiction and nonfiction. **Proposal Process:** No unsolicited manuscripts. Accepts agented queries only. **Sample Titles:** *Maniac Magee* by Jerry Spinelli; *The Jolly Pocket Postman* by Janet and Allen Ahlberg. **Contact:** Children's Editorial Dept.

LLEWELLYN PUBLICATIONS

P.O. Box 64383, St. Paul, MN 55164-0383. 612-291-1970.

E-mail: nancym@llewellyn.com. Web site: www.llewellyn.com. Nancy J. Mostad, Acquisitions Manager. **Description:** Specializes in both fiction and nonfiction in the New Age Sciences: alternative health, astrology, crafts, divination, magick and shamanism, nature religions and lifestyles, paranormal, spiritist, and mystery religions, spiritual science, and tantra. Also publishes fiction and nonfiction on occult, fantasy, and other metaphysical topics for middle grade and high school readers. **Books Statistics:** 100 titles/yr (2,500 submissions); 100% by first-time authors; 99% unagented. **Proposal Process:** Send complete manuscript or proposal with cover letter, outline, and sample chapters. Accepts simultaneous and electronic queries. See Web site for submission guidelines. **Payment:** Royalty. **Sample Titles:** (Adult nonfiction) *The Urban Primitive: Paganism in the Concrete Jungle* by Raven Kaldera; (YA Fiction) *The Lost Girl* by Dotti Enderle. **Tips:** "Interested in any story if the theme is authentic occultism, and the work is entertaining and educational."

LONE PINE PUBLISHING

1808 B St. NW, Suite 140, Auburn, WA 98001. 253-394-0400.

E-mail: hibach@lonepinepublishing.com. Web site: www.lonepinepublishing.com. **Description:** Nonfiction titles on nature, gardens, and outdoor recreation. Also ghost stories and popular history.

LONELY PLANET PUBLICATIONS

150 Linden St., Oakland, CA 94607. 510-893-8555.

E-mail: info@lonelyplanet.com. Web site: www.lonelyplanet.com. Eric Kettunen, U.S. Manager. **Description:** Travel guides, phrasebooks, maps, restaurant and activity guides, and other travel series.

LONGSTREET PRESS, INC.

2974 Hardman Ct. NE, Atlanta, GA 30305. 770-980-1488.

E-mail: info@longstreetpress.com. Scott Bard, Publisher/President. **Description:** General fiction and nonfiction, humor, sports, food/wine, art/photography, and children's books. **Proposal Process:** Query with outline, sample chapters, and SASE. Accepts very little fiction, and only through an agent. Responds in 5 months. **Payment:** Royalty. **Sample Titles:** *The Millionaire Next Door* by Thomas Stanley.

LOTUS PRESS INNER WORLDS MUSIC

P.O. Box 325, Twin Lakes, WI 53181. 262-889-8561.
E-mail: lotuspress@lotuspress.com. Web site: www.lotuspress.com. **Description:**
Publishes titles on alternative health, aromatherapy, and herbalism.

LOUISIANA STATE UNIVERSITY PRESS

P.O. Box 25053, Baton Rouge, LA 70894-5053. 225-578-6295.
E-mail: lsupress@lsu.edu. Web site: www.lsupress.edu. Sylvia Frank Rodrigue,
Editor-in-Chief. **Description:** Scholarly adult nonfiction, dealing mainly with the
U.S. South, its history, and its culture. **Proposal Process:** Query with outline and
sample chapters. **Payment:** Royalty.

THE LYONS PRESS

The Globe Pequot Press, 246 Goose Ln., Guilford, CT 06437. 800-962-0973.
E-mail: jcassell@lyonspress.com. Web site: www.lyonspress.com. **Description:** Jay
Cassell, Editorial Director (fishing, hunting, survival, military, history, gardening);
Lilly Golden, Editor-at-Large (fiction, memoirs, narrative nonfiction); Tom
McCarthy, Senior Editor (sports/fitness, history, outdoor adventure, memoirs);
George Donahue, Senior Editor (military history, martial arts, narrative nonfiction);
Jay McCullough, Editor (narrative nonfiction, travelogues, adventure, military, espi-
onage, international current events, fishing); Ann Treistman, Editor (narrative non-
fiction, travelogues, adventure, sports, animals, cooking); Lisa Purcell, Editor-at-
Large (history, adventure, narrative nonfiction, cooking, gardening). **Books
Statistics:** 240 titles/yr (200 submissions); 50% by first-time authors; 30% unagented.
Proposal Process: Send query with outline, sample chapters, or complete manu-
script. Accepts simultaneous queries, but not e-queries. Responds in 6 weeks.
Payment: Royalty.

MACADAM/CAGE PUBLISHING

155 Sansome St., Suite 550, San Francisco, CA 94104. 415-986-7502.
E-mail: info@macadamcage.com. Web site: www.macadamcage.com. Patrick Walsh,
Editor; Anika Streitfeld, Editor; Kate Nitze, Assistant Editor. **Description:**
Historical, mainstream, contemporary fiction and narrative nonfiction such as mem-
oirs. **Books Statistics:** 30-35 titles/yr; 75% first-time authors. **Proposal Process:**
Query with bio, cover letter with estimated word count, and 3 sample chapters. Does
not accept electronic submissions. Responds in 3-4 months. **Payment:** Royalty.
Sample Titles: *Ella Minnow Pea* by Mark Dunn; *Beautiful Girls* by Beth Ann
Bauman. **Tips:** No sci-fi, romance, religion, poetry, or New Age.

MACMILLAN REFERENCE USA

The Gale Group, 300 Park Ave. S, Fl. 9, New York, NY 10010. 917-534-2100.
E-mail: frank.menchaca@gale.com. Frank Menchaca, Vice President. **Description:**
Multi- and single-volume titles for junior high, high school, college, and public
libraries, primarily in science and social studies areas.

MADISON BOOKS

4720 Boston Way, Lanham, MD 20706. 301-459-3366.
Michael Dorr, Editorial Director/Acquisitions. **Description:** Adult trade nonfiction on music, art, biography, history, and literature. **Books Statistics:** 4 titles/yr **Proposal Process:** Query with outline, sample chapters, and SASE. Accepts simultaneous queries, but not e-queries. Responds in 2-4 months. **Payment:** Royalty. **Tips:** Submit work with a journalistic style. **Contact:** Ross Plotkin, Assistant Editor.

MANDALA PUBLISHING

354 Bel Marin Keys Blvd., Suite D, Novato, CA 94949. 415-460-6112.
E-mail: info@mandala.org. Web site: www.mandala.org. Lisa Fitzpatrick, Acquisitions Editor. **Description:** Books on East Indian art, culture, and philosophy. **Proposal Process:** Submit synopsis, TOC, and sample chapter. **Sample Titles:** *Prince of Dharma: The Illustrated Life of Buddha* by Ranchor Prime; *Practical Yoga: Yoga Cures for Daily Life* by James Bae.

MARION STREET PRESS, INC.

P.O. Box 2249, Oak Park, IL 60303. 708-445-8330.
E-mail: edavis@marionstreetpress.com. Web site: www.marionstreetpress.com. Ed Avis, Editor. **Description:** Books on writing and journalism. **Books Statistics:** 5 titles/yr (10 submission/yr); 50% by first-time authors; 100% unagented. **Proposal Process:** Send query via e-mail. Accepts simultaneous queries. Responds in 30 days. **Payment:** Royalty, 7%. **Sample Titles:** *Championship Writing: 50 Ways to Improve Your Writing* by Paula LaRocque; *Pen & Sword: A Journalist's Guide to Covering the Military* by Ed Offley. **Tips:** "We publish practical, how-to books for writers and journalists. Book proposals should have a specific, identifiable market."

MARVEL ENTERPRISES INC.

10 E 40th St., New York, NY 10016. 212-696-0808.
E-mail: jcollado@marvel.com. Web site: www.marvel.com. **Description:** Publisher of comic books. **Proposal Process:** Accepts artwork from letterers, pencilers, and inkers. Does not accept unsolicited written material or character ideas. Artists should submit story ideas with photocopies of work. Do not send originals. **Tips:** See Web site for specific submission guidelines.

MCFARLAND & COMPANY, INC.

P.O. Box 611, Jefferson, NC 28640. 336-246-4460.
E-mail: info@mcfarlandpub.com. Web site: www.mcfarlandpub.com. **Description:** Nonfiction, primarily scholarly and reference. Very strong lists in general reference, performing arts, baseball, and history (U.S., world, medieval, Civil War). Also has strong interest in automotive history. **Books Statistics:** 250 titles/yr. **Tips:** "We seek thorough, authoritative coverage of subjects not already exhausted by existing books. We sell mostly to libraries and individuals interested in specialized topics. See our Web site for submission guidelines." **Contact:** Steve Wilson, Senior Editor; Virginia Tobiassen, Editorial Development Chief; Gary Mitchem, Assistant Editor.

MCGRAW HILL/OSBORNE MEDIA

2100 Powell St., Fl. 10, Emeryville, CA 94608. 510-420-7700.
Web site: www.osborne.com. Roger Stewart, Editorial Director. **Description:** General computer books, from beginner to technical levels. Subject areas: networking, programming, databases, certification, applications, Internet, e-business, robotics, consumer technologies. **Books Statistics:** 200 titles/yr (1,000 submissions); 15% by first-time authors; 30% unagented. **Proposal Process:** Query. Prefers electronic format. Simultaneous queries accepted. Responds in 1-2 weeks. **Payment:** Royalty (10-15% of net). **Tips:** "Avoid over-published topics. Knowledge of audience and technical proficiency are crucial. First-time authors should be prepared to submit sample chapters." **Contact:** Roger Stewart (Consumer), Wendy Rinaldi (Programming), Tracy Dunkelberger (Networking), Gareth Hancock (Certification).

MCGREGOR PUBLISHING

4532 W Kennedy Blvd., Suite 233, Tampa, FL 33609. 813-805-2665.
E-mail: mcgregpub@aol.com. Dave Rosenbaum, Acquisitions. **Description:** Publishes only nonfiction, with an emphasis on sports and true crime. **Books Statistics:** 12 titles/yr (300 submissions); 50% by first-time authors; 50% unagented. **Proposal Process:** Query with outline, sample chapters, and SASE. Considers simultaneous queries and e-queries. Prefers hard copy. Responds in 2 months. **Payment:** Royalty.

MEL BAY PUBLICATIONS INC.

4 Industrial Dr., Pacific, MO 63069. 636-257-3970.
E-mail: email@melbay.com. Web site: www.melbay.com. **Description:** Music books, videos, CDs, DVDs, and material on instruments.

MENASHA RIDGE PRESS

P.O. Box 43673, Birmingham, AL 35243. 205-322-0439.
E-mail: info@menasharidge.com. Web site: www.menasharidge.com. Russell Helms, Acquisitions Editor. **Description:** How-to and where-to guidebooks to all outdoor, high adventure sports and activities. Limited nonfiction about adventure sports and general travel books. **Books Statistics:** 20 titles/yr (60 submissions); 15% by first-time authors; 90% unagented. **Proposal Process:** Query with outline and sample chapter. Considers simultaneous and electronic queries. Responds in 1-3 months. **Payment:** Royalty, 10% range. **Sample Titles:** *Mountain Bike! A Manual of Beginning to Advanced Techniques* by William Nealy; *The Best in Tent Camping: Wisconsin* by Johnny Molloy. **Tips:** "Examine the market to truly evaluate whether your book is unique."

MENTOR BOOKS

The Penguin Group/Penguin Putnam Inc.
375 Hudson St., New York, NY 10014. 212-366-2000.

Web site: www.penguinputnam.com. **Description:** Nonfiction for the college and high-school market. **Proposal Process:** Query required. **Payment:** Royalty.

MERIWETHER PUBLISHING LTD.

Contemporary Drama Service
885 Elkton Dr., Colorado Springs, CO 80907. 719-594-4422.
E-mail: merpcds@aol.com. Web site: www.meriwetherpublishing.com. Renee Congdon, Assistant Editor. **Description:** Nonfiction titles on theater and performing arts, mostly for educational markets. Also publishes plays and musicals for production. **Sample Titles:** *Playing Contemporary Scenes* by Gerald Lee Ratliff; *Characters in Action* by Marsh Cassady.

MICHIGAN STATE UNIVERSITY PRESS

1405 S Harrison Rd., Suite 25, East Lansing, MI 48823-5202. 517-355-9543.
E-mail: msupress@msu.edu. Web site: www.msupress.msu.edu. Martha Bates, Acquisitions Editor. **Description:** Scholarly nonfiction with concentrations in history, regional history, women's studies, African-American history, and contemporary culture. Also publishes series on Native American studies, rhetoric, and poetry. **Books Statistics:** 35 titles/yr (2,400 submissions); 75% first-time authors, 100% unagented. **Proposal Process:** Query with complete manuscript. Accepts simultaneous queries. Responds in 2 months. **Payment:** Royalty, range is negotiable. **Sample Titles:** *My Grandfather's Book: Generations of an American Family* by Gary Gildner. **Tips:** "We seek lucid writing, original perspective, and original scholarship."

MID-LIST PRESS

4324 12th Ave. S, Minneapolis, MN 55407-3218.
Web site: www.midlist.org. **Description:** Literary fiction (novels and short fiction collections), poetry, and creative nonfiction. Does not publish anthologies, so do not send individual short stories or poems. **Books Statistics:** 5 titles/yr (3,000 submissions); 80% first-time authors; 99% unagented. **Payment:** Royalty. **Sample Titles:** *The Last Cigarette* by Jason Waldrop; *The Sincere Cafe* by Leslee Becker. **Tips:** "We're interested in submissions of the highest literary quality." Guidelines available online or with SASE.

THE MIT PRESS

5 Cambridge Center, Cambridge, MA 02142. 617-253-5646.
Web site: http://mitpress.mit.edu. Larry Cohen, Editor-in-Chief. **Description:** Books on computer science/artificial intelligence; cognitive sciences; economics; finance; architecture; aesthetic and social theory; linguistics; technology studies; environmental studies; and neuroscience.

MONTANA HISTORICAL SOCIETY

P.O. Box 201201, Helena, MT 59620.
E-mail: mkohl@state.mt.us. Web site: www.montanahistoricalsociety.org. Martha

Kohl, Editor. **Description:** Publishes books on Montana history. **Books Statistics:** 3 titles/yr (20 submissions); 20% by first-time authors; 100% unagented. **Proposal Process:** Query with outline, sample chapters, and SASE. No simultaneous queries. Accepts e-queries, but prefers hard copy. **Payment:** Royalty. **Sample Titles:** *Mavericks: The Lives and Battles of Montana's Political Legends* by John Morrison and Catherine Wright Morrison; *Girl from the Gulches: The Story of Mary Ronan* edited by Ellen Baumier. **Tips:** Looking for well-researched, well-written regional history. Writers should avoid overexposed topics like western gunfighting.

MONTEREY BAY AQUARIUM PRESS

886 Cannery Row, Monterey, CA 93940. 831-648-4847.
E-mail: mgelizondo@mbayaq.org. Web site: www.montereybayaquarium.org.
Description: Publishes titles on natural history and conservation of the oceans for both adults and children.

WILLIAM MORROW AND CO., INC.

HarperCollins Publishers
10 E 53rd St., New York, NY 10022. 212-207-7000.
Web site: www.harpercollins.com. Michael Morrison, Editorial Director. **Description:** Adult fiction and nonfiction. **Proposal Process:** Query.

MOTORBOOKS INTERNATIONAL

Galtier Plaza, Suite 200, 380 Jackson St., St. Paul, MN 55101-3885.
E-mail: trade@motorbooks.com. Web site: www.motorbooks.com. **Description:** Books on automotive, motorcycle, tractor, railroading, truck, boating, aviation, and military.

MOUNTAIN PRESS PUBLISHING

1301 S Third W, P.O. Box 2399, Missoula, MT 59806. 406-728-1900.
E-mail: info@mtnpress.com. Web site: www.mountain-press.com. Kathleen Ort, Science Editor; Gwen McKenna, History Editor; Jennifer Carey, Geology Editor. **Description:** Nonfiction trade titles for general audiences, primarily adults. Considers proposals for projects in natural history (including field guides for plants, wildlife, etc.), western history, or frontier history. No technical earth science or ecology. **Books Statistics:** 12 titles/yr (150 submissions); 20% by first-time authors; 90% unagented. **Proposal Process:** Query with outline, sample chapters, and SASE. Simultaneous and electronic queries accepted. Responds in 1-12 weeks. **Payment:** Royalty. **Sample Titles:** *The Oregon Trail: A Photographic Journey* by Bill and Jan Mueller; *Organic Gardening in Cold Climates* by Sandra Perrin.

THE MOUNTAINEERS BOOKS

1001 SW Klickitat Way, Suite 201, Seattle, WA 98134. 206-223-6303.
E-mail: acquisitions@mountaineers.org. Web site: www.mountaineersbooks.org.
David Emblidge, Editor-in-Chief. **Description:** Nonfiction on the outdoors involving noncompetitive, non-motorized, self-propelled activities such as mountain climbing,

hiking, walking, skiing, canoeing, kayaking, and snow shoeing. Also publishes environmental and conservation subjects, narratives of expeditions, and adventure travel. **Books Statistics:** 50-60 titles/yr (400-500 submissions); 50% by first-time authors; 90% unagented. **Proposal Process:** Query with outline, sample chapters, and SASE. Accepts simultaneous and electronic queries. Prefers hard copy. Responds in 2-4 months. **Payment:** Royalty, typical range is $2,400-$4,500. **Sample Titles:** *Oregon State Parks: A Complete Recreational Guide* by Jan Bannan. **Contact:** Cassandra Conyers, Acquisitions Editor, Christine Hosler, Assistant Acquisitions Editor.

MUSEUM OF NEW MEXICO PRESS

228 East Palace Ave., Santa Fe, NM 87501. 505-827-6455.
E-mail: mwachs@oca.state.nm.us. Web site: www.mnmpress.org. Mary Wachs, Editorial Director. **Description:** Publisher of art and photography on Native America and the Hispanic Southwest. **Proposal Process:** Submit proposal with resume or curricular vita. Include TOC, a sample chapter, and samples of artwork if material is illustrated.

MUSTANG PUBLISHING CO., INC.

P.O. Box 770426, Memphis, TN 38177. 901-684-1200.
E-mail. mustangpub@aol.com. Web site: www.mustangpublishing.com. Rollin A. Riggs, Acquisitions Editor. **Description:** General nonfiction for an 18- to 50-year-old readership. **Books Statistics:** 4 titles/yr (1,000 submissions); 75% by first-time authors; 100% unagented. **Proposal Process:** Query with outline, sample chapters, and SASE. Accepts simultaneous queries, but not e-queries. Responds in 2-3 months. **Payment:** Royalty, 6-8% net. **Tips:** No travel or memoirs. No phone calls.

MY BYLINE MEDIA

P.O. Box 14061, Surfside Beach, SC 29587.
Web site: www.mybylinemedia.com; www.writingcareer.com. Brian S. Konradt, Publisher. **Description:** Nonfiction titles on the writing trade (screen, business, fiction, magazine, technical, corporate, copywriting, etc.), the publishing industry, journalism, public relations, freelancing, etc. No fiction or poetry. **Books Statistics:** 12 titles/yr; 0% by first-time authors; 100% unagented. **Proposal Process:** Query with complete manuscript. Prefers electronic format. Considers simultaneous submissions. Responds in 2-4 weeks. **Payment:** Royalty, 50%. **Sample Titles:** *Writing Industry Reports* by Jennie S. Bev; *Freelance Writing for Vet Hospitals* by Stanley Burkhardt. **Tips:** "Our books cover the entire spectrum of writing, to help freelancers, staff writers, or hobbyists with a passion for writing. We only accept material by experienced and published authors."

THE MYSTERIOUS PRESS

AOL Time Warner Book Group
1271 Avenue of the Americas, New York, NY 10020. 212-522-7200.
Web site: www.twbookmark.com. Sara Ann Freed, Editor-in-Chief. **Description:** Publishes mystery, suspense, and crime novels. **Books Statistics:** 45 titles/yr.

Proposal Process: Agented manuscripts only. **Payment:** Royalty. **Sample Titles:** *Death of a Village* by M.C. Beaton; *Epitaph* by James Siegel.

NATUREGRAPH PUBLISHERS

P.O. Box 1047, Happy Camp, CA 96039. 530-493-5353.
E-mail: nature@sisqtel.net. Web site: www.naturegraph.com. Barbara Brown, Editor.
Description: Publishes adult nonfiction books under two main categories: natural history and nature; and Native American culture, outdoor living, land, and Indian lore. **Books Statistics:** 2-3 titles/yr (400 submissions); 100% by first-time authors; 100% unagented. **Proposal Process:** Query with outline and SASE. Accepts simultaneous queries, but not e-queries. Responds in 1 month. **Payment:** Royalty. **Sample Titles:** *Anasazi Legends* by Lou Cuevas; *Greengrass Pipe Dancers* by Lionel Little Eagle. **Tips:** No children's books.

THE NAVAL INSTITUTE PRESS

291 Wood Rd., Annapolis, MD 21402-5035. 410-268-6110.
E-mail: esecunda@usni.org. Web site: www.usni.org. Paul Wilderson, Executive Editor. **Description:** Nonfiction (60,000-100,000 words) on naval history, seamanship and navigation, reference, professional guides, ship guides, biographies, textbooks, and other topics of current interest. Occasional military fiction (75,000-110,000 words). **Proposal Process:** Send detailed prospectus with sample chapters, chapter outlines, a list of sources, curriculum vitae, and cover letter. Hard copy only. Do not send original art/photographs; photocopies only. **Payment:** Royalty. **Sample Titles:** *Fight for the Sea: Naval Adventure from WWII* by John Frayn Turner; *Under Two Flags: The American Navy in the Civil War* by William M. Fowler.

NEW AMSTERDAM BOOKS

Ivan R. Dee, Publisher
1332 N Halsted St., Chicago, IL 60622-2694. 312-787-6262.
E-mail: editorial@ivanrdee.com. Web site: www.ivanrdee.com. **Description:** Art history, biography, cooking, politics, theater/drama, and international fiction.

NEW HARBINGER PUBLICATIONS

5674 Shattuck Ave., Oakland, CA 94609-1662. 510-652-0215.
E-mail: tesilya@newharbinger.com. Web site: www.newharbinger.com. Catharine Sutker, Acquisitions Manager. **Description:** Self-help psychology books, workbooks on life issues, women's topics, and balanced living. Read by lay people and used by mental health professionals. **Books Statistics:** 45 titles/yr (600+ submissions); 75% by first-time authors; 90% unagented. **Proposal Process:** Query with an outline and sample chapters. Responds in 1 month. **Payment:** Royalty 10% of net cash receipts. **Sample Titles:** *The Woman's Guide to Total Self-Esteem* by Stephanie Dillion, Ph.D., and M. Christina Benson, M.D. **Contact:** Tesilya Hanauer.

EW HORIZON PRESS
P.O. Box 669, Far Hills, NJ 07931. 908-604-6311.
E-mail: nhp@newhorizonpressbooks.com.
Web site: www.newhorizonpressbooks.com. Dr. Joan Dunphy, Editor-in-Chief.
Description: True stories of crime/justice, medical dramas, psychological thrillers, and courageous individuals in extraordinary circumstances. Also, nonfiction on current issues (self-help, minority concerns, politics, health, environment, animal rights) and books for children that teach tolerance, coping, and crisis skills. **Books Statistics:** 12 titles/yr; 90% first-time authors; 50% unagented. **Proposal Process:** Query with outline, sample chapters, and SASE. Accepts simultaneous and electronic queries. Prefers hard copy. Responds in 4 weeks. **Payment:** Royalty. **Sample Titles:** *Perilous Journey: A Mother's International Quest to Rescue Her Children* by Patricia C. Sutherland; *Shattered Bonds: A True Story of Suspicious Death, Family Betrayal, and A Daughter's Courage* by Cindy Band and Julie Malear. **Tips:** "Seeking nonfiction stories of courageous individuals with intense human-interest appeal; also, investigative journalism that probes important public issues." **Contact:** Lynda Hatch.

THE NEW PRESS
450 W 41st St., Fl. 6, New York, NY 10036. 212-629-8802.
Web site: www.thenewpress.com. Andre Schiffrin, Director. **Description:** Serious nonfiction in the fields of history, politics, African-American studies, economics, labor, multicultural education, media, and Latin-American studies. Does not publish U.S. fiction or poetry, but has a program in international fiction. **Books Statistics:** 50 titles/yr (several hundred submissions); 20% by first-time authors; 50% unagented. **Proposal Process:** Send query. Considers simultaneous queries, but not e-queries. Responds in 2 months. **Payment:** Royalty. **Sample Titles:** (Fiction) *Absolute Perfection of Crime* by Tanguy Viel; (Nonfiction) *American Power and the New Mandarins: Historical and Political Essays* by Noam Chomsky; **Tips:** "See Web site or request a print catalog to get an idea of the type of material we publish."

NEW VICTORIA PUBLISHERS
P.O. Box 27, Norwich, VT 05055. 802-649-5297.
E-mail: newvic@aol.com. Web site: www.newvictoria.com. Rebecca Béguin, Acquisitions Editor. **Description:** Publishes mostly mysteries and lesbian novels. **Books Statistics:** 6 titles/yr (150-200 submissions); 2-3% by first-time authors; 100% unagented. **Proposal Process:** Query with outline, sample chapters, and SASE. Accepts simultaneous queries, but not e-queries. Prefers hard copy. Responds in 2-3 weeks. **Payment:** Royalty, 10%.

NEW WORLD LIBRARY
14 Pamaron Way, Novato, CA 94949. 415-884-2100.
Web site: www.nwlib.com. Georgia Hughes, Editorial Director. **Description:** General trade nonfiction. No personal memoirs or fiction. **Books Statistics:** 30 titles/yr (2,000 submissions); 10% by first-time authors; 50% unagented. **Proposal**

Process: Send query with sample chapters or complete manuscript. Accepts simultaneous queries, but not e-queries. Prefers hard copy. Responds in 90 days. **Payment:** Royalty. **Tips:** "New World Library is dedicated to publishing nonfiction titles that inspire and challenge us to improve the quality of our lives and our world. Books must combine clear writing with a strong voice and unique message."

NEW YORK UNIVERSITY PRESS

838 Broadway, Fl. 3, New York, NY 10003. 212-998-2575.
E-mail: nyupress.info@nyu.edu. Web site: www.nyupress.org. **Description:** Scholarly nonfiction in history, law, religion, media studies, cultural studies, sociology, politics, anthropology, and psychology. No fiction or poetry. **Proposal Process:** Submit proposal with sample chapters and curriculum vitae. Enclose SASE for return of materials. Responds in 6 weeks. **Sample Titles:** *Irving Howe: A Life of Passionate Dissent* by Gerald Sorin; *Voicing Chicana Feminisms: Young Women Speak Out on Sexuality and Identity* by Aida Hurtado.

NEWCASTLE PUBLISHING

19450 Greenbriar Dr., Tarzana, CA 91356-5524. 818-787-4378. Daryl Jacoby. **Description:** Nonfiction manuscripts, 200-250 pages, for older adults on personal health, health care issues, psychology, and relationships. No fads or trends. We want books with a long shelf life. **Proposal Process:** Simultaneous queries considered. **Payment:** Royalty.

NEWMARKET PRESS

18 E 48th St., Fl. 15, New York, NY 10017. 212-832-3575.
E-mail: mailbox@newmarketpress.com. Web site: www.newmarketpress.com. Keith Hollaman, Executive Editor. **Description:** Nonfiction on health, psychology, self-help, child care, parenting, music, film, and personal finance. **Proposal Process:** Submit cover letter with concise 1-page summary of project and your qualifications, TOC, marketing analysis including similar or competing titles, and sample chapters (or complete manuscript). **Payment:** Royalty. **Sample Titles:** *Kids & Sports* by Eric Small, M.D., FAAP; *Stress Relief* by Georgia Witkin, Ph.D.; *The West Wing Script Book* by Aaron Sorkin. **Contact:** Editorial Department.

NICOLAS-HAYS INC.

P.O. Box 2039, York Beach, ME 03910-2039. 207-363-1558.
E-mail: nhi@ici.net. Web site: www.nicolashays.com.
Description: Books on Jungian psychology, Eastern philosophy, and women's psychospirituality.

NO STARCH PRESS

555 De Haro St., Suite 250, San Francisco, CA 94107. 415-863-9900.
E-mail: info@nostarch.com. Web site: www.nostarch.com. **Description:** Publisher of computer books. **Books Statistics:** 10 titles/yr.

NOLO
950 Parker St., Berkeley, CA 94710. 510-549-1976.
Web site: www.nolo.com/manuscripts.cfm.
Description: Publisher of do-it-yourself legal information. **Contact:** Marcia Stewart, Acquisitions Editor.

NORTH COUNTRY PRESS
P.O. Box 546, Unity, ME 04988-0546. 207-948-2208.
E-mail: ncp@unisets.net. Patricia Newell / Mary Kenney, Publishers.
Description: Nonfiction with a Maine and/or New England tie-in with emphasis on the outdoors; also limited fiction (Maine-based mysteries). **Proposal Process:** Query with SASE, outline, and sample chapters. No unsolicited manuscripts. **Payment:** Royalty. **Tips:** "We publish high-quality books for people who love New England."

NORTHEASTERN UNIVERSITY PRESS
360 Huntington Ave., 416 CP, Boston, MA 02115. 617-373-5480.
Web site: www.nupress.neu.edu. William Frohlich, Elizabeth Swayze, Robert Gormley. **Description:** Nonfiction trade and scholarly titles, 50,000-200,000 words, in music, criminal justice, women's studies, ethnic studies, law and society, political science, American studies, and American history. **Proposal Process:** Submit query with outline and sample chapter. **Payment:** Royalty.

NORTHERN ILLINOIS UNIVERSITY PRESS
310 N Fifth St., DeKalb, IL 60115. 815-753-1826.
Web site: www.niu.edu/univ_press. Mary L. Lincoln, Editorial Director.
Description: Publishes nonfiction titles on history, politics, anthropology, archaeology, and literary and cultural studies. **Books Statistics:** 18 titles/yr (500 submissions); 50% by first-time authors; 1% unagented. **Proposal Process:** Query with outline and sample chapters. Accepts simultaneous and electronic queries. Prefers hard copy. **Payment:** Varies.

NORTHWESTERN UNIVERSITY PRESS
625 Colfax St., Evanston, IL 60208-4210. 847-491-5313.
E-mail: nupress@northwestern.edu. Web site: www.nupress.northwestern.edu. Sue Betz, Executive Editor. **Description:** Trade and scholarly books. **Sample Titles:** *More Stories from the Round Barn* by Jacqueline Jackson; *Through the Poet's Eye* by Bozena Shallcross.

NORTHWORD PRESS
18705 Lake Dr. E, Chanhassen, MN 55317.
Web site: www.northwordpress.com. **Description:** Adult and children's nonfiction on nature and wildlife topics. **Books Statistics:** 15-20 titles/yr (500 submissions); 10% by first-time authors; 35% unagented. **Proposal Process:** Send query, outline, and sample chapters for adult nonfiction. Send query only for children's proposals. Accepts simultaneous queries. Responds in 90 days. **Payment:** Royalty on half of

projects, 5% list. Flat fee on half of projects; $3,000-$10,000. **Sample Titles:** (Adult) *America from 500 Feet!* by Bill and Wesley Fortney; (Children's) *Anna's Table* by Eve Bunting; **Tips:** "No poetry or personal memoirs/essays on nature. Also, no 'green' or animal rehabilitation stories." **Contact:** Bryan Tranden (adult titles) or Aimee Jackson (children's titles).

W.W. NORTON AND CO., INC.

500 Fifth Ave., New York, NY 10110.
E-mail: manuscripts@wwnorton.com. Web site: www.wwnorton.com. Starling Lawrence, Editor-in-Chief. **Description:** High-quality literary fiction and nonfiction. **Proposal Process:** Send outline, 1 sample chapter, and SASE to Editorial Department. Accepts brief e-mail submissions (no longer than 6 pages). **Tips:** No occult, paranormal, religious, genre fiction (formula romance, science fiction, westerns), arts and crafts, YA, or children's books.

O'REILLY & ASSOCIATES INC.

1005 Gravenstein Hwy N, Sebastopol, CA 95472. 707-827-7000.
E-mail: proposals@oreilly.com. Web site: www.oreilly.com.
Description: Nonfiction titles on computer technology. **Proposal Process:** Send formal proposal. State how you are qualified by outlining your technical experience as well as your experience as a writer. **Sample Titles:** *C++ in a Nutshell* by Ray Lischner; *Head First Java* by Kathy Sierra and Bert Bates. **Tips:** "A premier information source for leading-edge computer technologies, bringing to light the knowledge of innovators."

OHIO UNIVERSITY PRESS/SWALLOW PRESS

Scott Quadrangle, Athens, OH 45701. 740-593-1155.
Web site: www.ohiou.edu/oupress/. David Sanders, Director.
Description: Ohio University Press: Scholarly nonfiction, 300-400 manuscript pages. Especially interested in Victorian studies, contemporary history, regional studies, and African studies. Swallow Press: General-interest nonfiction and frontier Americana. **Proposal Process:** Query with outline and sample chapters. **Payment:** Royalty. **Sample Titles:** *Women, Work, and Representation: Needlewomen in Victorian Art and Literature* by Lynn M. Alexander; *Follow the Blue Blazes: A Guide to Hiking Ohio's Buckeye Trail* by Robert J. Pond. **Tips:** Also hosts annual Hollis Summers Poetry Award Competition. See Web site for guidelines.

ONJINJINKTA PUBLISHING

The Betty J. Eadie Press
909 SE Everett Mall Way, Suite A120, Everett, WA 98208. 425-290-7809.
E-mail: peter@onjinjinkta.com. Web site: www.onjinjinkta.com. Peter Orullian, Senior Editor. **Description:** Publishes nonfiction books with inspiration or spiritual content, must contain redeeming themes. Publishes nonfiction aimed at strengthening virtues, also books whose topics extol family values. **Books Statistics:** 8 titles/yr (2,000 submissions); 80% by first-time authors; 70% unagented. **Proposal Process:**

Query with outline and sample chapters. **Payment:** Royalty/advance. **Tips:** No New Age books or category fiction. "We seek books with clearly defined subject matter, authoritative writing, and original approaches to classic themes of spirituality." **Contact:** Tom Eadie, Submissions Editor.

OPEN COURT PUBLISHING CO.

332 S Michigan Ave., Suite 1100, Chicago, IL 60604. 312-939-1500.
Web site: www.opencourtbooks.com. David Ramsay Steele, Editor. **Description:** Scholarly books on philosophy, eastern thought, and related areas. Trade books of a thoughtful nature on pop culture, music, social issues, Jungian thought, psychology, education, social issues, and contemporary culture. **Books Statistics:** 20 titles/yr (1,200 submissions); 20% by first-time authors; 70% unagented. **Proposal Process:** Send sample chapters with outline, resume, and SASE. No simultaneous or electronic queries. Prefers hard copy. Response time varies. **Payment:** Royalty. **Sample Titles:** *The World of the Rings: Language, Religion, and Adventure in Tolkien* by Jared Lobdell; *The Logical Syntax of Language* by Rudolf Carnap.

ORCHISES PRESS

George Mason University
P.O. Box 20602, Alexandria, VA 22320-1602. 703-683-1243.
E-mail: lathbury@gmu.edu. Web site: http://mason.gmu.edu/~rlathbur. Roger Lathbury, Editor. **Description:** Original poetry, essays, some humor, textbooks, reprints. No fiction, children's books, or cookbooks. **Books Statistics:** 5-8 titles/yr (500 submissions); 20-40% by first-time authors; 90% unagented. **Proposal Process:** Query with sample chapters or complete manuscript, include SASE. Accepts simultaneous queries, but not e-queries. Hard copy only. **Payment:** Royalty. **Tips:** "For poetry, Orchises is a hard market—work must be technically adroit, intellectually precise, and sophisticated."

OREGON STATE UNIVERSITY PRESS

101 Waldo Hall, Corvallis, OR 97331-6407. 541-737-3166.
E-mail: mary.braun@oregonstate.edu. Web site: http://oregonstate.edu/dept/press. Mary Elizabeth Braun, Acquisitions Editor. **Description:** Scholarly nonfiction and books of importance to the Pacific Northwest, especially those dealing with the history, natural history, culture, and literature of the region; environmental history; or with natural resource issues. **Books Statistics:** 15 titles/yr. **Proposal Process:** Query with summary of manuscript. Responds in 10-12 weeks. **Payment:** Royalty. **Sample Titles:** *Gathering Moss: A Natural and Cultural History of Mosses* by Robin Wall Kimmerer. **Tips:** See guidelines on Web site.

THE OVERLOOK PRESS

141 Wooster St., Fl. 4, New York, NY 10012. 212-673-2210.
E-mail: overlook@netstep.net. Web site: www.overlookpress.com. Tracy Carns, Editor. **Description:** Literary fiction, fantasy/science fiction, and foreign literature in translation. General nonfiction, including art, architecture, design, film, history, biog-

raphy, crafts/lifestyle, gay/lesbian, martial arts, Hudson Valley regional interest, and children's books. **Proposal Process:** Query with outline, sample chapters, and SASE. Does not accept query letters or submissions via e-mail. **Payment:** Royalty. **Sample Titles:** *The Corruption of American Politics* by Elizabeth Drew; *Icons of the Twentieth Century* by Barbara Cady; *Hemingway vs. Fitzgerald* by Scott Donaldson.

PANTHEON BOOKS

Knopf Publishing Group/Random House, Inc.
1745 Broadway, New York, NY 10019. 212-782-9000.
Daniel Frank, Editorial Director. **Description:** Contemporary literary fiction, graphic novels, and nonfiction in the areas of current affairs, literature, the arts, business, travel, nature, science, and history. **Proposal Process:** Query with SASE. **Payment:** Royalty. **Sample Titles:** *Waiting* by Ha Jin; *Hidden Power: Presidential Marriages That Shaped Our Recent History* by Kati Marton.

PARA PUBLISHING

P.O. Box 8206-238, Santa Barbara, CA 93118-8206. 805-968-7277.
E-mail: info@parapublishing.com. Web site: www.parapublishing.com. Dan Poynter, Publisher. **Description:** Adult nonfiction books on parachutes and skydiving only. Author must present evidence of having made at least 1,000 jumps. **Proposal Process:** Query. **Payment:** Royalty.

PARAGON HOUSE PUBLISHERS

2285 University Ave. W, Suite 200, St. Paul, MN 55114-1635. 651-644-3087.
Web site: www.paragonhouse.com. Rose Yokoi, Editorial Director. **Description:** Reference and scholarly titles in the areas of biography, history, philosophy, psychology, religion, spiritual health, political science and international relations. **Books Statistics:** 12-15 titles/yr (2,500-3,000 submissions); 80% by first-time authors; 90% unagented. **Proposal Process:** Query with abstract of project. Include summary of your premise, main arguments, and conclusion. Does not accept e-mail submissions. Responds in 3 months. Guidelines available on Web site. **Payment:** Royalty, typically 10% net. **Sample Titles:** *Politics of Parenting* by William B. Irvine; *Oneness Perceived* by Jeffrey Eisen. **Tips:** "No fiction, poetry, or New Age materials. We seek scholarly nonfiction of cultural and intellectual appeal with international and interdisciplinary character."

PARENTING PRESS

P.O. Box 75267, Seattle, WA 98125. 206-364-290.
E-mail: office@parentingpress.com. Web site: www.parentingpress.com. Carolyn J. Threadgill, Publisher. **Description:** Publishes books offering practical life (social) skills to children, parents, and care-givers. Books offer concrete skills in modeling and problem-solving processes and acknowledge the importance of feelings and teaching responsibility. **Books Statistics:** 6 titles/yr (500+ submissions); 80% by first-time authors. **Proposal Process:** Query with outline, sample chapters, and SASE. Accepts simultaneous and electronic queries. Prefers hard copy. Responds in 6 weeks.

See Web site for detailed guidelines. **Payment:** Royalty. **Tips:** Niche is building social skills, dealing with feelings, and preventing abuse. Seeking authors with expertise derived from working with children.

PAUL DRY BOOKS

117 S 17th St., Suite 1102, Philadelphia, PA 19103. 215-732-9939. E-mail: editor@pauldrybooks.com. Web site: www.pauldrybooks.com. Paul Dry, Publisher. **Description:**Literary fiction and nonfiction. **Sample Titles:** *Hotel Kid: A Times Square Childhood* by Stephen Lewis; *For Solo Violin* by Aldo Zargani.

PAVEMENT SAW PRESS

P.O. Box 6291, Columbus, OH 43206. 614-445-0534. E-mail: editor@pavementsaw.org. Web site: www.pavementsaw.org. David Baratier, Editor. **Description:** Nonprofit organization publishing collections of poetry. **Books Statistics:** 7-8 titles/yr (700 manuscripts); 50% by first-time authors; 100% unagented. **Payment:** Royalty or flat fee ($1,000).

PEACHPIT PRESS

1249 Eighth St,. Berkeley, CA 94710. 510-524-2178. E-mail: proposals@peachpit.com. Web site: www.peachpit.com. **Description:** Books on computer and graphic-design topics. **Proposal Process:** Query with outline and sample chapters for manuscripts, 100-1,100 words, or submit proposal via e-mail.

PEARSON EDUCATION INC.

One Lake St., Upper Saddle River, NJ 07675. 201-236-7000. Web site: www.pearsoned.com. **Description:** Integrated educational textbooks, assessment tools, and educational services.

PELICAN PUBLISHING CO., INC.

P.O. Box 3110, Gretna, LA 70054. 504-368-1175. Web site: www.pelicanpub.com. Nina Kooij, Acquisitions Editor. **Description:** General trade. Travel guides (destination specific, no travelogues); children's (holiday, ethnic or regional); popular history (not scholarly); cookbooks (cuisine specific). **Books Statistics:** 90 titles/yr (5,000 submissions); 10% by first-time authors; 90% unagented. **Proposal Process:** Query with outline, sample chapters, and SASE. No simultaneous or electronic queries. Hard copy only. **Payment:** Royalty. **Tips:** No autobiographical material. See complete guidelines at Web site.

PENGUIN PUTNAM INC.

375 Hudson St., New York, NY 10014. 212-366-2000. Web site: www.penguinputnam.com. Phyllis Gran, President. **Description:** General-interest fiction and nonfiction paperbacks. Owns several imprints and trademarks including Berkley Books, Dutton, Grosset & Dunlap, New American Library, Penguin, Philomel, G.P. Putnam's Sons, Penguin Putnam Books for Young Readers, Riverhead Books, and Viking. **Payment:** Royalty.

THE PENNSYLVANIA STATE UNIVERSITY PRESS
University Support Bldg. 1, Suite C
820 N University Dr., University Park, PA 16802. 814-865-1327.
Web site: www.psupress.org. Peter Potter, Editor-in-Chief. **Description:** Scholarly nonfiction: art history, East European studies, gender studies, history, Latin American studies, law, philosophy, political science, religion, and sociology. **Proposal Process:** Query with outline and SASE. Considers simultaneous queries. **Payment:** Royalty.

THE PERMANENT PRESS
4170 Noyac Rd., Sag Harbor, NY 11963. 631-725-1101.
Web site: www.thepermanentpress.com. Judith Shepard, Editor. **Description:** Literary fiction. Original and arresting adult novels. **Books Statistics:** 12 titles/yr (6,000-7,000 submissions); 30-40% by first-time authors; 70% unagented. **Proposal Process:** Send query, sample chapters, and SASE. Accepts simultaneous queries, but not e-queries. Prefers hard copy. **Payment:** Royalty. **Sample Titles:** *Africa Speaks* by Mark Goldblatt; *The Spoiler* by Domenic Stansberry. **Tips:** "We seek distinctive writing style and original voice in adult fiction."

PERSPECTIVES PRESS
P.O. Box 90318, Indianapolis, IN 46290-0318. 317-872-3055.
E-mail: ppress@iquest.net. Web site: www.perspectivespress.com. Pat Johnston, Publisher. **Description:** Nonfiction books on infertility, adoption, and closely related reproductive health and child welfare issues (foster care, etc.). **Proposal Process:** Query. **Payment:** Royalty. **Tips:** "Writers must read our guidelines before submitting."

PETERSON'S
2000 Lenox Dr., Fl. 3, Princeton Pike Corporate Center
Lawrenceville, NJ 08648. 609-896-1800.
Web site: www.peterson.com. **Description:** Books and online products that offer information on colleges/universities, test preparation, study abroad, summer opportunities, grad programs, career exploration. **Books Statistics:** 200 titles/yr. Receives 250-300 submissions/yr. **Payment:** Royalty. **Contact:** Denise Rance, Acquisitions.

PHILOMEL BOOKS
Penguin Putnam Books for Young Readers/Penguin Putnam Inc.
345 Hudson St., New York, NY 10014. 212-414-3610.
Web site: www.penguinputnam.com. Patricia Lee Gauch, Editorial Director. **Description:** Juvenile picture books and young adult fiction, particularly fantasy and historical. Fresh, original work with compelling characters and sense of the dramatic. **Proposal Process:** Query. **Contact:** Michael Green, Senior Editor.

PINEAPPLE PRESS
P.O. Box 3889, Sarasota, FL 34230. 941-359-0886.
E-mail: info@pineapplepress.com. Web site: www.pineapplepress.com. June Cussen,

Editor. **Description:** Trade fiction and nonfiction about Florida. **Books Statistics:** 20 titles/yr (1,500 submissions); 75% by first-time authors; 99% unagented. **Proposal Process:** Query with outline, sample chapters, and SASE. Accepts simultaneous queries, but not e-queries. Prefers hard copy. **Payment:** Royalty. **Tips:** "We're looking for excellent books on Florida."

PLATYPUS MEDIA
627 A Street NE, Washington, DC 20002. 202-546-1674.
E-mail: info@platypusmedia.com. Web site: www.platypusmedia.com. Dia Michels, President. **Description:** Adult nonfiction titles on women's health, breastfeeding, and family life. Also publishes children's books (with accompanying activity guides) that explore the theme of families.

PLAYERS PRESS, INC.
P.O. Box 1132, Studio City, CA 91614. 818-789-4980.
Robert Gordon, Editor. **Description:** Publishes plays and musical books on the performing arts, theatre, film, television, costumes, makeup, technical theatre, technical film, etc. **Books Statistics:** 30 titles/yr (1,000 submissions); 60% by first-time authors; 80% unagented. **Proposal Process:** Query with manuscript-size SASE and 2 #10 SASEs for correspondence. Include bio/resume. No simultaneous or electronic queries. Responds in 3 weeks to queries, 1-3 months to submissions. **Payment:** Royalty.

POCKET BOOKS
Simon & Schuster, Inc.
1230 Avenue of the Americas, New York, NY 10020. 212-698-7000.
Maggie Crawford, V.P./Editorial Director. **Description:** Publisher of adult fiction. **Proposal Process:** Accepts material from literary agents only. **Payment:** Royalty. **Sample Titles:** *The Summerhouse* by Jude Deveraux.

POISONED PEN PRESS
6962 E First Ave., Suite 103, Scottsdale, AZ 85251.
E-mail: editor@poisonedpenpress.com. Web site: www.poisonedpenpress.com. **Description:** Adult mysteries on crime and detection. **Books Statistics:** 3-5 titles/yr **Proposal Process:** See Web site or send SASE for guidelines. **Payment:** Royalty. **Sample Titles:** *Midnight at the Camposanto* by Mari Ulmer; *Mad Dog and Englishman* by J.M. Hayes. **Contact:** Editorial Review Committee.

POLESTAR BOOK PUBLISHERS
Imprint of Raincoast Books
9050 Shaughnessy St., Vancouver, British Columbia V6P 6E5 Canada. 604-323-7100.
E-mail: info@raincoast.com. Lynn Henry, Managing Editor. **Description:** Poetry, fiction, sports, juvenile and teen nonfiction, and general trade nonfiction. **Proposal Process:** Submit outline and sample chapters. Accepts unsolicited manuscripts.

POMEGRANATE

Pomegranate Communications, Inc.
210 Classic Court, P.O. Box 6099, Rohnert Park, CA 94927-6099. 707-586-5500.
E-mail: info@pomegranate.com. Web site: www.pomegranate.com. **Description:**
Nonfiction titles on a variety of subjects including history, multicultural studies,
women's studies, photography, music, and humor. Special emphasis on art.

POPULAR PRESS

Bowling Green State University
Bowling Green, OH 43402. 419-372-7865.
Ms. Pat Browne, Editor. **Description:** Books of criticism on pop culture subjects
such as film, television, literature, and women's studies (200-450 pages). **Books
Statistics:** 15 titles/yr (350 submissions); 50% by first-time authors; 100% unagented.
Proposal Process: Query with outline and SASE. No simultaneous or electronic
queries. Send hard copy. Responds in 3-6 months. **Payment:** Flat fee or royalty.

POSSIBILITY PRESS

One Oakglade Circle, Hummelstown, PA 17036-9525. 717-566-0468.
E-mail: possibilitypress@aol.com. Web site: www.possibilitypress.com. Mike
Markowski, Publisher; Marjie Markowski, Editor-in-Chief. **Description:** How-to,
self-help, inspirational. Subjects include business, popular psychology, current significant events, success/motivation, entrepreneurship, sales/marketing, networking,
MLM, home-based business topics, and human-interest success stories. Also some
fiction that teaches lessons about life and success. **Books Statistics:** 5-10 titles/yr
(1,000 submissions); 90% by first-time authors; 95% unagented. **Proposal Process:**
Query with SASE. Prefers hard copy. Responds in 2 months. See Web site for guidelines. **Sample Titles:** (Nonfiction) *Awaken the American Dream* by Charles V.
Douglas, J.D., CFP; (Fiction) *The Millionaire Mentor* by Greg S. Reid. **Tips:** "Our
focus in on creating short to medium-length bestsellers by authors who speak and consult. We're looking for authors who are passionate about making a difference in the
world. To be considered, the author needs to be entrepreneurially minded and self-
motivated enough to promote his/her book's message via radio, TV, and print media."

PRAEGER PUBLISHERS

88 Post Rd. West, Westport, CT 06881-5007. 203-226-3571.
Web site: www.praeger.com. **Description:** Scholarly and professional nonfiction in
the humanities and social sciences. Particular interest in military/history, psychology,
business, current affairs, politics/international relations, performing arts, and literature. **Proposal Process:** Query with outline. **Payment:** Royalty. **Sample Titles:**
The United Nations and Iraq: Defanging the Viper by Jean E. Krasno and James S.
Sutterlin.

PRESIDIO PRESS

505-B San Marin Dr., Suite 300, Novato, CA 94945-1340. 415-898-1081.
E-mail: mail@presidiopress.com. Web site: www.presidiopress.com. Mr. E.J.

McCarthy, Executive Editor. **Description:** Publishes fiction and nonfiction military-related books. Specializes in military memoirs, biographies, unit histories, and battle and campaign books. **Books Statistics:** 42 titles/yr (1,500 submissions); 75% by first-time authors; 80% unagented. **Proposal Process:** Query with outline and SASE. Accepts simultaneous and electronic queries. Prefers hard copy. **Payment:** Royalty. **Sample Titles:** *Somalia on $5 a Day* by Martin Stanton; *Beyond the Rhine* by Donald R. Burgett. **Tips:** "Looking for well-written American military history that will make a contribution to the historiography of the subject."

PRICE STERN SLOAN, INC.
The Putnam Berkley Group/Penguin Putnam, Inc.
345 Hudson St., New York, NY 10014. 212-414-3610.
Web site: www.penguinputnam.com. Jon Anderson, Publisher. **Description:** Witty and quirky novelty juvenile titles. Imprints include Troubador Press, Wee Sing, and MadLibs. **Proposal Process:** No unsolicited manuscripts accepted. Query first. **Payment:** Royalty. **Sample Titles:** *The Ghost Hunter's Handbook* by Rachel Dickenson; *Haunted Mad Libs* by Roger Price, et al. **Tips:** No novels or picture books.

PRIMA PUBLISHING
3000 Lava Ridge Ct., Roseville, CA 95661. 916-787-7000.
Web site: www.primapublishing.com. Alice Feinstein, Editorial Director. **Description:** Nonfiction books in diverse areas including health, parenting and education, business, and current affairs. **Proposal Process:** Query with outline, sample chapter, and market research. Responds in 6-8 weeks. Hard copy format preferred. **Payment:** Royalty and flat fee, standard range. **Sample Titles:** *Maximize Your Presentation Skills* by Ellen A. Kaye; *Encyclopedia of Sports and Fitness Nutrition* by Liz Applegate, Ph.D.; *How to Plan an Elegant Second Wedding* by Julie Weingarden Dubin. **Contact:** David Richardson, Denise Sternad, Jamie Miller, Jennifer Base Sander.

PRIMER PUBLISHERS
5738 N Central Ave., Phoenix, AZ 85012. 602-234-1574.
E-mail: info@primerpublishers.com. Web site: www.primerpublishers.com. Bill Fessler, Acquisitions Editor. **Description:** Travel and regional subjects, especially about the Southwest U.S. Also publishes history (20th century, World War II, and Middle East conflicts), and "Living the Simple Life" philosophical writings. No fiction. General adult audience. **Books Statistics:** 5-10 titles/yr (20 submissions); 50% by first-time authors; 99% unagented. **Proposal Process:** Send query, outline, and sample chapters if available. Prefers hard copy. No simultaneous queries. Responds in 1 month. **Payment:** Royalty (8% net) or flat fee.

PRINCETON UNIVERSITY PRESS
41 William St., Princeton, NJ 08540. 609-258-4900.
Web site: www.pup.princeton.edu. Sam Elworthy, Editor-in-Chief. **Description:** Scholarly and scientific books on all subjects. **Proposal Process:** Submit brief pro-

posal with curriculum vitae. **Sample Titles:** *The Black Hole at the Center of Our Galaxy* by Fulvio Melia; *An Economic Analysis of the Family* by John F. Ermisch.

PROJECT MANAGEMENT INSTITUTE
Publishing Division
Four Campus Blvd., Newtown Square, PA 19073-3299. 610-356-4600.
E-mail: pmihq@pmi.org. Web site: www.pmi.org. **Description:** Books and resources on project management and general business/management.

PROMETHEUS BOOKS
59 John Glenn Dr., Amherst, NY 14228. 716-691-0133.
Web site: www.prometheusbooks.com. **Description:** Popular science, social sciences, New Age, religion, psychology, current events, humanism, health, biographies, politics, education and children's titles.

PRUETT PUBLISHING COMPANY
7464 Arapahoe Rd., Suite A-9, Boulder, CO 80303. 303-449-4919.
E-mail: pruettbks@pruettpublishing.com. Web site: www.pruettpublishing.com. Jim Pruett, Acquisitions Editor. **Description:** Nonfiction books and guides dealing with the Rocky Mountain West. Subjects include outdoor recreation travel and history, hiking, flyfishing, nature, and the environment. Also publishes textbooks on the history of Colorado for grade school students. **Books Statistics:** 10 titles/yr (300 submissions); 50% by first-time authors; 90% unagented. **Proposal Process:** Send proposal with brief summary, outline/TOC, 1-2 sample chapters, examples of artwork, market analysis, and bio/resume. Send electronic or hard copy. **Payment:** Royalty, net 10-12%. **Sample Titles:** *Yellowstone: Portraits of a Fly-Fishing Landscape* by John Juracek; *Montana Disasters: Fire, Floods, and Catastrophes* by Molly Searl.

PUCKERBRUSH PRESS
76 Main St., Orono, ME 04473-1430. 207-581-3832.
Constance Hunting, Editorial Director. **Description:** Publishes poetry, fiction, and belles lettres. **Books Statistics:** 3 titles/yr (500 submissions); 60% by first-time authors; 100% unagented. **Proposal Process:** Send query with complete manuscript and SASE. Accepts simultaneous queries, but not e-queries. Responds in 3 months **Payment:** Royalty, range 10% net. **Sample Titles:** (Poetry) *Settling* by Patricia Ranzoni; *A Night-Sea Journey* by Michael Alpert. (Fiction) *The Crow on the Spruce* by Chenoweth Hall. **Tips:** Literary only. Avoid crime, incest, prison, detective, police, mystery, and religious themes.

PURDUE UNIVERSITY PRESS
South Campus Courts, Building E, 509 Harrison St.
West Lafayette, IN 47907-2025. 765-494-2038.
E-mail: upress@purdue.edu. Web site: www.thepress.purdue.edu. **Description:** "Dedicated to the dissemination of scholarly and professional information, the Press

provides quality resources in several key subject areas including ageing, agriculture, business, technology, health, veterinary medicine, and other challenging disciplines in the humanities and sciences."

QED PRESS
155 Cypress St., Fort Bragg, CA 95437. 707-964-9520.
E-mail: publishing@cypresshouse.com. Web site: www.cypresshouse.com. Joe Shaw, Editor. **Description:** Books on health and healing, self-help, and how to fold paper airplanes. **Proposal Process:** Query with outline and sample chapters. **Payment:** Royalty.

QUILL DRIVER BOOKS/WORD DANCER PRESS, INC.
1831 Industrial Way, Suite 101, Sanger, CA 93657. 559-876-2170.
E-mail: info@quilldriverbooks.com. Web site: www.quilldriverbooks.com. Stephen Blake Mettee, Publisher. **Description:** Biographies and how-to books for seniors on self-help, parenting, the craft of writing, and California regional topics. **Books Statistics:** 12 titles/yr (500 submissions); 60% by first-time authors; 95% unagented. **Proposal Process:** Send query with nonfiction book proposal and SASE. Prefers hard copy. Considers simultaneous submissions. **Payment:** Royalty, 4-10%. **Sample Titles:** *It's Never Too Late to Be Happy: Repreparing Yourself For Happiness* by Muriel James; *The Fast Track Course on How to Write a Nonfiction Book Proposal* by Stephen Blake Mettee. **Tips:** No poetry, fiction, or children's books.

QUIXOTE PRESS
1854 345th Ave., Wever, IA 52658. 319-372-7480.
Bruce Carlson, President. **Description:** Adult fiction and nonfiction including humor, folklore, and regional cookbooks. **Proposal Process:** Query with sample chapters and outline. **Payment:** Royalty.

RAGGED MOUNTAIN PRESS
The McGraw-Hill Companies
P.O. Box 220, Camden, ME 04843-0220. 207-236-4837.
E-mail: alex_barnett@mcgraw-hill.com. Web site: www.raggedmountainpress.com. Jonathan Eaton, Editorial Director. **Description:** Nonfiction titles on a variety of outdoor activities (fishing, camping, sea kayaking, survival techniques, RV living, etc.) **Sample Titles:** *The Backpacker's Handbook* by Chris Townsend; *The Essential Wilderness Navigator: How to Find Your Way in the Great Outdoors* by David Seidman. **Contact:** Alex Barnett, Acquisitions Editor.

RAINBOW BOOKS, INC.
P.O. Box 430, Highland City, FL 33846-0430. 941-648-4420.
E-mail: rbibooks@aol.com. Betsy Lampe, Editor. **Description:** Primarily nonfiction with a small list of mystery fiction. **Books Statistics:** 15-20 titles/yr (600 submissions); 85% first-time authors; 99% unagented. **Proposal Process:** Query with outline, sample chapters, and SASE. Accepts simultaneous queries, but not e-queries.

Prefers hard copy. **Payment:** Royalty. **Tips:** Looking for a broad range of nonfiction books. In mystery fiction, primarily seeking "cozies" of no more than 70,000 words. Send SASE for guidelines. **Contact:** Betty Wright.

RAINCOAST BOOKS

9050 Shaughnessy St., Vancouver, British Columbia V6P 6E5 Canada. 604-323-7100. E-mail: wave@raincoast.com. Web site: www.raincoast.com. Brian Scrivener, Editorial Director. **Description:** Regional, national, and international titles on the environment, sports, travel, and cooking. Also, children's books, adult fiction, and nonfiction. **Proposal Process:** Submit query with outline and sample chapters. Include color photographs or slides or artwork for illustrated material. **Sample Titles:** *Mount Appetite* by Bill Gaston; *A Reckless Moon* by Dianne Warren.

RED CRANE BOOKS

P.O. Box 33950, Santa Fe, NM 87594. 505-988-7070.
E-mail: marianne@redcrane.com. Web site: www.redcrane.com. Marianne O'Shaughnessy, Acquisitions Editor. **Description:** Art and folk art, bilingual material with Spanish and English, cookbooks, gardening, herbal guides, natural history, novels, social and political issues, and social history. No children's books. **Proposal Process:** Send a short synopsis, 2 sample chapters, resume, and SASE. **Tips:** Topics vary each year. Write for guidelines.

RED HEN PRESS

P.O. Box 3537, Grand Hills, CA 91394. 818-831-0649.
E-mail: editors@redhen.org. Web site: www.redhen.org. Mark E. Cull, Editor; Kate Gale, Editor. **Description:** Literary fiction (novels, short fiction, gay/lesbian), poetry, memoirs, essays, literary criticism. **Books Statistics:** 12 titles/yr (2,000 submissions); 15% by first-time authors. **Proposal Process:** Send sample chapters via regular mail. **Payment:** Royalty, 10% of sales. **Sample Titles:** (Poetry) *Daphne's Lot* by Chris Albani; (Fiction) *Talking Heads: 77* by John Domini.

RED MOON PRESS

P.O. Box 2461, Winchester, VA 22604-1661. 540-722-2156.
E-mail: redmoon@shentel.net. **Description:** Publishes books, anthologies, and individual volumes of contemporary haiku.

THE RED SEA PRESS

11 Princess Rd., Trenton, NJ 08648. 609-844-9583.
E-mail: awprsp@africanworld.com. Web site: www.africanworld.com. Kassahun Checole, Publisher. **Description:** Adult nonfiction, 360 double-spaced manuscript pages. Focus on nonfiction material with a specialty on the Horn of Africa. **Proposal Process:** Query. **Payment:** Royalty.

RED WHEEL

Imprint of Red Wheel/Weiser, LLC

368 Congress St., Boston, MA 02210. 617-542-1324.

Web site: www.redwheelweiser.com. Ms. Pat Bryce, Editor. **Description:** Publishes spirituality, inspirational, and self-help books. **Proposal Process:** Submit outline, sample chapters, and 6½ x 9½-inch SASE. Hard copy only. Accepts simultaneous queries, but not e-queries. Responds in 3-6 months. **Payment:** Royalty. **Tips:** "Please visit our Web site for detailed submission guidelines. Before submitting any materials, please study our books in a bookstore, library, or publisher's catalog."

REGNERY PUBLISHING, INC.

One Massachusetts Ave., NW, Washington, DC 20001. 202-216-0600.

Web site: www.regnery.com. Harry Crocker, Executive Editor. **Description:** Nonfiction titles on current affairs, politics, history, biography, and other subjects. The Lifeline Press imprint publishes health titles. **Books Statistics:** 35 titles/yr. **Proposal Process:** Send query with outline and SASE. Hard copy only. Authors must have major media credibility or experience. **Payment:** Royalty.

RIO NUEVO PUBLISHERS

451 N Bonita Ave., Tucson, AZ 85745. 520-623-9558.

E-mail: info@rionuevo.com. Web site: www.rionuevo.com. **Description:** "Our mission is to publish compelling and visually exciting books about the places, people, and things that make the American Southwest so distinctive."

RISING TIDE PRESS

P.O. Box 30457, Tucson, AZ 85751. 520-888-1140.

E-mail: books@risingtidepress.com. Web site: www.risingtidepress.com. Brenda Kazen, Editorial Director. **Description:** Lesbian/feminist fiction and nonfiction. Books for, by, and about women. Fiction, romance, mystery, and young adult and adventure, science fiction/fantasy. **Books Statistics:** 6-10 titles/yr (3,000 submissions); 75% by first-time authors; 95% unagented. **Proposal Process:** Query with sample chapters and SASE. Responds in 2-3 months. **Payment:** Royalty.

RIVER CITY PUBLISHING

1719 Mulberry St., Montgomery, AL 36106. 877-408-7078.

E-mail: jdavis@rivercitypublishing.com. Web site: www.rivercitypublishing.com. Jim Davis, Editor. **Description:** Fiction, nonfiction, poetry, art, and children's books about life in America, today and yesterday (most books about the South). **Tips:** Generally publishes authors with extensive track records; no romances, science fiction, textbooks, YA novels, extremely religious books, or books about the Civil War.

RIVERHEAD BOOKS

Putnam Berkeley Group/Penguin Putnam, Inc.

375 Hudson St., New York, NY 10014.

Web site: www.penguinputnam.com. Julie Grau, Cindy Spiegel, Co-Editorial Directors. **Description:** Quality fiction and nonfiction. **Proposal Process:** Accepts material from literary agents only. **Payment:** Royalty. **Sample Titles:** *Blue Shoe* by Anne Lamott; *My Dream of You* by Nuala O'Faolain. **Contact:** Alex Morris, Editorial Assistant.

RIVEROAK PUBLISHING
Cook Communications Ministries
9412 S Darlington Ave., Tulsa, OK 74137. 918-688-5052.
E-mail: jeffd@riveroakpublishing.com. Web site: www.riveroakpublishing.com. **Description:** Christian fiction. **Books Statistics:** 15 titles/yr (1,000 queries and 500 mss/yr); 5% by first-time authors; 80% unagented. **Proposal Process:** Query with outline/summary, TOC, 3 sample chapters, brief author bio, contact info, and SASE. Responds in 2-3 months. **Payment:** Royalty. **Sample Titles:** *A Place Called Wiregrass* by Michael Morris; *Mutiny's Curse* by Dan Thrapp.

ROBINS LANE PRESS
A Division of Gryphon House, Inc.
P.O. Box 207, Beltsville, MD 20705. 301-595-9500.
E-mail: info@robinslane.com. Web site: www.robinslane.com. **Description:** "Timely, unique books on subjects of interest to today's parents." **Books Statistics:** 4 titles/yr (100 submissions); 75% by first-time authors; 90% unagented. **Proposal Process:** Query with outline and sample chapters if available. Considers simultaneous queries and e-queries. Prefers hard copy. Responds in 6-8 weeks. **Sample Titles:** *The Simpler Family: A Book of Smart Choices and Small Comforts for Families Who Do Too Much* by Christine Klein. **Contact:** Acquisitions Editor.

ROC
The Penguin Group/Penguin Putnam Inc.
375 Hudson St., New York, NY 10014. 212-366-2000.
Web site: www.penguinputnam.com. Laura Anne Gilman, Executive Editor; Jennifer Heddle, Editor. **Description:** Publisher of science fiction and fantasy. **Proposal Process:** Strongly discourages unsolicited submissions. "Most of our acquisitions come via reputable literary agents." **Payment:** Standard royalties. **Sample Titles:** *The Dragon Delasangre* by Alan F. Troop; *Conquistador* by S.M. Stirling.

RODALE BOOKS
400 S Tenth St., Emmaus, PA 18098. 610-967-5171.
Web site: www.rodale.com. **Description:** General trade nonfiction. No fiction, poetry, or screenplays. **Proposal Process:** Send complete proposal package that includes a book prospectus, outline (with headings and subheadings), 1 or more sample chapters, resume/bio listing credentials, market analysis with competing titles, and SASE. **Tips:** "Seeks to inspire and enable people to improve their lives and the world around them. We're looking for authors who can dig deeply for facts and details, report accurately, and write with flair." **Contact:** Jennifer Kushnier, Associate Editor

(general health, sports/fitness, self-help/inspiration, biography/memoir, relationships, current affairs, the environmental sciences, general business, psychology); Amy Super, Assistant Editor (women's health/fitness, organics, gardening, lifestyle, cooking, home arts, pet care, parenting); Jeremy Katz, Executive Editor (men's health, men's sports/fitness, science/technology, finance).

ROUGH GUIDES
345 Hudson St., Fl. 4, New York, NY 10014. 212-414-3635.
E-mail: mail@roughguides.com. Web site: www.roughguides.com. **Description:** Guides and phrase-books for independent travel. Also publishes reference titles on a wide range of subjects including music, film, the Internet, and computers.

ROYAL FIREWORKS PUBLISHING
One First Ave., P.O. Box 399, Unionville, NY 10988. 845-726-4444.
E-mail: rfpress@frontiernet.net. Charles Morgan, Editor. **Description:** Publishes books for gifted children, their parents and teachers. Also publishes teen and adult novels in the genres of science fiction, mystery, thriller, and historic Americana. **Books Statistics:** 100 titles/yr (2,000 submissions); 40% by first-time authors; 95% unagented. **Proposal Process:** Submit complete manuscripts with a brief plot overview. No simultaneous or electronic queries. Responds in 3 weeks. **Payment:** Royalty. **Tips:** "We're looking for historical fiction, books on growing up, books about kids solving problems, science fiction, and mystery-adventure." Extra Comments: Educational topics dealing with education or textbooks, student workbooks, etc.

RUMINATOR BOOKS
1648 Grand Ave., St. Paul, MN 55105. 651-699-7038.
E-mail: books@ruminator.com. Web site: www.ruminator.com. Pearl Kilbride, Editor. **Description:** Publishes fiction and memoirs on contemporary affairs, cultural criticism, travel essays, nonfiction, and international literature. No genre fiction, self-help, children's books, or poetry. Prefers books that examine the human experience or comment on social and cultural mores. **Proposal Process:** Query with outline and sample chapters. **Payment:** Royalty.

RUNNING PRESS
125 S 22nd St., Philadelphia, PA 19103-4399. 215-567-5080.
E-mail: comments@runningpress.com. Web site: www.runningpress.com. Jennifer Worick, Editorial Director. **Description:** Illustrated nonfiction titles for adults and children. Publishes educational, inspirational, pop culture-oriented, historical nonfiction, self-help, Miniature Editions (TM), and creative how-to kits for children and adults. **Proposal Process:** Query with outline/TOC and 2-3 page writing sample. Accepts simultaneous queries, but not e-queries. Prefers hard copy. Responds in 4 weeks. **Payment:** Royalty or flat fee. **Tips:** No fiction or poetry. **Contact:** Susan Phillips.

RUTGERS UNIVERSITY PRESS

100 Joyce Kilmer Ave., Piscataway, NJ 08854-8099. 732-445-7762.
Web site: rutgerspress.rutgers.edu. Leslie Mitchner, Editor-in-Chief. **Description:**
Scholarly publisher of religion, history of medicine, biological sciences, media studies, art, literature, history, gender studies, and multicultural studies. Also interested
in general studies that have a strong scholarly basis. **Books Statistics:** 90 titles/yr
(1,200 submissions); 35% by first-time authors; 85% unagented. **Proposal Process:**
Query with outline and sample chapters. Send Humanities proposals to Molly Baab;
Science and Social Sciences proposals to Adi Hovav. Accepts simultaneous queries,
but not e-queries. Hard copy only. Responds in 3-4 weeks. **Payment:** Royalty.
Sample Titles: *Born to Belonging: Writing on Spirit and Justice* by Mab Segrest;
Backroads, New Jersey: Driving at the Speed of Life by Mark Di Ionno. **Tips:**
"Avoid anything too jargon-laden. We are most interested in projects with a strong
scholarly foundation."

RUTLEDGE HILL PRESS

Division of Thomas Nelson Publishers
P.O. Box 141000, Nashville, TN 37214-1000. 615-902-2333.
E-mail: tmenges@rutledgehillpress.com. Web site: www.rutledgehillpress.com.
Lawrence M. Stone, Publisher. **Description:** General nonfiction, self-help, gift
books, cookbooks, regional history, and topics such as regional humor. **Books
Statistics:** 40 titles/yr (1,000 submissions); 35% by first-time authors; 70% una-
gented. **Proposal Process:** Query with outline, sample chapters and SASE. Accepts
simultaneous and electronic queries. Prefers hard copy. **Payment:** Flat fee. **Tips:**
Interested in adult nonfiction. **Contact:** Tracy Menges.

SAGE PUBLICATIONS, INC.

2455 Teller Rd., Thousand Oaks, CA 91320. 805-499-0721.
E-mail: info@sagepub.com. Web site: www.sagepub.com. **Description:** Nonfiction
books and materials for researchers, professionals, scholars, policymakers, and students. Subject matter includes aging/gerontology, anthropology/archaeology, the arts,
ethnic/cultural studies, business, communications, counseling/psychology, education,
social work, politics, engineering, history, science, and mathematics. **Books
Statistics:** 200 titles/yr. **Proposal Process:** Send formal book proposal to the appropriate editor. See Web site for staff listing and more specific guidelines. **Sample
Titles:** *Human Genetics for the Social Sciences* by Gregory Carey; *The Mating
Game: A Primer on Love, Sex, and Marriage* by Pamela C. Regan. **Contact:**
Editorial Acquisitions Department.

ST. MARTIN'S PRESS

175 Fifth Ave., New York, NY 10010. 212-674-5151.
Web site: www.stmartins.com. **Description:** Trade nonfiction (history, multicultural
studies, pop culture, the arts, science, business, professional), popular and literary fiction, and scholarly titles/reference titles/college textbooks. Also publishes a small list

for young readers. **Proposal Process:** No unsolicited submissions. Accepts work from literary agents only. **Payment:** Royalty. **Sample Titles:** (Fiction) *Sons of Fortune* by Jeffrey Archer; (Nonfiction) *Atkins for Life* by Robert C. Atkins, M.D.

J.S. SANDERS & CO.
Ivan R. Dee, Publisher
1332 N Halsted St., Chicago, IL 60622-2694. 312-787-6262.
E-mail: editorial@ivanrdee.com. Web site: www.ivanrdee.com. **Description:** General trade nonfiction, biographies, histories, and classics. Titles focus on the history, literature, and culture of the South.

SANTA MONICA PRESS
P.O. Box 1076, Santa Monica, CA 90406. 310-230-7759.
E-mail: books@santamonicapress.com. Web site: www.santamonicapress.com. **Description:** Lively and modern how to books, literary nonfiction, and books on pop culture, film, music, theater, and television. **Proposal Process:** Send cover letter and outline indicating the nature and scope of each chapter. Include 2 sample chapters and photocopies of any photographs or illustrations. State in cover letter the intended audience, explanation as to why book is unique, summary of competing books, anticipated length, brief bio, and complete contact info. Include SASE with appropriate postage. No phone calls. **Sample Titles:** *Footsteps in the Fog: Alfred Hitchcock's San Francisco* by Jeff Kraft and Aaron Leventhal; *Offbeat Museums* by Saul Rubin; *Letter Writing Made Easy!* by Margaret McCarthy. **Contact:** Acquisitions Editor.

SARABANDE BOOKS INC.
2234 Dundee Rd., Suite 200, Louisville, KY 40205. 502-458-4028.
E-mail: sarabandeb@aol.com. Web site: www.sarabandebooks.org. **Description:** Nonprofit literary press publishing poetry, short fiction, and creative nonfiction. **Proposal Process:** Open submissions during the month of September only. Query with 10 poems, a single story, or section of novella/short novel. Send complete manuscript only if requested. **Sample Titles:** (Fiction) *Bloody Mary* by Sharon Solwitz; (Poetry) *The Day Before* by Dick Allen. **Tips:** Also offers the Kathryn A. Morton Prize in Poetry and the Mary McCarthy Prize in Short Fiction.

SASQUATCH BOOKS
119 S Main St., Suite 400, Seattle, WA 98104. 206-467-4300.
E-mail: books@sasquatchbooks.com. Web site: www.sasquatchbooks.com. Gary Luke, Editor. **Description:** Regional titles covering the West Coast of the U.S. only. Topics include food, travel, gardening, pop culture, literary nonfiction, and children's books. **Books Statistics:** 40 titles/yr; 30% by first-time authors; 30% unagented. **Proposal Process:** Query with SASE. No e-queries or phone calls. Hard copy only. Responds in 3 months. **Payment:** Royalty. **Tips:** Regional only (Pacific Northwest, Alaska, and California).

SCARECROW PRESS
4501 Forbes Blvd., Suite 200, Lanham, MD 20706. 301-459-3366.
Web site: www.scarecrowpress.com. **Description:** Single-volume reference titles; historical dictionaries (of countries, religious, organizations, wars, movements, cities, and ancient civilizations); scholarly, professional, and textbooks in selected disciplines. **Contact:** Bruce Phillips (music); Rebecca Massa (film); Kim Tabor (YA literary criticism reference titles, historical dictionaries); Sue Easun (information studies, military history, children's literary criticism); Melissa Ray (all other inquiries). **Books Statistics:** 175 titles/yr; 20% by first-time authors; 95% unagented. **Proposal Process:** Query with subject matter, scope, and intended purpose of your manuscript. Accepts e-queries. Responds in 2-4 months. **Payment:** Royalty. **Tips:** See guidelines.

SCHIFFER PUBLISHING LTD.
4880 Lower Valley Rd., Atglen, PA 19310. 610-593-1777.
E-mail: info@schifferbooks.com. **Description:** Books on collectibles, antiques, military history, arts/crafts, art/design, and New Age topics.

SCOTT FORESMAN
1900 E Lake Ave., Glenview, IL 60025.
Web site: www.scottforesman.com. Susanne Singleton, Publisher. **Description:** Publisher of elementary textbooks on reading, language arts, science, mathematics, social studies, music, and biligual studies. **Proposal Process:** Considers authors with proper educational credentials only. Submit resume if qualified. Does not publish children's literature or unsolicited manuscripts. **Payment:** Royalty or flat fee.

SEAL PRESS
300 Queen Anne Ave. N, #375, Seattle, WA 98109. 206-722-1838.
E-mail: leslie.miller@avalonpub.com. Web site: www.sealpress.com. Leslie Miller, Senior Editor. **Description:** Publishes titles ranging from literary fiction to health, popular culture, women's studies, parenting and travel/outdoor adventure. Currently focusing acquisitions in two popular series: Adventura (focuses on women's travel/adventure writing) and Live Girls (showcases the voices of modern feminism). **Books Statistics:** 15 titles/yr (1,500 submissions); 20% by first-time authors; 20% unagented. **Proposal Process:** Query. No electronic or simultaneous queries. Hard copy only. Responds in 2-4 months. **Payment:** Royalty, 7% net. **Tips:** Does not accept unsolicited or unagented manuscripts.

SEVEN LOCKS PRESS
3100 W Warner Ave., Suite 8, Santa Ana, CA 92704. 714-545-2526.
E-mail: sevenlocks@aol.com. Web site: www.sevenlockspress.com. **Description:** Publishes nonfiction material on contemporary topics, self-help issues, public affairs, and critical issues of our time.

SEVEN STORIES PRESS

140 Watts St., New York, NY 10013. 212-226-8760.
E-mail: info@sevenstories.com. Web site: www.sevenstories.com. Daniel Simon,
Acquisitions Editor. **Description:** Small press publishing literary fiction and nonfiction in the areas of activism and politics. **Books Statistics:** 25 titles/yr; 20% by first-time authors; 15% unagented. **Proposal Process:** Does not read unsolicited manuscripts. Send query letter, synopsis, and no more than 1 sample chapter. Include SASE for response and return of materials. No e-queries. Responds in 10 weeks.
Payment: Royalty, 7-15%. **Sample Titles:** *Urban Injustice: How Ghettos Happen* by Dr. David Hilfiker; *Radical Walking Tours of New York City* by Bruce Kayton.

SHAMBHALA PUBLICATIONS, INC.

Horticultural Hall, 300 Massachusetts Ave., Boston, MA 02115. 617-424-0030.
E-mail: editors@shambhala.com. Web site: www.shambhala.com. Peter Turner,
Executive Editor. **Description:** Nonfiction titles on Eastern religion, especially Buddhism and Taoism, as well as psychology, self-help, arts, literature, health/healing, and philosophy. **Proposal Process:** Query with outline and sample chapters.
Payment: Flat fee and royalty. **Contact:** Laura Stone.

SIERRA CLUB BOOKS

85 Second St., San Francisco, CA 94105. 415-977-5500.
E-mail: danny.moses@sierraclub.org. Web site: www.sierraclub.org/books. Danny
Moses, Editor-in-Chief. **Description:** Nonfiction about nature, ecology, and environmental issues for a general audience. Also publishes children's books. **Books Statistics:** 15 titles/yr (1,000 submissions); 10-20% by first-time authors; 40-50% unagented. **Proposal Process:** Send outline and sample chapter. Considers simultaneous and electronic queries. Prefers electronic format. Responds in 1 month.
Payment: Royalty. **Sample Titles:** *Downhill Slide: Why the Corporate Ski Industry Is Bad for Skiing, Ski Towns, and the Environment* by Hal Clifford. **Tips:** Currently not accepting unsolicited manuscripts or proposals for children's books.

SIGNATURE BOOKS PUBLISHING

564 W 400 N, Salt Lake City, UT 84116-3411. 801-531-1483.
E-mail: people@signaturebooks.com. Web site: www.signaturebooks.com. George
Smith, President. **Description:** Fiction, nonfiction, essays, and humor on Western and Mormon Americana. Seeks to present history and culture in a scholarly, professional manner. **Proposal Process:** Submit query letter outlining thesis or plot with resume or curriculum vitae. Does not accept unsolicited manuscripts. **Payment:** Royalty. **Sample Titles:** *Mormon Mavericks* by John Sillito; *Being Different* by Stanford J. Layton. **Contact:** Ron Priddis, Editor.

SILMAN-JAMES PRESS

3624 Shannon Rd., Los Angeles, CA 90027. 323-661-9922.
E-mail: silmanjamespress@earthlink.net. Gwen Feldman, Jim Fox, Co-Publishers.

Description: Books on film, filmmaking, the motion picture industry, music, and the performing arts. Also includes Siles Press imprint, which publishes books on chess and other general nonfiction subjects. **Books Statistics:** 8 titles/yr; 40% by first-time authors; 90% unagented. **Proposal Process:** Query with outline and sample chapters. Accepts phone queries. Responds in 2-12 weeks. **Payment:** Royalty. **Sample Titles:** *Improvisation Technique for the Performing Actor in Film, Theatre, and Television* by Stephen Book; *In the Blink of an Eye: A Perspective on Film Editing* by Walter Murch; *Dealmaking in the Film & Television Industry,* by Mark Litwak.

SILVER LAKE PUBLISHING

2025 Hyperion Ave., Los Angeles, CA 90027. 323-663-3082.
E-mail: theeditors@silverlakepub.com. Web site: www.silverlakepub.com. James Walsh, Publisher. **Description:** Nonfiction on personal finance, small business management, consumer reference, and popular economics. **Books Statistics:** 8-10 titles/yr. **Proposal Process:** Send cover letter with outline, 2 sample chapters, and bio/resume. No electronic submissions. Responds in 6-8 weeks. **Sample Titles:** *Under 40 Financial Planning Guide: From Graduation to Your First Home* by Cornelius P. McCarthy; *Business Plans to Game Plans: A Practical System for Turning Strategies into Action* by Jan B. King. **Tips:** Study recent books published to get a sense of what material they are interested in. **Contact:** Kristin Loberg, Editor or Megan Thorpe, Editor.

SILVERBACK BOOKS INC.

55 New Montgomery St., Suite 503, San Francisco, CA 94105-3431. 415-348-8595.
E-mail: info@silverbackbooks.com. Web site: www.silverbackbooks.com. **Description:** Publisher of cookbooks. **Sample Titles:** *Moroccan Café* by Elisa Vergne; *Basic Italian* by Cornelia Schinharl and Sebastian Dickhaut.

SIMON & SCHUSTER

1230 Avenue of the Americas, New York, NY 10020. 212-698-7000.
Web site: www.simonsays.com. Alice Mayhew, Editorial Director. **Description:** High-quality fiction and nonfiction. **Proposal Process:** No unsolicited manuscripts. Accepts material from literary agents only. **Sample Titles:** (Fiction) *The Gold Swan* by James Thayer; *Down by the River: Drugs, Money, Murder, and Family* by Charles Bowden.

SMITH AND KRAUS, INC.

P.O. Box 127, Lyme, NH 03768. 603-643-6431.
E-mail: sandk@sover.net. Web site: www.smithkraus.com. Marisa Smith, Publisher. **Description:** Publishes monologue and scene anthologies, biographies of playwrights, translations, books on career development (in theater) and the art of theater, and teaching texts for young actors (K-12). **Books Statistics:** 30 titles/yr (500+ submissions); 20% by first-time authors; 50% unagented. **Proposal Process:** Query with SASE. No simultaneous queries. Accepts hard copy and brief e-queries (1-2 pages).

Responds in 1-2 months. **Payment:** Royalty and flat fee. **Tips:** "We seek material of interest to the theater community."

GIBBS SMITH, PUBLISHER
P.O. Box 667, Layton, UT 84041. 801-544-9800.
E-mail: info@gibbs-smith.com. Web site: www.gibbs-smith.com. Suzanne Taylor, Editorial Director. **Description:** Interior design books, cookbooks, gift books, architecture guides, monographs, children's picture and activity books, and other materials related to home and hearth and culture/lifestyle. **Tips:** "We're looking for fresh insights into home decorating and inspirational stories that can be illustrated and sold as adult gift books, suitable for any occasion."

SMITHSONIAN BOOKS
750 Ninth St. NW, Suite 4300, Washington, DC 20560-0950. 202-275-2300.
E-mail: inquiries@sipress.si.edu. **Description:** General trade and illustrated books in American studies, natural sciences, photography, aviation and spaceflight history, and anthropology.

SNOW LION PUBLICATIONS
P.O. Box 6483, Ithaca, NY 14851. 607-273-8519.
E-mail: tibet@snowlionpub.com. Web site: www.snowlionpub.com. **Description:** Publishes titles exclusively on Tibetan Buddhism. **Sample Titles:** *The Wheel of Time Sand Mandala* by Barry Bryant; *The Art of Peace* edited by Jeffrey Hopkin.

SOHO PRESS
853 Broadway, New York, NY 10003. 212-260-1900.
E-mail: soho@sohopress.com. Web site: www.sohopress.com. Juris Jurjevics, Publisher. **Description:** Adult literary fiction, mysteries, nonfiction memoirs, travel books, and materials on social and cultural history. **Books Statistics:** 50 titles/yr (2,000 submissions); 50% by first-time authors; 10% unagented. **Proposal Process:** Query with first 3 sample chapters, brief plot outline, and list of previously published credits. Considers simultaneous queries, but not e-queries Hard copy only. Responds in 2 months. **Payment:** Royalty (net 10%, 12.5%, 15%). **Sample Titles:** (Fiction) *After* by Phyllis Reynolds Naylor; (Crime Fiction) *Maisie Dobbs* by Jacqui Winspear; (Memoir) *Grace: An American Woman in China, 1934-1974* by Eleanor McCallie Cooper and William Liu. **Tips:** No mass-market, how-to, cooking, or religious titles.

SOUNDPRINTS
353 Main Ave., Norwalk, CT 06851. 203-840-2274.
E-mail: chelsea.shriver@soundprints.com. Web site: www.soundprints.com. Chelsea Shriver, Assistant Editor. **Description:** Publishes books on wildlife and history to educate and entertain. "Manuscript must have an exciting storyline—and be based on fact and supported by careful research." **Books Statistics:** 30 titles/yr (100 submissions); 100% unagented. **Proposal Process:** Does not accept unsolicited manuscripts; see specific guidelines for each series. Submit published writing samples for

review. **Payment:** Flat fee. **Sample Titles:** Currently publishes 8 series: *Smithsonian Oceanic Collection, Smithsonian's Backyard, Smithsonian Dinosaur Collection, Smithsonian Let's Go to the Zoo!, Soundprints Multicultural/Make Friends Around the World, Soundprints' Read-and-Discover, Early Reading Chapter Books*, and *Soundprints Amazing Animal Adventures*.

SOURCEBOOKS CASABLANCA

Sourcebooks, Inc., P.O. Box 4410, Naperville, IL 60567-4410. 603-961-3900.
E-mail: todd.stocke@sourcebooks.com. Web site: www.sourcebooks.com. Todd Stocke, Editorial Director. **Description:** The nonfiction, relationships/love imprint of Sourcebooks, Inc. **Proposal Process:** Query with outline and sample chapters. **Payment:** Royalty. **Sample Titles:** *1001 Ways to Be Romantic* by Gregory Godek; *Seduction* by Snow Raven Starborn; *365 Kisses* by Kathy Wagoner.

SOURCEBOOKS, INC.

P.O. Box 4410, Naperville, IL 60567-4410. 630-961-3900.
E-mail: todd.stocke@sourcebooks.com. Web site: www.sourcebooks.com. Todd Stocke, Editorial Director. **Description:** General-interest nonfiction titles in a wide rage of categories: reference, history, sports, self-help/psychology, personal finance, small business, marketing/management, parenting, health/beauty, relationships, biography, gift books, and women's issues. Launched a fiction imprint, Sourcebooks Landmark, in 2001. **Books Statistics:** 120 titles/yr (3,000+ submissions); 10% by first-time authors; 20% unagented. **Proposal Process:** Query with outline, sample chapters, and SASE. Accepts simultaneous queries, but not e-queries. **Payment:** Royalty. **Sample Titles:** (Fiction) *The Blue Moon Circus* by Michael Raleigh. (Nonfiction) *Bargain Beauty Secrets* by Diane Irons; *The Fiske Guide to Colleges* by Ted Fiske. **Tips:** "We work with our authors to develop great books that find and inspire a wide audience. We seek authors who are as committed as we are and we ask our prospective authors to do their research."

SOUTH END PRESS

7 Brookline St., Cambridge, MA 02139-4146. 617-547-4002.
Web site: www.southendpress.org. Jill Petty, Editor. **Description:** Nonprofit, collectively run book publisher with more than 200 titles in print. Committed to the politics of radical social change. Encourage critical thinking and consecutive action on the key political, cultural, social, economic, and ecological issues shaping life in the United States and in the world. **Books Statistics:** 10 titles/yr (1,000 submissions); 5% first-time authors; 95% unagented. **Proposal Process:** Query with sample chapters. Accepts simultaneous queries. Responds in 6-8 weeks. **Payment:** Royalty.

SOUTHERN ILLINOIS UNIVERSITY PRESS

P.O. Box 3697, Carbondale, IL 62902-3697. 618-453-2281.
E-mail: kageff@siu.edu. Web site: www.siu.edu/~siupress. Karl Kageff, Senior Editor. **Description:** Nonfiction on the humanities, 200-300 pages. **Proposal Process:** Query with outline and sample chapters. **Payment:** Royalty. **Sample Titles:** *Chicago*

Death Trap: The Iroquois Theatre Fire of 1903 by Nat Brandt; *Our Culture of Pandering* by Paul Simon.

SOUTHERN METHODIST UNIVERSITY PRESS
P.O. Box 750415, Dallas, TX 75275-0415. 214-768-1433.
E-mail: klang@mail.smu.edu. Web site: www.smu.edu/press. Kathryn Lang, Acquisitions Editor. **Description:** Publishes literary fiction, books on life in the Southwest (both fiction and nonfiction), and books on film, theater, and the performing arts. Also publishes nonfiction titles on medical humanities issues, ethics, and death/dying. **Books Statistics:** 10-12 titles/yr (2,500 submissions); 80% by first-time authors; 90% unagented. **Proposal Process:** Query with outline and sample chapters. Accepts simultaneous queries, but not e-queries. Hard copy only. Responds in 1 month. **Payment:** Royalty (net 10%).

SPHINX PUBLISHING
Imprint of Sourcebooks, Inc.
P.O. Box 4410, Naperville, IL 60567-4410. 630-961-3900.
E-mail: dianne.wheeler@sourcebooks.com. Web site: www.sourcebooks.com. Dianne Wheeler, Editor. **Description:** Nonfiction books on legal self-help in subjects including personal affairs, business, parenting, and real estate. **Proposal Process:** Query with outline and sample chapters. **Payment:** Royalty.

SPINSTERS INK
P.O. Box 22005, Denver, CO 80222. 303-761-5552.
E-mail: spinster@spinsters-ink.com. Web site: www.spinsters-ink.com. Sharon Silvas, Editorial Director. **Description:** Adult fiction and nonfiction books, 200+ pages, that deal with social justice and/or significant issues in women's lives from a feminist perspective and encourage change and growth. **Books Statistics:** 6 titles/yr; 50% by first-time authors; 80% unagented. **Proposal Process:** Query with outline and SASE. Considers simultaneous queries. Responds in 90 days. **Payment:** Royalty.

SPRINGHOUSE PUBLISHING
1111 Bethlehem Pike, P.O. Box 908, Springhouse, PA 19477. 215-646-8700.
E-mail: jrobinso@lww.com. Web site: www.springnet.com.
Description: Information for nursing students and other healthcare professionals.

SQUARE ONE PUBLISHERS INC.
115 Herricks Rd., Garden City Park, NY 11040. 516-535-2010.
E-mail: sq1info@aol.com. Web site: www.squareonepublishers.com. **Description:** Nonfiction on vintage poster art, collectibles, cooking, general interest, history, how-to, parenting, self-help, health, etc.

STACKPOLE BOOKS
5067 Ritter Rd., Mechanicsburg, PA 17055. 717-796-0411.
E-mail: jschnell@stackpolebooks.com. Web site: www.stackpolebooks.com. Judith

Schnell, Editorial Director. **Description:** Nonfiction on the outdoors, nature, birding, fishing, fly fishing, climbing, paddling, sports, sporting literature, history, and military reference. **Books Statistics:** 80 titles/yr (150 submissions); 20% by first-time authors; 70% unagented. **Proposal Process:** Submit queries with sample chapters to acquisitions editors: Mark Allison (nature), Judith Schnell (fishing/sports), Chris Evans (History), Kyle Weaver (Pennsylvania). No simultaneous or electronic queries. Hard copy only. **Payment:** Royalty; advance or flat fee. **Tips:** No poetry, cookbooks, fiction, or books on crafts. History books must have some original research involved.

STANFORD UNIVERSITY PRESS

1450 Page Mill Rd., Palo Alto, CA 94304. 650-723-9434.
Web site: www.sup.org. Norris Pope, Editor. **Description:** Furthers the university's research and teaching mission primarily through books of significant scholarship. Also publishes some professional books, advanced textbooks, and intellectually serious popular works. **Books Statistics:** 120 titles/yr (2,000 submissions); 35% by first-time authors; 95% unagented. **Proposal Process:** Query with outline and sample chapters. Accepts simultaneous queries, but not e-queries. Hard copy only. Response time varies. **Payment:** Royalty. **Tips:** No original fiction or poetry.

STARRHILL PRESS

1719 Mulberry St., Montgomery, AL 36106. 877-408-7078.
E-mail: jdavis@rivercitypublishing.com. Web site: www.rivercitypublishing.com. Jim Davis, Editor. **Description:** Nonfiction titles on art, gardening, health, history, literature, music, travel. **Tips:** Generally publishes authors with extensive track records.

STATE UNIVERSITY OF NEW YORK PRESS

90 State St., Suite 700, Albany, NY 12207. 518-472-5000.
Web site: www.sunypress.edu. James H. Peltz, Editor-in-Chief. **Description:** Publishes scholarly and trade books in the humanities and social sciences. **Books Statistics:** 200 titles/yr (1,200 submissions); 99% unagented. **Proposal Process:** Query with outline and sample chapters. Accepts simultaneous queries, but not e-queries. Responds in 4-6 weeks. **Payment:** Royalty (typically 5-10%). **Tips:** "We generally publish books for a scholarly audience, with perhaps some potential for crossover to general trade."

STEERFORTH PRESS

P.O. Box 70, South Royalton, VT 05068. 802-763-2808.
Web site: www.steerforth.com. Michael Moore, Editor. **Description:** Adult nonfiction and some literary fiction. Novels, serious works of history, biography, politics, current affairs. **Proposal Process:** No unsolicited proposals or manuscripts.

STEMMER HOUSE PUBLISHERS, INC.

2627 Caves Rd., Owings Mills, MD 21117. 410-363-3690.
E-mail: stemmerhouse@comcast.net. Web site: www.stemmer.com. Barbara Holdridge, Editorial Director. **Description:** Publishes the International Design

Book Series (illustrated books on the design and architecture of various countries including Africa, Asia, Native American, etc); general and multicultural nonfiction (cooking, gardening, nature); and nonfiction picture books, reference materials, and audio/book cassettes for children. **Books Statistics:** 4 titles/yr (2,000 submissions); 50% by first-time authors; 95% unagented. **Proposal Process:** Query with sample chapters and SASE. Considers simultaneous and electronic queries. Prefers hard copy. Responds in 2 weeks. **Payment:** Royalty, 5%-10% net. **Sample Titles:** (Design) *African Painted Textile Designs* by Diane V. Horn; *Chinese Flora and Fauna* Designs by Ming Sun; (Nonfiction) *The Bed & Breakfast Cookbook* by Martha W. Murphy; (Children's) *The Wide-Mouthed Frog* by Rex Schneider. **Tips:** "We look for books with at least 30 year's staying power, and therefore print on acid-free paper as part of that commitment."

STERLING PUBLISHING
387 Park Ave. S, New York, NY 10016. 212-532-7160.
Web site: www.sterlingpub.com. **Description:** Nonfiction on a wide variety of topics· how-to, hobby, woodworking, alternative health/healing, fiber arts, crafts, wine, nature, oddities, puzzles, juvenile humor and activities, juvenile nature/science, Celtic topics, gardening, pets, recreation, sports and games books, reference, and home decorating. **Proposal Process:** Query with outline, sample chapter, and sample illustrations. Include SASE for return of materials. No electronic submissions; hard copy only. **Payment:** Royalty. **Tips:** Unsolicited manuscripts accepted, please accompany with an SASE. **Contact:** Acquisitions Committee.

STONEYDALE PRESS PUBLISHING CO.
523 Main St., Stevensville, MT 59870. 406-777-2729.
E-mail: info@stoneydale.com. Web site: www.stoneydale.com. Dale A. Burk, Publisher. **Description:** Adult nonfiction, primarily how-to, on outdoor recreation with special emphasis on big game hunting. Also publishes some regional history of the Northern Rockies. Specialized market. **Proposal Process:** Query with outline and sample chapters. **Payment:** Royalty.

STOREY PUBLISHING
210 Mass Moca Way, North Adams, MA 01247. 413-346-2100.
Web site: www.storeybooks.com. Deborah Balmuth, Editorial Director. **Description:** Nonfiction how-to books in the areas of gardening, crafts, natural health, building, pets/animals, and nature. Also gift books and juvenile nature books. **Books Statistics:** 40 titles/yr; 50% by first-time authors; 80% unagented. **Proposal Process:** Send query with outline, sample chapters, and SASE. Accepts simultaneous queries, but not e-queries. Hard copy only. Responds in 2-3 months. **Payment:** Royalty or flat fee. **Tips:** Well-researched competitive analysis and clearly defined "hook" to make proposed book stand out from competition. Clear, hard-working content, with imaginative presentation. **Contact:** Deborah Burns (equine, animals, nature); Gwen Steege (gardening, crafts); Dianne Cutillo (cooking, wine, beer).

STORMLINE PRESS

P.O. Box 593, Urbana, IL 61801.

E-mail: ray@raybial.com. Raymond Bial, Publisher/Editor. **Description:** Publishes primarily regional nonfiction on language, literature, history, and photography. **Books Statistics:** 1-2 titles/yr; 10% first-time authors; 10% unagented. **Proposal Process:** Query with outline, sample chapters, and SASE. Accepts simultaneous queries, but not e-queries. Prefers hard copy. **Payment:** Royalty. **Sample Titles:** (Nonfiction) *When the Waters Recede* by Dan Guillory. (Fiction) *Silent Friends* by Margaret Lacey. **Tips:** "We publish distinctive works of literary and artistic value, with emphasis on rural and small town. Please review our books to gain a sense of the type of material we publish. We are a very small publisher and do not have the staff to respond to inquiries or submissions. We do not accept unsolicited manuscripts—publication by invitation only."

STRAWBERRY HILL PRESS

Strictly Book Promotions, Inc.

21 Isis St., Suite 102, San Francisco, CA 94103. 415-626-2665.

E-mail: strictly@bookpromo.com. Daniel F. Vojir, Editor. **Description:** Nonfiction: biography, autobiography, history, cooking, health, how-to, philosophy, performance arts, and the Third World. **Proposal Process:** Query with sample chapters, outline, and SASE. **Payment:** Royalty.

SUCCESS SHOWCASE PUBLISHING

131 W Sunburst Ln., Suite 220, Tempe, AZ 85284. 480-831-8334.

E-mail: info@confessionsofshamelessselfpromoters.com.

Web site: www.confessionsofshamelessselfpromoters.com. **Description:** Publishes books on successful marketing strategies.

SUMMIT BOOKS

Simon & Schuster Trade/Simon & Schuster, Inc.

1230 Avenue of the Americas, New York, NY 10020. 212-698-7000.

Web site: www.simonsays.com. **Description:** General-interest fiction and nonfiction of high literary quality. No category books. **Proposal Process:** Query through agents only. **Payment:** Royalty.

SUMMIT UNIVERSITY PRESS

P.O. Box 5000, Corwin Springs, MT 59030-5000. 406-848-9295.

E-mail: info@summituniversitypress.com.

Web site: www.summituniversitypress.com. **Description:** Books on spirituality and personal growth. **Sample Titles:** *Emotions: Transforming Anger, Fear, and Pain* by Marilyn C. Barrick, Ph.D.; *Your Seven Energy Centers* by Elizabeth Clare Prophet and Patricia R. Spadaro.

SUNDANCE PUBLISHING

P.O. Box 1326, Littleton, MA 01460. 800-343-8204.
Web site: www.sundancepub.com. M. Elizabeth Strauss, Director Publishing.
Description: Curriculum materials to accompany quality children's, young adult,
and adult literature. **Payment:** Flat fee only.

SYBEX INC.

1151 Marina Village Parkway, Alameda, CA 94501. 510-523-8233.
E-mail: proposals@sybex.com. Web site: www.sybex.com. Jordan Gold, VP/Publisher.
Description: Nonfiction titles on computers and software. **Books Statistics:** 180
titles/yr.

SYRACUSE UNIVERSITY PRESS

621 Skytop Rd., Suite 110, Syracuse, NY 13244-5290. 315-443-5534.
E-mail: msevans@syr.edu. Web site: http://sumweb.syr.edu/su_press/. Mary Selden
Evans, Executive Editor. **Description:** Scholarly general and regional nonfiction.
Proposal Process: Send formal prospectus with abstract, curriculum vitae, sample
chapter, TOC, and introduction Responds in 4-8 weeks. **Sample Titles:** *Painting the
Middle East* by Ann Zwicker Kerr; *Voices from Iran: The Changing Lives of Iranian
Women* by Mahnaz Kousha; *My War: A Memoir of a Survivor of the Holocaust* by
Edward Stankiewicz; *All in One Breath: Selected Poems* by Harry C. Staley.

THE TAUNTON PRESS INC.

63 S Main St., Newtown, CT 06470. 203-426-8171.
E-mail: tt@taunton.com. Web site: www.taunton.com. **Description:** Publishes books
on home design, fiber arts, woodworking, and gardening.

TAYLOR TRADE PUBLISHING

Rowman & Littlefield Publishing Group
4720 Boston Way, Lanham, MD 20706. 301-459-3366.
Web site: www.rlpgbooks.com. **Description:** Adult trade nonfiction on sports, gardening, history, entertainment, health, family matters, nature, regional interest.
Books Statistics: 100 titles/yr. **Proposal Process:** Send outline of manuscript with
sample chapters. **Contact:** Michael Dorr, Rick Rinehart, Jill Langford.

TEACHERS COLLEGE PRESS

1234 Amsterdam Ave., New York, NY 10027. 212-678-3929.
E-mail: tcpress@tc.columbia.edu. Web site: www.teacherscollegepress.com. Brian
Ellerbeck, Executive Acquisitions Editor. **Description:** Books and materials that
focus on all areas of education including curriculum, leadership, teacher education,
early childhood, child development, language, literacy, etc. Also publishes materials
on psychology, sociology/culture, history, philosophy, and women's studies. **Books
Statistics:** 60 titles/yr. **Sample Titles:** *Creating Solutions That Heal: Real-Life
Solutions* by Lesley Koplow; *The Children Are Watching: How the Media Teach
About Diversity* by Carlos E. Cortes; *Language of Learning* by Karen Gallas.

TEHABI BOOKS

4920 Carroll Canyon Road, San Diego, CA 92121-3735. 858-450-9100.
E-mail: nancy.cash@tehabi.com. Web site: www.tehabi.com. **Description:** Books on history, travel, sports, personalities, nature, and wildlife.

TEMPLE UNIVERSITY PRESS

1601 N Broad St., USB 306, Philadelphia, PA 19122-6099. 215-204-8787.
E-mail: tempress@temple.edu. Web site: www.temple.edu/tempress/. Janet Francendese, Editor-in-Chief. **Description:** Academic nonfiction in the fields of history, political science, sociology, anthropology, law, education, cinema, disabilities, multicultural studies, gay/lesbian, and women's studies. Also publishes a strong list of regional and sports titles for a general audience. **Proposal Process:** Send query or proposal with outline and sample chapters. Hard copy only. **Payment:** Royalty. **Sample Titles:** *Larry Kane's Philadelphia* by Larry Kane and Dan Rather; *The Sons and Daughters of Los: Culture and Community in L.A.* by David E. James; *Why I Burned My Book and Other Essays on Disability* by Paul K. Longmore.

TEN SPEED PRESS

P.O. Box 7123, Berkeley, CA 94707. 510-559-1600.
Web site: www.tenspeed.com. Kirsty Melville, Editorial Department. **Description:** Career and business books, cookbooks, and general nonfiction. **Books Statistics:** 150 titles/yr (5,000 submissions); 30% by first-time authors; 30% unagented. **Proposal Process:** Query with outline, sample chapters, and SASE. Responds in 6 weeks. **Payment:** Royalty. **Sample Titles:** *What Color Is Your Parachute?: A Practical Manual for Job-Hunters and Career Changes* by Richard Nelson Bolles; *The Breads of France: And How to Bake Them in Your Own Kitchen* by Bernard Clayton, Jr. **Tips:** "Familiarize yourself with our house and our list before submitting mss. Provide a rational for why we are the best publishing house for your work."

TEXAS A&M UNIVERSITY PRESS

John H. Lindsey Building
Lewis St., 4354 TAMU, College Station, TX 77843. 979-845-1436.
E-mail: dlv@tampress.tamu.edu. Web site: www.tamu.edu/upress. Mary Lenn Dixon, Editor-in-Chief. **Description:** American and military history, Eastern European studies, presidential studies, anthropology, natural history, literary fiction, and Southwestern and Western studies. **Proposal Process:** Submit proposal including synopsis, TOC, intended audience, competing titles currently on the market, resume or CV, and sample chapters. **Sample Titles:** *A Southern Family in White and Black* by Douglas Hales; *American Military Aviation in the 20th Century* by Charles J. Gross. **Contact:** Diana L. Vance, Editorial Assistant.

THAMES & HUDSON INC.

500 Fifth Ave., New York, NY 10110. 212-354-3763.
E-mail: info@thames.wwnorton.com. Web site: www.thamesandhudsonusa.com.
Description: Illustrated books on art, architecture, decorative arts, design, fashion,

photography, travel, history, archaeology, spirituality, and natural history. **Proposal Process:** Send letter of inquiry before submitting material.

THIRD WORLD PRESS
P.O. Box 19730, Chicago, IL 60619.
E-mail: twpress3@aol.com. Web site: www.thirdworldpressinc.com. Haki R. Madhubuti, Publisher. **Description:** Progressive Black Publishing. Adult fiction, nonfiction, poetry, and YA material. **Books Statistics:** 20 titles/yr; 20% by first-time authors; 80% unagented. **Proposal Process:** Query with outline. Send SASE or e-mail for guidelines. **Payment:** Royalty. **Contact:** Gwendolyn Mitchell, Editor.

THORSONS
4720 Boston Way, Lanham, MD 20706. 301-731-9526.
E-mail: karen.kreiger@harpercollins.uk. Web site: www.thorsons.com. **Description:** Publishes material on health, personal development, alternative health, inspiration, sex, parenting, psychology, religion, self-help, and spirituality.

THUNDER'S MOUTH PRESS
Avalon Publishing Group
161 William St., Fl. 16, New York, NY 10038. 212-614-7880.
Web site: www.avalonpub.com. **Description:** Publishes adult trade books in a variety of subject areas. Concentrates heavily on pop culture, current events, contemporary culture, fantasy and role-playing games, and biography. **Books Statistics:** 50 titles/year (thousands of submissions), 10% by first-time authors, 0% unagented. **Proposal Process:** Send query with complete manuscript. No simultaneous or electronic queries. Response time varies.

TILBURY HOUSE
2 Mechanic St., #3, Gardiner, ME 04345. 207-582-1899.
E-mail: tilbury@tilburyhouse.com. Web site: www.tilburyhouse.com. Jennifer Bunting, Publisher. **Description:** Small, independent publisher. Children's picture books (with possibility of teacher's guide) that deal with cultural diversity or nature/environment. Adult nonfiction titles on Maine and the Northeast. **Proposal Process:** Query with outline and sample chapters. Prefers hard copy format. Accepts unsolicited manuscripts. **Payment:** Pays on publication. **Sample Titles:** (Children's) *Saving Birds: Heroes Around the World* by Pete Salmansohn and Steve Kress; (Adult) *The Interrupted Forest: A History of Maine's Wildlands* by Neil Rolde.

TIMBER PRESS, INC.
133 SW Second Ave., Suite 450, Portland, OR 97204. 503-227-2878.
E-mail: info@timberpress.com. Web site: www.timberpress.com. Neal Maillet, Executive Editor. **Description:** High-quality books on plants and flowers for gardeners, horticulturists, and botanists. **Proposal Process:** Send proposal including cover letter outlining purpose and audience, TOC, 1-2 sample chapters, sample illustrations, bio/resume, and estimated timetable for completing the project. Responds

in 8-12 weeks. **Sample Titles:** *The Gardener's Guide to Growing Dahlias* by Gareth Rowlands; *Portraits of Himalayan Flowers* by Toshio Yoshida; *The American Woodland Garden: Capturing the Spirit of the Deciduous Forest* by Rick Darke.

TOKYOPOP
Mixx Entertainment, Inc.
5900 Wilshire Blvd., Suite 2000, Los Angeles, CA 90036-5020. 323-692-6700.
E-mail: info@tokyopop.com. Web site: www.tokyopop.com. **Description:** Japanese Manga, graphic novels, and comic books.

TOR BOOKS
Tom Doherty Associates
175 Fifth Ave., New York, NY 10010. 212-388-0100.
E-mail: inquiries@tor.com. Web site: www.tor.com. Patrick Nielsen Hayden, Senior Editor. **Description:** Science fiction, fantasy, and horror. From 80,000 words. **Proposal Process:** Send cover letter, complete synopsis, first 3 chapters, and SASE. Responds in 6-9 months. **Payment:** Advance and royalties. **Tips:** "For a complete listing of submission guidelines, please see our Web site."

TORCHLIGHT PUBLISHING INC.
P.O. Box 52, Badger, CA 93603. 559-337-2200.
E-mail: torchlight@spiralcomm.net. Web site: www.torchlight.com. **Description:** Features articles on health and vegetarianism, leadership, motivation and self-improvement, spirituality and religion, etc. **Contact:** Susanne Bolte.

TORMONT/BRIMAR PUBLICATIONS
338 Saint Antoine St. East, Montreal, Quebec H2Y 1A3 Canada. 514-954-1441.
E-mail: dianem@tormont.ca. Web site: www.tormont.com. Diane Mineau, Editorial Director. **Description:** Children's books, cookbooks, dictionaries, encyclopedias, and general-interest books.

TOUCHWOOD EDITIONS
#6-356 Simcoe St., Victoria, British Columbia V8V 1L1. 250-360-2031.
E-mail: touchwoodeditions@shaw.ca. Web site: www.touchwoodeditions.com. Vivian Sinclair, Managing Editor. **Description:** Nonfiction titles on nautical subjects, history, and biography with British Columbia focus. Emphasis on creative nonfiction; also interested in historical fiction. **Books Statistics:** 8-10 titles/yr; 50% by first-time authors; 100% unagented. **Proposal Process:** Submit query with outline and 2-3 sample chapters. No e-queries; hard copy only. **Payment:** Royalty.

TOWLEHOUSE PUBLISHING
1312 Bell Grimes Ln., Nashville, TN 37207. 615-822-6405.
E-mail: vermonte@aol.com. Web site: www.towlehouse.com. **Description:** Nonfiction publisher specializing in "Potent Quotables" and the Good Golf! series.

Also looking for timely and compelling books on American trends and issues from a conservative and/or Christian perspective. Also publishes sports books.

TRAFALGAR SQUARE PUBLISHING

P.O. Box 257, Howe Hill Rd., North Pomfret, VT 05053. 802-457-1911. E-mail: tsquare@sover.net. Web site: www.trafalgarsquarebooks.com or www.horseandriderbooks.com. **Description:** Specializes in books on horses, horse riding, and other equestrian topics. Also publishes books on crafts and home decorating, gardening and flower arranging, and mind, body, spirit. **Sample Titles:** *Centered Riding 2: Further Exploration* by Sally Swift; *Teach Your Horse Perfect Manners* by Kelly Marks; *Dressage Principles Illuminated* by Charles de Kunffy.

TRANSACTION PUBLISHERS

Rutgers State University
35 Berrue Circle, Piscataway, NJ 08854. 732-445-2280.
E-mail: trans@transactionpub.com. Web site: www.transactionpub.com. **Description:** Nonfiction titles on the social sciences: economics, political science, history, sociology, anthropology, psychology, etc. **Sample Titles:** *The First New Nation* by Seymour Martin Lipset; *Justice and the Politics of Memory* by Gabriel R. Ricci.

TRIUMPH BOOKS

601 South LaSalle St., Suite 500, Chicago, IL 60605. 312-939-3330.
Web site: www.triumphbooks.com. Thomas Bast, Editorial Director. **Description:** Books on sports, recreation, and popular culture. **Proposal Process:** Query with SASE or submit proposal with outline, 1-2 sample chapters, and art/illustrations. **Sample Titles:** *Few and Chosen* by Whitey Ford.

TUPELO PRESS

P.O. Box 539, Dorset, VT 05251. 802-366-8185.
E-mail: info@tupelopress.org. Web site: www.tupelopress.org. Jeffrey Levine, Editor-in-Chief. **Description:** Small, independent literary press publishing poetry, literary fiction, and anthologies. **Books Statistics:** 10 titles/yr. **Sample Titles:** *A House Waiting for Music* by David Hernadez; *The Next Ancient World* by Jennifer Michael Hecht. **Tips:** Also offers annual contests—see Web site for guidelines. **Contact:** Margaret Donovan, Managing Editor.

TURTLE POINT PRESS

103 Hog Hill Rd., Chappaqua, NY 10514. 914-244-3840.
Web site: www.turtlepoint.com. Jonathan D. Rabinowitz, President. **Description:** Forgotten literary fiction, historical and biographical; some contemporary fiction, poetry, 200-400 typed pages. Also publishes imprint "Books & Co." **Proposal Process:** Query with sample chapters. Considers simultaneous queries. **Payment:** Royalty.

TURTLE PRESS

P.O. Box 290206, Wethersfield, CT 06129-0206. 860-529-7770.
E-mail: editorial@turtlepress.com. Web site: www.turtlepress.com. Cynthia Kim,
Editor. **Description:** Publishes books on mind-body, Eastern philosophy, holistic fit-
ness, and martial arts. **Books Statistics:** 4-8 titles/yr (350 submissions); 40% by first-
time authors; 90% unagented. **Proposal Process:** Query with outline, sample chap-
ters, and SASE. Simultaneous and electronic queries accepted but prefers hard copy.
Responds in 2-4 weeks. **Payment:** Royalty. **Sample Titles:** *Martial Arts Instructor's
Desk Reference* by Sang H. Kim; *Fighting Science* by Martina Sprague; *Perfecting
Ourselves: Coordinating Body, Mind, and Spirit* by Aaron Hoopes.

TUTTLE PUBLISHING

153 Milk St., Fl. 5, Boston, MA 02109-4809. 617-951-4080.
E-mail: info@tuttlepublishing.com. Web site: www.tuttlepublishing.com.
Description: Publishes titles on various aspects of Asian culture such as cooking,
martial arts, spirituality, design, philosophy, travel, and language. **Contact:** Editorial
Acquisitions.

TWO-CAN PUBLISHING

234 Nassau St., Princeton, NJ 08542. 609-921-6700.
E-mail: tomhaworth@two-canpublishing.com.
Web site: www.two-canpublishing.com. **Description:** Publishes illustrated educational books and multimedia products for kids ages 3-13 on topics such as animals,
botany, geography, history, math, nature, reference, and science. **Sample Titles:** A
First Look at Animals series; Me and My Pet series; Sports Club series. **Tips:** "We
publish books that absorb, entertain, inform and explain for children, teachers, and
parents around the world."

ULYSSES TRAVEL GUIDES

4176 St.-Denis St., Montreal, Quebec H2W 2M5 Canada. 514-843-9882.
E-mail: info@ulysses.ca. Web site: www.ulyssesguides.com. **Description:** Travel
guidebooks that offer cultural and tourist information for various regions. **Sample
Titles:** *Canadian French for Better Travel* by Cindy Garayt; *Bed and Breakfast in
Ontario* by Julia Roles; *Hiking in Ontario* by Tracey Arial.

UNIVERSITY OF AKRON PRESS

374-B Bierce Library, Akron, OH 44325-1703. 330-972-5342.
E-mail: uapress@uakron.edu. Web site: www.uakron.edu/uapress. Michael J. Carley,
Editor. **Description:** Publishes 5 nonfiction series: poetry; Ohio history and culture;
technology and the environment; law, politics, and society; international, political, and
economic history. **Books Statistics:** 12 titles/yr (100 submissions); 40% by first-time
authors; 100% unagented. **Proposal Process:** Query with outline and sample chapters. Simultaneous and electronic queries accepted. Prefers hard-copy. Responds in
1-2 months. **Payment:** Royalty. **Tips:** See Web site for submission guidelines.

UNIVERSITY OF ALABAMA PRESS

20 Research Dr., Tuscaloosa, AL 35487-0380. 205-348-1561.
E-mail: jknight@uapress.ua.edu. Web site: www.uapress.ua.edu. Judith Knight, Acquisitions Editor. **Description:** Scholarly and general regional nonfiction. Submit work to appropriate editor: Daniel J.J. Ross (history, military history, Latin American history, and Jewish studies); Curtis Clark (African American, Native American and women's studies, public administration, theater, English, rhetoric and communication); Judith Knight (archaeology and anthropology). **Books Statistics:** 55 titles/yr; 50% by first-time authors; 90% unagented. **Proposal Process:** Send cover letter, curriculum vitae, outline, sample chapter(s), and a prospectus outlining the proposed length, illustrations, etc. **Payment:** Royalty, 5-10%.

UNIVERSITY OF ARIZONA PRESS

355 S Euclid Ave., Suite 103, Tucson, AZ 85719. 520-621-1441.
E-mail: szuter@uapress.arizona.edu. Web site: www.uapress.arizona.edu. Christine Szuter, Director/Editor-in Chief. **Description:** Scholarly and popular nonfiction: Arizona, American West, anthropology, archaeology, environmental science, geography, Latin America, Native Americans, natural history, space sciences, western and environmental history. **Proposal Process:** Query with outline, sample chapters, and current curriculum vitae or resume. **Payment:** Royalty. **Sample Titles:** *Science in the American Southwest: A Topical History* by George E. Webb; *Enduring Seeds: Native American Agriculture and Wild Plant Conservation* by Gary Paul Nabhan. **Contact:** Patti Hartmann or Yvonne Reineke, Acquiring Editors.

UNIVERSITY OF ARKANSAS PRESS

201 Ozark Ave., Fayetteville, AR 72701-1201. 479-575-3246.
E-mail: uaprinfo@cavern.uark.edu. Web site: www.uapress.com. Lawrence J. Malley, Director/Editor-in-Chief. **Description:** Scholarly nonfiction and poetry. **Proposal Process:** Send query with SASE. **Payment:** Royalty.

UNIVERSITY OF CALIFORNIA PRESS

2120 Berkeley Way, Berkeley, CA 94720. 510-642-4247.
E-mail: askucp@ucpress.edu. Web site: www.ucpress.edu. Lynne Withey, Director. **Description:** Scholarly and general-interest books in the fields of anthropology, art, art history, Asian studies, California natural history guides, classics, co-publications, film, food studies, history, Mark Twain series, Middle Eastern studies, music, poetry, public health, religion, regional studies, and sociology. **Proposal Process:** Send letter of introduction, curriculum vitae, TOC, and sample chapter. Proposals via e-mail or phone not accepted. **Sample Titles:** *Safe Food* by Marion Nestle; *Pathologies of Power* by Paul Farmer; *Winslow Homer* by Elizabeth Johns.

UNIVERSITY OF CHICAGO PRESS

1427 E 60th St., Chicago, IL 60637-2954. 773-702-7700.
Web site: www.press.uchicago.edu. **Description:** Scholarly, nonfiction, advanced texts, monographs, clothbound and paperback, reference books.

UNIVERSITY OF GEORGIA PRESS

330 Research Dr., Athens, GA 30602-4901. 706-369-6130.
E-mail: books@ugapress.uga.edu. Web site: www.ugapress.org. Nicole Mitchell, Director. **Description:** Scholarly and creative nonfiction with particular interests in Southern and American history and literature, environment/natural history, multicultural studies, women's studies, civil rights, folklore, biography/memoir, life sciences, pop culture, and regional topics. **Proposal Process:** Query with outline, sample chapters, and curriculum vitae. Responds in 1 month. **Sample Titles:** *The Lonely Hunter: A Biography of Carson McCullers* by Virginia Spencer Carr; *Beyond Atlanta: The Struggle for Racial Equality in Georgia, 1940-1980* by Stephen G.N. Tuck.

UNIVERSITY OF HAWAII PRESS

2840 Kolowalu St., Honolulu, HI 96822. 808-956-8694.
Web site: www.hawaii.edu/uhpress. Patricia Crosby, Pam Kelly, Keith Leber, Masako Ikeda, Editors. **Description:** Scholarly books on Asian, Southeast Asian, Asian American, Hawaiian and Pacific studies from disciplines as diverse as the arts, history, language, literature, natural science, philosophy, religion, and the social sciences. **Proposal Process:** Query with outline and sample chapters. **Payment:** Royalty.

UNIVERSITY OF ILLINOIS PRESS

1325 S Oak St., Champaign, IL 61820-6903. 217-333-0950.
E-mail: uipress@uiuc.edu. Web site: www.press.uillinois.edu. Willis G. Regier, Director/Editor-in-Chief. **Description:** Scholarly and regional nonfiction. **Proposal Process:** Query with cover letter, TOC, 1-2 sample chapters, and curriculum vitae. Does not accept simultaneous submissions. Responds in 3 weeks. **Payment:** Royalty. **Sample Titles:** *Art and Freedom* by E.E. Sleinis; *Contesting Identities: Sports in American Film* by Aaron Baker.

UNIVERSITY OF IOWA PRESS

119 W Park Rd., 100 Kuhl House, Iowa City, IA 52242-1000. 319-335-2000.
E-mail: holly-carver@uiowa.edu. Web site: www.uiowapress.org. Holly Carver, Director. **Description:** Scholarly nonfiction in the areas of poetry/literature, biography/memoir, theatre, archaeology/anthropology, Americana, natural history, and regional topics related to midwestern life and culture. **Payment:** Accepts book proposals from recognized experts. Send 300-500 word description of book, TOC, curriculum vitae, and market analysis. Responds in 5-6 weeks. **Sample Titles:** *Birth: A Literary Companion* by Kristin Kovacic and Lynne Barrett.

UNIVERSITY OF MASSACHUSETTS PRESS

P.O. Box 429, Amherst, MA 01004-0429. 413-545-2217.
E-mail: wilcox@umpress.umass.edu. Web site: www.umass.edu/umpress. Bruce Wilcox, Director. **Description:** Scholarly and general-interest books. Also material in African-American studies, American studies, architecture and environmental design. **Proposal Process:** Query with SASE.

UNIVERSITY OF MINNESOTA PRESS

111 Third Ave. S, Suite 290, Minneapolis, MN 55401-2520. 612-627-1970. Web site: www.upress.umn.edu. Doug Armato, Editorial Director. **Description:** Nonprofit publisher of selected general-interest books and academic books for scholars. Areas of emphasis include American studies, anthropology, art and aesthetics, cultural theory, film and media studies, gay/lesbian studies, geography, literary theory, political and social theory, race and ethnic studies, sociology and urban studies. Does not accept original fiction or poetry. **Books Statistics:** 110 titles/yr; 50% by first-time authors; 99% unagented. **Proposal Process:** Query with outline, detailed prospectus or introduction, TOC, sample chapter, and resume. Considers simultaneous queries, but not e-queries. Responds in 4-6 weeks. **Payment:** Royalty, 6-10% net. **Sample Titles:** *Inside the Ropes with Jesse Ventura* by Tom Hauser; *Harmful to Minors: Protecting Children from Sex* by Judith Levine; *Screenstyle: Fashion and Femininity in 1930's Hollywood* by Sarah Berry. **Tips:** "The Press maintains a long-standing commitment to publishing books that focus on Minnesota and the Upper Midwest, including regional nonfiction, history, and natural science."

UNIVERSITY OF MISSOURI PRESS

2910 LeMone Blvd., Columbia, MO 65201-8227. 573-882-7641. E-mail: upress@umsystem.edu. Web site: www.system.missouri.edu/upress. Beverly Jarrett, Clair Willcox, Acquisitions. **Description:** Scholarly books on American and European history; American, British, and Latin American literary criticism; political philosophy; intellectual history; regional studies; and short fiction.

UNIVERSITY OF NEBRASKA PRESS

233 N Eighth St., Lincoln, NE 68588. 402-472-3581. E-mail: lrandolph1@unl.edu. Web site: www.nebraskapress.unl.edu. Gary Dunham, Editor-in-Chief. **Description:** Scholarly and trade nonfiction in a wide range of areas including agriculture, Native studies, history, literature, music, sports history, political science, and multicultural studies. Also publishes titles on regional topics about the culture and history of the Great Plains and the American West. **Books Statistics:** 90 titles/yr; 20% first-time authors; 75% unagented authors. **Proposal Process:** Query with outline, sample chapters, and SASE. Accepts e-queries. No unsolicited mss; no simultaneous queries. **Payment:** Royalty. **Sample Titles:** *Monte Walsh* by Jack Schaefer; *Local Wonders: Seasons in the Bohemian Alps* by Ted Kooser; *Standing Up to the Rock* by Louise Freeman Toole. **Tips:** Does not accept poetry, fiction, or children's books. **Contact:** Ladette Randolph, Senior Editor.

UNIVERSITY OF NEVADA PRESS

MS 166, Reno, NV 89557. 775-784-6573. Web site: www.nvbooks.nevada.edu. Joanne O'Hare, Editor-in-Chief. **Description:** Publishes fiction, nonfiction, and poetry. Nonfiction topics include environmental studies, geography, anthropology, history, biography, natural history, regional (Nevada and the West), mining, gaming, and Basque studies. **Proposal Process:** Query first, with outline or TOC, synopsis, sample chapter, estimated length, completion date of manuscript, and resume. **Payment:** Royalty.

UNIVERSITY OF NEW MEXICO PRESS

1720 Lomas Blvd. NE, Albuquerque, NM 87131. 505-277-2346.
E-mail: unmpress@unm.edu. Web site: www.unmpress.com. Luther Wilson, Director. **Description:** Scholarly nonfiction on social and cultural anthropology, archaeology, Western history, art, and photography. **Proposal Process:** Query. **Payment:** Royalty.

UNIVERSITY OF NORTH CAROLINA PRESS

P.O. Box 2288, Chapel Hill, NC 27515-2288. 919-966-3561.
E-mail: uncpress@unc.edu. Web site: www.uncpress.unc.edu. David Perry, Editor-in-Chief. **Description:** General-interest books (75,000-125,000 words) on the lore, crafts, cooking, gardening, travel, and natural history of the Southeast. No fiction or poetry, or memoirs of living persons. **Proposal Process:** Query. **Payment:** Royalty.

UNIVERSITY OF NORTH TEXAS PRESS

P.O. Box 311336, Denton, TX 76203-1336. 940-565-2142.
Web site: www.unt.edu/untpress. Ronald Chrisman, Director. **Description:** Publishes titles on military history, Texas history, multicultural topics, and women's history. **Books Statistics:** 16 titles/yr (250 submissions); 95% unagented. **Proposal Process:** Query with sample chapters. Do not send complete manuscript. Accepts e-queries, but not simultaneous queries. Responds in 2 weeks. **Payment:** Royalty. **Sample Titles:** *The Light Crust Doughboys Are on the Air: Celebrating Seventy Years of Texas Music* by John Dempsey; *When Raccoons Fall Through Your Ceiling: The Handbook for Coexisting with Wildlife* by Andrea Lopez. **Tips:** "We prefer writing that has scholarly rigor, yet still appeals to a general audience. Avoid personal narrative, unless needed to make an analytical point. No memoirs. We prefer subjects of regional (Southwest) interest." **Contact:** Ronald Chrisman.

UNIVERSITY OF NOTRE DAME PRESS

310 Flanner Hall, Notre Dame, IN 46556. 219-631-6346.
Web site: www.undpress.nd.edu. Rebecca DeBoer, Executive Editor. **Description:** Academic books, hardcover and paperback; philosophy, Irish studies, literature, theology, international relations, sociology, and general interest.

UNIVERSITY OF OKLAHOMA PRESS

1005 Asp Ave., Norman, OK 73019-6051. 405-325-5111.
E-mail: cerankin@ou.edu. Web site: www.oupress.com. Charles E. Rankin, Associate Director/Editor-in-Chief. **Description:** Books, to 350 pages, on the history of the American West, Indians of the Americas, classical studies, literary criticism, natural history, women's studies, and Native American and Chicano literature. **Proposal Process:** Query. **Payment:** Royalty. **Sample Titles:** *Blood of the*

Prophets by Will Bagley; *Spain in the Southwest* by John Kessell; *Diminished Democracy* by Theda Skocpol.

UNIVERSITY OF PENNSYLVANIA PRESS
4200 Pine St., Philadelphia, PA 19104-4011. 215-898-6261.
E-mail: custserv@pobox.upenn.edu. Web site: www.upenn.edu/pennpress. Eric Halpern, Editor. **Description:** Scholarly nonfiction. **Proposal Process:** Query.

UNIVERSITY OF PITTSBURGH PRESS
3400 Forbes Ave., Pittsburgh, PA 15260. 412-383-2456.
Web site: www.pitt.edu/~press. Cynthia Miller, Director. **Description:** Scholarly nonfiction (philosophy of science, Latin American studies, political science, urban environmental history, culture, composition, and literacy).

UNIVERSITY OF TENNESSEE PRESS
Conference Center Bldg., Suite 110, Knoxville, TN 37996-4108. 865-974-3321,
E-mail: harrisj@utk.edu. Web site: www.utpress.org. Joyce Harrison, Acquisitions Editor. **Description:** Scholarly and general-interest titles in the areas of American studies: African-American studies, Appalachian studies, archaeology, architecture, Civil War studies, folklore, history, literary studies, material culture, and religion. Also publishes regional academic and trade books dealing with Appalachia, Tennessee, and the South. **Books Statistics:** 35-40 titles/yr; 99% unagented. **Proposal Process:** Query with SASE. Accepts simultaneous and electronic queries. **Payment:** Royalty. **Tips:** Scholarly treatment, unique contributions to scholarship. Readable style. Authors should avoid formatting their manuscripts (making them look like books).

UNIVERSITY OF TEXAS PRESS
P.O.Box 7819, Austin, TX 78713-7819. 512-232-7600.
E-mail: utpress@uts.cc.utexas.edu. Web site: www.utexas.edu/utpress. Theresa May, Editor-in-Chief. **Description:** Scholarly nonfiction in the areas of Latin American/Latino studies, Native American studies, anthropology, Texana, natural science and history, environmental studies, Classics, Middle Eastern studies, film and media studies, gender studies, Texas architecture, and photography/art. **Books Statistics:** 90-100 titles/yr (800 submissions); 5% by first-time authors; 98% unagented. **Proposal Process:** Query with proposal and SASE. Accepts simultaneous and electronic queries. Responds in 3 months. No phone calls. **Payment:** Royalty. **Tips:** No fiction (except occasional translation of literature, Latin American or Middle Eastern) or poetry. **Contact:** Allison Faust, Associate Editor.

UNIVERSITY OF TORONTO PRESS
10 St. Mary St., Suite 700, Toronto, Ontario M4Y 2W8 Canada. 416-978-2239.
E-mail: utpbooks@utpress.utoronto. Web site: www.utpress.utoronto.ca. Bill Harnum, Senior Vice-President . **Description:** Scholarly and general trade titles, and academic journals. Subjects include philosophy, social sciences, classical and

Medieval studies, language, literature and literary theory, gay and lesbian studies, religion, music, education, history, etc. **Books Statistics:** 140 titles/yr. **Proposal Process:** Submit query with outline and sample chapters. Accepts unsolicited manuscripts. **Sample Titles:** *Colour-Coded: A Legal History of Racism in Canada, 1900-1950* by Constance Backhouse; *On the Edge of Empire: Gender, Race, and the Making of British Columbia, 1849-1871* by Adele Perry.

UNIVERSITY OF UTAH PRESS
1795 E South Campus Dr., Rm. 101, Salt Lake City, UT 84112. 801-581-6771.
Web site: www.upress.utah.edu. Dawn Marano, Acquisitions Editor. **Description:** Scholarly nonfiction in anthropology/archaeology, linguistics, Mesoamerica, Native America, western history, and natural history. Also publishes Utah and regional guidebooks, nature writing, ecocriticism, and creative nonfiction relating to nature and the environment, and regional general-interest titles. **Proposal Process:** Submit curriculum vitae with either complete manuscript or book prospectus. **Payment:** Royalty. **Sample Titles:** *A Homeland in the West: Utah Jews Remember* by Eileen Hallet Stone; *The Aztec Tempo Mayor* by Antonio Serrato-Combe.

UNIVERSITY OF VIRGINIA PRESS
P.O. Box 400318, Charlottesville, VA 22904-4318. 434-924-1373.
E-mail: bz2v@virginia.edu. Web site: www.upress.virginia.edu. Boyd Zenner, Acquisitions Editor. **Description:** Generally scholarly nonfiction and regional general interest books with emphasis on history, literature and environmental studies. **Proposal Process:** Send 2-4 page narrative description stating book's purpose, intent, and audience, list of primary and secondary sources, chapter by chapter outline, estimated length, estimated schedule for completion, sample chapters, and updated curriculum vitae. **Sample Titles:** *An American Cutting Garden: A Primer for Growing Cut Flowers Where Summers Are Hot and Winters Are Cold* by Suzanne McIntire; *New England Silver and Silversmithing, 1620-1815* edited by Jeannine Falino and Gerald W.R. Ward.

UNIVERSITY OF WISCONSIN PRESS
1930 Monroe St., Fl. 3, Madison, WI 53711-2059. 608-263-1012.
E-mail: uniscpress@uwpress.wisc.edu. Web site: www.wisc.edu/wisconsinpress/. Raphael Kadushin, Acquisitions Editor. **Description:** Trade nonfiction (biography, natural history, poetry, social issues), scholarly nonfiction (anthropology, cinema, literature, rhetoric, multicultural studies, history, the environment, political science), and regional titles on the Midwest. **Books Statistics:** 80 titles/yr. **Proposal Process:** Submit formal book proposal with current curriculum vitae and list of 5 expert sources who could serve as potential readers. Be sure to address the essence or theme of manuscript along with intended audience and competing titles. **Sample Titles:** *Old World Wisconsin: Around Europe in the Badger State* by Fred L. Holmes; *Iran: From Religious Dispute to Revolution* by Michael M.J. Fischer. **Tips:** See Web site for specific guidelines.

UNIVERSITY PRESS OF COLORADO

5589 Arapahoe Ave., 206C, Boulder, CO 80303. 720-406-8849.
E-mail: sandy@upcolorado.com. Web site: www.upcolorado.com. Darrin Pratt, Editorial Director. **Description:** Scholarly nonfiction in archaeology, environmental studies, local interest titles, history of the American West, and mining history. **Books Statistics:** 16 titles/yr. **Proposal Process:** Query with outline and sample chapters. Accepts simultaneous and electronic queries. Prefers hard copy. **Sample Titles:** *Hiking Circuits in Rocky Mountain National Park* by Jack P. and Elizabeth D. Hailman; *Bats of the Rocky Mountain West: Natural History, Ecology, and Conservation* by Rick A. Adams. **Tips:** "We are currently not taking submissions for fiction, biographies, and memoirs." **Contact:** Sandy Crooms.

UNIVERSITY PRESS OF FLORIDA

15 NW 15th St., Gainesville, FL 32611-2079. 352-392-1351.
E-mail: mb@upf.com. Web site: www.upf.com. Meredith Morris-Babb, Editor-in-Chief. **Description:** Scholarly and general interest titles in archeology, anthropology, history, women's studies, literature, and regional topics. Does not accept fiction. **Books Statistics:** 80 titles/yr (800 submissions); 15% first-time authors; 95% unagented. **Proposal Process:** Query with outline, sample chapters, and SASE. Accepts simultaneous and electronic queries. Prefers hard copy. **Payment:** Royalty. **Sample Titles:** (History) *Colonial Plantations and Economy in Florida* edited by Jane G. Landers; (Archaeology) *Spanish Colonial Gold Coins in the Florida Collection* by Alan K. Craig; (General Interest) *Beyond Theme Parks: Exploring Central Florida* by Benjamin D. Brotemarkle.

UNIVERSITY PRESS OF KANSAS

2501 W 15th St., Lawrence, KS 66049-3905. 785-864-4154.
E-mail: upress@ku.edu. Web site: www.kansaspress.ku.edu. Michael Briggs, Editor-in-Chief. **Description:** General interest trade and academic books specializing in American history/culture, military history, legal studies, Western Americana, politics/presidential studies, and the Great Plains and Midwest regions. **Proposal Process:** Submit 500-2,500 word proposal outlining the thesis of the project, intended audience, overall significance, and methods of research. Include TOC and author bio with qualifications. Accepts proposals via e-mail, but not attached partial or complete manuscripts. **Sample Titles:** *The Modern American Presidency* by Lewis L. Gould; *In the Shadow of the Holocaust: Nazi Persecution of Jewish-Christian Germans* by James F. Tent.

UNIVERSITY PRESS OF KENTUCKY

663 S Limestone St., Lexington, KY 40508-4008. 606-257-8150.
E-mail: smwrin2@uky.edu. Web site: www.kentuckypress.com. Stephen Wrinn, Director. **Description:** Scholarly nonfiction in the areas of biography/memoir, environmental studies, medicine/health, folklore, history, literary criticism, military history, paranormal studies, and political science. Also publishes regional nonfiction related to Kentucky and the Ohio Valley, the Appalachians, and the South. **Proposal**

Process: Query with curriculum vitae, sample chapter, and SASE. **Sample Titles:** *Echoes of War: A Thousand Years of Military History in Popular Culture* by Michael C.C. Adams; *Haunted Houses and Family Ghosts of Kentucky* by Lynwood William Montell. **Tips:** Does not accept fiction, poetry, or drama.

UNIVERSITY PRESS OF MISSISSIPPI
3825 Ridgewood Rd., Jackson, MS 39211-6492. 601-432-6205.
E-mail: press@ihl.state.ms.us. Web site: www.upress.state.ms.us. Seetha Srinivasan. **Description:** Scholarly and trade titles in American literature, history, and culture, Southern studies, African-American, women's and American studies, pop culture, folklife, art/architecture, natural sciences, health, and other liberal arts.

UNIVERSITY PRESS OF NEW ENGLAND
One Court St., Suite 250, Lebanon, NH 03766. 603-448-1533.
E-mail: university.press@dartmouth.edu. Web site: www.upne.com. Phyllis Deutsch, Editor. **Description:** Nonfiction titles on nature and the environment, fiction of New England, Jewish studies, women's studies, American studies, and maritime studies. **Books Statistics:** 80 titles/yr (3,000 submissions); 30% by first-time authors; 80% unagented. **Proposal Process:** Send query. No simultaneous or electronic queries. Hard copy only. Responds in 3-6 months. **Payment:** Royalty, 0-10% net. **Sample Titles:** *The Bellstone: The Greek Sponge Divers of the Aegean* by Michael Kalafatas; *New England Weather, New England Climate* by Gregory A. Zielinski and Barry D. Keim; *The Jews of Prime Time* by David Zurawik. **Contact:** Ellen Wicklum, Editor; John Landrigan, Editor.

UPSTART BOOKS
P.O. Box 800, W5527 Hwy. 106, Fort Atkinson, WI 53538-0800. 920-563-9571.
Web site: www.highsmith.com. Matt Mulder, Publisher. **Description:** Publishes activity and curriculum resource books, 48-240 pages, for librarians and teachers of pre-K-12. Focuses on reading activities, Internet skills, library skills, and storytelling activity books. **Books Statistics:** 15 titles/yr (250 submissions); 30% by first-time authors; 100% unagented. **Proposal Process:** Query with outline and sample chapters. Accepts simultaneous and electronic queries accepted. Prefers hard copy. Responds in 1 month. **Payment:** Royalty. **Tips:** No books for children.

VAN DER PLAS PUBLICATIONS
1282 Seventh Ave., San Francisco, CA 94122. 415-665-8214.
E-mail: rob@vanderplas.net. Web site: www.vanderplas.net. Rob van der Plas, Publisher/Editor. **Description:** General and sports-related material on bikes/biking, golf, and baseball. **Sample Titles:** *Cycling for Profit: How to Make a Living With Your Bike* by Jim Gregory; *Lance Armstrong's Comeback from Cancer* by Samuel Abt; *Performance Cycling: The Scientific Way to Improve Your Cycling Performance* by Stuart Baird.

VANDAMERE PRESS

P.O. Box 17446, Clearwater, FL 33762. 727-556-0950.
Web site: www.vandamere.com. Arthur Brown, Publisher/Editor-in-Chief.
Description: History, biography, disability studies, health care issues, military, fiction, and the Nation's Capital for a national audience. **Books Statistics:** 10 titles/yr (2,500 submissions); 10% by first-time authors; 75% unagented. **Proposal Process:** Query with outline, sample chapters, and SASE. Simultaneous queries accepted. Does not accept material sent electronically or by registered/certified mail. Responds in 1-6 months. **Payment:** Royalty. **Sample Titles:** (regional) *Two Hundred Years: Stories of the Nation's Capital* by Jeanne Fogle; (History) *Americans Behind the Barbed Wire: WWII Inside a German Prison Camp* by J. Frank Diggs; (Disability) *Black Bird Fly Away: Disabled in an Able-Bodied World* by Hugh Gregory Gallagher.

VELOPRESS

1830 N 55th St., Boulder, CO 80301. 303-440-0601.
E-mail: velopress@7dogs.com. Web site: www.velopress.com. **Description:** Books for cyclists and multi-sport athletes. **Sample Titles:** *Tour de France 2002: The Official Guide* by Jacques Augendre; *Inside Triathlon Training Diary* by Joe Friel; *Eddy Merckx: The Greatest Cyclist of the 20th Century* by Rik Vanwalleghem.

VERSO

180 Varick St., Fl. 10, New York, NY 10014. 212-807-9680.
E-mail: versony@versobooks.com. Web site: www.versobooks.com. **Description:** Books with a radical or leftist perspective on topics in the social sciences, humanities, and politics. **Proposal Process:** Submit proposal with short overview of book's main themes, TOC, brief bio of author/contributors, target markets, potential competitors, and intended timetable. Limit proposal to 10 pages; do not send complete manuscript. Include SASE for response. **Sample Titles:** *Cultural Resistance Reader* edited by Stephen Duncombe; *Legalize This! The Case for Decriminalizing Drugs* by Douglas Husak; *Banking on Death: Or, Investing in Life: The History and Future of Pensions* by Robin Blackburn.

VIKING

The Penguin Group/Penguin Putnam Inc.
375 Hudson St., New York, NY 10014. 212-366-2000.
Web site: www.penguinputnam.com. Paul Slovak, Vice President/Publisher.
Description: Fiction and nonfiction, including psychology, sociology, child-rearing and development, cookbooks, sports, and popular culture. **Proposal Process:** Query with SASE. **Payment:** Royalty. **Sample Titles:** (Nonfiction) *Bamboozled at the Revolution: How Big Media Lost Billions in the Battle for the Internet* by John Motavalli; (Fiction) *Women About Town* by Laura Jacobs.

VINTAGE ANCHOR PUBLISHING

Knopf Publishing Group/Random House, Inc.

1745 Broadway, New York, NY 10019. 212-782-9000.

Web site: www.randomhouse.com. Martin Asher, Editor-in-Chief. **Description:** Adult trade paperbacks and reprints. Quality fiction, serious nonfiction, multicultural, sociology, psychology, philosophy, women's interest, etc. Includes Anchor Books and Vintage Books imprints. **Books Statistics:** 200 titles/yr (700 queries/yr); 5% by first-time authors; 0% unagented. **Proposal Process:** Accepts submissions from literary agents only. **Sample Titles:** (Nonfiction) *The Beauty of the Husband: A Fictional Essay in 29 Tangos* by Anne Carson; (Fiction) *On the Yankee Station* by William Boyd.

VITAL HEALTH PUBLISHING

P.O. Box 152, Ridgefield, CT 06877. 203-894-1882.

E-mail: info@vitalhealth.net. Web site: www.vitalhealth.net. David Richard, Publisher. **Description:** Promotes health and wellness through books, videos, and other products that focus on the integration of mind, body, and spirit. **Sample Titles:** *Healthy Living: A Holistic Guide to Cleansing, Revitalization, and Nutrition* by Susana Lombardi; *Trace Your Genes* by Chris Reading, M.D.; *Energy for Life: How to Overcome Chronic Fatigue* by George L. Redmond, Ph.D., N.D.

VOYAGEUR PRESS

123 N Second St., Stillwater, MN 55082. 651-430-2210.

E-mail: mdregni@voyageurpress.com. Web site: www.voyageurpress.com. Michael Dregni, Editorial Director. **Description:** Books, 15,000-100,000 words, on nature and the environment, country living and farm heritage, travel and photography, and regional history. "Photography—contemporary and/or historical—is very important for most of our books." **Proposal Process:** Query with outline and sample chapters. See guidelines. **Payment:** Royalty.

WALKER AND COMPANY

435 Hudson St., Fl. 8, New York, NY 10014. 212-727-8300.

Web site: www.walkerbooks.com. **Description:** Adult nonfiction on history, science, math, technology, biography, and health. Also books for young readers (picture books, middle grade fiction, YA novels). **Books Statistics:** 60 titles/yr; 5% by first-time authors. **Proposal Process:** Query with synopsis and SASE. Accepts simultaneous queries, but not e-queries. Prefers hard copy. **Payment:** Royalty. **Sample Titles:** (Adult Nonfiction) *Michelangelo & the Pope's Ceiling* by Ross King; *The Flying Books* by David Blatner; (Juvenile) *I.Q. Goes to School* by Mary Ann Fraser. **Tips:** No adult fiction, poetry, travel, photo books, or New Age. No juvenile fantasy, science fiction, series, folk tales, fairy tales, myths/legends, textbooks, novelties, or horror. **Contact:** Jacqueline Johnson (Adult Nonfiction), Emily Easton (Juvenile).

WARNER BOOKS

Time and Life Bldg.

1271 Avenue of the Americas, New York, NY 10020. 212-522-7200.

Web site: www.twbookmark.com. Maureen Egen, President. **Description:** Hardcover, trade paperback and mass market paperback, reprint and original, fiction and nonfiction, audio books and gift books. **Books Statistics:** 250 titles/yr. Publishes book 2 years after acceptance. **Payment:** Royalty. **Sample Titles:** *Land of the Living* by Nicci French; *amanda.bright@home* by Danielle Crittenden; *Native Dancer: The Grey Ghost* by John Eisenberg. **Tips:** Does not accept unsolicited manuscripts or proposals.

WARWICK PUBLISHING INC.

161 Frederick St., Suite 200, Toronto, Ontario M5A 4P3 Canada. 416-596-1555. E-mail: jennifer@warwickgp.com. Web site: www.warwickgp.com. **Description:** General-interest nonfiction with a focus on sports, food/wine, history, current events, art/architecture, photography, and personal finance. **Proposal Process:** Send query with brief outline/TOC, and SASE. Responds within 3 months. **Sample Titles:** *The World Cup of Hockey* by Joe Pelletier and Patrick Houda; *Icewine: The Complete Story* by John Schreiner. **Tips:** Does not accept proposals for fiction, poetry, drama, or children's picture books. **Contact:** Editor.

WASHINGTON STATE UNIVERSITY PRESS

P.O Box 045910, Pullman, WA 99164-5910. 800-354-7360. E-mail: wsupress@wsu.edu. Web site: www.wsupress.wsu.edu. Glen Lindeman, Editor. **Description:** Books on Northwest history, prehistory, natural history, culture and politics, 200-500 pages. Focus is on the greater Pacific Northwest region-Washington, Idaho, Oregon, western Montana, and Alaska. **Proposal Process:** Query. **Payment:** Royalty.

WASHINGTON WRITERS PUBLISHING HOUSE

P.O. Box 15271, Washington, DC 20003. **Description:** Poetry and fiction by writers in the greater Washington, D.C., and Baltimore area only. **Proposal Process:** Query with SASE. Guidelines available.

WATSON-GUPTILL PUBLICATIONS

770 Broadway, New York, NY 10003. 646-654-5000. E-mail: info@watsonguptill.com. Web site: www.watsonguptill.com. **Description:** Illustrated, nonfiction, instructional books on art, photography, graphic design, home decor, crafts, music, film, entertainment, performing arts, popular culture, architecture, and interior design. **Proposal Process:** Query to Editorial Department with proposal, detailed outline, author bio, sample text and artwork (no originals). No telephone or e-mail submissions or queries. Children's submissions: Nonfiction only, same categories as above. Include TOC and sample text. Send brief author bio and cover letter describing marketing considerations. Responds in 6-8 months. **Payment:** Royalty. **Tips:** "Demonstrate the need in the marketplace for your book." **Contact:** Editorial Department.

WAYNE STATE UNIVERSITY PRESS

4809 Woodward Ave., Detroit, MI 48201-1309.
Web site: wsupress.wayne.edu. Jane Hoehner, Director/Acquisitions. **Description:** Scholarly nonfiction in the areas of Judaica, African studies, film/television, folklore, literature (German and Renaissance), labor and urban studies, and speech language pathology. Also publishes regional titles on Michigan and the Great Lakes. **Books Statistics:** Approximately 50 titles/yr (150 submissions). **Proposal Process:** Send query with proposal, include SASE. Prefers hard copy. E-queries accepted. No simultaneous queries. **Sample Titles:** *Spirit Possession in Judaism* by Matt Goldish; *AIA Detroit: The American Institute of Architects Guide to Detroit Architecture* by Eric J. Hill and John Gallagher. **Tips:** No fiction. See Web site for details. **Contact:** Annie Marting, Assistant Acquisitions Editor.

WEISER BOOKS

Imprint of Red Wheel/Weiser, LLC
368 Congress St., Boston, MA 02210. 617-542-1324.
Web site: www.redwheelweiser.com. Ms. Pat Bryce, Editor. **Description:** Nonfiction titles on metaphysical topics such as Magic, Wicca, Tarot, Astrology, and Qabalah. **Proposal Process:** Submit outline, sample chapters, and 6½ x 9½-inch SASE. Hard copy only. Accepts simultaneous queries, but not e-queries. Responds in 3-6 months. **Payment:** Royalty. **Tips:** "Please visit our Web site for detailed submission guidelines. Before submitting any materials, please study our books in a bookstore, library, or publisher's catalog."

WESLEYAN UNIVERSITY PRESS

110 Mount Vernon St., Middletown, CT 06459-0433. 860-685-2420.
E-mail: tradko@wesleyan.edu. Web site: www.wesleyan.edu/wespress. Tom Radko, Director. **Description:** Scholarly press focusing on poetry, music, dance, performance arts, psychology, and science fiction. Also covers gay/lesbian, gender, cultural, regional, and American studies. **Books Statistics:** 40 titles/yr (1,500 submissions); 1% by first-time authors; 97% unagented. **Proposal Process:** Query with outline, sample chapters, and SASE. Accepts simultaneous and electronic queries. Prefers hard copy. Responds in 2-4 weeks. **Payment:** Royalty. **Tips:** Write for a complete catalog and submission guidelines. **Contact:** Suzanna Tamminen, Editor-in-Chief.

WESTCLIFFE PUBLISHERS

P.O. Box 1261, Englewood, CO 80150-1261. 303-935-0900.
E-mail: editor@westcliffepublishers.com. Web site: www.westcliffepublishers.com. Linda Doyle, Associate Publisher. **Description:** High-quality nature and landscape photography books, trail and travel guides, and books with regional focus. **Proposal Process:** Submit proposal with brief description of concept of book, TOC, sample chapter(s), bio/resume, and target market. **Sample Titles:** *Colorado Caves: Hidden Worlds Beneath the Peaks* by Richard J. Rhinehart; *Arizona's Best Wildflower Hikes: The Desert* by Christine Maxa; *Montana and Idaho's Continental Divide Trail* by Lynna and Leland Howard. **Contact:** Managing Editor.

WESTERN EDGE PRESS/SHERMAN ASHER PUBLISHING

P.O. Box 31725, Santa Fe, NM 87501. 505-988-7214.
E-mail: westernedge@santa-fe.net. Web site: www.shermanasher.com. Jim Mafchir, Publisher. **Description:** Small press publishing nonfiction (Jewish studies, Southwest studies, cats and humor, art, Latin American studies, literature, craft of writing, Northern New Mexico Hispanic and Pueblo culture, and erotica); poetry (collections and anthologies); and memoirs. Also publishes in bilingual format. **Books Statistics:** 4-8 titles/yr; 0% by first-time authors; 100% unagented. **Proposal Process:** Send query with outline, credentials, and no more than 50 pages of sample text, include SASE. E-mail queries accepted, but should be brief and should not contain attachments. Does not accept any unsolicited manuscripts. Responds in 3 months. **Payment:** Varies per project/author. **Sample Titles:** (Nonfiction) *Invisible Dreamer: Memory, Judaism, and Human Rights* by Marjorie Agosin; *Found Tribe: Jewish Coming Out Stories* edited by Lawrence Schimel. (Humor) *Vanity in Washington* by Peggy VanHulsteyn. (Poetry) *Written with a Spoon: A Poet's Cookbook* edited by Nancy Fay and Judith Rafaela. **Tips:** Currently not accepting poetry; send queries for nonfiction only.

WESTVIEW PRESS

Perseus Book Group
5500 Central Ave., Boulder, CO 80301. 303-444-3541.
E-mail: wvproposal@perseusbooks.com. Web site: www.westviewpress.com. **Description:** Academic, professional and reference books in the social sciences, humanities, and science. **Books Statistics:** 100 titles/yr. **Proposal Process:** Send query via e-mail. **Sample Titles:** *Blood Diamonds: Tracing the Deadly Path of the World's Most Precious Stones* by Greg Campbell; *A Delicate Balance: What Philosophy Can Tell Us About Terrorism* by Trudy Govier; *Kitchen Table Entrepreneurs: How Eleven Women Escaped Poverty and Became Their Own Bosses* by Martha Shirk and Anna Wadia.

WESTWINDS PRESS

Graphic Arts Center Publishing Co.
P.O. Box 10306, Portland, OR 97296-0306. 503-226-2402.
E-mail: tricia@gacpc.com. Web site: www.gacpc.com. Tricia Brown, Acquisitions Editor. **Description:** Regional nonfiction about the western United States for a general audience. Specializes in history, natural history, biography/memoir, travel, guidebooks, factbooks, cooking, and children's books. **Books Statistics:** 5-7 titles/yr (100 submissions); 10% by first-time authors; 90% unagented. **Proposal Process:** Send cover letter, complete outline with ideas for photos/illustrations, TOC, author bio with examples of previous publications, market analysis, photocopies or slides of artwork, and SASE. Responds in 6 months. **Payment:** Royalty (10-12% net). **Sample Titles:** *The Hidden Coast: Coastal Adventures from Alaska to Mexico* by Joel Rogers; *The Great Northwest Nature Factbook: A Guide to the Region's Remarkable Animals, Plants & Natural Features* by Susan Ewing. **Tips:** "Avoid poetry, adult fiction, and native 'legend' written by non-Native Americans.

Children's book authors should avoid partnering with an illustrator before submission has been accepted."

WHITE CLOUD PRESS
P.O. Box 3400, Ashland, OR 97520. 541-488-6415.
E-mail: sscholl@jeffnet.org. Web site: www.whitecloudpress.com. Steven Scholl, Publisher. **Description:** Nonfiction on religion, current events, travel, memoirs, and mythology. **Sample Titles:** *The Unlimited Mercifier* by S. Hirtenstein; *The Garden of Life* by Stephen Mason.

WHITECAP BOOKS
351 Lynn Ave., North Vancouver, British Columbia V7J 2C4 Canada. 604-980-9852. E-mail: whitecap@whitecap.ca. Web site: www.whitecap.ca. Robert McCullough, Publisher; Leanne McDonald, Rights/Acquisitions. **Description:** Juvenile fiction and nonfiction (nature-oriented), 32-84 pages. Also publishes adult books, varying lengths, on gardening, cookery, and regional subjects. **Proposal Process:** Query with TOC, synopsis, and 1 sample chapter. **Payment:** Royalty and flat fee. **Tips:** "Please visit our Web site to view our current catalog and submission guidelines."

WHITSTON PUBLISHING COMPANY
1717 Central Ave., Suite 201, Albany, NY 12205. 518-452-1900.
E-mail: whitston@capital.net. Web site: www.whitston.com. Michael Laddin, Editor. **Description:** Publishes nonfiction, scholarly, reference, indexes, literary criticism, and anthologies. **Books Statistics:** 20 titles/yr (200 submissions); 100% unagented. **Proposal Process:** Query with outline, sample chapters or complete manuscript, and SASE. No simultaneous or electronic queries. Hard copy only. Responds in 3-12 months. **Payment:** Royalty. **Sample Titles:** *Hustlers, Heroes & Hooligans* by Dan Lynch; *Mark Twain and His Illustrators: Volume II (1875-1883)* by Beverly R. David.

WILDCAT CANYON PRESS
2716 Ninth St., Berkeley, CA 94710. 510-848-3600.
E-mail: info@wildcatcanyon.com. Web site: www.wildcatcanyon.com. **Description:** Books on relationships, fashion, self-care, and parenting.

WILDERNESS PRESS
1200 Fifth St., Berkeley, CA 94710. 510-558-1666.
E-mail: mail@wildernesspress.com. Web site: www.wildernesspress.com. Jannie Dresser, Managing Editor. **Description:** Nonfiction books about outdoor activities and travel. **Books Statistics:** 12 titles/yr (250 submissions); 25% by first-time authors; 90% unagented. **Proposal Process:** Query with outline and SASE. Considers simultaneous and electronic queries. Prefers either electronic or hard copy. **Payment:** Royalty, typical is 10-12% of net. No flat fee.

JOHN WILEY & SONS, INC.

111 River St., Hoboken, NJ 07030. 201-748-6000.
E-mail: info@wiley.com. Web site: www.wiley.com. Gerard Helferich, Publisher, General Interest Books. **Description:** History, biography, memoir, popular science, health, self-improvement, reference, African American, narrative nonfiction, business, computers, cooking, architecture/graphic design, and children's nonfiction. **Books Statistics:** 1,500 titles/yr. **Proposal Process:** Query with outline. Prefers electronic format. Simultaneous queries accepted. Responds in 2-4 weeks. **Payment:** Royalty, range varies. **Sample Titles:** (Adult) *The Inextinguishable Symphony: A True Story of Love and Music in Nazi Germany* by Martin Goldsmith; *The Power of Gold: The History of an Obsession* by Peter L. Bernstein; *Splendid Soups* by James Peterson. (Children's) *New York Public Library Amazing Explorers* by Brendon January; *Revolutionary War Days* by David C. King.

WILEY/HALSTED

John Wiley & Sons, Inc.
111 River St., Hoboken, NJ 07030. 201-748-6000.
E-mail: info@wiley.com. **Description:** Publishes textbooks, educational materials, and reference books **Proposal Process:** Query. **Payment:** Royalty.

WILLOW CREEK PRESS

P.O. Box 147, Minocqua, WI 54548. 715-358-7010.
E-mail: books@willowcreekpress.com. Web site: www.willowcreekpress.com. Andrea Donner, Editor. **Description:** Trade nonfiction on outdoor sports/travel, wildlife, pets (dogs, cats, horses), gardening, food/wine, and other general-interest topics. **Books Statistics:** 20 titles/yr; 30% by first-time authors; 80% unagented. **Proposal Process:** Prefers to see detailed outline, sample chapter, and SASE instead of general query. Accepts simultaneous queries, but not e-queries. Responds in 4-6 weeks. **Payment:** Royalty. **Sample Titles:** *What Dogs Teach Us* by Glenn Droomgoole; *Garden Birds of America* by George H. Harrison; *Keller's Outdoor Survival Guide* by William Keller. **Tips:** "Avoid long letters explaining your work and what will be written; let the writing speak for itself."

WILSHIRE BOOK CO.

12015 Sherman Rd., North Hollywood, CA 91605-3781. 818-765-8579.
E-mail: mpowers@mpowers.com. Web site: www.mpowers.com. Melvin Powers, Publisher. **Description:** Nonfiction titles, from 50,000 words, on self-help, motivation/inspiration, recovery, psychology, personal success, entrepreneurship, humor, Internet marketing, mail order, horsemanship. Also publishes some fictional allegories, from 25,000 words, that teach principles of psychological growth or offer guidance in living. **Books Statistics:** 25 titles/yr (2,000 submissions); 80% by first-time authors; 75% unagented. **Proposal Process:** Query with SASE or submit outline, 3 sample chapters, author bio, or market analysis. **Payment:** Royalty and advance. **Sample Titles:** *The Princess Who Believed in Fairy Tales* by Marcia Grad; *The*

Knight in Rusty Armor by Robert Fisher; *Think & Grow Rich* by Napoleon Hill. **Tips:** "We suggest that you read successful books to discover what elements make them winners. Use those elements in your own style, using a creative approach and fresh material."

WINDSWEPT HOUSE PUBLISHERS

P.O. Box 159, Mount Desert, ME 04660. 207-244-5027.
E-mail: windswt@acadia.net. Web site: www.booknotes.com/windswept. Mavis Weinberger, Acquisitions Editor. **Description:** Adult and children's books (all ages), mostly relating to the Maine/New England region: novels, poetry, nature, history. **Books Statistics:** 4 titles/yr. **Proposal Process:** No unsolicited manuscripts. Send SASE for guidelines. **Payment:** Royalty, to 10%. No flat fee. **Tips:** Children's books needing pictures should come complete with illustrations.

THE WINE APPRECIATION GUILD LTD.

360 Swift Ave., South San Francisco, CA 94080. 415-866-3020.
E-mail: info@wineappreciation.com. Web site: www.wineappreciation.com. **Description:** Publishes books on wine.

WOODBINE HOUSE

6510 Bells Mill Rd., Bethesda, MD 20817. 301-897-3570.
E-mail: info@woodbinehouse.com. Web site: www.woodbinehouse.com. Nancy Gray Paul, Acquisitions Editor. **Description:** Publishes books for or about children with disabilities only. Current needs include parenting, reference, special education, and high-low books. **Proposal Process:** Query or submit complete manuscript with SASE. See guidelines. **Payment:** Royalty.

WORDWARE PUBLISHING

2320 Los Rio Blvd., Suite 200, Plano, TX 75074. 972-423-0090.
E-mail: gbivona@wordware.com. Web site: www.republicoftexaspress.com. Ginnie Bivona, Acquisitions Editor. **Description:** Publishes books related to Texas, history, ghost stories, humor, travel guides, and general-interest topics. No fiction or poetry. **Books Statistics:** 30 titles/yr (100+ submissions); 50% by first-time authors; 90% unagented. **Proposal Process:** Query with outline and SASE. Accepts simultaneous and electronic queries. Prefers hard copy. **Payment:** Royalty. **Sample Titles:** (Nonfiction) *Texas Money: All the Law Allows* by Mona D. Sizer; *Ghosts of North Texas* by Mitchel Whitington; (Children's) *Real Kids, Real Adventures in Texas* by Deborah Morris. **Tips:** "We are looking for interesting, entertaining books for the mainstream reader. We do not publish family memoirs unless they are famous, or better yet, infamous."

WORKMAN PUBLISHING CO., INC.

708 Broadway, New York, NY 10003-9555. 212-254-5900.
E-mail: info@workman.com. Web site: www.workman.com. Susan Bolotin, Editorial Director. **Description:** Nonfiction and calendars for adult and juvenile markets.

Books Statistics: 40 titles/yr. **Proposal Process:** Query with outline, sample chapters, and SASE. Considers simultaneous queries, but not e-queries. Hard copy only. Response time varies. **Payment:** Royalty or flat fee, range varies. **Sample Titles:** *Heal Your Headache* by David Buchholz, M.D.; *Antiques Roadshow Primer* by Carol Prisant. **Tips:** See Web site for details.

WORLD LEISURE CORPORATION
177 Paris St., Boston, MA 02128. 617-569-1966.
E-mail: editor@worldleisure.com. Web site: www.worldleisure.com. **Description:** Publishes nonfiction titles in the areas of travel and downhill skiing/snowboarding. Also publishes gift books. **Sample Titles:** *Great Nature Vacations with Your Kids* by Dorothy Jordan; *All-Terrain Skiing: Body Mechanics and Balance from Powder to Ice* by Dan Egan.

WORLDWIDE LIBRARY
Harlequin Enterprises, Ltd.
225 Duncan Mill Rd., Don Mills, Ontario M3B 3K9 Canada. 416-445-5860.
E-mail: feroze_mohammed@harlequin.ca. Feroze Mohammed, Senior Editor.
Description: Action adventure, paramilitary adventure, science fiction, and post-nuclear holocaust fiction. Imprints: Gold Eagle Books, Worldwide Mystery. **Books Statistics:** 36 titles/yr; 1% by first-time authors; 99% unagented. **Proposal Process:** Query with outline and sample chapters. Accepts simultaneous queries, but not e-queries. Hard copy only. Responds in 3 months. **Payment:** Flat fee. Typical range: $3,000-$6,000.

YALE UNIVERSITY PRESS
302 Temple St., New Haven, CT 06520-9040. 203-432-0960.
Web site: www.yale.edu/yup/. Jonathon Brent, Editorial Director. **Description:** Publishes scholarly texts and general-interest nonfiction. **Books Statistics:** 250 titles/yr; 15% by first-time authors; 85% unagented. **Proposal Process:** Send cover letter, prospectus, and curriculum vitae. If available, send TOC, a sample chapter, estimated length and intended audience, and accompanying artwork. Does not accept unsolicited manuscripts. **Payment:** Royalty. **Sample Titles:** *Why Terrorism Works* by Alan M. Dershowitz; *Benjamin Franklin* by Edmund S. Morgan; *New York: Capital of Photography* by Max Kozloff. **Contact:** Gretchen Ring, Assistant.

YANKEE PUBLISHING INC.
P.O. Box 520, Dublin, NH 03444. 603-563-8111.
E-mail: queries@yankeepub.com. Web site: www.almanac.com. Judson D. Hale, Sr., Editor-in-Chief. **Description:** Publishes *The Old Farmer's Almanac*.

YMAA
4354 Washington St., Roslindale, MA 02131. 617-323-7215.
E-mail: ymaa@aol.com. Web site: www.ymaa.com. **Description:** Nonfiction titles on Asian healing, health, spirituality, and martial art disciplines. **Sample Titles:** *Taiji*

Sword, Classical Yang Style by Dr. Yang, Jwing-Ming; *Inside Tai Chi: Hints, Tips, Training and Process for Students and Teachers* by John Loupos.

ZEPHYR PRESS

50 Kenwood #1, Brookline, MA 02445. 617-713-2813.
E-mail: editor@zephyrpress.org. Web site: www.zephyrpress.org. Christopher Mattison, Managing Editor. **Description:** Independent publisher of literature in English translation and contemporary English-language poetry. **Books Statistics:** 9 titles/yr (100 submissions); 40% by first-time authors; 100% unagented. **Proposal Process:** Submit sample chapters. Considers simultaneous queries **Payment:** Royalty 7%. **Sample Titles:** *The Boy Who Catches Wasps* by Duo Duo; *Salute—To Singing* by Gennady Aygi; *Courting Laura Providencia* by Jack Pulaski.

ZOO PRESS

P.O. Box 22990, Lincoln, NE 68542. 402-770-8104.
E-mail: editors@zoopress.org. Web site: www.zoopress.org. **Description:** A literary press, seeking work "that displays quality—originality, formal integrity, rhetorical variety, authenticity, and aesthetic beauty." **Books Statistics:** 10 titles/yr. **Proposal Process:** See Web site for guidelines. **Tips:** Publishes heavily from submissions to annual contests: The Paris Review Prize (poetry), The Kenyon Review Prize (poetry, for first book), and The Zoo Press Prizes (short fiction and novel).

JUVENILE BOOKS

Children's book publishing is big business, and getting bigger. With the blockbuster sales of the *Harry Potter* series by author J.K. Rowling, writing children's books has once again been shown to be a legitimate avenue to literary fame and, on occasion, fortune. In fact, curiously, some studies suggest that many children's books are sold to adults who intend to keep the books for themselves, making the question of what makes a children's book hit the bestseller lists an interesting one. For instance, the Dr. Seuss book, *Oh, The Places You'll Go!*, is a perennial favorite as a college graduation gift, although the sales show up in the children's book category.

The market for juvenile books is very diverse. Children's books range from colorful board books for toddlers to social-realism novels for young adults on subjects that just a few decades ago were taboo. Many books are issued in series, while others are released as stand-alone titles.

However, as in all areas of publishing, while there is tremendous diversity across the field, there is also increasing specialization by individual publishers. Each seeks to find its own profitable niche within that broad expanse of interest.

Before sending off materials, it is important to study each publisher under consideration very carefully. Start by getting a copy of their guidelines for author queries and submissions; often these can be found on their Web site. Also, request a catalog.

The publisher's catalog is one of the best vehicles to understand precisely the kind of books a publisher is acquiring. A marketing tool, a publisher's catalog reveals the special appeal that each book holds for the publisher and—it hopes—for bookstore buyers, librarians, and many eventual readers. A publisher's catalog tells how each book is different from (or similar to) others in the field. Reading a catalog carefully can help you understand clearly the kind of books a publisher is seeking.

As always, before you send a query letter or other materials, you may wish to get the name of the current editor at the publishing house who is in charge of the particular line or type of book that you are proposing. If this information is not available on the Web site, make a very brief phone call. Explain your project in just one or two sentences, ask whom to send the query (or manuscript) to, confirm the address, and then thank the receptionist and hang up. Do not try to harangue an editor or pitch your proposal on the phone; a busy editor seldom has time to listen to your idea, and you will not be as convincing as you can be by presenting a professional, well-written query that can be studied in leisure. Trying to pitch an idea on the phone is usually just the best way to annoy an editor.

Be polite, be professional, and remember to target your writing, making sure the language, style, and content are appropriate to your target readers.

ABBEVILLE PUBLISHING GROUP

116 W 23rd St., Suite 500, New York, NY 10011. 646-375-2039.
E-mail: abbeville@abbeville.com. Web site: www.abbeville.com. **Description:** Fine art and illustrated books on art/architecture, children's, decorative arts, design, music/media, animals, sports, gardening, travel, etc. **Proposal Process:** Does not accept unsolicited submissions or proposals.

ABDO PUBLISHING

Subsidiary of Abdo Consulting Group, Inc.
4940 Viking Dr., Suite 622, Edina, MN 55435. 612-831-1317.
E-mail: info@abdopub.com. Web site: www.abdopub.com. Paul Abdo, Editor-in-Chief. **Description:** Nonfiction material for children in grades pre-K through 8. Topics include biography, history, geography, science, social studies, and sports. **Books Statistics:** 200 titles/yr. **Proposal Process:** Send resume via e-mail. Does not accept unsolicited manuscripts. **Sample Titles:** Cats Series by Stuart A. Kallen; *Oceans & Seas* by Kate A. Furlong; *Holidays* by Julie Murray.

ACCORD PUBLISHING LTD.

1732 Wazee St., Suite 202, Denver, CO 80202-1284. 303-298-1300.
Web site: www.accordpublishing.com. Ken Fleck, Editor. **Description:** Children's books, calendars, and educational materials.

ADVANCE PUBLISHING

6950 Fulton St., Houston, TX 77022. 713-695-0600.
E-mail: info@advancepublishing.com. Web site: www.advancepublishing.com.
Description: Children's picture books, junior biographies, and educational texts and materials.

ALL ABOUT KIDS PUBLISHING

6280 San Ignacio Ave., Suite D, San Jose, CA 95119. 408-578-4026.
E-mail: mail@aakp.com. Web site: www.aakp.com. Linda Guevara, Editor.
Description: Publishes picture books, board books, chapter books, educational books, and how-to books. **Books Statistics:** 12 titles/yr. **Proposal Process:** Currently not accepting queries or submissions. **Sample Titles:** *The Moon Smiles Down* by Tony Waters; *A My Name Is Andrew* by Mary McManus Burke; *Swim, Swam, Swum* by Roy Marsaw.

ATHENEUM BOOKS FOR YOUNG READERS

Simon & Schuster Children's Publishing/Simon & Schuster, Inc.
1230 Avenue of the Americas, New York, NY 10020. 212-698-7200.
Web site: www.simonsays.com. **Description:** Picture books, juvenile fiction, and nonfiction as well as illustrated collections for preschool to high-school age children. **Proposal Process:** Query with SASE. No unsolicited manuscripts. **Sample Titles:** *Olivia* by Ian Falconer; *The House of the Scorpion* by Nancy Farmer; *Dovey Coe* by Francis O'Rourk Dowell; *Beautiful Blackbird* by Ashley Bryan. **Contact:** Ginee Seo, Associate Publisher; Caitlyn Dlouhy, Executive Editor.

AVISSON PRESS, INC.

3007 Taliaferro Rd., Greensboro, NC 27408. 336-288-6989.
Martin L. Hester, Editor. **Description:** YA biography only. Special interest in women and minorities, but is open to any good subject matter. **Books Statistics:** 6-8 titles/yr

(750 submissions); 25% by first-time authors; 80% unagented. **Proposal Process:** Query with outline or sample chapter, bio and SASE. Accepts simultaneous queries, but not e-queries. Responds in 2 weeks. **Payment:** Royalty. **Sample Titles:** *Eight Who Made a Difference: Pioneer Women in the Arts* by Erica Stux; *Prince of the Fairway: The Tiger Woods Story* by Allison Teague. **Tips:** Some literary topics and books by assignment only.

BENCHMARK BOOKS
Marshall Cavendish
99 White Plains Rd., P.O. Box 2001, Tarrytown, NY 1059. 914-332-8888.
Web site: www.marshallcavendish.com. Michelle Bisson, Editorial Director.
Description: Nonfiction school and library books for children K-12. **Books Statistics:** 135 titles/yr; 5% by first-time authors; 75% unagented. **Proposal Process:** Send query, outline, sample chapters, and SASE. Accepts simultaneous queries, but not e-queries. **Payment:** Flat fee. **Tips:** Quality treatment of curriculum-related topics. Series only; no single titles.

BLACK BUTTERFLY CHILDREN'S BOOKS
Writers and Readers Publishing, Inc.
62 E Starrs Plain Rd., Danbury, CT 06810. 203-744-6010.
Deborah Dyson, Editor. **Description:** Titles featuring black children and other children of color, ages 9-13, for Young Beginners series. Picture books for children to age 11; board books for toddlers. **Proposal Process:** Send query with SASE. **Payment:** Royalty.

BLACKBIRCH PRESS
Imprint of The Gale Group
10911 Technology Place, San Diego, CA 92117.
Description: Nonfiction series publisher for primary and middle grade readers, 2,500-13,000 words. Innovative series include Made in the U.S.A., Triangle Histories, Giants of Science, and History's Villains. **Proposal Process:** Seeks experienced freelance writers for work-for-hire projects. Send query letter, resume, brief writing sample, and/or list of publications. No unsolicited manuscripts. **Payment:** Flat fee. **Contact:** Chandra Howard, Senior Acquisitions Editor.

BLOOMSBURY CHILDREN'S BOOKS
175 Fifth Ave., Suite 712, New York, NY 10010.
Web site: www.bloomsbury.com/usa/childrens. Victoria Wells Arms, Editorial Director. **Description:** Picture books, literary nonfiction, and YA fiction (fantasy, mysteries, and historical fiction). **Proposal Process:** Send complete manuscript for picture books, query with synopsis and 10 sample pages for longer works (both fiction and nonficton). Include SASE. Responds in 20 weeks. **Sample Titles:** *Polly's Picnic* by Richard Hamilton; *Goodnight Lulu* by Paulette Bogan.

THE BLUE SKY PRESS

Scholastic Inc.

557 Broadway, New York, NY 10012. 212-343-6100.

Web site: www.scholastic.com. Bonnie Verburg, Editorial Director. **Description:** Children's picture books and novels for ages 0-12. **Books Statistics:** 12 titles/yr; 0% by first-time authors; 0% unagented. **Proposal Process:** Query with SASE. Considers simultaneous queries. **Tips:** Limited market.

BOOKS FOR YOUNG READERS

Henry Holt and Company

115 West 18th St., New York, NY 10011.

E-mail: info@henryholt.com. Web site: www.henryholt.com/byr. **Description:** Publishes a wide variety of books for children of all ages including picture books, fiction, and nonfiction. **Tips:** Manuscript should be typed and double-spaced. Complete manuscripts preferred. Do not submit textbooks or manuscripts written by children. Query letter and SASE required. Do not send original art.

BOYDS MILLS PRESS

Highlights for Children

815 Church St., Honesdale, PA 18431. 570-253-1164.

E-mail: admin@boydsmilllspress.com. Web site: www.boydsmillspress.com. **Description:** Children's books of literary merit, from picture books to novels. **Books Statistics:** 50 titles/yr (8,500 submissions); 40% by first-time authors; 60% unagented. **Proposal Process:** Send outline and sample chapters for YA novels and nonfiction. Send complete manuscripts for all other categories. Hard-copy only. No simultaneous queries. Responds in 30 days. **Sample Titles:** *Girls* by Eve Bunting; *A Cold Snap* by Audrey B. Baird; *Volcanoes* by David L. Harrison. **Tips:** Varied literary fiction. Avoid well-worn themes; no series or romances.

CANDLEWICK PRESS

2067 Massachusetts Ave., Cambridge, MA 02140. 617-661-3330.

E-mail: bigbear@candlewick.com. Web site: www.candlewick.com. Karen Lotz, President/Publisher; Elizabeth Bicknell, Editorial Director/Associate Publisher. **Description:** Humorous and/or non-rhyming picture-book texts about universal childhood experiences for ages birth to 8. Also high-quality literary fiction for YA readers. **Proposal Process:** Currently not accepting unsolicited manuscripts. **Sample Titles:** *Guess How Much I Love You* by Sam McBratney and Anita Jeram.

CAPSTONE PRESS

151 Good Counsel Dr., P.O. Box 669, Mankato, MN 56002.

E-mail: freelance.writing@capstone-press.com. Web site: www.capstone-press.com. Helen Moore, Acquisitions Editor. **Description:** Nonfiction children's books for schools and libraries. Content includes curriculum-oriented topics, sports, and pleasure-reading materials. **Books Statistics:** 400 title/yr **Proposal Process:** Send resume and writing sample only; does not accept submissions or proposals. E-queries okay for potential assignments. Send either electronic or hard copy. Responds in 4-6 weeks. **Payment:** Flat fee. **Sample Titles:** (Grades 3-9) *Stealth Bombers: The B-2 Spirits* by Bill Sweetman. (Grades 2-6) *The Boyhood Diary of Charles Lindbergh* by Megan O'Hara. (Grades 1-5) *Greece* by Janet Rienecky. (Grades K-3) *Frogs: Leaping Amphibians* by Adele Richardson. **Tips:** "We do not accept fiction or poetry. We do hire freelance authors to write titles on assignment."

CAROLRHODA BOOKS, INC.

Division of Lerner Publishing Group
241 First Ave. N, Minneapolis, MN 55401. 612-332-3344.
Web site: www.lernerbooks.com. Zelda Wagner, Submissions Editor. **Description:** Publishes hardcover originals for kids ages 4-12 in the areas of biography, science, nature, history, and historical fiction. **Books Statistics:** 50 titles/yr (2,000 submissions); 10% by first-time authors; 90% unagented. **Proposal Process:** Submissions are accepted in the months of March and October only. Work received in any other month will be returned unopened. SASE required for authors who wish to have their material returned. Responds in 2-6 months. **Sample Titles:** *Smile a Lot* by Nancy Carlson; *Emergency* by Margaret Mayo; *Ladybugs* by Mia Posada.

CARTWHEEL BOOKS

Scholastic, Inc.
557 Broadway, New York, NY 10012. 212-343-6100.
Web site: www.scholastic.com. Ken Geist, Editorial Director. **Description:** Picture, novelty, and easy-to-read books, to about 1,000 words, for children, preschool to third grade. No novels or chapter books. Royalty or flat fee.

CHARLESBRIDGE PUBLISHING

85 Main St., Watertown, MA 02472. 617-926-0329.
E-mail: tradeeditorial@charlesbridge.com. Web site: www.charlesbridge.com. **Description:** Nonfiction and fiction children's picture books. Children's nonfiction picture books under Charlesbridge imprint, fiction picture books under Talewinds or Whispering Coyote imprints. **Books Statistics:** 25 titles/yr (2,500-3,000 submissions); 10% by first-time authors; 20% unagented. **Proposal Process:** Send complete manuscript. Exclusive submissions only: must indicate on envelope and cover letter, include SASE. Hard copy. **Payment:** Royalty or flat fee. **Tips:** Not acquiring board books, folk tales, alphabet books, or nursery rhymes at this time.

CHELSEA HOUSE PUBLISHERS

1974 Sproul Rd., Suite 400, Broomall, PA 19008. 610-353-5166.
E-mail: sue_naab@chelseahouse.com. Web site: www.chelseahouse.com. Sally Cheney, Editorial Director. **Description:** Quality nonfiction books for children and young adults. Features biographies, sports, multicultural studies, science and high school/college-level literary criticism. Age range is 8-15 years for most materials with the exception of literary criticism, which is geared for readers of high school level and up. **Books Statistics:** 350 titles/yr (500+ submissions); 25% by first-time authors;

98% unagented. **Proposal Process:** No unsolicited manuscripts. Query with outline, 2 sample chapters, and SASE. Accepts simultaneous and electronic queries. Prefers electronic format. Do not send complete manuscript unless requested. **Payment:** Pays flat fee ($1,500-$3,500). **Tips:** No autobiographical or fictionalized biography. Writing should be clear and direct, but lively. **Contact:** Sue Naab, Editor.

CHILD AND FAMILY PRESS

Child Welfare League of America
440 First St. NW, Fl. 3, Washington, DC 20001-2085. 202-942-0263.
E-mail: ptierney@cwla.org. Web site: www.cwla.org. Peggy Porter Tierney, Assistant Director. **Description:** Positive, upbeat picture books for children. **Books Statistics:** 5 titles/yr (2,000 submissions); 25% by first-time authors; 90% unagented. **Proposal Process:** Send complete manuscript. Prefers hard copy. No query letters or phone calls. Considers simultaneous submissions. Responds in 6 months. **Payment:** Royalty. **Tips:** "Avoid anything too cutesy, moralistic, or patronizing."

CHILDREN'S BOOK PRESS

2211 Mission St., San Francisco, CA 94110.
E-mail: cbookpress@cbookpress.org. Web site: www.cbookpress.org. Ina Cumpiano, Senior Editor. **Description:** Bilingual and multicultural picture books, 750-1,500 words, for children in grades K-6. Publishes contemporary stories reflecting the traditions and culture of people of color and new immigrant communities in the U.S. Seeks to help encourage a more international, multicultural perspective on the part of all young people. **Proposal Process:** Query. **Payment:** Advance on royalty. **Tips:** See Web site for specific guidelines.

CHILDREN'S PRESS

Scholastic, Inc.
90 Sherman Turnpike, Danbury, CT 06816. 203-797-3500.
Web site: www.grolier.com. John Sefridge, Publisher. **Description:** Science, social studies, and biography, to 25,000 words, for supplementary use in libraries and classrooms. **Payment:** Royalty or outright purchase. **Tips:** Currently overstocked; not accepting unsolicited manuscripts. No phone inquiries.

CHOUETTE PUBLISHING

4710, Saint-Ambroise St., Bureau 225
Montreal, Quebec H4C 2C7 Canada. 514-925-3325.
Web site: www.chouettepublishing.com. Christine L'Heureux, President/Publisher.
Description: Picture and activity books for children ages 0-6.

CLARION BOOKS

A Division of Houghton Mifflin Co.
215 Park Ave. S, New York, NY 10003. 212-420-5889.
Web site: www.hmco.com. Dinah Stevenson, VP/Associate Publisher and Editorial Director. **Description:** Publishes picture books, nonfiction, and fiction for both chil-

dren and teens (birth to 18). **Books Statistics:** 50-60 titles/yr (1,000+ submissions); 5% by first-time authors; 50-75% unagented. **Proposal Process:** Send query with complete manuscript. No unsolicited material. Accepts simultaneous queries, but not e-queries. **Payment:** Royalty. **Sample Titles:** *The Secrets of Ms. Snickle's Class* by Laurie Miller; *A Pocketful of Poems* by Nikki Grimes. **Tips:** "Research the types of books we publish before submitting." **Contact:** Jennifer Greene, Jennifer Winjertzahn, Lynn Polvino.

COUNCIL FOR INDIAN EDUCATION
2032 Woody Dr., Billings, MT 59102. 406-652-7398.
E-mail: hapcie@aol.com. Web site: www.cie-mt.org. Hap Gilliland, Editor. **Description:** Books dealing with Native-American life and culture for children ages 5-18. Fiction, nonfiction, and YA titles, 100-300 pages. **Books Statistics:** 2 titles/yr (100 submissions); 75% by first-time authors; 100% unagented. **Proposal Process:** Query with complete manuscript. Accepts simultaneous queries, but not e-queries. Responds in 3 months. Manuscripts read from October 1-June 1. **Payment:** Flat fee for short stories in anthologies; royalty for books. **Sample Titles:** *Alone in the Wilderness* by Hap Gilliland; *Last Free Chief of the Modoc Nation* by Patricia Boyer; *My People or Myself: An Alaskan Story of Coming of Age in an Aleut Village* by Heather Miller. **Tips:** "We seek authentic Native American life (past or present) with good plot. No profanity, no condescending material for any culture. Books evaluated for authentic lifestyle by 20-member Intertribal Indian board."

CRABTREE PUBLISHING COMPANY
PMB 16A, 350 Fifth Ave., Suite 3308, New York, NY 10118. 212-496-5040.
E-mail: editor@crabtreebooks.com. Web site: www.crabtreebooks.com. **Description:** Colorful nonfiction children's books featuring sports, science, social studies, art, and biographies. **Sample Titles:** *Fun With Dolphins* by Robbie Kalman.

CREATIVE TEACHING PRESS
The Learning Works
15342 Graham St., Huntington Beach, CA 92649-1111. 714-895-5047.
E-mail: webmaster@creativeteaching.com. Web site: www.creativeteaching.com. **Description:** Publisher of educational books and materials.

CRICKET BOOKS
Carus Publishing Co.
332 S Michigan Ave., Suite 1100, Chicago, IL 60604. 312-939-1500.
Web site: www.cricketbooks.net. **Description:** Picture books, chapter books, middle-grade novels for children ages 7-14, and fiction/nonfiction for teens. **Books Statistics:** 25 titles/yr (5,000 submissions). **Proposal Process:** Nonfiction: send query with outline, sample chapters, and SASE. Fiction: send query with outline, complete manuscript, and SASE. Considers simultaneous queries, but not e-queries. Prefers hard-copy. Responds in 4 months to proposals, 6 months to manuscripts. **Payment:** Royalty, typical range 10%. **Tips:** "We're temporarily not accept-

ing unsolicited manuscripts. Please see our Web site for details and updates."
Contact: Submissions Editor.

CROWN BOOKS FOR YOUNG READERS

Random House Children's Media Group/Random House, Inc.
1540 Broadway, Fl. 19, New York, NY 10036. 212-782-9000.
Web site: www.randomhouse.com. **Description:** Children's nonfiction (science, sports, nature, music, and history) and picture books for ages 3 and up. Send complete manuscript and SASE for picture books. **Contact:** Editorial Department.

DAWN PUBLICATIONS

P.O. Box 2010, Nevada City, CA 95959. 800-545-7475.
Web site: www.dawnpub.com. Glenn J. Hovemann, Editor. **Description:** Nature-awareness/natural science illustrated picture-books for children. No talking animals, fantasies, or legends. **Books Statistics:** 6 titles/yr; 60% by first-time authors. **Proposal Process:** Submit complete manuscript. Hard-copy only. Responds in 2-3 months. Writer's guidelines available on Web site. **Payment:** Royalty. **Sample Titles:** *From Lava to Life: The Universe Tells Our Earth Story* by Jennifer Morgan; *Where Does the Wind Blow?* by Cindy Rink.

DIAL BOOKS FOR YOUNG READERS

Penguin Putnam Books for Young Readers/Penguin Putnam Inc.
345 Hudson St., New York, NY 10014.
Web site: www.penguinputnam.com. Lauri Hornik, Editorial Director. **Description:** Lively, unique picture books for children ages 2-8, and middle grade and young adult novels. Send complete manuscript for picture books; outline and two sample chapters for novels.

DOVER PUBLICATIONS, INC.

31 E 2nd St., Mineola, NY 11501. 516-294-7000.
E-mail: dover@inch.com. Web site: www.doverpublications.com. Paul Negri, Editor-in-Chief. **Description:** Children's books, coffee table books, cookbooks, biographies, and adult nonfiction on a wide variety of subjects. **Books Statistics:** 600 titles/yr. **Proposal Process:** Query with SASE. **Payment:** Offers advance. **Sample Titles:** *Engineering and Technology, 1650-1750: Illustrations and Texts from Original Sources* by Martin Jensen; *Tibetan Designs* by Marty Noble.

DUTTON CHILDREN'S BOOKS

Penguin Putnam Books for Young Readers/Penguin Putnam Inc.
345 Hudson St., New York, NY 10014. 212-414-3700.
Web site: www.penguinputnam.com. Stephanie Owens Lurie, Publisher. **Description:** Trade children's books for ages 0-18. Publisher's list includes board books, picture books, early readers, chapter books, novels, and nonfiction. Titles are sold to bookstores, schools, and libraries. **Tips:** "We're seeking clever wordsmiths who can tell a

compelling story, with distinctive style and memorable characters that learn or change in the course of the story." **Contact:** Stephanie Owens Lurie.

EDUPRESS

208 Avenida Fabricante, Suite 200, San Clemente, CA 92672-7536. 949-366-9499. E-mail: amanda@edupressinc.com. Web site: www.edupressinc.com. **Description:** Publishes hands-on, educational activities and materials for Pre-K through middle school teachers. Includes resources for language arts, math, reading, science, social studies, art, and early childhood. **Proposal Process:** Send partial or complete manuscript with cover letter that includes outline, synopsis, and author bio. Responds in 2-4 months. **Payment:** Purchases all rights to material; does not pay royalties. **Contact:** Amanda Meinke.

EERDMANS BOOKS FOR YOUNG READERS

William B. Eerdmans Publishing Co.
255 Jefferson Avenue, SE, Grand Rapids, MI 99503. 616-459-4591.
Web site: www.eerdmans.com/youngreaders. Judy Zylotia, Editor-in-Chief. **Description:** High-quality picture books, novels, and biographies for kids of all ages. Some titles have spiritual themes, others deal with historical events or social concerns. **Books Statistics:** 12-15/yr. **Proposal Process:** Send complete manuscript for picture books and those under 200 pages. For longer books, send query letter and 3-4 sample chapters. Responds in 2-3 months. **Tips:** Currently seeking stories with depth, "tales worth telling," works that delight in life's joys, but also offer honest hope and comfort in the face of life's challenges.

ENSLOW PUBLISHERS, INC.

40 Industrial Rd., P.O. Box 398, Berkeley Heights, NJ 07922-0398. 908-771-9400. Web site: www.enslow.com. **Description:** Juvenile and YA nonfiction for schools and public libraries. Primarily biography, holiday/customs, current issues, science, math, technology, sports, history, and health/drug education. No fiction or picture books. **Books Statistics:** 175 titles/yr; 50% by first-time authors; 99% unagented. **Proposal Process:** Send query with outline and sample chapters. No electronic or simultaneous queries. Prefers hard-copy format. **Payment:** Royalty or flat fee. **Sample Titles:** *American Women of Flight: Pilots and Pioneers* by Henry M. Holden; *Benjamin Franklin: Inventor and Patriot* by Carin T. Ford. **Tips:** "We're always seeking new or established authors who can write nonfiction in interesting and exciting manner. Propose a new title for an existing series, or possibly a new series idea."

EVAN-MOOR EDUCATIONAL PUBLISHERS

18 Lower Ragsdale Dr., Monterey, CA 93940. 831-649-5901.
E-mail: editorial@evan-moor.com. Web site: www.evan-moor.com. **Description:** Educational books and materials for grades PreK-6. Content covers reading, writing, math, geography, social studies, science, arts and crafts, dramatic plays, and thematic units. **Books Statistics:** 40-60 titles/yr.

FIREFLY BOOKS LTD.

3680 Victoria Park Ave., Toronto, Ontario M2H 3K1 Canada. 416-499-8412.
E-mail: valerie@fireflybooks.com. Web site: www.fireflybooks.com. Valerie Hatton,
Publicity Manager. **Description:** Publishes books on a variety of topics including
cooking, gardening, astronomy, health, natural history, reference, and sports. Also
publishes children's books and calendars.

FITZHENRY & WHITESIDE

195 Allstate Parkway, Markham, Ontario L3R 4T8 Canada. 905-477-9700.
Web site: www.fitzhenry.ca. **Description:** Adult nonfiction in a variety of subjects
including reference and natural science. Also publishes textbooks (geography and his-
tory) and children's books (biography, fiction, nonfiction). **Sample Titles:** (Adult) *Get
Back to Work: A No-Nonsense Guide for Finding Your Next Job Fast* by Charles
Grossner, Leo Spindel, and Harvey Glasner; (Children's) *Brady Brady* by Mary Shaw.

FREE SPIRIT PUBLISHING

217 Fifth Ave. N, Suite 200, Minneapolis, MN 55401-1724. 612-338-2068.
E-mail: help4kids@freespirit.com. Web site: www.freespirit.com. **Description:**
Award-winning publisher of books for parents, teens, educators, counselors, and
everyone else who cares about kids. **Tips:** "Our emphasis is on positive self esteem,
self awareness, stress management, school success, peacemaking and violence prevention, social action, creativity, family and friends, and special needs (i.e., gifted and
talented children with learning differences)."

FRONT STREET, INC.

20 Battery Park Ave., Suite 403, Asheville, NC 28801. 828-236-3097.
E-mail: contactus@frontstreetbooks.com. Web site: www.frontstreetbooks.com. Joy
Neaves, Editor. **Description:** An independent publisher of books for children and
young adults. **Books Statistics:** 10-15 titles/yr; 30% by first-time authors; 90% una-
gented. **Proposal Process:** Check Web site for submission guidelines. **Payment:**
Royalty. **Tips:** No longer accepting picture book manuscripts.

GARETH STEVENS PUBLISHING

330 West Olive St., Suite 100, Milwaukee, WI 53212. 414-332-3520.
E-mail: info@gspub.com. Web site: www.garethstevens.com. Mark Sachner, Creative
Director. **Description:** Quality educational books (arts/crafts, nature, science, social
studies, history, Spanish/bilingual, and atlas/reference) and fiction for children ages 4-
16. Specifically targets the school and public library educational market. **Books
Statistics:** 200 titles/yr. **Sample Titles:** *Animals I See at the Zoo* by JoAnn Early
Macken; *Courteous Kids* by Janine Amos; *Creature Features* by Nicola Whittaker.

GREENE BARK PRESS INC.

P.O. Box 1108, Bridgeport, CT 06601-1108. 203-372-4861.
Web site: www.greenebarkpress.com. Thomas J. Greene, Publisher. **Description:**
Children's picture books for ages 3-9. **Books Statistics:** 1-6 titles/yr **Proposal**

Process: Send cover letter with brief synopsis including the authors' background, name, address, etc. Send copies of artwork (do not send originals) if available. SASE required for response. **Payment:** Does not give royalty advances. Authors are given 10% royalty; illustrators are either paid flat fee or royalty between 3%-5%. **Tips:** Prefers artwork to accompany manuscript, but will not disqualify submissions without art. Do not send queries by telephone, fax, or e-mail. Rarely publishes juvenile novels. **Contact:** Michele Hofbauer, Associate Publisher.

GREENWILLOW BOOKS
HarperCollins Publishers
1350 Avenue of the Americas, New York, NY 10019. 212-261-6627.
Web site: www.harperchildrens.com. **Description:** Children's books and picture books for all ages. Fiction and nonfiction. **Books Statistics:** 50 titles per year, with 90% unagented authors; 2% first-time authors. **Proposal Process:** Currently not accepting unsolicited material. **Payment:** Royalty.

GROSSET & DUNLAP PUBLISHERS
Penguin Young Readers Group/Penguin Group (USA), Inc.
345 Hudson St., New York, NY 10014.
Web site: www.penguinputnam.com. Debra Dorfman, President/Publisher.
Description: Mass-market children's books. **Proposal Process:** Does not accept unsolicited manuscripts. Material from literary agents only. **Payment:** Royalty.
Sample Titles: *Anyone but Me* (Katie Kazoo Switcheroo) by Nancy Krulik; *Bless My Little Friends* (Christian Mother Goose) by Marjorie Ainsborough Decker.

HARCOURT TRADE CHILDREN'S BOOKS
Harcourt Inc.
525 B St., Suite 1900, San Diego, CA 92101-4495. 619-261-6616.
Web site: www.harcourtbooks.com. **Description:** Juvenile fiction and nonfiction for beginning readers through young adults. Imprints include Gulliver Books, Red Wagon Books, Odyssey Classics, Silver Whistle, Magic Carpet Books, Harcourt Children's Books, Harcourt Young Classics, Green Light Readers, Harcourt Paperbacks, Voyager Books/Libros Viajeros. **Proposal Process:** No unsolicited submissions or queries. Accepts work from agents only. **Sample Titles:** *lizards, frogs, and polliwogs* by Douglas Florian; *Stella's Dancing Days* by Sandy Asher.

HARPERCOLLINS CHILDREN'S BOOKS
1350 Avenue of the Americas, New York, NY 10019. 212-261-6500.
Web site: www.harperchildrens.com. Kate Morgan Jackson, Editor-in-Chief.
Description: Picture books, chapter books, and fiction and nonfiction for middle-grade and YA readers. **Books Statistics:** 300 titles/yr; 5% by first-time authors; 25% unagented. **Proposal Process:** Accepts submissions from literary agents only. **Payment:** Royalty **Sample Titles:** *I'm Gonna Like Me: Letting Off a Little Self-Esteem* by Jamie Lee Curtis; *And God Cried, Too: A Kid's Book of Healing and Hope* by Marc Gellman; *If You Give a Mouse a Cookie* by Laura Numeroff. **Tips:** "Our

imprints (Avon, HarperFestival, HarperTempest, HarperTrophy, Joanna Cotler Books, Laura Geringer Books, Greenwillow Books, and Katherine Tegen Books) are committed to producing imaginative and responsible children's books."

HOLIDAY HOUSE, INC.
425 Madison Ave., New York, NY 10017. 212-688-0085.
Description: General juvenile fiction and nonfiction. **Books Statistics:** 60 titles/yr (3,000 submissions); 2-5% by first-time authors; 50% unagented. **Proposal Process:** Query with SASE. **Payment:** Royalty. **Contact:** Suzanne Reinoehl, Acquisitions.

HOUGHTON MIFFLIN CO./TRADE & REFERENCE DIVISION
222 Berkeley St., Boston, MA 02116-3764. 617-351-5000.
Web site: www.hmco.com. **Description:** Quality adult and children's fiction, non-fiction and reference materials. Imprints include Houghton Mifflin, Mariner, Clarion, American Heritage, Chambers, Larousse, and Kingfisher.

HUMANICS PUBLISHING GROUP
P.O. Box 7400, Atlanta, GA 30357. 404-874-1930.
E-mail: humanics@mindspring.com. Web site: www.humanicspub.com. W. Arthur Bligh, Editor. **Description:** Self-help, philosophy, spirituality. Teacher resource (pre-K to 3). **Books Statistics:** 20 titles/yr (600 submissions); 70% by first-time authors; 90% unagented. **Proposal Process:** Query with outline, sample chapters, and SASE. Accepts e-querie, but not simultaneous queries. **Payment:** Royalty. **Tips:** Interested in books that provide help, guidance, and inspiration.

ILLUMINATION ARTS PUBLISHING
13256 Northup Way, Suite 9, Bellevue, WA 98005. 425-644-7185.
E-mail: liteinfo@illumin.com. Web site: www.illumin.com. Trey Bornmann, Marketing Director. **Description:** Publishes uplifting/spiritual children's picture books. **Books Statistics:** 4 titles/yr (2,000 submissions). **Sample Titles:** *All I See Is a Part of Me* by Chara M. Curtis; *The Tree* by Dana Lyons; *The Whoosh of Gadoosh* by Pat Skene; *Cassandra's Angel* by Gina Otto.

SARA JORDAN PUBLISHING
M.P.O. Box 490, Niagara Falls, NY 14302-0490. 905-938-5050.
Web site: www.songsthatteach.com. **Description:** Educational materials with particular emphasis on music and songs that teach. **Proposal Process:** Does not accept unsolicited manuscripts or illustrations.

JUST US BOOKS
356 Glenwood Ave., Fl. 3, East Orange, NJ 07017. 973-672-7701.
E-mail: justusbook@aol.com. Web site: www.justusbooks.com. Cheryl Willis Hudson, Editorial Director. **Description:** Specializes in Black-interest books for children: picture books, poetry, and chapter books for middle readers. **Books**

Statistics: 4-6 titles/yr **Proposal Process:** Query with a one-page synopsis and an SASE. **Sample Titles:** *Bright Eyes, Brown Skin* by Cheryl Willis Hudson; *Annie's Gift* by Angela Medearis.

KIDHAVEN PRESS
Imprint of The Gale Group
10911 Technology Place, San Diego, CA 92117.
Web site: www.gale.com/kidhaven. **Description:** Nonfiction series publisher for primary grade readers, 2,500-5,000 words. Popular series include Nature's Predators, Wonders of the World, Seeds of a Nation, and Animals with Jobs. **Proposal Process:** Seeks freelance writers for work-for-hire projects. Send query letter, resume, brief writing sample, and/or list of publications. No unsolicited manuscripts. **Payment:** Flat fee. **Contact:** Chandra Howard, Senior Acquisitions Editor.

ALFRED A. KNOPF BOOKS FOR YOUNG READERS
Random House Children's Media Group/Random House, Inc.
1745 Broadway, New York, NY 10019. 212-782-9000.
Web site: www.randomhouse.com/kids. **Description:** Distinguished juvenile fiction and nonfiction. **Proposal Process:** Query with SASE. No unsolicited manuscripts. Guidelines available. **Payment:** Royalty.

LEARNING HORIZONS
One American Rd., Cleveland, OH 44144. 216-252-7300.
Web site: www.learninghorizons.com. **Description:** Supplemental education materials for children in PreK-6 covering language, math, science, and social studies.

LEE & LOW BOOKS
95 Madison Ave., New York, NY 10016. 212-779-4400.
E-mail: lmay@leeandlow.com. Web site: www.leeandlow.com. Louise E. May, Executive Editor. **Description:** Quality children's book publisher specializing in multicultural themes. **Books Statistics:** 12-15 titles/yr (1,500 submissions); 35% by first-time authors; 80% unagented. **Proposal Process:** Send hard copy of manuscript with SASE. See Web site for details. **Payment:** Advance/royalty. **Tips:** No folk tales or animal stories. Seeking character-driven realistic fiction about children of color, with special interest in stories set in contemporary U.S. and nonfiction picture books with a multicultural focus. "Lee and Low is dedicated to publishing culturally authentic literature. The company makes a special effort to work with writers and artists of color and encourages new voices."

LEGACY PRESS
P.O. Box 261129, San Diego, CA 92196. 858-668-3260.
Web site: www.rainbowpublishers.com. Christy Scannell, Editorial Director. **Description:** Christian nonfiction for kids ages 2-12. **Books Statistics:** 10/yr (300 submissions); 50% by first-time authors; 100% unagented. **Proposal Process:** Submit

outline with sample chapters. Considers simultaneous queries. Responds in 3 months. **Sample Titles:** *The Christian Girl's Guide to Being Your Best*; *The Christian Kids Gardening Guide*. **Tips:** "Please request our guidelines and catalog before submitting. Visit a Christian bookstore and understand the niche market we work with."

LERNER PUBLICATIONS

241 First Ave. N, Minneapolis, MN 55401. 612-332-3344.
Web site: www.lernerbooks.com. Jennifer Zimian, Submissions Editor. **Description:** Publishes primarily nonfiction for readers of all grade levels. List includes titles encompassing nature, geography, natural and physical science, current events, ancient and modern history, sports, world cultures, and numerous biography series. No alphabet, puzzle, song or text books, religious subject matter, or plays. **Proposal Process:** Submissions are accepted in the months of March and October only. Work received in any other month will be returned unopened. SASE required for authors who wish to have their material returned. No phone calls. Responds in 2-6 months.

ARTHUR A. LEVINE BOOKS

Scholastic, Inc.
557 Broadway, New York, NY 10012. 212-343-4436.
Web site: www.scholastic.com. Arthur A. Levine, Editorial Director. **Description:** Picture books and literary fiction for children of all ages. **Books Statistics:** 15 titles/yr. **Proposal Process:** Query before sending submission. First-time authors welcome. **Sample Titles:** *The Hickory Chair* by Lisa Rowe Fraustino; *The Slightly True Story of Cedar B. Hartley* by Martine Murray.

LITTLE SIMON

Simon & Schuster Children's Publishing/Simon & Schuster, Inc.
1230 Avenue of the Americas, New York, NY 10020.
Web site: www.simonsayskids.com. Cindy Eng Alvarez, Vice President/Editorial Director. **Description:** Novelty books, board books, pop-up books, lift-the-flap, and touch-and-feel books. Audience is children 6 months-8 years. No picture or chapter books. **Proposal Process:** Query with SASE. **Sample Titles:** *A Is for Animals* by David Pelham; *A Charlie Brown Christmas* by Charles M. Schulz; *'Twas the Day After Christmas: A Lift-the-Flap Story* by Mavis Smith.

LOBSTER PRESS

1620 Sherbrooke St. W, Suite C, Montreal, Quebec H3H 1C9 Canada. 514-904-1100. E-mail: editorial@lobsterpress.com. Web site: www.lobsterpress.com. **Description:** High-quality children's books including picture books, travel guides for kids, Millennium Generation Series, and Pet-Sitters' Club Series. Also publishes travel guides, adult nonfiction, self-help, and illustrated titles. **Books Statistics:** 25 titles/yr (200 queries and 1,500 mss/yr); 90% by first-time authors; 75% unagented. **Payment:** Royalty.

LUCENT BOOKS
Imprint of The Gale Group
10911 Technology Place, San Diego, CA 92127.
Web site: www.gale.com/lucent. **Description:** Nonfiction series publisher for junior high and middle grade readers, 18,000-25,000 words. Highly regarded series include the Overview series, The Way People Live, Teen Issues, Modern Nations, and American War Library. Topics include current issues, political, social, historical, and environmental topics. **Proposal Process:** Seeks skilled freelance writers for work-for-hire projects. Send query letter, resume, brief writing sample and/or list of publications. No unsolicited manuscripts. **Payment:** Flat fee. **Contact:** Chandra Howard, Senior Acquisitions Editor.

MAGINATION PRESS
American Psychological Assn.
750 First St. NE, Washington, DC 20002. 202-218-3982.
Web site: www.maginationpress.com. Darcie Conner Johnston, Managing Editor. **Description:** Publishes illustrated story books and nonfiction of a clearly psychological nature for children. Picture books for children 4-11; fiction for children 8-12; nonfiction for children 8-18. **Books Statistics:** 8-12 titles/yr (700 submissions); 50% by first-time authors; 95% unagented. **Proposal Process:** Submit query with complete manuscript. Include SASE if material needs to be returned. No electronic submissions. Simultaneous queries accepted. Hard copy. Responds in 3-5 months. **Payment:** Royalty. **Sample Titles:** *The Magic Box: When Parents Can't Be There to Tuck You In* by Marty Sederman and Seymour Epstein; *Breathe Easy: Young People's Guide to Asthma* by Jonathan H. Weiss, Ph.D. **Tips:** "We're looking for strong self-help and psychological content in stories that focus on an issue that affects children, plus engaged writing. Many of our books are written by medical or mental-health professionals." No YA fiction or chapter books.

MARGARET K. MCELDERRY BOOKS
1230 Sixth Ave., New York, NY 10020. 212-698-2761.
Web site: www.simonsayskids.com. Emma D. Dryden, Vice President/Editorial Director. **Description:** Books for kids of all ages, infant through YA. Literary hardcover trade, fiction, nonfiction, and some poetry. **Books Statistics:** 25-30 titles/yr (4,000 queries); 35% by first-time authors; 50% unagented. **Proposal Process:** Query with outline and sample chapters. Accepts simultaneous and electronic queries. Prefers hard copy. Responds in 1-2 months. Guidelines available. **Payment:** Advance/royalty. **Tips:** "We're looking for unique perspectives on unique topics of interest to children. We don't accept science fiction, but we do publish some fantasy." **Contact:** Sarah Nielsen, Assistant Editor.

MEADOWBROOK PRESS
5451 Smetana Dr., Minnetonka, MN 55343. 952-930-1100.
E-mail: awiechmann@meadowbrookpress.com.
Web site: www.meadowbrookpress.com. Christine Zuchora-Walske, Editorial

Director. **Description:** Books on relationships, parenting, pregnancy/childbirth, party planning, humorous poetry for children, and children's activities. **Books Statistics:** 20 titles/yr (600 submissions); 80% by first-time authors; 90% unagented. **Proposal Process:** Send query with SASE via regular mail. Simultaneous queries accepted. Currently not accepting unsolicited manuscripts or queries for adult fiction, adult poetry, humor, and children's fiction. Responds in 4 months. **Payment:** Royalty or flat fee. **Sample Titles:** (Adult nonfiction) *Discipline Without Shouting or Spanking* by Jerry Wyckoff, Ph.D. and Barbara C. Unell; *Reflections for Expectant Mothers* by Ellen Sue Stern; (Children's) *Funny Little Poems for Funny Little People* by Bruce Lansky. **Contact:** Angela Wiechmann, Editor.

MILKWEED EDITIONS

1011 Washington Ave. S, Suite 300, Minneapolis, MN 55415. 612-332-3192. E-mail: editor@milkweed.org. Web site: www.milkweed.org. H. Emerson Blake, Editorial Director. **Description:** Literary fiction; literary nonfiction about the natural world; poetry; literary novels for middle graders (ages 8-13). **Books Statistics:** 15 titles/yr (3,000 submissions); 60% by first-time authors; 75% unagented. **Proposal Process:** Query with SASE. Accepts simultaneous queries, but not e-queries. Responds in 2-6 months. See Web site for specific submission guidelines. **Payment:** Royalty. **Sample Titles:** (Fiction) *Roofwalker* by Susan Power; (Nonfiction) *The Colors of Nature* edited by Alison H. Deming and Lauret E. Savoy; (Young Adult) *The Return of Gabriel* by John Armistead. **Tips:** "We're looking for a fresh, distinctive voice. No genre fiction, picture books, etc. We seek to give new writers a forum; publishing history isn't as important as excellence and originality." **Contact:** Elisabeth Fitz, First Reader.

THE MILLBROOK PRESS

P.O. Box 335, 2 Old New Milford Rd., Brookfield, CT 06804. 203-740-2220. Web site: www.millbrookpress.com. Kristin Vibbert, Manuscript Coordinator. **Description:** Children's book publisher, with 3 imprints: Copper Beech, Twenty-First Century, and Roaring Brook. Quality nonfiction for the school and library market for grades PreK-6. Main market is elementary schools, but titles range from infant picture books to YA historical fiction. **Books Statistics:** 150 titles/year (5,000 submissions), 50% by first-time authors, 75% unagented. **Proposal Process:** Query with outline, sample chapters, and SASE. Accepts simultaneous queries, but not e-queries. Responds in 1 month. **Payment:** Royalty or flat fee. **Sample Titles:** *Cats and Kids* by Allen H. Hudelhoff; *The Tooth Fairy Tells All* by Cynthia L. Copeland; *Apple Cider Making Days* by Ann Purmell. **Tips:** Send SASE for guidelines or catalog, or check Web site.

MONDO PUBLISHING

980 Avenue of the Americas, Fl. 2, New York, NY 10018. 212-268-3560. Don L. Curry, Executive Editor. **Description:** Children's trade and educational. Picture books, nonfiction, and early chapter books for readers ages 4-10. "We seek beautiful books that children can read on their own or have read to them, and enjoy

over and over." **Books Statistics:** 50 titles/yr (1,000 submissions); 30% by first-time authors. **Proposal Process:** Query with complete manuscript. No e-queries. Hard copy only.

NATIONAL GEOGRAPHIC SOCIETY
1145 17th St. NW, Washington, DC 20036-4688. 202-828-5492.
E-mail: jtunstal@ngs.org. Nancy Feresten, Editorial Director. **Description:** Nonfiction books in the areas of history, adventure, biography, multicultural themes, science, nature, and reference for children ages 4-14. **Books Statistics:** 25 titles/yr (1,000 submissions); 5% by first-time authors; 50% unagented. **Proposal Process:** Query with complete manuscript, and SASE. Accepts simultaneous queries. **Payment:** Royalty or flat fee. **Tips:** "We like a strong writer's voice telling an interesting story on a subject of interest to young people." **Contact:** Jo Tunstall, Editor.

THE OLIVER PRESS, INC.
Charlotte Square, 5707 W 36th St., Minneapolis, MN 55416-2510. 952-926-8981.
E-mail: queries@oliverpress.com. Web site: www.oliverpress.com. **Description:** Collective biographies for middle and high school students. Currently offering 6 different curriculum-based series such as Profiles, Business Builders, and Innovators (history of technology). Ages 10-young adult. **Proposal Process:** Submit proposals for books on people who have made an impact in such areas as history, politics, crime, science, and business. Include SASE. Accepts simultaneous and electronic queries. **Payment:** Royalty or flat fee. **Tips:** "Book proposals should fit one of our existing series; provide brief summaries of 8-12 people who could be included. We're looking for authors who thoroughly research their subject and are accurate and good storytellers." No fiction, picture books, or single-person biographies. **Contact:** Jenna Anderson, Editor; Denise Sterling, Editor.

ORCA BOOK PUBLISHERS
P.O. Box 468, Custer, WA 98240-0468. 250-380-1229.
E-mail: orca@orcabook.com. Web site: www.orcabook.com. **Description:** Publishes children's picture books, young readers and juvenile fiction, and YA fiction. **Proposal Process:** Considers work from Canadian authors only. Query with 1-page cover letter and SASE. Do not fax or e-mail. No simultaneous queries. **Tips:** Manuscripts can also be sent to Canadian office: P.O. Box 5626, Victoria, BC V8R 6S4.

RICHARD C. OWEN PUBLISHERS, INC.
Children's Book Dept., P.O. Box 585, Katonah, NY 10536. 914-232-3903.
Web site: www.rcowen.com. Janice Boland, Editor. **Description:** Fiction and nonfiction for kids in grades K-2 as well as professional resources for teachers and educators. **Books Statistics:** 15 titles/yr (1,000 submissions); 95% by first-time authors; 100% unagented. **Proposal Process:** Query with complete manuscript. Accepts simultaneous queries, but not e-queries. Prefers hard-copy format. Send SASE for guidelines. **Payment:** Royalty for writers. Flat fee for illustrators. **Sample Titles:** (Children's) *Star Pictures* by Julieanne Darling; (Professional) *How Children Learn*

to Read by John W.A. Smith and Warwick B. Elley. **Tips:** "We seek brief, original, well-structured children's books that youngsters in grades K-2 can read by themselves. Also short, high-interest articles, stories for children, ages 7-8. Writing should be fresh and energetic with a clear style and voice. We especially seek nonfiction about history, geography, and science for very young children ages 5-7."

PACIFIC VIEW PRESS
P.O. Box 2657, Berkley, CA 94702. Pam Zumwalt, Acquisitions Editor.
Description: Specializes in nonfiction for kids ages 8-12. Main focus in on the culture and history of countries of the Pacific Rim. Secondary focus is Asian and Chinese cookbooks and books on innovative aspects of Chinese history.

PEACHTREE PUBLISHERS
1700 Chattahoochee Ave., Atlanta, GA 30318-2112. 404-876-8761.
E-mail: hello@peachtree-online.com. Web site: www.peachtree-online.com.
Description: Fiction and nonfiction, children's, middle readers, young adults, adult nonfiction: regional, health, regional travel (Southeast only). **Proposal Process:** Send full manuscript or 3 sample chapters plus TOC and SASE. Send all submissions via U.S. mail; no e-mail or fax queries/submissions. Responds in 4-6 months. **Tips:** Strong writing with unique subject matter or approach. No adult fiction, fantasy, sci-fi, romance, anthologies, poetry, or short stories. **Contact:** Helen Harriss.

PINATA BOOKS
Arte Publico Press, University of Houston
452 Cullen Performance Hall, Houston, TX 77204-2004. 713-743-2841.
Web site: www.artepublicopress.com. Nicolas Kanellos, President. **Description:** Children's and YA literature by U.S. Hispanic authors. **Proposal Process:** Query with outline and sample chapters, or send complete manuscript. **Payment:** Royalty. **Sample Titles:** *Jumping Off to Freedom* by Anilu Bernardo; *Alicia's Treasure* by Diane Gonzales Bertrand; *Mexican Ghost Tales of the Southwest* by Alfred Avila.

PIPPIN PRESS
229 E 85th St., New York, NY 10028. 212-288-4920.
Barbara Francis, Editor-in-Chief. **Description:** Publishes early chapter books, middle group fiction, unusual nonfiction for children ages 7-12, and occasional picture books. Also publishes humor for all ages. **Books Statistics:** 6 titles/yr (3,000 submissions); 10% by first-time authors; 90% unagented. **Proposal Process:** Query with SASE. No unsolicited manuscripts. No simultaneous or electronic queries. **Payment:** Royalty. **Tips:** "We're looking for childhood memoirs and small chapter books (64-96 pages) on historical events in which young people are the heroes." **Contact:** Joyce Segal, Senior Editor.

PLEASANT COMPANY PUBLICATIONS
8400 Fairway Pl., Middleton, WI 58562-0998. 608-836-4848.
Web site: www.americangirl.com/corp. **Description:** Historical fiction, contempo-

rary fiction, and contemporary advice and activity for girls ages 7-13. Also publishes books on parenting and family issues. **Proposal Process:** Fiction: send complete manuscript of 25,000-40,000 words. Nonfiction: send query with outline, sample chapters, and list of previous publications. Include SASE with all submitted material. Responds in 12-16 weeks. **Payment:** Royalty or flat fee. **Sample Titles:** The American Girls Collection series by Valerie Tripp; The Amelia series by Marissa Moss; The Girls of Many Lands series; *What I Wish You Knew* by Dr. Lynda Madison. **Tips:** Small "concept-driven" list. Does not accept picture books or manuscripts for The American Girls Collection. See Web site for specific guidelines. **Contact:** Submissions Editor.

PUFFIN BOOKS
Penguin Young Readers Group/Penguin Group (USA), Inc.
345 Hudson St., New York, NY 10014-3647. 212-414-3600.
Web site: www.penguinputnam.com/yreaders. Tracy Tang, President/Publisher. **Description:** Children's novels, picture books, chapter books, easy-to-reads, and lift-the-flap books. **Proposal Process:** Query or send complete manuscript, include SASE. No picture book manuscripts. **Contact:** Kristin Gilson, Executive Editor; Sharyn November, Senior Editor.

G.P. PUTNAM'S SONS BOOKS FOR YOUNG READERS
Penguin Putnam Books for Young Readers/Penguin Putnam Inc.
345 Hudson St., Fl. 14, New York, NY 10014. 212-366-2000.
Web site: www.penguinputnam.com. Nancy Paulsen, President/Publisher. **Description:** Publishes general trade nonfiction and fiction for ages 2-18. Mostly picture books and middle-grade novels. **Books Statistics:** 45 titles/yr (12,000 submissions); 5% by first-time authors; 50% unagented. **Proposal Process:** Children's novels: query with synopsis and 3 sample chapters. Picture books: send complete manuscript (if less than 10 pages). Considers simultaneous queries, but not e-queries. Prefers hard copy. Responds in 1-3 months. **Payment:** Royalty. **Sample Titles:** *Saving Sweetness* by Diane Stanley; *Amber Brown Sees Red* by Paula Danziger. **Tips:** "Multicultural books should reflect different cultures accurately, but unobtrusively. Stories about children who are physically or cognitively disabled should portray them accurately, without condescension. Avoid series, romances. We accept very little fantasy."

RAINBOW BRIDGE PUBLISHING
323 West Martin Lane, P.O. Box 571470, Salt Lake City, UT 84157-1470.
800-598-1441. E-mail: rainbow@xmission.com. Web site: www.rbpbooks.com. **Description:** Parent and teacher resource materials for students in grades PreK-8. Topics include math, reading, writing, science, geography, and language arts.

RAINBOW PUBLISHERS
P.O. Box 261129, San Diego, CA 92196. 858-668-3260.
Web site: www.rainbowpublishers.com. Christy Scannell, Editorial Director.

Description: Reproducible activity books for Christian teachers in church, school, and home settings. Materials target kids ages 2-12. **Books Statistics:** 16/yr (300 submissions); 50% first-time authors; 100% unagented. **Proposal Process:** Submit outline and sample chapters. Considers simultaneous queries. Responds in 3 months. **Payment:** Flat fee of $640 or more. **Sample Titles:** *Undercover Heroes of the Bible* (4-book series); *Instant Bible Lessons* (7-book series). **Tips:** "Please request our guidelines and catalog before submitting. We only accept book proposals; we do not buy individual ideas such as 1 game or 1 craft."

RAINTREE
15 E 26th St., New York, NY 10010. 646-935-3702.
Web site: www.raintreesteckvaughn.com. Eileen Robinson, Editorial Director.
Description: Children's nonfiction in series only. No single titles. All published books are curriculum-oriented. **Books Statistics:** 200 titles/yr (500 submissions). Considers some first-time authors; almost all unagented. **Proposal Process:** Query with outline, sample chapters, and SASE. Accepts simultaneous queries with notice. No e-queries. Responds in 2-4 months. **Payment:** Flat fee (varies).

RANDOM HOUSE BOOKS FOR YOUNG READERS
Random House Children's Media Group/Random House, Inc.
1540 Broadway, New York, NY 10036. 212-782-9000.
Web site: www.randomhouse.com/kids. Kate Klimo, Vice President/Publisher.
Description: Fiction and nonfiction for beginning readers; paperback fiction line for kids ages 7-9. **Proposal Process:** No unsolicited manuscripts. Agented material only.

THE READER'S DIGEST ASSOCIATION, INC.
Readers Digest Rd., Pleasantville, NY 10570-7000. 914-238-1000.
Web site: www.rd.com. **Description:** Do-it-yourself books on home improvement, gardening, cooking, etc; children's books; Select Editions; reading series; Young Families products; music collections, home videos, and other special-interest magazines.

MORGAN REYNOLDS, INC.
620 S Elm St., Suite 223, Greensboro, NC 27406. 336-275-1311.
E-mail: editors@morganreynolds.com. Web site: www.morganreynolds.com. John Riley, Publisher. **Description:** Lively, well written biographies and histories for young adults. Suitable subjects include important historical events and important historical and contemporary figures. **Books Statistics:** 20 titles/yr (300 submissions); 50% by first-time authors; 90% unagented. **Proposal Process:** Query with outline, sample chapters, and SASE. Considers simultaneous and electronic queries. Prefers hard-copy. Responds in 1 month. **Payment:** Royalty. **Sample Titles:** *Curious Bones: Mary Anning and the Birth of Paleontology* by Thomas W. Goodhue; *Remarkable Journeys: The Story of Jules Verne* by William Schoell; *Gwendolyn Brooks: Poet from Chicago* by Martha E. Rhynes. **Tips:** YA nonfiction only. Avoid eccentric topics, autobiographies, and "cute" writing styles. Market includes libraries, both public and middle/high school. **Contact:** Laura Shoemaker, Editor.

RISING MOON

Northland Publishing

2900 N Fort Valley Rd., Flagstaff, AZ 86001. 928-774-5251.

E-mail: editorial@northlandpub.com. Web site: www.northlandpub.com. Theresa Howell, Children's Editor. **Description:** Picture books for children ages 5-8. Interested in material with Southwest themes and contemporary bilingual Spanish/English themes. **Books Statistics:** 10-12 titles/yr (3,000 submissions); 25% unagented. **Proposal Process:** Accepts unsolicited manuscripts. Considers simultaneous queries, but not e-queries. Prefers hard-copy. Responds in 3 months. **Payment:** Royalty or flat fee. **Sample Titles:** *Kissing Coyotes* by Marcia Vaughan; *Do Princesses Wear Hiking Boots?* by Carmela LaVigna Coyle; *My Best Friend Bear* by Tony Johnston. **Tips:** "Please submit through your agent, and review our guidelines carefully first."

THE ROSEN PUBLISHING GROUP

29 E 21st St., New York, NY 10010. 212-777-3017.

Kathy Kuhtz Campbell, Managing Editor. **Description:** Publishes nonfiction children and YA titles for the school and library market. Rosen books encompass a wide variety of topics and issues that affect young people's lives in the areas of careers, guidance, science, health, history, social studies, art, culture, and sports. Imprints: PowerPlus Books, a 12-book series of nonfiction titles correlated to the curriculum for students in grades 4-8. Buenas Letras, books designed for Spanish-speaking students and students learning Spanish in the U.S. **Books Statistics:** 200 titles/yr. **Proposal Process:** Query via regular mail. No e-queries. **Payment:** Royalty and/or flat fee. **Tips:** Nonfiction work-for-hire series format (6 books to a series).

SANDCASTLE PUBLISHING

1723 Hill Dr., P.O. Box 3070, South Pasadena, CA 91031-6070.

E-mail: www.sandcastle-online.com. **Description:** Specializes in books that introduce children to the performing arts. Fiction and nonfiction titles range from easy reading to young adult. **Sample Titles:** *Sensational Scenes for Teens* by Chambers Stevens; *African American Heritage Cookbook* by Vanessa Roberts Stevens.

SCHOLASTIC PRESS

Division of Scholastic, Inc.

557 Broadway, New York, NY 10012. 212-343-6100.

Web site: www.scholastic.com. Elizabeth Szabla, Editorial Director; Dianne Hess, Executive Editor; Tracy Mack, Executive Editor; Lauren Thompson, Senior Editor. **Description:** Picture book fiction and nonfiction; literary middle grade and young adult fiction (no genre or series); books dealing with key relationships in children's lives; and books with unique approaches to biography, history, math, or science. **Books Statistics:** 40-60 titles/yr (4,000+ submissions); 5-10% by first-time authors; 1-2% unagented. **Proposal Process:** Prefers to receive submissions from literary agents or previously published authors. Query with outline and sample chapters. Hard copy only. Considers simultaneous submissions. Responds to queries 1-4 weeks, submissions 6-12 months. **Sample Titles:** *Dear Mrs. LaRue* by Mark Teague; *A Corner of the Universe* by Ann M. Martin; *Shatterglass* by Tamora Pierce. **Tips:** No board books/flap books, resources for teachers or librarians, genre or series fiction, poetry, fairy tales, books similar to existing successful titles, or didactic books that carry heavy moral theme. **Contact:** Jennifer Rees, Assistant Editor.

SCHOLASTIC PROFESSIONAL BOOKS

524 Broadway, New York, NY 10012-3999. 212-965-7287.

Web site: www.scholastic.com. Adriane Rozier, Editorial/Production Coordinator. **Description:** Books by and for K-8 teachers. Instructor Books: practical, activity/resource books on teaching reading and writing, science, math, etc. Teaching Strategies Books: 64-96 pages on new ideas, practices, and strategies for teaching. **Proposal Process:** Query with outline, sample chapters or activities, contents page, and resume. Considers simultaneous queries. **Payment:** Flat fee or royalty. **Tips:** "Our theory and practice books are written by academic professionals, thoroughly discuss current research, and show research in practice."

SHOE STRING PRESS

2 Linsley St., North Haven, CT 06473-2517. 203-239-2702.

E-mail: books@shoestringpress.com. Web site: www.shoestringpress.com. Diantha C. Thorpe, Editor. **Description:** Books for children and teenagers, including juvenile nonfiction for ages 10 and older. Resources that share high standards of scholarship and practical experience for teachers and librarians. Imprints include Linnet Books, Archon Books, and Linnet Professional Publications. **Proposal Process:** Submit outline and sample chapters. **Payment:** Royalty.

SILVER MOON PRESS

160 Fifth Ave., Suite 622, New York, NY 10010. 212-242-6499.

E-mail: mail@silvermoonpress.com. Web site: www.silvermoonpress.com. Hope Killcoyne, Editor; David S. Katz, Publisher. **Description:** American historical/biographical fiction with young protagonists, for children ages 8-12. Also educational test prep material/English language arts, and social studies. **Books Statistics:** 6-12 titles/yr (75-100 submissions); 80% by first-time authors; 80% unagented. **Proposal Process:** Query with outline and sample chapters. Accepts simultaneous and electronic queries. Prefers hard copy. Responds in 1-3 months. **Payment:** Royalty. **Contact:** Karin Lillebo.

SIMON & SCHUSTER BOOKS FOR YOUNG READERS

Simon & Schuster Children's Publishing/Simon & Schuster, Inc.

1230 Avenue of the Americas, New York, NY 10020. 212-698-2851.

Web site: www.simonsays.com. Steve Geck, Vice President/Associate Publisher. **Description:** Fiction (picture books and YA novels) and nonfiction for kids in grades PreK-12. **Proposal Process:** Query with SASE. Guidelines available. **Sample Titles:** (Nonfiction) *Elizabeth Taylor's Nibbles and Me* by Elizabeth Taylor; (Fiction)

Eloise Takes a Bawth by Kay Thompson. **Contact:** David Gale, Editorial Director; Paula Wiseman, Editorial Director; Kevin Lewis, Executive Editor.

SPORTS PUBLISHING
804 N Neil, Champaign, IL 61820. 217-363-2072.
E-mail: srauguth@sportspublishingllc.com. Web site: www.sportspublishingllc.com. Scott Rauguth, Editor. **Description:** Leading publisher of regional sports covering a wide range of sports. Kids Superstars series for readers in grades 3-5.

STORY LINE PRESS
Three Oaks Farm, P.O. Box 1240, Ashland, OR 97520-0055. 541-512-8792.
Web site: www.storylinepress.com. Robert McDowell, Editorial Director. **Description:** Fiction, nonfiction, and poetry of varying lengths. **Books Statistics:** 12 titles/yr (8,000 submissions); 10% by first-time authors; 80% unagented. **Proposal Process:** Query with outline, sample chapters and SASE. Accepts simultaneous and electronic queries. Prefers hard copy. **Payment:** Royalty.

TEACHER CREATED MATERIALS
6421 Industry Way, Westminster, CA 92683.
Web site: www.teachercreated.com. **Description:** Quality resource books covering all areas of the educational curriculum. Books are created by teachers for teachers and parents. **Proposal Process:** Send 10-12 sample pages, tentative TOC, summary of audience, content, and objectives, and SASE. Mail materials to P.O. Box 1040, Huntington Beach, CA, 92647. Does not accept electronic submissions.

TIME-LIFE FOR CHILDREN
Time-Life, Inc.
2000 Duke St., Alexandria, VA 22314. 703-838-7000.
Web site: www.timelife.com. Mary J. Wright, Managing Editor. **Description:** Juvenile books. Publishes series of 12-36 volumes (no single titles). Author must have a series concept. **Proposal Process:** Does not accept unsolicited material.

MEGAN TINGLEY BOOKS
Little, Brown & Co. Children's Publishing
1271 Avenue of the Americas, New York, NY 10020.
Web site: www.twbookmark.com/childrens. Megan Tingley, Editor-in-Chief. **Description:** Fiction and nonfiction for preschoolers through young adults. Mainly picture books. No mystery or romance. **Proposal Process:** Agented submissions only.

TRICYCLE PRESS
Ten Speed Press
P.O. Box 7123, Berkeley, CA 94707. 510-559-1600.
Web site: www.tenspeed.com. Nicole Geiger, Publisher. **Description:** Publishes activity books (ages 3-12); novels for young readers (ages 8-12); picture books (ages

3+); and "real life" books (ages 3-13) for kids and parents on important growing-up issues. **Books Statistics:** 20 titles/yr (8,000-10,000 submissions); 15-20% first-time authors; 50% unagented. **Proposal Process:** No queries. Send outline and sample chapters for novels and activity books; complete mss for picture books. No electronic queries or faxed submissions. Hard-copy format only. Responds in 12-24 weeks. **Payment:** Royalty, 15-20% net. **Sample Titles:** *G is for Googol: A Math Alphabet Book* by David M. Schwartz; *Pretend Soup and Other Real Recipes: A Cookbook for Preschoolers* by Mollie Katzen and Ann Henderson; **Tips:** See Web site for specific submission guidelines.

TROLL COMMUNICATIONS
100 Corporate Dr., Mahwah, NJ 07430. 201-529-4000.
Web site: www.troll.com. M. Francis, Editor. **Description:** Juvenile fiction and non-fiction. **Proposal Process:** Submit query letter. **Payment:** Royalty or flat fee. **Sample Titles:** *Treasures in the Dust* by Tracy Porter; *In the Forest of the Night* by Amelia Atwater-Rhodes.

TUNDRA BOOKS
McClelland & Stewart
481 University Ave., Suite 900, Toronto, Ontario M5G 2E9 Canada. 416-598-4786. E-mail: mail@mcclelland.com. Web site: www.tundrabooks.com. Kathy Lowinger, Publisher. **Description:** Fiction, nonfiction, books for young adults, myths and legends, history, and picture books. **Tips:** Currently not accepting unsolicited manuscripts.

TURTLE BOOKS
866 United Nations Plaza, Suite 525, New York, NY 10017. 212-644-2020.
Web site: www.turtlebooks.com. John Whitman, Publisher. **Description:** Children's picture books only. **Proposal Process:** Submit complete manuscript with SASE. **Payment:** Royalty. **Sample Titles:** *The Lady in the Box* by Ann McGovern; *The Legend of Mexicatl* by Jo Harper.

TWENTY-FIRST CENTURY BOOKS
The Millbrook Press
P.O. Box 335, 2 Old New Milford Rd., Brookfield, CT 06804. 203-740-2220.
Web site: www.millbrookpress.com. Kristen Vibbert, Manuscript Coordinator. **Description:** Curriculum-oriented publisher for the school and library market, focusing on current issues, U.S. history, science, biography and social studies, etc. **Books Statistics:** 135 titles/yr (2,000 submissions). **Proposal Process:** Query with outline. Considers simultaneous queries, but not e-queries. Hard copy only. Responds in 2-3 months. **Payment:** Royalty. **Tips:** Accepts full submissions through agents only. Requires proposals with strong tie to curriculum for grades 5 and up. Picture books, activity books, parent's guides, etc., will not be considered. Send SASE for guidelines or catalog.

VIKING CHILDREN'S BOOKS

Division of Penguin Young Readers Group
345 Hudson St., New York, NY 10014.
Web site: www.penguinputnam.com.
Description: "Viking Children's Books is currently not accepting unsolicited manuscripts. Thank you."

ALBERT WHITMAN & CO.

6340 Oakton St., Morton Grove, IL 60053. 847-581-0033.
Web site: www.albertwhitman.com. Kathleen Tucker, Editor-in-Chief.
Description: Picture books for ages 2-8. Also novels, biographies, mysteries, and nonfiction for middle-grade readers. **Proposal Process:** Send complete manuscript for picture books, 3 chapters and outline for longer fiction; query for nonfiction.

WILEY CHILDREN'S BOOKS

John Wiley & Sons, Inc.
111 River St., Hoboken, NJ 07030. 201-748-6088.
E-mail: info@wiley.com. Web site: www.wiley.com. **Description:** Nonfiction books, 96-128 pages, for children 8-12. **Proposal Process:** Query. **Payment:** Royalty.

WILLIAMSON PUBLISHING CO.

P.O. Box 185, Charlotte, VT 05445. 802-425-2102.
Web site: www.williamsonbooks.com. Susan Williamson, Editorial Director.
Description: How-to-do-it learning books based on a philosophy that says "learning is exciting, mistakes are fine, and involvement and curiosity are wonderful." **Books Statistics:** 15 titles/yr (800-1,000 submissions); 50% by first-time authors; 90% unagented. **Proposal Process:** Query with outline and sample chapters. No simultaneous or electronic queries. Hard copy only. Responds in 3-4 months. **Payment:** Royalty or flat fee. **Tips:** "We're looking for knowledgeable writers who know their subject and understand how kids learn. Writing should be filled with information supported by how-to activities that make learning a positive and memorable experience. All of our books are written directly to kids, although they are also often used by teachers and parents. We're also looking for illustrators who work in B&W and can combine how-to illustrations along with a sense of 'kid' humor."

WIZARDS OF THE COAST, INC.

P.O. Box 707, 1801 Lind Avenue, SW, Renton, WA 98055. 425-226-6500.
Web site: www.wizards.com/books. **Description:** Publisher of shared-world fantasy and science fiction series. **Proposal Process:** Series are developed in-house and writers are hired on work-for-hire basis only. Send writing sample (short stories accepted), cover letter with brief description, credentials, and SASE. No phone calls. Responds in 12-18 weeks. **Sample Titles:** *Lord of Stormweather* by Dave Gross; *Emperor's Fist* by Scott McGough.

ZINO PRESS CHILDREN'S BOOKS
2348 Pinehurst Dr., Middleton, WI 53562. 608-836-6660.
Web site: www.zinopress.com. Dave Schreiner, Acquisitions/Production Editor.
Description: Original fiction that tells an unusual story and composed in rhyme.
Also publishes nonfiction or fiction on multicultural issues that promote positive
images and tolerance. **Proposal Process:** Send complete manuscript with SASE.
Responds within 1 month. **Sample Titles:** *A Drawing in the Sand: The Story of
African American Art* by Jerry Butler; *How to Be the Greatest Writer in the World*
by Matt Cibula; *Fall Is Not Easy* by Marty Kelley. **Tips:** Does not accept folk tales or
descriptive rhymes on food or animals.

RELIGIOUS BOOKS

Religious book publishing is growing in leaps and bounds. In the 21st century, it ranges from books on Jewish traditions to Christian devotionals, from picture books for children to religious romances, from scholarly works on theology to the popular prophesy of the fictional *Left Behind* series (published by Tyndale House), found high on *The New York Times* bestseller lists.

Clearly, each publisher of religious books has a distinctive mission, often with a specialized sense of ideal approach and language to be used. Publishers expect their authors to be knowledgeable about readers' needs, to be familiar with the appropriate methods and concerns required for any book in this field to succeed.

Perhaps even more so than for other markets, before sending off materials, research each publisher under consideration carefully. Request a catalog, and get a copy of their guidelines for queries and submissions (often found on publisher Web sites). Be sure to send an SASE with your query, as well as sufficient return postage for any subsequent materials or illustrations sent.

JASON ARONSON, INC.

230 Livingston St., Northvale, NJ 07647-1726. 201-767-4093.

Web site: www.aronson.com. Dana Salzman, Associate Publisher. **Description:** Nonfiction on all aspects of Jewish life, including such topics as anti-semitism, the Bible, Hasidic thought, genealogy, medicine, folklore and storytelling, interfaith relations, the Holocaust, the Talmud, women's studies, and travel. **Proposal Process:** Send complete manuscript or query with outline and sample chapters. **Payment:** Royalty.

BAKER BOOKS

P. O. Box 6287, Grand Rapids, MI 49516-6287. 616-676-9185.

Web site: www.bakerbooks.com. Don Stephenson, Director of Publications. **Description:** Publishes hardcover and trade paperbacks in both fiction and nonfiction categories: trade books for the general public; professional books for church and parachurch leaders; texts for college and seminary classrooms. Topics include contemporary issues, women's concerns, parenting, singleness, children's books, Bible study, Christian doctrine, reference books, books for pastors and church leaders, textbooks for Christian colleges and seminaries, and literary novels focusing on women's concerns. **Books Statistics:** 250 titles/yr; 10% by first-time authors; 65% unagented. **Sample Titles:** *I Am with You Always* by Chip Ingram; *Transformed for Life* by Derek Prince; *Night Whispers* by Jennie Afman Dimkoff. **Tips:** Does not accept unsolicited proposals. See Web site for guidelines.

BETHANY HOUSE PUBLISHERS

11400 Hampshire Ave. S, Minneapolis, MN 55438. 952-829-2500.

Web site: www.bethanyhouse.com. **Description:** Religious fiction and nonfiction. Adults: personal growth, devotionals, women's issues, spirituality, contemporary issues. Adult manuscripts should be 75,000 words or longer. Typical novels range up to 125,000 words. Children and teens: first chapter books, 6,000-7,500 words, of biblical lessons and Christian faith for ages 7-10; imaginative stories and believable characters, 20,000-40,000 words, for middle grade readers; and at least 40,000-word stories with strong plots and realistic characters for teens of ages 12-17. **Proposal Process:** Does not accept unsolicited manuscripts or book proposals. Does accept 1-page fax proposals (see Web site for current number), directed to Adult Nonfiction, Adult Fiction, or YA/Children editors. Accepts queries, proposals, and manuscripts through literary agents, manuscript services, and writer's conferences attended by editorial staff. **Sample Titles:** (Nonfiction) *The Eyes of the Heart* by Tracie Peterson; (Fiction) *The Covenant* by Beverly Lewis; (Youth) *Long Shot* by Sigmund Brouwer.

BLUE DOLPHIN PUBLISHING, INC.

P.O. Box 8, Nevada City, CA 95959-0008. 530-265-6925.
E-mail: bdolphin@nutshel.net. Web site: www.bluedolphinpublishing.com. Paul M. Clemens, President. **Description:** Books, 200-300 pages, on comparative spiritual traditions, lay and transpersonal psychology, self-help, health, healing, and whatever helps people grow in their social awareness and conscious evolution. **Proposal Process:** Query with outline, sample chapters, and SASE. **Payment:** Royalty.

BROADMAN AND HOLMAN PUBLISHERS

127 Ninth Ave. N, Nashville, TN 37234-0115.
Web site: www.broadmanholman.com. Leonard G. Goss, Editorial Director. **Description:** Trade, academic, religious, and inspirational fiction and nonfiction. **Books Statistics:** 100 titles/yr **Proposal Process:** Query with SASE. Guidelines available. **Payment:** Royalty. **Sample Titles:** *Jesus the One and Only* by Beth Moore; *Mission Compromised* by Oliver North.

CHRISTIAN PUBLICATIONS

3825 Hartzdale Dr., Camp Hill, PA 17011. 717-761-7044.
E-mail: editors@christianpublications.com.
Web site: www.christianpublications.com. Lauraine Gustafson, Managing Editor. **Description:** Adult nonfiction from an evangelical Christian viewpoint, centering on personal spiritual growth often with a "deeper life" theme. **Books Statistics:** 20 titles/yr (250 submissions); 30% by first-time authors; 99% unagented. **Proposal Process:** Query with outline, proposal, sample chapters, and SASE. Accepts simultaneous and electronic queries. Prefers hard copy. Responds in 6-8 weeks. **Payment:** Royalty, 10% net. **Tips:** Seeking writing that grows out of author's personal relationship with Christ and experience in Christian service, whether lay or ordained. Especially interested in books on spiritual growth, Christian living, family, marriage, home schooling, leadership, inspirational, devotional. May consider theological and Bible study books, but no Bible commentaries.

CONCORDIA PUBLISHING HOUSE

3558 S Jefferson Ave., St. Louis, MO 63118-3968. 314-268-1187
E-mail: brandy.overton@cph.org. Web site: www.cph.org. **Description:** Nonfiction

on Christian living, inspiration, parenting, literature/arts, spirituality, and culture. Also publishes children's/YA titles, devotionals, pastoral/professional resources, day school and Sunday school curriculum and resources, multiethnic materials, music/hymnals, and Bible study/Bible reference materials. **Proposal Process:** Submit brief cover letter with resume, outline, short sample of manuscript, and SASE. Responds in 8-12 weeks. **Payment:** Royalty. **Sample Titles:** (Adult Nonfiction) *Christianity in an Age of Terrorism* by Gene Edward Veith. (YA) *Teens Pray* by Edward C. Grube. (Children's) *The Very First Christmas* by Paul L. Maier. **Tips:** Does not accept poetry, drama, adult fiction, biographies, or short stories. See Web site for submission guidelines. **Contact:** Editorial Assistant.

COOK COMMUNICATIONS MINISTRIES

4050 Lee Vance View, Colorado Springs, CO 80918. 719-536-3271. Web site: www.cookministries.com. **Description:** Nonfiction Christian titles on business, Christian living, marriage/relationships, parenting, leadership, stewardship, inspiration, Bible reference, and women's studies. Also publishes children's and juvenile titles under the Faith Kids Books imprint. **Books Statistics:** 120 titles/yr; 10% by first-time authors; 50% unagented. **Proposal Process:** Submit outline, sample chapters, and SASE. **Sample Titles:** *Taking the High Ground* by Jeff O'Leary; *When Your World Falls Apart* by Mike MacIntosh; *Courage to Connect* by Rich Hurst.

DEVORSS & COMPANY

1046 Princeton Dr., Marina del Rey, CA 90292. 310-822-8940. E-mail: service@devorss.com. Web site: www.devorss.com. **Description:** Nonfiction titles on metaphysical, spiritual, inspirational, New Age, and self-help topics. **Proposal Process:** Write for guidelines. Send SASE for reply and return of materials. **Sample Titles:** *The Little Book of Candle Power* by Carli Logan; *How to be Healthy Wealthy Happy* by Raymond Charles Barker.

WILLIAM B. EERDMANS PUBLISHING CO., INC.

255 Jefferson Ave. SE, Grand Rapids, MI 49503. 616-459-4591. E-mail: info@eerdmans.com. Web site: www.eerdmans.com. Jon Pott, Editor-in-Chief. **Description:** Publishes nonfiction books that focus on Christian theology, religious history and biography, ethics, philosophy, literary studies, and spiritual growth. Also publishes children's books, Biblical reference, and ministry resources. **Proposal Process:** Send query letter explaining the content of the book, intended audience, estimated length, and your qualifications for writing the material. Also state how the book is different from other books currently available on the subject. Include TOC, sample chapters, and SASE. **Payment:** Royalty. **Sample Titles:** *Who Were the Early Israelites and Where Did They Come From?* by William G. Dever; *Scarred by Struggle, Transformed by Hope* by Joan Chittister; *God's Diary* by Joaquin Antonio Peñalosa. **Tips:** Does not respond to submissions sent by e-mail or fax.

FORTRESS PRESS

P.O. Box 1209, Minneapolis, MN 55440. 612-330-3300.
E-mail: submissions@augsburgfortress.org. Web site: fortresspress.com.
Description: Academic and ecumenical publisher of books in religion, with focus in the following: biblical studies, Christian theology (including historical, feminist, and contextual theologies), ethics, history of Christianity, Judaism, religion and science, African-American religion, and pastoral resources. **Books Statistics:** 60 titles/yr; 10% or less by first-time authors. **Proposal Process:** Send bio with curriculum vitae, working title, 250-word description stating thesis, TOC, intended audience, list of competing titles currently on the market, 1-3 sample chapters, and SASE. **Payment:** Royalty. **Sample Titles:** *Writings of the New Testament* by Luke Timothy Johnson; *The Prophetic Imagination* by Walter Brueggemann; *Models of God* by Sallie McFague.

GENESIS PUBLISHING CO., INC.

1547 Great Pond Rd., North Andover, MA 01845-1216. 978-688-6688.
Web site: www.genesisbook.com. Gerard M. Verschuuren, President. **Description:** Adult fiction and nonfiction, especially on the topics of religion and philosophy. **Proposal Process:** Query with SASE. **Payment:** Royalty.

GOOD NEWS PUBLISHERS/CROSSWAY BOOKS

1300 Crescent St., Wheaton, IL 60187. 630-682-4300.
E-mail: editorial@gnpcb.org. Web site: www.crosswaybooks.org. **Description:** Publishes books with an Evangelical Christian perspective. Fiction (historical, action/adventure, contemporary/Christian realism, YA), nonfiction (Christian living, Biblical teaching, evangelism, Christian truth), and a select number of academic/professional volumes. **Books Statistics:** 85 titles/yr. **Proposal Process:** Send 1-2 page synopsis (preferably chapter by chapter), 2 sample chapters, and SASE. Does not accept e-mail or fax submissions. Do not send complete manuscript. Responds in 4-6 months. **Sample Titles:** *Jesus Driven Ministry* by Ajita Fernado; *Holiness by Grace: Delighting in the Joy That is Our Strength* by Bryan Chapell. **Tips:** See guidelines on Web site before submitting. **Contact:** Jill Carter, Editorial Administrator.

GOSPEL LIGHT PUBLICATIONS

2300 Knoll Drive, Ventura, CA 93003-7383. 805-644-9721.
Web site: www.gospellight.com. **Description:** Sunday school curriculum, teacher training resources, and inspirational biblical books for pastors and church leaders. **Proposal Process:** Send cover letter with outline, 2-3 sample lessons, and SASE. Currently not accepting manuscripts for Regal imprint. **Sample Titles:** *Blessing Your Children: How You Can Love the Kids in Your Life* by Jack W. Hayford; *The Worship Warrior: How Your Prayer and Worship Can Protect Your Home and Community* by Chuck D. Pierce. **Tips:** Does not accept unsolicited manuscripts.

HACHAI PUBLISHING
156 Chester Ave., Brooklyn, NY 11218. 718-633-0100.
E-mail: info@hachai.com. Web site: www.hachai.com. D.L. Rosenfeld, Editor.
Description: Publishes Judaica children's picture books for readers ages 2-8.
Interested in stories that convey traditional Jewish experience in modern times, traditional Jewish observance such as holidays and year-round mitzvahs, and positive
character traits. **Books Statistics:** 4 titles/yr (300 submission); 60% by first-time
authors; 90% unagented. **Proposal Process:** Query or send complete manuscript,
and SASE. Accepts simultaneous queries, but not e-queries. Hard copy only.
Responds in 6 weeks. **Payment:** Flat fee. **Tips:** "We do not accept fantasy, animal stories, romance, violence, or preachy sermonizing."

HARPER SAN FRANCISCO
HarperCollins Publishers
353 Sacramento St., Suite 500, San Francisco, CA 94111-3653. 415-477-4400.
Web site: www.harpercollins.com. **Description:** Books on spirituality and religion.
Strives to publish important books "across the full spectrum of religion and spiritual
literature, adding to the wealth of the world's wisdom by respecting all traditions."
Books Statistics: 70 titles/yr; 5% by first-time authors. **Proposal Process:** No unso-
licited manuscripts. Accepts material from literary agents only. **Sample Titles:** *The
Brother of Jesus* by Hershel Shanks and Ben Witherington III; *When Religion
Becomes Evil* by Charles Kimball; *Christmas in Harmony* by Philip Gulley; *100
Simple Secrets of Great Relationships* by David Niven. **Contact:** Acquisitions Editor.

HARVEST HOUSE PUBLISHERS
990 Owen Loop N, Eugene, OR 97402-9173. 541-343-0123.
Web site: www.harvesthousepublishers.com. **Description:** Publisher of Evangelical
Christian books. **Books Statistics:** 160 titles/yr **Proposal Process:** Does not accept
unsolicited submissions. Recommends using Evangelical Christian Publishers
Association (ECPA). Web site www.ecpa.org or the Writer's Edge, P.O. Box 1266,
Wheaton, IL. 60189 **Tips:** "We provide high-quality books and products that glorify
God, affirm biblical values, help people grow spiritually strong, and proclaim Jesus
Christ as the answer to every human need."

JOURNEYFORTH BOOKS
Bob Jones University Press
1700 Wade Hampton Blvd., Greenville, SC 29614.370-1800 x 4350.
E-mail: jb@bjup.com. Web site: www.bjup.com/books. **Description:** Christian publisher. Books for young readers, ages 6-teen, that reflect "the highest Christian standards of thought, feeling, and action." Also adult nonfiction titles on home/family,
Christian living, theology, church ministries, church history, etc. Also textbooks,
Bible-study tools, and other resources for educators and clergy. **Books Statistics:** 10
titles/yr (500 submissions). **Proposal Process:** Query with outline and sample

chapters or complete manuscript. Accepts simultaneous queries. **Payment:** Negotiable—royalty or flat fee. **Sample Titles:** (Children's) *Arby Jenkins Meets His Match* by Sharon Hambrick. (Adult) *In Search of God's Man: A Help for Pulpit Committees* by Douglas S. DeVore. **Tips:** "Secular conflicts considered, but only within a Christian worldview. Avoid modern humanistic philosophy in stories; instead, emphasize a biblically conservative lifestyle. The writing must be excellent and the story engaging." For adult nonfiction line, prefers KJV. **Contact:** Nancy Lohr, Youth Manuscript Editor; Suzette Jordan, Adult Manuscript Editor.

JUDSON PRESS

American Baptist Churches
P.O. Box 851, Valley Forge, PA 19482-0851.610-768-2109.
E-mail: randy.frame@abc-usa.org. Web site: www.judsonpress.com. Randy Frame, Editor. **Description:** Publishes resources to enhance individual Christian living and the life of the church. **Books Statistics:** 30 title/yr (700 submissions); 20% by first-time authors; 90% unagented. **Proposal Process:** Query with proposal, TOC, estimated length of book, sample chapters, target audience, expected completion date, and bio. Simultaneous queries accepted. Electronic queries okay, but not for proposals. Prefers hard copy. **Payment:** Royalty. **Tips:** Avoid life stories or poetry. Looking for unusually good writing and original ideas.

KREGEL PUBLICATIONS

P.O. Box 2607, Grand Rapids, MI 49501-2607. 616-451-4775.
E-mail: acquisitions@kregel.com. Web site: www.kregelpublications.com. Dennis Hillman, Publisher. **Description:** Evangelical Christian publisher interested in pastoral ministry, Christian education, family and marriage, devotional books, and biblical studies. Also publishes adult and juvenile fiction (with solid Christian message), children's literature, and academic titles. No poetry, general fiction, or cartoons. **Proposal Process:** Query with summary, target audience, brief bio, outline/TOC, 2 sample chapters, and SASE. Allow 2-3 months for response. See Web site for guidelines. **Payment:** Royalty. **Sample Titles:** *Eusebius* translated by Paul Maier; *A Different Kind of Laughter: Finding Joy and Peace in the Deep End of Life* by Andy Cook; *Unveiling Islam* by Ergen Caner and Emir Caner. **Contact:** Acquisitions Editor.

LOYOLA PRESS

3441 N Ashland Ave., Chicago, IL 60657-1397. 773-281-1818.
E-mail: editorial@loyolapress.com; durepos@loyolapress.com.
Web site: www.loyolapress.org. Jim Manney, Editorial Director. **Description:** Publishes Christian books and resources for the general trade. Titles cover gift/inspiration, prayer, spirituality, Catholic life, history, theology, Jesuit or Ignatian spirituality, and spiritual direction. **Books Statistics:** 40 titles/yr (500-600 submissions); 25% by first-time authors; 50% unagented. **Proposal Process:** Send proposal with 1-2 sample chapters and SASE. Simultaneous and electronic queries accepted. Prefers

hard copy. Responds in 6-8 weeks. **Payment:** Royalty, typically industry standard. **Sample Titles:** *The New Faithful* by Colleen Carroll; *Mystics & Miracles* by Bert Ghezzi; *Waiting with Gabriel* by Amy Kuebelbeck. **Tips:** Does not accept academic material, poetry, children's books, or fiction. See Web site for guidelines. **Contact:** Joseph Durepos, Acquisitions Editor.

MOODY PUBLISHERS
820 N LaSalle Blvd., Chicago, IL 60610-3284. 312-329-8047. E-mail: acquisitions@moody.edu. Web site: www.moodypublishers.org. **Description:** Evangelical Christian books in categories such as Christian living, women, marriage/family, finances, and fiction. **Proposal Process:** Considers agented proposals only. No phone calls. **Tips:** Seeks "to educate the Christian and to evangelize the non-Christian by ethically publishing conservative, evangelical Christian literature and other media for all ages around the world." **Contact:** Acquisitions Coordinator.

MOREHOUSE PUBLISHING
4775 Linglestown Rd., Harrisburg, PA 17112. 717-541-8130. E-mail: dfarring@morehousegroup.com. Web site: www.morehousepublishing.com. Debra Farrington, Publisher and Editorial Director. **Description:** An Episcopal publisher specializing in books on spirituality, Anglican studies, professional books for clergy, and Episcopal adult formation materials. **Books Statistics:** 30-35 titles/yr (500-750 submissions); 60% by first-time authors; 90% unagented. **Proposal Process:** Query with cover letter, brief proposal, resume, short book description, outline, market analysis, sample chapters (20 pages). Accepts simultaneous queries, but not e-queries. Responds in 4-6 weeks. **Tips:** No fiction or poetry. "We are currently not accepting children's book manuscripts."

MULTNOMAH PUBLISHERS, INC.
P.O. Box 1720, Sisters, OR 97759. 541-549-1144. Web site: www.multnomahbooks.com. David Webb, Managing Editor. **Description:** Evangelical, Christian publishing house. "Multnomah Books are message-driven, clean, moral, uplifting fiction and nonfiction." Does not accept unsolicited manuscripts. **Proposal Process:** Submit 2-3 sample chapters with outline, cover letter, and SASE. **Payment:** Royalty.

THOMAS NELSON PUBLISHERS
P.O. Box 141000, Nashville, TN 37214-1000. Web site: www.thomasnelson.com. **Description:** Publishes nonfiction adult inspirational, motivational, devotional, self-help, Christian living, prayer, and evangelism titles. Also, fiction from a Christian perspective. **Books Statistics:** 40-50 titles/yr **Proposal Process:** Send query with SASE. **Payment:** Royalty. **Sample Titles:** *Wild at Heart* by John Eldredge; *Seeking His Face* by Charles F. Stanley. **Tips:** Does not accept unsolicited manuscripts. All material must be submitted through a literary agent. **Contact:** Acquisitions Editor.

NEW CANAAN PUBLISHING COMPANY

P.O. Box 752, New Canaan, CT 06840.

E-mail: djm@newcanaanpublishing.com. Web site: www.newcanaanpublishing.com. Kathy Mittelstadt, Editor. **Description:** Children's books for readers ages 5-16. Also YA fiction/nonfiction and Christian titles. **Books Statistics:** 3-4 titles/yr (120 submissions); 50% by first-time authors; 100% unagented. **Proposal Process:** Submit complete manuscript with SASE. Accepts simultaneous queries, but not e-queries. Hard copy only. Responds in 6 months. **Sample Titles:** (Nonfiction) *Dynamic Evangelism* by Luke Tamu. (Children's) *Little Red Baseball Stockings and Other Stories* by Nathan Zimelman. **Tips:** Seeks strong educational and moral content.

NEW LEAF PRESS, INC./MASTER BOOKS

P.O. Box 726, Green Forest, AR 72638. 870-438-5288.

E-mail: nlp@newleafpress.net. Web site: www.newleafpress.net. Roger Howerton, Acquisitions Editor. **Description:** New Leaf Press: nonfiction titles, 100-400 pages, on Christian living as well as gift books and devotionals. Master Books: nonfiction titles related to creationism, including children's books, scholarly works, and books for the layman. No poetry, fiction, or personal stories. **Books Statistics:** 15-20 titles/yr (500-600 submissions); 15% by first-time authors. **Proposal Process:** Query with outline and sample chapters. Accepts simultaneous queries. Responds in 3 months. **Payment:** Royalty, 10% of net. **Sample Titles:** (New Leaf Press) *G.I. Joe & Lillie* by Joseph S. Bonsall; (Master Books) *Grand Canyon: A Different View* by Tom Vail. **Tips:** "Tell us why this book is marketable and to which market(s) it is directed. How will it fulfill the needs of Christians?"

OUR SUNDAY VISITOR PUBLISHING

200 Noll Plaza, Huntington, IN 46750. 219-356-8400.

E-mail: booksed@osv.com. Web site: www.osv.com. Jacquelyn M. Lindsey, Mike Dubruiel, Beth McNamara, Acquisitions Editors. **Description:** Catholic-oriented nonfiction of various lengths. **Books Statistics:** 20-30 titles/yr (500+ submissions); 10% by first-time authors; 90% unagented. **Proposal Process:** Query with proposal, outline, market analysis, and SASE. Responds in 3 months. **Payment:** Royalty.

PARACLETE PRESS

P.O. Box 1568, Orleans, MA 02653. 508-255-4685.

E-mail: mail@paracletepress.com. Web site: www.paracletepress.com. Editorial Review Committee. **Description:** An ecumenical publisher specializing in full-length, nonfiction works for the adult Christian market. **Books Statistics:** 16 titles/yr (150-250 submissions). **Proposal Process:** Query with summary of proposed book and its target audience, estimated length of book, TOC, and 1-2 sample chapters. Accepts simultaneous queries. Responds in 8 weeks. **Payment:** Royalty.

PAULINE BOOKS & MEDIA

Daughters of St. Paul

50 Saint Paul's Ave., Jamaica Plain, MA 02130-3491. 617-522-8911.

Web site: www.pauline.org. **Description:** Roman Catholic publications for both adults and children.

PAULIST PRESS
997 Macarthur Blvd., Mahwah, NJ 07430. 201-825-7300.
Web site: www.paulistpress.com. Lawrence Boadt, Publisher. **Description:** Adult nonfiction, 120-250 pages, on ecumenical theology, Roman Catholic studies, liturgy, spirituality, church history, ethics, religious education, and Christian philosophy. Also publishes a limited number of story books for children. HiddenSpring imprint publishes general religious trade books. **Proposal Process:** For adult books, query with SASE. For juvenile books, submit complete manuscript, with one sample illustration. No simultaneous submissions. **Payment:** Flat fee or royalty. **Contact:** Paul McMahon, Managing Editor.

QUEST BOOKS
Theosophical Publishing House
306 W Geneva Rd., P. O. Box 270, Wheaton, IL 60189-0270. 630-665-0130.
Web site: www.questbooks.net. Brenda Rosen, Acquisitions Editor. **Description:** Nonfiction books on Eastern and Western religion and philosophy, holistic health, healing, transpersonal psychology, men's and women's spirituality, creativity, meditation, yoga, ancient wisdom. **Proposal Process:** Query with outline and sample chapters. **Payment:** Royalty or flat fee. **Contact:** Anna Urosevich.

ST. ANTHONY MESSENGER PRESS
28 W Liberty St., Cincinnati, OH 45202. 513-241-5615.
E-mail: stanthony@americancatholic.org. Web site: www.americancatholic.org. Lisa Biedenbach, Editorial Director. **Description:** Inspirational nonfiction for Catholics. Supports a Christian lifestyle in our culture by providing material on scripture, church history, education, practical spirituality, parish ministries, and family-based religious education programs. Also publishes liturgy resources, Franciscan resources, prayer aids, and children's books. **Proposal Process:** Query with 500-word summary. **Payment:** Royalty.

SAINT MARY'S PRESS
Christian Brothers of the Midwest Province
702 Terrace Heights, Winona, MN 55987-1320. 800-533-8095.
Web site: www.smp.org. Lorraine Kilmartin, Editor-in-Chief. **Description:** Nonprofit Catholic publisher developing materials in 5 lines: Catholic high school religion textbooks and resources; parish religious education and youth ministry resources; the Bible and supplemental resources; family faith-life resources; and teen spirituality resources.

SCHOCKEN BOOKS
Knopf Publishing Group/Random House, Inc.
299 Park Ave., New York, NY 10171. 212-572-2838.

Web site: www.schocken.com. Susan Ralston, Editorial Director. **Description:** Fiction and nonfiction books of Jewish interest. **Books Statistics:** 9 titles/yr. **Proposal Process:** Query with outline and sample chapters. Accepts simultaneous queries, but not e-queries. Prefers hard copy. Responds in 1 month. **Payment:** Royalty. **Sample Titles:** *Living a Life That Matters* by Harold Kushner; *The Jewish Holiday Kitchen* by Joan Nathan; *How to Be a Jewish Parent* by Anita Diamant. **Tips:** Looking for well-written fiction, history, biography, current affairs of Jewish interest for general readers. **Contact:** Altie Karper, Editor; Cecelia Cancellaro, Editor.

SHAW BOOKS

WaterBrook Press
2375 Telstar Dr., Suite 160, Colorado Springs, CO 80920-3669. 719-590-4999.
Web site: www.shawbooks.com. Elisa Fryling Stanford, Editor. **Description:** Nonfiction books with a Christian perspective. **Books Statistics:** 25 titles/yr; 20% by first-time authors; 50% unagented. **Proposal Process:** Query with SASE. **Payment:** Flat fee or royalty. **Sample Titles:** *Penguins and Golden Calves* by Madeleine L'Engle; *Simple Acts of Moving Forward* by Vinita Hampton Wright.

STANDARD PUBLISHING

8121 Hamilton Ave., Cincinnati, OH 45231. 513-931-4050.
Web site: www.standardpub.com. **Description:** Christian children's materials: books, board books, picture books, coloring books, and Christian church curriculum/teacher resources. **Books Statistics:** 70 titles/yr (2,000 submissions); 15% by first-time authors; 80% unagented. **Proposal Process:** Query with outline. Simultaneous queries accepted. Responds in 3 months. **Payment:** Royalty (typically 5-10%) and flat fee (varies). **Tips:** "Study our products before submitting. Call or write for up-to-date guidelines."

TRINITY PRESS INTERNATIONAL

4775 Linglestown Rd., Harrisburg, PA 17112. 717-541-8130.
Web site: www.trinitypressintl.com. Henry L. Carrigan, Jr., Editorial Director. **Description:** Serious studies and research in Bible and theology/religion, interfaith studies, African-American religious life and thought, biblical interpretation, and methodology. **Books Statistics:** 30 titles/yr. **Proposal Process:** Query with outline and sample chapters, or send complete manuscript. Considers simultaneous and electronic queries. Prefers hard copy. Responds in 4-6 weeks. **Payment:** Royalty.

TYNDALE HOUSE PUBLISHERS, INC.

351 Executive Dr., Carol Stream, IL 60188. 630-668-8300.
E-mail: manuscripts@tyndale.com. Web site: www.tyndale.com. **Description:** General-interest titles for the evangelical Christian market including fiction (romance, suspense, historical), general nonfiction (home/family, devotional, motivational, Christian growth, humor), Bibles and Bible reference, and children's books. **Books Statistics:** 300+ titles/yr; 5% by first-time authors; 0% unagented. **Proposal**

Process: Does not accept unsolicited manuscripts or proposals; agented material only. Responds in 3-4 months to queries. Send SASE or see Web site for guidelines. **Payment:** Royalty. **Sample Titles:** (Fiction) *Unspoken* by Francine Rivers; (Nonfiction) *Beyond Belief to Convictions* by Josh D. McDowell and Bob Hostetler; (Children's) *Before I Dream Bible Storybook* by Karyn Henley. **Tips:** Does not accept curriculum, plays, poetry, sermons, or music.

UAHC PRESS

633 Third Ave., New York, NY 10017. 212-650-4120.
E-mail: uahcpress@uahc.org. Web site: www.uahcpress.com. Rabbi Hara Person, Editorial Director. **Description:** Trade books and textbooks of Jewish interest for preschool through adult readers. **Books Statistics:** 18 titles/yr (300 submissions); 17% by first-time authors; 100% unagented. **Proposal Process:** Query with outline and sample chapters. Considers simultaneous queries. Prefers hard copy. Responds in 4-8 weeks. **Payment:** Royalty. **Sample Titles:** (Nonfiction) *Jewish Living: A Guide to Contemporary Reform Practice* by Mark Washofsky; (Children's) *Solomon and the Trees* by Matt Biers-Ariel. **Tips:** Seeks books dealing with Jewish topics in areas of textbooks for religious classrooms, children's trade, and adult nonfiction.

UPPER ROOM BOOKS

Division of Upper Room Ministries
1908 Grand Ave., Nashville, TN 37212. 615-340-7332.
Web site: www.upperroom.org. JoAnn Miller, Executive Editor. **Description:** Focuses on Christian spiritual formation (families, churches, small groups, congregational leaders, and individuals). **Books Statistics:** 15 titles/yr (300 submissions); 2% by first-time authors; 100% unagented. **Proposal Process:** Query with outline, 2 sample chapters, and SASE. Prefers electronic submissions. Considers simultaneous queries. See guidelines on Web site. **Payment:** Royalty. **Sample Titles:** *Called by a New Name: Becoming What God Has Promised* by Gerrit Scott Dawson; *Abundance: Joyful Living in Christ* by Marilyn Brown Oden. **Tips:** Keep these categories in mind: Opening Our Hearts and Minds to God, Walking Together with Christ, Preparing the Spiritual Way for Emerging Generations, Maturing as Spiritual Leaders, and Realizing Our Oneness in Christ. No fiction or poetry.

W PUBLISHING GROUP

Thomas Nelson, Inc.
545 Marriott Dr., Suite 750, P.O. Box 141000, Nashville, TN 37214. 615-902-3602.
Web site: www.wpublishinggroup.com. David L. Moberg, Publisher. **Description:** Christian titles on apologetics/theology, Bible/Bible reference, career/personal finance, Christian living, devotionals, fiction, marriage/family, men, ministry, women, and youth. **Proposal Process:** Does not accept unsolicited manuscripts. **Payment:** Royalty. **Sample Titles:** *A Love Worth Giving* by Max Lucado; *Great Lives Volume 6: Paul* by Charles R. Swindoll; *Strong Women, Soft Hearts* by Paula Rinehart.

WESTMINSTER JOHN KNOX PRESS

Presbyterian Publishing Corporation

100 Witherspoon St., Louisville, KY 40202-1396. 502-569-5613.

E-mail: ldowell@presbypub.com. Web site: www.presbypub.com. **Description:** Academic nonfiction in Biblical studies, theology, church history, homiletics, ethics, and religious studies. "Books that inform, interpret, challenge, and encourage religious faith and living." **Proposal Process:** Send curriculum vitae, TOC, one-page summary, introduction or sample chapter, and SASE. Do not send via e-mail. Responds in 6-8 weeks. **Payment:** Royalty. **Sample Titles:** *Soul Feast: An Invitation to the Christian Spiritual Life* by Marjorie Thompson; *The Gospel According to the Simpsons* by Mark I. Pinsky. **Contact:** Lori Dowell, Editorial Department.

ZONDERKIDZ

Zondervan Publishing

5300 Patterson Avenue SE, Grand Rapids, MI 49530. 616-698-6900.

Web site: www.zondervan.com. **Description:** Publishes children's books based on Christian values. **Tips:** See Web site for specific submission guidelines. Prospective writers must follow guidelines exactly, or submissions will go unread. **Contact:** Julie Marchese, Editorial Assistant.

ZONDERVAN

HarperCollinsPublishers

5300 Patterson SE, Grand Rapids, MI 49530. 616-698-6900.

E-mail: zpub@zondervan.com. Web site: www.zondervan.com. Diane Bloem, Manuscript Editor. **Description:** General fiction and nonfiction for children and adults in the Christian publishing market. **Books Statistics:** 150 titles/yr. **Proposal Process:** Query with outline and sample chapters. Considers simultaneous queries. Does not accept manuscripts or queries via e-mail. No poetry, drama, sermons, cookbooks or dissertations. **Sample Titles:** *Purpose Driven Life* by Rick Warren; *Courageous Leadership* by Bill Hybels. **Tips:** Does not accept unsolicited manuscripts and proposals sent by air or surface mail. Authors may fax proposals to 616-698-3454, c/o Book Proposal Review Editor; or submit work electronically to First Edition, The ECPA Manuscript Service, at www.ecpa.org.

OTHER MARKETS
& RESOURCES

AGENTS

As the number of book publishers that will consider only agented submissions grows, more writers are turning to agents to sell their manuscripts. The following list includes agents that handle literary work, agents that handle dramatic work, and those that handle both. Submission procedures, commission rates, and organizations to which the agent(s) is a member are also included in each listing. Since agents derive their income from the sales of their clients' work, they must represent writers who are selling fairly regularly to good markets. Nonetheless, many of the agents listed here note they will consider unpublished writers. Always query an agent first, and enclose a self-addressed, stamped envelope—most agents will not respond without it. Do not send any sample material until the agent has requested it.

Be wary of agents who charge fees for reading manuscripts. The agents listed below have indicated they do not charge reading fees, however it is typical for many agents to charge their clients for copyright fees, manuscript retyping, photocopies, copies of books for use in the sale of other rights, and long-distance calls.

To learn more about agents and their role in publishing, the Association of Authors' Representatives, Inc., (AAR) publishes a canon of ethics as well as an up-to-date list of members. Write to: Association of Authors' Representatives, P.O. Box 237201, Ansonia Station, New York, NY 10023, or visit their Web site: www.aar-online.org.

Another good source which lists agents and their policies is *Literary Market Place*, a directory found in most libraries.

ABRAMS ARTISTS AGENCY

275 Seventh Ave., Fl. 26, New York, NY 10001. 646-486-4600.
Description: Plays and screenplays. Receives 1,000 queries/submissions per year. Unpublished writers considered. **Submissions:** Query with synopsis, up to 10 sample pages, bio/resume, and SASE. Accepts simultaneous queries, but not e-queries. **Commission:** 10%. **Contact:** Charmaine Ferenczi.

MIRIAM ALTSHULER LITERARY AGENCY

53 Old Post Rd N, Red Hook, NY 12571. 845-758-9408.
Description: Serious literary fiction, serious commercial fiction and nonfiction, memoirs, general nonfiction, and narrative nonfiction. Receives 3,000 queries/yr; 275 submissions/yr. Accepts unsolicited queries, but not manuscripts. Unpublished writers considered. **Submissions:** Query with SASE. Accepts simultaneous queries and e-queries (no attachments). Responds in 3 weeks. **Commission:** 15% domestic, 20% foreign. **Member:** AAR. **Tips:** No romance, sci fi, self-help, spiritual, mystery, fantasy, poetry, screenplays, how-to, or techno-thrillers. **Contact:** Miriam Altshuler.

MICHAEL AMATO AGENCY

1650 Broadway, Suite 307, New York, NY 10019-6833. 212-247-4456.
Web site: www.amatoagency.tvheaven.com. **Description:** Screenplays. **Submissions:** Query or send complete manuscript with SASE. **Commission:** 10%.

MARCIA AMSTERDAM AGENCY

41 W 82 St., #9A, New York, NY 10024-5613. 212-873-4945.

Description: Adult and YA fiction, mainstream nonfiction, and screenplays and teleplays in the categories of comedy, romance, and psychological suspense. Receives 14,000 submissions/yr. Accepts 5-6% of unsolicited material. Accepts unsolicited queries, but not manuscripts. Considers unpublished writers. **Submissions:** Query with bio/resume and SASE. Accepts simultaneous queries, but not e-queries. Responds within 2 weeks. **Commission:** 10% screen/television, 15% books, 20% foreign. **Member:** WGA signatory. **Contact:** Marcia Amsterdam.

THE AXELROD AGENCY

49 Main St., P.O. Box 357, Chatham, NY 12037. 518-392-2100.

E-mail: steve@axelrodagency.com. **Description:** Fiction and nonfiction. No unsolicited manuscripts. **Submissions:** Query with SASE. Responds in 3-6 weeks. **Commission:** 15% domestic, 20% foreign. **Member:** AAR. **Contact:** Steven Axelrod.

MALAGA BALDI LITERARY AGENCY

204 W 84th St., Suite 3C, New York, NY 10024. 212-579-5075.

E-mail: mbaldi@aol.com. **Description:** Quality literary adult fiction and nonfiction. Receives 1,000+ queries/submissions per year. Accepts 2% of unsolicited material. Considers unsolicited queries/manuscripts. **Submissions:** "Send query first; if we are interested, we will ask for proposal, outline, and sample pages for nonfiction, complete manuscript for fiction." Accepts simultaneous queries, but not e-queries. Responds in 10 weeks. **Commission:** 15%. **Contact:** Malaga Baldi.

THE BALKIN AGENCY, INC.

P.O. Box 222, Amherst, MA 01004. 413-548-9835.

E-mail: balkin@crocker.com. **Description:** Specializes in adult nonfiction, professional books, and college textbooks. Does not accept unsolicited manuscripts. **Submissions:** Query with outline, 1 sample chapter, and SASE. **Commission:** 15% domestic, 20% foreign. **Member:** AAR. **Contact:** Rick Balkin.

LORETTA BARRETT BOOKS, INC.

101 Fifth Ave., Fl. 11, New York, NY 10003. 212-242-3420.

Description: Fiction and nonfiction. No unsolicited manuscripts. **Submissions:** Query with SASE. For fiction, include synopsis; for nonfiction, include outline and sample chapters. No e-mail or fax queries. **Member:** AAR. **Contact:** Loretta Barrett, Nick Mullendore.

BERMAN, BOALS & FLYNN, INC.

208 W 30th St., Suite 401, New York, NY 10001. 212-868-1068.

E-mail: bbf@earthlink.net. **Description:** Full-length stage plays and musicals. Considers unsolicited queries, but not manuscripts. **Submissions:** Query with bio/resume and SASE. **Commission:** 10%. **Contact:** Judy Boals, Jim Flynn, Zack Loeb.

BIG SCORE PRODUCTIONS

P.O. Box 4575, Lancaster, PA 17604. 717-293-0247.
E-mail: bigscore@bigscoreproductions.com.
Web site: www.bigscoreproductions.com. **Description:** Nonfiction and fiction.
Specializes in inspiration and self-help nonfiction, and commercial fiction. No poetry.
Represents 30-50 clients. 25% of clients are new or previously unpublished writers.
Welcomes new writers. **Submissions:** Send query or proposal with outline and TOC.
Prefers to receive submissions via e-mail (no attachments). **Commission:** 15%
domestic. **Contact:** David Robie, Sharon Hanby-Robie, Deb Strubel.

BLEECKER STREET ASSOCIATES, INC.

532 LaGuardia Place, Suite 617, New York, NY 10012. 212-677-4492.
Description: Represents 25% fiction (mystery/suspense, women's novels, literary)
and 75% nonfiction (biography, business, parenting, cooking/food, current affairs,
Judaica, military, finance, health/medicine, nature/environment, history, how-to, New
Age, pop culture, psychology, science/technology, self-help, sociology, sports, women's
studies, politics). Receives 5,000+ queries/yr; 200 submissions/yr. Accepts 2% of
unsolicited material. Accepts unsolicited queries, but not manuscripts. Unpublished
writers considered. **Submissions:** Query with bio/resume and SASE. Accepts simultaneous queries. No phone, fax, or e-queries. Responds in 2-4 weeks. **Commission:**
15% domestic, 25% foreign. **Member:** AAR, MWA, RWA. **Comments:** "Do not call
us with book ideas. Contact us via a query letter. Ditto on fax and e-mail—we will not
respond." **Contact:** Agnes Birnbaum.

REID BOATES LITERARY AGENCY

69 Cooks Crossroad, Pittstown, NJ 08867-0328. 908-730-8523.
Description: Adult mainstream nonfiction only. No unsolicited manuscripts or proposals. Unpublished writers considered. **Submissions:** Send query with SASE via
regular mail. Does not accept simultaneous queries or e-queries. **Commission:** 15%
domestic, 20% foreign. **Contact:** Reid Boates.

BOOK DEALS, INC.

244 Fifth Ave., Suite 2164, New York, NY 10001-7604. 212-252-2701.
E-mail: cfcarney@bookdeals.com. Web site: www.bookdealsinc.com. **Description:**
Commercial fiction, narrative nonfiction, commercial nonfiction (personal finance,
nutrition/fitness, parenting, lifestyle, relationships, self-help, women's health,
mind/body/spirit), and serious nonfiction (American studies, history, science, current
affairs, health/medicine, psychology, religion, ethnic studies, and business). No children's books, cookbooks, poetry, screenplays, or genre fiction. Receives 6,000
queries/submissions per year. Accepts less than 1% of unsolicited material. Considers
unsolicited queries, but not manuscripts. **Submissions:** Query with SASE. Accepts
simultaneous queries, but not e-queries. Responds in 2-6 weeks. **Commission:** 15%
domestic, 20% foreign. **Member:** AAR. **Tips:** "We consider unpublished book
authors with exceptional credentials, a fresh perspective, and quality work." See Web
site for specific guidelines. **Contact:** Caroline Carney.

BOOKSTOP LITERARY AGENCY

67 Meadow View Rd., Orinda, CA 94563. 925-254-2664.
E-mail: info@bookstopliterary.com. Web site: www.bookstopliterary.com.
Description: Juvenile and young adult fiction and nonfiction, also illustration for children's books. Unpublished writers considered. **Submissions:** No queries; send complete manuscript for fiction, sample chapters and outline for nonfiction. **Commission:** 15% **Tips:** Manuscript evaluation services available. **Contact:** Kendra Marcus, Jennifer Rosen.

GEORGES BORCHARDT, INC.

136 E 57th St., New York, NY 10022. 212-753-5785.
Description: Fiction and nonfiction. Does not accept unsolicited manuscripts. **Commission:** 15% domestic **Member:** AAR.

BRANDT & HOCHMAN LITERARY AGENTS

1501 Broadway, New York, NY 10036. 212-840-5760.
Description: Fiction and nonfiction. Does not accept unsolicited manuscripts. **Submissions:** Send query with SASE via regular mail. **Commission:** 15% domestic, 20% foreign. **Member:** AAR. **Contact:** Carl D. Brandt, Gail Hochman, Marianne Merola, Charles Schlessiger, Meg Giles.

ANDREA BROWN LITERARY AGENCY, INC.

1076 Eagle Dr., Salinas, CA 93905. 831-422-5925.
E-mail: ablitag@pacbell.net. **Description:** Children's and YA fiction and nonfiction only. **Submissions:** Query with outline, sample pages, bio/resume, and SASE; no faxes. **Commission:** 15% domestic, 20% foreign. **Member:** SCBWI, WNBA. **Contact:** Andrea Brown, Laura Rennert.

CURTIS BROWN LTD.

10 Astor Place, New York, NY 10003. 212-473-5400.
Description: General trade fiction and nonfiction in a variety of categories. Also represents juvenile material, short stories, poetry, and screenplays. **Submissions:** Query first with SASE. Submit outline or sample chapters. No e-mail or fax queries. Responds in 3 weeks to queries, 5 weeks to manuscripts. **Member:** AAR. **Contact:** Timothy Knowlton, CEO; Peter L. Ginsberg, President.

KNOX BURGER ASSOCIATES LTD

425 Madison Ave., New York, NY 10017. 212-759-8600.
Description: Adult fiction and nonfiction. No science fiction, fantasy, or romance. Accepts unsolicited queries, but not manuscripts. **Submissions:** Query with SASE. No simultaneous or electronic queries. **Commission:** 15% **Member:** AAR. **Tips:** Highly selective in choosing clients. **Contact:** Knox Burger.

SHEREE BYKOFSKY ASSOCIATES, INC.

16 W 36th St., Fl. 13, New York, NY 10018.

Web site: www.shereebee.com. **Description:** Adult fiction (literary and commercial) and nonfiction (popular reference, business, self-help, humor, biography, women's interest, spiritual, multicultural, parenting, gay/lesbian, and cooking). **Submissions:** Query with outline, up to 3 sample pages or proposal, and SASE. Accepts simultaneous queries with notice. Responds in 1 week to queries, 1 month to manuscripts. **Commission:** 15% domestic, 15% foreign. **Member:** AAR, ASJA. **Tips:** No e-mails, phone calls, or unsolicited manuscripts. **Contact:** Sheree Bykofsky.

MARTHA CASSELMAN, LITERARY AGENT

P.O. Box 342, Calistoga, CA 94515-0342. 707-942-4341.

Description: Trade nonfiction, food books, and cookbooks. No fiction, poetry, short stories, children's, or YA. Does not accept unsolicited manuscripts. **Submissions:** Query first with brief writing sample, synopsis, and SASE. Do not send query by fax or e-mail. Accepts simultaneous submissions with notice. **Member:** International Association of Culinary Professionals.

JULIE CASTIGLIA LITERARY AGENCY

1155 Camino del Mar, Suite 510, Del Mar, CA 92014. 858-755-8761.

Description: Fiction (ethnic, commercial, and literary) and nonfiction (science, biography, psychology, women's issues, business/finance, popular culture, health, and niche markets). **Submissions:** Query via regular mail; does not accept phone or fax queries. **Member:** AAR, PEN. **Contact:** Julie Castiglia, Winifred Golden.

HY COHEN LITERARY AGENCY

66 Brookfield Rd., Upper Montclair, NJ 07043-1327. 973-783-9494.

E-mail: cogency@comcast.net. **Description:** Quality adult and YA fiction and nonfiction. Receives several hundred queries/submissions per year; little unsolicited material accepted. Considers unsolicited queries and manuscripts. Unpublished writers considered. **Submissions:** Query with SASE. Simultaneous submissions encouraged. Accepts e-queries. Responds within 2 weeks. **Commission:** 10% domestic, 20% foreign. **Contact:** Hy Cohen, Director.

DON CONGDON ASSOCIATES

156 Fifth Ave., Suite 625, New York, NY 10010. 212-645-1229.

E-mail: dca@doncongdon.com. **Description:** Trade books, both fiction and nonfiction, by professional writers. **Submissions:** Query with SASE. Responds in 1 week to queries, 1 month to manuscripts. **Commission:** 15% domestic. **Member:** AAR. **Contact:** Don Congdon, Susan Ramer, Michael Congdon, Cristina Concepcion.

DOE COOVER AGENCY

P.O. Box 668, Winchester, MA 01890. 781-721-6000.

Web site: www.doecooveragency.com. **Description:** Literary fiction and a broad range of nonfiction (biography/memoir, business, social science, cooking, and gardening). Receives 500 queries/submissions per year. Accepts 2% of unsolicited material. Considers unsolicited queries, but not manuscripts. Unpublished writers considered. **Submissions:** Query with outline, sample pages, bio/resume, and SASE. Accepts simultaneous queries, but not e-queries. Responds in 2 weeks. **Commission:** 15% **Contact:** Frances Kennedy.

RICHARD CURTIS ASSOCIATES, INC.
171 E 74th St., New York, NY 10021.
Web site: www.curtisagency.com. **Description:** Commercial adult nonfiction and commercial fiction by published authors. Receives 3,000 submissions/queries per year. Accepts less than 1% of unsolicited material. No unsolicited manuscripts. Considers unpublished writers in nonfiction only. **Submissions:** Query with 1-2 sample chapters, bio/resume, and SASE. No simultaneous, fax, or e-queries. Responds in 4-6 weeks. **Commission:** 15% domestic, 20% foreign. **Member:** RWA, MWA, WWA, SFWA. **Tips:** Guidelines available on Web site. **Contact:** Pamela Valvera.

THE CYPHER AGENCY
816 Wolcott Ave., Beacon, NY 12508-4261. 845-831-5677.
E-mail: jimcypher@prodigy.net. Web site: http://pages.prodigy.net/jimcypher. **Description:** Represents nonfiction in the areas of biography/autobiography, current affairs, pop culture, gay/lesbian, government/politics/law, health/medicine, history, how-to, psychology, science/technology, sports, true crime, self-help, and women's studies. Receives 1,500 queries/yr; 200 submissions/yr. Accepts 30% of unsolicited material. Considers unpublished writers. Accepts unsolicited queries and manuscripts. **Submissions:** Submit book proposal with 2 sample chapters and SASE. Accepts simultaneous and e-queries. Responds in 1 week to queries, 1 month to manuscripts. **Commission:** 15% domestic, 20% foreign. **Member:** AAR. **Contact:** Jim Cypher.

DARHANSOFF, VERRILL, FELDMAN LITERARY AGENTS
236 W 26th St., Suite 802, New York, NY 10001. 917-305-1300.
Description: Fiction and nonfiction, literary fiction, history, science, biography, pop culture, and current affairs. Does not accept unsolicited manuscripts. **Submissions:** Query with SASE. **Member:** AAR. **Contact:** Rosalyn Perrotta.

SANDRA DIJKSTRA LITERARY AGENCY
PMB 515, 1155 Camino del Mar, Del Mar, CA 92014. 858-755-3115.
E-mail: sdla@dijkstraagency.com. **Description:** Adult literary and commercial fiction, historical and inspirational nonfiction, and mysteries. Accepts unsolicited queries and manuscripts. Unpublished writers considered. **Submissions:** Query with outline, bio/resume, and SASE. Include first 50 pages and synopsis for fiction or formal proposal for nonfiction. Accepts simultaneous queries, but not e-queries. Responds in 4 weeks to queries, 6-8 weeks to submissions. **Commission:** 15% domestic, 20% foreign. **Member:** AAR, Authors Guild, WMA. **Contact:** Jill Marr.

JONATHAN DOLGER AGENCY

49 E 96th St., 9B, New York, NY 10128. 212-427-1853.
Description: Adult fiction, nonfiction, and illustrated books. Does not accept unsolicited manuscripts. **Submissions:** Query with SASE. **Member:** AAR. **Contact:** Herbert Erinmore.

DOUGLAS & KOPELMAN ARTISTS, INC.

393 W 49th St., Suite 5G, New York, NY 10019. 212-445-0160.
Description: Represents stage plays only. No unsolicited scripts. **Member:** AAR.

DUNHAM LITERARY, INC.

156 Fifth Ave., Suite 625, New York, NY 10010.
Web site: www.dunhamlit.com. **Description:** Adult literary fiction/nonfiction and children's books. Receives 10,000+ queries/yr; 300+ submissions/yr. Accepts less than 1% of unsolicited material. No unsolicited manuscripts. **Submissions:** Query with SASE. No phone, fax, or e-queries. Responds in 2 weeks. **Commission:** 15% domestic, 20% foreign. **Member:** AAR. **Tips:** "We highly recommend that writers review our Web site before submitting." **Contact.** Jennie Dunham.

DIANE DURRETT AGENCY

727 22nd St., Sacramento, CA 95816. 916-492-9003.
Description: New agency specializing in screenplays and novels with strong motion picture potential. Accepts unsolicited queries, but not manuscripts. Unpublished writers considered. **Submissions:** Query with SASE. Accepts simultaneous queries, but not e-queries. Responds in 2-4 weeks. **Commission:** 10% domestic, 10% foreign. **Member:** WGA signatory. **Contact:** Diane Durrett.

JANE DYSTEL LITERARY MANAGEMENT, INC.

One Union Square W, Suite 904, New York, NY 10003. 212-627-9100.
Web site: www.dystel.com. **Description:** Adult fiction and nonfiction. Receives 15,000 queries/submission per year. Accepts 10% of unsolicited material. Considers unsolicited queries, but not manuscripts. Unpublished writers considered. **Submissions:** Query with bio/resume. Accepts e-queries, but not simultaneous queries. Respond in 3-5 weeks to queries, 2 months to submissions. **Commission:** 15% domestic, 19% foreign. **Member:** AAR. **Contact:** Jane Dystel, Miriam Goderich, Stacey Kendall Glick, Michael Bourret, James McCarthy.

EDUCATIONAL DESIGN SERVICES, INC.

P.O. Box 253, Wantaugh, NY 11793-0253.
Description: Educational texts (K-12 only). Receives 300 queries/submissions per year; accepts 3% of unsolicited material. Considers unsolicited queries and manuscripts. Unpublished writers considered. **Submissions:** Query with outline, sample pages or complete manuscript, bio/resume, and SASE. Simultaneous queries accepted, but not e-queries. Responds in 4-6 weeks. **Commission:** 15% domestic, 25% foreign. **Contact:** Bertram L. Linder.

ETHAN ELLENBERG LITERARY AGENCY

548 Broadway, Suite #5E, New York, NY 10012. 212-431-4554.

E-mail: agent@ethanellenberg.com. Web site: www.ethanellenberg.com.

Description: All types of commercial fiction (thrillers, mysteries, children's, romance, women's fiction, ethnic, science fiction, fantasy, general fiction); literary fiction with strong narrative; and nonfiction (current affairs, health, science, psychology, cookbooks, New Age, spirituality, pop science, pop culture, adventure, true crime, biography, and memoir). No poetry or short stories. Receives 10,000 queries/ submission per year. Accepts 5% of unsolicited material. Accepts unsolicited queries and manuscripts. **Submissions:** For fiction, query with first 3 chapters, synopsis, SASE. For nonfiction, send proposal with sample material and SASE. Accepts simultaneous and e-queries (no attachments). No phone calls. Responds 1-2 weeks for queries, 4-6 weeks for submissions. **Commission:** 15% domestic, 20% foreign. **Member:** AAR. **Tips:** "We seek established and new writers in wide range of genres." **Contact:** Ethan Ellenberg, Michael Psaltis.

ANN ELMO AGENCY, INC.

60 E 42nd St., New York, NY 10165. 212-661-2880.

Description: Fiction (literary, contemporary, mystery, romance, thriller) and nonfiction (business, cooking, biography/memoir, self-help, pop culture, science, technology). **Submissions:** Query with SASE. Responds in 3 months. **Member:** AAR, MWA, Author's Guild. **Contact:** Lettie Lee, Andree Abecassis, Mari Cronin.

FELICIA ETH LITERARY REPRESENTATION

555 Bryant St., Suite 350, Palo Alto, CA 94301-1700. 650-375-1276.

Description: Selective mainstream literary fiction and diverse nonfiction in the areas of psychology, health, popular science, women's issues, investigative journalism, and biography. Does not accept unsolicited manuscripts. **Submissions:** Send query for fiction, proposal for nonfiction. **Commission:** 15% domestic, 20% foreign. **Member:** AAR. **Contact:** Felicia Eth.

FARBER LITERARY AGENCY, INC.

14 E 75th St., New York, NY 10021. 212-861-7075.

E-mail: farberlit@aol.com. Web site: www.donaldfarber.com. **Description:** Adult fiction and nonfiction, YA and children's literature, and plays. Receives 4,000 queries/submissions per year. Accepts unsolicited queries and manuscripts. Unpublished writers considered. **Submissions:** Query with outline, 3 sample chapters, and SASE. Accepts simultaneous queries, but not e-queries. Responds in 2 weeks to queries, 3-10 weeks to submissions. **Commission:** 15%, includes legal services of Donald C. Farber. **Contact:** Ann Farber, Seth Farber, Donald Farber.

FLANNERY LITERARY

1140 Wickfield Ct., Naperville, IL 60563-3300. 630-428-2682.

E-mail: flanlit@aol.com. **Description:** Fiction and nonfiction for children and young adults, all genres, infant to college age. Accepts unsolicited queries/manuscripts.

Unpublished writers considered. **Submissions:** Query by letter only (no phone, fax, or e-queries), include SASE. Accepts simultaneous queries. Responds in 2 weeks to queries, 3-4 weeks to submissions. **Commission:** 15% domestic, 20% foreign. **Contact:** Jennifer Flannery.

THE FOGELMAN LITERARY AGENCY

7515 Greenville Ave., Suite 712, Dallas, TX 75231. 214-361-9956. E-mail: info@fogelman.com. Web site: www.fogelman.com. **Description:** Women's fiction, romance, mystery, suspense, and thrillers. Nonfiction that targets a female audience, or has commercial/pop-culture appeal. **Submissions:** Published authors may call, unpublished authors are invited to submit a query (1-2 pages) with SASE. Responds in 3 days. **Commission:** 15% domestic, 10% foreign. **Member:** AAR, RWA. **Contact:** Evan M. Fogelman, Linda Kruger.

ROBERT A. FREEDMAN DRAMATIC AGENCY, INC.

1501 Broadway, Suite 2310, New York, NY 10036. 212-840-5760. **Description:** Screenplays, teleplays, and stage plays. Does not accept unsolicited manuscripts. **Submissions:** Send query with SASE. Accepts simultaneous queries. Responds in 2 weeks. **Commission:** 10% domestic **Member:** AAR. **Contact:** Robert A. Freedman, Selma Luttinger, or Marta Praeger for stage plays; Robin Kaver for screenplays or teleplays.

GELFMAN SCHNEIDER LITERARY AGENTS, INC.

250 W 57th St., Suite 2515, New York, NY 10107. 212-245-1993. E-mail: mail@gelfmanschneider.com. **Description:** Contemporary women's commercial fiction, literary and commercial fiction, mystery and suspense, and some nonfiction. Receives 2,000 queries/submissions per year. Considers unsolicited queries, but not unsolicited manuscripts. Unpublished writers considered. **Submissions:** Query with outline, sample pages, bio, and SASE. Does not accept simultaneous queries or e-queries. Responds in 4-6 weeks to queries. **Commission:** 15% domestic, 20% foreign, 15% film/dramatic. **Member:** AAR. **Contact:** Jane Gelfman, Deborah Schneider.

GOODMAN ASSOCIATES

500 West End Ave., New York, NY 10024-4317. 212-873-4806. **Description:** Adult book-length fiction and nonfiction. No plays, screenplays, poetry, textbooks, science fiction, or children's books. Does not accept unsolicited manuscripts. **Submissions:** Query with SASE. **Commission:** 15% domestic, 20% foreign. **Member:** AAR. **Tips:** Accepts new clients on a highly selective and limited basis. **Contact:** Arnold P. Goodman, Elise Simon Goodman.

GRAYBILL & ENGLISH LLC

1875 Connecticut Ave. NW, Suite 712, Washington, DC 20009. 202-558-9798. Web site: www.graybillandenglish.com. **Description:** 20% adult fiction, 80% adult nonfiction. Nina Graybill: serious nonfiction, literary fiction. Elaine English: commercial women's fiction, including romance (single titles). Kristen Auclair: nonfiction, women's issues, literary fiction. Jeff Kleinman: creative nonfiction, especially historical; prescriptive nonfiction, especially health; literary/commercial fiction. Lynn Whittaker: nonfiction, literary fiction, mystery. Receives 3,000 queries/submissions per year; accepts less than 10% of unsolicited material. Does not accept unsolicited manuscripts. Considers unpublished writers. **Submissions:** Send query letter with bio, proposal or up to 3 sample chapters, and SASE. Simultaneous queries accepted. Responds in 2-3 weeks to queries, up to 8 weeks for requested submissions. **Commission:** 15% domestic, 20% foreign and dramatic. **Member:** AAR.

SANFORD J. GREENBURGER ASSOCIATES, INC.

55 Fifth Ave., Fl. 15, New York, NY 10003. 212-206-5600.
Web site: www.greenburger.com. **Description:** All types of fiction and nonfiction (sports, health, business, psychology, parenting, science, biography, gay/lesbian) juvenile books. Considers unsolicited queries and manuscripts. Unpublished writers with strong credentials considered. **Submissions:** Query with proposal, including 3 sample chapters, bio/resume, and SASE. Accepts simultaneous queries, but not e-queries. Responds in 6-8 weeks. **Commission:** 15% domestic, 20% foreign. **Contact:** Heide Lange, Faith Hamlin, Beth Vesel, Elyse Cheney, Theresa Park, Daniel Mandel, Peter McGuigan, Julie Barber.

CHARLOTTE GUSAY LITERARY AGENCY

10532 Blythe Ave., Los Angeles, CA 90064. 310-559-0831.
E-mail: gusay1@aol.com. Web site: www.mediastudio.com/gusay.
Description: Fiction, nonfiction (humor, travel, gardening, gender issues, biography/memoir, parenting, psychology), children's/YA material, and screenplays. Receives 2,000 queries/submissions per year. Accepts unsolicited queries, but not manuscripts. Unpublished writers considered. **Submissions:** Submit 1-page query only, with bio/resume and SASE. Simultaneous queries discouraged. Responds in 3-6 weeks to queries, 6-8 weeks to submissions. **Commission:** 15% **Member:** Author's Guild, PEN/West, WGA. **Contact:** Charlotte Gusay.

THE JOY HARRIS LITERARY AGENCY

156 Fifth Ave., Suite 617, New York, NY 10010. 212-924-6269.
E-mail: gen.office@jhlitagent.com. **Description:** Adult fiction and nonfiction. **Submissions:** Query first with SASE. Submit outline or sample chapters. Responds in 2 months. **Member:** AAR. **Contact:** Joy Harris.

THE JEFF HERMAN LITERARY AGENCY LLC

332 Bleecker St., Suite G-31, New York, NY 10014.
E-mail: jeff@jeffherman.com. Web site: www.jeffherman.com.
Description: General adult nonfiction in the categories of business, reference, self-help, computers, recovery/healing, and spirituality. Also represents a growing list of fiction titles. Receives 5,000 queries/submissions per year. Accepts less than 1% of unsolicited material. Accepts unsolicited queries and manuscripts. Unpublished writ-

ers considered. **Submissions:** Query with SASE. Simultaneous submissions and e-queries accepted. **Commission:** 15% domestic, 10% foreign. **Member:** AAR. **Contact:** Jeff Herman, Deborah Levine, Amanda White.

THE BARBARA HOGENSON AGENCY, INC.
165 West End Ave., Suite 19-C, New York, NY 10023. 212-874-8084.
Description: Adult fiction, nonfiction, and stage plays. **Submissions:** Send query with bio, synopsis, and SASE. Accepts simultaneous queries. **Commission:** 10% plays, 15% books **Member:** AAR, WGA, Author's Guild, Society of Stage Directors & Choreographers. **Tips:** Client recommendations preferred. **Contact:** Barbara Hogenson.

JCA LITERARY AGENCY
27 W 20th St., Suite 1103, New York, NY 10011. 212-807-0888.
Web site: www.jcalit.com. **Description:** Adult fiction (thrillers, mysteries, commercial) and nonfiction (narrative, history, science, true crime). No children's books, romance, or screenplays. Unpublished writers considered. **Submissions:** Query with 50 sample pages, synopsis, and SASE. Simultaneous queries accepted. **Commission:** 15% domestic, 20% foreign. **Member:** AAR. **Tips:** "Be straightforward, to-the-point. Don't try to hype us or bury us in detail." **Contact:** Jeff Gerecke, Tony Outhwaite, Peter Steinberg.

NATASHA KERN LITERARY AGENCY
P.O. Box 2908, Portland, OR 97208-2908. 503-297-6190.
Web site: www.natashakern.com. **Description:** Commercial adult fiction (thrillers, mysteries, women's fiction, historical, romance) and nonfiction (health, natural science, investigative journalism, inspirational, New Age, psychology, self-help, parenting, gardening, business, current affairs, and women's issues). No horror, true crime, children's/YA, short stories, poetry, scripts, software, sports, photography, cookbooks, gift books, or scholarly works. Receives 10,000 queries/submissions per year; 1% of unsolicited material accepted. Considers unsolicited queries, but not manuscripts. Considers unpublished writers. **Submissions:** Query with SASE, include writing history. Responds in 3-4 weeks to queries, 8 weeks to submissions. Considers simultaneous queries. **Commission:** 15% domestic, 20% foreign. **Contact:** Natasha Kern.

KIDDE, HOYT & PICARD
335 E 51st St., New York, NY 10022. 212-755-9465.
E-mail: khp@worldnet.att.net. **Description:** Mainstream fiction, literary fiction, romance, mysteries, and general nonfiction. Receives 10,000 queries/submissions per year. Will consider authors who have published short stories, articles, essays, or other short works. Consideration is also given to participants of writing workshops and related degree programs. Unsolicited queries considered, but not unsolicited manuscripts. **Submissions:** Send query with short synopsis, list of previous publishing experience, and SASE. Simultaneous queries accepted. Responds in 2 weeks to queries, 1-2 months to submissions. Do not fax queries. **Commission:** 15% domes-

tic, 20% foreign. **Tips:** "Looking for exciting, witty, compelling characters, in psychologically suspenseful plot (fiction)—and the counterpart of that in nonfiction." **Contact:** Katharine Kidde, Kristen Fuhs.

KIRCHOFF/WOHLBERG, INC.

866 United Nations Plaza, Suite 525, New York, NY 10017. 212-644-2020. Web site: www.kirchoffwohlberg.com. **Description:** Children's and YA fiction and nonfiction. No adult titles. **Submissions:** Query with outline, sample chapter, and SASE. **Member:** AAR, AAP, Society of Illustrators. **Contact:** Lisa Pulitzer-Voges.

HARVEY KLINGER, INC.

301 W 53rd St., New York, NY 10019. 212-581-7068. E-mail: queries@harveyklinger.com. Web site: www.harveyklinger.com. **Description:** Mainstream adult fiction and nonfiction, literary and commercial. Unpublished writers considered. Receives 5,000 queries/year; 1% of unsolicited material accepted. Does not accept unsolicited manuscripts. **Submissions:** Query with outline, sample pages, bio/resume, and SASE. No simultaneous queries, phone calls, or faxes. Responds in 4-6 weeks to queries, 2-3 months to submissions. **Commission:** 15% domestic, 25% foreign. **Tips:** "We critique clients' work carefully to get manuscript in best possible form before submitting to publishers." **Contact:** Jenny Bent, David Dunton, Wendy Silbert, Lisa Dicker.

THE KNIGHT AGENCY

P.O. Box 550648, Atlanta, GA 30355. E-mail: knightagency@msn.com. Web site: www.knightagency.net. **Description:** Currently seeking romance (contemporary, historical, time travel, paranormal, futuristic, science fiction, romantic suspense), women's fiction, commercial fiction, literary and multicultural fiction. Also nonfiction in the areas of business, self-help, finance, entertainment, media-related, pop culture, how-to, psychology, health, inspiration/religious. Accepts unsolicited queries, but not manuscripts. Unpublished writers considered. **Submissions:** Query with SASE. Accepts e-queries, but not simultaneous queries. Responds in 1-3 weeks to queries, 8-12 weeks to submissions. **Commission:** 15% domestic, 20-25% foreign. **Member:** AAR. **Contact:** Deidre Knight.

LINDA KONNER LITERARY AGENCY

10 W 15th St., Suite 1918, New York, NY 10011. 212-691-3419. E-mail: ldkonner@cs.com. **Description:** Adult nonfiction in the areas of self-help, fitness/nutrition, relationships, parenting, pets, celebrities, pop culture. Writers must be experts in their field. Receives 1,500 queries/yr. Does not accept unsolicited manuscripts. **Submissions:** Query with SASE. Accepts simultaneous submissions and e-queries. Responds in 1-2 weeks. **Commission:** 15% domestic, 25% foreign **Member:** AAR, ASJA, signatory of WGA. **Comments:** "The vast majority of projects I take on come from authors with a national profile, media experience and contacts, and appropriate academic credentials." **Contact:** Linda Konner.

ELAINE KOSTER LITERARY AGENCY LLC

55 Central Park W, Suite 6, New York, NY 10023. 212-362-9488.
Description: Fiction (commercial and literary), narrative nonfiction, self-help, and memoir. Receives 1,000+ queries/yr. Accepts 15% of unsolicited material. Accepts unsolicited queries, but not manuscripts. Rarely considers unpublished writers. **Submissions:** Query with SASE. Accepts simultaneous queries, but not e-queries. Responds in 2 weeks. **Commission:** 15% domestic, 25% foreign. **Member:** AAR.

BARBARA S. KOUTS LITERARY AGENCY LLC

P.O. Box 560, Bellport, NY 11713. 631-286-1278.
Description: Children's fiction and nonfiction. Receives 1,500 queries/year. Accepts 10% of unsolicited material. Accepts unsolicited queries, but not manuscripts. Unpublished writers considered. **Submissions:** Query with bio/resume and SASE. Accepts simultaneous queries, but not e-queries. Responds in 1 week to queries, 6-8 weeks to submissions. **Commission:** 15% domestic, 20% foreign. **Member:** AAR. **Contact:** Barbara Kouts.

OTTO R. KOZAK LITERARY & MOTION PICTURE AGENCY

P.O. Box 152, Long Beach, NY 11561.
Description: Represents novice and professional scriptwriters for TV and film. Seeks docudramas, true stories, and work that is family-oriented or appeals to female audiences. Receives 800 queries/submission per year. Accepts 3% of unsolicited material. Considers unsolicited queries (with outline) and simultaneous queries. Does not accept e-queries or complete manuscripts. **Submissions:** Query with SASE. Responds in 2 weeks to queries, 6 weeks to submissions. **Commission:** 10% **Contact:** Rob Kozak.

EDITE KROLL LITERARY AGENCY, INC

12 Grayhurst Park, Portland, ME 04102. 207-773-4922.
Description: Feminist and issue-oriented nonfiction, humor, children's fiction, and picture books written and illustrated by artists. No genre fiction. Unpublished writers considered. **Submissions:** Query with outline and sample chapter (dummy for picture books), a brief note about the author, and SASE; simultaneous queries accepted. Keep queries brief; no phone, fax, or e-queries. **Commission:** 15% domestic, 20% foreign. **Contact:** Edite Kroll.

THE LA LITERARY AGENCY

P.O. Box 46370, Los Angeles, CA 90046. 323-654-5288.
E-mail: laliteraryag@aol.com. **Description:** Adult fiction and nonfiction. **Submissions:** Send query with outline, 50 sample pages, bio/resume, and SASE. Does not accept unsolicited manuscripts or electronic submissions. **Contact:** Ann Cashman.

PETER LAMPACK AGENCY, INC.

551 Fifth Ave., Suite 1613, New York, NY 10176-0187. 212-687-9106.
E-mail: renbopla@aol.com. **Description:** Commercial and literary fiction and non-fiction by experts in a given field (especially autobiography, biography, law, finance, politics, history). No horror, sci-fi, westerns, or romance. No original screenplays. Receives 3,000 queries/submissions per year. Accepts less than 1% of unsolicited material. Considers unsolicited queries, but not manuscripts. Unpublished writers considered. **Submissions:** Send query with synopsis, sample chapter, credentials, and SASE. Include e-mail address if available. Simultaneous queries accepted, but not e-queries. Responds in 3 weeks. **Commission:** 15% domestic, 20% foreign. **Contact:** Loren Soeiro.

MICHAEL LARSEN/ELIZABETH POMADA LITERARY AGENCY

1029 Jones St., San Francisco, CA 94109-5023. 415-673-0939.
E-mail: larsenpoma@aol.com. Web site: www.larsen-pomada.com. **Description:** Seeks new voices and fresh ideas in literary/commercial fiction and general nonfiction for adults. Receives 5,000 queries/submissions per year. Accepts 1% of unsolicited material. Considers unpublished writers and unsolicited queries. **Submissions:** For fiction, send query with synopsis, first 10 pages, complete contact info, and SASE. Accepts simultaneous queries with notice; does not accept e-queries. Responds in 6-8 weeks to queries, 4-6 weeks to submissions. **Commission:** 15% domestic, 20-30% foreign. **Member:** AAR, ASJA, Author's Guild. **Tips:** "For nonfiction, follow Michael Larsen's book *How to Write a Book Proposal*, then send by mail or e-mail the title or promotion plan." **Contact:** Elizabeth Pomada (fiction), Michael Larsen (nonfiction).

LESCHER & LESCHER, LTD.

47 E 19th St., New York, NY 10003. 212-529-1790.
E-mail: rl@lescherltd.com or mc@lescherltd.com. **Description:** A broad range of serious nonfiction, including current affairs, history, biography, memoir, government, politics, law, contemporary issues, sociology, psychology, pop culture, and food/wine. Also represents literary and commercial fiction, including mysteries/thrillers and some children's books. **Submissions:** Query with SASE. Accepts simultaneous queries and e-queries. Responds in 1-2 weeks to queries, 2-4 weeks to submissions. **Commission:** 15% domestic, 20% foreign. **Member:** AAR. **Contact:** Robert Lescher, Mickey Choate.

ELLEN LEVINE LITERARY AGENCY, INC.

Trident Media Group, LLC
15 E 26th St., Suite 1801, New York, NY 10010. 212-889-0620.
E-mail: info@ellenlevineagency.com. Web site: www.ellenlevineagency.com. **Description:** General fiction and nonfiction. Handles film and TV rights for clients only. Does not accept unsolicited manuscripts. **Submissions:** Query with SASE first. If requested, send outline and sample chapters. Responds in 2 weeks to queries, 6 weeks to manuscripts. **Member:** AAR. **Contact:** Ellen Levine, Diana Finch.

LINDSEY'S LITERARY SERVICES
7502 Greenville Ave., Suite 500, Dallas, TX 75231. 214-890-9262.
Description: Quality fiction (mystery/suspense/thriller, mainstream, romance, women as strong heroines) and nonfiction (self-help, psychology, women's issues, some metaphysical). Accepts 5% of unsolicited material. Considers unsolicited queries and unpublished writers. Rarely considers unsolicited manuscripts. **Submissions:** Fiction: query with synopsis, first 3 chapters, and brief bio. Nonfiction: query with proposal, writing sample, brief bio detailing credentials and platform. Include SASE with all materials. Responds in 2-4 weeks to queries, 6-12 weeks to manuscripts. **Commission:** 15% domestic, 20% foreign. **Tips:** "As a small agency, we will aggressively represent our clients. Getting published in today's market is difficult. We look for quality work, and writers who are willing to go the extra mile." **Contact:** Emily Armenta, Bonnie James.

NANCY LOVE LITERARY AGENCY
250 E 65th St., Suite 4A, New York, NY 10021. 212-980-3499.
Description: Adult nonfiction in the areas of health, self-help, parenting, medical, psychology, women's issues, memoirs (literary), current affairs, pop science. Popular reference if by an authority, with a fresh slant. Also represents adult fiction (mysteries/thrillers only). Receives 2,000 queries/submissions per year; 1% unsolicited material accepted. Considers unsolicited queries, but not manuscripts. **Submissions:** Query with SASE. Accepts simultaneous queries, but not e-queries. Responds in 4 weeks to queries. **Commission:** 15% domestic, 20% foreign. **Tips:** "Looking for brands, authorities with a track record." **Contact:** Miriam Taqer.

DONALD MAASS LITERARY AGENCY
160 W 95th St., Suite 1B, New York, NY 10025. 212-757-7755
Description: Represents fiction only. Does not accept unsolicited manuscripts. **Submissions:** Query first with 1-page letter, first 5 pages, and SASE. Responds in 2 weeks to queries, 3 months to manuscripts. **Member:** AAR, SFWA, MWA, RWA. **Contact:** Donald Maass, Jennifer Jackson, Michelle Brummer, Andrea Somberg.

GINA MACCOBY LITERARY AGENCY
P.O. Box 60, Chappaqua, NY 10514. 914-238-5630.
Description: Fiction and nonfiction for adults and children. Does not accept unsolicited manuscripts. **Submissions:** Query with SASE. Responds in 2 months.

CAROL MANN LITERARY AGENCY
55 Fifth Ave., New York, NY 10003. 212-206-5635.
E-mail: kim@carolmannagency.com. **Description:** General nonfiction and literary fiction. Specializes in current affairs, self-help, popular culture, psychology, parenting, history. No genre fiction. Unpublished writers considered. **Submissions:** Query with outline and SASE. Does not accept queries via fax or e-mail. Responds in 3 weeks to queries. **Commission:** 15% domestic, 20% foreign. **Member:** AAR. **Contact:** Carol Mann, Kim Goldstein, Jim Fitzgerald, Leylha Ahuile.

MANUS & ASSOCIATES LITERARY AGENCY, INC.

375 Forest Ave., Palo Alto, CA 94301. 650-470-5151.

E-mail: manuslit@manuslit.com. Web site: www.manuslit.com. **Description:** General fiction and dramatic nonfiction. No poetry, children's books, science fiction/fantasy, romance, screenplays, or magazine articles. Does not accept unsolicited manuscripts. **Submissions:** For nonfiction, send query, formal proposal, sample chapters, bio, and SASE. For fiction, send query, first 30 pages, bio, and SASE. Responds in 8 weeks. **Commission:** 15% domestic **Member:** AAR. **Tips:** See Web site for more information regarding genres, writing proposals, and deal points. **Comments:** Also has NYC office: 445 Park Ave., Fl. 10, New York, NY 10022. 212-644-8020. **Contact:** Jillian Manus, Janet Manus, Jandy Nelson, Stephanie Lee, Christian Cummings.

DENISE MARCIL LITERARY AGENCY, INC.

685 West End Ave., Suite 9C, New York, NY 10025. 212-932-3110.

Description: Commercial fiction, especially thrillers, suspense, and contemporary mainstream women's fiction. Nonfiction in the areas of self-help, how-to, reference, business, parenting/relationships, and health. Receives 3,000+ queries/submissions per year. Accepts less than 1% of unsolicited material. Unpublished writers considered. **Submissions:** Send 1-page query with SASE. Accepts simultaneous queries with notice. Responds in 4 weeks. **Commission:** 15% domestic, 20% foreign. **Member:** AAR. **Contact:** Denise Marcil, President.

JED MATTES, INC

2095 Broadway, Suite 302, New York, NY 10023-2895. 212-595-5228.

E-mail: general@jedmattes.com. **Description:** Fiction and nonfiction. Does not accept unsolicited manuscripts. **Submissions:** Query with SASE. **Member:** AAR. **Contact:** Jed Mattes, Fred Morris.

MARGRET MCBRIDE LITERARY AGENCY

7744 Fay Ave., Suite 201, La Jolla, CA 92037. 858-454-1550.

E-mail: staff@mcbridelit.com. Web site: www.mcbrideliterary.com. **Description:** Specializes in fiction (particular interest in legal thrillers) and nonfiction (business, health, self-help). No poetry, romance, or screenplays. Accepts unsolicited queries, but not manuscripts. Unpublished writers considered. **Submissions:** Query with 1-2 page synopsis, bio, and SASE. Accepts simultaneous queries, but not e-queries. Responds in 4-6 weeks to queries, 6-8 weeks to requested submissions. **Member:** AAR. **Tips:** Do not phone, fax, or e-mail. **Contact:** Michael J. Daley.

CLAUDIA MENZA LITERARY AGENCY

1170 Broadway, Suite 807, New York, NY 10001. 212-889-6850.

Description: Fiction and nonfiction. Emphasis on African-American themes and topics. No poetry, short stories, romance, or juvenile material. **Submissions:** Query first, include SASE. Accepts simultaneous queries, but not e-queries. Responds in 1-4 weeks to queries, 2-4 months to submissions. **Commission:** 15%, 20% co-agent. **Member:** AAR. **Tips:** "Please do not call to check on submissions made."

DORIS S. MICHAELS LITERARY AGENCY, INC.

1841 Broadway, Suite 903, New York, NY 10023.

Web site: www.dsmagency.com. **Description:** Represents high-quality literary fiction; women's literary fiction; and nonfiction in the areas of current affairs, biography/memoirs, self-help, business, history, health, classical music, sports, women's issues, computers, and pop culture. Receives 5,000 queries/yr. Accepts .5% of unsolicited material. **Submissions:** Send query with short bio and credentials via e-mail (no attachments). Does not accept queries via mail, phone, or fax. See Web site for specific guidelines. **Commission:** 15% domestic, 20% foreign. **Member:** AAR, Women's National Book Association, Women in Publishing.

WILLIAM MORRIS AGENCY, INC.

1325 Avenue of the Americas, New York, NY 10019. 212-586-5100.

Web site: www.wma.com. **Description:** Fiction and nonfiction. No screenplays, children's books, or poetry. Does not accept unsolicited manuscripts. **Submissions:** Send query with synopsis, publication history, and SASE. No fax or e-queries. **Commission:** 15% domestic, 10% foreign. **Contact:** Book Department Coordinator.

HENRY MORRISON, INC.

P.O. Box 235, Bedford Hills, NY 10507-0235. 914-666-3500.

Description: Fiction, nonfiction, and screenplays. **Submissions:** Send query, outline, and SASE. Responds in 2 weeks to queries, 3 months to manuscripts. **Commission:** 15% domestic, 25% foreign. **Contact:** Henry Morrison.

JEAN V. NAGGAR LITERARY AGENCY

216 E 75th St., Suite 1E, New York, NY 10021. 212-794-1082.

Description: "Strong adult mainstream fiction and nonfiction, from literary to commercial, with a good story told in a distinctive voice." Receives 6,000 queries/submissions per year. Considers unsolicited queries, but not unsolicited manuscripts. Unpublished writers considered. **Submissions:** Query with outline, bio/resume, and SASE. No electronic or simultaneous queries. Responds in 48 hours to queries, several weeks to requested submissions. **Commission:** 15% domestic, 20% foreign. **Contact:** Jean Naggar, Alice Tasman.

NEW ENGLAND PUBLISHING ASSOCIATES

P.O. Box 5, Chester, CT 06412. 860-345-7323.

E-mail: nepa@nepa.com. Web site: www.nepa.com.

Description: General-interest nonfiction for adult markets in the areas of biography/memoir, business, true crime, science, law, reference, nature, parenting, women's issues, current events, history, and politics. Receives 3,000 submissions/yr. **Submissions:** Send book proposal with 1-2 page summary, description of intended audience and competing titles, chapter outline, one sample chapter, bio/resume, list of previous publications, and SASE. Check "Tips on Proposal Development" on Web site for complete guidelines. Accepts simultaneous queries with notice. Responds in

3-4 weeks. **Commission:** 15% domestic, 20% foreign. **Member:** AAR, ASJA, Authors Guild. **Tips:** "We provide editorial guidance, representation, and manuscript development for book projects." **Contact:** Elizabeth Frost-Knappman, Edward W. Knappman, Kris Schiavi, Vicki Harlow, Ron Formica.

BETSY NOLAN LITERARY AGENCY

224 W 29th St., Fl. 15, New York, NY 10001. 212-967-8200.
E-mail: 74731.2172@compuserve.com. **Description:** Adult nonfiction, especially popular psychology, child care, cookbooks, African-American and Jewish issues. Does not accept unsolicited manuscripts. **Submissions:** Submit outline, no more than 3 sample chapters, author bio/resume, and SASE. **Commission:** 15% domestic, 20% foreign. **Contact:** Donald Lehr, Carla Glasser.

HAROLD OBER ASSOCIATES, INC.

425 Madison Ave., New York, NY 10017. 212-759-8600.
Description: General fiction and nonfiction. Does not handle scripts. **Submissions:** Query with SASE. No simultaneous or e-queries. Responds in 1 week to queries, 6 weeks to manuscripts. **Commission:** 15% **Member:** AAR. **Contact:** Phyllis Westberg, Emma Sweeney.

THE RICHARD PARKS AGENCY

138 E 16th St., Fl. 5, New York, NY 10003-3561. 212-254-9067.
Web site: www.richardparksagency.com. **Description:** General trade adult nonfiction with special emphasis on narrative nonfiction. Accepts fiction by referral only. Accepts unsolicited queries, but not manuscripts. **Submissions:** Query with SASE. Accepts simultaneous queries with notice. No phone calls, faxes, or e-mails. Responds in 2-4 weeks to queries, 4-6 weeks to requested submissions. **Commission:** 15% domestic, 20% foreign. **Member:** AAR. **Contact:** Richard Parks.

JAMES PETER ASSOCIATES, INC.

P.O. Box 358, New Canaan, CT 06840. 203-972-1070.
E-mail: gene_brissie@msn.com. **Description:** Adult nonfiction, all subject areas. Considers unsolicited queries, but not manuscripts. Unpublished writers considered. **Submissions:** Query with outline, sample pages, bio/resume, and SASE. Accepts simultaneous queries, but not e-queries. Responds in 2-3 weeks. **Commission:** 15% domestic, 20% foreign. **Contact:** Gene Brissie, President.

ALISON PICARD, LITERARY AGENT

P.O. Box 2000, Cotuit, MA 02635. 508-477-7192.
E-mail: ajpicard@aol.com. **Description:** Adult fiction, nonfiction, and children's/YA. No poetry, short stories or plays. Receives 3,000 queries/submissions per year. Accepts 5% of unsolicited material. Considers unsolicited queries, but not manuscripts. **Submissions:** Send query via mail or e-mail. Accepts simultaneous queries, but not phone or fax queries. Responds in 1 weeks to queries, 3 months to submissions. **Commission:** 15% domestic, 20% foreign. **Contact:** Alison Picard.

PINDER LANE & GARON-BROOKE ASSOCIATES, LTD.

159 W 53rd St., Suite 14E, New York, NY 10019. 212-489-0880.
Description: Fiction and nonfiction. Does not accept unsolicited manuscripts.
Submissions: Query with short synopsis and SASE. **Commission:** 15% domestic,
30% foreign. **Member:** AAR. **Contact:** Dick Duane, Robert Thixton, Roger Hayes.

SUSAN ANN PROTTER LITERARY AGENT

110 W 40th St., Suite 1408, New York, NY 10018. 212-840-0480.
Description: Fiction (mysteries, thrillers, science fiction) and nonfiction
(health/medicine, how-to, science, psychology, biography, reference, self-help). No
children's/YA material. Does not accept unsolicited manuscripts. **Submissions:**
Query first with SASE. Does not accept queries by phone, fax, or e-mail. **Member:**
AAR, Authors Guild. **Contact:** Susan Ann Protter.

HELEN REES LITERARY AGENCY

123 N Washington St., Fl. 5, Boston, MA 02114-2113. 617-227-9014.
E-mail: reesliterary@aol.com. **Description:** Literary fiction and nonfiction. No short
stories, science fiction, or poetry. Unpublished writers considered. **Submissions:**
Query with outline, bio/resume, sample text (to 50 pages), and SASE. No simultaneous queries. **Commission:** 15% **Member:** AAR. **Contact:** Joan Mazmanian.

REECE HALSEY NORTH

98 Main St., Suite 704, Tiburon, CA 94920. 415-789-9191.
E-mail: info@reecehalseynorth.com. Web site: www.kimberleycameron.com.
Description: Represents adult fiction and nonfiction. Receives 1,000+ queries/
submissions per year. Accepts 50% of unsolicited material. Unpublished writers considered. **Submissions:** Query with SASE. Accepts simultaneous queries and
e-queries. **Commission:** 15% domestic, 20% foreign. **Member:** AAR, MWA, Sisters
in Crime. **Comments:** "We take this writing life very seriously. We don't get paid by
the hour– please be patient and polite!" **Contact:** Kimberley Cameron.

JODY REIN BOOKS, INC.

7741 S Ash Ct., Littleton, CO 80122. 303-694-4430.
Web site: www.jodyreinbooks.com. **Description:** Commercial and narrative nonfiction, by writers with media contacts, experience, and expertise in their field. Also, outstanding works of literary fiction by award-winning short-story writers and commer-
cially viable screenplays. Receives 2,000 queries/submissions per year. Accepts less
than 1% of unsolicited material. Considers unsolicited queries, but not manuscripts.
Unpublished writers considered. **Submissions:** Query with SASE. Accepts simultaneous queries, but not e-queries. Responds in 2-4 weeks to queries, 4-6 weeks to submissions. **Commission:** 15% domestic, 25% foreign. **Member:** AAR, Author's
Guild. **Contact:** Jody Rein.

JODIE RHODES LITERARY AGENCY

8840 Villa La Jolla Dr., Suite 315, La Jolla, CA 92037. 858-625-0544.
E-mail: jrhodes1@san.rr.com. **Description:** Fiction (multicultural, African American, literary, mystery, suspense, thrillers), nonfiction (parenting, fitness/health, science, medicine, pop culture, politics, military, memoirs), and YA literature. Receives 9,000 queries/submissions per year. Accepts 1-2% of unsolicited material. Considers unpublished writers. **Submissions:** Send query with up to first 50 pages and SASE. Accepts simultaneous queries, but not e-queries. Responds in 1-2 weeks. **Commission:** 15% domestic, 20% foreign. **Member:** AAR. **Comments:** "I seek writers who care passionately about their books and have something worth saying about the human condition. I have no interest in romance novels, erotica, horror, science fiction, or children's books."

ANGELA RINALDI LITERARY AGENCY

P.O. Box 7877, Beverly Hills, CA 90212-7877. 310-842-7665.
E-mail: amr@rinaldiliterary.com. **Description:** Adult fiction (commercial and literary) and nonfiction (narrative and practical/proactive). No cookbooks, screenplays, science fiction, romance, western, fantasy, or children's literature. Receives 6,000 queries/submissions per year. Accepts 1-2% of unsolicited material. Considers unpublished writers. Accepts unsolicited queries and manuscripts. **Submissions:** Send first 3 chapters with short synopsis and SASE. Accepts simultaneous queries (with notice) and e-queries (no attachments). Responds in 6-8 weeks. **Commission:** 15% domestic, 20% foreign. **Member:** AAR. **Contact:** Angela Rinaldi.

ANN RITTENBERG LITERARY AGENCY, INC

1201 Broadway, Suite 708, New York, NY 10001. 212-684-6936.
E-mail: info@rittlit.com. Web site: www.rittlit.com. **Description:** Upmarket contemporary fiction and serious narrative nonfiction. Receives 1,000 queries/yr; 200 submissions/yr. Accepts 2% of unsolicited material. Accepts unsolicited queries, but not manuscripts. Unpublished writers considered. **Submissions:** Query with first chapter and SASE. Accepts simultaneous queries, but not e-queries. Responds in 4 weeks to queries; 8 weeks to submissions. **Commission:** 15% domestic, 20% foreign. **Member:** AAR. **Contact:** Ann Rittenberg, Ted Gideonse.

B.J. ROBBINS LITERARY AGENCY

5130 Bellaire Ave., North Hollywood, CA 91607. 818-760-6602.
E-mail: robbinsliterary@aol.com. **Description:** Literary fiction, women's fiction, narrative nonfiction, and trade nonfiction (parenting, health, medicine, and self-help). Receives thousands of queries/submissions per year. Accepts 1% of unsolicited material. Accepts unsolicited queries, but not manuscripts. Unpublished writers considered. **Submissions:** Query with 3 sample chapters for fiction, proposal for nonfiction; SASE required. No e-queries. Considers simultaneous submissions. Responds in 2-4 weeks to queries, 8-12 weeks to manuscripts. **Commission:** 15% domestic, 20% foreign. **Member:** AAR. **Contact:** B.J. Robbins, Rob McAndrews.

RITA ROSENKRANZ LITERARY AGENCY

440 West End Ave., Suite 15D, New York, NY 10024-5358.
Description: General nonfiction in the areas of biography, business, parenting, cooking, current affairs, health, history, how-to, military/war, theater, nature, pop culture, religious/inspirational, science/technology, women's issues, humor, and decorative arts. Accepts 2% of unsolicited material. Accepts unsolicited queries and manuscripts. **Submissions:** Submit outline, sample chapter, and SASE. No e-queries. Considers simultaneous submissions. Responds in 2 weeks. **Commission:** 15% domestic, 20% foreign. **Member:** AAR, Authors Guild, IWWG. **Contact:** Rita Rosenkranz.

ROSENSTONE/WENDER

38 E 29th St., Fl. 10, New York, NY 10016. 212-725-9445.
Description: Represents adult fiction and nonfiction, juvenile fiction and nonfiction, and stage plays. Accepts unsolicited queries, but not manuscripts. Unpublished writers considered. **Submissions:** Send query with SASE. **Member:** AAR. **Contact:** Phyllis Wender, Susan Cohen, Sonia Pabley.

GAIL ROSS LITERARY AGENCY, LLC

1666 Connecticut Ave. NW, Suite 500, Washington, DC 20009.
Web site: www.gailross.com. **Description:** Adult nonfiction. Unpublished writers considered. **Submissions:** Query with outline, sample pages, resume, and SASE. Accepts simultaneous queries. **Commission:** 15% **Member:** AAR. **Contact:** Gail Ross, Jennifer Manguera.

PETER RUBIE LITERARY AGENCY

240 W 35 St., Suite 500, New York, NY 10001. 212-279-1776.
E-mail: peterrubie@prlit.com. **Web site:** www.prlit.com. **Description:** Literate fiction and nonfiction, all types, for adults. Seeks authors with strong writing backgrounds or recognized experts in their fields. No romance or children's books. Receives 800 queries/submission per month. Accepts 5% of unsolicited material. Considers unsolicited queries, but not manuscripts. Unpublished writers considered. **Submissions:** Query with outline, sample pages, bio/resume, and SASE. Accepts simultaneous queries and e-queries. Responds in 6-8 weeks to queries, 12-14 weeks to submissions. **Commission:** 15% domestic, 20% foreign. **Member:** AAR. **Tips:** See Web site for details. **Contact:** Peter Rubie or June Clark.

RUSSELL & VOLKENING, INC.

50 W 29th St., Suite 7E, New York, NY 10001. 212-684-6050.
Description: General fiction and nonfiction. No screenplays, romance, science fiction, children's, or juvenile submissions. **Submissions:** Send outline with two sample chapters. **Member:** AAR.

VICTORIA SANDERS & ASSOCIATES

241 Avenue of the Americas, Suite 11H, New York, NY 10014. 212-633-8811.
E-mail: vsanders@victoriasanders.com. **Web site:** www.victoriasanders.com.

Description: Fiction, both literary and commercial, and nonfiction in the areas of biography, history, autobiography, psychology, gay studies, politics, and African-American, Asian, Latin, and women's studies. Receives 5,000 queries/yr; 300 submissions/yr. Accepts 40% of unsolicited material. Accepts unsolicited queries and manuscripts. Unpublished writers considered. **Submissions:** Submit outline, 2 sample chapters, and SASE. Responds in 2-4 weeks. **Commission:** 15% domestic, 20% foreign. **Member:** AAR. **Contact:** Victoria Sanders.

SANDUM & ASSOCIATES
144 E 84th St., New York, NY 10028. 212-737-2011.
Description: Primarily nonfiction and literary fiction. **Submissions:** Query with sample pages, bio/resume, and SASE. Accepts simultaneous queries. **Commission:** 15% domestic, 20% foreign. **Tips:** New clients by referral only. **Contact:** Howard E. Sandum, Director.

WENDY SCHMALZ AGENCY
P.O. Box 831, Hudson, NY 12534-0831.
E-mail: wschmalz@earthlink.net. **Description:** Adult fiction/nonfiction and children's books. Receives 1,250 queries/yr. Accepts unsolicited queries, but not manuscripts. Unpublished writers considered. **Submissions:** For fiction, send complete manuscript; for nonfiction, send overview with sample chapters. SASE required for all materials. Responds in 2 days to queries, 4 weeks to submissions. **Commission:** 15% domestic, 20% foreign. **Member:** AAR. **Contact:** Wendy Schmalz.

THE SEYMOUR AGENCY
475 Minor Street Rd., Canton, NY 13617-3256.
E-mail: marysue@slic.com. Web site: www.theseymouragency.com.
Description: Represents nonfiction, literary fiction, and genre fiction in the areas of thrillers, romance, and westerns. Considers unsolicited manuscripts and unpublished writers. Accepts 5% of unsolicited material. **Submissions:** For nonfiction, send proposal and first chapter. For fiction, send synopsis and first 50 pages. SASE required for all materials. Accepts e-queries and simultaneous submissions. Responds in 2 weeks to queries, 2-3 months to submissions. **Commission:** 15% **Member:** AAR, Author's Guild. **Contact:** Mary Sue Seymour.

THE SHUKAT COMPANY, LTD.
340 W 55th St., Suite 1A, New York, NY 10019-3744. 212-582-7614.
E-mail: staff@shukat.com. **Description:** Represents playwrights. Personal management of composers, lyricists, and directors. Does not accept unsolicited manuscripts. **Submissions:** Query with outline and 10-page sample. **Member:** AAR. **Contact:** Scott Shukat, Maribel Rivas, Lysna Scriven-Marzani.

BOBBE SIEGEL, LITERARY AGENT
41 W 83rd St., New York, NY 10024. 212-877-4985.
Description: Adult fiction and nonfiction. No plays (dramatic or screen), romances,

juvenile, cookbooks, humor, or short stories. Considers unsolicited queries, but not manuscripts. Unpublished writers considered. **Submissions:** Query with SASE. Accepts simultaneous queries, but not e-queries. Responds in 2-3 weeks to queries, 2-3 months to submissions. **Commission:** 15% domestic, 10% foreign. **Contact:** Bobbe Siegel.

JACQUELINE SIMENAUER LITERARY AGENCY
P.O. Box A.G., Mantoloking, NJ 08738. 941-597-9964.
Description: Fiction (literary and mainstream commercial) and nonfiction (health/medicine, popular psychology, how-to/self-help, women's issues, alternative health, spirituality, New Age, fitness/nutrition, current issues, true crime, business, celebrities, reference, social issues). Unpublished writers considered. **Submissions:** Query with first 3 chapters, synopsis, and SASE. Accepts simultaneous queries and e-queries. **Commission:** 15% domestic, 20% foreign. **Contact:** Jacqueline Simenauer (nonfiction), Fran Pardi (fiction).

THE SPIELER AGENCY
154 W 57th St., Fl. 13, Room 135, New York, NY 10019. 212-757-4439.
Description: Nonfiction and literary fiction. No romance or thrillers. Receives 1,000 queries/submissions per year. Accepts less than 1% of unsolicited material. Considers unsolicited queries, but not manuscripts. Unpublished writers considered. **Submissions:** Query with outline and SASE (or material will not be returned). Does not accept simultaneous queries or e-queries. Responds in 2 weeks to queries, 6-8 weeks submissions. **Commission:** 15% domestic, 20% foreign. **Contact:** Katya Balter.

PHILIP G. SPITZER LITERARY AGENCY
50 Talmage Farm Ln., East Hampton, NY 11937. 631-329-3650.
E-mail: spitzer516@aol.com. **Description:** Adult fiction (literary and suspense/mystery) and nonfiction. No unsolicited manuscripts. **Submissions:** Query with outline and sample chapters. **Member:** AAR. **Contact:** Philip Spitzer.

STIMOLA LITERARY STUDIO
210 Crescent Ave., Leonia, NJ 07605. 201-944-9886.
E-mail: ltrystudio@aol.com. **Description:** Preschool through YA fiction/nonfiction. Receives 100 queries/yr; 60 submissions/yr. Accepts 5% of unsolicited material. Considers unsolicited queries and manuscripts. **Submissions:** Send query with SASE. Accepts e-queries. No simultaneous submissions. Responds in 2-4 weeks. **Commission:** 15% **Member:** AAR. **Contact:** Rosemary B. Stimola.

PATRICIA TEAL LITERARY AGENCY
2036 Vista del Rosa, Fullerton, CA 92831-1336. 714-738-8333.
Description: Represents women's fiction and commercial nonfiction. Receives 400 queries/yr; 75 submissions/yr. Accepts 10% of unsolicited material. Accept unsolicited queries, but not manuscripts. **Submissions:** Send query with SASE via regular mail.

Accepts simultaneous queries, but not e-queries. Responds in 1 week to queries, 60 days to submissions. **Commission:** 15% domestic, 20% foreign. **Member:** AAR. **Tips:** Not accepting new clients at this time. **Contact:** Patricia Teal.

SCOTT TREIMEL

434 Lafayette St., New York, NY 10003. 212-505-8353.
E-mail: st.ny@verizon.net. **Description:** Represents juvenile/YA fiction and nonfiction. Receives 3,500 queries/submissions per year. Unpublished writers considered. **Submissions:** Send query for works 60+ pages; send complete manuscript for picture books and works fewer than 60 pages. No simultaneous queries or e-queries. Responds in 90 days; SASE required. **Commission:** 15% domestic, 20% foreign. **Member:** AAR. **Tips:** No unicorns, fairies, or rainbows. **Contact:** Scott Treimel.

THE VINES AGENCY, INC.

648 Broadway, Suite 901, New York, NY 10012. 212-777-5522.
E-mail: jv@vinesagency.com. Web site: www.vinesagency.com.
Description: Women's fiction, romantic suspense, thrillers, historical, supernatural thrillers, mainstream fiction, literary, political thrillers, legal thrillers. Also commercial nonfiction, both prescriptive and narrative. Receives 25,000 queries/yr; 1,000 submissions per year. Represents 11-12 submissions per year. Accepts unsolicited queries, but not manuscripts. Unpublished writers considered. **Submissions:** Submit outline, sample chapters, and SASE. Accepts e-queries. Simultaneous submissions accepted. Responds in 6 weeks. **Commission:** 15% domestic, 25% foreign. **Member:** Authors Guild, WGA. **Comments:** "We represent authors whose work we feel passionate about." **Contact:** James C. Vines.

WALES LITERARY AGENCY, INC.

P.O. Box 9428, Seattle, WA 98109-0428. 206-284-7114.
E-mail: waleslit@aol.com. **Description:** Mainstream and literary fiction and narrative nonfiction. Does not accept unsolicited manuscripts. **Submissions:** Query with brief description, outline, and writing sample(s). **Commission:** 15%. **Member:** AAR. **Contact:** Elizabeth Wales or Meg Lemke.

JOHN A. WARE LITERARY AGENCY

392 Central Park W, New York, NY 10025. 212-866-4733.
Description: Adult fiction (noncategory, thrillers, and mysteries) and nonfiction (biography, history, current affairs, investigative journalism, social criticism, nature, Americana and folklore, "bird's eye views" of phenomena, science, medicine, and sports). Receives 2,000 queries/yr. Accepts 1-2% of unsolicited material. Accepts unsolicited queries, but not manuscripts. Unpublished writers considered. **Submissions:** Query with SASE. Do not call or fax. Accepts simultaneous queries. **Commission:** 15% domestic, 20% foreign. **Contact:** John Ware.

WATKINS/LOOMIS AGENCY, INC.

133 E 35th St., Suite 1, New York, NY 10016. 212-532-0080.
Description: Adult literary fiction and nonfiction (biography/memoir and cookbooks). Receives 500 queries/submissions per year. Accepts 5% of unsolicited material. Considers unsolicited queries and manuscripts. Considers unpublished writers.
Submissions: Query with first 3 chapters for fiction, and a query letter plus synopsis for nonfiction; SASE required. No electronic or simultaneous queries. Responds in 2-6 weeks. **Tips:** No romance, self-help, or novelty books. **Contact:** Katherine Fausset.

SANDRA WATT & ASSOCIATES

1750 N Sierra Bonita, Los Angeles, CA 90046. 323-874-0791.
Description: Adult fiction and nonfiction. Receives 200 queries/submissions per year. Accepts 2% of unsolicited material. Unpublished writers sometimes considered.
Submissions: Query with bio/resume and SASE. Accepts simultaneous queries, but not e-queries. Responds in 1 week to queries, 3 weeks to submissions. **Commission:** 15% domestic, 25% foreign. **Member:** WGA West. **Contact:** Sandra Watt.

WIESER & WIESER, INC.

25 E 21st St., Fl. 6, New York, NY 10010. 212-260-0860.
Description: Specializes in trade and mass market adult fiction and nonfiction. Unpublished writers considered. **Submissions:** Query with outline, 25 sample pages, bio/resume, and SASE. **Commission:** 15% **Contact:** Olga Wieser, Jake Elwell.

WITHERSPOON ASSOCIATES, INC.

235 E 31st St., New York, NY 10016. 212-889-8626.
Description: Adult fiction and nonfiction. Unpublished writers considered.
Submissions: Query with sample pages and SASE. Does not accept simultaneous queries. Responds in 6 weeks. **Commission:** 15% domestic, 20% foreign. **Contact:** Kimberly Witherspoon, Maria Massie, David Forrer.

ANN WRIGHT REPRESENTATIVES

165 W 46th St., Suite 1105, New York, NY 10036-2501. 212-764-6770.
E-mail: danwrightlit@aol.com. **Description:** Fiction and screenplays with strong film potential, varied subjects. Considers only queries or referrals, with SASE. Receives 6,000 queries/submissions per year. Accepts .5% of unsolicited material. Considers unsolicited queries, but not manuscripts. Unpublished writers considered.
Submissions: Responds: 1-2 weeks to queries, 4-8 weeks for submissions. No electronic queries. Accepts simultaneous queries (agency only). **Commission:** 10% film/tv, 10-20% literary. **Tips:** "Always open to new writers of screen material and to new authors of fiction with strong film potential." **Contact:** Dan Wright.

WRITERS HOUSE

21 W 26th St., New York, NY 10010. 212-685-2400.
Description: Represents trade books of all types, fiction and nonfiction, including all rights. No plays, screenplays, teleplays, or software. **Submissions:** Send 1-page query first. **Member:** AAR. **Tips:** "State in query the subject of your book and why you are qualified to write it." **Contact:** Submissions Department.

ZACHARY SHUSTER HARMSWORTH LITERARY AGENCY

1776 Broadway, Suite 1405, New York, NY 10019. 617-262-2400.
Web site: www.zshliterary.com. **Description:** Adult fiction (commercial and literary) and nonfiction (biography/memoir, business, psychology, and medicine). Receives 2,000 queries/submissions per year. Accepts less than 1% of unsolicited material. Unpublished writers considered. **Submissions:** Query with sample pages (up to 30) and SASE. Accepts simultaneous queries, but not fax or e-queries. Responds in 1-2 months to queries, 2-4 months to submissions. **Commission:** 15% domestic, 20% foreign.

THE ZACK COMPANY, INC.

243 W 70th St., Suite 8-D, New York, NY 10023-4366.
Web site: www.zackcompany.com. **Description:** Represents adult fiction (commercial, thrillers, action, science fiction/fantasy, horror, historical fiction—*no women's fiction*) and nonfiction (narrative, military/history, politics, current affairs, science/technology, biography/memoir by political figures and celebrities, personal finance, parenting/relationships, health/medicine). Authors of nonfiction must be recognized experts in their field and have prior publishing credits. Receives 25,000 queries/yr; 500-750 submissions/yr. Accepts 1% of unsolicited material. Unpublished writers considered. **Submissions:** Query with SASE. **Member:** AAR, Author's Guild, SFWA. **Comments:** "Before submitting, you should visit our Web site and read our submission guidelines. Send all material via regular mail; we do not accept e-queries." **Contact:** Andrew Zack.

SUSAN ZECKENDORF ASSOCIATES INC.

171 W 57th St., Suite 11B, New York, NY 10019. 212-245-2928.
Description: Commercial fiction (mysteries, thrillers, literary) and nonfiction (science, biography, health, parenting, social history, and classical music). Considers unsolicited queries, but not manuscripts. Unpublished writers considered. **Submissions:** Query with outline, bio/resume and SASE. Accepts simultaneous queries, but not e-queries. Responds in 1 week to queries, 2 weeks to submissions. **Commission:** 15% domestic, 20% foreign. **Tips:** "We're a small agency providing individual attention." **Contact:** Susan Zeckendorf.

ARTS COUNCILS

State arts councils are a resource frequently overlooked by writers, but they offer useful services that can boost a writer's career. First of all, many offer cash awards of various sorts. One type of award is a "project" grant; that is, a specific award to complete a specified piece of work. These are awarded based on details of a proposal the individual author or a sponsoring arts group submits. The criteria for project grants are the quality of writing (based on sample poems or pages of fiction or nonfiction submitted), the clarity of the project, and some indication of community support, such as a letter of support from a community group. For instance, a project to publish an anthology of multicultural writers from your state might qualify for a grant. Other projects can be as diverse and creative as printing poems on placards to place in public transit vehicles, or on billboards or in other nontraditional venues.

The other type of cash support is a fellowship award. Many states offer awards for writers based on the general quality of their work. There is no "project" requirement; the money awarded is simply to further the author's career and is "unrestricted"; that is, it may be used for any purpose at all.

The review process involves peer groups of writers, creative artists, and arts administrators from around the state. The important thing to know is that these panels constantly rotate their membership. Review is somewhat subjective; a panel that hated your work one year may love it the next. Don't give up applying for fellowships in particular, as these are the easiest to apply for. Keep sending in your 1-page form and 10 best poems (or whatever is requested) each year. You may be pleasantly surprised one year to be selected for a writing fellowship award.

For project grants, after you get a rough idea of your desired project, you may wish to call the arts council to talk briefly with a grants officer. This person may be able to help you think through some key elements of your project that will need to be covered in a proposal. Many arts councils also offer regional grants-writing workshops and sometimes fund local agencies that in turn offer awards to authors.

Finally, arts councils have a variety of other services, such as newsletters which publish information on regional and national competitions, requests for submissions for regional collections of writing, and so on.

All writers should contact their state agencies and get on their mailing list, to keep abreast of these valuable services.

ALABAMA STATE COUNCIL ON THE ARTS

201 Monroe St., Suite 110, Montgomery, AL 36130-1800. 334-242-4076. Web site: www.arts.state.al.us. **Description:** Newsletter, workshops, conferences, and grants. **Contact:** Randy Shoults, Community Program Manager.

ALASKA STATE COUNCIL ON THE ARTS

411 W 4th Ave., Suite 1E, Anchorage, AK 99501-2343. 907-269-6610. E-mail: aksca_info@eed.state.ak.us. Web site: www.aksca.org. Charlotte Fox, Director. **Description:** Offers grants to Alaska artists and arts organizations. **Contact:** Pat Oldenburg.

ALBERTA FOUNDATION FOR THE ARTS
901 Standard Life Centre
10405 Jasper Avenue NW, Edmonton, Alberta T5J 4R7 Canada. 780-427-2921.
Web site: www.affta.ab.ca. **Description:** Grant programs and competitions.
Contact: Paul Pearson.

ARIZONA COMMISSION ON THE ARTS
417 W Roosevelt, Phoenix, AZ 85003-1226. 602-255-5882.
E-mail: general@ArizonaArts.org. Web site: www.arizonaarts.org. **Description:**
Newsletter, workshops, conference, grants, and fellowships for Arizona writers.
Contact: Paul Morris, Public Information/Literature Director.

ARKANSAS ARTS COUNCIL
1500 Tower Bldg., 323 Center St., Little Rock, AR 72201. 501-324-9766.
E-mail: info@arkansasarts.com. Web site: www.arkansasarts.com. **Description:**
Supports programs and services for arts organizations, schools, and individual artists.
Also offers individual artists fellowships and grants. **Contact:** James E. Mitchell,
Executive Director.

ASSOCIATED WRITING PROGRAMS
George Mason University, Mail Stop 1E3, Fairfax, VA 22030. 703-993-4301.
Web site: www.awpwriter.org. **Description:** Nonprofit organization of teachers, writers, writing programs, and lovers of literature. Awards: for poetry, short fiction, creative nonfiction, and novels. Prague Summer Seminars Fellowship Competition.
Annual conferences. See Web site for contest guidelines. Annual dues: $59 ($37 for
students), $20 for subscription to *AWP Chronicle* only.

BRITISH COLUMBIA ARTS COUNCIL
P.O. Box 9819, Stn Prov Govt
Victoria, British Columbia V8W 9W3 Canada. 250-356-1718.
E-mail: walter.quan@gems9.gov.bc.ca. Web site: www.bcartscouncil.ca. **Description:**
Provides opportunities and support for professional writers in British Columbia.
Contact: Walter Quan, Coordinator–Arts Awards Programs.

CALIFORNIA ARTS COUNCIL
1300 I St., Suite 930, Sacramento, CA 95814. 916-322-6395.
Web site: www.cac.ca.gov. Barry Hessenius, Executive Director. **Description:**
Supports small presses and writers with fellowships. Currently inaugurating a Poet
Laureate Program. Does not offer grants to writers to finish or publish books.
Applications available online. **Contact:** Ray Tatar, Literature Coordinator.

COLORADO COUNCIL ON THE ARTS
750 Pennsylvania St., Denver, CO 80203-3699. 303-894-2617.
E-mail: coloarts@state.co.us. Web site: www.coloarts.state.co.us. **Description:**
Newsletter and grants. **Contact:** Fran Holden, Executive Director.

COMPAS: WRITERS & ARTISTS IN THE SCHOOLS

304 Landmark Center, 75 W Fifth St., St. Paul, MN 55102. 651-292-3249.
E-mail: dei@compas.org. Web site: www.compas.org. **Description:** Nonprofit organization that collaborates with a wide of variety of arts, education, government, business, and philanthropic partners to employ professional artists, provide technical assistance, and offer grants to artists and agencies. **Contact:** Daniel Gabriel, Director.

CONNECTICUT COMMISSION ON THE ARTS

755 Main St., One Financial Plaza, Hartford, CT 06103. 860-566-4770.
E-mail: artsinfo@ctarts.org. Web site: www.ctarts.org. Linda Dente, Artist Fellowships Manager. **Description:** Dedicated to developing and strengthening Connecticut's cultural resources. Offers fellowships to Connecticut creative writers biannually. The next opportunity for writers will be in 2004. Awards are $5,000 and $2,500. **Contact:** Douglas C. Evans, Executive Director.

DELAWARE DIVISION OF THE ARTS

Carvel State Bldg., 820 N French St., Wilmington, DE 19801. 302-577-8278.
Web site: www.artsdel.org. **Description:** Offers fellowships and grants to individual artists from Delaware. **Contact:** Kristin Pleasanton, Art/Artist Services Coordinator.

FLORIDA ARTS COUNCIL

1001 De Sota Park Dr., Tallahassee, FL 32301. 858-245-6470.
E-mail: culturalaffiars@mail.dos.state.fl.us. Web site: www.florida-arts.org. **Description:** Encourages the development of culture and the arts statewide and provides cultural grant funding. **Contact:** JuDee L. Pehijohn, Director.

GEORGIA COUNCIL FOR THE ARTS

260 14th St., Suite 401, Atlanta, GA 30318. 404-685-2787.
E-mail: bbaker@gaarts.org. Web site: www.gaarts.org. Betsy Baker, Executive Director. **Description:** Offers funding, programs, and services to both support and encourage excellence in the arts. **Contact:** Ann Davis, Grants Manager, Literature.

HAWAII STATE FOUNDATION ON CULTURE AND THE ARTS

250 S Hotel St., Fl. 2, Honolulu, HI 96813. 808-586-0307.
E-mail: sfca@sfca.state.hi.us. Web site: www.hawaii.gov/sfca. David C. Farmer, Executive Director. **Description:** Programs include Art in Public Places, Arts in Education, Community Outreach, Foundation Grants, Folk Arts, Individual Artists Fellowships, and History and Humanities. **Contact:** Ronald Yamakawa.

IDAHO COMMISSION ON THE ARTS

P.O. Box 83720, Boise, ID 83720-0008. 208-334-2119.
E-mail: cconley@ica.state.id.us. **Description:** The state's principal cultural agency supports Idaho writers through annual grants and awards, readings and workshops. Grants are possible every year, but awards are given every three years (fellowships and writer-in-residence). **Contact:** Cort Conley, Director.

ILLINOIS ARTS COUNCIL

James R. Thompson Center

100 W Randolph, Suite 10-500, Chicago, IL 60601. 312-814-6750.

E-mail: susan@arts.state.il.us; info@arts.state.il.us.

Web site: www.state.il.us/agency/iac. Sue Eleuterio, Director of Literature Programs. **Description:** Biannual fellowships in poetry (odd-numbered fiscal years) and prose (even-numbered fiscal years). Deadline: September 1. Literary Arts Award for authors published in nonprofit Illinois literary publications. Deadline: March 1. Also offers a newsletter, workshops, grants, and prizes to Illinois organizations and writers.

INDIANA ARTS COMMISSION

402 W Washington St., Room W072, Indianapolis, IN 46204-2741. 317-232-1268.

E-mail: arts@state.in.us. Web site: www.in.gov/arts/. **Description:** Promotes and encourages the arts throughout Indiana. Goals are to support the Regional Partnership Initiative, increase public awareness of the arts, and support arts education and individual artists. **Contact:** Dorothy Ilgen, Executive Director.

IOWA ARTS COUNCIL

State Historical Building, 600 E Locust, Des Moines, IA 50319-0290. 515-281-4011.

E-mail: sarah.oltrogge@dca.state.ia.us. Web site: www.culturalaffairs.org/iac. **Description:** Seeks to make the arts available to individuals living in Iowa. Offers grants for artists in arts education, technical assistance and professional development, community development, and support for arts organizations. **Contact:** Sarah Oltrogge, Public Relations Specialist.

KANSAS ARTS COMMISSION

700 SW Jackson, Suite 1004, Topeka, KS 66603-3761. 785-296-3335.

E-mail: kac@arts.state.ks.us. Web site: http://arts.state.ks.us. David M. Wilson. **Description:** Offers programs, services, and grants to the citizens of Kansas and works to encourage and promote the celebration of the arts statewide. **Contact:** Robert T. Burtch, Editor.

KENTUCKY ARTS COUNCIL

Old Capitol Annex, 300 W Broadway, Frankfort, KY 40601-1980. 502-564-3757.

E-mail: kyarts@mail.state.ky.us. Web site: www.kyarts.org. **Description:** Offers programs, grants, virtual exhibits, and arts education. **Contact:** Gerri Combs, Executive Director.

LOUISIANA DIVISION OF THE ARTS

P.O. Box 44247, Baton Rouge, LA 70804-4247. 225-342-8180.

E-mail: jborders@crt.state.la.us; arts@crt.state.la.us. Web site: www.crt.state.la.us. **Description:** Workshops, conference, grants, and newsletter. **Contact:** James Borders, Executive Director.

MAINE ARTS COMMISSION
25 State House Station, 193 State St., Augusta, ME 04333-0025. 207-287-2724.
E-mail: kathy.shaw@state.me.us. Web site: www.mainearts.com. **Description:**
Newletter, workshops, and grants. **Contact:** Alden C. Wilson, Director.

MANITOBA ARTS COUNCIL
525-93 Lombard Ave., Winnipeg, Manitoba R3B 3B1 Canada. 204-945-0422.
E-mail: jthomas@artscouncil.mb.ca. Web site: www.artscouncil.mb.ca. **Description:**
Provides grants to professional writers working in poetry, fiction, creative nonfiction,
theater, and filmscripts. Manitoba residency required. Program guidelines available
on Web site. **Contact:** Joan Thomas, Program Officer: Literary, Film and Video.

MARYLAND STATE ARTS COUNCIL
Literature Program, 175 W Ostend St., Suite F,
Baltimore, MD 21230. 410-767-6555.
E-mail: pdunne@mdbusiness.state.md.us. Web site: www.msac.org. Theresa M.
Colvin, Executive Director. **Description:** Grants, awards, newsletter. **Contact:**
Pamela Dunne, Literature Program Director.

MASSACHUSETTS CULTURAL COUNCIL
10 St. James Avenue, Fl. 3, Boston, MA 02116. 617-727-3668.
E-mail: mcc@art.state.ma.us. Web site: www.massculturalcouncil.org. Mary Kelley,
Director. **Description:** Newsletter and grants. **Contact:** Charles Coe, Literature
Coordinator.

MICHIGAN COUNCIL FOR ARTS AND CULTURAL AFFAIRS
525 W Ottawa, P.O. Box 30705, Lansing, MI 48909-8205. 517-241-4011.
Web site: www.cis.state.mi.us/arts. **Description:** Strives to increase public awareness
of the arts, strengthen the arts and culture statewide, and support art education, communities, and artists. **Contact:** Betty Boone, Executive Director.

MINNESOTA STATE ARTS BOARD
Park Square Court, Suite 200, 400 Sibley St.
St. Paul, MN 55101-1928. 651-215-1600, 800-8MN-ARTS.
E-mail: msab@arts.state.mn.us. Web site: www.arts.state.mn.us. Robert Booker,
Executive Director. **Description:** Offers newsletter, workshops, and grants.
Contact: Amy Frimpong, Artist Assistance Program Officer.

MISSISSIPPI ARTS COMMISSION
239 N Lamar St., Suite 207, Jackson, MS 39201. 601-359-6030.
Web site: www.arts.state.ms.us. **Description:** Supports and promotes the arts in both
community life and education. **Contact:** Beth Batton, Arts-Based Community
Development Center.

MISSOURI ARTS COUNCIL
Wainwright Office Complex, 111 N Seventh St., Suite 105
St. Louis, MO 63101-2188. 314-340-6845.
E-mail: nboyd@mail.state.mo.us. Web site: www.missouriartscouncil.org. Norree Boyd, Executive Director. **Description:** Newsletter, conferences, grants. **Contact:** Beverly Strohmeyer, Assistant Director for Programs.

MONTANA ARTS COUNCIL
P.O. Box 202201, Helena, MT 59620-2201. 406-444-6430.
E-mail: mac@state.mt.us. Web site: www.art.state.mt.us. **Description:** Strives to promote and expand the Montana culture and the arts by offering support to individuals, organizations, schools, and communities in Montana. Only Montana residents are eligible for most programs. **Contact:** Kristin Han Burgoyne, Grants & Database Director.

NEBRASKA ARTS COUNCIL
3838 Davenport St., Omaha, NE 68131-2329. 800-341-4067.
Web site: www.nebraskaartscouncil.org. Jennifer Severin, Executive Director. **Description:** Offers grants and other opportunities, and provides access to numerous resources.

NEVADA ARTS COUNCIL
716 N Carson St., Suite A, Carson City, NV 89701. 775-687-6680.
E-mail: cjnemania@clan.lib.nv.us. Web site: www.nevadaculture.org. **Description:** Workshops, conferences, newletter, and grants.

NEW BRUNSWICK ARTS BOARD
P.O. Box 6000, Fredericton, New Brunswick E3B 5H1 Canada. 506-453-4307.
E-mail: artsnb@gov.nb.ca. Web site: www.artsnb.ca. **Description:** Offers programs, scholarships, and artist-in-residence program.

NEW HAMPSHIRE STATE COUNCIL ON THE ARTS
Phenix Hall, 40 N Main St., Concord, NH 03301-4974. 603-271-2789.
E-mail: jmento@nharts.state.nh.us. Web site: www.state.nh.us/nharts. Rebecca Lawrence, Director. **Description:** Newsletter, workshops, conference, grants, and prizes. **Contact:** Julie Mento, Artist Services Coordinator.

NEW JERSEY STATE COUNCIL ON THE ARTS
Artist Services, P.O. Box 306, Trenton, NJ 08625. 609-292-6130.
E-mail: Beth@arts.sos.state.nj.us. Web site: www.njartscouncil.org. **Description:** Workshops, newletter, conferences, grants. **Contact:** Beth Vogel, Program Officer.

NEW MEXICO ARTS
P.O. Box 1450, Santa Fe, NM 87504-1450. 505-827-6490.
E-mail: aweisman@oca.state.nm.us. Web site: www.nmarts.org. Ann Weisman, Local

Arts Councils/Arts Education Coordinator. **Description:** State arts agency that provides grants to New Mexico nonprofit organizations to implement arts and cultural programs in their communities.

NEW YORK STATE COUNCIL ON THE ARTS

175 Varick St., New York, NY 10014. 212-387-7000.
E-mail: kmasterson@nysca.org. Web site: www.nysca.org.
Description: Offers support to a wide range of literary and multi-disciplinary writing or literary organizations in the state of New York through the Literature Program (LIT). Objective is to develop and support public literary activity around the state. New applicants are encouraged to apply. Applicants must provide completed NYSCA application forms and specific additional narrative for the category in which they are applying. Application deadline: March 1. **Tips:** Does not offer funding for individual writers or a separate writer-in-residence. Does offer translation grants and guest editorships. **Contact:** Kathleen Masterson, Director, Literature Program.

NEWFOUNDLAND & LABRADOR ARTS COUNCIL

P.O. Box 98, St. John's, Newfoundland A1C 5H5 Canada. 709-726-2212.
E-mail: nlacmail@newcomm.net. Web site: www.nlac.nf.ca. **Description:** Supports the arts by providing financial assistance programs, services, resources, and grants to individuals and groups with an interest in the arts.

NORTH CAROLINA ARTS COUNCIL

Dept. of Cultural Resources, Raleigh, NC 27699-4632. 919-733-2111.
E-mail: debbie.mcgill@ncmail.net. Web site: www.ncarts.org. **Description:** On-line newsletter, grants. **Contact:** Deborah McGill, Literature Director.

NORTH DAKOTA COUNCIL ON THE ARTS

1600 E Century Ave., Suite 6, Bismarck, ND 58503. 701-328-7590.
E-mail: comserv@state.nd.us. Web site: www.discovernd.com/arts. **Description:** Newsletter and grants. **Contact:** Janine Webb, Director.

OHIO ARTS COUNCIL

727 E Main St., Columbus, OH 43205-1796. 614-466-2613.
E-mail: bob.fox@oac.state.oh.us. Web site: www.oac.state.oh.us.
Description: Dedicated to encouraging the development of the arts and to preserving Ohio's cultural heritage. Offers grants to organizations, fellowships to individuals, and service programs. **Contact:** Bob Fox, Literature Program Coordinator.

OKLAHOMA ARTS COUNCIL

P.O. Box 52001-2001, Oklahoma City, OK 73152-2001. 405-521-2931.
E-mail: jennifer@arts.state.ok.us. Web site: www.state.ok.us/~arts. Betty Price, Executive Director. **Description:** Workshops, conferences, newsletters, grants. **Contact:** Jennifer James.

ONTARIO ARTS COUNCIL
151 Bloor St. W, Fl. 5, Toronto, Ontario M5S 1T6 Canada. 416-969-7413.
E-mail: jstubbs@arts.on.ca. **Description:** Awards, grants, and scholarships.
Contact: Janet Stubbs.

OREGON ARTS COMMISSION
775 Summer St. NE, Salem, OR 97301-1284. 503-986-0086.
E-mail: oregon.artscomm@state.or.us . Web site: www.oregonartscommission.org.
Christine T. D'Arcy, Executive Director. **Description:** Dedicated to fostering the
arts in Oregon. Offers grants and programs. **Contact:** Susan Hanf, Assistant Director.

PENNSYLVANIA COUNCIL ON THE ARTS
Room 216, Finance Bldg., Harrisburg, PA 17120. 717-787-6883.
E-mail: http://artsnet.org/pca/. Web site: www.artsnet.org/pca. **Description:** Strives
to foster the excellence and appreciation of the arts in Pennsylvania. Offers grants,
awards, and services. **Contact:** James Woland, Literature Program.

PRINCE EDWARD ISLAND COUNCIL OF THE ARTS
115 Richmond St.
Charlottetown, Prince Edward Island C1A 1A7 Canada. 902-368-4410.
Description: Contests and grants. **Contact:** Ferne Taylor.

RHODE ISLAND STATE COUNCIL ON THE ARTS
83 Park St., Fl. 6, Providence, RI 02903-1037. 401-222-3880.
E-mail: randy@risca.state.ri.us. Web site: www.risca.state.ri.us. **Description:** Offers
workshops and grants. **Contact:** Karolye Cunha.

SASKATCHEWAN ARTS BOARD
2135 Broad St., Regina, Saskatchewan S4P 3V7 Canada. 306-787-4056.
E-mail: sab@artsboard.sk.ca. Web site: www.artsboard.sk.ca/. **Description:**
Programs, services, consultation, and grants to assist artists and arts organizations.

SOUTH CAROLINA ARTS COMMISSION
1800 Gervais St., Columbia, SC 29201. 803-734-8696.
E-mail: goldstsa@arts.state.sc.us. Web site: www.state.sc.us/arts. Suzette M.
Surkamer, Executive Director. **Description:** Offers grants, programs, and resources
to art organizations and South Carolina artists. **Contact:** Sara June Goldstein,
Program Director for Literary Arts.

SOUTH DAKOTA ARTS COUNCIL
800 Governors Dr., Pierre, SD 57501-2294. 605-773-3131.
E-mail: sdac@stlib.state.sd.us. Web site: www.sdarts.org. **Description:** Offers grants
to South Dakota writers. Also offers workshops, conferences, and a newsletter.
Contact: Dennis Holub, Executive Director.

TENNESSEE ARTS COMMISSION

401 Charlotte Ave., Nashville, TN 37243-0780. 615-741-1701.
Web site: www.arts.state.tn.us. **Description:** Provides access to the arts in Tennessee. Various grants available. **Contact:** Literary Arts Director.

TEXAS COMMISSION ON THE ARTS

P.O. Box 13406, Austin, TX 78711-3406. 512-475-3327.
E-mail: front.desk@arts.state.tx.us. Web site: www.arts.state.tx.us. **Description:** Newsletter, workshops, conferences, grants. **Contact:** Gaye Greever McElwain, Director of Marketing.

UTAH ARTS COUNCIL

617 E South Temple, Salt Lake, UT 84102-1177. 801-236-7555.
E-mail: glebeda@utah.gov. Web site: www.dccd.state.ut.us/arts. Bonnie Stephens, Director. **Description:** Fosters creativity and diversity in the arts in Utah. Provides funding, training and development services, and educational programs in the arts. **Contact:** Guy Lebeda, Literature Coordinator.

VERMONT ARTS COUNCIL

136 State St., Drawer 33, Montpelier, VT 05633-6001. 802-828-3294.
E-mail: mbailey@vermontartscouncil.org. Web site: www.vermontartscouncil.org. **Description:** Workshops, newsletter, conferences, grants. **Contact:** Michele Bailey, Director of Creation & Presentation Programs.

VIRGINIA COMMISSION FOR THE ARTS

223 Governor St., Lewis House, Fl. 2, Richmond, VA 23219-2010. 804-225-3132.
E-mail: pbaggett.arts@state.va.us. Web site: www.arts.state.va.us. Donna Champ Banks, Program Coordinator. **Description:** Workshops, conferences, and grants. **Contact:** Peggy J. Baggett, Executive Director.

WASHINGTON STATE ARTS COMMISSION

234 E Eighth Ave., P.O. Box 42675, Olympia, WA 98504-2675. 360-586-2421.
E-mail: bitsyb@wsac.wa.gov. Web site: www.arts.wa.gov. Kris Tucker, Director. **Description:** Newsletter, workshops, grants (for nonprofit organizations only, no individuals). **Contact:** Bitsy Bidwell, Community Arts Development Manager.

WEST VIRGINIA COMMISSION ON THE ARTS

West Virginia Division of Culture & History
The Cultural Center, 1900 Kanawha Blvd. E, Charleston, WV 25305. 304-558-0220.
E-mail: gordon.simmons@wvculture.org. Web site: www.wvculture.org.
Description: Strives to promote and preserve West Virginia's culture and the arts. **Contact:** Gordon Simmons, Individual Artist Services.

WISCONSIN ARTS BOARD

101 E Wilson St., Fl. 1, Madison, WI 53702. 608-266-0190.
E-mail: artsboard@arts.state.wi.us. Web site: www.arts.state.wi.us. George Tzougros, Executive Director. **Description:** Newsletter, workshops, conferences, and grants. **Contact:** Mark Fraire.

WYOMING ARTS COUNCIL

2320 Capitol Ave., Cheyenne, WY 82002. 307-777-7742.
E-mail: mshay@state.wy.us. Web site: www.wyoarts.state.wy.us. John G. Coe, Executive Director. **Description:** Offers three literary contests to writers from Wyoming: The Literary Fellowship Awards, the Warren Alder Fiction Award, and the Neltje Blanchan/Frank Doubleday Memorial Awards. **Contact:** Michael Shay, Literature Program Manager.

COLONIES

Writers' colonies offer solitude and freedom from everyday distractions so that writers can concentrate on their work. Though some colonies are quite small, with space for just three or four writers at a time, others can provide accommodations for as many as 30 or 40. The length of a residency may vary, too, from a couple of weeks to five or six months. These programs have strict admissions policies, and writers must submit a formal application or letter of intent, a resume, writing samples, and letters of recommendation. As an alternative to the traditional writers' colony, a few of the organizations listed offer writing rooms for writers who live nearby. Write for application information first, enclosing a stamped, self-addressed envelope. Residency fees are subject to change.

EDWARD F. ALBEE FOUNDATION

14 Harrison St., New York, NY 10013. 212-226-2020.
Description: On Long Island, "The Barn" (William Flanagan Memorial Creative Persons Center), offers 1-month residencies to 12 writers each season, from June 1-October 1. Applicants are chosen based on artistic talent and need. Applications (writing samples, project description, and resume) are accepted January 1-April 1. **Fees:** None, but residents are responsible for food/travel. **Contact:** Jacob Holder.

ALTOS DE CHAVÓN

66 Fifth Ave., Room 604A, New York, NY 10011. 212-229-5370.
Description: Nonprofit center for the arts in the Dominican Republic, for design innovation, international creative exchange, and the promotion of Dominican culture. Residencies average 12 weeks, offering emerging or established artists a chance to live and work in a setting of architectural and natural beauty. Selects 2-3 writers each year. Send letter of interest, writing sample, and resume by July 15. **Fees:** $400/month. **Contact:** Stephen D. Kaplan, Arts/Education Director.

MARY ANDERSON CENTER

101 St. Francis Dr., Mount St. Francis, IN 47146. 812-923-8602.
E-mail: maca@iglou.com. Web site: www.maryandersoncenter.org.
Description: Residencies (1-8 weeks) and retreats on the grounds of a Franciscan friary with 400 acres of rolling hills and woods. Private rooms for up to 6 writers, musicians, and visual artists. Includes working space and a visual artist's studio. Applicants selected based on project proposal and artist's body of work. Apply year-round (with $15 application fee). **Fees:** $30/day. Work exchange program available. **Contact:** Debra Carmody, Executive Director.

ATLANTIC CENTER FOR THE ARTS

1414 Art Center Ave., New Smyrna Beach, FL 32168. 386-427-6975, 800-393-6975.
E-mail: program@atlanticcenterforthearts.org.
Web site: www.atlanticcenterforthearts.org. **Description:** Residencies (2-3 weeks) on Florida's east coast, with 67 acres of pristine land on tidal estuary. Unique envi-

ronment for sharing ideas, learning, and collaborating on interdisciplinary projects. Master artists meet with talented artists for readings and critiques, with time for individual work. Residents are selected by Master Artist in-Residence. Application deadlines vary. **Fees:** None. **Contact:** Nicholas Conroy, Program and Residency Manager.

BLUE MOUNTAIN CENTER
P.O. Box 109, Blue Mountain Lake, NY 12812.
E-mail: bmcl@telenet.net. Web site: www.bluemountaincenter.org. **Description:** Residencies (4 months) for writers, artists, and activists from mid-June through late October. Send brief biographical sketch, a plan for work at BMC, 5-10 slides or writing sample (approx. 30 pages, designate 10 pages for preliminary reading), and $20 application fee. **Fees:** None, contributions encouraged. **Tips:** "The admissions committee is particularly interested in applicants whose work demonstrates social or ecological concern. Students are discouraged from applying." **Contact:** Admissions Committee.

BYRDCLIFFE ARTS COLONY
Woodstock Guild, 34 Tinker St., Woodstock, NY 12498. 845-679-2079.
E-mail: wguild@ulster.net. Web site: www.woodstockguild.org. **Description:** The Villetta Inn, at a 400-acre arts colony, offers 1-month residencies (June-September) to fiction writers, poets, playwrights, and visual artists. Private studios, separate bedrooms, communal kitchen, and a peaceful environment. Submit application, resume, writing sample, 2 letters of recommendation, and $5 application fee by April 1. **Fees:** $600/month. **Contact:** Carla T. Smith, Director.

CAMARGO FOUNDATION
125 Park Square Ct., 400 Sibley St., St. Paul, MN 55101-1982. 202-302-7303.
E-mail: camargo@jeromefdn.org. **Description:** Maintains a center of studies in France for 9 scholars and grad students each semester to pursue projects in humanities and social sciences on France and Francophone culture. Also, one artist, one composer, and one writer accepted each semester. Research should be at advanced stage. Send application form, curriculum vitae, 3 letters of recommendation, and project description by February 1. Writers, artists, and composers must send work samples. **Contact:** Michael Pritina, Director; Ellen Guettler, U.S. Secretariat.

CENTRUM
P.O. Box 1158, Port Townsend, WA 98368. 360-385-3102.
E-mail: sally@centrum.org. Web site: www.centrum.org. **Description:** Residencies (1-4 weeks) for writers and other creative artists, September-May. Selected applicants receive free housing. Some stipends ($300 or less) available for Seattle area artists. Send application package (see Web site) and $20 application fee by August 1. **Contact:** Sally Rodgers, Coordinator.

DJFR∧OЗI RESIDENT ARTISTS PROGRAM

2325 Bear Gulch Rd., Woodside, CA 94062. 650-747-1250.
E-mail: drap@djerassi.org. Web site: www.djerassi.org. **Description:** Residencies
(4 weeks) for artists in literature (prose, poetry, playwrights/screenwriters), choreography, music composition, visual arts, and media arts/new genres. Located in rural
setting in Santa Cruz Mountains. Submit application (send SASE or see Web site) and
$25 application fee by February 15 (for residency the following year). **Fees:** None.

DORLAND MOUNTAIN ARTS COLONY

P.O. Box 6, Temecula, CA 92593. 909-302-3837.
E-mail: dorland@ez2.net. Web site: www.ez2.net/dorland/. **Description:**
Residencies (1-2 months) for novelists, playwrights, poets, nonfiction writers, composers, and visual artists. Located in the Palomar Mountains of Southern California.
Submit application (send SASE or see Web site) by March 1 or September 1. **Fees:**
$450/month (includes cottage, fuel, and firewood). **Tips:** "Without electricity, residents find a new, natural rhythm for their work."**Contact:** Karen Parrott, Director.

DORSET COLONY HOUSE

P.O. Box 510, Dorset, VT 05251. 802-867-2223.
E-mail: theatre@sover.net. Web site: www.dorsetcolony.org. **Description:**
Residencies (2-3 weeks) for writers and playwrights (up to 9 at a time) in the fall and
spring. Low-cost rooms with kitchen facilities at historic Colony House. Applications
accepted year-round. **Fees:** $120/week, limited financial aid. Send SASE for details.

FINE ARTS WORK CENTER IN PROVINCETOWN

24 Pearl St., Provincetown, MA 02657. 508-487-9960.
Web site: www.fawc.org. **Description:** Offers fellowships to 10 writers and 10 visual
artists to work independently from October 1-May 1. Includes studio apartment, studio space for visual artists, and monthly stipends. Writer's deadline: December 1.
Visual artists deadline: February 1. Send SASE for application/guidelines.

GLENESSENCE WRITERS COLONY

1447 W Ward Ave., Ridgecrest, CA 93555. 760-446-5894.
Description: Luxury villa in the Upper Mojave Desert (private rooms with bath,
pool, spa, courtyard, shared kitchen, fitness center, and library). No children, pets,
smoking. Seasonal (January through May). Reservations on a first-come basis. **Fees:**
$565/month, meals not provided. **Contact:** Allison Swift, Director.

TYRONE GUTHRIE CENTRE

Annaghmakerrig, Newbliss, County Monaghan, Ireland. 353-47-54003.
E-mail: thetgc@indigo.ie. Web site: www.tyroneguthrie.ie/. **Description:**
Residencies (1-3 months) on a 450-acre forested estate, offering peace and seclusion
to writers and other artists. Writers chosen based on CV, samples of published work,
and outline of intended project. **Fees:** £2,550/month. Some longer-term residencies
in old farmyard are available at £380/week. **Contact:** Sheila Pratschke, Director.

THE HAMBIDGE CENTER

P.O. Box 339, Rabun Gap, GA 30568. 706-746-5718.
E-mail: center@hambidge.org. Web site: www.hambidge.org. **Description:**
Residencies (2-8 weeks) for artists in all disciplines. The center is on 600 pristine acres
of quiet woods in the north Georgia mountains. Eight private cottages available. All
fellowships partially underwritten, residents contribute $125/week. Download appli-
cation from Web site or send SASE. Deadlines: October 1 for February to August;
May 1 for September to December.

HEADLANDS CENTER FOR THE ARTS

944 Fort Barry, Sausalito, CA 94965. 415-331-2787.
E-mail: staff@headlands.org. **Description:** On 13,000 acres of open coastal space,
residencies are available to current residents of Ohio, New Jersey, North Carolina,
and California. Application requirements vary by state. Deadline: June. Decisions
announced October for residencies beginning March. No residency or application
fees. Send SASE for details. **Contact:** Allison Rasin, Public Relations Manager.

HEDGEBROOK

2197 Millman Rd., Langley, WA 98260. 360-321-4786.
E-mail: hedgebrk@whidbey.com. Web site: www.hedgebrook.org.
Description: Residencies (1-8 weeks) on 48 acres of farmland/woods on Whidbey
Island in Washington State. Provides women writers (published or not) of all ages and
from all cultural backgrounds, with a natural place to work. Stipend program available
for low income, without college degree, or aged 55 and over. See Web site for more
information or to download application. **Fees:** None. **Contact:** Janice Kennedy.

KALANI OCEANSIDE RETREAT CENTERs

Artist-in-Residence Program
RR2, Box 4500 Beach Rd., Pahoa, HI 96778. 808-965-7828, 800-800-6886.
E-mail: kalani@kalani.com. Web site: www.kalani.com. **Description:** Residencies (2-
8 weeks) in rural coastal setting of 113 botanical acres. Hosts and sponsors educational programs to bring together creative people from around the world in culturally
and artistically stimulating environment. Offers housing, B&W darkroom, various studio spaces. Applications accepted year-round. **Fees:** $50 to $105/day, meals extra.

THE MACDOWELL COLONY

100 High St., Peterborough, NH 03458. 603-924-3886.
E-mail: info@macdowellcolony.org. Web site: www.macdowellcolony.org.
Description: Residencies (up to 8 weeks) for 80-90 writers each year. Stipend available, up to $1,000 depending on financial need. Selection is competitive. Apply by
January 15 for May-August; by April 15 for September-December; by September 15
for January-April. Travel grant of up to $1,000 also available. Send SASE for applica-
tion or e-mail for details. **Contact:** Courtney Bethel, Admissions Coordinator.

THE MILLAY COLONY FOR THE ARTS
454 East Hill Rd., P.O. Box 3, Austerlitz, NY 12017-0003. 518-392-3103.
E-mail: application@millaycolony.org. Web site: www.millaycolony.org. **Description:**
Residencies (1 month), April-November at Steepletop (former home of Edna St.
Vincent Millay). Provides studios, living quarters, and meals at no cost. Applications
reviewed by independent jurors, selection based on talent. Send SASE or e-mail for
application. Submit by November 1 for the coming season. **Contact:** Martha
Hopewell, Executive Director or Nikki Hayes, Executive Assistant.

MILLETT FARM: AN ART COLONY FOR WOMEN
295 Bowery, New York, NY 10003.
Description: Summer residencies for women writers and visual artists at picturesque tree farm in rural New York. For housing, all residents contribute 5 hours of
work each weekday morning and $300/month for meals. Preference given to writers
who can stay all summer or at least 6 weeks. Also, 1-week master class ($500) avail-
able with Kate Millett. Send SASE for details. **Contact:** Kate Millett, Director.

MOLASSES POND WRITERS' RETREAT AND WORKSHOP
15 Granite Shore, Milbridge, ME 04658. 207-546-2506.
Description: This 1-week workshop held in June is led by published authors who
teaching writing at the Univ. of New Hampshire. Up to 10 writers stay in colonial
farmhouse with private bed/work rooms. Applicants must be serious about their work.
No children's literature or poetry. Submit statement of purpose and 15-20 pages of
fiction or nonfiction between February 1-March 1. **Fees:** $450 (lodging, meals,
tuition). **Contact:** Martha Barron Barrett or Sue Wheeler, Coordinators.

MONTANA ARTISTS REFUGE
P.O. Box 8, Basin, MT 59631. 406-225-3500.
E-mail: mar@mt.net. Web site: www.montanarefuge.org. **Description:** Offers living
and studio space in rural environment to self-directed artists in all disciplines. Writers
can work with other artists or in solitude. The length of a residency may be 1 month
to 1 year; with rents ($495-$550/month). Financial aid available, but limited. Send
SASE for details. **Contact:** Jennifer Pryor, Residency Coordinator.

NEW YORK MILLS ARTS RETREAT
AND REGIONAL CULTURAL CENTER
24 N Main Ave., New York Mills, MN 56567. 218-385-3339.
E-mail: nymills@kulcher.org. Web site: www.kulcher.org. Heather Humbert Price,
Arts Retreat Coordinator. **Description:** A small house and studio are provided to 6-8
selected professional, emerging artists in all disciplines. Applicants may be eligible for
Jerome Foundation Fellowships, which provide stipends of $750-$1,500. Special
emphasis is given to providing opportunities for artists of color. Each fellowship artist
returns a minimum of 8 hours of community service, usually teaching in area schools.
Deadlines: April 1 and October 1. **Contact:** Heather Price.

NORTHWOOD UNIVERSITY

Alden B. Dow Creativity Center

4000 Whiting Dr., Midland, MI 48640-2398. 989-837-4478.

E-mail: creativity@northwood.edu. Web site: www.northwood.edu/abd.

Description: Four 10-week residencies (early-June to mid-August) awarded yearly to individuals who wish to pursue project ideas without interruption. A project idea should be innovative, creative, and have potential for impact in its field. A $750 stipend plus room/board are provided. No spouses or families. Submit application materials and $10 fee by December 31. **Contact:** Liz Drake, Assistant Director.

OX-BOW

37 S Wabash Ave., Chicago, IL 60603. 800-318-3019.

E-mail: ox-bow@artic.edu. Web site: www.ox-bow.org. **Description:** Residencies (1-2 weeks) in mid-June to mid-August for writers to reside and work in a secluded, natural environment in Michigan. "Primarily for the visual arts, Ox-Bow nurtures the creative process through instruction, example, and community." Resident writers are encouraged to present a reading of their work and to participate in the community life. Submit application by mid-February. **Fees:** $425/week.

RAGDALE

1260 N Green Bay Rd., Lake Forest, IL 60045. 847-234-1063.

E-mail: mosher@ragdale.org. Web site: www.ragdale.org. **Description:** Nonprofit artists' community that supports emerging and established artists, writers, and composers. Provides room/board, as well as peaceful space where writers and artists can focus on their work. Facilities include 8 writer's rooms, 3 visual art studios, and one composer's studio. Submit application and $20 fee by January 15 or June 1. **Fees:** $15/day. **Contact:** Melissa Mosher, Director of Admissions.

SASKATCHEWAN WRITERS/ARTISTS
COLONIES AND INDIVIDUAL RETREATS

P.O. Box 3986, Regina, Saskatchewan S4P 3R9 Canada. 306-565-8785.

E-mail: skcolony@attglobal.net. Web site: www.skwriter.com/colonies.html.

Description: Offers a 6-week summer colony (July-August) and a 2-week winter colony (February). Also offers individual retreats (for Canadian residents only) year-round, up to 3 residents at a time. Submit application by December 1 for winter, May 1 for summer. **Fees:** $150/week ($200 for nonmembers). **Contact:** Shelley Sopher, Colony Coordinator.

JOHN STEINBECK ROOM

Long Island University

Southampton College Library, Southampton, NY 11968. 631-287-8382.

E-mail: library@southampton.liu.edu. **Description:** Provides a basic research facility to writers with either a current book contract or a confirmed magazine assignment. The room is available for a period of 6 months with one 6-month renewal permissible. Send SASE for application. **Contact:** Robert Gerbereux, Library Director.

THURBER HOUSE RESIDENCIES

c/o Thurber House, 77 Jefferson Ave., Columbus, OH 43215. 614-464-1032.
E-mail: thurberhouse@thurberhouse.org. Web site: www.thurberhouse.org.
Description: Residencies in the restored home of James Thurber are awarded to creative fiction and nonfiction writers, journalists, poets, playwrights, and children's fiction writers. Residents work on their own writing projects, and in addition to other duties, some teach a class at the Ohio State University. Send letter of interest, CV, and other materials by November 15. **Contact:** Trish Houston, Residencies Director.

TWO WHITE WOLVES RETREAT

8561 De Soto Ave., #191, Canoga Park, CA 91304. 818-464-3727.
E-mail: twowhitewolvesretreat@yahoo.com. **Description:** Residency at the beautiful and peaceful 15.7 acre Maine retreat. Property is being made into a fauna sanctuary. Writers welcome to apply for residency for short- or long-term stay. One-time fee of $25 for guest application with no fee for entire stay. No hunting is allowed and residents must be self-contained during their stay. **Contact:** Kate Alexander, Director.

UCROSS FOUNDATION

Residency Program, 30 Big Red Ln., Clearmont, WY 82835. 307-737-2291.
E-mail: ucross@wyoming.com. Web site: ucrossfoundation.org. **Description:** Residencies (2-8 weeks) in the foothills of Big Horn Mountains for writers, artists, and scholars. Residency sessions offered in fall (August-December) and spring (February-June). Send application and $20 fee by March 1 for fall, October 1 for spring. Send SASE for details. **Fees:** None. **Contact:** Sharon Dynak, Executive Director.

VERMONT STUDIO CENTER

P.O. Box 613, Johnson, VT 05656. 802-635-2727.
E-mail: info@vscvt.org. Web site: www.vermontstudiocenter.org. **Description:** Independent residencies (4-12 weeks) offered year-round, for up to 12 writers of fiction, nonfiction, and poetry. Includes studio space, room, meals, and community interaction. Also optional readings and private conferences with prominent visiting writers. Full fellowships, grants, and work-exchange aid are available. Send application and $25 fee by February 15, June 15, or September 30. **Fees:** $3,200/month.

VILLA MONTALVO ARTIST RESIDENCY PROGRAM

15400 Montalvo Rd., P.O. Box 158, Saratoga, CA 95071. 408-961-5818.
E-mail: kfunk@villamontalvo.org. Web site: www.villamontalvo.org. **Description:** Residencies (1-3 months) in the foothills of the Santa Cruz Mountains for writers, visual artists, and composers. Several merit-based fellowships available. Send application and $20 fee by September 1 or March 1. Send self-addressed label and $.55 postage for applicaton and details. **Fees:** None. **Contact:** Kathryn Funk, Artist Residency Director.

VIRGINIA CENTER FOR THE CREATIVE ARTS

154 San Angelo Dr., Amherst, VA 24521.
E-mail: vcca@vcca.com. Web site: www.vcca.com. **Description:** Residencies (2-8 weeks) available year-round for writers, composers, and visual artists at this working retreat in Virginia's Blue Ridge Mountains. About 300 residents accepted each year, 22 at any one time. Submit application by January 15, May 15, or September 15. Send SASE or visit Web site for details. **Contact:** Suny Monk, Executive Director.

THE WRITERS ROOM

740 Broadway, Fl. 12, New York, NY 10003. 212-254-6995.
E-mail: writersroom@writersroom.org. Web site: www.writersroom.org.
Description: In the East Village, the Writers Room offers a quiet work space for all types of writers, at all stages of their careers. Holds 43 desks separated by partitions, a typing room, kitchen, and library. Open 24 hours/day, 365 days/year. See Web site for application guidelines and fees. Currently a 1-year wait for fulltime membership.

THE WRITERS STUDIO

Mercantile Library Assn., 17 E 47th St., New York, NY 10017. 212-755-6710.
E-mail: mercantile_library@msn.com. **Description:** A quiet place for writers to rent space to allow them to produce good work. A carrel, locker ($15 fee), small reference collection, electrical outlets, and membership in the Mercantile Library are available for $200 for 3 months. Submit application, resume, and writing samples; applications considered year-round. Must have proof of previously published work and current contract with a publisher. **Contact:** Ann Keisman.

HELENE WURLITZER FOUNDATION OF NEW MEXICO

P.O. Box 1891, Taos, NM 87571. 505-758-2413.
E-mail: hwf@taosnet.com. Michael A. Knight, Director. **Description:** Rent-free, fully furnished houses, with free utilities, in Taos on 18-acre campus, offered to writers and artists in creative (not performing) media. Residency is usually 3 months, April 1-September 30, and on a limited basis October-March. Send SASE for application and guidelines. **Contact:** Michael A. Knight, Director.

YADDO

P.O. Box 395, Saratoga Springs, NY 12866-0395. 518-584-0746.
E-mail: chwait@yaddo.org. Web site: www.yaddo.org. **Description:** A 400-acre estate, with private bedrooms and studios for each visiting artist. All meals provided. Visual artists, writers, choreographers, film/video artists, performance artists, composers, and collaborators, working at a professional level, are invited for stays for 2-8 weeks. Submit application and $20 fee by January 15 or August 1. **Fees:** None. **Contact:** Candace Wait, Program Coordinator.

CONFERENCES & WORKSHOPS

Each year, hundreds of writers' conferences are held across the country. The following list, arranged by state, represents a sampling of conferences; each listing includes the location of the conference, the month during which it is usually held, and the name and address of the person from whom specific information may be received. Writers are advised to write (always enclose an SASE) or e-mail directly to conference directors for full details, or check the web sites. Additional conferences are listed annually in the April issue of *The Writer* magazine (Kalmbach Publishing Co., 21027 Crossroads Circle, P.O. Box 1612, Waukesha, WI 53187-1612).

Writers' conferences are a great opportunity not only to develop writing skills in specific areas but also to hear presentations by leading professionals in your field. It's also a chance to meet and develop lasting friendships with other writers, as well as with agents and editors.

Writer workshops are a smaller gathering, focused on a specific topic; often these are sponsored by individual writing instructors or site-specific organizations.

ALABAMA

HOW TO BE PUBLISHED WORKSHOPS
Location/dates vary.
Details: Learn how to develop a career as a fiction writer from Michael Garrett ("Stephen King's first editor"). Topics include marketing, components of a successful novel, what editors really want, finding an agent, manuscript critique, etc.
Contact: Writing 2 Sell, 3606 Bermuda Dr., Birmingham, AL 35210. Auburn University: 334-244-3929.
E-mail: mike@writing2sell.com.
Web site: www.writing2sell.com.

WRITING AND ILLUSTRATING FOR KIDS
Birmingham, Ala., Spring & Fall conferences.
Details: Speakers offer advice and inspiration, tips on the trade, and information to help improve your writing or illustration. Mss. critiques and portfolio review available for additional fee.
Contact: Jo S. Kittinger, Southern Breeze, SCBWI, P.O. Box 26282, Birmingham, AL 35260.
E-mail: jskittinger@bellsouth.net.
Web site: www.southern-breeze.org.

WRITING TODAY
Birmingham, Ala., March.
Details: Explores poetry, playwriting, children's books, novels, short stories, magazine writing, e-publishing, biography and memoir writing, historical fiction, scriptwriting, publishing, editing, and library resources.

Contact: Birmingham-Southern College, Special Events Office, BSC 549003, Birmingham, AL 35254. 800-523-5793.
E-mail: dcwilson@bsc.edu.

ALASKA

SITKA SYMPOSIUM
Sitka, Alaska, June.
Details: A forum that uses written and oral traditions to explore a selected theme. Faculty talks, group discussions, readings, and optional manuscript critiques.
Contact: Carolyn Servid, The Island Institute, Box 2420, Sitka, AK 99835. 907-747-3794.
E-mail: island@ak.net.

ARIZONA

ARIZONA STATE POETRY SOCIETY
ANNUAL FALL CONFERENCE
Location/date varies each year.
Details: Winners of ASPS Annual National/Poetry Contests are read (prizes awarded); also workshops, speaker and/or reader, panel of poets, open readings, etc.
Contact: Genevieve Sargent, 1707 N Sunset Dr., Tempe, AZ 85281-1551. 480-990-7300.

HASSAYAMPA INSTITUTE FOR CREATIVE WRITING
Prescott, Ariz., July.
Details: Writers gather in the mountains of Prescott, Ariz. for 5 days of intensive workshops, talks, readings, and editor and agent panels. Intimate atmosphere.
Contact: Susan Lang, Rex Ijams, Yavapai College, 1110 E Sheldon St., Prescott, AZ 86301. 928-776-2281.
E-mail: yescwi@yc.edu.
Web site: www.yc.edu/hassayampa.nsf.

SPRING POETRY FESTIVAL
Location/date varies each year.
Details: Free, may include workshops, guest speaker/reader, advance contest, and open readings. Hosted by branches of the Arizona State Poetry Society located in various cities in Arizona.
Contact: Genevieve Sargent, 1707 N Sunset Dr., Tempe, AZ 85281-1551. 480-990-7300.

WRANGLING WITH WRITING

Tucson, Ariz., January.

Details: 30 workshops, plus keynote speakers, and one-on-one interviews with editors, agents, and publishers.

Contact: Alan M. Petrillo, Society of Southwestern Authors, P.O. Box 30355, Tucson, AZ 85751. 520-546-9382.

E-mail: excalibureditor@earthlink.net.

Web site: www.azstarnet.com/nonprofit/ssa.

WRITERS' ROUNDUP

North West Valley, Ariz., October.

Details: One full day of workshops, networking, and book signings.

Contact: Sandra L. Lagesse, Valley of the Sun Romance Writers, Inc., P.O. Box 1201, Glendale, AZ 85318-2012.

E-mail: vos@azauthors.com.

WRITING THE BREAKOUT NOVEL

Phoenix, Ariz., May.

Details: Intensive day-and-a-half workshop covering storylines, characterization, voice, themes, etc.

Contact: Lorin Oberweger, Free Expressions, 2420 W Brandon Blvd., #198, Brandon, FL 33511. 866-497-4832.

E-mail: lorin@free-expressions.com.

Web site: www.free-expressions.com.

ARKANSAS

ARKANSAS WRITERS' CONFERENCE

Little Rock, Ark., June.

Details: Sponsored by the National League of American Penwomen, Arkansas Pioneer Branch.

Contact: Barbara Longstreth Mulkey, Director, 17 Red Maple Ct., Little Rock, AR 72211. 501-312-1747. E-mail: blm@aristotle.net.

OZARK CREATIVE WRITERS CONFERENCE

Eureka Springs, Ark., October.

Details: Workshops with well-known authors, agents, and editors in several fields.

Contact: Marcia Camp, 75 Robinwood Dr., Little Rock, AR 72227. 501-225-8619.

E-mail: ocwinc@earthlink.net.

Web site: www.ozarkcreativewriters.org.

WRITER'S WORKSHOP

Eureka Springs, Ark., May.

Details: One day workshop at The Writers' Colony at Dairy Hollows, located in the

Ozark Mountains.
Contact: Daily Hollows, 501-253-7444.
E-mail: execdir@writerscolony.org.
Web site: www.writerscolony.org.

CALIFORNIA

ADVANCED FICTION WORKSHOP
San Francisco, Calif., February.
Details: One-week intensive workshop for short story writers, novelists, and authors of creative nonfiction. Includes individual consultation.
Contact: Tom Jenks and Carol Edgarian. 415-346-4477.
E-mail: tj@narrativemagazine.org.
Web site: www.narrativemagazine.org.

ANNUAL CONFERENCE ON WRITING AND ILLUSTRATING FOR CHILDREN
Los Angeles, Calif., August.
Details: Gathering of children's authors and illustrators. Attendees can participate in mss./portfolio consultations, and break-out sessions with separate tracks for illustrators, beginning writers, and professional writers or illustrators.
Contact: Kate Goodman, SCBWI, 8271 Beverly Blvd., Los Angeles, CA 90048. 323-782-1010.
E-mail: kategoodman@scbwi.com.
Web site: www.scbwi.com.

BOOK PASSAGE TRAVEL WRITERS & PHOTOGRAPHERS CONFERENCE
Corte Madera, Calif., August.
Details: Annual conference for travel writers and photographers.
Contact: Karen West, 51 Tamal Vista Blvd., Corte Madera, CA 94925. 415-927-0960.
E-mail: conferences@bookpassage.com.
Web site: www.bookpassage.com.

CENTRAL COAST BOOK AND AUTHOR FESTIVAL
San Luis Obispo, Calif., June.
Details: A free family event celebrating reading, writing, and literacy; held in San Luis Obispo's Mission Plaza. Features celebrity author panels and speakers, book signings, book sales, free workshops, readings, and kids' stories and activities.
E-mail: info@ccbookfest.org.
Web site: www.ccbookfest.org.

CREATIVE WRITING

Berkeley, Calif., June.

Details: A one-week intensive workshop offered at the Graduate Theological Union, Berkeley, CA.

Contact: Sharon A. Bray, 350-325-0680.

E-mail: sharon@wellspringwriters.org.

Web site: www.wellspringwriters.org.

EARLY SPRING IN CALIFORNIA CONFERENCE

Santa Cruz, Calif., March.

Details: Weekend workshops in the Redwoods.

Contact: Hannelore Hahn, International Women's Writing Guild, P.O. Box 810, Gracie Station, New York, NY 10028. 212-737-7536.

E-mail: iwwg@iwwg.com.

Web site: www.iwwg.com.

HOLLYWOOD FILM CONFERENCE

Hollywood, Calif., October.

Details: Networking opportunities with industry professionals who can assist writers in finding, packaging, and selling their projects. Executives from BBC, Columbia/TriStar, Paramount, Walt Disney, Miramax, New Line, Fox Searchlight, the Samuel Goldwyn Co., NBC, Overseas Filmgroup, Showtime Networks, Fox 2000, and Buena Vista Home Video, and agents from CAA, ICM, Metropolitan, William Morris, and Writers & Artists among others.

Contact: Hollywood Network, Hollywood Film Festival, 433 N Camden Dr., Suite 600, Beverly Hills, CA 90210. 310-288-1882.

E-mail: awards@hollywoodawards.com.

Web site: www.hollywoodawards.com.

JEFF KITCHEN'S SCREENWRITING SEMINARS

Los Angeles, Calif., Ongoing.

Details: Weekend intensives, 10-week classes, and private one-on-one classes, offering advanced structural technique.

Contact: Jeff Kitchen, Development Heaven, 843 16th St., #101, Santa Monica, CA 90403. 213-243-3817.

E-mail: info@developmentheaven.com.

Web site: www.developmentheaven.com.

ROBERT MCKEE'S STORY SEMINAR

Los Angeles, Calif., March.

Details: Teaches the essential principles of screenwriting and story design that studios and publishers demand from their writers.

Contact: Two Arts, Inc., P.O. Box 452930, Los Angeles, CA 90045. 888-676-2533.

E-mail: contact@mckeestory.com.

Web site: www.mckeestory.com.

MENDOCINO COAST WRITERS CONFERENCE
Fort Bragg, Calif., June.
Details: Writer's conference in friendly, seaside setting. Presenters are dedicated writing teachers.
Contact: Stephen Garber, College of the Redwoods, 1211 Del Mar Dr., Fort Bragg, CA 95437. 707-964-7735.
E-mail: stephengarber@earthlink.net.
Web site: www.mcwcwritewhale.com.

MYSTERY WRITERS CONFERENCE
Corte Madera, Calif., July.
Details: Features authors, teachers, and panelists from around the country, creating an atmosphere where mystery writers learn all the clues to a successful writing career.
Contact: Karen West, 51 Tamal Vista Blvd., Corte Madera, CA 94925. 415-927-0960.
E-mail: conferences@bookpassage.com.
Web site: www.bookpassage.com.

OPENING THE DOORS TO HOLLYWOOD
Los Angeles, Calif., June.
Details: Offers two days of intensive networking with Hollywood pros, and the chance to pitch ideas, stories, books, or scripts.
Contact: Hollywood Network, Hollywood Film Festival, 433 N Camden Dr., Ste. 600, Beverly Hills, CA 90210. 310-288-1882.
E-mail: awards@hollywoodawards.com.
Web site: www.hollywoodawards.com.

THE PUBLISHING GAME
Location/dates vary.
Details: Workshops on self-publishing and promotion, with Fran Reiss.
Contact: Peanut Butter and Jelly Press, P.O. Box 590239, Newton, MA 02459. 800-408-6226.
E-mail: workshops@publishinggame.com.
Web site: www.publishinggame.com.

THE SAN FRANCISCO ALGONKIAN
San Francisco, Calif., March, May.
Details: Workshop for novel planners, beginners, and veterans. Study and apply techniques of craft, style, and complication culled from over 20 novelists (and dramatists). Workshop leader will review novel concepts and pass them on to an agent who works with Algonkian.
Contact: Web Del Sol, 2020 Pennsylvania Ave., NW, Suite 443, Washington, DC 20006. 703-281-4426.
E-mail: algonkian@webdelsol.com.
Web site: www.webdelsol.com.

SANTA BARBARA CHRISTIAN WRITERS' CONFERENCE

Santa Barbara, Calif., October.

Details: Workshop and speakers suitable for all levels of writers. New this year: bookkeeping and tax laws.

Contact: Opal Mac Dailey or Pam Sneddon, P.O. Box 42429, Santa Barbara, CA 93140. 805-969-3712.

E-mail: info@wisdomtoday.org.

SANTA BARBARA WRITER'S CONFERENCE

Santa Barbara, Calif., June.

Details: Covers all genres of writing.

Contact: Mary Conrad, P.O. Box 304, Carpinteria, CA 93014. 805-684-2250.

Web site: www.sbwc-online.com.

SCREENWRITING EXPO

Los Angeles, Calif., November.

Details: Features Michael Hauge, author of *Writing Screenplays that Sell*.

Contact: 323-727-6978.

E-mail: info@screenwritingexpo.com.

Web site: www.screenplaymastery.com.

SCREENPLAY MASTERY WORKSHOPS

Locations/dates vary.

Details: Michael Hauge and Christopher Vogler, two of Hollywood's top story experts, present their unique approaches to structure, character, and theme to screenwriters, novelists, and playwrights.

Contact: Hilltop Productions, P.O. Box 55728, Sherman Oaks, CA 91413. 818-995-8118.

E-mail: mhauge@juno.com.

Web site: www.screenplaymastery.com.

SOUTHERN CALIFORNIA WRITERS' CONFERENCE

Los Angeles, Calif., October.

San Diego, Calif., February.

Details: Devoted to the art, craft, and business of writing professionally; emphasis on interactive troubleshooting and critiquing.

Contact: 1010 University Ave., #54, San Diego, CA 92103. 619-233-4651.

E-mail: wewrite@writersconference.com.

Web site: www.writersconference.com.

SQUAW VALLEY COMMUNITY OF WRITERS WORKSHOPS

Squaw Valley, Calif., August.

Details: Assists writers by exploring the craft and business sides of writing. Offers

regular morning workshops, craft lectures, panel discussions on editing and publishing, staff readings, and brief individual conferences.
Contact: Brett Hall Jones, P.O. Box 1416, Nevada City, CA 95959. 530-470-8440.
E-mail: svcw@oro.net.
Web site: www.squawvalleywriters.org.

STORYCON
Palm Springs, Calif., September.
Details: Offers advanced discussions on story creation techniques, models, strategies, concepts, application, and philosophy.
Contact: StoryCon, 211 N Sycamore St., Newtown, PA 18940. 215-504-1700.
E-mail: rob@storycon.org.
Web site: www.storycon.org.

WELLSPRING WRITERS WORKSHOPS
Locations/dates vary.
Details: Creative writing workshops for women, also for lay ministers, ministers, and helping professionals who wish to incorporate writing as a tool for emotional healing and self-discovery in group work.
Contact: Sharon A. Bray, 350-325-0680. E-mail: sharon@wellspringwriters.org.
Web site: www.wellspringwriters.org.

WRITING THE BREAKOUT NOVEL
San Diego, Calif., March.
Details: Workshops offering advice on storylines, characterization, voice, themes, etc.
Contact: Lorin Oberweger, Free Expressions, 2420 W Brandon Blvd., #198, Brandon, FL 33511. 866-497-4832.
E-mail: lorin@free-expressions.com.
Web site: www.free-expressions.com.

COLORADO

ASPEN SUMMER WORDS
Aspen, Colo., June.
Details: Five-day intensive writing retreat featuring hands-on workshops in fiction, creative nonfiction, poetry, and magazine writing. Also includes readings, industry panels, and agent meetings.
Contact: Julie Comins, Aspen Writers' Foundation, 110 E Hallam St., Suite 116, Aspen, CO 81611. 970-925-3122.
E-mail: info@aspenwriters.org.
Web site: www.aspenwriters.org.

COLORADO CHRISTIAN WRITERS CONFERENCE

Estes Park, Colo., May.
Details: 6 sessions, 36 workshops, etc., to encourage and equip Christian writers.
Contact: Marlene Bagnull, 316 Blanchard Rd., Drexel Hill, PA 19026.
610-626-6833.
E-mail: mbagnull@aol.com.
Web site: www.writehisanswer.com.

COLORADO GOLD CONFERENCE

Boulder, Colo., September.
Details: Fiction conference, featuring editors and agents as speakers and workshop presenters.
Contact: Diana Rowe Martinez, Rocky Mountain Fiction Writers, 6526 Torrey Ct., Arvada, CO 80007. 303-422-6903.
E-mail: diana10277@aol.com.
Web site: www.rmfw.org.

NATIONAL WRITERS ASSOCIATION
FOUNDATION CONFERENCE

Denver, Colo., June.
Details: Workshops taught by professionals in the business (film producers, authors, editors, agents, publishers, and marketing specialists, etc.).
Contact: Anita Whelchel, 3140 S Peoria St., #295, Aurora, CO 80014. 303-841-0246.
E-mail: conference@nationalwriters.com.
Web site: www.nationalwriters.com.

NATURE AND THE SUBLIME

Ouray, Colo., June.
Details: Writers will explore the spiritual influence of the landscape upon their writing, their characters, their voices.
Contact: Leslie Jill Patterson, Inkwell Literary Services, San Juan Workshops, P.O. Box 841, Ridgeway, CO 81432. 970-626-4125.
Email: inkwellliterary@mac.com.
Web site: http://homepage.mac.com/inkwellliterary.

STEAMBOAT SPRINGS WRITERS CONFERENCE

Steamboat Springs, Colo., July.
Details: Workshops sponsored by Steamboat Springs Arts Council.
Contact: Harriet Freiberger, P.O. Box 774284, Steamboat Springs, CO 80477.
970-879-8079.
E-mail: harriet@freiberger.com.

SUMMER WRITING PROGRAM

Boulder, Colo., June/July.
Details: Four-week long workshop covering composition of poetry, prose fiction,

cross-genre possibilities, inter-arts, translation, and writing for performance.
Contact: Lisa Birman, Naropa University, Summer Writing Program, 2130 Arapahoe Ave., Boulder, CO 80302. 303-546-5296.
E-mail: lisab@naropa.edu.
Web site: www.naropa.edu.

WOMEN WRITERS
Ouray, Colo., June.
Details: Female writers will study their craft. Participants should be prepared to write, learn, and renew the energy behind their work.
Contact: Leslie Jill Patterson, Inkwell Literary Services, San Juan Workshops, P.O. Box 841, Ridgeway, CO 81432. 970-626-4125.
E-mail: inkwellliterary@mac.com.
Web site: http://homepage.mac.com/inkwellliterary.

CONNECTICUT

WESLEYAN WRITERS CONFERENCE
Middletown, Conn., June.
Details: Covers the novel, short story, fiction techniques, poetry, memoir, and literary journalism; also special sessions covering freelance writing and publishing.
Contact: Anne Greene, Wesleyan University, Middletown, CT 06459. 860-685-3604.
E-mail: agreene@wesleyan.edu.
Web site: www.wesleyan.edu/writing/conferen.html.

YALE SUMMER PROGRAMS
New Haven, Conn., July/August.
Details: College-level creative writing courses in journalism, play-writing, poetry, fiction, and nonfiction.
Contact: P.O. Box 208355, New Haven, CT 06520. 203-432-2430.
E-mail: summer.programs@yale.edu.
Web site: www.yale.edu/summer.

DISTRICT OF COLUMBIA

NLAPW BIENNIAL CONVENTION
Washington, D.C., April.
Details: Includes workshops, seminars, competitions, motivational speakers, sightseeing, and the election of national officers.
Contact: Mary Haliburton, National League of American Pen Women, Inc. 202-785-1997.
E-mail: mewriter@mindspring.com.
Web site: www.americanpenwomen.org.

WASHINGTON WRITERS CONFERENCE
Washington, D.C., May.
Details: Sponsored by Washington Independent Writers; offers panels and workshops on a broad array of writing-related topics, meetings with agents, and manuscript critiques.
Contact: Aishling McGinty, 733 15th St. NW, #220, Washington, DC 20005. 202-347-4973.
E-mail: info@washwriter.org.
Web site: www.washwriter.org.

FLORIDA

CLASSEMINAR
Tampa, Fla., March.
Details: CLASS (Christian Leaders, Authors & Speakers Services) offers intensive three-day seminars: training in communication skills for both the spoken and written word.
Contact: Linda Jewell, P.O. Box 66810, Albuquerque, NM, 87193. 800-433-6633.
E-mail: mary@classervices.com; or linda@classervices.com.
Web site: www.glorietacwc.com; or www.classervices.com.

INSTITUTE FOR TRAVEL AND GUIDEBOOK WRITING
Orlando, Fla., May/June.
Details: For writers, experienced travelers, and others considering careers in article and guidebook work. Topics include a survey of travel and guidebook writing, article queries and book proposals, contracts and negotiations, editor-publisher relations, how the work gets done, Webzines and e-guidebooks, self publishing, marketing, and photography.
Contact: Herb Hiller, Society of American Travel Writers, 1500 Sunday Dr., Suite 102, Raleigh, NC 27607. 919-787-5181.
E-mail: satw@satw.org.
Web site: www.satw.org.

KEY WEST WRITERS' WORKSHOPS
Key West, Fla., January.
Details: Brings aspiring writers from all over the country into creative contact with major writers in this literary setting.
Contact: Miles Frieden, 4 Portside Ln., Searspoint, ME 04974. 888-293-9291.
E-mail: mail@keywestliteraryseminar.org.
Web site: www.keywestliteraryseminar.org.

MIAMI BOOK FAIR INTERNATIONAL

Miami, Fla., November.

Details: Eight days celebrating the written word. World-renowned authors address hundreds of book lovers and discuss their latest books, the art of writing, and life as an author, among other topics.

Contact: M-DCC Wolfson Campus, 300 NE 2nd Ave., Suite 1515, Miami, FL 33132. 305-237-3258.

E-mail: wbookfair@mdcc.edu.

Web site: www.miamibookfair.com.

TOUCH OF SUCCESS WRITING SEMINAR

Ocala, Fla., March.

Details: Learn how to write nonfiction article leads, book proposals, captions for photos, and query letters.

Contact: Bill Thomas, P.O. Box 59, Glendale, KY 42740. 270-769-1823.

Web site: www.touchofsuccess.com.

WRITING THE REGION:
MARJORIE KINNAN RAWLINGS WRITERS WORKSHOP

Gainesville, Fla., July.

Details: Five-day workshop featuring fiction, nonfiction, poetry, and memoir.

Contact: Norma M. Homan, P.O. Box 12246, Gainesville, FL 32604. 888-917-7001.

E-mail: shakes@ufl.edu.

Web site: www.writingtheregion.com.

GEORGIA

SANDHILLS WRITERS CONFERENCE

Augusta, Ga., March.

Details: For writers of fiction, poetry, nonfiction, plays, children's literature, and song lyrics. Activities include talks on the writer's craft, awards, advice from regional and national agents and editors, and mss consultations.

Contact: Augusta State University, Division of Continuing Education, 2588 Walton Way, Augusta, GA 38984.

E-mail: akellman@aug.edu.

Web site: www.sandhills.aug.edu.

SOUTHEASTERN WRITERS WORKSHOP:
EPWORTH-BY-THE-SEA

St. Simon's Island, Ga., June.

Details: Week-long workshop covering all areas of writing, including fiction, nonfiction, poetry, and the business of writing. Agents-in-residence to meet with students; free manuscript critiques; contests.

Contact: Amy Munnell, P.O. Box 774, Hinesville, GA 31310.
E-mail: purple@southeasternwriters.com.
Web site: www.southeasternwriters.com.

HAWAII

MAUI WRITERS CONFERENCE
Wailea, Hawaii, August/September.
Details: More than 125 agents, editors, bestselling authors, and renowned writing teachers on faculty. 100 seminars and workshops in fiction, nonfiction, screenwriting, children's books, cookbooks, playwriting, magazine writing, poetry, and more. While the conference highlights the fields of fiction, nonfiction, and screenwriting, we are also proud to present insightful specialty workshops on the business of writing, children's books, journalism, food and cookbook writing, travel writing, and poetry.
Contact: Shannon Tullius, P.O. Box 1118, Kihei, HI 96753. 808-879-0061.
E-mail: writers@maui.net.
Web site: www.mauiwriters.com.

MAUI WRITERS RETREAT
Wailea, Hawaii, August.
Details: Learn from the masters during this six-day intensive program. Teaching in small, intimate, hands-on groups, the emphasis will be on how to shape and present a saleable manuscript. **Contact:** Shannon Tullius, P.O. Box 1118, Kihei, HI 96753. 808-879-0061. E-mail: writers@maui.net. Web site: www.mauiwriters.com.

IDAHO

MURDER IN THE GROVE
Boise, Idaho, May.
Details: A conference for readers and writers of mystery fiction. The conference ends with an interactive mystery play and reception. Sponsored by Partners in Crime.
Contact: Log Cabin Literary Center, 801 S Capitol Blvd., Boise, ID 83702.
208-331-8000.
Web site: www.sistersincrimeboise.org.

ILLINOIS

AUTUMN AUTHORS' AFFAIR
Lisle, Ill., October.
Details: Includes all types of writing for beginners to pros. We usually have approximately 40 speakers as well as a couple of editors.

Contact: Nancy McCann, 1507 Burnham Ave., Calumet City, IL 60409.
708-862-9797.
E-mail: vadew9340@aol.com.
Web site: www.rendezvousreviews.com.

MISSISSIPPI VALLEY WRITERS CONFERENCE

Rock Island, Ill., June.
Details: Offers workshops in fiction, nonfiction, short story, and poetry; also one-on-one mss critique.
Contact: B.J. Elsner, Midwest Writing Center, 1629 2nd Ave., Suite 2, Rock Island, IL 61201. 309-788-2711.
E-mail: mwcqc@qconline.com.
Web site: www.midwestwritingcenter.org.

MISSISSIPPI VALLEY YOUNG AUTHORS CONFERENCE

Rock Island, Ill., June.
Details: One-day conference for young authors grades 8-12.
Contact: B.J. Elsner, Midwest Writing Center, 1629 2nd Ave., Ste. 2, Rock Island, IL 61201. 309-786-3406.
E-mail: beej@qconline.com.
Web site: www.midwestwritingcenter.org.

RAGDALE FOUNDATION

Lake Forest, Ill., ongoing.
Details: Non-profit artists' community.
Contact: Melissa Mosher, 1260 N Green Bay Rd., Lake Forest, IL 60045. 847-234-1063.
E-mail: admissionragdale@aol.com.
Web site: www.ragdale.org.

INDIANA

BUTLER UNIVERSITY
CHILDREN'S LITERATURE CONFERENCE

Indianapolis, Ind., January.
Details: Meet award-winning children's book authors and illustrators and attend sessions for teachers, librarians, writers, and illustrators.
Contact: 4600 Sunset Ave., Indianapolis, IN 46208.
317-940-9861.

INDIANA UNIVERSITY WRITERS' CONFERENCE

Bloomington, Ind., June.
Details: A week-long conference offering classes and workshops in fiction, poetry, creative nonfiction, and playwriting.

Contact: Amy Lockin, IUWC, 464 Ballantine Hall, Bloomington, IN 47401. 812-855-1877.
E-mail: writecon@indiana.edu.
Web site: www.indiana.edu/~writecon.

MIDWEST WRITERS WORKSHOP
Muncie, Ind., July.
Details: For aspiring and published writers.
Contact: Jama Rehoe Bigger, 2106 N Colson Dr., Muncie, IN 47304. 765-282-1055.
E-mail: info@midwestwriters.org.
Web site: www.midwestwriters.org.

ROPEWALK WRITERS RETREAT
New Harmony, Ind., June.
Details: Gives participants an opportunity to attend workshops and to confer privately with one of six prominent writers.
Contact: Linda Cleek, USI Extended Services, 8600 University Blvd., Evansville, IN 47712. 812-464-1932.
E-mail: ropewalk@usi.edu.
Web site: www.ropewalk.org.

IOWA

IOWA SUMMER WRITING FESTIVAL
Iowa City, Iowa, June/July.
Details: Short-term, noncredit writing programs for adults, offered by The University of Iowa. 137 week-long and weekend workshops across the genres, including novel, short fiction, poetry, essay, memoir, humor, playwriting, writing for children, and more.
Contact: Amy Margolis, 100 Oakdale Campus, W310, University of Iowa, Iowa City, IA 52242. 319-335-4160.
E-mail: iswfestival@uiowa.edu.
Web site: www.uiowa.edu/~iswfest.

KANSAS

BEWARE THE JABBERWOCK:
CONFRONTING MONSTERS IN CHILDREN'S LITERATURE
Wichita, Kan., February.
Details: A conference for writers and teachers of children's literature. Writing workshops, panel discussions, and illustrator presentations.
Contact: Debra Seely, Newman University, Milton Center, 3100 McCormick, Wichita, KS 67213. 316-942-4291. E-mail: miltonc@newmanu.edu.

WRITERS WORKSHOP IN SCIENCE FICTION

Lawrence, Kan., June/July.

Details: Intensive workshop involving critiquing of four stories each, aimed at preparing writers to publish regularly.

Contact: James Gunn, English Dept., University of Kansas, Lawrence, KS 66045. 785-864-3380.

E-mail: jgunn@ku.edu.

Web site: www.ku.edu/~sfcenter.

KENTUCKY

APPALACHIAN WRITERS WORKSHOP

Hindman, Ky., July/August.

Details: Well-known authors who are from and/or write about Appalachia teach workshops in several genres. Includes seminars, conferences with staff, nightly readings and book signings, readings by participants, sharing, and learning.

Contact: Mike Mullins, Hindman Settlement School, P.O. Box 844, Hindman, KY 41822. 606-785-5475.

E-mail: hss@tgtel.com.

Web site: www.hindmansettlement.org.

GREEN RIVER SUMMER RETREAT

Louisville, Ky., July.

Details: Eclectic writers' retreat with activities generated by participants: sharing, critiquing, freewriting.

Contact: Mary O'Dell, 703 Eastbridge Ct., Louisville, KY 40223. 502-245-4902.

E-mail: mary_odell@ntr.net.

GREEN RIVER WINTER RETREAT

Louisville, Ky., January.

Details: Eclectic writers' retreat with activities generated by participants: sharing, critiquing, freewriting.

Contact: Mary O'Dell, 703 Eastbridge Ct., Louisville, KY 40223. 502-245-4902.

E-mail: mary_odell@ntr.net.

KENTUCKY WOMEN WRITERS CONFERENCE

Lexington, Ky., March.

Details: A Feast of Words: Nourishing the Mind and Body.

Contact: Dr. Brenda Weber, The Kentucky Women Writers Conference, 213-215 Bowman Hall, Lexington, KY 40506. 859-257-8734.

E-mail: kywwc@hotmail.com.

Web site: www.uky.edu/conferences/kywwc.

NATIONAL FEDERATION OF PRESS WOMEN COMMUNICATIONS CONFERENCE
Location/date TBA.
Details: Designed to enhance the skills of professional communicators by focusing on the needs of journalists, public relations specialists, freelance writers, and authors.
Contact: Carol Pierce, P.O. Box 5556, Arlington, VA 22205. 703-534-2500.
E-mail: presswomen@aol.com.
Web site: www.nfpw.org.

NOVELS-IN-PROGRESS WORKSHOP
Louisville, Ky., March.
Details: Seven instructors, one-on-ones with agents and editors, instruction and mss reading by instructors. 40-50 participants selected.
Contact: Mary O'Dell, 703 Eastbridge Ct., Louisville, KY 40223. 502-245-4902.
E-mail: mary_odell@ntr.net.

TOUCH OF SUCCESS WRITING SEMINAR
Louisville, Ky., October.
Details: Targets writing nonfiction story leads, captivating query letters, and photo captions. Some training on producing marketable book proposals and children's books. Located in quaint Amish country.
Contact: Bill Thomas, P.O. Box 59, Glendale, KY 42740. 270-769-1823.
Web site: www.touchofsuccess.com.

WRITERS RETREAT WORKSHOP
Erlanger, Ky., May/June.
Details: A ten-day intensive workshop for beginning and published novelists. Classes, workshops, discussions, and writing time.
E-mail: wrwwisi@cox.net.
Web site: www.writersretreatworkshop.com.

LOUISIANA

TENNESSEE WILLIAMS
NEW ORLEANS LITERARY FESTIVAL
New Orleans, La., March.
Details: A gathering of novelists, poets, playwrights, journalists and bibliophiles. Offers master classes, discussions, theater performances, walking tours, music performances, special food events, and a book fair.
Contact: Shannon Stover, 938 Lafayette St., #328, New Orleans, LA 70113.
504-581-1144.
E-mail: info@tennesseewilliams.net.
Web site: www.tennesseewilliams.net.

WORDS & MUSIC:
A LITERARY FEAST IN NEW ORLEANS
New Orleans, La., December.
Details: Five days of literary discussions, master classes, drama, poetry readings, evening music events, and dance. Manuscript critiques and one-on-one consultations with agents and editors are available.
Contact: Rosemary James, Faulkner House, 624 Pirate's Alley, New Orleans, LA 70116. 504-586-1609.
E-mail: faulkhouse@aol.com.
Web site: www.wordsandmusic.org.

WRITING SHORT STORIES AND NOVELS
New Orleans, La., October.
Details: Small-group workshop tour.
Contact: John Lehman. 1-800-7-TO-KNOW.
Web site: www.writerjourney.com.

MAINE

STONECOAST WRITERS' CONFERENCE
Freeport, Maine, July.
Details: Offers workshops in six genres and draws on a strong writing faculty who regularly publish and are recognized for their excellence.
Contact: B. Lee Hope, 37 College Ave., Gorham, ME 04038. 207-780-5617.
E-mail: summer@usm.maine.edu.
Web site: www.usm.maine.edu/summer.

MARYLAND

MID-ATLANTIC CREATIVE NONFICTION
SUMMER WRITERS CONFERENCE
Baltimore, Md., August.
Details: Offers intensive workshops devoted to creative nonfiction.
Contact: Noreen Mack, Goucher College, 1021 Dulaney Valley Rd., Baltimore, MD 21204. 800-697-4646 or 410-337-4646.
E-mail: center@goucher.edu. Web site: www.goucher.edu/cnf.

MASSACHUSETTS

ALICE FURLAUD: WRITING FOR RADIO
Truro, Mass., August.
Details: Workshops on writing for radio.

Contact: Castle Hill Workshops, P.O. Box 756, Truro, MA 02666. 508-349-7511.
E-mail: castelhilltruro@aol.com.
Web site: www.castlehill.org.

AMHERST WRITERS & ARTISTS
Mass., dates/locations vary.
Details: Offers retreats, workshops, and certification training in leading writers' workshops.
Contact: Daphne Slocombe, P.O. Box 1076, Amherst, MA 01004. 413-253-3307.
E-mail: awapress@amherstwriters.com.
Web site: www.amherstwriters.com.

BUST INTO FREELANCE WRITING
Arlington, Mass., February.
Details: Learn how write a winning query letter, make your writing profitable, negotiate better fees, and determine when, how and where to pitch your article. Also what to expect from editors and how to communicate with them.
Contact: NewsJobs.Net, 5 Marvel Ave., Burlington, MA 01803.
E-mail: seminar@newsjobs.net.
Web site: www.newsjobs.net/seminar.asp.

CAPE COD WRITERS CONFERENCE
Cape Cod, Mass., August.
Details: Covers children's books, screenplays, romance, mystery, memoir, fiction, nonfiction, and poetry. Also offers a scholarship workshop for young writers, ages 12-16.
Contact: Jacqueline M. Loring, Box 186, Barnstable, MA 02630. 508-375-0516.
E-mail: ccwc@capecod.net.
Web site: www.capecodwriterscenter.com.

CASTLE HILL SUMMER WORKSHOPS
Truro, Mass., July–August.
Details: Writing workshops with Marge Piercy, Justin Kaplan, Wendy Kesselman, Anne Bernays, Toby Olsen, and many more.
Contact: Cherie Mittenthal, P.O. Box 756, Truro, MA 02666. 508-349-7511.
E-mail: castelhilltruro@aol.com.
Web site: www.castlehill.org.

DOCUMENTATION & TRAINING
Tyngsboro, Mass., October.
Details: Brings together leading experts in the technical writing and online training fields.
Contact: Julia Doyle, PUBSNET, 1 Bridgeview Cir., Tyngsboro, MA 01879.
978-649-8555.
E-mail: julia@pubsnet.com.
Web site: www.doctrain.com.

HARVARD SUMMER SCHOOL WRITING PROGRAM

Cambridge, Mass., June-August.

Details: For writers at all levels, this program offers small classes, college credit, student-faculty readings, a published journal of student work, and workshops on special topics, such as Writing With Sources and Writing College Application Essays.

Contact: Harvard Summer School Writing Program, 51 Brattle St., Cambridge, MA 02138. 617-496-5000.

E-mail: summer@hudce.harvard.edu.

Web site: www.summer.harvard.edu.

LET YOUR IMAGINATION TAKE FLIGHT CONFERENCE

Natick, Mass., April.

Details: Speakers and workshops on point of view, structure, characterization, and more.

Contact: Jessica Andersen.

E-mail: drjsandersen@aol.com

Web site: www.geocities.com/necrwa.

SCREENWRITING FOR HOLLYWOOD

Boston, Mass., May-June.

Details: An intensive weekend seminar on the art, craft, and business of screenwriting.

Contact: Michael Hague, Hilltop Productions, P.O. Box 55728, Sherman Oaks, CA 91413. 800-477-1947.

E-mail: contact@screenplaymastery.com.

Web site: www.screenplaymastery.com.

SHOW TIME!

Boston, Mass., May.

Details: Aims to preview the pitfalls, and spare you the pratfalls, of filmmaking.

Contact: Micheline Cote, The Writers Retreat, 15 Canusa St., Stanstead, Quebec, J0B 3E5, Canada. 819-876-2065.

E-mail: info@writersretreat.com.

Web site: www.writersretreat.com/workshops.htm.

THE PUBLISHING GAME

Boston, Mass., April.

Details: On self-publishing and promotion, with Fran Reiss.

Contact: Peanut Butter and Jelly Press, P.O. Box 590239, Newton, MA 02459. 800-408-6226.

E-mail: workshops@publishinggame.com. Web site: www.publishinggame.com.

WEEKEND RETREATS AT PATCHWORK FARM

Westhampton, Mass., ongoing.

Details: Guided writing sessions. Typically 8-9 participants.

Contact: Patricia Lee Lewis, Patchwork Farm Retreat, 292 Chesterfield Rd., Westhampton, MA 01027. 413-527-5819.
E-mail: patricia@writingretreats.org.
Web site: www.writingretreats.org.

WRITING THE BREAKOUT NOVEL
Boston, Mass., September.
Details: With Donald Maass; teaches writers to rev up their storylines, plumb the depths of character, develop a strong voice, deepen themes, and more.
Contact: Lorin Oberweger, Free Expressions, 2420 W. Brandon Blvd., #198, Brandon, FL 33511. 866-497-4832.
E-mail: lorin@free-expressions.com.
Web site: www.free-expressions.com.

MICHIGAN

ANNUAL MIDWEST POETS & WRITERS CONFERENCE
Detroit, Mich., August.
Details: Two-day conference covering poetry, fiction, nonfiction, playwriting, screenwriting, e-publishing, writing for children, entertainment law, and technology.
Contact: Heather Buchanan, P.O. Box 23100, 9710 W Outer Dr. #202, Detroit, MI 48223. 313-897-2551.
E-mail: detroitwriters@aol.com.
Web site: www.detroitwritersguild.org.

ANNUAL WRITERS' CONFERENCE
Rochester, Mich., October.
Details: Features private and group manuscript evaluations, writing laboratories, and a choice of 36 presentations conducted by published authors, agents, and editors.
Contact: Gloria J. Boddy, 221 Varner Hall, Oakland Univ., Rochester, MI 48309. 248-370-3125.
E-mail: gjboddy@oakland.edu.
Web site: www.oakland.edu/contin-ed/writersconf.

CLARION SCIENCE FICTION & FANTASY WRITERS' WORKSHOP
East Lansing, Mich., June/July.
Details: Six weeks of intensive training in short story form science fiction and fantasy.
Contact: Mary Sheridan, E-193 Holmes Hall, Michigan State University, East Lansing, MI 48825. 517-355-9598.
E-mail: sherida3@msu.edu.
Web site: www.msu.edu/~clarion.

CRITICAL CONNECTION FICTION WORKSHOPS

Ann Arbor, Mich., June.

Details: Workshop for fiction writers who want to improve their craft and increase understanding of what is working or not working in their writing; offers getting published seminars and fiction workshops.

Contact: 3096 Williamsburg, Ann Arbor, MI 48108.

E-mail: keith@criticalconnection.org.

Web site: www.criticalconnection.org.

MIDLAND WRITERS CONFERENCE

Midland, Mich., June.

Details: Annual event providing a forum for beginning and established writers to exchange ideas with professionals.

Contact: Ann C. Jarvis, 1710 W St. Andrews, Midland, MI 48640. 989-837-3435.

E-mail: ajarvis@midland-mi.org.

Web site: www.midland-mi.org/gracedowlibrary.

RETREAT FROM HARSH REALITY

Stanwood, Mich., April.

Details: Sponsored by the Mid-Michigan chapter of Romance Writers of America. Offers a casual atmosphere with a chance for learning, sharing, and one-on-one conversations about writing.

Contact: Pam Trombley, 6845 Forest Way, Harbor Springs, MI 49740. 231-526-2153.

E-mail: ptrombley@voyager.net.

Web site: www.midmichiganrwa.com.

WALLOON WRITERS' RETREAT

Boyne City, Mich., September.

Details: Writers and poets, new and established, attend workshops, readings and provocative panel discussions.

Contact: John D. Lamb, Springfed Arts, P.O. Box 304, Royal Oak, MI 48068. 248-589-3913.

E-mail: johndlamb@ameritech.net.

Web site: www.springfed.org.

MINNESOTA

ANNUAL INTENSIVE WEEKEND OF WRITING

St. Paul, Minn., March.

Details: Four concentrated class sessions on the theory of literary psychology and the craft of writing fiction and nonfiction.

Contact: Carol Bly, 1668 Juna Ave., St. Paul, MN 55116. 651-699-5427.

E-mail: carolbly@visi.com. Web site: www.carolbly.com.

CLASSEMINAR

Minneapolis, Minn., August.

Details: CLASS (Christian Leaders, Authors & Speakers Services) offers intensive three-day seminars: training in communication skills for both the spoken and written word.

Contact: Linda Jewell, P.O. Box 66810, Albuquerque, NM, 87193. 800-433-6633.

E-mail: mary@classervices.com; or linda@classervices.com.

Web site: www.glorietacwc.com; or www.classervices.com.

DULUTH WRITERS' WORKSHOP

Duluth, Minn., June.

Details: Six days of creative writing sessions in poetry, fiction, playwriting, and the memoir and personal essay. Workshop sessions, special events, panel discussions, and presentations. Limited space is available.

Contact: Pauline Nuhring, UMD Continuing Education, 1049 University Dr., 104 Darland Admin. Bldg., Duluth, MN 55812. 218-726-6361.

E-mail: pnuhring@d.umn.edu.

Web site: www.d.umn.edu/goto/writers

SPLIT ROCK ARTS PROGRAM

Duluth, Minn., June/August.

Details: Workshops in creative writing (poetry, short stories, memoirs, novels, etc), visual arts, design, and creativity enhancement.

Contact: Vivien Oja, University of Minnesota, 360 Coffey Hall, 1420 Eckles Ave., St. Paul, MN 55108. 612-625-8100.

E-mail: srap@cce.umn.edu.

Web site: www.cce.umn.edu/splitrockarts.

MISSISSIPPI

HOW TO BE PUBLISHED WORKSHOPS

Long Beach, Miss., November.

Details: Learn how to develop a career as a fiction writer from Michael Garrett ("Stephen King's first editor"). Topics include marketing, components of a successful novel, what editors really want, finding an agent, manuscript critique, and much more.

Contact: Writing 2 Sell, 3606 Bermuda Dr., Birmingham, AL 35210. U of South Mississippi Gulf Coast: 228-867-8777.

E-mail: mike@writing2sell.com.

Web site: www.writing2sell.com.

MISSOURI

TO MARKET, TO MARKET
Jefferson City, Mo., April.
Details: Sponsored by the Missouri Writers Guild. Includes seminars on both fiction and nonfiction.
Contact: Vicki Cox, Missouri Writers Guild, P.O. Box 1895, Lebanon, MO 65536.
E-mail: vcox01@yahoo.com.

MONTANA

WRITING ROMANTIC SUSPENSE
Big Timber, Mont., April.
Details: Workshops on writing supsense. Features in-depth discussions and new markets for this genre.
Contact: Gwen Peterson, Sagebrush Writers, P.O. Box 1255, Big Timber, MT 59011. 406-932-4227.
E-mail: sagebrsh@ttc-cmc.net.

NEBRASKA

NEBRASKA SUMMER WRITERS' CONFERENCE
Lincoln, Neb., July.
Details: Features workshops and panels in novel, short story, poetry, travel and nature writing, mystery, memoir, screenwriting, publishing, and mss. consultation.
Contact: Jonis Agee, 202 Andrews Hall, Department of English, University of Nebraska, Lincoln, NE 68588. 402-472-1834.
E-mail: nswc@unl.edu.
Web site: www.nswc.org.

NEVADA

AUTHOR'S VENUE JOURNEY CONFERENCE
Lake Tahoe, Nev., April.
Details: Offers workshops with top authors, editor and agent appointments, banquets, and more.
Contact: Suzanne Spletzer or Stephanie Dooley, Author's Venue, 600 Central Ave. SE, Suite 235, Albuquerque, NM 87102. 505-244-9337.
E-mail: info@authorsvenue.com.
Web site: www.authorsvenue.com.

TMCC WRITERS' CONFERENCE
Reno, Nev., March.
Details: Four-day critique workshops and weekend seminars that teach solid writing and marketing techniques for fiction, nonfiction, and poetry.
Contact: Kathy Berry, Truckee Meadows Community College, 7000 Dandini Blvd., RTMAI, Reno, NV 89512. 775-829-9010.
E-mail: kberry@tmcc.edu.
Web site: www.tmccwriters.com.

NEW HAMPSHIRE

FIRSTNOVELFEST
Jackson, N.H., October.
Details: For first-time writers with or without a completed manuscript.
Contact: P. Elizabeth Collins, Gardenia Press, P.O. Box 18601, Milwaukee, WI 53218. 866-861-9443.
E-mail: pressgdp@gardeniapress.com.
Web site: www.gardeniapress.com.

ODYSSEY FANTASY WRITING WORKSHOP
Manchester, N.H., June/July.
Details: Six-week workshop for writers of fantasy, science fiction, and horror.
Contact: Jeanne Cavelos, 20 Levesque Ln., Mont Vernon, NH 03057. 603-673-6234.
E-mail: jcavelos@sff.net.
Web site: www.sff.net/odyssey.

SEACOAST WRITERS SPRING CONFERENCE
Chester, N.H., May.
Contact: Pat Parnell, 59 River Rd., Stratham, NH 03885. 603-778-1470.
E-mail: riverrd@tiac.net.

NEW JERSEY

TECHNIQUES OF FICTION
Princeton, N.J., June.
Details: Workshops that teach the techniques of successful fiction authors.
Contact: Micheline Cote, The Writers Retreat, 15 Canusa St., Stanstead, Quebec, J0B 3E5, Canada. 819-876-2065.
E-mail: info@writersretreat.com.
Web site: www.writersretreat.com/workshops.htm.

NEW MEXICO

THE GLEN WORKSHOP
Santa Fe, N.M., August.
Details: Week-long arts festival and workshop with classes in writing and the visual arts, sponsored by *Image: A Journal of the Arts and Religion*.
Contact: Mary Kenagy, Image, 3307 3rd Ave. W, Seattle, WA 98119. 206-281-2988.
E-mail: glenworkshop@imagejournal.org.
Web site: www.imagejournal.org.

GLORIETA CHRISTIAN WRITERS CONFERENCE
Glorieta, N.M., October.
Details: Offers classes, sessions, roundtables, and individual interviews with a faculy of nearly 60 editors, professional writers, and other experts.
Contact: Linda Jewell, P.O. Box 66810, Albuquerque, NM, 87193. 800-433-6633.
E-mail: linda@classervices.com.
Web site: www.glorietacwc.com; or www.classervices.com.

IWWG SANTA FE CONFERENCE
Santa Fe, N.M., March.
Details: Workshops with Anya Achtenberg on writing through the mystery of human behavior in fiction and memoir.
Contact: Hannelore Hahn, International Women's Writing Guild, P.O. Box 810, Gracie Station, New York, NY 10028. 212-737-7536.
E-mail: iwwg@iwwg.com. Web site: www.iwwg.com.

MEMOIR INTENSIVE
Santa Fe, N.M., March.
Details: Day-long program on the craft and art of the memoir. Features hands-on writing exercises, critique, and more.
Contact: Santa Fe Workshops and Tours, 304 Calle Oso, Santa Fe, NM 87501. 800-821-5145.
E-mail: wordharvest@yahoo.com.
Web site: www.sfworkshops.com.

SANTA FE WRITERS CONFERENCE
Santa Fe, N.M., August.
Details: Five-day conference featuring workshops, discussions, and individual meetings with writers and teachers of fiction, poetry, and creative nonfiction.
Contact: Robert Wilder, Southwest Literary Center of Recursos de Santa Fe, 826 Camino de Monte Rey #A-6, Santa Fe, NM 87505. 505-577-1125.
E-mail: litcenter@recursos.org.
Web site: www.santafewritersconference.com.

SOUTHWEST WRITERS ANNUAL CONFERENCE

Albuquerque, N.M., September.

Details: Multi-genre conference with lectures by authors, editors, agents, and publicists. Opportunity for one-on-one appointments.

Contact: Jo Ann Hamlin, SWW, 8200 Mountain Rd. NE, Suite 106, Albuquerque, NM, 87110. 505-265-9485.

E-mail: swriters@aol.com.

Web site: www.southwestwriters.org.

TAOS SUMMER WRITERS' CONFERENCE

Taos, N.M., July.

Details: Features writing workshops, readings, craft panels, and special events.

Contact: Sharon Oard Warner, University of New Mexico, Taos Writers, Humanities 255, Albuquerque, NM 87131. 505-277-6248.

E-mail: taosconf@unm.edu.

Web site: www.unm.edu/~taosconf.

THE WRITER'S LANDSCAPE

Santa Fe, N.M., April.

Details: For writers of all abilities, this workshop focuses on the natural landscape as a source of inspiration. Writers will learn to use nature and its metaphors to create compelling fiction, poetry, or essays.

Contact: Santa Fe Workshops and Tours, 304 Calle Oso, Santa Fe, NM 87501. 800-821-5145.

E-mail: wordharvest@yahoo.com. Web site: www.sfworkshops.com.

NEW YORK

THE ART OF REVISION

New York, N.Y, March.

Details: Through lectures and writing exercises, fiction writers gain techniques in macro/micro revision, how to establish checkpoints, how and when to cut and edit, how to determine when to revise, etc.

Contact: Gotham Writers' Workshop, 1841 Broadway, #809, New York, NY 10023. 212-974-8377 or 877-974-8377.

E-mail: office@write.org.

Web site: www.writingclasses.com.

ASJA WRITERS CONFERENCE

New York, N.Y., May.

Details: For freelance nonfiction writers; includes panels and workshops.

Contact: Brett Harvey, ASJA, 1501 Broadway, Suite 302, New York, NY 10036.
212-997-0947.
E-mail: staff@asja.org.
Web site: www.asja.org.

BIG APPLE CONFERENCE & OPEN HOUSE
New York, N.Y., April.
Contact: Hannelore Hahn, International Women's Writing Guild, P.O. Box 810,
Gracie Station, New York, NY 10028. 212-737-7536. E-mail: iwwg@iwwg.com.
Web site: www.iwwg.com.

THIS BUSINESS OF WRITING
New York, N.Y., May.
Details: For writers that plan to make writing a profession. Examines the business of
writing through the perspectives of the writer, the editor, the agent, and the publish-
er. Closes with panel discussion and Q&A.
Contact: Micheline Cote, The Writers Retreat, 15 Canusa St., Stanstead, Quebec,
J0B 3E5, Canada. 819-876-2065.
E-mail: info@writersretreat.com.
Web site: www.writersretreat.com/workshops.htm.

CATSKILL POETRY WORKSHOP
Oneonta, N.Y., June/July.
Details: Workshops, classes, readings, and individual instructional conferences.
Covers traditional meters, free verse lineation, and the uses of metaphor.
Contact: Carol Frost, English Dept., Hartwick College, Oneonta, NY 13820.
607-431-4448.
E-mail: frostc@hartwick.edu.
Web site: www.hartwick.edu/library/catskill/poetry.htm.

CHENANGO VALLEY WRITERS' CONFERENCE
Hamilton, N.Y., June.
Details: Workshops that develop writing skills in fiction, poetry, and nonfiction.
Contact: Matthew Leone, Colgate Univ., Office of Summer Programs, 13 Oak Dr.,
Hamilton, NY 13346. 315-228-7771.
E-mail: mleone@mail.colgate.edu.
Web site: http://clark.colgate.edu/cvwritersconference.

CHILDREN'S BOOK WRITING
New York, N.Y, February, March, May.
Details: Covers plot, structure, voice, characterization, description, and dialogue as
applied to all forms of fiction and nonfiction for pre-schoolers through young adults.
Contact: Gotham Writers' Workshop, 1841 Broadway, #809, New York, NY 10023.
212-974-8377.
E-mail: office@write.org. Web site: www.writingclasses.com.

CHILDREN'S BOOK WRITING AND ILLUSTRATING WORKSHOPS
New York, N.Y., July.
Details: Five-day intensive focusing on writing and illustrating children's picture books.
Contact: Robert Quackenbush, 460 E 79th St., New York, NY 10021. 212-744-3822.
E-mail: rqstudios@aol.com.
Web site: www.rquackenbush.com.

CHILDREN'S LITERATURE CONFERENCE: TRUTH IN FACT & FICTION
Hempstead, N.Y., April.
Details: Covers writing and illustrating picture books, contemporary fiction, fantasy and science fiction, and nonfiction. Mss. critiques available.
Contact: Marion Flomenhaft, 250 Hofstra University, Hempstead, NY 11549. 516-463-5016.
E-mail: uccelibarts@hofstra.edu.
Web site: www.hofstra.edu/writers.

CREATIVITY WORKSHOPS
New York, N.Y., ongoing.
Details: Aims to help writers believe in and develop their unique creative processes, using memoir, creative writing, visual arts, and storytelling exercises.
Contact: Shelley Berc and Alejandro Fogel, 245 E 40th St., Suite 25H, New York, NY 10016. 212-922-2153.
E-mail: info@creativityworkshop.com.
Web site: www.creativityworkshop.com.

FALL BIG APPLE WRITING WORKSHOP AND OPEN HOUSE
New York, N.Y., October.
Details: One-day workshop, plus an open house with editors and agents.
Contact: Hannelore Hahn, International Women's Writing Guild, P.O. Box 810, Gracie Station, New York, NY 10028. 212-737-7536.
E-mail: iwwg@iwwg.com.
Web site: www.iwwg.com.

GOTHAM WRITERS' WORKSHOP
New York, N.Y, various dates.
Details: Offers 10-week, one-day intensive, and on-line workshops in fiction, nonfiction, memoir, poetry, songwriting, screenwriting, playwriting, science fiction, business writing, romance, mystery, children's writing, and TV/comedy writing.
Contact: Dana Miller, 1841 Broadway, #809, New York, NY 10023. 212-974-8377 or 877-974-8377.
E-mail: office@write.org.
Web site: www.writingclasses.com.

GROWING AS AUTHORS AND ILLUSTRATORS

Watertown, N.Y., April.

Details: Offers individual manuscript critiques and presentations by editors and authors involved in children's publishing.

Contact: Aline A. Newman, RD #1 Box 43 East Rd., Turin, NY 13473.

HOW TO SELL YOUR SCREENPLAY

New York, N.Y, February and May.

Details: Covers the current film market, agents, production companies, the development process, the business of screenwriting, pitching ideas, and the most effective steps and strategies for selling a script.

Contact: Gotham Writers' Workshop, 1841 Broadway, #809, New York, NY 10023. 212-974-8377.

E-mail: office@write.org.

Web site: www.writingclasses.com.

IWWG'S ANNUAL SUMMER CONFERENCE

Saratoga Springs, N.Y., August.

Details: Offers 65 workshops on networking, critiquing, etc.

Contact: Hannelore Hahn, International Women's Writing Guild, P.O. Box 810, Gracie Station, New York, NY 10028. 212-737-7536.

E-mail: iwwg@iwwg.com.

Web site: www.iwwg.com.

MARYMOUNT MANHATTAN COLLEGE'S WRITERS CONFERENCE

New York, N.Y., June.

Details: Covers fiction and nonfiction; includes writers, editors, and agents.

Contact: Lewis Burke Frumkes, Marymount Manhattan College, 221 E 71st St., New York, NY 10021. 212-774-0780.

E-mail: l.frumkes@mmm.edu. Web site: www.mmce.edu.

MEMOIR WRITING

New York, N.Y, February, March, May.

Details: Covers plot, structure, voice, description, character development, point of view, and dialogue.

Contact: Gotham Writers' Workshop, 1841 Broadway, #809, New York, NY 10023. 212-974-8377.

E-mail: office@write.org.

Web site: www.writingclasses.com.

MID-YEAR CONFERENCE

New York, N.Y., February.

Details: Featuring the top professionals in the field of writing and illustrating children's books.

Contact: SCBWI NY Conference, 8271 Beverly Blvd., Los Angeles, CA 90048. Web site: www.scbwi.org.

NONFICTION WRITING

New York, N.Y, February, March, May.

Details: Covers magazine and newspaper articles, essays and travel pieces, memoirs and profiles. **Contact:** Gotham Writers' Workshop, 1841 Broadway, #809, New York, NY 10023. 212-974-8377. E-mail: office@write.org.

Web site: www.writingclasses.com.

PEOPLE'S POETRY GATHERING

New York, N.Y., April.

Details: Focuses on epics, ballads, and oral poetries from around the world, featuring performances, music, panels, lectures, and readings.

Contact: Elena Martinez, Poets House, 72 E 1st St., Fl. 2, New York, NY 10012. 212-431-7920.

E-mail: info@poetshouse.org.

Web site: www.peoplespoetry.org.

POETRY WRITING

New York, N.Y, March.

Details: Covers voice, imagery, music and sound, structure and syntax, and figurative language.

Contact: Gotham Writers' Workshop, 1841 Broadway, #809, New York, NY 10023. 212-974-8377.

E-mail: office@write.org.

Web site: www.writingclasses.com.

POLISH YOUR PITCH

New York, N.Y., May.

Details: For writers of novel, memoirs, short stories, or screenplays. Writers should come prepared to pitch story or screenplay.

Contact: Micheline Cote, The Writers Retreat, 15 Canusa St., Stanstead, Quebec, J0B 3E5, Canada. 819-876-2065.

E-mail: info@writersretreat.com.

Web site: www.writersretreat.com/workshops.htm.

ROBERT MCKEE'S STORY SEMINAR

New York, N.Y., March.

Details: Teaches the essential principles of screenwriting and story design.

Contact: Two Arts, Inc., P.O. Box 452930, Los Angeles, CA 90045. 888-676-2533.

E-mail: contact@mckeestory.com.

Web site: www.mckeestory.com.

SCREENWRITING
New York, N.Y, February, March, May.
Details: Covers plot, act structure, character development, conflict, dialogue, and format.
Contact: Gotham Writers' Workshop, 1841 Broadway, #809, New York, NY 10023. 212-974-8377.
E-mail: office@write.org.
Web site: www.writingclasses.com.

SITCOM WRITING
New York, N.Y, February, May.
Details: Covers storyline, plot, dialogue, scene and act structure, development, and consistency of characters.
Contact: Gotham Writers' Workshop, 1841 Broadway, #809, New York, NY 10023. 212-974-8377.
E-mail: office@write.org.
Web site: www.writingclasses.com.

SOUTHAMPTON WRITERS CONFERENCE
Southampton, N.Y., July.
Details: Provides a forum for authors of all genres to study and discuss writing.
Contact: Carla Caglioti, Summer Programs, Southampton College of Long Island Univ., Southampton, NY 11968. 631-287-8175.
E-mail: summer@southampton.liu.edu.
Web site: www.southampton.liu.edu.

SUMMER SEMINAR FOR WRITERS
Bronxville, N.Y., June.
Details: Intensive week of workshops, conferences, and readings with nationally-known writers and Sarah Lawrence faculty members.
Contact: Grant Grastorf, Sarah Lawrence College, Bronxville, NY 10708. 914-395-2412.
E-mail: grant@sarahlawrence.edu.
Web site: www.sarahlawrence.edu.

TRAVEL WRITING
New York, N.Y, March, May.
Details: Covers the full spectrum of travel writing, from destination guides to literary travel essays and memoirs. Topics include finding an angle, research and preparation, capturing the essence of places and people, what consumers want to know, and tips on how to break into the business.
Contact: Gotham Writers' Workshop, 1841 Broadway, #809, New York, NY 10023. 212-974-8377.
E-mail: office@write.org.
Web site: www.writingclasses.com.

WRITING FOR CHILDREN
Chautauqua, N.Y., July.
Details: Intensive workshop for individuals interested in writing and illustrating children's literature; includes individual and group sessions.
Contact: Kent L. Brown, Jr., Highlights Foundation, 814 Court St., Honesdale, PA 18431. 570-253-1192.
E-mail: contact@highlightsfoundation.org.
Web site: www.highlightsfoundation.org.

YOUNG PLAYWRIGHTS URBAN RETREAT
New York, N.Y., July.
Details: Weeklong intensive playwriting program for writers ages 14-21. Writers attend workshops, develop new material, and collaborate with professional directors, dramaturgs, and actors on short plays created during the retreat.
Contact: Young Playwrights, Inc., 306 W 38th St., Suite 300, New York, NY 10018. 212-594-5440.
E-mail: writeaplay@aol.com.
Web site: www.youngplaywrights.org.

NORTH CAROLINA

ANNUAL WRITER'S WEEK
Wilmington, N.C., March.
Details: Activities include workshops, panels, readings, and manuscript conferences.
Contact: Creative Writing Department, University of North Carolina at Wilmington, 601 S College Rd., Wilmington, NC 28403.
Web site: http://www.uncwil.edu/writers/WRITERS_WEEK.HTM

ASSOCIATION FOR WOMEN IN COMMUNICATIONS PROFESSIONAL CONFERENCE
Charlotte, NC
Details: Professional conference focusing on current topics in communications disciplines. Includes Clarion Awards.
Contact: Patricia H. Troy, 780 Ritchie Hwy., Suite S-28, Severna Park, MD 21146. 410-544-7442.
E-mail: pat@womcom.org. Web site: www.womcom.org.

BLUE RIDGE MOUNTAIN CHRISTIAN WRITERS CONFERENCE
Ridgecrest, N.C., April.
Details: Designed to train, encourage, equip, and inspire Christian writers.
Contact: Robin Hawkins, LifeWay Ridgecrest Conference Ctr., P.O. Box 128, Ridgecrest, NC 28770. 828-669-3596.
E-mail: robin.hawkins@lifeway.com.
Web site: www.lifeway.com/conferencecenters.

N. C. WRITERS' NETWORK FALL CONFERENCE

Wilmington, N.C., November.

Details: Features prominent writers, editors, publishers, and agents during a full weekend of workshops, panel discussions, and readings.

Contact: The North Carolina Writers' Network, P.O. Box 954, Carrboro, NC 27510. 919-967-9540.

E-mail: mail@ncwriters.org.

Web site: www.ncwriters.org.

READING BETWEEN THE LINES: WORDCRAFTING WITH THE PROS

Winston-Salem, N.C., April.

Details: One-day workshop on the craft of writing. Covers poetry, fiction, children's literature, screenwriting, and creative nonfiction.

Contact: Salem College, 601 S Church St., Winston-Salem, NC 27101. 336-721-2669.

Web site: www.salem.edu/community.

WILDACRES WRITERS WORKSHOP: ADULT WRITING

Little Switzerland, N.C., June/July.

Details: Covers novel, short story, creative nonfiction, sudden fiction, and poetry.

Contact: Judi Hill, 233 S Elm St., Greensboro, NC 27401. 336-370-9188.

E-mail: judihill@aol.com.

Web site: www.wildacres.com.

WILDACRES WRITERS WORKSHOP: CHILDREN'S WRITING

Little Switzerland, N.C., July.

Details: Covers picture book, middle grades, and young adult writing.

Contact: Judi Hill, 233 S Elm St., Greensboro, NC 27401. 336-370-9188.

E-mail: judihill@aol.com.

Web site: www.wildacres.com.

WOMEN, WRITING, PLACE

Wilson, N.C., April.

Contact: Jim Clark, Barton College Creative Writing Symposium, Department of English and Modern Languages, Box 5000, Wilson, NC 27893. 252-399-6450.

E-mail: jclark@barton.edu.

Web site: www.barton.edu.

OHIO

ANTIOCH WRITERS' WORKSHOP
Yellow Springs, Ohio, July.
Details: Talented faculty presenting lectures, sessions, and panel discussions on fiction, nonfiction and poetry.
Contact: Jordis Ruhl, P.O. Box 494, Yellow Springs, OH 45387. 937-475-7357.
E-mail: info@antiochwritersworkshop.com.
Web site: www.antiochwritersworkshop.com.

COLUMBUS WRITERS CONFERENCE
Columbus, Ohio, August.
Details: Offers a wide range of writing topics presented by writers, editors, and literary agents. Includes manuscript critiques by editors and one-to-one consultations with literary agents. Also offers open-mike sessions for poetry, fiction, and nonfiction.
Contact: Angela Palazzolo, P.O. Box 20548, Columbus, OH 43220. 614-451-0216.
E-mail: angelapl28@aol.com. Web site: www.creativevista.com

FEBRUARY THAW
Cleveland, Ohio, February.
Details: Northern Ohio SCBWI Annual Conference. Workshops on picture books, YA novels, historical/nonfiction material, photography for writers, and illustration markets. Manuscript and portfolio critiques available.
Contact: 225 N Willow St., Kent, OH 44240. 330-678-2900.
E-mail: conference2003@sp-ds.com. Web site: www.geocities.com/scbwioh.

KENYON REVIEW WRITERS WORKSHOP
Gambier, Ohio, June.
Details: Workshops in poetry, fiction, and creative nonfiction. Instructors use challenging exercises and lead the groups in close readings and discussions of participants' work.
Contact: Ellen Sheffield, Walton House, Kenyon College, Gambier, OH 43022. 740-427-5207.
E-mail: kenyonreview@kenyon.edu.
Web site: www.kenyonreview.org.

OKLAHOMA

OKLAHOMA FALL ARTS INSTITUTES
Lone Wolf, Okla., October.
Details: Workshops in writing led by top writers in fiction, nonfiction, and poetry.

Contact: Gayla Foster or Jessica Buzzard, 105 N Hudson, Suite 101, Oklahoma City, OK 73102. 405-319-9019.
E-mail: okarts@okartinst.org.
Web site: www.okartinst.org.

OWFI CONFERENCE
Oklahoma City, Okla., May.
Details: Writers, editors, and agents meet for informative programs teaching authors skills to write well and get published.
Contact: Lou Mansfield, 2302 Brandeis Ct., Hall Park, OK 73071.
Web site: http://owfi.tripod.com/.

SHORT COURSE ON PROFESSIONAL WRITING
Norman, Okla., June.
Details: Sessions on writing for publication: mystery, screenwriting, romance writing, and other genres.
Contact: J. Madison Davis, Univ. of Oklahoma, 860 Van Vleet Oval, Norman, OK 73019. 405-325-4171.
E-mail: jmadisondavis@ou.edu.
Web site: http://jmc.ou.edu.

OREGON

ASHLAND WRITERS CONFERENCE
Ashland, Ore., July/August.
Details: Covers poetry, fiction, and nonfiction.
Contact: Jonah Bornstein, 404 Wilson Rd., Ashland, OR 97520. 866-482-2783.
E-mail: mail@ashlandwriters.com.
Web site: www.ashlandwriters.com.

FISHTRAP, INC.
Wallowa Lake, Ore., Dates vary.
Details: Summer and winter writing workshops on a wide variety of topics including writing about nature, history, humor, and the West.
Contact: Rich Wandschneider, 400 Grant St., P.O. Box 38, Enterprise, OR 97828. 541-426-3623.
E-mail: rich@fishtrap.org
Web site: www.fishtrap.org

HAYSTACK SUMMER PROGRAM IN THE ARTS
Cannon Beach, Ore., July/August.
Details: Creative arts workshops in fiction, poetry, nonfiction, essay, memoir,

children's books, and screenplays.
Contact: Elizabeth Snyder, P.O. Box 1491, Portland State Univ. Portland, OR 97207.
503-725-4186.
E-mail: snydere@pdx.edu.
Web site: www.haystack.pdx.edu.

TIN HOUSE SUMMER WRITERS WORKSHOP
Portland, Ore., July.
Details: Seminars, workshops, panels, and readings on fiction, nonfiction, poetry, and film.
Contact: *Tin House Magazine*, P.O. Box 10500, Portland, OR 97210. 503-219-0622.
E-mail: summerworkshop@tinhouse.com.
Web site: www.tinhouse.com.

PENNSYLVANIA

CONFLUENCE
Pittsburgh, Pa., July 25-27, 2003.
Details: Panel discussions and talks focused on the literature and art of science ficton and fantasy.
Contact: Confluence, P.O. Box 3681, Pittsburgh, PA 15230.
412-344-0456.
E-mail: confluence@spellcaster.org.
Web site: http://trfn.clpgh.org/parsec/conflu.

A CRASH COURSE IN THE BUSINESS OF CHILDREN'S PUBLISHING
Honesdale, Pa., Spring.
Details: Informative sessions and opportunities for writers and illustrators to meet with children's book publishing professsionals.
Contact: Jo Lloyd, Highlights Foundation, 814 Court St., Pa. 18431.
570-251-4557.
E-mail: contact@highlightsfoundation.org.
Web site: www.highlightsfoundation.org.

GREATER PHILADELPHIA CHRISTIAN WRITERS CONFERENCE
Langhorne, Pa., August.
Details: Sessions and workshops to encourage and equip Christian writers.
Contact: Marlene Bagnull, 316 Blanchard Rd., Drexel Hill, PA 19026.
610-626-6833.
E-mail: mbagnull@aol.com.
Web site: www.writehisanswer.com.

THE HEART OF THE NOVEL:
DEVELOPING CHARACTERS THAT READERS CARE ABOUT

Honesdale, Pa., Fall.

Details: Designed for experienced fiction writers. Writers will create an unforgettable character and make that character grow throughout several chapters of a book. Provides opportunity to work with a professional editor.

Contact: Jo Lloyd, Highlights Foundation, 814 Court St., Honesdale, PA 18431. 570-251-4557.

E-mail: contact@highlightsfoundation.org.

Web site: www.highlightsfoundation.org.

LIFE IN THE SPOTLIGHT:
POLISHING YOUR PRESENTATIONS
AND PROMOTING YOUR BOOKS

Honesdale, Pa., Spring.

Details: Offers useful tips and stategies for making polished presentations and promoting yourself to schools, libraries, and bookstores.

Contact: Jo Lloyd, Highlights Foundation, 814 Court St., Honesdale, PA 18431. 570-251-4557.

E-mail: contact@highlightsfoundation.org.

Web site: www.highlightsfoundation.org.

MIXING RESEARCH WITH IMAGINATION:
THE ART OF WRITING HISTORY AND HISTORICAL FICTION

Honesdale, Pa., Spring.

Details: Designed for experienced nonfiction or historical fiction writers. Features lectures, discussion, and mss. critique sessions.

Contact: Jo Lloyd, Highlights Foundation, 814 Court St., Honesdale, PA 18431. 570-251-4557.

E-mail: contact@highlightsfoundation.org.

Web site: www.highlightsfoundation.org.

MONTROSE CHRISTIAN WRITERS CONFERENCE

Montrose, Pa., July.

Details: Classes and workshops for all writers, beginner through experienced. Manuscript review and editorial appointments available.

Contact: Donna Kosik, Montrose Bible Conference, 5 Locust St., Montrose, PA 18801. 570-278-1001 or 800-598-5030.

E-mail: mbc@montrosebible.org.

Web site: www.montrosebible.org.

NATURE AND SCIENCE WRITING FOR KIDS

Honesdale, Pa., Spring.

Details: Lectures, nature walks, and hand-on critiques for writing nature/science stories for kids. Lecture topics include where to find good story ideas, how to use

characters and plotting to create good nonfiction, the importance of solid research, and working with nonfiction editors.
Contact: Jo Lloyd, Highlights Foundation, 814 Court St., Honesdale, PA 18431. 570-251-4557.
E-mail: contact@highlightsfoundation.org.
Web site: www.highlightsfoundation.org.

NONFICTION—IT'S MORE THAT JUST THE FACTS!

Honesdale, Pa., Fall.
Details: Workshops geared towards writers of children's nonfiction. Past faculty include Carolyn P. Yoder and Liza Ketchum.
Contact: Jo Lloyd, Highlights Foundation, 814 Court St., Honesdale, PA 18431. 570-251-4557.
E-mail: contact@highlightsfoundation.org.
Web site: www.highlightsfoundation.org.

PHILADELPHIA WRITERS' CONFERENCE

Philadelphia, Pa., June.
Details: Offers workshops, contests, meetings with agents/editors, etc.
Contact: W. Haggerty, 535 Fairview Rd., Medford, NJ 08055. 215-497-9445.
E-mail: info@pwcwriters.org. Web site: www.pwcwriters.org.

PICTURE BOOKS A-Z

Honesdale, Pa., Spring.
Details: Conference for writers with strong interest in publishing picture books. Topics include coming up with the right ideas, using lively, stimulating language and pictures to involve readers, creating storyboards and page layouts to visualize your picture book, and working with illustrators/art directors.
Contact: Jo Lloyd, Highlights Foundation, 814 Court St., Honesdale, PA 18431. 570-251-4557.
E-mail: contact@highlightsfoundation.org.
Web site: www.highlightsfoundation.org.

WORD PLAY: WRITING POETRY FOR CHILDREN

Honesdale, Pa., Fall.
Details: Workshops that focus on the art of writing poetry for children's markets. Past faculty include Eileen Spinelli, Jerry Spinelli, and Wendy Murray.
Contact: Jo Lloyd, Highlights Foundation, 814 Court St., Honesdale, PA 18431. 570-251-4557.
E-mail: contact@highlightsfoundation.org. Web site: www.highlightsfoundation.org.

WRITE HERE, WRITE NOW!

Pittsburgh, Pa., May.
Details: Workshops and panel discussions cover multi-genre topics for writers at every level of experience and interest.

Contact: Mike Crawmer, 6306 Stanton Ave., Pittsburgh, PA 15206. 412-361-0936.
E-mail: mcrawmer@aol.com.
Web site: www.pennwriters.org.

WRITING FROM THE HEART:
A GUIDED WRITERS' RETREAT

Honesdale, Pa., Spring.
Details: For writers of children's books who seek a supportive environment to complete a new work or a work-in-progress.
Contact: Jo Lloyd, Highlights Foundation, 814 Court St., Honesdale, PA 18431. 570-251-4557.
E-mail: contact@highlightsfoundation.org.
Web site: www.highlightsfoundation.org.

WRITING NOVELS FOR YOUNG ADULTS

Honesdale, Pa., Spring/Fall.
Details: Lectures, hands-on writing sessions, and mss. critiques with an expert in the field. Workshop sessions include tapping into memories to find ideas for stories, writing dialogue, creating an internal monologue, voice, and revision.
Contact: Jo Lloyd, Highlights Foundation, 814 Court St., Honesdale, PA 18431. 570-251-4557.
E-mail: contact@highlightsfoundation.org.
Web site: www.highlightsfoundation.org.

WRITING YOUR FIRST NOVEL

Honesdale, Pa., Spring/Fall.
Details: Workshops and mss. critiques for writers developing their first children's novel. Past faculty include Sandy Asher.
Contact: Jo Lloyd, Highlights Foundation, 814 Court St., Honesdale, PA 18431. 570-251-4557.
E-mail: contact@highlightsfoundation.org.
Web site: www.highlightsfoundation.org.

YOU REALLY SHOULD PUBLISH THAT

Bangor, Pa., July.
Details: A writing workshop especially for clergy, but open to all who have heard the words, "You really should publish that." Offers techniques for turning sermons into op-eds, prayers into poems, and good stories into radio, written features, or memoirs.
Contact: Janet Lewis, Kirkridge Retreat Center, 2495 Fox Gap Rd., Bangor, PA 18013. 610-588-1793.
E-mail: kirkridge@fast.net.
Web site: www.kirkridge.org.

SOUTH CAROLINA

CLASSEMINAR

Spartanburg, S.C., May.

Details: CLASS (Christian Leaders, Authors & Speakers Services) offers intensive three-day seminars: training in communication skills for both the spoken and written word.

Contact: Linda Jewell, P.O. Box 66810, Albuquerque, NM, 87193. 800-433-6633.

E-mail: mary@classervices.com; or linda@classervices.com.

Web site: www.glorietacwc.com; or www.classervices.com.

SOUTH CAROLINA BOOK FESTIVAL

Columbia, S.C., February.

Details: Annual festival featuring nationally-known authors for readings and signings, as well as booksellers and exhibitors. Also festival-related book clubs and library discussion groups from around the state, free showings of films based on books by festival authors, and Late Night Readings.

Contact: The Humanities Council SC, P.O. Box 5287, Columbia, SC 29204. 803-771-2477.

E-mail: bookfest@schumanities.org.

Web site: www.schumanities.org/bookfestival.htm.

SOUTH CAROLINA WRITERS WORKSHOP CONFERENCE

Myrtle Beach, S.C., October.

Details: Features agents, editors, and bestselling authors. Workshop sessions will focus on the craft of writing and practical information on how to become established in the literary industry.

Contact: Steve Vassey, SCWW, P.O. Box 7104, Columbia, SC 29202. 803-794-0832.

E-mail: vasseyws@hotmail.com.

Web site: www.scwriters.com.

TENNESSEE

AMERICAN CHRISTIAN WRITERS CONFERENCE

Chattanooga, Tenn., January.

Details: Offers instruction, networking opportunites, and one-on-one time with editors and professional freelance writers. **Contact:** Reg A. Forder, P.O. Box 110390, Nashville, TN 37222. 800-219-7483. E-mail: acwriters@aol.com.

Web site: www.acwriters.com.

AMERICAN CHRISTIAN WRITERS: MENTORING RETREAT

Nashville, Tenn., July.

Details: Offers instruction, networking opportunites, and one-on-one time with editors and professional freelance writers. **Contact:** Reg A. Forder, P.O. Box 110390, Nashville, TN 37222. 800-219-7483. E-mail: acwriters@aol.com.

Web site: www.acwriters.com.

SEWANEE WRITERS' CONFERENCE

Sewanee, Tenn., July.

Details: Features workshops in poetry, fiction, and playwriting. Over 100 contributors, scholars, and fellows meet with renowned faculty members and visitors to discuss their work and aspects of craft.

Contact: Cheri B. Peters, 735 University Ave., Sewanee, TN 37383. 931-598-1141. E-mail: cpeters@sewanee.edu.

Web site: www.sewaneewriters.org.

TENNESSEE MOUNTAIN WRITERS CONFERENCE

Oak Ridge, Tenn., April.

Details: Includes workshop sessions, book fair/writer's block, exhibits, mss. evaluations and readings, and awards banquet.

Contact: TMWI, P.O. Box 5435, Oak Ridge, TN 37831-5435. 865-671-6046. E-mail: mail@tmwi.org.

Web site: www.tmwi.org.

TEXAS

AGENTS! AGENTS! AGENTS! & EDITORS TOO

Austin, Texas, July.

Details: Provides writers an opportunity to exchange ideas and network with agents, editors, and authors. Panel and workshop discussions led by a wide range of published professional writers.

Contact: Stephanie Sheppard, Writers' League of Texas, 1501 W 5th St., Suite E2, Austin TX 78703. 512-499-8914.

E-mail: ssheppard@writersleague.org.

Web site: www.writersleague.org.

CAT WRITERS' ASSOCIATION ANNUAL CONFERENCE

Houston, Texas, November.

Details: Seminar topics are of interest to all writers and include contract advice, media training, creating and selling a nonfiction project, manuscript critiques, and more.

Contact: Karen Commings, 6225 Blue Bird Ave., Harrisburg, PA 17112.

Web site: www.catwriters.org.

CELEBRATING WOMEN & WRITING

Arlington, Texas, February.

Details: Experienced and emerging writers unite to write. Offers workshops and keynote presentations.

Contact: Sheri' McConnell, Founder/President, National Association of Women Writers, P.O. Box 183812, Arlington, TX 76096. 866-821-5829.

E-mail: naww@onebox.com.

Web site: www.naww.org.

CLASSEMINAR

Granbury, Texas, November.

Details: CLASS (Christian Leaders, Authors & Speakers Services) offers intensive three-day seminars: training in communication skills for both the spoken and written word.

Contact: Linda Jewell, P.O. Box 66810, Albuquerque, NM, 87193. 800-433-6633.

E-mail: linda@classervices.com.

Web site: www.glorietacwc.com, or www.classervices.com.

CREATIVE WRITING & YOGA RETREAT

Austin, Texas, May/June.

Details: Three-day creative writing and yoga retreat at Barsana Dham Retreat Center near Austin, Texas. Co-led by Patricia Lee Lewis and Charles MacInerney.

Contact: Patricia Lee Lewis, Patchwork Farm Retreat, 292 Chesterfield Rd., Westhampton, MA 01027. 413-527-5819.

E-mail: patricia@writingretreats.org.

Web site: www.writingretreats.org.

GEMINI INK SUMMER LITERARY FESTIVAL

San Antonio, Texas, July.

Details: Held in San Antonio's vibrant Southtown Arts District during Contemporary Arts Month. Writers meet with editors and agents from major publishing houses.

Contact: 513 S Presa St., San Antonio, TX 78205. 877-734-9673.

E-mail: info@geminiink.org.

Web site: www.geminiink.org.

INDIAN PAINTBRUSH WRITING

Fort Davis, Texas, May.

Details: An intensive children's writing workshop, teaching the art of literature from the illustrator's and writer's viewpoints.

Contact: Melanie Chrismer, Roger Williamson, 12330 Barryknoll Ln., Houston, TX 77024. 281-855-9561.

E-mail: phoebe5@pdq.net; or vroeder@earthlink.net.

Web site: http://scbwi-houston.org.

RWA NATIONAL CONFERENCE

Dallas, Texas, July.

Details: Offers workshops, author signings, Golden Heart and RITA contest awards, and more.

Contact: Jane Detloff, 3707 FM 1960 W, Suite 555, Houston, TX 77068. 281-440-6885.

E-mail: jdetloff@rwanational.com.

Web site: www.rwanational.com.

TEXAS CHRISTIAN WRITERS CONFERENCE

Houston, Texas, August.

Details: One-day conference featuring workshops and large group sessions.

Contact: Martha Rogers, 6038 Greenmont, Houston, TX 77092. 713-686-7209.

E-mail: rrogersll@houston.rr.com.

WRITING FOR FILM AND TELEVISION

Austin, Texas, April.

Details: Focuses on dialogue, plot, character, structure, tricks of the trade and more.

Contact: Lorin Oberweger, Free Expressions, 2420 W Brandon Blvd., #198, Brandon, FL 33511. 866-497-4832.

E-mail: lorin@free-expressions.com.

Web site: www.free-expressions.com.

WRITING THE MYSTERY NOVEL

Austin, Texas, June.

Details: Focuses on dialogue, plot, character, structure, tricks of the trade, finding an agent, and more.

Contact: Lorin Oberweger, Free Expressions, 2420 W Brandon Blvd., #198, Brandon, FL 33511. 866-497-4832.

E-mail: lorin@free-expressions.com.

Web site: www.free-expressions.com.

UTAH

DESERT WRITERS WORKSHOP

Bluff, Utah, October.

Details: Five-day workshop focusing on inspirational and creative writing, related to the natural world and the ethic of responsible stewardship.

Contact: Karla VanderZanden, Canyonlands Field Institute, P.O. Box 68, Moab, UT 84532. 435-259-7750.

E-mail: cfiinfo@canyonlandsfieldinst.org. Web site: www.canyonlandsfieldinst.org.

LEAGUE OF UTAH WRITERS ROUNDUP

Ogden, Utah, September.

Details: League of Utah Writers annual roundup including speakers, workshops, and more.

Contact: Kathy Jones, 5879 Cranston Cove, West Valley City, UT 84128.
801-969-9351.

E-mail: kathy.jones3@attbi.com.

Web site: www.luwrite.com.

SOUTHERN UTAH UNIVERSITY WRITERS CONFERENCE

Cedar City, Utah.

Details: Workshop for beginning and advanced writers, English teachers, and college students to learn the techniques of writing and understanding fiction, poetry, etc.

Contact: David Nyman, Southern Utah University, Cedar City, UT 84720.
435-586-1995.

E-mail: nyman@suu.edu.

Web site: www.suu.edu.

WRITERS AT WORK

Salt Lake City, Utah, June.

Details: Workshops in which students discuss writing techniques with nationally renowned instructors and writers, and participate in lectures, panels, readings, and one-on-one manuscript consultations with professional editors/agents.

Contact: Lisa Peterson, P.O. Box 540370, North Salt Lake, UT 84054. 801-292-9285.

E-mail: lisa@writersatwork.org.

Web site: www.writersatwork.org.

VERMONT

ANNUAL NEW ENGLAND WRITERS CONFERENCE

Windsor, Vt., July

Details: Includes a distinguished panel, seminars in poetry and fiction, awards, book sales, and open readings.

Contact: Dr. Frank and Susan C. Anthony, P.O. Box 5, Windsor, VT 05089.
802-674-2315. E-mail: newvtpoet@aol.com.

Web site: www.newenglandwriters.org

VERMONT COLLEGE POSTGRADUATE WRITERS' CONFERENCE

Montpelier, Vt., August.

Details: Conference for postgraduate writers (or individuals with comparable experience) featuring workshops and consulations.

Contact: Rick Zind, Vermont College, 36 College St., Montpelier, VT 05602.
802-828-8764. E-mail: rick.zind@tui.edu.

Web site: www.tui.edu/vermontcollege.

WILDBRANCH WORKSHOP IN OUTDOOR, NATURAL HISTORY, AND ENVIRONMENTAL WRITING

Craftsbury Common, Vt.
Details: Week-long workshop of classes, lectures, discussion groups, and readings in the craft and techniques of fine writing about the world outdoors.
Contact: Sterling College, P.O. Box 72, Craftsbury Common, VT 05827. 800-648-3591.
E-mail: wldbrnch@sterlingcollege.edu.
Web site: www.sterlingcollege.edu/wildbranch.htm.

VIRGINIA

ALGONKIAN PARK NOVEL CAMP

Algonkian Park, Va., March, April, June.
Details: Cross-genre craft and prose workshop for novel planners, beginners, and veterans. Students will study and apply techniques of craft and style. The workshop leader will review promising novel concepts and pass them on to an agent who works with Algonkian, and will also devote workshop time to film adaptation, high concept pitching, and other aspects of novel-to-film.
Contact: Web Del Sol, 2020 Pennsylvania Ave., NW, Suite 443, Washington, DC 20006. 703-281-4426.
E-mail: algonkian@webdelsol.com.
Web site: www.webdelsol.com.

HIGHLAND SUMMER CONFERENCE: APPALACHIAN WRITING AND CULTURE

Radford, Va., June.
Details: Two-week intensive workshop in creative and expository writing.
Contact: JoAnn Asbury, Radford University, Appalachian Regional Studies Center, Box 7014, Radford, VA 24142. 540-831-6152.
E-mail: jasbury@radford.edu.
Web site: www.radford.edu/~arsc.

MALICE DOMESTIC

Arlington, Va., April/May.
Details: An international array of mystery authors, academics, fans, dealers, agents, and others come together for an annual celebration of the traditional mystery.
Contact: Marie O'Day, P.O. Box 31137, Bethesda, MD 20824. 301-681-4875.
E-mail: registrar@malicedomestic.org.
Web site: www.malicedomestic.org.

VIRGINIA FESTIVAL OF THE BOOK

Charlottesville, Va., March.
Details: Annual public festival for children and adults featuring over 200 programs.

Offers readings, along with panels and discussions with authors, illustrators ,and publishing professionals to celebrate books and promote reading and literacy.
Contact: Virginia Foundation for the Humanities, 145 Ednam Dr., Charlottesville, VA 22903. 434-924-6890.
E-mail: vabook@virginia.edu.
Web site: www.vabook.org.

WASHINGTON

CENTRUM'S PORT TOWNSEND WRITERS' CONFERENCE
Port Townsend, Wash., July.
Details: Seaside retreat community exploring diverse opinions, styles, and genres. Critiqued and open-enrollment workshops are available.
Contact: Carla Vander Ven, Centrum, P.O. Box 1158, Port Townsend, WA 98368. 360-385-3102.
E-mail: info@centrum.org.
Web site: www.centrum.org.

CHRISTIAN WRITERS WEEKEND
Seattle, Wash., May.
Details: Offers 19 workshops and three general sessions. Past instructors include Liz Curtis Higgs.
Contact: Linda Wagner, Center for Learning, Seattle Pacific University, 3307 Third Ave. W, Seattle, WA 98119. 206-281-2492.
E-mail: lwagner@spu.edu.
Web site: www.spu.edu/fellows.

CLARION WEST WRITERS WORKSHOP
Seattle, Wash., June-August.
Details: Instensive six-week workshop for writers interested in pursuing careers in sceince fiction, fantasy, and horror.
Contact: Nisi Shawl, Clarion West, 340 15th Ave. E, Suite 350, Seattle, WA 98112. 206-720-1008.
E-mail: nisis@aol.com. Web site: www.clarionwest.org.

PACIFIC NORTHWEST WRITERS ASSOCIATION SUMMER CONFERENCE
Seattle, Wash., July.
Details: Offers workshops, seminars, and master classes that are geared for every experience level, genre, and style. Writers may also schedule appointments with agents and editors.
Contact: Dennis Globus, PNWA, P.O. Box 2016, Edmonds, WA 98020. 425-673-2665.
E-mail: staff@pnwa.org. Web site: www.pnwa.org.

WHIDBEY ISLAND WRITERS CONFERENCE
Langley, Wash., February/March.
Details: Features nearly every genre and over 40 presenters annually. Known for its unique features (Fireside Chats, Bedtime Stories, Readings), this conference also has traditional offerings such as panels, workshops, and agent/editor consultations.
Contact: Celeste Mergens, P.O. Box 1289, Langley, WA 98260. 360-331-6714.
E-mail: writers@whidbey.com.
Web site: www.whidbey.com/writers.

WEST VIRGINIA

THE SYMPOSIUM FOR PROFESSIONAL FOOD WRITERS
White Sulpher Springs, W.V., March.
Details: Limited to 90 professional food writers and editors, this conference includes workshops, private group coaching sessions, open readings, roundtables, and more.
Contact: Lynn Swann, The Greenbrier, 300 W Main St., White Sulpher Springs, WV 24986. 800-624-6070.
E-mail: lynn_swann@greenbrier.com.
Web site: www.greenbrier.com/foodwriters.

WISCONSIN

ANNUAL WRITERS INSTITUTE
Madison, Wis., July.
Details: Sessions focus on fiction and nonfiction topics, as well as marketing and career issues. Sessions for beginners and advanced. Agents and editors also attend.
Contact: Christine DeSmet, 610 Langdon St., Rm. 621, Madison, WI 53703. 608-262-3447.
E-mail: cdesmet@dcs.wisc.edu.
Web site: www.dcs.wisc.edu/lsa/writing.

THE CLEARING WRITING WORKSHOPS
Ellison Bay, Wis., Dates vary.
Details: Workshops on various forms of writing including story writing, journaling, and poetry. Past instructors include Barbara Fitz Vroman, Darlene Cole, Jerry Apps, Robin Chapman, Judith Strasser, Ellen Kort, and John Lehman. See Web site for specific dates.
Contact: Kathy Vanderhoof, The Clearing, P.O. Box 65, Ellison Bay, WI 54210. 920-854-4088.
E-mail: clearing@theclearing.org.
Web site: www.theclearing.org.

CREATING CHARACTERS WE CARE ABOUT

Madison, Wis., February.

Details: Teaches techniques for creating characters in novels and movie scripts that evoke emotion in readers/viewers. Learn what editors, agents, producers, and actors look for in characters.

Contact: University of Wisconsin-Madison, Liberal Studies & the Arts, 610 Langdon St., Rm. 616, Lowell Center, Madison, WI 53703. 608-262-3447.

E-mail: cdesmet@dcs.wisc.edu.

Web site: www.dcs.wisc.edu/lsa/writing.

HOW TO WRITE AND DESIGN
GREAT NEWSLETTERS AND BROCHURES

Madison, Wis., April.

Details: Teaches techniques on creating effective headlines, writing creative copy, and making decisions on content for newsletters and brochures. Also teaches the fundamentals of design.

Contact: University of Wisconsin-Madison, Liberal Studies & the Arts, 610 Langdon St., Rm. 616, Lowell Center, Madison, WI 53703. 608-262-3447.

E-mail: cdesmet@dcs.wisc.edu.

Web site: www.dcs.wisc.edu/lsa/writing.

THE POWER OF POINT OF VIEW: A FICTION WORKSHOP

Madison, Wis., March.

Details: Sessions cover how point of view delivers exposition, plot and theme.

Contact: University of Wisconsin-Madison, Liberal Studies & the Arts, 610 Langdon St., Rm. 616, Lowell Center, Madison, WI 53703. 608-262-3447.

E-mail: cdesmet@dcs.wisc.edu.

Web site: www.dcs.wisc.edu/lsa/writing.

THE ROOTS OF THE POEM:
A POETRY WORKSHOP ON FERTILIZING, WEEDING, AND MORE

Madison, Wis., April.

Details: Offers analysis of published poems—both classic and contemporary—publication tips, discussion of participant poems (optional), and instructor written critique of one poem. (Send one or two poems by March 15 to instructor Laurel Yourke at the address below.)

Contact: University of Wisconsin-Madison, Liberal Studies & the Arts, 610 Langdon St., Rm. 616, Lowell Center, Madison, WI 53703. 608-262-3447.

E-mail: cdesmet@dcs.wisc.edu. Web site: www.dcs.wisc.edu/lsa/writing.

SCBWI-WISCONSIN FALL RETREAT

Racine, Wis., October.

Details: Focus in on children's literature. Includes one-on-one critiques, lectures, breakout sessions, and First Pages on Saturday night.

Contact: 15255 Turnberry Dr., Brookfield, WI 53005.

7 WAYS TO TELL YOUR STORIES IN FICTION AND NONFICTION

Madison, Wis., February.

Details: For fiction and creative nonfiction writers, this conference explores 7 ways to tell compelling stories. Topics include setting, characterization, theme, abstractions, tone, etc.

Contact: University of Wisconsin-Madison, Liberal Studies & the Arts, 610 Langdon St., Rm. 616, Lowell Center, Madison, WI 53703. 608-262-3447.

E-mail: cdesmet@dcs.wisc.edu.

Web site: www.dcs.wisc.edu/lsa/writing.

THE STORY ONLY YOU CAN TELL: NEW TOOLS FOR AUTOBIOGRAPHY

Madison, Wis., April.

Details: Apply the techniques and structure of storytelling to your own experiences. Use character development, scenes, thematic conflict, drama, and dialogue to give shape and meaning to the events of your life and make your story interesting to others.

Contact: University of Wisconsin-Madison, Liberal Studies & the Arts, 610 Langdon St., Rm. 616, Lowell Center, Madison, WI 53703. 608-262-3447.

E-mail: cdesmet@dcs.wisc.edu.

Web site: www.dcs.wisc.edu/lsa/writing.

WISCONSIN REGIONAL WRITERS ASSOCIATION FALL CONFERENCE

Oshkosh, Wis., September.

Details: Co-sponsored with the Wisconsin Fellowship of Poets.

Contact: Don Derozier, 2491 Security Dr., Oshkosh, WI 54904.

E-mail: dbderozier@cs.com. Web site: www.wrwa.net.

WISCONSIN REGIONAL WRITERS SPRING CONFERENCE

Milwaukee, Wis., May.

Details: Includes breakout sessions with practical applications of writing and publishing strategies. A book fair and publishers' tables complement the program.

Contact: Don Derozier, 2491 Security Dr., Oshkosh, WI 54904.

E-mail: dbderozier@cs.com. Web site: www.wrwa.com.

WRITE-BY-THE-LAKE WRITER'S WORKSHOP & RETREAT

Madison, Wis., June.

Details: Each section limited to 15: Poetry, Fiction/Plotting, Fiction/Character, Writing from Your Life, Screenwriting, Unleashing Your Creativity, Writing the Modern Mystery or Thriller, and Building Blocks of Children's Literature.

Contact: Christine DeSmet, 610 Langdon St., Rm. 621, Madison, WI 53703. 608-262-3447.

E-mail: cdesmet@dcs.wisc.edu.

Web site: www.dcs.wisc.edu/lsa/writing.

WRITING A SUCCESSFUL SCREENPLAY

Madison, Wis., March.

Details: Learn how to write a screenplay that gets attention from producers, agents, actors, or studios. Covers tips for better characterization, dialogue, story concepts, structure, cinematic value, and formatting.

Contact: University of Wisconsin-Madison, Liberal Studies & the Arts, 610 Langdon St., Rm. 616, Lowell Center, Madison, WI 53703. 608-262-3447.

E-mail: cdesmet@dcs.wisc.edu.

Web site: www.dcs.wisc.edu/lsa/writing.

WYOMING

JACKSON HOLE WRITERS CONFERENCE

Jackson, Wyo., June.

Details: Offers programs relevant to fiction, screenwriting, and creative nonfiction. Topics include story structure, narrative thrust, character development, work habits, and business techniques.

Contact: University of Wyoming, P.O. Box 3972, Laramie, WY 82071. 877-733-3618.

E-mail: kguille@uwyo.edu.

Web site: www.jacksonholewriters.org.

CANADA

BLOODY WORDS

Ottawa, Ont., June.

Details: Covers the mystery genre. Panels, discussions, readings, workshops, and banquet.

Contact: Barbara Fradkin, 40 Glendenning Dr., Nepean, ON, K2H 7Y9, Canada. 613-238-2583.

E-mail: prime.crime@rogers.com.

Web site: www.bloodywords.com.

DYNAMICS OF THE DRAMATIC STRUCTURE

Quebec, Canada, April, March, July.

Details: Intensive five-day conference on dramatic structure. Work-in-progress is not essential, but a detailed synopsis or treatment (for screenplays) is a prerequisite to attend.

Contact: Micheline Cote, The Writers Retreat, 15 Canusa St., Stanstead, Quebec, J0B 3E5, Canada. 819-876-2065.

E-mail: info@writersretreat.com.

Web site: www.writersretreat.com/workshops.htm.

SCREENWRITING DYNAMICS

Quebec, Canada, July, October.

Details: Intensive five-day conference teaching the techniques for developing screenplays into marketable property. Covers current industry practices and formats, the requisite elements of the screenplay, and the techniques of successful screenwriters.

Contact: Micheline Cote, The Writers Retreat, 15 Canusa St., Stanstead, Quebec, J0B 3E5, Canada. 819-876-2065.

E-mail: info@writersretreat.com.

Web site: www.writersretreat.com/workshops.htm.

SELF-EDITING FOR PUBLICATION

Quebec, Canada, June, April, August, October.

Details: Five-day conference featuring one-on-one editorial consultation of work-in-progress, manuscript critique, readings, writing/editing sessions, instruction and discussion.

Contact: Micheline Cote, The Writers Retreat, 15 Canusa St., Stanstead, Quebec, J0B 3E5, Canada. 819-876-2065.

E-mail: info@writersretreat.com.

Web site: www.writersretreat.com/workshops.htm.

STORY REALIZATION

Quebec, Canada, June, August, November.

Details: Five-day conference featuring tips on how to pitch an editor or agent in a conference setting. Morning sessions of formal instruction, discussion, and feedback; afternoons of group readings and private writing time.

Contact: Micheline Cote, The Writers Retreat, 15 Canusa St., Stanstead, Quebec, J0B 3E5, Canada. 819-876-2065.

E-mail: info@writersretreat.com.

Web site: www.writersretreat.com/workshops.htm.

THE MANULIFE FINANCIAL LITERARY ARTS FESTIVAL

Victoria, British Columbia, May.

Details: Features the newest and best voices in contemporary fiction and poetry. Presents 20 authors in readings, on-stage discussions, interviews, and Q&A.

Contact: Rainbow Wilson, P.O. Box 8606, Victoria, BC, V8W 3S2, Canada. 250-381-6722.

E-mail: literary@writeme.com.

Web site: www.literaryartsfestival.org.

WRITING WITH STYLE

Banff, Alberta, April, September.

Details: Week-long workshop for writers of all levels. Writers are given the opportunity to edit and shape a ms. under the guidance of an experienced writer/editor.

Contact: Office of the Registrar, The Banff Centre, Box 1020, 107 Tunnel Mountain Rd. Banff, AB, T1L 1H5, Canada. 800-565-9989.
E-mail: arts_info@banffcentre.ca.
Web site: www.banffcentre.ca.

MEXICO

ART WORKSHOP INTERNATIONAL
Oaxaca City, Mexico, February/March
Puerto Escondido, Mexico, March.
Details: Courses include fiction, nonfiction, poetry, memoir, playwriting, visual arts, and art history.
Contact: 463 West St., 1028H, New York, NY 10014. 212-691-1159.
E-mail: bk@artworkshopintl.com.
Web site: www.artworkshopintl.com.

CREATIVE WRITING & YOGA RETREAT
Yelapa, Mexico, February.
Details: Writing and yoga on Yelepa Bay.
Contact: Patricia Lee Lewis, Patchwork Farm Retreat, 292 Chesterfield Rd., Westhampton, MA 01027. 413-527-5819.
E-mail: patricia@writingretreats.org.
Web site: www.writingretreats.org.

DYNAMICS OF THE DRAMATIC STRUCTURE
Zihuatanejo, Guerrero, Mexico, February.
Details: Intensive five-day conference on dramatic structure. Work-in-progress is not essential, but a detailed synopsis or treatment (for screenplays) is a prerequisite to attend.
Contact: Micheline Cote, The Writers Retreat, 15 Canusa St., Stanstead, Quebec, J0B 3E5, Canada. 819-876-2065.
E-mail: info@writersretreat.com.
Web site: www.writersretreat.com/workshops.htm.

SAN MIGUEL POETRY WEEK
San Miguel de Allende, Mexico, January.
Details: An intimate poetry conference which includes U.S., British, and Mexican poets. The conference consists of workshops, readings, and poetry classes.
Contact: Barbara Sibley, P.O. Box 171, Cooper Station, New York, NY 10276. 212-439-5104.
E-mail: info@sanmiguelpoetry.com.
Web site: www.sanmiguelpoetry.com.

SCREENWRITING DYNAMICS

Zihuatanejo, Guerrero, Mexico, March.

Details: Intensive five-day conference teaching: the techniques for developing screenplays into marketable property. Covers industry practices and formats, screenplay elements, and successful screenwriting tips.

Contact: Micheline Cote, The Writers Retreat, 15 Canusa St., Stanstead, Quebec, J0B 3E5, Canada. 819-876-2065.

E-mail: info@writersretreat.com.

Web site: www.writersretreat.com/workshops.htm.

SELF-EDITING FOR PUBLICATION

Zihuatanejo, Guerrero, Mexico, January.

Details: Five-day conference featuring one-on-one editorial consultation of work-in-progress, manuscript critique, readings, writing/editing sessions, instruction, and discussion.

Contact: Micheline Cote, The Writers Retreat, 15 Canusa St., Stanstead, Quebec, J0B 3E5, Canada. 819-876-2065.

E-mail: info@writersretreat.com.

Web site: www.writersretreat.com/workshops.htm.

CONTESTS & AWARDS

Writers seeking the thrill of competition should review this list of literary prize offers, many designed to promote the as-yet-unpublished author. Most of the competitions listed here are for unpublished manuscripts and usually offer publication in addition to a cash prize. The prestige that comes with winning one of the more established awards can do much to further a writer's career, as editors, publishers, and agents are likely to consider the future work of the prize winner more closely.

There are hundreds of literary contests open to writers in all genres, and the following list covers a representative number of them. The summaries given below are intended merely as guides; since submission requirements are more detailed than space allows, writers should send an SASE for complete guidelines before entering any contest. Writers are also advised to check the monthly "Prize Offerings" column of *The Writer* magazine (Kalmbach Publishing Co., 21027 Crossroads Circle, P.O. Box 1612, Waukesha, WI 53187-1612) for additional contest listings and up-to-date contest requirements. Deadlines are annual unless otherwise noted.

AKRON POETRY PRIZE

University of Akron Press
374 B Bierce Library, Akron, OH 44325-1703. 330-972-6896.
E-mail: uapress@uakron.edu. Web site: www3.uakron.edu/uapress. **Details:** Offered annually for a collection of poems, 60-100 pages. Include list of previously published poems. **Submission Period:** May 15-June 30. **Entry Fee:** $25/submission. **Prizes:** $1,000 and publication.

WARREN ALDER FICTION AWARD

Wyoming Arts Council
2320 Capitol Ave., Cheyenne, WY 82002. 307-777-7742.
E-mail: mshay@state.wy.us. Web site: http://wyoarts.state.wy.us. **Details:** Honors the best short story. **Deadline:** November 3. **Prizes:** $1,000. **Contact:** Michael Shay, Literature Program Manager.

NELSON ALGREN AWARDS FOR SHORT FICTION

Chicago Tribune
435 N Michigan Ave., Fl. 5, Chicago, IL 60611.
Details: A first prize of $5,000, and three runner-up prizes of $1,000, for outstanding unpublished short stories, 2,500-10,000 words, by American writers. **Submission Period:** November 1-January 31.

ALLIGATOR JUNIPER'S NATIONAL WRITING CONTEST

Alligator Juniper
Prescott College, 301 Grove Ave., Prescott, AZ 86301. 928-778-2090.
E-mail: aj@prescott.edu. Web site: www.prescott.edu/highlights/aj.html.
Details: Open to previously unpublished short fiction, creative nonfiction, and poetry. Stories and essays can be up to 30 pages; poetry up to five poems or five pages. See

Web site for specific guidelines. Entrants are required to agree to all submission guidelines in order for work to be considered. **Submission Period:** May 1-October 1. **Entry Fee:** $10/entry. **Prizes:** $500 and publication. **Contact:** Melanie Bishop.

AMERICAN MARKETS NEWSLETTER COMPETITION

American Markets Newsletter, 1974 46th Ave., San Francisco, CA 94116.
Details: Fiction and nonfiction to 2,000 words, both published and unpublished. All entries will be considered for worldwide syndication. **Deadline:** July 31 and December 31. **Entry Fee:** AMN subscribers, $6 /1 entry, $9 /2 entries, $12/3 entries; non subscribers, $7.50/entry. **Prizes:** $250, $50, $30.

ANHINGA PRIZE FOR POETRY

Anhinga Press, P.O. Box 10595, Tallahassee, FL 32302-0595. 850-521-9920.
E-mail: info@anhinga.org. Web site: www.anhinga.org. **Details:** Offered annually to an unpublished full-length collection of poetry, 48-72 pages, by a poet who has published no more than one full-length collection. **Submission Period:** February 15-May 1. **Entry Fee:** $20. **Prizes:** $2,000 and publication.

ARTS AWARDS

National Foundation for Advancement in the Arts
800 Brickell Ave., Suite 500, Miami, FL 33131. 1-800-970-2787.
E-mail: info@nfaa.org. Web site: www.artsawards.org. **Details:** Identifies young artists—high school seniors or 17-18 years of age—in the disciplines of dance, film and video, classical, pop and jazz music, photography, theater, visual arts, voice, and writing, for scholarships and financial support toward their continued arts education. See Web site for more details. **Deadline:** November 1. **Entry Fee:** Before June 2: $25 online, $30 by mail. After June 2: $35 on-line, $40 by mail. **Prizes:** $10,000, $3,000, $1,500, $1,000, $500, $100.

ASF TRANSLATION PRIZE

American-Scandinavian Foundation
58 Park Ave., New York, NY 10016. 212-879-9779.
E-mail: ahenkin@amscan.org. Web site: www.amscan.org. **Details:** Translations of literary prose (50+ pages) or poetry (25+ pages) originally written after 1800 in Danish, Finnish, Icelandic, Norwegian, or Swedish. Send SASE or e-mail for guidelines. **Deadline:** June 1. **Prizes:** $2,000, publication in *Scandinavian Review*, and bronze medallion. **Contact:** Audrey Henkin.

THE AUSTIN FILM FESTIVAL SCREENWRITERS COMPETITION

Austin Film Festival, 1604 Nueces St., Austin, TX 78701-1106. 512-478-4795.
E-mail: austinfilm@aol.com. Web site: www.austinfilmfestival.com. **Details:** Offers two first prizes for unpublished screenplays in the Adult/Family category and the Comedy category. **Deadline:** May 15. **Entry Fee:** $40. **Prizes:** $5,000, reimbursement of travel expenses, the AFF Bronze Typewriter award, and admission to the Film Festival and Heart of Film Screenwriters Conference.

AUTHORS IN THE PARK SHORT STORY CONTEST

P.O. Box 85, Winter Park, FL 32790-0085.
E-mail: foley@magicnet.net. **Details:** Offers three monetary prizes ($1,000, $500, and $250) and publication in *Fine Print* for short stories written in English up to 5,000 words. E-mail or send SASE for guidelines. **Deadline:** April 30.

AWP AWARD SERIES

Associated Writing Programs, Tallwood House
Mail Stop 1E3, George Mason University, Fairfax, VA 22030. 703-993-4301.
E-mail: awo@gmu.edu. Web site: www.awpwriter.org. **Details:** Open to all authors writing in English. Only book-length manuscripts are eligible: for poetry, 48 pages minimum text; short story collections and creative nonfiction, 150-300 manuscript pages; novels at least 60,000 words. Send SASE for guidelines. **Submission Period:** January 1-February 28. **Entry Fee:** $20 ($10 for AWP members). **Prizes:** $10,000 advance against earnings for novel; $2,000 honorarium for poetry, short fiction, and nonfiction. **Contact:** Katherine Perry.

MURIEL CRAFT BAILEY MEMORIAL AWARD

Comstock Review, 4956 St. John Dr., Syracuse, NY 13215.
Web site: www.comstockreview.org. **Details:** For a single poem, up to 40 lines. **Deadline:** July 1. **Entry Fee:** $3. **Prizes:** $1,000, $250, $100.

BARNARD NEW WOMEN POETS PRIZE

Barnard College, Dept. of English, 3009 Broadway, New York, NY 10027-6598.
E-mail: jdidonato@hotmail.com. **Details:** Honors a book of poems by a female poet who has already published one book of poetry. **Deadline:** October 15. **Entry Fee:** $20. **Prizes:** $1,500 and publication by W.W. Norton & Co. **Contact:** Jill Di Donato.

BARROW STREET PRESS BOOK CONTEST

Barrow Street Press, Old Chelsea Station, P.O. Box 1831, New York, NY 10156.
E-mail: info@barrowstreet.org. Web site: www.barrowstreet.org. **Details:** For the best previously unpublished poetry manuscript (50-70 pages) in English. **Deadline:** July 1. **Entry Fee:** $25. **Prizes:** $1,000 and publication by Barrow Street Press.

BATTLE OF THE BARDS POETRY CONTEST

WriteLink, The Competition Secretary
7 Melbourne Road, Newbold, Coleorton, Leicestershire LE67 8JH, UK.
E-mail: sue@writelink.co.uk. Web site: www.writelink.co.uk. **Details:** On-line poetry contest designed to put an end to procrastination: theme and word count are provided with 24 hours to complete the entry. Limited to 100 competitors; e-mail entries only. **Deadline:** May 17. **Entry Fee:** £4.50 or $8. **Prizes:** £50 for winner and £25 each for two runners up.

THE BEATRICE HAWLEY AWARD
Alice James Books
University of Maine at Farmington, 238 Main St., Farmington, ME 04938.
207-778-7071. E-mail: ajb@umf.maine.edu. Web site: www.alicejamesbooks.org.
Details: Open to poetry manuscripts 50-70 pages. Include TOC and list of acknowledgments for previously published poems with submission. See Web site for detailed guidelines. **Deadline:** December 1. **Entry Fee:** $20. **Prizes:** $2,000 and publication by Alice James Books.

ELINOR BENEDICT POETRY PRIZE
Passages North
Northern Michigan University, 1401 Presque Isle Ave., Marquette, MI 49855.
906-227-1203. E-mail: passages@nmu.edu. **Details:** Poetry contest offered in even-numbered years. **Deadline:** February 15. **Entry Fee:** $4 for first two poems; $3 for each additional poem. **Prizes:** $500.

BEVERLY HILLS THEATRE GUILD
PLAYS FOR CHILDREN'S THEATRE COMPETITION
Beverly Hills Theatre Guild, 2815 N Beachwood Dr., Los Angeles, CA 90068-1923.
323-465-2703. **Details:** Open to plays suitable for kids in grades 6-8 or grades 9-12.
Material should be 45-75 minutes long. **Submission Period:** January 15-February 28. **Prizes:** $500, $300, and $200.

NELTJE BLANCHAN MEMORIAL AWARD
Wyoming Arts Council
2320 Capitol Ave., Cheyenne, WY 82002. 307-777-7742.
E-mail: mshay@state.wy.us. Web site: http://wyoarts.state.wy.us. **Details:** Honors a writer whose work is insprired by nature. Any genre. **Deadline:** August 1. **Prizes:** $1,000. **Contact:** Michael Shay, Literature Program Manager.

THE BLUESTEM POETRY AWARD
Emporia State University, English Dept., Emporia, KS 66801-5087. 620-341-5216.
E-mail: bluestem@emporia.edu. Web site: www.emporia.edu/bluestem/. **Details:** Open to U.S. authors. Submit a previously unpublished book of poems at least 48 pages, written in English. **Deadline:** March 1. **Entry Fee:** $18. **Prizes:** $1,000 and publication. **Contact:** Philip Heldrich, Director.

BOSTON REVIEW POETRY CONTEST
Boston Review, MIT, 30 Wadsworth St., E53, Room 407, Cambridge, MA 02139.
617-253-3642. Web site: www.bostonreview.net. **Details:** Annual poetry contest for original, unpublished poems. Submit up to five poems, no more than 10 pages.
Deadline: June 1. **Entry Fee:** $15. **Prizes:** $1,000 and publication in *Boston Review*.

BOSTON REVIEW SHORT STORY CONTEST

Boston Review, MIT, 30 Wadsworth St., E53-407 Room 407, Cambridge, MA 02139. 617-494-0708. Web site: www.bostonreview.net. **Details:** Annual fiction contest for previously unpublished short stories up to 4,000 words. **Deadline:** October 1. **Entry Fee:** $20. **Prizes:** $1,000 and publication in *Boston Review*.

BARBARA BRADLEY AWARD

New England Poetry Club, 11 Puritan Rd., Arlington, MA 02476-7710. E-mail: info@nepoetryclub.org. Web site: www.nepoetryclub.org. **Details:** Open to female poets; submit an unpublished lyric poem under 21 lines. Entrants may submit up to three entries total out of all the contests sponsored by NEPC, but no more than one poem per contest. Send SASE or see Web site for specific guidelines and fees. **Submission Period:** April 1-June 30. **Entry Fee:** Free for members; $10 for non-members. **Prizes:** $200. **Contact:** Virginia Thayer.

JOSEPH E. BRODINE/BRODINSKY POETRY CONTEST

Connecticut Poetry Society, P.O. Box 4053, Waterbury, CT 06704 0053. 203-753-7815. E-mail: wtarzia@nvctc5comment.edu. Web site: http://hometown.aol.com/ctpoetrysociety. **Details:** Original, unpublished poetry up to 40 lines. Maximum five poems/contest. Identify each submission as Brodine/Brodinsky Contest. All entries will be considered for publication unless "For Contest Only" is marked on submission. Does not accept simultaneous submissions. **Deadline:** July 31. **Entry Fee:** $2/poem. **Prizes:** Three monetary prizes ($150, $100, $50) and publication in *Connecticut River Review*.

ROBERT BURNS POETRY AWARD/
TERRY SEMPLE MEMORIAL CONTEST

Knoxville Writers' Guild, P.O. Box 10326, Knoxville, TN 37939. E-mail: m.boyanton@att.net. Web site: www.knoxvillewritersguild.org. **Details:** Open to Tennessee residents 18 years of age or older. Submit up to three poems/entry on the subject of heritage, ancestry, ethnicity, community, or discovery of self. **Deadline:** December 15. **Entry Fee:** $15/entry; KWG members may submit first three poems for free, $15 for each additional entry (set of two) thereafter. **Prizes:** $200 and free admission to the Scottish Society of Knoxville's Robert Burns Night Celebration. **Contact:** Marybeth Boyanton, Director.

HAYDEN CARRUTH AWARDS

Copper Canyon Press, P.O. Box 271, Port Townsend, WA 98368. 360-385-4925. E-mail: poetry@coppercanyonpress.org. Web site: www.coppercanyonpress.org. **Details:** Prize for new and emerging poets in honor of Hayden Carruth. Open to writers who have published no more than two books of poetry. Manuscripts should be 46-150 pages. **Submission Period:** November 1-November 30. **Entry Fee:** $25. **Prizes:** $1,000, publication by Copper Canyon Press, and one-month residency at the Vermont Studio Center.

CHELSEA AWARDS

P.O. Box 773, Cooper Station, New York, NY 10276-0773.
Details: Awards for Fiction and Poetry. Traditional and experimental fiction, previously unpublished, up to 30 typed pages or 7,500 words. Collection of 4-6 poems, not to exceed 500 lines. Focus is on quality and fresh, original use of language. Send SASE for guidelines. **Deadline:** June 15 (fiction), December 15 (poetry). **Entry Fee:** $10. **Prizes:** $1,000 each and publication in *Chelsea*.

THE CHESTERFIELD WRITER'S FILM PROJECT

Chesterfield Film Co.
PMB 544, 1158 26th St., Santa Monica, CA 90403. 213-683-3977.
E-mail: info@chesterfield-co.com. Web site: www.chesterfield-co.com. **Details:** Offers a $20,000 fellowship for fiction, theatre, and film writers who are pursuing a career in screenwriting. Five writers are chosen each year based on prose and dramatic writing samples. **Deadline:** June 21. **Entry Fee:** $39.50.

CHICAGO LITERARY AWARDS

Another Chicago Magazine, 3709 N Kenmore, Chicago, IL 60613.
Details: Submit a short story up to 6,500 words or up to three poems no more than 300 lines. **Deadline:** December 15. **Entry Fee:** $10. **Prizes:** $1,000 and publication in *Another Chicago Magazine*.

DOROTHY CHURCHILL CAPPON CREATIVE NONFICTION PRIZE

New Letters, University of Missouri-Kansas
University House, 5101 Rockhill Rd., Kansas City, MO 64110. 816-235-1168.
E-mail: newletters@umkc.edu. Web site: www.umkc.edu/newletters. **Details:** Offers $1,000 and publication for the best expository nonfiction. **Deadline:** May 15. **Entry Fee:** $10.

CNW/FFWA FLORIDA STATE WRITING COMPETITION

Florida Freelance Writers Assn., P.O. Box A, North Stratford, NH 03590.
603-922-8338. Web site: www.writers-editors.com. **Details:** Contest open to all writers. Categories include fiction, nonfiction, children's and poetry. Send SASE for guidelines and entry form, or visit Web site. **Deadline:** March 15. **Entry Fee:** $5-$20. **Prizes:** $50-$100. **Contact:** Dana K. Cassell.

COLORADO PRIZE FOR POETRY

Colorado Review, Colorado State University,
Dept. of English, Fort Collins, CO 80523. 970-491-5449.
E-mail: creview@colostate.edu. Web site: www.coloradoreview.com. **Details:** A prize of $1,500, plus publication, for a book-length collection of original poems. See Web site or send SASE for guidelines. **Deadline:** January 13. **Entry Fee:** $25 (includes subscription to *Colorado Review*).

THE COLUMBINE AWARDS
Moondance International Film Festival, 6472 Robin Dr., Niwot, CO 80503.
E-mail: contest@moondancefilmfestival.com.
Web site: www.moondancefilmfestival.com. **Details:** Open to writers of feature screenplays that display a non-violent resolution to conflict. See Web site for details. **Deadline:** January 31. **Entry Fee:** $25-$75.

THE COMSTOCK REVIEW ANNUAL POETRY CONTEST
The Comstock Review, 4956 St. John Dr., Syracuse, NY 13215.
Web site: www.comstockreview.org. **Details:** Submit original, unpublished poems.
Deadline: July 1. **Entry Fee:** $3/poem. **Prizes:** $1,000, $250, and $100.

CONNECTICUT RIVER REVIEW POETRY CONTEST
Connecticut Poetry Society
P.O. Box 4053, Waterbury, CT 06704-0053. 203-753-7815.
E-mail: editorcrr@yahoo.com (for queries only). **Details:** Submit up to three poems, 40 lines max. Include two copies (only one with contact info) and SASE for results. No e-mail submissions **Submission Period:** December 1-March 1. **Entry Fee:** $10. **Prizes:** 3 monetary prizes ($25, $50, and $100) and publication in *Connecticut River Review*.

THE CONTEMPORARY POETRY SERIES
University of Georgia Press
330 Research Dr., Athens, GA 30602-4901. 706-369-6130.
E-mail: books@ugapress.uga.edu. Web site: www.ugapress.org. **Details:** Four books of poetry are selected each year for publication by both emerging and established poets. Manuscripts must be at least 50 pages. **Submission Period:** Poets who have not published a full-length collection must submit during the month of September. Poets who have published at least one full-length collection must submit during the month of January. **Entry Fee:** $20. **Prizes:** Publication by the University of Georgia Press.

CSU POETRY CENTER PRIZES
Cleveland State University
2121 Euclid Ave., Cleveland, OH 44115-2214. 216-687-3986.
E-mail: poetrycenter@csuohio.edu. Web site: www.csuohio.edu/poetrycenter.
Details: Award of $1,000 and publication for a previously unpublished book-length volume of poetry in two categories: First Book and Open Competition (for poets who have published a collection of at least 48 pages with a press run of at least 500).
Deadline: February 1. **Entry Fee:** $20.

JANE CUNNINGHAM CROLY/
GFWC PRINT JOURNALISM CONTEST
General Federation of Women's Clubs
1734 N St. NW, Washington, DC 20036. 202-347-3168.

E-mail: skranz@gfwc.org. Web site: www.gfwc.org. **Details:** Award offered for excellence in covering issues of concern to women. Submit three stories published in 2002 that demonstrate a concern for the rights and advancement of women, an awareness of women's sensitivity and strength, and/or an attempt to counteract sexism. **Deadline:** March 3. **Entry Fee:** $50. **Prizes:** $1,000. **Contact:** Sally Kranz.

A CUP OF COMFORT FOR COURAGE

Adams Media Corporation, 57 Littlefield St., Avon, MA 02322. 800-872-5627. E-mail: cupofcomfort@adamsmedia.com. Web site: www.cupofcomfort.com. **Details:** Submit narrative essays or creative nonfiction, 1,000-2,000 words. Positive and poignant stories about extraordinary acts of heroism, people who are heroes of their own lives or in the lives of others, and facing life's challenges with courage, dignity, and inner strength. **Deadline:** May 1. **Prizes:** $100, $500, and publication.

A CUP OF COMFORT FOR INSPIRATION

Adams Media Corporation, 57 Littlefield St., Avon, MA 02322. 800-872-5627. E-mail: cupofcomfort@adamsmedia.com. Web site: www.cupofcomfort.com. **Details:** Submit narrative essays or creative nonfiction, 1,000-2,000 words. Soul-stirring stories about inspiring people and enlightening experiences. Possible themes include (but are not limited to): triumph over tragedy; grace under fire; significant doing for others; making dreams come true; making a difference; affecting positive change; surviving and/or thriving in the face of serious illness. **Deadline:** April 1. **Prizes:** $100, $500, and publication.

A CUP OF COMFORT FOR SISTERS

Adams Media Corporation, 57 Littlefield St., Avon, MA 02322. 800-872-5627. E-mail: cupofcomfort@adamsmedia.com. Web site: www.cupofcomfort.com. **Details:** Submit narrative essays or creative nonfiction, 1,000-2,000 words. Uplifting true stories celebrating the unique bond shared by sisters—the blessings sisters share, the bridging of distance sisters can have, and the extraordinary acts of kindness and support sisters have together. **Deadline:** June 1. **Prizes:** $100, $500, and publication.

A CUP OF COMFORT FOR TEACHERS

Adams Media Corporation, 57 Littlefield St., Avon, MA 02322. 800-872-5627. E-mail: cupofcomfort@adamsmedia.com. Web site: www.cupofcomfort.com. **Details:** Submit narrative essays or creative nonfiction, 1,000-2,000 words. Heartwarming stories that honor exceptional teachers and mentors, celebrate the joys and rewards of teaching, or honor dedicated teachers overcoming challenges and helping difficult students. **Deadline:** May 1. **Prizes:** $100, $500, and publication.

DOROTHY DANIELS HONORARY WRITING AWARDS

National League of American Pen Women
P.O. Box 1485, Simi Valley, CA 93062. 805-493-1081.
E-mail: cdoering@adelphia.net. **Prizes:** $100 in three categories. **Details:** Original,

unpublished poetry to 50 lines, fiction to 2,000 words and nonfiction to 1,500 words. **Deadline:** July 31. **Entry Fee:** $5/poem or $5/fiction or nonfiction entry.

EDWARD DAVIN VICKERS POETRY CONTEST

Georgia Poetry Society, 3822 Clubhouse Place, Gainesville, GA 30501. 770-531-9473. **Details:** Original, unpublished poetry. 80 lines maximum. Send two copies of each poem with contest name in upper right-hand corner, entry name and address on one copy only. **Deadline:** July 15. **Entry Fee:** $5 for one poem, $1 for each additional poem. **Prizes:** $250, $100, and $50.

MARGUERITE DE ANGELI CONTEST

Delacorte Press/Random House, Inc., 1745 Broadway, New York, NY 10019. Web site: www.randomhouse.com/kids. **Details:** Contemporary or historical fiction manuscripts, 80-144 pages for readers ages 7-10. Open to U.S. and Canadian writers who have not previously published a novel for middle-grade readers. **Submission Period:** April 1-June 30. **Prizes:** $1,500 cash, book contract for hardcover and paperback edition, and $7,500 advance.

DELACORTE PRESS
CONTEST FOR A FIRST YOUNG ADULT NOVEL

Delacorte Press/Random House, Inc., 1745 Broadway, Fl. 9, New York, NY 10019. Web site: www.randomhouse.com/kids. **Details:** Open to writers who have not previously published a YA novel. Submit a book-length manuscript with a contemporary setting, for readers ages 12-18. **Deadline:** December 31. **Prizes:** $1,500, book contract for hardcover and paperback edition, and $6,000 advance.

DER-HOVANESSIAN PRIZE

New England Poetry Club, 11 Puritan Rd., Arlington, MA 02476-7710. E-mail: info@nepoetryclub.org. Web site: www.nepoetryclub.org. **Details:** Open to unpublished translations from any language. Send copy of original with submission. Entrants may submit up to 3 entries total out of all the contests sponsored by NEPC, but no more than 1 poem per contest. Send SASE or see Web site for specific guidelines and fees. **Submission Period:** April 1-June 30. **Entry Fee:** Free to members; $10 for non-members. **Prizes:** $100. **Contact:** Virginia Thayer.

ANNIE DILLARD AWARD FOR NONFICTION

Bellingham Review
Mail Stop 9053, Western Washington University, Bellingham, WA 98225. Web site: www.wwu.edu/~bhreview. **Details:** Open to nonfiction essays on any topic and in any style, up to 10,000 words. **Submission Period:** December 1-March 15. **Entry Fee:** $15 for first entry; $10 for each additional entry. **Prizes:** $1,000 and publication in *Bellingham Review*.

THE DOLPHIN AWARDS

Moondance International Film Festival, 6472 Robin Dr., Niwot, CO 80503.
E-mail: contest@moondancefilmfestival.com.
Web site: www.moondancefilmfestival.com. **Details:** Open to. children and young adults who are 18 years of age or younger. This category accepts short narratives and short screenplays. **Deadline:** January 31. **Entry Fee:** $25-$75.

DAVID DORNSTEIN MEMORIAL
CREATIVE WRITING CONTEST FOR YOUNG ADULT WRITERS

Coalition for the Advancement of Jewish Education
261 W 35th St., Fl. 12A, New York, NY 10001. 212-268-4210.
E-mail: cajeny@caje.org. Web site: www.caje.org. **Details:** Offered annually to authors ages 18-35. Submit original, previously unpublished short stories, no more than 5,000 words, on a Jewish theme or topic. **Deadline:** December 31. **Prizes:** Three monetary prizes ($700, $200, $100) and publication in the *CAJE Jewish Education News*.

FRANK DOUBLEDAY MEMORIAL AWARD

Wyoming Arts Council
2320 Capitol Ave., Cheyenne, WY 82002. 307-777-7742.
E-mail: mshay@state.wy.us. Web site: http://wyoarts.state.wy.us. **Details:** Honors a woman writer of exceptional talent in any creative writing genre. **Deadline:** August 1. **Prizes:** $1,000. **Contact:** Michael Shay, Literature Program Manager.

DRURY UNIVERSITY PLAYWRITING CONTEST

900 N Benton Ave., Springfield, MO 65802. 417-873-6821.
E-mail: msokol@drury.edu. **Details:** Prizes of $300 and two $150 honorable mentions, plus possible production (Open Eye Theatre), for original, previously unproduced one-act plays. **Deadline:** December 1. **Contact:** Mick Sokol, Assistant Professor of Theatre.

DUBUQUE FINE ARTS PLAYERS
ONE-ACT PLAYWRITING CONTEST

1686 Lawndale Dr., Dubuque, IA 52001. 563-582-5502.
E-mail: garms@clarke.edu. **Details:** Open to original one-act plays up to 40 minutes. **Deadline:** January 31. **Entry Fee:** $10. **Prizes:** Three monetary prizes of $600, $300, and $200, plus full production of all winning scripts.

SUE SANIEL ELKIND POETRY CONTEST

Kalliope, FCCJ-South Campus, 11901 Beach Blvd., Jacksonville, FL 32246. 904-646-2081. Web site: www.fccj.org/kalliope. **Details:** Poetry, any style, any subject. Entrants may submit unlimited number of poems, but no longer than 50 lines/poem. **Deadline:** November 1. **Entry Fee:** $4/poem, or $10 for three poems. **Prizes:** $1,000 and publication in *Kalliope*.

EVENT CREATIVE NONFICTION CONTEST

P.O. Box 2503, New Westminister, British Columbia V3L 5B2 Canada. 604-527-5293.
E-mail: event@douglas.bc.ca. Web site: http://event.douglas.bc.ca. **Details:** Previously
unpublished creative nonfiction up to 5,000 words. **Deadline:** April 15. **Entry Fee:**
$25 (includes subscription to *Event* magazine). **Prizes:** Three $500 prizes and publication.

WILLIAM FAULKNER CREATIVE WRITING COMPETITION

Pirate's Alley Faulkner Society
Faulkner House, 624 Pirate's Alley, New Orleans, LA 70116. 504-586-1609.
E-mail: faulkhouse@aol.com. Web site: www.wordsandmusic.org. **Details:**
Unpublished works of fiction, nonfiction, or poetry. Send SASE or see Web site for
guidelines and entry form. **Deadline:** April 30. **Entry Fee:** $10-$35. **Prizes:** $250-
$7,500.

FELLOWSHIPS FOR HISTORICAL RESEARCH
BY CREATIVE AND PERFORMING ARTISTS AND WRITERS

American Antiquarian Society
James David Moran, 185 Salisbury St., Worcester, MA 01609-1634. 508-471-2131.
E-mail: jmoran@mwa.org. Web site: www.americanantiquarian.org.
Details: At least three fellowships, for creative and performing artists, writers, film-
makers, and journalists, for research on pre-20th century American history.
Residencies 4-8 weeks; travel expenses and stipends of $1,200 per month. Write for
guidelines. **Deadline:** October 5.

FICTION FELLOWSHIPS COMPETITION

Heekin Group Foundation, Box 1534, Sisters, OR 97759.
Details: Awards fellowships to beginning career writers: two $1,500 Tara Fellowships
in Short Fiction; two $3,000 James Fellowships for Novel in Progress; a $2,000 Mary
Molloy Fellowship for Juvenile Novel in Progress (address H.G.F., P.O. Box 209,
Middlebury, VT 05753); and a $2,000 Cuchulain Fellowhip for Rhetoric (Essay).
Writers who have never published a novel, a children's novel, more than five short sto-
ries in national publication, or an essay are eligible to enter. **Deadline:** December 1.

FICTION OPEN

Glimmer Train Press, Inc.
710 SW Madison St., Suite 504, Portland, OR 97205. 503-221-0836.
E-mail: info@glimmertrain.com. Web site: www.glimmertrain.com.
Details: Contest for short fiction of any length on any theme. All stories must be submitted on-line; see Web site for specific submission guidelines. **Submission Period:**
May 1-June 30, November 1-January 11. **Entry Fee:** $15/story. **Prizes:** 1st place
wins $2,000, publication in *Glimmer Train Stories*, and 20 copies. 2nd place wins
$1,000; 3rd place wins $600.

FIELD POETRY PRIZE
FIELD: Contemporary Poetry and Poetics
Oberlin College Press, 10 N Professor St., Oberlin, OH 44074. 440-775-8408.
E-mail: oc.press@oberlin.edu. Web site: www.oberlin.edu/~ocpress. **Details:**
Unpublished poetry manuscripts of 50-80 pages. See Web site for details. **Entry Fee:**
$22 (includes a 1-year subscription to *FIELD*). **Prizes:** $1,000 and publication.

THE FILM IN ARIZONA SCREENWRITING COMPETITION
Arizona Film Commission
3800 N Central Ave., Suite 1500, Phoenix, AZ 85012. 602-280-1386.
E-mail: wendy@azcommerce.com.
Web site: www.azcommerce.com/azfilmcommission.htm. **Details:** Open to screen-
plays that are set in Arizona and feature the state's landscape and geography.
Deadline: April 15. **Entry Fee:** $30. **Prizes:** $1,000 and meetings with film indus-
try professionals. **Contact:** Wendy Carroll.

FLASH FICTION CONTEST
NLAPW Pikes Peak Branch, 1015 Valley Rd., Colorado Springs, CO 80904.
E-mail: warnerwrit@aol.com. **Details:** Submit a complete story of 100 words or less.
All genres welcome, including contemporary, historical, romance, mystery, sci-fi, hor-
ror, western, adventure, and inspirational. **Deadline:** May 7. **Entry Fee:** $6. **Prizes:**
$60, $25, $15. **Contact:** Marylin Warner.

THE FLORIDA REVIEW EDITOR'S AWARDS
University of Central Florida
Dept. of English, P.O. Box 6222950, Orlando, FL 32816. 407-823-2038.
Web site: http://pegasus.cc.ucf.edu/~english/floridareview. **Details:** Open to unpub-
lished fiction and memoirs to 10,000 words and poetry to 40 lines. **Submission
Period:** January 1-April 2. **Entry Fee:** $12. **Prizes:** Three $1,000 awards.

LESLIE GARRETT FICTION CONTEST
Knoxville Writers' Guild, P.O. Box 10326, Knoxville, TN 37939.
Web site: www.knoxvillewritersguild.org. **Details:** Fiction contest open to Tennessee
residents 18 years of age or older. **Deadline:** January 31. **Prizes:** $250, $150, $100.
Contact: Don Williams.

JOHN GASSNER MEMORIAL PLAYWRITING AWARD
The New England Theatre Conference, Inc.
Northeastern University, 360 Huntington Ave., Boston, MA 02115. 617-424-9275.
E-mail: mail@netconline.org. Web site: www.netconline.org. **Details:** New, unpublished full-length plays that have not been produced by a professional or Equity company. Open to New England residents and NETC members. Guidelines and applications available on Web site. **Deadline:** April 15. **Entry Fee:** $10. **Prizes:** $1,000 and
$500. **Contact:** Tara McCarthy, Director.

ALLEN GINSBERG POETRY AWARDS

Poetry Center at Passaic County Community College
1 College Blvd., Paterson, NJ 07505. 973-684-6555.
Web site: www.pccc.cc.nj.us/poetry. **Details:** Up to five previously unpublished poems, up to two pages each. Send four copies of each entry. Do not submit poems that imitate Allen Ginsberg's work. **Deadline:** April 1. **Entry Fee:** $13. **Prizes:** $1,000, $200, and $100. **Contact:** Maria Mazziotti Gillan.

THE GREAT BLUE BEACON POETRY CONTEST

1425 Patriot Dr., Melbourne, FL 32940.
E-mail: ajircc@juno.com. **Details:** Poetry, any style, up to 24 lines. Send SASE or e-mail to request specific guidelines. **Deadline:** June 20. **Entry Fee:** $3. **Prizes:** $25, $15, $10. **Contact:** Andy J. Byers.

THE GREAT BLUE BEACON SHORT-SHORT STORY CONTEST

1425 Patriot Dr., Melbourne, FL 32940.
E-mail: ajircc@juno.com. **Details:** Submit short fiction, up to 1,000 words. Send SASE or e-mail to request specific guidelines. **Deadline:** June 20. **Entry Fee:** $5. **Prizes:** $50, $25, $10. **Contact:** Andy J. Byers.

GROLIER POETRY PRIZE

6 Plympton St., Cambridge, MA 02138. 617-547-4648.
Web site: www.grolier-poetry.com. **Details:** Poetry manuscripts (up to 10 pages), including no more than five previously unpublished poems, by writers who have not yet published a book of poems. **Deadline:** May 1. **Prizes:** Two $150 honorariums.

GREG GRUMMER POETRY AWARD

Phoebe: A Journal of Literary Arts
George Mason University, 4400 University Dr., Fairfax, VA 22030-4444.
E-mail: phoebe@gmu.edu. **Details:** A prize of $500, plus publication, for an outstanding previously unpublished poem. **Deadline:** December 15. **Entry Fee:** $10.

HACKNEY LITERARY AWARDS

Birmingham-Southern College
P.O. Box 549003, Birmingham, AL 35282-9765. 205-226-4921.
E-mail: dcwilson@bsc.edu. Web site: www.bsc.edu. **Details:** Awards, open to writers nationwide, presented as part of Birmingham-Southern College "Writing Today" Conference. Awards $5,000 in annual prizes for poetry and short fiction (in national and state categories), plus a $5,000 prize for an unpublished novel. Write or request by e-mail for details (include mailing address for guidelines).

MARILYN HALL AWARDS

Beverly Hills Theatre Guild, P.O. Box 39729, Los Angeles, CA 90039-0729.
Details: Awards $200, $300, and $500 for plays for young and adolescent audiences 45-90 minutes in length. Authors must be U.S. citizen or legal resident and may sub-

mit up to two English-written scripts that have not been previously submitted or published. Plays must be original, adaptations, or translations; no musicals. Plays may have had one non-professional or educational theatre production. Send SASE for guidelines. Materials will not be returned. **Submission Period:** January 15-last day of February.

AURAND HARRIS MEMORIAL PLAYWRITING AWARD

The New England Theatre Conference, Inc.
Northeastern University, 360 Huntington Ave., Boston, MA 02115. 617-424-9275.
E-mail: mail@netconline.org. Web site: www.netconline.org. **Details:** New, unpublished full-length plays for young audiences. Open to New England residents and NETC members. Guidelines and applications available on Web site. **Deadline:** May 1. **Entry Fee:** $20. **Prizes:** $1,000 and $500. **Contact:** Tara McCarthy, Director.

JULIE HARRIS PLAYWRIGHT COMPETITION

Beverly Hills Theatre Guild, P.O. Box 39729, Los Angeles, CA 90039-0729.
Details: Annual award for original, full-length play 90 minutes or more. Authors must be U.S. citizen or legal resident and may submit one English-written manuscript that has not been previously submitted, published, or produced. Send SASE for guidelines. **Submission Period:** August 1-November 1. **Prizes:** Three monetary prizes of $5,000, $2,000, and $1,000.

DRUE HEINZ LITERATURE PRIZE

University of Pittsburgh Press
Eureka Building, Fl. 5, 3400 Forbes Ave., Pittsburgh, PA 15260. 412-383-2456.
Web site: www.pitt.edu/~press. **Details:** Short fiction contest open to writers who have published a book-length collection of short fiction or at least three short stories or novellas in a literary or national magazine. Submit manuscripts of 150-300 pages. See Web site for specific guidelines. **Deadline:** May 1-June 30. **Prizes:** $15,000 and publication by University of Pittsburgh Press.

HIGHLIGHTS FOR CHILDREN FICTION CONTEST

Highlights for Children, 803 Church St., Honesdale, PA 18431-1824. 570-253-1080.
Web site: www.highlightsforchildren.com. **Details:** Annual contest with a different theme each year. Open to stories for beginning readers up to 500 words, for more advanced readers up to 800 words. No stories that glorify war, crime, or violence. **Submission Period:** January 1-February 28. **Prizes:** Three prizes of $1000 each and publication in *Highlights*. **Contact:** Marileta Robinson, Senior Editor.

HOLLIS SUMMERS POETRY PRIZE COMPETITION

Ohio University Press, Scott Quadrangle, Athens, OH 45701.
Web site: www.ohiou.edu/oupress. **Details:** Submit unpublished collections of original poems, 60-95 pages. **Deadline:** October 31. **Entry Fee:** $15. **Prizes:** $500 and publication.

THE HOLLYWOOD SCREENPLAY AWARDS

CCS Entertainment Group

433 N Camden Dr., Suite 600, Beverly Hills, CA 90210. 310-288-1881.

E-mail: awards@hollywoodawards.com. Web site: www.hollywoodawards.com.
Details: Selects one unproduced screenplay each month. All selected screenplays
become finalists in the annual contest where first, second, and third place winners are
chosen. **Deadline:** May 30. **Entry Fee:** $55. **Prizes:** Cash prizes ($1,000, $500, and
$250) and opportunity to meet with industry professionals.

JOHN HOLMES AWARD

New England Poetry Club, 11 Puritan Rd., Arlington, MA 02476-7710.

E-mail: info@nepoetryclub.org. Web site: www.nepoetryclub.org. **Details:** Open to
an unpublished poem written by a New England college student. Entrants may submit up to three entries total out of all the contests sponsored by NEPC, but no more
than one poem per contest. Send SASE or see Web site for specific guidelines and
fees. **Submission Period:** April 1-June 30. **Entry Fee:** Free to members; $10 for
non-members. **Prizes:** $100. **Contact·** Virginia Thayer.

FIRMAN HOUGHTON AWARD

New England Poetry Club, 11 Puritan Rd., Arlington, MA 02476-7710.

E-mail: info@nepoetryclub.org. Web site: www.nepoetryclub.org. **Details:** Open to
an unpublished lyric poem in honor of the former NEPC president. Entrants may
submit up to three entries total out of all the contests sponsored by NEPC, but no
more than one poem per contest. Send SASE or see Web site for specific guidelines
and fees. **Submission Period:** April 1-June 30. **Entry Fee:** Free to members; $10
for non-members. **Prizes:** $250. **Contact:** Virginia Thayer.

HUMANITAS PRIZE

17575 Pacific Coast Hwy, P.O. Box 861, Pacific Palisades, CA 90272.

E-mail: humanitasp@aol.com. Web site: www.humanitasprize.org. **Details:** Awards
screenplays and teleplays that emphasize human values. Awards are given in the categories of: 30-minute program; 60-minute program; 90-minute program; PBS/cable;
feature film; Sundance feature; children's live action; children's animation; and documentary. **Deadline:** April 1. **Prizes:** Cash prizes ranging from $10,000-$25,000.

INTERNATIONAL HAIKU CONTEST

NLAPW Palomar Branch, 11929 Caminito Corriente, San Diego, CA 92128.

E-mail: helensherry1@aol.com. **Details:** All proceeds from this contest provide a
scholarship for a student entering college. **Deadline:** March 1. **Entry Fee:** $5/2
haiku. **Prizes:** $100, $40, $20. **Contact:** Helen J. Sherry.

IOWA POETRY PRIZES

University of Iowa Press

119 W Park Rd., 100 Kuhl House, Iowa City, IA 52242. 319-335-2000.

E-mail: holly-carver@uiowa.edu. Web site: www.uiowa.edu/~uipress. **Details:** Open to new as well as established poets of book-length collections of poetry. Poems must be written originally in English and be 50-150 manuscript pages. **Submission Period:** April 1-April 30. **Entry Fee:** $20. **Prizes:** Publication by University of Iowa Press under standard royalty contract. **Contact:** Holly Carver, Director.

IOWA SHORT FICTION AWARD

University of Iowa Press
102 Dey House, Iowa City, IA 52242. 319-335-2000.
E-mail: holly-carver@uiowa.edu. Web site: www.uiowa.edu/~uipress. **Details:** Open to writers who have not previously published a volume of prose fiction. Submit a collection of short stories totalling at least 150 pages. **Submission Period:** August 1-September 30. **Contact:** Holly Carver, Director.

JESSE BRYCE NILES CHAPBOOK CONTEST

Comstock Review, 4956 St. John Dr., Syracuse, NY 13215.
Web site: www.comstockreview.org. **Details:** Submit poetry chapbooks, 25-34 pages. Accepts previously published poems with credit(s) given. **Submission Period:** August 1-September 30. **Entry Fee:** $15/chapbook.

JAMES JONES FIRST NOVEL FELLOWSHIP

James Jones Literary Society, P.O. Box 111, Wilkes University, English Dept.
Wilkes-Barre, PA 18766. 570-408-4530. E-mail: english@wilkes.edu.
Web site: www.wilkes.edu//humanities/jones.html. **Details:** "Honors the spirit of unblinking honesty, determination, and insight into modern culture exemplified by the late James Jones, author of *From Here to Eternity*." Open to all American writers who have not published a novel. Submit two-page (maximum) outline and first 50 pages. **Deadline:** March 1. **Entry Fee:** $15. **Prizes:** $5,000 first prize and attendance at the society's annual conference; $250 honorarium for runner-up.

MARC A. KLEIN PLAYWRITING AWARD

Case Western Reserve University
Dept. of Theater Arts, 10900 Euclid Ave., Cleveland, OH 44106-7077. 216-368-4868.
E-mail: ksg@po.cwru.edu. Web site: www.cwru.edu. **Details:** A prize of $1,000, plus production, for an original, previously unproduced full-length play by a student currently enrolled at an U.S. college or university. **Deadline:** March 15. **Contact:** Ron Wilson.

THE KNOXVILLE WRITERS' GUILD ESSAY CONTEST

Knoxville Writers' Guild, P.O. Box 10326, Knoxville, TN 37939.
Web site: www.knoxvillewritersguild.org. **Details:** Open to Tennessee residents 18 years of age or older. **Deadline:** January 31. **Entry Fee:** $15/submission; KWG members may submit first entry for free, $15 for each additional entry thereafter. **Prizes:** $200, $100, $50.

E.M. KOEPPEL SHORT FICTION AWARD

WriteCorner Press, P.O. Box 16369, Jacksonville, FL 32245-6369. Web site: www.writecorner.com. **Details**: Submit any number of unpublished short stories, any genre. Stories may be no longer than 3,000 words. **Submission Period:** October 1-April 30. **Entry Fee:** $15/story or two stories for $25. **Prizes:** $1,100. **Contact:** Mary Sue Koeppel, Editor.

THE LEDGE ANNUAL POETRY AWARDS CONTEST

The Ledge, 78-44 80th St., Glendale, NY 11385.
Details: Awards 3 monetary prizes ($1,000, $250, and $100) and publication in *The Ledge* for unpublished poetry. Accepts simultaneous submissions. **Deadline:** April 30. **Entry Fee:** $10. **Contact:** Timothy Monaghan, Editor.

THE LEDGE ANNUAL POETRY CHAPBOOK CONTEST

The Ledge, 78-44 80th St., Glendale, NY 11385.
Details: Authors may submit 16-28 pages of poetry with title page, bio, and acknowledgements. No restrictions on form or content. Accepts simultaneous submissions. **Deadline:** October 31. **Entry Fee:** $12. **Prizes:** $1,000. **Contact:** Timothy Monaghan, Editor.

THE LENORE MARSHALL POETRY PRIZE

The Academy of American Poets
588 Broadway, Suite 604, New York, NY 10012. 212-274-0343.
E-mail: rmurphy@poets.org. Web site: www.poets.org. **Details:** For the most outstanding book of poems published in the United States during 2002; open to books by living American poets published in a standard edition (40 pages or more and 500 or more copies). **Submission Period:** April 1-June 15. **Entry Fee:** $25. **Prizes:** $25,000. **Contact:** Ryan Murphy, Awards Coordinator.

LEVIS POETRY PRIZE

Four Way Books, P.O. Box 535, Village Station, New York, NY 10014. 212-619-1105.
E-mail: four_way_editors@yahoo.com. Web site: www.fourwaybooks.com.
Details: Open to all U.S. poets. Electronic submissions strongly encouraged; see Web site for details. **Deadline:** March 31. **Entry Fee:** $25/manuscript. **Prizes:** $1,000 honorarium, book publication, a reading at Readings on the Bowery in New York City, and residency at The Fine Arts Work Center in Provincetown, MA (sponsered by FWB). **Contact:** David Doddlee, Contest Coordinator.

LIMERICK CONTEST

NLAPW Santa Clara Branch, 15724 Adams Ridge, Los Gatos, CA 95033.
E-mail: ralph_susan@juno.com. **Details:** Submit previously unpublished limericks.
Deadline: March 17. **Entry Fee:** $4. **Prizes:** Monetary awards for 1st, 2nd and 3rd place. **Contact:** Susan Zerweck.

THE LITERATURE FELLOWSHIP AWARDS

Wyoming Arts Council, 2320 Capitol Ave., Cheyenne, WY 82002. 307-777-7742.
E-mail: mshay@state.wy.us. Web site: http://wyoarts.state.wy.us. **Details:** Three
$3,000 fellowships are awarded to Wyoming literary artists. Poetry accepted in odd-
numbered years, prose accepted in even-numbered years. **Contact:** Michael Shay,
Literature Program Manager.

NAOMI LONG MADGETT POETRY AWARD

Lotus Press, Inc., P.O. Box 21607, Detroit, MI 48221. 313-861-1280.
E-mail: lotuspress@aol.com. **Details:** Open to African American poets. Submit man-
uscripts approximately 60-80 pages. E-mail or send SASE for complete guidelines.
Submission Period: April 1-June 30. **Prizes:** $500 and publication.

DEANN LUBELL PROFESSIONAL WRITERS' COMPETITION

NLAPW Palm Springs Branch, P.O. Box 1166, Palm Desert, CA 92261.
Details: Categories: Published magazine articles, essays and editorials, poetry, short
stories, and web-based articles. Entries must have been published within the past five
years. **Deadline:** March 15. **Entry Fee:** $15. **Prizes:** $100, $75 and $50 in each category. **Contact:** Kristin Johnson.

BARBARA MANDIGO KELLY PEACE POETRY AWARDS

Nuclear Age Peace Foundation
PMB 121, 1187 Coast Village Rd., Suite 1, Santa Barbara, CA 93108-2794.
805-965-3443. E-mail: wagingpeace@napf.org. Web site: www.wagingpeace.org.
Details: Original, unpublished poetry. Open to all writers. All poems must be the
original work of the poet, unpublished, and in English. Honorable mentions in each
category. Encourages poets to explore and illuminate positive visions of peace and the
human spirit. Maximum of 40 lines per poem. **Deadline:** July 1. **Entry Fee:** $12 for
up to three poems; waived for youth entries. **Prizes:** $1,000 for adults; $200 for ages
13-18; $200 for under age 12.

RICHARD J. MARGOLIS AWARD FOR ESSAYISTS

Blue Mountain Center
c/o ElderLaw Services, 294 Washington St., Suite 610, Boston, MA 02108.
Web site: www.bluemountaincenter.org. **Details:** "Award given each year to an essay-
ist whose work recalls Richard Margolis's warmth, humor, and a concern for social
issues." Apply with up to 30 pages of published or unpublished work. Include short
bio, description of current and anticipated work, and three writing samples.
Deadline: July 1. **Prizes:** $4,000 grant and 1-month residency at the Blue Mountain
Center in the Adirondacks.

MIGUEL MARMOL PRIZE

Curbstone Press, 321 Jackson St., Willimantic, CT 06226.
Details: Annual prize for a first work of fiction in English by a Latina/o writer.
Manuscript must reflect a respect for intercultural understanding and human rights.

Writers who have previously published poetry or nonfiction in book form are eligible. Submit book-length manuscript or collections of stories. **Deadline:** December 15. **Entry Fee:** $15. **Prizes:** Publication by Curbstone Press and $1,000 advance against royalties.

MARY MCCARTHY PRIZE IN SHORT FICTION

Sarabande Books, 2234 Dundee Rd., Suite 200, Louisville, KY 40205. 502-458-4028. E-mail: sarabandeb@aol.com. Web site: www.sarabandebooks.org. **Details:** Submit manuscript (collections of short stories, novellas, or short novel), 150-250 pages. Material that has previously appeared in magazines or anthologies is eligible. Translations and self-published collections are not eligible. **Submisson Period:** January 1-February 15. **Entry Fee:** $20. **Prizes:** $2,000 cash award, publication, and standard royalty contract.

MID-LIST PRESS FIRST SERIES
AWARDS FOR POETRY AND THE NOVEL

Mid-List Press, 4324 12th Ave. S, Minneapolis, MN 55407-3218. E-mail: guide@midlint.org. Web site: www.midlist.org. **Details:** Unpublished poetry collections and novels by writers who have not previously published in the category under submission. Poetry manuscripts must be at least 60 pages; novels must be at least 50,000 words. Include SASE. All submissions must follow guidelines exactly and include entry form. See Web site for detailed guidelines. **Deadline:** February 1. **Entry Fee:** $30. **Prizes:** Publication and advance against royalties.

MID-LIST PRESS FIRST SERIES
AWARDS FOR SHORT FICTION AND CREATIVE NONFICTION

Mid-List Press, 4324 12th Ave. S, Minneapolis, MN 55407-3218. E-mail: guide@midlist.org. Web site: www.midlist.org. **Details:** Unpublished short fiction collections and creative nonfiction by writers who have not published collections in the category under submission. Manuscripts must be at least 50,000 words. See Web site for detailed guidelines or send SASE. All submissions must follow guidelines exactly and include entry form. **Deadline:** July 1. **Entry Fee:** $30. **Prizes:** Publication and advance against royalty.

MILL MOUNTAIN THEATRE NEW PLAY CONTEST

Mill Mountain Theatre
One Market Square SE, Fl. 2, Roanoke, VA 24011. 540-342-5749. E-mail: outreach@millmoutain.org. Web site: www.millmountain.org. **Details:** Open to full-length, unpublished theatrical scripts. Scripts must be submitted by an agent or accompanied by a professional letter of recommendation by a director, literary manager, or dramaturg. **Submission Period:** October 1-January 1. **Prizes:** $1,000, staged reading, and possibility of full production. **Contact:** Julianne Homokay, Literary Coordinator.

MISSISSIPPI REVIEW PRIZE

The Center for Writers, University of Southern Mississippi
P.O. Box 5144, Hattiesburg, MS 39406. 601-266-4321.
E-mail: rief@netdoor.com. Web site: www.mississippireview.com. **Details:** Offers two prizes for unpublished works in fiction and poetry. Submit a short story up to 5,000 words or three poems up to 10 pages total. **Submission Period:** April 1-October 1. **Entry Fee:** $15. **Prizes:** $1,000 and publication.

MISSISSIPPI VALLEY POETRY CONTEST

Midwest Writing Center, P.O. Box 3188, Rock Island, IL 61204. 319-359-1057.
E-mail: mwc@midwestwritingcenter.org. Web site: www.midwestwritingcenter.org.
Details: Up to five unpublished poems, to 50 lines each. Nine categories. K-12 poets encouraged to submit. **Deadline:** April 1. **Entry Fee:** $3 (students), $5 (adults).
Prizes: $1,500-$1,700. **Contact:** Max Molleston, Chairman.

MONTEREY COUNTY FILM COMMISSION
SCREENWRITING COMPETITION

P.O. Box 111, Monterey, CA 93955. 831-646-0910.
E-mail: filmmonterey@redshift.com. Web site: www.filmmonterey.org.
Details: Screenwriting contest open to all genres. Competition is limited to the first 500 entries received. See Web site for contest guidelines prior to submitting.
Deadline: January 31. **Entry Fee:** $55. **Prizes:** $2,003. **Contact:** Ann Quamen.

MONTEREY COUNTY ON LOCATION AWARD

Monterey County Film Commission, P.O. Box 111, Monterey, CA 93955.
831-646-0910. E-mail: filmmonterey@redshift.com.
Web site: www.filmmonterey.org. **Details:** Annual contest open to screenplays that include at least 50% Monterey County locations. Open to writers who do not earn a living writing screenplays. See Web site for contest guidelines prior to submitting.
Deadline: December 31. **Entry Fee:** $55. **Prizes:** $1,000. **Contact:** Ann Quamen.

MOONDANCE INTERNATIONAL FILM FESTIVAL
SCREENWRITING CONTEST

6472 Robin Dr., Niwot, CO 80503. E-mail: contest@moondancefilmfestival.com.
Web site: www.moondancefilmfestival.com. **Details:** Open to feature screenplays, short screenplays, feature and short screenplays for children, short stories, and stageplays. **Deadline:** January 31. **Entry Fee:** $25-$75.

MOONLIGHT & MAGNOLIA FICTION WRITING CONTEST

P.O. Box 180489, Richland, MS 39218-0489. 601-825-7263.
E-mail: hoover59@aol.com. **Details:** Annual competition for writers of science fiction, fantasy, and horror stories. Open to unpublished writers or those who have not published more than two stories in a national, 5,000+ circulation magazine.
Submissions must be unpublished and not under contract. Submit stories up to 10,000 words, include SASE. E-mail for specific submission guidelines before send-

ing material. **Deadline:** December 15. **Entry Fee:** $7.50/story, $2.50 for each additional story (three entries per contest maximum). **Prizes:** $250 first prize, $100 second prize, and $50 third prize. **Contact:** K. Mark Hoover, Contest Administrator.

LIBBA MOORE GRAY POETRY COMPETITION

Knoxville Writers' Guild, P.O. Box 10326, Knoxville, TN 37939.
Web site: www.knoxvillewritersguild.org. **Details:** Open to Tennessee residents 18 years of age or older. **Deadline:** January 31. **Entry Fee:** $15/submission; KWG members may submit first three poems for free, $15 for each additional entry thereafter. **Prizes:** $300, $200, and $100.**Contact:** Judy Loest.

KATHRYN A. MORTON PRIZE IN POETRY

2234 Dundee Rd., Suite 200, Louisville, KY 40205. 502-458-4028.
E-mail: sarabandeb@aol.com. Web site: www.sarabandebooks.org. **Details:** Open to any U.S. citizin writing in English. Submit poetry manuscript of at least 48 pages. Individual poems may have been previously published, but the collection as a whole must be unpublished. **Submission Period:** January 1-February 15. **Entry Fee:** $20. **Prizes:** $2,000 and publication under standard royalty contract.

SHEILA MARGARET MOTTON PRIZE

New England Poetry Club, 11 Puritan Rd., Arlington, MA 02476-7710.
E-mail: info@nepoetryclub.org. Web site: www.nepoetryclub.org. **Details:** Open to a book of poetry published in the last two years. Send two copies of book with $5 handling fee for non-members. Entrants may submit up to three entries total out of all the contests sponsored by NEPC, but no more than one entry per contest. Send SASE or see Web site for specific guidelines and fees. **Submission Period:** April 1-June 30. **Entry Fee:** Free to members; $10 for non-members. **Prizes:** $500. **Contact:** Virginia Thayer.

ERIKA MUMFORD PRIZE

New England Poetry Club, 11 Puritan Rd., Arlington, MA 02476-7710.
E-mail: info@nepoetryclub.org. Web wise: www.nepoetryclub.org. **Details:** Open to an unpublished poem in any form on the subject of travel or foreign cultures. Entrants may submit up to three entries total out of all the contests sponsored by NEPC, but no more than one poem per contest. Send SASE or see Web site for specific guidelines and fees. **Submission Period:** April 1-June 30. **Entry Fee:** Free to members; $10 for non-members. **Prizes:** $250. **Contact:** Virginia Thayer.

NATIONAL CHILDREN'S THEATRE FESTIVAL

Actors' Playhouse at the Miracle Theatre
280 Miracle Mile, Coral Gables, FL 33134. 305-444-9293.
E-mail: maulding@actorsplayhouse.org. Web site: www.actorsplayhouse.org. **Details:** Literary prize offering $500, full production, and author's transportation and lodging to the Festival based upon availability. See Web site for complete rules and guidelines. **Deadline:** June 1. **Entry Fee:** $10. **Contact:** Earl Maulding, Festival Director.

NATIONAL TEN-MINUTE PLAY CONTEST

Actors Theatre of Louisville, 316 W Main St., Louisville, KY 40202. 502-584-1265. E-mail: mail@actorstheatre.org. Web site: www.actorstheatre.org. **Details:** Submit a previously unproduced 10-minute play, 10 pages or less. Submissions must not have had a previous Equity production. Limit 1 script per person. Open to U.S. citizens or residents. Send SASE or see Web site for guidelines. **Deadline:** December 1. **Prizes:** $1,000 Heideman Award. **Contact:** Tanya Palmer, Literary Manager.

HOWARD NEMEROV SONNET AWARD

The Formalist, 320 Hunter Dr., Evansville, IN 47711. **Details:** Original and unpublished sonnets. No translations. Place name, address, and phone number on the back of each entry, include SASE. **Deadline:** June 15. **Entry Fee:** $3/sonnet. **Prizes:** $1,000 and publication.

NEVADA SCREENWRITERS COMPETITION

Nevada Film Office, 555 E Washington Ave., Suite 5400, Las Vegas, NV 89101. 877-638-3456. E-mail: lvnfo@bizopp.state.nv.us. Web site: www.nevadafilm.com. **Details:** Open to writers who have not sold or optioned a feature screenplay. Script must allow 75% of all scenes to be shot in Nevada. **Submission Period:** May 1-June 30. **Entry Fee:** $15 for Nevada residents; $30 for nonresidents. **Prizes:** Cash and prizes, consideration from industry professionals, and film festival admission.

THE NEW ENGLAND/NEW YORK AWARD

Alice James Books, University of Maine at Farmington, 238 Main St., Farmington, ME 04938. 207-778-7071. E-mail: ajb@umf.maine.edu. Web site: www.alicejames-books.org. **Details:** Open to poets who reside in New England or New York State. Submit poetry manuscript (50-70 pages) with TOC and list of acknowledgments for previously published work. Winners serve three-year term on the Alice James Books Editorial Board. **Deadline:** October 1. **Entry Fee:** $20. **Prizes:** $2,000, publication, and 1-month residency at the Vermont Studio Center.

NEW LETTERS POETRY PRIZE

New Letters, University of Missouri-Kansas
University House, 5101 Rockhill Rd., Kansas City, MO 64110. 816-235-1168. E-mail: newletters@umkc.edu. Web site: www.umkc.edu/newletters. **Details:** Offers $1,000 and publication to the best collection of 3-6 poems. **Deadline:** May 15. **Entry Fee:** $10/entry.

NEW YORK STORIES FICTION PRIZE

New York Stories, LaGuardia Community College/CUNY, English Dept. E-103, 31-10 Thomson Ave., Long Island City, NY 11101. E-mail: nystories@lagcc.cuny.edu. Web site: www.newyorkstories.org. **Details:** Submit previously unpublished short stories, no longer than 6,500 words. **Deadline:** September 15. **Entry Fee:** $15/submission. **Prizes:** $500 and publication in *New York Stories*. **Contact:** Daniel Caplice Lynch.

DON AND GEE NICHOLL SCREENWRITING FELLOWSHIPS

Academy of Motion Picture Arts & Sciences
8949 Wilshire Blvd., Beverly Hills, CA 90211. 310-247-3000.
E-mail: nicholl@oscars.org. Web site: www.oscars.org/nicholl. **Details:** Accepts original feature film scripts by writers who do not make their living writing screenplays. No translations. **Deadline:** May 1. **Entry Fee:** $30. **Prizes:** Up to five fellowships of $30,000 each.

FLANNERY O'CONNOR AWARD FOR SHORT FICTION

University of Georgia Press
330 Research Dr., Athens, GA 30602-4901. 706-369-6130.
E-mail: books@ugapress.uga.edu. Web site: www.ugapress.org. **Details:** Open to collections of short fiction written in English, 200-275 pages. Collections that include long stories or novellas accepted, however no novels or single novellas. Accepts pieces that have appeared in magazines or anthologies, but not those which have been published in a full-length collection by the author. **Submission Period:** April 1-May 31. **Entry Fee:** $20. **Prizes:** $1,000 and publication by the University of Georgia Press.

PARALLEL AWARD FOR POETRY

Bellingham Review
Mail Stop 9053, Western Washington University, Bellingham, WA 98225.
Web site: www.wwu.edu/~bhreview. **Details:** Submit previously unpublished poems of any length. **Submission Period:** December 1-March 15. **Entry Fee:** $15 for first entry of three poems; $10 for each additional poem. **Prizes:** $1,000 and publication in *Bellingham Review*.

IRENE I. PARISI AWARD

Greater Philadelphia Film Office
100 S Broad St., Suite 600, Philadelphia, PA 19110. 215-686-2668.
E-mail: joanb@film.org. Web site: www.film.org. **Details:** Awards an outstanding screenwriter 21 years old or younger. **Deadline:** December 2. **Entry Fee:** $45. **Prizes:** $2,000 and admission to Philadelphia Film Festival. **Contact:** Joan Bressler, Director.

ALEXANDER PATTERSON CAPPON FICTION PRIZE

New Letters, University of Missouri-Kansas
University House, 5101 Rockhill Rd., Kansas City, MO 64110. 816-235-1168.
E-mail: newletters@umkc.edu. **Details:** Offers $1,000 and publication for the best short story. **Deadline:** May 15. **Entry Fee:** $10.

PEARL POETRY PRIZE

Pearl Editions, 3030 E Second St., Long Beach, CA 90803.
Web site: www.pearlmag.com. **Details:** Open to all poets, with or without previous book publication. Submit poetry manuscript of 48-64 pages. **Submission Period:** May 1-July 15. **Entry Fee:** $20. **Prizes:** $1,000 and publication in *Pearl*.

PEARL SHORT STORY PRIZE

Pearl Editions, 3030 E Second St., Long Beach, CA 90803.
Web site: www.pearlmag.com. **Details:** Submit previously unpublished short stories, no longer than 4,000 words. Accepts simultaneous submissions with notice. All submissions considered for publication. Submission Period: April 1-May 31. **Entry Fee:** $10/story. **Prizes:** $250 and publication in *Pearl*.

PERUGIA PRESS INTRO AWARD

Perugia Press, P.O. Box 60364, Florence, MA 01062.
E-mail: info@perugiapress.com. Web site: www.perugiapress.com. **Details:** Annual contest for a first or second book of poetry. Open to female poets only. Individual poems may be previously published, but not the collection as a whole. Send 48-72 page manuscript via regular mail. Include SASE for notification. **Submission Period:** August 1-November 15. **Entry Fee:** $20/submission. **Prizes:** $1,000 and publication. **Contact:** Susan Kan, Director.

PHILBRICK POETRY AWARD

251 Benefit St., Providence, RI 02903. Web site: www.providenceathenaeum.org.
Details: Open to residents of New England (CT, ME, MA, NH, RI, VT) who have not had a book of poetry published. One manuscript per entrant, 15-25 pages.
Submission Period: June 15-October 15. **Entry Fee:** $8. **Prizes:** $500, publication of chapbook, and opportunity to read at the Providence Athenaeum.

PLAYHOUSE ON THE SQUARE

51 S Cooper in Overton Square, Memphis, TN 38104.
Details: Full-length comedies and dramas; cast up to 15. **Deadline:** April 1. **Prizes:** $500 and production.

PLAYWRIGHTING CONTEST

LDI Productions, 4470 Sunset Blvd., Suite. 497, Hollywood, CA 90027.
E-mail: edward@ldiproductions.com. Web site: www.ldiproductions.com. **Details:** Original, unpublished full-length scripts, cast up to 8. Small musicals accepted. SASE required. **Deadline:** May 31. **Entry Fee:** $10. **Prizes:** $1,000 and production.

POCKETS FICTION-WRITING CONTEST

Pockets Magazine, 1908 Grand Ave., P.O. Box 340004, Nashville, TN 37203-0004.
E-mail: pockets@upperroom.org. Web site: www.upperroom.org/pockets. **Details:** Open to unpublished short stories, 1,000-1,600 words. No historical fiction. **Submission Period:** March 1-August 15. **Prizes:** $1,000 and publication in *Pockets*.

POETRY OPEN

Glimmer Train Press, Inc.
710 SW Madison St., Suite 504, Portland, OR 97205. 503-221-0836.
E-mai: info@glimmertrain.com. Web site: www.glimmertrain.com.
Details: Open to original, unpublished poetry. All poems must be submitted on-line;

see Web site for specific submission guidelines. **Submission Period:** April and October. **Entry Fee:** $6/poem. **Prizes:** 1st place wins $500, publication in *Glimmer Train Stories*, and 20 copies; 2nd place wins $250; 3rd place wins $100.

POETS OUT LOUD

Fordham University at Lincoln Center
113 W 60th St., Room 924, New York, NY 10023. 212-636-6792.
E-mail: pol@fordham.edu. Web site: www.fordham.edu/english/pol.
Details: Open to previously unpublished, full-length poetry manuscripts, 50-80 pages. **Prizes:** $1,000, publication by Fordham University Press, and invitation to read at Poet's Out Loud Reading Series. **Entry Fee:** $25. **Deadline:** October 15.

PRISM INTERNATIONAL SHORT FICTION CONTEST

University of British Columbia, Dept. of Creative Writing, Buch E462-1866 Main Mall, Vancouver, British Columbia V6T 1Z1 Canada. 604-822-2514.
E-mail: prism@interchange.ubc.ca. Web site: http://prism.arts.ubc.ca. **Details:** Annual short fiction contest, $3,000 in prizes. Send request with SASE for rules to register for new drama contest. Include IRC's.

PRISM INTERNATIONAL NONFICTION CONTEST

University of British Columbia, Dept. of Creative Writing, Buch E462-1866 Main Mall, Vancouver, British Columbia V6T 1Z1 Canada. 604-822-2514.
E-mail: prism@interchange.ubc.ca. Web site: http://prism.arts.ubc.ca. **Details:** Annual nonfiction contest, $1,500 in prizes. Pays $40 per published page of poetry, $20 per page of prose, $10 per page Web rights. Send request with SASE for rules to register for new drama contest. Include IRC's.

RED ROCK POETRY AWARD

English Dept. 12A, Community College of Southern Nevada, 3200 E Cheyenne Ave., North Las Vegas, NV 89030. **Details:** Submit entry of three poems, no more than 20 lines each. No previously published poems or simultaneous submissions. **Deadline:** October 31. **Entry Fee:** $6/entry. **Prizes:** $500 and publication in *Red Rock Review*. **Contact:** Dr. Richard Logsdon.

RIVER OAK REVIEW POETRY CONTEST

River Oak Arts, P.O. Box 3127, Oak Park, IL 60303.
E-mail: info@riveroakarts.org. Web site: www.riveroakarts.org. **Details:** Poets may submit up to four previously unpublished poems no more than 500 lines total. **Deadline:** December 31. **Entry Fee:** $15/entry (includes subscription). **Prizes:** $500 and publication in *River Oak Review*.

RICHARD RODGERS AWARDS

American Academy of Arts and Letters, 633 W 155th St., New York, NY 10032. **Details:** Offers subsidized productions or staged readings in New York City by a nonprofit theater for a musical, play with music, thematic review, or any comparable work. Send SASE for application and guidelines. **Deadline:** November 1.

S.C. PLAYWRIGHTS CENTER

S.C. Playwrights Center, 1001 Bay St., Suite 101, Beaufort, SC 29902. 843-524-7773. **Details:** Submit three copies of a play in play format with a synopsis. Reading time should be 30-90 minutes. No previous productions, musicals, or translations; must be original with a maximum of 8 characters. Selected playwrights will attend the Annual South Carolina Playwrights Conference. Send SASE for details. **Deadline:** March 31. **Entry Fee:** $10.

BENJAMIN SALTMAN POETRY AWARD

Red Hen Press, P.O. Box 3537, Granada Hills, CA 91394. 818-831-0649. E-mail: editors@redhen.org. Web site: www.redhen.org. **Details:** Submit poetry manuscript, 48-80 pages. **Deadline:** October 31. **Entry Fee:** $20/entry. **Prizes:** $1,000 and publication by Red Hen Press.

THE SEAHORSE AWARDS

Moondance International Film Festival, 6472 Robin Dr., Niwot, CO 80503. E-mail: contest@moondancefilmfestival.com. Web site: www.moondancefilmfestival.com. **Details:** Open to male writers of feature screenplays that depict women and girls in a positive manner and/or have lead roles for female actors over 40. **Deadline:** January 31. **Entry Fee:** $25-$75.

SERPENTINE ANNUAL SHORT STORY CONTEST

Serpentine, 1761 Edgewood Rd., Redwood City, CA 94062. E-mail: publisher@serpentinia.com. Web site: www.serpentinia.com. **Details:** Annual contest for original, unpublished short stories up to 10,000 words. **Deadline:** December 31. **Entry Fee:** $18/manuscript. **Prizes:** First prize of $1,000, second prize of $200, third prize of $100, and four $50 honorable mentions. **Contact:** Robert Burdette Sweet, Editor.

SET IN PHILADELPHIA,
BY A PHILADELPHIAN SCREENWRITING COMPETITION

Greater Philadelphia Film Office, 100 S Broad St., Suite 600, Philadelphia, PA 19110. 215-686-2668. E-mail: joanb@film.org. Web site: www.film.org. **Deadline:** December 2. **Entry Fee:** $45. **Prizes:** $2,500, critique from judges, and admission to Philadelphia Film Festival. **Details:** Open to screenplays written by Philadelphia residents. **Contact:** Joan Bressler, Director.

SET IN PHILADELPHIA SCREENWRITING COMPETITION

Greater Philadelphia Film Office, 100 S Broad St., Suite 600, Philadelphia, PA 19110. 215-686-2668. E-mail: joanb@film.org. Web site: www.film.org. **Details:** Open to all screenwriters who submit an original feature-length screenplay set primarily in Philadelphia. **Deadline:** December 2. **Entry Fee:** $45. **Prizes:** $10,000, opportunity to meet with industry professionals, critique from judges, and free admission to Philadelphia Film Festival. **Contact:** Joan Bressler, Director.

SHORT STORY AWARD FOR NEW WRITERS

Glimmer Train Press, Inc., 710 SW Madison St., Suite 504, Portland, OR 97205. 503-221-0836. E-mail: edsd@glimmertrain.com. Web site: www.glimmertrain.com. **Details:** Open to original, unpublished stories, up to 8,000 words. All stories must be submitted on-line; see Web site for specific submission guidelines. **Deadline:** (Spring) February 1-March 31; (Fall) August 1-September 30. **Entry Fee:** $12. **Prizes:** $1,200 and publication; $500; $300.

SLIPSTREAM ANNUAL POETRY CHAPBOOK COMPETITION

Slipstream Press, P.O. Box 2071, Niagara Falls, NY 14301. Web site: www.slipstreampress.org. **Details:** Send up to 40 pages of poetry with any style, format, or theme. Accepts previously published material and simultaneous submissions with notice. All entrants receive free copy of winning chapbook. **Deadline:** December 1. **Entry Fee:** $10. **Prizes:** $1,000 and 50 copies.

SNAKE NATION PRESS AWARD FOR SHORT FICTION

Snake Nation Press, 110 W Force St., Valdosta, GA 31601. 229-244-0752. E-mail: jeana@snakenationpress.org. Web site: www.snakenationpress.org. **Details:** Awards $1,000 plus publication for a collection of published or unpublished short stories by a new or underpublished writer. **Deadline:** June 15. **Entry Fee:** $20.

SONORA REVIEW ANNUAL CONTEST

University of Arizona, Dept. of English, Tucson, AZ 85721. 520-321-7759. E-mail: sonora@u.arizona.edu. Web site: www.coh.arizona.edu/sonora. **Details:** Prize for original and unpublished short stories. No novel chapters or simultaneous submissions. Send SASE for return of manuscript. See Web site for detailed guidelines. **Deadline:** December 1. **Entry Fee:** $10. **Prizes:** $250 and publication in *Sonora Review*.

SOUL-MAKING LITERARY COMPETITIONS

NLAPW Nob Hill Branch, Webhallow, 1544 Sweetwood Dr., Colma, CA 94015. Web site: www.soulmakingcontest.us. **Details:** Categories are: the Janice Farrel Poetry Prize, Sheila K. Smith Short Story Prize, Rosalie Fleming Memorial Essay and Creative Nonfiction Prize, Joanna Catherine Scott Novel Excerpt Prize, Kathryn Handley Prose Poem Prize, Carolyn A. Clark Short-Short Story/Flash Fiction Prize, and Clarence Douglas Wright Song/Lyric Prize. **Deadline:** November 30. **Entry Fee:** $5. **Prizes:** $100, $50 and $25 in each category.

SOUTH CAROLINA FICTION PROJECT

The South Carolina Arts Commission, 1800 Gervais St., Columbia, SC 29201. 803-734-8696. E-mail: goldstsa@arts.state.sc.us. Web site: www.state.sc.us/arts. **Details:** Offers an annual short story competition. Up to 12 previously unpublished stories of 2,500 words or less. Stories are not required to have Southern theme or to be set in South Carolina. Only legal South Carolina residents are eligible to apply. **Deadline:** January 15. **Prizes:** $500 and publication in *The Post and Courier*. **Contact:** Sara June Goldstein, Program Director for Literary Arts.

SOW'S EAR CHAPBOOK COMPETITION
Sow's Ear Poetry Review
19535 Pleasant View Dr., Abingdon, VA 24211-6827. 276-628-2651.
E-mail: owens017@bama.ua.edu. **Details:** Send 22-26 pages of poetry with a title page and TOC. No length limit on poems, but no more than one poem/page. Accepts previously published poems if writer holds publication rights. Send SASE or e-mail address for notification. **Deadline:** May 1. **Entry Fee:** $10. **Prizes:** Publication, $1,000, 25 copies; $200 and $100. **Contact:** James Owens, Editor.

SOW'S EAR POETRY COMPETITION
Sow's Ear Poetry Review
19535 Pleasant View Dr., Abingdon, VA 24211-6827. 276-628-2651.
E-mail: owens017@bama.ua.edu. **Details:** "Seeking poems that make the strange familiar or the familiar strange, that connect the little story of the text and the big story of the human situation." No length limit. Accepts simultaneous submissions. Poets who submit five+ poems receive free subscription. Include SASE or e-mail address for notification. **Deadline:** November 1. **Entry Fee:** $2/poem. **Contact:** James Owens, Editor.

THE SPIRIT OF MOONDANCE AWARDS
Moondance International Film Festival, 6472 Robin Dr., Niwot, CO 80503.
E-mail: contest@moondancefilmfestival.com.
Web site: www.moondancefilmfestival.com. **Details:** Open to female writers of feature screenplays, short screenplays, feature and short screenplays for children, short stories, and stageplays. **Deadline:** January 31. **Entry Fee:** $25-$75.

THE SPOON RIVER POETRY PRIZE
4241 Dept. of English, Publications Unit, Illinois State University, Normal, IL 61790-4241. Web site: www.litline.org/spoon. **Details:** Submit two copies (one with name and address, the other without) of three unpublished poems, up to 10 pages total. Include SASE for notification. Does not accept submission via e-mail or fax. **Deadline:** April 15. **Entry Fee:** $16. **Prizes:** $1,000 and publication in *The Spoon River Poetry Review*.

SPRING POETRY CONTEST
Montgomery Chapter NLAPW, 91 Cloverfield Rd., Hope Hull, AL 36043.
Details: Submit poetry of up to 50 lines. **Deadline:** April 1. **Entry Fee:** $5. **Prizes:** Dependent upon number of entries. **Contact:** Mary Halliburton.

ANN STANFORD POETRY PRIZE

Professional Writing Program, University of Southern California, WPH 404, Los Angeles, CA 90089. 213-740-3252. E-mail: mpw@mizar.usc.edu. **Details:** Send up to five unpublished poems with SASE. All entrants receive free issue of the anthology. **Deadline:** April 15. **Entry Fee:** $10. **Prizes:** Three monetary prizes ($1,000, $200, and $100) and publication in *Southern California Anthology*. **Contact:** James Ragan, Director.

HOLLIS SUMMERS POETRY PRIZE COMPETITION

University of Georgia Press, Scott Quadrangle, Athens, OH 45701. 740-593-1155. Web site: www.ohiou.edu/oupress/. **Details:** Submit 60-95 manuscript pages of original, unpublished poetry. Open to both those who have published a collection and those who have not. See guidelines at Web site. **Deadline:** October 31. **Entry Fee:** $15. **Prizes:** $500 and publication by Ohio University Press.

SUNDANCE INSTITUTE SCREENWRITING LABORATORIES

Sundance Institute, 8857 W Olympic Blvd., Beverly Hills, CA 90211. 310-360-1981. E-mail: featurefilmprogram@sundance.org. Web site: www.sundance.org. **Details:** Provides the opportunity for 10-12 artists to work on their feature scripts with the support of established screenwriters. The Institute selects 15-20 projects each year. Interested applicants should send first five pages of script, cover letter, bio, two-page synopsis, and application. **Deadline:** May 1. **Entry Fee:** $30. **Prizes:** Participation at five-day Sundance screenwriting lab.

TANTALUS POETRY CONTEST

Tantalus Magazine

P.O. Box 189, Clarion, PA 16214. E-mail: submissions@tantalusmagazine.com. Web site: www.tantalusmagazine.com. **Details:** Original, previously unpublished poetry. **Deadline:** March 1. **Entry Fee:** $2/poem. **Prizes:** $500, $200, $100.

SYDNEY TAYLOR MANUSCRIPT COMPETITION

Assn. of Jewish Libraries, 315 Maitland Ave., Teaneck, NJ 07666. 201-862-0312. E-mail: rkglasser@aol.com. Web site: www.jewishlibraries.org. **Details:** Open to writers who have no previously published fiction works. Submit book-length manuscript of 64-200 pages. Stories must have a positive Jewish focus, universal appeal, and be for readers ages 8-11. **Deadline:** December 1. **Prizes:** $1,000.

PETER TAYLOR PRIZE FOR THE NOVEL

Knoxville Writers' Guild, Brian Griffin, P.O. Box 2565, Knoxville, TN 37901-2565. Web site: www.knoxvillewritersguild.org. **Details:** Open to U.S. residents writing in English. Submit unpublished novel manuscripts 40,000 words or more. See Web site for details. **Submission Period:** February 1-April 30. **Entry Fee:** $20. **Prizes:** $1,000 and publication by the University of Tennessee Press.

THE TEN-MINUTE MUSICALS PROJECT

Box 461194, West Hollywood, CA 90046. Web site: www.tenminutemusicals.org. **Details:** Submit complete original stage musicals (any musical style) which run 7-20 minutes. Cast limited to 10 members—five men, five women. "Start with a strong story, even it if means postponing work on music and lyrics until dramatic foundation is complete." See Web site for complete guidelines. **Deadline:** August 31. **Prizes:** $250 royalty advance. **Contact:** Michael Koppy, Producer.

LENA-MILES WEVER TODD POETRY SERIES

Pleiades Press, LMWT Poetry Series, Dept. of English
Central Missouri State Univ., Warrensburg, MO 64093.
Web site: www.cmsu.edu/englphil/pleiades. **Details:** Open to all U.S. writers. Submit poetry manuscript, at least 48 pages. **Submission Period:** July 30-October 30. **Entry Fee:** $15/entry. **Prizes:** $1,000 and publication by Pleiades Press. **Contact:** Kevin Prufer.

KATE TUFTS DISCOVERY AWARD

Claremont Graduate University, 160 E 10th St., Harper East B7, Claremont, CA 91711. 909-621-8974. Web site: www.cgu.edu/tufts. **Details:** For an emerging poet whose work shows extraordinary promise. See Web site for detailed guidelines. **Deadline:** September 15. **Prizes:** $10,000.

KINGSLEY TUFTS POETRY AWARD

Claremont Graduate University, 160 E 10th St., Harper East B7, Claremont, CA 91711. 909-621-8974. Web site: www.cgu.edu/tufts. **Details:** Open to emerging American poets. See Web site for detailed guidelines. **Deadline:** September 15. **Prizes:** $100,000.

TUPELO PRESS ANNUAL CHAPBOOK COMPETITION

Tupelo Press, P.O. Box 539, Dorset, VT 05251. 802-366-8185.
E-mail: editors@tupelopress.org. Web site: www.tupelopress.org. **Details:** Accepts poetry manuscripts of 20-30 pages by poets who have not published a full-length book. **Deadline:** October 31. **Entry Fee:** $15. **Prizes:** $1,000, publication, and 50 copies. **Contact:** Margaret Donovan.

TUPELO PRESS DORSET PRIZE

Tupelo Press, P.O. Box 539, Dorset, VT 05251. 802-366-8185.
E-mail: editors@tupelopress.org. Web site: www.tupelopress.org. **Details:** Open to all poets writing in English. Submit a previously unpublished, full-length poetry manuscript between 50-80 pages. **Deadline:** November 15. **Entry Fee:** $25. **Prizes:** $3,000, publication, and two-week stay at Dorset Writers Colony. **Contact:** Margaret Donovan.

TUPELO PRESS POETRY AWARDS

Tupelo Press, P.O. Box 539, Dorset, VT 05251. 802-366-8185.
E-mail: editors@tupelopress.org. Web site: www.tupelopress.org. **Details:** Open to unpublished, full-length collections of poetry by poets who have not yet published a full collection. **Submission Period:** January 1-April 15. **Entry Fee:** $25. **Prizes:** Judge's prize of $3,000 and editor's prize of $1,000. Both winners also receive publication and are invited to read at the Great River Arts Institute. **Contact:** Margaret Donovan.

DANIEL VAROUJAN AWARD

New England Poetry Club, 11 Puritan Rd., Arlington, MA 02476-7710.
E-mail: info@nepoetryclub.org. Web site: www.nepoetryclub.org. **Details:** Open to unpublished poems (no translations) echoing the work and/or memory of Daniel Varoujan, a poet killed by Turks in 1915. Entrants may submit up to three entries total out of all the contests sponsored by NEPC, but no more than one poem per contest. Send SASE or see Web site for specific guidelines and fees. **Submission Period:** April 1-June 30. **Entry Fee:** Free to members; $10 for non-members. **Prizes:** $1,000. **Contact:** Virginia Thayer.

VERY SHORT FICTION AWARD

Glimmer Train Press, Inc., 710 SW Madison St., Suite 504, Portland, OR 97205. 503-221-0836. E-mail: info@glimmertrain.com. Web site: www.glimmertrain.com. **Details:** Short stories up to 2,000 words. All stories must be submitted on-line; see Web site for specific submission guidelines. **Submission Period:** (Summer) June 1-July 31; (Winter) November 1-January 31. **Entry Fee:** $10/story. **Prizes:** 1st place wins $1,200, publication in *Glimmer Train Stories*, and 20 copies; 2nd place wins $500; 3rd place wins $300.

VOILET REED HAAS POETRY CONTEST

Snake Nation Press, 110 W Force St., Valdosta, GA 31601. 229-244-0752.
E-mail: jeana@snakenationpress.org. Web site: www.snakenationpress.org. **Details:** Awards $500 plus publication for poetry manuscript of 50-75 pages. **Deadline:** June 15. **Entry Fee:** $10.

THE WASHINGTON PRIZE

The Word Works, P.O. Box 42164, Washington, DC 20015. E-mail: editor@wordworksdc.com. Web site: www.wordworksdc.com. **Details:** Original poetry by a living American writer. Send 48-64 page manuscript with TOC, acknowledgments page, and a brief bio. See Web site for complete submission guidelines. **Deadline:** March 1. **Entry Fee:** $20. **Prizes:** $1,500 and publication.

WALT WHITMAN AWARD

The Academy of American Poets, 588 Broadway, Suite 1203, New York, NY 10012-3250. 212-274-0343. E-mail: mtyrell@poets.org. Web site: www.poets.org. **Details:** Open to American poets who have never before published a book of poetry.

Manuscripts should be 50-100 pages of original poems, one poem/page. **Submission Period:** September 15-November 30. **Entry Fee:** $25. **Prizes:** $5,000, publication by Louisiana State University Press, and one-month residency at Vermont Studio Center.

WALLACE W. WINCHELL POETRY CONTEST

Connecticut Poetry Society, P.O. Box 4053, Waterbury, CT 06704-0053. 203-753-7815. E-mail: wtarzia@nvctc5comment.edu. Web site: http://hometown.aol.com/ctpoetrysociety. **Details:** Original, unpublished poetry up to 40 lines. Maximum five poems per contest. All entries will be considered for publication unless "For Contest Only" is marked on submission. Does not accept simultaneous submissions. Identify each submission as Wallace W. Winchell Poetry Contest. **Deadline:** December 31. **Entry Fee:** $2/poem. **Prizes:** Three monetary prizes ($150, $100, $50) and publication in *Connecticut River Review*.

TOBIAS WOLFF AWARD FOR FICTION

Bellingham Review, Mail Stop 9053, Western Washington University, Bellingham, WA 98225. www.wwu.edu/~bhreview. **Submission Period:** December 1-March 15. **Entry Fee:** $15 for first entry, $10 for each additional entry. **Prizes:** $1,000 and publication in *The Bellingham Review*. **Details:** Submit a short story or novel excerpt up to 10,000 words.

YOUNG WRITERS' AWARD

Turning Wheel, Journal of the Buddhist Peace Fellowship, P.O. Box 4650, Berkeley, CA 94704. 510-655-6169. E-mail: sue@bpf.org. Web site: www.bpf.org. **Details:** Open to writers of essays who are 30 years of age or younger and who have not been previously published in *Turning Wheel*, on the theme of an issue. Themes and guidelines available on Web site. Do not submit material by fax. **Prizes:** $500. **Contact:** Marianne Dresser, Associate Editor.

YOUNG WRITERS' PRIZE IN POETRY

Knoxville Writers' Guild, Laura Still, Director, P.O. Box 10326, Knoxville, TN 37939. E-mail: eunicehat@aol.com. Web site: www.knoxvillewritersguild.org. **Deadline:** December 15. **Entry Fee:** $15/submission; KWG members may submit first three poems for free, $15 for each additional entry (set of two) thereafter. **Prizes:** $200 and free admission to the Scottish Society of Knoxville's Robert Burns Night Celebration.

ZOETROPE SHORT FICTION CONTEST

Zoetrope: All Story
916 Kearny St., San Francisco, CA 94133. 415-788-7500. E-mail: contests@all-story.com. Web site: www.all-story.com. **Details:** Awards three monetary prizes for an unpublished short story no longer that 5,000 words. Do not submit material via e-mail or fax. **Submission Period:** June 1-October 1. **Entry Fee:** $15. **Prizes:** $1,000, $500, and $250. **Contact:** Francis Ford Coppola, Publisher.

DRAMA & THEATER

Community, regional, and civic theaters and college dramatic groups offer the best opportunities today for playwrights to see their work produced, whether on the stage or in dramatic readings.

Indeed, aspiring playwrights will be encouraged to hear that many well-known playwrights received their first recognition in the regional theaters. Payment is generally nominal, but regional and university theaters usually buy only the right to produce a play, and all further rights revert to the author. Since most directors like to work closely with authors on any revisions necessary, theaters will often pay the playwright's expenses while in residence during rehearsals.

The thrill of seeing your play come to life on the stage is one of the pleasures of being on hand for rehearsals and performances. In addition to producing plays and giving dramatic readings, many theaters also sponsor competitions or new-play festivals. Aspiring playwrights should query college and community theaters in their region to find out which ones are interested in seeing original scripts.

Dramatic associations of interest to playwrights include the Dramatists Guild (1501 Broadway, Suite 701, New York, NY 10036), and Theatre Communications Group, Inc. (355 Lexington Ave., New York, NY 10017), which creates the annual *Dramatists Sourcebook: The Playwright's Companion*, published by Feedback Theatrebooks (305 Madison Ave., Suite 1146, New York, NY 10165), is an annual directory of theaters, play publishers, and prize contests seeking scripts. See Organizations for Writers listings (in Other Resources section of this book) for details on dramatists' associations.

Some of the theaters on this list require that playwrights submit all or some of the following with scripts—cast list, synopsis, resume, recommendations, and return postcard—and with scripts and queries, SASEs must always be enclosed.

Also, writers who want to try their hand at writing screenplays for television or film may find it helpful to gain experience in playwriting and further their knowledge of dramatic structure by working in amateur, community, or professional theaters.

The following list also includes a number of publishers of full-length or one-act plays for use by juvenile and adult drama programs.

A. D. PLAYERS

2710 W Alabama, Houston, TX 77098. 713-439-0181.
E-mail: adtour@hern.org. Web site: www.adplayers.org.
Description: Full-length plays or musicals (12 actors max.), or one-act children's plays or musicals (8 actors max.) with Judeo-Christian world view. **Proposals:** Send synopsis and/or brief scene or demo tape/CD to Literary Manager. Submit scripts and cast list with SASE. **Payment:** Negotiable rates.

ACTORS' PLAYHOUSE AT THE MIRACLE THEATRE

280 Miracle Mile, Coral Gables, FL 33134. 305-444-9293.
E-mail: jchacin@actorsplayhouse.org. Web site: www.actorsplayhouse.org.

Description: Seeking new readings for comedy, drama and musicals. Smaller casts preferred. Minimal set restrictions for readings/workshop productions. Looking to expand Reading Series, 6-10 readings/ season. A new black box space allows workshop performances of already read material, and small performance pieces. **Plays/season:** 6 (average 200 submissions). **Proposals:** Send recommendations, synopsis and SASE. Sponsors National Call to Competition/Children's Theatre. Accepts unsolicited manuscripts. Responds in 1 month (queries), 6 months (submissions). Accepts electronic queries. **Payment:** Negotiable pay, on production. **Comments:** Mainstage subscribers are conservative; avoid controversial material.

ACTORS THEATRE OF LOUISVILLE

316 W Main St., Louisville, KY 40202. 502-584-1265.
Web site: www.actorstheatre.org. **Description:** Seeks full-length and one-act plays.
Proposals: Send query with synopsis and 10 sample pages from script. Prefers to receive submissions from literary agents or recommendations from an artistic director, literary manager, or some other qualified source. Responds in 1 month. **Tips:** Also hosts the National Ten-Minute Play Contest to identify new playwrights.

ALABAMA SHAKESPEARE FESTIVAL

The State Theatre, 1 Festival Dr., Montgomery, AL 36117-4605. 334-271-5300.
E-mail gorel@asf.net. Web site: www.asf.net. **Description:** Southern and African-American themes/writers. Seeking new full-length plays for production. Sponsors local young playwrights' contest (new). Offers workshops/readings; 1-2 will see full production. **Plays/season:** 10 (average 200-400 submissions). **Proposals:** Send synopsis, resume, recommendations, cast list and SASE. Accepts unsolicited manuscripts. No e-queries. Responds in 10 months. **Tips:** Be familiar with Southern writing. Avoid cliché, plays that recall the movies. "We cannot do edgy or urban-style plays with language and themes that offend a conservative audience, but are contemporary in outlook and will embrace difficult subjects." See our list of productions on Web site. Avoid cinematic styles, gritty subject/language. No musicals.

THE ALLEY THEATRE

615 Texas Ave., Houston, TX 77002. 713-228-9341.
Web site: www.alleytheatre.org. **Description:** Full-length plays, including translations and adaptations. No unsolicited scripts; agent submissions or professional recommendations only.

ALLIANCE THEATRE COMPANY

1280 Peachtree St. NE, Atlanta, GA 30309. 404-733-4650.
Web site: www.alliancetheatre.org. **Description:** New full-length children's plays, comedy or drama. Plays for a culturally diverse community told in stylish or adventurous ways. **Plays/season:** 11 (average 500 submissions), some freelance material. **Proposals:** Send synopsis, 10 page sample, SASE. No unsolicited mss. Responds in 2-3 months (queries), 6-9 months (submissions). Electronic queries accepted. **Tips:**

"As the premier theatre of the Southeast, the Alliance Theatre sets the highest artistic standards, creating the powerful experience of shared theatre for diverse people."

AMERICAN LITERATURE THEATRE PROJECT

Fountain Theatre, 5060 Fountain Ave., Los Angeles, CA 90029.
Web site: www.fountaintheatre.com. **Description:** One-act and full-length stage adaptations of classic and contemporary American literature. Sets and cast size unrestricted. **Proposals:** Send synopsis and SAS postcard. **Payment:** Standard pay, set by Dramatists Guild.

AMERICAN LIVING HISTORY THEATER

P.O. Box 752, Greybull, WY 82426.
Description: One-act dramas, ideally, one or two characters, about American historical and literary characters and events. Nonfiction, historically accurate, primary source material. **Proposals:** Submit treatment and letter with SASE. Responds in 6 months.

AMERICAN STAGE

211 Third St. S, St. Petersburg, FL 33731. 727-823-7529.
Web site: www.americanstage.org. **Description:** Full-length comedies and dramas. Send synopsis with short description of cast and production requirements. Include SAS postcard. **Payment:** negotiable. Submit September-January.

AMERICAN THEATRE OF ACTORS

314 W 54th St., New York, NY 10019.
Description: Full-length dramas for a cast of 2-6. Submit complete play with SASE. Responds in 1-2 months.

ANCHORAGE PRESS PLAYS, INC.

International Agency of Plays for Young People
P.O. Box 2901, Louisville, KY 40201. 502-583-2288.
E-mail: applays@bellsouth.net. Web site: www.applays.com. **Description:** Publishes plays, proven in multiple production, for children in grades K-12.

MAXWELL ANDERSON PLAYWRIGHTS SERIES

P.O. Box 671, W. Redding, CT 06896.
Description: Produces six professional staged readings of new plays each year. Send complete script with SASE.

ARKANSAS REPERTORY THEATRE COMPANY

601 S Main St., P.O. Box 110, Little Rock, AR 72203-0110. 501-378-0445.
E-mail: therep@alltel.net. Web site: www.therep.org. **Description:** Full-length comedies, dramas, and musicals; prefer up to 8 characters. **Proposals:** Send synopsis, cast list, resume, and SASE; do not send complete manuscript. Responds in 3 months.

BAKER'S PLAYS

P.O. Box 69922, Quincy, MA 02269-9222. 617-745-0805.
E-mail: editor@bakersplays.com. Web site: www.bakersplays.com.
Description: Prefers produced plays for high school, community and regional theatres. Publishes full-length or one-act plays for young audiences, musicals and chancel dramas. **Proposals:** Send complete play (no samples) c/o the editor. Include cover letter, resume, and press clippings if available. CD, tape, or sheet music must accompany musical submissions. Include SASE with pre-paid priority shipping for return of scripts. Responds in 6-8 months.

BARTER THEATER

P.O. Box 867, Abingdon, VA 24212-0867. 267-628-2281
E-mail: barter@naxs.com. Web site: www.bartertheatre.com.
Description: Full-length dramas, comedies, adaptations, and children's plays. **Proposals:** Submit synopsis, dialogue sample, and SASE. Responds in 6-8 months. **Payment:** Standard royalty.

BERKELEY REPERTORY THEATRE

2025 Addison St., Berkeley, CA 94704. 510-647-2900.
E-mail: info@berkeleyrep.org. Web site: www.berkeleyrep.org. **Description:** Seeking new full-length plays for production, five mainstage/two parallel season productions, mid-level career and above. Some work commissioned. No restrictions on cast or set. Agent submissions only; no unsolicited scripts accepted. See website for guidelines. **Plays/season:** 7 (400 submissions). **Proposals:** No unsolicited manuscripts. Accepts submissions only from agents and professional colleagues. Submit resume with SASE. Responds in 3-4 months. No e-queries.

BERKSHIRE THEATRE FESTIVAL

P.O. Box 797, Stockbridge, MA 01262.
E-mail: kate@berkshiretheatre.org. Web site: www.berkshiretheatre.org.
Description: Full-length comedies, musicals, and dramas; cast to 8. **Proposals:** Submit through agent only.

BOARSHEAD THEATER

425 S Grand Ave., Lansing, MI 48917. 517-484-7800.
E-mail: boarshead-admin@boarshead.org. Web site: www.boarshead.org.
Description: Seeking new full-length plays, comedy and drama, cast of 4-10. Single or unit set preferred. SASE. Send only 10 pages of representitive dialogue, cast list (with descriptions), number of sets, and a one page (only) précis. **Plays/season:** 6 (1,000 submissions); 100% freelance. **Proposals:** Send synopsis, return postcard, 10 pages of dialogue. No unsolicited manuscripts or electronic queries. Responds in 2-3 months (queries), 6-12 months (submissions). **Payment:** Varies, on acceptance. **Tips:** Sponsors Michigan-wide UPF, high school, middle school, and elementary school playwriting contests. Five staged readings/year.

BRISTOL RIVERSIDE THEATRE

P.O. Box 1250, Bristol, PA 19007.
Web site: www.brtstage.org. **Description:** Seeks full-length plays, up to 15 actors, with simple set.

CENTER STAGE

700 N Calvert St., Baltimore, MD 21202. 410-685-3200.
E-mail: jmagruder@centerstage.org. Web site: www.centerstage.org. **Description:** Full-length comedies, dramas, translations, and adaptations. **Proposals:** Send cover letter with brief synopsis, 10 pages of sample dialogue, resume or bio, cast list, production history, and SASE. Submit tape or selection of songs for musicals. Responds in 3-6 weeks. Does not accept unsolicited manuscripts.

CHILDSPLAY INC.

P.O. Box 517, Tempe, AZ 85280-0517. 480-858-2127.
E-mail: childsplayaz@juno.com. Web site: www.childsplayaz.org.
Description: Seeking new full-length and one act children's plays, multi-generational, 45-120 minutes: dramas, musicals, and adaptations for family audiences. Cast up to 12. Set: no restrictions. Productions may need to travel. Prefer visual, theatrical pieces rather than didactic message plays. SASE. **Plays/season:** 8 (50 submissions), 2-3% freelance. **Proposals:** Send query with synopsis, resume, cast list, SASE/return postcard. Accepts unsolicited manuscripts and e-queries. Responds in 2 months. Offers workshops/readings. **Tips:** "We are a major theatre for youth company and we deal with serious subjects: AIDS, illiteracy, Vietnam War. We also produce musicals, comedies, and historical drama."

CIRCLE IN THE SQUARE THEATRE SCHOOL

1633 Broadway, New York, NY 10019-6795.
E-mail: circleinthesquare@att.net. Web site: www.circlesquare.org.
Description: Accepts scripts, tapes, and sheet music for children's theatre using 4-6 adult actors. Prefers multi-cultural or American historical themes, 35-45 minutes long; may include music.

CITY THEATRE COMPANY

1300 Bingham St., Pittsburgh, PA 15203.
Web site: www.citytheatrecompany.org. **Description:** Commissions, develops, and produces contemporary plays of substance and ideas that engage diverse audiences. Interests: new plays; compelling stories; unconventional form, content, and use of language; under-represented voices (women, writers of color, writers who are disabled). Full-length dramas, comedies, musicals, adaptations, translations, solo plays. Prefers cast limit of 8. **Proposals:** No unsolicited or e-mail submissions. Agented submissions, or query with resume, synopsis, character breakdown, dialogue sample (15 pages), development/production history, music demo, and SASE. No phone calls.

I. E. CLARK PUBLICATIONS

P.O. Box 246, Schulenburg, TX 78956.

E-mail: ieclark@cvtv.net. Web site: www.ieclark.com. **Description:** Publishes one-act and full-length plays and musicals for children, young adults, and adults, that have been produced. Serious drama, comedies, classics, fairytales, melodramas, and holiday plays. **Proposals:** Send SASE with submissions. Responds in 2-6 months. **Payment:** Royalty.

THE CONSERVATORY THEATRE ENSEMBLE

Tamalpais High School, 700 Miller Ave., Mill Valley, CA 94941.

E-mail: directors@ctetam.org. Web site: www.ctetam.org. **Description:** Comedies, dramas, children's plays, adaptations, and scripts on high school issues, for casts of 8-20. Plays with flexible casting, adaptable to "ensemble" style. One-act, 30-minute plays are especially needed; produce 50 short plays each season using teenage actors. **Proposals:** Send synopsis and resume.

CONTEMPORARY DRAMA SERVICE

Meriwether Publishing Co.

885 Elkton Dr., Colorado Springs, CO 80907.

E-mail: merpcds@aol.com. Web site: meriwetherpublishing.com.

Description: Publishes plays and supplemental textbooks on theatrical subjects for middle school, high school, and college students. Accepts new full-length and one-act plays—comedy or musical. Prefers large-cast scripts with limited staging requirements. No obscene language, unsuitable subject matter, or violence. Prefers comedic material, but publishes some serious work appropriate to educational markets. Include SASE. **Plays/season:** Approx. 800 submissions, 100% freelance. **Proposals:** Send query with synopsis, return postcard, SASE. Accepts unsolicited mss. Responds in 2 weeks (queries), 4 weeks (submissions). Accepts electronic queries. **Payment:** Royalties.

CROSSROADS THEATRE CO.

7 Livingston Ave., New Brunswick, NJ 08901. 732-729-9559.

Web site: www.crossroadstheatre.net. **Description:** Full-length and one-act dramas, comedies, musicals, and adaptations; issue-oriented experimental plays with honest, imaginative, and insightful examinations of the African-American experience. Also interested in African and Caribbean plays and plays exploring cross-cultural issues. **Proposals:** No unsolicited scripts; query first with synopsis, cast list, and resume. Include SASE.

DELAWARE THEATRE COMPANY

200 Water St., Wilmington, DE 19801-5030.

Web site: www.delawaretheatre.org. **Description:** Full-length comedies and dramas. Cast up to 10. **Proposals:** Responds in 6 months. Unsolicited manuscripts from local authors only. Agent submissions considered. Include SASE.

DETROIT REPERTORY THEATRE

13103 Woodrow Wilson Ave., Detroit, MI 48238.

Description: Full-length comedies and dramas. Scripts accepted October-April.

DORSET THEATRE FESTIVAL

P.O. Box 510, Dorset, VT 05251. 802-867-2223.

E-mail: theatre@sover.net. Web site: www.theatredirectories.com.

Description: Seeking new full-length scripts with general audience appeal, comedy and drama. Cast: Prefer less than 8. Prefer unit set. Also operates a writers' colony, Dorset Colony for Writers. **Proposals:** No unsolicited mss. Send query with synopsis, resume, professional recommendations, cast list, 10 pages of dialogue. Responds in 1 month. Accepts electronic queries. **Payment:** Royalty on production. **Tips:** "Most new plays come from professional contacts or through our writers' colony."

DRAMATIC PUBLISHING COMPANY

311 Washington St., Woodstock, IL 60098. 815-338-7170.

E-mail: plays@dramaticpublishing.com. Web site: www.dramaticpublishing.com.

Description: Publishes full-length and one-act plays and musicals for professional, stock, amateur, and children's theater market. **Payment:** Royalty.

EAST WEST PLAYERS

120 N Judge John Aiso St., Los Angeles, CA 90012. 213-625-7000.

E-mail: info@eastwestplayers.org. Web site: www.eastwestplayers.org.

Description: Seeking new full-length plays in comedy, drama, musicals and special material dealing with Asian/Asian Pacific/Asian American issues. Offers periodic contests and workshops/readings. **Plays/season:** 4 (100 submissions), 10% freelance. **Proposals:** Send query with synopsis, return postcard, resume, cast list, SASE. Accepts unsolicited manuscripts. No e-queries. Responds in 2-4 months (queries), 3-9 months (submissions). **Tips:** Avoid Asian stereotypes.

ELDRIDGE PUBLISHING CO.

P.O. Box 14367, Tallahassee, FL 32317. 800-447-8243.

E-mail: info@histage.com. Web site: www.histage.com. **Description:** Publishes one-act and full-length plays and musicals for schools, churches, and community theatre groups. Comedies, tragedies, dramas, children's theatre, adaptations, interactive plays, and religious plays (all holidays). **Proposals:** Submit complete manuscript with cover letter. Responds in 2 months. **Payment:** Flat fee for religious plays, royalty for all else.

ENSEMBLE STUDIO THEATRE

549 W 52nd St., New York, NY 10019. 212-247-4982.

Web site: www.ensemblestudiotheatre.org. **Description:** Seeking new full-length and one-act plays: comedy, drama, science/technology, and plays by African-American women writers. New one-act plays, 15-45 minutes (annual spring one-act play marathon; deadline, November 8). New full-length plays by African-American women ("Going to the River Series"; deadline, November 1). New readings of plays in development. **Proposals:** Send resume, cast list, SASE. Accepts unsolicited manuscripts. Responds in 6 months.

FLORIDA STAGE
Plaza Del Mar, 262 S Ocean Blvd., Manalapan, FL 33462. 561-585-3404.
Web site: www.floridastage.org. **Description:** Full-length comedies, dramas, and musicals. **Proposals:** Agent submissions only. Responds in 9 months. **Payment:** Royalty.

WILL GEER THEATRICUM BOTANICUM
P.O. Box 1222, Topanga, CA 90290.
E-mail: theatricum@earthlink.net. Web site: www.theatricum.com. **Description:** Seeking new full-length plays: comedy, drama, and musicals for large outdoor rustic stage. All types of scripts for outdoor theater. Playreading performances. **Plays/season:** 4 (175 submissions), 1% freelance. **Proposals:** Send synopsis, sample pages, SASE. Accepts e-queries. Revisions/criticisms offered. Occasional contests. Responds sooner if sent in September-December. **Tips:** New play series—Botanicum Seedlings. Year round. 9 showings/year selected.

THE GLOBE THEATRES
P.O. Box 122171, San Diego, CA 92112-2171.
Description: Full-length comedies, dramas, and musicals. **Proposals:** No unsolicited manuscripts. Submit through agent, or query with synopsis.

THE GOODMAN THEATRE
170 N Dearborn St., Chicago, IL 60601. 312-443-3811.
E-mail: staff@goodman-theatre.org. Web site: www.goodman-theatre.org.
Description: Accepts queries for full-length comedies or dramas from recognized literary agents or producing organizations only. **Proposals:** Does not accept unsolicited scripts.

THE GUTHRIE THEATER
725 Vineland Place, Minneapolis, MN 55403. 612-377-2224.
E-mail: joh@guthrietheater.org. Web site: www.guthrietheater.org.
Description: Produces full-length dramas and adaptations of world literature, classic masterworks, oral traditions, and folktales. **Proposals:** No unsolicited scripts; accepts new play submissions from literary agents only. Responds in 3-6 months.

HEUER PUBLISHING COMPANY
210 2nd St., Suite 301, Cedar Rapids, IA 52406-0248. 319-364-6311.
E-mail: editor@hitplays.com. Web site: www.hitplays.com. **Description:** Publishes new full-length and one-act plays for comedy, drama, musicals, and adaptations. Prefers large cast, mostly female, and simple sets. **Plays/season:** 15 (200 submissions), 100% freelance. **Proposals:** Send query with synopsis, cast list, and SASE. See

guidelines. Accepts unsolicited mss. Responds in 1 month (queries), 1-2 months (submissions). **Payment:** Royalty. **Tips:** No violence or derogatory, racist, or sexist language or situations. "We publish plays for middle, junior, and senior high schools and community theatres. Creative dialogue and intriguing characters crucial."

HONOLULU THEATRE FOR YOUTH

2846 Ualena St., Honolulu, HI 96819. www.htyweb.org.
Description: Plays, 60-90 minutes, for young people and family audiences. Adult casts. Contemporary issues, Pacific themes, etc. Unit sets, small cast. **Proposals:** Query or send cover letter with synopsis, cast list, and SASE. **Payment:** Royalties negotiable. **Tips:** See Web site for more information about season.

ILLINOIS THEATRE CENTER

371 Artists' Walk, P.O. Box 397, Park Forest, IL 60466. 708-481-3510.
E-mail: ilthctr@bigplanet.com. Web site: www.ilthctr.org. **Description:** Full-length comedies, dramas, musicals, and adaptations, for unit/fragmentary sets, up to 8 cast members. Also offers workshops and readings. **Proposals:** Send summary and SAS postcard. No unsolicited manuscripts. **Payment:** Negotiable rates.

JEWISH REPERTORY THEATRE

1395 Lexington Ave., New York, NY 10128. 212-415-5550.
E-mail: mail@jrt.org. Web site: www.jrt.org. **Description:** Full-length comedies, dramas, musicals, and adaptations, with up to 10 cast members, relating to the Jewish experience. **Proposals:** Enclose SASE. **Payment:** Pays varying rates.

KUMU KAHUA THEATRE

46 Merchant St., Honolulu, HI 96813. 808-536-4222.
Description: Full-length plays, especially relevant to life in Hawaii. Prefers simple sets for arena productions. Offers reading and contests. **Proposals:** Submit resume and synopsis. **Payment:** Pays $50/performance.

LOS ANGELES DESIGNERS' THEATRE

P.O. Box 1883, Studio City, CA 91614-0883. 323-650-9600.
E-mail: ladesigners@juno.com. **Description:** Seeking proposals for new, full-length plays: comedy, drama, musicals, and adaptations. Can incorporate religious, social or political themes, street language, nudity, etc. No cast or set restrictions. Looking to commission scripts on work-for-hire basis. Has produced over 400 original works since 1970. **Plays/season:** 6-18 (1,200 submissions/month), 100% freelance. **Proposals:** Query with proposal. Responds in 4-5 months. Accepts electronic queries.**Payment:** Pays royalties on performance. **Tips:** "We want proposals we can commission into highly commercial shows for our use. No guidelines, just send proposal."

THE MAGIC THEATRE

Fort Mason Ctr., Bldg. D, San Francisco, CA 94123. 415-441-8001.
Web site: www.magictheatre.org. **Description:** Comedies and dramas, interested in

political, non-linear, and multicultural work for mainstage productions. **Proposals:** Query with synopsis, resume, first 10-20 pages of script, and SASE. Accepts unsolicited manuscripts by Bay area playwrights. **Payment:** Pays varying rates. **Tips:** Smaller casts preferred (6 and under).

MANHATTAN THEATRE CLUB

311 W 43rd St., Fl. 8, New York, NY 10036. 212-399-3000.

E-mail: lit@mtc-nyc.org. Web site: www.manhattantheatreclub.com.

Description: Seeking new plays: comedy, drama, musicals, and adaptations. **Proposals:** Accepts submissions from agents and by invitation only.

MARK TAPER FORUM

601 W Temple St., Los Angeles, CA 90012. 213-972-8033.

E-mail: scritps@ctgla.org. Web site: www.taperahmanson.com. **Description:** Seeks new full-length plays. Annual New Work Festival, offering selected playwrights resources to work on their plays. Each play gets at least one open public rehearsal in a small Los Angeles theater. Deadline: March 1. **Plays/season:** 6 (900 submissions), 5% freelance. **Proposals:** No unsolicited manuscripts. Send query with synopsis, resume, recommendations, 5-10 pages of sample dialogue, and SASE. Accepts e-queries. Responds in 8-10 weeks.

MCCARTER THEATRE COMPANY

91 University Pl., Princeton, NJ 08540. 609-258-6500.

Web site: www.mccarter.org. **Description:** Seeks new full-length plays (comedies, dramas, and adaptations). **Plays/season:** 6. **Proposals:** Send query with synopsis, resume, cast list, and SASE. **Tips:** Does not accept unsolicited manuscripts or e-queries.

METROSTAGE

1201 N Royal St., Alexandria, VA 22314. 703-548-9044.

Web site: www.metrostage.org. **Description:** Seeking new full-length plays in comedy, drama, and small musicals. Prefers unit sets and cast of 2-3. Workshops/readings offered. Interested only in plays with history of readings and development. **Plays/season:** 5-6 plays produced/season (300 submissions), 80% freelance. **Proposals:** Send query with synopsis, production/reading history, resume, cast breakdown, 10-page dialogue sample, and SASE.

MILL MOUNTAIN THEATRE

One Market Square SE, Fl. 2, Roanoke, VA 24011. 540-342-5749.

E-mail: outreach@millmountain.org. Web site: www.millmountain.org.

Description: Seeking new full-length plays: comedy, drama, musicals, and children's. **Plays/season:** 15-18 (200-500 submissions), 50% freelance. **Proposals:** Send queries with return postcard, resume, recommendations, SASE. Accepts unsolicited manuscripts. Responds in 6 weeks (queries), 6-8 months (submissions). Accepts electronic queries. **Payment:** On production. **Tips:** Send query and dialogue sample. Does not accept queries or submissions by e-mail. See Web site for specific guidelines.

MISSOURI REPERTORY THEATRE

4949 Cherry St., Kansas City, MO 64110. 816-235-2727.
E-mail: theatre@umkc.edu. Web site: www.missourirep.org. **Description:** Seeks full-length classical, contemporary, African-American, Asian-American, Hispanic-American, and Mid-Western comedies and dramas. **Proposals:** Send letter of interest to Literary Dept. with synopsis, full script, cast list, resume, and SASE. Response may take more than 6 months.

NATIONAL BLACK THEATRE, INC.

2033 Fifth Ave., Harlem, NY 10035.
Description: Drama, musicals, and children's plays. Scripts should reflect African and African-American lifestyle. Historical, inspirational, and ritualistic forms appreciated. Workshops and readings.

NATIONAL DRAMA SERVICE

LifeWay, One LifeWay Plaza, Nashville, TN 37234-0160.
E-mail: terry.terry@lifeway.com. Web site: www.lifeway.com. **Description:** Publishes dramatic material (drama in worship, puppet and clown scripts, Christian comedy, mime/movement scripts, readers theater, creative worship services, and monologues) used in Christian ministry. **Proposals:** Submit scripts 2-10 minutes long. E-mail or write for specific submission guidelines. **Comments:** "We seek scripts that communicate the message of Christ and that help even the smallest churches enhance their ministry with drama."

NEW YORK SHAKESPEARE FESTIVAL/
JOSEPH PAPP PUBLIC THEATER

425 Lafayette St., New York, NY 10003. 212-539-8500.
Web site: www.publictheater.org. **Description:** Full-length plays, translations, adaptations, musicals, operas, and solo pieces. **Proposals:** Submit synopsis, 10-page sample scene, letter of inquiry, and CD or cassette of 3-5 songs for musicals or operas.

NEW YORK STATE THEATRE INSTITUTE

37 First St., Troy, NY 12180.
Web site: www.nysti.org. **Description:** Emphasis on new, full-length plays and musicals for family audiences. **Proposals:** Query with synopsis and cast list.

ODYSSEY THEATRE ENSEMBLE

2055 S Sepulveda Blvd., Los Angeles, CA 90025. 310-477-2055.
E-mail: odyssey@odysseytheatre.com. Web site: www.odysseytheatre.com.
Description: Seeking new full-length comedies, dramas, musicals, and adaptations

with provocative subject matter, or plays that stretch and explore the possibilities of theater. Cast: limit to 10. Offers workshops/readings. **Plays/season:** 9 (200-300 submissions). **Proposals:** No unsolicited mss. Send synopsis, resume, 10 pages of dialogue, cast list, SASE. Responds in 2 weeks (queries), 6 months (submissions). Accepts electronic inquiries. **Payment:** Varies.

OLDCASTLE THEATRE COMPANY
Bennington Center for the Arts, P.O. Box 1555, Bennington, VT 05201.
Description: Full-length comedies, dramas, and musicals for small cast (up to 10). Offers workshops and readings. **Proposals:** Submit synopsis and cast list in the winter. Responds in 6 months. **Payment:** Royalty.

PAPER MILL: THE STATE THEATRE OF NEW JERSEY
Brookside Dr., Millburn, NJ 07041. 973-379-3636.
E-mail: pparker@papermill.org. Web site: www.papermill.org. **Description:** Produces full-length plays and musicals. **Proposals:** Submit completed work, including script, synopsis, resume, and tape for musicals. Responds in 6-12 months.

PENGUIN REPERTORY COMPANY
P.O. Box 91, Stony Point, Rockland County, NY 10980.
Description: Full-length comedies and dramas, cast size to 4. **Proposals:** Submit script, resume, and SASE. **Payment:** Varies.

PEOPLE'S LIGHT AND THEATRE COMPANY
39 Conestoga Rd., Malvern, PA 19355.
Description: Full-length comedies, dramas, and adaptations. **Proposals:** Query with synopsis and ten pages of script. No unsolicited manuscripts. **Payment:** Varies.

PIER ONE THEATRE
Box 894, Homer, AK 99603-0894. 907-235-2333.
E-mail: lance@xyz.net. Web site: www.pieronetheatre.org. **Description:** Seeking new full-length and one-act comedies, dramas, musicals, children's plays, and adaptations. Offers workshops/readings. **Plays/season:** 5-7 (300 submissions), 1-2% freelance. **Proposals:** Submit complete script; include piano score with musicals, SASE. Responds in 4-6 months. Accepts electronic queries. **Payment:** Royalty on production. **Tips:** "Do not start the play with a phone call! No AIDS plays, New Age plays, etc. Your work must have something wonderful and unique to offer."

PIONEER DRAMA SERVICE
P. O. Box 4267, Englewood, CO 80155. 303-779-4035.
E-mail: editors@pioneerdrama.com. Web site: www.pioneerdrama.com.
Description: Publishes full-length and one-act plays, musicals, melodramas, and children's theatre. No un-produced plays. Simple costumes and sets, and large, flexible casts with mostly female roles preferred. **Proposals:** Query or submit manuscript with SASE. **Payment:** Royalty.

PLAYWRIGHTS HORIZONS

416 W 42nd St., New York, NY 10036. 212-564-1235.
Web site: www.playwrightshorizons.org. **Description:** Full-length, original comedies, dramas, and musicals by American authors. No one-acts, adaptations, or screenplays. **Proposals:** Synopses discouraged; send script, resume and SASE, include cd
or tape for musicals. Off-Broadway contract.

PLAYWRIGHTS' PLATFORM

P.O. Box 35151, Boston, MA 02135.
Web site: www.playwrightsplatform.org. **Description:** Full-length and one-act plays
of all kinds. Script development workshops and public readings for Massachusetts
playwrights only. **Plays/season:** 55 readings/season (100 submissions), 100% free-
lance. **Proposals:** Send scripts with short synopsis, resume, SAS postcard, and SASE.
Readings held 3x/month at Hovey Theater in Waltham, MA. Responds in 1-2 months.
No electronic queries. **Tips:** Massachusetts residents only. No sexist or racist material.
"We have readings every Sunday evening. We're always looking for scripts."

POPLAR PIKE PLAYHOUSE

7653 Old Poplar Pike, Germantown, TN 38138. 901-755-7775.
E-mail: efblue@aol.com. Web site: www.ppp.org. **Description:** Full-length and one-
act comedies, dramas, musicals, and children's plays. We are in a high school; most
plays feature high school students, with characters that students can realistically portray and understand. **Plays/season:** 4. **Proposals:** Send synopsis with SAS postcard
and resume.

PRINCETON REP COMPANY/
PRINCETON REP SHAKESPEARE FESTIVAL

One Palmer Square, Suite 541, Princeton, NJ 08542. 609-921-3682.
E-mail: prcreprap@aol.com. Web site: www.princetonrep.org. **Description:** Seeks
full-length plays which address contemporary issues in challenging and provocative
terms, and adaptations/translations of classical plays especially the Greeks and
Shakespeare. Particular interest: plays by or about women. Considered for reading,
workshop and production. **Proposals:** Submit 10 page dialogue sample, 2-page synopsis, cast list, set requirements, and resume. Responds within 9-12 months.

THE REPERTORY THEATRE OF ST. LOUIS

P.O. Box 191730, St. Louis, MO 63119.
E-mail: sgregg@repstl.org. Web site: www.repstl.org.
Description: Query with brief synopsis, technical requirements, and cast size.
Unsolicited manuscripts are returned unread.

ROUND HOUSE THEATRE

P.O. Box 30688, Bethesda, MD 20824. 301-933-9530.
E-mail: dcrosby@roundhousetheatre.org. Website: www.roundhousetheatre.org.
Description: Seeking new full-length plays, translations, adaptations, musicals, solo

pieces, and plays for young audiences. Cast: 8-10 actors max. Unit set preferred. Offers workshops/reading, revisions for New Works series (November and June, readings of local playwrights). **Proposals:** No unsolicited scripts; will accept synopsis. Send 10-page dialogue sample, cast, tech requirements, resume and SASE. Address all submissions c/o Production Department.

SAMUEL FRENCH, INC.
45 W 25th St., New York, NY 10010.
E-mail: samuelfrench@earthlink.net. Web site: www.samuelfrench.com.
Description: Publishes full-length plays and musicals. One-act plays, 20-45 minutes. Children's plays, 45-60 minutes. Stage plays. Unpublished writers considered. **Proposals:** Query with complete manuscript; unsolicited and multiple queries okay. No fees.

SEATTLE REPERTORY THEATRE
155 Mercer St., P.O. Box 900923, Seattle, WA 98109. 206-443-2210.
Web site: www.seattlerep.org. **Description:** Produces full-length comedies, dramas, and adaptations. **Proposals:** Submit letter of inquiry, resume with previous writing experience, synopsis, 10 sample pages of script, and SASE. Does not accept unsolicited submissions.

SINISTER WISDOM
P.O. Box 3252, Berkeley, CA 94703.
Description: Publishes one-act (15 pages or less) lesbian drama that reflects diverse and multicultural experiences. Responds in 3-9 months to submissions. Send SASE for upcoming themes.

SOCIETY HILL PLAYHOUSE
507 S 8th St., Philadelphia, PA 19147-1325. 215-923-0210.
Web site: www.societyhillplayhouse.com. **Description:** Full-length dramas, comedies, and musicals, up to 6 cast members, simple set. **Proposals:** Submit synopsis and SASE. Responds in 6 months. **Payment:** Nominal payment.

SOUTH COAST REPERTORY
P. O. Box 2197, Costa Mesa, CA 92628-2197. 714-708-5500.
Web site: www.scr.org. **Description:** Full-length plays, adaptations, translations, musicals, and theatre for young audiences. COLAB (Collaboration Laboratory) New Play Program: developemental program culminating in staged readings, workshop productions, and full productions. **Proposals:** No unsolicited scripts; send synopsis, dialogue sample, and letter of inquiry. **Payment:** playwright receives grant, commission, and/or royalties depending on nature of project.

SOUTHERN APPALACHIAN REPERTORY THEATRE
P.O. Box 1720, Mars Hill, NC 28754. 828-689-1384.
E-mail: sart@mhc.edu. Web site: http://sart.mhc.edu. **Description:** Seeking new

full-length plays: comedy, drama, and musicals—plays that explore and celebrate the culture, history, or life in the Southern Appalachian region are especially welcomed. Enclose SASE for return of script. Musicals must include the book and tape or CD of four songs. New plays are defined as unproduced and unpublished. Workshops are ok. Adaptations of books are not accepted. Southern Appalachian Playwrights Conference in spring; 4 plays read and discussed; playwrights get room and board. One play may receive full production during the following SART season. First-time authors welcome. Scripts received all year, but cut-off is October 31 for each year's submissions. **Plays/season:** 5-6 (500 submissions), 5% freelance. **Proposals:** Submit resume, recommendations, full script, and SASE. Responds in 2 weeks (queries), 3-4 months (submissions). Accepts electronic queries. **Payment:** Honorarium to produce script and present 5-10 performances in two-week period. Residency in Mars Hill. Some travel expenses. **Tips:** "Avoid scripts that read like screenplays, and use of profanity for shock value only."

STAGE LEFT THEATRE

3408 N Sheffield, Chicago, IL 60657. 773-883-8830.
E-mail: sltchicago@aol.com. Web site: www.stagelefttheatre.com.
Description: Produces and develops plays that raise the level of debate on social and political issues. Full-length comedies, dramas, and adaptations for cast of 1-12. Productions include post-show discussion. **Plays/season:** 4 (300 submissions). **Proposals:** Send synopsis, 10-page excerpt, resume, and SASE. No unsolicited scripts or e-queries. Responds in 3-5 months. **Payment:** On acceptance and on production. Purchases rights for one Chicago production. **Tips:** Welcomes new authors. Offers workshops/readings and new-play development program, Downstage Left.

STAGE ONE: PROFESSIONAL
THEATRE FOR YOUNG AUDIENCES

501 W Main St., Louisville, KY 40202. 502-589-5946.
E-mail: stageone@stageone.org. Web site: www.stageone.org. **Description:** Seeking new children's plays, adaptations of classics and original plays for young audiences (ages 4-18). No restrictions on cast or set. **Plays/season:** 8 (100-200 submissions), 10-20% freelance. 3 plays/year in reading series. **Proposals:** Submit script with resume and SASE. Responds in 4 months. **Payment:** Purchases performance rights. **Tips:** "We seek plays relevant to young people and their families, related to school curriculum, and classic tales of childhood, ancient and modern."

STAGES REPERTORY THEATRE

3201 Allen Pkwy., #101, Houston, TX 77019. 713-527-0220.
E-mail: stagestheatre.com. Web site: www.stagestheatre.com. **Description:** Southwest Festival of New Plays. Divisions: Children's Theatre, Texas Playwrights, Women Playwrights, and Hispanic Playwrights. Seeking new plays: comedy and drama (full-length). Cast: 6-8 max. Unit set with multiple locations preferable. **Plays/season:** 6 plays (250 submissions). **Proposals:** Send query with synopsis, return postcard, resume, cast list, SASE. Accepts unsolicited manuscripts. No e-queries. Responds in

2-6 months. **Payment:** Purchases performance rights. **Tips:** "We're not interested in realistic domestic dramas; prefer theatrically told stories."

STATE THEATER COMPANY

Austin Theatre Alliance, 719 Congress Ave., Austin, TX 78701. 512-472-2901. Web site: www.austintheatrealliance.org. **Description:** Seeks new full-length plays, both comedy and drama. **Plays/season:** 6 (200 submissions). **Proposals:** Send query with resume, synopsis, and 10-page dialogue sample. Does not accept material via e-mail. Responds in 1-6 months. Submit between December 1-March 1.

STOREFRONT

66 E Randolph St., Chicago, IL 60601. 312-744-2000 Web site: www.storefronttheater.org. **Description:** Publishes and produces performing arts programs that strive to expose the need for cultural awareness. **Proposals:** Submit completed proposal form, brief synopsis of manuscript, list of characters, proposed length, biographical information, proposed project budget, and company reference materials.

STUDIO ARENA THEATRE

710 Main St., Buffalo, NY 14202-1990. **Description:** Comedies and dramas, cast up to 8. Interested in plays of theatrical/nonrealistic nature. **Proposals:** Include synopsis, resume, cast list, and sample dialogue. Do not send full script.

THEATER OF THE FIRST AMENDMENT

George Mason University, Center for the Arts MSN 3E6, Fairfax, VA 22030. **Description:** Full-length comedies, drama, and adaptations. Send synopsis, resume, and 10 sample pages. **Tips:** "Cultural history made dramatic as distinct from history dramatized; large battles joined; hard question asked; word and image stretched."

THEATRE BUILDING CHICAGO

1225 W Belmont Ave., Chicago, IL 60657-3205. 773-929-7367. E-mail: jsparks@theatrebuildingchicago.org. Web site: www.theatrebuildingchicago.org. **Description:** New musicals only, all styles, full-length and one-act (10 min.), for children, young adults, opera and Broadway audiences, etc. No restrictions on cast. Writers workshop meets monthly (fee based). Write, call or e-mail for submission application. **Plays/season:** 20 readings; 3-4 skeletal productions/season (average 150-200 submissions), 50% freelance. **Proposals:** Send synopsis, resume, tape or CD along with piano/vocal score of threesongs, cast list, SASE. Responds in 3-6 months. **Tips:** Discourages single author projects.

THEATRE/TEATRO

Bilingual Foundation of the Arts 421 N Ave. 19, Los Angeles, CA 90031. 323-255-4044. E-mail: bfa99@earthlink.net. Web site: www.bfatheatre.org. **Description:** Produces four full-length mainstage productions each season with alternate weeks in Spanish and English. Plays include new translations and adaptations of classic Hispanic plays, plays by recognized Hispanic playwrights, and new plays by emerging Hispanic writers. Prefers small casts. **Proposals:** Submit manuscript with SASE. Pay varies.

THEATREWORKS

P.O. Box 50458, Palo Alto, CA 94303-0458. 650-463-1950.
E-mail: jeannie@theatreworks.org. Web site: www.theatreworks.org.
Description: Full-length comedies, dramas, and musicals. **Proposals:** Submit complete script or synopsis with SAS postcard and SASE, cast list, theatre resume, production history. For musicals, include cassette of up to 6 songs, with lyrics. Responds in 4-5 months. **Payment:** Varies.

THEATREWORKS/USA

151 W 26th St., Fl. 7, New York, NY 10001. 212-647-1100.
E-mail: info@theatreworksusa.org. Web site: www.theatreworksusa.org.
Description: Seeks one-act (60-90 minute) plays and musicals for family/young audiences/teens. Accepts adaptations of literary classics and contemporary work. Material should celebrate history's heroes/heroines, or dramatize historical events. Cast: 8 actors. **Plays/season:** Four (60-100 submissions), 3% freelance. **Proposals:** Send query with synopsis, cast list, SASE. Accepts unsolicited manuscripts and e-queries. Responds in 3-6 months. **Tips:** "We commission most work, but evaluate submitted scripts to find good writers. We want to encourage writers who have never written for this audience. Please submit your best work; it does not have to be a play or musical written specifically for children."

WALNUT STREET THEATRE COMPANY

825 Walnut St., Philadelphia, PA 19107. 212-574-3550.
Web site: www.wstonline.org. **Description:** Mainstage: Full-length comedies, dramas, musicals, and popular, upbeat adaptations; also, plays for studio stage, cast of 1-4. **Proposals:** Submit 10-20 sample pages with SAS postcard, character breakdown, synopsis. Musical submissions must include audio cassette or CD. Responds in 6 months with SASE. Pay varies.

WOOLLY MAMMOTH THEATRE COMPANY

917 M St. NW, Washington, DC 20001. 202-312-5270.
E-mail: mary@woollymammoth.net. Web site: www.woollymammoth.net.
Description: "We're looking for language-driven plays that deal with edgy situations through complex and intense character engagement." **Proposals:** Does not accept unsolicited scripts. **Payment:** Varies.

GREETING CARD PUBLISHERS

Companies selling greeting cards and novelty items (T-shirts, coffee mugs, buttons, etc.) often have their own specific requirements for the submission of ideas, verse, and artwork. In general, however, each verse or message should be typed double-space on a 3x5 or 4x6 card. Use only one side of the card, and be sure to put your name and address in the upper left-hand corner. Keep a copy of every verse or idea you send. (It's also advisable to keep a record of what you've submitted to each publisher.) Always enclose an SASE, and do not send out more than ten verses or ideas in a group to any one publisher. Never send original artwork unless a publisher indicates a definite interest in using your work.

AMBERLEY GREETING CARD COMPANY

11510 Goldcoast Dr., Cincinnati, OH 45249-1695. 513-489-2775.
E-mail: dcronstein@amberleygreeting.com. Web site: www.amberleygreeting.com.
Dan Cronstein, Editor. **Description:** Humorous ideas for cards: birthday, illness, friendship, anniversary, congratulations, "miss you," etc. Short, humorous verse ok. SASE for guidelines. **Payment:** $150. Rights: All. **Contact:** Chuck Marshall.

BLUE MOUNTAIN ARTS

P.O. Box 1007, Boulder, CO 80306. 303-449-0536.
E-mail: editorial@spsstudios.com. Web site: www.sps.com. **Description:** Poetry and writings suitable for publication on greeting cards and in books. Looking for original, heartfelt poetry and prose on love, friendship, family, special occasions, positive living, aspirations, self-help, and other similar topics. Submit seasonal material (Christmas, Valentine's Day, Mother's Day, etc.) 5 months in advance. Full book manuscripts also accepted. **Payment:** $300 for the first work chosen for publication on a card (payment scale escalates after that) and $50 if poem is used only in a book anthology. Guidelines available on request. **Tips:** "Definitely get a feel for what we publish by trying to find our cards and books in stores, but don't study them too closely, as we're looking for fresh, new ideas—not rewrites of existing cards."

BRILLIANT ENTERPRISES

117 W Valerio St., Santa Barbara, CA 93101-2927.
Web site: www.ashleighbrilliant.com. **Description:** Illustrated epigrams emphasizing truth, wit, universality, and originality. This line of greeting cards is very unusual and should be studied carefully before material is submitted. Payment is $60. Send $2 for catalog and samples. **Tips:** "Writers will be wasting their time and ours unless they first study our very unusual line. We supply a catalogue for $2." Rights: All. **Payment:** On acceptance. **Contact:** Ashleigh Brilliant.

COMSTOCK CARDS

600 S Rock, Suite 15, Reno, NV 89502-4115. 775-856-9400.
Web site: www.comstockcards.com. **Description:** Adult humor, outrageous or sexu-

al content, for greeting cards, invitations, and notepads. SASE required. **Payment:** varies, on publication. Guidelines on website. **Contact:** Production Department.

DAYSPRING GREETING CARDS

P.O. Box 1010, Siloam Springs, AR 72761.
E-mail: info@dayspring.com. **Description:** Inspirational material for everyday occasions and most holidays. Currently only accepting freelance copy submissions from published greeting card authors. Qualified writers should print "Previously Published" on lower left corner of mailing envelope containing the submissions. No more than 10 pieces/submission. **Payment:** $50 on acceptance. Send SASE or e-mail for guidelines. **Contact:** Freelance Editor.

DESIGN DESIGN, INC.

P.O. Box 2266, Grand Rapids, MI 49501-2266.
Tom Vituj, Creative Director. **Description:** Short verses for both humorous and sentimental concepts for greeting cards. Everyday (birthday, get well, just for fun, etc.) and seasonal (Christmas, Valentine's Day, Easter, Mother's Day, Father's Day, Graduation, Halloween, Thanksgiving) material. **Payment:** flat fee payment on publication. Include SASE with submission.

DUCK & COVER

P.O. Box 21640, Oakland, CA 94620.
E-mail: duckcover@aol.com. Jim Buser, Editor. **Description:** Does not produce any greeting cards. However, makes buttons, magnets and stickers with fresh, original and outrageous slogans. Send SASE for writer guidelines.

EPHEMERA, INC.

P.O. Box 490, Phoenix, OR 97535. 541-535-4195.
E-mail: mail@ephemera-inc.com. Web site: www.ephemera-inc.com. **Description:** Provocative, irreverent, and outrageously funny slogans for novelty buttons, magnets, and stickers. Submit a typed list of slogans. SASE. **Payment:** $40 per slogan. Pays on acceptance. **Tips:** "We're looking for satirical slogans about pop culture, free speech, work attitudes, women's and men's issues, coffee, booze, pot, drugs, food, politics, aging boomers, teens, gays and lesbians. Surprise us! Make us laugh out loud!"

FRAVESSI GREETINGS, INC.

P.O. Box 1800, Enfield, CT 06083-1800. 800-223-0963.
E-mail: info@fravessi.com. Web site: www.fravessi.com. **Description:** Short verse, mostly humorous or sentimental; cards with witty prose. Christmas and everyday material. **Payment:** varying rates, on acceptance.

FREEDOM GREETING CARDS

Plesh Creative Group, Inc., 75 West St., Walpole, MA 02081. 508-668-1224.
Web site: www.freedomgreetings.com. Suzanne Comeau, Editorial Department.

Description: Traditional and humorous messages for everyday occasions and all major seasons. **Payment:** negotiable rates, on acceptance. Query with SASE.

GALLANT GREETINGS CORPORATION

P.O. Box 308, Franklin Park, IL 60131. (P) 847-671-6500, (F) 847-233-2499.
E-mail: info@gallantgreetings.com. Web site: www.gallantgreetings.com.
Jack Lackouitz, Vice President Product Development. **Description:** Seeks ideas for seasonal, humorous and traditional greeting cards.

KATE HARPER DESIGNS

E-mail: kateharp@aol.com. **Description:** Edgy humor about everyday life. Young writers encouraged to submit. Also needs submissions by kids for "Kid Quote" line. **Payment:** $25-$50 and in sample cards ($18 worth). Contact via e-mail only. For standard guidelines, type "guidelines/adult" in subject line; for "Kid Quote" guidelines, type "guidelines/kids." Buys 100% freelance work several times/year.

OATMEAL STUDIOS GREETING CARD COMPANY

Box 138 TW, Rochester, VT 05767. 802-767-3171.
Web site: www.awoc.com/guidelines. Dawn Abraham, Editor.
Description: Humorous ideas for all occasions. Pays $75/idea purchased. **Tips:** "Your ideas must be original! We look forward to seeing your work!"

P.S. GREETINGS

5730 North Tripp, Chicago, IL 60646.
Web site: www.psgreetings.com. **Description:** Manufacturer of Everyday greeting cards. Seeks material for all major holidays, particular interest in Christmas. Writers should send verses or poems applicable to product line. **Payment:** one-time, flat fee; buys exclusive rights for all greeting and/or stationary products for indefinate use. Only submissions accompanied by an SASE will be returned. Responds within 30 days. **Contact:** Art Director.

PARAMOUNT CARDS, INC.

P.O. Box 6546, Providence, RI 02940-6546.
Web site: www.paramountcards.com. **Description:** Light humor, traditional, and inspirational sentiments for everyday occasions, Christmas, Valentine's Day, Easter, Mother's Day, Father's Day, Graduation and Thanksgiving. Submit each idea (5-10 per submission) on a 3x5 card with name and address on each; include SASE. No e-mail submissions. **Payment:** varies on acceptance. **Contact:** Editorial Freelance Coordinator.

RECYCLED PAPER GREETINGS, INC.

3636 N Broadway, Chicago, IL 60613-4488.
Web site: www.recycledpapergreetings.com. **Description:** Seeks original copy that is hip, flip, and concise. Risqué material considered. Send up to 10 pieces; mock-up ideas complete with artwork required. Will not consider ideas without appropriate

artwork included with submission. Allow 12 weeks for response. Payment made if design tests well and is picked up for distribution. Send SASE for guidelines. **Contact:** Gretchen Hoffman, John LeMoine.

ROCKSHOTS, INC.

20 Vandam St., Fl. 4, New York, NY 10013. 212-243-9661.
Web site: www.rockshots.com. Bob Vesce, Editor. **Description:** Humorous, soft line of greeting cards. Combination of sexy and humorous come-on type greeting and "cute" insult cards. Card gag can adopt a sentimental style, then take an ironic twist and end on an offbeat note. No sentimental or conventional material. Put gag lines on 8x11 paper with name, address, phone, and social security numbers in right corner, or individually on 3x5 cards. Submit 10 ideas/batch. **Payment:** $50 per copy upon acceptance. Send SASE for guidelines. Response: SASE required. Rights: Greeting Card. **Payment:** On acceptance.

MARCEL SCHURMAN COMPANY

101 New Montgomery, Fl. 6, San Francisco, CA 94105. 415-284-0133.
Web site: www.schurmanfinepapers.com. **Description:** Seeking sincere, positive, and clever text ideas for traditional and humorous greeting cards. Seeking text that goes beyond the standard generic verse. Poetry and off-color humor are not appropriate for this line. **Payment:** flat fee per text purchase. Send SASE or see Web site for submission guidelines. **Contact:** Text Editor.

VAGABOND CREATIONS, INC.

2560 Lance Dr., Dayton, OH 45409. 937-298-1124.
E-mail: vagabond@siscom.net. Web site: www.vagabondcreations.com.
Description: Greeting cards with graphics only on cover (no copy) and short punch line inside: birthday, everyday, Valentine's Day, Christmas, and graduation. Mildly risqué humor with double entendre acceptable. Ideas for illustrated theme stationery. **Payment:** $20, on acceptance. Response: SASE required. Rights: All. Payment: On acceptance. **Contact:** George F. Stanley, Jr.

ORGANIZATIONS

AMERICAN SOCIETY OF JOURNALISTS AND AUTHORS
1501 Broadway, Suite 302, New York, NY 10036. 212-997-0947.
E-mail: execdir@asja.org. Web site: www.asja.org. Brett Harvey, Executive Director.
National organization of independent writers of nonfiction, promoting high standards
of writing. ASJA benefits include referral services, many discount services, and ways
to explore professional issues and concerns with other writers; also produces a free
electronic bulletin board for freelancers on contract issues in the new-media age.
Members receive a monthly newsletter with confidential market information.
Membership open to professional freelance writers of nonfiction; qualifications
judged by the membership committee. Call or write for application details. Also hosts
annual writers conference with buying editors, publishers, and agents.

ARIZONA BOOK PUBLISHING ASSOCIATION
975 East Guadalupe Rd., Suite 20, Tempe, AZ 85283. 602-274-6264.
Web site: www.azbookpub.com. Serves the needs of Arizona book publishers and promotes the publishng industry in this state. Offers a newsletter and awards.

ASSITEJ/USA-INTERNATIONAL ASSOCIATION
OF THEATRE FOR CHILDREN AND YOUNG PEOPLE
724 Second Ave. S, Nashville, TN 37210. 615-254-5719.
E-mail: usassitej@aol.com. Promotes development of professional theater for young
audiences and international exchange. Provides a link between professional theaters,
artists, directors, training institutions, and arts agencies; sponsors festivals and forums
for interchange among theaters and theater artists. Annual dues: $65 (individual),
$35, (retiree), $30 (student).

ASSOCIATION OF AMERICAN PUBLISHERS
71 Fifth Ave., New York, NY 10003-3004. 212-255-0200.
E-mail: sbrandwein@publishers.org. Web site: www.publishers.org. Sara Brandwein,
Deputy Director, PSP Division. National trade organization for the U.S. publishing
industry.

THE AUTHORS GUILD
31 E 28th St., Fl. 10, New York, NY 10016. 212-563-5904.
E-mail: staff@authorsguild.org. Web site: www.authorsguild.org or www.authors-
guild.net. Paul Aiken, Executive Director. The largest organization of published writers in America. Membership offers access to web site-building software for writers
with discounted site-hosting fees, free reviews of publishing and agency contracts,
access to group health insurance, and seminars on subjects of concern. Authors Guild
also lobbies on behalf of authors on issues such as copyright, taxation, and freedom of
expression. A writer who has published a book in the last 7 years with an established

publisher, or has published three articles in general-circulation periodicals in the prior 18 months is eligible for active membership. An unpublished writer with a contract offer may be eligible for associate membership. First-year annual dues: $90.

THE AUTHORS LEAGUE OF AMERICA

31 E 28th St., Fl. 10, New York, NY 10016. 212-564-8350.
National organization representing 14,000 authors and dramatists on matters of joint concern, such as copyright, taxes, and freedom of expression. Membership is restricted to authors and dramatists who are members of the Authors Guild and the Dramatists Guild.

CATHOLIC BOOK PUBLISHERS ASSOCIATION

8404 Jamesport Dr., Rockford, IL 61108. 815-332-3245.
Web site: www.cbpa.org. Organization for Catholic book publishers in the U.S. and abroad. Offers newsletter, member directory, and professional resources.

DRAMATISTS GUILD OF AMERICA

1501 Broadway, Suite 701, New York, NY 10036-3909. 212-398-9366 Ext. 11.
E-mail: membership@dramatistsguild.com. Web site: www.dramaguild.com. Tom Epstein, Director of Membership Services. Professional association of playwrights, composers, and lyricists who work to protect author rights and to improve working conditions. Services include use of guild contracts; a toll-free number for members in need of business advice; discount tickets; access to health insurance and group term-life insurance plans; many seminars. Frederick Loewe room is available to members for readings and rehearsals at a nominal fee. Publishes *Dramatists Guild Resource Directory* and *The Dramatist Magazine*. All playwrights, produced or not, are eligible for membership. Annual dues: $125 (active), $75 (associate), $35 (student).

INTERNATIONAL ASSOCIATION OF CRIME WRITERS/
NORTH AMERICAN BRANCH

P.O. Box 8674, New York, NY 10116-8674. 212-243-8966.
E-mail: mfrisque@igc.org. Mary A. Frisque, Executive Director.
Description: Promotes communications among crime writers worldwide, encourages translation of crime writing into other languages, and defends authors against censorship. The North American branch of IACW also sponsors conferences, publishes a quarterly newsletter, *Border Patrol*, and awards the annual Hammett prize for literary excellence in crime writing (fiction or nonfiction) by a U.S. or Canadian author. Membership open to published authors of crime fiction, nonfiction, and screenplays. Agents, editors, critics and booksellers are also eligible to apply. Annual dues: $60.

INTERNATIONAL WOMEN'S WRITING GUILD

Box 810, Gracie Station, New York, NY 10028-0082. 212-737-7536.
E-mail: iwwg@iwwg-com. Web site: www.iwwg.com. Hannelore Hahn, Executive

Director. A network for personal and professional empowerment of women through writing. Services include 6 issues of a 32-page newsletter, a list of literary agents, independent small presses, and publishing services, access to group health insurance plan, reduced rates at writing conferences, referral services, and events, including an annual summer conference at Skidmore College in Saratoga Springs, NY, regional writing clusters, and year-round supportive networking. Any woman may join regardless of portfolio. Annual dues: $45.

MYSTERY WRITERS OF AMERICA
17 E 47th St., Fl. 6, New York, NY 10017. 212-888-8171.
Mary Beth Becker, Executive Director. Works to raise the prestige of mystery and detective writing, to encourage the reading of mysteries, and to defend the rights and increase the income of all writers in mystery, detection, and fact-crime writing. Each year, presents the Edgar Allan Poe Awards for the best mystery writing in a variety of fields. Membership classes: "active" (open to any writer who has made a sale in mystery, suspense, or crime writing), "associate" (professionals in allied fields), "corresponding" (writers living outside the U.S.), and "affiliate" (general members). Annual dues: $80 ($60 for "corresponding").

NATIONAL ASSOCIATION OF SCIENCE WRITERS
P.O. Box 890, Hedgesville, WV 25427. 304-754-5077.
E-mail: diane@nasw.org. Web site: www.nasw.org. Diane McGurgan, Executive Director. Promotes and helps to improve the flow of accurate information about science through all media. Anyone actively engaged in the dissemination of science information is eligible to apply. Members must be principally involved in reporting on science through newspapers, magazines, TV, or other media that reach the public directly. Annual dues: $75, students $30.

NATIONAL ASSOCIATION OF WOMEN WRITERS
P.O. Box 183812, Arlington, TX 76096. 866-821-5829.
E-mail: naww@onebox.com. Web site: www.naww.org. Sheri' McConnell, Founder/President. "NAWW is where women unite to write. We strive to support, encourage, and teach women writsers of all levels." Members have access to writing resources, participation in workshops and conferences, and access to online writing forums. Dues are $55 (US) and $65 (outside the US). See website for current listing of member benefits.

NATIONAL CONFERENCE OF EDITORIAL WRITERS
3899 N Front St., Harrisburg, PA 17110. 717-703-3015.
E-mail: ncew@pa-news.org. Web site: www.ncew.org. Nonprofit organization working to improve the quality of editorial pages and broadcast editorials, and to promote high standards among opinion writers and editors. Offers networking opportunities, regional meetings, page exchanges, foreign tours, educational opportunities and seminars, annual convention, and a subscription to the quarterly journal, *The Masthead*. Membership is open to opinion writers and editors for general-circulation newspa-

pers, radio or television stations, and syndicated columnists; teachers and students of journalism; and others who determine editorial policy. Annual dues (based on circulation or broadcast audience), $90-$200 (journalism educators: $100; students: $25).

THE NATIONAL LEAGUE OF AMERICAN PEN WOMEN, INC.

National Headquarters-Pen Arts Building
1300 17th St. NW, Washington, DC 20036-1973. 202-785-1997.
E-mail: nlapwi@juno.com. Web site: www.americanpenwomen.org. Wanda A. Rider, PhD., National President. Promotes development of creative talents of professional women in the arts. Membership is through local branches, in categories of Art, Letters, and Music.

NATIONAL WRITERS ASSOCIATION

3140 S Pooria, Suite 295, Aurora, CO 80014. 303-841-0246.
E-mail: sandywrter@aol.com. Web site. www.nationalwriters.com. Sandy Whelchel, Executive Director. Full-service organization assisting writers, from formatting a manuscript to assistance finding agents and publishers. Awards cash prizes in 5 contests each year. Published book contest, David R. Raffelock Award for Publishing Excellence. Referral services, conferences, and financial assistance also offered. Annual dues: $65 Individual, $35 Student, $85 Professional.

NATIONAL WRITERS UNION

113 University Place, Fl. 6, New York, NY 10003. 212-254-0279.
E-mail: nwu@nwu.org. Web site: www.nwu.org. Jonathan Tasini, President. Works for equitable payment and fair treatment for freelance writers through collective action. Membership over 6,000, includes authors, poets, cartoonists, journalists, and technical writers in 17 chapters nationwide. Offers contract and agent information, group health insurance, press credentials, grievance handling, a quarterly magazine, and sample contracts and resource materials. Sponsors workshops and seminars. Membership open to writers who have published a book, play, three articles, five poems, a short story, or an equivalent amount of newsletter, publicity, technical, commercial, government, or institutional copy, or have written unpublished material and are actively seeking publication. Annual dues: $95-$260.

NEW DRAMATISTS

424 W 44th St., New York, NY 10036.
Web site: www.newdramatists.org. Service organization for playwrights, providing time, space, and other resources to develop their craft. Services include readings and workshops; a director-in-residence program; national script distribution for members; artist work spaces; international playwright exchange programs; script copying facilities; and a free ticket program. Membership open to residents of New York City and surrounding tri-state area. National memberships for those outside the area who spend time in NYC. Apply between July 15 and September 15. No annual dues. See website for more information.

NORTHWEST PLAYWRIGHTS GUILD
318 SW Palatine Hill Rd., Portland, OR 97219. 503-452-4778.
E-mail: bjscript@teleport.com. Web site: www.nwpg.org. Barbara Callander, Director. Chapters in Portland, OR and Seattle, WA. Encourages the creation and production of new plays. Support through play development, staged readings, and networking for play competitions and production opportunities. Oregon chapter offers Page to Stage and Living Room Theater to help playwrights develop new work. Monthly and quarterly newsletters. Annual dues: $25.

OUTDOOR WRITERS ASSOCIATION OF AMERICA
121 Hickory St., Suite 1, Missoula, MT 59801. 406-728-7434.
E-mail: owaa@montana.com. Web site: www.owaa.org. William H. Geer, Executive Director. Non-profit organization of outdoor communicators. Awards: Ham Brown Award, Jade of Chiefs, Excellence in Craft, Mountain of Jade Award, Jackie Pfeiffer Memorial Award. Also, referral services and conferences. Dues: $100 individual, $30 student, $300 supporting.

PEN AMERICAN CENTER
568 Broadway, New York, NY 10012. 212-334-1660.
E-mail: pen@pen.org. Web site: www.pen.org. Michael Roberts, Executive Director. One of over 130 centers worldwide of International PEN. Members are poets, playwrights, essayists, editors, and novelists, also literary translators and agents who have made a substantial contribution to the literary community. Main office in New York City; branches in Boston, Chicago, New Orleans, Portland, Oregon, and San Francisco. Programs and services include literary events and awards, outreach projects, assistance to writers in financial need, and international and domestic human-rights campaigns on behalf of literary figures imprisoned because of their writing. Membership open to writers who have published two books of literary merit, also editors, agents, playwrights, and translators who meet specific standards; apply to membership committee. Annual dues, $75.

THE PLAYWRIGHTS' CENTER
2301 Franklin Ave. E., Minneapolis, MN 55406. 612-332-7481.
E-mail: info@pwcenter.org. Web site: www.pwcenter.org. Kristen Gandrow, Playwright Services Director. Provides services to support playwrights and playwriting, nurtures artistic excellence and new visions, fosters initiative and leadership, practices cultural pluralism, discovers emerging artists, and connects playwrights with audiences. Annual awards: McKnight Residency and Commission, McKnight Advancement Grant, Jerome fellowships, Many Voices residencies, Many Voices Cultural Collaboration Grants. Members may apply for all programs and participate in special activities, including classes, outreach programs, and PlayLabs. Annual dues: $75 local member, $30 student/senior, $40 low-income, $40 member over 100 miles.

POETRY SOCIETY OF AMERICA

15 Gramercy Park, New York, NY 10003. 212-254-9628.

Web site: www.poetrysociety.org. Alice Quinn, Executive Director.

Seeks to raise awareness of poetry, to deepen understanding of it, and to encourage more people to read, listen to, and write poetry. Presents more than 40 readings and events across the country each year, and places posters on busses and subways through "Poetry in Motion." Also offers annual contests for poetry, seminars, conferences, poetry festivals, and publishes a journal. Annual dues: $40 ($25 for students).

POETS & WRITERS

72 Spring St., New York, NY 10012. 212-226-3586.

Web site: www.pw.org. Elliot Figman, Executive Director. Fosters the professional development of poets and fiction writers and promotes communication throughout the literary community. Also publishes *Poets & Writers* magazine (which contains information on markets for writers) and *A Directory of American Poets and Fiction Writers*, and supports readings and writing workshops at varied venues.

PUBLICATION RIGHTS CLEARINGHOUSE

National Writers Union

113 University Pl., Fl. 6, New York, NY 10003. 212-254-0279.

Web site: www.nwu.org/nwu. The collective-licensing agency of the National Writers Union created in 1996 to help writers license and collect royalties for the reuse of their published works in electronic databases and other media. It is modeled after similar organizations in the music industry. Writers license non-exclusive secondary rights to the PRC; the PRC licenses those rights to secondary users and distributes payment to writers. Enrollment open to NWU members and to non-members.

ROMANCE WRITERS OF AMERICA

3707 FM 1960 West, Suite 555, Houston, TX 77068. 281-440-6885.

E-mail: info@rwanational.com. Web site: www.rwanational.org. Allison Kelley, Executive Director. Nonprofit organization for published or unpublished writers interested in romantic fiction. Offers conferences, and awards: RITA (for published romance novels), Golden Heart (for unpublished manuscripts). Annual dues, $75.

SCIENCE FICTION AND FANTASY WRITERS OF AMERICA

P.O. Box 877, Chestertown, MD 21620.

E-mail: execdir@sfwa.org. Web site: www.sfwa.org/org/sfwa_info.htm. Jane Jewell, Executive Director. Promotes the professional interests of science fiction and fantasy writers. Presents annual Nebula Award for excellence in the field; publishes the *Bulletin* and *SFWA Handbook* for members (also available to non-members). Any writer who has sold a work of science fiction or fantasy is eligible. Annual dues: $50 (active), $35 (affiliate), plus $10 installation fee; send for application.

SISTERS IN CRIME
P.O. Box 442124, Lawrence, KS 66044-8933.
E-mail: sistersincrime@juno.com. Web site: www.sistersincrime.org. Eve K. Sandstrom, President. Fights discrimination against women in the mystery field, educates publishers and the public about inequalities in the treatment of female authors, and increases awareness of their contribution to the field. Membership open to all: writers, readers, editors, agents, booksellers, librarians. Publishes a quarterly newsletter and *Books in Print* membership directory. Annual dues: $35 (U.S.), $40 (foreign).

SOCIETY OF AMERICAN TRAVEL WRITERS
1500 Sunday Dr., Suite 102, Raleigh, NC 27607. 919-787-5181.
E-mail: nshore@satw.org. Web site: www.satw.org. Cathy Kerr, Executive Director. Represents writers and other professionals who strive to provide travelers with accurate reports on destinations, facilities, and services. Active membership limited to travel writers and freelancers with a steady volume of published or distributed work about travel. Application fees: $250 (active), $500 (associate). Annual dues: $130 (active), $250 (associate).

SOCIETY OF CHILDREN'S BOOK WRITERS & ILLUSTRATORS
8271 Beverly Blvd., Los Angeles, CA 90048. 323-782-1010.
E-mail: scbwi@scbwi.org. Web site: www.scbwi.org. Lin Oliver, Executive Director. A national organization of authors, editors, publishers, illustrators, librarians, and educators; for beginners and established professionals alike. Offers varied services: referrals, conferences, grants program. Full memberships open to anyone who has had at least 1 children's book or story published. Associate memberships open to all interested in children's literature. Annual dues: $50. Annual awards: Golden Kite Book Award, Magazine Merit Award.

SOCIETY OF ENVIRONMENTAL JOURNALISTS
P.O. Box 2492, Jenkintown, PA 19046. 215-884-8174.
E-mail: sej@sej.org. Web site: www.sej.org. Beth Parke, Executive Director. **Description:** Dedicated to improving the quality, accuracy, and visibility of environmental reporting. Serves 1,200 members and the journalism community with a quarterly newsletter, annual and regional conferences, *EJToday* news digest service, Tipsheet, comprehensive website, awards, mentor programs, and membership directory. Annual dues: $40, $30 (student).

SOCIETY OF PROFESSIONAL JOURNALISTS
3909 N Meridian St., Indianapolis, IN 46208. 317-927-8000.
E-mail: spj@spj.org. Web site: www.spj.org. Terrence Harper, Executive Director. **Description:** Serves the interests of print, broadcast, and wire journalists (10,000+ members and 300 chapters). Services: Journalists' legal defense fund, freedom of information resources, professional development seminars, and awards. Members

receive *Quill*, a magazine on current issues in the field. Also promotes ethical reporting. Annual dues: $72 (professional), $36 (student).

THE SONGWRITERS GUILD OF AMERICA

1560 Broadway, Suite 1306, New York, NY 10036.
E-mail: songnews@aol.com. Web site: www.songwriters.org. Provides published and unpublished songwriters with sample contracts, contract review, and a service that collects royalties from publishers. Additionally, SGA offers group health and life insurance plans, conducts workshops and critique sessions, and provides newsletters. Annual dues: $70 (associate membership), $85 and up (full membership).

THEATRE COMMUNICATIONS GROUP

520 Eighth Ave., New York, NY 10018. 212-609-5900.
Web site: www.tcg.org. Terence Nemeth, Vice President. Offers a wide array of services to strengthen, nurture, and promote the not for-profit American theatre (artistic and management programs, advocacy activities, International programs and publications). Seeks to increase organizational efficiency of member theatres, encourages artistic talent and achievement, and promotes public appreciation for the theatre field. Individual members receive *American Theatre* magazine. Annual dues: $35.

WESTERN WRITERS OF AMERICA

1012 Fair St., Franklin, TN 37064. 615-791-1444.
E-mail: tncrutch@aol.com. Web site: www.westernwriters.org. James A. Crutchfield, Secretary/Treasurer/Managing Editor. Open to professional writers of fiction and nonfiction on the history and literature of the American West. Promotes distribution, readership, and appreciation of the West and its literature. Annual convention last week of June. Sponsors annual Spur Awards, Owen Wister Award, and Medicine Pipe Bearer's Award for published work and produced screenplays. Annual dues: $75.

WRITERS GUILD OF AMERICA

East: 555 W 57th St., Suite 1230, New York, NY 10019-2967. 212-767-7806.
Web site: www.wgaeast.org. Mona Mangan, Executive Director.
West: 7000 W 3rd St., Los Angeles, CA 90048. 323-951-4000.
Web site: www.wga.org. Victoria Riskin, President.
Represents writers in motion pictures, broadcast, cable and new media industries, including news and entertainment. To qualify for membership, writers must meet requirements for employment or sale of material. Basic dues: $25/quarter + 1.5% of earnings. Also, quarterly dues based on percentage of the member's earnings in any of the fields over which the guild has jurisdiction. Initiation fee: $1,500 for WGAE (writers living east of the Mississippi), $2,500 for WGAW (for those west of the Mississippi). Also publishes *Written By*, an official publication for screen and television writers.

WRITERS INFORMATION NETWORK (WIN)
Professional Assn. for Christian Writers
P.O. Box 11337, Bainbridge Island, WA 98110. 206-842-9103.
E-mail: writersinfonetwork@juno.com. Web site: www.bluejaypub.com/win. Elaine Wright Colvin, Founder/Director. Provides a link between Christian writers and the religious publishing industry and offers professional development in writing, marketing, and speaking. Also publishes the *WIN-INFORMER*, a magazine reporting on industry news and trends. Annual dues: $40. Submit resume or biographical sketch with application. Go to website to download membership application.

SYNDICATES

Syndicates buy material from writers and artists to sell to newspapers all over the country and the world. Authors are paid either a percentage of the gross proceeds or an outright fee. Of course, features by people well known in their fields have the best chance of being syndicated. In general, syndicates want columns that have been popular in a local newspaper or magazine. Since most syndicated fiction has been published previously in magazines or books, beginning fiction writers should try to sell their stories to magazines before submitting them to syndicates.

Always query syndicates before sending manuscripts, since their needs change frequently, and be sure to enclose SASEs with queries and manuscripts.

AGEVENTURE NEWS SERVICE
Demko Publishing
19432 Preserve Dr., Boca Raton, FL 33498. 561-182-6271.
E-mail: editor@demko.com. Web site: www.demko.com. David Demko, Editor.
Description: Presents work to international audience of three million readers in 29 countries. Topics must address baby-boomer and retiree concerns. Submissions should be 250-500 words; specify costs for use at time of submission. 25% freelance. Submit manuscripts, 200-500 words, as e-mail text (no attachments).

AMERICAN PRESS SERVICE
P.O. Box 917, Van Nuys, CA 91408. 818-997-6497.
E-mail: iscs1assoc@aol.com. Isreal I. Bick, Vice President/General Manager.
Description: Features on all subjects especially arts, entertainment, hobbies, and books. Send query with SASE before submitting.

AMPERSAND COMMUNICATIONS
2311 S Bayshore Dr., Miami, FL 33133-4728. 305-285-2200.
E-mail: amprsnd@aol.com. Web site: www.ampersandcom.com. George Leposky, Editor. **Description:** Feature material for online use, and for newspapers, magazines, and special-interest publications. Sells content to end-users directly and through marketing agreements with other online syndication services. Topics include: book reviews, humor, business, medicine and health, business travel, pets, cooking, food and wine, senior lifestyles, environmental issues, timesharing and vacation ownership, home improvement, and travel. 5% freelance. Query or send manuscript, 800-1,000 words. **Tips:** "We are most interested in receiving freelance submissions for our business travel column."

ASK THE BUILDER
3166 N Farmcrest Dr., Cincinnati, OH 45213-1112. 513-531-9229.
E-mail: tim@askthebuilder.com. Web site: www.askthebuilder.com. Tim Carter, Editor.
Description: Features articles on residential building and remodeling. Submit elec-

tronic press-release or product information via e-mail; lead with a 100-word (max.) summary of the press release. Color images for the Ask the Builder e-zine should be in .gif or .jpg format (width: 250 pixels; height: proportional; resolution: 72 dpi; send as e-mail attachment). Note: Only submit news and information if it is relevant to home building and remodeling.

COPLEY NEWS SERVICE

Box 120190, San Diego, CA 92112. 619-293-1818.
E-mail: infofax@copleynews.com. Web site: www.copleynews.com. Glenda Winders, Editorial Director. **Description:** Features columns on: music, books, cars, fashion, films, sports, gardening, home improvement, and other special interests. 1,500 subscribers. 75% freelance. Accepts unsolicited mss. **Tips:** "The market is tight at the moment and we are buying very little. Still, we like to know what is available in case there is a change in our lineup."

HISPANIC LINK NEWS SERVICE

1420 N St. NW, Washington, DC 20005. 202-234-0280.
E-mail: charles@hispaniclink.org. Mr. Charles A. Ericksen, Editor. **Description:** Trend articles, opinion and personal experience pieces, and general features with Hispanic focus, 650-700 words; editorial cartoons. Pays $25 for op-ed columns and cartoons, on acceptance. **Tips:** Send SASE for guidelines.

THE HOLLYWOOD INSIDE SYNDICATE

P.O. Box 49957, Los Angeles, CA 90049. 818-509-7840.
E-mail: hollywood@ez2.net. Web site: www.ez2.net/hollywood. John Austin, Director. **Description:** Short pieces on world-class celebrities, or column type items for internationally syndicated "Hollywood Inside" column.

KING FEATURES SYNDICATE

888 Seventh Ave., New York, NY 10019. 212-455-4000.
E-mail: kfscartoonists@hearst.com. Web site: www.kingfeatures.com. Jay Kennedy, Editor-in-Chief. **Description:** Columns, comics. Does not buy individual articles; looking for ideas for nationally syndicated columns. Submit cover letter, six sample columns of 650 words each, bio sheet and any additional clips, and SASE. No simultaneous submissions. Send SASE for guidelines. **Contact:** Glenn Mott, Managing Editor.

MOTOR NEWS MEDIA CORPORATION

7177 Hickman Rd., Suite 11D, Urbandale, IA 50322. 515-270-6782.
E-mail: mnmedia@quest.net. Web site: www.motornewsmedia.com.
Description: New or unique automotive stories and features. Automotive reviews not needed. 30% freelance. Submit manuscript, 650-800 words, by mail with sample, print references, and SASE. Pays $125/feature.

NATIONAL GAY LESBIAN
BISEXUAL TRANSGENDER TRAVEL DESK

2790 Wrondel Way, PMB #444, Reno, NV 89502. 775-348-7990.
E-mail: nglbtraveldesk@aol.com. Sylvia Seltzer, Ira Gruber, Editors. **Description:** Looking for "rookie" travel writers to write only about cities in their state. Also looking for stringers for national gay/lesbian guidebook to North America. Send e-mail to editors with author bio. Articles run 1,200-2,400 words. 80% freelance. Pays $25/story. **Tips:** "You must get a local gay/lesbian newspaper in your area to accept stories and then we will give you assignments. We prefer people who travel rather than those who have experience."

NATIONAL NEWS BUREAU

P.O. Box 43039, Philadelphia, PA 19129. 215-849-9016.
E-mail: nnbfeature@aol.com. Web site: www.nationalnewsbureau.com. Harry Jay Katz, Publisher. **Description:** Articles, 500-1,500 words, celebrity interviews, consumer news, how-tos, travel pieces, reviews, entertainment pieces, features, etc. Pays on publication. **Contact:** Andy Edelman, Features Editor.

NEW DIMENSIONS RADIO

P.O. Box 569, Ulkiah, CA 95482. 707-468-5215.
E-mail: info@newdimensions.org. Web site: www.newdimensions.org. Rose Holland, Associate Producer. **Description:** Programming presents a diversity of views from many different traditions and cultures, and strives to provide listeners with practical knowledge and perennial wisdom. New Dimensions fosters living a more healthy life of mind, body and spirit while deepening their connections to self, family, community, the natural world, and the planet. No unsolicited manuscripts; query first.

NEW YORK TIMES SYNDICATION SALES

122 E 42nd St., Fl. 14, New York, NY 10168. 212-499-3300.
E-mail: nytsf@nytimes.com. Web site: www.nytsyn.com/syndicate. Mr. Cristian Edwards, Executive Vice President. **Description:** Articles on international, seasonal, health, lifestyle, and entertainment topics, to 1,500 words (previously published or unpublished). Query with published article or tear sheet and SASE. No calls please. Pays 50% royalty on collected sales.

NEWSPAPER ENTERPRISE ASSOCIATION/
UNITED FEATURE SYNDICATE

200 Madison Ave., Fl. 4, New York, NY 10016. 212-293-8500/800-221-4816.
Web site: www.unitedfeatures.com. **Description:** National features and columns on news, politics, sports, business, entertainment, books, and lifestyles, for over 600 daily newspapers. Payment varies. **Tips:** Send submissions c/o Submissions Editor. See Web site for guidelines.

TRIBUNE MEDIA SERVICES
435 N Michigan Ave., Suite 1500, Chicago, IL 60611. 312-222-4444/800-245-6536. E-mail: tms@tribune.com. Web site: www.tmsfeatures.com. Eve Becker, Managing Editor. **Description:** Continuing columns, comic strips, features, editorial cartoons, puzzles, and word games. Query with clips. Guidelines at www.comicspage.com.

GLOSSARY

Advance—The amount a publisher pays a writer before a book is published; it is deducted from the royalties earned from sales of the finished book.

Agented material—Submissions from literary or dramatic agents to a publisher. Some publishing companies accept agented material only.

All rights—Some magazines purchase all rights to the material they publish, which means that they can use it as they wish, as many times as they wish. They cannot purchase all rights unless the writer gives them written permission to do so.

Assignment—A contract, written or oral, between an editor and writer, confirming that the writer will complete a specific project by a certain date, and for a certain fee.

B&W—Abbreviation for black-and-white photographs.

Book outline—Chapter-by-chapter summary of a book, frequently in paragraph form, allowing an editor to evaluate the book's content, tone, and pacing, and determine whether he or she wants to see the entire manuscript for possible publication.

Book packager—Company that puts together all the elements of a book, from initial concept to writing, publishing, and marketing it. Also called **book producer** or **book developer.**

Byline—Author's name as it appears on a published piece.

Clips—Copies of a writer's published work, often used by editors to evaluate the writer's talent.

Column inch—One inch of a typeset column; often serves as a basis for payment.

Contributor's copies—Copies of a publication sent to a writer whose work is included in it.

Copy editing—Line-by-line editing to correct errors in spelling, grammar, and punctuation, and inconsistencies in style. Differs from **content editing,** which evaluates flow, logic, and overall message.

Copy—Manuscript pages before they are set into type.

Copyright—Legal protection of creative works from unauthorized use. Under the law, copyright is secured automatically when the work is set down for the first time in written or recorded form.

Cover letter—A brief letter that accompanies a manuscript or book proposal. A cover letter is not a query letter (see definition).

Deadline—The date on which a written work is due at the editor's office, agreed to by author and editor.

Draft—A complete version of an article, story, or book. First drafts are often called **rough drafts.**

Electronic rights—Refers to the use of an article in electronic form, rather than hard-copy formats. The term is not very precise, and it is a good idea to pin down exactly what the publisher means by electronic rights, and consider what rights are reasonable to allow considering the fee, advance, or royalty amount being offered.

Fair use—A provision of the copyright law allowing brief passages of copyrighted material to be quoted without infringing on the owner's rights.

Feature—An article that is generally longer than a news story and whose main focus is an issue, trend, or person.

Filler—Brief item used to fill out a newspaper or magazine column; could be a news item, joke, anecdote, or puzzle.

First serial rights—The right of a magazine or newspaper to publish a work for the first time in any periodical. After that, all rights revert to the writer.

FNASR (First North American Serial Rights)—This refers to the specific right to use an author's work in a serial periodical, in North America, for its first appearance. Thereafter, rights to reprint the work remain with the author.

Ghostwriter—Author of books, articles, and speeches that are credited to someone else.

Glossy—Black-and-white photo with a shiny, rather than a matte, finish.

Hard copy—The printed copy of material written on a computer.

Honorarium—A modest, token fee paid by a publication to an author in gratitude for a submission.

International reply coupon (IRC)—Included with any correspondence or submission to a foreign publication; allows the editor to reply by mail without incurring cost.

Internet rights—See also electronic rights. This refers to the rights to post an author's work on a Web site, and possibly to distribute or allow the distribution of the article further via the Internet.

Kill fee—Fee paid for an article that was assigned but subsequently not published; usually a percentage of the amount that would have been paid if the work had been published.

Lead time—Time between the planning of a magazine or book and its publication date.

Libel—A false accusation or published statement that causes a person embarrassment, loss of income, or damage to reputation.

Little magazines—Publications with limited circulation whose content often deals with literature or politics.

Mass market—Books appealing to a very large segment of the reading public and often sold in such outlets as drugstores, supermarkets, etc.

Masthead—A listing of the names and titles of a publication's staff members.

Ms—Abbreviation for manuscript; mss is the plural abbreviation.

Multiple submissions—Also called **simultaneous submissions.** Complete manuscripts sent simultaneously to different publications. Once universally discouraged by editors, the practice is gaining more acceptance, though some still frown on it. **Multiple queries** are generally accepted, however, since reading them requires less of an investment in time on the editor's part.

NA (North American)—Sometimes appears as 1st NA; refers the right to publish the North American appearance of a piece of work, leaving the author free to market other appearances of the same work elsewhere.

On speculation—Editor agrees to consider a work for publication "on speculation," without any guarantee that he or she will ultimately buy the work.

One-time rights—Editor buys manuscript from writer and agrees to publish it one time, after which the rights revert to the author for subsequent sales.

Op-ed—A newspaper piece, usually printed opposite the editorial page, that expresses a personal viewpoint on a timely news item.

Over-the-transom—Describes the submission of unsolicited material by a freelance writer; the term harks back to the time when mail was delivered through the open window above an office door.

Payment on acceptance—Payment to writer when manuscript is submitted.

Payment on publication—Payment to writer when manuscript is published.

Pen name—A name other than his or her legal name that an author uses on written work.

Public domain—Published material that is available for use without permission, either because it was never copyrighted or because its copyright term is expired, Works published at least 75 years ago are considered in the public domain.

Q-and-A format—One type of presentation for an interview article, in which questions are printed, followed by the interviewee's answers.

Query letter—A letter—usually no longer than one page—in which a writer proposes an article idea to an editor.

Rejection slip—A printed note in which a publication indicates that it is not interested in a submission.

Reporting time—The weeks or months it takes for an editor to evaluate a submission.

Reprint rights—The legal right of a magazine or newspaper to print an article, story, or poem after it has already appeared elsewhere.

Royalty—A percentage of the amount received from retail sales of a book, paid to the author by the publisher. For hardcovers, the royalty is generally 10% on the first 5,000 copies sold; 12 ½% on the next 5,000 sold; 15% thereafter. Paperback royalties range from 4% to 8%, depending on whether it's a trade or mass-market book.

SASE—Self-addressed, stamped envelope, required with all submissions that the author wishes returned—either for return of material or (if you don't need material returned) for editor's reply.

Slush pile—The stack of unsolicited manuscripts in an editor's office.

Tear sheets—The pages of a magazine or newspaper on which an author's work is published.

Unsolicited submission—A manuscript that an editor did not specifically ask to see.

Vanity publisher—Also called **subsidy publisher.** A publishing company that charges an author all costs of printing his or her book. No reputable book publisher operates on this subsidy basis.

Web rights—See Internet rights.

Work for hire—When a work is written on a "for hire" basis, all rights in it become the property of the publisher. Though the work-for-hire clause applies mostly to work done by regular employees of a company, some editors offer work-for-hire agreements to freelancers. Think carefully before signing such agreements, however, since by doing so you will essentially be signing away your rights and will not be able to try to resell your work on your own.

Worldwide—Refers to the right to publish an article anywhere in the world (however, this right may be limited by other wording in a contract to publication in the English language only, or in-print only, or in electronic form only, etc.).

Writers guidelines—A formal statement of a publication's editorial needs, payment schedule, deadlines, and other essential information.

INDEX